The Palgrave Handbook of Contemporary Irish Theatre and Performance

Eamonn Jordan • Eric Weitz
Editors

The Palgrave Handbook of Contemporary Irish Theatre and Performance

palgrave
macmillan

Editors
Eamonn Jordan
School of English, Drama and Film
University College Dublin
Dublin, Ireland

Eric Weitz
School of Creative Arts
Trinity College Dublin
Dublin, Ireland

ISBN 978-1-137-58587-5 ISBN 978-1-137-58588-2 (eBook)
https://doi.org/10.1057/978-1-137-58588-2

Library of Congress Control Number: 2018952933

Cover illustration: 'The Seagull & Other Birds' Robert Altman Photography

This Palgrave Macmillan imprint is published by the registered company Springer Nature Limited
The registered company address is: The Campus, 4 Crinan Street, London, N1 9XW, United Kingdom

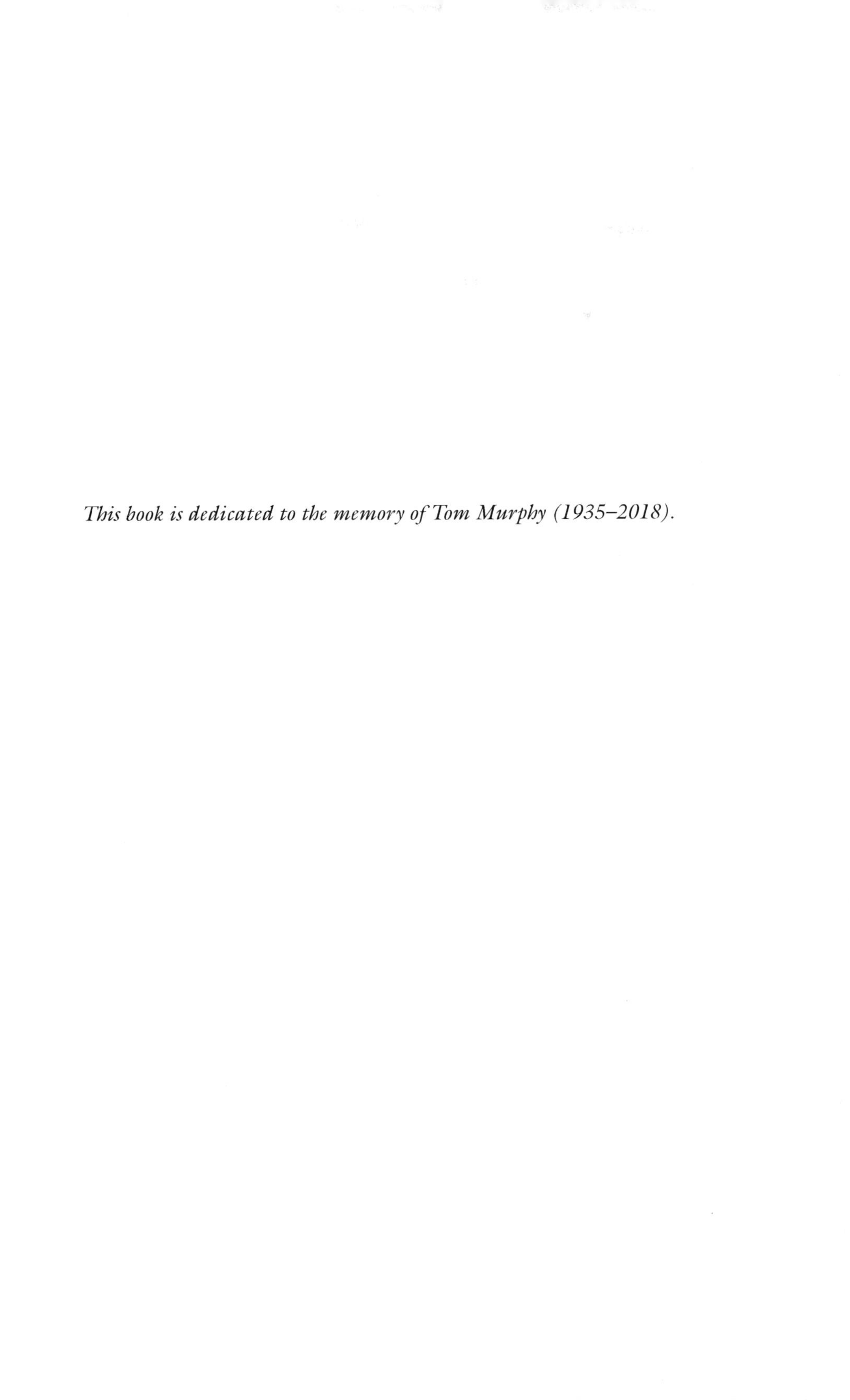

This book is dedicated to the memory of Tom Murphy (1935–2018).

Acknowledgements

A collection such as this, which attempts to assemble a wide range of original contributions, comes more and more to lean upon not only the expertise but the altruism of (1) scholars, subject in the current climate to third-level institutions insisting they produce research with a minimum of meaningful support (in terms of time and money), while in many cases minimizing the official worth of contributions to such collections; and (2) practitioners who have little, if anything, to gain professionally from such endeavours and who are all too accustomed to having their time and energy exploited. A massive amount of gratitude must therefore go to each and every one of our contributors for somehow carving out time and brain space in overstuffed, underpaid lives for the good of the project.

We owe particular thanks to Angie Butler who served as a first line of editorial organization for the manuscript. We also owe an extreme debt of thanks to Palgrave for its interest, support, co-operation and, inevitably, its understanding and patience—in particular, the people who have worked with us directly: Peter Cary, Jen McCall, Vicky Bates and Tomas René, as well as Dhana and her editorial team. We would like to put on record our thanks to Robert Altman for the use of his photograph in the cover design, and Pan Pan for facilitating such permission, also including the actors pictured; to the Irish Society for Theatre Research, at whose conferences some of these ideas were first aired and to which most of the contributors belong; and to our respective schools and departments for their support.

Contents

Notes on Contributors

Bisi Adigun is originally from the Yoruba nation in western Nigeria but has made Ireland home since 1996. He holds a PhD in Drama from Trinity College Dublin, where he is currently a visiting lecturer. Bisi is a playwright, theatre director/producer and the artistic director of Arambe Productions, Ireland's first African theatre company, which he founded in 2003. His productions with Arambe include *The Gods Are Not to Blame* (2004), *Dilemma of a Ghost* (2007), *Through a Film Darkly* (2008), *Haba Pastor Jero!* (2009), *The Butcher Babes* (2010) and *The Paddies of Parnell Street* (2013). Bisi was also a co-presenter on the first three series of RTE's intercultural television programme, *Mono.*

Maha Alatawi is a Lecturer in English at Prince Sattam Bin Abdulaziz University in Saudi Arabia. She was awarded an MA in English Literature from Al-Imam Muhammad Ibn Saud Islamic University with a thesis examining two plays by Arthur Miller and Marsha Norman. She is currently a PhD student and works as a tutor for the School of English, Drama, and Film at University College Dublin. The focus of her research is Contemporary Irish Theatre, particularly the work of Conor McPherson.

Ruth Barton is Associate Professor in Film Studies at Trinity College Dublin. She is the author of a number of publications on Irish cinema, including *Irish National Cinema* (2004) and *Acting Irish in Hollywood* (2006). She has written critical biographies of the Hollywood star, Hedy Lamarr: *Hedy Lamarr, The Most Beautiful Woman in Film* (2010) and the Irish silent era director, Rex Ingram: *Rex Ingram, Visionary Director of the Silent Screen* (2014). She is currently preparing a monograph on Irish cinema.

Csilla Bertha (University of Debrecen, Hungary) is a member of the International Advisory Board of *Irish University Review*, the Editorial Board of *Hungarian Journal of English and American Studies* and a founding director of *Centre for the International Study of Literatures in English.* She has published widely (in English and Hungarian) on interart relations, memory, sites of memory, space in Irish drama and theatre. Her *A drámaíró Yeats* (Yeats the Playwright, 1988) was the first on Yeats's drama in Hungary. She co-authored and co-edited volumes, including, *More Real than Reality* (1991), *The Celebration of the Fantastic* (1992), *A Small Nation's Contribution to the World* (1993), *Worlds Visible and Invisible* (1994), and *Brian Friel's Dramatic Artistry* (2006). Her latest edited special Irish drama issues are *IUR*, 2015 and *HJEAS*, 2017. Her co-translated Transylvanian-Hungarian plays include *Silenced Voices* (2008) and her latest editing of Hungarian literature in English is *Down Fell the Statue of Goliath*, 2017.

Angela Butler is a final year PhD student in the Department of Drama at Trinity College Dublin. Her doctoral research presents a phenomenologically guided study of immersive performance and digital culture. Her research considers the affective aesthetic experience offered by a certain strand of immersive theatre which she has identified and termed "sensory spectacle performance" and investigates it within the context of digital culture. Angela's research interests include immersive performance, digital/post-digital culture, aesthetic experience, affect theory, perception, attention and phenomenology.

Máirtín Coilféir is Assistant Professor in Celtic Studies at St Michael's College in the University of Toronto. Originally from Navan, Co. Meath, he has previously worked in the National University of Ireland, Galway, and University College, Dublin. He is also editor of *Comhar Taighde*, an Irish-language academic journal.

Susanne Colleary is Lecturer/Theatre Practitioner and researcher in the Humanities Department at Sligo Institute of Technology and Adjunct Lecturer in Trinity College Dublin. Susanne was awarded her PhD in 2011 (University College Dublin) and published her first book, *Performance and Identity in Irish Stand-Up Comedy: The Comic 'i'* (Palgrave Macmillan, 2015), She has published on Irish theatre, stand-up comedy and televisual satire. Susanne has been working on practice-based research focussed on Irish popular theatre and performance for five years. Recent theatre projects include *Marian and Joseph: A Revolutionary Love Story* (Dublin, 2016). Written and directed by the author, the work deals with political melodrama in early twentieth-century Ireland. In collaboration with Sue Morris, the two produced a multimedia work, *'Here We Are At The Risk Of Our Lives'*, dealing with Irish Music Hall during Easter Week 1916 (2016). Susanne is currently writing her second book, *The Subversive Comic Impulse of Rough Theatre: Irish Political Melodrama 1900–1923* (Palgrave Macmillan, forthcoming).

Christopher Collins is an Assistant Professor of Drama at the University of Nottingham, UK. He has published widely on Irish theatre, including two monographs on the work of J.M. Synge (*Theatre and Residual Culture* [Palgrave, 2016], and *J.M. Synge's The Playboy of the Western World* [2016]), and a co-edited collection of essays on the performance of history and memory in Irish theatre, *Ireland, Memory and Performing the Historical Imagination* (2014).

Finola Cronin is Head of Drama Studies at University College Dublin (UCD). She studied dance in Dublin and at the London School of Contemporary Dance. She performed most recently with Raimund Hogue (Germany/France), and previously in Germany with Vivienne Newport (Frankfurt) and Pina Bausch (Wuppertal). She was Dance Specialist at the Arts Council/An Chomhairle Ealaíon from 2003–2007. She teaches choreography, and drama & performance studies at UCD, and is director of the UCD/GSA MA in Theatre Practice. She co-curates Corp_Real | Galway Dance Days with Dr. Ríonach Ní Néill and Dr. Aoife McGrath and serves on the boards of Siamsa Tíre—The National Folk Theatre, and Dublin Dance Festival (as vice-chair). With Eamonn Jordan she edited *The Contemporary Irish Theatre and Performance Studies Reader* (2016).

Jim Culleton is Artistic Director of Fishamble: The New Play Company, for which he has directed productions which have won Olivier, The Stage, Fringe First, Herald Angel, Argus Angel, 1st Irish, Adelaide Fringe and Irish Times Theatre awards, on tour throughout Ireland, the UK, Europe, Australia, New Zealand and the US. He has also directed for the Abbey Theatre, Woodpecker/the Gaiety, 7:84 (Scotland), Project Arts Centre, Amharclann de hIde, Amnesty International, Tinderbox, The Passion Machine, The Ark, Second Age, RTE Radio 1, The Belgrade, TNL Canada, Dundee Rep Ensemble, Draíocht, Barnstorm, Trinity College Dublin School of Drama, Frontline Defenders, Gúna Nua, Origin (New York), Vessel (Australia), Little Museum of Dublin, Symphony Space Broadway & Irish Arts Center (New York) and RTE Lyric FM. Jim has taught for NYU, NUIM, GSA, Notre Dame University, Trinity College Dublin and University College Dublin.

Brian Devaney holds a PhD in English Language and Literature from Mary Immaculate College, Limerick, Ireland. He is the author of one of the most comprehensive studies of the Irish dramatist John B. Keane, titled *What Lies Beneath: Social, Cultural, and Psychological Resonance in John B. Keane's The Field*. He has worked as a tutor and departmental assistant for the department of English Language and Literature in Mary Immaculate College, and also as an English language teacher at Killarney School of English, Co. Kerry, Ireland. He hails from the "village" of Lisselton, Co. Kerry, Ireland, and is currently working as an English-language teacher in the city of Huelva, on the south-west coast of Spain.

Kate Donoghue is a PhD student in the University of Manchester, UK, where her research concerns trauma representation in the performance work of the former Yugoslavia, and live performance as a means of trauma relief in post-conflict communities. Her research interests include; bodies in performance, memory and memorialization, acts of violence, and physical theatres. Kate earned her MA in Drama and Performance Studies from University College Dublin, and her BA from Knox College in Galesburg, Illinois, USA.

Conor Doyle is an author, radio presenter and historian of the Theatre Royal. As Ireland's leading expert on Dublin's long-lost Theatre Royal, he lectures and has assembled an extensive collection of Theatre Royal programmes, photos and film archive. In recent years, he has also performed in "sell out" concerts in the National Concert Hall, remembering this iconic Dublin institution. Producer and presenter of four one-hour radio programmes, which commemorated the fiftieth anniversary of the closing of the Royal. His passion for theatre history was triggered upon inheriting his uncle Jimmy O'Dea and aunt Ursula Doyle's memorabilia from their stage, radio, film and radio careers, which he subsequently donated to the Irish Theatre archives.

Bernard Farrell is a playwright whose first play, *I Do Not Like Thee Doctor Fell*, opened at the Abbey Theatre in 1979 and is still produced in many translations throughout the world. His following twenty plays were premiered at the Abbey, Gate and Red Kettle theatres in Ireland and the Laguna Playhouse in California, and include *Canaries*, *The Last Apache Reunion*, *Kevin's Bed*, *Lovers At Versailles*, *Happy Birthday Dear Alice*, *Stella By Starlight*, *The Verdi Girls* and *Bookworms*. His work for television includes *Lotty Coyle Loves Buddy Holly* (RTE) and, with Graham Reid, the eighteen-part BBC series *Foreign Bodies*. For radio, his plays have represented Ireland at the Prix Italia and his *Greta At The Gresham* received the 2016 Zebbie Award for Best Play of the Year. He has won the Rooney Prize For Irish Literature, the Sunday Tribune Comedy of the Year Award, and the Best Production Award in the Dublin Theatre Festival. He is a member of Aosdana, was Writer-in-Association and also served on the Board of Directors of the Abbey Theatre and, in 2014, received the John B. Keane Lifetime Achievement Award for his services to the Arts.

Lisa Fitzpatrick is Senior Lecturer in Drama at Ulster University, where she also has responsibility for the research students in the Faculty of Arts. She studied in Trinity College and University College Dublin prior to completing her PhD at the Graduate Centre for Study of Drama, University of Toronto. She has published on performance and violence, post-conflict theatre and gender, and has been funded by the British Academy and the Canadian High Commission. She has been an invited speaker at a number of events, including the International Association for the Study of Irish Literatures (IASIL), the Warwick Politics and Performance Network, and the Irish Theatrical Diaspora project. She convened the conference "The North: Exile, Diaspora, Troubled Performance", held in Derry in 2012 and, worked with the Playhouse on the International Culture Arts Network Festival in the same city in 2013. She is a founding member of the Irish

Society for Theatre Research, and convenes the Gender and Performance Working Group.

Ciara Fleming is a recent graduate of Trinity College Dublin, where she studied Drama and Theatre Studies, with a focus on directing. As part of this study, she completed her dissertation on the realities of feminist readings of musical theatre. These interests are reflected in the work that she contributes to as a director and theatremaker. Ciara has worked extensively within the wardrobe departments of the Gate Theatre and Abbey Theatre since leaving university, as well as undertaking projects as an Assistant Director with META productions and Landmark Productions.

Anne Fogarty is Professor of James Joyce Studies at University College Dublin and co-founder with Luca Crispi of the *Dublin James Joyce Journal*. She has been Academic Director of the Dublin James Joyce Summer School since 1997 and was President of the International James Joyce Foundation, 2008–2012. She is co-editor of *Joyce on the Threshold* (2005), *Bloomsday 100: Essays on 'Ulysses'* (2009), *Imagination in the Classroom: Teaching and Learning Creative Writing in Ireland* (2013) and *Voices on Joyce* (2015). She has edited special issues of the *Irish University Review* on Spenser and Ireland, Lady Gregory, Eiléan Ní Chuilleanáin, and Benedict Kiely and has published widely on aspects of twentieth- and twenty-first-century Irish literature, especially fiction. She is currently co-editing a collection of essays on the novelist, Deirdre Madden, and completing a study of the historical and political dimensions of *Ulysses*, entitled *James Joyce and Cultural Memory: Reading History in 'Ulysses'*.

Nicholas Grene is Emeritus Professor of English Literature at Trinity College Dublin and a Member of the Royal Irish Academy. His books include *Shakespeare's Tragic Imagination* (1992), *The Politics of Irish Drama* (1999), *Shakespeare's Serial History Plays* (2002), *Yeats's Poetic Codes* (2008) and *Home on the Stage* (2014). The *Oxford Handbook of Modern Irish Theatre*, which he co-edited with Chris Morash, was published in 2016. *The Theatre of Tom Murphy: Playwright Adventurer* was published in 2017.

J. Paul Halferty is Assistant Professor in Drama Studies at University College Dublin. He has taught at York University, the University of Toronto, and at Brock University, mainly in the areas of theatre history, acting, gender and sexuality studies. His work has been published in *Theatre Research in Canada*, *Canadian Theatre Review*, and in the anthology *Queer Theatre in Canada*. He is associate editor and contributor to *TRANS(per) FORMING NinaArsenault: An Unreasonable Body of Work*, and co-editor of the "Views and Reviews" section of *Canadian Theatre Review*. His current book project is a history of gay theatre in Toronto from the mid-1960s to the mid-1990s.

Richard Hayes lectures in English at Waterford Institute of Technology where he is also Vice President for Strategy. He is a graduate of Maynooth University and University College Dublin, where he completed doctoral research on twentieth-century American theatre. His current research interests include an interest in charting the relationship between regional identity and theatre practice, a project called "Performing the Region". He has published a number of articles on American theatre and American cinema, on Irish poetry, and on aspects of contemporary film culture.

Barry Houlihan is an Archivist at the James Hardiman Library, NUI Galway. There he manages theatre and performance archives such as Druid Theatre Company and the Galway Arts Festival and is Project Board member of the Abbey Theatre and Gate Theatre Digital Archives. Barry is editor of the forthcoming volume *Navigating Ireland's Theatre Archive: Theory, Performance, Practice* (2018). Barry holds a PhD from NUI Galway, based on research investigating archives of plays at the intersection of Irish theatre and society in Modern Ireland. He is also President of the International Association of Libraries, Museums, Archives and Documentation Centres of the Performing Arts (SIBMAS).

Elizabeth Howard studied Drama and Theatre Studies with Counselling Skills at the University of Chester before completing an MA in Performance Making at Goldsmiths College, London. In 2013, she was awarded a PhD scholarship from Waterford Institute of Technology for research into Red Kettle Theatre Company using the company's archive as a primary research source. In between and during academic engagements Elizabeth has worked extensively in the theatre industry in both Ireland and the UK. She continues to make her own performance work.

Kellie Hughes is a theatremaker based in Dublin. Recent work includes the adaptation and direction of José Saramago's *Death at Intervals* (Galway International Arts Festival, Dublin Theatre Festival) and co-direction of Beckett's *Lessness* (Barbican International Beckett Festival) and Olwen Fouéré's *riverrun* (world tour). Kellie was an ensemble performer with Blue Raincoat Theatre for seven years, collaborating on the creation of new works, interpreting classic texts and directing on occasion, most notably the *Yeats Project*. Interested in the expressive potential of the body, Kellie wrote and performed two shows for the Science Museum, London: *Art, Science and the Moving Body* and *The Brain and the Body* (televised on the BBC). She trained at the Ecole de Mime Corporel Dramatique, London and the Centre Artistique International Roy Hart, Maleragues. Kellie holds a first-class BA (Hons) in Theatre and History and an MA (Hons) in Physical Theatre. She is currently Director in Residence at University College Dublin.

Eamonn Jordan is Associate Professor in Drama Studies at the School of English, Drama and Film, University College Dublin. His book *The Feast of Famine: The Plays of Frank McGuinness* (1997) is the first full-length study on

McGuinness's work. In 2000, he edited *Theatre Stuff: Critical Essays on Contemporary Irish Theatre*. More recently, he co-edited with Lilian Chambers *The Theatre of Martin McDonagh: A World of Savage Stories* (2006). His book *Dissident Dramaturgies: Contemporary Irish Theatre* was published in 2010. In 2012, he co-edited with Lilian Chambers *The Theatre of Conor McPherson: 'Right beside the Beyond'*. In 2014 *From Leenane to LA: The Theatre and Cinema of Martin McDonagh* was published. He will publish *The Theatre of Conor McPherson: Conspicuous Communities* in 2019.

Úna Kavanagh holds a BA and MA from the National College of Art & Design, Dublin. She is a figurative artist whose work includes sculpture, text, painting, drawing, performance, film, installation, animation, script writing, music composition, performance art and live art durational performances. Her practice ranges from extensive work in theatre, film, television and radio to her artistic collaborations. She has been a company member with multi-award-winning ANU Productions since 2010, collaborating on three performance artworks, eleven live art theatre works and film works. Úna has exhibited in both solo and group exhibitions for the last twenty years. Her work is held in private collections both here and the Middle East. She has been awarded The Art's Council Theatre Bursary award 2017 and represented Ireland in "Art By Country" in Abu Dhabi in 2014. She is an award-winning actress and has received international nominations for her work on screen. She was shortlisted for the SKY Arts Ignition award as part of TATSOI (Art/Science Collaboration) and was the first Artist In Residence for the inaugural Festival Of Curiosity in 2013.

Úna Kealy currently lectures in Theatre Studies and English at Waterford Institute of Technology (WIT). She has worked in professional theatre as a company, venue and festival manager, workshop facilitator and dramaturg. Her current research projects include "Performing the Region", which aims to critically examine the place of playwrights and practitioners from the south-east of Ireland within the narrative of Irish theatre; "Performing Women", which considers the representation of women in plays by women staged at the Abbey Theatre during the 1900s; and "Letters from the Past", a research project around the correspondence between Waterford playwrights Teresa Deevy and James Cheasty. Details of publications, curatorial achievements, workshops and public lectures available at: www.wit.ie/about_wit/contact_us/staff_directory/una_kealy.

Gavin Kostick is an internationally produced playwright and Literary Officer for Fishamble: The New Play Company. Through Fishamble and as an independent dramaturg he has worked with hundreds of writers for the stage. He is currently a tutor in both the Samuel Beckett Centre, Trinity College Dublin and the Lír. He performed Joseph Conrad's *Heart of Darkness: Complete*, a six-hour show in Dublin and London.

Mária Kurdi is Professor in the Institute of English Studies at the University of Pécs, Hungary. Her main area of research is Irish and anglophone theatre. She is author of five books, including *Representations of Gender and Female Subjectivity in Contemporary Irish Drama by Women* (2010). She is editor or co-editor of several volumes of essays, the latest one being the collection *Radical Contemporary Theatre Practices by Women in Ireland*, co-edited with Miriam Haughton (2015). In various journals and edited collections, she has published numerous scholarly articles and interviews with Irish playwrights.

Luke Lamont is a PhD candidate in the School of English, Drama and Film at University College Dublin having received his BA in English and Philosophy from the same institution in 2013. He then completed an MPhil. in Irish Writing at Trinity College Dublin in 2014, writing his dissertation on the representations of memory and trauma in Irish theatre. His current research project is entitled "Act of Witnessing: Analysing the Rise of Documentary Theatre in Irish Drama", and is funded by the Irish Research Council Government of Ireland Postgraduate Scholarship. Luke's research interests include socially engaged theatre, "theatre of the real" and memory studies.

Kasia Lech is a scholar, actor, storyteller, puppeteer, and a Senior Lecturer in the School of Music and Performing Arts at Canterbury Christ Church University, UK. She holds a PhD from University College Dublin, with her research being supported by the Irish Research Council. She has published on verse and verse drama in contemporary performance, theatre translation, multilingual theatre, multilingual actor, Spanish, Polish, and Irish theatres, theatre and animal rights, and puppetry. Her research interests also include actor training and performance of poetry. Kasia trained as an actor at the Ludwik Solski State Drama School in Poland and has performed in numerous productions in Poland and Ireland, including starring as the Grey Cat, a puppet that co-hosted the awarded live TV show for children *CyberMysz* on Polish national television. Kasia is a co-founder and the Artistic Liaison of Polish Theatre Ireland—a multicultural theatre company based in Dublin. Kasia also runs a project *Bubble Revolution* that engages with the process of performing translation and looks at the role of non-native speaking actors in staging translation.

Cathy Leeney is currently Adjunct Assistant Professor in Drama Studies at University College Dublin, where she lectured in theatre and performance for twenty years and established the first Irish postgraduate programme in Directing for Theatre, now running in partnership with the Gaiety School of Acting as The MA in Theatre Practice. She initiated the project that led to Ireland's first national entry into the Prague Quadrennial International Exhibition of Theatre Scenography and Architecture in 2007, which was supported by Culture Ireland and the Arts Council. Her publications and research range across Irish theatre and Performance in the twentieth and twenty-first centuries, focussing largely on the work of women playwrights and feminist analysis. *Irish Women Playwrights 1900–1939: Gender and Violence on Stage* was published in 2010.

Tom Maguire is a Senior Lecturer in Theatre Studies and Research Unit Coordinator at Ulster University. He teaches on undergraduate and postgraduate programmes and supervises research students in Drama and in Museums and Cultural Heritages. His research engages with the relationships between performance, identity, place and power, particularly in Britain and Ireland. Current projects are focused on Theatre for Young Audiences and the performance of post-conflict places. In addition to over 30 essays and chapters, he has published *Making Theatre in Northern Ireland: Through and Beyond the Troubles* (2006) and *Performing Story on the Contemporary Stage* (2015). With Karian Schuitema, he co-edited *Theatre for Young Audiences in the UK: A Critical Handbook* (2013); and April 2015 saw the launch of *The Theatre of Marie Jones: Telling Stories from the Ground Up*, which he co-edited with Eugene McNulty. He serves on the Peer Review College of the Arts and Humanities Research Council. He is a member of the Board of the International Theatre for Young Audiences Research Network and the Editorial Board for *About Performance*. He is Chair of the Board of Big Telly Theatre Company, Northern Ireland.

Una Mannion teaches a Live Art module in the Performing Arts programme at IT Sligo and is programme chair of the new BA in Literature and Writing. She is a writer and in the past year she is the winner of Ambit Fiction Prize, Cuirt Short Story prize, Doolin short story prize and was winner of the Hennessy Emerging poetry award. Her work has been published in *Bare Fiction, The Irish Times, Ambit* and *The Incubator*.

Kate McCarthy is Lecturer in Drama at Waterford Institute of Technology. Her research interests include educational drama, contemporary theatre practice, in particular participatory performance, and the arts and education. Current research projects at WIT include Performing the Region, the Waterford Memories Project, which is an interdisciplinary oral history project that aims to document cultural heritage in the south-east region of Ireland, and "Letters from the Past", a research project around the correspondence between Waterford playwrights Teresa Deevy and James Cheasty. Kate is also a member of the Arts Education Research Group at Trinity College Dublin. As a practitioner, Kate has facilitated and devised numerous contemporary theatre projects.

John McCormick has taught at Åbo Akademi, Finland, and lectured in French at Glasgow University and Trinity College, Dublin, where he was associate professor and first director of the Drama Department (1984). He is a founder of the Irish Theatre Archive (1981) and also a member of the executive committee of UNIMA (International puppetry association) 2000–2002. Author of various books and articles on nineteenth- and twentieth-century

French and British theatre. An active amateur puppeteer and author of *Popular Puppets in Europe 1800–1914* (with Bennie Pratasik) (1998); *The Victorian Marionette Theatre* (2004); *The Italian Puppet Theater—A history* (with Alfonso Cipolla and Alessandro Napoli) (2010); *Pupazzi—Glove Puppets and Marionettes in the Castello dei Burattini Museo Giordano Ferrari in Parma* (with Paolo Parmiggiani) (2015). He is currently in the process of preparing for publication *The Holdens—Monarchs of the Marionette Theatre.*

Rosaleen McDonagh is a Traveller woman with a disability, and the fourth eldest in a family of twenty children. She is a board member of Pavee Point Traveller & Roma Centre, where she previously managed its Violence Against Women programme for ten years. Rosaleen's theatre work includes *The Baby Doll Project, She's Not Mine* and *Rings*. Her play, *Mainstream*, was directed by Jim Culleton. Her latest project, *Protégée*, is based on Colum McCann's Booker Prize-winning novel, *Zoli*. In 2012, *Beat Him Like a Badger* was commissioned as part of the *Tiny Plays for Ireland* series. Rosaleen has worked with Graeae Theatre, and also spent two weeks on attachment in the Royal Court Theatre. Rosaleen has a BA in Biblical & Theological Studies, an MPhil in Ethnic & Racial Studies, and an MPhil in Creative Writing, all from Trinity College Dublin. She is currently a PhD candidate in Northumbria University.

Aoife McGrath is a lecturer in Drama at the School of Arts, English and Languages, Queen's University Belfast. After a professional dance career in Germany and Ireland, Aoife has worked as a choreographer and dance critic, and as Dance Advisor for the Irish Arts Council. Recent publications include work on: dance and affect; improvisation and feminism; dance, modernity and politics; and creativity in contemporary re-imaginings of traditional Irish dance. Aoife's book publications include her monograph, *Dance Theatre in Ireland: Revolutionary Moves* (2013), and a forthcoming co-edited collection (with Dr. Emma Meehan, CDaRe), *Dance Matters in Ireland: Contemporary Processes and Practices* (2017). She is currently developing a project on dance and the maternal. Aoife is a co-convenor of the Choreography and Corporeality Working Group of the IFTR, an executive committee member of the Irish Society for Theatre Research, a member of the board of directors of Dance Limerick, and a performer/choreographer member of Dance Ireland.

Charlotte McIvor is a Lecturer in Drama and Theatre Studies at the National University of Ireland, Galway. She is the author of *Migration and Performance in Contemporary Ireland: Towards A New Interculturalism* (Palgrave Macmillan) and the co-editor of *Staging Intercultural Ireland: Plays and Practitioner Perspectives* (with Matthew Spangler) and *Devised Performance in Irish Theatre: Histories and Contemporary Practice* (with Siobhán O'Gorman). She has published in *Theatre Topics, Modern Drama, Irish University Review, Irish Studies Review* and multiple edited volumes on contemporary theatre and performance.

Audrey McNamara was awarded her PhD in Drama from University College Dublin and now lectures there. Her monograph *Bernard Shaw: From Womanhood to Nationhood—The Irish Shaw* is forthcoming from Palgrave Macmillan. Her publications include essays on the work of Bernard Shaw, Conor McPherson, Enda Walsh and Benjamin Black. She wrote the programme note for the Abbey Theatre's production of *Pygmalion* (2014), and was a plenary speaker for the National Theatre (London) production of *Man and Superman*. She was guest co-editor with Nelson O'Ceallaigh Ritschel for *Shaw 36.1: Shaw and Money* (2016) and *Shaw and Modern Ireland* (Palgrave Macmillan, 2017). She is also guest co-editor of *The Eugene O'Neill Review Spring 2018 Edition*.

Erika Meyers earned her MA in Creative Writing from University College Dublin and her PhD from the University of Edinburgh. Her first book, *Strangers in America*, won first place in the Great Lakes Novel Contest.

James Moran is Professor of Modern English Literature and Drama at the University of Nottingham, UK. His recent books include *The Theatre of D.H. Lawrence* (2015); *The Theatre of Sean O'Casey* (2013); and—as co-editor with Neal Alexander—*Regional Modernisms* (2013).

Ciara L. Murphy is a PhD student at the Centre for Drama, Theatre and Performance at NUI Galway. Ciara's research is an interrogation of contemporary participatory performance practice in public space on the island of Ireland, with a specific focus on immersive and site-responsive performance. This research is supported by the Galway Doctoral Scholarship scheme. Ciara previously obtained a BA in Drama and English and an MA in Theatre and Performance Studies from University College Dublin.

Eimer Murphy received her primary degree is in film, but on graduation Eimer found her way into theatre work and has yet to find her way back. As a stage manager on Fringe shows with miniscule budgets, necessity forced Eimer to discover a previously unsuspected aptitude for making things, and it was this ability which led to her early work with Barabbas… the Company, where madcap invention, ingenuity and artistry were involved in the creation of almost every single prop. As a freelance stage manager/prop maker, Eimer made props for companies such as Barabbas, Calypso, TEAM, Opera Theatre Company, Rough Magic, Cois Ceim, Passion Machine, Lane Productions, and four successive Gaiety Pantomimes, before joining the Abbey Theatre to work alongside the legendary Stephen Molloy as a full-time prop maker/set dresser in 2007. She has recently completed an MA in Material Culture Design History in NCAD, where she submitted a thesis on props entitled *When Are We Getting the Real Thing?*—a title which initially perplexed her tutor but to which her colleagues instantly related.

Christopher Murray is Emeritus Professor of English, Drama and Film at University College Dublin. He is a former editor of *Irish University Review.* His books include *Twentieth-Century Irish Drama: Mirror up to Nation* (1997); *Seán O'Casey: Writer at Work, A Biography* (2004); and *The Theatre of Brian Friel: Tradition and Modernity* (2014). In addition, he has edited *Samuel Beckett: 100 Years, Centenary Essays* (2006); *Brian Friel: Essays, Diaries, Interviews 1964–1999* (1999); and *'Alive in Time': The Enduring Drama of Tom Murphy, New Essays* (2010), and he has also contributed many articles and chapters to journals and books on Irish drama and theatre history.

Cormac O'Brien is Assistant Professor of Anglo-Irish Drama in the School of English, Drama and Film at University College Dublin. He is a specialist in modern and contemporary Irish drama with a comparative focus on British and American theatre, investigating the relations between governance and citizenship, and gender, sexuality and national identities. Cormac further specializes in the interdisciplinary field of Medical Humanities, comparatively exploring Irish and other western cultural responses to HIV and AIDS, predominantly in drama, fiction, cinema and television. He has recently expanded this research into dramatic and literary representations of epidemics and pandemics. Cormac has published widely on masculinities and queer sexualities in Irish theatre, as well as on HIV and AIDS in Irish culture and performance, including in journals such as *Journal of Medical Humanities, The Irish Review, Irish University Review*, and *Theatre Research International.* Together with John M. Clum (of Duke University), Cormac has recently co-edited the collection, *Gender and Sexuality in the Theatre of Edward Albee* (2017). He is also co-editor, with Shonagh Hill, of a special edition Irish Society for Theatre Research's journal, *Performance Ireland: Gender, Sexuality, and the City.* He is currently preparing his first monograph, *Masculinities and Manhood in Irish Contemporary Irish Drama*, for publication in 2018.

Siobhán O'Gorman is a Senior Lecturer at the School of Fine & Performing Arts, University of Lincoln. She also has taught and researched theatre and performance at NUI Galway, Trinity College Dublin and the University of Derby. She held a Government of Ireland Postdoctoral Fellowship from 2013 to 2015. Her work has appeared in several books and such journals as *Scene, Irish Studies Review* and the *Journal of Adaptation in Film and Performance.* She is on the executive committee of the Irish Society for Theatre Research, and the editorial board of *Studies in Costume & Performance*, and was part of the curatorial team for Ireland's participation in the Prague Quadrennial 2015. She is co-editor of *Devised Performance in Irish Theatre: Histories and Contemporary Practice* (2015) and her monograph, *Theatre, Performance and Design: Scenographies in a Modernizing Ireland*, is forthcoming with Palgrave Macmillan.

Emilie Pine is Associate Professor of Modern Drama in the School of English, Drama and Film at University College Dublin. Emilie is editor of the *Irish*

University Review and Director of the Irish Memory Studies Network (www.irishmemorystudies.com). She is PI of the Irish Research Council New Horizons project *Industrial Memories* (2015–2018), and was a judge for the *Irish Times* Theatre Awards 2014. Emilie has published widely in the field of Irish studies, theatre and memory studies, including *The Politics of Irish Memory: Performing Remembrance in Contemporary Irish Culture* (Palgrave Macmillan, 2011) and *Performing in the Memory Marketplace: Witnessing in World Theatre* (forthcoming). Emilie is also the author of a collection of personal essays, *This is Not on the Exam* (2018).

Carole Quigley is a Teaching Fellow in the Department of Drama and Theatre Studies at Mary Immaculate College, Limerick. She recently completed her PhD dissertation in the Department of Drama at Trinity College Dublin. Her dissertation title is *The Fourth Wave Fights Back: Deconstructing the Performativity of Rape Culture Through Contemporary Irish Theatre, Performance and Society.* She graduated from an MPhil. in Theatre and Performance at Trinity College Dublin in 2015, and a BA in English with Drama from University College Dublin in 2013. Her specific research interests include; women on the contemporary Irish stage, the female body in performance, representations of feminisms and femininities in Ireland, sexual violence against women and the construction of a global "rape culture", and navigating the sexual and sexualized female performer.

Shaun Richards is Emeritus Professor of Irish Studies at Staffordshire University, UK. He is the author (with Chris Morash) of *Mapping Irish Theatre: Theories of Space and Place* (2013) and editor of the *Cambridge Companion to Twentieth-Century Irish Drama* (2004). He has published on Irish drama in major journals and edited collections, most recently a chapter on realism in early twentieth-century Irish drama in *The Oxford Handbook of Modern Irish Theatre* (2016).

Noelia Ruiz is a native of Barcelona now based in Dublin. She graduated from her research PhD programme in 2013 (University College Dublin) and also holds an MA in Directing for Theatre (University College Dublin, 2007). Her research interests focus on contemporary theatre and performance aesthetics and its processes of creation, having published a number of articles, including "Mapping Contemporary European Theatre(s): Reconsidering Notions of Devised and Postdramatic Theatre" in *Devised Performance in Irish Theatre: Histories and Contemporary Practice* (2015). She is an occasional lecture in University College Dublin and works as a freelance producer, digital marketer and communications manager for different artistic entities.

Melissa Sihra is Assistant Professor of Drama and Theatre Studies at Trinity College Dublin and editor of *Women in Irish Drama: A Century of Authorship and Representation* (Palgrave Macmillan). She is also co-editor (with Paul Murphy) of *The Dreaming Body: Contemporary Irish Theatre* and (with Pirkko Koski) of *The Global Meets the Local in Performance.* She researches in the field of women in Irish theatre, gender, feminism, Marina Carr and Augusta Gregory. She is former President of the Irish Society for Theatre Research (2011–2015).

Bernadette Sweeney has a PhD from the School of Drama, Trinity College, Dublin. Previously, she was lecturer at University College Cork's drama and theatre studies programme, and is now associate professor of theatre at the School of Theatre & Dance at the University of Montana. Practice as research has been a foundation of her work in her performance research, teaching and directing. She directed the 2014 Montana Repertory Theatre national tour and will direct for Bare Bait Dance later this year. Recent productions include *Translations*, *Romeo and Juliet* and a film adaptation of *Krapp's Last* Tape called *Be Again*.

She has published a monograph *Performing the Body in Irish Theatre* with Palgrave Macmillan, co-edited, with Marie Kelly, a collection *The Theatre of Tom Mac Intyre: Strays from the Ether*, and is currently co-editing *The Routledge Companion to Performance Practitioners* and *The Routledge Handbook of Studio Practice* with Franc Chamberlain. She was a founder member of the Irish Society for Theatre Research.

Ashley Taggart studied in the USA for many years, lecturing on topics such as *Irish Novel*, and *The Literature of the Northern Irish Troubles*. He has also taught courses in Creative Writing, Playwriting and Screenwriting, and has recently taken on a lecturing post at UCD. He has an MA and PhD in Literature from the University of York and has worked as a script editor and screenwriter. His films have been accepted by the Chicago Film Festival, the Cork Film Festival and the Boston Film Festival. He has also been a winner of the P.J. O'Connor Radio Drama Award. He has recently completed a book with Chris Comer on neuroscience and literature, entitled *Enchanting the Loom*, which is shortly to be published.

Rhona Trench is Programme Chair and lecturer in Performing Arts at IT Sligo. Her research interests include theatre design (set, sound and lighting), actor training in Ireland, women playwrights and performance, and the body in performance. Her books include *Bloody Living: The Loss of Self in the Plays of Marina* (2010); *Staging Thought: Essays on Irish Theatre, Scholarship and Practice* (edited, 2012) and *Blue Raincoat Theatre Company* (2015). She is Treasurer of the Irish Society for Theatre Research.

Shelley Troupe worked for a diverse range of Broadway and off-Broadway producers in New York City, including the Irish Repertory Theatre, the National Asian American Theatre Company, and Dodger Endemol. She completed her PhD in Irish Theatre at the National University of Ireland, Galway, and is an occasional lecturer at Maynooth University. Her publication contributions include the *Oxford Handbook of Modern Irish Theatre* and *The Great Irish Famine: Visual and Material Cultures*. In recent years, she has returned to theatre production as Social Media Manager for Co-Motion Media and as dramaturg for London's Ardent Theatre. A member of Ballina Textiles Group and Craftworks Mayo, she is also a craftsperson who specializes in bespoke lifestyle items.

Eva Urban is Senior Research Fellow at Queen's University, Belfast. Previously, she was a Région de Bretagne Postdoctoral Research Fellow at the Centre de Recherche Bretonne et Celtique (CRBC), Université de Rennes 2, France. She recently completed a British Academy Postdoctoral Research Fellowship at the University of Cambridge and is a Life Member of Clare Hall, Cambridge. The author of *Community Politics and the Peace Process in Contemporary Northern Irish Drama* (2011), she has also published many research articles in the journals *New Theatre Quarterly, Etudes Irlandaises* and *Caleidoscopio*, and essays in edited book collections. Publications include "Reification and Modern Drama: an Analysis, a Critique, and a Manifesto" (2016); "'Actors in the same Tragedy': Bertrand Russell, Humanism, and *The Conquest of Happiness*" (2015); "From the Enlightenment to the Berliner Ensemble: Lessing's *Nathan the Wise*" (2014).

Kevin Wallace is the Head of Department of Humanities and Arts Management in Dun Laoghaire Institute of Art, Design & Technology. He lectures in contemporary and twentieth-century Irish literature and drama. He has published on various British and Irish theatremakers, including Marina Carr, Sarah Kane, Conor McPherson, Katie Mitchell and Enda Walsh.

Ian R. Walsh is a Lecturer in Drama and Theatre Studies at NUI Galway. He has a PhD from University College Dublin and has published widely on Irish theatre in peer-reviewed journals and edited collections. In 2012, his monograph, *Experimental Irish Theatre: After W.B. Yeats*, was published by Palgrave Macmillan. He has co-edited (with Mary Caulfield) *The Theatre of Enda Walsh* (2015) and co-written (with Charlotte McIvor) *Contemporary Irish Theatre and Performance* (2018) for Palgrave Macmillan. Ian has been a Theatre Reviewer for *Irish Theatre Magazine* and RTE Radio 1 and has also worked as a freelance director of theatre and opera.

Eric Weitz lectures in Comedy and Acting at Trinity College Dublin. Publications include *Theatre & Laughter* (2016) and *The Cambridge Introduction to Comedy* (2009), as well as two edited collections, *For the Sake of Sanity: Doing Things with Humour in Irish Society* (2014) and *The Power of Laughter: Comedy and Contemporary Irish Theatre* (2004). He has contributed to *Performance Research*, the *Irish University Review*, the *Encyclopedia of Humor Studies* and the *Oxford Encyclopedia of Theatre and Performance.* He edited the *European Journal of Humour* Research Special Issue on "Humour and Social Media" (2016) and he has also contributed a chapter to the *Routledge Handbook of Language and Humor*, with the title "Online and Internet Humor" (2017). He is currently President of the Irish Society for Theatre and Performance Research.

Willie White has been Artistic Director of Dublin Theatre Festival since 2011 and was previously Artistic Director of Project Arts Centre, Dublin from 2002 to 2011. He was a board member of IETM, the international network for the contemporary performing arts, from 2010 to 2017 and its President for four years.

List of Figures

Children of the Revolution: 1916 in 2016

Introductions/Orientations

Eamonn Jordan and Eric Weitz

The *Palgrave Handbook of Contemporary Irish Theatre and Performance* was originally envisaged as a raft of commissioned chapters based on two general categories. First, a large collection of sustained scholarly arguments covering a thematized group of people, companies, theatres and other entities relevant to the volume's title. Second, a gathering of short pieces by practitioners reflecting upon process—creative and pragmatic—regarding a past project of personal import. This second type of chapter would afford a number of people whose work would likely come to attention in the longer pieces the chance to think back upon a seminal production in his or her professional journey and to try to articulate something of that moment through seasoned eyes. This two-pronged initial model was neat and straightforward, conveying a sense of organized academic industry that would contribute to a clean proposal.

We, the editors, aspired from the start to think beyond the strictures imposed by encyclopaedic coverage—beyond the usual analytical "hard borders" (to draw resonance from a phrase very much of the current moment as negotiations for Great Britain's exit from the European Union—known popularly as 'Brexit'—continue in early 2018, carrying important implications for the ease or difficulty of future border crossings between Northern Ireland and the Republic of Ireland), which we came to realize have been stamped on academic thought by familiar, timely and discrete critical positions. As will be evident from the chapter titles in the table of contents, we did not altogether abandon these critical lenses, but neither did we allow ourselves to be enslaved by them.

E. Jordan (✉)
School of English, Drama and Film, University College Dublin, Dublin, Ireland
e-mail: eamonn.jordan@ucd.ie

E. Weitz
School of Creative Arts, Trinity College Dublin, Dublin, Ireland
e-mail: weitzer@tcd.ie

E. Jordan, E. Weitz (eds.), *The Palgrave Handbook of Contemporary Irish Theatre and Performance*,
https://doi.org/10.1057/978-1-137-58588-2_1

Through our invitations to potential contributors we hoped to attract a spread of sensibilities, so that previously unexamined surfaces would come to light both directly and by refraction through other entries. As it happened, and not undesirably, our collection came to acquire a mind of its own, showing few signs of categorical orderliness. Gradually, and with patient support from Palgrave, we surrendered to a more open model of invitation and assignment for prospective chapters. From the beginning, we approached potential writers with chapter titles in mind, but we soon realized that the themes and stances of the chapters would be constrained by what we could think of in advance, so in some cases we invited potential contributors to propose subjects of interest to them and to comment, revise, reimagine or even propose alternatives. We relaxed our thinking on what subject matter or voice might be appropriate in a long or short chapter or, indeed, the necessity to meet a word count.

We came to realize that the practice-based, or practice-leaning, chapters were more valuable in their own right than we originally anticipated. Practitioners think as hard as they work and are diligent researchers. The recording and articulation of their experiences represent important contributions to the archive of performance-related literature and are of no less scholarly value than academic analysis or historical documentation of theatrical productions. We sought other insights from spectators and social observers, which merit attention and would fall through the cracks of a more regimented approach.

We decided that a productive consideration of contemporary theatre and performance could stand in the present while taking within its gaze the preceding sixty years or so (see below), reaching further back when fruitful. You will find chapters of varying lengths, some of which theorize, some of which historicize, some of which summarize, some of which scrutinize, and many of which do more than one of the above. You will find pieces guided by personal reflections of varying kinds and lengths, and not always from the people involved. We have, fortuitously, ended up with a wide range of generational voices from a practitioner-to-scholar spectrum.

The handbook, then, presents a certain amount of information and thought particular to theatre and performance in an Irish context, but would serve most handily as a spur to discussions on the subject. Each chapter comes with a full bibliography (when the use of sources applies), so in most cases the reader has ample opportunity to pursue avenues of interest.

We have abandoned any pretence towards a "complete" enumeration of practitioners, companies and other entities relevant to the title of this volume. The organizing principle of this handbook means that some people, theatres, companies and other features of the theatrical landscape receive attention from more than one viewpoint. We also acknowledge that the vicissitudes of the editorial process for a project like this have led to the omission of players we earnestly wish we had noted. We realize the strong possibility that blind spots will come to light only after the collection has acquired concrete form. We have tried to index as usefully as possible, but for the sake of space have adopted a general policy that declines most single-reference entries.

All of this brings us to the ultimate content of the handbook: a multiform sweep of theoretical, historical, practical and personal glimpses of aspects of a landscape roughly characterised as contemporary Irish theatre and performance. There is, of course, no prescribed or ideal method of approaching this volume. In an attempt to advance some manner of structure rather than a single string of fifty-nine chapters, we have adopted four section headings for the purpose of clustering pieces with certain affinities: Histories, Close-ups, Interfaces, and Reflections. Within each section, we have sought to order the chapters so that successive contributions can speak to one another; in other cases, we have consciously assigned seemingly tangential chapters to different sections. Some readers may wade into a particular section, while others may prefer to see where their curiosity takes them, as this or that chapter title strikes their fancies. Having by this point offered some background, rationale and advice, we will supply some general context for the chapters that follow.

Theatrical Contexts

This part of the introduction offers a brief overview of the political, socio-economic and cultural contexts of the period under analysis, it makes some tentative observations about texts and performances, and signals some of the evolutions that have taken place over the sixty or so years under the focus of this collection. We also point to existing publications that could help broaden, deepen and otherwise supplement the perspectives articulated by the chapters in this handbook. (We do not provide a summary of the volume's chapters, sometimes undertaken for a compilation like this.)

Undoubtedly, the history of Irish theatre is complex. Publications in the field take as their starting points the establishment of the Irish Literary Theatre in 1899 by Augusta Gregory, Edward Martyn, and W.B. Yeats; the establishment of Inghinidhe na hÉireann/Daughters of Ireland in 1900 by Maude Gonne; or the founding of the Ulster Branch of the Irish Literary Theatre by Bulmer Hobson and David Parkhill in 1902, reconstituted as the Ulster Literary Theatre in 1904.[1] Most commentators focus on the foundation in 1904 of the Irish National Theatre Society—or as it is better known, the Abbey Theatre—by Gregory and Yeats.[2] There is, of course, a far longer history that is not limited to the establishment of theatre venues in Dublin from the early seventeenth-century onward.[3] This would cover other forms of indigenous theatrical practice including, in addition to plays, the games, rituals and ceremonies that come under the broader rubric of performance.[4]

However, because of the local and international attention warranted by the work of Augusta Gregory, Sean O'Casey, John Millington Synge and W.B. Yeats during the Abbey Theatre's formative years, and because of the ongoing legacies of these writers, the early Abbey is the most functional starting point for many scholars. The controversies surrounding the premieres of Synge's *The Playboy of the Western World* (1907) and O'Casey's *The Plough and the Stars* (1926) remain critical talking points to this day; each is fascinating for different reasons, as each exposes particular cultural and political tensions.

Outraged responses to the first staging of Synge's *Playboy* and the riots that followed seem to have stemmed from tensions in the play that threatened the values and perspectives that were politically, religiously and socially dominant in Ireland at the time. Given that O'Casey's *Plough* offers a harsh view of revolutionary nationalism to which many did not subscribe, it is understandable that it caused such offence when it was first staged. It continues to exercise critics, many of whom have allegiances to a different brand of politics to O'Casey's. Yet, for some critics, this period produced a notable body of work limited by its allegiances to cultural nationalism, and by its subservience to the agenda of the elite classes.[5] Dublin-born Samuel Beckett's writings for theatre were hugely influenced by works of Synge and O'Casey, which he saw during his early adult life in Dublin.[6] The influences of Irish-born playwrights Oscar Wilde and George Bernard Shaw upon world theatre remain significant, yet, interestingly, their Irish backgrounds are often occluded, repressed or even erased in discussions and analysis of their works.

Although anything but a unified tradition, the overall standing of the work of all of these playwrights is evident not only in its initial impact, but also in the influence it has had on international peers and those who followed. Enticing opportunities and challenges remain to those staging their plays across a range of contemporary contexts up to, and more than, a hundred years later.[7] Their works have been interpreted in various ways, including gendered interventions in the staging of *The Importance of Being Earnest*, or the supplementation of texts with contemporary features, as Seán Holmes did with a production of *The Plough and the Stars* at the Abbey in 2016. To date, however, productions of their works are seldom reconceived with significant textual deconstructions or reinventions. Bisi Adigun and Roddy Doyle's version of *The Playboy of the Western World* (2007) is a good example of such a reinvention, as they relocated the play to contemporary West Dublin, where Christy Mahon becomes Christopher Malomo, a Nigerian refugee.

Their longevity may well account for the plays' ability to emanate an aura of relevance through successive generations, as well as the reassurance, comfort and even pride that has arisen from people's familiarity with the texts. But this relevance is surely also a result of the complexity of the writing, the challenges they pose for actors and directors, and the ways that the dilemmas and conflicts faced down by their characters materialize to striking effect under difficult and fraught circumstances. In addition, there are notable and compelling intricacies of form in these writings, often realised through an innovative mingling of genres by the likes of Gregory, O'Casey and Beckett. Critical responses to this body of work are informed by diverse theoretical frames. The plays by Gregory, O'Casey and Beckett have proven rich and diverse enough to bear the burden of persistent and varied critical scrutiny.

Those who followed the early Abbey writers, including Teresa Deevy, Denis Johnston, Mary Manning and Lennox Robinson, each became canonical figures in different ways. The Northern Irish playwrights worth noting from this early period include Joseph Campbell, Alice Milligan, George Shiels, St. John Ervine, Rutherford Mayne, Gerald MacNamara and Joseph Tomelty. The eventual founding of the Lyric Players Theatre in 1951 by Mary O'Malley in Belfast was also a significant initiative.

The Briefest Political Contexts

The writings and performances of the early twentieth century ran in tandem with—and some would argue influenced, if not shaped—the wider political realities that were emerging across the island. The rebellion of Easter of 1916 saw a bitter and overwhelming defeat for the Irish revolutionaries. However, the poor treatment of those captured by or who had surrendered to the British forces swung public opinion towards both the rebels and the revolutionary act itself. In the main, public opinion had initially been hostile towards the revolution. The Government of Ireland Act of 1920 would partition the island and The Anglo-Irish Treaty of 1922 that followed the War of Independence (1919–1921) led to a harrowing civil war between two rival factions. One side could not countenance a divided island under any conditions. The other saw the treaty as the best deal available, a stepping stone to a united Ireland.[8]

The twenty-six county Free State was a complex socio/political entity, shaped by its joy in ridding itself of colonial subjugation after close to 800 years of occupation. It also resulted in power transitioning from the British state to an indigenous Irish bourgeois/elite, a cohort keen to serve its own agenda by reinforcing its rank and status and perpetuating its own privileges. As the nascent state evolved, conservative social and isolationist economic policies and the persistence of a mutually self-serving church/state relationship meant that socio-economic advances were negligible for most citizens.

Indeed, the failure to meet the aspirations of the proclamation of 1916, or to instigate the ambitions of the 1922 Constitution, left the country in a conformist position. The Constitution of 1937, despite its rigor and many fine ambitions, remains a bugbear into the twenty-first century, particularly because of how it reinforces gender hierarchies and promotes patriarchal subservience. Yet there has been far less critical probing into how this Constitution substantiates gross material inequalities. Ireland's neutrality during the Second World War still divides opinion.

While the region of Ulster experienced a more advanced industrialization, especially throughout the nineteenth century, the establishment of the

Northern Irish state was a major turning point in the history of the island. The province of Ulster was divided, three counties to be included within the Free State, and six counties would remain part of the United Kingdom.

After the Second World War, the political situation in Northern Ireland was fraught and complex. There was an intermittent campaign by the Irish Republican Army, political practices such as Gerrymandering (the shaping of political boundaries to ensure unionist election dominance), a series of state practices that left many Catholics and Nationalists discriminated against when accessing healthcare, education, employment and social welfare provision. Sectarianism, civic unrest, internment, and crucial events such as (what became known as) Bloody Sunday on 28 January 1972 (the killing of fourteen people and the wounding of many others by the British army during their attack on a civil rights protest) led to a sectarian political situation that seemed intractable.[9]

The Troubles, as the period from 1968 to 1994 came to be known, saw over 3,000 people die, twice as many injured, and exponentially more impacted by violence.[10] The Downing Street Declaration of 1994 and the Good Friday Agreement of 1998 were landmarks in a Peace Process that brought ceasefires from Loyalist and Republican paramilitaries, the decommissioning of weapons, and a series of protracted negotiations that led to an evolving political settlement. Peace brought huge dividends, even if the formal cessation of the conflict did little to heal either community divisions or the wounds of many—especially those bereaved, injured or traumatized. Indeed, conflict situations elsewhere have since looked to Northern Ireland for the strategies employed in the evolution of a political resolution.

During the Troubles and even during the post-conflict period, many Northern Irish plays remained occupied with contentious ideologies, sectarianism, breaches of human rights, the sinister actions effectively sanctioned by the state, the intransigence of some political sensibilities, and the lingering influence of paramilitary organizations and their associated criminal elites. Legacy issues continue to complicate the political situation. As Mark Phelan notes, "[i]f Troubles drama has been largely defined by the expectation that artists deal with the conflict, perhaps post-conflict theatre in the North can be similarly defined by an expectation that it should play some sort of role in the processes of truth and reconciliation".[11] Teya Sepunick's Theatre of Witness project is a pertinent example. Troubles plays are not going away; neither are they the sole prerogative of Irish writers. English-born Jez Butterworth's *The Ferryman* (2017), set in 1981 during the Hunger Strikes, deals with the disappeared, paramilitary intimidation, and scrutinizes but also maintains a particular sympathy for a republican position.

Stacey Gregg's work includes and moves well beyond the Northern Irish conflict. Her work in *Shibboleth* (2015) deals with peace-wall extensions, migration and post-conflict politics; *Overdrive* (2013) considers medical and technological augmentation; *Perve* (2011) dramatizes the impact of deception and manipulation through the use of social media platforms; and *Scorch* (2015) is a monologue about gender curiosity and the legal implications of gender fraud, narrated by a female teenager, Kes, who wants to be a boy—and deals with how Kes establishes an online relationship with a young woman, who assumes Kes is male.

Poverty and mass emigration were significant features in the Republic of Ireland of the 1950s. The end of that decade saw a shift in economic policy, and the Seán Lemass-led Government oversaw a period of industrial development. This was prompted by a key document written by civil servant, T.K. Whitaker, which led to the First Programme for Economic Expansion under the Industrial Development Act in 1958. Donogh O'Malley's announcement of universal free second-level education in 1966 was a game changer in terms of educational access and social mobility.

Ireland's accession to the European Economic Community in 1972 was another important advancement. The global oil crisis of the early 1970s led to another recessionary period in Ireland. Major government indebtedness saw the 1980s blighted by economic stagnation, industrial unrest, high levels of inflation, substantial levels of unemployment, and, again, mass emigration. In the early part of the 1990s, the Republic of Ireland went through a hugely significant economic boom; this period was euphemistically known as the Celtic Tiger (1993–2008). The boom brought radical changes to society, which included a Peace Process dividend, more liberal-leaning social legislation, a decrease in the influence of a Catholic church that had been blighted by scandal, enhanced education provision, better employment opportunities thanks to Direct Foreign Investment, rises in standards of living, an increase in immigration, better travel opportunities and extensive globalization. Most of these changes were welcomed. Many citizens were the first generation in their families to own their own homes, and, temporarily, emigration was no longer an imperative but an option.

However, access to cheap credit from international money markets, and the opportunity to increase profitability, turned the banking sector from its traditional prudent orientation into a reckless, often rogue, industry. Government policy was increasingly driven by neo-liberal ideology, leading to less regulation, lower taxes, and a reluctance for economic intervention by the state, all of which increasingly left transactions (and not only financial ones) at the mercy of market mechanisms. Prosperity for all proved a myth—all boats did not rise, by any means. Poverty was not eradicated, even though economic indicators trumpeted a boom time.

The greed, narcissism and conspicuous consumption associated with this period have been well outlined, but it is worth considering how reckless behaviour and excesses could have been prompted by the fact that previous generations never had access to such material resources or economic freedoms. The delusion that things could only get better was constantly reinforced by media soundbites and government pronouncements. And so, the global financial crisis of 2008 and the bursting of the Irish property bubble led to economic collapse in late 2008, although key economic indicators were already flagging problems at least a year earlier. A bank guarantee was offered by the government to depositors and those bond holders who lent money to the bank. A massive bank bailout, huge increases in national debt, suffocating personal debt for many, negative equity, a significant rise in unemployment figures, business and personal insolvencies and, again, mass emigration were the fallout from the economic collapse.

A temporary loss of economic sovereignty ensued. After the government requested intervention and financial bailout from the Troika (the European Union, European Central Bank and the International Monetary Fund) Ireland's national debt spiralled, and whatever rainy-day funds had been squirreled away disappeared. Inadequate governance, prompted by the persistence of a neo-liberal rationale, was a substantial part of the problem. Government did little to stabilize the economy or to put a halt to the rampant property speculation that gripped the country.

While Northern Irish plays appeared to be Troubles-obsessed in the main, in contrast few plays that premiered in the Republic during the Celtic Tiger period spoke directly to this period of plenty. Indeed, the most successful plays of this period were historic in focus, and poverty-orientated in their dramaturgies. However, the post-boom environment saw multiple works all too willing to dramatize the fallout from the economic collapse. McPherson's works, *The Veil* (2011), even though it is set in 1822, and *The Night Alive* (2013) are pertinent examples of post-boom plays.

Dramaturgical and Performance Practices

For the sake of clarity and convenience, we identify the contemporary period of Irish Theatre and performance as starting from the post-Second World War era,[12] even if it is only from the late 1950s and early 1960s that a significant new generation of writers emerged.[13] Brendan Behan, Eugene McCabe, Brian Friel, John B. Keane, Thomas Kilroy, Hugh Leonard, and Tom Murphy were the most prominent figures to arise during this early contemporary period. These playwrights would have their work widely produced, garnering substantial critical acclaim nationally and internationally. Behan's plays brought a remarkable vivacity to the stage, partly prompted by his work with Joan Littlewood at the Theatre Royal, Stratford East in London. Kilroy's writings stand out for many reasons, not least for his inclination to allow his dramaturgy to be open to the influence of radical theatrical forms, ranging from Brechtian technique to Bunraku puppet theatre. Keane is noted for transposing a basic naturalism by way of folk drama, and Leonard is respected not only for his willingness to experiment with form, for his championing of comedy, but also because of his commitments to serve as the Abbey's Literary Editor (1976–1977) and as programme director of the Dublin Theatre Festival (1979). Of course, Leonard's play *Da* (1973) won four Tony Awards in 1979.

In Northern Ireland, the controversy surrounding Sam Thompson's *Over the Bridge* (1960) was an important historical event, arising from the play's left-leaning ideology and exposure of rampant sectarianism in the pre-Troubles era.

As Ophelia Byrne notes, "[i]n the difficult 1970s and early 1980s, plays were staged at the Lyric by writers such as John Boyd, Patrick Galvin, Christina Reid, Graham Reid, Stewart Parker and Martin Lynch which directly addressed the socio-political realities around them".[14]

Stewart Parker exerted a profound impact upon playwriting on this island in a life cut tragically short by cancer, writing with inspired dramaturgical invention from a Northern Irish orientation, from his first stage play, *Spokesong* (1975), and including *Catchpenny Twist* (1977), *Northern Star* (1984) and *Pentecost* (1987).[15] Later, Anne Devlin's blending of gender into class antagonisms and sectarian politics in plays like *Ourselves Alone* (1985) and *After Easter* (1994), relies on mystical and imaginative ways of evading or circumventing the real by theatricalizing a shunt into an alternative dimension, to cross borders and boundaries. (It should be emphasized that a simple Green/Orange binary oversimplifies the politics we are discussing—there are, of course, multiple communities in existence, not ones that simply align as Nationalist/Republican/Catholic and Loyalist/Unionist/Protestant.[16])

Brian Friel and Frank McGuinness regularly positioned their writing in relation to Northern Ireland, its histories and conflicts, and the consequences of British imperialism. The writings of Murphy and Friel stand out for various reasons: Both forged extensive careers, both kept challenging themselves as writers, and both became benchmark writers for so many others in Ireland and elsewhere. Not surprisingly, several chapters in this handbook include reflections upon their work.

To that end, Friel's *Philadelphia, Here I Come!* (1964) is an important landmark in twentieth-century Irish theatre. Within the frame of a more traditional play, it splits between two actors the play's main character, Gar O'Donnell, represented as Gar Private and Gar Public. Friel's *Faith Healer* (1979) is another groundbreaking play, which established the "monologue play" as a popular contemporary form. Three characters offer different accounts of key events in their shared lives, and two characters narrate from beyond the grave. And of course, *Translations* (1980) and *Dancing at Lughnasa* (1990) are works of world renown and influence. The former is known for the conceit that the Irish characters are supposedly speaking in their native Gaelic tongue, which the English characters cannot understand, whereas in performance, they are speaking not Gaelic, but Hiberno-English. The latter takes a conventional family situation and distorts it with acts of narrative recollection that are inconsistent to the extent that they embody the reassurance, need, unreliability and instability of memory itself. Friel's role in the establishment of the Field Day Theatre company with Stephen Rea is also significant. The company's remit was to intervene in and reimagine the politics of Northern Ireland and the Republic of Ireland. The Nationalist/Republican leanings of the company led to critical disparagements from some quarters.

Murphy has had a varied career, writing initially for an amateur group in Tuam, Co. Galway, before having *A Whistle in the Dark* produced in London at the Theatre Royal in 1961, after its rejection by the Abbey. (The influence of *A Whistle in the Dark* on Harold Pinter's *The Homecoming* (1968) has been considered by many scholars.) Murphy's groundbreaking work like the Brechtian *Famine* (1968) and the surrealistic/impressionistic *A Crucial Week in the Life of a Grocer's Assistant* (1969), are notable and important dramaturgical experiments. Later in his career, productions of *Conversations on a Homecoming* (1983) and *Bailegangaire* (1985) would see Murphy as a house playwright (Writer-in-Association) for Druid Theatre Company. Geraldine Aron is another playwright who had a number of plays premiered by Druid, including *Same Old Moon* (1984), *The Donahue Sisters* (1990) and *My Brilliant Divorce* (2001).

Druid was set up by director/playwright Garry Hynes and two actors, Mick Lally and Marie Mullen; they had made their initial mark with a memorable production of Synge's *Playboy of the Western World* (1975) and subsequent stagings of the same play in the early 1980s.[17] Sadly, Lally passed away in 2010, and to this day Mullen plays a hugely influential role in the company's many productions; Hynes, apart from a short stint as the Artistic Director of the Abbey Theatre, remains at the helm of Druid. The emergence of Druid parallels a shift in the policy of the Republic's Arts Council (An Chomhairle Ealaíon) to increase its support for theatre in the regions. Many other companies were to benefit from such a change in policy, as chapters in this *Handbook* explore.

The 1980s, 1990s and early 2000s would see almost all of the writers mentioned above continuing to write and would also see the emergence of a broad and diverse cohort of writers, including: Sebastian Barry, Dermot Bolger, John Breen, Patricia Burke Brogan, Mary Elizabeth Burke-Kennedy, Pom Boyd, Marina Carr, Lucy Caldwell, Daragh Carville, Amy Conroy, Anne Devlin, Neil Donnelly, Claire Dowling, Roddy Doyle, Dave Duggan, Grace Dyas, Bernard Farrell, Stella Feehily, Gerard Mannix Flynn, Stacey Gregg, Michael Harding, Declan Hughes, David Ireland, Rosemarie Jenkinson, Marie Jones, Jennifer Johnston, Deirdre Kinahan, Tim Loane, Martin Lynch, Owen McCafferty, Martin McDonagh, Rosaleen McDonagh, Lisa McGee, Frank McGuinness, Tom Mac Intyre, Una McKevitt, Philip McMahon, Nicola McCarthy, Conor McPherson, Paul Mercier, Gary Mitchell, Jimmy Murphy, Jim Nolan, Máiréad Ní Ghráda, Joe O'Byrne, Antoine Ó Flatharta, Donal O'Kelly, Mark O'Rowe, David Rudkin, Ursula Rani Sarma, Christina Reid, Graham Reid, Arthur Riordan, Billy Roche, Stewart Parker, Stefanie Preissner, Jim and Peter Sheridan, Abbie Spallen, Gerard (Gerry) Stembridge, Colin Teevan, Enda Walsh, Michael West and Vincent Woods.

As this is a script-driven writing tradition—and as critical commentaries grew up around these key playwrights over the past decades—the inputs of directors, theatre managers, actors, designers and performers are often signalled and individual productions referenced, but such analysis places insufficient emphasis on performance as a central factor. There are a few obvious reasons for this: much of the criticism grew out of those teaching in English and Languages Departments in universities; and, apart from production images and reviews, in some cases there is no record of a performance event. Texts offer the most accurate and stable record of a performance. The absence of critical methodologies to deal with the ephemerality of performance proved another obstacle. Usage of and access to video recordings of productions changed approaches, but still could not preserve some of the vital elements of live performance—neither could they address the night-to-night variation of a performance text and the on-the-spot audience response. Analysis of Irish plays too easily and invariably spoke to and of Ireland, another limiting perspective.

Having attempted a roll call of playwrights, above, the emergence of theatre companies and theatres from the 1970s forward is also vital to discussions of contemporary Irish theatre. Such a listing would include ANU, An Taibhdhearc, Barabbas, Bedrock, Bickerstaffe, Big Telly, Blue Raincoat, Branar, Brokentalkers, Calypso, Charabanc, CoisCéim, Collapsing Horse, Company SJ, Corcadorca, Druid, Dubbeljoint, Field Day, Fabulous Beast, Fishamble, Galloglass, Glasshouse, Graffiti, Irish Modern Dance Theatre, Island, Kabosh, Loose Canon, Macnas, Meridian, Passion Machine, Muted Cupid, Red Kettle, Rough Magic, Operating Theatre, Ouroborous, Pan Pan, Performance Corporation, Prime Cut, Replay, Smashing Times, Siamsa Tíre, the National Folk Theatre, Storytellers, TEAM Educational Theatre, Tinder Box, The Corn Exchange, THEATREclub, THISISPOPBABY, Wet Paint, and Yew Tree. Companies like Desperate Optimists and Gare St Lazare Players were formed outside Ireland by Irish performance makers.

Directors, designers and actors are of equal consequence in any survey of Irish Theatre. The importance of people like Hilton Edwards and Tyrone Guthrie to Friel's development are well documented, and we have briefly signalled the significance of Hynes's contribution to Murphy's career already. Patrick Mason's contribution to Irish theatre cannot be undervalued, having directed the premieres of work as varied and significant as Kilroy's *Talbot's Box* (1977), McGuiness's *The Factory Girls* (1982) and *Observe the Sons of Ulster Marching Towards the Somme* (1985), Murphy's *The Gigli Concert* (1983), Stewart Parker's *Pentecost* (1987), Thomas Kilroy's *The Secret Fall of Constance Wilde* (1997) and Marina Carr's *By the Bog of Cats* (1998). The production for which he received most acclaim is Friel's *Dancing at Lughnasa* (1990). Mason also served two terms as artistic director of the Abbey theatre (1993–1999).[18]

Alongside Mason, actor Tom Hickey and designers Bronwen Casson and later Monica Frawley, were crucial collaborators with Tom Mac Intyre. Inasmuch as the island of Ireland is the holding frame for much of the work discussed here, it is imperative to see that work not only within the confines of a national tradition and context, but also from an international perspective—especially as globalized culture has led to the increasing problematisation of national identities. Like Irish-American Deirdre O'Connell, who brought her Stanislavsky-based training experiences from New York to Ireland, many people who make or have made theatre in Ireland were born elsewhere. Key figures like the Gate Theatre's Hilton Edwards and Micheál Mac Liammóir, born Alfred Willmore, who reinvented himself as Irish, were born in England. Likewise, Patrick Mason and Selina Cartmell, the new Artist Director of the Gate Theatre, were born in England. And writer/

actor/scholar Elizabeth Kuti, has written about the challenges of being born outside Ireland, yet is perceived to be working within that tradition.[19]

The categorization of Martin McDonagh as an Irish playwright has raised all kinds of questions, even objections, not least from the writer himself, who was born in London to Irish-born parents. A writer like Gary Mitchell, born in Belfast in the unionist tradition, unsurprisingly does not think of himself as an Irish writer.[20] Mitchell's early career is notable for work staged by the Abbey Theatre. Somewhat differently, early in his career Conor McPherson refuted the notion that he was an Irish playwright, although more recently he has regarded this self-positioning as naive and has become increasingly aware of how his Irish background shaped his work. Two notable productions of *The Weir*—at the Royal Court in 1997 directed by Ian Rickson and at the Donmar Warehouse in 2013 directed by Josie Rourke—had actors with Irish and non-Irish backgrounds, had design inputs from non-Irish practitioners, and were seen by audiences around the world. A play written by an Irish writer and set in Ireland becomes something altogether different when staged by companies with some or no associations with the country, or with little concern for its "Irishness" (in, for example, productions of Marina Carr's work in the Netherlands or McDonagh's plays in Turkey or the Middle-East).

In both past and current times, the reputations of Irish companies have been enhanced by productions toured abroad. The Abbey Theatre toured to Britain and America almost from its founding. The reputation of the Gate Theatre is partially built on the successes of its tours, again going back to its early years, under the stewardship of Hilton Edwards and Micheál Mac Liammóir, who took work to Europe from the early 1930s forward. More recently under Michael Colgan's directorship, the Gate mounted key productions of plays by Brian Friel, Harold Pinter and Sean O'Casey to be staged in Dublin and abroad. The Gate's co-productions of Conor McPherson's plays with the Royal Court is also significant.

Part of Field Day's remit was to tour work to non-traditional venues across the island; they also brought their work to London in partnership with the Hampstead Theatre, Royal Court and the National Theatre. Apart from the Abbey, Gate and Druid Theatres, companies like Charabanc, the Lyric, Galloglass, Rough Magic, Dubbeljoint and Passion Machine brought work to various London venues, such as Riverside Studios, Drill Hall, The Bush, Tricycle, Rough Court, Donmar Warehouse, and Almedia Theatres. Work also toured beyond London, as well, Mac Intyre's plays going to Russia, for example.[21] Pan Pan have produced work in China, while Company SJ have transplanted site-specific and environmental readings of Beckett to New York City.

Druid Theatre Company has always been active in touring. In the 1980s, tours of Synge's *Playboy of the Western World* enhanced the company's reputation, and recently their production of Enda Walsh's *The Walworth Farce* (2006) toured to Britain, Australia, New Zealand, Canada, and the United States. Druid's concept projects, DruidSynge (2004) and DruidMurphy (2012) have been large scale, ambitious initiatives, with DruidShakespeare (2015) touring Ireland and New York.

Apart from Druid's co-productions, with the Royal Court, of McDonagh's *Leenane* trilogy, and the transfers of *The Beauty Queen of Leenane* and *The Lonesome West* to Broadway, Druid has twice toured with McDonagh's *The Cripple of Inishmaan* in 2008–2009 and 2011.[22] Additionally, Hynes's twenty-year anniversary production of McDonagh's *The Beauty Queen of Leenane* toured across America and Ireland in 2016. The Druid/Royal Court co-production of Marina Carr's unnerving work, *On Raftery's Hill* (2000), staged at the Kennedy Centre in Washington DC, was programmed as part of a celebration of Irish arts (a thematic umbrella under which it may not have stood entirely comfortably).

Pat Kinevane's *Silent* (2011), directed by Jim Culleton for Fishamble, has toured Europe, the US and Australia, picking up numerous accolades including an Olivier Award in 2016. Brokentalker's *The Blue Boy* (2011) and Pan Pan's shows, including *The Crumb Trail* (2008) and *The Seagull and Other Birds* (2014) are other examples of work that has toured productively. As suggested above, Pan Pan has regularly collaborated with international partners, and their work in Germany and China is notable. When such non-traditional work by the likes of Brokentalkers or Pan Pan is performed in Europe, it stands up to the scrutiny of peers and critics. It is received not simply as work grounded or inflected by its country of origin, but lauded for how it affirms, aligns with (or fails to) and contests broader international theatrical practices and processes.

Versions/Adaptations/Appropriations

Writers and directors adapt, translate or perform versions of existing work for a variety of reasons. Sometimes it may be out of curiosity, at others it is about allowing another's work to influence their creative writing or to pursue a thematic connection; it may be about working on a project that boosts their reputation; and, of course, it may be pragmatically opportune to undertake a commission that is financially rewarding.

Adaptations are likely to cast marquee actors in central roles if the work aspires to commercial reward or artistic prestige. Staging adaptations of tried and tested work is presumably less risky than performances of new writing. The adaptations of Greek drama by Irish writers has been an important enterprise in the history of Irish theatre. Indeed, the adaptations of Greek plays by Tom Paulin, Derek Mahon and Seamus Heaney were central to the Field Day initiative. Greek drama has been used to comment on the conflict in Northern Ireland, and this use has been addressed by many commentators to date. Somewhat differently, Marina Carr has suffused her dramaturgy with various Greek myths, and Billy Roche has done likewise.

Of contemporary significance, Frank McGuinness's versions of Greek plays commissioned by Irish and English companies has been prominent achievements. His version of *Electra*, featuring Zoë Wanamaker at the Donmar Warehouse in 1997, and more recently the Old Vic in 2015 with Kristin Scott Thomas, were highly regarded productions, as was his version of *Oedipus* (2008), which starred Ralph Fiennes at London's National Theatre. McGuinness's reputation has been bolstered by his versions of Ibsen and Chekhov plays, as well, and his work on Ibsen in particular has been important, including versions of *Peer Gynt* (1988), *A Doll's House* (1996), *Rosmersholm* (1987) and *John Gabriel Borkman* (2010).[23] Friel, Murphy and Kilroy have also adapted a range of classic plays by Ibsen and Chekhov. Kilroy's *Christ Deliver Us!* (2010) at the Abbey, inspired by Frank Wedekind's *Spring Awakening*, is a notable transformation of a classic work into an Irish context.

Adaptations of novels are also popular. Tolstoy's *Anna Karenina* was recently adapted by Carr (2016), Saltykov-Shchedrin's *The Golovlyov Family* reworked as *The Last Days of a Reluctant Tyrant* (2009) by Tom Murphy, and Friel's work on both Turgenev's *Father and Sons* (1987) and *A Month in the Country* has been widely produced. Dostoevsky's *The Brothers Karamazov* (1992) was adapted by Enda Walsh as *Delirium* (2008); Michael West adapted Vladimir Nabokov's *Lolita* (2002) for the stage as did Declan Hughes for Wilkie Collins's *The Woman in White* (1986); while Olwen Fouéré's *riverrun* (2013) derives directly from an extract of James Joyce's *Finnegans Wake*. Blue Raincoat's production history includes multiple adaptations of various novels and biographies, directed by Niall Henry, with Joycelyn Clarke playing a major role as adaptor/dramaturg on work ranging from Lewis Carroll to Flann O'Brien.

Across Platforms

Increasingly over the past few decades actors have sought to ply their trade on stage, screen and television, while writers, directors and designers increasingly move between various media. Similarly, it is not uncommon for practitioners to wear different hats, working interchangeably as actors, directors, dramaturgs, playwrights, novelists, poets and screenwriters. A handful of examples are sufficient here. Hugh Leonard has had success across various artforms, including radio, fiction, journalism, television and film. Sebastian Barry is an accomplished novelist, poet and playwright. Emma Donoghue is a novelist and playwright. Paula Meehan is foremost a poet, yet she has made some important interventions in theatre. Gerard Stembridge has moved fluidly between theatre, television, film and fiction writing. Frank McGuinness has always published poetry and written for television and screen, he has had two novels published, *Arimathea* (2013) and *The Woodcutter and his Family* (2017). Stella Feehily started out as an actor and became a playwright, as has Elaine Murphy, Pat Kinevane and many others. Pauline McLynn, a veteran actor of stage, radio and screen—perhaps most widely known for her portrayal of Mrs Doyle in the *Father Ted* (1995–1998) television series—is also a novelist. Richard Dormer is a particularly good example: he trained as an actor, is remembered for a remarkable, award-winning performance as Younger Pyper in McGuinness's *Observe the Sons of Ulster Marching Towards the*

Somme at the Abbey in 2004, wrote plays like *Hurricane* (2003) and *Drum Belly* (2012) and continues to take major roles in film and television, including *Games of Thrones* (2013, ongoing) and *Fortitude* (2015). Additionally, Ian McElhinney has worked as an actor and director, as has Adrian Dunbar and others.

Marina Carr's recent work includes a translation of Verdi's *Rigoletto* (2015) for Opera Theatre Company, and *Mary Gordon* (2016), an oratorio with music by Brian Irvine and Neil Martin. Apart from his work as artistic director, producer, director and actor with Arambe Productions, Bisi Adigun worked in television, and, holding a Ph.D., has taught in academic and community contexts. Recently, Stacey Gregg wrote three episodes of *Riviera* (2017) the Sky mini-series, she is also an actor, poet and screenwriter. Ursula Rani Sarma wrote for the television series *Raw* and soap opera, *Red Rock* (2015–2017). Mark O'Halloran, who was often seen in leading stage roles in the early part of his acting career, wrote films like *Adam and Paul* (2004) (in which he also starred), *Garage* (2007) and *Viva* (2016). He also wrote the much-discussed play *Trade* (2011).[24] Then there is someone like Úna Kavanagh, who has worked across a phenomenal number of forms, including painting, sculpture, performance art, script-writing, music composition, theatre, film and television.

Mark O'Rowe wrote the screenplays for *Intermission* (2003) and *Perrier's Bounty* (2009). Martin McDonagh may now be known more for his film than his theatre work.[25] Conor McPherson has been involved in many film projects.[26] His three-part drama *Paula* was broadcast by the BBC/RTE in 2017. His *Girl from the North Country* opened at the Old Vic, London, in July 2017 to critical acclaim. This piece of work includes a selection of Bob Dylan songs, and was a project initiated by Dylan's management company. Enda Walsh's collaborations also have been numerous. He worked with Steve McQueen on the film *Hunger* (2008), on the musical adaptation of the film *Once* (2011) and on the stage version of Roald Dahl's *The Twits* (2015). Additionally, Walsh's work with David Bowie on *Lazarus* (2016) and Donnacha Dennehy on the operas, *The Last Hotel* (2015) and *The Second Violinist* (2017), attests to his versatility. Walsh, McPherson and Mark O'Rowe have all directed their own theatre work, with the latter two directing the work of others. Finally, John Crowley had initial experience as a writer and director of theatre, with companies like Bickerstaff, the Abbey, and later in London at the RSC and National Theatre, followed by work on Broadway. He has also directed episodes of the television series *True Detective* (2015) and films like *Intermission* (2003) and *Brooklyn* (2015). Derry-born Lisa McGee came to prominence as a playwright, but is now better known for her television work on *Raw* (RTE) (2008–13), *Being Human* (BBC) (2010–12), *London Irish* (2013) and *Derry Girls* (2018) (both Channel 4).

A different example is the career of Jo Mangan, who serves as the Artistic Director of The Performance Corporation, is Director of Carlow Arts Festival and Chairs the National Campaign for the Arts. She also works in creative consultancy and served as the International Programmer for Limerick's City of Culture. The likes of Róisín McBrinn, Caroline Byrne and Oonagh Murphy have established active directing careers in Britain, as well as closer to home.

Cross-Cultural Dynamics

Irish performance makers have long been influenced by practices from other countries and cultures. Earlier writers like Gregory, Yeats, Synge and O'Casey allowed influences as varied as French comedy, melodrama, Nôh Theatre, Shakespeare, music hall, and Adolphe Appia and Edward Gordon Craig's work with mask and puppets to impact on their work. Alternatively, Synge's *Playboy* has inspired various versions of it in other cultural contexts, and O'Casey's impact on Brecht's dramaturgy is well known. The influence of modern American drama on early post-Second World War Irish playwriting is considerable, namely work produced by Tennessee Williams, Eugene O'Neill and Arthur Miller—Marina Carr has credited Shakespeare, Williams and Ibsen as influences. Brecht's staging techniques have informed works by Kilroy and McGuinness, and Tom Mac Intrye's indebtedness, amongst many others, to Pina Bausch's Tanztheater practices are also well documented. More recently, Jason Byrne's productions for Loose Canon in the late 1990s and early 2000s owed much to the works of key contemporary theatre makers such as Eugenio Barba, Romeo Castellucci, and Jerzy Grotowski. Many practitioners name and signal an array of influences, without being necessarily wedded to the theoretical vocabularies that are circulated in academic discussion about such practices. Community and educational drama practitioners are far more likely to reflect, document and theorize their practices than professional performance makers.

Theatre for young people, community theatre, educational and youth theatre allow for a certain amount of experimentation. Over the past forty years, a number of performers and practitioners have come of age in youth theatre and amateur environments. Some of the more innovative work seen today on Irish stages seems to come from a generation of theatre-makers challenged by and introduced to expanding notions of theatre from those formative years. Alumni from Dublin Youth Theatre (DYT), founded in 1977 by Paddy O'Dwyer, with Eilís Mullan serving as an early artistic director, include Aiden Gillen, Enda Walsh, Sarah Jane Shiels, as well as the founders of THEATREclub, Grace Dyas, Shane Byrne, Lauren Larkin, and Doireann Coady. Emmet Kirwan, Phillip McMahon, Camille O'Sullivan were also past members.[27] Mullan went on to become director of the National Association for Youth Drama (NAYD), which was established in 1980. Now known as Youth Theatre Ireland, the organization supports scores of youth theatres around the country. It is worth noting that the non-professional Dublin Shakespeare Society (known by its members as 'The Shakes') was founded in 1907 and is still active—and one can find within its cast lists venerated names such as Milo O'Shea, Brenda Fricker, Donal McCann and Betty Ann Norton, the last of whom has run her own theatre school for over fifty years.

Many of the companies currently making work in Ireland have been heavily influenced, intra-culturally as well, by three key Irish companies, Pan Pan led by Aedín Cosgrove and Gavin Quinn, the Corn Exchange under Annie Ryan's leadership and Barabbas.... the Company. These companies bring various intercultural practices to bear on their work. Their influences are as varied as Jacques Le Coq, Ariane Mnouchkine, *commedia dell'arte* and Second City improvisation from Chicago. All three companies offer workshops, training and mentorships to many performance makers and such contributions speak to the spirit of collegiality and the generosity that exists within the sector. The direct and indirect influence of Britain's Forced Entertainment on the practices of companies like Pan Pan, Brokentalkers and THEATREclub is also substantial. These points are made simply to demonstrate that influences are exchanged in complex and sometimes convoluted ways between theatre-makers.

Intercultural influences have been brought to bear on contemporary theatre practices in Ireland by other means, as well, as when practitioners and facilitators train abroad, or when practitioners teach masterclasses and workshops, either on a visiting basis or when taking up an extended residence. In recent times, non-Irish national practitioners have migrated to Ireland, bringing with them skills that serve as an important component of intercultural exchange. The impact of companies like Arambe Productions and the Polish Theatre Company are only two examples.

Equally, international productions seen during festivals in Dublin, Galway, Kilkenny and Belfast have had a far-reaching impact.[28] For instance, the Dublin Theatre Festival, across its sixty-year history, has hosted the work of many renowned companies from Britain, America, Australia, Canada, Japan, Russia, Romania, Hungary, and numerous companies from across mainland Europe.[29]

The Belfast Festival at Queens, now the International Arts Festival, established in 1962, has attracted work as various as Robert Wilson, Japanese Theatre company Ishinha, Philip Glass, the Royal National Theatre and the Royal Shakespeare Company. More recently the Happy Days Enniskillen International Beckett Festival has attracted high-profile figures from abroad. The Galway and Kilkenny Arts Festivals, Cork's Midsummer Festival, Dublin's Fringe Theatre Festival, the International Dublin Gay Theatre Festival and the Dublin Dance Festival also draw productions from outside Ireland.

In many respects, Project Arts Centre has been one of the more innovative and consistent of hosting venues, both for Irish and international work, including the Gay Sweatshop productions, developmental initiatives with Rough Magic, partnerships with emerging artists, and events like Pan Pan's Dublin International Theatre Symposia (1997–2003, first held at the Samuel Beckett Centre, Trinity College Dublin). Its direct and indirect influence on writing and performance practices has been phenomenal, currently under Cian O'Brien, and prior to him, under Willie White's stewardship. Since 2012, the MAC in Belfast has served as a similar sort of cultural hub.

Beginning in the 1930s, when Abbey actors had considerable success in Hollywood, actors who trained or first worked in Ireland have gone on to work internationally. An ever-growing list of actors grew up, trained, studied or worked in Ireland initially, before making names for themselves through work further afield: Caitriona Balfe, Eva Birthistle, Colin Blakley, Kenneth Branagh,

Bríd Brennan, Niall, Buggy, Gabriel Byrne, Lorcan Cranitch, Kerry Condon, Dermot Crowley, Liam Cunningham, Sinead Cusack, Laura Donnelly, Richard Dormer, Jamie Dornan, Adrian Dunbar, Caoilfhionn Dunne, Colin Farrell, Michelle Fairley, Tara Fitzgerald, Michael Gambon, Aiden Gillen, Brian, Brendan and Domhnall Gleeson, Dan Gordon, Denise and Kelly Gough, Sarah Greene, Stuart Graham, Conleth Hill, Ciarán Hinds, Sharon Horgan, Rory Keenan, Dervla Kirwan, John and Susan Lynch, Des McAleer, Donal McCann, Stella McCusker, Peter McDonald, Pauline McGlynn, Siobhán McKenna, T.P. McKenna, Ray McNally, Dearbhla Molloy, Charlie Murphy, Cillian Murphy, Ruth Negga, Liam Neeson, James Nesbitt, Jim Norton, Brian F. O'Byrne, Stephen Rae, Jack Raynor, Sorcha Ronan, Andrew Scott, Fiona Shaw, Frances Tomelty, Stewart Townsend, Aidan Turner and Eileen Walsh.

It is possible to see actors like these offering distinctive cross-cultural contributions to theatre and film, even if this is difficult or impossible to measure. This, of course, is not to dismiss actors who have done most of their work in Ireland, such as John Kavanagh, Ingrid Craigie, Owen Roe, Andrew Bennett, Derbhle Crottty, Lalor Roddy, Rosaleen Linehan, Marie Mullen, Barry McGovern, Johnny Murphy, Aisling O'Sullivan, John Kavanagh Sean McGinley, and many others. It is worth noting here some of the performers who do not sit solidly in the theatre-centric context established in this volume. They include the Nualas, who started life in 1995 as a musically inclined take-no-prisoners comedy trio, originally comprised of Susan Collins, Anne Gildea and Tara Flynn. They toured extensively until their farewell in 2001, to be reborn in 2011 with Maria Tecce taking Flynn's place. Little John Nee defies description as a street performer and poet, as well as a singing clown, storyteller and actor. Notably, he portrayed one of his inspirations in the 2010 production by Barabbas of *Johnny Patterson the Singing Irish Clown*, directed by Raymond Keane.

The role of actors in the formation of theatre companies is not highlighted as extensively as it could be. A few important examples include Stephen Rea's involvement in the establishment of Field Day and Marie Jones, Maureen McAuley, Eleanor Methven, Carol Scanlan (Moore) and Brenda Winter's collective investment in the establishment of Charabanc in Belfast. Actor Olwen Fouéré along with musician Roger Doyle founded Operating Theatre, and performers Feidlim Cannon, Damien Fenty, Gary Keegan and Faye Munns set up Brokentalkers in Dublin after graduating from De Montfort University, Leicester.

Funding

Apart from the commercial wing of the theatre sector, monies raised from box office receipts, benefactors, sponsorship and partnership arrangements are seldom enough to cover running costs at any level of production.[30] Most often municipal or state funding is necessary to make productions financially viable and to ensure that the activities of production companies can be sustainable and not entirely risk-averse in their programming. State support is premised on the rights of citizens to have access to the arts and the idea that arts organizations have a civic obligation to develop an audience base and to be as socially inclusive as possible by overcoming structural and financial barriers to the arts.[31] Such supports vary from country to country but, in the main, the arts sectors and creative industries in Ireland have been reliant on state supplements to fund and maintain their practices. It is safe to say that the Irish theatre sector has always been underfunded, perhaps radically so, even if some individual companies and theatres have been in receipt of what seems like considerable amounts of financial support relative to others.

Governments, particularly Irish ones, are not slow to leverage public relations opportunities by piggybacking on prominent artists and arts activities. The utilization of such achievements—alongside the categorical valorization of the Arts in Irish history for purposes of attracting tourism and corporate relocation—can seem like grandstanding at best, and callous opportunism at worst.

In both the Republic of Ireland and Northern Ireland from the 1970s, policies aimed to develop and promote theatre in areas outside of the main cities.[32] They led to support for new companies and investment in the construction of theatres and arts centres in different communities across the island. During the 1980s and 1990s, this process evolved further. Victor Merriman maps the evolution of the Arts Council's policy in terms of changes that include regionalism, support for companies and the development of new performing Arts.[33]

The combination of a Peace Process dividend and healthy economies in both the North and South led to further expansion. Chris Morash and Shaun Richards identified the existence of sixty-six theatre venues by 2014.[34] Apart from the longer established venues in Belfast, Derry, Galway, Sligo, Tralee, Cork, Waterford and Dublin, places as various as Ballina, Bray, Carlow, Castleblaney, Coleraine, Cookstown, Drogheda, Dundalk, Ennis, Enniskillen, Letterkenny, Lisburn, Mullingar, Navan, Newbridge, Portlaoise, Thurles, Tralee, Navan, Strabane, and Wexford have benefited from infrastructural investment. Some are theatres, some are arts venues that house a theatre.[35]

These new spaces were built to host touring shows and generate their own work, to maximize usage and the impact of the space on the community. Such spaces facilitated work by professionals, community groups, amateurs and students. They also offered lab, rehearsal, residency and exhibition spaces. Only on occasion were theatre companies directly associated with such spaces. Belfast's Lyric Theatre is the only producing venue in Northern Ireland, and Sligo's Blue Raincoat have their own venue, called the Factory Performance Space.

The amounts of revenue funding distributed annually by the Arts Councils increased significantly between 1993 and 2007, which gave rise to more secure employment conditions for some arts staff, and led to an expansion of activities. Some companies in the Republic acquired the status of a Regularly Funded Organisation (RFO), meaning that they could make plans that were not just yearly, but structure them as part of a three-year cycle. The amount of funding allocated to both the Abbey and Gate theatres has long been contentious, given the significant chunk of the overall funding available that they receive, in contrast to the totals granted to those in the independent sectors. During the Celtic Tiger period, even newly formed companies, relatively speaking, with small track records in professional programming were awarded funding, in contrast to previous years when companies needed to have been operating with some measure of quality and "success" for a considerable time before they received a place on the funding ladder.[36]

As for the Abbey, the financial crisis that emerged during its centenary year in 2004, "AbbeyOneHundred", with Ben Barnes at the helm, proved just how precarious budgeting and planning can be. An impressive season was scheduled, based on ambitious revenue projections that were not achieved. Further anticipated costs for novel initiatives went well beyond what was initially budgeted.[37] There were many unknowns, and not enough foresight or contingency planning. Ambition led to decisions which proved chaotic in practice. 2004 emerged as a period of financial mismanagement and poor governance. Barnes was forced to resign and a bailout was required from the Government to address a deficit of €1.85 million.[38]

While the Celtic Tiger period put many theatre companies on a safer footing, the economic crash of 2008 took things in an altogether different direction. Some companies that had been long-term recipients of funding lost out. The effective demise or reduction in the activities of companies as various as Storytellers, Loose Canon, Red Kettle and Barabbas had major impacts on the sector, even though many of the individuals involved with these companies managed to persist in their involvement in the theatre. The effective dormancy of Arambe Productions was another loss.

Of course, some companies have a shelf life; no company can assume funding will continue in perpetuity, and if money is limited not everyone can be funded. The demands on funding are widespread and relentless, with the criteria under which funding decisions are made appearing to undergo continual mutation. It is now a fact of theatre production that companies spend most of their time and energy pursuing funding, especially as it has become largely project based rather than sustained. It is not just the case that small companies are finding it impossible to establish the administrative and managerial structures necessary to evolve and maintain themselves into the medium term; the routine precarity of their financial situations leaves huge question marks about the ability of these companies to plan.

It would appear that the generation of established practitioners—once modestly funded but brutally undercut by the economic crash—have found individual ways of persisting and, indeed, of producing extraordinary work. Witness, for example, *City of Clowns* (2010), a Barabbas collaboration between Raymond Keane, performer, and Maria Fleming, director. The piece arose out of the profound despair brought about by the sudden withdrawal of Arts Council support from established companies. Ultimately, it led in Keane's performance to an innovative if downbeat variation on the clowning persona and its social resonance. In it, twenty to thirty red-nose clowns amongst whom the spectators strolled performed short loops of everyday activity. For a touring context, Keane worked with local volunteers to cultivate their own, personalized performances for a "city of clowns" that became part of the show. This is one example of how, having been put to the economic sword, persistence and invention led practitioners to valuable, timely work as well as new models for flexible production and touring. An artistically impassioned wave of young theatre-makers with shoestring budgets a necessary part of their vision was another result of the recession. These companies include Collapsing Horse with their infusion of energetic, wide-eyed wonder (sometimes with puppets), and THEATREclub with their unflinching confrontation both of theatrical form and social stasis.

From an endemically conservative government point of view, in a country with a huge national debt—which in recent memory temporarily lost its economic sovereignty, needing a bailout—the arts have not been a priority, at best receiving lip service and minimal funding. In this low hum of ideological priority, a way of thinking about the arts as in thrall to neo-liberal imperatives is unnerving. The methodologies of the corporate world and its so-called best practices are inform funding criteria, evaluations, and decisions. This is not by any means meant to imply that theatre companies should be absolved of any financial accountability by the government, nor that they should not be encouraged to track down alternative income streams. Currently, companies shepherded towards programming based on the latest funding criteria shelve work they might be motivated or inspired to do outside the necessary buzz-word proposals that foreground trends of the moment, but which can be every bit as valuable and necessary.

Needless to say, viable working lives for artists are not easy to come by in this and recent economic climates. Gender disparities commonplace in Irish society and ingrained in the theatre workplace carry harsh economic implications for women trying to work in the theatre. The recent controversies over the Abbey Theatre's 2016 programming to mark the centenary of the Easter Rising led to the #WakingTheFeminists initiative and movement, out of which came the recent report, Gender Counts: An Analysis of Gender in Irish Theatre 2006–2015.[39] This foregrounding of systemic gender imbalance in the theatre industry gathered personalized force amid a wave of accusations levelled at powerful men in Hollywood towards the end of 2017. In November 2017, the Gate theatre appointed an independent Human Resources advisor to investigate charges by seven women against longtime artistic director Michael Colgan for sexual harassment and abuse of power. The public prominence of this issue has led to an initiative taken by the Arts Council to tighten the conditions it sets for the institutions it funds, including an implicit demand on theatre companies and arts-related organizations to publish and enforce standards for the elimination of sexual harassment, bullying and abuse of power in the workplace.

How and Why Theatre

Why people write and create work and how they have done so has clearly evolved over the decades considered in this collection. The early writers within the contemporary period had concerns about identity, religion, nationhood, rival versions of the past, inequality and injustices, but many of these issues modified significantly over time because of economic change, liberalisation, legislative changes, secularisation, social mobility, greater transparency, access to systems of justice beyond the island, technology and knowledge growth.

While the writing of plays remains central to the more established or conventional theatres, the number of productions originating from a text written in advance by a sole writer seems to be on the wane—and this is a pattern repeated across Europe. Directors are not necessarily reducing the significance of writing in the production hierarchy—although, increasingly, theatre-making involves creative constellations in which the dramaturg figures more prominently. We have not, in any case, gotten to the point where there are discussions about the death of the director in ways that we have about the death of the playwright.

It is, however, increasingly common for performers, directors, dramaturgs, musicians, choreographers, designers and sound and visual artists to make work based on devised and/or collaborative practices. Moreover, it is not only the collegial and eclectic means of making such work that makes it distinctive, but also the sheer range of inputs available: from the inclusion of pre-recorded content, videos, sound art, live web links, interactive music and even the creation of work that is performed in multiple languages. More and more, such work receives invitations to tour abroad. There is not, however, a tradition of other companies remounting such work thus far—it is less likely to be picked up by a company elsewhere, as with a Marina Carr play. Moreover, such companies are less likely to receive funding for the remounting of past projects.

In addition, considerable developments in live art, performance art, street art, circus, spectacle, street theatre, durational work, flashmobs, invisible theatre, parades, drag performance and alternative pageants suggest a broadening of the definitions of mainstream and/or popular theatre and performance is taking place. Site-specific productions shaped by the likes of Sarah Jane Scaife for Company SJ, and the work by ANU productions, led by Owen Boss and Louise Lowe, have provided templates and practices for others. Of course, Tinderbox's production of *Convictions* (2000), a collection of seven twelve-minute plays staged in various locations in Belfast's Crumlin Road Courthouse led the way for an increasingly recognizable type of off-site work, as performances are more likely to take spectators outside conventional theatre buildings.

The Ireland of this kind of work reveals the island as a complex, evolving and mutating entity, encompassing diverse currents at home and abroad and incapable of any singular characterization—there can be nothing uniform or easily classifiable about the body of theatre work it has generated over the last sixty years and more.

A fixation on identarian politics and the "Irishness" of Irish theatre and on the aspects that seemingly make it distinctive and enriching for some, cliched and pejorative for others, has prompted numerous critical debates, as the politics of identity have become more prominent globally in the academic sphere. In any one production, the concept of Irishness can be supplemented, undermined, transposed, and erased, effectively imagined and constituted in divergent ways. As Patrick Lonergan has proposed, Irishness is an utterly porous, unstable concept, suitably adopted and invariably localized. Lonergan suggests that "branding", "reflexivity", and "an audience's enjoyment of a theatrical production is determined by that audience's capacity to relate the action to their own preoccupations and interests, as those preoccupations and interests are determined locally [...] *Irishness acts as a deterritorialized space* in which audiences may explore local preoccupations."[40]

Sometimes, theatre can be perceived as radical, contestational and resistant to a dominant ideology; sometimes theatre can be appeasing, inclined to collude, manipulate, reinforce or discretely align itself to hegemonic practices.

Increasingly, there is no simple binary between conventional and experimental forms, fringe or mainstream, established and found spaces. Experimental work can be radical in form, but conservative in its ideology; other work can be conservative in form, and radical in its content. While the spaces in which work is made determine much of the material conditions, nothing is predetermined by space per se.

Collectively, the chapters here identify a topography for the history of recent (and not-too-distant) Irish theatre, its practices, its evolutions and its ideologies. The analysis counters hegemonic thinking and uses plays and performances to substantiate its point of view, particularly in tracing gender, sexualities, ethnicities, race or class, prejudices and discriminations. These writings reflect, expose and critique, but they also explicate and celebrate the significance of this body of work. We trust that the range of the chapters, the insights and reflections offered, will prompt further engagement, reflection and comment from various readers.

Notes

1. See Eugene McNulty's *The Ulster Literary Theatre and the Northern Revival* (Cork: Cork University Press, 2008).
2. For overviews see Nicholas Grene's *The Politics of Irish Drama: Plays in Context from Boucicault to Friel* (Cambridge: Cambridge University Press, 1999), Mária Kurdi's, *Representations of Gender and Female Subjectivity in Contemporary Irish Drama by Women* (Lewiston, Queenston, Lampeter: Edwin Mellen Press, 2011), Cathy Leeney's, *Irish Women Playwrights, 1900–1939: Gender & Violence on Stage* (New York: Peter Lang, 2010), Christopher Murray's *Twentieth-Century Irish Drama: Mirror Up to Nation* (Manchester: Manchester University Press, 1997), and Lionel Pilkington's, *Theatre and the State in Twentieth-Century Ireland: Cultivating the People* (London: Routledge, 2001).
3. See Christopher Morash's, *A History of Irish Theatre: 1601–2000* (Cambridge; CUP, 2002).

4. Lionel Pilkington, *Theatre and Ireland* (Basingstoke: Palgrave Macmillan, 2010), 26–7, citing Alan J. Fletcher, *Drama and the Performing Arts in Pre-Cromwellian Ireland: A Repertory of Sources and Documents from the Earliest Times* (Cork: Cork University Press, 2000), 6.
5. The construction of the poor and marginalized in the writings of Gregory, Synge, and Yeats is articulated in Paul Murphy's, *Hegemony and Fantasy in Irish Drama, 1899–1949* (Basingstoke: Palgrave, 2008).
6. For an extensive analysis see Anthony Roche, *Synge and the Making of Modern Irish Drama* (Dublin: Carysfort Press, 2013).
7. See Catherine Morris, *Alice Milligan and the Irish Cultural Revival* (Dublin: Four Courts, 2013). Primarily because of the institutionalized stature of these figures, modern Irish theatre tends to be overly associated with the impact of writers, at the expense of the input of directors, designers, actors, and administrators, and, indeed, women more widely. More recent decades have seen attempts by critical commentators to redress this imbalance, noting, for example, the influence of Alice Milligan on stage design during the Irish Cultural Revival.
8. See overview of the partition of the Island at http://www.irishborderlands.com/ireland/index.html, accessed 10 August, 2017.
9. See Tom Maguire's comprehensive study, *Making Theatre in Northern Ireland: Through and Beyond the Troubles* (Exeter: University of Exeter Press, 2006). Maguire discusses distinctions between and usage of the terms Ulster, the North and Northern Ireland, 6–7.
10. See CAIN Web Service—Conflict and Politics in Northern Ireland, accessed 20 August, 2017, http://cain.ulst.ac.uk/.
11. Mark Phelan, "From Troubles to Post-Conflict Theatre", in *The Oxford Handbook of Modern Irish Theatre*, eds. Nicholas Grene and Christopher Morash (Oxford: OUP, 2016), 372–388, 384.
12. What is clear is that the period from the 1930s to the 1940s is not the dramatic wasteland it was once considered to be, and more recent scholarship has been forensic in pointing this out. Much of the writing of the late 1940s and 1950s seemed stuck in a conservative dramaturgy, and few of these plays remain influential apart from the works of George Fitzmaurice and M.J. Molloy.
13. Of course, the period of the 1940s and 1950s is increasingly researched and many of the activities on that ground, particularly in Dublin's Little Theatres, were significant to their own time, laying the ground for what was to follow. That fact that such work seldom gets produced ensures that such a period is more likely to be covered by theatre historiographers and those interested in archival activities.
14. See Ophelia Byrne, "Northern Irish Theatre." Extract from Ophelia Byrne, *The Continuum Companion to Twentieth Century Theatre*, ed. Colin Chambers (London: Continuum, 2002), accessed 21 July, 2017. http://www.dramaonlinelibrary.com/genres/northern-irish-drama-iid-21658.
15. Marilynn Richtarik's biography of Stewart Parker offers a wonderful assessment of the interfaces between a writer and his socio-cultural context, comprising the theatre community, production histories, cultures and funding and commission environments. That way, theatre is not just a narrative about plays and performances but something where many forces interconnect. See *Stewart Parker: A Life* (Oxford: Oxford University Press, 2012).
16. Fiona Coleman Coffey offers a substantial theatre history of Northern Irish women writers. She notes how the handshake between the Queen of England and Martin McGuinness, Northern Ireland's Deputy First Minister, an

Republican leader, took place on 27 June, 2012 at the Lyric Theatre, and this exchange emphasized, according to Coleman Coffey "the highly theatrical and symbolic nature of politics, violence and the peace process in Northern Ireland." See *Women in Northern Irish Theatre, 1921–2012* (Syracuse, Syracuse University Press, 2016), 1.

17. Like Murphy, Martin McDonagh and later Enda Walsh would become, in effect, Druid house playwrights, premiering a series of significant works in the late 1990s and the mid to late 2000s, respectively.
18. In many instances, Joe Vaněk's scenographic work was crucial to many of Mason's productions.
19. Elizabeth Kuti, "'strangeness made sense': reflections on being a non-Irish playwright positioned in the Irish tradition", in *Irish Drama: Local and Global Perspectives*, eds. Nicholas Grene and Patrick Lonergan (Dublin: Carysfort, 2012), 141–162.
20. See Maguire, *Making Theatre in Northern Ireland*, 8.
21. For more information see Peter James Harris, "Chronological Table of Irish Plays Produced in London 1920–2006", in *Irish Theatre in England*, eds. Richard Cave and Ben Levitas (Dublin: Carysfort Press, 2007), 195–286.
22. See Druid Theatre Company website to view how extensive the tours were and the awards that the awards won, August, 2017, http://archive.druid.ie/websites/2009-2017/productions/the-cripple-of-inishmaan-2011. Accessed 10 August 2017.
23. Further, McGuinness has produced adaptations of work by Lorca, Valle-Inclan, de Molina, Brecht, Ostrovsky, Racine, Strinberg and Pirandello; he also reimagined *The Dead*, James Joyce's short story, and adapted novels by Bram Stoker and Daphne Du Maurier for the stage.
24. O'Halloran's recent appearance in Pan Pan's *The Importance of Nothing* (2016) is a reminder of just how good an actor he can be.
25. Playwrights working as directors in film become relatively accomplished at financing and resolving distribution challenges that they do not face in the theatre.
26. These would include McPherson's screenplay for Paddy Breathnach's *I Went Down* (1997). He wrote and directed *Saltwater* (2000) and *The Actors* (2003). McPherson directed and also co-wrote *The Eclipse* (2009) with Billy Roche.
27. See Maggie Armstrong, "Theatre: Young guns rising to the challenge of 1916", *Irish Independent*, 14 August, 2016, accessed 17 June, 2017, http://www.independent.ie/entertainment/theatre-arts/theatre-young-guns-rising-to-the-challenge-of-1916-34958271.html.
28. More commercial-orientated venues like the Grand Opera House in Belfast, the Gaiety and Bord Gáis Theatre in Dublin have been more inclined to host touring productions that have broad audience appeal and often productions sourced from the West-End.
29. See Nicholas Grene, Patrick Lonergan with Lilian Chambers, *Interactions, Dublin Theatre Festival 1957–2007* (Dublin, Carysfort Press, 2008).
30. The Gate Theatre, while Arts Council funded, has always been very commercially minded. It has cast highly regarded actors in their shows, such as Frances McDormand in a production of *Street Car Named Desire* or Ralph Fiennes in *Faith Healer*. Michael Gambon, John Hurt, Lia Williams also spring to mind. The novel production of Walsh's *The Walworth Farce* at the Olympia Theatre in 2015 with Brian, Brendan, and Domhnall Gleeson is a particularly good example of the theatre using big names and a novel concept in casting three members

of the one family in a play about acting. A recent production of Mark O'Rowe's *Howie the Rookie* had Tom Vaughan-Lawlor, playing the two narrators, the Howie and the Rookie Lee, a major acting achievement in and of itself, but the public interest that arose from Vaughan-Lawlor having been the lead in Stuart Carolan's hit television series *Love/Hate* was very notable. Big name draw Sinead Cusack has appeared regularly on the Irish stage since 2009 most recently at the Gate in McPherson's adaptation of *The Birds*, at the Abbey in *Juno and the Paycock* and in Mark O'Rowe's *Our Few and Evil Days*. Ciarán Hinds has starred opposite her in each of these productions.

31. Over the years audiences for the Abbey and the Gate theatre productions have been reluctant to evolve their tastes, and the prompting of audiences to expand their horizons of expectations has not always been well received. Theatres like the Project Arts Centre in Dublin or the Metropolitan Arts Centre (MAC) in Belfast attract greater social and age-diverse audiences.
32. The Republic of Ireland's Arts Council [founded in 1951] has evolved through various Arts Acts, and its strategy has altered accordingly. See http://www.artscouncil.ie/about/. Accessed 2 September, 2017.

    In Northern Ireland, "The Arts Council was originally established in 1962 as a successor to the Committee for the Encouragement of Music and the Arts (CEMA) which had operated since 1942." See http://artscouncil-ni.org/about-us. Accessed 21 July, 2017.
33. See Victor Merriman's account of developments south of the border in "'As We Must': Growth and Diversification in Ireland's Theatre Culture 1977–2000", in *The Oxford Handbook of Modern Irish Theatre*, 389–403.
34. Chris Morash and Shaun Richards, *Mapping Irish Theatre: Theories of Space and Place* (Cambridge: Cambridge University Press, 2013), 15.
35. Longer established venues in Belfast include the Grand Opera house, Belfast Civic Arts, and Lyric Players Theatre. In the Republic of Ireland these would include the Belltable Arts Centre, Limerick, Cork Opera House, Druid Lane, Everyman Playhouse, Hawk's Well Theatre Sligo, Siamsa Tíre, the National Folk Theatre and in Dublin, Abbey and Gate Theatres and venues as varied as the Project Arts Centre to the New Theatre.
36. See the following report: "The Living and Working Conditions of Artists in the Republic of Ireland and Northern Ireland", accessed 20 August, 2017, http://www.artscouncil.ie/uploadedFiles/LWCA_Study_-_Final_2010.pdf.
37. Ben Barnes compellingly accounts for his tenure in *Plays and Controversies: Abbey Theatre Diaries 2000–2005* (Dublin: Carysfort Press, 2008).
38. Sara Keating's review of *Plays and Controversies: Abbey Theatre Diaries 2000–2005* in "The Years of Living Dangerously", *The Irish Times*, November 25, 2008, accessed 21 August, 2017, http://www.irishtimes.com/culture/the-years-of-living-dangerously-1.914545.
39. Report available at http://www.irishtheatreinstitute.ie/attachments/2ec80fd4-3289-43db-b810-57bd44a370fa.PDF. Accessed 25 July, 2017. See also Chris McCormack's fine summation of the report "#WakingTheFeminists: The Numbers are Out", at http://exeuntmagazine.com/features/wakingthefeminists-report-now/. Accessed 25 July, 2017.
40. See *Theatre and Globalization: Irish Drama in the Celtic Tiger Era* (Basingstoke: Palgrave, 2008), 92.

Bibliography

Armstrong, Maggie. "Theatre: Young Guns Rising to the Challenge of 1916." *Irish Independent*, August 14, 2016. Accessed June 17, 2017. http://www.independent.ie/entertainment/theatre-arts/theatre-young-guns-rising-to-the-challenge-of-1916-34958271.html.

Barnes, Ben. *Plays and Controversies: Abbey Theatre Diaries 2000–2005*. Dublin: Carysfort Press, 2008.

Byrne, Ophelia. "Northern Irish Theatre." Extract from Ophelia Byrne, *The Continuum Companion to Twentieth Century Theatre*, edited by Colin Chambers. London: Continuum, 2002. Accessed July 21, 2017. http://www.dramaonlinelibrary.com/genres/northern-irish-drama-iid-21658.

CAIN Web Service—Conflict and Politics in Northern Ireland. Accessed August 20, 2017. http://cain.ulst.ac.uk/.

Coffey, Fiona Coleman. *Women in Northern Irish Theatre, 1921–2012*. Syracuse: Syracuse University Press, 2016.

Grene, Nicholas and Patrick Lonergan with Lilian Chambers, eds. *Interactions, Dublin Theatre Festival 1957–2007*. Dublin: Carysfort Press, 2008.

Grene, Nicholas. *The Politics of Irish Drama: Plays in Context from Boucicault to Friel*. Cambridge: Cambridge University Press, 1999.

Harris, Peter James. "Chronological Table of Irish Plays Produced in London 1920–2006." In *Irish Theatre in England*, edited by Richard Cave and Ben Levitas. Dublin: Carysfort Press, 2007.

Keating, Sara. "The Years of Living Dangerously." (A Review of Ben Barnes's *Plays and Controversies: Abbey Theatre Diaries 2000–2005*). *The Irish Times*, November 25, 2008. Accessed August 21, 2017. http://www.irishtimes.com/culture/the-years-of-living-dangerously-1.914545.

Kurdi, Mária. *Representations of Gender and Female Subjectivity in Contemporary Irish Drama by Women*. Lewiston, Queenston, Lampeter: Edwin Mellen Press, 2011.

Kuti, Elizabeth. "'Strangeness Made Sense': Reflections on Being a Non-Irish Playwright Positioned in the Irish Tradition." In *Irish Drama: Local and Global Perspectives*, edited by Nicholas Grene and Patrick Lonergan. Dublin: Carysfort, 2012.

Leeney, Cathy. *Irish Women Playwrights, 1900–1939: Gender & Violence on Stage*. New York: Peter Lang, 2010.

Lonergan, Patrick. *Theatre and Globalization: Irish Drama in the Celtic Tiger Era*. Basingstoke: Palgrave, 2008.

Maguire, Tom. *Making Theatre in Northern Ireland: Through and Beyond the Troubles*. Exeter: University of Exeter Press, 2006.

McCormack, Chris. "#WakingTheFeminists: The Numbers are Out." Accessed July 25, 2017. http://exeuntmagazine.com/features/wakingthefeminists-report-now/.

McNulty, Eugene. *The Ulster Literary Theatre and the Northern Revival*. Cork: Cork University Press, 2008.

Merriman, Victor. "'As We Must': Growth and Diversification in Ireland's Theatre Culture 1977–2000." In *The Oxford Handbook of Modern Irish Theatre*, edited by Nicholas Grene and Christopher Morash. Oxford: OUP, 2016.

Morash, Christopher. *A History of Irish Theatre: 1601–2000*. Cambridge; CUP, 2002.

Morash, Chris and Shaun Richards. *Mapping Irish Theatre: Theories of Space and Place*. Cambridge: Cambridge University Press, 2013.

Morris, Catherine. *Alice Milligan and the Irish Cultural Revival.* Dublin: Four Courts, 2013.

Murphy, Paul. *Hegemony and Fantasy in Irish Drama, 1899–1949.* Basingstoke: Palgrave, 2008.

Murray, Christopher. *Twentieth-Century Irish Drama: Mirror Up to Nation.* Manchester: Manchester University Press, 1997.

Phelan, Mark. "From Troubles to Post-Conflict Theatre." In *The Oxford Handbook of Modern Irish Theatre*, edited by Nicholas Grene and Christopher Morash. Oxford: OUP, 2016.

Pilkington, Lionel. *Theatre and the State in Twentieth-Century Ireland: Cultivating the People.* London: Routledge, 2001.

———. *Theatre and Ireland.* Basingstoke: Palgrave Macmillan, 2010.

Report. "The Living and Working Conditions of Artists in the Republic of Ireland and Northern Ireland." Accessed August 20, 2017. http://www.artscouncil.ie/uploadedFiles/LWCA_Study_-_Final_2010.pdf.

Report. "Gender Counts: An Analysis of Gender in Irish Theatre 2006–2015." Accessed July 25, 2017. http://www.irishtheatreinstitute.ie/attachments/2ec80fd4-3289-43db-b810-57bd44a370fa.PDF.

Richtarik, Marilynn. *Stewart Parker: A Life.* Oxford: Oxford University Press, 2012.

Roche, Anthony. *Synge and the Making of Modern Irish Drama.* Dublin: Carysfort Press, 2013.

PART I

Histories

The Mainstream: Problematising and Theorising

Shaun Richards

In his 1955 article "The Future of the Irish Theatre" Gabriel Fallon gave a gloomy prognosis, lamenting the fact that the Abbey, "a theatre begun in poetry should find itself after fifty years deeply sunk in the pit of naturalism".[1] While he claimed that his essay was written "in the optative mood" it is the sense of frustration at the failure of Irish theatre as a whole that is most striking, for as there was "little sign [...] of the promise of lively new dramatists" the theatre seemed condemned to "a further term of naturalism" as the dominant form of Irish theatre.[2] Fallon was writing from the perspective of conservative Catholicism, his hope being that naturalism would be replaced by verse drama of a spiritual nature, but his analysis captures a more widespread sense that "a spiraling entropy [...] had existed since the mid-1920s" and the national theatre was its paradigmatic expression.[3]

Fallon focused on the Abbey because "the Irish theatre is the Abbey Theatre",[4] but as Ernest Blythe, the theatre's managing director from 1941 to 1967, "didn't want anything that wasn't a three wall set",[5] the result was an "oleaginous conformity".[6] Although this lack of innovation was resisted by Ria Mooney, the Abbey's artistic director from 1948 to 1963, she acknowledged that often the only set decision was where to place the door and, indeed, recalled that "many of the plays were so monotonously alike that I honestly can't remember even the names of many of them".[7] However, despite this creative inertia at the heart of the theatrical establishment, there was a resistance to formulaic naturalism. The Pike theatre produced Beckett's *Waiting for Godot* in 1955 and in 1957 gave the Irish premier of Tennessee Williams's sexually outspoken *The Rose Tattoo*, which led to the arrest of the theatre's

S. Richards (✉)
Staffordshire University, Stoke-on-Trent, UK
e-mail: c.s.richards@staffs.ac.uk

E. Jordan, E. Weitz (eds.), *The Palgrave Handbook of Contemporary Irish Theatre and Performance*,
https://doi.org/10.1057/978-1-137-58588-2_2

director, Alan Simpson, and ultimately the closure of the theatre itself. But although the Pike, the 37 Theatre Club and above all the Gate, refused to conform to the naturalism which was "the signature tune of Irish theatre",[8] the reality, as the Gate's co-founder Micheál Mac Liammóir observed in 1959, was that "the search goes on for those authors who will deliver [Irish theatre] from the cumbersome drawingroom and library set, [...] from the limitations of those literal and representative surroundings".[9] In the same year, the playwright and critic Thomas Kilroy noted that "During the last twenty years few Irish dramatists have been in any way exciting technically" and so the challenge was to "create an environment which will help to inspire new Irish plays and keep playwrights alive to the experiments and advances of modern stagecraft".[10] The mainstream of Irish theatre flowed through the 1950s as sluggishly as the Liffey.

The reasons for this state of relative stasis are clear. As noted by Nicholas Grene, "In so far as Irish drama is centrally concerned with the explanation and interpretation of Ireland there is a bias towards the representational within it" and this had a specific impact on Irish women as dramatic form underwrote state policy in an effective denial of female agency.[11] As Melissa Sihra argues, "The recurring interior of the home on the Irish stage has come to signify an enduring association and conflation of family and nation"[12] in which, as in Article 41 of the Irish Constitution, women's domestic life "gives to the State a support without which the common good cannot be achieved" and therefore they "shall not be obliged by economic necessity to engage in labour to the neglect of their duties in the home".[13] Any dramatic denials of this orthodoxy were largely suppressed during the autarchic 1930s and 1940s, when the stage was expected to present an indivisible people united within a common culture.[14] However by 1958—when the parlous state of the economy established emigration as a fact of Irish life that fragmented families—state policy on the family and its theatrical confirmation were under strain. The conclusion of T.K. Whitaker's 1958 *Programme for Economic Expansion* was that "It would be well to shut the door on the past and to move forward"; an injunction that applied to more than the economy.[15] Irish society was changing and its theatre needed to engage with that fact. Indeed, as argued by Fintan O'Toole, "From the late 1950s onwards, 'Ireland' as a single, simple notion which might underlie and give coherence to a work of theatre began to seep away [...] The theatre of naturalism [...] became virtually impossible."[16]

Cultural change, however, was rarely as absolute and, as Raymond Williams observed in *Marxism and Literature* (1977), nearly always involves a mix of dominant, residual and emergent forms—a factor that would lend complexity to Irish theatre over the next several decades. But there was a sense that Irish society was in a state of upheaval and Brian Friel wanted to dramatize that moment: "I would like to write a play that would capture the peculiar spiritual, and indeed material, flux that this country is in at the moment."[17]

Friel's comment was made in the course of a discussion published in the *Irish Times* on 12 February 1970 whose title, "The Future of Irish Drama", echoed that of Fallon's article some fifteen years earlier—and again naturalism was the issue. It was not, however, a case of a frustrated yearning for a poetic theatre, rather it was a search for, in Seamus Heaney's phrase, a form "adequate to our predicament".[18] Hugh Leonard, who participated in the discussion, along with Friel and John B. Keane, identified the question of form as central, noting that "Brian Friel and I share a desperate search for form [...] Irish playwrights as a whole are trying to break away from a naturalistic form".[19]

Friel did not respond to Leonard on this point and appeared to refute it in his 1972 statement that "[m]atter is our concern, not form".[20] But his 1974 comment to Seamus Deane, "I'm as sick of the naturalistic style as I'm sure you are", makes clear that he was significantly concerned with the dominance of naturalism, but in a way which sought its modification rather than its outright rejection.[21] The two plays that ushered in contemporary Irish drama, Hugh Leonard's *Stephen D.* (1962) and Friel's *Philadelphia, Here I Come!* (1964), were staged at the Gate theatre during the Dublin Theatre Festival—a major influence on the development of Irish theatre through its introduction of international drama. Kilroy noted that they had many traditional features in terms of situations and characters, "but the sensibility of both writers is what is striking: modern, alive to the dislocating perspectives of the mid-century and the fluidity of expression possible on stage with modern lighting, design and direction".[22]

Stephen D., an adaptation of James Joyce's novels concerning Stephen Daedalus, was described by Leonard as "a very flexible piece of stage material" but one which was clearly non-naturalistic as, in the first production, "the dialogue between Stephen and the President was delivered as they walked down into the auditorium and completed a circuit of the stalls, during which time the house lights were switched on".[23] Friel's play is seemingly less radical in staging the kitchen set with all its resonance of "Peasant Quality"—the criterion of dramatic value in the Literary Revival—but it then fragments it. In addition to the kitchen, the set also contains a bedroom, which are lit according to whether they are the location of action, and "[t]hese two areas – kitchen and Gar's bedroom – occupy more than two-thirds of the stage. The remaining portion is fluid: in Episode I for example, it represents a room in Senator Doogan's home". The protagonist is also divided, on-stage as Public Gar and Private Gar, the latter is "the man within [...] the secret thoughts". When the play concludes with Gar's response to the question as to why he is emigrating, "I don't know. I—I—I don't know", Friel articulates the uncertainty of both his character, the society and its theatrical expression, poised between traditional themes and modern forms.[24]

Friel then interrogates these themes—emigration, generational conflict, the clash of tradition and modernity—through the disaggregation of the rural, naturalist set. Tom Murphy also tackles these issues in *A Whistle in the Dark* (1961), which was distinguished by its ruthless honesty rather than an experimental use of set. Indeed Murphy acknowledged that while he had wanted to "break away from the naturalism to which the Irish theatre [was] clinging" he "cheated": "I had told myself it would not be a play set in the traditional Irish kitchen; I didn't go much further when I set it in an English kitchen."[25] But *A Crucial Week in the Life of a Grocer's Assistant* (1969) featured a number of dream sequences signalled by a "pool of unreal light", frequently heightened language and, in one scene, "[t]he stage is peopled with grotesque whispering figures".[26] Murphy followed this with *The Morning After Optimism* (1971) a surrealistic fairy tale set in a forest where "[t]he tree-trunks reach up so high that we do not see the branches" and "the roars of anonymous wild animals" can be heard.[27] The fact that the play opens with Berlioz's *Symphonie Fantastique* signals Murphy's non-naturalistic intent. While this is the furthest he was to move in that direction his plays expand the naturalist frame to incorporate the metaphysical, especially in *The Gigli Concert* (1983) in which JPW King unplugs the record-player—so that it is clear that he is not miming—and then sings an aria in Gigli's voice.

For all their innovations, however, both Friel and Murphy largely remained within the world of rural Ireland and nowhere more so than in *Translations* (1980) and *Bailegangaire* (1985). But, as argued by Kilroy, despite the power and impact of these plays, they are theatrical elegies alert to the tradition in which they are located with a clear sense that what they have inherited is "at the end of its tether".[28] In this sense both the themes and the form, to adapt Hugh's phrase from *Translations*, "no longer match the changing landscape of fact"[29] that had been created by a society moving rapidly "from the thatched cottage to the bliss of the bungalows".[30] The consequence, Kilroy concludes, was that "the most durable of all Irish theatrical genres, the Irish peasant play" was no longer relevant and so Friel and Murphy's great plays of the 1980s began "to finally exhaust the form".[31]

Kilroy is not only an acute critic but, over a career of some five decades, one of the most relentlessly experimental of Irish dramatists. From *Talbot's Box*, (1967) to *Christ Deliver Us!* (2010), an adaptation of Wedekdin's *Spring Awakening* (1906), his work, as noted by Anna McMullan, "is a radical refusal of realism".[32] His experimentation is seen at its most imaginative in *The Secret Fall of Constance Wilde* (1997) which opens on a dark stage into which four figures "roll a great white disk, a performance space like a circus ring, into place down-stage under a brilliant spot". There are also a "set of stairs which may become an elaborate staircase with bannisters, a court room, a railway carriage" and while there are only three speaking parts there are six mute attendants and a number of full-sized puppets, including "two child puppets for the Wilde children [and] Puppets of several Victorian gentlemen in frock-coats".[33] However, in the same year that Kilroy's play was staged, Christopher Murray noted that "postmodernism is not congenial to Irish audiences" and Kilroy's drama, whose influences ranged from Brecht to Bunraku, remained the exception rather than the rule within the evolving theatrical mainstream.[34] Nevertheless, and despite Murray's note of caution with regard to audience attitudes to experimentation—postmodern or otherwise—the three decades from *Philadelphia, Here I Come!* to *The Secret Fall of Constance Wilde* saw a progressive shift in Irish theatre as established play forms and their traditional pieties were reappraised.

One of the unifying influences in terms of plays of this period is Patrick Mason, who even prior to becoming artistic director of the Abbey from 1993 to 1999, in which capacity he staged *The Secret Fall of Constance Wilde*, was a crucial force in introducing innovative staging to the Irish stage. Experimental in all senses of the word, including a script in which stage directions rather than dialogue dominate, Tom Mac Intyre's *The Great Hunger*, produced on the Peacock stage of the National Theatre in 1983, was a dramatization of Patrick Kavanagh's 1942 poem developed in rehearsal by Mac Intyre, Mason and the actor Tom Hickey. Highly influenced by the modern dance of Meredith Monk, Merce Cunningham and Pina Bauch, Mac Intyre celebrated what he termed "the saboteur energy" of the image.[35] The play, accordingly, moves across twenty-one scenes that are "played, ideally, without an interval", in a setting which is "[l]oosely defined, fluid as possible".[36] While Mac Intyre works with the traditional material of peasant life, its dramatization is decisively innovative. The Mother is a large wooden effigy set between a bucket and a kettle in a representation, rather than realisation, of the kitchen; the scene of potato picking has the rhythmic work and delivery of the lines interrupted by the appearance of a girl so that "*[t]he heads of the men dive*—Three heads between wide-apart legs—*to see,* Too late. *Slowly they rise from that position and become scarecrows stirring lightly in the wind, scarecrows that swivel and stare vacantly into the audience*". As in this instance, the movements of the actors are frequently choreographed rather than naturalistic, the better to reveal the repressed passions of this life. Maguire's imitations of farm-yard fowls are copied by a school girl, in what the stage directions term a "*mirror-game*" whose "*natural climax is that she leaps boldly into his embrace: her arms around his neck, her legs about his waist. The two whirl, brief release, then a jolt. There's a mutual realization of the sexual voltage*". And when Maguire takes up a bellows he "*works it to climax in an image of masturbation*".[37]

As Vincent Hurley noted, the production's "Theatre of the Image" acknowledged the Irish dramatic tradition "while taking it a step, or even several steps, farther, challenging our perceptions of the 'action' and the modes chosen to express it".[38] However, the extent to which it marked a significant advance towards the experimental theatre of directors such as Kazimierz Braun, whose Wroclaw Contemporary Theatre Company had been in the Dublin Theatre Festivals of 1981 and 1982, was queried by Fintan O'Toole's comment that "Director Patrick Mason seems not to have been prepared to cut off the anchor in naturalism".[39] Despite this caveat, the production established a clear benchmark, not only for a theatre of images that were physical and visual rather than just verbal, but for a frank engagement with sexuality that, as in the case of *The Rose Tattoo* in 1957, had been one of the shibboleths of Irish theatre for decades.

However, the rural location of Irish drama was still as much a site of struggle as it had been in the 1950s, when Noel O'Donoghue said to Tom Murphy that "[o]ne thing is fucking sure" about the play they were discussing writing: "it's not going to be set in a kitchen". That, said Murphy, "was the most progressive thing anyone had ever said to me".[40] Consequently, while *Bailegangaire* is set in "a country kitchen in the old style" this is "stylized to avoid cliché".[41] Similarly Friel's *The Secret Fall of Constance Wilde* is set in "*a 'traditional' Irish cottage*" in which "*[e]very detail of the kitchen and its furnishings is accurate of its time (from 1900 to 1930). But one quickly senses something false about the place. It is too pat, too 'authentic'*". What we see in these set directions is both playwrights' acute awareness that they are working within a traditional set, but one which can too easily become a stale convention whose artificiality suggests an irrelevance to the contemporary moment. But, while Murphy highlights the stylised nature of his traditional set, Friel destroys it. The final stage directions of *The Communication Cord* read "*[t]he sound of cracking timbers increases*". For the house, as the character Nora cries out, is collapsing.[42]

The move away from the rural as both set and theme was celebrated by playwright Clare Dowling who noted that "In the late Eighties and early Nineties, modern urban Dublin finally booted boggy bits of land off the Irish stage, page and screen. Suddenly people were writing about dole queues and housing estates and southside dinner parties".[43] While the urban world had been staged before now, it was presented in a clearly oppositional sense in which a bleak rejection of any remnants of the rural was dominant. Dermot Bolger's *The Lament for Arthur Cleary* (1989) is set in a Dublin where "[e]verywhere [is] closed except the burger huts, all the buses gone, everyone milling around drunk, taking to the glittering lights like the aborigines to whiskey".[44] The play is fluid in its use of time and space to stage the story of the already dead Arthur Cleary whose spirit, on the border of life and death, returns to a Dublin ravaged by poverty and drug addiction. The fact that it was first staged at the Project Arts Centre Dublin, rather than the Abbey or Peacock stages of the National Theatre, was a further indicator of the opening up of Irish theatre to new stories, styles and stages. And even when plays were premiered at the National Theatre they were often equally diverse in terms of style and theme, as in Frank McGuiness's *Observe the Sons of Ulster Marching Towards the Somme* (1985). The play is innovative in its use of space and time, as the elderly Pyper emerges from a dream only to inhabit the carnage of the First World War, from which he has just awoken. The play's significance lies in the fact that he is a survivor of the Somme. The battle of 1916—in which the 36th Ulster Division fought, and died, for King and Country only months after the Easter Rising—had seen fellow Irishmen rebel against the symbols of British power. McGuinness's sympathetic rendering of the fate of those written out of national commemoration, and the production of the play at the Peacock, anticipated Mary Robinson's presidential aspiration in 1990 that a "pluralist, open Ireland" would not see "the replacement of one set of power structures for another but [the] willingness on the part of each to learn from the other".[45] With a similar blurring of time-past and time-present, and the on-stage presence of a son who died in the British army in World War One, Sebastian Barry's

The Steward of Christendom (1995) stages the world of the senile Thomas Dunne, an inhabitant of a county hospital who, in his prime, was a chief superintendent in the Dublin Metropolitan Police. Dunne is a Catholic who loved queen and country and in their name broke up resistance to their rule but who, in the play's present—1932—is a man becalmed in an Ireland whose values he does not share. But, while Barry enables Dunne "to escape history's relentless drive to obliterate [his] memory",[46] so complicating a monocultural national narrative, the play also fractured any sense of a single theatrical mainstream as it was premiered at the Royal Court Theatre, London. As Barry acknowledged, "[t]he new Irish theatre is a moveable feast that moves quite naturally and lightly between Dublin, Belfast, London, New York".[47]

This global context was also claimed by Declan Hughes for the culture as a whole, arguing that "The village is no longer the objective correlative for Ireland: the city is, or to be more precise, *between* cities is".[48] As the protagonist of his *Digging for Fire* (1991) recalls, "[w]hen I arrived in New York for the first time [...] and I got my first glimpse of the Manhattan skyline, I felt that I was coming home" because, he tells his doubting friends, "*there* is just as much *here* as *here* is [...] and I don't believe the *here* you're describing exists here. To me, *here* is more like [...] *there*".[49] Given this embrace of globalisation, Hughes's comment, "I could live a long and happy life without seeing another play set in a Connemara kitchen, or a country pub",[50] seems anomalous coming at the end of a decade which opened with Friel's *Dancing at Lughnasa* (1990) and moved to a close with Martin McDonagh's *Leenane Trilogy* (1996–1997), Conor McPherson's *The Weir* (1997) and Marina Carr's *By the Bog of Cats* (1998), all of which all of which have a rural setting and, in the case of McDonagh and McPherson, the kitchen and pubs disparaged by Hughes. What distinguishes these plays from their more traditional predecessors, however, is the way that they disrupt those inherited sets and certainties and suggest their gradual passing from the world of social reality into that of parodic stage presence or disturbed states of mind and being.

When *Dancing at Lughansa* opens "Michael is downstage in a pool of light. The rest of the stage is in darkness", but immediately he speaks the lights slowly come up on the rest of the stage to reveal that "Slightly more than half of the stage is taken up by the kitchen [...] The rest of the stage is the garden adjoining the house".[51] Here Friel extends his disaggregation of the naturalist set, incorporating the off-stage into an on-stage presence and, moreover, operating in two historical periods; the physically enacted world of 1936 and the 1960s, from which Michael nostalgically re-inhabits that of his childhood. Given that *Lughnasa* is a play that remembers and mourns both a way of life and the naturalist set in which it found its fullest expression, it might appear surprising that one of the most successful theatrical events of the 1990s, which appeared only four years after Kilroy's comments on a form "at the end of its tether", was Martin McDonagh's *Leenane Trilogy* which began with *The Beauty Queen of Leenane* in 1996. Staged in the single set of "*the living-room/kitchen of a rural cottage in the west of Ireland*" that was maintained with only minor variations across the other two plays, *A Skull in Connemara* (1997) and *The Lonesome West* (1997), McDonagh appeared to prove that the traditional set still had theatrical power and cultural relevance.[52] However, as Fintan O'Toole observed, "[i]t is easy to be fooled by the apparently traditional, naturalistic form of the plays",[53] which are actually parodic demolitions of the plots of peasant plays from *Playboy of the Western World* (1907) to *Bailegangaire*. McDonagh simultaneously pushed the detailed set to a decidedly non-naturalist extreme in *The Cripple of Inishmaan* (1996), using that of a village shop with "shelves of canned goods, mostly peas"[54]; his plays being less concerned with social realities in the west of Ireland than their comic potential. But, as noted by Declan Hughes, even when the naturalist kitchen set was used in an iconoclastic way "the iconography remains powerfully the same", still able to haunt the Irish stage.[55]

While McDonagh made the rural set the place of black comedy in which Mag, an incontinent "Poor Old Woman", is beaten to death with a poker by her daughter, Carr's *The Mai* (1994) is a seemingly conventional domestic drama set in a "room with a huge bay window". However, it undercuts naturalism in its fluid use of time and the mythic echoes in its plot. Most significantly, the house has been built by The Mai to try and retain her philandering husband. Faced with his recurring infidelity, she describes the house as one "you build to keep out neuroses, stave off nightmares. But they come in anyway" as the domestic home—and by implication its naturalist set—proves to be a restriction to the self-realization of the female protagonist.[56] In a more overt rejection of naturalism, *The Bog of Cats* has a set of disturbing otherness in which fated lives stalk a world akin to that of Greek tragedy: "Dawn. On the Bog of Cats. A bleak white landscape of ice and snow. Music, a lone violin. HESTER SWAYNE trails the corpse of a black swan after her, leaving a trail of blood in the snow."[57] Carr's objective across her work is quite other than naturalism and as Eamonn Jordan notes "[a]lthough the superficial impression created is of theatrical realism, the disparate elements do not coalesce into meaningful mimetic structures".[58] In this context *The Weir* stands as an anomaly. While set in the "Present day"—a contemporaneity confirmed by its references to German tourists—its stage set of "a small rural bar", complete with turf fire, "in a rural part of Ireland, Northwest Leitrim or Sligo" stands for the seeming solidity of traditional forms with regard to which McPherson's attitude is neither parodic nor destabilizing.[59] Fintan O'Toole identified the play's "profound sense of dignity"[60] as an attraction for a global audiences, but Clare Wallace, following "ecstatic tributes" from figures such as Michael Billington of the UK's *Guardian*, argued that *The Weir* appeals "to the more conservative critical establishment … as a welcome antidote to In-Yer-Face theatre"; a comment which suggests that Irish theatre has an influential constituency outside of the country itself.[61]

As traditional sets and themes were progressively disrupted, so too was the idea that Irish drama had a single point of origin and reception. The establishment of Druid Theatre, Galway in 1975 as only the second professional company in the Republic; the creative flourish of the Derry-based Field Day theatre company from 1980 to 1991; the opening of the new Lyric in Belfast in 2011 (the Lyric had a professional company from 1968); and the creation of companies such as Waterford's Red Kettle (1985), Cork's Corcadorca (1991), and Sligo's Blue Raincoat (1991), altered the profile of Irish theatre.[62] And its location was no longer necessarily Ireland. McDonagh's Trilogy premiered at The Town Hall Theatre, Galway, but in a co-production with London's Royal Court, which premiered *The Weir* prior to its commercial and critical success in London's West End and New York's Broadway. Other London premieres for Irish plays include Frank McGuiness's *Mutabilitie* (1997) at the English National Theatre; Mark O'Rowe's *Howie the Rookie* (1999) at the Bush Theatre; Tom Murphy's *Alice Trilogy* (2005) and Marina Carr's *Woman and Scarecrow* (2006) at the Royal Court; with Martin McDonagh's *The Lieutenant of Inishmore* (2001) premiering at the Royal Shakespeare Company, Stratford-upon-Avon. All these changes pointed to a range of companies and cities staging original Irish drama that defied narrow definitions of a uniform mainstream.

But this diversification of theatre in terms of form, theme and location cannot be regarded in isolation from the society in which and for which it is created. In 1997 John Fairleigh noted the financial support for drama enabled by the fact that "the economy is developing at one of the fastest rates in the European Union" with the result that artists were "warmly embraced as confirmation of the country's new dynamism and diversity".[63] Sixteen years later, Fintan Walsh observed that since 2007 Ireland had "plummeted from the heady heights of neoliberal abundance and excess into political, economic, social and cultural turmoil" as a result of which there had been a "severance of subsidy" which impacted most severely on the theatre.[64] However he noted that many new companies had been established in the wake of the financial crisis including THISISPOPBABY (2007), ANU Productions (2009) and HotForTheatre (2010), whose work was frequently innovative of economic necessity, featuring only one or two performers in bare or stripped-down sets. The work in two recent collections demonstrates the creativity of this "poor theatre" and includes: Amy Conway's *I ♥ Alice ♥ I* (2010), a "show which is fictional but presented as a documentary piece"[65] in which two middle-aged, working-class lesbians speak directly to the audience about their relationship and how they were persuaded to tell them their story—only to have one of the women (in the first production the playwright herself) remove her wig and make-up to reveal that it was actually a performance, and ANU Productions' site-specific *The Boys of Foley Street* (2012) which gave audiences an immersive experience of the violent heroin epidemic in North Side Dublin during the 1970s.[66] More recently, Annie Ryan's adaptation of Eimear McBride's *A Girl is a Half-formed Thing* (2014), first performed by the Corn Exchange Theatre Company at the Samuel Beckett Centre during Dublin's Theatre Festival, was also new in company, location and form. Conceived "for a solo performer on a spare set with no props or furniture" it captures the anguished adolescence, sexual abuse and suicide of a teenage girl who, through voice and gesture, captures all the characters who impacted on her short life.[67] It is as engaged with contemporary reality as any naturalist drama, but achieves this while eschewing all of its formal aspects, leaving only the truths articulated by the performer's voice and body.

Within this diversity of forms, in works that address lives previously deemed socially and theatrically marginal, two productions by established companies demonstrate how the reconfigured mainstream of Irish theatre now accommodates both naturalist and non-naturalist dramas in a pluralistic theatrical culture: Enda Walsh's *Ballyturk* and Mark O'Rowe's *Our Few and Evil Days*, which won Best Production and Best New Play respectively in the *Irish Times* theatre awards for 2014.

In Galway, Enda Walsh's work with Druid already included *The Walworth Farce* (2006), whose set is "*three square spaces. Essentially a living room at its centre, a kitchen to stage left and a bedroom to stage right*". This is occupied by a "*Farce*" in a "*performance style [that] resembles The Three Stooges*" for,[68] as Walsh commented, he knew that he had to "explode" the naturalist play of the Irish diaspora "and bring it somewhere else".[69] Unsurprisingly, then, he dismantled every aspect of the naturalist set in *Ballyturk*, staging "a very large room—too large" in which "the back wall looks vast—its painted surface powdery to the touch. On this wall a large mustard curtain is drawn—where possibly a window is". This suggests that this could be a naturalist set, but when the back wall slowly tears off with ripping wallpaper, aggressively sparking power cables and buckling water pipes what is revealed is "a beautiful blue light—onto a small hill of perfect grass". The stage directions state (somewhat doubtfully) that this is "what must be the outside" and that this is the "real life behind that wall". But *Ballyturk*'s objective is theatricality rather than reality. As one of the characters says, "it's filling rooms with words, not real life".[70]

In his review of the Abbey production of *Our Few and Evil Days*, the drama of a middle-class Dublin family, Peter Crawley noted that the dialogue was so "fastidiously naturalistic" that he wondered if O'Rowe had "genuinely fallen for realism". "The impression is enforced by Paul Wills' set", Crawley continued, "so staggeringly convincing in construction, from its ceiling to functioning kitchen taps, it's almost surprising he stopped short of a fourth wall".[71] This "hyper-realist" set was striking from a playwright whose previous work had been resolutely non-naturalistic and whose *Terminus* (2007) had a set composed of broken shards of mirror on which the three performers stood to deliver their monologues. But as O'Rowe observed, "sometimes the subject dictates the form" and in *Our Few and Evil Days* the family drama of buried secrets demanded a "very traditional form" in "the conventional proscenium arch".[72]

In 1955, Fallon lamented the fact that naturalism, which he felt was "only a phase in the drama's long and varied history", seemed to be "even more strongly entrenched in the Irish theatre today".[73] That is no longer the case. As

O'Rowe's comment makes clear, naturalism is now an option rather than an obligation in a theatre culture which no longer has a single, exclusionary mainstream but is multiple in its forms, themes and theatres.

Notes

1. Gabriel Fallon, "The Future of the Irish Theatre", *Studies,* Vol. 44, No. 173 (1955): 99. Although some of the quotations use "realism" but as "naturalism" is the term used by Fallon I retain that throughout the chapter. Both "advocated a total reproduction of unstylized, unembellished reality, stressing the material aspects of human existence." Patrice Pavis, *Dictionary of Theatre: Terms, Concepts, and Analysis* (Toronto: University of Toronto Press, 1998), 236.
2. Fallon, "The Future of the Irish Theatre", 100, 99, 95.
3. Christopher Morash, *A History of the Irish Theatre 1601–2000* (Cambridge University Press: Cambridge 2002), 209
4. Fallon, "The Future of the Irish Theatre", 98.
5. Vincent Dowling quoted in James P. McGlone, *Ria Mooney: The Life and Times of the Artistic Director of the Abbey Theatre, 1948–1963* (Jefferson, North Carolina, 2002).
6. Lionel Pilkington, *Theatre and the State in Twentieth-Century Ireland, Cultivating the People* (Routledge: London, 2001), 149
7. McGlone, 139.
8. Lionel Pilkington, *Theatre and Ireland* (London: Palgrave Macmillan, 2010), 55.
9. Michael Mac Liammóir, *Theatre in Ireland* (Dublin: Cultural Relations Committee, 1950), 42.
10. Thomas Kilroy, "Groundwork for an Irish Theatre", *Studies*, 48 (190) (1959): 195–196.
11. Nicholas Grene, *The Politics of Irish Drama: Plays in Context from Boucicault to Friel* (Cambridge: Cambridge University Press, 1999), 171.
12. Melissa Sihra, "Introduction: Figures at the Window", in *Women in Irish Drama: A Century of Authorship and Representation,* ed. Melissa Sihra (London: Palgrave Macmillan, 2007), 2.
13. www.constitution.ie/Documents/Bhunreacht_na_hEireann_web.pdf. Accessed 4 April, 2016.
14. The protagonists of Teresa Deevy's plays such as *Katie Roche* (1936), resist social conformity but ultimately succumb to its pressure. Revivals of the play in 1975 and 1994, along with a special issue of *Irish University Review* on Deevy (Spring/Summer 1995) attested to the increasing relevance of her drama.
15. T. K. Whitaker, *Programme for Economic Expansion* (Dublin: Government Papers, 1958), pr. 4808, 9
16. Fintan O'Toole, "Irish Theatre: The State of the Art", in *Theatre Stuff: Critical Essays on Contemporary Irish Theatre*, ed. Eamonn Jordan (Dublin: Carysfort Press, 2000), 51.
17. Fergus Linehan, "The Future of Irish Drama: A discussion between Fergus Linehan, Hugh Leonard, John B. Keane and Brian Friel", *The Irish Times*, February 12, 1970, 14.

18. Seamus Heaney, *Preoccupations: Selected Prose 1968–1978* (London: Faber and Faber, 1980), 56.
19. Linehan, 14.
20. Brian Friel, "Plays Peasant and Unpeasant", in.), *Brian Friel: Essays, Diaries, Interviews: 1964–1999,* ed. Christopher Murray (London: Faber and Faber, 1999), 55.
21. Ciarán Deane, "Brian Friel's *Translations*: The Origins of a Cultural Experiment", *Field Day Review* 5 (2009): 12.
22. Thomas Kilroy, "A Generation of Playwrights", *Irish University Review* 22 (1) (1992): 136
23. Hugh Leonard, "Production Note", *Stephen D* (London: Evans and Brothers Ltd., 1964), 5, 7.
24. Brian Friel, *Philadelphia, Here I Come!, Plays One* (London: Faber and Faber, 1996), 27, 99.
25. Tom Murphy, "Two Playwrights with a Single Theme", in *A Paler Shade of Green,* eds. Des Hickey and Gus Smith (London: Leslie Frewin, 1972), 226.
26. Tom Murphy, *A Crucial Week in the Life of a Grocer's Assistant, Plays: 4* (London: Methuen, 1997), 142.
27. Tom Murphy, *The Morning After Optimism, Plays: 3* (London: Methuen, 1994, 5, 12.
28. Kilroy, "A Generation of Playwrights", 140.
29. Brian Friel, *Translations, Plays One*, 419.
30. Fintan O'Toole, *The Politics of Magic: The Work and Times of Tom Murphy* (Dublin: Raven Arts Press, 1987), 21.
31. "A Generation of Playwrights", 137, 139.
32. Anna McMullan, "Masculinity and Masquerade in Thomas Kilroy's *Double Cross* and *The Secret Fall of Constance Wilde*", *Irish University Review: Special Issue, Thomas Kilroy*, 32 (1) (2002): 136.
33. Thomas Kilroy, *The Secret Fall of Constance Wilde* (Loughcrew, County Meath: 1997), 11, 18.
34. Christopher Murray, *Twentieth-Century Irish Drama: Mirror Up to Nation* (Manchester: Manchester University Press, 1997), 233.
35. Catriona Ryan, *Border States in the Work of Tom Mac Intyre: A Paleo-Postmodern Perspective* (Newcastle-upon-Tyne: Cambridge Scholars Press, 2012), 233.
36. Patrick Kavanagh and Tom Mac Intyre, *The Great Hunger* (Gigginstown, Mullingar: Lilliput Press, 1988), 33.
37. Ibid., 37, 46, 39.
38. Ibid., 82.
39. Julia Furay and Redmond O'Hanlon eds., *Critical Moments: Fintan O'Toole on Modern Irish Theatre* (Dublin: Carysfort Press, 2003), 21.
40. "A Generation of Playwrights", 139.
41. Tom Murphy, *Bailegangaire, Plays: Two* (London: Methuen, 1993), 90–91.
42. Brian Friel, *The Communication Cord* (Loughcrew, Co. Meath: The Gallery Press, 1983), 11, 93.
43. Caroline Williams, Katy Hayes, Siân Quill and Clare Dowling, "People in Glasshouse: An Anecdotal History of an Independent Theatre Company", in *Druids, Dudes and Beauty Queens: The Changing Face of Irish Theatre*, ed. Dermot Bolger (Dublin: New Island Books, 2001), 133.

44. Dermot Bolger, *The Lament for Arthur Cleary, A Dublin Quartet* (Harmondsworth: Penguin, 1992), 26
45. Fergus Finlay, *Mary Robinson: A President with a Purpose* (Dublin: O'Brien Press, 1990), 156.
46. Fintan O'Toole, "Introduction", *Three Plays by Sebastian Barry,* ix.
47. Sebastian Barry, "Foreword", *Far from the Land: Contemporary Irish Plays*, ed. John Fairleigh (London: Methuen, 1998), xi.
48. Declan Hughes, "Who the Hell Do We Think We Still Are?: Reflections on Theatre and Identity", *Theatre Stuff,* 12.
49. Declan Hughes, *Digging for Fire, Plays 1* (London: Methuen, 1998), 37–38.
50. Hughes, "Who the Hell Do We Think We Still Are?", 13.
51. Brian Friel, *Dancing at Lughnasa* (London: Faber and Faber, 1990), 1, np.
52. Martin McDonagh, *The Beauty Queen of Lenane, Plays:1* (London: Bloomsbury, 2008), 1.
53. Fintan O'Toole, "Introduction", McDonagh, *Plays:1*, xii.
54. Martin McDonagh, *The Cripple of Inishmaan* (London: Methuen, 1997), 1.
55. Hughes, "Who the Hell Do We Think We Still Are?", 12.
56. Marina Carr, *The Mai* (Loughcrew, Co. Meath: Galley Press, 1995), 11, 51.
57. Marina Carr, *By the Bog of Cats* (Loughrew, Co Meath: Gallery Press, 198), 13
58. Eamonn Jordan, *Dissident Dramaturgies: Contemporary Irish Theatre* (Dublin: Irish Academic Press, 2010), 7.
59. Conor McPherson, *The Weir* (London: Nick Hern Books, 1997), np.
60. Furay and O'Hanlon, *Critical Moments*, 185.
61. Clare Wallace, *Suspect Cultures: Narrative, Identity and Citation in 1990s New Drama* (Prague: Literaria Pragensia, 2006), 40.
62. The company went into liquidation in 2014 because of a reduction in Arts Council funding.
63. John Fairleigh, "Introduction", *Far From the Land*, xi-xii.
64. Fintan Walsh, *"That Was Us": Contemporary Irish Theatre and Performance* (London: Oberon Books, 2013), 2–3.
65. Amy Conroy, *I ♥ Alice ♥ I*, in *"This is Just This. It isn't Real. It's Money": The Oberon Anthology of Contemporary Irish Plays*, ed. Thomas Conway (London: Oberon, 2013), 187.
66. Louise Lowe, *The Boys of Foley Street*, in *Contemporary Irish Plays*, ed. Patrick Lonergan (London: Methuen, 2015), 347–376.
67. Eimear McBride, *A Girl is a Half-formed Thing* (London: Faber and Faber, 2015), 11.
68. Enda Walsh, *The Walworth Farce* (London: Nick Hearn Books, 2007), 5, 7.
69. Jordan, 248.
70. Enda Walsh, *Ballyturk*, *Plays: Two* (London: Nick Hearn Books, 2014), 221, 269, 272.
71. Peter Crawley, Review of *Our Few and Evil Days*, *The Irish Times*, October 4, 2014. www.irishtimes.com/culture/stage/review-our-few-and-evil-days. Accessed 4 April, 2016.
72. Response to a question from the author. Mark O'Rowe in conversation with Annabelle Comyn, "Theatre of Change Symposium", Abbey Theatre Dublin, 22 January 2016. www.youtube.com/watch?v=e9g6dLDiJVA. Accessed 4 April 2016.
73. Fallon, "The Future of the Irish Theatre", 92–93.

Bibliography

Conway, Thomas, ed. *"This Is Just This. It isn't Real. It's Money": The Oberon Anthology of Contemporary Irish Plays* London: Oberon, 2013.

Furay, Julia and Redmond O'Hanlon, eds. *Critical Moments: Fintan O'Toole on Modern Irish Theatre*. Dublin: Carysfort Press, 2003.

Hughes, Declan. "Who the Hell Do We Think We Still Are?: Reflections on Theatre and Identity." In *Theatre Stuff: Critical Essays on Contemporary Irish Theatre*, edited by Eamonn Jordan. Dublin: Carysfort Press, 2000.

Jordan, Eamonn. *Dissident Dramaturgies: Contemporary Irish Theatre*. Dublin: Irish Academic Press, 2010.

Lonergan, Patrick, ed. *Contemporary Irish Plays*. London: Methuen, 2015.

Mac Liammóir, Michael. *Theatre in Ireland*. Dublin: Cultural Relations Committee, 1950.

Morash, Christopher. *A History of the Irish Theatre 1601–2000*. Cambridge University Press: Cambridge, 2002.

O'Toole, Fintan. *The Politics of Magic: The Work and Times of Tom Murphy*. Dublin: Raven Arts Press, 1987, 21.

———. "Irish Theatre: The State of the Art." In *Theatre Stuff: Critical Essays on Contemporary Irish Theatre*, edited by Eamonn Jordan. Dublin: Carysfort Press, 2000.

Pilkington, Lionel. *Theatre and Ireland*. London: Palgrave Macmillan, 2010.

Sihra, Melissa, ed. *Women in Irish Drama: A Century of Authorship and Representation*. London: Palgrave Macmillan, 2007.

Wallace, Clare. *Suspect Cultures: Narrative, Identity and Citation in 1990s New Drama*. Prague: Literaria Pragensia, 2006.

Whitaker, T. K. *Programme for Economic Expansion*. Dublin: Government Papers, 1958.

Williams, Caroline, Katy Hayes, Siân Quill and Clare Dowling, "People in Glasshouse: An Anecdotal History of an Independent Theatre Company." In *Druids, Dudes and Beauty Queens: The Changing Face of Irish Theatre*, edited by Dermot Bolger. Dublin: New Island Books, 2001.

The Theatre Royal: Dublin

Conor Doyle

Overview

From 1820, three Theatre Royals fronted onto Dublin's Hawkins Street. The final incarnation was opened on 23 September 1935. Ownership of the third Royal changed hands three times during its relatively short, but illustrious, existence. The Pearce family were the original owners, followed by Maurice Elliman in 1938, who added the "Jewel in their Crown" to his family's Irish theatre and cinema empire. Lastly the Royal was acquired in the mid 1950s by the UK's Rank Organisation, led by industrialist J. Arthur Rank. Designed by Leslie Norton, the theatre had capacity for 4,000 patrons—3,700 seated and 300 standing. It was billed as the largest theatre in Europe. At the time of its last acquisition, the city was still recovering from the devastation of civil strife and the Economic War with the UK in the early 1930s. The structure had a magnificent art deco edifice and dwarfed every building in the surrounding area. Its size was artificially magnified by the narrowness of the streets it stood on. The interior was Moorish in style and was truly exquisite.

The new Royal was to be part of the "New Ireland" described by Sean Lemass TD—the Minister for Commerce and Trade—at the gala opening night, who noted that "[a]ll the materials and construction were made in Ireland". To reinforce the "Irishness" of the building, three hand-carved statues by Laurence Campbell RHA (1911–2001) depicting a Celtic warrior, Eire and the mythic Celtic muse of imagination were placed on the outside. The city's air pollution—caused by coal fires, leaded petrol and smog—blackened these statues within a year or two and their beauty was lost from street level. The Pearce family aimed at an upmarket classical concert audience and held

C. Doyle (✉)
Independent Researcher, Dublin, Ireland

E. Jordan, E. Weitz (eds.), *The Palgrave Handbook of Contemporary Irish Theatre and Performance*,
https://doi.org/10.1057/978-1-137-58588-2_3

celebrity concerts in 1936 and early 1937. The principle artists were Paul Robeson, Sergei Rachmaninov, Toti Dal Monte, Fritz Kreisler, Beniamino Gigli and, of course, Count John McCormack. In this period the Royal also staged the variety show format.

The pre-war years saw a huge number of US stars appear at the Royal, including Jimmy Durante, The Nicholas Brothers, The Three Stooges, Dizzy Gillespie, Nina Mae McKinney—the first African American film star—and The Mills Brothers. Then there were the "cowboy" actors/singing stars Tom Mix and Gene Autry. Autry was the last international star to appear on the Royal stage, at the start of the Second World War: 6 September 1939. Many of the film stars were from the US film company RKO (Radio-Keith-Orpheum) Pictures and were on publicity tours of Europe to promoter their films. RKO specialized in films that featured vaudeville theatre stars of the late 1920s and 1930s. It was reported at the time that Dublin had the highest cinema-going public per capita than any other city in Europe, no wonder these stars came to the Royal.

There were, of course, artists from the UK: George Formby, Gracie Fields, Jack Hylton and his Orchestra, Vera Lynn and comedians Tommy Trinder and the notoriously risqué Max Millar. These performers would have been familiar to audiences in Ireland from their popular films and their BBC radio broadcasts. Millar appeared at the Royal before the Elliman ownership as they never allowed risqué material or what they deemed as inappropriate dress on stage. Even in the late 1950s management dropped the main stage curtain on pop star Billy Idol mid-performance and had him escorted from the theatre, as they thought he had been making sexual gestures with the microphone and stand.

In the 1930s the Royal carved out a reputation as one of the four major variety theatres in the British Isles, the others were London's Palladium, Blackpool's Opera House and Glasgow's Empire. After the 1938 change of ownership, the Elliman's soon altered the shows and introduced a "cine-variety" format to the theatre. Cine-variety was a variant of the typical variety shows that were being performed in other theatres in Dublin and the UK. The format ran as follows: a short show, a film, a community sing-a-long with the organ, and a full-length show. The first show was usually a shortened version of the later full show. This was followed by a film—usually a B film. As the Elliman's owned over thirty cinemas in Ireland, the A films usually went to Dublin's Savoy and Metropole. A large screen would have been wheeled out onto the stage of the Royal to show the films. This was followed by organ playing with a community sing-a-long. Alban Chambers, Gordon Spicer, Norman Medcalfe and Tommy Dando were the famous organists in the Royal at different times. The large Compton organ would rise from the side of the orchestra pit in a blaze of light. The organ had a glass Perspex console and coloured light emerged from within the organ itself. The words of popular songs would be projected onto the screen and a black dot would dance across it so that patrons could sing in time, like an early version of karaoke. The format would finish with a full ninety-minute show, which changed every week as did the sets, scripts and costumes.

The Royal soon became the heart and soul of the bleak, grey Dublin of the 1930s and 1940s. Patrons of any social group could spend a few pennies and be entertained from early afternoon to 10:15 p.m. each night, without having to leave the theatre. There were bars on every floor, with the added draw that the top-floor bar's license allowed it stay open thirty minutes later than any other bar in the city. This license had been granted to the previous Royal. To ensure its continuation, large parts of the back-gable wall of the theatre was built using red brick from the earlier building. The majority of Dubliners and Royal patrons lived in a four-mile radius of the theatre, no more than thirty minutes' walk. Many of them inhabited near-tenement conditions and saw the Royal a place of sheer escapism from life.

The War Years

With the outbreak of the Second World War, during which Ireland declaring neutrality, the country was cut off from international acts. The Elliman family decided to keep the Royal open during these years and kept the ticket prices very low in order to make it affordable for ordinary Dubliners. This gave Irish acts a chance to hone their stagecraft and Dubliners flocked to the Royal each week. Performers like Jimmy O'Dea, Noel Purcell, Peggy Dell, Eddie Byrne, Frankie Blowers and Maureen Potter took full advantage of the lack of overseas competition. They became firm favourites with audiences, and held this status for the rest of their careers. Noel Purcell proclaimed that the Royal was full during the war for the simple reason that "[g]oing to the Royal was the best way of keeping your family warm on a Sunday as your coal ration had run out". The cine-variety formula remained in place—it had proved very popular with audiences—and the shows still changed each week, as did the material.

During the period from 1920's to 1965 the influence of the Roman Catholic Church in Ireland extended to places of entertainment, the Theatre Royal was no exception. The Archbishop of Dublin, John Charles McQuaid, appointed a chaplain to the theatre to ensure high moral values and a religious ethos were maintained. To this end, the theatre's famous, permanent, all-female dance troupe—The Royalettes—were instructed to say the rosary at six o'clock each evening. A chaplain was available at all times to hear confession, in case they had any "impure thoughts" while dancing; he had unrestricted access to their dressing rooms. All this took place while the theatre owners were a Jewish family.

Post-War Royal

After the end of the war, international acts resumed touring Irish theatres. Louis Elliman or "Mr Louis", as he was known to Dubliners, took over the running of the Elliman cinema and theatre portfolio after his father, Maurice, died. The portfolio then held over thirty venues across the country. In 1950, Elliman went on a business trip to Hollywood and Los Angeles. He met the agents of many high-profile artists and—the stars themselves—securing agreements that they would appear at the Royal during tours of the UK and Europe. This copper-fastened the future and reputation of the Royal as one of the "Big 4" theatres for the next three to four years.

The cine-variety format continued during this period, except when a visiting superstar was appearing. In July 1951, Judy Garland came to the Royal and reportedly entertained 50,000 patrons in a week. There was such demand for tickets that up to 200 Dubliners without tickets stood on Poolbeg Street each night while Garland sang to them out the window of the number one dressing room. A succession of superstars played the Royal over the next few years including Bob Hope (May 1951), Danny Kaye (June 1952), Gracie Field (December 1952), Maurice Chevalier (January 1953), Frankie Laine (September 1953), Roy Rogers and Trigger—Trigger the horse even appeared on stage—(March 1954), and Nat King Cole (April 1954).

The flow of superstars started to dry up during the remainder of the 1950s. There were only a few rays of light, such as Dame Margot Fonteyn and the Royal Ballet from London (May 1957), the Israel Philharmonic Orchestra (June 1955) and the film première of Disney's *Darby O' Gill and the Little People* (June 1959), with Walt Disney and Sean Connery in attendance. The glory days of the Royal were starting to be a distant memory. In the late 1950s, Dubliners continued to flock to the Royal, but things were about to change for many reasons.

The Decline and Fall of the Royal

In the mid-1950s, the Ellimans decided to sell the majority of their cinema and theatre portfolio—including the Royal—to the Rank Organisation. Rank had no real interest in the Royal, except for its property development potential as an office block or the newly required multistorey car parks. Younger patrons did not want to see a full variety show, with their pop idols only coming on at the end of the night for eight to ten minutes. In 1957, Bill Haley and the Comets were not part of a variety show, instead appearing as a standalone act.

In 1957, during Jimmy O'Dea's run at the Royal, the film to be shown was Elvis Presley's *Loving You*. The younger audience eagerly awaited Presley's film and were not interested in the show that preceded it. They chatted and disturbed the performers on stage. O'Dea eventually stopped the show and remonstrated with them. O'Dea and Presley never appeared on the same bill again.

In the early 1960s, home-grown showbands were becoming more popular with young people. This was a phenomenon unique to Ireland. With the increasing number of dancehalls, more pressure was put on the limited financial resources of the Royal. Many of the Irish stage performers were getting older and their style of entertainment did not appeal to the increasingly affluent younger audiences. Young Irish artists travelled to England and the USA to advance their show-business careers and did not join Irish variety theatre companies.

The social housing schemes, started in Dublin during the 1930s to help alleviate the chronic housing problems, were interrupted by the war. These projects were not restarted until near the end of the 1950s and beginning of the 1960s, due to financial constraints. However, once restarted, Dubliners were rehoused in suburbs well outside walking distance of the Royal. In May–June 1961, a five-week musicians' strike took place, after which a substantial pay demand was made. This added to the already high overheads that the Rank Organisation in London were increasing reluctant to fund.

The introduction of television to Ireland in January 1962 sounded the death knell for the Royal. Many people on the east coast were now able to pick up the BBC and ITV's Ulster TV signal that was broadcast from Northern Ireland. With TV sets becoming cheaper, a Dublin viewer could now pick up three stations and watch "Sunday Night at the London Palladium" and not go to the Royal.

Despite all of this, Louis Elliman maintained that the Royal as a venue was making money in 1962. However, J. Arthur Rank sent a blunt message: "Close the joint." On the 30 June 1962, the Theatre Royal closed. Dubliners never thought that it would close, but to their shock it was demolished a few months later. The great bastion of variety in Dublin had fallen. The cine-variety formula has not been used in Dublin since. It was not just the building that was lost but a way of life, for its very loyal patrons who had grown up, socialized, made friends and formed relationships in this grand, escapist paradise.

The Politics of Performance: Theatre in and about Northern Ireland

Lisa Fitzpatrick

Introduction

Theatre in Northern Ireland has frequently engaged with the social and cultural turmoil colloquially referred to as the Troubles: the civil violence that dominated life in the region between 1969 and the 1995 Ceasefires which preceded the Good Friday Agreement in 1998. Since then, the theatre has been actively engaged in mapping the changing society, in commemorating the history of the conflict, and in commenting on the emergence of the new post-conflict culture. This has sometimes been an explicitly political process, as in the production of new writing like Martin Lynch's *Chronicles of Long Kesh* (2010), Seamus Keenan's *Over the Wire* (2013) or Dave Duggan's *Denizen* (2014). The first two of these commemorate events in Long Kesh/the Maze (as the prison is variously known), while Duggan's verse drama gives voice to the dissident Republican movement as its representative, the denizen, struggles to decide between the Armalite and the ballot box. Other productions that engage with the politics of Northern Ireland include revivals of plays written during and about the conflict: in 2007 Lynch's *The Interrogation of Ambrose Fogarty* (originally staged in 1982); in 2012 Frank McGuinness's *Carthaginians* (premiered 1988); and, also in 2012, Brian Friel's *The Freedom of the City* (premiered 1973). In each of these, the original reception and meanings generated by the production have shifted over the course of time, as discussed below. The result is that *Ambrose Fogarty* played largely as comedy, while *Carthaginians* and *Freedom* both commemorated the publication of the Saville Report and

L. Fitzpatrick (✉)
University of Ulster, Derry, Northern Ireland, UK
e-mail: L.Fitzpatrick@ulster.ac.uk

E. Jordan, E. Weitz (eds.), *The Palgrave Handbook of Contemporary Irish Theatre and Performance*,
https://doi.org/10.1057/978-1-137-58588-2_4

David Cameron's apology for the killings on Bloody Sunday in Derry in 1972.[1] Another tranche of work that has emerged on the Northern Irish stage since 1998 uses the metaphor of the buried or submerged to express the need to reconcile and find a way of healing the trauma of the past so that a new society can emerge. Some of Tinderbox Theatre Company's new writing addresses this issue, as does work by Big Telly Theatre Company, Prime Cut Productions, and Kabosh. This work seems in particular to speak to a local audience about lingering concerns, most explicitly the fate of the "disappeared" whose burial sites are still sought by their families. To a lesser extent, site has played a part in recent Northern Irish theatre. Tinderbox's important site-specific performance *Convictions* (2000) in the Crumlin Road Courthouse and Replay Theatre Company's use of the Crumlin Road Gaol to stage *Macbeth* (2007) reclaimed and opened to the public sites that had previously been closed and forbidden. Both these places are significant in Republican and paramilitary histories of Northern Ireland. Finally, and most recently, verbatim theatre productions from the "Theatre of Witness" Project have sought to explicitly engage with the history of the conflict and bring accounts of the conflict to a community as well as a theatrical audience.

This chapter defines political performance very broadly, to include a range of thematically and formally varied work. I am concerned with theatrical efficacy only in a few instances; my main interest is in the affective qualities of the work and the audience response.[2] I am particularly interested in work that evokes a sense of a private conversation between stage and auditorium, and that addresses shared histories to create an ephemeral moment of "feeling together", which Jill Dolan describes as the "utopian performative". She coins the term to describe ways in which

> theatre and performance can articulate a common future, one that's more just and equitable, one in which we can all participate more equally, with more chances to live fully and contribute to the making of culture [...] such desire to be part of the intense present of performance offers us, if not expressly political then usefully emotional, expressions of what utopia might feel like.[3]

Representing Bloody Sunday: *Freedom of the City*, *Carthaginians*, *Heroes with Their Hands in the Air*

Of the three plays discussed in this section, two were written during the conflict. Brian Friel's *Freedom of the City* was the most immediate response to the events on Bloody Sunday, and Frank McGuinness's *Carthaginians* was written during the late 1980s and first staged in 1988, after the Hunger Strikes, during some of the most violent and hopeless years of the conflict. Fintan Brady's *Heroes with their Hands in the Air* was first staged in 2007 and was remounted in 2012 following the publication of the Saville Report into the events on Bloody Sunday. In addition, Richard Norton Taylor's *Scenes from the Saville Inquiry* also played in Derry to a mixed reception, touring from the Tricycle

Theatre in London in Autumn 2005. *Freedom of the City* had premiered in Dublin at the Abbey Theatre in July 1973, directed by Tómas Mac Anna and running for twelve performances. Richard Rankin Russell's discussion of the play quotes Eavan Boland's 1973 interview with Friel, in which he reveals that he was writing a different play before Bloody Sunday happened. Entitled *John Butt's Bothy*, it was set in the 1700s and explored evictions and poverty. Friel tells Boland that *Freedom* is "about poverty" primarily, using the events in Derry as a base to explore that theme.[4] Reviewing for the *Irish Times*, David Nowlan argues that it is "patently not meant to be" a documentary on Bloody Sunday, but that some of the spectators seemed unaware of this and uncertain how to respond. He also notes the irony of the premieres taking place almost simultaneously in London and Dublin, while the play was not performed in Belfast or Derry. The play was staged again at the Abbey in 1999, touring to the Friel Festival at the Lincoln Centre, in a production directed by Conall Morrison with Sorcha Cusack in the role of Lily. In 2005 it was performed at the Finborough Theatre in London, and following the publication of the Saville Report it was given a rehearsed reading at the Elmwood Hall in Belfast in October 2010, directed by Adrian Dunbar. The play was produced again in an amateur production that toured in the North West of Ireland in early 2013, playing to packed houses in Derry and Donegal.

While details of the text mark the play as an angry response to Bloody Sunday, the passing of time has drawn out its wider significance. The stage directions give the setting defiantly as "Derry City, Ireland" (when the Judge speaks he names "the City of Londonderry, Northern Ireland") and the staging indicates Bloody Sunday with the woman's voice (Bernadette Devlin McAliskey) exhorting the crowd to stand firm, and the assault by the armored cars, gas canisters and baton rounds. The Judge is clearly a representation of Widgery and his judgment is equally clearly a deliberate miscarriage of justice. But between the first staging of the play and the 2010 reading and 2013 production, a number of significant things changed. The political landscape in Northern Ireland changed dramatically, with the end to the armed conflict and the establishment of a power-sharing executive cementing the primacy of political over military struggle. The publication of the Saville Report, which was accompanied by an apology from the Prime Minister at the time, David Cameron, was another significant event. This allowed different productions of *Freedom* to foster the interpretation of the work as "a meditation on how politics can crush innocent people"[5] and "a politically pertinent play [that] shows this siege of three innocent Catholics as an assault of the powerful on the poor".[6] Joe Nawaz's review argues, "It's no surprise that *Freedom of the City* was sharpened to a point by the real-life events that took place in Derry in January 1972—the spectre of that massacre hangs everywhere. *Freedom of the City* isn't just timely. In the wake of belated justice of a kind for the families of the 13[7] innocents gunned down 38 years ago, it's also timeless. One can only hope this is a trial run for a full revival at the new Lyric of this bleak, beautiful and fiercely righteous play."[8] Wilborn Hampton states that "[t]he play is still timely. The geography may have changed, but a glance at today's headlines will testify to its continuing relevance".[9]

There is an annual Bloody Sunday Memorial Weekend in Derry city, which includes a march along the original route, a laying of wreaths at the memorial in the Bogside, speeches by local politicians and, often, performances or staged readings of plays that address the tragedy. Sheila McCormick points out that this annual reproduction is a way of "constructing and conforming the participants' communal memory".[10] David Cameron's apology was itself stage-managed in Derry as a piece of public theatre. The widespread speculation about Saville's findings had become public optimism that at last the dead would be exonerated and the culpability of the British Army acknowledged. On 13 June 2010 in the afternoon, the Guildhall Square (where the original march had been heading) was linked live to the Westminster parliament and huge screens were erected outside the Guildhall. The event began with a silent march that followed the original route, with marchers carrying large banners depicting the faces of the dead. An estimated 10,000 people gathered in the square in the sunshine, including many people who had been on the march on that day in 1972. The families of the victims were inside the hall to hear the key findings before they were made public. The families indicated to the crowd that they were satisfied with the findings by waving from an upstairs window, holding up copies of the report and giving a thumbs-up. The crowd responded with loud cheers and with some singing of "We shall overcome", the ballad of the civil rights movement internationally. After the Guildhall clock chimed the half hour, at 3:30 p.m., the broadcast from Westminster began. The square was largely silent to receive the apology, with loud cheering greeting the key findings. The speeches from Westminster were followed by speeches from the family members outside the Guildhall, and the crowd slowly dispersed. However, the event had much of the quality of Dolan's utopian performative. It was a large public gathering of people "feeling together": sharing the dignity of the silent march, the grief of the original event and of the families, the emotional release of eventual justice, and another step in a process of recovering from the trauma of the decades of conflict.

This public expression is part of the reception of post-Saville productions of *Freedom* and *Carthaginians*. The reception is also shaped by the fact that the events of Bloody Sunday are no longer really contested; the plays are therefore freed from some of the controversy that previously shaped audiences' responses. The production of *Carthaginians* at the Millennium Forum in Derry, directed by Adrian Dunbar, evoked a meditative response from theatre critics and played to full houses. Stuart Marshall's set was a minimalist pair of raked platforms set before a blazing blue trapezium of sky. The white stone facings on the platforms evoked Derry's famous walls, a graveyard, and a bleak, sun-bleached place of classical tragedy. The three women who are the first characters on the stage, one of them nursing a sick bird, also suggest mythic figures: the three Graces at the judgement of Paris; their presence in the graveyard recalls the three Marys at the tomb of Christ. As the plot unfolds, the goddesses in the

Judgement of Paris—Hera goddess of marriage and childbirth, Aphrodite goddess of love and Athene goddess of wisdom—suggest the particular qualities and histories of these three female characters. Meanwhile they wait for the dead to rise.

The opening scene, in its setting and in the presence of the women, evokes tragedy, grief, and the potential for resurrection. *Carthaginians* tells the story of seven men and women from Derry and their individual responses to the events of Bloody Sunday. Maela camps by the grave of her daughter who died of cancer, aged 13, on Bloody Sunday. Refusing to admit that her daughter is dead, she insists that nobody died that day, and that her daughter will rise again. Hark joined the IRA after Bloody Sunday and served time in prison; Seph was an informer and will no longer speak; Greta is childless and despairing; Sarah is a former drug addict and prostitute, ex-girlfriend to Hark; and Paul spends his time building a pyramid of garbage. The master of ceremonies is a young gay man, nicknamed Dido. Dido occupies a liminal space, both part of this grieving community and outside it: he brings in supplies of food and cigarettes each day in a pram, intervenes to move the action along, elicits confidences from the characters, and scripts a play within the play called *The Burning Balaclava* under his drag persona of Fionnuala McGonigle. As Dido he is Queen of Carthage, and therefore not the Queen of a ruined city but the founder and defender of a famous city. Dido, by his name, recalls destruction but also signifies the creation and founding of new, great possibilities. Staged post-Saville, the play responds to the grief of the characters—and through them, of the city of Derry/Carthage—with the promise that letting go of grief will bring new opportunities for joy. Moving beyond the closed history of Bloody Sunday, Dido's entrance in drag and his announcement of his new work *The Burning Balaclava* is a theatrical set-piece that mocks and inverts sectarian and gender stereotypes. Through this, Dido challenges the characters—and McGuinness challenges the audience—to confront their prejudices and recognize how limiting and reductive they are.

Although *Carthaginians* is clearly concerned with memorializing Bloody Sunday, the play primarily fits within a body of translations and adaptations of ancient Greek tragedy in the Irish theatre of the 1980s and 1990s. These plays—including Tom Paulin's *Riot Act* and Seamus Heaney's *Cure at Troy* which were Field Day productions in 1985 and 1990 respectively—explore the history of Northern Ireland through the metaphor of Greek tragedy.[11] Like them, McGuinness borrows the classical form, but he incorporates elements of popular culture such as drag performance, the musical and burlesque. The use of music comments on the setting and the characters: Sarah's repeated singing of "In the Port of Amsterdam" reveals her past experience more powerfully than her pushing up her sleeves to show that the tracks on her arms have now faded; the singing of "We Shall Overcome" immediately recalls the Civil Rights movements in Northern Ireland and elsewhere, while Don McLean's "American Pie" and "Waters of Babylon" express the play's thematic exploration of grief, memory and forgetting. The review in the local paper comments,

> The violence associated with the blackest day in the city's history occurs offstage, but is replayed over and over again in the minds of these characters, each fighting their own war, not sure if they even want a truce, never mind how to get there. These characters struggle to live life while moving among the dead, and the remedies on offer from McGuinness are those of truth, friendship and love [...] If the arts community is examining the state of our city ahead of City of Culture, then this production offers as much food for thought today as it did before the Saville Report was commissioned.[12]

Significantly, the local critic identifies the production as being about the present and future of the city. These productions of *Freedom* and *Carthaginians* commemorate the past in order to liberate the characters and the audience from it; their production post-Saville begins the process of stilling the ghosts.

Unlike these other plays, *Heroes with their Hands in the Air* was first performed in 2007, while the Saville inquiry was ongoing. It is based on Eamonn McCann's book *The Bloody Sunday Inquiry—The Families Speak Out* (2006), which captured the testimonies of the families relating to their experiences of the Saville inquiry as well as the events of the day, and the unfolding of their decades-long fight for justice for the dead. The first performance of the work in 2007 involved people who had been on the march or who were directly involved with the families of the dead, emphasizing the authenticity of their testimonies. The production of the work again in 2012—by Fahy Productions—to commemorate the fortieth anniversary included the families' responses to the findings of Saville. It also focused on the continuing efforts to clear Gerald Donaghey, a teenager who was killed and whom Saville found was "probably" carrying a nail bomb—a claim his family refutes.

Examples of verbatim theatre are discussed further below; but the staging of Friel and McGuinness's plays was part of an emerging interpretation and response to work written during and about the conflict, that seeks to depoliticize the work or, alternatively, to refocus the central argument to make it address contemporary world events. Thus, *Freedom*'s thematic focus on the power of the state crushing the impoverished and powerless individual citizen, and *Carthaginians* classical references, both originally interpreted as work about Bloody Sunday, can also be read in reference to contemporary international events. While these playwrights write for an international audience, they are closely connected to the geography and social history of Northern Ireland. Friel's *Translations*, first staged in Derry's Guildhall in 1980, addresses the history of colonization and crystallizes Field Day's post-colonial project. The quadricentennial of the Flight of the Earls in 2007 saw Ouroboros's production of Friel's *Making History* tour to the Guildhall, where it had premiered in 1999. As with *Translations*, Friel uses the historical event as an opportunity to reflect upon the tragedies of the Northern Irish conflict. *Dancing at Lughnasa* is also frequently revived and toured, most recently by the Lyric Theatre in 2015. McGuinness's *The Factory Girls* (1982) and *Observe the Sons of Ulster Marching Towards the Somme* (1985) both engage with the social history of the region. *The Factory Girls*, set in Donegal, addresses a cross-border history of more than 3000 people, mostly women, working in the shirt factories in Derry, Donegal and Tyrone. Their contribution to the local economy was immense, as was the social impact of women working and earning a reasonable wage. *Observe the Sons* was remounted and toured by the Abbey in 2016 for the anniversary of the Battle of the Somme, and offers a sympathetic portrait of the Unionist community. But Pyper emerges ever more strongly as part of a pre-Ceasefire generation in contemporary productions, compared with the early stagings of the play amid opposition to the Anglo-Irish Agreement. The death of Ian Paisley, a figure that the Older Pyper powerfully recalls, and Pyper's embrace of his dead comrades at the end, suggests a shift in the interpretation of the work. Patrick Mason's 1994 production sees the young soldiers marching downstage and down concealed steps at the back of the theatre space, lit so that their long shadows are cast upwards over the stage, expressed their immense influence on the development of Northern Ireland's political and social frameworks. They literally cast long shadows. But in Jeremy Herrin's 2016 production, Pyper and his comrades are caught in a freeze-frame that represents their going over the top in the trenches. This staging consigns them more absolutely to the past: to images from the war memorials familiar in most Northern Irish cities. Post-Ceasefire, the play becomes more poignantly an elegy for a dead or dying culture as Unionism itself abandons Craig's project of a "Protestant government for a Protestant people" and turns its energies towards building a viable future in partnership with the various communities in the region.

"Troubles Nostalgia": Representing the Conflict

Martin Lynch emerged as a significant Northern Irish writer during the 1980s, with *A Roof Over Our Heads (reworked and performed in 1983 as Castles in the Air), Dockers* (1981) and *The Interrogation of Ambrose Fogarty* (referred to here as *Fogarty*) (1982). He had left school at fifteen and began writing for performance after some experiences of theatre—he names John Arden and Margaretta D'Arcy's *The Non-Stop Connolly Show* as a particular influence.[13] He was writer in residence at the Lyric Theatre in Belfast when he wrote *Fogarty*, which premiered there in 1982, directed by Sam McCready. It was also performed at the Peacock theatre in Dublin and at the Irish Arts Centre in New York before being remounted at the Lyric in 1984. The play, which ran for seven weeks at its premiere, was a controversial one. It deals with the abuse of suspects in RUC custody.[14] Ambrose Fogarty is from the Nationalist community and is arrested and interrogated over a three-day period, on a charge of armed robbery. The action is set in the Springfield Road Police Barracks. In the cell next to him is Willie Lagan, a country and western singer who has a mild learning disability and who has been arrested on a charge of rioting. It is immediately clear that Fogarty, who is finally released without charge, may well be involved in a minor way in paramilitary activities; but Willie, who is clearly innocent, is held and prosecuted. The other characters are three RUC officers who fit into clear types: Knox with his old-fashioned sense of duty; Lundy, a woman, who is looking for a way out of Belfast; and the upwardly-mobile McFadden. There are also three Special Branch officers, two of whom fit neatly into stereotypes of sectarian police officers: Stanley who is a staunch Paisley-ite and Jackie who is short tempered and violent. Peter, the third, has more in common with Fogarty and is psychologically more skilled in his manipulation of the prisoner.

Lynch said of the play that "I want Catholics to have a better understanding of the police, and I want Protestants to have a better understanding of how people end up Republicans."[15] To do this, he creates police characters who are at least partly sympathetic, and explores the interrogation techniques in use in Northern Ireland. At its premiere, this was the first play to address the issue of police brutality in Northern Ireland, and it is set against the social and political backdrop of internment without charge (1971), the European Commission of Human Rights ruling on a case taken by the Irish government that Britain was guilty of "inhuman and degrading treatment" of suspects (1976), reports of abuse of prisoners from Amnesty International, and the dirty protest and Hunger Strikes in Long Kesh (1981). Maguire argues that the high level of verisimilitude in the costuming, set, props, and behavioural codes that distinguish the security forces from the civilians is Lynch's key strategy. Because the play is realistic, the audience have access to the police officers' motivations and circumstances, which shape their behaviours. They provide the main focus for an exploration of individual responsibility, because they are aware that they have some immunity from prosecution and that they have greater social and hegemonic credibility than either Fogarty or Willie. The audience is given access to Fogarty's internal thoughts through his soliloquies when he is alone in the police cell: this situates the spectators in an empathetic relationship with him. The realistic aesthetic also, arguably, positions the audiences as witnesses. The play clearly seeks to inform and engage the audience in a discussion about policing practices in Northern Ireland with the aim of promoting understanding and encouraging people to seek change. The re-staging of Fogarty by Lynch's company in 2007, nine years after the Good Friday Agreement, provoked a markedly different reaction in both Belfast where the play opened, and Derry while it was on tour.

In 2007, *Fogarty* played as comedy to audiences in Northern Ireland. This was partly catalysed by the casting of Conor Grimes in the role of Willie Lagan. Grimes is a very popular comic, well known from regional television as well as stage work. Though the text sets Willie as a comic foil for Ambrose, the casting tended to position Willie as the comic star turn. The review on *Culture Northern Ireland* describes Lagan as a "half-witted pub-musician caught between the rioters and the police" setting the tone for this interpretation. The reviewer notes that "from the moment Grime steps on the stage at the Grand Opera House the audience are in stitches. And for the next 90 minutes every gag is ruthlessly milked, ensuring that rarely is Grimes on a stage not filled with laughter". Even the scenes of beating are met with laughter. The reviewer, Brendan Deeds, is critical of the decision to play the work as purely comic, describing it as "a brave and important play" and this production as a "weak and soulless affair".[16] He likens the play to other manifestations of "Troubles Tourism", such as the tours of the murals; these offer "a comfortable glimpse at the dark days of our recent past". The *Belfast Telegraph* interviewed Lynch, who describes it as a humorous play and a political one; and the Unionist *Newsletter* describes it as a "fiery play" that was "close to home" when it was first written. "Nowadays we can sit back and enjoy it safely. But as this week's packed house shows, it is as relevant and incisive as it ever was."[17]

The play performed to full houses across the region and, despite the criticisms of the *Culture Northern Ireland* reporter, the audience responded enthusiastically to the work. Grimes' well-advertised participation in the show would certainly have been read by the audience as a sign that this was a comedy. Yet the play text has moments of real pathos, and Willie's humanity comes through clearly in a number of scenes. Towards the end of the play, he tells Ambrose "I'm alright, but they beat up my guitar, smashed it".[18] The line can be played for laughs, but the earlier scenes establish Willie's love for his guitar and its importance in allowing him to earn a little extra money. He is too poor to easily replace it. Even if not beaten by the Special Branch, Willie is certainly bullied and intimidated by them, and just as he thinks he is going home he is taken to court to face three more charges.[19] Lynch's representation of Willie is humorous, but its more serious point is that the system and its injustices crush people like Willie, who have no effective intellectual or financial capacity to defend themselves.

While audience reception is notoriously difficult to analyse, several responses to the original production were apparent from the documentation of the time. Some spectators walked out, offended by what they saw as either overly negative or overly positive representations of the RUC. In response to the scene where Fogarty is beaten and forcibly stripped, an audience may laugh to reject the notion of RUC abuse and from a refusal to empathize with Fogarty. But contemporary productions may also provoke uncertainty about the meaning of the play in a post-conflict society, and discomfort at the theatrical performance of issues that are generally avoided in everyday life and conversation because of their potential to provoke disagreement. The response to *Fogarty* in 2007 might therefore be read as evidence of Northern Irish society reaching a midpoint, where the play is no longer controversial but where, equally, it cannot yet be considered as authentic material about the conflict and some of the sources of that conflict. Instead, the audience are caught in a moment where empathy with Fogarty suggests a political stance that is not in keeping with the imperative of maintaining conflict-free public interactions. Paul Devlin's 2009 essay, using Foucault's concept of heterotopias to propose the staging of Fogarty against the recent history of Abu Ghraib and Camp X-Ray, identifies a future point where the Northern Irish audience might read *Fogarty* beyond the local conflict, and with resonances of international abuses of human rights.

Lynch's *History of the Troubles (According to my Da)* (2003, 2009) and *Chronicles of Long Kesh* (2009), both of which toured, recount potted versions of the history of the conflict using humour, music, movement, and Lynch's characteristic mixing of tragedy with comedy to speak largely to an audience with memories of the conflict. The dates of the first productions would suggest this, since the Good Friday Agreement predates *History of the Troubles* by just five years and *Chronicles* by eleven; though there was a ceasefire most of the time since late 1994. This is obviously important in the reception of the work. The use of humour in both these plays suggests an audience that is able to recognize humour as a coping strategy, though when it is over-played it depoliticizes the performance, emphasizing a kind of nostalgia for a bygone era. This nostalgia is based, not on the daily, lived experience of the conflict but on the idea that the conflict heightened a sense of community cohesion—the "blitz spirit" often referred to when discussing the British experience during the Second World War—where individuals are drawn into a close sense of community to enable them to endure difficult circumstances.

Lynch's plays use colloquialisms and in-jokes to appeal to a local audience and create a sense of a private, family conversation that excludes those outside the group. He uses this technique in *History* and in *Chronicles*, making comic reference to events that are very familiar to a Northern Irish audience, such as the dubbing of Gerry Adam's voice on television or Iris Robinson's notorious love affair. *Chronicles* was produced by Bruiser Theatre Company for its 2009 premiere, which brought the company's trademark physical style to the work. The cast also sing well-known songs from the 1970s and 1980s (the plays cover the period from 1971 to 1984), which one critic describes as "a curious yet effective jarring technique which causes the audience, stopping just short of clapping along, to spontaneously applaud each number".[20] Like the use of local dialect, humour, and references to local events, the use of familiar songs heightens the sense of community in the theatre space.

The sense of nostalgia evoked by Lynch's work is absent from Dave Duggan's verse-drama *Denizen*, which was performed at the Bishop Street Court House in Derry and then toured locally and to Liverpool in 2014. *Denizen* is the last dissident Republican, delivering his speech from the dock. He defends his actions and poses important questions for this point in Northern Ireland's development as a peaceful society. Describing himself as the "pariah part of yourself", he challenges the audience to interrogate their assumptions about peace and war, placing the Northern Irish conflict against the background of international realpolitik:

Forced regime changes, and the lies, proceed

Daily, under cover of denials

Each night on broadcast news, across the globe.

So why not my desire for regime change?

By brute force, if that be necessary?[21]

While Denizen's eventual decision is to break the pike over his knee and to accept that the time for war is past, the play presents its audience with an unsentimental commentary that, as in Lynch's plays, asks what all the bloodshed was for and whether it was all worthwhile. This is a question not only for paramilitaries, but also for politicians who resisted power-sharing for decades, and the Westminster government with its various ill-thought-out policies on the region.

Verbatim Theatre and the Troubles

Fintan Brady's *Heroes with their Hands in the Air* (2007) belongs to a body of verbatim theatre that sets out to commemorate significant events in the community's history, through witness testimony. Verbatim theatre, as defined by Derek Paget, uses recorded material "from the 'real-life' originals of the characters and events to which it gives dramatic shape".[22] As McCormick notes, quoting Paget, documents are vulnerable to postmodern doubts about truth and authenticity, and to widespread suspicion in the digital age of tampering using technology; but "the witness's claim to authenticity can still warrant a credible perspective".[23] Some of this work has the explicit aim of healing the community through the act of remembering and sharing experience. Indeed, "Healing through Remembering" is an extensive cross-community project in Northern Ireland, which is predicated on the idea that remembrance is an important factor in mutual understanding, and moving towards reconciliation. A significant contribution to this body of work comes from American dancer and therapist Teya Sepunick, who was based at the Playhouse Theatre in Derry from 2009 to 2013. During this time, she translated her method of working with marginalized groups in the United States to working with former paramilitaries, members of the security forces, and civilians whose lives had been altered by the conflict. In an interview, Sepunick commented that she had originally expected former paramilitaries to express regret for their actions. Her work in prisons and with violent abusers in the USA had prepared her for the participants to express sorrow and penitence, or to be brought to those emotions through the workshop process. This of course did not happen in Northern Ireland, where former paramilitaries expressed grief for the events of the past and talked of the pain of living with their former actions, but saw those actions as taking place within a just war.

The project produced four shows under the title "Theatre of Witness", which toured Northern Ireland and the Border areas playing in small halls and community centres as well as theatres to reach a wide audience. The work included talkback sessions at the end of each performance and gathered written feedback and testimonies from the spectators. Sepunick also ran training events to pass on her working method, and other smaller productions using the same technique have been performed since the formal end of the project.

"Theatre of Witness" relies on affect for its efficacy. Building initially on Spinoza's *Ethics* and on potential collaborations between performance studies, queer theory and cognitive science, the concept of "affect" has become popular in the scholarship of the past decade. Sara Ahmed's work explores the role of the emotions in shaping bodies and social interactions, and examines the physical, visceral aspects of felt emotion.[24] Teresa Brennan explores affect as something that is communicated between people, a non-verbal "atmosphere" that is both psychological and physiological.[25] This idea of affect—of the communication of emotion through non-verbal as well as verbal means—is a feature of dramatic theatrical performance, where the actor elicits a physiological, emotional response from the audience through his or her physicality and voice. As spectators, we do not only recognize the character's fear when it is mimetically presented to us, we also feel in our own bodies the tension evoked by a skilful performance of fear or the effective creation of suspense and threat; or indeed of joy or sympathy. Thus "affect" is a feature of theatrical reception, though not always configured in those terms or in that language. Dolan's "utopian performative" circles this concept of affect through its exploration of moments of "feeling together", when the audience at a live performance experience a shared moment of unity, of "present-ness", that she specifies is pre-political.[26] Affective and effective, these moments are about a glimpse of utopian possibility, brief instances of shared grief or pleasure, and this seems to be true of the "Theatre of Witness" project in those moments that are largely devoid of sentimentality.

Dolan's concept of a "fleeting intimation" or "moment" resonates with Lehmann's concept of the "absolute present" of post-dramatic theatre, the moment that he links to the "aesthetic of startling" or "aesthetic of responsibility". Lehmann argues that postdramatic theatre (a genre to which "Theatre of Witness" belongs) is "*a theatre of the present*" (original emphasis). "The presence of the actor is not an object, an objectifiable present but a co-presence in the sense of the unavoidable implication of the spectator"; this extra-aesthetic encounter with "the presence of the actor as the presence of a living human being" can be described as "shock". He draws upon Bohrer's concept of the "absolute present" to conceive of presence as a process or verb, rather than as an object. The presence of the performer therefore does not demand mimesis or representation and does not function "according to the registers of representation and interpretation".[27] Rather than assuming the co-presence of actor and character, post-dramatic theatre assumes the co-presence of performer and spectator in a moment of "absolute present".

Lehman refers to "responsibility", rendered by Kelly Oliver as "response-ability", meaning the encounter with the Other in the moment of performance. This is potentially an ethical moment—though pre-political and not necessarily lasting. This moment of response-ability and address-ability is connected, for Oliver, with the process of witnessing and with the witnesses' capacity to recognize the testifying other as a being like them. This ethical engagement arguably offers opportunities to create change in the spectators' political or moral lives by offering a glimpse of a shared humanity. Equally, to return to Dolan, it offers the possibility of "fleeting intimation" or alliance.

As Paget points out, the testimony of witnesses has a particular power, and the performers in these shows are all witnessing events that happened to them or their family members. Across the four shows, the stories include near escapes from bomb attacks, the murder of loved ones, various paramilitary or military activities, and in the final show the testimony of refugees seeking asylum in Northern Ireland. Notably, amongst the women, testimonies of sexual abuse as children or as adults recur. The multimedia performances, which include film footage, live and recorded music, song, movement sequences and puppets, appeal directly to the audience's emotions through the evocation of shared memories, shared grief, and hope for the future. What might be regarded as an ongoing disagreement about the causes and justifications for the conflict is incorporated into the productions, finding a resonance in the audiences' own understandings of the matter. But amidst such disagreements, a sense of shared history does tend to emerge in performance, and this is key to the utopian possibilities that the performances create.

Conclusions

Post-conflict, the theatre in Northern Ireland has engaged with both contemporary classics by major Irish writers and new plays by emerging playwrights, to address the creation of the new civil society. A significant portion of this work engages with the history of the Troubles, through a wide range of aesthetic forms and with a variety of political and social motivations. The remounting of plays by Friel and McGuinness increasingly explores the international resonances of the texts rather than focusing primarily on the local situation. This is clear in recent productions of plays inspired by Bloody Sunday: though they commemorate the event, their main function is to explore issues of power, powerlessness, grief, and hope. While these texts retain a strong political sense of engagement, other work by popular playwright Martin Lynch plays to audiences eager to set aside the painful memories of the past. Lynch's *Interrogation of Ambrose Fogarty* and his more recent productions blend the comedic with the tragic to commemorate the past while celebrating the future. Finally, Duggan's *Denizen* asks a question that underlies much of the recent Northern Irish work: was it worth it, after all? This question strongly echoes in the verbatim theatre productions of the "Theatre of Witness" project, where individual citizens explain what the conflict meant to them and to their families. Throughout this body of work is a strong sense of the efficacy of affect: the importance of creating a community in the theatre, however briefly, to contemplate the possibility of a different and better future. This is particularly evident in the examples of verbatim theatre, which shares stories of the conflict with the purpose of arriving at an understanding of opposing viewpoints and cross-community experience. Though not political theatre in the Brechtian sense, the body of work emerging in performance and in writing utilizes affective responses to utopian ends.

Notes

1. Bloody Sunday refers to the events of 30 January 1972, when the First Battalion, Parachute Regiment of the British Army opened fire on a peaceful Civil Rights protest in Derry city, killing fourteen people (many of them teenage boys) and injuring twelve others. The first inquiry immediately after the event by Lord Widgery exonerated the soldiers. It was widely decried as a cover-up and led to a long campaign by family members of the dead for another inquiry. In 1998 Tony Blair appointed Lord Saville to head a tribunal that released its report in June 2010. This report described the killings as "unjustified and unjustifiable" and the public reporting of the Tribunal uncovered unambiguous evidence of soldiers' lying under oath. To date, there have been no prosecutions of the soldiers involved, and the family of one of the dead continues to campaign to clear his name (the report concluded that it was possible that he was carrying a nail bomb).
2. Baz Kershaw uses the term theatrical efficacy to describe "the potential that theatre may have to make the immediate effects of performance influence, however minutely, the general historical evolution of wider social and political realities" in *The Politics of Performance* (London: Routledge, 1992), 1.
3. Jill Dolan, "Performance, Utopia, and the 'Utopian Performative'", *Theatre Journal* 53:3 (2001): 455.
4. Brian Friel, *The Freedom of the City and Translations* in *Plays One* (London: Faber & Faber, 2013).
5. Terry Teachout, "A Tragedy of Irish Proportions", *Wall Street Journal*, 25 October 2012.
6. Joe Nawaz, "Freedom of the City", review of *Freedom of the City*, by Brian Friel, *Culturenorthernireland.org*, 23 October 2010.
7. A fourteenth victim, 59 year-old John Johnson, died four months later of his injuries.
8. Nawaz, "Freedom of the City".
9. Wilborn Hampton, "Brian Friel's Requiem on Bloody Sunday", *Huffington Post*, 15 October 2012.
10. Sheila McCormick, "Heroes with Their Hands in the Air: Memory and Commemoration in Contemporary Documentary Theater", *Kritika Kultura* 21/22 (2013): 500–515.
11. See, for example, Danine Farquharson "The force of law in Seamus Heaney's Greek translations", in *Performing Violence in Contemporary Ireland*; Tony Roche "Ireland's Antigones: Tragedy North and South", in *A Century of Irish Drama*; or Des O'Rawe "(Mis)translating Tragedy: Irish Poets and Greek Plays", online http://www2.open.ac.uk/ClassicalStudies/GreekPlays/Conf99/Orawe.htm.
12. Laurence McClenaghan, "Watch Yourself Derry", review of *Carthaginians* by Frank McGuinness. *Derry Journal*, 28 February 2012.
13. See Tom Maguire, *Making Theatre in Northern Ireland* (Exeter: Exeter University Press, 2006).

14. The Royal Ulster Constabulary (RUC) was the police force in Northern Ireland from 1922 to 2001. It was replaced by the Police Service of Northern Ireland (PSNI) in 2001. The PSNI pursues stringent recruitment policies to ensure cross-community representation on the force, and has been largely successful in building a working relationship with most communities in the region. The RUC had a reputation for collusion with Loyalist terrorists and for privileging the Protestant community in its everyday work. In the 1970s and 1980s there were repeated accusations of the abuse and torture of Republican prisoners and Catholic suspects in RUC custody at Castlereagh Holding Centre in East Belfast.
15. Maguire, *Making Theatre in Northern Ireland*, 26.
16. Brendan Deeds. Review, *The Interrogation of Ambrose Fogarty*, http://www.culturenorthernireland.org/features/performing-arts/interrogation-ambrose-fogarty
17. Ibid.
18. Martin Lynch, *The Interrogation of Ambrose Fogarty* and *Castles in the Air* (Belfast: Lagan Press, 2003), 69.
19. Ibid., 81.
20. Unnamed Critic, Chronicles of Long Kesh, http://www.culturenorthernireland.org/features/performing-arts/chronicles-long-kesh-0
21. Dave Duggan, *Denizen*, (Derry: Guildhall Press, 2014).
22. Derek Paget, "'Verbatim Theatre': Oral History and Documentary Techniques", *New Theatre Quarterly*, Volume 3, Issue 12 (1987): 317.
23. Derek Paget, "The 'Broken Tradition' of Documentary Theatre and Its Continued Powers of Endurance", in *Get Real: Documentary Theatre Past and Present*, ed. Alison Forsyth and Chris Megson (Basingstoke: Palgrave Macmillan 2009), 235–236 quoted in Sheila McCormick, "Heroes with Their Hands in the Air: Memory and Commemoration in Contemporary Documentary Theater", *Kritika Kultura*, 21/22 (2013): 501.
24. Sara Ahmed, *Cultural Politics of Emotion* (Edinburgh: Edinburgh University Press, 2004).
25. Teresa Brennan, *The Transmission of Affect* (Ithaca, NY: Cornell University Press, 2004), 1.
26. Dolan, "Performance, Utopia, and the 'Utopian Performative'" and *Utopia in Performance: finding hope at the theatre* (Chicago: University of Michigan Press, 2005).
27. Lehmann, *Postdramatic Theatre* (London: Routledge, 2006), 143–4.

Bibliography

Ahmed, Sara. *Cultural Politics of Emotion*. Edinburgh: Edinburgh University Press, 2004.

Brady, Fintan. *Heroes with Their Hands in the Air*. Unpublished. 2007.

Brennan, Teresa. *The Transmission of Affect*. Ithaca, NY: Cornell University Press, 2014.

Devlin, Paul "Restaging Violence: H-Block as Abu Ghraib, Castlereagh as Camp X-Ray." In *Performing Violence in Contemporary Ireland* ed. Lisa Fitzpatrick. Dublin: Carysfort Press, 2010.

Dolan, Jill. "Performance, Utopia, and the 'Utopian Performative'." *Theatre Journal* 53:3 (2001): 455–479.

———. *Utopia in Performance: Finding Hope at the Theatre*. Chicago: University of Michigan Press, 2005.

Duggan, Dave. *Denizen*. Derry: Guildhall Press, 2014.

Fitzpatrick, Lisa. "The Utopian Performative in Post-Conflict Northern Irish Theatre." In *Performing Violence in Contemporary Ireland* ed. Lisa Fitzpatrick. Dublin: Carysfort Press, 2010.

Fricker, Karen. "Freedom of the City" Review *Variety*. 1999. Available online at http://variety.com/1999/film/reviews/the-freedom-of-the-city-1200457880/. Last accessed 20 May 2018.

Friel, Brian. *The Freedom of the City* and *Translations* in *Plays One*. London: Faber & Faber, 2013.

———. *Dancing at Lughnasa*. London: Faber & Faber, 2011.

———. *Making History*. London: Faber & Faber, 2013.

Hampton, Wilborn. "Brian Friel's Requiem on Bloody Sunday" *Huffington Post*. US edition. 2012. Available online at http://www.huffingtonpost.com/wilborn-hampton/freedom-of-the-city-review_b_1967292.html. Last accessed 20 May 2018.

Keenan, Seamus. *Over the Wire*. Performed at the Playhouse Theatre, Derry, 14–19 January 2013. Unpublished. 2010.

Kershaw, Baz. *The Politics of Performance*. London: Routledge. 1992.

Lehmann, Hans-Thies. *Postdramatic Theatre* trans. Karen Jurs-Munby. London & New York: Routledge, 2006.

Lynch, Martin. *The Interrogation of Ambrose Fogarty* and *Castles in the Air*. Belfast: Lagan Press, 2003.

———. *The History of the Troubles (According to my Da)*. Belfast: Lagan Press, 2005.

———. *Chronicles of Long Kesh*. London: Oberon, 2012.

Maguire, Tom. *Making Theatre in Northern Ireland*. Exeter: Exeter University Press, 2006.

McAleavey, Jimmy. *The Sign of the Whale* and *The Virgin Father*. Belfast: Tinderbox Theatre Company. Scripts published with theatre programme, 2010.

McCann, Eamonn. *The Bloody Sunday Inquiry: The Families Speak Out*. London: Pluto Press, 2005.

McClenaghan, Laurence. "Watch Yourself Derry" Review of *Carthaginians. Derry Journal*, 28 February 2012. Available at http://www.derryjournal.com/news/watch-yourself-derry-1-3568693. Last accessed 20 May 2018.

McCormick, Sheila. "Heroes with Their Hands in the Air: Memory and Commemoration in Contemporary Documentary Theater". *Kritika Kultura*, 21/22 (2013): 500–515.

McGuinness, Frank. *Plays One: Factory Girls, Observe the Sons of Ulster Marching Towards the Somme, Innocence, Carthaginians, Baglady*. London: Faber & Faber, 2013.

Nawaz, Joe. "Freedom of the City" Review *Culturenorthernireland.org*. 2010. Available online at http://www.culturenorthernireland.org/reviews/performing-arts/freedom-city. Last accessed 20 May 2018.

O'Rawe, D. "(Mis)Translating Tragedy: Irish Poets and Greek Plays." In *Theatre: Ancient and Modern* eds. L. Hardwick, P. Easterling, S. Ireland, N. Lowe & F. Macintosh. Berkshire: Open University, 1999, 109–124.

Oliver, Kelly. *Witnessing: Beyond Recognition*. Minneapolis: University of Minnesota Press, 2001.

Paget, Derek. "'Verbatim Theatre': Oral History and Documentary Techniques," *New Theatre Quarterly*, Volume 3, Issue 12 (1987): 317–336.

———. "The 'Broken Tradition' of Documentary Theatre and Its Continued Powers of Endurance." In *Get Real: Documentary Theatre Past and Present* ed. Alison Forsyth & Chris Megson. Basingstoke: Palgrave Macmillan, 2009, 224–238.

Rankin Russell, Richard. *Modernity, Community, and Place in Brian Friel's Drama*. Syracuse, NY: Syracuse University Press, 2013.

Sepunick, Teya. *Theatre of Witness*. London: Jessica Kingsley, 2013.

Teachout, Terry. "A Tragedy of Irish Proportions" *Wall Street Journal*. 2012. Available online at http://www.wsj.com/articles/SB10001424052970203406404578074741956698664. Last accessed 20 May 2018.

The Literary Tradition in the History of Modern Irish Drama

Christopher Murray

Introduction

It is perhaps axiomatic that Irish drama in the twentieth century is distinctive because it is in some sense poetic. What that sense may be, and what the argument may be for its endurance, are questions still to be settled. They form the basis of this chapter, which, chronologically, is concerned mainly with the period from the early 1960s, when Brian Friel and Tom Murphy first appeared on the scene, and the early 1990s, when a new generation, headed by Stewart Parker, Frank McGuinness and a youthful Marina Carr, seemed to interrogate the older tradition and yet stay within its parameters. An initial danger lodged within any analysis of this broad topic is the assumption that the history of Irish drama from its initiation by W.B. Yeats, Lady Gregory and Edward Martyn in 1899, under the significant title the Irish Literary Theatre, forms a continuum; that the decades that followed, right down to the present, manifest a through-line, from which certain subplots may be allowed but which nevertheless has served to keep alternative theatre in its place while mainstream or "traditional drama"—whatever that term may denote—consistently stepped forward to take the curtain calls. Inherent in that simplistic reading rests the inference that Irish drama is basically conservative, serving an orthodox realist aesthetic that tends to ignore the experimentalism and theatrical innovations that characterize the dramatic output of other nations, the French or the Polish, for example.

To offset these dangerous oversimplifications of the historical narrative, this chapter will first attempt to clarify the sophisticated aesthetic the founders

C. Murray (✉)
School of English, Drama and Film, University College Dublin, Dublin, Ireland
e-mail: christopher.murray@ucd.ie

E. Jordan, E. Weitz (eds.), *The Palgrave Handbook of Contemporary Irish Theatre and Performance*,
https://doi.org/10.1057/978-1-137-58588-2_5

established and then to indicate how the influence of Yeats—to this day and in spite of many attempts to correct misleading opinion a figure regarded as a hopeless amateur in the business of steering Irish theatre towards artistic excellence—deserves to be seen as a far-seeing and well-informed force for good. The chapter will then briefly indicate how, after Yeats's death in 1939, the decline of the national theatre into the creation of stereotypes and repetition of worn-out forms through total distortion of artistic priorities was compounded by the misfortune of the Abbey fire in July 1951, which meant the abandonment of a small, intimate theatre seating just over 500, supplemented by the Peacock annex seating 100. For fifteen years before the new Abbey was opened on the site of the old in July 1966, the Abbey Company played at the Queen's Theatre on Pearse Street, a decrepit nineteenth-century commercial venue (now extinct) with almost twice the capacity of the old Abbey and no experimental annex; the Company could do little more than survive by repeating old dramatic successes, and Yeats's aesthetic largely went by the board. Opened in the year of the golden jubilee of the 1916 Rising, the new Abbey entered a well-endowed period, with a newly-designed theatre and annex and the provision for the first time of an artistic director, who could confront the board of directors to defend his or her (Lelia Doolan was one of the first artistic directors) vision. It is during this period of revival that, it can be argued, Yeats's aesthetic came once again—albeit with little acknowledgement—to underpin production values and the acceptance of new plays.

The Yeatsian Paradigm

The Yeatsian paradigm, then, is what may be said to underlie the Irish dramatic movement. As just indicated, the aesthetic was not usually adverted to. Brian Friel, for instance, more than once appeals to T.S. Eliot's seminal essay "Tradition and the Individual Talent" in the assertion of his own ideas on dramatic art, but never refers to Yeats's body of essays on this theme.[1] Tom Murphy's work, from *Famine* (1968) through *The Morning after Optimism* (1972) and *The Sanctuary Lamp* (1975), reveals a strong kinship with Yeats's spiritual values. Thomas Kilroy, whose plays, particularly those dealing self-consciously with artists and visionaries, such as *Tea, Sex and Shakespeare* (1976), *Talbot's Box* (1977), *Double Cross* (1986), and *The Secret Fall of Constance Wilde* (1997), provide an excellent example of the modern Irish playwright who has carefully attended to Yeats's ideas for an artistic theatre.

In order to sift through these ideas and place them in historic context, it is useful to refer to Una Ellis-Fermor's study, *The Irish Dramatic Movement* (1939, revised edition 1954), taking the title Yeats himself had used for his Nobel lecture in Sweden in 1924. It is significant that Yeats chose on that prestigious occasion to speak about drama and not about his poetry, for which he is best known. We bear in mind here the line from one of his last poems, "Players and painted stage took all my love".[2] Ellis-Fermor was a formidable scholar of Elizabethan and Jacobean drama, author of a challenging book of essays titled *The Frontiers of Drama* (1945, second edition 1964), and was in addition a translator of Ibsen's plays. It was her admiration for Yeats that drew her to take a look at Irish drama, where she was in pursuit of the quality of the Irish imagination, seen as original and poetic. "[B]y some strange stirring of the spirit which in part eludes analysis, that poetic drama was a means of bringing back to the drama of the other English-speaking races the habit of high poetry which it had lost for two hundred years."[3] By poetic drama she did not exclusively mean verse drama, as Yeats's was, but also the whole range of peasant drama initiated by Lady Gregory and J.M. Synge. She saw a shared aesthetic of which she greatly approved. She also saw a new historic phase beginning with Lennox Robinson and carried on by Seán O'Casey, a form of realism which was satiric but retaining the earlier poetic force: "Both [phases] combine [...] with intermediate moods and positions to make a whole which is indivisible, a living and representative body of national drama, which by virtue of its scope and attitude, is also international."[4] The value of such an authoritative view lies partly in its objectivity—Ellis-Fermor had no axe to grind—and partly in the emphasis on wholeness, her sense that, "[t]he Irish drama has been a continuous movement, showing continuous development from its beginnings in 1899 to the present day."[5] By "present day" she meant 1954, and it shows. One has to concede that, although her book was reprinted in 1964, the year of the premiere in Dublin of *Philadelphia, Here I Come!*, it is out of date in its assumption that Irish drama was a continuum. She passes over the doldrums of the years 1940–64. But she was not to know that after 1964 came a second renaissance, and that it would renew the links she had shown as binding poetry and realism in a highly theatrical fashion.

In spite of this shortcoming, Ellis-Fermor's study still provides a valuable starting point for the interpretation of later twentieth-century Irish drama, whose roots are now often invisible. In a chapter headed "Ideals in the Workshop", emphasizing the practical and the theoretical, Ellis-Fermor stresses both Yeats's originality and his influence upon the modern literary theatre:

> Against a background of English drama in the serious discussion play [...] stands the figure of Yeats, the man who from his own innate wisdom and with no help from any dramatic tradition then at work in Europe, led the drama of the English-speaking people back to the paths of poetry and power, making way, in both countries, for the first body of plays which can seriously compare with the Elizabethans.[6]

Her point is perhaps overstressed. After all, Yeats was part of a *European* movement in theatre and drama which looked to symbolism as a counter-expression to naturalism. In that regard, Katharine Worth's *The Irish Drama of Europe from Yeats to Beckett* is a salutary balancing of this issue of "tradition" and "influence." The workshop spirit that Yeats fostered at the Irish Literary Theatre, and more practically when the Abbey was founded in 1904, contained more than poets. It contained, in a word, Ibsenists who also admired the ideals of André Antoine at the *Théâtre Libre* in Paris. In particular, the Fay brothers, Frank and Willy, saw in Antoine and the French tradition a way of counteracting the stilted acting style which was standard in serious English theatre at that time. To Yeats's immense delight, the Fays also had an interest in the recitation of poetry; he cast them in his own plays and between them they evolved an Abbey style of acting that fused naturalism and the French tradition, which had descended from Talma to Coquelin (a frequent visitor to Dublin, as was Sarah Bernhardt).[7] Stillness, a musical delivery, and ensemble playing became the main features of the Abbey acting style.

Ellis-Fermor's main emphasis falls on the language itself. For Yeats, poetry as a kind of spirit "lived still in the Irish peasants whose attitude to common life was like that of the great ages" and "this spirit reveals itself in the living language which they still spoke."[8] It was the rhythm, the musicality of the speech that Yeats fastened upon and made the basis of how the Abbey plays should be written and performed. Yeats insisted on the "sovereignty of language" in the hierarchy of theatrical values, but the actor's skill came next. He wanted plays "that will make the theatre a place of intellectual excitement" and "if we are to restore words to their sovereignty we must make speech even more important than gesture upon the stage."[9] He found his best disciple in Synge, whose dramatic language was solidly based on the language and lilt of the Irish country people, as he proclaimed in his preface to *The Playboy of the Western World* (1907). Indeed, in spite of her admiration for Yeats, Ellis-Fermor declared that "Synge is the only great poetic dramatist of the movement; the only one, that is, for whom poetry and drama were inseparable, in whose work dramatic intensity invariably finds poetic expression and the poetic mood its only full expression in dramatic form" (163). In his own pursuit of a modern poetic drama, T.S. Eliot rather ruefully accepts that Synge, whose plays "form rather a special case", could be no model for him, because Synge's language "is not available except for plays set among that same people" that gave him his inspiration.[10] Eliot saw no problem in regarding Synge as a poetic playwright. And so with the rest of the Irish dramatists who wrote in prose: since they availed of speech patterns already, in Synge's words, "rich and copious" because "the imagination of the people" in Ireland "is rich and living", stage speech is just a heightened form of the ordinary. "In a good play", Synge insisted, "every speech should be as flavoured as a nut or apple, and such speeches cannot be written by anyone who works among people who have shut their lips on poetry."[11] This was precisely Yeats's view also.

It was also part of Yeats's aesthetic that Irish playwrights should be steeped in the works of great predecessors. They should be well-read in the classics and in Shakespeare. In addition, were it not for the regulations governing the granting of a theatre patent in 1904, Lady Gregory (who as the person with connections in Dublin Castle was the one who applied for a patent) would have asked for permission to perform plays in English from all ages and countries. The established Dublin theatres objected to this and she had to be satisfied with a licence to perform mainly Irish plays by Irish authors, together with "such dramatic works of foreign authors as would tend to educate and interest the Irish public in the higher aspects of dramatic art".[12] The phrasing is pure Yeats. "It is of the first importance that those among us who want to write for the stage should study the masterpieces of the world [...] if Irish drama is to mean anything to Irish intellect" (Yeats, *Explorations* 78). He hoped that the loophole in the terms of the patent would allow a version of *Oedipus the King* he was working on. It didn't happen then, but it would happen in 1926, with the great F.J. McCormick in the leading role. In the early days, however, Synge was very much against the notion of an international repertoire.[13] His argument was so intense that Yeats and Lady Gregory backed off. Years later, when Synge was dead and Lennox Robinson wanted to introduce modern foreign plays into the repertory, Yeats refused permission out of loyalty to the memory of Synge. During a public debate on the matter in 1919 Yeats commented:

> I had all this out with Synge years ago. I was of your opinion, and he convinced me that I was wrong. [...] He argued that the municipal theatres of Germany gave excellent performances of every kind of masterpiece, picked the whole world through, and that Germany herself remained sterile and produced no great creative school, and that such a school could only arise out of an absorbing interest in the country one lived in and perpetual attempts to put that interest on the stage.[14]

That explains the narrow range of Abbey drama in the first twenty years, but it doesn't explain its continuance after it became free of the British-style patent restrictions after 1922. What happened was that Lennox Robinson had formed the Dublin Drama League to stage modern European and American drama (that is, Eugene O'Neill) and Yeats allowed these productions to go up on the Abbey stage on Sunday evenings. As has been shown, this new venture was "always a complement, never a rival, to the Abbey".[15] Ironically, what it achieved in its "active decade" (1919–1929), when it staged sixty-six plays originally written in eleven languages by thirty-six authors from fifteen countries (Clarke and Ferrar 14) was to create an appetite and an audience for new, modern, experimental work. In short, it paved the way for the Gate Theatre to be founded in Dublin by Hilton Edwards and Micheál MacLiammóir in 1928 with much the same purpose. Here was definitely a rival to the Abbey, as time would tell, to Yeats's chagrin. Even though the Abbey gradually started to stage Shakespeare, beginning in 1928 with *King Lear*, and going on in the 1930s to stage *Macbeth* and *Coriolanus*, it was obvious the Abbey actors were mainly out of their depth, so well were they trained in their individualistic "peasant-drama" style. Thus Yeats's "people's theatre", as he liked to describe it, had its disadvantages. After his death, when the Abbey had Ernest Blythe as general manager, no productions of Shakespeare took place, and the repertory reverted to an all-Irish one, with the addition of plays and even pantomimes in the Irish language, since such was the predilection of Blythe the keen nationalist. To his shame, he also cut off the supply of women playwrights, chief among them Teresa Deevy, and set a precedent for their exclusion. It was in part the prejudice of the times. At the Gate, too, women playwrights were all too few, among whom Mary Manning, Christine Longford and Maura Laverty stand out for merit and rarity alike.

I would now reiterate my premise, that the literary tradition underpinning the development of twentieth-century Irish drama derives from a Yeatsian aesthetic which lay fallow within the Abbey in spite of its deviation into complacency and mediocrity in the 1940s and 1950s. It was claimed by Peter Kavanagh when he published *The Story of the Abbey Theatre* in 1950 that—one year before the disastrous fire of 1951—after Yeats came the deluge:

> Every possible degrading influence from within and from without was exerted on the Abbey. Every little society, from the Catholic Truth Society and the Children of Mary to the government's Fianna Fáil party pushed and shoved that they might be in on the spoils. Nothing was left unsaid or undone to make certain the Abbey would never again defame the holy name of Ireland.[16]

This reading, however, whereby social, religious and political changes arrested the fearless attitude of Yeats towards his audience—"not what you want but what we want"—is post-dated.[17] Already, by 1935, the Free State had installed censorship, had ruled out divorce as a possibility in Catholic Ireland and was drafting a new constitution to inscribe Catholic doctrine into daily life.[18] In 1935, O'Casey's *The Silver Tassie* had its Irish premiere at the Abbey, to a chorus of disapproval from church and pious citizens alike. It was not to be seen again until 1951, at the new venue in the Queen's Theatre, and once again there were protests condemning the play as blasphemous. It is odd, in this context, that Yeats had rejected this play when O'Casey submitted it to the Abbey in 1928. His conservatism related to his neo-classical aesthetic theory, however, and not at all to the possibility of opposition: he had gloried in the riotous protests over both *The Playboy* and *The Plough* and had asserted in his Nobel speech that "we were from the first a recognized public danger".[19] The tragedy was that in turning down *The Silver Tassie* Yeats was sending into exile the one playwright who was capable of carrying through Yeats's ideal of poetic realism. Yeats completely missed the significance of expressionism lurking behind O'Casey's Dublin plays and when he had to face it full-on in 1928 he was not equal to it. The result was that O'Casey stayed in England writing political allegories when he might have been in Dublin defying the forces closing in on the Free State. Already, in his 1937 essay "Green Goddess of Realism" O'Casey shows clear signs of how his presence at home would have resisted the deadening hold of Abbey realism that was closing on the Irish dramatic movement: "This rage for real, real life on the stage has taken all the life out of the drama."[20] Blythe did the rest.

1966 and All That

It was to be after 1966, when the 1916 Rising was commemorated "with a mixture of nationalistic and Catholic fervour that would be incomprehensible today",[21] that the new generation of playwrights recovered something of the Yeatsian bravery and contempt for orthodoxy necessary to a free theatre. Dates, of course, tend to be fluid where shifts in cultural epochs are concerned, and yet 1958 was the year when Archbishop McQuaid, protesting against planned productions of an adaptation of *Ulysses* and of a new play by O'Casey, *The Drums of Father Ned*, scuppered the Dublin Theatre Festival. This was a turning point in Irish theatre history. The year 1962, when Hugh Leonard's *Stephen D*, a daring adaptation of *Stephen Hero* and *A Portrait of the Artist as a Young Man*, became the hit of that year's Theatre Festival and transferred to London, marks the prelude to Ireland's theatrical *glasnost*. It was to be Brian Friel's *Philadelphia, Here I Come!*, however, through its combination of innovation and tradition, that ushered in the second renaissance in modern Irish drama. "The drive for innovation and formal experiment so evident in Friel has been characteristic of the modern Abbey"[22]—even if *Philadelphia* was actually a Gate Theatre production.

Friel's long career in the theatre—during which he switched back and forth between Abbey and the Gate theatres, for they were no longer aesthetically at odds—best illustrates the literary quality of Irish drama at this time. He began as a short story writer and was adopted by the *New Yorker* as a regular contributor. His success in this mode led to two collections, *A Saucer of Larks* (1962) and T*he Gold in the Sea* (1967), both published outside Ireland. Although his Broadway success with *Philadelphia* made his transfer from writer of prose fiction to playwright—as *Waiting for Godot* had pressed Beckett in a similar direction—it can be said that Friel always retained the skills of the short story. In an essay he argued that the playwright's technique "is the very opposite of the short-story writer's or the novelist's", the former writes for an audience, the collective, while the fiction writer "functions privately, man to man, [in] a personal conversation" (*Essays, Diaries, Interviews* 18). Yet such is the intimacy of Friel's plays and the prevalence of the monologue in many that although they require an audience, certainly, the effect of such success on stage as *Faith Healer* (1979) and *Molly Sweeney* (1996) is very much of the story recited aloud. Friel became the father of the monologue in Irish drama of the last quarter of the twentieth century. Indeed, by 2010 the Literary Director at the Abbey, Aideen Howard, could remark: "There's no denying that we now certainly have a tradition of the monologue play [...] even if it's a recent one".[23] Further, in many respects *Dancing at Lughnasa*, with its narrator firmly in control, is a long short story transferred to the stage (if the Irish bull can be permitted). It is the skill of the writing, needless to say, that contrives the stage illusion of action, for which, incidentally, the well-written stage directions in the published text carry a huge burden. In a later piece written as a programme note for a festival showcasing his plays in 1999, Friel returned to the question that seems always to have fascinated him, of the special quality *words* carry within the hierarchy of the playwright's work, with actors and music coming next in order. It is a Yeatsian diagram:

> In the theatre that has engaged me words are at the very core of it all. The same words that are available to the novelist, to the poet; and used with the same precision and with the same scrupulous attention not only to the exact kernel meaning but to all those allusive meanings that every word hoards. But there is a difference. The playwright's words aren't written for solitary engagement—they are written for public utterance. They are used as the story-teller uses them, to hold an audience in his embrace and within that vocal sound. So, unlike the words of the novelist or poet, the playwright's words are scored for a very different context. And for that reason they are scored in altogether different keys and in altogether different tempi. And it is with this score that the playwright and the actor privately plot to work their public spell.[24]

The emphasis on music and the musical is also significant. With good actors, for Friel's idea of a play "what is written to be sung is now being sung" and the language "fully realizes itself".[25] At this point the private and the public fuse into a duet "where both voices [the author's private voice and the publicly uttered speeches] are distinctly audible." This, for Friel, is "what makes the experience of theatre unique".[26] The technique is to be first found in *Philadelphia*, through the extraordinary use of two actors, Public and Private Gar (the protagonist), representing the conscious and unconscious mind interacting antiphonally. It is found in a more sophisticated form in the four monologues which make up *Faith Healer*, where each is discrete and private but in the audience's perception must dialogue with each of the three individual and isolated characters. When *Faith Healer* premiered on Broadway in 1979 many of the New York reviewers dismissed it as too literary to be dramatic. But this is Friel's great achievement: to invent a form which by using a literary mode in the theatre transcends traditional genres. Its influence has been enormous.

Friel would play a different game in *Translations* (1980), the play which inaugurated the Field Day Theatre Company. It is well to take note that in his most successful plays Friel is always in some sense at play, toying with the nature of the stage, the empty space, and toying also with the challenge presented by time and relativity. This reckless behaviour is quite traditional. Beckett, too, is full of it, but before Beckett Denis Johnston—a neglected playwright—mocked all sorts of traditional discourses, songs, poetry, the voices of patriots and established cultural icons in *The Old Lady Says No!* (1929) to weave an expressionist clash of Robert Emmet's mad romantic stance in 1803 with Dublin's new society of republicans and pretenders in the late 1920s. For Johnston, space-time was an enduring fascination; its duality and ambiguity pervade all of his work. In Beckett a similar but less scientifically or philosophically based interest in the fusion of time and space is often bound up with autobiography and is always elegiac in tone; for Johnston the tone is satiric. If we say Friel's *Translations* is also preoccupied with such binaries, including the alienation effect of making one language, English, serve for two, Irish and English, we have also to say that the tone is political. When, in the aftermath of Bloody Sunday, Friel wrote the angry *The Freedom of the City* with withering irony, he knew he had overstepped the mark he usually set down for himself between art and politics. In an interview nine years after the play's premiere, he beat his breast in regret: "[T]he experience of Bloody Sunday [Friel was present at the march] wasn't *adequately* distilled in me. I wrote [*The Freedom of the City*] out of some kind of heat and some kind of immediate passion that I would want to have quieted a bit before I did it."[27] Contrariwise, in spite of Friel's frequent attempts to deny a political intent, *Translations* was enthusiastically received as deeply political. It is Friel's *Cathleen Ni Houlihan* (1902), a play Conor Cruise O'Brien (no mean political dramatist himself) described as "probably the most powerful piece of nationalist propaganda that has ever been composed".[28] But Yeats abhorred propaganda. Even in his "Advice to playwrights who are sending plays to the Abbey, Dublin", sent out to novice writers, he included a caveat on this point: "We do not desire propagandist plays, nor plays written to serve some obvious moral purpose; for art seldom concerns itself with those interests or opinions."[29] Like Yeats, again, in his work Friel strove to prioritise art, with the declaration "I do not believe that art is a servant of any movement.".[30] It is an ideal most Irish dramatists, O'Casey excepted, strive to maintain. It stems from a reluctance to accept that social drama is in itself, by its nature, political. Ireland is perhaps unique in this regard in the Anglo-centric world.

What we get in later twentieth-century Irish drama is politics by default. Characterization, well-turned speeches and a plot that is either resolved in reconciliation or goes all the way into the tragic mode, provide sufficient audience interest. The Troubles are explored only obliquely. Tom Murphy's *The Patriot Game* (Peacock 1991) is about the only play staged at this time which openly dramatized a political event: the 1916 Rising. It was not very good.[31] In an earlier play, *Conversations on a Homecoming* (1985), written for the Druid Theatre, a play about disillusion among young Irishmen in their late thirties, the returned exile asks during the night's drinking if his mates had ever thought of "marching on the North". They prevaricated: "We nearly did. [...] Shoot us a few Prods. [...] It's very bad up there. [...] We nearly did, one night."[32] Murphy exposes the fraudulent politics of a whole generation in one satiric scene. But the North is not his theme here or elsewhere in his work, because, in truth, it was not really a deep concern to denizens of the Republic anyway. It was merely a cue for pub talk. In a magnificent tribute to Murphy's genius, Friel has written that Murphy's imagination is essentially Gaelic: "antic, bleak, agitated, bewildered, capable of great cruelty and great compassion. [...] Language and character are a unity. Each is a creation of the other. That is an achievement that Synge would have been proud of."[33] But Synge, as Yeats testified, "seemed by nature unfitted to think a political thought".[34]

It is only those writers, then, either born in Northern Ireland or close to its border with the Republic who can honestly and passionately write plays about its sufferings. Frank McGuinness's 1985 *Observe the Sons of Ulster* is the prime example after Friel. It is set in 1916 but focused on the Northern Unionist tradition and the insecurity of identity within that community. Its revival in 1995 on the main Abbey stage, again directed by Patrick Mason, then artistic director of the Abbey, elevated the play into a dual role: a daring call for the acceptance of gay sexuality and a fruitful commentary on the ceasefire tentatively introduced in the North and marked in the Republic by attendance at this Abbey production by political figures from both communities. In that instance, the whole context of the play was politically heightened so that it spoke to audiences in challenging tones directed towards expanding consciousness. McGuinness has the gift of seizing upon a moment to deliver such challenges. *Carthaginians* (Peacock 1988) daringly commemorated Bloody Sunday in a meta-theatrical fashion at one of the worst periods of violence in the North; even O'Casey's *Juno* is parodied here to deconstruct the language of traditional grief. But McGuinness (a borderline northerner) was soon to find that southern audiences had limited patience with plays reminding them of northern tragedy. Even the revered novelist Benedict Kiely found that his 1977 novel *Proxopera*, while successful critically as a bleak comment on bombing in the North, proved a disaster on the Gate stage when subsequently adapted.

On the other hand, many Northern writers, resident in Belfast and its environs, successfully intervened in the political debate in the 1970s and after. These would include Martin Lynch, Pam Brighton, Anne Devlin, John Wilson Haire, Robin Glendinning, and Christina Reid, whose plays were staged mainly at the Lyric Players Theatre. Stewart Parker was staged north and south of the border; being as meta-theatrical as Friel he too strove to make art, or entertainment, dominate over politics. He gloried in music-hall techniques and subject matter but only his *Northern Star* (Lyric 1984) and *Pentecost* (Field Day 1987) are serious reflections on the Troubles, although *Catchpenny Twist* (Peacock 1977) projects a dark comedy in that direction. The only playwrights from the unionist community to write for the Abbey during this period were Graham Reid and Gary Mitchell. Reid's 1979 play, *The Death of Humpty Dumpty* (with Liam Neeson) was a huge success at the Peacock, to be followed by *The Closed Door* (1980). Neither is set in the North, but both deal with violence arising out of frustration and terror. A third play, *Dorothy* (1981) was not deemed suitable for the Peacock but found a home in the Oscar, an experimental theatre in Ballsbridge (now extinct). It is set in Belfast, and again deals with extraordinary violence not of a directly political nature. It is thus British in approach, out of the same stable as Edward Bond's *Saved* (1965). Apart from the "Billy" plays, which are set as well as staged only in Belfast (and on television), there is only one Reid play which could be said to intervene in the Northern debate and offer at least some kind of analysis. This is *The Hidden Curriculum* (1982), set in Belfast but premiered at the Peacock in Dublin. The action takes place in a

Protestant secondary school and its environs in West Belfast in the late 1970s. The thesis is that if pupils are taught only English history, and taught it with prejudice, there is a bias that will turn the young in a direction bound to oppose their counterparts being indoctrinated with a Republican version of history. The inference is that segregated education breeds segregated minds likely to turn to hatred of difference. Even today such an argument bears weight. Gary Mitchell is a less subtle playwright, whose work would later on land him in trouble in the North. *In a Little World of Our Own* (Peacock 1997) deals with working-class loyalism, its immersion in corruption and violence in Belfast after the ceasefire. It is a brave, outspoken play, which in spite of crudities in style and structure deserves the critical acclaim it has achieved. Mitchell's outlook is uncompromising: "The loyalist community is deeply self-destructive. It's suspicious of culture and suspicious of education."[35] His role is thus an unenviable one, at work in an environment where art can be totally misunderstood and the consequences can be deadly.

Conclusion

By the 1990s the Abbey's artistic director could once again invoke the "high ambition" articulated by Yeats, Gregory and Martyn as founding fathers.[36] "It has been my task over the last six years", Patrick Mason said in a lecture in 1999, "to try and move the Abbey towards a new and fuller understanding of itself and its role, and I have tried to do that both through the practical work of the theatre—defining and expanding its artistic and cultural remit—and by looking back, creatively I hope, to the origins of this idea of a National Theatre."[37] At much the same time Thomas Kilroy wrote: "An Irish playwright even remotely concerned with tradition is faced with a tri-furcated past with such tenuous connections between the three strands that the very notion of tradition becomes questionable."[38] His three divisions are the Anglo-Irish theatre of the Ascendancy, Yeats's theatre, and the period between 1922 and the end of the 1950s. Kilroy sees a difficulty in the sectarian division between the last-mentioned division, in which the playwrights were mainly Catholic, and the preceding two when they were mainly Protestant and proud of it. Kilroy argues that the new Catholic generation of the 1920s and after were dedicated to naturalism. Being of this generation, alongside Friel, Leonard, Keane and Murphy, who matured after 1960, Kilroy sees tradition as significant. "My own may be the last generation with such a sense of continuity with the past. [...] But it is also a generation of originality."[39] He associates this quality with the stand he and his fellow playwrights took against cultural totems and taboos in an effort to delineate the features of an emergent culture which would throw off the strictures of Catholicism forever. It is a way of redefining Irishness. Kilroy is very aware of the Yeatsian precedent here. Elsewhere he writes of Yeats as "at one of the centers [*sic*] of the modern dramatic tradition".[40] In turn, Kilroy's generation struggled for decades to give expression to a changing

Ireland, creating thereby a significant extension to the literary tradition which had distinguished Irish drama since 1899.

Notes

1. Brian Friel, *Essays, Diaries, Interviews: 1964–1999*, ed. Christopher Murray (London: Faber, 1999), 53.
2. W. B. Yeats, "The Circus Animals' Desertion", *Collected Poems*, second edn. (London: Macmillan, 1950), 392.
3. Una Ellis-Fermor, *The Irish Dramatic Movement* (London: Methuen, 1964), 1.
4. Ibid., 8.
5. Ibid., 200.
6. Ibid., 61.
7. Frank Fay, *Towards a National Theatre: The Dramatic Criticism of Frank J. Fay*, ed. Robert Hogan (Dublin: Dolmen Press, 1970), 15–20, 90–94. See also Gabriel Fallon, "The Abbey Theatre Acting Tradition", *The Story of the Abbey Theatre*, ed. Sean McCann (London: New English Library/Four Square Books, 1967), 101–125.
8. Ibid., 62.
9. W. B. Yeats, "*Samhain* 1903: The Reform of the Theatre", *Explorations* (London: Macmillan, 1962), 107, 108.
10. T. S. Eliot, "Poetry and Drama", *Selected Prose of T.S. Eliot*, ed. Frank Kermode (London: Faber, 1975), 137.
11. J. M. Synge, *Collected Works, Volume IV: Plays Book II*, ed. Ann Saddlemyer (Gerrards Cross: Colin Smythe, 1982), 53–54.
12. Peter Kavanagh, *The Story of the Abbey Theatre: A Facsimile Reprint*, Appendix D, "Warrant for Letters Patent for a new Theatre in the City of Dublin" (Orono, ME: National Poetry Foundation/University of Maine at Orono, 1984), 214.
13. In 1906 the patron of the Abbey, Annie Horniman, proposed the German Municipal Theatre as a model for the Abbey to emulate. Synge disagreed and won over Yeats and Lady Gregory. See Ann Saddlemyer, ed., *Theatre Business: The Correspondence of the First Abbey Theatre Directors: William Butler Yeats, Lady Gregory and J.M. Synge* (Gerrards Cross: Colin Smythe, 1982), 168–80.
14. Lennox Robinson, *Curtain Up: An Autobiography* (London: Michael Joseph, 1942), 118.
15. Brenna Katz Clarke and Harold Ferrar, *The Dublin Drama League 1919–1941* (Dublin: Dolmen Press, 1979), 19.
16. Peter Kavanagh, *The Story of the Abbey Theatre* (New York: Devin-Adair, 1950), Facsimile reprint (Orono, ME: University of Maine at Orono, 1984), 179.
17. W. B. Yeats, *Explorations. Selected by Mrs. W. B. Yeats* (London and New York: Macmillan, 1962), 414.
18. Lauren Arrington, *W. B. Yeats, the Abbey Theatre, Censorship, and the Irish State: Adding the Half-Pence to the Pence* (Oxford: Oxford University Press, 2010).
19. W. B. Yeats, "The Irish Dramatic Movement", Autobiographies (London: Macmillan, 1961), 566.
20. Seán O'Casey, *The Green Crow* (New York: Grosset & Dunlap, 1956), 83. The essay was first published in O'Casey, *The Flying Wasp* (London: Macmillan, 1937), 123.

21. Michael O'Regan, "Nationalism and Catholicism dominated 50th commemoration", *Irish Times* 16 March 2016: 4. See also Anthony Roche, "Staging 1916 in 1966: Pastiche, Parody and Problems of Representation", *1916 in 1966: Commemorating the Easter Rising*, eds. Mary E. Daly and Margaret O'Callaghan (Dublin: Royal Irish Academy, 2007), 303–22.
22. Augustine Martin, *Anglo-Irish Literature* (Dublin: Department of Foreign Affairs, 1980), 52.
23. Christine Madden, "The music of the lone voice on the Irish stage", *Irish Times* 3 August 2010: 9. See also Eamonn Jordan, "The Glut of Monologues: Look Who's Talking, Too", *Dissident Dramaturgies: Contemporary Irish Theatre* (Dublin: Irish Academic Press, 2010), 218–238.
24. Brian Friel, *Essays, Diaries, Interviews: 1964–1999*, ed. Christopher Murray (London: Faber, 1999), 173.
25. Ibid.
26. Ibid., 174.
27. Ibid., 110. Italics added for "adequately."
28. Conor Cruise O'Brien, *Ancestral Voices: Religion and Nationalism in Ireland* (Dublin: Poolbeg, 1994), 61.
29. Lady Gregory, *Our Irish Theatre* (Gerrards Cross: Colin Smythe, 1972), 62. This history was first published in 1913.
30. Ibid., 56.
31. But see also Shaun Richards, "The Work of a "Young Nationalist"?: Tom Murphy's *The Patriot Game* and the Commemoration of Easter 1916", *Irish University Review* 45.1 (2015): 39–53.
32. Tom Murphy, *Plays: Two* (London: Methuen Drama, 1993), 13. See also pp. 43, 49.
33. Ibid., 89–90.
34. W. B. Yeats, *Essays and Introductions* (London and New York: Macmillan, 1961), 319.
35. Gary Mitchell in interview with Una Bradley, "A peace of the action", *Irish Times* 2 January 2013: 12.
36. Gregory, *Our Irish Theatre*, 20.
37. Patrick Mason, *Playing with Words: A Fantasy on the Themes of Theatre, the National Theatre, and Post-Modernism* (Dublin: Royal Irish Academy, in Association with the National Theatre Society Ltd., 2000), 20.
38. Thomas Kilroy, "A Generation of Playwrights", *Irish University Review* 22.1 (1992): 135–41 (135).
39. Thomas Kilroy, *Irish University Review Special Issue: Thomas Kilroy*, ed. Anthony Roche 32.1 (2002): 136.
40. Thomas Kilroy, "Two Playwrights: Yeats and Beckett", in *Myth and Reality in Irish Literature*, ed. Joseph Ronsley (Waterloo, Ont.: Wilfrid Laurier University Press, 1977), 183–195 (184).

Bibliography

Arrington, Lauren. *W. B. Yeats, the Abbey Theatre, Censorship, and the Irish State: Adding the Half-Pence to the Pence*. Oxford: Oxford University Press, 2010.

Bort, Eberhard, ed. *The State of Play: Irish Theatre in the 'Nineties*. Trier: Wissenschaftlicher Verlag Trier, 1996.

Brown, Terence. *Ireland: A Social and Cultural History 1922–2002*. London: Harper Perennial, 2004.

Cave, Richard Allen, ed. *W. B. Yeats: Selected Plays*. London and New York: Penguin, 1997.

Clarke, Brenna Katz and Harold Ferrar. *The Dublin Drama League 1919–1941*. Dublin: Dolmen Press, 1979.

Dean, Joan Fitzpatrick and José Lanters, eds. *Beyond Realism: Experimental and Unconventional Irish Drama Since the Revival*. Amsterdam and New York: Rodopi, 2015.

Dubost, Thierry. *The Plays of Thomas Kilroy: A Critical Study*. Jefferson, NC: McFarland, 2007.

Ellis-Fermor, Una. *The Irish Dramatic Movement*. Revised edition. London: Methuen, 1964.

Fitz-Simon, Christopher. *The Boys: A Double Biography* [of Micheál MacLiammóir and Hilton Edwards]. London: Nick Hern Books, 1994.

Flannery, James W. *W. B. Yeats and the Idea of a Theatre: The Early Abbey Theatre in Theory and Practice*. New Haven and London: Yale University Press, 1989.

Friel, Brian. *Essays, Diaries, Interviews: 1964–1999*. Ed. Christopher Murray. London: Faber, 1999.

Grene, Nicholas. *The Politics of Irish Drama*. Cambridge: Cambridge University Press, 1999.

Hogan, Robert. *After the Irish Renaissance: A Critical History of the Irish Drama Since The Plough and the Stars*. Minneapolis: University of Minnesota Press, 1967; London: Macmillan, 1968.

Hunt, Hugh. *The Abbey Theatre 1904–1979*. Dublin: Gill and Macmillan, 1979.

Jordan, Eamonn, ed. *Theatre Stuff: Critical Essays on Contemporary Irish Theatre*. Dublin: Carysfort Press, 2000.

Jordan, Eamonn. *Dissident Dramaturgies: Contemporary Irish Theatre*. Dublin: Irish Academic Press, 2010.

Kavanagh, Peter. *The Story of the Abbey Theatre*. New York: Devin-Adair, 1950. Facsimile reprint, Orono, ME: University of Maine at Orono, 1984

Kilroy, Thomas. *Irish University Review Special Issue: Thomas Kilroy*, ed. Anthony Roche 32.1 (2002).

Kosok, Heinz. *Plays and Playwrights from Ireland in International Perspective*. Trier: WVT Wissenscaftlicher Trier, 1995.

Kurdi Mária. *Codes and Masks: Aspects of Identity in Contemporary Irish Plays*. Frankfurt a.m.: Peter Lang, 2000

Lojek, Helen. *The Spaces of Irish Drama: Stage and Place in Contemporary Plays*. New York: Palgrave Macmillan, 2011.

Lonergan, Patrick and Riana O'Dwyer, eds. *Echoes Down the Corridor*. Dublin: Carysfort Press, 2007.

McMinn, Joseph, ed. *The Internationalism of Irish Literature and Drama*. Gerrards Cross: Colin Smythe, 1992.

Madden, Tom. *The Making of an Artist: Creating the Irishman Micheál MacLiammóir*. Dublin: Liffey Press, 2015.

Merriman, Victor. *"Because We Are Poor": Irish Theatre in the 1990s*. Dublin: Carysfort Press, 2011.

Miller, Liam. *The Noble Drama of W. B. Yeats*. Dublin: Dolmen Press, 1977.

Morash, Christopher. *A History of Irish Theatre*. Cambridge: Cambridge University Press, 2002.
Morash, Chris and Shaun Richards. *Mapping Irish Theatre: Theories of Space and Place*. Cambridge: Cambridge University Press, 2013.
Morse, Donald E., ed. *Irish Theatre in Transition: From the Late Nineteenth Century to the Early Twenty-First Century*. London: Palgrave Macmillan, 2015.
Murray, Christopher. *The Theatre of Brian Friel: Tradition and Modernity*. London: Bloomsbury, 2014.
Murray, Christopher, ed. *"Alive in Time": The Enduring Drama of Tom Murphy*. Dublin: Carysfort Press, 2010.
O'Casey, Seán. *The Green Crow*. New York: George Braziller, 1956.
O'Neill, Michael. *The Abbey at the Queen's: The Interregnum Years 1951–1966*. Nepean, ONT: Borealis Press. 1999.
Pilkington, Lionel. *Theatre and the State in Twentieth-Century Ireland: Cultivating the People*. London and New York: Routledge, 2001.
Pilny, Ondřej. *Irony and Identity on Modern Irish Drama*. Prague: Litteraria Pragensia, 2006.
Pine, Richard. *Brian Friel and Ireland's Drama*. London and New York: Routledge, 1990.
Richtarik, Marilynn J. *Stewart Parker: A Life*. Oxford: Oxford University Press, 2014.
Robinson, Lennox. *Curtain Up: An Autobiography*. London: Michael Joseph, 1942.
Robinson, Lennox. *The Abbey Theatre: A History 1899–1951*. London: Sidgwick and Jackson, 1951.
Roche, Anthony. *Contemporary Irish Drama*. Second edition. Basingstoke: Palgrave Macmillan, 2009.
Roche, Anthony. *The Irish Dramatic Revival 1899–1939*. London: Bloomsbury, 2015.
Synge, J.M. *Collected Works Volume IV: Plays Book II*. Ed. Ann Saddlemyer. Gerrards Cross: Colin Smythe; Washington, DC: Catholic University of America Press, 1982.
Walsh, Ian R. *Experimental Irish Theatre after W.B. Yeats*. London: Palgrave Macmillan, 2012.
Watt, Steve et al, eds. *A Century of Irish Drama: Widening the Stage*. Bloomington and Indianapolis: Indiana University Press, 2000.
Welch, Robert. *The Abbey Theatre 1899–1999*. Oxford University Press, 1999.
White, Harry. *Music and the Irish Literary Imagination*. Oxford: Oxford University Press, 2008.
Worth, Katharine. *The Irish Drama of Europe from Yeats to Beckett*. London: Athlone Press, 1978.
Yeats, W. B. *Essays and Introductions*. London and New York: Macmillan, 1961.
Yeats, W. B. *Explorations. Selected by Mrs W. B. Yeats*. London and New York: Macmillan, 1962.

#WakingTheFeminists

Carole Quigley

On 28 October 2015, Ireland's National Theatre, the Abbey Theatre, announced its programme of events, entitled "Waking the Nation," to commemorate the 1916 centenary. Of the ten plays listed in the 2016 programme, there featured only one play written by a woman and all but three of the ten plays were due to be directed by men. The message portrayed by this programme was blatantly clear for the theatre makers of Ireland—women and their artistic work do not belong on the national stage, and they do not represent a part of the nation deemed worthy of "waking". The one play written by a woman, entitled *Me, Mollser,* was listed as, "a specially commissioned monologue play to introduce *The Plough and the Stars* by Sean O'Casey to a younger audience, telling the story of the Easter Rising 1916 through the magical power of a performance and workshop in their own school or local community".[1] It was written by Ali White, and directed by Sarah Fitzgibbon. This play toured schools in Ireland from January to March 2016. It was never performed on either the Abbey Theatre's main stage, or its smaller stage, the Peacock.[2] This meant that the commemorative season would not present any writing by women in the theatre building itself. The irony in the press release was palpable as a short promotional video released alongside the programme featured only female theatre makers, and began with a quote from Helena Molony, a 1916 Rebel and an Abbey Theatre actress that read, "[w]e saw a vision of Ireland, free, pure, happy. We did not realise this vision, but we saw it".[3] One hundred and twelve years since the Abbey was founded, then Director of the Abbey, Senator Fiach Mac Conghail, presented a programme to commemorate the

C. Quigley (✉)
Mary Immaculate College, University of Limerick, Limerick, Ireland
e-mail: QUIGLEC6@tcd.ie

E. Jordan, E. Weitz (eds.), *The Palgrave Handbook of Contemporary Irish Theatre and Performance*,
https://doi.org/10.1057/978-1-137-58588-2_6

centenary of the 1916 Easter Rising that was exclusive, divisive and inherently sexist.

In the days that followed the announcement of this programme, many people involved in theatre and the arts in Ireland took to social media sites including Facebook and Twitter to voice their concerns and disappointment at such a subjective programme. Lian Bell, a freelance set designer and arts manager, initiated and led the discussion. This led to the coining of the hashtag #WakingTheFeminists (or #WTF) by director Maeve Stone in response to the idea of "Waking The Nation". This hashtag began trending on social media sites both in Ireland and abroad as it was used to highlight disappointment in the sexist nature of the programme itself, and also to discuss the systemic under-representation of women and minority groups throughout the theatre industry as a whole. The poignant link between the established use of the letters "WTF" to convey feelings of disbelief and annoyance with the use of the same letters for the #WakingTheFeminists campaign was not lost on those involved in the campaign, who reacted with anger and exasperation to the news of the programme.

On 29 October 2015, Mac Conghail took to his personal Twitter account to field questions about the "Waking The Nation" programme. His Twitter reaction to the backlash over his choice of works showed an audacious disregard for the work of women in the theatre.[4] Some of the Tweets from his twitter handle @fmacconghail on 29 October read, "All my new play choices are based on the quality of the play, form and theme. It's my call and I'm pleased with the plays I picked for #wtn", "I don't and haven't programmed plays or productions on a gender basis. I took decisions based on who I admired and wanted to work with"[5] and the since deleted but now infamous final response, "Thems the breaks,"[6] as he defiantly claimed that there were no appropriate new plays written by women, or old plays in The Abbey Theatre archives. He claimed this as fact even though, as Melissa Sihra points out, there are over 600 known Irish plays written by women since 1663.[7]

The #WakingTheFeminists movement was driven by a need to challenge this form of patriarchal, oppressive, phallocentric, offensive and misogynist thinking. #WakingTheFeminists began as a platform from which to combat systemic prejudice in the Irish theatre industry and to give a voice to those silenced by this pervading oppression. It is of vital importance that this response was initially ignited by the actions of the national theatre, as the Abbey routinely receives half of the Arts Council's funding for theatre in Ireland, and it was awarded €6.2 million for the 2015/2016 season. Comparatively, The Gate Theatre received €860,000, and the Druid Theatre Company received €762,000 for the same time period.[8] That such a comparatively well-funded theatre could fail to address the issue of gender diversity within its programming highlights the systemic prejudice against female theatre makers working in the industry. The lack of gender diversity at Ireland's national theatre sets a precedent for bias on the grounds of gender identity, and trains theatre makers to expect this bias throughout the industry's hierarchy.

As #WakingTheFeminists garnered viral attention, Lian Bell wrote on her Facebook page on 3 November 2015,

> If all these posts about wanting equality in the arts mean something to you, say something. Even if you don't want to bang a drum. Even if you don't know what to say. Even if your comment is 'I stand with you'. Say something. It helps us to know you're out there. If possible—say it on Twitter (it's louder). #WakingTheFeminists.[9]

This was a call to arms for the feminists and women within the Irish theatre community as the movement escalated dramatically. The reaction to the exclusionary programming and the explosion of interest in, and support for, the #WakingTheFeminists movement culminated in a public meeting staged at the Abbey on November 12th 2015, chaired by Senator Ivana Bacik and theatre producer Sarah Durcan.[10] Durcan was subsequently elected to the Board of Directors of The Abbey in 2016. Thirty women spoke of their experiences in the theatre industry.[11] These women spoke as actors, writers, directors, producers, designers, academics, dramaturgs and theatre makers. The Abbey was chosen as a suitable, if not ironic, location for this meeting, as it was highly symbolic to have so many women discuss problems within the Irish theatre industry on the country's National Stage. As the Abbey also kindly offered the theatre space to those involved in the campaign, it showed its willingness to engage in this conversation. Soon after this meeting, the board and director of the Abbey issued a public statement pledging their support for striving towards a gender balance in Irish theatre, and Fiach Mac Conghail stated:

> I am determined to programme the work of women artists in the latter half of 2016. An exciting and innovative programme of plays will be confirmed when we announce our Autumn/Winter Season. A national conversation is underway; one which I look forward to participating further in with members of the theatre community. The Abbey Theatre looks forward to leading the way in achieving a much-needed cultural shift in gender equality in the years to come.[12]

Since this inaugural meeting, the #WakingTheFeminists founders have gone on to host numerous other events including follow up meetings to discuss their progress in investigations into gender equality within the theatre.[13] In December 2015, #WakingTheFeminists put out a call for feminists to organize meetings for 6 January 2016, a day also known as "Nollaig na mBan", or "Women's Christmas".[14] Their open call looked for people to meet up, socialize and plan events for #WakingTheFeminists,

> Nollaig na mBan is traditionally a day for women to gather socially and chat, a quiet celebration of women and their work. We thought it would be the perfect time for all feminists, women and men, who have been following and supporting the WakingTheFeminists campaign to get together locally over a drink or a cup of tea. It's a chance to kick start the year by meeting each other, discussing the issues, telling their stories and having a bit of craic.[15]

On International Women's Day (8 March) 2016, #WakingTheFeminists hosted its second public meeting in Dublin's Liberty Hall.[16] This meeting was entitled "Spring Forward" and discussed the progress of the movement. It featured reactions from seven key Irish theatre organizations as they discussed their response to the call of #WakingTheFeminists to work towards gender equality in Irish theatre. The seven speakers represented the Abbey Theatre, Druid, Dublin Fringe Festival, Dublin Theatre Festival, Gate Theatre, Project Arts Centre and Rough Magic Theatre Company. The meeting also featured an update from Lian Bell on the work of the movement and a presentation from Brenda Donohue and Sarah Durcan on the research plans for #WakingTheFeminists.

On 7 June 2017, the #WakingTheFeminists research team launched their report entitled *Gender Counts*.[17] This report provides an analysis of gender in Irish theatre from 2006–2015, focusing, "on ten of the top Arts Council-funded organisations that produce or present theatre in Ireland".[18] The six members of the research team, led by Brenda Donohue, sourced data on 1,155 productions[19] and found that "women are underrepresented in every role studied[20] except costume design,"[21] and, "[t]o achieve parity in all roles, women face a gap of between 8 and 41 percentage points".[22] They also found that the four highest-funded organizations in their sample have the lowest female representation and, in general, the more funding an organization receives, the lower its female representation throughout.[23] In conjunction with their research project, as stated by the campaign, "#WakingTheFeminists have also begun to engage with the Arts Council to ensure that gender equality is addressed across the sector at policy level, in a way that will be practical, significant and long-lasting."[24] The #WTF campaign has also led to other events such as the Irish Women Playwrights and Theatremakers' Conference held at Mary Immaculate College in Limerick in June 2017. This curated conference gathered academics and theatre makers alike in a bid to, "[h]ighlight women's overlooked contribution to Irish theatre from the 1700s to today".[25] The conference featured talks and presentations on a wide range of female playwrights and theatremakers, from re-examining the positioning of seminal playwrights such as Lady Gregory and Marina Carr as "token female playwrights," to uncovering the hidden histories of writers such as Teresa Deevy and Mary Manning, to looking at the new work of emerging Irish theatremakers such as Caitríona Daly and Amanda Coogan. This conference looked at re-inventing the Irish dramatic canon post #WakingTheFeminists.

In addition to the #WakingTheFeminists campaign highlighting the visibility of women working in the theatre industry along with their access to it, the campaign also aims to speak out against and tackle workplace bullying and harassment. Many of the voices speaking out in favour of the movement initially cited stories of exposure to abuse as a result of being a woman in the theatre industry. A huge amount of this abuse had previously been silenced and normalized. In a statement published by the campaign regarding the issue of bullying and harassment, #WakingTheFeminists said,

> We at #WakingTheFeminists are saddened and angered by recent posts by theatre professionals talking openly about what has long been rumoured and whispered about: that women in theatre are experiencing bullying or harassment in the workplace on the basis of their gender. Everyone is entitled to feel safe at work, and bullying and sexual harassment are illegal.[26]

The website goes on to provide a series of links to resources about workplace rights and how to deal with such abuse. The existence of #WakingTheFeminists affords those affected the opportunity to speak about their experiences and their work pushes towards greater transparency within the theatre industry in regards to such injustices.

Public meetings, gatherings, presentations and discussions remain a critical part of the #WakingTheFeminists work. What has become so apparent from this movement, and the subsequent work of those involved directly in it, is that this kind of sexism still exists and needs to be tackled immediately. Such workplace sexism remains evident in the fact that on average, women are paid 14% less than men for the same jobs in Ireland.[27] This percentage rises to 24.6% for those in the top 10% of earners, showing that there is still a "glass ceiling" in place for women in the workforce in Ireland today.[28] Sexism in Ireland also remains potent in the Eighth Amendment of The Irish Constitution, which denies the right to full reproductive freedom and comprehensive healthcare for pregnant people living in Ireland. While 2015 saw the success of the landmark Marriage Equality Referendum, the need for a #WakingTheFeminists campaign further highlights the lack of equality for women in Ireland as they continue to experience gender discrimination in various ways.

#WakingTheFeminists serves as a prime example of the ways in which Irish feminists, both in Ireland and abroad, are mobilizing to reject gender discrimination and fight against flagrant sexism in the twenty-first century. It is clear from the outrage sparked by #WakingTheFeminists, and the subsequent momentum garnered by the movement, that the drive for full equality for all people living in Ireland, regardless of gender, creed, race, class or sexual orientation, is a contemporary revolution and driving force of cultural progression in Ireland. The evidence is clear: sexism and gender discrimination remain at large in contemporary society. However, a wholly positive movement such as #WakingTheFeminists aims to tackle and eradicate such issues. Sexism is not a new issue in Ireland, or in the theatre world. From the opening of the Abbey in 1904, when Lady Augusta Gregory was denied her rightful recognition for co-authorship of one of its inaugural plays *Cathleen Ni Houlihan*, right through to the current moment, women in Ireland have experienced patriarchal oppression in a myriad of forms. Women have been routinely erased from all areas of Irish theatre. This includes exclusion from the canon for playwrights, a lack of opportunity afforded to female directors and producers and the devaluation of the work of costumiers, makeup and technical designers. It is also not a new idea for women to stand up to such oppression. Scholars such as Melissa Sihra, Cathy Leeney and Lisa Fitzpatrick, to name but a few, have routinely spoken out against such erasure and its implications for how we critically analyse theatre history, along with how such discrimination is impacting women working in the industry today. The "Irish Women Playwrights and Theatremakers" Conference presented the research of such women engaged in the conversation around tackling systemic sexism and uncovering hidden histories. The feminists of Ireland are very much awake, and their sheer number proves that change is slowly but surely coming to Irish society.

Notes

1. "Priming the Canon: Me, Mollser", Abbey Theatre, http://www.abbeytheatre.ie/engage/projects/priming-the-canon-me-mollser/, accessed 28 July 2016.
2. Correct at the time of writing.
3. "Waking the Nation – 2016 at the Abbey Theatre" Abbey Theatre, https://www.youtube.com/watch?v=HL6_Bh2nQd0&feature=youtu.be. Accessed 8 February 2016.
4. Fiach Mac Conghail, Twitter Post, 29 October, 2015, https://twitter.com/fmacconghail.
5. Ibid.
6. Ibid.
7. Melissa Sihra, Twitter Post, 4 November 2015, https://twitter.com/MelissaSihra.
8. Interactive map of Arts Council Funding for 2015/2016, http://www.artscouncil.ie/map-of-funding-decisions/. Accessed 28 July 2016.
9. Lian Bell, Facebook Post, 3 November 2015, https://www.facebook.com/lianbell?fref=ts.
10. Full video of #WakingTheFeminists first public meeting available on #WakingTheFeminists website, http://www.wakingthefeminists.org/2015/11/03/public-meeting-video/. Accessed 28 July 2016.
11. A full list of speakers is available at, http://www.wakingthefeminists.org/public-meeting-women-irish-theatre/. Accessed 1 December 2016.
12. A statement from the Board and Director of the Abbey Theatre, http://www.abbeytheatre.ie/a-statement-from-the-board-and-director-of-the-abbey-theatre/, published 22 December 2015, accessed 28 July 2016.
13. A full list of the events that took place to celebrate Nollaig na MBan both in Ireland and internationally can be found at: http://www.wakingthefeminists.org/2015/12/10/celebrate-wakingthefeminists-on-nollaig-na-mban/
14. Ibid.
15. "#WakingTheFeminists celebrated Nollaig na mBan", #WakingTheFeminists website, http://www.wakingthefeminists.org/2015/12/10/celebrate-wakingthefeminists-on-nollaig-na-mban/. Accessed 28 July 2016.
16. "International Women's Day Meeting", #WakingTheFeminists website, accessed 29 July 2016, http://www.wakingthefeminists.org/international-womens-day/.
17. "Gender Counts", published 6 June 2017, accessed 14 June 2017, https://www.dropbox.com/s/gawewk3dq43rqnd/Gender_Counts_WakingTheFeminists_2017.pdf?dl=0.
18. Ibid., 7.

19. Ibid.
20. For the purpose of this research project, there were seven roles within the theatre studied. They are: Director, Author, Cast Member, Set Designer, Lighting Designer, Sound Designer and Costume Designer.
21. "Gender Counts", 25.
22. Ibid.
23. Ibid., 7.
24. "Story So Far", #WakingTheFeminists Website, accessed 29 July 2016, http://www.wakingthefeminists.org/about-wtf/how-it-started/
25. David Clare, "Fired from the canon: Waking the Feminists, the conference", *The Irish Times*, May 16, 2017, accessed 16 May 2017, http://www.irishtimes.com/culture/books/fired-from-the-canon-waking-the-feminists-the-conference-1.3084729
26. "Bullying And Sexual Harassment In The Theatre Workplace", #WakingTheFeminists Website, accessed 29 July 2016, http://www.wakingthefeminists.org/2015/12/10/bullying-and-sexual-harassment-in-the-theatre-workplace/
27. National Council for Women in Ireland website, accessed 16 January 2016, http://www.nwci.ie/?/discover/what_we_do/womens_economic_independence/women_and_employment/gender_pay_gap/
28. Ibid.

Bibliography

Abbey Theatre. Accessed July 28, 2016. http://www.abbeytheatre.ie/engage/projects/priming-the-canon-me-mollser/

———. "Waking the Nation–2016 at the Abbey Theatre." Accessed February 8, 2016. https://www.youtube.com/watch?v=HL6_Bh2nQd0&feature=youtu.be YouTube,

———. "A Statement from the Board and Director of the Abbey Theatre." Accessed July 28, 2016. http://www.abbeytheatre.ie/a-statement-from-the-board-and-director-of-the-abbey-theatre/

Bell, Lian. Facebook Post. November 3, 2015. https://www.facebook.com/lianbell?fref=ts

Clare, David. "Fired from the Canon: Waking the Feminists, the Conference." *The Irish Times*. May 16, 2017. Accessed May 16, 2017. http://www.irishtimes.com/culture/books/fired-from-the-canon-waking-the-feminists-the-conference-1.3084729

Donohue, Brenda, Ciara O'Dowd, Tayna Dean, Ciara Murphy, Kathleen Cawley, Kate Harris. "Gender Counts." Accessed June 14, 2017. https://www.dropbox.com/s/gawewk3dq43rqnd/Gender_Counts_WakingTheFeminists_2017.pdf?dl=0

Interactive Map of Arts Council Funding for 2015/2016. Accessed July 28, 2016. http://www.artscouncil.ie/map-of-funding-decisions/

Mac Conghail, Fiach. Twitter Post. October 29, 2015. https://twitter.com/fmacconghail.

Sihra, Melissa. Twitter Post. November 4, 2015. https://twitter.com/MelissaSihra.

National Council for Women in Ireland website. Accessed January 16, 2016. http://www.nwci.ie/?/discover/what_we_do/womens_economic_independence/women_and_employment/gender_pay_gap/

#WakingTheFeminists website. Accessed July 28, 2016. http://www.wakingthefeminists.org

Live Art in Ireland

Una Mannion

What Is Live Art?

"What exactly is live art and how is it different from performance art?" is one of the first questions I am invariably asked in a live art module that I teach. It is a difficult, and potentially impossible, question to answer. Performance art is a precursor to live art but also an example of it, its practice based on the "liveness" of the performance, the presence of the artist and the audience who witness it in a particular time and space. Live art, a more recent category with a broader taxonomy, includes site-specific art, land art, experimental film, social sculptures, immersive and living installations and performance—these multiple practices often "live" by means of the embodied presence of the spectator.

Performance art emerged during the 1970s as a distinct area of artistic expression although preceded by many avant-garde movements and "happenings". At a historical juncture marked by resistance to mediatized culture, hyper-realities and multinational capitalism, performance artists insisted on the reality and presence of their own bodies and the bodies of others as an assertion of the real. They broke conventions of both visual arts and theatre, trying to work outside traditional spaces and beyond marketplace values.

Serbian born Marina Abramović, the self-proclaimed godmother of performance art, began a series of performances in which her own body was the material that she exposed to mutilation, pain and risk. In 1974, she performed *Rhythm O* where she arranged seventy-two objects on a table including a feather, a rose, a knife, a gun, for the audience to use upon her as they wished. Her clothes were cut, a thorn stuck into her, a loaded gun put in her hand and pointed at her head. In the United States, other artists were also using bodily

U. Mannion (✉)
Institute of Technology Sligo, Sligo, Ireland

E. Jordan, E. Weitz (eds.), *The Palgrave Handbook of Contemporary Irish Theatre and Performance*,
https://doi.org/10.1057/978-1-137-58588-2_7

violence to explore the complicated relationship between performer and audience and the unspoken contract by which society passively accepts violence. In Chris Burden's *Shoot* (1971), his assistant shoots him in the arm with a rifle from five metres away.

According to Abramović, by the 1990s "there was an increasing awareness of the body, of the vulnerability of the body, of temporality and death". The experience of AIDS, famines and wars, she argues, generated interest in temporary performances.[1] In England, Franko B began a series of performances in the 1990s during which he bled. In *I Miss You* (1999–2005), he walked up and down a white catwalk naked, his body painted white, and the red blood spilling from veins opened by inserted cannula, "confronting the human form at its most existential and essential".[2]

There is a visceral immediacy in the space of performance art as the spectator experiences the smell, the heat, the body and the pain of the performer in a durational action. The performance demands something different from the spectator, who is implicated in the action through the experiential space that generates some level of inter-subjectivity or empathy. Michelle Browne, a practitioner and performance scholar writes: "[t]he actual physical embodied act of viewing performance in the live moment is as important as the live presence of the performer: as the actual effect and consequence of experiencing performance opens up new aspects of its meaning and its function".[3]

Live art as a category or strategy has stretched the parameters of performance art to include other forms of 'liveness.' In the *Histories and Practices of Live Art*, Deirdre Heddon discusses the term live art "as an expanded and expanding category". Áine Phillips in her "Introduction" to *Performance Art in Ireland: A History* observes a "resurgence of performance practices" at the turn of the millennium in Ireland, designated as live art, a term that "allows for diverse performance tactics".[4]

In Ireland, the emergence of work designated as live art parallels a time of profound change in Irish society that has been accompanied by a growing commitment to presence and "liveness" in performance practices. In an essay examining "moments of change" in Irish theatre, performance and culture, Miriam Haughton refers to the "recent surge in radicalising the role of presence in live performance to achieve a visceral and affective end", and she notes the shift in the "role and form of *presence* and *expectation* in live performances and encounters" (emphasis in original).[5] The element of presence in live art, and other performance practices, crucially references the embodied spectator whose role is no longer passive viewer but active participant.

This chapter will explore live art practices in Ireland since 2000 through the work of four Irish practitioners. Amanda Coogan, Dominic Thorpe, Áine Phillips and Aideen Barry have been performing live work since the turn of the millennium, a time when Ireland has experienced seismic shifts in the landscape, demographics and identity brought about by the Celtic Tiger, European expansion, immigration, the economic crash and the crisis in meaning and identity precipitated by revelations of pervasive and systemic abuse of children and adults in Irish institutions. This chapter will examine how their work engages with these issues, interrogates space and facilitates immersive encounters where the spectator is no longer a detached observer in a darkened auditorium but is repositioned as participant or witness in the visceral immediacy of the space and the actions encountered.

Amanda Coogan

In October 2001 at the Irish Museum of Modern Art, Amanda Coogan opened *Marking the Territory*, a three-day international performance event curated by Marina Abramović. Coogan performed *The Fountain* on a stage, front and centre in the Great Hall. She sat down, her knees bent, her bare legs parted, while a spotlight illuminated her open thighs and exposed genitalia. She then urinated before the audience for two and a half continuous minutes, the stream of liquid darkening the ground in front of her as it spread and ran off in trickling streams. The performance embodied a disturbing paradox: an image of the uncontained, undisciplined female body in an act that required exceptional control and containment. As Kerstin Mey writes, "[t]he performance suggests a loss of body control and yet could only be staged through the exertion of extreme corporeal discipline".[6]

Each year in a live art module that I teach, we look at the extant photograph of the above and discuss the performance. Invariably, it inflames students who are more disturbed by Coogan's action than, say, by Franko B's catwalk performances or Stelarc's body suspensions where he hangs by hooks inserted through his stretched skin. What is it about staging the incontinent female body that is so transgressive? Coogan's allusion to Duchamp's *Fountain* from 1917 might be read as an assertion of her own body as "readymade" material or as a challenge to artistic canons, just as Duchamp's iconic piece was. But it is not her interrogation of site, gendered art canons or aesthetic value that upsets the students; it is exhibiting the leaking female body that makes them deeply uncomfortable. "Losing control over one's bodily functions and putting the body on display as incontinent infringes one of the strictly guarded taboos in contemporary sanitised western society", observes Mey in her discussion of Coogan's piece, "particularly where it concerns women".[7] *The Fountain* conjures the disordered, uncontained female body and, in so doing, draws us into our own complicated psychic space. Women, particularly, are taught shame in relation to physiological and emotional leakage as well as sexuality and desire and Coogan's performance perhaps activates internalized shame.

Coogan has said that the piece "directly references" the story of Ann Lovett, the fifteen-year-old girl who died alone giving birth in a grotto in Granard, County Longford on the 31 January 1984. It was a cold and wet day and Lovett walked alone to the top of the town to a grotto dedicated to Our Lady and there gave birth. She was found semi-conscious, in shock and haemorrhaging beneath a statue of the Blessed Mother, her dead newborn son beside her. In the preceding months, when Lovett must have agonized over her condition,

Ireland was in the middle of the divisive abortion referendum which took place on the 7 September 1983. A month later, the Eighth Amendment of the Constitution was enacted by law which constitutionally banned abortion and gave explicit recognition to the unborn child's right to life but remained unclear about the rights of the mother.

In 2001, when Coogan performed *The Fountain* reproduction rights and access to abortion had again become a pressing issue. In June, just months before the IMMA Event, the Dutch ship *The Aurora*, which proposed to offer Irish women abortions on international waters, docked in Dublin. In conjunction with this, Coogan showed a video of *The Fountain*. She had been reluctant to perform the piece live in Ireland but changed her mind given the urgency of access to abortion for Irish women. Coogan's performance speaks to the regulation and control of women's bodies in Ireland through legislation and the shaming of women. Brenda O'Connell, in her incisive analysis of *The Fountain*, suggests that Coogan's performance "makes public what is considered a private bodily function" and "confronts the audience with bodily fluids, forcing them to consider the isolation and vulnerability of Lovett and the circumstances of her death".[8] The proximity of artist and audience and the provocative action refuses the audience the habitual stance of detachment; rather, it repositions them as witnesses. Coogan's "use of transgressive corporeal strategies in *The Fountain* implicates the audience with the shame, humiliation and suffering of Lovett and also the shame of the Irish nation who allowed it to happen".[9] The story and the extreme isolation inflicted upon Lovett, who was only a child, shocked the nation as did the refusal of people to talk about it. Coogan's act, its shamelessness, can be read as her refusal to conceal her body and its functions and her insistence that we reconsider our public gaze and what we hide from view.

In 2001, Coogan staged another durational piece at the Irish Museum of Modern Art. For *Medea*, Coogan wore a long blue gown and reclined majestically on a chaise longue, looking imperious and classical in a room of comparable grandeur. Coogan's eyes, magnetic blue, gazed back at audience members, emotionless and impenetrable, challenging our spectatorship and its assumption of its own agency and its object's passivity. Her dress was splayed out on the floor below her like a caudal fin. She looked serpentine, cold blooded and powerful, a poised or restrained version of the mythical Medea, witch, female transgressor and destroyer of her children.

Throughout the performance, Coogan retained a distant and impassive posture but simultaneously narrated emotional testimonies through Irish Sign Language (ISL) from deaf children who had suffered sexual and physical abuse in Irish institutions.[10] Coogan's first language is ISL as both her parents are deaf.[11] The performance created a dynamic tension between contained surfaces and underlying pain. "The use of a minority non-sonic discourse enables the silencing of those abused by the Catholic clergy to come into focus", writes Helena Walsh. Moreover, it also suggested to the majority of spectators, who could not understand the language, "what it is like to be rendered outside of discourse".[12]

Coogan's choice of an infamous mother and the colour blue also suggests the Madonna, the virgin mother of Christ. In Irish nationalism, the Virgin Mary or Blessed Mother and Mother Ireland are frequently conflated, their iconographies confused. "The concept of a special relationship between Ireland and the Virgin Mary was heavily promoted in the early decades of southern independence", notes Gerardine Meaney, citing Pope Pius XI's reference to "the Virgin Mary, Queen of Ireland".[13] Coogan's *Medea* as both the destructive mother of Greek myth and Mother Ireland interrogates the nationalist conceit that aligns the idea of national identity with the pure mother. What kind of mother, figured here as both the State and the Church, destroys her children, forcing them into institutions where they suffer terrible abuse? What kind of mother refuses to see or hear that abuse and will not let her children speak about what has happened to them?

There were other elements in this performance that further disrupted the initial picture of maternal purity. As Frances Ruane has observed, the "serene image" is "subverted by the placement of her hand, the staining of her dress and the physically limiting placement of the lower body".[14] Coogan's hand at times was near to or covering her genitalia and the stained dress—a motif that will recur in her work—connotes both the uncontrolled or leaking female body, the desiring female body and the immoral or stained one. These dissenting gestures, signs and narratives refuse to participate in the use of women's bodies as virginal cyphers for womanhood, motherhood or nation and the inherent denial of female embodiment and sexuality.

Coogan returned to the motif of the woman's uncontained body in Dublin Contemporary (2011) where she performed a durational piece entitled *Spit Spit Scrub Scrub* with two other performers in a small room upstairs in the former Medical School on Earlsfort Terrace. The three women were costumed in one single piece of blue fabric that engulfed the entire room. Each of their bodies possessed its own bodice that emerged from the shared skirt. The audience watched from the hallway. The women made stylized movements to a soundtrack by Handel while saliva, foam and drool collected at their mouths. Bubbled spit dribbled slowly down the front of their dresses in what Kate Antosik-Parsons refers to as a "disturbing oral incontinence".[15] The three bodices were stained from previous performances. One of the performers opened her mouth as she leaned towards me, her tongue out, her lips bright red, a long thread of drool hanging from them. The trio suggested gorgons, fates or furies: female chthonic energies that are disruptive and irrepressible. They could also be maenads, suggestive of other destructive mothers and choral groups—the Dionysian irrational, undisciplined and feminine straining against the Apollonian effort to control, conceal and create illusion.

Coogan's chosen title, *Spit Spit Scrub Scrub,* is evocative. "Spit Spit", its liquid suggestion of openness, leakage or outpouring threatens the safe paradigm of femininity, the disembodied Madonna or Mother Ireland. "Scrub Scrub" connotes the sense of stain and need for purification or cleansing that has been a tragic reality in Irish history, as thousands of so called "stained"

Fig. 1 Amanda Coogan, *Yellow*, RHA Dublin, October 2015. (Photo credit: Paddy Cahill)

women were sent away to scrub in laundries. Cleansing is also connected to ideas of catharsis, and Coogan's live performance hints at its illusory quality.

These themes are pursued in Coogan's *Yellow Series*, a number of durational pieces all of which involve the colour yellow. *Yellow (Pieta)* was first performed in 2008 and again in 2010, this time with five other performers. In October 2015 as part of the Coogan retrospective *I'll sing you a song from around the town* at the Royal Hibernian, *Yellow* was again performed (Fig. 1). In this incarnation, there were five yellow dresses behind Coogan, presumably those worn by the women in the 2010 performance.[16] The dresses were moulded into the shapes of upright figures that mimicked Coogan's posture, so that they sat straight up as if possessed by bodies, an evocative sculptural installation suggesting both the presence of other women and their absence.

Coogan, dressed in a billowing yellow dress, sat astride a bucket filled with water and suds. Over the course of four hours, she washed and scrubbed the material of her dress, dipping her hands repeatedly into the water and drawing up suds. Intermittently, she twisted the yellow fabric into a phallic cone with suds spewing out of the top of it, alluding to ejaculation. At times, she blew the suds from her fingertips or took the tip of fabric between her teeth. She snapped the material out flat as if it were laundry. She looked at members of the audience. She rhythmically moved her hands under the material, a suggestive action that sometimes she seemed disconnected from and at other times intently focused on. I was reminded of Lady Macbeth's tortured scrubbing—"will these hands n'er be clean"—as the performer scrubbed maniacally at stains we could not see. The stains seemed sexual, and she repeatedly submerged her hands between her legs drawing up the material and suds as if she were cleaning her own genitalia.

The incessant scrubbing and suggestion of laundry and detergent in *Yellow* conjures the Magdalene Laundries and other institutions where "fallen women" were forced out of public sight and into unwaged labour. The triangle of female forms, dressed uniformly, their invisible legs spread across buckets suggested the countless work of women, and their disembodied shapes created a ghostly presence.

Coogan's live durational performances, her embodiment and presence, recall those absences and elisions in Irish cultural memory. Her performances stage the competing discourses around women's bodies, the illusion of containment and the materiality of her body that upsets this illusion: her spit, urine, pain, her desire, her exclusion.

Dominic Thorpe

Like Coogan, Dominic Thorpe's performances are invested in the idea of presence and its potential to narrate or witness the trauma of others. While Coogan's pieces complicate the act of looking for the spectator or witness, Thorpe's durational performances attempt to reposition the audience member from detached observer to active participant. Thorpe creates intimate and immersive encounters "making it difficult or impossible", as he says, "to sustain a position of detached observer".[17]

In 2010, Thorpe performed *Redress State: Questions Imagined* in a small gallery in Galway City (Fig. 2). Visitors were greeted by a receptionist who

Fig. 2 Dominic Thorpe, *Redress State—Questions Imagined*, Performance at 126 Gallery Galway 2010. (Photo credit: Jonathon Salmon)

gave background to the Irish Residential Institutions Redress Act (2002), particularly the controversial "gagging" clauses prohibiting survivors who have given their statement to the Redress Board from recounting their experience before the Board. The receptionist then handed the viewer a torch before they entered the performance space.

Thorpe performed in a completely dark room, the only light projected into the space was the handheld torch of the spectator. Sheepskins were piled on a table, the air earthy and damp. His breathing was audible, as was the sound of chalk connecting with the wall as he furiously wrote, a noise reminiscent of school, the chalk aggressively hitting the board. Directing the torch towards the wall, the questions became visible: "Why didn't you hit back?" "Are you sure you remember?" Traces of previous questions were barely legible in the confusion of overlaying words. "Why should we believe you?" Or, more intrusively, "Was the pubic hair grey or black?" Silence was the largest and most repeated word on the wall. Sometimes Thorpe rang a hand-bell and, in the light of the torch, his mouth opened in a scream but no sound came out.

Because it took place in the dark with only a small torch to illuminate what was happening, the performance refused any perspective or vantage point that was all encompassing. As Áine Phillips writes, "Thorpe's performance is porous; we enter and absorb. Like victims, the viewer is kept in the dark, able to see only fragments of a whole".[18] What the audience saw was fleeting, revealed through indefinite glimpses caught in torchlight. Holding the torch gave the spectator a certain agency in choosing to shine the light or not. The space and lighting disallowed any privileged perspective where the spectator could see everything at once; but there was an impression of having seen something disturbing, a painful shard of a narrative. Thorpe's performance questions not only the forced silence of victims and the brutality of their experiences, but our own complicity in a collective, national silence, then and now.

In a talk given at the National College of Art and Design, Thorpe discusses the relationship between proximity and responsibility. "How far away would you have to be from a thing", he asks, "before you are not involved?" In his work, he says, he is "trying to think about the idea of an ethical memory and challenging the kind of memory that mostly just reinforces forgetting".[19] Thorpe's performance positions us as belated witnesses, immersing us in a sensory experience and asks us to listen and to remember because the State and the Church have failed to.

Thorpe's performance in the Galway space was durational, lasting five hours a day for a period of nine days. His work explores the potential of the live body in action, the presence of the artist engaged in an exchange with the spectator who is positioned within the performance itself, methodologies increasingly visible in immersive and participatory Irish theatre practices.

Thorpe has also performed many site-responsive works. In 2014, he was invited to contribute to *These Immovable Walls: Performing Power* at Dublin Castle. Given the opportunity to choose his own space, he unwittingly selected a room that he subsequently discovered was the former Children's Court from the 1930s until the 1980s, meaning that virtually every child sent on to industrial schools spent time in that room, where their fates were decided. The room was not part of the tour of Dublin Castle and no plaques signalled its history. Thorpe's *Proximity Mouth* drew a parallel between the kind of institutional power wielded in the children's court during that period and the direct provision asylum system in Ireland today.

The performance began when an individual audience member was taken by the hand by an assistant with experience of the direct provision system and who acted as a guide, holding the spectator's hand for the duration of the performance. Thorpe performed with a long mirror balanced on his feet, angling and moving it to reflect audience members as within the institutional space or, indeed, within the system. He opened and shut windows. "All I was trying to do was to visually take the veneer of innocence off the place."[20] In the room of the Children's Court, an eleven-year old Ugandan girl sat in the judge's chair, and she asked each visitor their name and then printed out a sheet of paper which listed all the direct provision reception centres in Ireland. The child then asked if the visitor would like the sheet turned into a boat or plane and she folded the paper accordingly.

On leaving, the audience member is found holding their folded boat or aircraft, uncertain of what exactly has just transpired. This is how power is exercised in the system; this is how the asylum system and reception centres are a direct echo of the way children were disappeared into institutes; and so, this is another instance of cultural forgetting. While some may argue that live art's presentational methods tend toward the literal, what it offers is something else: proximity, contact, touch. Someone in that system held your hand and walked you through a space that is a part of Irish history that has deeply impacted and disturbed our sense of who we are. That person has been through a system that has similarly concealed them. You are holding a small symbol of their journey and a list of the spaces where they are now being held.

Áine Phillips

In November 2010, Dominic Thorpe along with Amanda Coogan and Niamh Murphy curated *Right Here Right Now*, a live exhibition of 20 artists performing simultaneously on one night over a four-hour period, throughout the cells and open areas of the historical Kilmainham Gaol's East Wing. The curators imagined this as a site-specific event and, walking into Kilmainham Gaol's East Wing, most audience members were probably aware of the building's significance in Irish revolutionary history. It has an interesting architectural and social history as well. Added in 1862, the East Wing adheres to philosopher Jeremy Bentham's panopticon prison design, a space that enforced discipline through surveillance. The hypothetical prison, like Kilmainham, would have a central vantage point from which prisoners could be watched and from which they felt they were always being observed. The architecture was designed as a tool of corporeal and psychological control, isolating and inciting

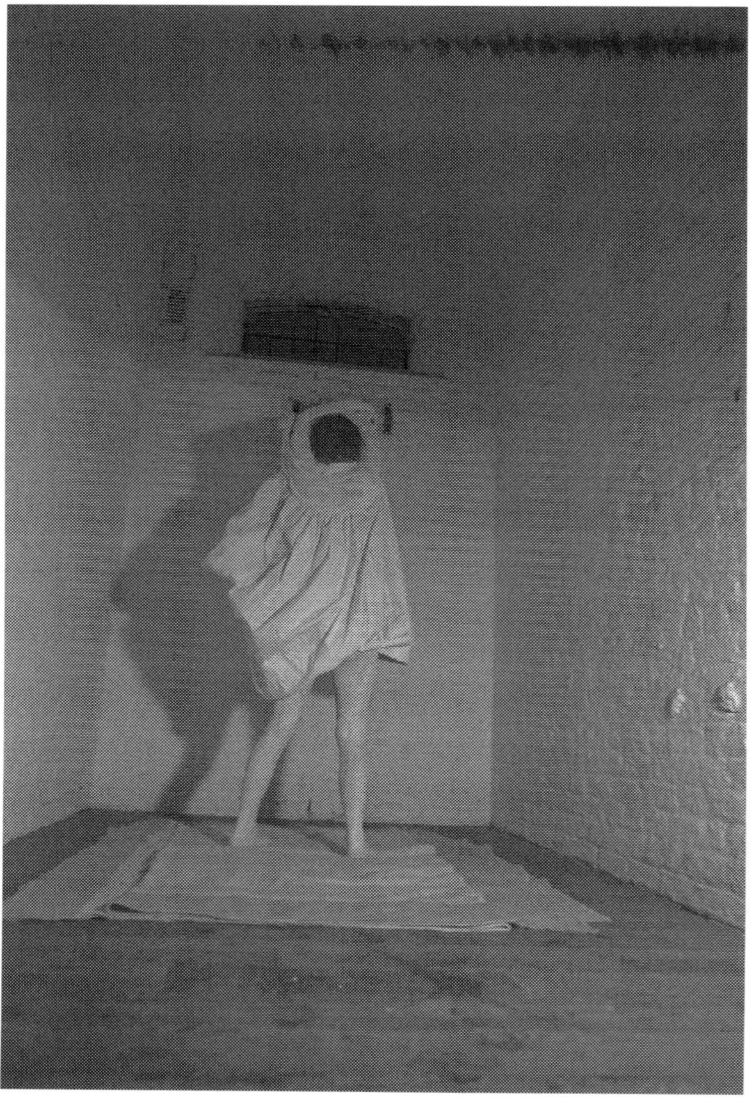

Fig. 3 Áine Phillips, *Redress*, Right here Right Now, Kilmainham Gaol 2010. (Photo credit: T. O'Brien)

anxiety in the inmate through the institutional, all-seeing gaze. Like Dublin Castle, the Kilmainham site raises questions about institutional and state power and its relationship to its marginal or aberrant citizens.

In one of the cells, behind a closed door, Phillips performed *Redress* (Fig. 3). "I dress and redress myself with a garment that will not fit properly", Phillips explains, and she struggles with the "unfitting dress so that my form becomes a live sculptural image of contorted body and dress merged together".[21] A line of visitors queued outside Phillips's cell and, one at a time, observed the performance through the cell door's peephole. Inside the cell, the walls were stone and painted chalk white. The performer had whitened her body and face, creating a phantom presence that almost mimicked the contained space. Helena Walsh describes its spectral quality, "referential of those negated or vanished from discourses of power".[22] Phillips's dress was off white and, wrangling with it, she looked at times immobilized, or even hanged, her arms stretched above her, the hands crossed, her head down. She struggled again to wear the dress, her body a form that could not, or would not, or just did not fit. The white dress suggested many of the cultural assignations available to Irish women historically, and their limited options: baptism, communion, virgin, marriage, prison, laundries. Phillips offered us a body that cannot conform in a space that symbolizes a state that could not imagine or accommodate other possibilities. Sometimes, she struggled; other times, she slumped, exhausted.

As in Thorpe's *Redress State*, the vantage point offered through the peephole is limited but, in this instance, suggests an uncomfortable power differential between spectator and performer. The audience is forced into an act of seeing that is both voyeuristic and intrusive. The all-seeing eye of the prison architecture and systems is re-enacted in the subjugating gaze of the audience, who occupy the position of authority or institutional policing. It perhaps also speaks to "the overt scrutinizing of the body in Irish culture", as Helena Walsh suggests.[23]

Phillips's performance complicates the act of looking as audiences are asked to consider what it means to spectate and to witness, a question particularly relevant within the context of institutions and redress, to which the title of her piece refers. "The Ryan Report" was published less than a year before the Kilmainham performances, and its findings were an indictment of not only the clerics and teachers who abused in state-funded institutions but a society at large who failed to look. An *Irish Times* editorial from the time captures the systemic and pervasive nature of the abuse: "over 800 known abusers in over 200 institutions during a period of 35 years".[24] "The Ryan Report" imputes the failure of organizations and the public itself to see or to question. Emilie Pine cites a remarkable passage from the Report that catalogues the failure of the media, the Oireachtas, interest groups and the general public who did not want to see. The paragraph concludes, "all these pools of unknowing reinforced each other".[25] "Unknowing" possesses a certain charge; it suggests a wilful effort to forget what is known, a refusal to see, an erasure. This "mind blindness", as Pine phrases it, was a perceptual blind-spot within communities. "Because these institutions were seen", she says. "They were seen by the communities that abutted their walls, by the families who sent members to them, by the courts who sentenced children and women to them, by the government inspectors who visited them." It was, Pine provocatively writes, "a failure of spectatorship".[26]

We might ask: does live art performance, with its insistence on embodiment and presence, its durational commitment, its effort to choreograph an intimate encounter between performer and spectator, help us to see, to know again, to remember—to remember, as Pine asks, how we forgot?

Phillips's performances, like Thorpe's, use embodiment and presence as a method to stave off erasure. *Emotional Labour* (2012) was part of the live event *Labour* held in Dublin's LAB Gallery, where eleven female artists performed for eight hours, the average length of a working day. Like Kilmainham, the event was site specific, reflecting the types of female labour endured in this area of Dublin, which historically had been one of the largest red light districts in Europe. As the exhibition catalogue observes, the site "in the historic Monto and around the corner from the Gloucester Street Magdalene Convent layers the composition of the eleven bodies of the artists with potent shadows".[27]

"My piece deals with the Magdalen laundries and female confinement in Ireland", writes Phillips.[28] In the first part of the performance, Phillips walked through the gallery space leaking black ink as if from the inside out, staining her white garments. She wandered around the LAB seemingly distressed about the source of this stain and her inability to stop its flow. She held herself where the black liquid bled into her clothes. *Emotional Labour* suggests the psychic damage done to Magdalene women and "working women" as they internalized the corrosive social gaze, the stain projected upon them that labelled them as fallen, dirty and that caused them to be removed out of the public eye. The audience witness pain, confusion and self-censure. The piece also suggests the psychic damage done to a society that has concealed, refused to recognize or rationalized how women were disappeared. "What is hidden is seeping out", Phillips explains.[29]

In his 2013 apology to the Magdalenes who were excluded from seeking redress in the 2002 Act, Taoiseach Enda Kenny said that as a society Ireland failed the women. "We forgot you", he said, and this forgetting was Ireland's "national shame".[30] The apology came on the heels of the controversial McAleese Report or the "Report of the Inter-Departmental Committee to establish the facts of State involvement with the Magdalen Laundries", which the Taoiseach refers to as a "document of truth", an assessment contested by multiple organizations. Most notably, the Report excluded 796 pages of testimony from Magdalene women submitted by the Justice for Magdalenes organization that had been gathered under rigorous academic and ethical guidelines. The elisions and omissions of the McAleese Report and its failure to provide a thorough and comprehensive investigation, along with the silence imposed on those seeking redress under the Redress Act, complicate our acceptance of official narratives.

Aideen Barry

Like Phillips and Thorpe, Galway-based artist Aideen Barry could also be said to perform site-responsive work in her domestic performances inside a suburban housing estate in Clare-Galway. Barry's work focuses on contemporary anxieties brought about by the Celtic Tiger and the subsequent recession. Beneath seemingly stable, uniform facades of the suburban housing estate, Barry records emotional and psychological instability, paranoia and delusion. In her work, the suburban house is an architecture that both estranges and imprisons its inhabitants. While Barry's focus is on the anxieties facing contemporary middle-class Irish women, obsessive cleaning and scrubbing are also motifs in her work. We repeatedly encounter the modern Irish housewife disinfecting and decontaminating invisible germs, much like the immaterial stains of Coogan's *Yellow*.

Levitating (2007), a stop motion film made for the Galway Arts Festival, captures Barry as she undertakes domestic work: she cleans, takes out the bins, goes to the supermarket, dusts, hoovers and performs other rituals/compulsions associated with suburban life. As she performs her housework, she looks as though she is levitating several inches above the ground. The film was made from stills of Barry undertaking the domestic tasks while jumping. The stop motion editing effects in the final film are pronounced with the result that her movements look spasmodic, automated and disturbing.

According to Barry, the piece comments "on this ridiculous strain we put on ourselves to have this veneer of perfection". She says "[w]e have to be so perfect, we have to levitate six inches above the ground in order to achieve it".[31] Here, the Irish housewife mystically levitates as she hoovers. Barry's protagonist is uncanny, both familiar and strange, as she floats and jerks through her domestic rituals. Barry has also made work in zero gravity as part of her residency at the NASA Kennedy Space Centre, including a film *Vacuuming in a Vacuum*, in which she floats in a weightless environment, her body melded with a sterile hoover. Futuristic and surreal, the hose extends from her mouth as she floats through space cleaning, her verbal and creative agency supplanted by her capacity to clean.

In 2006, Barry was diagnosed with Obsessive Compulsive Disorder brought on, she argues, by the strain of living in Celtic Tiger suburbia: "these estates of cookie cutter homes that grew up out of the [Irish] boom of the '90s. It's a very un-Irish landscape. [...] The domesticity that I'm interested in came out of this space."[32] She began to find herself in a spiral of cleaning, exhaustion and constant anxiety. She sought help and, after her diagnosis, became interested in the obsessive domestic rituals she, and others, practise in order to stabilize anxieties. In the context of the recession, the tension between the impression of success and stability and other realities became more profound as people attempted to sustain illusions about who they were and meanwhile their "electricity has been cut off and the bank is talking about re-possessing the house".[33] Barry's work responds to the shift in how Irish people live, the idea of the suburb itself and the anxiety it has generated, particularly for women. Women increasingly compete in the workplace, are primary earners in the household but, simultaneously, are trying to manage domestic spaces including hiring labour to assume roles they would have traditionally fulfilled. Barry's housing estate in Claregalway became the site of many performances that capture her sense of "unstable domesticity".[34]

Levitating was one of eleven videos installed in Barry's first major survey show, *Brittlefield*, at the RHA in August 2016. To show the films, she created "a forest of shards", as Aidan Dunne describes it in the *Irish Times*: "looming, teeth-like spikes. Stick your head through a circular opening in each shard and you are into a video".[35] The eleven videos signal her playful preoccupation with neuroses, domestic rituals and, as the RHA exhibition notes reference, monachopsis.[36] According to the *Dictionary of Obscure Sorrows*, monachopsis "is the subtle but persistent feeling of being out of place".[37] In the videos, in which Barry performs for the camera, we see this persistent sense of alienation and the uncanny. Garage doors opening and shutting to slice bread, a woman is trapped inside a house on a ghost estate sucking up dust through her mouth, an open oven becomes a self-tanning mechanism.

This preoccupation with domestic spaces and monachopsis is evident in an earlier work in which Barry collaborated with artist Anne Ffrench. *Heteratopic Glitch* was first performed for Kinsale Arts Week 2008 and was brought to the Dock in Carrick-on-Shannon, County Leitrim the following year and performed along the Carrick Marina on the River Shannon (Fig. 4). The performance in Leitrim began as twelve transparent balls floated down the river to Strauss's "Blue Danube". Inside each bubble, a woman reclined in a red dress, red leggings and red gloves. Through the initial subdued movement of the

Fig. 4 Anne Ffrench and Aideen Barry, *Heteratopic Glitch*. (Photo credit: John Allen)

waltz, the women remained lying in their bubbles, making what looked like choreographed dance movements first with their arms and, as the performance continued, their legs. As the music escalated, the women attempted to rise to a kneeling position. Some managed this briefly with great effort, arms extended out to the sides of their clear walls as they sought balance on a fluid surface, while others tottered and fell. When the music reached crescendo, the women attempted to stand inside. One of the performers fell and hit her face at the front of the ball and nearly made a full flip as the ball spun. Across the river, the twelve women fell, rose, grasped and clutched for balance, but they could not find any, and so fell inside their plastic spheres, upended and entirely powerless.

Somewhere beneath the hilarity and public comedy was a disturbing counter-strain of apprehension and distress as the audience watched women in their own microcosms visibly struggle to stay upright and realized the absurdity of their effort in the profoundly unstable spaces. On display, their costumes and movements were choreographed to make them appear 'pretty' and synchronized, but their splayed bodies before us were in frantic and ridiculous poses, on their bums, legs straight up or flipping or scrambling up the side of the sphere to try and stay standing. The tension between their efforts to make elegant classical dance gestures—intrinsically feminine moves—and their inability to even stand up or control how they fell, heightened the pathos as did the suggestion that in their red dresses and repeated falls, these were "fallen women". The performance suggested their tenacity, isolation and endurance and perhaps the futility of it all. Watching created other anxieties: What if the ball got punctured and sank with a woman trapped inside? What if they cannot breathe?

Like Coogan's *Spit Spit Scrub Scrub*, *Heteratopic Glitch* enacts the tension between the ostensibly feminine, graceful pretty dance gestures, and an underlying contradictory reality. If the former performance unleashes a powerful choral energy, the latter ultimately discloses a latent desperation and loss of agency. Spectators, too, are powerless to help.

Heteratopias

The title of Barry and French's *Heteratopic Glitch* plays on a term used by Foucault, who explains heterotopias as alternative or "counter-spaces" that reflect, contrast, invert, and contest the experience of our own spaces.[38] He uses the examples of prisons, asylums and other substitute or surrogate spaces, worlds within worlds. The spaces of Coogan's tableaus confront us with oppressive emblems of femininity and subvert them; the site-specific and durational work of Thorpe and Phillips situate spectators in the counter-spaces of twentieth-century Ireland: state institutions, industrial schools and Magdalen Laundries where the most vulnerable citizens were detained. These encounters radically trouble the experience of being Irish in the twenty-first century and raise questions about our spectatorship. Dominic Thorpe's *Proximity Mouth* suggests direct parallels between architectures of containment then and now.[39] Finally, Aideen Barry's somewhat quirky domestic "heteratopias", female counter-spaces, expose the glitches and ultimately the illusory nature of stability inside Irish suburbia. Live art practice in Ireland creates environments, heteratopic architectures, that bring performer and spectator into proximity, a shared presence for a duration of time that repositions audiences and interrogates and contest how we spectate, remember and forget.

Notes

1. Marina Abramovic, quoted in "The Art of Living Dangerously", *The Irish Times*, Wednesday November 28th 2001, accessed 6 November 2016, http://www.irishtimes.com/culture/the-art-of-living-dangerously-1.339464
2. Franko B, Artist's Website, accessed November 6, 2016, http://www.franko-b.com/I_Miss_You.html
3. Michelle Browne, "Performance Art in Ireland: The New Millennium", in *Performance Art in Ireland: A History,* ed. Áine Phillips (London: Live Art Development Agency, 2015), 248.
4. Áine Phillips, ed., *Performance Art in Ireland: A History* (London: Live Art Development Agency, 2015), 10.
5. Miriam Haughton, "Flirting with the Postmodern: Moments of Change in Contemporary Irish Theatre, Performance and Culture" *Irish Studies Review* 22:3 (2014), 374–392, 375, 379.
6. Kerstin Mey, *Art and Obscenity* (London: I.B. Tauris, 2007), 32.
7. Ibid.
8. Brenda O'Connell, "'The horror, the horror': Performing 'The Dark Continent' in Amanda Coogan's *The Fountain* and Samuel Beckett's *Not I*", in *Radical Contemporary Theatre Practices by Women in Ireland*, eds. Miriam Haughton and Mária Kurdi (Dublin: Carysfort Press, 2015), 130.
9. Ibid.
10. Frances Ruane, "A Provocative Performance", *Irish Arts Review* 21:2 (2004): 52–35, 52.
11. Mike Fitpatrick, "Through my eyes and my body", in *Amanda Coogan*, ed., John O'Regan (Kinsale: Profile, 2005), 21.
12. Helena Walsh, "Medea", in *Brutal Silences: Live Art and Irish Culture* ed. Ann Maria Healy and Helena Walsh, A Study Room Guide for the Study Room of the Live Art Development Agency, London, 2011, accessed April 28, 2016, http://www.thisisliveart.co.uk/uploads/documents/SRG_brutal_silences_2011_reducedsize.pdf
13. Gerardine Meaney, *Gender, Ireland and Cultural Change: Race, Sex and Nation* (New York: Routledge, 2010), 13.
14. Ruane, "A Provocative Performance", 53.
15. Kate Antosik-Parsons, "A Review of Dublin Contemporary", *Artefact: The Journal of Irish Association of Art Historians* 5 (2012), accessed April 30, 2016. http://www.kateap.com/kap/Writing_files/KAP%20Dublin%20Contemporary%20Review%20.pdf
16. Each week Coogan performed a new piece, culminating in six performances. On the 8th October 2015 when we attended, five pieces were being staged and Coogan was performing *Yellow*.

17. Dominic Thorpe, "Working with stories of other people's traumatic experiences: Questions of responsibility as an artist", *Arts in Health* (2015), artsinhealth.ie, accessed April 5, 2016. http://www.artsandhealth.ie/perspectives/working-with-stories-of-other-peoples-traumatic-experiences-questions-of-responsibility-as-an-artist/
18. Áine Phillips, "Dominic Thorpe| Hardy Langer: The Artist Will be Present Galway May 2010", *Paper Visual Art Journal*, July 21, 2010. Accessed November 25, 2016.
19. Dominic Thorpe, NCAD lecture, 8 December 2016 https://media.heanet.ie/page/679225cdd1a9265c498badfe53c5f0d5
20. Dominic Thorpe, Talking about Perpetrators, Irish Memory Studies Network, UCD, at Dublin Castle 29th October 2015. Accessed December 16, 2016. http://irishmemorystudies.com/index.php/memory-cloud/#thorpe
21. Áine Phillips, Website, accessed April 19, 2016, ainephillips.com/section/237254_REDRESS.html
22. Helena Walsh, "Redress", in *Brutal Silences: Live Art and Irish Culture* ed. Ann Maria Healy and Helena Walsh, A Study Room Guide for the Study Room of the Live Art Development Agency, London, 2011, accessed April 28, 2016, http://www.thisisliveart.co.uk/uploads/documents/SRG_brutal_silences_2011_reducedsize.pdf
23. Walsh, *Brutal Silences*, 13.
24. "The savage reality of our darkest days", Opinion, *Irish Times*, Thursday May 2, 2009. Accessed April 26, 2016. http://www.irishtimes.com/opinion/the-savage-reality-of-our-darkest-days-1.767385
25. *The Report of the Commission to Inquire into Child Abuse (Ryan Report)*, 2009, Vol. IV, chapter 3 'Society and the Schools,' Part 4, 'Independent Monitoring, compiled by Professor David Gwyn http://www.childabusecommission.ie/rpt/04-03.php. Qtd in Emilie Pine, "Commemorating Abuse: Gender Politics and Making Space", *UCD Scholarcast Series 8* (Spring 2013) Irish Memory Studies Research Network Lectures Series editor Emilie Pine, General Editor P.J. Matthews, 6. http://www.ucd.ie/scholarcast/transcripts/Gender_politics_and_making_space.pdf
26. Pine, "Commemorating Abuse", 6.
27. *Labour*, Catalogue, accessed April 27, 2016, http://www.dublincity.ie/main-menu-services-recreation-culture-arts-office-lab-previous-exhibitions/labour
28. Áine Phillips, artist's website, *Áine Phillips*, Accessed April 26, 2016, http://ainephillips.com/section/314535_EMOTIONAL_LABOUR_2012.html
29. Ibid.
30. Enda Kenny, full text of speech before Dail Eireann, February 19 2013, qtd in "In full: Enda Kenny's State apology to the Magdalene women,' *The Journal.ie* http://www.thejournal.ie/full-text-enda-kenny-magdalene-apology-801132-Feb2013/
31. Aideen Barry, Graduate Showcase Conference, GMIT 2013, accessed March 28, 2016, https://www.youtube.com/watch?v=4wJhe3jVWy4
32. Bean Gilsford, "At Home on the Edge: Interview with Aideen Barry", *Daily Serving: An International Publication for Contemporary Art*, accessed February 28, 2016, http://dailyserving.com/2011/08/at-home-on-the-edge-interview-with-aideen-barry/
33. Kernan Andrews, "Aideen Barry Exploring Gothic Terror in Suburbia", *Galway Advertiser*, July 14, 2011, retrieved February 28, 2016, http://www.advertiser.ie/galway/article/41704/aideen-barry-exploring-gothic-terror-in-suburbia

34. The phrase "unstable domesticity" was used by Bean Gilsford in an interview with Aideen Barry. "At Home on the Edge: Interview with Aideen Barry", *Daily Serving: An International Publication for Contemporary Art*, http://dailyserving.com/2011/08/at-home-on-the-edge-interview-with-aideen-barry/
35. Aidan Dunne, "Five Star Review: Domesticity Rendered Wonderfully Weird", *Irish Times*, August 2, 2016, accessed October 30, 2016, http://www.irishtimes.com/culture/art-and-design/visual-art/five-star-review-domesticity-rendered wonderfully-weird-1.2737454
36. RHA, Brittlefield, accessed October 30, 2016, http://www.rhagallery.ie/exhibitions/brittlefield-a-solo-survey-of-the-work-of-aideen-barry/
37. Dictionary of Obscure Sorrows, accessed October 30, 2016, http://www.dictionaryofobscuresorrows.com/post/36505968156/monachopsis
38. Michel Foucault, "Of Other Spaces: Utopias and Heterotopias, "in *Architecture /Mouvement/ Continuité* (March 1967, "Des Espace Autres", Translated from the French by Jay Miskowiec), accessed February 26, 2016, http://web.mit.edu/allanmc/www/foucault1.pdf
39. The phrase "architecture of containment" is James Smith's in his book *Ireland's Magdalen Laundries and the Nation's Architecture of Containment* (Notre Dame Indiana: University of Notre Dame Press, 2007).

Bibliography

"The Art of Living Dangerously", *The Irish Times*, Wednesday November 28, 2001. Accessed 6 November 2016. http://www.irishtimes.com/culture/the-art-of-living-dangerously-1.339464

"The savage reality of our darkest days." Opinion, *Irish Times*, May 21, 2009. Accessed April 26, 2016. http://www.irishtimes.com/opinion/the-savage-reality-of-our-darkest-days-1.767385

"In full: Enda Kenny's State apology to the Magdalene women." *The Journal.ie*. Accessed October 30, 2016. http://www.thejournal.ie/full-text-enda-kenny-magdalene-apology-801132-Feb2013/

Andrews, Kernan. "Aideen Barry Exploring Gothic Terror in Suburbia." *Galway Advertiser*, July 14, 2011. Retrieved February 28, 2016. http://www.advertiser.ie/galway/article/41704/aideen-barry-exploring-gothic-terror-in-suburbia

Antosik-Parsons, Kate. "A Review of Dublin Contemporary." *Artefact: The Journal of Irish Association of Art Historians* 5 (2012). Accessed April 30, 2016. http://www.kateap.com/kap/Writing_files/KAP%20Dublin%20Contemporary%20Review%20.pdf

Barry, Aideen. Graduate Showcase Conference, GMIT, 2013. Accessed March 28, 2016. https://www.youtube.com/watch?v=4wJhe3jVWy4

Browne, Michelle. "Performance Art in Ireland: The New Millennium." In *Performance Art in Ireland: A History,* edited by Áine Phillips. London: Live Art Development Agency, 2015.

Dictionary of Obscure Sorrows. Accessed October 30, 2016. http://www.dictionaryofobscuresorrows.com/post/36505968156/monachopsis

Dunne, Aidan. "Five Star Review: Domesticity Rendered Wonderfully Weird." *Irish Times*, August 2, 2016. Accessed October 30, 2016. http://www.irishtimes.com/culture/art-and-design/visual-art/five-star-review-domesticity-rendered wonderfully-weird-1.2737454.

Fitpatrick, Mike. "Through My Eyes and My Body." In *Amanda Coogan*, edited by John O'Regan, Kinsale: Profile, 2005.

Foucault, Michel. "Of Other Spaces: Utopias and Heterotopias." In *Architecture / Mouvement/ Continuité* (March 1967, "Des Espace Autres", Translated from the French by Jay Miskowiec. Accessed February 26, 2016. http://web.mit.edu/allanmc/www/foucault1.pdf

Franko B. Artist's Website. Accessed November 6, 2016, http://www.franko-b.com/I_Miss_You.html

Gilsford, Bean. "At Home on the Edge: Interview with Aideen Barry." *Daily Serving: An International Publication for Contemporary Art*. Accessed February 28, 2016. http://dailyserving.com/2011/08/at-home-on-the-edge-interview-with-aideen-barry/.

Haughton, Miriam. "Flirting with the Postmodern: Moments of Change in Contemporary Irish Theatre, Performance and Culture" *Irish Studies Review* 22:3 (2014): 374–392.

Labour, Catalogue. Accessed April 27, 2016. http://www.dublincity.ie/main-menu-services-recreation-culture-arts-office-lab-previous-exhibitions/labour.

Meaney, Gerardine. *Gender, Ireland and Cultural Change: Race, Sex and Nation*. New York: Routledge, 2010.

Mey, Kerstin. *Art and Obscenity*. London: I.B. Tauris, 2007.

O'Connell, Brenda. "'The Horror, the Horror': Performing 'The Dark Continent' in Amanda Coogan's *The Fountain* and Samuel Beckett's *Not I*." In *Radical Contemporary Theatre Practices by Women in Ireland*, edited by Miriam Haughton and Mária Kurdi. Dublin: Carysfort Press, 2015.

Phillips, Áine, ed. *Performance Art in Ireland: A History*. London: Live Art Development Agency, 2015.

———. "Dominic Thorpe| Hardy Langer: The Artist Will be Present Galway May 2010." *Paper Visual Art Journal*, July 21, 2010. Accessed November 25, 2016.

———. Website. Accessed April 19, 2016. ainephillips.com/section/237254_REDRESS.html.

———. Artist's Website, *Áine Phillips*. Accessed April 26, 2016. http://ainephillips.com/section/314535_EMOTIONAL_LABOUR_2012.html.

Pine, Emilie. "Commemorating Abuse: Gender Politics and Making Space." *UCD Scholarcast Series 8* (Spring 2013) Irish Memory Studies Research Network Lectures Series editor Emilie Pine, General Editor P.J. Matthews, 6. Accessed April 26, 2016. http://www.ucd.ie/scholarcast/transcripts/Gender_politics_and_making_space.pdf

RHA, Brittlefield. Accessed October 30, 2016. http://www.rhagallery.ie/exhibitions/brittlefield-a-solo-survey-of-the-work-of-aideen-barry/.

Ruane, Frances. "A Provocative Performance." *Irish Arts Review* 21:2 (2004): 52–35.

Smith, James. *Ireland's Magdalen Laundries and the Nation's Architecture of Containment*. Notre Dame Indiana: University of Notre Dame Press, 2007.

Thorpe, Dominic. "Working with stories of other people's traumatic experiences: Questions of responsibility as an artist." *Arts in Health* (2015). artsinhealth.ie. Accessed April 5, 2016. http://www.artsandhealth.ie/perspectives/working-with-stories-of-other-peoples-traumatic-experiences-questions-of-responsibility-as-an-artist/.

———. Talking About Perpetrators. Irish Memory Studies Network, UCD, at Dublin Castle, October 29, 2015. Accessed December 16, 2016. http://irishmemorystudies.com/index.php/memory-cloud/#thorpe.

———. NCAD Lecture. December 8, 2016. Accessed 16th December 2016. https://media.heanet.ie/page/679225cdd1a9265c498badfe53c5f0d5.

Walsh, Helena. "Medea", in *Brutal Silences: Live Art and Irish Culture*, edited by Ann Maria Healy and Helena Walsh. A Study Room Guide for the Study Room of the Live Art Development Agency, London, 2011. Accessed April 28, 2016. http://www.thisisliveart.co.uk/uploads/documents/SRG_brutal_silences_2011_reduced-size.pdf.

———. "Redress." In *Brutal Silences: Live Art and Irish Culture*, edited by Ann Maria Healy and Helena Walsh. A Study Room Guide for the Study Room of the Live Art Development Agency, London, 2011. Accessed April 28, 2016. http://www.thisisliveart.co.uk/uploads/documents/SRG_brutal_silences_2011_reducedsize.pdf

Gestures of Resistance: Dance in 1990s Ireland

Finola Cronin

Conditions of dance practice and production in Ireland in the last decades of the twentieth century interfaced most forcefully (and often problematically) with the state in the guise of the Arts Council of Ireland/An Chomhairle Ealaíon. In 1989, tensions between dance artists and the Arts Council escalated due to funding decisions that terminated Arts Council support for a number of well-established companies. This chapter introduces five choreographers whose work was supported to various degrees by the Arts Council in the immediate aftermath of that period: Adrienne Brown, Fiona Quilligan, John Scott, Robert Connor and Loretta Yurick.[1] These choreographers formed independent dance companies and experimented with dance in ways that echoed the investigations of their European and American contemporaries. In mapping these choreographers' approaches to their work, I highlight the value they placed on dance training (all had some engagement with pioneers of modern and post-modern practice). I trace how they adapted these influences in the formation of their dance aesthetic and suggest that an embodied internationalism lay at the core of their dance practice in the Irish republic at that time.[2] This international dimension, I argue, provided not only opportunities for exchange and collaboration but can be posited as a factor that helped mobilise these dance artists to forebear certain prescriptive Arts Council policies in a period where the art form was under severe strain due to lack of investment.

In 1985, it was noted that "dance occupied the lowest rung on the ladder of Irish education and the Irish arts", and that attitudes to dance discounted its position as a "significant element of Irish life".[3] The absence of dance from state educational settings and its omission from successive Arts Acts put

F. Cronin (✉)
University College Dublin, Dublin, Ireland
e-mail: finola.cronin@ucd.ie

E. Jordan, E. Weitz (eds.), *The Palgrave Handbook of Contemporary Irish Theatre and Performance*,
https://doi.org/10.1057/978-1-137-58588-2_8

particular pressure on the Arts Council as, arguably, dance artists relied on that body not only for grant aid but also for its imprimatur. The low status of dance in Ireland was not a unique case. In the USA, dance was appraised as "the most economically fragile and publically marginal of the performing arts".[4] However, a growing diversity of dance expression from the mid-twentieth century onward was followed by an "explosion" of interest in critical dance studies and the emergence of dance as a discipline aligned with cultural studies frameworks where its value as embodied practice was recognised in the making visible of relations of power in political, social and cultural contexts.[5]

Dance scholar Randy Martin identifies as pivotal Susan Leigh Foster's positing of dance as a "condition for the production of a certain knowledge":[6]

> It is with her work that the project of thinking through dance—rather than identifying dance—receives its seminal articulation. That knowledge is more not less than, what the various hyphenations of dance (history, anthropology, aesthetics, notation, kinesiology) provide, namely, a foregrounding of how a given form of knowledge gets produced.[7]

Martin, addressing the implication of Foster's ideas, points out that: "once dance is established as a condition and not merely a location [...] the issue of its production and its product is thereby raised", and he argues that understanding dance not purely as an object to be interpreted brings emphasis to dancing as "an activity that must be produced through incessant process where the product of that process is itself a cultural practice".[8] Practice, Martin concludes, is "what emerges at the juncture between [...] a particular historical moment and what is generated though forms of agency".[9] Writing on ideas of agency, history and practice, Ramsay Burt notes the power of dancing bodies to reveal "the very matter of historical inscription".[10] Drawing on Michel Foucault's ideas of the body as "the inscribed surface of events",[11] Burt suggests: "sometimes troubling and disturbingly material dancing bodies [...] both uncover the process of history's destruction of the body *and* the possibilities of agency and resistance".[12]

Dancers clearly acquire a range of technical abilities through their training and practice, and Martin argues that the learning of diverse techniques is a process of "self-governance" through which "dancers generate their own authority".[13] To this end, Martin posits that the practice of dance is a political practice because through techniques that are grounded in disciplined authoritarian practices, dancers are given the opportunity to "move for and against that very authority".[14] Within Irish contexts, to conceive the works of the choreographers under discussion as practices of embodied self-determination is to draw attention to those practices as corporeally inscribed and in dialogue with socio-political contexts, and as creative practices that mark artistic autonomy and agency.

Withstanding Dance: The Arts Council and Dance's Recent History

At a public consultation forum hosted by the Arts Council in 1998, Patricia Quinn, described dance as a "beleaguered art form".[15] For some dance artists present, the acknowledgement of deficits in dance by the Arts Council director was welcome. Other dance artists, however, might have held the view that successive Arts Council policies on dance had contributed to the serious challenges facing dance in the 1990s and that, in fact, little had progressed since the publication of the Arts Plan 1995–1997, in which the Arts Council noted dance as the "weakest of artforms in the country", and articulated its resolve to accord "the highest priority to dance development".[16]

John Scott has referred to the Arts Council's withdrawal of funding to dance companies at the end of the 1980s as a "dance genocide".[17] The Dance Council of Ireland, as the representative body for dance at the time, stated its dismay and concern "at the pre-emptive decision of the Arts Council to effectively destroy the infrastructure of professional dance in the country", and noted that the decision marked a "deviation from the adopted policy of the Arts Council on dance as embraced in the Brinson Report".[18]

Peter Brinson's *The Dancer and the Dance: Developing Theatre Dance in Ireland* was commissioned by the Arts Council, and its terms of reference—specifically focussed on professional dance development—required consideration of "three dance companies: Irish National Ballet Company, Dublin City Ballet and Dublin Contemporary Dance Theatre".[19] These companies—along with Daghdha Dance based in Limerick, and Barefoot Dance Theatre in Wexford—formed the public face of dance at the time and, as they focused on professional dance practice, were strictly speaking the proper remit for support from the Arts Council. Brinson's final recommendation was to "reallocate resources to try to develop a more balanced, therefore modest, dance profession with wider choices for dancers and public than at present".[20] However, four years later the Arts Council decided to withdraw funding from Irish National Ballet (INB) and Dublin Contemporary Dance Theatre (DCDT),[21] and thereby implemented the nuclear action that Brinson had counselled against, namely to "throw away everything already achieved".[22]

Doubtless the Brinson report proposed a rigorous set of strategies to develop dance in the 1980s, but crucially and perhaps understandably, the report failed to fully understand successive Irish Governments' approaches to funding the Arts, and the lack of political will in Ireland to fund the Arts adequately. The report was to become a cornerstone of policy for dance in the years that followed. In 1989, the Arts Council's cherry picking of Brinson's recommendations unsettled relations between that body and the dance community, and led to a legacy of unease between dance artists and their chief funder.

In the *Irish Times* in 1998, Michael Seaver's article "No Dancing" asks: "Why has the buzz gone from dance?"[23] Lamenting the dearth of performances in that season compared to the number of productions mid-decade, Seaver berates dance policy as outlined in the Arts Plan of 1995–1997 for its lack of "courage and imagination".[24] Seaver argues that the Arts Council's plan "had sought to develop dance by making major changes, with little concern for existing work", and he claims that this strategy revealed "a curious unwillingness to evolve practices organically [...] each difficulty is addressed by scrapping existing work and starting again".[25] I'd like to dwell on the idea that the Arts Council's 1995–1997 Plan included the aspiration to arrive "ultimately at a distinctive form of Irish dance".[26] Seaver interprets this statement as the Council's intention to foster the development of a "distinctive character" of "indigenous dance" and he correctly assesses that this line of thinking is taken from Brinson's report.[27] But Seaver deduces from the Arts Plan the Arts Council's intention to select a dance company to operate as a national company from among the three companies it had pledged funding to: Dance Theatre of Ireland (DTI), Irish Modern Dance Theatre and Rubato Ballet. This is a point that Seaver returns to in 2003, writing: "when debate around a national ballet company re-emerged in the 1990s many believed that any company's relevance lay in its ability to be 'Irish'".[28] While Seaver in 1998 dismisses certain trends followed by the companies chosen for support over the duration of the Arts Plan 1995–1997, he commends their "choreographic craft" and adds that neither DTI nor Irish Modern Dance Theatre had "succumbed to trying to find the Arts Council's desired distinctive style".[29,30]

I refer to Seaver's *Irish Times* article at length because I think it reveals two critical and contiguous issues that resonated with dance artists in the 1990s, namely: the proposition from the Arts Council of a notional distinct Irish dance style and the concept of one singular expression of that style in the form of a company to be recognised as a national company. Ironically, in retrospect, and in the context of post-Celtic Tiger Ireland, the 1990s emerged as a period of pronounced activity in dance marked by significant productions from an increasing number of choreographers working in the field. Many productions of the period were startlingly innovative in their drive towards interdisciplinary creative processes, their use of site-specific performance locations, and their embrace of advances in technology. Most notable perhaps is the sheer diligence of dance artists who collectively established the Association of Professional Dancers of Ireland (APDI) to lobby on behalf of dance artists and the art form.[31] The five choreographers profiled below were founder members and served as officers on the board of the APDI. They carried out these positions in addition to their roles in dance in education settings, and their professional work as artists, performers, producers and teachers of emerging dance artists. The question that Seaver alludes to, and one that Patricia Quinn in some respects fails to acknowledge, is, what if these artists had decided to quit Ireland in 1989 in the face of evidential lack of support for the art form and their livelihoods?[32]

The Chance of Dance: Picking up the Pieces

Adrienne Brown

Adrienne Brown studied Graham technique at the London School of Contemporary Dance from 1979–1981, and became the first Irish dancer to gain a teacher-training certificate from the Martha Graham Centre of Dance in New York.[33] Brown studied classical ballet, which she admits was her "first love", but was introduced to the Graham technique by Terez Nelson in Dublin and was stimulated by "this new and exciting technique aesthetic—its earthiness, and its fire and punch in the body", and she later studied and performed with Joan Davis.[34] For Brown, the move to London to The Place brought her into contact with a range of teachers, dance artists and choreographers who had come from Graham's company and dance centre in New York to establish a school in London at the invitation of Robin Howard.[35,36]

Brown moved back to Ireland in the mid-1980s and observes that "by then, the Graham aesthetic was on the wane in Dublin", as Joan Davis and DCDT signalled increased interest "in experimentation and in general somatic practices".[37] Brown was exercised by the body's ability to be "athletic, virtuosic and dynamic", and, in 1987, in partnership with Annalise Schmidt she formed New Balance Dance Company with the aim "to bring strong contemporary dance to Irish audiences".[38] Brown admits that she struggled to find her own voice and that this may have been because of her deep immersion in Graham's technique and dance vocabulary. Brown was drawn to expression of the body as mastered by Graham, who was known for her mining of the psychological and the emotional in her work, and while Brown concedes that Graham's "rigid autocracy" did not appeal to her, Graham's attention to the structuring of myth and narrative did.[39]

While Brown was interested in what can be termed a modern dance aesthetic, her work *The Sin Eater* (1995) signals her intent to interrogate themes that explored events particular to Irish social history. Based on a short work *For Delia*, which was performed at the New Music/New Dance Festival in 1993, *The Sin Eater*—presented at Coláiste Mhuire, Parnell Square, Dublin—was a full-length two-act work for eleven performers. These included, among others: J'Aime Morrison, Steve Blount, Alexandra Diana and Philip Connaughton. The work had a commissioned score by Michael Seaver, and set and costume design by Irene O'Brien. The programme notes that the work was based on the "true story" of a young woman who lived in a rural town in 1930s Ireland and who, through a series of tragic events, suffered mental illness and was incarcerated in a mental asylum where she eventually died. The work draws attention to the notion of the "sin eater" as "one who eats the sins of others and becomes mad" (*The Sin Eater* Programme). Brown's acknowledgement of the role of the eleven performers in the creation of the work in the programme marked her leaning towards a democratisation of the rehearsal space, while the use of text to explore "themes of isolation, secrecy and grief" followed developments in dance theatre expression internationally.[40] As the decade progressed, Brown says that her aesthetic shifted: "I moved away from narrative and biographical and personal impulses to create work, and I became interested in exploring more abstract ideas [...] I needed to address what I perceived was a lack of structure—an organizing principle—Kim showed me how to use structure."[41]

Kim Brandstrup, artistic director of Arc Dance Company London, had been invited by Brown to act as a mentor on the Institute of Choreography and Dance (ICD) "Righting Dance" programme. The brainchild of Mary Brady, director of ICD, "Righting Dance" was designed to create a safe environment for choreographers to research work without the pressures of production and with the support of a mentor.[42] Under Brandstrup's guidance, Brown researched her craft with an ensemble of dancers for eleven weeks from 1997–1999, but took the decision to devote her final research period to building the foundation of a new production commissioned by ICD in 1999. Brandstrup agreed to direct the work, *Colmcille*, which premiered at ICD on the 25 February 2000. The work was choreographed for seven dancers: Ríonach Ní Néill, Fearghus O'Conchuir, Lisa McLoughlin, Beccy Reilly, Jonathan Poole, Alfonso Bordi and Rebecca Walters. Music was by John Travener, Ian Wilson and Arvo Part, and costumes and set design was by Patrick Murray, with lighting by Paul Keoghan.[43]

Brown's articulated aims for her research included the desire to "challenge her choreographic practice" and, specifically, to examine "timing and response to music, repetition and development of phrasing" and, importantly, her research facilitated professional development opportunities for all concerned to learn from Brandstrup, who set daily composition tasks for dancers and choreographer alike.[44] The research for *Colmcille* clearly enabled Brown to test her aesthetic of athleticism with dancers who had the technical ability to deliver "body shape as expression" and to reveal "full extension of limb and the torso as gateways to the body's organs" and, in hindsight, Brown identifies the period of Brandstrup's mentorship as a time in which "she felt supported during the creative process".[45]

Among the most vocal of choreographers of the period, Brown regularly voiced her opinion of the Arts Council's remit to support the professional development of dance artists. In 1994, in a submission to the Working Party on Dance, a committee gathered by the Arts Council to help it develop policy on dance, Brown wrote that "choreographers are not given proper recognition for work they do—they are not being funded or else only in a sporadic way".[46] Brown also criticized the Arts Council for what she saw as its "neglect" of dance artists and was clearly unsympathetic to the Arts Council, which she claimed "has always worked to its own agenda".[47]

In conversation with Diana Theodores, in 2003, Brown admits that she faced her own "death" as a choreographer. "I have not been funded by the Arts Council [...] it is very hard for me to talk about choreography [...] when you actually don't think that you exist as a choreographer any more."[48] To date,

Brown has created over forty works and continues to make new work in dance, most recently attracted to working in Screendance. She is a faculty member of the Dance Department at Inchicore College of Further Education in Dublin, and returned to formal education earning a PhD from University College Dublin in 2012.

Fiona Quilligan

Fiona Quilligan also ceased to create new work for a period in the early 2000s, but has latterly received Arts Council Project Awards for new productions in film and for the stage, and has most recently been elected to Aosdána.

> I was 16 or 17 and I remember seeing Joan [Davis] doing Terez Nelson's class – you could see her embodiment and commitment to the Graham technique. I quickly started training with Joan and she asked me to choreograph a solo for her. That was my first choreography. I designed a double frame and choreographed her body within. It was set it to music of Eric Satie.[49]

Following her initial study of visual art at Dun Laoghaire of Art and Design and the National College of Art and Design, and dance with Joan Davis, Quilligan left Dublin to study at the London School of Contemporary Dance. She recalls: "full time training really exposed me to the depth of Graham technique with Jane Dudley, Bill Louther, Juliet Fisher and other original members of the Martha Graham Company".[50,51] When an injury forced her to abandon study at LCDS, Quilligan turned her focus to classical ballet and she thrived under the tuition of Hungarian ballet master Maria Fay. She returned to Ireland to work with Dublin City Ballet (DCB) and its artistic director, American dancer and choreographer, Anne Courtney.[52] While at DCB, Quilligan was cast in the lead role of visiting guest choreographer Anna Sokolov's revival of her seminal work *Dreams*—a work that interrogates the horrors of the Holocaust and was originally conceived in 1961. The *New York Times* dance critic, Anna Kisselgoff, described Sokolov as an abstract expressionist "whose aesthetic of stillness played a large part of her choreography" and whose work had the capacity to "sum up a state of being—an entire society—in an arrested pose".[53]

Following the Brinson Report, reduced funding to Dublin City Ballet from the Arts Council forced its closure. Quilligan, with her sister, the dancer Zelda Quilligan (who used the stage name Francesca), formed Rubato Ballet in 1986 chiefly to make original works with a group of former colleagues from Dublin City Ballet. Quilligan claims that she wanted "to stay to make something in Ireland: I'm an artist who wanted to make work here. On reflection I think we had something to prove; we were not going to emigrate or lie down defeated".[54] Among the dancers that Quilligan drew to her work were Zelda Francesca, Muirne Bloomer, Roy Galvin, Aideen Gohery and James Hosty, and they were often joined by David Bolger, Alexandra Diana and Daire O'Dunlaing, to name but a few. But Quilligan's ambition was to create and perform new works in collaboration with composers, musicians, painters, poets and sculptors, she notes: "I was concerned with work that reflected what was emerging in the arts scene in Dublin".[55]

Quilligan describes her aesthetic as an attempt "to find a resolution to classicism through ballet's idiom rather than an interest in classical ballet per say".[56] On a study trip to Pina Bausch and Tanztheater Wuppertal in Germany in 1992, Quilligan observed Bausch's use of stiletto heels and was inspired to consider how soft pointe shoes (where the stiff insole is removed) might "require of dancers a similar transition between barefoot work and dancing in flexible pointe shoes".[57] Bausch's work also informed and influenced Quilligan's aesthetic: "[Bausch's] scale of work—her non-linear dramaturgy and the monumental scale of costume design took my breath away."[58]

Quilligan worked extensively in site-specific venues and art galleries throughout the 1990s (and indeed later in her career). She admits she sought out these venues "to enable the confluence of artists of all disciplines to become involved in her projects."[59] Quilligan indeed attracted an impressive range of collaborators to Rubato Ballet productions. In 1990, her work, *Dance Strokes: Images of Nijinsky* was presented at the RHA Gallagher Gallery, Dublin. This event comprised a series of lunchtime readings from Vaslav Nijinsky's diary, and a performance inspired by Nijinsky's work and life danced by Zelda Quilligan and Barry Murray. To accompany the readings and performances Quilligan curated the exhibition: *Dance Strokes: The Artist and The Dancer*, for the RHA Gallery, with works by twenty-five leading Irish visual artists including Brian Bourke, Elizabeth Cope, Janet Mullarney, Felim Egan and Eamonn Coleman, among others. In recognition of her work on this project, Quilligan was awarded the prestigious Nijinsky Medal by the Polish Artists Agency Warsaw in 1990.

Many of Quilligan's works were inspired by the poems of Paula Meehan, and Meehan herself read her poem *The Wounded Child* live during a performance of the 1992 eponymously titled work at the RHA Gallagher Gallery. For her work *Bull Dance*, Quilligan was inspired by Meehan's poem *Crete-A Journey*, and by Minoan art. This work, presented at the RHA Gallagher Gallery in 1994, included the backdrop of a massive canvas by Michael Mulcahy and a series of life-size sculpted figures from James McKenna, who was a frequent collaborator (and friend) and visitor to her rehearsal studio. Long-term music collaborators included the contemporary composers Raymond Dean and Fergus Johnston, traditional musicians Emer Maycock and Liam O'Maonlai, and the jazz artist Richie Buckley. For *A Close Shave* (1990), programmed by the Dublin Theatre Festival at Whelan's Wexford Street, Dublin, and at Project Arts Centre, music was composed and played live by the Jazz Quartet of Patrick Carayannis.[60] In a piece for *In Dublin* magazine, Mic Moroney described the improvisation process in progress in the rehearsal studio: "[The Carayannis Quartet] has to keep their eyes on the moves, and respond accordingly. It is a rich environment for improvisational ideas."[61] Quilligan notes "it was exciting to explore new music compositions live in rehearsal with the musicians and dancers—I always worked closely with the composers and studied the score".[62]

Of her work in the 1990s, Quilligan comments: "As I look back, I see these works as very ambitious. Despite the lack of funding from the Arts Council it was a very fertile and creative time. There was a sense of artistic freedom, a feeling of experimentation and pushing boundaries."[63] Photographs and production programmes indicate Quilligan's attention to the presentation of bodies; her interest in the anatomy of the performer; and her design of dancing bodies' shape in space. A study of these images and photographs also reveals Quilligan's resolute classicism in terms of balance, symmetry and harmony.

John Scott

John Scott claims also to have been influenced by Anna Sokolov:

> Anna Sokolow, a teacher of Pina Bausch at Julliard School, was the first world-class choreographer I got to witness working in the studio. In Dublin City Ballet, she created two works *Homage to John Field* and *Transfigured Night* and mentored Anne Courtney in a duet she [Courtney] was making.[64]

Sokolov was a member of Martha Graham's dance company in the early 1930s and counted as a member of the so-called left-wing radical faction of that company, whose own work "could satisfy the demands of both dance and politics".[65] Of Sokolov's work in the studio in 1980s Dublin, Scott notes her "remarkable ability to watch dancers as they worked with material she had created and her instinct to intervene with new possibilities, to guide, to push a bit more, to trust and use the natural inclinations of the dancers to sense and inhabit the space. This opened doors for me".[66]

Scott came to dance through Anne Courtney's workshops in Contemporary Jazz Dance for Dramsoc at UCD, where he was studying for a BA. Marsha Paludin also delivered workshops in Alexander alignment at UCD and her use of pedestrian movement and contact improvisation, honed from her study with Anna Halprin, introduced Scott to an aesthetic developed by American post-modern dance artists. Scott would later study with Pablo Vela, a member of Meredith Monk's The House. Monk was a leading member of the Judson Church Group of post-modern choreographers, who were to have significant influence on international developments in dance in the latter decades of the twentieth century.

But when Scott came to create *Macalla* in 1995, it was Julian Beck's *The Life of the Theatre* that struck a chord: "[Beck] writes that 'with theatrical means we could hear the sound of a bullet–thuck–entering the body, hear the sound of the world turning'—I thought of the Anglo Irish peace talks taking place and used images of two lines uniting/merging during the prologue in the downstairs space of the RHA Gallery".[67] Scott had seen productions by The Living Theatre in France and studied their stagecraft, particularly their use of

Brechtian alienation techniques "to create real situations and audience dialogue. What I got was [their] ignoring of scenography—using a bare stage complete with ladders, exit signs, tools, all visible—an acknowledgement of the beauty of the bare stage".[68]

Scott was born into the theatre. His father Leslie Scott was lighting designer at the Abbey Theatre, and his brother Michael Scott is a theatre director and producer. Scott has always acknowledged his almost insatiable interest in theatre, dance and music (he is also a fine tenor), as impulses to feed his choreography and began choreographing in 1985, while still a member of Dublin City Ballet. In 1990, *Earthwalk* was presented as part of the New Music/New Dance Festival and Scott's contribution, which was well received, was the catalyst for him to form his company, Irish Modern Dance Theatre, in 1991.

Scott's work *Macalla*, which he describes as a "sprawling opera", was a promenade performance using various spaces of the RHA Gallagher Gallery on Dublin's Ely Place. It was born out of "an imagining of the RHA Gallery to conceive a performance on a big scale. Most stages are too small and it was liberating to have access to vast spaces".[69]

Macalla is the Irish for echo, and Scot's impulse for the work arose from "the peace developments in Northern Ireland and the new permission to think about Irish independence, unity, reconciliation".[70] Scott's work offered an array of images—the opening scene, mentioned above, suggested the all too familiar image from the early 1990s Ireland of communities gathering at a graveside. Some performers held black umbrellas aloft and wore overcoats. Roy Galvin played an Irish lament on the tin whistle. Later, the performers led spectators to other spaces in the Gallery, and Joanna Banks (who was to become a long-time collaborator of Scott's), dressed in black with a black veil, played an ominous 'ghost' in the performance. Dance critic Carolyn Swift's review of the work for the *Irish Times* mentioned that ideas of tragedy and violence were counterpointed by comedy, and she noted: "among the evocations of lost youth, lost loved ones and lost opportunities are unexpected glimpses of loss of nerve or loss of face, the funnier for being juxtaposed with gothic drama".[71]

The work, however, that Scott maintains propelled him towards finding his own individual aesthetic was *Slam*, created in the same year. That work did not find favour with the *Irish Times* critic, but did enjoy success when presented in France. Scott acknowledges his interest in the so-called "new French dance" of the 1980s in works, by among others, Jean-Claude Galotta. *Slam* signals Scott's interest in non-linear narrative and ruptured and abstracted scenes, and his increasing lack of interest in codified dance moves.[72] Swift's review mentions the production's "off the wall humour" and she adds that "it seemed wasteful [...] to use two good Irish male dancers to stick plaster on each other and kick the walls for what seemed an eternity".[73] The emergence of everyday pedestrian movement in *Slam* and the charged energy that Swift describes, suggests that the work was a breakthrough piece for Scott and signalled what would become characteristic elements of his artistic signature.

Mark Franko writes that "dance does not only become political when the choreographer adopts a political legible content: the cultural politics of dance are always embedded in form".[74] From 2002 onward, Scott began working with survivors of torture seeking asylum in Ireland and has since created a number of works that have been critically acclaimed, and which foreground ideas of multiculturalism. But Scott's use of avant-garde structures in works such as *Slam* and his continued use of such resistant dramaturgy can be read as markers of his works' inherently political strategies and are perhaps a legacy of Sokolov and Monk's influences, where bodies as sites of embodied experience operate in opposition to normative ideologies.

Robert Connor and Loretta Yurick

Perhaps the best-known dance company of the 1990s was DTI, founded by Robert Connor and Loretta Yurick in 1989, ostensibly to secure the delivery of a project that had been already submitted to the Arts Council under the auspices of the DCDT in 1989.[75] And, in fact, it might be proposed that their decision to follow through on commitments made by DCDT, and the element of serendipity surrounding the timing of the funding award for their new company, indicate the fragility of dance in that period. Connor and Yurick are American and moved to Ireland to dance with Joan Davis (founder of DCDT) in 1980. Both studied with Nancy Hauser at her Center for the Performing Arts in Minneapolis. Hauser had been among the first Americans to be trained by Hanya Holm, who was a member of Mary Wigman's company in Dresden, Germany. Wigman was known as an expressionist choreographer, who had in turn been influenced by Rudolf von Laban's pedagogic principles that espoused the value of creative improvisation as a teaching technique. Following her successful tour to the United States in 1930, Wigman was invited by the impresario Sol Hurok to open a school of dance in New York and she appointed Holm to establish the school which duly opened in 1931. Holm gradually adapted Wigman's pedagogy to suit American teaching methods which focussed on rigorous dance techniques, such as those offered by Graham and Humphreys. Holm's choreographies would continue to be noted for their traces of Wigman's expressionist aesthetic, but Holm's status was to be secured in America when she became known as one of the "Big Four" choreographers of modern dance.[76] Connor and Yurick were conscious of Holm's legacy while working with Hauser: "from the moment you began to dance, you took improvisation and composition classes equally" recalls Yurick, and later Connor and Yurick would invite Sara and Jerry Pearson, both of whom had worked with Hauser, to work with them at DTI. This further consolidated the role of improvisation as a creative tool in their practice.[77] Joan Davis had initiated a policy of inviting international choreographers to teach and choreograph for DCDT, and Connor and Yurick continued Davis's policy of international engagement and developed close ties with dance artists internationally. Connor acknowledges that he was "very conscious of developments in the European dance culture", and mentions that both he and Yurick "not only invited international artists to work with them but travelled to see work, and read up on it".[78]

DTI's first production, *La Beauté des Fleurs*, was an invitation to French choreographers Isabelle Dubouloz and Pierre Douissant to mount their work mount on the new company. The work was premiered at the Dublin Theatre Festival in 1989 at Lombard Street Studio and was nominated for a Sunday Tribune/Dublin Theatre Festival Award.[79] Other notable international links in the 1990s forged by DTI included their invitation to Les Carnets Bagouet Company to reconstruct and stage Dominique Bagouet's *Deserts d'Amour*. This was a coup for DTI, who were then invited to open the prestigious Montpellier Dance Festival in 1996 with their production.[80] In 1996, DTI invited Suzy Blok (NL) and Chris Steel (UK) to create *Deseo* on the company.

As regards training, Connor notes that in the 1990s "daily class was very important".[81] Yurick clarifies however, that the work dictated what associated dance training would be required for the company:

> For *La Beauté des Fleurs* for example our training was based in Butoh (Japanese) dance, but training was always there to serve the work. We always wanted well-trained dancers, but dancers with anima, visceral, physical appetites and who could go into and out of the floor. These days these are assumed qualities (for dancers), but in the early 1990s these weren't so prevalent. There were a lot of ballet dancers but very few contemporary dancers in Ireland so we would have a few Irish dancers but also employ dancers from around the world.[82]

Connor and Yurick acknowledge that their aesthetic changed over the course of the 1990s: "in the early part of the decade, we had strong theatrical impulses, making works driven by strong central themes".[83] By the mid-1990s, Connor notes: "our interests shifted to more physical explorations and we had a desire to explore a multi-directional, multi-articulation physicality".[84] This artistic shift in focus might be interpreted as the result of DTI's work with Blok and Steel, and the Portuguese choreographer Rui Horta who created *Made to Measure* for DTI in 1999: "choreographers whose work was fast-paced and physically demanding".[85] Towards the end of the decade, Connor and Yurick's interests included exploration of the "emerging new possibilities of visual and digital technology and motion-capture animation".[86] Their final work of the decade, *Soul Survivor* (1999), was very well received—Seona MacReamoinn reviewing for the *Sunday Tribune* noted the work's "exciting multi-media collaboration and original three dimensional animation".[87] With digital projections by Ted Redfern, the work was presented at the Galway Arts Festival and toured nationally and internationally to great acclaim.

Connor and Yurick are prolific choreographers, and are renowned as excellent producers. Yurick asserts that she and Connor were determined to "move dance out of the Fringe and into the mainstream and into bigger venues", and from the outset DTI presented their work at the Samuel Beckett Theatre and in the 350-seater Tivoli Theatre, and "remained in those venues for the decade: commissioning designers such as Rupert Murray, Robert Ballagh and Marc O'Neill.[88] Connor and Yurick also established the first purpose-built dance studio in the greater Dublin area in 2000, and the studio in Dun Laoghaire continues to house their company. It is where Connor and Yurick offer support for professional dance artists, and an extensive teaching programme based on their teaching philosophy, which is strongly influenced by international practice:

> Hanya's [Holm] abstract expressionism was understood as an expression of the distilled essence brought to life by the expressive qualities of the dancer—their passion for emotion—this was related to Laban's work through Hauser and the Pearsons, and today is fundamental to how I introduce dance to people.[89]

Conclusion

This chapter has introduced the work of five choreographers and offers insight into the environment of dance in 1990s Ireland. These were not the only choreographers working in the field, as I've mentioned. Other dance artists include Cindy Cummings, Mary Nunan, David Bolger, Paul Johnston, Kalichi, Cathy O'Kennedy (formerly Hayes) and Diana Richardson. Among the emerging artists of that period, future stalwarts of dance in Ireland in the new millennium included Michael Keegan-Dolan, Liz Roche, Ríonach Ní Néill, Fearghus O'Conchuir, Catherine Young, Niamh Condron and Nick Bryson, to name but a few. Infrastructural supports for dance expanded throughout the 1990s: Shawbrook Dance's Summer Schools for aspiring professional dancers initiated in 1984 were well established by the mid-1990s and began to have increased impact on professional dance artists' development, while Catherine Numes championed the establishment of an international dance festival that would have its inaugural outing in 2002. The Arts Council also showed signs of greater commitment to dance development as the decade wore on, with increased funding allotted to the art form. Gaye Tanham, an expert in dance education matters and former secretary of the Dance Council of Ireland, was appointed to the post of Arts Council Dance Officer and, perhaps most significantly, at the end of the decade the Arts Council pledged to build a suite of studios in the capital. This initiative, which became Dance House, was finally opened to professional dance artists in 2006.

Critically, the decade changed the face of dance. Its diverse expression and aesthetic autonomy in Ireland signalled a broadening among dance artists and dance audiences of what dance could be. As the artists' profiles indicate, their works were heavily influenced by international approaches to dance but also explored a range of themes in dialogue with Irish arts, music and culture, entirely on their own terms. This suggests that the Arts Council's aspirations to establish an "Irish" dance company were not only at odds with international practices in dance at that time, but were also arguably at odds with the trend of globalization palpable in Ireland's growing Celtic Tiger economy and increasingly multi-cultural demographic. What becomes clear is that dance artists opposed the state's resistance to the art form. They occupied the vacuum where authoritarian or prescribed dance practices might have operated—practices that, in retrospect, might well have pursued a narrow or singular expression of "Irish" dance. Instead, in the lacuna created by the state, dance artists seized the opportunity to forge their artistic signature inspired by international links, and engagement with Irish-based transdisciplinary collaboration.

Notes

1. The choreographers are selected for a number of reasons. Firstly, they were chosen in the early 1990s for funding by the Arts Council. Secondly, a number of significant choreographers who were to emerge later in the decade danced with the five selected for interview. For example: David Bolger who established CoisCéim Dance Theatre in 1992, worked with Fiona Quilligan on a number of occasions and was an original cast member in *Bull Dance* which is referenced here. Liz Roche worked with DTI (and CoisCéim) and formed Rex Levitates in 1999. Fearghus O'Conchuir and Ríonach Ní Néill worked with Adrienne Brown and emerged as exciting artists at the end of the decade. This is not to suggest that Bolger, Roche, Ní Néill, and O'Conchuir danced exclusively with the choreographers I interviewed (in fact all mentioned had significant experience of training and practice abroad), or that these dancers necessarily practiced the style or choreographic vocabulary of those I foreground, but this chapter does not allow space to include all choreographers of the period. A further very significant choreographer is Michael Keegan-Dolan who has enjoyed considerable success in Ireland and abroad. See Aoife McGrath's *Dance Theatre in Ireland: Revolutionary Moves* (Palgrave, 2013), for an excellent account of Keegan-Dolan and David Bolger's work, and for a scholarly appraisal of selected Irish dance history and aesthetics. For note, discussion of two important choreographers of the period, Mary Nunan who founded Daghdha Dance Company, and Cathy O'Kennedy (formally Hayes), was beyond the scope of this chapter. Hence I acknowledge the chapter's Dublin-centric focus, as both Daghdha Dance Company and Barefoot Dance Company were located in Limerick and Wexford respectively. Another important choreographer is the American-born dance artist Cindy Cummings who has been based in Ireland since 1990 and whose career has focused particularly on trans-disciplinary collaboration.
2. I encountered a lack of consensus from among the five choreographers interviewed with regard to their description of their work. Connor and Yurick refer to their work as dance theatre and Quilligan refers to her work as modern ballet, while Scott and Brown use the terms dance theatre, dance and/or contemporary dance interchangeably. For note, dance terminology forms an ongoing debate in dance studies and for further reading see: Sally Banes, *Terpsichore in Sneakers: Modern and Post-Modern Dance,* Middletown (CT: Wesleyan University Press, 1977, 1989).
3. Peter Brinson, *The Dancer and the Dance: Developing Theatre Dance in Ireland* (Dublin: The Arts Council/An Chomhairle Ealaíon, 1985), 15.

4. Randy Martin, *Critical Moves: Dance Studies in Theory and Politics* (Durham and London: Duke University Press 1998), 10.
5. Jane C. Desmond, "Introduction" in *Meaning in Motion: New Cultural Studies in Dance* ed. Jane C. Desmond (Durham and London: Duke University Press, 1997), 1.
6. Martin, *Critical Moves: Dance Studies in Theory and Politics*, 204.
7. Ibid., 203–204.
8. Ibid.
9. Ibid., 205.
10. Ramsay Burt, "Genealogy and Dance History: Foucault, Rainer, Bausch and de Keersmaeker" in *Of The Presence Of The Body: Essays on Dance and Performance Theory*, ed. André Lepecki (Middletown, CT: Wesleyan University Press, 2004), 30.
11. Michel Foucault, "Nietzsche, Genealogy, History" in *Language Counter-Memory, Practice: Selected Essays and Interviews* (Oxford: Basil Blackwell, 1977), 148.
12. Burt, "Genealogy and Dance History: Foucault, Rainer, Bausch and de Keersmaeker", 34.
13. Martin, *Critical Moves: Dance Studies in Theory and Politics*, 175.
14. Ibid., 156.
15. Patricia Quinn, Arts Council director, speaking in 1998 at a Public Consultation Forum for the development of the New Arts Plan, Malahide, Co. Dublin.
16. *The Arts Plan: 1995–1997* (Dublin: 1994), 43.
17. John Scott in *Dancing on the Edge of Europe: Irish Choreographers in Conversation*, ed. Diana Theodores (Cork: Institute of Choreography and Dance ICD, 2003), 220.
18. *Dance News Ireland: The Newsletter of the Dance Council of Ireland*, Vol. 5 No. 1, 1989, 1.
19. Brinson, Peter, *The Dancer and the Dance: Developing Theatre Dance in Ireland* (Dublin: The Arts Council/An Chomhairle Ealaíon, 1985), 21.
20. Brinson's recommendations are given separately for each company. The report was particularly favourable to DCDT and recommended that resources be given to employ an administrator and one further dancer, and that the company be included in any plans to develop a National Dance School (34). The achievements of DCB were duly recorded but it was noted that within the context "of limited Government funding there seems to be no way that funds can be argued for to support a company of this size and programme" (30). Brinson recommended a root and branch overhaul of INB's governance and company structures but argued: "there is no question an Irish National ballet should exist. Present problems are not insoluble" (27). This chapter cannot do justice to the breath of commentary, analysis and recommendations articulated by Brinson. Under "National Considerations" Brinson turns his attention to Government funding for the Arts in Ireland and urges that: "the Irish Government should as a matter of urgency and equity, reconsider its attitude to the arts [...] and increase immediately its annual subvention to the Arts Council with consequential benefit to dance" (15). And one can speculate whether section 1.1.2., on the same page, was carefully considered by the Arts Council with regard to its decision to withdraw funds to dance in 1989: "Since no short term solution to underfunding seems in sight [...] we are compelled in this report to access what

sacrifices will be necessary to achieve the objective of a balanced theatre dance profession able to contribute with increasing vigour to cultural life in Ireland" ibid.

21. Dublin City Ballet ceased to operate in 1986 due to decreased financial support from the Arts Council.
22. The first of three options for the Arts Council as articulated by Brinson was: "Accept that present funds available to the Arts Council are insufficient to allow support for dance in any meaningful way." Brinson discounted this option however arguing: "we do not believe [...] that nothing can be done for dance with £375,000" 21.
23. Michael Seaver, "No Dancing", The *Irish Times*, 5 August 1998, 9.
24. Ibid.
25. To illustrate Seaver's points on the Arts Council's changing policy in the 1990s, I quote this paragraph, which prefaces the section on Dance in its Annual Report: "1997 saw the final phase of a three-year funding cycle, which was set up in 1994 as one of the development strategies for theatre dance. Three dance companies (Rubato Ballet, Irish Modern Dance Theatre and Dance Theatre of Ireland) had been in receipt of guaranteed funding for the years 1994, 1995 and 1996. In the course of the Arts Plan, two other revenue-funded companies (New Balance and CoisCéim), were seen as part of the revenue-support framework for theatre dance. The Council made the decision to carry three of these five companies (Dance Theatre of Ireland, Irish Modern Dance Theatre and CoisCéim) forward on a revenue basis into 1997" *Annual Report 1997*, Dublin: The Arts Council/An Chomhairle Ealaíon, 1997 22.
26. The Arts Council of Ireland/An Chomhairle Ealaíon, *The Arts Plan: 1995–1997*, 44.
27. Michael Seaver, "No Dancing", *The Irish Times*, 5 August 1998.
28. Michael Seaver "Afterword-Edging Towards Centre Stage: Living Dance History in Contemporary Ireland" in Theodores, *Dancing on the Edge of Europe: Irish Choreographers in Conversation*, 233.
29. Seaver, "No Dancing."
30. For note, Rubato Ballet had already been removed from the cohort of companies (see note 25 above). This decision was indicative of inconsistent Arts Council funding policies. For reaction among dance artists, see Paul Johnston "Dancing in the Dark" in *Irish Theatre Magazine* May 2000, and Finola Cronin "The Time has Come to Dance: The International Dance Festival of Ireland 2002" in Finola Cronin and Eamonn Jordan eds. *The Contemporary Irish Theatre and Performance Studies Reader*, 2016.
31. Dance was marginalised at the very core of the Arts Council in so far as it was not a named art form until the Arts Act of 2003. Hence, it was not until 2006 that choreographers were deemed eligible for election to Aosdána. At the time of writing, three choreographers are members of that body but are not entitled to artists' tax exemption in contrast to other artist members.
32. Brinson notes the "absence of any member with dance knowledge within the Council itself" (18). The Arts Council's *Annual Reports* in 1988 and 1989 record the drop in the Dance budget from IR£417,114 to IR£214,607 in the period 1988–1989. In the same period, funding for Film rose from IR£125,000 to IR£211,600.

33. Brown studied on the London School of Contemporary Dance Evening School programme led by American dance teacher Karen Bell-Kanner. On her return to Dublin, Brown continued to attend Summer Schools at the Graham centre in New York City throughout the 1990s and was awarded a teacher certificate in 1996.
34. The quotes in this section are from Brown and emanate from a live interview on 28 February, 2017 and one recorded interview on 3 March 2017 with the author.
35. London Contemporary Dance School, which also housed the London Contemporary Dance Theatre (the professional company), is located on Flaxman Terrace off the Euston Road, London, and was also known as The Place.
36. Philanthropist Robin Howard saw the Martha Graham Dance Company in performance in London in 1954 and financed the company's tour to Edinburgh Festival in 1963. He was determined to bring her teaching method and dance style to London. Graham agreed to have the school formally associated with her work and sent one of her leading dancers, Robert Cohen, to guide the project. Among the dance artists who taught at The Place were Jane Dudley, a member of the Graham Company from the 1930s and a significant choreographer in her own right, Juliet Fisher, Bill Louther, Nina Fonaroff and the Argentinean dancer Naomi Lapzeson. All of these artists were instrumental in establishing The Place's reputation as among the most exciting dance schools in Europe in the late twentieth century whose alumni includes leading choreographers and filmmakers Siobhan Davis, Richard Alston, Kim Brandstrup and Sally Potter, among many others.
37. Brown, in conversation.
38. Ibid.
39. Seminal works of Graham based on interpretation of Greek myth include: *Cave of the Heart* (1946), *Night Journey* (1947) and *Errand into the Maze* (1947). Mark Franko records the dramaturgy of these works as exemplars of Graham's approach to "universalizing narrative and its mythical symbolism" and notes that that Graham's aim was to encourage the spectator to "project their own life experience into [the] choreography." Mark Franko, *Martha Graham in Love and War: The Life in the Work*, 2012, 6.
40. Brown, in conversation.
41. Brown, interview.
42. Dance artists in Ireland have long been aware of the need to nurture their craft, and are all too aware of the resources required to do so. The first "National Choreographic Course" took place in Wexford in 1985. Organized by Cathy Hayes (O'Kennedy) it afforded dance artists the live bodies and appropriate rehearsal spaces in which to create and research their work.
43. Brady commissioned this writer to document the research process of Adrienne Brown's *Righting Dance* programme. The research process included curated events where the material created was shared with invited audiences. A second *Righting Dance* programme was initiated in January 1999 with choreographers Mary Nunan and Paul Johnson under the mentorship of Canadian choreographer Tedd Senmon-Robinson. The accompanying publication/documentation sets out the aims of ICD's *Righting Dance* programme: "To engineer circumstances that test and try current practice, helping to invigorate stronger work

and proposals for fresh approaches in making dance." Mary Brady in Theodores, *Writing Dancing Righting Dance*, 5.

44. Finola Cronin, *Righting Dance: 'Time Out' Choreographer: Adrienne Brown, December 1997–April 1999* (Cork: Institute of Choreography and Dance (ICD), 2000), 6.
45. Brown, in interview.
46. Adrienne Brown, letter to Mary Brady, of the Arts Council sub-committee on Dance, dated 10 February 1994. The Adrienne Brown Papers. Accessed 6 July 2016.
47. Ibid.
48. Brown in *Dancing on the Edge of Europe: Irish Choreographers in Conversation*, 62.
49. Fiona Quilligan, written correspondence with FC. Quotations from Fiona Quilligan are from written correspondence and one interview conducted on 1 March 2017.
50. Ibid.
51. The Place's Head of Technique was Jane Dudley, but classes in composition and choreography were also core. Nina Fonaroff was head of the Department of Choreography and, as Stephanie Jordan points out, she espoused a training method "devised by Louis Horst, Graham's long-time musical director." In *Striding Out: Aspects of Contemporary and New Dance in Britain*, 1992 (15).
52. American dancer and choreographer Anne Courtney was invited to Dublin to act as artistic director of Dublin City Ballet and lead its dance in education brief. Dublin City Ballet was first established in 1979 by entrepreneur Louis O'Sullivan under the name of The Oscar Ballet Company with Ian Montague appointed as artistic director.
53. Anna Kisselgoff, "Review/Dance; Anna Sokolow: Takes a Bow for 50 Years", *New York Times*, 20 January 1991. For note, Sokolov is also written Sokolow. I have used Sokolov except when inserting quotations from other writers.
54. Quilligan, written correspondence.
55. Ibid.
56. Quilligan, interview.
57. Ibid.
58. Quilligan, correspondence.
59. Ibid.
60. The Jazz Quartet of Patrick Carayannis included Mike Nielsen, Ray McCann and Dave Flemming.
61. Mic Moroney, 'Rubato in Rehearsal', in *In Dublin*, 11–24 October 1990, 117.
62. Quilligan, correspondence.
63. Ibid.
64. John Scott written correspondence with FC February 2017. The author conducted one interview with Scott and written correspondence on 20 February 2017. Sokolov created two new works for Dublin City Ballet: *Homage to John Field* which had its premiere in The Place, London, in June 1985, and *Transfigured Nights* which premiered at the Peacock Theatre Dublin in July 1985.
65. Ellen Graff, quoted in Mark Franko's *The Work of Dance: Labor, Movement, and Identity in the 1930s*, 2002, 57.

66. Scott, written correspondence.
67. Ibid.
68. Scott, interview.
69. Scott, written correspondence.
70. Ibid.
71. Carolyn Swift, "Emotion in Motion: Macalla RHA Gallagher Gallery", *The Irish Times*, 11 January 1995, 12.
72. The establishment of a number of *Centres Chorégraphic Nationale* (National Choreographic Centres) throughout France in the late 1970s, and spearheaded by culture minister Jack Lang in the 1980s, was instrumental in creating a boom in dance practice in France. So-called 'New French Dance' built on American modern and post-modern dance as brought to France by among others Alwin Nikolais (a protégée of Hanya Holm, and from 1978 director of the Centre Chorégraphic at Angers) and Carolyn Carlson (a dancer with Nikolais and later choreographer for the Paris Opera Ballet among other companies). New French Dance's leading figures included: Jean-Claude Galotta director of Group Emile Dubois, who studied in New York with Merce Cunningham from 1976–1978, Régine Chopinot, Joelle Bovier and Régis Obadia to name but a few. In 1988, Group Emile Dubois presented *Docteur Labus* by Galotta at the Olympia Theatre as part of the Dublin Theatre Festival.
73. Carolyn Swift, "Dancers in Search of a choreographer: Irish Modern Dance Theatre Project Arts Centre", *The Irish Times*, 7 June 1995, 10.
74. Mark Franko, *The Work of Dance: Labor, Movement, and Identity in the 1930s* (Middletown CT: Wesleyan University Press, 2002), 57.
75. Robert Connor and Loretta Yurick in conversation with FC 6 March 2017. Quotations from Connor and Yurick emanate also from written correspondence with the author, 25 February 2017.
76. The 'Big Four' included: Holm, Martha Graham, Doris Humphreys and Charles Wideman and had enormous influence in the 1930s–1950s. Particularly noteworthy was the popularizing of modern dance through the Bennington School of Dance summer programme, established in 1934 at Benningtom College, Vermont, which operated as an incubation laboratory for emerging dancers and choreographers.
77. Davis had invited Sara and Jerry Peason to work with DCDT in the 1980s and commissioned among other works *Acid Rain* (1982) and *Lunar Parables* (1984).
78. Connor, written correspondence.
79. Douissant and Dubuloz won the prestigious Prix de Bagnolnet choreographic competition in 1988 and *La Beauté* was subsequently premiered in France (with a different cast) at Theatre de la Ville, Paris in 1991.
80. Dominique Bagouet (1951–1992) was a towering figure at the heart of so-called 'New French Dance' in the 1980s. A further collaboration followed in 1997 when Les Carnets Bagouet co-produced and restaged *Jours Etranges* with DTI.
81. Connor, written correspondence.
82. Yurick, written correspondence.
83. Connor, written correspondence.
84. Ibid.

85. Ibid.
86. Ibid.
87. Seona Mac Réamoinn, "Soul Survivor", *The Sunday Tribune* 18 July 1999. Dance Theatre of Ireland Collected Papers. Accessed 27 July 2016.
88. Yurick, written correspondence.
89. Connor, written correspondence.

Bibliography

Banes, Sally. *Terpsichore in Sneakers: Modern and Post-Modern Dance*. Middletown, CT: Wesleyan University Press, 1977, 1989.

Brinson, Peter. *The Dancer and the Dance: Developing Theatre Dance in Ireland*. Dublin: The Arts Council/An Chomhairle Ealaíon, 1985.

Cronin, Finola, and Eamonn Jordan. eds., *The Contemporary Irish Theatre and Performance Studies Reader*. Dublin: Carsyfort Press, 2016.

Cronin, Finola *Righting Dance: 'Time Out' Choreographer: Adrienne Brown December 1997–April 1999*. Cork: Institute of Choreography and Dance (ICD), 2000. (Unpublished).

Dance News Ireland: The Newsletter of the Dance Council of Ireland, Vol. 5 No. 1, 1989 (Winter).

Desmond, Jane C., ed. *Meaning in Motion: New Cultural Studies in Dance*. Durham & London: Duke University Press, 1997.

Franko, Mark. *The Work of Dance: Labor, Movement, and Identity in the 1930s*. Middletown CT: Wesleyan University Press, 2002.

Franko, Mark. *Martha Graham in Love and War: The Life in the Work*. Oxford: Oxford University Press, 2012.

Foucault, Michel. *Language Counter-Memory, Practice: Selected Essays and Interviews* edited with an Introduction by Donald F. Bouchard, translated by Donald F. Bouchard and Sherry Simon, Oxford: Basil Blackwell, 1977.

Johnston, Paul. "Dancing in the Dark." *Irish Theatre Magazine*, May, 2000.

Jordan, Stephanie. *Striding Out: Aspects of Contemporary and New Dance in Britain*. London: Dance Books, 1992.

Kisselgoff, Anna. "Review/Dance; Anna Sokolow: Takes a Bow for 50 Years." *New York Times*, January 20, 1991.

Lepecki, André, ed. *Of The Presence Of The Body: Essays on Dance and Performance Theory*. Middletown, CT: Wesleyan University Press, 2004.

Martin, Randy. *Critical Moves: Dance Studies in Theory and Politics*. Durham & London: Duke University Press, 1998.

McGrath, Aoife. *Dance Theatre in Ireland: Revolutionary Moves*. Basingstoke: Palgrave Macmillan, 2013.

Mac Réamoinn, Seona. Review, *Sunday Tribune*, November 6, 2000.

Moroney, Mic. "Rubato in Rehearsal." *In Dublin*, October 11–24, 1990.

Seaver, Michael. "No Dancing." *The Irish Times*, August 5, 1998.

Swift, Caroline. "Emotion in Motion: Macalla RHA Gallagher Gallery." *The Irish Times*, January 11, 1995.

Swift, Caroline. "Dancers in Search of a Choreographer: Irish Modern Dance Theatre Project Arts Centre." *The Irish Times*, June 7, 1995.

Theodores, Diana. *Writing Dancing Righting Dance.* Cork: Institute of Choreography and Dance ICD, 2000.

Theodores, Diane, ed. *Dancing on the Edge of Europe: Irish Choreographers in Conversation.* Cork: Institute of Choreography and Dance (ICD), 2003.

The Arts Council of Ireland/An Chomhairle Ealaíon, *The Arts Plan: 1995–1997*, Dublin: 1994.

The Arts Council of Ireland/An Chomhairle Ealaíon. *Annual Report, 1988*, Dublin: 1989.

The Arts Council of Ireland/An Chomhairle Ealaíon. *Annual Report, 1989*, Dublin: 1990.

The Arts Council of Ireland/An Chomhairle Ealaíon. *Annual Report, 1997*, Dublin: 1998.

Contemporary Theatre in the Irish Language

Máirtín Coilféir

For practitioners and scholars alike, theatre in the Irish language has long been considered problematic.[1] It is a marginalized art form in a marginalized vernacular, "the poor relation", as Alan Titley puts it, "of prose and poetry, indeed of music and of song, and even now of journalism and of discursive writing".[2] It has no obvious tradition to draw on nor canon to sustain it—although we have evidence of earlier works written for performance,[3] it is generally recognized that the first organized effort at developing the theatre stemmed from the cultural revival little more than one hundred years ago.[4] It relies heavily on state subsidy and has never had a full-time professional company of actors,[5] both of which are significant disadvantages to writers, performers and directors who would engage with theatre on any basis beyond the short-term. Then there is the perennial problem of audience, or lack thereof—"the absence", as Máirín Nic Eoin has it, "both historically and in a contemporary context, of an urban, Irish-speaking, theatre-going bourgeoisie".[6] These are the stultifying conditions that frame contemporary Irish-language theatre, the social and economic realities that shape all potential productions and their reception, largely independent of merit or circumstance. And yet theatre in Irish is as varied as could be hoped for. Averaging over sixty professional or semi-professional productions each decade since 1960,[7] it spans everything from one-man monologues on a bare stage to simultaneously-translated, full-cast shows with visual and audio special effects. It is so varied, in fact, that no one chapter can do it justice and I make no claim to a comprehensive account of its practice here. Instead, I aim to use the difficulties inherent in Irish-language theatre making to offer one explanation as to its impetus, its market and some of its production strategies. In order to make these

M. Coilféir (✉)
University of St. Michael's College, University of Toronto, Toronto, Canada
e-mail: COLFERMA@tcd.ie

E. Jordan, E. Weitz (eds.), *The Palgrave Handbook of Contemporary Irish Theatre and Performance*,
https://doi.org/10.1057/978-1-137-58588-2_9

abstract points more concrete, I will draw on two well-known works that illustrate my argument; these, however, are only explicit manifestations of generally implicit determinants and they cannot reflect the diversity of contemporary drama. What follows, then, is a conceptual framework that seeks to explain fundamental aspects of Irish-language theatre in light of the challenges its practitioners must face.

The framework I have in mind is based on applied theatre, itself an increasingly prevalent idea in performance studies. It is a fluid concept, variously used,[8] but at its core is an emphasis on the social, political and emotional effects of theatre (as opposed to its spectacle, entertainment value or aesthetic experience). Theatre here is a vehicle for identification: through performance, participants engage imaginatively and empathetically with issues and with others in order to come to a clearer understanding of their place and their role in any given community. Ideally it is pedagogic, democratic, holistic, leading to a more generous and nuanced understanding of how we are shaped by past events and by present social structures.

Such an idea, of course, is not new. Versions of applied theatre have long been practiced in local and grassroots drama movements, and the fact that organizers often work towards some sort of emotional catharsis suggests a deliberate continuation of the principles of antiquity. What marks the term off from previous labels for socially-engaged theatre, however, is its scope: it encompasses not only community-based drama but the whole range of performance initiatives that would promote empathy, education and social co-operation. In one of the earliest book-length accounts of the concept, which I use as my point of reference, Helen Nicholson gives a succinct explanation: "What makes theatre 'applied', however, rather than just 'theatre' is not only the pedagogical processes, but understanding the educational, institutional or community settings in which it takes place."[9] Nicholson's wording in this passage is particularly useful in understanding Irish-language plays for two reasons. Firstly, it describes applied theatre, not simply as a practice or ideal consciously pursued by cast and crew, but as a quality to be inferred or appreciated by the viewer. In other words, it is not the performance of applied theatre that is foregrounded here so much as an "understanding" of its context and, indeed, the social effects of performance within that context. My contention is that the social context of the Irish language—its marginalized and contested status in the discourse of the country—is also the single most important factor in understanding its theatre. The local or national standing of Irish itself is always implicitly attended to in the staging of a play and often openly examined in the productions themselves.

Secondly, Nicholson provides us with two touchstones that are key to understanding the production, demands and aesthetics of theatre in the Irish language: that of education and that of community. These are very broad categories that will need disentangling but, by way of anticipation, my argument will be that the educational and the communitarian potential of theatre is the biggest force in determining script, staging and audience alike.

It is on this latter point, however, that existing accounts of applied theatre must be tailored to better suit the specificities of the subject at hand. Adapting the work of Nicholson and other theorists, I use the words "community" and "communitarian" here to denote populations defined, not primarily by their shared sense of place or history, but by their conscious commitment to the language of performance. That is to say, Irish-language theatre communities can be helpfully understood as sociolinguistic "communities of practice"—social "aggregates" who, "united by a common enterprise, develop and share ways of doing things, ways of talking, beliefs, and values".[10] The enterprise or practice in question here is, of course, Irish-language theatre itself, which in turn has a unifying effect on the individuals who participate in the language conventions of that community:

> In the course of regular joint activity, a community of practice develops ways of doing things, views, values, power relations, ways of talking. And the participants engage with these practices in virtue of their place in the community of practice, and of the place of the community of practice in the larger social order. The community of practice is thus a rich locus for the study of situated language use, of language change, and of the very process of conventionalization that underlies both.[11]

With the focus here on "situated language use", theatre is presented as a site for the expression of the dynamics of linguistic "change" and "conventionalization". It is a medium through which participants affirm, assess or renew their membership in their speech communities and the social principle that makes the performance "applied" is the commitment to the minority language itself. With this as our paradigm, we can begin to explicate fundamental aspects of contemporary theatre in Irish, from the centres of performance to the dialogue, presentation and appreciation of individual plays. These will be the focus for the remainder of this chapter as I discuss them in the context of the communitarian and educational ideals mentioned above.

Beginning with centres of performance, the sociolinguistic framework is particularly useful for contextualizing the recognized division of Irish-language theatre communities into two overlapping groups. On the one hand there is the folk theatre movement of the *Gaeltacht* areas, relatively small groupings of (usually) native speakers whose work often draws on local affairs, history and, importantly, dialects, which are very pronounced in the Irish language and not always readily understood by learners and speakers from other areas.[12] The *Gaeltacht* regions are usually divided into three large provincial groups—Munster, Connaught and Ulster—and each of these has its own distinct dialect and provincial theatre centre (in Dingle, Co. Kerry; Inverin, Co. Galway; and Gweedore, Co. Donegal, respectively). On the other hand there is the urban theatre movement. The cities of Belfast, Dublin and Galway are its main centres and its participants' sociolinguistic backgrounds tend to more varied, with learners of the language mixing with native speakers of the different dialects. Although popular plays often tour all of the venues just mentioned (as well as some others unsaid), the linguistic dynamic of these communities of practice are naturally very different, with divergent acting and writing styles.

To illustrate this we can take as examples two of the most successful plays in the last fifty years, one from the *Gaeltacht* tradition and the other from the urban. The first of these is *Níor Mhaith Linn do Thrioblóid* [We're Sorry for your Trouble], a popular three-act work that was staged multiple times in Ireland as well as for the expatriate community in Boston.[13] It was written by Joe Steve Ó Neachtain, a well-known actor and writer from the Conamara Gaeltacht, and is set in the area. The play revolves around the death of a local woman, the wife of the School Master, and focusses on the different ways in which the characters understand the time-honoured rituals surrounding death and in which they offer support for the widower. Although it is essentially a comedy, much of the humour is rooted in the decaying sense of community that should, in theory, sustain the bereaved in their hour of hardship. The two main characters are small farmers unrelated to the deceased; they are middle-aged, sharp-tongued and immersed in the cultural traditions they expect will be followed in the days after death—the wake, the rosary, the digging of the grave and so on. The School Master himself is of a higher social standing and senile. He too would fall back on local customs in his time of grief but is dependent on his three children, all of whom have left the *Gaeltacht* to pursue different life paths and are now, to varying degrees, out of touch with traditional etiquette. What makes the play such an excellent representative of Irish-language theatre in general, however, is that it dramatizes the linguistic and cultural conditions that shape both the *Gaeltacht* and its dramatic tradition. In *Níor Mhaith Linn do Thrioblóid* the older generation speak an extremely rich Irish—in their mourning rituals they are, in fact, a community of practice in themselves and their idiom both expresses and symbolizes their cultural values. Their striking vocabulary does not lend itself well to English translation, but Irish readers will recognize a density in the dialogue:

Tom: (*ag gáire*) Cogar mé seo leat. (*ag an doras*) An mbeidh tú ag dul ar an tórramh?

Séamas: Hea? Cén tórramh í seo, 'rú?

Tom: A dheabhail, ab in a bhfuil a fhios a'd? Bean an tseanmháistir. Ní raibh snig ar maidin inti nuair a dhúisigh sé.

Séamas: Is, an bhfuil sí básaithe uilig?

Tom: Nach ndeirim leat go raibh sí ina pleainc lena thaobh sa leaba! Deir siad go raibh sí básaithe ó thús oíche ach nár thug sé faoi deara é.

Séamas: Is, ar ndóigh, Jasus… ní fhéadfadh sí a bheith strompaithe lena thaobh i ngan fhios dó.

Tom: Bhí. Chaith sé chúig nóiméad dhá craitheadh ag iarraidh uirthi éirí ag déanamh tae dhó…

Séamas: Á muise, beannacht Dé lena hanam… más síos fhéin atá an striapach imithe…[14]

Tom: (*laughing*) C'mere to me. (*at the door*) Are you going to the wake?
Séamas: Hah? What wake's this?
Tom: God, do you know anything? The old master's wife. There wasn't a breath left in her this morning when he woke up.
Séamas: And is she dead altogether?
Tom: Amn't I telling you she was like a plank beside him in the bed! They say she was gone from the previous night only he never noticed.
Séamas: All the same, Jaysus… she couldn't be gone stiff there right beside him without him knowing.
Tom: She was. He spent five minutes shaking her, telling her to get up and make the tea…
Séamas: Ah, God be good to her… even if it *is* down below the bitch has gone…[15]

As for the younger generation in the play, ostensibly—and, indeed, in the eyes of the community as represented by the farmers—they have done well for themselves for leaving the *Gaeltacht*. One daughter is a manager in Brussels, the other seemingly happily married in Dublin, and the son is a missionary priest. In truth, their upwardly mobile life paths will lead the family to destruction. Two of the children are miserable, the other is bilious, and their abandonment of the community and its ways will have disastrous consequences for their father in particular, who is to be promptly shipped off to a nursing home. As with the older generation, the cultural values the children represent are given a linguistic dimension by Ó Neachtain. They speak a more "modern" Irish with English exclamations and loan words much more prevalent (shown by italics in the dialogue below):

Lisa: *Oh, for God's sake,* abair amach é. Níl maith ar bith a bheith ag ceilt rud a bhí a fhios a'inn uilig ón tús.
Móna: Tá sé tinn, sin an méid.
Éamonn: Bhuel, níl Dad ag dul in áit ar bith anocht. Tá a dhóthain de *shock* faighte aige.
Móna: *Yeah*, socróidh muid rud éicint théis na sochraide amáireach.
Lisa: Móna, dúirt mé leat cheana nach mbeidh mé anseo théis na sochraide amáireach. Beidh *taxi* do mo bhailiú ag an séipéal ag a dó dhéag. Ní féidir liom a dhul ag an reilig nó caillfidh mé mo *flight* ar ais.
Éamonn: Lisa, cop op. Tá níos mó ná sin ómóis do do mháthair a'd.[16]

Lisa: Oh for God's sake, out with it. There's no point hiding something we already knew about from the start.
Móna: He's sick, that's all.
Éamonn: Well, Dad's not going anywhere tonight. He's had enough shock for one day.

Móna: Yeah, we'll sort something out after the funeral tomorrow.
Lisa: Móna, I told you that I won't be here after the funeral tomorrow. A taxi's picking me up at the chapel at twelve. I can't go to the graveyard or I'll miss my flight back.
Éamonn: Lisa, cop on. You've more respect for your mother than that.

In *Níor Mhaith Linn do Thrioblóid*, the new and traditional ways of seeing and of speaking about the world are fundamentally at odds with one another. The modern way of life (as epitomized by Lisa) eventually wins out and the School Master is left confused and afraid by the change that awaits him. The community of practice to which the farmers belong, however long-established, cannot intervene and the play ends with the widower begging his deceased wife, and the social stability she stands for, not to desert him.

Ó Neachtain's work enacts local modes of life and speech while highlighting the difficulties in sustaining them. In that, it has much to offer us in understanding the current and future conditions of *Gaeltacht* theatre. As in the writing of many *Gaeltacht* authors, the major artistic virtue of *Níor Mhaith Linn an Trioblóid* is the dialogue, particularly that of the older characters. Yet, precisely because of its brilliance, the dialogue is also arguably the most constrictive aspect of the play: it demands a linguistic competence that is beyond the capacity of most self-identifying Irish speakers, not just to perform but even to understand without aid.[17] Adepts of the Conamara dialect may appreciate the crafted repartee but, localized as it is, much of it will be lost on others, perhaps especially urban speakers. Indeed, the gap of linguistic and cultural understanding that exists between the younger and older generation in *Níor Mhaith Linn do Thrioblóid* will also be a factor among members of the audience, made increasingly obvious as the language of the *Gaeltacht* undergoes rapid change (as is happening now).[18] Needless to say, such a delicate language balance has very profound consequences for script-writers, actors and spectators: it immediately limits effective writing and acting opportunities, while also leaving any informed appreciation of the work's merits to a minority of speakers. In other words, the community of practice that can fully engage with this kind of work is necessarily quite small, and this means that even the finest plays of the *Gaeltacht* tradition are likely to remain on the margins of the discourse in Ireland.

Obscurity, however, bears little relation to excellence and this masterful and somewhat exclusivist exhibition of language is also what makes the work of Gaeltacht playwrights both important and—within their given communities of practice—popular. The hall in Inverin, Co. Galway and the nearest urban theatre, An Taibhdearc in Galway City, are often filled to capacity when new works by Conamara writers are shown there.[19] The same goes for the drama venues in Donegal and Kerry (although their writers are perhaps not as well known nationally). Attending shows in any of these venues, there is a palpable sense of being present at an important local event which both portrays and brings together the speech communities at which they are aimed. Indeed, these plays (and other related art forms such as the *agallamh beirte* and *lúibín*) are among the most effective expressions of living *Gaeltacht* speech and no small part of their appeal is their public showcasing of language registers seldom seen in the arts. This, I believe, is the defining quality of the folk theatre tradition: the abundant language resources of its community give it huge artistic potential but genuine appreciation of its work is limited by the sociolinguistic realities of the *Gaeltacht*. Ó Neachtain is our example here but we could have as easily taken the work of a number of other writers who are popular in Irish media and almost unknown in English-speaking Ireland: Johnny Chóil Mhaidhc Ó Coisdealbha, Darach Ó Scolaí, Noel Ó Gallachóir, Tomás Mac Giolla Bhríde (to list but a few). If these names are among the most arcane in this volume, it serves as a further illustration of the profound gap between the arts in the two national languages.

As a counterpoint to the folk tradition represented by *Níor Mhaith Linn do Thrioblóid*, Máiréad Ní Ghráda's *An Triail* [The Trial] is not only the most well-known work associated with the urban theatre movement, but also the most consistently popular work of the last sixty years.[20] As is the case in so much Irish-language drama, the play focuses on the idea of a community failing one of its more vulnerable members, but it predates Ó Neachtain's play by some forty years and takes up very different social issues. The catalyst for the action here once more is the death of a character—in this case the main character, Máire, a single mother in mid-twentieth century Ireland who has killed herself and her child after suffering the cruelty of a narrow-minded society. In a series of flashbacks, the audience is shown the events leading up to the tragedy while various characters testify to the young woman's ethics and actions. It is left to us to judge who, if anyone, is ultimately responsible for her death.

The play was first staged in 1964; it was very controversial and very successful, showing in Dublin and Belfast to packed houses before being televised by the national broadcaster in 1965.[21] Ní Ghráda had been writing short one-acts for the Abbey Theatre in Dublin for some time before and, as with *Níor Mhaith Linn do Thrioblóid*, the audiences and locations that she was attending to inform the dialogue and action of the work.[22] The scenes take place in different locations, covering a range different social codes and classes: a small town school, a city factory, a suburban boarding house, a Magdelene laundry. Regardless of the geography, all the characters speak fluent Irish, yet it is telling that the play makes no reference to the *Gaeltacht*, which is the only region in the country where one is actually likely to encounter an organic and well-knit population of speakers. On the whole the dialogue is simple—bland, even—and in its grammar and vocabulary it is much closer to the standardized version of Irish used by educational and state bodies (sometimes called the *lárchanúint* or middle dialect). This makes it at once more stilted and more accessible for Irish speakers of all abilities, as this passage between Máire and her wooer shows:

Pádraig: A Mháire Ní Chathasaigh, an rincfidh tú liom—nó an gá dom cead a fháil ó do mháthair? Nó ó do dheartháir Liam?

Máire: Ní gá, ach caithfidh tú a bheith foighneach liom. Nílim go rómhaith chuige. Níl mórán taithí agam air.

Pádraig:	Cailín deas óg agus gan taithí aici ar an rince!
Máire:	Ní ligeann mo mháthair dom dul ar na rincí.
Pádraig:	Eagla atá uirthi roimh na mic tíre.
Máire:	Ní hea… Is amhlaidh… is amhlaidh is dóigh léi go rachaidh mé sna mná rialta.[23]

Pádraig:	Máire Ní Chathasaigh, will you dance with me—or must I get permission from your mother? Or your brother Liam?
Máire:	No, but you'll have to be patient with me. I'm not very good at it. I don't have a lot of practice.
Pádraig:	A nice young girl who doesn't know how to dance!
Máire:	My mother doesn't let me go to dances.
Pádraig:	She's afraid of the wolves.
Máire:	No… It's… It's that she thinks I'm going to join the nuns.

An Triail was originally performed by the Damer theatre company, which, for the majority of the 1960s, enjoyed a period of sustained creativity and relatively high audience numbers.[24] Although the play's immediate and enduring popularity makes it in many ways exceptional, it too can tell us a lot about other works in the urban drama tradition. Thematically and stylistically, for example, it addresses the (inter)national issue of unwed mothers and draws on hyper-realistic stage techniques to engage the audience in its social review. The local and naturalistic are passed over here in favour of the universal and experimental. This scope in subject and ambition in design is in itself one of the lasting legacies of the urban theatre groups, anticipated and continued by major writers such as Seán Ó Tuama in Cork[25] and Alan Titley in Dublin.[26]

The community for which *An Triail* was written is, correspondingly, more diverse than the implied audience of *Gaeltacht* theatre. In 1964 the Damer group was under the aegis of Gael Linn, an organization based in Dublin whose aim is to promote the Irish language nationwide.[27] In that sense, the work is clearly rooted in a metropolitan Irish-speaking community of practice: a conglomerate whose members share a commitment to the language but not necessary the same social or linguistic background. It is important to note that, for its original run, the lead part was played by Conamara writer Caitlín Maude, a point that conveniently highlights the overlap between the two theatre traditions. The other twenty-six members of the cast, however, spoke various dialects variously well, and this linguistic mixture is a hallmark of urban theatre productions in general. Dramas by city troupes such as Aisteoirí Bulfin in Dublin (the Damer group is no longer active) tend to be much more representative of the national Irish-speaking demographic, much more inclusive, than any individual provincial organization. This comes with practical advantages such as increased casting opportunities and the satisfying sense of collaborating on a national project. At the same time, this linguistic diversity is the Achilles heel in many amateur productions, with characters of similar stock sometimes sporting a bizarre range of accents and varieties of grammar and syntax constantly challenging the audience's suspension of disbelief. This is an intrinsic weakness in urban Irish-language theatre. Compounded by low levels of funding and few stable resources, it mitigates against any wide-spread, sustained support for development and effectively relegates much hard work and some genuine talent to the sphere of "pastime" rather than "art".

For all that, *An Triail* is still shown annually in venues around the country and is probably the most frequently staged play ever written in Irish. This is in part down to its germane social message and its clear dialogue. A much more important factor in its longevity, however, is that it has been directed away from its original community of practice—the theatre-going city dwellers of the 1960s—and towards another: Leaving Certificate students in the Irish education system. Although not many works intended for the stage are taken onto the national secondary school reading list, the tailoring of drama to the needs of language learners is the third of the three major engines driving Irish-language theatre. If the two communities of practice discussed above are equally hamstrung by the linguistic limitations of audience and cast, works directed at students and non-speakers are best understood by the strategies they employ to reduce, or bypass altogether, verbal communication on the stage. Uncomfortable a truth as it is, these strategies have been so successful as to make theatre for children and learners the most exciting sector of performance in the Irish language in recent years. The three most important companies are Fíbín, Branar and Moonfish, and it is notable that they are all located in Galway in close proximity to both *Gaeltacht* and city, and run by bilingual staff familiar with folk tradition. Each employs inventive stage techniques to make their work as visual as possible, using puppets and pantomime to great effect. Moonfish in particular perform bilingual shows that monolinguals can easily follow by virtue of context and visual clues. The result is that these troupes can well cater for the whole spectrum of Irish speakers, avoiding the sociolinguistic pitfalls of traditional amateur theatre. In terms of cultural capital and scholarly recognition, however, the price paid for that privilege is quite high: children's theatre is nowhere near as readily accepted into the pantheon as, for example, children's literature. This is evidenced by the fact that, in the first international conference held on Irish-language drama in 2015, no youth productions were included in the tentative canon of works discussed over two days. For the moment, at least, this strand of theatre also looks set to remain in the margins of discourse, yet for very different reasons.

Although the educational theatre groups mentioned above have honed their craft in the absence of a stable target audience, they are not alone in their attempt to circumvent the language problem. Urban and *Gaeltacht* productions have also tried various methods to bridge the potential linguistic gap between actor and spectator, and on this point of production strategy I re-join the two traditions in order to come to some closing remarks on theatre in the Irish language in general.

The marginalization of Irish as a spoken language in largely Anglophone Ireland has meant that, from its very inception in the late nineteenth century, the theatre project has been rolled out in the shadow of the English-language tradition. An initial result of this was a place of significant prestige for translations, particularly translations of English texts, and this is still the case today.[28] This is, of course, not to suggest that theatre groups have not looked further afield—works from Italian, Russian, German, French, Greek, Latin, Norwegian, Danish and Dutch writers have all been performed in Irish.[29] But because all Irish players and producers are also fluent speakers of English, the vast majority of translations since 1960 have come from that language—some 130 out of 182, according to the database of Irish-language theatre.[30] Whether the ratio between composition and translation is avoidable, unhealthy, pragmatic or something else is debatable but, regardless, the idea of accessing Irish-language performances via English is an enduring one. It underlies the fundamental, infuriating problem of boosting attendance; it has also brought forth some ingenious attempts at solution. How popular and successful these attempts become will, I believe, dictate the prevailing aesthetic of Irish-language theatre in the future.

One of the most obvious methods for reconciling the two languages, as has been already mentioned, is the macaronic script. The Moonfish company is perhaps the most creative in this regard, but special mention should be made here of the writers who, like Ó Neachtain's young generation in *Níor Mhaith Linn do Thrioblóid*, give a more realistic portrayal of contemporary speech inside and outside of the *Gaeltacht*. Chief among these is Antaine Ó Flatharta, a prolific playwright from Conamara whose bilingual characters code-switch effortlessly in hybrid worlds often bereft of monolithic cultural networks and monolingual communities.[31] As Máirín Nic Eoin has pointed out, however, Ó Flatharta's work has been criticized for being perhaps too realistic in its dialogue and bilingual scripts of "serious drama" remain relatively uncommon.[32] More recently, the macaronic approach was successfully taken up by Breandán Ó hEaghra in *Gaeilgeoir Deireanach Charna* [The Last Irish Speaker of Carna] and, as the title of the play suggests, the method may well become more accepted in Irish-language theatre as traditional Gaeltacht speech recedes.[33]

A more ambitious approach to bridging the language divide entails a company of actors performing the same play in Irish and in English on alternating nights during a production run. The only writer to have tried this, to my knowledge, is Seán Mac Mathúna whose play *Gadaí Géar na Geamhoíche* or *The Winter Thief* was performed in the Peacock in both languages by the same actors in April 1992. This is unlikely to be tried again any time soon: not only does it place exorbitant demands on the cast but, in a sobering reflection of the comparative status of Irish-language theatre, over a dozen reviews were published on the English version without a single reference to the Irish one.[34]

Finally, there is the increasingly common method of simultaneous translation. This is becoming more and more feasible in well-equipped city theatres, not least when the Irish-language play being performed is a translation of an English work and the original script can be displayed on screen near the stage.

An excellently produced recent example of this is *An Tíoránach Drogallach*, Mac Dara Ó Fátharta's translation of Tom Murphy's *The Last Days of a Reluctant Tyrant*.[35] The cast were mostly native speakers and Ó Fátharta's rendering of Murphy's language was wonderfully dense, so much so that the monitors showing the English were an integral part of the performance for many of the viewers. And yet, however well-intended, this too carries potentially grave consequences for the sustaining essence of Irish-language performance: the speech community around which it is built. To borrow Philip Auslander's term, simultaneous translation has the effect of "mediatising" the live spectacle,[36] of virtualizing the dialogue, distracting the audience from actorly presence and thereby blunting its most powerful artistic tool: the connection of charisma that joins audience and actor in a shared community of practice, a community of language. The more prevalent simultaneous translation becomes, the more difficult it will be to establish the paradox of dramatic intimacy that lies at the heart of the best live performance.

At root, all bilingual strategies are essentially applied theatre techniques directed at solving the founding riddle of Irish-language drama: how to cultivate an engaged, stable—or, at the very least, a predictable—community of practice. Perhaps no one solution will gain enough currency to energize the theatre as much as its practitioners or advocates would hope for. In the meantime, it remains a small art form for a splintered speech community, persevering towards further recognition.

Notes

1. In this chapter I use the terms "theatre in the Irish language" and "Irish-language theatre" to denote scripted and staged plays performed in Irish. Some recent scholarship on the Irish dramatic tradition has broadened the terms of the debate, including traditional forms of performance such as *lúibíní* and *agallaimh beirte*. These are popular forms of dramatic dialogue long practiced in the *Gaeltacht* (the Irish-speaking areas in Ireland) and, although much of the following discussion could be applied to them as well, they fall outside the scope of this chapter. For a study of traditional Irish modes of performance as drama, see Éadaoin Ní Mhuircheartaigh, "Drámaíocht ó Dhúchas? Stáitsiú na nEalaíon Béil san Fhichiú hAois" [Native Drama? Staging of the Oral Arts in the Twentieth Century] (PhD diss., National University of Ireland, Galway, 2013).
2. Alan Titley, "Neither the Boghole nor Berlin: Drama in the Irish Language from Then until Now", in *Players and the Painted Stage*, ed. Christopher Fitz-Simon (Dublin: New Island, 2004), 111–112.
3. See Titley's overview mentioned in the previous note.
4. Philip O'Leary, *Prose Literature of the Gaelic Revival* (Pennsylvania: Pennsylvania State University Press, 1994), 84–88.
5. Máiréad Ní Chinnéide gives an account of The Damer theatre's ultimately unsuccessful attempt at founding and sustaining a professional troupe in *An Damer: Stair Amharclainne* [The Damer: A Theatre's History] (Baile Átha Cliath: Gael Linn, 2008).

6. Máirín Nic Eoin, "Contemporary Prose and Drama in Irish 1940–2000", in *The Cambridge History of Irish Literature*, eds. Margaret Kelleher and Philip O'Leary (Cambridge: Cambridge University Press, 2005), 299.
7. This figure is based on the comprehensive catalogue of *Playography na Gaeilge* [The Irish-Language Playography], http://gaeilge.irishplayography.com, accessed 12 April 2016. The highest numbers were in the 1960s (69) and the Celtic Tiger 2000s (98), with the lowest in the 1980s (41). The 1970s (50), 1990s (50) and, it seems, 2010s (28 as at April 2016) straddle the middle ground.
8. For an overview of the various approaches and theorists that can be gathered under the banner of applied theatre, see Tim Prentki and Shiela Preston, eds., *The Applied Theatre Reader* (London: Routledge, 2009); Monica Prendergast and Juliana Saxton, eds., *Applied Theatre: International Case Studies and Challenges for Practice* (Bristol: Intellect, 2009).
9. Helen Nicholson, *Applied Drama: The Gift of Theatre* (Basingstoke: Palgrave Macmillan, 2014), 60.
10. Penelope Eckert and Sally McConnell-Ginet, "New Generalizations and Explanations in Language and Gender Research", *Language in Society* 28: 2 (1999), 186.
11. Penelope Eckert, "Communities of Practice", in *Encyclopedia of Language & Linguistics*, ed. Keith Brown (Amsterdam: Elsevier, 2006), 683.
12. As evidence of this, see Máirín Breatnach Uí Choileáin's account of the dialogue changes made by native speakers from Conamara when staging a script written in Munster Irish: *Aisteoirí an Spidéil* [The Actors of Spiddal] (Indreabhán: Cló Iar-Chonnacht, 2015), 69–70. Dialect issues are also mentioned *passim* in Ní Chinnéide, *An Damer*.
13. Joe Steve Ó Neachtain, *In Ainm an Athar & Níor Mhaith Linn do Thrioblóid* [In The Name of the Father & We're Sorry for your Trouble] (Indreabhán: Cló Iar-Chonnacht, 2006). It was first staged in An Taibhdhearc theatre in Galway in 2000. It is not common for Irish-language plays to tour in the United States.
14. Ó Neachtain, *Níor Mhaith Linn do Thrioblóid*, 101.
15. All translations here are my own except where otherwise indicated.
16. Ó Neachtain, *Níor Mhaith Linn do Thrioblóid*, 150. The italics are not in the original.
17. The alarming disappearance of traditional Irish speech in the *Gaeltacht* is charted by Conchúr Ó Giollagáin and Martin Charlton, *Nua-Shonrú ar an Staidéar Cuimsitheach Teangeolaíoch ar Úsáid na Gaeilge sa Ghaeltacht: 2006–2011* [An Update on the Comprehensive Linguistic Study on the Use of Irish in the *Gaeltacht*: 2006–2011] (2015), http://www.udaras.ie/media/pdf/002910_Udaras_Nuashonr%C3%BA_FULL_report_A4_FA.pdf, accessed 12 April 2016. See also Feargal Ó Béarra, "Late Modern Irish and the Dynamics of Language Change and Language Death", in *The Celtic Languages in Contact: Papers from the Workshop Within the Framework of the XIII International Congress of Celtic Studies* (2008), ed. Hildegard L.C. Tristram (Potsdam: Potsdam University Press), 260–269. For a representative overview of the linguistic abilities of non-*Gaeltacht* Irish speakers, see John Walsh, Bernadette O'Rourke and Hugh Rowland, eds., *Research Report on New Speakers of Irish* (2015), http://www.gaeilge.ie/wp-content/uploads/2015/10/New-speakers-of-Irish-report.pdf, accessed 12 April 2016.

18. In the *Nua-Shonrú* referenced above, which is the most recent and comprehensive study done to date, Ó Giollagáin and Charlton estimate that in ten years' time Irish will no longer be a sustainable community language in the majority of *Gaeltacht* areas. Anecdotally, it is also worth alluding here to the stage (1996) and film (2007) adaptations of Máirtín Ó Cadhain's novel, *Cré na Cille* (1949). The two productions featured many of the same actors, most of whom were between 45 and 80, and both media commentators and cast remarked that they were the last generations who could do justice to the Irish dialogue in Ó Cadhain's original.
19. See Breathnach Uí Choileáin, *Aisteoirí an Spidéil* for a comprehensive account of plays performed by a long-standing amateur theatre group from Conamara.
20. Máiréad Ní Ghráda, *An Triail* (Baile Átha Cliath: An Gúm, 1978).
21. A succinct account of the play's initial run and reception is in Ní Chinnéide, *An Damer*, 48–49.
22. For an overview of Ní Ghráda's work, see Siobhán Ní Bhrádaigh, *Máiréad Ní Ghráda: Ceannródaí Drámaíochta* (Indreabhán: Cló Iar-Chonnacht, 1996).
23. Ní Ghráda, *An Triail*, 23.
24. See Nic Eoin, "Contemporary Prose and Drama", 300–302 and Ní Chinnéide, *An Damer*, 40–54.
25. Seán Ó Tuama, *Ar Aghaidh Linn a Longadáin* [Off We Go, Longadán] (Indreabhán: Cló Iar-Chonnacht, 1991). It was first staged by the Cork group Compántas Chorcaí in the Damer theatre in 1959.
26. Alan Titley, *Tagann Godot* [Godot Arrives] (Indreabhán: Cló Iar-Chonnacht, 1991). It was first staged in the Peacock in 1990.
27. See Ní Chinnéide, *An Damer*.
28. This effects even the most independent of the *Gaeltacht* theatre companies such as Aisteoirí an Spidéil. In her catalogue of their work Breathnach Uí Choileáin counts seventeen translations in forty-six productions between 1910 and 2015.
29. Between 1926 and 1960 most of these translations were commissioned by the state publishing house called An Gúm; some of these were then staged during our period—see Antain Mag Shamhráin, *Foilseacháin an Ghúim: liosta de na leabhair a d'fhoilsigh an Gúm ó 1926 i leith* [An Gúm's Publications: a list of the books published by an Gúm from 1926 onwards] (Baile Átha Cliath: An Gúm, 1997). For an account of some of the early cultural debates surrounding the translation of plays, see Philip O'Leary, *Gaelic Prose in the Irish Free State 1922–1939* (University Park, PA: Pennsylvania State University Press), 391–395 and 458–503. For a catalogue of all professional and semi-professional productions (but not necessarily publications) of plays translated into Irish, see http://gaeilge.irishplayography.com.
30. *Playography na Gaeilge*, http://gaeilge.irishplayography.com, accessed 12 April 2016.
31. Perhaps Ó Flatharta's most well-known plays are *Gaeilgeoirí* [Irish Speakers] (Indreabhán: Cló Iar-Chonnacht, 1981) and *An Solas Dearg* [The Red Light] (Indreabhán: Cló Iar-Chonnacht, 2002). They were both staged in the Peacock, *Gaeilgeoirí* in 1981 and *An Solas Dearg* in 1995.
32. Nic Eoin, "Contemporary Prose and Drama", 305.
33. Micheál Ó Conghaile, Breandán Ó hEaghra and Caitríona Ní Chonaola, *Jude, Gaeilgeoir Deireanach Charna, Incubus* [Jude, The Last Irish Speaker of Carna,

Incubus] (Indreabhán: Cló Iar-Chonnacht, 2007). Ó hEaghra's play was first staged in the Taibhdhearc in 2005.

34. This point was made by Brian Ó Conchubhair at a conference on Irish-language drama held in Boston College House, Dublin, in February 2016. The author was present and confirmed it; the proceedings of the conference are expected to be published in 2018.
35. The play was first staged in Galway's An Taibhdhearc in 2013 but the translation has not yet been published.
36. Philip Auslander, "Liveness, Mediatization, and Intermedial Performance", *Degrés: Revue de synthèse à orientation sémiologique* 101 (2000): 1–12.

Bibliography

Auslander, Philip. "Liveness, Mediatization, and Intermedial Performance." *Degrés: Revue de synthèse à orientation sémiologique* 101 (2000): 1–12.

Eckert, Penelope and Sally McConnell-Ginet. "New Generalizations and Explanations in Language and Gender Research." *Language in Society* 28:2 (1999): 185–201.

Eckert, Penelope. "Communities of Practice." In *Encyclopedia of Language & Linguistics*, edited by Keith Brown, 683–685. Amsterdam: Elsevier, 2006.

Mag Shamhráin, Antain. *Foilseacháin an Ghúim: liosta de na leabhair a d'fhoilsigh an Gúm ó 1926 i leith.* Baile Átha Cliath: An Gúm, 1997.

Ní Bhrádaigh, Siobhán. *Máiréad Ní Ghráda: Ceannródaí Drámaíochta.* Indreabhán: Cló Iar-Chonnacht, 1996.

Ní Chinnéide, Máiréad. *An Damer: Stair Amharclainne.* Baile Átha Cliath: Gael Linn, 2008.

Ní Ghráda, Máiréad. *An Triail.* Baile Átha Cliath: An Gúm, 1978.

Ní Mhuircheartaigh, Éadaoin. "Drámaíocht ó Dhúchas? Stáitsiú na nEalaíon Béil san Fhichiú hAois." PhD diss., National University of Ireland, Galway, 2013.

Nic Eoin, Máirín. "Contemporary Prose and Drama in Irish 1940–2000." In *The Cambridge History of Irish Literature*, edited by Margaret Kelleher and Philip O'Leary, 270–316. Cambridge: Cambridge University Press, 2005.

Nicholson, Helen. *Applied Drama: The Gift of Theatre.* Basingstoke: Palgrave Macmillan, 2014.

Ó Béarra, Feargal. "Late Modern Irish and the Dynamics of Language Change and Language Death." In *The Celtic Languages in Contact: Papers from the Workshop Within the Framework of the XIII International Congress of Celtic Studies*, edited by Hildegard L.C. Tristram, 260–269. Potsdam: Potsdam University Press, 2008.

Ó Conghaile, Micheál, Breandán Ó Eaghra and Caitríona Ní Chonaola. *Jude, Gaeilgeoir Deireanach Charna, Incubus.* Indreabhán: Cló Iar-Chonnacht, 2007.

Ó Flatharta, Antaine. *Gaeilgeoirí.* Indreabhán: Cló Iar-Chonnacht, 1981.

———. *An Solas Dearg.* Indreabhán: Cló Iar-Chonnacht, 2002.

Ó Giollagáin, Conchúr and Martin Charlton. *Nua-Shonrú ar an Staidéar Cuimsitheach Teangeolaíoch ar Úsáid na Gaeilge sa Ghaeltacht: 2006–2011.* Accessed 12 April 2016. http://www.udaras.ie/media/pdf/002910_Udaras_Nuashonr%C3%BA_FULL_report_A4_FA.pdf.

Ó Neachtain, Joe Steve. *In Ainm an Athar & Níor Mhaith Linn do Thrioblóid.* Indreabhán: Cló Iar-Chonnacht, 2006.

Ó Tuama, Seán. *Ar Aghaidh Linn a Longadáin.* Indreabhán: Cló Iar-Chonnacht, 1991.

O'Leary, Philip. *Prose Literature of the Gaelic Revival*. Pennsylvania: Pennsylvania State University Press, 1994.

Playography na Gaeilge. Accessed 12 April 2016. http://gaeilge.irishplayography.com/.

Prentki, Tim and Shiela Preston, eds. *The Applied Theatre Reader*. London: Routledge, 2009.

Prendergast, Monica and Juliana Saxton, eds. *Applied Theatre: International Case Studies and Challenges for Practice*. Bristol: Intellect, 2009.

Titley, Alan. "Neither the Boghole nor Berlin: Drama in the Irish Language from Then until Now." In *Players and the Painted Stage*, edited by Christopher Fitz-Simon, 111–125. Dublin: New Island, 2004.

———. *Tagann Godot*. Indreabhán: Cló Iar-Chonnacht, 1991.

Walsh, John, Bernadette O'Rourke and Hugh Rowland, eds. *Research Report on New Speakers of Irish*. Accessed 12 April 2016. http://www.gaeilge.ie/wp-content/uploads/2015/10/New-speakers-of-Irish-report.pdf.

Theatre for Young Audiences in Ireland

Tom Maguire

Introduction

This chapter examines the developing sector of Theatre for Young Audiences (TYA) from its roots in educational theatre for children in the 1970s into one of the most innovative and flourishing fields of contemporary theatrical practice across the island of Ireland. As noted in Sara Keating's 2014 article for the *Irish Times*, "Baboró and beyond: Irish kids' theatre comes of age", children's theatre in Ireland has a strong aesthetic identity, dedicated venues and a deep connection with Irish audiences. Today in Ireland, a TYA production may be explicitly local in its engagement with a specific audience yet draw on models of practice that are shared widely internationally, within an aesthetic form the lineage of which owes little to specifically Irish theatrical traditions. Such aesthetic forms might include Theatre in Education (TiE) models that originated in Coventry's Belgrade Theatre; approaches to visual theatre or modes of performance adopted from continental Europe; or texts that have been adapted, translated or imported from any number of contexts and sources. Critical to this international exchange is the function of festivals in Ireland and abroad in showcasing and sharing theatrical practices and issues. Nonetheless, the sector is distinctively organized through separate organizations on each side of the border. In this sense then, this sector of Irish theatre serves to work against any sense of "Irishness" as a globalized commodity and the function of theatre to reflect national rather than local concerns, while simultaneously drawing strength from collaboration across Ireland that make it distinctive.

T. Maguire (✉)
Ulster University, Derry, Northern Ireland
e-mail: tj.maguire@ulster.ac.uk

E. Jordan, E. Weitz (eds.), *The Palgrave Handbook of Contemporary Irish Theatre and Performance*,
https://doi.org/10.1057/978-1-137-58588-2_10

Origins

It is not possible within the scope of this chapter to chart exhaustively the precise origins of a professional sector of theatre for children. Eimear Beardmore suggests examples in Georgian pantomime as precursors, with the annual pantomime season at theatres like Dublin's Gaiety and the founding of the Lambert Puppet Theatre in 1972 providing more recent precedents. The proposition here is that the contemporary field draws on the heritage of three specific companies that were focused, at least initially, on using theatre's power for educational purposes: TEAM Educational Theatre Company in Dublin, Graffiti Theatre Company in Cork and Replay in Belfast. These pioneering companies initiated and established many of the parameters for practices within the sector today and the issues that they have faced remain perennial for contemporary companies.

As Beardmore notes, TEAM was founded after the disbanding of the Young Abbey, Ireland's first TiE company in 1975.[1] In its early days, it was able to avail of ongoing support from the Abbey, so that for example, *Wonder Ponder Time* in December 1975 was directed by Nuala Hayes and Joe Dowling and was produced in association with the Abbey, being staged in its rehearsal room. When Martin Drury took over as artistic director of TEAM in 1981, he sharpened the focus of the company's work by commissioning and developing new work by writers such as Frank McGuinness, Bernard Farrell (both of whom were appointed as writer in residence) and John McArdle. The company published works by these writers in the volume *Three Team Plays* (Drury 1985): these were *Borderlands* (1984) by McGuinness, Farrell's *Then Moses Met Marconi* (1983) and McArdle's *Jacko* (1979). McGuinness would also contribute *Gatherers* in 1985, while McArdle's *Two Houses* was staged in 1984 and remounted in 1987 and 1990. The company mounted two further plays by Farrell: his adaptation from the German of *Max und Milli* by Volker Ludwig as *One, Two, Three, O'Leary* in 1985 and *Because Just Because* in 1986. Drury extended the reach of TEAM's touring to the Midlands, North East and North West of Ireland. Perhaps core to the company's success under him was that he pulled together a core company of actors committed to TiE practice, a number of whom would later be influential in the development of the TYA sector. These included Philip Hardy, artistic director of Barnstorm Theatre Company at the time of writing, and Patrick Sutton, who was to take over as artistic director for TEAM in 1989. Drury himself was to go on to be the founding director of The Ark (1992–2001), Ireland's only arts centre specifically for children. Sutton went on to take up the role of director of the Gaiety School of Acting in 1993.

TEAM's aim was primarily educational in the broadest sense, producing theatre for children and young people that challenged, inspired and met the concerns of its audience. There was an emphasis on providing an authentic experience that would resonate with the lives of its audiences and thereby challenge them to feel, think, interact and do within the dramatic context. This set of ambitions has been one of the legacies of the company to those making theatre for children today. In meeting these aims, TEAM produced both original commissions from playwrights and devized work, annually staging two new tours and running interactive workshops with children, primarily in primary and post-primary schools. TEAM nurtured a number of writers who would go on to write for young audiences or adult theatre. Jim Nolan's *Round and Round the Garden* was mounted in 1981, *Heartstone* in 1986 and *Dear Kenny* in 1988. Amongst other endeavours, he would go on to found Red Kettle Theatre Company producing theatre in Waterford for over thirty years until its closure in 2014. Antoine Ó Flatharta was writer in residence, contributing *Dream Walker* and *The Native Ground* in 1989. Nonetheless, although TEAM by the end of the 1980s was firmly established and had a track record of work with many of Ireland's leading playwrights, the company's activities remained largely unseen by the general public. It was rendered doubly so by almost complete omission from critical accounts of Irish theatre practice, professional reviews and academic analyses of the work produced, a major historiographical obstacle in writing this chapter.

Although TEAM was by then running successfully in Dublin, the inspiration for the founding of the Cork-based Graffiti company in 1984 came from a workshop undertaken by Emelie Fitzgibbon at the Goethe Institute run by a TiE company from Berlin.[2] From its inception, Graffiti's aim was to provide a permanent professional, educational theatre company for Munster (extending later to South Leinster). The materials for its productions came from a number of sources and through different processes. While early work featured pre-existing material from established educational theatre companies, including Duke's Playhouse in Lancaster and the Belgrade TiE Team in Coventry, soon the company was producing scripts from writers in Ireland such as Roger Gregg, including his *Silence in the Ravens* (1985) and later *The Dogs of Chulainn* (1992). A number of early productions were also devized and developed by the company. Some were based on Shakespeare plays, such as *A Modern Othello* (1985) and *Merchant's Club* (1986); while others were issue-based contemporary pieces, such as the 1987 *A World of a Difference*, which focused on the representations of underdeveloped countries in the media. Many of these productions were supplemented by workshops and resource materials, something further developed with the creation of an Outreach Department to offer workshops both to children and as a contribution to teacher education and professional development.

The significance of Graffiti's foundational contribution to TYA as a sector within its first five years was to extend its scope, setting up strands of activity on which later companies would pick up. The first was to make work for early years, initiated in 1984 with *Hospitals*, a TiE programme for nursery schools. The second was to take work out of schools and into both mainstream theatre venues and the streets. It had established the Ivernia Theatre as its home venue by the second year of its existence (Emelie Fitzgibbon was a founder member of The Cork Theatre Company, which had begun leasing the venue in 1982). With *Graffiti in the Gallery* in 1984 it showed its willingness to develop new spaces for performance, providing a TiE programme for 11- to 14-year-olds on attitudes to art in the Crawford Municipal Art Gallery. In 1988, it took to the streets with *It's Not Fair*, which was performed as part of the Dublin Street Carnival, the Cork City Carnival and at the Hammersmith Multicultural Festival in London. A third innovation by Graffiti was a concern with the Irish language; in 1986 it mounted *Teanga*, a play designed to heighten awareness of its importance.

In her article, "Tie Hits Back" for *Theatre Ireland*, Emelie Fitzgibbon calculates that by 1989, TEAM and Graffiti were between them playing to over 130,000 spectators in some twenty counties. Together these two companies had proved that there was a year-round audience for professional theatre for children in Ireland. They had established themselves as part of their immediate communities, but a further aspect also widened the span of their activities. Both companies not only toured to their local schools, but quite early on also began to make links internationally. In 1987 and 1988, Graffiti toured *Circles* to schools in the Poitou-Charentes region of France, and in 1993 toured *Infidel* to the United States as well as remounting *Frog & Toad* as part of the Scottish International Children's Festival. Under Martin Drury, TEAM had already toured to London, representing Ireland twice at the international TiE festival in Stratford East, and Fitzgibbon (1989) noted that the company had also toured to Leeds and to France in the 1980s.

Fitzgibbon notes that this international dimension was consolidated when the two companies came together with Wet Paint to found, the Irish Centre for the Association Internationale du Théâtre de l'Enfance et la Jeunesse (ASSITEJ). However, despite its initial energy, the collaboration was to go into dormancy for several years until it was revived in 2007 as TYA-Ireland. Since then it has served as the national association representing and promoting professional organizations and individual artists whose work primarily focuses on engaging Irish children and young people through theatre. It provides a crucial link between members, the arts sector, the wider community and government, addressing the relative invisibility of the sector and, crucially, fostering the training of its own members and an international dimension to its work. With TYA companies such as Graffiti and Barnstorm also running their own youth theatres, there is a degree of cross-over with the National Association of Youth Drama, which since its founding in 1980 has both supported the development of youth theatre and acted as an advocate for the benefits of the involvement of young people in theatre.

It was in 1988 that the first northern counterpart was added with the founding of Replay Productions in Belfast. Artistic director Brenda Winter had been one of the founding members of Charabanc Theatre Company, a pioneering collective of women making plays for working-class audiences across Northern Ireland. She had initially conceived of the new company as "a kind of Charabanc for schools. In other words, it was to be a group that privileged the language of this place, the culture and history of this place—and brought that work into the schools".[3] Thus, just as with TEAM and Graffiti, a focus on the lived experiences of audiences within a specific geographical locale was a defining characteristic of Replay's work from the outset. This was articulated within its early years through devized work and site-specific performances such as Brenda Winter's *Timetrekker To Tea Lane* (1989) at the Ulster Folk and Transport Museum and *The Normans at Carrick* (1992) at Carrickfergus Castle.

However, the company's first production in 1988 was Marie Jones's *Under Napoleon's Nose*, directed by Ian McElhinney, bringing back together some of the former Charabanc team in a play set in Belfast and revisiting the experience of the Blitz of 1941. In many respects, the production provided a model to which the company was to return repeatedly in charting the relationship between Belfast's history and the present day of its audiences within a dramatic frame. The response to that first production convinced Winter of the demand from schools for high-quality professional theatre. Winter, however, did not see it as a TiE company in the mode of Coventry's Belgrade TiE company; rather, it was to produce theatre for an audience that happened to be in an educational setting.[4] Such a description might not only be applied to much of the work of its two contemporary sister companies, but also indicates a shift from the practices of TiE to those more closely associated with TYA; although within Ireland the distinction between the two fields is far from absolute.

While there are rarely single watershed moments in any cultural practice, one can see that by 1989, the main characteristics of the Irish theatre for children sector had been established, so that it was with some justification that Emelie Fitzgibbon could champion the contribution of TEAM and Graffiti (here extended to Replay, though not in her original) as

> a substantial force within an Irish theatre scene which does not confine itself to received images of performance, audience and space. It is a force which philosophically is not inward looking and which concerns itself with topics, modes and methodologies which are internationally recognized but rooted by the companies' expertise in the audience's own experience.[5]

The Contemporary Sector

From those roots the sector has grown rapidly to become what it is today. Writing, performing or directing theatre for children is no longer an apprenticeship for proper grown-up theatre-making. Although TEAM was wound up in 2013, over the course of its history it nourished a number of writers who would go on to make a significant contribution to the sector. Maeve Ingoldsby had her first play, *Firestone*, produced by the company in 1990, with three further plays staged by TEAM, before going on to spend ten years as writer in residence and then script editor with Barnstorm. Graffiti too has commissioned and engaged with a large number of writers. Raymond Scannell scripted a number of productions for the company, including *Striking Distance* (2001), *A Day in the Life of a Pencil* (2004), *Closed Circuit* (2006) and *Permutations & Palpitations* (2009). Graffiti has also sought to make such work available by publishing playscripts, including Scannell's *A Day in the Life of a Pencil* and *The Lost Ones* by Laurie Brooks, a script for professional production to younger teenagers.

Replay has a similar track record of commissioning a range of new writers and supporting their development through a variety of projects. There have been original commissions of plays from Northern Irish playwrights, including Winter herself. Marie Jones has written six plays for the company, including *It's a Waste of Time, Tracey* (1989), *The Cow, The Ship and The Indian* (1991) and *Hiring Days* (1992). Damian Gorman has contributed four plays, including *Ground Control to Davy Mental* (1992) and *Sometimes* (1998). Other notable Northern Irish writers producing original work for the company include Nicola McCartney and Gary Mitchell.

Both Graffiti and Replay have been eager too to extend the repertoire of work beyond Ireland. Graffiti has commissioned new plays from writers such as Mike Kenny, including *The Lost Child* (2002) and *Cloud Pictures* (2008) (some of which were also produced in Irish translation) and producing existing scripts from other anglophone contexts, including the Canadian Joan MacLeod's *The Shape of a Girl* (2011) and *Hoods* (2014) by Australian playwright Angela Betzien. The company also commissioned an original piece from Betzien, *Where in the World is Frank Sparrow?*, in 2012. Replay too has turned to existing repertoire elsewhere, producing works such as *The Lost Child* by Mike Kenny (1998) and Moira Buffini's *Marianne Dreams* (2012).

Alongside Graffiti and Replay, the range of companies working currently includes Barnstorm Theatre Company, Branar, Cahoots NI, Cups and Crowns, Fíbín, Meitheal na mBeag, Monkeyshine Theatre, Moonfish, Pignut Productions, Púca Puppets, Sticky Fingers and Theatre Lovett. There is scarcely a region or county where children will now not have access to high-quality professional theatre made specifically for them. These companies have each in their own way followed the precedents that TEAM, Graffiti and Replay pioneered. The rest of this chapter, then, will explore how they have maintained a fundamental commitment to local audiences; developed an international perspective; and engaged in cross-sectoral collaboration. I will argue too that these features are most fully expressed in the growth of an additional feature: international festivals of theatre for children.

Performing the Local

The commitment to local audiences within TYA does not just involve returning repeatedly to the same set of schools for audiences (though such relationships are important), but is expressed in a number of other ways. Replay's Brenda Winter notes, for example, parallels between the tastes of audiences for popular political performance advocated by John McGrath and the tastes of the school children in Replay's audiences, including localism of place and identity.[6] Thus, the most straightforward expression of localism is in choosing subject material that engages with and matters to the audience.

One example of an approach to this is Gary Owen's play *Bulletproof* mounted by Replay Productions, then under the directorship of David Fenton, in 2010. The piece was in response to increasing concern in the local media about mental health issues amongst young people; the company's own growing awareness of these issues through their work in secondary schools; and Owen's own experience of suicide by young people in his home town of Bridgend, Wales. These were given sharp focus in a government report on mental health in 2007. Owen interviewed young people in Belfast and used their words and stories to construct an adapted form of Verbatim Theatre, in which real experiences were fictionalized in the mouths of his two central characters, brother and sister Michael and Alex. Using the technique of direct audience narration, the play recounts the events leading up to and the aftermath of Michael's suicide. This use of verbatim and its close references to Belfast provided a compelling sense of authenticity that tied the play to both a specific geographical location and an issue of vital concern to its audiences.

The strongest commitment to a locale is evident where companies have set down roots in running venues specifically for children's theatre. Graffiti now runs its administrative offices, its outreach department, an auditorium and studio space in its premises on Assumption Road in Cork. It also has two attached youth theatres, blurring the lines between theatre *for* and theatre *by* young people. Barnstorm's commitment to its home locale in Kilkenny for over twenty years similarly includes running its own venue, The Barn Theatre, close to the city centre. From that base, the company not only mounts its own productions and outreach activity, but supports its youth theatres, Community Theatre and adult theatre clubs.

The development of The Ark as a specialist, purpose-built cultural centre for pre-teen children might be seen as the boldest initiative in providing a home for theatre for children. When the Irish government was considering how to regenerate the area of Dublin's Temple Bar in 1991, Martin Drury was engaged to conduct a feasibility study for just such a venue. With the support of the city council, national government and European funding, The Ark opened its doors in 1995 as Europe's first custom-designed arts centre for children. It commissions and hosts professional work, activities and workshops across all art forms. It has had notable successes in commissioning theatre work, premiering *The Giant Blue Hand* by Marina Carr, which received a nomination for an *Irish Times* Theatre Award in 2009, for example. In 2010, Louis Lovett was appointed The Ark's first theatre-maker in residence, and *The Girl who Forgot to Sing Badly* was presented by The Ark in association with Theatre Lovett in the spring of 2011 and as part of the Ulster Bank Dublin Theatre Festival, followed by a national tour.

A further dimension of the localism of Ireland's TYA sector is the way in which companies engage in sustained outreach projects with their local communities. One example of this is Barnstorm's engagement with the Townlands Project (2010), a creative exploration of the north Kilkenny landscape within the nine townlands of the old civil parish of Rathcoole. Barnstorm's involvement culminated in a production of *The Spooky Feast in the Scary Field* on 24 June. This was a collaborative project between artist Alan Counihan, Johnswell National School and Barnstorm's Outreach Officer, Anna Galligan, that used material that had been generated by pupils of the school some seventy years previously as the basis of a performance by the contemporary pupils. As documented on Barnstorm's website, the overall aim of the drama strand was to present the local place to local people in a new way. To achieve this each class group worked in a different way. The youngest worked primarily through movement, visuals and group rhymes. They devized around the idea of seasons and what happens to the land throughout the year. The largest group with the widest age range was the first to third class group. Six of the stories taken from the pupils of 1937–38 were chosen to be presented in storytelling form with a narrator and characters speaking the lines; as well as the whole group working to create a story, which they then performed as a chorus.

A more distinctively Irish expression of localism has been in the turn toward the Irish language. In 1999, Graffiti produced its first show *as Gaelige*: *Scéal faoi Bhláth*, which toured to Irish-medium schools and schools in the Munster, Connemara and Donegal Gaeltachts. However, of all the companies that have produced work in the Irish language, it is Galway's Branar Téatar do Pháistí founded by Marc Mac Lochlainn in 2001 that has generated the most sustained output. Its mission statement is "Insíonn muid scéalta móra do shaoránaigh Beaga / We tell big stories to little citizens", neatly summarizing both its ambition and its commitment. As with many of its sister companies, Branar's work is multi-faceted involving professional productions, outreach activities and a commitment to training artists and teachers.

Their productions (one or two new shows opening annually alongside productions in the repertoire) play in schools that may be Irish-medium or where Irish is just part of the broader curriculum. This has had implications for the work, which although performed in the Irish tongue, cannot rely on its audiences having even a basic knowledge of the language. This awareness has prompted experimentation with different visual forms, including object manipulation, mask, commedia dell'arte, physical theatre and puppetry. One benefit of both the company's development of its repertoire of puppet shows and its highly visual performance modes has been the facility to tour the work internationally.

Clann Lir (2010) exemplifies this link between local rootedness in Irish language and culture and the international. A re-telling of the myth of the Children of Lir, the performance uses puppetry and newly composed traditional Irish music by Michael Chang and Freda Nic Giolla Chatháin to create a vividly visual and hauntingly beautiful sonic experience for audiences from six years of age upwards. It was developed initially as a music-led piece but was reworked subsequently to give greater prominence to a poetic text that would match the music and movement of the puppets. As part of the Branar repertoire, it has been remounted in a number of tours across Ireland. In 2012, for example, it was presented at six venues and festivals across Ireland, and was performed internationally for the first time at the Cologne Children's Literature Festival in Germany.

If work in the Irish language represents one way of engaging with the specifics of the local audience, a further way has been the creation of bespoke forms of performance that have extended the understanding both of who the audience of TYA might be, and what might even count as *theatre* for such an audience. Under Anna Newell's artistic directorship, from 2011 to 2016, Replay evolved two new strands of work that saw the company making even more bespoke forms of work for children. *Babble* (2013) was the first in a series of works engaging with babies that included *Tiny* (2014) and culminated in BabyDay in 2015, which saw the staging of over eighty events at more than twenty venues all over Belfast, focusing on families with babies and young children.

A second focus of bespoke theatre-making under Newell was a return to a strand of work that the company had initiated in the 1990s, making work for children with special needs. Projects such as Paul Boyd's *Smelly Won't Behave!* (2001) usually involved bringing a short play into designated special schools and then working as a company-in-residence to make a performance piece with the pupils. Newell reviewed that model and after a period of consultation, the company changed direction to embark on the task of making work for children with profound and multiple learning disabilities that would blend participation and performance, through projects such as *Bliss* (2012), *Closer* (2014) and *Into the Blue* (2015).

Such opening up of the performance process to the participation of the audience as a means of creating bespoke theatre was also developed for more mainstream audiences in *Once Upon a Time*, by performer/illustrator Patrick Sanders and performer Mary Jordan. This interactive piece for 5- to 8-year-olds finds Sanders and Jordan as The Very Trusted and Nearly Excellent Guardians of Tall Tales and Small Stories, who look after a magical library containing all the stories ever made. Following a fire, the guardians have had to reconstruct the library and they have managed to do this with one last exception. Unfortunately, neither of the guardians can remember the details of the story and they enlist the audience to construct it for them. With Jordan engaging the audience through a series of guided questions and suggestions, the mute Sanders communicates by drawing out the suggestions as an extended sequence of cartoons. Once the story has been created and the drawing finished, Jordan is then able to retell it in its completeness. While the process for this work is fundamentally the same, the outcome is a bespoke performance for the particular audience in that place and time: a uniquely local production.

An International Perspective

While in the previous section I emphasized the ways in which TYA in Ireland is resolutely local, such localism is informed by and engages with practices drawn from other countries and theatre cultures in a way that has been largely resisted by mainstream theatrical and dramatic practice in Ireland. This internationalism has had several effects: it has informed the choice of dramatic repertoire;

collaborations with artists from other countries and contexts have led to the adoption of models of practice from other theatrical cultures; and the engagement with audiences outside of Ireland through touring and appearances at festivals and events in other countries has developed the confidence and expertise of Irish TYA makers.

As discussed earlier, each of the pioneering companies turned to works or writers from outside Ireland to develop their repertoire. In some instances, this has produced longer-term relationships that mean companies repeatedly commission the same writer or produce their work. Thus, Barnstorm has staged a range of works by Mike Kenny including *Big Sister, Little Brother* (2008), *Boy with a Suitcase* (2009), *The Song from the Sea* (2011) and *Ice Child* (2014). It has also collaborated with Sarah Argent from Welsh company Theatr Iolo to write *The Bockety World of Henry & Bucket* (2013) and *Me Too!* (2015), for example. CAHOOTS NI has a similar track record of working with Charles Way, staging his *A Spell of Cold War* (2012) and *Nivelli's War* (2013) and commissioning *The Gift* (2015).

A more significant aspect of internationalism is that is has enabled companies to collaborate directly with artists from other countries and contexts. In 2009, Marc Mac Lochlainn invited Bjarne Sandborg of Denmark's Teater Refleksion to work through an extended rehearsal period for *An Seanfhear Beag*, itself an adaptation of *The Story of the Little Old Man* by Swedish writer Barbro Lindgren (a staple source for TYA performances in continental Europe). This collaboration was picked up again in the 2012 production of *Croí á Mhúscailt*, a version of the book *The Heart and the Bottle* by Oliver Jeffers for children between 7 and 12 years old. Again using custom-made wooden puppets, it was co-directed by Mac Lochlainn and Sandborg. The project deepened the collaboration, since the Branar company worked with Teater Refleksion for a week in Denmark, opening the show for a short run of four performances in Aarhus, before a ten-venue tour in Ireland. A third collaboration between Branar and Teater Refleksion, again involving an adaptation of a book by Jeffers, *The Way Back Home*, premiered at the Dublin Theatre Festival in 2014. The designer for the production was Teater Refleksion's Mariann Agaard. Such collaborations have developed the practice of Branar as the Irish host company in the field of puppetry as well as broadening its visual aesthetic. They have also encouraged and supported the company's confidence in undertaking collaborations with other Irish artists, both working within theatre and in other art forms. So, for example, for the 2014 adaptation of John Light's book *The Flower*, produced as *Bláth*, the company commissioned paper artist Maeve Clancy to design and build the paper set and Colm Mac Con Iomaire of the pop group The Frames to compose the original score.

A similar example of collaboration can be seen in the process by which Sligo-based Monkeyshine developed its original show *Losha* in 2011. The show was created over a year as part of the theatre-maker in residence scheme with Roscommon Arts Centre and Roscommon County Council. Under a mentoring scheme through which young Irish groups were paired with established companies in other countries, the artistic director of Baboró, Lali Morris, arranged for Kareen Pennefather and James Jobson of Monkeyshine Theatre to be mentored by Charlot Lemonine of the acclaimed French company Theatre Vélo. *Losha* is the story of an unusual creature who collects other people's forgotten moments. She finds them stuck in a variety of discarded objects, which she gathers during the night. A lost shoe holds a love story, a birthday candle still holds the wish that blew it out and a soft toy is filled with forgotten fears of the dark. The influence of Theatre Vélo's long history of creating performances where actors interact with objects to create images, using few or no words, is evident in what has become a signature piece for Monkeyshine.

Irish TYA has further benefitted from its engagement with audiences in other cultures and contexts through touring and appearances at festivals. Most straightforwardly, this has involved extending tours to other parts of the British Isles to take in festivals and events, such as when Barnstorm's *Boy with a Suitcase* toured to the Opening Doors International Festival in Wales in 2010, or following its original runs of *The Bockety World of Henry & Bucket* with stagings at the Imaginate Festival in Edinburgh and then a tour across the UK in 2015. Similarly, The Ark/Theatre Lovett's *The Girl who Forgot to Sing Badly* toured to Scotland as part of The Bank of Scotland Imaginate Festival in May 2011. Companies have also taken up invitations further afield, such as when TEAM's *Devotion* by Leo Butler toured to South Africa in September 2010 or when Fíbín travelled to Malawi to perform *An Rón Dall* and conduct puppeteering workshops with the local children in March 2011.

Perhaps unsurprisingly, the TYA sector of the United States has also provided opportunities for Irish TYA artists to engage internationally. New Visions, New Voices at the Kennedy Centre, Washington DC is a biennial national festival for plays-in-progress that has supported the development of projects by Irish theatre-makers. In 2014, the festival invited Graffiti to bring *Gile na Gealaí* and CAHOOTS NI *The Gift* as part of the development of each of these new works. The United States has also become a more feasible option for the touring of Irish TYA work. In 2013, Replay remounted its co-production with Assault Events of *Wobble* for five days at the Irish Arts Center in New York, alongside workshops and seminars. It followed this, in 2015, with a remount of another of its shows for babies, *Babble*, at the New Victory Theatre on New York's 42nd Street for a run of seventeen performances. In 2016, CAHOOTS NI undertook a sixteen-venue tour of the States with its production *Egg*.

Such internationalism has been championed too by the involvement of both TYA-Ireland and TYA-Northern Ireland (a constituent member of TYA-UK) with the work of ASSITEJ. Representatives attend the organization's congress, interim events, artistic gatherings and festivals. They contribute too to its organization and policy development, as well as participating in its networks such as Small Size, for example. In collaboration with TYA-UK, the Irish organizations won the right to stage *On the Edge*, a week-long programme of showcase performances, seminars and workshops as an ASSITEJ Artistic Gathering in Birmingham in 2016.

Festivals

One of the key developments in the sector in Ireland that has supported both this international exchange and the consolidation of the cross-sectoral collaboration that is distinctive about TYA in Ireland has been the creation of festivals across the country. Although TEAM had participated in the Dublin Theatre Fringe from its early days, it was Graffiti that led the development of festivals for children with its ACTIVATE Festival in 1992 in conjunction with the Everyman Theatre in Cork. From this precedent have grown festivals across the country. Since then children's arts festivals have sprung up across the country, including Roscommon Arts Centre's *Lollipops*, a programme of events for children and young people; Castlebar's RoolaBoola Children's Arts Festival; the Sticky Fingers Festival in Newry; and Hullabaloo! in Offaly. October 1997 saw the first festival in Galway, Baboró, now one of the biggest festivals in the country. Initially an off-shoot of the Galway Arts Festival, under the fourteen-year leadership of Lali Morris it established an international reputation when it became a stand-alone event, attracting children's artists, dramatists and educationalists from all over the world. A similar trajectory can be seen in Young at Art's annual Belfast Children's Festival under the leadership of Ali Fitzgibbon, who took over the role in 2003 after six years as the producer at Replay, stepping down in 2016. From programming theatre performances, she also expanded the experience of performance for its audiences, including through transforming the large-scale space of the Waterworks park in North Belfast as Festival Goes to the Waterworks (2008 and 2010) and creating the world's first Baby Rave in 2005.

Such festivals not only showcase the best of Irish TYA, but also open up the field for both artists and audiences to the influence and example of the best of work from across the globe. Thus, for example, Belfast Children's Festival has programmed work by La Baracca, Italy; Compagnia RODISIO, Italy; Daniel Morden and Oli Wilson-Dickson, Wales; Erfreuliches Theatrefurt, Germany; Het Filiaal, The Netherlands and Junges Ensemble, Germany. A further effect of such festivals is to provide a focused and concentrated opportunity for audiences to see work of the highest quality. As Hautpfleisch notes, "[t]he arguments for the festivalization of culture in the world today … seem to suggest that the arts festival circuit may actually in some cases have come to represent the theatrical 'season' in certain countries".[7] Collaborating with other festivals across both Ireland and the whole of the United Kingdom has also made it possible in some cases to combine costs and make tours viable.

Conclusions

In this chapter, I have charted the development of TYA on what might appear to be an untroubled linear path to success. Each and every artist and company has nonetheless faced different challenges and obstacles that have conditioned the work, including the inevitable processes of applying for and securing funding from private sponsors, public agencies and third-sector partners. That they have managed to shape a sector of practice the quality of which is recognized internationally within these conditions is praiseworthy. Yet its significance is much more than that: this sector has expanded the conception of what constitutes Irish theatre. Rather than focusing on specific dramatic tropes or thematic concerns that might hitherto have been regarded as distinctively or uniquely Irish, or returning to the lineage of Irish literary theatre, TYA has embraced a diverse range of forms of expression, topics and modes of practice, reaching a wide range of audiences, across the country (and abroad) and across a wide social demographic. Its internationalism has engaged with and mirrored the fracturing of hitherto dominant conceptions of a homogeneous Irish identity in the last twenty years in particular. By doing so while retaining a commitment to its specific audiences, it has simultaneously brought the global to the local, recognizing and validating the lives and experiences of its spectators as important; a counter-narrative to the sense within mass media that the universal is elsewhere. Yet, these achievements remain obscured in Irish theatre history and historiography. Few scripts are published and even fewer studied in formal educational settings, despite a substantial legacy of new writing. By comparison with other sectors, there is little formal training at higher-level education institutions. TYA may have come of age, but it remains a hidden gem.

Notes

1. Eimear Beardmore, "And the Adults Came Too! Dublin Theatre Festival and the Development of Irish Children's Theatre", in *'That Was Us': Contemporary Irish Theatre and Performance*, ed. Fintan Walsh (London: Oberon, 2013).
2. Aidan Harman, "Graffiti", *Theatre Ireland* 23 (1990): 37.
3. Brenda Winter, "Brenda Winter interviewed by Eugene McNulty", in *The Theatre of Marie Jones*, ed. Eugene McNulty and Tom Maguire (Dublin: Carysfort Press, 2015), 68.
4. Ibid., 69.
5. Emelie Fitzgibbon, "TiE Hits Back", *Theatre Ireland* 19 (1989): 17.
6. Winter, "Brenda Winter interviewed by Eugene McNulty", 69.
7. Temple Hauptfleisch, "Festivals as Eventifying Systems" in *Festivalising! Theatrical Events, Politics and Culture*, ed. Temple Hauptfleisch et al. (Amsterdam and New York: Rodopi, 2007), 39.

Bibliography

Beardmore, Eimear. "And the Adults Came Too! Dublin Theatre Festival and the Development of Irish Children's Theatre." In *'That Was Us': Contemporary Irish Theatre and Performance*, edited by Fintan Walsh, 115–29. London: Oberon, 2013.

Coyle, Jane. "TiE." *Theatre Ireland* 18 (1989): 13–14.

Cremona, Vicki Ann. "Introduction—The Festivalising Process." In *Festivalising! Theatrical Events, Politics and Culture*, edited by Temple Hauptfleisch et al., 5–16. Amsterdam and New York: Rodopi, 2007.

Drury, Martin. *Three Team Plays*. Dublin: Wolfhound Press, 1985.
Egan, Eliz. *Voices from The Glen: A Research Report by Graffiti Theatre Company*. 2013. http://graffiti.ie/wp-content/uploads/2013/08/Voice-From-The-Glen-A-Research-Project.pdf. Accessed March 18, 2016.
Fitzgibbon, Emelie. "TiE Hits Back." *Theatre Ireland* 19 (1989): 16–18.
Harman, Aidan. "Graffiti." *Theatre Ireland* 23 (1990): 36–37.
Hauptfleisch, Temple. "Festivals as Eventifying Systems." In *Festivalising! Theatrical Events, Politics and Culture*, edited by Temple Hauptfleisch et al., 39–47. Amsterdam and New York: Rodopi, 2007.
TYA Ireland. *TYA Ireland Newsletter*. 2011. http://www.barnstorm.ie/assitej.php
TYA Northern Ireland. *Theatre for Young Audiences Northern Ireland*. 2011. http://tya-uk.org/norther-ireland/
Walsh, Fintan. "Child's Play: Making Theatre for Young Audiences." *Irish Theatre Magazine*, 2009.
Winter, Brenda. "Brenda Winter Interviewed by Eugene McNulty." In *The Theatre of Marie Jones*, edited by Eugene McNulty and Tom Maguire, 63–70. Dublin: Carysfort Press, 2015.

Performance in the Community: Amateur Drama and Community Theatre

Elizabeth Howard

Writing about the patterns of theatre-related activity that emerged in Britain during the earlier part of the twentieth century, theatre historian Claire Cochrane contends, "amateur theatre has represented a major experience of performance for a significant proportion of the population".[1] Amateur drama allowed local British communities to perform together and become involved in making theatre.

The Irish experience was similar to the British situation Cochrane describes, as before the 1980s most theatre available to regional and rural Irish communities came from amateur groups. Work that was made in the community by local amateur drama groups was rooted in and influenced by that particular place, if only because of the involvement of local people and the wider effects that their gathering had on the community. However, despite the growth of amateur theatre activity during the twentieth century and its position as a community-based cultural phenomenon, to date it has remained on the periphery of academic interest. Cochrane attributes the lack of interest in amateur drama as being a "consequence of advanced capitalism" which puts "an increasing emphasis on professionalism in all sectors of society".[2] Nonetheless, the amateur drama movement remains a rich source of local and national cultural expression, making it worthy of scholarly attention.

Community theatre, a trend in theatre that emerged during the late 1960s and throughout the 1970s, has also received a shortage of attention from Irish scholars. Community theatre is often used as a tool for social development and encourages the exploration of issues such as gender equality, human rights,

E. Howard (✉)
Waterford Institute of Technology, Waterford, Ireland

E. Jordan, E. Weitz (eds.), *The Palgrave Handbook of Contemporary Irish Theatre and Performance*,
https://doi.org/10.1057/978-1-137-58588-2_11

environmental concerns and democracy. Like amateur theatre, community theatre is made by, with and for particular communities. Communities occur when a certain group of people comes together because those people have something in common, and for this reason community theatre can be practiced in many different settings such as prisons, care homes, addiction centres, social clubs and schools. The leader of the theatre project is often an individual or a group of full-time professional artists, although the community itself sometimes leads the project. Community theatre is often process-based, meaning that the experience of creating the work is seen to be more beneficial to those involved than the effect the end product has on an audience. This process can mean that new texts are generated by the group that relate directly to the concerns of the community, although sometimes established texts are used to explore emotions and situations. For example, the American group Shakespeare Behind Bars exclusively uses the texts of Shakespeare to assist incarcerated juveniles to understand and express the emotions that led to their imprisonment and develop life skills to reintegrate into society.

The process-focused element of community theatre differs from amateur drama in that the latter is mainly product-oriented: rehearsals are set for a number of people who prepare work, often from established texts, which becomes valued by the artistic experience it offers an audience. It can be argued that this process still has beneficial effects for those involved. For example, amateur drama inspires a coming together of communities that is based in a mutual form of expression, and can, for instance, facilitate group healing after a shared tragedy such as civil war. Indeed, the amateur drama movement flourished in Ireland in the decades after the Irish War of Independence. This war was a national experience that fractured local communities, but amateur drama offered a cultural outlet for these communities to express the commonality of their humanity. Thus, although community drama has developed as a theatrical form that can facilitate social rehabilitation, reconstruction and political activism, amateur drama has the ability to achieve similar results. Amateur drama practitioners tend to be seen as non-professional hobbyist artists, while community theatre workers are seen to use the artistic process to develop social capital.

Yet both community theatre and amateur drama are frequently sidelined in artistic and scholarly circles due to being classed outside what community theatre scholar Eugene van Erven calls "legitimate arts milieux".[3] The end products of these grass-roots theatres are often regarded as inferior to the socially constructed forms that shape recognized artistic tastes, like high-art products, commercial mainstream performances, or avant-garde work. However, as Cochrane argues above, amateur drama has provided a way for many people to participate in theatre practice, and community theatre has offered the same. These acts of social and political expression provide insights into waves of cultural interests and enable the performance of identities.

This chapter aims to outline the development of the Irish amateur drama movement alongside the later advancements of community theatre. Considering the cultural impact of these theatres on the ways in which local and national identities are formed and expressed, the chapter also explores how the practice of community theatres was representative of the wider sociopolitical and sociocultural climates within which they performed and developed.

Amateur Drama's Beginnings

Plotting the history of amateur drama in Irish society, theatre historian Christopher Morash highlights the emergence of amateur theatre performances in aristocratic circles during the 1700s, but states that amateur drama really took hold in Irish society during the last years of the 1800s, when commemorations of the 1798 Rebellion took place and land reform was introduced. In the run-up to 1916 most of these organizations had evolved into political groups, and had completely disappeared by 1920. Yet in the years after Independence during the 1920s and 1930s, there was a sharp rise in the number of operational amateur dramatic associations, and by 1932 there were enough amateur companies around Ireland to form a national Amateur Dramatic Association.[4]

In areas where there were clusters of companies, competitive amateur drama festivals emerged, and by 1946 there was a network of thirteen festivals throughout the island. The Bundoran, Enniskillen, Sligo, Tubercurry and Cavan festivals provided the northwest with an active theatre infrastructure, while the Killarney festival provided the southwest region with the same function. Other festivals included Belfast, Dundalk, Dublin, Bray, New Ross, Waterford and Limerick, which were towns on the established professional theatre touring routes.[5] Thus, amateur theatre flourished in areas where there was a notable lack of professional theatre activity, and in towns that enjoyed regular visits from professional touring companies. This suggests that while a lack of professional theatre may have been one reason for the development of these groups, another, more fundamental reason relating to the development of cultural identity inspired people to join in the making of such work.

Positioning the post-Independence developments in amateur drama as a reflection of a recalibration of community identity after a period of political unrest, Morash states that some people "turned to the Gaelic Athletic Association, some to lay religious confraternities [...] but others were forming amateur theatre companies".[6] After the civil war, national and local identities were formed and reformed through the performance of community activities, such as sport, religion and theatre. Performance theorist Baz Kershaw argues that the idea of communal identity can be the "conceptual lynch-pin which links the experience (and action) of individuals—including that of performance—to major historical changes in society".[7] Thus, the creation of strong community associations and identities allows individuals to cope with and support major historical societal changes. The grass-roots nature of the amateur drama movement called for a gathering of local people at which they could express and release the tensions that surrounded the articulation of post-war and post-colonial identities. Interestingly, similar motivations for the creation of post-colonial cultural identities at a national level were behind the original work of Ireland's National Theatre, the Abbey, during previous decades. The development of the amateur drama movement in post-Independence Ireland can therefore be seen as a quest to establish communal cultural identities at a local level, which were filtered down from the theatrical influences and concerns of national identity formation projected by the Abbey.

Arts Council Funding

One year after the first Arts Act was passed in 1951, a new Tourist Traffic Act was implemented, and what was formerly known as the Irish Tourism Association was renamed An Bord Fáilte. In April 1953 An Bord Fáilte created a national cultural festival entitled An Tóstal (The Gathering) which celebrated Irish culture and took place in various locations around the country. An Tóstal was specifically targeted at the diaspora and aimed to draw people to Ireland during the Easter off-season. Building on the theatre infrastructure provided by the established network of regional amateur drama festivals, the An Tóstal organizing committee decided that an all-Ireland amateur drama festival would be an appropriate event to promote. Due to its Midlands location and the amenity that was the Sportex Hall, Cecil Ffrench-Salkeld, the cultural director of An Tóstal, chose Athlone as the town that would host the all-Ireland amateur drama festival.[8] While offering a central focus to the national amateur drama scene, this festival was promoted as a cultural tourism pursuit, encouraging increased spending on travel and accommodation, and contributing to national economic development.

Notably, the Arts Council funded the first festival with IEP £500 and between 1953 and 1960 the Council granted the Athlone Festival a total of IEP £7287. An amount of IEP £3154 went directly to the Amateur Drama Council of Ireland (ADCI), a thirty-two county organization which was founded in 1954, and separate funding was granted to construct a purpose-built theatre called the Dean Crowe Memorial Hall which opened in 1959.[9]

Arts Council involvement in the Athlone Festival not only demonstrated the co-operation between the offices of government to invest in the Festival as a tourist attraction, but was also a way for the Council to fulfil its functions as outlined in the Arts Act, 1951, to

> (a) stimulate public interest in the arts; (b) promote the knowledge, appreciation and practice of the arts; (c) assist in improving the standards of the arts; (d) organise or assist in the organising of exhibitions (within or without the State) of works of art and artistic craftsmanship.[10]

Arts Council assistance encouraged the Athlone Festival to develop, while the event itself drew public attention to theatre as an art form. The Festival's competitive nature stimulated a more critical engagement with theatre, resulting in an inevitable rise in standards. Therefore, public investment in the All-Ireland

Festival allowed the amateur drama movement to advance, and enabled the Council to facilitate and shape the activity of the amateur theatre-maker to the country's economic advantage.

The Quest for High Standards

At the close of the 1960 Athlone Festival a meeting was held by the Arts Council during which Council secretary Mervyn Wall stated:

> There are something like seven hundred amateur drama societies in Ireland and it is obvious to everyone that the amateur drama movement has been very successful. I suggest therefore that the time may have come for the amateur drama movement throughout the country to become self-supporting and not seek further assistance from public funds.[11]

Unsurprisingly, Wall's statement echoed an alteration in the Arts Council's standing order which occurred that year. When formulated in 1957, the standing order read "future policy, while not failing to encourage local enterprise, would insist on high standards", but it was changed in 1960 to read "the Council's main function is to maintain and encourage high standards in the arts".[12] The revised version went on to state that future applications from a number of categories which were not considered to be fine or applied arts would be refused. "Amateur dramatic activity other than courses for producers, actors and playwrights, and by way of assistance towards lighting" was one of the categories facing exclusion.[13] The Council argued that the excluded categories were practiced for enjoyment rather than offering audiences an accomplished form of artistic expression and aesthetic satisfaction, which meant that they were of less monetary value to the nation and required less investment. This tenet of the Council's new standing order meant that the work of the professional would be prioritized because of the associated presumption that the professional would produce higher standards of work than the amateur—hence, the subsequent withdrawal of public funding from the Athlone Festival.

Conversations around standards in the arts featured heavily in cultural policy papers over the following decades due to the manifestos put forward by the Arts Council. The amateur drama movement reflected these conversations and the divisions which shaped the movement's structures often arose from concerns relating to production standards. When the first Athlone Festival was launched, the programme consisted of thirty plays, and there were three competitive categories: Three-Act Plays, One-Act Plays and Verse. Both the Three-Act and One-Act categories had two further divisions, named "Open" and "Rural". Work that was considered to be more advanced technically was entered into the Open category, while the Rural category, also known as the Confined category, was judged more leniently. The Open category was predominantly associated with drama groups from urban locations because it was presumed that these groups would display higher standards due to having a greater population to choose from and a higher chance of seeing professional theatre on a regular basis than those from rural areas.[14] Following this logic it was thought that groups from rural areas would make work that was less technically competent than those in urban areas, and the festival was divided accordingly.

After the announcement of the Arts Council's withdrawal of sponsorship from the Athlone Festival in 1960, the Rural category was removed from the competition and another festival in Loughrea was created to accommodate those groups that wished to enter at this level. The creation of the Loughrea Festival sidelined the groups that were felt to display more modest standards, and this move reflected wider government policies that placed less value on those sections of artistic practice considered to exhibit less accomplished technical standards.

Commenting on the Athlone Festival in 1962, the *Irish Times* theatre critic David Nowlan lamented the loss of the Rural groups, stating that they were "like football teams travelling with all their supporters" and created much of the "atmosphere" of the festival.[15] Nowlan's observation relates to the idea of a practiced collective identity put forward by cultural theorist Stuart Hall. Hall argues that "identification is constructed on the back of a recognition of some common origin or shared characteristics with another person or group, or with an ideal, and with the natural closure of solidarity and allegiance established on this foundation".[16] Supporting something local is a demonstration of allegiance that is built on a common identity related to place; the drama group acts as a catalyst that can bring a community together for the shared cause of following their local drama group to the All-Ireland finals.

Nowlan goes on to say that it was not just the Rural groups that had this sort of dedicated local support, because even though the Rural groups were removed from Athlone it was still evident that the groups in the Open finals went there largely to "[represent] their respective towns rather than [present] plays for the audiences' entertainment". However, while Nowlan's statement suggests that preoccupation with representing a local community may take away from concern with technical proficiency, he argues that "during the last week or so in Athlone we have been watching settings, lighting and make-up infinitely better than anything that could have been thought of even ten years ago".[17]

An attempt to raise standards in amateur drama was made in 1966 with the establishment of a new representative body called the Amateur Drama League (ADL). In April 1967, at the first congress of the ADL, the aims and purposes of the organization were outlined as follows:

> To improve standards of acting, production and stage presentation among its member groups [...] To hold a residential top quality drama course for affiliated members and to found a library for the use of its members [...] To hold writer courses in rural areas and to improve communication between groups.[18]

Various winter weekend training courses were initiated in areas around the country, and Gormanston Summer School in County Meath became a regular event on the amateur drama calendar. This was a week-long training course for which professional theatre workers were employed to give classes in different aspects of stagecraft. Additionally, a central collection of books and plays intended to increase members' knowledge of theatre was created and continually expanded upon. Attempts to raise standards by bringing people together non-competitively instigated further acts of community, as the ADL provided a greater programme of activities and resources through which its groups could be represented beyond their locality. However, the creation of the ADL caused a split between the national network of amateur groups, as some continued to belong to the Amateur Drama Council of Ireland.

Further Divisions

Initially, both the Rural and Open categories in the One-Act and Three-Act Festivals were held under the aegis of the Amateur Drama Council of Ireland. However, during the late 1960s tensions grew between the ADL and the ADCI due to the ongoing problems with access, technical inefficiency and poor catering experienced at the Loughrea Festival during the Rural finals.[19] In order to ease the pressure on the Loughrea and Athlone festivals, in 1969 the One-Act and Three-Act circuits became separate, and different festivals began to take place for each, with both the Open and Rural categories for the All-Ireland One Act Festival held at one event in Naas. However, the stated problems at Loughrea continued to cause distress.

The tensions between the ADL and the ADCI led to further disputes during the 1970s about adjudicators and perceived favouritism at festivals, and the lack of agency awarded to the ADL. At the time, the ADL represented between ninety and one hundred groups nationwide, and 85% of the seventy-four festival-going groups. In 1979 seven of the ten groups that qualified for the All-Ireland Festival in Loughrea voted to hold the Rural finals in Sligo, while the three remaining groups refused to join them and stayed in Loughrea.[20]

In late 1979 a meeting was held in Athlone in an attempt to prevent a permanent split between the ADL and the ADCI. It was proposed that bi-annual meetings should be held between both organizations to establish areas of common interest, and create a joint committee of four to six representatives from each side. However, the ADL refused to accept Loughrea as the venue for the 1980 Rural finals and the ADCI was not willing for the location to change.[21] Because of the inability to agree, it was decided to bring in a neutral party to the next meeting in the hope of resolution.

Another meeting was held in January 1980 chaired by Arthur Lappin of the Arts Council, who represented a neutral party through whom negotiations could be made. At this meeting, it was agreed that the Rural finals for 1980 would be held in Loughrea, but in the name of fairness and equal representation, the overall directorate for the festival would consist of a member of the ADL, a member of the ADCI and Arthur Lappin. The directorate was to "operate in conjunction with the Festival Committee in Loughrea and [the] committee

[was] responsible to the directorate". Arrangements were made to accommodate the access and technical requirements of all groups, and the local women's committee undertook to ensure that there would be "no cause for complaint" with catering.[22] In subsequent years, Loughrea ceased to be the regular venue for the Three-Act Rural finals, and instead, the event rotated around the provinces on an annual basis.

Tensions between the ADL and the ADCI were eased further in 1981 when the two groups formed a joint committee known as the "6 & 6" to steer the direction of the One-Act Festivals. That year, the One-Act finals moved from Naas and began to change venue on an annual basis. The One-Act finals took place over a long weekend in December as opposed to the twelve nights of the Athlone Festival. This was because the short length of the plays meant that more could be seen in a shorter time.

In his history of British theatre, Simon Trussler attributes the continued popularity of the one-act play in the twentieth century to its proliferation in amateur theatre circles. He states that its short length could offer more prospects of engaging in the form for those with limited rehearsal time or groups with "the need to offer as many acting opportunities as possible to their members through double- or triple-bills".[23] Thus, the one-act play circuit was developed due to the nature of the life of the amateur theatre maker, for whom time away from work for which money was earned may have been limited. Additionally, the one-act play could provide a more democratic structure to groups in that a double or triple bill made roles and duties more plentiful and less time-consuming.

North–South Connections

The Association of Ulster Drama Festivals (AUDF) was founded in 1949, and there has been consistent cross-border co-operation between festivals since their inception during the 1920s and 1930s, suggesting that no "hard border" exists in the operational structure of the amateur drama circuits. Since 1953 a three-act festival entitled the Ulster Drama Festival has been held annually in Northern Ireland that brings together groups from north and south of the border, and this remains the main remit of the AUDF organizing committee. Its Northern Ireland One-Act Festival began in 1959, and ran intermittently until 1974, when it began to take place on an annual basis. This festival is organized by the AUDF, but some regional Northern Irish festivals are affiliated to both the AUDF and the ADCI, and Northern Irish groups can be affiliated with the ADCI, the ADL and the AUDF.

Claire Cochrane postulates that in Northern Ireland during the 1970s the violent conditions made it unfavourable for professional theatre to occur systematically, and it was the amateur movement that helped to sustain theatrical activity.[24] However, when sectarian tensions escalated in Northern Ireland in the late 1960s the amateur drama scene there was not immune to the suffering. Because of the ongoing risks of violence the Newry and Carrickmore festivals were cancelled in 1973 and 1974. Keeping the cross-border communication open, in 1974 a non-competitive reciprocal arrangement was made between the ADCI and the AUDF, whereby a Northern Irish group would present a play at the Athlone Festival and a group from the Republic would present at the Northern Ireland Festival in Ballymena.[25] Both the British prime minister and the Irish taoiseach wrote letters that congratulated and approved of the exchange, because it showed how the act of bringing people together can transcend the wars that tear communities apart. Amateur drama became a symbol of solidarity and togetherness in a climate of political violence. Furthermore, continued cross-border policies between the three main amateur drama organizations on the island can be seen to be symbolic of the wider sociopolitical efforts towards peace in Northern Ireland.

Changes to Public Funding Structures

Soon after Ireland officially joined the European Economic Community (EEC) in 1972, the first social action programme of the EEC was established, whereby recommended social standards of living and working for school leavers, women and the elderly were implemented across member states, and initiatives to combat poverty aimed to create more job opportunities and improve economic development within poorer areas.[26] These initiatives filtered into the various sectors of society and the general cultural push was for inclusivity with a focus on strong economic development.

Inclusivity in the arts became a popular "anti-establishment" agenda during the 1960s with the rise of cultural democracy and the wide spectrum of political activism that occurred. According to Eugene van Erven, various forms of "counter-cultural, radical, anti- and post-colonial, educational, and liberational theatres" appeared across the United States, Africa, Australia, Asia and Britain, influenced by the "improvisation-based collectively oriented community theatre", such as that based on the work of Augusto Boal, which emerged in South America at that time.[27] These theatres were part of the overall community arts movement and formed the nucleus of the global community theatre movement as we know it.

Following in the footsteps of the worldwide community arts trend, the Dublin art world revolted and Project 67, later to become the Project Arts Centre, was established in the city centre area of Temple Bar in 1967. The Project accused the Dublin art world of "class bigotry, racial prejudice and pernicious art snobbery", and in an attempt to rectify this, the Project's stated aim was "to allow ideas to interact freely between artists and their public who have become separated from the arts".[28] This aim positioned the Project as an entity that would make art for and with culturally disenfranchised communities, and a wave of community theatre practice in Ireland emerged.

One year after Ireland officially joined the EEC, the government passed the 1973 Arts Act. The new Act empowered local authorities to make funding decisions which contributed to the development of arts activity at grass-roots level and in regional areas. Regional development was on the EEC's agenda, and cultural activity was seen as a way in which opportunities for social and economic advancement could be created. Even with the new Arts Act, regions in Ireland suffered from poor facilities and lack of funding; however, the revamped 1970s Arts Council aimed to rectify this through encouraging and facilitating infrastructural growth and expansion. In 1976, the Arts Council commissioned a report entitled "Provision for the Arts". This report aimed to

> clarify the current situation in the various arts in the Irish Republic and how they are organised and financed, and to make recommendations with a view to helping the Arts Council to formulate its future programmes, to assess its priorities and to allocate its funds in the most positive and effective way; also to help the Irish Government to take the best steps to ensure that the arts in the Republic flourish.[29]

"Provision for the Arts" documented the current situation of arts practice in Ireland and provided the Council with an overview of the situation it aimed to develop and change.

The report found that there was an urgent requirement to extend arts activities into the regions outside Dublin, and recommended the appointment of arts development officers in main centres, and the assistance of the development and improvement of the arts in small towns and rural areas. Notably, the Gulbenkian Foundation, a grant-giving foundation that worked in the Republic of Ireland and Northern Ireland, was synonymous with a commitment to experiment in and develop the arts, particularly in the domains of arts education and community arts.[30] The promotion of community arts and arts in education then became a tactic used by the Arts Council during the 1970s to increase regional participation in and knowledge of the arts. Pockets of arts practice that focused on local sociopolitical circumstances emerged, notably in areas where ports and docks operated but no longer thrived. These included the Neighbourhood Open Workshops in Belfast, Grapevine, City Workshop and Moving Theatre in Dublin and the Waterford Arts-for-All Project.[31] Fulfilling a community arts brief, these groups brought theatre into the community, which was created and produced within a local context.

Waterford Arts-for-All is an interesting example of how a community arts project initiated further artistic activity and development in a particular region. The initiative emerged in 1979 from a group forum held by the Waterford branch of the Combat Poverty Network. With the assistance of Combat Poverty and financial support from the Arts Council, Waterford Arts-for-All began to host annual arts festivals in the city. The theatre made for these festivals consisted of plays written by local people that addressed issues such as unemployment and mental health, and were staged in spaces other than established theatre buildings, such as pubs, hospitals, factories, beaches and housing estates. Companies like Footsbarn Travelling Theatre from Cornwall, England, took part in these festivals and outside artists were commissioned to give workshops.

Waterford Arts-for-All Theatre Company emerged and began to make productions all year round. Influenced by the work of Peter Sheridan and City Workshop, in 1983 Waterford Arts-for-All applied to the Department of Education for a grant to begin a community theatre project in Waterford.[32] This project was called Ciotóg, and the group developed different facets of its operation such as drama in education and drama classes for young people. Ciotóg ran for eighteen months and closed due to lack of funding, but in 1985 two further theatre groups emerged from Waterford Arts-for-All. These were Red Kettle Theatre Company, which closed its mainstage company in 2014 but continues to run the children's branch of its operation, and Waterford Youth Drama, which runs now as Waterford Youth Arts. Red Kettle was Waterford's first professional theatre company, and Waterford Youth Arts is the city's longest-running youth arts service. Spraoi, Waterford's annual street theatre festival, grew in the 1990s from those involved with Red Kettle, and many people involved in the arts in Waterford were involved in Waterford Youth Arts as teenagers. Thus, through its legacies, Waterford Arts-for-All was the foundation for a longstanding relationship Waterford has had with theatre and the arts, and the Arts Council's aim of ongoing wider participation in the arts was achieved by using community arts as a strategic starting point.

Community arts scholar Jan Cohen-Cruz maintains that community arts often find themselves in a "hyphenated relationship" with education, in that the transmission of cultural values and knowledge is aimed for, or with politics, in that local organisation of performance is required.[33] Community arts practice, therefore, becomes a cultural performance of human endeavour, making links between personal and political transformation and art. Plugging into community arts as a form of community and regional development, as the Arts Council began to do in the 1970s, acted in tandem with the principles of the art form, in that it aimed to achieve social change through educating those who were distanced from arts practice. Because of the perceived accessibility associated with community arts, the form provided a stronger base from which cultural barriers that prevented people from participating in the arts could be broken down.

It can be argued that establishing community arts organizations as clients of the Arts Council reduces the autonomy of these groups, compromising the principles of freedom and equality on which the movement is founded by making the groups answerable to the government. Government funding subverts the operation of movements that are strongly rooted in political change into specific and determinate modes of social and cultural production. Somewhat paradoxically, government funding is often seen as a necessity for community arts to operate, and many companies and projects would cease to exist if this funding was withdrawn. While it is beyond the scope of this chapter to discuss this matter in detail, structures of funding for community arts have caused much debate within the sector and have been discussed by authors such as Ciarán Benson in the 1989 report "Art and the Ordinary" and his 1992 article "Towards a Cultural Democracy", and Rhona Henderson in "Community Arts as Socially Engaged Art", featured in Sandy Fitzgerald's 1994 community arts reader *An Outburst of Frankness.*

Notable developments in the field of community arts in Ireland have emerged from community initiatives. In 1983, for instance, a collective of cross-border community arts practitioners formed Creative Activity for Everyone (CAFE). CAFE aimed to create a dialogue between those engaged in community arts activity across the whole island by

> encouraging an exchange of information and ideas; formulating a coherent policy to finance groups and individuals – generating funds for pilot projects – compiling a directory of groups/individuals participating in creative community arts and a list of resources at their disposal; [and taking] action in support of community arts initiatives.[34]

CAFE acted as an administrative base for community arts, thus reinforcing and further establishing the movement. In 1985 the Arts Community Education (ACE) project was established as a joint project between the Arts Council and the Gulbenkian Foundation to develop both arts in education and community arts, as the sector was now seen to be a "vital and growing practice".[35] Benson records how ACE attempted to foster the experience of the arts as part of everyday life and developed projects in community arts and arts in education, in that the project was a way in which participation in community theatre could be expanded further. From ACE six projects emerged: three in arts education and three in community arts. *The Big Game* by Galway-based Macnas was one of these projects. Macnas was formed in Galway in 1986 by Páraic Breathnach, Tom Conroy, Ollie Jennings and Pete Sammon. The four responded to the ACE call for projects, and *The Big Game* was a large-scale theatre event staged during the Connacht Football Final in 1986. The company went on to be known for this type of large-scale work made accessible through the use of outdoor public places as performance spaces, and it still operates from Galway today.

Later Developments

Over the subsequent decades, community theatre practices developed further in Ireland under various auspices, assisted by the continuous funding awarded to the field by the Arts Council. Individual artists and projects are selected for funding, which is a different format from the way in which public funding for the amateur movement has evolved. During the 1970s and 1980s the amateur movement remained largely unfunded by the Arts Council. However, in the early 1990s the Arts Council agreed to fund the ADL's administration and continues to do so.

In 1989, under increasing administrative pressure, the ADL submitted an application to the Arts Council on behalf of the amateur theatre movement, requesting a grant to "support amateur theatre activity and organisation".[36] After much deliberation and an examination of other countries' policies regarding funding the amateur arts, such as those of Holland and Wales, in 1991 the Arts Council agreed to provide £7500 for an administrator if the ADL agreed to match the sum, and in 1992 an advertisement for an administrator was posted.[37] A professional administrator was subsequently employed by the ADL, which in 1994 became the Drama League of Ireland (DLI). The discontinuation of the term "amateur" in its title can be surmised to have been a deliberate relabelling by the organization to encourage a new perception of its artistic ability. As Cochrane points out, society has come to value the professional over the amateur,[38] and the removal of the term amateur suggests a wish to be disassociated from the sense the word has come to have.

Going On, an Arts Council policy document for drama published in 1996, which promotes the use of amateurs by professional groups, states that in regard to supporting the artistic and technical development of the amateur the Council would "consider applications for support towards the costs of engaging theatre professionals who would conduct seminars or workshops" with amateur groups and organisations, and it would "examine sympathetically" on a "very selective and limited basis" proposals for experimental projects involving both professional production companies and amateurs. Additionally, the Council pledged to "support umbrella organisations which can demonstrate substantial representation and affiliation with the amateur movement".[39] Thus, in becoming a client of the Arts Council, the DLI could expand and become more ambitious, while the professional theatre was encouraged with rewards in grant aid to use the amateur as a resource for employment and experimentation.

The amateur movement continued to change and develop in the coming years. In 2017 there were more than 600 drama groups throughout the island, and thirty-eight three-act festivals and twenty-six one-act festivals were organized. RTE now sponsors the finals from Athlone and broadcasts from the festival through television and radio. Residential winter schools run in Coole Park, County Galway, and the residential summer school is now held at the University of Limerick, after being based at Maynooth University in the early years of the new millennium. Gormanston summer school also runs annually, although it is organized privately by the O'Donoghue family, who have extensive experience in theatre and drama. Due to the increasing demands of work, the rise of professional and community theatre and the ever-growing possibilities for leisure pursuits, the amateur movement may or may not have the same community impact it had during the 1960s and 1970s. Yet it remains a mainstay of cultural activity in Ireland, engaged in for the most part—as *amare*, the Latin root of the word amateur, suggests—out of love.

Notes

1. Claire Cochrane, "The Pervasiveness of the Commonplace: The Historian and Amateur Theatre", *Theatre Research International* 26, no.3 (2001): 233.
2. Ibid.
3. Eugene Van Erven, *Community Theatre. Global Perspectives* (London: Routledge, 2001), 2.

4. Christopher Morash, *A History of Irish Theatre: 1601–2000* (Cambridge: Cambridge University Press, 2002).
5. Morash, *A History of Irish Theatre*, 193.
6. Ibid.
7. Baz Kershaw, *The Politics of Performance. Radical Theatre as Cultural Intervention* (London: Routledge, 1992), 29.
8. Gus Smith, *Festival Glory in Athlone* (Tralee: The Kerryman Ltd., 1977).
9. Arts Council, "All Ireland Amateur Drama Festival", accessed April 10, 2016, http://archivestories.artscouncil.ie/all-ireland-amateur-drama-festival/.
10. Arts Act (Republic of Ireland) 1951, accessed March 13, 2016, http://www.irishstatutebook.ie/1951/en/act/pub/0009/index.html.
11. Arts Council, "Closing of all Ireland Drama Festival at Athlone", accessed April 10, 2016, http://archivestories.artscouncil.ie/all-ireland-amateur-drama-festival/.
12. Brian P. Kennedy, *Dreams and Responsibilities: The State and the Arts in Independent Ireland* (Dublin: The Arts Council, 1990), 136.
13. Ibid., 137.
14. John Travers (Chairman of the Amateur Drama Council of Ireland, 2016) in discussion with the author, January 2016.
15. As cited by Smith 1977, 104.
16. Stuart Hall "Who Needs 'Identity'?" In *Questions of Cultural Identity*, ed. Stuart Hall, and Paul du Gay (London: Sage, 1996), 2.
17. As cited by Smith, *Festival Glory in Athlone*, 104.
18. Amateur Drama League, "Newsletter" (April 1980): 2, accessed November 16, 2015, Drama League of Ireland files, 2062/1977/1, Arts Council Archives, Merrion Square, Dublin.
19. Arts Council, "Procedures surrounding the 1980 confined festival at Loughrea" (1980), accessed November 16, 2015, Drama League of Ireland files, 2062/1977/1, Arts Council Archives, Merrion Square, Dublin.
20. Amateur Drama League, "Official statement resulting from meeting with Amateur Drama Council of Ireland" (November, 1979), accessed November 16, 2015, Drama League of Ireland files, 2062/1977/1, Arts Council Archives, Merrion Square, Dublin.
21. Amateur Drama League 1979.
22. Arts Council 1980.
23. Simon Trussler, *Cambridge Illustrated History of British Theatre* (Cambridge: University of Cambridge Press, 1994), 296.
24. Cochrane, "The Pervasiveness of the Commonplace", 236.
25. Smith, *Festival Glory in Athlone*, 44.
26. See Pauline Conroy, "From the Fifties to the Nineties: Social Policy Comes Out of the Shadows", in *Irish Social Policy in Context*, ed. Gabriel Kiely, Anne O'Donnell, Patricia Kennedy and Suzanne Quin (Dublin: University College Dublin Press, 1999), 33–50.
27. Van Erven, *Community Theatre*, 1–2.
28. Paula Clancy, "Rhetoric and Reality. A Review of the Position of Community Arts in State and Cultural Policy in the Irish Republic", in *An Outburst of Frankness. Community Arts in Ireland: A Reader*, ed. Sandy Fitzgerald (Dublin: Tasc at New Island, 2004), 86.

29. J.M. Richards, *Provision for the Arts* (Dublin: The Arts Council/Calouste Gulbenkian Foundation, 1976), 5.
30. Ciarán Benson, *Art and the Ordinary—the Report of the Arts Community Education Committee* (Dublin: The Arts Council, 1989).
31. Sandy Fitzgerald, "The Beginning of Community Arts and the Irish Republic" in *An Outburst of Frankness. Community Arts in Ireland: A Reader*, ed. Sandy Fitzgerald (Dublin: Tasc at New Island, 2004), 64–79.
32. Waterford Arts-for-All, "Proposal to the Department of Education to Establish a Community Theatre Project for Waterford City" (February1983), accessed March 14, 2016, Waterford Arts-for-All Archive, Waterford Youth Arts, Barrack Street, Waterford.
33. Jan Cohen-Cruz, *Local Acts: Community Based Performance in the United States* (New Jersey: Rutgers University Press, 2005), 5.
34. CAFE, "CAFE Seminar Report—First National Conference" (Dublin: CAFE, 1984): 4, accessed March 14, 2016, Waterford Arts-for-All Archive, Waterford Youth Arts, Barrack Street, Waterford.
35. Arts Council, "A Note on the Funding of Community Arts" (1985), accessed March 14, 2016, Waterford Arts-for-All Archive, Waterford Youth Arts, Barrack Street, Waterford.
36. Amateur Drama League, "Application for Funding on Behalf of the Amateur Theatre Movement" (1989), accessed November 16, 2015, Drama League of Ireland files, 2062/1983/1, Arts Council Archives, Merrion Square, Dublin.
37. Padraig O'Farrell, "Amateur Administrator Sought", *The Irish Times,* January 3, 1992, accessed November 16, 2015, Drama League of Ireland files, 2062/1991/1, Arts Council Archives, Merrion Square, Dublin.
38. Cochrane, "The Pervasiveness of the Commonplace".
39. Arts Council, *Going On* (Dublin: The Arts Council, 1996), 8.

Bibliography

Amateur Drama League. "Official Statement Resulting from Meeting with Amateur Drama Council of Ireland," November, 1979. Accessed November 16, 2015, Drama League of Ireland files, 2062/1977/1, Arts Council Archives, Merrion Square, Dublin.

Amateur Drama League. "Newsletter," April 1980. Accessed November 16, 2015, Drama League of Ireland files, 2062/1977/1, Arts Council Archives, Merrion Square, Dublin.

Amateur Drama League. "Application for Funding on Behalf of the Amateur Theatre Movement," 1989. Accessed November 16, 2015, Drama League of Ireland files, 2062/1983/1, Arts Council Archives, Merrion Square, Dublin.

Arts Act (Republic of Ireland). 1951. "Office of the Attorney General, Government of Ireland." Accessed March 13, 2016, http://www.irishstatutebook.ie/1951/en/act/pub/0009/index.html.

Arts Council. "All Ireland Amateur Drama Festival." Accessed April 10, 2016, http://archivestories.artscouncil.ie/all-ireland-amateur-drama-festival/

Arts Council. "Closing of all Ireland Drama Festival at Athlone." Accessed April 10, 2016, http://archivestories.artscouncil.ie/all-ireland-amateur-drama-festival/

Arts Council. "Procedures Surrounding the 1980 Confined Festival at Loughrea," 1980. Accessed November 16, 2015, Drama League of Ireland files, 2062/1977/1, Arts Council Archives, Merrion Square, Dublin.

Arts Council. "A Note on the Funding of Community Arts," 1985. Accessed March 14, 2016, Waterford Arts-for-All Archive, Waterford Youth Arts, Barrack Street, Waterford.

Arts Council. *Going On*. Dublin: The Arts Council, 1996.

Benson, Ciarán. *Art and the Ordinary—The Report of the Arts Community Education Committee*. Dublin: The Arts Council, 1989.

CAFE. "CAFE Seminar Report—First National Conference." Dublin: CAFE, 1984. Accessed March 14, 2016, Waterford Arts-for-All Archive, Waterford Youth Arts, Barrack Street, Waterford.

Clancy, Paula. "Rhetoric and Reality. A Review of the Position of Community Arts in State and Cultural Policy in the Irish Republic." In *An Outburst of Frankness. Community Arts in Ireland: A Reader*, edited by Sandy Fitzgerald, 83–114. Dublin: Tasc at New Island, 2004.

Cochrane, Claire. "The Pervasiveness of the Commonplace: The Historian and Amateur Theatre." *Theatre Research International* 26, no.3 (2001): 223–242.

Cohen-Cruz, Jan. *Local Acts: Community Based Performance in the United States*. New Jersey: Rutgers University Press, 2005.

Conroy, Pauline. "From the Fifties to the Nineties: Social Policy Comes Out of the Shadows." In *Irish Social Policy in Context*, edited by Gabriel Kiely, Anne O'Donnell, Patricia Kennedy and Suzanne Quin, 33–50. Dublin: University College Dublin Press, 1999.

Fitzgerald, Sandy. "The Beginning of Community Arts and the Irish Republic." In *An Outburst of Frankness. Community Arts in Ireland: A Reader*, edited by Sandy Fitzgerald, 64–79. Dublin: Tasc at New Island, 2004.

Hall, Stuart. "Who Needs 'Identity'?" In *Questions of Cultural Identity*, edited by Stuart Hall and Paul du Gay, 1–17. London: Sage, 1996.

Henderson, Rhona. "Community Art as a Socially Engaged Art." In *An Outburst of Frankness. Community Arts in Ireland: A Reader*, edited by Sandy Fitzgerald, 159–178. Dublin: Tasc at New Island, 2004.

Kennedy, Brian P. *Dreams and Responsibilities: The State and the Arts in Independent Ireland*. Dublin: The Arts Council, 1990.

Kershaw, Baz. *The Politics of Performance. Radical Theatre as Cultural Intervention*. London: Routledge, 1992.

Morash, Christopher. *A History of Irish Theatre: 1601–2000*. Cambridge: Cambridge University Press, 2002.

O'Farrell, Padraig. "Amateur Administrator Sought." *The Irish Times*, January 3, 1992. Accessed November 16, 2015, Drama League of Ireland files, 2062/1991/1, Arts Council Archives, Merrion Square, Dublin.

Richards, J.M. *Provision for the Arts*. Dublin: The Arts Council/Calouste Gulbenkian Foundation, 1976.

Smith, Gus. *Festival Glory in Athlone*. Tralee: The Kerryman Ltd., 1977.

Travers, John (Chairman of the Amateur Drama Council of Ireland, 2016) in Discussion with the Author, January 2016.

Trussler, Simon. *Cambridge Illustrated History of British Theatre*. Cambridge: University of Cambridge Press, 1994.

Van Erven, Eugene. *Community Theatre. Global Perspectives*. London: Routledge, 2001.

Waterford Arts-for-All. "Proposal to the Department of Education to Establish a Community Theatre Project for Waterford City," February, 1983. Accessed March 14, 2016, Waterford Arts-for-All Archive, Waterford Youth Arts, Barrack Street, Waterford.

Performing Politics: Queer Theatre in Ireland, 1968–2017

J. Paul Halferty

Theatrical performance is a cultural activity through which people assemble to engage in public discourse and to form—however provisionally—a community. It is a public, performative, and political art, and it is not, therefore, surprising that it has played an important role in the changing representations of sex, sexuality, and gender in the latter half of the twentieth century, when these issues became politicized and new social movements arose around them. In Ireland, theatre has played a central role in how the sexuality of queer people—the lesbian, gay, bisexual, transgender or queer (LGBTQ) community—has been represented, and how they have represented themselves, from the 1960s to the present day.[1] In this period, theatrical performance has been deployed to interrogate and challenge sexual repression of all kinds, to negotiate sexual and gender politics, and to foster a shared and continuing sense of identity and community.

Focusing on the public and political nature of theatrical performance, this chapter conducts an analysis of theatre in Ireland that has represented LGBQT people from the late 1960s to the present day. It examines how plays from this period have intervened into the changing issues and concerns of queer life in Ireland. This chapter is not, however, an exhaustive survey of plays and performances produced by, or that represent, LGBTQ people during this period. Rather, it focuses on published plays that have garnered some critical attention, and contextualizes them in relation to their contemporary politics. What emerges from this study is an awareness of the changing use of theatrical representations of LGBTQ people on Irish stages.[2] During this period, Irish artists

J. P. Halferty (✉)
University College Dublin, Dublin, Ireland
e-mail: paul.halferty@ucd.ie

E. Jordan, E. Weitz (eds.), *The Palgrave Handbook of Contemporary Irish Theatre and Performance*,
https://doi.org/10.1057/978-1-137-58588-2_12

have exploited theatre's public forum to explicitly and collectively address repressed sexualities, shame, and various forms of injustice in Irish life. This study charts how representations of queer sexualities and genders have transformed in this period from a trope employed by mostly straight/heterosexual playwrights to investigate broader issues of sexual repression in Irish culture into a social, aesthetic, and political tool used by openly LGBTQ artists to raise consciousness, foster community, reclaim history, and expand both current and historical conceptions of Irishness.

Queer theatre and activism in Ireland exists in broader, international contexts that have seen significant transformation since the late 1960s, when a new social movement known as gay liberation emerged and developed across the English-speaking world. The Stonewall Riots, which took place in New York City after police raided the Stonewall Inn on 28 June 1969, are generally thought of as the birth of the gay liberation movement. Prior to 1969, there had been various forms of "homophile" political organization in the United States and elsewhere,[3] but following the Stonewall Riots, and the formation of the short-lived but inspiring Gay Liberation Front in New York, gay liberation as a political ideology and movement took root in cities across the English-speaking world. This followed in the wake of the new social movements of the 1950s and 1960s, such as the civil rights movement in the United States, and the women's, peace/anti-war, and students' movements internationally. In Ireland and elsewhere, the primary aim of gay liberationists in this period was the establishment of visible, politicized gay communities, and their most common political tactic was "coming out": being open about their existence as gay men and lesbian women, and rejecting the shame and stigma—accusations of deviancy, sin, criminality or pathology—and discriminatory practices, social, legal, political and otherwise, that had traditionally attended same-sex desire.

In Ireland, the extreme social conservatism that had characterized the 1950s began to thaw and break by the late 1960s. In this context, two plays, staged in the late 1960s and early 1970s—just prior to the emergence of the women's and gay liberation movements in Ireland—mark a complex and, when compared to the British and American theatre of the same period, relatively unique beginning for contemporary representation of homosexuality in theatre in Ireland.[4] These plays are Thomas Kilroy's *The Death and Resurrection of Mr. Roche* (1968) and Brian Friel's *The Gentle Island* (1971). Though written by heterosexual playwrights, both include gay characters in a similar and surprisingly positive manner, eschewing the trope of degeneracy, which was common at this time, as well as what Alan Sinfield has characterized as a desire for "zany humour".[5]

The Death and Resurrection of Mr. Roche tells the story of Kelly and a group of his friends who arrive drunkenly at his Dublin flat after the pub. The group of men continue to party there, but their mirth and drunken bonhomie shifts in tone with the arrival of Mr. Roche and his young and very drunk friend, Kevin. Kelly in particular is not happy that Mr. Roche, "the queer", has arrived but the others welcome him for the alcohol he has brought, and they enjoy making jokes at his expense.[6] While in the flat, Mr. Roche is not only the victim of homophobic slurs, but also a violent attack. Preying upon his claustrophobia, the men forcibly push Mr. Roche into what Kelly calls the "holy hole", a crawlspace beneath a set of stairs. In the holy hole, begging to be set free, Mr. Roche suffers a seizure and dies. Faced with this emergency, the group of men quickly sober up and concoct a plan to dispose of Mr. Roche's body, with Kevin and the Medical Student departing the flat to execute it.

Left alone in his flat, Kelly and his oldest, married friend Seamus speak about their humble beginnings in rural Ireland and their new lives in Dublin. But something larger is bothering Kelly, for which Mr. Roche is a clear trigger. While alone with Seamus he confides that he hasn't "looked at a woman sideways" in a long time, and that he thinks there may be something wrong with him when it comes to women.[7] When pressed about his relationship to Mr. Roche, he admits to Seamus that they have a history. He tells Seamus that in his loneliness he has socialized with Mr. Roche, and that on one occasion he allowed him to stay the night and that, "I let him handle me".[8] Seamus is quite thrown by the confession and quickly departs, leaving Kelly alone in his flat. Kelly's revelation is followed by another when Kevin and the Medical Student return to the flat with Mr. Roche, who is not dead after all. Kevin is very tired and crashes on Kelly's bed. The others begin to leave, but Mr. Roche insists that he wait until Kevin wakes up. It is Sunday morning and Kelly and the other characters decide they will go to mass, but Mr. Roche remains in Kelly's apartment, "facing [the] audience" with an "enigmatic smile" as the play ends.[9]

In the titular character's resurrection, Alan Sinfield sees a Pinteresque vogue for menace in the 1960s: "[Mr. Roche's return] is either a sinister move—he is blackmailing Kelly—or the stirring of Kelly's conscience".[10] But, as Anthony Roche argues in his book *Contemporary Irish Drama*, "Mr. Roche presents them with the threat, not just of homosexuality but of sexuality per se", which is "notably absent from the lives of a group of bachelors pushing forty".[11] In his confession to Seamus, Kelly's emphatic disgust for Mr. Roche and homosexuals functions as a symptom of his own repressed homosexual desire and the self-loathing he experiences because of it. Rather than Pinteresque menace, Mr. Roche's death and resurrection represent sexual violence and repression in Irish culture, as Anthony Roche suggests, and homophobia, depicting its malignant effects in the lives of both Kelly and Mr. Roche.

Friel's ironically titled play *The Gentle Island* opens with a rather grand exit, followed by an entrance. With the exception of Manus Sweeney and his family, sons Joe and Philly, and Philly's wife Sarah, the inhabitants of the island of Inishkeen, off the coast of county Donegal, are in the process of leaving—moving on to lives of labour in the factories of Scotland and England. Following the islanders' exit, and a short scene that establishes Philly's lack of sexual desire for his still-childless wife, Sarah, Shane Harrison and Peter Quinn arrive on the island, two Dublin tourists on the last leg of their summer holiday. The two are met with both puzzlement and delight by the Sweeneys, with Manus and Sarah encouraging them to stay for a few days to see and enjoy the island.

In scene two, which takes place a few days later, we find Shane has endeared himself to the Sweeneys by fixing the island's broken machinery, outboard motors, gramophones, and radios. Looking for either sexual fulfilment or a chance to get pregnant, Sarah propositions Shane. She has been spying on the pair in their tent and tells Shane that she will come at 10 o'clock to lie with him while Peter goes for his nightly walk. But Shane refuses. When Sarah asks why, he says Philly's name, to which she responds that Philly is of no use to her, and presses again for an answer: "Why not? Tell me why not?"[12] Peter then arrives on the scene and, their conversation interrupted, Sarah runs off. Later that same evening, Shane and Philly have gone off fishing, but Sarah returns and reports to Manus that she has seen the two men in the boat house "stripped naked" and that Philly was "doing for the tramp [Shane] what he couldn't do for me".[13] Sarah encourages Manus to kill Shane for this trespass, but when Shane returns, he cannot bring himself to shoot him. Sarah takes the gun from Manus and shoots Shane herself as he attempts to run away. Shane is transferred to the mainland for medical attention, but the islanders don't know if he will survive. In the final scene, Philly returns the next day from fishing to find his brother Joe has left to join the others islanders in Glasgow, and that the two visitors have also departed. Neither Manus nor Sarah confront him about the alleged sexual encounter with Shane, homosexuality being an almost unutterable subject. The play ends with a sense of continued stagnation as the islanders are unable to confront both homo- and heterosexuality.

As these plays suggest, Ireland was slowly beginning to address sex and sexuality as social and political issues in the late 1960s and early 1970s in the public sphere. Founded in 1971, the Irish Women's Liberation Movement (IWLM) was a political organization on the vanguard of social and political critique, and paved the way for future political, social, and cultural change. At its inception, and despite the participation of lesbian and bisexual women, such as founding member Nell McCafferty, "lesbian issues were not on the core feminist agenda" of the IWLM.[14] But lesbian and bisexual women's participation and presence was registered, though quite indirectly, when Irish Women United, founded in 1975, published their "seven minimum demands", the final point of which read: "The right of all women to our own self-determined sexuality".[15] In 1978, the first Irish lesbian conference took place in Dublin, bringing lesbian issues to greater prominence within feminist activism.[16]

According to Kieran Rose, the work of the IWLM was fundamental in "creat[ing] the space in which a gay movement could form".[17] The Irish Gay Rights Movement (IGRM), Ireland's first gay organization, was formed in 1974 in "a blaze of energy and optimism, when radical change seemed possible, necessary and immediate".[18] In 1976, the IGRM teamed up with Project Arts Centre to bring Gay Sweatshop, Britain's first gay and lesbian theatre company, to Dublin to perform a double bill of plays: *Any Woman Can*, written by Jill Posner, and *Mister X*, written by Roger Baker and Drew Griffiths. Espousing the politics of gay liberation through coming out and consciousness raising, *Any Woman Can* is based on the author's own life: it is "a tale of one woman's pride and acceptance of her homosexuality".[19] *Any Woman Can* is a performance of consciousness raising, depicting a personal story that will resonate with others. Adopted from feminists in the United States, consciousness raising "brought about collective knowledge about the reality of women's lived experience still 'invisible' and unexplored in Irish public discourse at this time" and was a common practice in Irish feminist circles.[20] As the title suggests, and as the author experienced, "any woman can" come out, liberate herself, and live a happy life as a lesbian. As a piece of autobiographical performance, the play also follows the more broadly feminist dictum of the time, "the personal is political", and focuses on the true story of a single woman as an example that others can follow.

According to Gay Sweatshop member Philip Osment, "*Mister X* was a positive gay play that attacked the sort of apolitical gay man who would go to gay bars but ridicule the idea of Gay Liberation and pretend that he didn't need it".[21] Also an exercise in gay consciousness raising, the play ends with "Mister X walk[ing] centre stage, fac[ing] the audience and sa[ying], 'My name is Mister [...] My name is Alan Pope and I live at 10 Marius Mansions, Marius Road, London SW17 and I'm gay".[22] With Mister X naming himself publicly and coming out as a gay man, he espouses a politics of visibility and community, essentially rehearsing and performing coming out as political action for gays and lesbians in the theatre and in the real world.

Performing these plays at Project Arts Centre caused huge controversy, with the theatre losing and then regaining its funding from the Dublin Corporation. Opponents of the play took particular umbrage with *Mister X*, calling it "pornographic", referring to the play's opening scene where a group of fully clothed men simulate masturbation, each saying whom he was imagining as he pursued his onanistic pleasure. In his memoir, David Norris recalls: "the resulting publicity proved a great advantage as people queued around the block in the hope of seeing what they expected would be a truly shocking obscene production".[23] More than *Mister X*'s perceived pornography, the furore caused by these plays is due to their forthright and open assertion of gay and lesbian identities in a public forum, and their call for the unashamed living of gay and lesbian lives in the public sphere.

Gay civil rights came to political prominence nationally in 1977, when activist and Trinity professor David Norris mounted a legal challenge to the laws prohibiting homosexual acts between men, represented by Mary Robinson, who would become Ireland's first woman president in 1990. The trial was heard in 1980, but Norris and Robinson were unsuccessful. Norris appealed, taking his case to the Supreme Court, but in April 1983, in a 3:2 decision, the High Court "also found that the laws did not contravene the Constitution having regard to the Christian nature of the State, the immorality of the deliberate practice of homosexuality, the damage that such practices cause to the health of citizens and the potential harm to the institution of marriage".[24] Although homosexuality had been decriminalized in most other western European countries, the frameworks of Irish law were not yet able to assimilate gay men and lesbians as subjects, finding them still beyond the pale of Irish citizenship.

In 1980, Joni Sherrin, later Joni Crone, became the first lesbian woman to speak openly on Irish television when she appeared on *The Late, Late Show*. Crone was active in the women's movement and gay activism in Britain and Ireland before appearing on *The Late, Late*, and wrote a play, *Anna Livia Lesbia,* produced in 2017 by Splódar Theatre company, about her experience. A memory play that depicts the lead-up to and aftermath of her appearance on *The Late, Late Show*—among other issues that I will address below—the play concerns the ramifications for Crone's domestic and family life of her public declaration of lesbian identity. Taking up classic feminist issues, the play depicts how Crone's declaration of lesbian identity challenges a patriarchal order that is maintained by men controlling women's access to the public sphere. According to Crone, "I did suffer personally but not professionally … I suffered rejection from my family, received threats of violence and experienced ostracism. My parents had feared that their house would be set on fire or that they would be shunned by the neighbours".[25] While gay men have traditionally been subject to legal censure, as well as social and cultural mores, lesbian women's lives have been more acutely shaped by the effects of the patriarchy and misogyny they endure as women, as well as the homophobia they encounter as lesbians. But, as Marian Duggan suggests,[26] "while social homophobia can be psychologically and physically damaging, legal and political homophobia can destroy family units and cause women significant distress and alarm".[27] For lesbian women, the primary danger the law threatened was not incarceration, but rather being deemed unfit mothers to their children because of their sexual identity.

In 1982, Frank McGuinness, one of Ireland's most significant gay playwrights, had his first major success with *The Factory Girls*. Despite the highly conservative social and cultural politics in which McGuinness was writing, nearly all of his plays, from the 1980s to the present, deal with homosexuality in some way. In *Frank McGuiness's Dramaturgy of Difference and the Irish Theatre*, David Cregan sees in McGuiness' oeuvre a "queering" of the Irish theatrical cannon. For Cregan, McGuinness's plays "fit nicely into the Irish theatrical tradition in their comparable narrative choices and their traditional literary techniques",[28] but his plays are made unique by the ways in which he "plac[es] homosexual characters into historical memories […] establishing new 'realities' that elucidate the fiction of hegemonic regimes of normativity".[29] In the simplest sense, McGuinness's historical plays insert gay and lesbian characters into contexts within which dominant, heterosexist discourses would presume them not to exist. For example, *Factory Girls* depicts a group of women who go on strike and occupy the offices of the shirt factory in Donegal in which they work, protesting for better wages. Among its cast of women are Rebecca and Vera, who are lovers—though this can be diminished or emphasized according to how the play is staged. As McGuinness suggests: "[…] Rebecca and Vera is a gay relationship. In the first production it was completely ignored, there was no way they […] were going to deal with it. But then when Garry Hynes did the Druid production […] it was finally dealt with".[30]

Similarly, in *Observe the Sons of Ulster Marching Towards the Somme* (1985) the primary action charts how enlisting in the British army and surviving the Battle of the Somme transforms its central character, Pyper, from the politically apathetic, black-sheep scion of a respectable Ulster family into a staunch Unionist and defender of the province of Northern Ireland from Irish Republicanism. For Cregan, McGuinness queers a narrative of political transformation such as this by making Pyper a homosexual who engages in a loving and sexual relationship with another patriotic son of Ulster, "one of Carson's men", David Craig. A similar strategy is employed in *Innocence* (1986), *Carthaginians* (1988), and *Dolly West's Kitchen* (1999), wherein gay and lesbian characters appear in what might be thought of as the most unlikely historical places—sixteenth-century, Catholic Italy, post-Bloody-Sunday Derry, rural Donegal during the Second World War—though McGuiness's later plays feature more overtly queer characters who nominate themselves as gay, and whose sexuality cannot, therefore, be ignored in production.

The broad-ranging effects of homophobia in the 1980s, and especially the ways in which legal discourses that criminalized gay men contributed to homophobic violence, were demonstrated in the shocking murders of Charles Self and Declan Flynn. Born in England in 1949, Self moved to Dublin in 1978 to take a job as a set designer for Raidió Teilifís Éireann (RTÉ). Self was gay man who participated in Dublin's gay sub-culture, and was stabbed to death in his home in Dublin on 20 January 1982. It was a gruesome murder that caught the attention of national media. Seeking justice, the Irish Gay Rights Movement and the National Gay Federation "called for collaboration with the police in charge of the investigation".[31] But rather than seriously pursing the perpetrator of the crime (the case remains unsolved), gay rights activists have accused Gardaí of using the murder as an opportunity to collect information about and harass gay men living in Dublin.[32] According to Kieran Rose, "the investigation led to almost 1,500 gay men being questioned, photographed and fingerprinted at Pearse Street Garda station".[33]

This distrust of the legal system was confirmed to be well founded later that same year, when Declan Flynn, a gay man, was murdered in Fairview Park by five youths. The young men admitted to the assault that resulted in Flynn's death, and that they had been "queer bashing" for a few weeks that summer as they wanted to rid the park of the gay men who went there to meet. Shockingly, each man was given a suspended sentence with the warning from Justice Sean Gannon that "they would serve the sentences if they got into trouble again".[34] The leniency of their sentences was the catalyst for the first major gay rights demonstration in March 1983, when gays and lesbians marched from the city centre to Fairview Park to protest against violence against them and their communities.

With striking similarities to the Flynn case, Aodhán Madden's play *Sea Urchins* is an investigation of the social factors that lead to this kind of homophobic assault. Produced at Hawk's Well in Sligo in 1988, the play's central character is "Huey", an orphan brought up in state care who "hates himself and violently resists his own homosexual nature".[35] Focusing on Huey and his group of friends—other alienated youth who loiter and drink on Dun Laoghaire pier—the play represents the causes and effects of the young people's marginalization and homophobic violence in a State that continues to criminalize homosexuality.

The play dramatizes how combined forces of poverty, addiction, and restlessness lead the youths to assault and rob The Duke, a middle-aged, married man who cruises the pier for gay sex. Alluding to the suspended sentences of the youths who attacked Flynn, Brian Singleton suggests, the play's dialogue "makes it crystal clear" that the youths know their harassment and violence against gay men will be condoned by the police: "they are fully aware that the law, for once, is on their side".[36] Through the central character of Huey, the play also illustrates how societal homophobia leads to violence and death, when the sexually conflicted and psychologically traumatized Huey does not stop when The Duke's wallet is taken, but kicks him to death. And like the Flynn case, these youths are let off with suspended sentences for the murder of a gay man.

A significant difference between Flynn's murder and *Sea Urchins* is the historical context in which the play is set.[37] Rather than set the play in the present, or in the same year as the Flynn murder, Madden chooses "Sept [*sic*] 1979, during the Pope's visit to Ireland" as the backdrop for his play's action.[38] In doing so, Madden represents the causes and effects of homophobia in Irish life and society: a Church and State that are entirely enmeshed in their homophobia and patriarchy, and in their failure to care for those who are young and poor. Within this context, Huey's and the Duke's similarly repressed homosexual desires beget a violent confrontation and murder that, when brought before the law, goes unpunished because the man murdered was gay, and he was killed in a place where he was looking for sex.

Although the 1980s were a difficult decade for LGBTQ people in Ireland, the 1990s saw a number of social, cultural, and political victories that changed the lives of many gay men and lesbians for the better. First, as mentioned above, Mary Robinson was elected President in 1990. To signal her commitment to human rights and equal citizenship she "invit[ed] thirty-five representatives of the lesbian and gay community from all parts of the country, north and south, to Áras an Uachtarán in December 1992", signalling that they were valued and welcome within Irish political life.[39] Second, in 1993, homosexuality was finally decriminalized. Decriminalization meant that it was now possible to begin to look for antidiscrimination legislation in housing and employment, and for the government to begin supporting gay men and lesbians publicly, in areas such as health and wellbeing—especially important given the ongoing AIDS crisis. Finally, the 1990s saw the rise of the "Celtic Tiger", the expansion of the Irish economy that saw greater employment and a stemming of the almost continuous tide of emigration. For gay men and lesbians, these changes made the idea of staying in Ireland possible, and much more inviting.

The 1990s also saw the emergence of Ireland's first gay theatre company, Muted Cupid. The company billed itself as "The National Gay and Lesbian

Theatre of Ireland", and produced a number of queer plays from the international canon, including Caryl Churchill's Cloud Nine (1993), Joe Orton's What the Butler Saw (1993), Harvey Fierstein's Torch Song Trilogy (1994), Brad Fraser's Poor Superman (1998), Martin Sherman's Bent (1999), and Alan Kinsella's The New Lesbian Vampires Of Sodom (1999), an an adaptation of Charles Busch's Lesbian Vampires Of Sodom.

Novelist and historian Emma Donoghue also began to produce plays in the 1990s, most of which do the important work of imaginatively reclaiming lesbian history and offering these historical figures as examples for lesbians living in the present. *I Know My Own Heart*, Donoghue's first play, was produced by Glasshouse Theatre, a company dedicated "to present[ing] and promot[ing] the work of women in the theatre".[40] It is based on the life of Anne Lister (1791–1849), whose diaries (written in code) detail her lesbian love affairs. Lister, who was known as "Fred" and "Gentleman Jack" is the "butch" woman who broke "all the rules of Regency ladyhood. She cropped her hair short, travelled unchaperoned, studied Greek and geometry, and refused to even consider marriage".[41]

The play concerns Lister's life and especially her sexual relationships with a number of other mostly "fem" women. It focuses particularly on her love affair with a farmer's daughter named Marianne Brown, and the complications caused by their status as women in love in Regency Yorkshire, and by Lister's affairs with her best friend Tib, and Marianne's sister, Nancy. Among its concerns are the ways in which women's lives are limited by a patriarchal culture that generally denies them access to employment and money, and the self-determination they afford—with Tib, "a woman of independent means", providing the exception that proves the rule. In a pivotal scene that brings these issues to the fore, Marianne proposes that she and Anne run off together when she learns that she has contracted a venereal disease from her philandering husband, Charles.

Marianne: I shall send Charles a note informing him of my decision [to leave].

Anne: He'd toss it in the fire. Think, Marianne. Even if you did manage to run away and hide in London, you'd lose all you call precious—your house, your friends, your reputation even.

Marianne: But not you. You're the most precious thing I have, and I wouldn't lose you. We can leave in the morning.

Anne: With what? Seven pounds and ten shillings, that's the sum total of my worldly wealth. So don't taunt me with impossibilities.[42]

The scene ends with Anne writing in her diary, having sent Marianne home to Charles: "I never asked her to leave him. I wanted only a fair share of her", but she also berates herself for her inability to match Marianne's courage.[43] The play, and Anne and Marianne's relationship, ends with Anne inheriting her uncle's fortune and leaving for Paris, where she will make her own life and live as she chooses.

Anne's inability to settle with Marianne is due not just to financial and social constraints, but also her desire for personal and sexual autonomy. Anne is something of a womanizer, and in the final scene Marianne castigates her for her infidelities.

Anne:	All I want is you.
Marianne:	That's a damn lie. You want money and freedom and a wife and a mistress, a string of mistresses. You want me, and Tib [...] and every pretty servant you lay eyes on...[44]

In this way the play does not offer a happy-ever-after, monogamous love story; but Donoghue does not impose any such moral on this tale. As Cathy Leeney suggests, she "refuses to punish her characters, and [at the play's end] Lister leaves the audience in a mood of optimistic excitement as she sets off alone on a new adventure".[45]

Glasshouse Theatre and the Irish Arts Council commissioned Donoghue to write her second play, *Ladies and Gentlemen*, which premiered at The Project Arts Centre in 1996. Like *I Know My Own Heart*, *Ladies and Gentleman* is based on historical fact: the life of Annie Hindle, a male impersonator who worked on the late nineteenth-century vaudeville stage in the United States. The play focuses on Annie's relationship with a young Irish immigrant named Annie Ryan, who works backstage as a dresser in the travelling act of which Hindle is star, and who is called Ryanny on account that she and Hindle share a first name. In this case, the financially successful Hindle has a house that she has bought herself in New Jersey, and in which she would like to settle after many years on the road. In a scene similar to that of *I Know My Own Heart*, the "fem" in this relationship, Ryanny, courageously proposes that they leave the theatre and move into the house in New Jersey as a married couple. Hindle doesn't understand how this could be possible, but Ryanny convinces the male impersonator to also live as a man offstage, so they might marry, and settle together as husband and wife.

Annie:	You've been all I want for as long as I can remember.
Ryanny:	Well then. Doesn't that give us as much right to a wedding as any pair of persons?
Annie:	It never struck me quite that way before.
Ryanny:	I get a lot of time to think while you're up there prancing about in the limelight.[46]

Following the historical record, the play sees the pair marry in Grand Rapids, Michigan, and live happily together until Ryanny's untimely death from breast cancer, bringing this tale of romantic love to a sadly tragic conclusion.

In an essay titled "Mad about the Butch", Donoghue examines the personal and political motivations for writing about masculine women, butch-femme couples, and reclaiming lost lesbian history. She suggests that her return to "butch women", emerges out of her own sexual awakening as a young woman: "It finally clicked for me that I wanted girls who didn't dress like me, and that if same-sex desire, like the heterosexual kind, is sometimes a matter of opposites attracting, that doesn't make it a pathetic copy of the real thing."[47] Donoghue's personal desires are attended by a simultaneously artistic and political determination to reclaim lesbian history. She describes her work as

> a peculiarly geekish form of historical fiction, which tries to work as history as well as fiction, because when you're writing about those who've been left out of capital-H History, you feel a burning obligation to put the facts on the record as well as spinning a memorable story.[48]

Donoghue's work in this period echoes the work of feminist theatre scholar Sue-Ellen Case, who published her essay "Toward a Butch-Femme Aesthetic" in 1988. Case suggests that the butch-femme couple, both historically and currently, is a politically empowering example for lesbians to follow. She argues that their sense of camp and role-play on stage and in the world gives both the butch and the femme "the power to self-determine her role and her conditions on the micropolitical level".[49] The drama and conflicts of Donoghue's historical plays enact these struggles for self-determination. In doing so Donoghue's plays participated in the process of "bring[ing] the lesbian subject out of the closet of feminist history"[50] and putting the butch-femme couple centre stage: performatively effecting new possibilities for lesbian lives in the contemporary moment.

In the new millennium, queer theatre and performance festivals became important sites for local and international work. The Dublin International Gay Theatre Festival was founded in 2004. At the inaugural festival its founder, Brian Merriman, said, "I would be proud to see this festival develop into an event that would continue to increase the visibility, and celebrate the contribution of gay people to theatre in Ireland and abroad".[51] The festival has achieved this goal as it has produced hundreds of plays by local Irish as well as international companies and continues to run annually in May.

The Outburst Festival in Belfast is an interdisciplinary arts festival, including theatre and performance, as well as film and visual arts, which began in 2007. In the ten years since its birth, it has fostered important local queer artists, and brought a range of queer work from around the world to Belfast.[52] The Queer Notions festival ran for two years, produced by THISISPOPBABY and Calipo Theatre Company in 2009, and THISISPOPBABY and Project Arts Centre in 2010. According to THISISPOPBABY's artistic director Philip McMahon, the festival emerged out of work they had done at Electric Picnic, where the company programmed a stage that hosted important international queer cabaret performers. With Queer Notions they wanted to create, as their by-line for the

2009 festival articulates, "a platform for glorious outsiders".[53] The TheatreofplucK, which was originally founded in Philadelphia in 1998, migrated with its two of its founders, Niall Rea and Karl Schappell, to Europe, mounting shows in Amsterdam and London, before settling with Rea in his home city, Belfast. It has been producing and touring work in Belfast since 2003, and acquired a venue there, The Barracks, in 2015.[54]

Panti Bliss, the drag alter ego of Rory O'Neill, has played a seminal role in recent LGBTQ history in Ireland, on stage and off. To date, she has written and performed four plays, *In These Shoes?* (2007), *All Dolled Up* (2007), *A Woman in Progress* (2009), and *High Heels in Low Places* (2014). Panti's was an important voice in the Equal Marriage referendum, in which Ireland became the first jurisdiction to extend the right to marry to same-sex couples through public plebiscite in a vote held on 22 May 2015.

Anthologies of essays and plays are important vehicles for documenting queer theatre and performance in Ireland. While dedicated to literature more broadly, Eibhear Walshe's (1997) *Sex, Nation and Dissent in Irish Writing* is a pioneering text that includes writing on queer theatre, including Oscar Wilde and Micheál Mac Liammóir. David Cregan's (2009) *Deviant Acts: Essays on Queer Performance* and Fintan Walsh's (2010) *Queer Notions: New Plays and Performances from Ireland* are the first Irish anthologies dedicated to criticism of queer performance respectively. Walsh's anthology includes plays by Loughlin Deegan, Deirdre Kinahan, Neil Watkins, Verity-Alicia Mavenawitz, Philip McMahon, and Panti Bliss. In 2016, Walsh also published an excellent book of essays called *Queer Performance and Contemporary Ireland: Dissent and Disorientation.*

Queer theatre's contemporary importance in Ireland, and the extent to which recent Irish theatre has been concerned with queer sexual identities, is confirmed by the recently published Oberon Anthology of Contemporary Irish Plays, titled *This Is Just This. It Isn't Real. It's Money*, edited by Thomas Conway. Unlike *Queer Notions*, this anthology's focus is not dedicated specifically to queer work, and yet four of the of the eight plays published in the anthology deal with gay, lesbian, and trans subjects: *Trade* by Mark O'Halloran, *I (Heart) Alice (Heart) I* by Amy Conroy, *The Big Deal* by Una McKevitt, and *The Year of Magical Wanking* by Neil Watkins. In the anthology's introduction, Conway addresses the number of queer plays by suggesting that each play published concerns "unfinished business in Ireland" and "it becomes astonishing, in this light, to reflect just how often these plays revolve around the question of sexual identity".[55]

Trade by Mark O'Halloran received a workshop production as part of the Queer Notions festival at Project Arts Centre during the second instalment of the festival in 2010. The play was then staged site-specifically, in a room of the Clifden Guesthouse on Gardiner Place in Dublin's North Inner City, as part of the Dublin Theatre Festival in September 2011.[56] *Trade* has two characters, Older Man and Younger Man, who are meeting to have sex, for which Older Man pays Younger Man. On its broadest level, the play is about love, intimacy, and contact within a male, working-class context. It details how both men struggle with their identities, with connection to their families, with homosexual desire/sex, and with the pressures of life in an economically depressed Ireland. In his discussion of the play, Fintan Walsh sees in *Trade* a critique of the failures of the Celtic Tiger economy and supposed liberalization of Irish attitudes toward gay men. For Walsh, the restrictions imposed at the intersection of heteronormative masculinity and class mean that this kind of individual liberation is not available to all gay men.[57]

The conceit of *I (Heart) Alice (Heart) I* by Amy Conroy is that a long-term but closeted lesbian couple are spotted sharing a simple kiss in a Tesco supermarket. An actress and writer approaches them and wants to interview them to create a show about their relationship. *I (Heart) Alice (Heart) I* is a fictional story, but it uses the form and performance conventions associated with verbatim and documentary theatre, genres that incorporate words spoken by actual people, and sometimes cast these people in their performances. The couple, Alice Kinsella and Alice Slattery, are retired, have known each other all their lives, and have lived together as a couple for decades, but have not come out publicly as a couple or as lesbians. Rather, they have lived their lives quietly and invisibly in a misogynistic and homophobic culture within which coming out would have serious consequences—the pros and cons of which they detail in the course of the performance. *I (Heart) Alice (Heart) I* thus tells a fictional story that *could* be true. It uses the conventions of verbatim theatre as the genre of performance currently most associated with lived reality to tell its imagined, but highly plausible narrative. In this sense, the play enacts a fictional narrative performed in the idiom of verbatim theatre to imagine and, in the feminist sense, reclaim a forgotten or marginalized example of women's history by openly suggesting that while not based on real people, there must have been—and still are—women like Alice and Alice in Ireland quietly living out their lives.[58]

Una McKevitt's *The Big Deal* is a verbatim play that charts the experiences of two trans women "Cathy" and "Deborah", focusing on the journey that each of them takes toward their sex reassignment surgery, which is to be performed outside Ireland. The performance is "scripted from original material provided by the contributors—including journals, poems, songs and interviews", and McKevitt is listed as "editor" in the anthology.[59] The two trans women whose stories are represented worked with McKevitt to "produce the script and direct the production".[60] When it premiered at the Kilkenny Arts Festival in August 2011, the play was performed by two cisgender women actors performing as Cathy and Deborah, rather than the two women whose stories are told—which has been the case in McKevitt's other work. *The Big Deal* is thus a kind of verbatim and autobiographical performance at one remove. In his discussion of the play, Fintan Walsh notes that, according to McKevitt, "this decision emerged from the fact that one of the subjects did not want to perform, and the presence of the other woman on stage would have jeopardized her anonymity. And in staging cisgendered identity, the choice also reflected the subjects' wishes to pass".[61] In addition to anonymity and a desire to pass, the decision of the subjects *not* to perform on stage also represents one of the central issues of gender recognition as they have been articulated by the Transgender Equality Network of Ireland (TENI): the ability to self-determine one's gender and when to disclose, or not disclose, one's status as a trans person.

While not addressed directly, the play's political context is the battle for gender recognition in Ireland. The legal fight for the right to determine one's gender began in 1997, when Lydia Foy began court proceedings to have the Registrar General issue her with a new birth certificate that stated her gender as female. This right was not achieved until July 2015, when, after several court cases, the Gender Recognition Act was passed by the Oireachtas. This allows individuals to declare their gender, and to have all government documents reflect this declaration.[62]

Neil Watkins' *The Year of Magical Wanking* is a one-man, autobiographical performance in which Watkins confronts personal demons. The title is a reference to Joan Didion's *The Year of Magical Thinking*, but, as Fintan Walsh suggests, "unlike Didion, Watkins does not mourn the loss of a spouse, but describes coming to terms with his queer sexuality, his abuse as a child, current dependencies on porn and cannabis, and HIV infection".[63] Written in rhyming couplets, the play takes the form of ritual healing through storytelling, prompted by a meeting with an indigenous healer from Oregon named Sweet Medicine Horse Nation, who gets Watkins to confront his life and its difficulties without shame. It begins in November, with a monologue for each month, ending with a spiritual encounter in which Watkins is told to tell his story, a revelation that transforms the play itself into an exercise in healing through storytelling.

In 2016–17, the paradoxical place of LGBTQ identities and sexualities in the nation and the state, simultaneously mainstream and still marginal, and the ways performance can be deployed to remember the past, were taken up by two performances. The first is in *Butterflies and Bones: The Casement Project*, a dance performance choreographed by. Fearghus Ó Conchúir.

> *The Casement Project* is inspired by the queer body of Roger Casement, British peer, Irish rebel and international humanitarian, whose experience reminds us that Ireland's flourishing has always been linked to the flourishing of disadvantaged people around the world.[64]

With this, Ó Conchúir signals the paradoxical position Casement himself occupied in life—British peer and Irish rebel—and in history, hero of the 1916 revolution and a homosexual in a time of virulent homophobia and criminalization. For Ó Conchúir, "Casement's body offers the model for a national body whose identity is dynamic and open to otherness".[65]

The second performance is one mentioned above: Joni Crone's play, *Anna Livia Lesbia*, produced by Splódar Theatre Company. In addition to depicting the homophobia and patriarchy of the late 1970s and early 1980s in Ireland, *Anna Livia Lesbia*'s performance in the present functions as a public opportunity for collective remembering. It is structured as a memory play, with the contemporary Crone, played by Deirdre O'Meara, remembering her life in the

1970s and 80s, as it is acted out by a cast of younger women. On the evening I attended the play, its status and structure as a memory play was one that was quite uniquely shared by the majority of its audience, most of whom were women, presumably queer, and contemporaries of Crone. In its structure, it invites its audience, especially Irish women, and Irish lesbians and bisexual women, to recall the past in the present. On the evening I attended *Anna Livia Lesbia* in Liberty Hall, the play was a performance of a community coming together to remember the joys and pains of a shared, lived history.

The sentiments encapsulated by *Butterflies and Bones* and by *Anna Livia Lesbia* exemplify much of what the queer performances discussed here have aimed to achieve over the last fifty years: to question sexual repression and expand conceptions of Irishness, to foster and create queer communities, to reclaim queer histories, and to negotiate these histories in the present and presence of others as a means to create a (hopefully) more inclusive and queer future.

Notes

1. Once a term of abuse, "queer" was reclaimed in the late 1980s and early 1990s as an inclusive term that does not denote a specific sex or gender, and that launches a critique of normative identity categories, including, potentially, lesbian and gay. In the academy, the field of queer theory has impacted on a diverse array of fields from art history to law. It is often used as an umbrella term for lesbian, bisexual, gay, and trans men and women, and for others who challenge hetero-normative identities. In this chapter, I will use specific identity categories whenever possible, and use queer as either a term to denote gay, lesbian, bisexual and trans people, or to denote a crisscrossing and blurring sexual and gender identity. For more on queer theory and the re-definition of the term, see (Jagose 1996).
2. This chapter does not address plays that represent HIV/AIDS. For work on this subject see (O'Brien 2016, 2017).
3. The first homosexual emancipation movement emerged in Germany in 1897 when Magnus Hirschfeld and colleagues founded The Scientific–Humanitarian Committee, a group that sought to conduct scientific research and to advocate for the legal protection of gay, lesbian, bisexual and transgender men and women. When the National Gay Federation was founded in 1979 in Dublin, it named its resource centre the Hirschfeld Centre in recognition of his pioneering work in queer rights.
4. As this study focuses on the relationship between the political emergence of gay liberation and activism from the late 1960s and early 1970s to the present, it does not look at Brendan Behan's *The Hostage*, which includes gay characters, Princess Grace and Rio Rita. It was staged in Dublin in Irish as *An Giall* at the Damer Theatre in Dublin in June 1958, though the Irish text does not include the homosexual characters and is set in a tenement rather than a brothel. These changes were made when it was rewritten in English for Joan Littlewood's Theatre Workshop in Stratford East, London, where it premiered in October 1958. See Ann Marie Adams, "The Sense of an Ending: The Representation of Homosexuality in Brendan Behan's the Hostage", *Modern Drama* 40, no. 3 (1997); Nicholas Grene, *The Politics of Irish Drama: Plays in Context from*

Boucicault to Friel, Cambridge Studies in Modern Theatre (Cambridge: Cambridge University Press, 1999).

5. Alan Sinfield, *Out on Stage: Lesbian and Gay Theatre in the Twentieth Century* (New Haven: Yale University Press, 1999), 271.
6. Thomas Kilroy, *The Death and Resurrection of Mr. Roche*, rev. edition (Oldcastle, Co. Meath: Gallery Books, 2002), 30.
7. Ibid., 57.
8. Ibid., 63.
9. Ibid., 81.
10. Sinfield, 183.
11. Kilroy, 135.
12. Brian Friel, *The Gentle Island* (Oldcastle, Co. Meath: Gallery Press, 1993), 39.
13. Ibid., 61.
14. Linda Connolly and Tina O'Toole, *Documenting Irish Feminisms: The Second Wave* (Dublin: Woodfield, 2005), 174.
15. Ibid., 176.
16. Ibid., 179.
17. Kieran Rose, *Diverse Communities: The Evolution of Lesbian and Gay Politics in Ireland* (Cork: Cork University Press, 1994), 11.
18. Ibid.
19. Unfinished Histories, "Any Woman Can", Unfinished Histories: Recording the History of Alternative Theatre, http://www.unfinishedhistories.com/history/companies/gay-sweatshop/any-woman-can/.
20. Connolly and O'Toole, 27.
21. Philip Osment, *Gay Sweatshop: Four Plays and a Company* (London: Methuen Drama, 1989), xx.
22. Ibid., xx.
23. David Norris, *A Kick against the Pricks: The Autobiography* (London: Transworld Ireland, 2012), 143.
24. Rose, 36.
25. Joni Crone cited in Connolly and O'Toole, 186.
26. Duggan writes specifically about women in Northern Ireland; however, in this instance, lesbian women's experience in relation to the law is not impacted by patrician, and the same experience can be seen in the lives of Irish lesbians in the Republic of Ireland.
27. Marian Duggan, Queering Conflict: Examining Lesbian and Gay Experiences of Homophobia in Northern Ireland (Burlington, VT: Ashgate, 2012). 103.
28. David Cregan, *Frank McGuinness's Dramaturgy of Difference and the Irish Theatre* (New York: Peter Lang, 2011), 1.
29. Ibid., 3.
30. Ibid., 214.
31. Chrystel Hug, *The Politics of Sexual Morality in Ireland* (Basingstoke: Macmillan, 1999), 213.
32. Ibid.
33. Rose, 19.
34. "Manslaughter Sentence Suspended on Five Youths", *The Irish Times*, March 9, 1983.
35. Aodhán Madden, "Sea Urchins", (Unpublished Script, 1988), 1.

36. Brian Singleton, *Masculinities and the Contemporary Irish Theatre* (Basingstoke: Palgrave Macmillan, 2011), 108.
37. This date makes the play's references to HIV and AIDS historical anachronisms, as the syndrome was first reported on in the press in 1981 with Lawrence Altman's article "Rare Cancer Seen in 41 Homosexuals" in *The New York Times*.
38. Madden, 1.
39. Rose, 33.
40. Caroline Williams et al., "People in Glasshouse: An Anecdotal History of an Independent Theatre Company", in *Druids, Dudes, and Beauty Queens: The Changing Face of Irish Theatre*, ed. Dermot Bolger (Dublin: New Island, 2001), 134.
41. Emma Donoghue, "I Know My Own Heart", in *Seen and Heard: Six New Plays by Irish Women*, ed. Cathy Leeney (Dublin: Carysfort Press, 2001), 160.
42. Ibid., 137.
43. Ibid., 138.
44. Ibid., 158.
45. Cathy Leeney, "Introduction", in *Emma Donoghue Selected Plays*, ed. Emma Donoghue (London: Oberon Books, 2015), xii.
46. Emma Donoghue, *Ladies and Gentlemen* (Dublin: New Island Books, 1998), 57.
47. "Mad About the Butch: Emma Donoghue Pursues Women in Pants", https://oberonbooks.wordpress.com/2015/06/23/mad-about-the-butch-emma-donoghue-pursues-women-in-pants/.
48. Ibid.
49. Sue-Ellen Case, "Toward a Butch-Femme Aesthetic", in *The Lesbian and Gay Studies Reader*, ed. Henry Abelove, Michèle Aina Barale, and David M. Halperin (New York; London: Routledge, 1993), 295.
50. Ibid.
51. Brian Merriman, *Wilde Stages in Dublin: A Decade of Gay Theatre* (Dublin, Ireland: International Dublin Gay Theatre Festival Ltd, 2013), 93–4.
52. Outburst Queer Arts Festival, http://outburstarts.com/about-us/.
53. J. Paul Halferty, "Phillip McMahon Interview" (Dublin 2016).
54. "TheatreofplucK: Queer Theatre for Belfast and Beyond", http://www.theatreofpluck.com/about/.
55. Thomas Conway, ed. *This Is Just This. It Isn't Real. It's Money: The Oberon Anthology of Contemporary Irish Plays*, Oberon Modern Playwrights (London: Oberon Books, 2012), 7.
56. J. Paul Halferty, "Tom Creed Interview" (Dublin 2017).
57. Fintan Walsh, *Queer Performance and Contemporary Ireland: Dissent and Disorientation*, Contemporary Performance Interactions (Palgrave Macmillan, 2016), 116.
58. The play was restaged at the Abbey's sister stage The Peacock in 2012, was recorded for radio by Raidió Teilifís Éireann (RTÉ), and toured extensively in Ireland as debates continued over the merits of civil partnerships versus equal marriage. It was restaged at Project Arts in March 2015, ahead of the successful referendum on equal marriage held in May, and as a fundraiser for the Marriage Equality Campaign.

59. Una McKevitt, "The Big Deal", in *This Is Just This. It Isn't Real. It's Money: The Oberon Anthology of Contemporary Irish Plays*, ed. Thomas Conway (London: Oberon Books, 2012), 222.
60. Ibid., 96.
61. Walsh, 96.
62. TENI, "Gender Recognition: Dr. Lydia Foy's Case", Transgender Equality Network Ireland, http://www.teni.ie/page.aspx?contentid=588.
63. Walsh, 65.
64. Fearghus Ó Conchúir, "Ireland 2016—the Casement Project", Fearghus Ó Conchúir, http://www.fearghus.net/ireland-2016-the-casement-project/.
65. Ibid.

Bibliography

About. "TheatreofpluK Queer Theatre for Belfast and Beyond." http://www.theatreofpluck.com/about/.

Adams, Ann Marie. "The Sense of an Ending: The Representation of Homosexuality in Brendan Behan's the Hostage." *Modern Drama* 40, no. 3 (1997).

Altman, Lawrence. "Rare Cancer Seen in 41 Homosexuals." *New York Times*, July 3, 1981.

Case, Sue-Ellen. "Toward a Butch-Femme Aesthetic." In *The Lesbian and Gay Studies Reader*, edited by Henry Abelove, Michèle Aina Barale and David M. Halperin, 294–306. New York; London: Routledge, 1993.

Connolly, Linda, and Tina O'Toole. *Documenting Irish Feminisms: The Second Wave*. Dublin: Woodfield, 2005.

Conway, Thomas, ed. *This Is Just This. It Isn't Real. It's Money: The Oberon Anthology of Contemporary Irish Plays*, Oberon Modern Playwrights. London: Oberon Books, 2012.

Cregan, David. *Frank McGuinness's Dramaturgy of Difference and the Irish Theatre*. New York: Peter Lang, 2011.

Donoghue, Emma. *Ladies and Gentlemen*. Dublin: New Island Books, 1998.

———. "I Know My Own Heart." In *Seen and Heard: Six New Plays by Irish Women*, edited by Cathy Leeney, 99–160. Dublin: Carysfort Press, 2001.

———. "Mad About the Butch: Emma Donoghue Pursues Women in Pants." https://oberonbooks.wordpress.com/2015/06/23/mad-about-the-butch-emma-donoghue-pursues-women-in-pants/.

Duggan, Marian. *Queering Conflict: Examining Lesbian and Gay Experiences of Homophobia in Northern Ireland*. Burlington: Ashgate, 2012.

Friel, Brian. *The Gentle Island*. Oldcastle, Co. Meath: Gallery Press, 1993.

Grene, Nicholas. *The Politics of Irish Drama: Plays in Context from Boucicault to Friel*. Cambridge Studies in Modern Theatre. Cambridge: Cambridge University Press, 1999.

Halferty, J. Paul. "Phillip McMahon Interview." Dublin, 2016.

———. "Tom Creed Interview." Dublin, 2017.

Histories, Unfinished. "Any Woman Can." Unfinished Histories: Recording the History of Alternative Theatre, http://www.unfinishedhistories.com/history/companies/gay-sweatshop/any-woman-can/.

Hug, Chrystel. *The Politics of Sexual Morality in Ireland*. Basingstoke: Macmillan, 1999.

Jagose, Annamarie. *Queer Theory: An Introduction*. New York: New York University Press, 1996.

Kilroy, Thomas. *The Death and Resurrection of Mr Roche*. Rev. edition. Oldcastle, Co. Meath: Gallery Books, 2002.

Leeney, Cathy. "Introduction." In *Emma Donoghue Selected Plays*, edited by Emma Donoghue, vii–xxii. London: Oberon Books, 2015.

Madden, Aodhán. "Sea Urchins." Unpublished Script, 1988.

"Manslaughter Sentence Suspended on Five Youths." *The Irish Times*, March 9, 1983, 1.

McKevitt, Una. "The Big Deal." In *This Is Just This. It Isn't Real. It's Money: The Oberon Anthology of Contemporary Irish Plays*, edited by Thomas Conway, 221–49. London: Oberon Books, 2012.

Merriman, Brian. *Wilde Stages in Dublin: A Decade of Gay Theatre*. Dublin: International Dublin Gay Theatre Festival Ltd, 2013.

Norris, David. *A Kick Against the Pricks: The Autobiography*. London: Transworld Ireland, 2012.

Ó Conchúir, Fearghus. "Ireland 2016 – The Casement Project." Fearghus Ó Conchúir, http://www.fearghus.net/ireland-2016-the-casement-project/.

O'Brien, Cormac. "HIV and Aids in Irish Theatre: Queer Masculinities, Punishment, and Post-Aids Culture." *Journal of the Medical Humanities* (2017).

———. "Ireland in the Age of Aids: The Cultural Politics of Stigma." *Irish Review*, no. 53 (2016): 45–59.

Osment, Philip. *Gay Sweatshop: Four Plays and a Company* [in English]. London: Methuen Drama, 1989.

Outburst Queer Arts Festival, http://outburstarts.com/about-us/.

Rose, Kieran. *Diverse Communities: The Evolution of Lesbian and Gay Politics in Ireland*. Cork: Cork University Press, 1994.

Sinfield, Alan. *Out on Stage: Lesbian and Gay Theatre in the Twentieth Century*. New Haven: Yale University Press, 1999.

Singleton, Brian. *Masculinities and the Contemporary Irish Theatre*. Basingstoke: Palgrave Macmillan, 2011.

TENI. "Gender Recognition: Dr. Lydia Foy's Case." Transgender Equality Network Ireland. http://www.teni.ie/page.aspx?contentid=588.

Walsh, Fintan. *Queer Performance and Contemporary Ireland: Dissent and Disorientation*. Contemporary Performance Interactions. Palgrave Macmillan, 2016.

Williams, Caroline, Katy Hayes, Siân Quill, and Clare Dowling. "People in Glasshouse: An Anecdotal History of an Independent Theatre Company." In *Druids, Dudes, and Beauty Queens: The Changing Face of Irish Theatre*, edited by Dermot Bolger, 132–47. Dublin: New Island, 2001.

Long Flame in the Hideous Gale: The Politics of Irish Popular Performance 1950–2000

Susanne Colleary

> The question for the "alternative" is how far it can accept the complexities of reality, merge this with its dramatic method, and infer, without recourse to polemics a political way forward.
>
> —Peter Sheridan[1]

Popular Politics

In his essay "The Politics of the Popular?—From Melodrama to Television", Bernard Sharratt describes the relationship between an art form and class struggle as difficult to define. He acknowledges that any connections between the production of the artefact and its conditions of reception, that is, between the art work and the audience to which it speaks, cannot be reduced to any simplistic characterization. Building on the work of Lucien Goldmann, *Le Dieu caché* (1966) and Pierre Macherey's *Pour une théorie de la production littéraire* in the same year, Sharatt suggests that one way of understanding that relationship is to see the art object as "expressing, embodying, working through or otherwise containing the ideology of a social class", through its world view or from its clefts and silences, which seek to expose the dominant credo of the period.[2]

While Sharratt is concerned with complexities when attempting to define the popular political art form, more broadly, John Fiske argues for the inherent politicism of popular culture in society, and uses Laclau's analysis of populism to make his point.[3] He defines populism in relation to the state as constituting three main forms in capitalist societies: democratic populism, popular opposition and populist opposition. Democratic populism can be under-

S. Colleary (✉)
Sligo Institute of Technology, Dublin, Ireland

E. Jordan, E. Weitz (eds.), *The Palgrave Handbook of Contemporary Irish Theatre and Performance*,
https://doi.org/10.1057/978-1-137-58588-2_13

stood as instances in which "the differences between the state and various formations of the people are [...] as complementarities, not antagonisms".[4]

Popular opposition arises in order to cope with the challenges that the dominant system offers, while populist opposition arises during "social crises", where change or revolution becomes possible.[5] In other words, popular oppositional forces are described as peoples or groupings whose interests are in "necessary conflict with that of the state [...] they never allow the forces of domination to relax or feel secure in their control"; the potential to tip over into confrontation with the state transforms popular opposition into a direct populist challenge to the status quo.[6] That said, in Fiske's view popular oppositional politics remains in the progressive rather than the radical realm, with the potential to raise sociocultural awareness, and even to effect change within the micro–macro political spectrum in society.

I make these points here, as I want to explore the nature of the popular political art form when brought up close to aspects of Irish theatre in recent years. Specifically, I want to connect ideas of popular theatre to the performance work of both the community arts and independent theatre sectors as flashpoints or key moments, from the 1970s on to the turn of the century. In order to do so, I want to temporarily fuse the two sectors together by creating an "ideological hybrid" for the timeline. Working as a loose formulation, and encapsulating the two, the hybrid constitutes a conceptual framework with which to interrogate those theatre and performance flashpoints as counter or alternative narratives to the dominant political and cultural coda of the time.

To begin then, I would like to look to the story of independent theatre and the community arts sectors in Ireland. Then I want to look to ideas of cultural democracy, to flesh out the bones of the hybrid outlined here, before moving on to examine particular companies and their works as exemplary of popular theatre and performance in the timeframe. Towards the end of the chapter I will return to the politics of popular theatre and to the hybrid as a way to understand the cultural and political significance of the performance work produced through both sectors in recent Irish theatre history.

A Potted History of Independent Theatre and Community Arts in Ireland

Contextualized within their discussion of Samuel Beckett's work at the Gate Theatre in Dublin, Anna McMullan and Trish McTighe stress that the independent theatre sector in Ireland can be understood as "theatre outside commercial venues [...] and the heavily subsidized National Theatre, as well as the subsidized Gate Theatre in Dublin".[7] Acknowledging that drawing neat boundaries is a difficult task "in such a small and severely under-funded sector where theatre practitioners work across different theatrical contexts", the authors briefly chart a history from the Drama League to contemporary companies including Druid in Galway and Rough Magic in Dublin.[8] In their view, the sector continues to place itself within experimental European theatre, "one which seeks intellectual, social and artistic liberation in addition to national autonomy". Although it can be hard to differentiate between well-established independent theatre companies and more heavily subsidized theatre, the authors argue that the independent sector has carried, staged and characterized countercultural and at times radical histories of Irish life.[9]

Arguably, the first independent theatre to influence the theatrical landscape in Dublin within the timeframe was the Pike Theatre Club. Formed in 1953 by Carolyn Swift with her husband, Alan Simpson, the Pike was much in line with the pattern and substance of international theatre. Stylish and satirical late-night revues (*Pike Follies*) were a staple along with avant-garde plays including works by Sartre and Ionesco. In a short time, the Pike became famous for staging the premieres of Brendan Behan's *The Quare Fellow* (1954), (rejected by the Abbey) and Samuel Beckett's *Waiting for Godot* in 1955.[10]

In many respects the Pike fits well within what Ulick O'Connor described as a basement-theatre, that is "a movement [that was] partly 'professional […] [with] just enough amateurs in it to keep the spirit of dedication alive".[11] If so, what Fintan O'Toole terms the "second wave" of Irish theatre was fast approaching. Writers including John B. Keane, Brian Friel, Thomas Kilroy, Tom Murphy and Hugh Leonard came to the fore, making alliances with the emerging independent theatre world. Among them, Phyllis Ryan's Gemini Productions with Norman Rodway, formed in 1958, became one of the leading producers of new Irish writing. The company forged strong bonds with Hugh Leonard, who gave them a play for every (Dublin Theatre) festival and with John B. Keane, staging productions of several of his plays, including *The Field* and *Big Maggie*. The company exerted a significant force on the national and international circuit and through the 1960s; Ryan produced the premiere of Eugene McCabe's *King of the Castle* (1964), Máiréad Ni Ghráda's *An Triail* (1964) and Tom Murphy's *The Orphans* (1968).

Across town, the Project Arts Centre was coming into life as a festival at the Gate Theatre known as Project 67, with the Project Gallery opening in Lower Abbey Street as an artists' co-operative. In 1969, it expanded its alternative remit, becoming the Project Arts Centre, attracting writers and directors including Jim and Peter Sheridan, and Neil Jordan. By 1974, the Project had found a permanent home in East Essex Street.[12] It has since evolved from a voluntary co-operative to a full-time artist-led organization, one which has attempted to capture the complexities of Irish social, cultural and political life over the past four or so decades. In describing the growth of the independent theatre scene from the mid-1980s, the noted theatre director, performer and writer Declan Gorman accounts for it as a

> social movement of reaction to emigration, rejection by the young middle class of archaic moral law and idealistic anxiety about urban poverty [that] all fed into the birth of a first wave of modern independent theatre in Ireland.[13]

The sector continued to expand and diversify into the 1990s, creating a rich field of companies and works so that the independent scene became more confident, as emerging theatre companies were articulating contemporary experience on national and international stages. While for some, transfer to more established theatres and lines of funding remained a primary goal, this was no longer the only route available to younger theatre makers. That said, the call from within the sector also spoke to the difficulties of ongoing resourcing of the work as well as the expansion of the sector to adopt and embrace new ideas, training and forms of theatre across international horizons.

Arguably, and not unlike independent theatre in certain respects, the beginnings of the community arts sector, as recognisable today, can be traced to the sociopolitical contexts emerging from the decades spanning the 1950s to 1970s in Ireland. Successive governments sought to cultivate Ireland as modernized and progressive in the eyes of the wider European community. However, political aspirations and international goals had, in many respects, little effect at local level. The country was still held in the vice-like grip of material forces including crippling poverty and the ravages of emigration, so that by the 1970s, "working class communities [...] were barely surviving, struggling under layer upon layer of bad decisions".[14] These communities (as in England) were not part of the larger and primarily middle-class counter-cultural movement that sparked across Europe and America in the 1960s. Increasingly sidelined in a post-industrial world, the old certainties that had sustained the labour market were disappearing fast in the face of the growing technological era, so

> while the hippies were animated and enthused by their vision of a new future, enabled by education and their families' wealth, the working-class vision was crumbling and from London's Bermondsey to Dublin's Sheriff Street, the future looked pretty bleak.[15]

Staring down such bleakness in the face of institutional apathy mobilized local communities to protest and to find other ways to draw attention to issues including housing, health and education for the working classes in Ireland. Alternative means of raising awareness toward better standards of living for neglected or ghettoized communities entered the cultural field. Connections began to be forged between those working from within the community from the ground up and those in the creative field, as a means of challenging the power bloc to act. Events began to take place; poster making, film making, marches, theatre, festivals and photography, connecting across class lines, so that, as Sandy Fitzgerald argues, these collaborations mark out "the point where the counter-culture movement and working-class struggle formed an uneasy alliance out of which grew 'community arts.'"[16]

As was happening in England, community arts began to gain a strong foothold from the late 1970s. People began to forge their own sets of relationships with artists built on an understanding that community action and protest for change could be expressed creatively. Such a movement could speak to the most pressing issues of the day as well as give voice to ideas of cultural identity in opposition to or separate from the pervasive hegemonic tone.[17] Early examples of community arts practice in Ireland, in terms of that which drew on its own experiences creatively, driven by the desire to make work based on the local (realpolitik), included the work of Waterford Arts for All, Grapevine and Moving Theatre in Dublin, all of which were in existence by the end of the 1970s.[18] In the capital the Community Arts For Everyone (CAFE) organization was established in 1984 as an advocacy and support organization, "ensur[ing] that the essentially political project of integrating arts and culture into the wider society should be kept to the fore".[19] Indeed, the Grapevine Arts Centre housed the CAFE organization and itself was the forerunner to the City Arts Centre, which occupied various locations in Dublin, probably the most well known of which was the centre's residence in Moss Street from 1988 to 2003.

Histories and the Hybrid

Paula Clancy argues that up until the middle of the 1960s in Ireland, the Arts Council's function was understood to be the promotion of excellence, mostly in the form of the "high arts", increasing the grant aid for a variety of flagship cultural institutions.[20] She locates Project 67 with the emergence of a counter-dialogue by the artistic community who, angered by the lack of state support, accused the Dublin art world of "symptoms of class bigotry, racial prejudice and pernicious art snobbery".[21] The introduction of the 1973 Arts Act responded in some measure to those pressures, so that by the mid-1980s "access" to the arts became something of a cornerstone of Arts Council policy. Through the 1980s, those policy shifts in thinking were reflected through broader approaches to supporting the arts, including the growth of regional arts centres, local authority commitment to the arts, the establishing of arts officers and more support for locally based theatre companies around the country.

In 1989, Ciarán Benson made the argument for community arts clear: community arts is "explicitly political; it opposes hierarchical control of the many by the few and is in favour of democratic collective action over individualistic action".[22] The Arts Council continued to mirror this thinking, describing community arts as the "process of creation in concert with one's audience as opposed to the traditional view of the work of art as an end it itself divorced from the social context of its making".[23] Despite such rhetoric, however, subsequent Arts Council publications became more guarded in their vision for community arts, and Fitzgerald suggests that community groups continued to be locked out of the elitist world of the established arts. So too, the independent theatre scene was in the business of "producing work of a contrast and quality that mounted a challenge to the [heavily subsidised] Abbey and the Gate, which had until then almost totally dominated the theatrical landscape".[24] Collective spaces began to come to the fore, which allied the community arts and the independent scene. Chief, perhaps, among them (although by no means alone) was the City Arts Centre, mentioned earlier, which strongly identified with both the community arts scene and the growing independent theatre sector at the time.

Declan Gorman makes the point that the open-door policy of the Project in the 1980s along with the work of the City Arts Centre through the 1990s attempted to

> create concerted links between the fringe theatre development and its radical community arts activities platforming the early work of Conor McPherson, Conall Morrison, Gerry Morgan, Katy Hayes, John Crowley and Jimmy Fay, among others.[25]

The connecting of the community arts sector to the independent theatre scene during the period speaks to ideas of cultural democracy; that is

> learning to tell your own story on an equal footing with all the other stories [...] discovering ways of giving expression to your own values and heritage and joining with others to do this in some sort of action.[26]

In many ways, the ideas inherent in the conceptual framework of cultural democracy resonated strongly with both sectors and fused independent theatre and the community arts together, producing key moments in recent Irish theatre and performance histories. That fusion, as outlined earlier, constitutes the hybrid here, as a means to explore the creative expression at work through both sectors as flashpoints along that timeline. In other words, the hybrid constitutes an intertwining of the ideals and beliefs of community arts with those of the independent theatre sector from the 1970s to the turn of the century. This loose ideological lynchpin joins together the theatre and performance work produced across both scenes and stands for those ideals held within the ethics of a cultural democracy, contesting hierarchical control. It is to those snapshot moments that this chapter now turns, before coming back to the politics of popular performance, and what the hybrid formulation might stand for in the discussion.

Passion Machines

If plays like James McKenna's *The Scatterin'* (1960) and Heno Magee's *Hatchet* (1972) reflected the political and social estrangement of the working classes in Dublin, by the late 1970s, Jim and Peter Sheridan were also staging plays at the Project Arts Centre. For the brothers, "the inequalities evident in the rougher side of Dublin provid[ed] the major theme of their left leaning work".[27]

Embodying a social realist approach, works included *Mobile Homes* (1976), by Jim Sheridan, which charted low-income lives lived in caravans through Dublin's accommodation crises, and *The Liberty Suit* (1977), a story of prison life by Peter Sheridan and Mannix Flynn. *The Lost Post*, which dealt with internment in Ireland, was a Communist Party production and went to Cuba in 1981, and James Plunkett's *The Risen People* (1958) has been revived several times, including by the National Theatre, in the years since its Project/Sheridan production. In time, Jim Sheridan went on to film, and Peter to community theatre, where he formed the City Workshop in the early 1980s with Mick Rafferty as part of the North City Centre Community Action Programme (NCCCAP). At about the same time, in 1982, the inner city *Looking On* festival took place, and was a major milestone for the emerging community arts sector in the capital. The festival was staged within the deprived area of the north inner city of Dublin as a month-long event showcasing the issues and problems facing the community at that time. NCCCAP also succeeded in mobilizing communities and activists in several directions including training, information services and cultural activities, all of which "recognised the necessity of identifying and exploring your roots and of finding ways to develop your community [...] to actively engage in positive change".[28]

Ideas of active engagement in community theatre drove Peter Sheridan's work for the City Workshop and as a collective was peopled by non-actors from the local area. Together, they produced a trilogy of "ould" Dublin, *The Kips, The Digs* and *The Village* (1983), about the "Monto", *Pledges and Promises* (1983) about the collapse of the Docks in Dublin in the 1950s, and *A Hape of Junk* (1983),[29] so that more traditional ideas of theatre performance were reshaped to include work produced by, with and for localized audiences. Throughout the 1980s, the ideas inherent in NCCCAP were reflected in the growing community arts momentum countrywide, and that energy also began to forge connections across, with and into the independent theatre scene. That fusion created a symbiotic atmosphere, so that "fragments of theatre, isolated pieces of the whole story that no one really knows" were being made which challenged the idea that the established arts could (or would) accommodate those experiences.[30]

The work of the Sheridan brothers in the early days of community theatre and the Project would, in their turn, make way for the work of the Passion Machine company in the late 1980s. Founded by writer and director Paul Mercier, the company wanted to "give voice to the weaker sections of society [...] a minority view or a threatened way of life", as well as understanding that "you live in Dublin [...] this is where you're from—why even attempt to write about other experiences".[31] According to Joseph Long, Passion Machine was driven to

> widen the social base of theatre audiences [...] [Mercier] writes and produces for a public who would otherwise look on theatre as something remote from their own class culture and he offers that public representations of their own concerns and experiences [...] reflecting Dublin working class life with energy and humanity.[32]

Passion Machine created theatre of "everyday life",[33] for those, according to Redmond O'Hanlon, who "do not think of alternative theatre, who do not think of the fringe, [or] the Dublin Theatre Festival [...] they come to be entertained, to see something about themselves".[34] In Fintan O'Toole's opinion, Mercier's work succeeds because "there is a huge theatrical impulse going together with the political one", centring in many respects on "the way people's fantasies reflect on their lives."[35]

Early examples of the works include Mercier's *Wasters* (1985) and *Studs* (1986), both staged at the SFX centre, which was not a theatre at all, but an all-purpose hall that hosted everything from heavy metal gigs to bingo on Friday nights. *Wasters* is set literally on wasteland in a Dublin Corporation estate, where three men and three women meet to welcome the return of one of their own, Bonzo, who has arrived from the building-site world of London. On bare ground and stage, they play out their fantasies through sex, drink and games in the face of harsh realities, and with the encroaching grown-up world of marriage, emigration and incarceration looming over them. If, as O'Toole suggests, the cast of working-class characters in *Wasters* were the "disenfranchised of Irish society and of Irish literature", it remains so in Mercier's next play, *Studs* (1986).[36] The premise of *Studs* revolves around the Emmet Rovers, a local housing-estate working-class football team, whose fantasy it is to land a place in the upcoming Cup Final. The ragbag team are led on by Moses, a stranger in their midst, who appoints himself as their manager. With vague hints of past glories on the field, Moses promises to lead them on to victory. But the hard realities rehearsed in *Wasters* also turn this "fantasy into a harsh bitter enactment of the reality of being a loser"—so that *Studs* builds on Mercier's earlier works, "creating a collective portrait of the urban dispossessed".[37]

As Passion Machine was creating "Northside Realist" urban dramaturgy for a widening Irish stage, others were also in the running. Victor Merriman suggests that Wet Paint Arts and Calypso Productions are amongst the clearest examples in the late twentieth century of Irish "cultural workers engaged in explicit confrontation with the betrayal and silences of the state and the national bourgeoisie".[38]

A contemporary of Passion Machine, Wet Paint Arts was founded in 1984 by David Byrne and "sought to interrogate the dynamics of inner city decay and suburban alienation in the capital city".[39] Within the ambitious ethos along class lines, the company was also interested in devising work, positioning the actor as creative artist in democratic alliance with writer and director. In addition, and for Byrne, spectators did not inhabit a peripheral stance, but were central to the theatre-making as creative collaborators, with an emphasis on widening access to the arts for young audiences.

While the work spans several years, Merriman describes the "commissioning, development and production" of Dermot Bolger's first play *The Lament for Arthur Cleary* (1989) as a "significant chapter" in the company's performance arc. Described as an "urban drama of intranational betrayal" it was based on Bolger's reworking of an eighteenth-century Gaelic poem, written by Eileen O'Connell on the death of her husband Art O'Leary.[40] In Bolger's vision, the working-class Arthur Cleary has finally come back home to Dublin after years of working as a *gastarbieter*—a "guest worker", one with permission to work temporarily in another country—on the continent. Yet, he returns to a Dublin he no longer recognizes or understands, a city that has changed irrevocably since Arthur's childhood—a Dublin ravaged by unemployment and heroin, and harbouring a "new viciousness" and a brutality which Arthur cannot grasp.

The play was a critical success at the Dublin Theatre Festival, and with reviews from the *Sunday Tribune*, the *Irish Times* and the *Irish Independent* describing the work as "a joyous celebration of old Strumpet city itself [while] [...] exposing the underbelly of a city seething with violence [...] written in a language both brutal and lyrical". The success of the work also echoed the commitment by Wet Paint to its theatre-making processes and its audiences during the development and the production of *Lament*. The actors held open workshops with people from communities where the play would be staged, and for whom the contemporary nature of the subject matter held real resonance. This meant that *Lament* played to both the general theatre-going public and to those for whom theatre-going was less relevant. In this way, the play's sense of immediacy was tested by audiences "for whom dispossession, exile and fruitless return are experiences first and metaphors second", and from whom at times the cast had to face down nightly hostility.[41]

In many respects, Arthur's statelessness and exile in unrecognisable cities spoke in part to Ireland's emergent relationship with the EU during the 1980s. The shifting dynamics of a changing sociopolitical culture were high on the agenda of Calypso Productions, formed in 1993 by Donal O'Kelly and Kenneth Glenaan with Charlie O'Neill. Their mission statement of 1995 is unequivocal:

> We want to change the world [...] Too often art and artists travel a journey where landscapes [...] and the people they encounter [...] become ideas to be used. Other artists travel as participants in their landscapes [...] Our landscape covers the planet. Our family is global. Our creativity is a critical one.[42]

In the same year, the company produced *The Business of Blood* by Donal O'Kelly and Kenneth Glenaan. The story tells of Chris Cole, a Christian pacifist who broke into a British Aerospace base at Stevenage and destroyed components in the nose cones of Hawk fighter jets. Cole wanted to highlight the use of weapons against the people of East Timor and the British government's doublespeak on its sale of arms to those involved in human rights abuses. Stylistically linked to workers' theatre in the 1930s, it divided critical opinion: David Nowlan for the *Irish Times* stated that "this is theatre being used to make a point rather than a point being used to create drama".[43] O'Toole argued for the work's political power, suggesting that "pointing the finger of blame may not be the most complex [...] gesture that can be performed on a stage but [...] with a steady hand [...] it will always be a powerful one".[44]

That spirit of a politicized voice continued with the company's production of *Rosie and Starwars* (1997) by Charlie O'Neill and directed by Garret Keogh. Written as a contribution to the European Year Against Racism, the play deals with the "implications of cultural representation for the lived experience of marginal groups, specifically Travellers".[45] *Rosie and Starwars* was first staged in a marquee at Meeting House Square, Temple Bar, Dublin, before going on to tour and conducting a series of seminars and discussions with the Irish

Travelling community in audiences and workshops. The production also produced an information package entitled *Information and Action on Racism*. A review in the *Irish Times* had some issues with structure and dialogue, but argued that the play clearly

> has its heart in the right place and eschews any studied neutrality; the Travellers are persecuted and the tormentors act from bigoted and mercenary motives [...] [it] appeals directly to those who espouse or sympathise with the Travellers' cause.[46]

In situating the audience as integral to the experience (not unlike the approaches of Passion Machine and Wet Paint), *Rosie and Starwars* dealt with racism among, and not apart from, the opinions and concerns of the Irish Travelling community.

Insofar as *Rosie and Starwars* dealt with the lived experience of the Travelling community in Irish society, *Farawayan* (1998) extended the focus to the experience of refugees and asylum seekers in late 1990s Ireland. Staged at the Olympic Ballroom and written by Donal O'Kelly, the play recounts the experience of being unwelcome. It centres on the experience of refugees and asylum seekers in Ireland while also echoing the country's own emigratory trails. The *Irish Times* described the work as a "passionate propaganda piece that challenges thinking and feeling on the treatment of asylum seekers in Ireland". As with other works by the company, the reviewer acknowledges its "limitations" as theatre, while making the point that such thinking becomes irrelevant in the face of Calypso's commitment to the significance of the subject matter.[47]

Calypso's dedication to the poetics of "creative criticism" and the "glocal" family echoed the work of Passion Machine and Wet Paint Arts. These companies made no bones about wanting to politicize the dynamics of Irish theatre, representing the voices of the dispossessed, the exiled, the marginalized and the undervalued in society, while democratizing the traditionalized relationships between actor, author and audience that were so well established on Irish stages. And they were not alone. A feminist collective of women writers and performers was on the move. Glasshouse Theatre Company was about to create its own set of feminist poetics for the Irish stage, intent on unsettling and upsetting the conventional cart of ideas involved in the "staging" of Irish women.

> Hollow of cheek with poverty
> And the whippings of history[48]

Glasshouse was founded in Dublin in 1990, producing ten shows between 1990 and 1996 including new works by Claire Dowling, Trudy Hayes and Emma Donoghue. The all-women theatre company was influenced by others, including Charabanc in Northern Ireland and Trouble and Strife in the UK, that were focussed on presenting and promoting the work of women in the theatre.[49] Before an established and male-dominated professional backdrop, the company was unapologetic about "give[ing] Irish women a voice in theatre

[...] [and stating] that fight was informed by feminism".[50] Glasshouse was clear in its intention to produce plays by and about women, and understood that as a radical act it challenged the existing Irish theatre system.[51] Early productions (1990–91) included *Ficky Stingers* (Eve Lewis), which dealt with a woman's experience of rape, and *Low Level Panic* (Claire McIntyre), which explored sexuality, pornography and eating disorders. Both were staged at Andrews Lane Theatre in Dublin and both received mixed reviews, some of which suggested that the work had limitations, with the capacity to speak to, but not beyond, an audience made up of "the sisters".[52]

That said, at the City Arts Centre in 1991 Glasshouse showcased its new work entitled *Out of My Head*, by Trudy Hayes, which documented a woman's experience of alcoholism and was shortlisted for the Stewart Parker Theatre Award. Later in the same year, the company staged a rehearsed reading of *Burn Both Ends*, by Claire Dowling, again at the City Arts Centre; written in a comic vein, the play tackled the experience of "women and private enterprise written in a Dublin idiom".[53] The play went on to a full production at the Project Arts Centre in 1992.

In that year and the next, the company also staged a showcase of historical and emerging women writers in the ironically titled "THERE ARE no Irish Women Playwrights" festival to counteract the historical and contemporary omission of writing by and of women. Working with Emma Donoghue, the company staged the lunchtime piece *I Know My Own Heart: A Lesbian Regency Romance* (1993) at the Project, going into full production in Andrews Lane in October of the same year. The play detailed Anne Lister's experience as a lesbian in Regency England, as a woman interested in "geometry and Greek [...] [who] had a vigorous sexual appetite and wrote intimate details of her "romantic relationships" in her diary".[54] The play garnered good critical and popular support and was nominated for the Stewart Parker Award for "Best Irish Debut Play". Another of Donoghue's plays, *Ladies and Gentlemen*, is considered a high point for the company; directed by David Byrne, it was staged in 1996 and was based on the real life of the male impersonator or "masher" of vaudeville, Annie Hindle, who eloped with her dresser Annie Ryan.[55] In what has been described as a "lesbian version of a female biography play", the piece divided critical opinion at the time.[56] Luke Clancy described the play's exploration of how "fundamentally malleable characteristics, such as gesture, gait, posture and voice, come to define gender".[57] The *Sunday Tribune* described it as a wonderful playing of "theatrical games, gently blurring the sexual boundaries",[58] and more recent literary criticism makes a strong argument for the play as "stand[ing] among the few works, whether on stage or in film, that attempt to narrate any kind of queer Irish female history".[59]

By 1997 Glasshouse was beginning to fragment, not least because of the necessity to make a living wage after an intense period of plays and productions; meanwhile, Rough Magic was about to produce the Irish working-class poet Paula Meehan's first play for adults at the Project. Meehan initially wrote *Mrs Sweeney* as a poem, based on the Irish myth of Buile Suibhne (the Madness of Sweeney) which tells of a pagan king who, on angering St. Ronan, is cursed by the abbot to wander the world, naked and birdlike, condemned to exile and insanity. The legend is often used as a metaphor for "poetic exile and creative inspiration".[60] When initially writing the poem as the wife of Sweeney, Meehan found herself thinking: "Get a grip woman, it wouldn't be songs cast on water at all, at all. Scraping shite off a mantelpiece you'd be", and immediately the play structure came to her mind.[61] Described as a "feminist take" on the Irish myth, the play is set in the working-class Fatima Mansion flats in Dublin, where Meehan used to live, and "envisages a marginalised Ireland, where crime, drugs, domestic violence and AIDS prey on the lives of three women".[62] In review, O'Toole recognizes "extraordinary moments of theatre", yet takes issue with the formal experiment of placing the stylistic elements of the myth alongside contemporary social realities. However, Anna McMullan argues that the confines of realism in the play make poignant the socioeconomic entombment of people who have little or no means of escape. The culture of "upward mobility" and "self-actualization" alive in Irish mainstream society through the 1990s belongs to others—those who are more advantaged—and not to Meehan's women. For these women, the day-to-day work of survival for a community and its people within the prevailing order takes all that a body has got.[63]

Meehan's next play was commissioned by Calypso, and was shortlisted for Best New Play at the *Irish Times* Theatre Awards in the same year. Performed at the City Arts Centre, *Cell* (1999) is about the experience of prison of four women and is loosely based on Meehan's own history as a writer working within women's prisons for several years. Indeed, *Cell* has been described as "artistic witness…to the voices and the spirit of the women prisoners [Meehan] met".[64] The play also chimes with Calypso's own known commitment (as discussed earlier) to tackling social issues and to raising public awareness through theatre and performance.

In keeping with that ethos, Calypso received funding from the Department of Justice, and created an information pack in collaboration with the Penal Reform Trust. The pack documented prison conditions in Ireland and was handed out to audience members nightly before each performance. *Cell*'s four central characters each have their own back story: Delo (42) is in prison for heroin dealing, Alice (49) for murder, Martha (26) for shoplifting, and Lila (19) for possession of heroin. There is also the constant presence of a disembodied voice, controlling access into and out of the cell; and the cell is run by Delo, who controls Martha and Lila through their drug addictions. Alice, however, a newcomer from Leitrim, is not wise to the drug culture that dominates the other women's worlds. The play focuses on the power struggle between the women in the cell, heightened by the arrival of the outsider, while exposing the ultimate power that the prison wields over the lives of all the women inmates.[65]

In the *Irish Times*, Meehan spoke of those she had met in prison:

> I'm from the same social background as a lot of these women...These people aren't invisible to me. What's happening to them in prison is only a more extreme version of what's happening to them in their community [...] Few of the women I worked with I would describe as criminal. Most were victims of social forces, of the same class background as myself.[66]

Journalist Rosita Boland described the play as "unwatchable if it were not so powerful",[67] with the blackest of humour—like watching Martha going cold turkey while learning to crochet the Leitrim flag with Alice. Discussing her work, Meehan describes her vision: "I began to realize how powerfully healing the making path could be, you could actually transform what was oppressive into something very powerful".[68] Meehan identifies her obsessions as relating to class, and the level at which disparities in access and opportunities define and shape the story of people's lives. In *Cell*, Meehan exposes the grim mechanics of prison for these women, illuminating their lives as they are warped and wrought by the experience of being cogs in that machine. Such "theatre of commitment" clearly identifies Meehan's theatre, alongside that of the women performers and writers of Glasshouse, as theatre that defies the narrower strictures of staged female representation in mainstream theatre during the period.[69] *Cell* demonstrates that commitment in its positioning within Meehan's own background and community, its staging at the City Arts Centre, and its powerful telling of women's stories as a rebellious act of communication in the Irish theatre system.

Class Acts: Popular Politics and the Hybrid

I spoke earlier of the politics of popular performance in recent Irish theatre and performance histories, and outlined a loose formulation called the hybrid. I characterized the hybrid as an "ideological lynchpin", fused to capture the creative expression at work across the independent theatre and community arts scene from the 1970s to the millennium as a rough timeline. I want now to return to that discussion and to what the hybrid might stand for by looking to ideas of class in recent Irish cultural and political criticism.

Micheal Pierse quotes Maura Adshed who points out the failure of the "protagonists recorded and the political scientists recording—to explicitly recognise [...] class dimensions [...] the steadfast refusal to acknowledge class in popular political discourse", in Ireland.[70] In Pierce's view, "classless" Ireland is an historical misremembering with a legacy that has, over time, denied working-class people "access to their own histories and to the cultural production that mirrors their experiences".[71] And he is incisive on the question of why the study of Irish cultural production is not more attuned to the rigour of class analysis.[72]

In many respects, his thinking echoes the community arts story in Ireland. From its first day, the CAFE organization as advocate body for the sector was severely underfunded by the Arts Council. At the same time, it took on the impossible task of being all things to all people and groupings while meeting state organizational demands.[73] CAFE did create a rallying point for the sector, supported by the Council's remit to deal with one representative body, yet over time "so many activities had fallen under its umbrella", that "community arts itself had become indefinable".[74] There were those who resisted, as Annie Kilmartin believes: "We didn't actually want to be labelled as community arts, because we knew that it would become marginalised and it would be undervalued and underfunded".[75] It was felt that a community arts 'brand' would allowed the Arts Council to sideline the sector with small budgets and alternative funding, while retaining its rhetoric on the value of cultural democracy. As a consequence, the sector became involved in one-off and non-art aims that took it away from its advocacy and artistic role in the community. Successive Arts Plans (1995–1998; 1999–2001) reported sectoral attitudes on the 'ongoing marginalised position of the community arts' with calls for more value to be placed on the sector [...] "supporting long term projects [...] and fulfilling higher standards of practice".[76] Paula Clancy argues that while some movement forward in policy was apparent, with some real allocation of resources, in the main the Arts Council continued to keep the community arts outside the real power structures, with an ethos that meant the work fell into the category of "worthy", certainly, but not art. It was felt by sections of the sector that the Arts Council was intent on protecting art from community arts itself, which should be kept "at arm's length from the centre...rather than as a strategy for change" in the cultural, social and political power relationships of the period.[77]

In contrast, writing at the turn of this century, Joseph Long attests to the vigorous and continuing growth ofindependent theatre in Ireland. Experimental modes of theatre have developed, horizons have become international and more traditional goals have been usurped as newer ways of seeing and being seen are created.[78] Declan Gorman suggests that while more established theatres such as the Abbey have absorbed some of the independent sector's talent and spirit, he welcomes that symbiosis, pointing out the "national neglect of the leading independent innovators of the 1980s".[79] By the end of the 1990s in Ireland, state funding for the arts came to almost eight million Irish punts. There were somewhere in the region of fifty professionally run venues and over forty professional theatre companies, so that

> there are now more theatre buildings, more people involved in creating theatre, better training and a greater variety of performance to be seen than ever before. This is the most obvious manifestation of a healthy theatre culture.[80]

That said, the healthy state of millennial theatre culture cannot fully reflect the continuous chronic underfunding of the independent theatre sector, in which the inability to make a living and the struggle to produce work became untenable for many, and many a good company has vanished, including some companies discussed in this chapter. In something of a parallel trajectory, community-arts sectoral support perhaps reached its peak in the early to mid-1990s. However, the continual separation of artistic practice from alternative objectives and outcomes ultimately undermined and stripped the sector of its artistic ideals and political agency.

Fintan O'Toole suggests a stock answer for the cultural exclusion of support for community arts in Ireland: "great art is of its nature elitist [...] complex, challenging and almost always out of line with the assumptions of everyday life". So its audiences will always be in the minority, but "why should that minority be so easy to define in terms of its socio-economic class?"[81] O'Toole's observation of this oversimplification brings the discussion back to one of popular politics. Sharratt describes the popular political art form as that which contains or expresses in some way the "ideology of a social class", and which seeks to expose the controlling coda of the period. Fiske, too, argues for a popular politics as an oppositional force, necessarily in conflict with the ruling order, never allowing those in control to feel safe. However, drawing on Bourdieu and Barthes, Fiske suggests that popular art cannot be radical art, for "radical art is bourgeois and lies outside the bounds of popular taste"; "radical art may cause conflict between sections of the bourgeoisie, but it can never be part of a class war".[82] Perhaps. Yet, I would argue that this does not have to be the case. Fiske does suggest that radical art and popular art can bleed into each other, finding influences across stratifications. And maybe that is what the formulation of this hybrid can mean for the purpose of this analysis. It can describe the relationship between the community arts and the independent theatre sector in Ireland at particular flashpoints in recent theatre history. It can embody the two as an ideological concept from across the traditions, growth and fortunes of both, and encompass their spirit, ethos and drive. It allows for the interrogation of the performance work across those blurred boundaries over the timeframe under discussion. But most importantly, the formulation creates a way to understand how both forms fused into one another to represent "fragments of the whole story" in recent Irish theatre and performance. The story of a community finding its voice to tell the unseen or unheard stories of its experiences, equally, and joining with others to do so as a creative expression and as an action for change. The story of a community attempting to come to grips with its past, its present moment and its imagined future in the full glare of the advancing European project.

Finally, the tradition of community arts in Ireland over the last thirty-odd years is an ethnographic case study on its relationship with those who never shook off a collective uncertainty about the artistic value of the local arts. Those who, with quiet power, continually resist the truly radical struggle for cultural democracy, in which all voices are equally valued. That said, both the independent theatre and the community arts world have taken action by blurring those boundaries to speak from within the hybrid space for a time. From that space, they have spoken about the "right of people to contribute to and participate fully in culture, [they speak to] the right to have a voice and the right to give voice".[83] Peter Sheridan believed that the "alternative" is about being able to interrogate the "complexities of reality", and to create artistic work that tries to represent or envisage a political way forward.[84] It is doubtful, certainly within the timeframe considered in this chapter, that the ideal (or nettle for some) of cultural democracy in Irish society has been fully grasped. And that requires vigilant watching.

Notes

1. *Peter Sheridan, "The Theatre and Politics," in The Crane Bag Book of Irish Studies, 1977–1981, ed. M.P. Hederman et al. (Dublin: The Blackwater Press, 1982), 75.*
2. Bernard Sharratt, "The politics of the popular?—From melodrama to television", in *Performance and Politics in Popular Drama*, ed. David Bradby et al. (Cambridge: Cambridge University Press, 1980), 275.
3. John Fiske, *Understanding Popular Culture* (London: Routledge, 1989).
4. Ibid., 160.
5. Ibid., 160.
6. Ibid., 160.
7. Anna McMullan and Trish McTighe, "Samuel Beckett, the Gate Theatre Dublin and the Contemporary Irish Independent Theatre Sector: Fragments of Performance History", *Breac: A Digital Journal of Irish Studies* (2014): 2, accessed March 1, 2017, https://breac.nd.edu/articles/samuel-beckett-the-gate-theatre-dublin-and-the-contemporary-irish-independent-theatre-sector-fragments-of-performance-history.
8. McMullan and McTighe, "Samuel Beckett", 3.
9. Ibid.
10. Beckett's play transferred to the Gate Theatre and subsequently toured the country into 1956, while *The Quare Fellow* was later produced at the Abbey and Joan Littlewood's Theatre Workshop in London. The Pike Theatre caused controversy when it staged the Irish premiere of Tennessee Williams' *The Rose Tattoo* in 1957 as its contribution to the inaugural Dublin Theatre Festival. Simpson was prosecuted for obscenity for including a mimed representation of a condom on stage. The costly and tedious process of going through the Irish courts before Simpson was exonerated caused irrevocable damage to the Pike's fortunes, which closed its doors in 1961.
11. O'Connor cited in Morash, "*A History of Irish Theatre*", 217.
12. The centre became the home of independent theatre company Rough Magic in the 1980s. Loose Canon and Bedrock developed their craft there, along with Dagdha Dance Company, among others.
13. Declan Gorman, "Long Live the Fringe", *Irish Theatre Magazine* 1:1 (1998): 3.
14. Fitzgerald, "The Beginnings of Community Arts", 70.
15. Ibid., 68.
16. Ibid., 69.
17. Ibid., 68–70.
18. Ibid., 70, 77.
19. Paula Clancy, "Rhetoric and Reality: A Review of the Position of Community Arts in State Cultural Policy in the Irish Republic" in *An Outburst of Frankness*, ed. Sandy Fitzgerald (Dublin, New Island, 2004), 106.
20. Ibid., 85.
21. Brian Kennedy cited in Clancy, "Rhetoric and Reality", 86.
22. Ciarán Benson cited in Clancy, "Rhetoric and Reality", 90. The ACE Report was the result of a four-year action research project undertaken by the Arts Community Education Committee and funded by the Arts Council and the Gulbenkian Foundation. The project researched six Education and Community Arts Projects funded by ACE between 1985 and 1989. Indeed, CAFE, as the "representative body" for the Community Arts in Ireland, was partly funded by ACE.

23. Lar Cassidy cited in Clancy, "Rhetoric and Reality", 92.
24. Karen Fricker, "Travelling Without Moving: True Lines and Contemporary Irish Theatre Practice", in *Druids, Dudes and Beauty Queens: The Changing Face of Irish Theatre*, ed. Dermot Bolger (Dublin: New Island, 2001), 117.
25. Gorman, "Long Live the Fringe", 3.
26. Jenny Harris cited in Clancy, "Rhetoric and Reality", 108.
27. Mic Moroney, "The Twisted Mirror: Landscapes, Mindscapes, Politics and Language on the Irish Stage", in *Druids, Dudes and Beauty Queens: The Changing Face of Irish Theatre*, ed. Dermot Bolger (Dublin: New Island, 2001), 264.
28. Fitzgerald, "The Beginnings of Community Arts", 72.
29. The 'Monto' was a famous red-light district in Dublin. The collective was also involved in the North Star Conferences of 1983/84, which led to the formation of CAFE, as discussed earlier.
30. Fintan O'Toole cited in Morash, "*A History of Irish Theatre*", 262.
31. Jim Culleton, "Paul Mercier in Conversation with Jim Culleton", in *Theatre Talk: Voices of Irish Theatre Practitioners*, ed. Lillian Chambers et al. (Dublin: Carysfort Press, 2001), 336.
32. Joseph Long, "Come Dance with Me in Ireland: Current Developments in the Independent Theatre Sector", in *Theatre Stuff: Critical Essays on Contemporary Irish Theatre*, ed. Eamonn Jordan (Dublin: Carysfort Press, 2000), 90.
33. The work produced with the company also helped to launch the careers of both Roddy Doyle and Brendan Gleeson; both were teachers at the same school as Mercier, Greendale Community School in Kilbarrack, North Dublin.
34. Lauren Onkey, "The Passion Machine Theatre Company's Everyday Life", in *A Century of Irish Drama: Widening the Stage*, ed. Stephen Watt et al. (Indiana: Indiana University Press, 2000), 225.
35. Redmond O'Hanlon, "In Conversation with Redmond O'Hanlon", in *Critical Moments: Fintan O'Toole on Modern Irish Theatre*, ed. Julia Furay and Redmond O'Hanlon (Dublin: Carysfort Press, 2003), 336.
36. *Critical Moments: Fintan O'Toole on Modern Irish Theatre*, 45.
37. Ibid., 54.
38. Victor Merriman, *Because We Are Poor: Irish Theatre in the 1990s* (Dublin: Carysfort, 2011), 12.
39. Ibid., 156.
40. Ibid.
41. Merriman, *Because We Are Poor*, 157–160; Martine Pelletier, "Dermot Bolger's Drama", in *Theatre Stuff: Critical Essays on Contemporary Irish Theatre*, ed. Eamonn Jordan (Dublin: Carysfort Press, 2000), 250.
42. Merriman, *Because We Are Poor*, 166–68.
43. Nowlan in Merriman, *Because We Are Poor*, 167.
44. *Critical Moments: Fintan O'Toole on Modern Irish Theatre*, 323–4.
45. Merriman, *Because We Are Poor*, 167.
46. Gerry Colgan, "Rosie and Starwars", *Irish Times*, February 28, 1997, accessed March 1, 2017, https://www.irishtimes.com/culture/rosie-and-starwars-html.
47. For full review, see *Irish Times*, September 25, 1998, accessed March 3, 2017, https://www.irishtimes.com/culture/farawayan-html.
48. Paula Meehan, "The Apprentice", in Return and No Blame (Dublin: Beaver Row Press, 1984), 27.

49. Caroline Williams, Katie Hayes, Siân Quill and Clare Dowling, "People in Glasshouse: An Anecdotal History of an Independent Theatre Company", in *Druids, Dudes and Beauty Queens: The Changing Face of Irish Theatre*, ed. Dermot Bolger (Dublin: New Island, 2001), 132.
50. Williams et al, "People in Glasshouse", 135.
51. Ibid., 135–37.
52. Ibid., 137.
53. Ibid., 140.
54. Cathy Leeney, "I Know My Own Heart; Ladies and Gentlemen", in *The Methuen Drama Guide to Contemporary Irish Playwrights*, ed. Martin Middeke and Peter Paul Schnierer (London: Methuen, 2010), 77.
55. Williams et al, "People in Glasshouse", 145–6.
56. Charlotte McIvor, "Albert Nobbs, Ladies and Gentlemen, and Quare Irish Female Erotohistories", *Irish University Review*, 43 (2013): 1.
57. Luke Clancy, "Ladies and Gentlemen", *Irish Times*, April 19, 1996, accessed February 20, 2017, https://www.irishtimes.com/culture/ladies-and-gentlement-html.
58. *Sunday Tribune*, April 1996, accessed February 20, 2017.
59. Charlotte McIvor, "Albert Nobbs, Ladies and Gentlemen", 5–6.
60. Anna McMullan, "Unhomely Stages: Women Taking (a) Place in Irish Theatre", in *Dudes and Beauty Queens: The Changing Face of Irish Theatre*, ed. Dermot Bolger (Dublin: New Island, 2001), 83.
61. Paula Meehan in McMullan "Unhomely Stages", 83.
62. *Critical Moments: Fintan O'Toole on Modern Irish Theatre*, 177–8.
63. McMullan "Unhomely Stages", 85.
64. Eileen Denn Jackson, "The Lyricism of Abjection in Paula Meehan's Drama of Imprisonment", *An Sionnach: A Journal of Literature, Culture, and the Arts*, 5 (2009): 177.
65. Mountjoy Prison–Dóchas is a medium security prison for women aged over eighteen years, located in Dublin, Ireland.
66. Rosita Boland, "Out of the Joy", *Irish Times*, September 11, 1999, accessed February 26, 2017, https://www.irishtimes.com/news/out-of-the-joy-html.
67. Boland, "Out of the Joy", [n.p].
68. Jackson, "The Lyricism of Abjection", 177.
69. Ibid.
70. Michael Pierse, "From Yeatsian Nightmares to Tallifornian Dreams: Reflections on Classism and Culture in 'Classless' Ireland", in *Locked Out: A Century of Irish Working-Class Life*, ed. David Convery (Kildare: Irish Academic Press, 2013), 196.
71. Ibid., 204.
72. Ibid., 197–205.
73. Through the 1980s the community arts were successful at funding outside the confines of a limited budgetary line from the Arts Council, including European funding and Department of Labour and Community Employment Schemes, at times far surpassing the budget offered by the Council for the community arts.
74. Fitzgerald, "The Beginnings of Community Arts", 75.
75. Annie Kilmartin is the founder of Moving Theatre and one of the founders of Community Arts For Everyone (CAFE). See Peter Crawley, "What on Earth is Community Art?" in *Irish Times*, December 7, 2004, accessed February 28, 2017, https://www.irishtimes.com/culture/what-on-earth-is-community-art.html.

76. The third Arts Plan (2002–2006), while listing "concerns about the state of the arts", makes no mention of the clear "disparity of access and participation between different groupings". Clancy, "Rhetoric and Reality", 98–9.
77. Cocking cited in Clancy, "Rhetoric and Reality", 107.
78. Long, "Come Dance with Me in Ireland", 93.
79. Gorman, "Long Live the Fringe", 4.
80. Morash, *A History of Irish Theatre*, 271.
81. *Critical Moments: Fintan O'Toole on Modern Irish Theatre*, 325.
82. John Fiske, *Understanding Popular Culture*, 161.
83. Fitzgerald, "The Beginnings of Community Arts", 79.
84. Peter Sheridan, "The Theatre and Politics," in *The Crane Bag Book of Irish Studies*, 1977–1981, ed. M.P. Hederman et al. (Dublin: The Blackwater Press, 1982), 75.

Bibliography

Boland, Rosita. "Out of the Joy." *Irish Times*, September 11, 1999. Accessed February 26, 2017. https://www.irishtimes.com/news/out-of-the-joy-html.

Colgan, Gerry. "Rosie and Starwars." *Irish Times*, February 28, 1997. Accessed January 13, 2017. http://www.irishtimes.com/culture/rosie-and-starwars-html.

Clancy, Luke. "Ladies and Gentlemen." *Irish Times*, April 19, 1996. Accessed February 20, 2017.

Clancy, Paula. "Rhetoric and Reality: A Review of the Position of Community Arts in State Cultural Policy in the Irish Republic." In *An Outburst of Frankness*, edited by Sandy Fitzgerald, 83–114. Dublin: New Island, 2004.

Crawley, Peter. "What on Earth Is Community Art?" *Irish Times*, December 7, 2004. Accessed February 28, 2017. https://www.irishtimes.com/culture/what-on-earth-is-community-art.html.

Critical Moments: Fintan O'Toole on Modern Irish Theatre, edited by Julia Furay and Redmond O'Hanlon. Dublin: Carysfort Press, 2003.

Culleton, Jim. "Paul Mercier in Conversation with Jim Culleton." In *Theatre Talk: Voices of Irish Theatre Practitioners*, edited by Lillian Chambers et al., 331–341. Dublin: Carysfort Press, 2001.

Fitzgerald, Sandy. "The Beginnings of Community Arts and the Irish Republic." In *An Outburst of Frankness*, edited by Sandy Fitzgerald. 64–79. Dublin: New Island, 2004.

Fiske, John. *Understanding Popular Culture*. London: Routledge, 1989.

Fricker, Karen. "Travelling Without Moving: True Lines and Contemporary Irish Theatre Practice." In *Druids, Dudes and Beauty Queens: The Changing Face of Irish Theatre*, edited by Dermot Bolger, 104–119. Dublin: New Island, 2001.

Gorman, Declan. "Long Live the Fringe." In *Irish Theatre Magazine*. 1:1 (1998): 3–4.

Jackson, Eileen Denn. "The Lyricism of Abjection in Paula Meehan's Drama of Imprisonment." *An Sionnach: A Journal of Literature, Culture, and the Arts*, 5 (2009): 169–179.

Laclau, E. *Politics and Ideology in Marxist Theory*. London: New Left, 1977.

Leeney, Cathy. "I Know My Own Heart; Ladies and Gentlemen." In *The Methuen Drama Guide to Contemporary Irish Playwrights*, edited by Martin Middeke and Peter Paul Schnierer, 73–88. London: Methuen, 2010.

Long, Joseph. "Come Dance With Me in Ireland: Current Developments in the Independent Theatre Sector." In *Theatre Stuff: Critical Essays on Contemporary Irish Theatre*, edited by Eamonn Jordan, 89–94. Dublin: Carysfort Press, 2000.

McIvor, Charlotte. "Albert Nobbs, Ladies and Gentlemen, and Quare Irish Female Erotohistories." *Irish University Review* 43 (2013): 1–25.

McMullan, Anna. "Unhomely Stages: Women Taking (a) Place in Irish Theatre." In *Dudes and Beauty Queens: The Changing Face of Irish Theatre*, edited by Dermot Bolger, 72–90. Dublin: New Island, 2001.

McMullan, Anna and Trish McTighe. "Samuel Beckett, the Gate Theatre Dublin and the Contemporary Irish Independent Theatre Sector: Fragments of Performance History." *Breac: A Digital Journal of Irish Studies* (2014): 1–13. Accessed March 1, 2017, https://breac.nd.edu/articles/samuel-beckett-the-gate-theatre-dublin-and-the-contemporary-irish-independent-theatre-sector-fragments-of-performance-history.

Meehan, Paula. "The Apprentice." In *Return and No Blame*. Dublin: Beaver Row Press, 1984.

Merriman, Victor. *Because We Are Poor: Irish Theatre in the 1990s*. Dublin: Carysfort, 2011.

———. "Settling for More: Excess and Success in Contemporary Irish Drama." In *Druids, Dudes and Beauty Queens: The Changing Face of Irish Theatre*, edited by Dermot Bolger, 55–71. Dublin: New Island, 2001.

Morash, Christopher. *A History of Irish Theatre*. Cambridge: Cambridge University Press, 2002.

Moroney, Mic. "The Twisted Mirror: Landscapes, Mindscapes, Politics and Language on the Irish Stage." In *Druids, Dudes and Beauty Queens: The Changing Face of Irish Theatre*, edited by Dermot Bolger, 250–275. Dublin: New Island, 2001.

O'Hanlon, Redmond. "In Conversation with Redmond O'Hanlon." In *Critical Moments: Fintan O'Toole on Modern Irish Theatre*, edited by Julia Furay and Redmond O'Hanlon, 341–377.Dublin: Carysfort Press, 2003.

Onkey, Lauren. "The Passion Machine Theatre Company's Everyday Life." In *A Century of Irish Drama: Widening the Stage*, edited by Stephen Watt, Eileen Morgan, and Shakir Mustafa, 223–238. Indiana: Indiana University Press, 2000.

Pelletier, Martine. "Dermot Bolgers Drama." In *Theatre Stuff: Critical Essays on Contemporary Irish Theatre*, edited by Eamonn Jordan, 249–256. Dublin: Carysfort Press, 2000.

Pierse, Michael. "From Yeatsian Nightmares to Tallifornian Dreams: Reflections on Classism and Culture in 'Classless' Ireland." In *Locked Out: A Century of Irish Working-Class Life*, edited by David Convery, 193–209. Kildare: Irish Academic Press, 2013.

Sharratt, Bernard. "The Politics of the Popular?—From Melodrama to Television." In *Performance and Politics in Popular Drama*, edited by David Bradby, Louis James and Bernard Sharratt, 275–291. Cambridge: Cambridge University Press, 1980.

Sheridan, Peter. "The Theatre and Politics." In *The Crane Bag Book of Irish Studies, 1977–1981*, edited by M.P. Hederman and R. Kearney, 73–77. Dublin: The Blackwater Press, 1982.

Williams, Caroline, Katie Hayes, Siân Quill & Clare Dowling. "People in Glasshouse: An Anecdotal History of an Independent Theatre Company." In *Druids, Dudes and Beauty Queens: The Changing Face of Irish Theatre*, edited by Dermot Bolger, 132–147. Dublin: New Island, 2001.

Other Theatres

Christopher Collins

Contemporary Irish theatre has a diverse investment in performance and place that necessarily demands different spatial practices: work may be staged in ornate Victorian theatres or immersed in city streets. What is critically apparent is that very few companies in contemporary Irish theatre have their own space for rehearsal, let alone their own place for performance. On the one hand, this trend clearly demonstrates the growth and diversification of contemporary Irish theatre and performance practitioners; on the other, it demonstrates that contemporary Irish theatre operates within a funding infrastructure that privileges the larger houses over smaller ones, and by corollary those companies whose work can fill these houses. There are, however, one hundred and three other theatres and arts centres on the island (in 2018) that are filling an invaluable role in supporting the sector, particularly when it comes to offering spaces for rehearsal and places to perform.

This chapter seeks to foreground the unique places and spaces of these "other theatres", so that the conversation about place, space and theatre and performance on the island can be more inclusive. Although my focus will largely be on the other theatres south of the border, I will also discuss other theatres in Ulster. Pat Kiernan, artistic director of Corcadorca Theatre Company based in Cork, points out that in Ireland "there's still that chocolate-box image that can inhibit a first-time theatre-goer".[1] First-timers can feel that while the conventional theatre might look inviting, visiting it is too much of a risk because they do not know what to expect. All of the other theatres in this chapter use space to create a unique sense of place that directly challenges that idealized but intimidating image. From providing space for experimental work

C. Collins (✉)
University of Nottingham, Nottingham, UK
e-mail: christopher.collins@nottingham.ac.uk

E. Jordan, E. Weitz (eds.), *The Palgrave Handbook of Contemporary Irish Theatre and Performance*,
https://doi.org/10.1057/978-1-137-58588-2_14

to being actively involved in their respective communities, other theatres on the island have an individual place in contemporary Irish theatre.

Other Theatres in Context

The late 1970s brought a change in the infrastructure that continues to support contemporary Irish theatre to this day. As Christopher Morash points out, "until the late 1970s, virtually all theatre funding on the island went to the three main theatres: the Abbey, the Lyric and the Gate. However, policy changes in arts funding in both jurisdictions in the late 1970s initiated a new regional awareness".[2] In 1979 in Ireland, An Chomhairle Ealaíon (The Arts Council) introduced the Independent Theatre Management Scheme, which offered extra funding to different companies that were caught having "to choose between the maintenance of the institutions where creative work can be performed or developing the conditions for the creation of art".[3] With financial support from the Council, companies were able to tour their work to regional theatres across the island. For example, in 1980 Field Day Theatre Company received support from the scheme so that Brian Friel's *Translations* (1980) could tour from Derry/Londonderry to Galway, Tralee, Cork and Dublin. The Council's annual report for that year reflected on the importance of the scheme because it made a "contribution—both financial and artistic—to theatres outside Dublin", while acknowledging that they had a responsibility to create "a network of adequately equipped theatres".[4] Consequently, the annual report for 1981 documents increased funding for the Everyman Theatre in Cork, Siamsa Tíre in Tralee and Hawk's Well Theatre in Sligo because "the most important development which the Council can assist in the area of theatre" was growing "the number and professionalism of theatres outside of Dublin".[5]

As Victor Merriman notes, throughout the 1980s and 1990s there was an exponential growth in new places of performance "from nineteen (eleven theatres and eight arts centres) in 1983 to fifty-five (twenty-eight theatres and twenty-seven arts centres) by 2001".[6] Collectively, between 1990 and 2008, seventy-five new places of performance were built on the island and, as Merriman suggests, "companies were involved either in generating performance spaces or in occupying them, once built".[7] These theatres were all built and/or renovated in line with the Council's commitment to public access and participation, which is why there was an increase in arts centres (multi-purpose venues that include a theatre space) across this period; for example, in 1997 there was a significant increase (12%) in funding to arts centres, and the annual report for that year justifies the expenditure on the basis that arts centres can be "directed towards serving the needs of a particular interest group, such as children and young people, or a local community".[8]

The rapid increase in places of performance from 1980 to 2008 was an essential support to the infrastructure of Irish theatre. However, since the economic downturn in 2008, places of performance on the island have been significantly affected due to the lack of funding from the Arts Councils in Ireland and Northern Ireland. If companies were once at the heart of building and restoring theatre venues, then by 2008 many of these companies were homeless as their funding had been cut. Nevertheless, companies and practitioners continued to emerge. What this has meant for the sector is that the number of venues that commission, receive and produce work is at odds with the number of spaces for performance and rehearsal. By corollary, the artistic visions of some venues are restricted; in order to keep the lights switched on, venues must make an effective use of their space. Likewise, the same can be said for theatre companies and practitioners who have to curate their practice with care to respond to the competition over space.

Some theatres on the island with distinctive artistic visions have not been affected by the funding cuts. The New Theatre, founded in Dublin in 1997, is an example of one theatre that had not been drastically affected by the funding cuts because its artistic vision was already bespoke: the theatre solely supports new writing. Yet the uniqueness of the New Theatre highlights the fact that the privilege of space results in a limited and limiting artistic vision. Enda Walsh, who first directed his play *Bedbound* in the New Theatre in 2000, puts the situation in apposite terms: When asked "What's your favourite theatre space in Ireland?", Walsh replied: "I must say I had a great experience in the New Theatre in Dublin doing *Bedbound*, because everyone had forgotten it is a venue. [...] there aren't places like that now".[9] There aren't many theatres like the New Theatre because of the financial demands placed on theatres: new writing is a potentially risky business. For example, Bewley's Cafe Theatre, founded in Dublin in 1999, stages new writing, but the theatre also stages the lesser-known works of canonical playwrights and writers such as Tennessee Williams and Oscar Wilde.

With a lack of venues that have specific artistic remits, it is unsurprising that many of the theatres on the island act as receiving venues that are supported either by local companies or as part of a touring network. If contemporary Irish theatre is to continue to flourish—particularly outside of the major towns and cities—then it is vitally important that the sector is supported by a healthy combination of venues that serve the community, while at the same time facilitating contemporary practice on a touring network. The Strollers Touring Network is the largest touring network on the island, comprised of nine theatres/arts centres: Draíocht Arts Centre (Dublin), Hawk's Well (Sligo), Linenhall Arts Centre (Mayo), Riverbank Arts Centre (Kildare), Siamsa Tíre, the National Folk Theatre and Arts Centre (Kerry), Solstice Arts Centre (Meath), The Source Arts Centre (Tipperary), the Visual Centre for Contemporary Art & the George Bernard Shaw Theatre (Carlow) and the Watergate Theatre (Kilkenny). The Network has a production award that offers companies and practitioners €10,000 to facilitate the tour, with a further fee guaranteed from each of the nine venues that cumulates in approximately €20,000 for each recipient.

The diversity of theatres across the island is an important material point. Morash and Shaun Richards have questioned: "If theatre in performance creates an event that is by definition local, why is theatre—particularly Irish theatre—so often considered in the context of the national?"[10] Other theatres in contemporary Ireland are no longer concerned with staging the national from the urban centre, but staging the local, often from the rural periphery. This is reflected by work that regularly engages with a local sense of place, as well as the fact that regional theatres engage with their communities through youth theatre and/or amateur dramatics. For example, the Waterside Arts Centre in Derry/Londonderry has two youth theatre groups. It is therefore possible to ascertain an ideological reading of space based upon the distribution of these theatres across the island: contemporary Irish theatre privileges the local over the national. However, Morash and Richards have suggested that

> the spread of physical spaces for theatre around the national space [does] not necessarily reinforce the idea of a national theatre; it could, in fact, have the opposite effect, highlighting regional difference over national solidarity [...] For an audience in Navan, for instance, there is a difference between watching a play that has been produced in their home town at the Solstice Theatre by a locally based company, and one that is on tour from a national theatre based in the capital.[11]

While this is certainly true, it is also equally important to think about how a local theatre relates to a national sense of theatre. A regional, local sense of place is always intricately and inextricably interrelated to a national sense of place. As geographer Doreen Massey has argued, if we consider space as a multiplicity of connections, then this allows for contemporary Irish theatres to embody "a politics of outwardlookingness, from place to place".[12] The local, regional spaces of contemporary Irish theatre should not be reductively bound to a fixed sense of locale, or a territorial sense of place.

This alternative spatial reading of contemporary Irish theatre is most evident in amateur theatre. Amateur theatre on the island is fostered by the Amateur Drama Council of Ireland, which holds regional festivals, the winners of which proceed to the annual All Ireland Drama Festival in Athlone. The emphasis here is on staging the local in the national, or in other words, finding the ways in which a local theatre constellates into a national sense of theatre. In the professional sector other theatres on the island have emerged as playing an integral role in supporting the sector, while at the same time remaining active, engaged participants in their local communities. This is due in large part to the specific role that arts centres have played in supporting companies and practitioners with space to research, develop and emerge. These artists then go on to present their work in local theatres before touring them across the island. For example, WillFredd Theatre's *Follow* (2011) by Shane O'Reilly and Jack Cawley, about deaf and hard-of-hearing culture on the island, was developed in a short twenty-minute performance at the Project Arts Centre in Dublin in 2010 under a scheme called Project Brand New, before premiering in 2011 at a local theatre in Dublin, the Lír. The production then toured to theatres and arts centres across the island, finally arriving at the Abbey Theatre in 2014. In this way, other theatres on the island are instrumental in ensuring that contemporary Irish theatre is not restricted by place, or that companies are not restricted by artistic vision. Other theatres facilitate a collective, shared sense of space in contemporary Irish theatre. As Massey points out, space is "the sphere of a dynamic simultaneity, constantly disconnected by new arrivals, constantly waiting to be determined (and therefore always underdetermined) by the construction of new relations. It is always being made and always therefore, in a sense, unfinished".[13] The same could be said for the use of spaces in other theatres in contemporary Ireland.

Theatres and Arts Centres

Theatres that commission or produce their own work are accordingly at liberty to curate their own spaces, and there are diverse curatorial policies on the island. Located in Galway city centre is An Taibhdhearc, the national Irish language theatre. Founded in 1928, An Taibhdhearc plays an invaluable role in allowing access to theatre for speakers of Ireland's national language (Gaeilge). Brian Ó Conchubhair has argued that An Taibhdhearc "faces many of the problems it confronted in the 1930s and 1940s: the need to procure new scripts and strike a balance between translations and original work".[14] Yet, in 2014 Galway-based Moonfish Theatre worked with the theatre to stage an adaptation of Joseph O'Connor's novel *Star of the Sea*. The bilingual production premiered at the theatre during the International Galway Arts Festival before heading to the Dublin Theatre Festival. Ó Conchubhair points out that "the fundamental problem is a mismatch between supply—a limited number of theatre companies—and demand—a fractured audience, scattered throughout the country, unaccustomed to attending semi/professional productions".[15]

The difficulties that places like An Taibhdhearc face are very real, but the promise of space does result in a consistent artistic vision. The same can be said for Siamsa Tíre National Folk Theatre and Arts Centre, founded in Tralee in 1991. As the island's National Folk Theatre, the theatre engages with Ireland's folk heritage by predominantly staging work from its extensive repertoire. For example, the theatre performs *Fadó Fadó* (1968)—a production that celebrates Irish rural life past—almost on an annual basis. However, while it is important that both An Taibhdhearc and Siamsa Tíre have their own dedicated theatres that directly support national language and collective heritage, the point remains that the work of these theatres is not regularly incorporated into dialogue about contemporary Irish theatre practice, despite the success of the adaptation of *Star of the Sea* by An Taibhdhearc and Moonfish Theatre. This is another example of how a theatre's artistic vision can be potentially limited by its own specific use of space. However, this is not always the case. The Factory Performance Space in County Sligo is the home of Blue Raincoat Theatre Company. The theatre was founded in 1991, the same year in which the company was formed. Prior to becoming a theatre the Factory was a slaughterhouse throughout the 1980s, and Rhona Trench points out that "the notion of the performance space as abattoir figuratively represents Blue Raincoat's rejection of the predominantly text-based theatrical style that dominated Irish theatre in the 1980s and 1990s".[16] The company regularly brings a heightened sense of physicality and corporeality to its productions, as evidenced in its 2014 production of J.M. Synge's *The Playboy of the Western World*. Furthermore, as Trench points out, the company "play[s] a key role in the development of community access to and participation in the arts in Sligo".[17]

Two integral arts centres on the island are Project Arts Centre in Dublin and the Metropolitan Arts Centre in Belfast. Project Arts Centre in Dublin uses its space to programme national and international contemporary art, theatre and performance. While Project has certainly had to adapt to changing economic markets, its artistic vision for theatre and performance has remained intact: Project is synonymous with contemporary style and form. Founded in 1967 and finding its permanent home in Temple Bar in 1975, Project is a multidisciplinary venue with one art gallery and two theatre spaces that nurture new work just as much as they revive and restage historical and contemporary drama. What makes Project an innovative arts centre is its insistence on working with emerging and established theatre makers to give them a larger stage on which to present their work. Often these theatre makers have staged their work in smaller theatres; the spaces that Project provides facilitate wider audience access to work that grew from more modest origins.

Project does not have any official relationship with theatres in Ireland, but current Artistic Director Cian O'Brien is always in dialogue with other theatres and theatre makers who might be interested in working with Project. "We have always sought out new voices and artists; whether they are artists making their first work or experienced artists who wish to experiment with their practice", O'Brien explains, "and Project Arts Centre is a place where artists can expand and develop their work, and bring it to new audiences and evolve their practice over long periods of time".[18] For example, Emmet Kirwan's *Dublin Oldschool* opened at Project in 2014; it had premiered at Bewley's Cafe Theatre at the Tiger Dublin Fringe Festival earlier that year. The roots of the production are relatively humble: it was first developed by the Show in a Bag programme, an initiative run by the Dublin Fringe Festival and Fishamble: The New Play Company, and the Irish Theatre Institute. However, Project gave the production a larger platform and supported a tour to international festivals and to the Royal National Theatre in London. Indeed, the production also appeared at the Metropolitan Arts Centre (MAC) in Belfast, which is, in some respects, Belfast's answer to Project in Dublin.

Located in Belfast's Cathedral Quarter, the MAC is similar to Project in that it programmes national and international contemporary art, theatre and performance. Like Project, the MAC also has two theatre spaces. However, the venue is considerably larger: it has three art galleries, one rehearsal space, one dance studio, three education and workshop rooms, as well as one artist-in-residence studio. MAC's spaces are invested with the history and heritage of Belfast. For example, Owen McCafferty's *Titanic: Scenes from the British Wreck Commissioner's Inquiry, 1912* opened at the MAC in April 2012, a month after the museum Titanic Belfast opened. The MAC is committed to outreach and public engagement. Since its opening in 2012, the arts centre has had over 29,000 people take part in community group activities—encompassing a variety of art, music and theatre workshops—from cross-community groups to school and youth groups in Belfast.[19]

The MAC is an example of how arts centres on the island use contemporaneous styles and forms of theatre to engage with local communities. For example, Moonfish Theatre was the 2016 company resident at the Riverbank Arts Centre, Newbridge, Kildare, where it created *Pop-Up Worlds* (2016) This production created mini pop-up audio storybooks in which actors recounted stories of Kildare people who were active in the 1916 Easter Rising. As part of the residency, the company hosted community workshops on "Electric Theatre", in which people of all ages and backgrounds explored the relationship theatre and performance has with scenography, sound design, electronics and coding. It is because of their wider artistic visions that arts centres are able to use their spaces to cater to wider demographics. Indeed, some arts centres, like the Ards Arts Centre in County Down, offer their own small-scale funding to local practitioners. In many respects, regional arts centres both north and south of the border lie at the heart of their communities, offering a dialogue with a local sense of place, while at the same time allowing companies and practitioners to stage their own work. Often these arts centres are in the larger towns in counties such as Armagh, Wexford and Omagh. As the example of Moonfish Theatre at the Riverbank Arts Centre demonstrates, arts centres are instrumental in supporting the sector by offering artist in residency schemes that practitioners and companies apply for through the Arts Councils of Ireland and Northern Ireland. While not an arts centre proper, the Tyrone Guthrie Centre in Monaghan provides residencies to practitioners of all disciplines, and it is supported by the Arts Council of Northern Ireland and the Arts Council of Ireland. The Centre hosts a week-long residency programme called MAKE that gives theatre practitioners and companies the space and time to generate new performance work.

The division between arts centres and theatres is far from simple. Theatres and arts centres rarely produce their own work, but they do co-produce work by offering a box-office split or a guaranteed fee. However, much more than this, theatres and arts centres accommodate a broad spectrum of contemporary practice while at the same time striving to be at the heart of their local communities. In Sligo, Hawk's Well Theatre, founded in 1982 (and renovated in 1986), provides a performance space for local drama groups, such as the St. Farnan's Drama Group and the Sligo Everyman, while at the same time continuing to be a space for established companies to stage new work. For example, in 2014 the theatre co-produced *The Second Coming* with Fidget Feet, an aerial dance theatre company from Donegal. Based on W.B. Yeats's poem,

"The Second Coming", the theatre became a space to interrogate Yeats's legacy in the very heart of Yeats country. In Dublin, Collapsing Horse Theatre was resident at The Civic Theatre in Tallaght from 2013 to 2014, where it developed and had work-in-progress showings of its production of *The Aeneid* before it premiered in 2016 at Smock Alley Theatre in Dublin—the oldest theatre on the island. The company was also resident at Draíocht Arts Centre in Blanchardstown from 2016 to 2017, where it developed *Conor at the End of the Universe* (2016), a Theatre for Young Audiences production about astrophysics. Both residencies involved community engagement: in Tallaght the company held puppetry workshops with different age groups; in Blanchardstown the company worked with D15 Youth Theatre. Similarly, in Carlow WillFredd Theatre was company in residence at the Visual Centre for Contemporary Art and the George Bernard Shaw Theatre, where it developed and premiered *Jockey* (2015) in collaboration with local racing and equestrian communities. In many respects, other theatres and arts centres are the lifeblood of contemporary Irish theatre, particularly because they offer laboratory spaces for practitioners and companies to test out new ideas. However, arts centres have a specifically pluralist artistic vision, which means they are able to accommodate a broader spectrum of contemporary Irish theatre and performance. Consequently, arts centres are clearly at the forefront of nurturing and supporting new work from both emerged and emergent practitioners that can then be taken into theatres.

In Cork, Corcadorca established the Theatre Development Centre in the Triskel Arts Centre. The Theatre Development Centre led to the creation of another Centre in Waterford in 2016: A Little Room. A Little Room is housed in Garter Lane Arts Theatre, which is predominantly a receiving venue. The symbiosis between Garter Lane and the Development Centre affords the opportunity for work to be developed before transferring to a venue that is more public-facing. Indeed, the Theatre Development Centre is a fully-equipped space in which organizations can rehearse and take up residence. The Centre holds the annual SHOW festival, a work in progress festival that is run over one weekend and offers a platform for companies to show their work to wider audiences. A company that has been resident at the Centre and has participated in the festival is BrokenCrow Theatre Company. BrokenCrow has staged work in other theatres in Cork: the Granary Theatre, the Half Moon Theatre (Cork Opera House) and the Everyman. Emerging companies like BrokenCrow are able to present work in these places because of the support they have received from places like the Triskel Arts Centre.

Such support is not always as forthcoming from established theatres under pressure to make a return at the box office. The largest and oldest theatre in Cork is the ornate Victorian theatre, the Everyman, founded in 1897. The theatre has a diverse programme ranging from various forms and styles of theatre to music and comedy. However, a theatre like the Everyman is in an awkward artistic position due to its sheer size, in that it has a box-office responsibility to sell 650 seats, and at the same time it wishes to be a receiving and producing theatre. Programming consistency is often dictated by economics, which is why journalist Rachel Andrews argued in 2011 that "it's a long time since Cork felt theatrically exciting, at least on anything more than a sporadic basis".[20] It is clear, then, that arts centres are more able to take risks whereas theatres are not. However, risks are essential to contemporary practice: they catalyse style and form. Risks give space to practitioners to research, develop, emerge and grow. Taking risks on new work is important, particularly because only one theatre in Ireland has a permanent, professional, full-time venue-based ensemble: Blue Raincoat.[21] Not only do arts centres fulfil the Arts Council's objective of supporting practice and engaging with particular interest groups and communities, they also support established theatre buildings.

Other Spaces

The lack of available space has resulted in companies radically altering their relationship with space and place. What is becoming increasingly important on the island is the specificity of site when making contemporary work; there is a very real shift from work presented in theatre buildings to site-generic and site-specific work. Fiona Wilkie's taxonomy of site suggests that performance can be placed in theatre buildings, outside theatres (for example, theatre in the park), or it can engage with site in three ways: performances at site can be site-sympathetic, site-generic or site-specific. Site-sympathetic includes an "existing performance text physicalized in a selected site"; site-generic work includes "performance generated for a series of like sites (eg: car parks, swimming pools)"; and site-specific work includes "performance specifically generated from/for one selected site".[22]

Based in Galway, Macnas has been making site-generic performances since 1986. Macnas turns public places into sites of performance in an attempt to question the perception of public space and place. For example, its 2012 production of *The Cockroach and the Inventor* saw an ensemble of clown-scientists perform wacky experiments for bemused spectators in public places across the island. ANU Productions mounts site-specific work that immerses spectators in public places where they are forced to peel away the layers of history and collective memory at site. Its 2014 production of *Vardo* used collective memories and anecdotal evidence of sex work, human trafficking, asylum and migration in the Monto, a quarter-square-mile of Dublin's north inner city. As Brian Singleton points out, ANU Productions' 'site-specificity lies in its political efficacy to emerge from and engage with communities in the present but mindful of their past, and to engage communities of spectators in the lives and histories of a community's spaces and places respectfully but also to challenge them ethically in their intimate encounters'.[23] For Macnas and ANU, the otherness of the city street is the new other theatre.

What Macnas and ANU demonstrate is that their spatial practices interrogate the public conception of place by creating what geographer Edward Soja terms a Thirdspace. Building on the work of Henri Lefebvre and Michael Foucault, Soja understands a Thirdspace "as an-Other way of understanding and acting to change the spatiality of human life, a distinct mode of critical spatial awareness that is appropriate to the new scope and significance being brought about in the re-balanced trialectics of spatiality-historicality-sociality".[24] What Soja is modelling here is way of seeing space that is not just physically real, or mentally imagined, but both. Thirdspaces are limitless and constantly evolving, and they have the power to break down preconceived historical binaries and expectations about space in society. The work of Macnas and ANU creates Thirdspaces that directly engage with our spatial sense of history and society in order to interrogate our categorization of other places. However, could not the same be said about other theatres on the island?

Other theatres on the island are real because they exist; imagined because they involve diverse acts of artistic creation; and both real and imagined because they use their respective spaces to create a unique sense of place that breaks down all of those idealized binaries about contemporary Irish theatre. Other theatres support artists and their communities and actively engage with a national sense of theatre. In so doing, they use their spaces to reconsider embedded, historical attitudes to theatre as being elitist in contemporary Irish theatre.

The critical importance of other theatres on the island, then, can hardly be overstated. At a time of disproportionate funding for the larger houses, at a time of restricted spaces and artistic visions, other theatres—particularly arts centres—allow companies and practitioners the freedom to create the work that they want to make, and the freedom to engage with local communities. It is true that all of the other theatres will always have a carefully curated programme, but with one hundred and three other theatres on the island offering different programmes in 2018, there is a broad spectrum of places of performance. Accordingly, other theatres on the island engage with the very crux of contemporary Irish theatre. Other theatres provide financial viability and aesthetic visibility to practitioners and companies across the island.

In 2017 the new directors of the Abbey Theatre, Neil Murray and Graham McLaren, stated that "we believe in the concept of a national theatre that reaches all of the country. This applies to touring work, but also addresses the issue of where shows and projects are rooted and made, regardless of geographical remoteness or perceived social barriers".[25] Murray and McLaren were previously the executive producer (Murray) and associate director (McLaren) of the National Theatre of Scotland, a national theatre without walls that used diverse spaces to form a national theatre. There is precedent, then, for the other theatres, south of the border at least, to be future national theatres. A national theatre without walls encapsulates Massey's emphasis on space being a multiplicity of voices. However, there is a sense that the other theatres on the island already constitute a national sense of theatre without walls. As Massey argues, "without space, no multiplicity; without multiplicity, no space. If space is indeed the product of interrelations, then it must be predicated upon the existence of plurality".[26] The multiplicity of other spaces on the island testifies to the plurality and interrelatedness of contemporary Irish theatre. According to Massey, space is always under negotiation by the material practices that take place in it, and the material practices of other theatres in contemporary Irish theatre connect audiences in the smallest of ways: from the company on tour, to the practitioner who takes up residency in the local theatre, to the company giving a community engagement workshop. "Perhaps we could imagine space as a simultaneity of stories-so-far",[27] Massey suggests. Space in other theatres on the island connects the local stories-so-far to a national sense of place; a local story in a national conversation.

Notes

1. Pat Kiernan, "Ben Hennessy, Pat Kiernan and Ger Fitzgibbon in Conversation", in *Theatre Talk: Voices of Irish Theatre Practitioners*, eds. Lillian Chambers, Ger Fitzgibbon, Eamonn Jordan, Dan Farrelly and Cathy Leeney (Dublin: Carysfort Press, 2001), 169.
2. Chris Morash, "Places of Performance" in *The Oxford Handbook of Modern Irish Theatre*, ed. Nicholas Grene and Chris Morash (Oxford: Oxford University Press, 2016), 442.
3. *An Chomhairle Ealaíon/the Arts Council Annual Report*, 1980, 29.
4. *An Chomhairle Ealaíon/the Arts Council Annual Report*, 1980, 29–30.
5. *An Chomhairle Ealaíon/the Arts Council Annual Report*, 1981, 24.
6. Victor Merriman, "'As We Must': Growth and Diversification in Ireland's Theatre Culture 1977–2000", in *The Oxford Handbook of Modern Irish Theatre*, 401.
7. Ibid.
8. *An Chomhairle Ealaíon/the Arts Council Annual Report*, 1987, 38.
9. Enda Walsh, "Enda Walsh in Conversation with Emelie Fitzgibbon", in *Theatre Talk: Voices of Irish Theatre Practitioners*, 473.
10. Chris Morash and Shaun Richards, *Mapping Irish Theatre: Theories of Space and Place* (Cambridge: Cambridge University Press, 2016), 18.
11. Ibid., 16.
12. Doreen Massey, *For Space* (London: Sage, 2010), 192.
13. Ibid., 107.
14. Brian Ó Conchubhair "Twisting in the Wind: Irish-Language Stage Theatre 1884–2014" in *The Oxford Handbook of Modern Irish Theatre*, 268.
15. Ibid., 267.
16. Rhona Trench, *Blue Raincoat Theatre Company* (Dublin: Carysfort Press, 2015), 10.
17. Ibid., 12.
18. Cian O'Brien, interview with Christopher Collins, August 31, 2016.
19. https://themaclive.com/about-us. Accessed June 7, 2017.
20. Rachel Andrews, "A New Direction for Corcadorca", *Irish Theatre Magazine*, April 27, 2011, accessed September 2, 2016, http://itmarchive.ie/web/Features/Current/A-new-direction-for-Corcadorca.aspx.html.

21. Rhona Trench, "Blue Raincoat: Pushing the Boundaries of Theatre from WB Yeats to Étienne Decroux", *Irish Times*, October 27, 2014.
22. Fiona Wilkie, "Mapping the Terrain: A Survey of Site-Specific Performance in Britain", *New Theatre Quarterly*, vol. 18, no. 2 (2002): 150.
23. Brian Singleton, *ANU Productions: The Monto Cycle* (London: Palgrave, 2016), 7.
24. Edward Soja, *Thirdspace: Journeys to Los Angeles and Other Real-and-Imagined Places* (Cambridge, Massachusetts: Blackwell, 1996), 10. Emphasis added.
25. https://www.abbeytheatre.ie/new-directors-of-the-abbey-theatre-appointed/. Accessed June 9, 2017.
26. Massey, *For Space*, 9.
27. Ibid.

Bibliography

An Chomhairle Ealaíon/the Arts Council Annual Report, 1980.

An Chomhairle Ealaíon/the Arts Council Annual Report, 1981.

An Chomhairle Ealaíon/the Arts Council Annual Report, 1987.

Andrews, Rachel. "A New Direction for Corcadorca." *Irish Theatre Magazine*, April 27, 2011.

Kiernan, Pat. "Ben Hennessy, Pat Kiernan and Ger Fitzgibbon in Conversation." In *Theatre Talk: Voices of Irish Theatre Practitioners*, eds. Lillian Chambers, Ger Fitzgibbon, Eamonn Jordan, Dan Farrelly and Cathy Leeney, 167–180. Dublin: Carysfort Press, 2001.

O'Brien, Cian. Interview with Christopher Collins. August 31, 2016.

Ó Conchubhair, Brian. "Twisting in the Wind: Irish-Language Stage Theatre 1884–2014". In *The Oxford Handbook of Modern Irish Theatre*, eds. Nicholas Grene and Chris Morash, 251–268. Oxford: Oxford University Press, 2016.

Massey, Doreen. *For Space*. London: Sage, 2010.

Merriman, Victor. "'As We Must': Growth and Diversification in Ireland's Theatre Culture 1977–2000." In *The Oxford Handbook of Modern Irish Theatre*, eds. Nicholas Grene and Chris Morash, 389–403. Oxford: Oxford University Press, 2016.

Morash. "Places of Performance" In *The Oxford Handbook of Modern Irish Theatre*, eds. Nicholas Grene and Chris Morash, 425–442. Oxford: Oxford University Press, 2016.

———. and Shaun Richards. *Mapping Irish Theatre: Theories of Space and Place*. Cambridge: Cambridge University Press, 2016.

Singleton, Brian. *ANU Productions: The Monto Cycle*. London: Palgrave, 2016.

Soja, Edward. *Thirdspace: Journeys to Los Angeles and Other Real-and-Imagined Places*. Cambridge, MA: Blackwell, 1996.

Trench, Rhona. "Blue Raincoat: Pushing the Boundaries of Theatre from WB Yeats to Étienne Decroux." *The Irish Times*. October 27, 2014.

———. *Blue Raincoat Theatre Company*. Dublin: Carysfort Press, 2015.

Walsh, Enda. "Enda Walsh in Conversation with Emelie Fitzgibbon." In *Theatre Talk: Voices of Irish Theatre Practitioners*, eds. Lillian Chambers, Ger Fitzgibbon, Eamonn Jordan, Dan Farrelly and Cathy Leeney, 471–480. Dublin: Carysfort Press, 2001.

Wilkie, Fiona. "Mapping the Terrain: A Survey of Site-Specific Performance in Britain." *New Theatre Quarterly* 18, no. 2 (2002): 140–160.

Independent Theatre and New Work

Gavin Kostick

Julian Gough, Toasted Heretic and now novelist and playwright, once told the following story. I had asked him in front of a pleasant group of playwriting students in Trinity College why Galway felt like such a creative place in the late 1980s and early 1990s. He said simply that it was the cheap rents: you could live in the middle on very little. Then he said that he had earned a small amount of regular money by writing a column for the Galway edition of a *Buy & Sell* type paper. As the editor of the paper had no real interest in the column, other than requiring that there should be one, Julian, who is a natural provocateur, wrote increasingly bizarre, surreal and satirical pieces. Then he noticed that a different writer for the Cork edition was also writing bizarre, surreal and wildly imaginative columns. Although they did not communicate directly, Julian liked to think of the two of them reading each other's work, exchanging ideas and encouraging each other on to go further. The other writer turned out to be the playwright Enda Walsh.

I like this story as it captures something of the strangeness and chance of the time. Younger writers mainly started out poor and often in environments of little money. But the upside was the ability to live in the centres of towns and cities and have some kind of turbulent social life. I myself lived off Grafton Street in Dublin in this period. Temple Bar was a place that still had genuine artists living there with actual garret studios because it was dingy, rat-infested and cheap. When I worked box office for Project Arts Centre on a government community scheme I was on nodding terms with some of the rats. I also like the story as it shows for me how precarious the starts of careers are. Without the chance encounter, the moment of discovery, perhaps some now very established playwrights would never have written. Certainly I imagine that for many people

G. Kostick (✉)
Fishamble Theatre Company, Dublin, Ireland
e-mail: Gavin@fishamble.com

E. Jordan, E. Weitz (eds.), *The Palgrave Handbook of Contemporary Irish Theatre and Performance*,
https://doi.org/10.1057/978-1-137-58588-2_15

who might have written, something didn't quite click and a career didn't happen. There was, in short, very little infrastructure and, of course, no mobile phones or emails.

The main moral of the story, though, is that when one tries to put some shape on new writing over the last twenty-five years it is as well to remember that many of us didn't see much in the way of a shape at all at the time. Talking about the twentieth century towards the end of his life, the historian Eric Hobsbawm talks about the past-in-the-present, those past events that are still alive in us today and which we can perceive and discuss at some distance but with the awareness that our subjective involvement with them, our emotional connection to them, is likely to influence our take on them.

But we can see some patterns. For example, Dublin Youth Theatre was founded in 1977 and again we can see that Enda Walsh was a member. The rise of the youth theatres, including the arrival of the umbrella organization the National Association of Youth Drama in 1980, now called Youth Drama Ireland, provided a conduit for young people to find their way in theatre. The Gaiety School of Acting, with its policy of producing a new play at the end of its two-year course, was founded in 1986. Michael West, Marina Carr and Mark O'Rowe, for example, have all written for the GSA.

The first full-time Drama undergraduate degree course began at Trinity College, Dublin, in 1984. This marked the beginning of a whole raft of courses at undergraduate and postgraduate levels across the country, and naturally attracted students who were making a more conscious and significant decision to commit to drama and seek out like-minded people. An aside: I find it interesting that whilst many profession practitioners came out of drama courses—directors, designers, actors and so on—in the early days very few writers did. Michael West, Marina Carr and Conor McPherson took Humanities courses at Trinity or UCD. They were, however, involved in the student drama groups (e.g. Players at Trinity and Dramsoc at UCD). The most recent institution to come on the scene is the Lír, The National Academy of Dramatic Art, which opened in 2011 and is a conservatoire institution offering Trinity undergraduate degrees in acting, based on a RADA-style model. It also offers master's degrees in Playwriting, Design and Direction and an undergraduate qualification in Technical Theatre.

What Ireland has seen, then—and the coinage is ugly—is a kind of formalization and academicization of the route into drama for many practitioners. Naturally this has caused some discomfort for those who came first into theatre through chance and the traditional learning-on-the-job approach.

Another key influence on the development of writing in the independent sector is the changing pattern of funding. The Abbey Theatre is notable for being the first National Theatre in Europe to receive state funding from 1925. The Gate Theatre under MacLiammóir and Edwards followed suit, after the Abbey had become somewhat moribund, and innovated Irish theatre.

Naturally, many independent companies that existed from the 1950s on are now lost in time. The Focus Theatre (founded 1963) brought a certain liveliness to the sector, particularly with regard to introducing Stanislavski for actors. But it is really the foundation and success of the Druid theatre in Galway in 1975 that sets the scene and template for the development of the independent sector. This is true in one very tangible way in that Garry Hynes remains the original and current artistic director (with one sabbatical when she was artistic director of the Abbey from 1991 to 1994). Of the surviving theatre companies from the 1980s and 1990s, it is commonly the case that the founding director is the current director. The next company to found itself lastingly in a similar model was Rough Magic, under Lynne Parker's stewardship, founded in 1984 with the help of Declan Hughes. Again, she remains the current artistic director.

Druid and Rough Magic preceded the academic, university-level courses, even if both were formed by graduates of University College Galway and Trinity, respectively. But what happened then is that students who had immersed themselves in drama saw these companies as a natural way to go. They were in some way seen as the hip older siblings to emulate and challenge. I graduated in 1988. Although that was only four years after Rough Magic they were already legends and I was somewhat intimidated, somewhat jealous and determined to do better. One of the most ferociously witty conversations I was ever part of was at a Rough Magic opening at the Project Arts Centre. It was between Anne Enright, Pauline McLynn and Gerry Stembridge, all of whom were around Rough Magic at the time. I say I was part of—I considered it sensible to remain largely silent as the pace was such that one risked sounding like a blurting idiot if one interjected unwisely. At the same time, the Arts Council was looking to see the further professionalization of theatre and so naturally very young graduates began to form theatre companies of their own.

It is worth reinforcing the fluidity, messiness and odd ways in which things happened at that time. For example, the Players Theatre in Trinity had a rule that if you had, as I recall, three Players members in your company you could use the Players Theatre, then in Front Square, during the summer for cheap. This meant that members of UCD Dramsoc who wanted a city centre theatre would need to find three Trinity students, and a number of creative relationships were formed. Also, a lot of it was to do with personal as well as artistic issues: who liked whom, who didn't like whom, and indeed, who was going out or breaking up with whom. Annie Ryan and Michael West of Corn Exchange (founded by Annie in 1995) are married, and the company contains a long history of their working relationship. Pan Pan is, in a way, the history of the tremendous relationship of co-artistic directors Gavin Quinn and Aedín Cosgrove. I should say that I would like to think that Fishamble (founded as Pigsback in 1988) contains the story of Jim Culleton's and my enduring (and tactful) friendship. But as the two of us are so tactful one never really knows. And I should add that it is an asymmetric partnership (unlike Pan Pan) as Jim is definitely the artistic director to my literary manager.

You can see why this might cause a problem for an Arts Council. If every wave of graduates (and theatre people from other sources) brought new companies, how many would there be? Could they all be omnium theatre companies, as Druid and Rough Magic were and are—that is, they can produce what they please? Could they all, by and large, be in limited locations such as Temple Bar in Dublin? In practice they began to encourage specialization and geographic spread. The mission statement of the company became vital. Corcadorca was established in Cork in 1991, Bickerstaff in Kilkenny and Blue Raincoat in Sligo. Barabbas became the Lecoq/physical clown company; the Corn Exchange a modern *commedia*; Fishamble was The New Play Company; Performance Corporation produced site-specific work; Bedrock championed difficult works from abroad; Second Age brought Shakespeare to school-age audiences, and so on. In many cases this was a happy fit—the artistic director(s) wanted the specialization and the gap was there—but it did also cause frustrations as ambitious directors were told certain projects were "not within their remit" and, of course, later generations might find that a company already occupied a space where they might want to be. But in general, through to 2007 this was a golden (or at least good-quality silver) period for the independent sector, with about thirty companies being supported on an annual basis (and at one point multi-annually). It also had the odd feature, which had come about naturally, that on the whole, the older the company was the more funding it was likely to receive. To this day, the Abbey, the Gate, Druid and Rough Magic still receive the most public subvention in that order, with the Abbey taking half of all Arts Council Theatre funding.

From the 1990s, this was backed by the rise of the festivals: Dublin Fringe, Cork Misdsummer, Galway International, Kilkenny, and so on. These initially provided seasonal work and presentational possibilities, but then, both of their own volition and as a consequence of the economic crash, began to see themselves more as year-round creative centres. The same period also saw the rise of venues (often linked to the local authority), usually as civic amenities—indeed, the Tallaght venue is actually called "The Civic"—with over sixty venues being built or refurbished right across the country. Funding, as ever, was tight and many of these sought ways to avoid white-elephant status by innovating with schemes established to benefit local artists and ignite community initiatives. A further piece was the professionalization of the support for theatre, with the Irish Theatre Institute (and its Playography) and Theatre Forum providing much greater support for production, national and international, and a forum for debate and lobbying. In total, Irish theatre could now be said to have a rich and even thriving eco-system: though still at levels of public support far below the European average.

Then came the crash, and along with it a severe reduction in public subsidy between 2009 and 2013.

It was the companies that took the brunt of this. This is still a much debated and heated issue: in the Hobsbawm sense, this recent past is so much in the present that there are very few impartial observers who can write this history objectively. We are all still very much engaged with it.

Roughly, of thirty companies then annually funded, about twenty lost that status, and generally the cuts went from the smaller companies upwards, though all were affected. This meant that the older a company was, the more chance it had of survival. But neither was venerability enough; the remaining companies underwent more scrutiny to see what value they offered, what their artistic quality was like, what they contributed to the sector as a whole and how younger theatre practitioners were to be supported.

The next part of the story is one of a wounded ecosystem, but one still being fed by a tremendous amount of young people who have sought a career in the arts and, indeed, by audiences steadily returning after the initial shock, and by adapted and newly developed ways of working.

Funding, Sponsorship and Touring: Causing a Co-Motion

Shelley Troupe

A Short Story About Arts Funding Through the Ages

Imagine yourself in the throng of people celebrating the City Dionysia in the fifth century BCE. It is a beautiful day for Athen's ancient dramatic festival. Perched on the slope of the Acropolis, you enjoy the magnificent view of the Aegean Sea as well as the sun, the chat, the wine, and the food. In front of you, the Chorus performs in one of the tragedian's offerings in the contest. Although you are located a fair distance from the stage, you catch a glimpse of the front row of spectators. The important people are all there—the politicians, the statesmen, the visiting dignitaries. Among them sits the *choregos*: the Chorus's sponsor who costumed them, provided props, and sheltered them while they prepared for the play.[1] As a member of one of the wealthiest families in Athens, his service as *choregos* is not entirely philanthropic but is a public duty required and expected of him due to his financial circumstances. You have also heard that, in the event of legal trouble, reminding the jury of a man's former civic service as a *choregos* can assist him in winning his case, underscoring the fact that the public service is not an entirely altruistic measure. If the play wins the City Dionysia, his patronage will be remembered, as that of so many others has been, when the commemorative base etched with his name and topped with a bronze tripod or a relief is erected for all to see.

Fast-forward now and you head to the north and west. Bypassing the civic-funded passion plays, Michelangelo's privately supported paintings, and the court-sponsored European theatres, you find yourself in Dublin at the turn of the twentieth century. Here, in Ireland's capital, the folklore historian Augusta

S. Troupe (✉)
Independent Researcher, County Mayo, Republic of Ireland

E. Jordan, E. Weitz (eds.), *The Palgrave Handbook of Contemporary Irish Theatre and Performance*,
https://doi.org/10.1057/978-1-137-58588-2_16

Gregory, the poet W.B. Yeats, and others are setting up shop, or rather, a theatre. They have been toiling away for a while, at first under the auspices of the Irish Literary Theatre. Now, though, you see that a new person is associated with their enterprise: Miss Annie Horniman. The wealthy English woman had previously put together tours of Yeats's plays in England and now has leased and refurbished a building on the corner of Abbey and Marlborough Streets, just north of the River Liffey.[2] Upon entering the theatre, you notice Horniman's portrait hanging prominently in the lobby, a memorialization of her part in the making of the new Irish National Theatre Society. It reminds you of an updated version of the Grecian monuments dedicated to the *choregi*. You observe that both are visual reminders of each person's monetary contribution to theatre.

You read in the *Freeman's Journal* that Horniman's aim in supporting a theatre in Ireland is "the cultivation of the dramatic art in general and of Irish dramatic art in particular".[3] That goal sounds wonderful, but the next sentence sends a bit of a jolt through you: "This aesthetic object is solely what she has had in view, any element of a political or religious nature being entirely excluded."[4] Such a sentiment directly contrasts with your understanding of the theatre's intention, particularly with the famous (or, perhaps, *in*famous) production of Yeats and Gregory's *Kathleen Ni Houlihan* (1902), which became a theatrical nationalist anthem. You sense a tension between the creators' aims for the theatre and the money behind it. This observation makes you wonder if money actually *is* power, and whether or not Yeats and Gregory will compromise the form and content of the Abbey Theatre's productions to meet Horniman's demands. As the years pass, you are aware of the protests against John Millington Synge's *The Playboy of the Western World* in 1907, and think it is quite possible that, in part, they precipitated Horniman's withdrawal of funding from the Abbey Theatre a couple of years later.[5]

By the mid-1920s, as the nation reels from the tumultuous events of the past decade, the Abbey has cultivated its image as a well-established theatre and has a number of touring productions under its belt (some of which were box-office successes and some of which were not). Looking back on the eve of the Irish government's first public subsidy of the Abbey in the mid-1920s, you ponder the ramifications of government sponsorship of the arts. If the *choregi* and Horniman were not immune from wielding their monetary influence, it follows that the Irish state might do so as well. You discern, perhaps a bit cynically, that the directors of the Abbey are now highlighting the theatre's educative qualities rather than its political aims. Such a shift suggests an attempt to distance the theatre's repertoire, such as the fiery February 1926 production of Sean O'Casey's *The Plough and the Stars*, from political commentary. You sense a similar tension between funding and programming as you did earlier in the century.

After Gregory's death in 1932 and Yeats's death in 1939, Ernest Blythe takes the reins at the Abbey, assuming the position of managing director in 1941. As the country's former finance minister, you know Blythe as the person who deducted a shilling from the old-age pension in 1924. Interesting, you think: maybe that explains, at least in part, his role as co-architect of the Abbey's first governmental subsidy the year after his arrival. Maybe he was aiming for a little positive publicity, a little "symbolic capital", as sociologist Pierre Bourdieu would refer to it later in the century.[6] Regardless of his motivation for assisting with the subsidy and his commitment to Irish language programming at the Abbey, you observe Blythe's penchant for turning down the work of writers such as Teresa Deevy, John B. Keane, Tom Murphy, and many others. When he leaves the job in the 1960s, you hope it is the end of what you and your friends call "the age of darkness at the Abbey".

You identify one step forward in Irish arts policy during Blythe's tenure at Ireland's National Theatre: the establishment of the government's Arts Act of 1951. You are delighted to see a clause stipulating funding for the arts in Ireland.[7] Great stuff, you think, the Irish nation is dedicated to funding artistic endeavours. The Act is revised and expanded in 1973, explicitly outlining a commitment to the regions outside Dublin, including "the cinema" as an art form, and weakening the ties between politicians and the Council.[8,9] As a result, you note with great delight that several regional companies pop up during the ensuing years; Galway's Druid Theatre, for example, receives its first Arts Council support in 1976, just one year after its establishment.

The 1980s see a burst of independent theatrical activity around the island, but there is one Dublin theatre, helmed by two young men, that grabs your attention. Joe O'Byrne and Declan Gorman establish Dublin-based Co-Motion Theatre Company in 1985, and their aesthetic is a bit unusual: very European, very visual, very of the continent. You watch their venture grow from small shows to large shows, from Dublin performances to an international tour. A little more than a decade later, in 1996, you are disappointed to see Co-Motion's final show. However, in 2015, thirty years after its initial premiere, O'Byrne re-teams with Gorman and in January 2016 the duo formally announce a new company, Co-Motion Media. You are delighted. At the same time, you wonder how the changes in Irish funding structures from 1985 to 2015 will influence its artistic product.[10]

Co-Motion Theatre Company in the 1980s and 1990s

The early to mid-1980s saw an increase of independent theatres with the establishment of companies such as Waterford's Red Kettle and Dublin-based companies Rough Magic, Passion Machine, Co-Motion, and Pigsback (now known as Fishamble: The New Play Company). As a basis for examining how funding works in terms of a company's organizational life, this section focuses on Co-Motion Theatre Company and provides an artistic and administrative history of the theatre to showcase the importance of infrastructure development and funding to the company's success and its demise. Joe O'Byrne, Co-Motion's Artistic Director, breaks the company into three phases, primarily based on the company's funding history.

Phase One, 1985–1990: Gaining Momentum and Funding

Joe O'Byrne posits that the growth of independent theatre in the 1980s was, in part, a response to a lack of sustained artistic experimentation at Ireland's monolithic theatres: the Abbey and the Gate.[11] A niche existed for theatre that challenged the conventions of the Irish literary theatre tradition; and the work of this new independent theatre sector challenged such practices by providing, as Declan Gorman observes, a "quiet revolution—an intellectual movement".[12] In the case of O'Byrne and Gorman, that revolution was, in part, inspired by the time they independently spent abroad in Germany in the late 1970s and early 1980s. Gorman trained in theatre in Munich and worked for an Irish theatre company in Berlin, while O'Byrne trained at the Milan Sladek School of Mime in Cologne and worked with the English Theatre Workshop in Aachen. After returning to Ireland, each man entered academia—Gorman as a mature student at Trinity College Dublin and O'Byrne as a Master's student at University College Dublin. In 1985, they were directing German-language student productions at their respective colleges and met at "German Weekend", an intervarsity competition for these productions. The concept of Co-Motion Theatre was proposed one evening over pints in a local pub.

The duo sought to develop their artistic vision, one that was inspired by their time in Germany. Those experiences introduced them to cultural reference points that shaped their theatrical sensibilities, and so Co-Motion Theatre Company commenced operations in October 1985 with a production of Iwan Goll's avant-garde satire of middle-class greed, *Methusalem* (1922), at that year's Dublin Fringe Festival. An assault on the bourgeoisie that incorporates cinematic dream projections, *Methusalem* aligned with Co-Motion's "intention to present theatre of a strong visual character exploiting modern visual drama".[13] Amy Garvey of the *Irish Press*, unimpressed with the fledgling company's first show, criticized it as "[a]n ambitious production that sadly lacks coherent vision and direction".[14] Undeterred, Co-Motion returned in June 1986 with an adaptation of Peter Weiss's 1965 play *Song of the Lusitanian Bogey*, which delves into Angola's struggle under Portuguese colonialism. Retitled *Song of the White Man's Burden* and presented at Temple Bar Studios, Co-Motion's version is set in South Africa and reflects that country's contemporary fight to rescind apartheid. *White Man's Burden* was remounted twice: once more at Temple Bar Studios in December 1986 and then at the Project Arts Centre in March 1988. The latter year marked a turning point in the company's history, both artistically and administratively.

Between 1985 and 1988, Co-Motion had produced between three and five shows per year, all of which were self-funded. Productions such as the aforementioned *Song of the White Man's Burden*, Ntozake Shange's *For Colored Girls Who Have Considered Suicide When the Rainbow is Enuf* (1975), and Caryl Churchill's *Vinegar Tom* (1976) spurred one critic to proclaim Co-Motion "a committed company with political and theatrical guts".[15] Co-Motion's infrastructure was tenuous, but the men began to establish systems, records, and checklists so that prior work such as casting sheets and budgets did not require re-creation for subsequent productions. The most onerous administrative task was promotion and marketing. With no funding to hire a press officer, actor/manager Gorman performed that function in a neighbourly way, handwriting notes to critics urging them to attend productions. Although the actors were paid on a shares basis, virtually no wages were generated. Gorman subsisted through acting, directing, teaching, and the occasional visit to the Social Welfare office; O'Byrne taught Art History to make ends meet.

1988 saw two important changes at Co-Motion. First, Joe O'Byrne emerged as a playwright and director with Co-Motion's production of his original script *Gerrup!* The play, which revolves around a set of Dublin youths and their gritty urban problems, did not garner great critical acclaim. For many reviewers, the juxtaposition between the harsh realities of the characters' lives—substance abuse, abortion, and domestic violence—and the production's expressionistic presentation of those issues did not work. However, a few months later, Fintan O'Toole found O'Byrne's sophomore effort, *Departed,* an Irish Land War story that interrogates the eviction of a pair of siblings from Mayo to Dublin, "impressive and effective".[16] Within a few short years, and in response to Co-Motion's production of *The Sinking of the Titanic* (1990), O'Byrne's writing and directing prowess prompted O'Toole to call the show "a remarkable feat of theatrical storytelling", "wonderfully confident, disciplined and resourceful".[17] Artistically, then, Co-Motion was in the ascendant.

The second development was the receipt of a £5000 corporate grant from Allied Irish Banks (AIB) in March 1988. At that time, as Lorcan Roche reported, corporate sponsorship was on the rise, and AIB had earned a reputation as an arts ally with its sponsorship of the Dublin Theatre Festival, among other arts organizations.[18] The funds allowed Co-Motion, as Declan Gorman explains, to "take our shows to established venues and reach a much wider audience. We can even begin to think seriously about advertising and publicity".[19] A remount of *Song of the White Man's Burden* was the first production to significantly benefit. Originally presented at Temple Bar Studios, the show found a new home at the more established Project Arts Centre. Signalling the company's development, Co-Motion received its Dublin Theatre Festival debut with Joe O'Byrne's *Departed* in September 1988. Previously, the company had presented at the annual Fringe Festival rather than the main Festival. The AIB grant, along with the organization's body of work, gave Co-Motion access to Arts Council funding when, in 1989, the company received its first award from the national agency in the amount of £5000. The following year, 1990, saw a 300% increase in Arts Council funding for Co-Motion with an award of £15,000. The funds received were, simultaneously, a blessing and a curse.

Artistically and organizationally, 1990 marked another watershed moment for Co-Motion Theatre Company. That year's sole production, the world premiere of Joe O'Byrne's *The Sinking of the Titanic and Other Matters,* marked the apex of Co-Motion's productions in terms of scale. Like the actual ship and its legend, *Titanic* was enormous. Staged at the SFX Centre as part of the Dublin Theatre Festival, a recreation of the ship's hull and a cast of over twenty people filled the cavernous space. The show was a critical success. Administratively, the Arts Council funding allowed Co-Motion to expand its productions, but brought with it a poverty trap. Upon acceptance of those monies, Co-Motion found itself becoming more institutionalized and regulated. Organizations in receipt of Arts Council monies were required to conform to certain business practices, such as registering as a charitable organization; paying payroll taxes, legal fees and insurance coverage; and completing annual financial audits. With no solid infrastructures, these administrative changes overwhelmed the company. "There is", Declan Gorman remarked in 2006, "a pressure inherent in the evolution from two guys putting on shows to running a theatre company".[20] The knock-on effect of increased administrative costs was a decrease in productions. As a self-funded company, Co-Motion generated between three and five productions per year. After Arts Council funding, it produced one or two shows per year until O'Byrne closed the company in 1997.

Phase II, 1991–1994: Pressures of Success

Co-Motion's success in the late 1980s created administrative burdens that were amplified when Declan Gorman left in 1990 to accept a full-time position as theatre director at Dublin's City Arts Centre. Although Gorman continued to serve as a board member and to assist in producing shows from 1991 to 1993, the company's direction was primarily led by O'Byrne; and Arts Council funding was not sufficient to allow him to hire a proper administrative staff (Gorman and O'Byrne in separate interviews 2006). These circumstances led O'Byrne to take the company in a new artistic direction. In 1992, Co-Motion produced only two shows, both with small casts. O'Byrne's play *The Man in the Iron Mask* utilized four actors; and *Frank Pig Says Hello*, adapted by Pat McCabe from his Booker Prize-nominated novel *The Butcher Boy*, was a two-hander starring David Gorry and Sean Rocks. *Frank Pig Says Hello* opened to rave reviews at the Dublin Theatre Festival, garnering a Festival Choice Award for Best New Irish Play. With the support of a £30,000 Theatre Touring Grant from the Arts Council, Co-Motion presented the play nationally and internationally in places such as Dublin's Gate Theatre, Monaghan, Cork, Thurles, Belfast, Glasgow, and London's Royal Court Theatre. For that effort, *Frank Pig Says Hello* received two nominations in the London Fringe Awards: Best Production, and Best Actor for David Gorry, who won his category.

In a retrospective piece on Co-Motion that appeared in advance of *Frank Pig Says Hello*'s presentation at the Gate Theatre, Helen Meany described the hallmark of Co-Motion's work, which "drew on aspects of German Expressionism as well as other non-naturalistic influences—political cabaret, mime, dance, music, video, puppetry—in a manner which distinguished the company from the other independent theatre groups that emerged in the late

1980s".[21] In that same article, Gorman candidly reveals the tension between funding and creative pursuits. Speaking about the change in the company's artistic policy, he states that *The Sinking of the Titanic*

> marked the end of that strand of experimentation [...]. We felt we had exhausted that particular direction and began to ask: 'Where can we go from here?' It was a crisis of morale, and in our concerns about funding we made a mistake. Instead of trying to find new ways to develop, we looked to where the sources of funding were and tried to fit in.[22]

Here, Gorman expands the idea of an organizational poverty trap, as discussed above, to an artistic poverty trap in which organizations apply for and accept monies for initiatives that are not organic to the company. This issue is not isolated to companies like Co-Motion or to companies in Ireland. For example, in the 1980s and 1990s, American funding agencies issued calls for theatre education initiatives, and certain producing companies that did not have an education remit took the bait to prop up organizational budgets. In Ireland a similar situation occurred in the late 1990s and early 2000s, when Ireland's political leaders accepted European Union funding for the construction of performance arts venues around Ireland without careful consideration of the needs of such venues upon their completion, such as future capital improvements, audience base, and the availability of programming. In both examples, more forethought and stronger planning would have been required to achieve a successful realization of such projects. For Co-Motion, chasing funding resulted in the obfuscation of a clear artistic vision.

Upon reflection, Joe O'Byrne sees the aftermath of *Frank Pig Says Hello* as the beginning of the end of Co-Motion Theatre.[23] In May 1993, he remounted a revised version of Co-Motion's successful 1987 production of Gorman and O'Byrne's *Cabaret/Kabarett*, a contemporary satire featuring sketches and songs in the German kabarett tradition. That show was followed by a bitter disappointment with serious consequences. The company was slated to premiere Joe O'Byrne's *Para* at the 1993 Dublin Theatre Festival; the play concerns a paramilitary loyalist and his lover. The principal actor, himself a former loyalist paramilitary soldier who had spent six years in Maze Prison, was so affected by the memories of his experiences that it caused him to withdraw from the production. In the end, *Para* was never staged.

The following year, 1994, saw renewed enthusiasm for Co-Motion's work with the excitement surrounding a second Pat McCabe play, *Loco County Lonesome*. Set in the Midlands of Ireland and based on country and western ballads, it received much publicity, opening in County Monaghan and touring extensively throughout Ireland with the assistance of a £35,000 Theatre Touring Grant from the Arts Council. The tour concluded in Dublin, where it was presented at the Dublin Theatre Festival. Critical acclaim eluded the show and reviewers put the blame squarely on the shoulders of the playwright. Fintan O'Toole noted that the play was "a bold attempt, and Joe O'Byrne's confident, supple staging nearly pulls it off, but the play itself is too weak to bear its own ambitions".[24] *Loco County Lonesome*, then, marked the beginning of the end of Co-Motion Theatre Company.

Phase III, 1995–1997: Winding Down

Joe O'Byrne recalls that Co-Motion's artistic growth faltered after *Loco County Lonesome*.[25] There was neither an increase in box office receipts nor in Arts Council funding, while the administrative needs of the company continued as an administrator hired in 1994 was made redundant the following year.[26] Co-Motion produced the world premiere of Tony Kavanagh's *The Drum* in 1995; the show was a critical failure for the company. That year, O'Byrne also oversaw an improvised piece called *Terra Incognita*. Created as a Spanish, Finnish, and Irish co-production, the show was presented in Spain and Finland, but never mounted in Ireland. In 1996, Co-Motion toured *Frank Pig Says Hello* to New York City's Irish Repertory Theatre, where it received critical acclaim; and later that year, the company produced Manuel Puig's *Kiss of the Spider Woman* (1993). The December 1996 premiere of Joe O'Byrne's *The History of the World at 3am* at Andrews Lane Theatre was the company's finale, bringing Co-Motion Theatre Company's contribution to Dublin's independent theatre movement to an end.

O'Byrne and Gorman: The Intervening Years

In the latter years of Co-Motion's lifespan, Joe O'Byrne engaged in new creative ventures, emerging as a screenwriter with his script for Cathal Black's *Korea* (1995). He subsequently wrote and directed his feature film debut, *Pete's Meteor* (1998). Starring Brenda Fricker, Mike Myers, and Alfred Molina, *Pete's Meteor* won the Crystal Bear Special Mention award for Best Feature Film at the 1999 Berlin International Film Festival. O'Byrne received his Abbey Theatre debut in 2002 with his play *En Suite*. Emer O'Kelly of the *Sunday Independent* did not care for it, but did find that "[t]he overriding impression that comes out of Joe O'Byrne's work is that he cares passionately about the human condition, and the mauling it frequently receives at the hands of society".[27] He continues writing for film, television, radio, and the stage, and maintains his artistic relationship with Pat McCabe. Most recently, for Co-Motion Media, he directed the world premiere of McCabe's original play *The Leaves of Heaven* (2016), a follow-up to *Frank Pig Says Hello*.

Declan Gorman moved on from the City Arts Centre to take up the role of artistic director at Drogheda's Upstate Theatre Project, where he remained from 1997 until 2010. He wrote and directed several plays in this period, including *Hades* (1999), which was awarded the Stewart Parker Trust's Northern Ireland Community Relations Council Award. For a one-year period prior to this, between 1995 and 1996, Gorman served as theatre review co-ordinator for The Arts Plan, an Arts Council initiative that sought to review and set out an active arts policy for theatre in Ireland. He has since taught theatre courses for the National University of Ireland, Galway, and New York University's Steinhardt School of Culture, Education, and Human Development. *The Dubliners Dilemma* (2012), Gorman's one-man show about James Joyce, toured in Ireland and internationally; his most recent solo work *Eye Witness: Casement* (2016), drawing on Roger Casement's Congo Report, was commissioned by and performed for Irish Art Oslo's "Meeting Casement" celebration in Norway.

Co-Motion Media: The Phoenix is Risen

Re-formed in late 2015, Co-Motion Media "is an artist-led platform for new and innovative theatrical productions, audiovisual projects, and occasional publishing".[28] In 2016, the focus was on live theatre and five productions were presented under the Co-Motion Media banner. Joe O'Byrne produced three plays during the first quarter of 2016. His adaptation of J.M. Synge's *The Aran Islands* premiered at Dublin's Viking Theatre in January and was followed by a ten-stop tour to Cork, Galway, Belfast, Armagh, and Letterkenny, among other locations. He presented two shows, one a premiere and one a revival of a 2014 production, for Dublin's Five Lamps Arts Festival in February and March: *Nighttown*, his adaptation of the Circe chapter in James Joyce's *Ulysses*, was co-produced with Carnation Theatre and presented in February, while *The Rising and By Way of Interludes World War I* was revived and co-produced by Powerscourt Productions. O'Byrne ended the year by producing and directing the premiere of Pat McCabe's *The Leaves of Heaven* in a co-production with the presenting venue: Dublin's The Complex. Declan Gorman's *The Big Fellow*, an adaptation of Frank O'Connor's biography of Michael Collins, was co-produced by and premiered at the Drogheda Arts Festival in May, followed by a short tour on the outskirts of Dublin and five performances in Dublin itself. It is important to keep in mind that, while Gorman and O'Byrne assist each other with administrative and production tasks, they work independently of each other artistically. Co-Motion Media, although not a registered company, serves as an umbrella organization for each man's artistic pursuits.

This seemingly mundane list of performances reveals two important trends in the contemporary theatre scene. These developments are not singular to Co-Motion Media, but suggest key changes in Ireland's theatrical landscape since Co-Motion Theatre Company wrapped up activities in 1997. Notice that, except for O'Byrne's *The Aran Islands*, every show is a co-production. Although the terms of each deal differ, it is striking that Co-Motion Media, unlike Co-Motion Theatre, does not produce shows under its name only. This shift is not borne by Co-Motion alone. Take, for example, Galway's Druid Theatre, the third highest-funded company in Ireland (beaten only by the Abbey and the Gate). In 2012, the company's gigantic production *DruidMurphy* allowed audiences the chance to see three of Tom Murphy's plays performed in repertory on the same day or as individual shows over the course of three separate evenings. The production premiered in Galway and toured to London, New York, Oxford, various venues around Ireland, and Washington DC. Two separate sets were built to accommodate this touring schedule, which gave seventeen actors and several crew members employment for many months. It was the most ambitious theatre project of 2012 both for Druid and for Irish theatre generally, requiring no less than four co-producers: Quinnipiac University in Connecticut, home to Ireland's Famine Museum; the National University of Ireland, Galway; the Lincoln Center Festival; and Galway Arts Festival. Theatrical co-productions are on the rise in a period that is saturated by both theatrical veterans and neophytes who are seeking funding.

A second trend that Co-Motion's 2016 productions points up is an emphasis on touring in the present day. In the 1980s and 1990s, Co-Motion Theatre spent very little time on the road, in part because, as Gorman recollects, "We acknowledged that the kind of work we had in repertoire at the time was not particularly suited to the regional circuit," and in part because the company did not have the funding or personnel to tour.[29] In fact, until 1993 and 1994 when Co-Motion Theatre received Arts Council funds specifically allocated to touring *Frank Pig Says Hello* and *Loco County Lonesome*, the company had only toured two shows. In 1989, Co-Motion Theatre brought Georg Büchner's *Woychek* to Germany, and a double bill of O'Byrne's *Departed* and O'Byrne and Gorman's *Cabaret/Kabarett* to Waterford; these efforts were supported by its first Arts Council funds and an increased contribution from AIB. In 2016, however, three of the five shows produced under the Co-Motion Media banner toured extensively. Gorman reveals the reason why: "Touring [is] pretty much the only way to make income."[30] Even so, his short tour of *The Big Fellow* left him with personal debt.[31]

The prevalence of co-productions and the rationale behind touring aside, other shifts in funding issues are revealed in independent interviews with Gorman and O'Byrne, including the integration of commercial business practices with the arts and increased funding bureaucracy. Gorman observes a change in the attitude of the Arts Council that occurred between the end of Co-Motion Theatre in the 1980s and the present period. At one point in the late 2000s, while he was artistic director of the Upstate Theatre Project, Gorman met with a member of the Arts Council staff:

> [T]he language was language I had not heard used in that building before [… and it] really resonated [with me]. One was that we were now talking about what he called the *highly competitive environment*. Another expression that was used was, "What was your USP?" I didn't understand what the abbreviation meant. It means your *unique selling point* […]. I was asked what was the USP of my company and the project I was proposing […]. The other word[s] that came up again and again [… were] the need to make a *compelling case*. This is not the language of the arts sector, the arts world, the arts climate in which I grew up.[32]

Joe O'Byrne gives a good example of a consequence of this "highly competitive environment", which arose when he applied for Arts Council funding in 2015 under the auspices of Co-Motion Media. He completed the application, gathered the required supporting material, and submitted the application, which could only be done online (a significant but predictable change from the hard-copy applications of the 1980s and 1990s). Shortly after pressing "Submit", O'Byrne realized he made an error: he had forgotten to attach the project budget.[33] Although the Council does have a formal appeals process, it only applies after an application has been assessed and rejected. A forgotten attachment means that the application will not reach the assessment stage, as mentioned in the application guidelines: "If you do not submit the required supporting material, your application will be deemed ineligible.... Applications are assessed for eligibility, and any that are ineligible are excluded."[34] With a limited budget and an ever-increasing applicant pool, it appears that the Arts Council may have found a way to decrease the number of applications by instituting administrative technicalities. Co-Motion Media, then, is operating in a "highly competitive environment"; an era in which ticking boxes supersedes the opportunity to showcase a "unique selling point" that would give it a "compelling case" for funding.[35]

The integration of commercial business practices with theatre funding results in added bureaucracy, which is also evidenced by the changes made to the 1951 Arts Act in 1973 and 2003. The 1951 Act sets out a national arts policy in simple, but not simplistic terms. The remit of the Act is "to stimulate public interest in, and to promote the knowledge, appreciation, and practice of the arts, and, for these and other purposes, to establish an Arts Council".[36] In eight sections and one additional schedule, the Act defined the arts as "painting, sculpting, architecture, music, the drama, literature, design in industry and the fine arts and applied arts". Early in the document, specifically in the third paragraph of Section 3, funding is dealt with thus: "The Council may co-operate with and assist any other persons concerned directly or indirectly with matters relating to the arts, *and the assistance may include payments by the Council* upon such terms and conditions as they think fit."[37] The important point to remember for the moment is that the Council's role in funding artists and organizations is placed at the forefront of the document. The Council's aim is to support the arts by funding them. The overarching goal of the 1973 Arts Act is to "amend and extend the Arts Act, 1951".[38] To do so, it expands the remit of the Arts Council to include cinema and fleshes out members' appropriateness by excluding politicians from participating as Arts Council members. The Act systematizes the Council's infrastructure development and adds a section that specifically addresses regional arts development. In Section 13 of 15, several amendments are made to the original 1951 act. Notably, although one change is made to Section 3 of the original act, that section is held intact, indicating that funding continues as a priority within the Act's framework. Rather than expanding or amending the 1951 and 1973 Arts

Acts, the 2003 Act repeals them outright. As written, the Act champions the agency's own bureaucratic structure over funding Ireland's artistic development. First, the act is four times longer than the original 1951 Act, consisting of 32 sections. Perhaps the most conspicuous change is the placement of a section entitled "Funding of the Arts", which has been demoted from Section 3 in 1951 to Section 24 in 2003.[39] Five years after the Act was instituted, and in the wake of the international banking crisis and ensuing recession, the Irish government slashed the Art Council's budget. As a result, the agency decreased its own budget and staff. Further, over the next six years, longstanding independent companies that had flourished such as Tipperary's Galloglass, Dublin's Barabbas, and Waterford's Red Kettle, lost their Arts Council funding and ceased operations in 2009, 2012, and 2014, respectively.

Irish Arts Funding: A Coda

Now back to our story of arts funding through the ages. You sadly observe that the demise of Galloglass, Barabbas, and Red Kettle was to the detriment of audiences throughout the island and your own theatre-going activities. Yet, you see that other theatrical stalwarts and Co-Motion Theatre contemporaries, such as Fishamble and Rough Magic, have endured budget cuts and continue to succeed with the help of funding outside of the Arts Council. You notice that both organizations have benefited from the assistance of Culture Ireland, an organization committed to helping Irish companies tour internationally, and that Fishamble has also forged a relationship with New York City's Irish Arts Center, presenting a number of shows there.

New companies are also on your radar. One example is Galway's Moonfish Theatre, which has utilized a relatively new fundraising tool, FundIt, to crowd-source monies for at least one show. When you saw its adaptation of Joseph O'Connor's novel *The Star of the Sea* on tour at Sligo's Hawk's Well Theatre in 2015, you were extremely impressed: artistically and administratively. A co-production with Galway's An Taibhdhearc that was a critical and box office success at the 2014 Galway Arts Festival, *The Star of the Sea* adapted extremely well to the stage, was gorgeous to look at, and provided a unique approach to subtitling. (They were handwritten, and very helpful since your Irish is a bit rusty.) You spot the acknowledgement for the show's funders on the production programme. Among the logos for the Arts Council's Touring Scheme, Galway City Council, and others, you observe that the incorporation of the Irish language into the production, and the company's commitment to helping audiences speak Irish, allowed it to seek assistance from Foras na Gaeilge, the cross-border agency charged with promoting the Irish language. Perhaps even more importantly, you see that this younger company has quite a bit in common with veterans like Co-Motion. Both companies are presenting shows in co-production and both are touring quite quickly after the initial presentation of their shows, indicating to you that this is not the end of the story: it is the beginning of a new funding age.

Notes

1. For further information on the responsibilities and memorialization of the *choregos*, see Wilson, *The Athenian Institution*, and Csapo, *Actors and Icons*.
2. For a detailed analysis of Horniman's sponsorship of the Abbey Theatre, see Frazier, *Behind the Scenes*, and Flannery, *Miss Annie F. Horniman*. The studies diverge, as Frazier remarks, with Flannery 'stress[ing] the positive, liberating effects of [Horniman's] generosity' while Frazier concentrates on 'its determinative effects' (Frazier, *Behind the Scenes*, 239n83).
3. "New Dublin Theatre", *Freeman's Journal*, December 15, 1904, 5.
4. Ibid.
5. Adrian Frazier, *Behind the Scenes: Yeats, Horniman, and the Struggle for the Abbey Theatre* (London and Berkeley, CA: University of California Press, 1990), 205–40.
6. Pierre Bourdieu, "The Forms of Capital", in *Readings in Economic Sociology*, ed. Nicole Woolsey Biggart, 280–291 (Malden, MA and Oxford: Blackwell, 2002), 289n3.
7. "Arts Act, 1951", *Irish Statute Book* (Dublin: Office of the Attorney General, Government of Ireland), accessed February 12, 2016, http://www.irishstatutebook.ie/eli/1951/act/9/enacted/en/html.
8. "Arts Act, 1973", *Irish Statute Book* (Dublin: Office of the Attorney General, Government of Ireland), accessed February 12, 2016, http://www.irishstatutebook.ie/eli/1973/act/33/enacted/en/html.
9. See also Merriman, "'As We Must'", 389–403, for a good accounting of the ways in which the government policy has shaped Irish theatre companies.
10. To provide transparency, please note that I serve, on a volunteer basis, as social media manager for Co-Motion Media. I also previously worked with Joe O'Byrne in 2001 when he directed his stage adaptation of Oscar Wilde's *The Picture of Dorian Grey* at New York City's Irish Repertory Theatre, where I worked as general manager.
11. Joe O'Byrne, Interview (Dublin: 2006).
12. Declan Gorman, Interview (Dublin: 2006).
13. "Methusalem", Production Programme (Dublin: Co-Motion Theatre Company, 1985).
14. Amy Garvey, "Spur to the Imagination", *Irish Press*, October 3, 1985, 16.
15. Peter Thompson, "'Black' theme in café theatre", *Irish Press*. December 1, 1986, 2.
16. Fintan O'Toole, "A Leap Beyond the Dark", *Irish Times*, October 1, 1988, A11.
17. Fintan O'Toole, "Roll Up! Roll Up! A New Playwright Comes to Town", *Irish Times*, October 6, 1990, A5.
18. Lorcan Roche, "Big business bails out the arts", *Irish Independent*, March 9, 1988, 8.
19. Lorcan Roche, "Banking on a dramatic future", *Irish Independent*. March 9, 1988, 8.
20. Gorman, Interview (Dublin: 2006).
21. Helen Meany, "Perpetual Co-Motion", *Irish Times*, February 6, 1993, A5.
22. Ibid.
23. O'Byrne, Interview (Dublin: 2006).

24. Fintan O'Toole, "Embracing a bigger stage", *Irish Times*, October 11, 1994.
25. O'Byrne, Interview (Dublin: 2006).
26. Ibid.
27. Emer O'Kelly, "O'Byrne's En Suite is off the map", *Sunday Independent*, Living Section, March 24, 2002, 20.
28. "About", *Co-Motion Media (Ireland)*, accessed 1 April 2017, https://co-motionmedia.com/about/.
29. Gorman, Interview, 2016.
30. Ibid.
31. Ibid.
32. Ibid., emphasis added.
33. O'Byrne, Interview (Dublin: 2016).
34. "Open Call Award: Guidelines for Applicants", Arts Council/*An Chomhairle Ealaíon*, accessed April 1, 2017, http://www.artscouncil.ie/Funds/Open-Call/, 4, 9.
35. For a specific perspective on the complex interconnection between funding and artistic product, see also McIvor, "Interview with Declan Gorman and Declan Mallon: Upstate Theatre Project", especially Declan Gorman's comments on page 365.
36. "Arts Act, 1951".
37. Ibid., emphasis added.
38. "Arts Act, 1973".
39. "Arts Act, 2003", *Irish Statute Book* (Dublin: Office of the Attorney General, Government of Ireland), accessed February 12, 2016, http://www.irishstatutebook.ie/eli/2003/act/24/enacted/en/html.

Bibliography

"About." *Co-Motion Media (Ireland)*. Accessed April 1, 2017. https://co-motionmedia.com/about/

"Arts Act, 1951." *Irish Statute Book*. Dublin: Office of the Attorney General, Government of Ireland. Accessed February 12, 2016. http://www.irishstatutebook.ie/eli/1951/act/9/enacted/en/html

"Arts Act, 1973." *Irish Statute Book*. Dublin: Office of the Attorney General, Government of Ireland. Accessed February 12, 2016. http://www.irishstatutebook.ie/eli/1973/act/33/enacted/en/html

"Arts Act, 2003." *Irish Statute Book*. Dublin: Office of the Attorney General, Government of Ireland. Accessed February 12, 2016. http://www.irishstatutebook.ie/eli/2003/act/24/enacted/en/html

"Methusalem." Production Programme. Dublin: Co-Motion Theatre Company, 1985.

"New Dublin Theatre." *Freeman's Journal*. December 15, 1904.

"Open Call Award: Guidelines for Applicants." Arts Council/ *An Chomhairle Ealaíon*. Accessed April 1, 2017. http://www.artscouncil.ie/Funds/Open-Call/

Bourdieu, Pierre. "The Forms of Capital". In *Readings in Economic Sociology*, edited by Nicole Woolsey Biggart, 280–291. Malden, MA and Oxford: Blackwell, 2002.

Csapo, Eric. *Actors and Icons of the Ancient Theatre*. Chichester: Wiley-Blackwell, 2010.

Flannery, James W. *Miss Annie F. Horniman and the Abbey Theatre*. Dublin: Dolmen Press, 1970.

Frazier, Adrian. *Behind the Scenes: Yeats, Horniman, and the Struggle for the Abbey Theatre*. London and Berkeley, CA: U of California P, 1990.
Garvey, Amy. "Spur to the Imagination." *Irish Press*. October 3, 1985.
Gorman, Declan. *Interview*. Dublin: May, 2006.
Gorman, Declan. *Interview*. Dublin: May, 2016.
McIvor, Charlotte. "Interview with Declan Gorman and Declan Mallon: Upstate Theatre Project." In *Staging Intercultural Ireland: New Plays and Practitioner Perspectives*, edited by Charlotte McIvor and Matthew Spangler, 359–366, Cork: Cork UP, 2014.
Meany, Helen. "Perpetual Co-Motion." *Irish Times*. February 6, 1993.
Merriman, Victor. "'As We Must': Growth and Diversification in Ireland's Theatre Culture." In *The Oxford Handbook of Modern Irish Theatre*, edited by Nicholas Grene and Chris Morash, 389–403. Oxford: Oxford UP, 2016.
O'Byrne, Joe. *Interview*. Dublin: May, 2006.
O'Byrne, Joe. *Interview*. Dublin: May, 2016.
O'Kelly, Emer. "O'Byrne's En Suite Is Off the Map." *Sunday Independent*, Living Section. March 24, 2002.
O'Toole, Fintan. "A Leap Beyond the Dark." *Irish Times*. October 1, 1988.
———. "Roll Up! Roll Up! A New Playwright Comes to Town." *Irish Times*. October 6, 1990.
———. "Embracing a Bigger Stage." *Irish Times*. October 11, 1994.
Roche, Lorcan. "Banking on a Dramatic Future." *Irish Independent*. March 9, 1988.
———. "Big Business Bails Out the Arts." *Irish Independent*. March 9, 1988.
Thompson, Peter. "'Black' Theme in Café Theatre." *Irish Press*. December 1, 1986.
Wilson, Peter. *The Athenian Institution of the of Khoregia: The Chorus, The City, and the Stage*. Cambridge: Cambridge UP, 2000.

New Century Theatre Companies: From Dramatist to Collective

Cormac O'Brien

Introduction: Ireland's Shape Shifting Theatre

Since the establishment in 1904 of Ireland's National Theatre, the Abbey, the nation's theatrical culture has taken many shapes, evolving and shifting and evolving again into what can be identified as several dramatic movements or schools. Each of these distinct yet intertwined movements can be understood as both a reaction to what came before and a laying of the groundwork for what would follow in its wake. That the state of the nation and Irish identities have been of primary concern to each of these movements there is no doubt. In our present moment, the question of where Irish theatre has taken itself since the beginning of the twenty-first century, especially with regards to exploring the state of the nation and Irish identities, is, of course, the primary concern of this chapter.

However, to understand fully the latest shape-shift in our national theatrical culture, some consideration must be given to the dramatic structure and theatrical form of what has come before. Over the course of the twentieth century, Irish theatre established itself as a world leader of captivating and socially aware drama, with plays that relied to a great degree on the "situation-conflict-resolution" paradigm of Ibsenite dramatic narrative; itself a theatrical structure that stems from the Aristotelian model of tragedy. For the spectator, this is a familiar dramatic structure of linear, performed storytelling with an engaging plot that, in keeping with the Irish National Theatre's manifesto of being

C. O'Brien (✉)
University College Dublin, Dublin, Ireland
e-mail: cormac.obrien@ucd.ie

E. Jordan, E. Weitz (eds.), *The Palgrave Handbook of Contemporary Irish Theatre and Performance*,
https://doi.org/10.1057/978-1-137-58588-2_17

"a writers' theatre", positions both the playwright and their written text as the primary, centrifugal forces from which all other elements of the drama—directing, acting, scenography, lighting—must emanate.

Since the turn of the new millennium, however, Irish theatre has been undergoing a renaissance in terms of moving away from Ibsenite dramatic narratives and into more radical performance structures and theatrical forms. This renaissance had been spearheaded by a small but ever-growing cohort of theatre companies that were all founded in the last eighteen years, and can be thus identified as New Century Irish theatre companies. And while these New Century companies still have the state of the nation and Irishness as central concerns, these theatre makers are creating ensemble works that not only eschew any over-reliance on a central text, but also make strange the familiar structures of narrative drama that have long been entrenched. Bound up with this new-millennium thrust towards more total theatre experiences for spectators is a decentring of the role of the dramatist. Collaboration with associate artists from outside the realm of theatre, as well as local communities, drives this latest cohort of theatre makers as they endeavour to both speak and respond to an ever-changing Ireland in the opening decades of the twenty-first century. Yet, while they might disregard the traditional role of singular dramatist as storyteller, they still tell stories: stories of less visible communities and those marginalized by mainstream society. In this sense, New Century companies pay homage to the entrenched Irish tradition of storytelling: a tradition, one should remember, that was mobilized frequently to subversive, political aims during the struggle for Irish independence and, after the Republic had made the transition from colony to nation state, as a means of destabilizing oppressive authoritarian governments and institutions.

The aim of this chapter, then, is to embark upon a critical survey of five New Century Irish theatre companies, interrogating the ways in which their radical dramaturgical strategies and rehearsal and performance practices make comment on Irish identities and the state of the nation. The chapter is organized into three sections. The first elaborates a critical survey of three companies, Talking Shop Ensemble, WillFredd and Brokentalkers. While there is a wide variety of New Century companies to choose from, such as TheatreCLUB, Hot for Theatre, Gonzo and Collapsing Horse, to name but a few, these three were chosen because their theatre practice—in terms of both how they create their shows and how those shows are presented—captures three distinct methods of theatre-making and audience engagement. The second and third sections of this chapter each present a case study of a New Century company, namely Dead Centre and THISISPOPBABY. These companies were chosen as case studies because each has, respectively, taken one of those two primary themes of modern Irish theatre—the state of the nation or Irish identities—and has produced, to great critical and public acclaim, radical dramaturgical approaches to these themes.

Embracing Our Future, Paying Homage to Our Past

Irish theatre has always been a cultural expression that both comes from and speaks to social movements and concerns. Each of the New Century companies discussed below has, through radical theatre-making and performance practices, voiced the concerns and challenges of a broad cohort of disparate and less visible communities across Ireland. Rather than address a monolithic notion of a nationwide Irish identity that could somehow encompass all of those living on the island, what we see with New Century companies is an intersectional sensitivity that recognizes and contributes to the sustainability of the plurality and multi-culturalism of today's Ireland.

The first of the New Century theatre companies to emerge was Brokentalkers, founded at the start of the new millennium in 2001 by Feidlim Cannon, Damien Fenty, Gary Keegan and Faye Munns. Brokentalkers paradoxically embraces and simultaneously critiques the globalized, multi-platform, media-drenched nature of today's Ireland by producing its work in an eclectic variety of places, ranging from theatres to public spaces, disused sites and the Internet. Under the artistic directorship of Cannon and Keegan since 2003, and having earned an international reputation as one of Ireland's most innovative and original theatre companies, such is the diverse nature of its output that Brokentalkers' work is difficult to categorize. Its work is nothing if not structurally and formally ambitious, encompassing song, movement, video, live music, masks and mime.

Reinforcing Charlotte McIvor's view that Brokentalkers provides "witness to the broken nation",[1] is the way in which its work often brings into sharp focus Irish familial, religious and sociopolitical structures, and their often negative impact on the individual's progress through society. This focus is underwritten by an examination of the ways in which contemporary relationalities of kinship and bonding that form outside the family can often provide more nurturing support systems. The company's output has been prolific indeed, with some sixteen shows to its name as of 2018. The following list of recent key productions demonstrates, by the volume of names in the writing and production credits, the truly collaborative nature of the work: *The Circus Animals' Desertion* by Feidlim Cannon and Gary Keegan (2016); *This Beach* by Feidlim Cannon and Gary Keegan (co-produced by the Goethe Institute, Munich Kammerspiele and Tiger Dublin Fringe, 2016); *It Folds* by Feidlim Cannon, Gary Keegan, Jessica Kennedy and Megan Kennedy (co-produced with LÓKAL Theatre Festival Reykjavík, and supported by Culture Ireland, Dance Ireland, Dublin City Council, Project Arts Centre and FRINGE LAB (Tiger Dublin Fringe, 2015)); *Have I No Mouth* by Feidlim Cannon and Gary Keegan (Project Arts Centre; Dublin Theatre Festival, 2012); *The Blue Boy* by Feidlim Cannon and Gary Keegan (Dublin Theatre Festival, 2011); *Silver Stars* by Sean Miller (Project Arts Centre, 2008, with subsequent international tour).

Brokentalkers' practice and performance methods are diverse, with its online manifesto declaring its aim to "explore new forms that challenge traditional ideologies of text-based theatre".[2] Its central theatre-making ethos lies in immersive and inclusive collaborative processes that draw from the skills and experiences of multitudinous artists, performers, designers and writers. Crucial to its theatrical idiom is its collaboration with people who do not usually work in the arts, which thus brings authentic lived experiences to its work. Its performance events therefore respond to twenty-first century Ireland by utilizing the many platforms through which society communicates—original writing, dance, classic texts, film, interviews, found materials and music—and then offering that back as a searing critique of the current state of the nation.

Founded in 2008 by theatre makers Oonagh Murphy, Aisling Byrne, Lisa Walsh and Robbie Sinnott, Talking Shop Ensemble is a theatre-making collective with a manifesto that stemmed from, its website states, "a shared wish to make work that pushed at the definition of theatre".[3] Talking Shop frequently collaborates with Shaun Dunne, an upcoming playwright and performer whose work has garnered both critical and audience acclaim in recent years. (Dunne's 2014 drama, *The Waste Ground Party*, was produced by and staged at the Abbey.) With all its work, Taking Shop seeks to uncover the truth of what it means to be an ordinary person struggling to survive in today's Ireland as ever-encroaching neoliberal precarity and economic austerity measures, such as water charges and property taxes, dispel any notions of a population in recovery from recession, even as the economy booms for the second time in twenty years. With its dramaturgical idiom manifesting primarily in the documentary theatre genre, as with the majority of New Century companies, Talking Shop's work draws heavily from performance art, music and installations. Carrying echoes of the socially aware "agitprop theatres" of the 1960s, such as Joan Littlewood's Theatre Workshop in Stratford East, London, the company's performance events are firmly rooted in the workshop paradigm of rehearsal practice, which lends itself easily to its highly collaborative model of working with associate artists and musicians.

In accordance with its statement that "We believe theatre should speak about what it is to live here and now",[4] Talking Shop's key performance events since its establishment demonstrate that its primary concerns lie with issues of identity and belonging in the Ireland of today. Its 2010 show, *FAT*, was devised in collaboration with Stephen Quinn, Dan Bergin and Louise Melinn, and explored the ways in which globalized notions of body fascism, celebrity obsession and dieting culture play out in Ireland. October 2010 saw Dunne's first collaboration with Talking Shop, which resulted in *I am a Home Bird (It's Very Hard)*, a performance piece that explored Irish emigration since the recession and its impact on contemporary understandings of home and the home-place. *Home Bird* was originally produced by TheatreCLUB as part of its "The Theatre Machine Turns You On" programme and later toured Ireland in 2011. Continuing with themes of twenty-first century Irish identities, and working in collaboration with Robbie Lawlor, an HIV-positive man who won the "Mr Gay Ireland" context in 2015, the company's most recent piece *Rapids* explores what it means to live with HIV in today's Ireland. This project is timely indeed: with new diagnoses of HIV in Ireland reaching an all-time high, higher even than in the "AIDS crisis years" of 1981–1996, several leading experts have warned that Ireland is heading for an HIV catastrophe.[5] Little surprise then that the Abbey picked up on *Rapids* by providing support, space and resources for a series of five development workshops, which Dunne and Lawlor facilitated in February 2017.[6] *Rapids* then saw a full scale production at The Project Arts Centre, Dublin, as part of the 2017 Dublin Theatre Festival.

Dispelling the cultural perception of theatre as an elitist art and bringing it to broader, quotidian audiences is the key concern of WillFredd, founded in 2011 by Sophie Motley, Sarah Jane Shiels and Kate Ferris. With a committed community ethos and strong ethical impetus, WillFredd's aim is simple: to create locally produced performances that engage with contemporary culture while simultaneously inviting new audiences into the theatre. Unlike its 1980s counterpart Passion Machine, which also sought to bring theatre to the masses, rather than have a dramatist write plays about less visible populations in Ireland, WillFredd has eschewed both the role of the playwright and incumbent traditional theatre spaces by taking its work to the communities involved and making the performances with them.

WillFredd has created five productions to date: *FOLLOW* (2011), *FARM* (2012), *CARE* (2014), *JOCKEY* (2015), and BEES—which is a theatre-in-education piece about environmental awareness that has been touring Irish schools since 2016. *FOLLOW* presents the experiences of the Irish Deaf Community through sound, light, Irish Sign Language and traditional storytelling. With its timely status as the first piece of theatre in Ireland created for both a Deaf and Hearing audience, *FOLLOW* won the Spirit of the Fringe Award at Dublin Fringe Festival in 2011. For *FARM*, WillFredd worked with communities of farmers, beekeepers, allotment owners and city dwellers. Conceptualizing the city as a space where the urban and rural intersect and can potentially flourish together, *FARM* is an immersive event that invites spectators, as the company's website says, to "get your hands dirty and unearth your roots" by taking a playful performative approach to the "cycles of life and death, land and machines, animals and insects, dawn and dusk".[7] Through a kaleidoscope of music, song and live testimonial, *CARE* seeks to disrupt common misperceptions about hospices, the lives of those who work as hospice carers and those who go to die in them. *JOCKEY* gives voice to, through movement and music, the lives of those who work in the horse-racing industry by exploring an original idea from dancer Emma O'Kane, who was struck by the similarities between jockeys and dancers.

WillFredd's commitment to the collective theatre-making that speaks for and is inclusively representative of twenty-first century Irish communities manifests in its constant evaluation and interrogation of work in progress. Performances are constantly re-evaluated, oscillating between workshop practice and subsequent periods of extended research. As such, to consider its in-development shows as not yet ready for public consumption is to misunderstand its work. Because of its community-focused practice, from the moment of a show's conception right though to its final performance, WillFredd's work is fulfilling its mission of exploring the issues of what it means to belong to less visible populations in Ireland. In this sense then, the company disrupts that well-intentioned but often misguided idea of the relatively well-positioned dramatist and theatre company giving voice to the voiceless without ever fully knowing or understanding exactly who those voices belong to, or anything of their lives and concerns. Its work can never be considered as mere lip service to less empowered communities; rather, WillFredd can be understood as providing a vital community service.

Speaking Truth to Post-Truth Power: Dead Centre

As the lights darken to signal the start of Dead Centre's *Lippy* (2013), a man onstage speaks but his words become distorted as if in a horror movie. His lips and face stop moving, yet still his voice continues, echoing from place to place around the auditorium.[8] Random noises conglomerate to become a cacophonous soundscape, as rich and beautiful as it is terrifying and haunting. Suddenly, the lighting becomes normal as the sounds stop. Two men sit centre stage in front of a closed curtain. These men facilitate a post-show discussion of a play that the spectator has never seen, nor will ever see. *Lippy*, as it careers along, becomes chaotic: the curtain opens on an eerily lit stage and frightening figures in hazmat suits appear, only to morph into four tragically doomed women—the central protagonists of this piece—who then subject themselves to violent harm. A man suddenly pops out of a black plastic bin-liner. A Snickers bar becomes the gateway between life and death. The spectator has been taken, courtesy of Dead Centre's surreal and chaotic dramaturgy, on a nightmare journey based on the final days of four women in the Dublin suburb of Leixlip, County Kildare, who, according to the coroner's reports, shut away the outside world and starved themselves to death in 2000.

As grim as this may sound, Dead Centre's work represents New Century Irish theatre-making at its most probing, most polemic, and, crucially, most political. Dead Centre was founded in 2012 by artistic directors Bush Moukarzel and Ben Kidd, with producers Matthew Smyth and Rachel Murray, and technical manager Nic Ree. Thus far it has worked with several Irish and UK-based associate artists, including Adam Welsh, Jason Booher and Ailbhe Wakefield-Drohan, as well as Mark O'Halloran, a successful Irish playwright and screenwriter. In keeping with the globalized nature of our contemporary, post-modern world, it is based between Dublin and London and has, to date, staged four theatre events: *Souvenir*, which opened in September 2012 at the New Theatre, Dublin, as part of the Dublin Fringe Festival; *Lippy* (2013), which opened at the Lír in Dublin as part of the Dublin Fringe Festival and has won a remarkable four awards[9]; *(S)quark!* (2013), which was a joint commission between the James Joyce Centre in Dublin and the Garden of Geniuses festival in Yasnaya Polyana, Russia; *Chekhov's First Play* (2015), which opened at the Samuel Beckett Theatre in Trinity College Dublin as part of the Dublin Theatre Festival and garnered Dead Centre its second Irish Times Irish Theatre Award; *Hamnet*, which was co-produced with and had its Irish premiere at the Abbey for the 2017 Dublin Theatre Festival; and most recently,

Shakespeare's Last Play, which premiered at the Schaubuhne Theatre, Berlin, in April 2018. Their first five projects have toured throughout the world, playing at venues in New York, Russia, Australia, France, Estonia and Holland; at theatres across the UK, including the Bristol Old Vic, London's Young Vic and Edinburgh's Traverse; and at the Schaubühne theatre in Berlin.

It is significant that Dead Centre was established in 2012, at a time when Irish society was reeling from the 2008 global financial meltdown, the brutal cutbacks of austerity politics and the economic policies enacted by three successive governments under the watchful eye of the International Monetary Fund, which had been invited by our political masters to intervene into and "structurally reform" a broken Irish economy at the end of 2010. Contemporary politics, not just in Ireland but globally, is nothing if it is not based on spin, rhetoric and propaganda, some of which is based on falsehoods. As ordinary citizens spiral into the sort of financial precarity from which there is often no recovery, with homeless numbers reaching crisis levels while an epidemic of suicide becomes ordinary, politicians and governments attempt (often successfully) to justify the shocking conditions in which they force people to live by presenting ideologically laden "truisms" that are little more than thinly disguised excuses for the massive transfer of wealth from those who have very little to those who already have far too much. All that is required for this rhetoric to work is that its witnesses—in other words we the people—are willing to enter a state of suspended disbelief and embrace cognitive dissonance by feeling, and therefore somehow believing, that this highly emotive political spin is, by some bizarre twist of fate and contrary to all evidence, proof of our society's betterment. Indeed, there is a new term for this phenomenon of spin-based political rhetoric, which is so often built not just on lies, but on its witnesses' willingness to believe them: "post-truth", which entered the lexicon of the *Oxford English Dictionary* in 2016.[10]

Of course, it is the job of contemporary theatre makers to speak truth to post-truth power. One of Dead Centre's primary concerns, then, is to provide a dramaturgical critique of post-truth politics and the ways in which it encourages citizens to vote with their feelings rather than cast their ballots based on facts and statistics. By provoking spectators to engage with a non-linear and often confusing theatrical narrative which itself is undergirded with questions of what Irish governance might now mean in a post-truth world, Dead Centre's work thus lays bare the mechanics of theatrical and, by extension and most importantly, political artifice. Essentially, in political terms, what Dead Centre endeavours to uncover is the truth of what it means to be both an Irish and a world citizen after the global financial meltdown. That it undertakes this through a dramaturgy and scenography that is as brutal as it is chaotic, and that is theatrically dazzling while simultaneously achieving the highest standards of technical excellence, is, I want to argue, what makes Dead Centre one of the most important of the New Century Irish companies.

Confusion and chaos are a vital element of Dead Centre's stagecraft as well as being a key dramaturgical tool for questioning the state of the nation. In *(S) quark!*, for example, a play which purports to answer the question of whether James Joyce was a genius, the spectator is informed before the show starts that they will witness "a duet for one performer"—a theatrical and cultural contradiction in terms if ever there was one. *Lippy*, through the device of a Beckett-inspired closing monologue performed by a mouth on a screen and written by Mark O'Halloran, brings dignity and honour to the four Irish women who chose death over living. We can never know exactly why these three sisters and their elderly aunt chose to leave this world, and nor is this the question that Dead Centre attempts to answer. Instead, Dead Centre questions the role of the traditional dramatist and dramatic storytelling—and by extension media and political storytelling—through meta-theatrical staging (this is theatre offering a comment on itself as theatre) and an overarching trope of lip-reading. What, then, this trope asks, are the moral and political implications of mapping your own words onto someone else's life? The urgency of seeking meaning beyond the words that someone utters is thus evoked, while culturally mediated truisms are disrupted, negated and must be reconstructed by the spectator.

In Dead Centre's 2015 production, *Chekhov's First Play*, each spectator wears headphones. The show starts, but nothing happens. After a while, long enough for the audience to feel uneasy, artistic director Bush Moukarzel, wearing jeans, checked shirt and messy hair, wanders onstage. In his right hand he carries a microphone, in his left, a gun. And this gun is, indeed, Chekhov's gun. Moukarzel tries to explain to the audience the premise of Chekhov's gun, but he fails, unable to articulate what he means. He then elaborates that, because the show about to be presented is an early work by Chekhov and largely considered unstageable, the audience will hear in their headphones his personal running commentary throughout, explaining the performance as it unfolds.

> Moukarzel/Director: Personally, I always need things explained to me, especially art. I'm the kind of guy who goes to an art gallery and spends all the time reading the writing on the wall next to the paintings. I hardly ever look at the paintings.[11]

This patrician, over-reaching conceit of telling a group of interested witnesses that they need to have what they are about to witness explained to them because otherwise they would lose interest, or not understand, or draw conclusions that the event organizers do not want them to draw, cuts to the heart of what Dead Centre is about. Its work provokes spectators to ask not what the questions of the day are, but more precisely who has set those questions, how they have been framed, and whose agenda they are expected to serve. Pinpointing the essence of post-truth politics, at one particularly complicated point in Chekhov's text, Moukarzel's voiceover proclaims: "Fuck's sake! This play is getting in the way of me explaining it"[12]; just as real-life issues such as homelessness get in the way of easily digested, glorified political rhetoric. By telling the untellable tale of Platonov, the protagonist of this earliest work by Chekhov, and yet informing the spectator that "you're probably missing all the key themes",[13] Dead Centre provokes an awareness of the media-saturated, reality-show nature of contemporary politics.

Evident in Dead Centre's work are strong influences drawn from non-text-based European theatre makers, such as German director Sebastian Nübling, as well as from UK "devised theatre" companies such as Complicité and the David Glass Ensemble. But beyond this, in many ways Dead Centre's work resonates with the 1990s wave of experientialist "in-yer-face" British playwrights, also known as "the new brutalists", such as Sarah Kane, Mark Ravenhill, Jez Butterworth and Tracy Letts. But to this argument I want to add a caveat—this is what in-yer-face theatre has now evolved into in the second decade of the twenty-first century. In-yer-face has grown up and matured. Indeed, this is a studied, intellectual approach to in-yer-face dramaturgy, especially when one considers that Moukarzel and his main collaborators, sound designer Adam Welsh and director Ben Kidd, are too young to have witnessed in-yer-face first hand. Thus, they have the benefit of studying it as a genre rather than living through the original controversy and shock-horror hype back in the day whereby reviewers like Michael Billington eviscerated playwrights such as Sarah Kane.[14]

Dead Centre, therefore, has taken the best of in-yer-face, discarded its less helpful aspects, and created a theatrical tour de force that is capable of haunting its audience's dreams while simultaneously bringing them a sense of political truth and social understanding. In the last analysis, Dead Centre's performance work provides, despite its disruptive brutality, a paradoxical sense of theatrical peace.

Bringing the Mainstream to the Queer: THISISPOPBABY

Founded in 2007 by Jennifer Jennings and Phillip McMahon, THISISPOPBABY is, alongside Brokentalkers, the most polemic and prolific of Ireland's New Century theatre companies. THISISPOPBABY embraces collective theatre-making imbued with a strong performance art tradition. Upbeat, punkish, rebellious, politically irreverent, and with an ever-questioning finger on the pulse of the Irish cultural zeitgeist, THISISPOPBABY is fully invested in and committed to providing an immersive, total performance experience for both its theatre spectators and those who attend its non-theatrical events such as its performance space at the annual Electric Picnic music festival. What is most remarkable about THISISPOPBABY's work is that this invigorating sense of collective theatre-making—which, one should note, also showcases the oft-forgotten theatricality of scenography and set design—resonates through not only its communally created theatre events, but more importantly is ever-present when it produces single-authored plays. That THISISPOPBABY can meld seamlessly these two seemingly disparate sources of theatre-making—the collective and the dramatist—is testament to its ever-growing status as one of the most important companies producing performance events in Ireland today.

THISISPOPBABY identifies itself, in its online manifesto, as "a theatre and events production company that rips up the space between popular culture, counter culture, queer culture and high art—providing both a vehicle for our associate artists' dreams and an electrifying access point to the arts".[15] One of its most singular contributions to both theatrical art and the state of the nation is, I want to argue, the ways in which it has foregrounded queer culture and Irish LGBTQ lives and identities while never yet pandering to those easily digestible and asexual versions of gayness that heteronormative culture so often demands. Its first show, staged in Dublin's Red Box nightclub, *Danny and Chantelle (still here)* (2007), albeit demonstrating the harshness and difficulties of coming out as gay in contemporary Ireland, still managed through an upbeat dramaturgy infused with dance music to celebrate both the queerness and the counter-normative lives of its characters as joyous things that its heterosexual counterparts could never experience. Likewise, its camp musical fantasia *Alice in Funderland*, which started life as a workshop reading in 2010 and received a main-stage production as the Abbey Theatre's summer show of 2012, melded a queer aesthetic with a camp, fantastical plot. *Elevator* (2012), written and directed by McMahon, mobilized its singular queer dramaturgy—including carnivalesque sequences with traditional characters donning horse-heads to perform scenes of bacchanalian excess—to question received notions of wealth, privilege and masculine bisexuality at a time when the country is being fed a political narrative of conservative austerity. THISISPOPBABY has also queered theatrical space with a series of "Performance. Art. Club" events, called "WERK", which take place in the lobby of the Abbey Theatre's studio space, The Peacock, and constitute a mish-mash of monologues, poetry slam, solo singers, bands, performance art and idiosyncratic "personalities" from the Dublin alternative scene who mingle with spectators, just being queer. The company's offering for the 2016 Dublin International Theatre Festival, *Riot*, is a mash-up of circus, polemic monologues, satirical takes on traditional Irish song and dance, and acrobatics, which played in a non-traditional theatre space and headlined drag queen Panti Bliss. Operating as a political call to arms for ordinary, everyday people and, if audience reactions on the nights I attended are anything to go by, very much succeeding in its aim of consciousness raising, *Riot* is, as McMahon asserts, "THISISPOPBABY's most entertaining show to date, uniting the brightest talents of Irish stage and screen in a glittering roulette of the brilliant, brazen and downright bizarre".[16] *Riot* was staged again in revival in July 2017, and is currently touring several venues on the East Coast of the United States.

THISISPOPBABY's queer-themed work avoids an overarching trend to which many presentations of queerness in Irish theatre tend to fall prey, in that however progressive and well-intentioned these presentations may be, such work often highlights the challenges, difficulties and victimhood status frequently visited on LGBTQ individuals and communities by Ireland's overreaching heteronormative sociopolitical and healthcare structures. THISISPOPBABY's performances of queer lives and living, on the other hand, celebrate the gloriously excessive, outrageous and very different elements of queer culture while simultaneously acknowledging the similarities between LGBTQ and heterosexual lives and living. Indeed, one might think of its performances as a theatrical gay pride parade. Hence its work both nurtures and maintains those counter-normative aspects of queer cultures and sexualities—the largely unknown pockets of queerness that heteronormative subjects can never experience—that make queers queer and keep them queer. Indeed, when dissecting its sizeable canon of work, one could argue that THISISPOPBABY has reversed the usual processes of raising queer awareness in Irish society: rather than bringing celebrations of queer culture to mainstream Ireland, it has carried mainstream Ireland to a unique discursive space where it can celebrate queer culture.

This celebratory queerness is best exemplified in the company's strong and by-now entrenched tradition of international touring. Perhaps its most successful tour to date has been drag queen Panti Bliss's biographical monologue, *High Heels in Low Places* (2014), which toured internationally on and off from 2014 until 2017 when the show was given a special farewell performance at the Abbey, billed as *High Heels: The Last Hurrah*. *High Heels* is the culmination of a decade-long partnership between Panti and THISISPOPBABY; the company has staged a series of Panti-authored monologues since 2007, *In These Shoes* (2007), *All Dolled Up* (2007), *A Woman in Progress* (2009) and *Restitched* (2013–15), with each one being a reboot of its predecessor, while the latest version of *High Heels* attends to Panti's recent rise to international acclaim by virtue of her leading role as a spokesperson for a Yes vote in Ireland's 2015 equal marriage referendum.

Meanwhile, its international tour of Neil Watkins' dark and polemic autobiographical monologue, *The Year of Magical Wanking* (2010), brought to the world as a searing queer critique of the ways in which, despite a gloss of progressive tolerance for LGBTQ rights in Ireland, there still exists a dark underbelly of HIV-related stigma and homophobia in the nation's social welfare and healthcare structures, particularly in terms of meeting or even understanding the mental health needs of queer citizens. And yet, despite its darkness, *Magical Wanking* still manages to celebrate Watkins' journey from being shamed for his radically alternative lifestyle into embodying and performing a profound sense of queer pride. The shaming of queer subjects has, since the first gay-themed play to appear on the Irish stage, Thomas Kilroy's *The Death and Resurrection of Mr. Roche* (1968), been of primary concern to any dramatists and theatre makers who have tackled the topic of being LGBTQ identified in Ireland. Queer shame, as Eve Sedgwick contests, moves beyond mere negation of identity and into the realms of both political and subjective identity formation. For queer subjects, "shame is simply the first, and remains a permanent, structuring fact of identity: one that [...] has its own powerfully productive and powerfully social metamorphic possibilities".[17] And while under Sedgwick's formulation queer shame can never be dispelled fully, THISISPOPBABY has, with *Magical Wanking*, chronicled a journey from shame to pride. What I want to argue here, then, is that Watkins' monologue, under the direction of McMahon, can be considered one of the most probing and satisfying performances seen on the stage in terms of tackling queer shame while simultaneously presenting an autobiographical account (and thus a suggested route for others) of one Irish man's negotiation of what former President of Ireland Mary McAlesse has called "Ireland's architecture of homophobia".[18]

THISISPOPBABY, in keeping with its queer dramaturgical ethos, continues to make strange, indeed continue to queer, the traditional format of narrative drama. Where the entrenched Ibsenite model is employed, it is mobilized in meta-theatrical and Brechtian ways, thus ensuring that its audiences come away with questions about Ireland and official narratives of Irish identity. For example, McMahon's recent Abbey play *Town is Dead* (2016, with music by Raymond Scannell) seems on the surface to be a rather typical realist narrative of an underclass, inner-city Dublin woman who has endured deprivation, violence, addiction and tragedy. Certainly the main protagonist, Ellen (played by Irish stage veteran Barbara Brennan) resonates with O'Casey's Juno; however, this show has a prescient twenty-first century twist in that Ellen is about to lose her home, which is falling prey to globalization and property vulture funds. Adding to the overarching and jarring dissonance of quotidian Irish identity since the recession, not only is the ghost of Ellen's dead son an onstage presence, but furthermore all the dialogue is sung like an opera while the stage movement is choreographed as slow dance; thus provoking spectator awareness of disingenuous mainstream political and media-driven narratives about what makes poor people poor and keeps them poor.

By focusing on touring and festivals while simultaneously pushing the boundaries of narrative realism, as well as constantly showcasing the work of emerging theatre artists, THISISPOPBABY—as with all of the New Century companies discussed—thus exemplifies to other independent and fringe theatre makers and playwrights that there are alternative routes to success to the typical blind submission of scripts to a theatre company or festival or acceptance onto a new writing programme. To be sure, THISISPOPBABY did, eventually, produce its work on the Abbey stage. But this was no compromise on the company's part; indeed, the ways in which it achieved its place at the National Theatre table were most certainly on its own terms while never losing its singular vision and queer atheistic. THISISPOPBABY's access to mainstream theatre in Ireland has always been in keeping with its own agenda, and as the company grows from success to success, it seems set to continue to steer its own theatrical course.

Notes

1. Charlotte McIvor, "Witnessing the Broken Nation: Theatre of the Real and Social Fragmentation in Brokentalkers' *Silver Stars, The Blue Boy*, and *Have I No Mouth*", in *That Was Us: Contemporary Irish Theatre and Performance*, ed. Fintan Walsh, (London: Oberon, 2013), 37.
2. "About Us," Brokentalkers, accessed January 4, 2017, http://www.brokentalkers.ie/.
3. "What Do We Do?," Talking Shop Ensemble, accessed January 6, 2017, https://talkingshopensemble.wordpress.com/about/company/.
4. Ibid.
5. Cormac O'Brien, "Ireland in the Age of AIDS: The Cultural Politics of Stigma, *The Irish Review*, 53 (2016): 45–59.

6. "Shaun Dunne and Robbie Lawlor: HIV Workshops," Abbey Theatre, accessed January 7, 2017, https://www.abbeytheatre.ie/shaun-dunne-and-robbie-lawlor-hiv-workshops/.
7. "FARM," WillFredd, accessed January 9, 2017, http://willfredd.com/productions-2care/farm/.
8. Bush Moukarzel & Dead Centre, *Lippy* (London: Oberon, 2014).
9. Dead Centre's awards to dates include: "Best Production," Irish Times Irish Theatre Awards 2013, Fringe First 2014, Herald Angel 2014, Total Theatre Award 2014, OBIE (Off Broadway awards) 2014.
10. Alison Flood, "Post-truth named word of the year by Oxford Dictionaries," *The Guardian*, 15 November 2016, accessed January 4, 2017, https://www.theguardian.com/books/2016/nov/15/post-truth-named-word-of-the-year-by-oxford-dictionaries.
11. Bush Moukarzel & Dead Centre, *Chekhov's First Play* (London: Oberon Books, 2015), 14.
12. Moukarzel & Dead Centre, *Chekhov's First Play*, 12.
13. Moukarzel & Dead Centre, *Chekhov's First Play*, 9.
14. Michael Billington, 'Blasted, Review, *The Guardian*, 20 January, 1995.
15. "THISISPOPBABY," Irish Theatre Institute, accessed January 4, 2017, http://www.irishtheatre.ie/company-page.aspx?companyid=425.
16. Philip McMahon, email communication with author, January 9, 2017.
17. Eve Sedgwick, "Shame, Theatricality, and Queer Performativity: Henry James's The Art of the Novel" in *Gay Shame*, eds. David Halperin & Valerie Traub (Chicago: University of Chicago Press, 2009), 15.
18. Fiach Kelly, "Mary McAleese calls for Yes vote in marriage referendum," *The Irish Times*, April 13, 2015, 2.

Bibliography

"About Us." Brokentalkers. Accessed January 4, 2017. http://www.brokentalkers.ie/.

"FARM." WillFredd. Accessed January 9, 2017. http://willfredd.com/productions-2care/farm/.

"Shaun Dunne and Robbie Lawlor: HIV Workshops." Abbey Theatre. Accessed January 7, 2017. https://www.abbeytheatre.ie/shaun-dunne-and-robbie-lawlor-hiv-workshops/.

"THISISPOPBABY." Irish Theatre Institute. Accessed January 4, 2017. http://www.irishtheatre.ie/company-page.aspx?companyid=425.

"What Do We Do?." Talking Shop Ensemble. Accessed January 6, 2017. https://talkingshopensemble.wordpress.com/about/company/.

Flood, Alison. "Post-truth Named Word of the Year by Oxford Dictionaries." *The Guardian*, November 15, 2016. Accessed January 4, 2017. https://www.theguardian.com/books/2016/nov/15/post-truth-named-word-of-the-year-by-oxford-dictionaries.

Heaney, Mick. "Review: Dublin Oldschool." *The Irish Times*, September 10, 2014.

Hughes, Declan. "Who the Hell Do We Think We Still Are? Reflections on Irish Theatre and Identity." in *Theatre Stuff: Critical Essays on Contemporary Irish Theatre*, edited by Eamonn Jordan. Dublin: Carysfort Press, 2000.

Kelly, Fiach. "Mary McAleese Calls for Yes Vote in Marriage Referendum." *The Irish Times*, April 13, 2015.

McIvor, Charlotte. "Witnessing the Broken Nation: Theatre of the Real and Social Fragmentation in Brokentalkers' *Silver Stars, The Blue Boy,* and *Have I No Mouth.*" in *That Was Us: Contemporary Irish Theatre and Performance*, edited by Fintan Walsh. London: Oberon, 2013.
Moukarzel, Bush & Dead Centre. *Lippy*. London: Oberon, 2014.
———. *Chekhov's First Play*. London: Oberon Books, 2015.
O'Brien, Cormac. "Ireland in the Age of AIDS: The Cultural Politics of Stigma." *The Irish Review*, 53 (2016): 45–59.
Sedgwick, Eve. "Shame, Theatricality, and Queer Performativity: Henry James's The Art of the Novel in *Gay Shame,* edited by David Halperin & Valerie Traub. Chicago: University of Chicago Press, 2009.

PART II

Closeups

The Joyful Mysteries of Comedy

Bernard Farrell

Comedy is full of mystery. And that is why psychologists can spend years trying to discover why we laugh and how we laugh. Retired comedians can make money teaching would-be comedians how to tell jokes. (Trevor Griffiths had fun with that in his biting play, *The Comedians.*) Theatre managers sit scratching their heads as they stare at empty seats when another sure-fire comedy mysteriously fails. And dramaturgs persist in trying to crack the code and teach aspiring playwrights how to write these sure-fire comedies. All fruitless exercises because, I would suggest, comedy defies theory, experience or education. Instead, it relies on instinct, attitude and inspiration. And can anything be more mysterious (or mercurial) than these three strange bedfellows?

Many years ago, when I decided to write a play, I wrote a comedy. I don't know why. To me, there was no option. I had a story to tell, a story that, at times, angered or intrigued or puzzled me, and the only way I could tell that story was to coat it with comedy. And so I have continued in my career, dealing with my frustrations in play after play, sometimes lacing them with lashings of laughter, sometimes with less. But never with none.

In 1978, at the rehearsals of my play *I Do Not Like Thee Doctor Fell*, I overheard one of the actors saying to another: "You know, I think there could be a few laughs in this". This was the first play that I had ever written and, by good fortune, it had been accepted by the Abbey Theatre and was due to open in three weeks. When I heard that comment, far from being encouraged, I was immediately plunged into a silent whirlpool of panic. This was not only because the actors in question were actors of some experience and reputation—the cast included Liam Neeson, Tom Hickey, Garrett Keogh and Billie Morton—but

B. Farrell (✉)
Playwright, Dublin, Ireland

E. Jordan, E. Weitz (eds.), *The Palgrave Handbook of Contemporary Irish Theatre and Performance*,
https://doi.org/10.1057/978-1-137-58588-2_18

also because, while the play was indeed very serious, it was also intended as a comedy, and would be nothing if it didn't have a lot more than "a few laughs". Clearly, from the unperformed script that they still held in their hands, there was little to indicate much laughter.

If I knew then what I know now (twenty plays later), perhaps I would not have been so worried. I would, at the very least, have recognized the process.

The play, as written, does not have any obviously funny lines. There are certainly no jokes. And the issues that hold and harness the drama—betrayal, bullying, suicide, attempted murder—are more the stuff of tragedy than comedy. And, presented with this subject matter, the play's first director, Paul Brennan, gave the play what I would, in later years, recognize as his precise, analytical exploration of each character, each sub-plot, each action. Thus the play was rehearsed in an atmosphere of forensic examination, truthful seriousness, with little hint of comedy.

The actor's comments, therefore, clearly reflected the mood of that rehearsal room and it was not until the first preview in the Abbey's Peacock Theatre that the play was allowed to reveal its true self. Then, in presenting the characters' anguish, terror and dilemma with absolute seriousness, the story mysteriously emerged in all its hilarious glory.

So Paul Brennan's astute method of telling the story through laughter—and not *for* laughter—allowed this, my first play, to make its mark, attract its audience, please the critics and keep the Abbey box office ticking over nicely. And the lesson for me was that the darker the play (and *Doctor Fell* is dark), the more light it will require. The secret is that this light (the comedy) should be subtle, allowed to almost emerge unannounced, never to dominate; in short, it should be (that word again) "mysterious". And if the playwright has done his/her work in the writing, the laughter will enhance—but never unbalance—the drama, and nothing will be lost.

If, in 1979, the reaction of the audience took some of the actors by surprise, it was nothing to the surprises that awaited me following that opening. Many of my friends, who never imagined that I could write a play, were astounded by my theatrical emergence and often, out of desperation, asked which parts did I write and which parts were written by the actors. One friend—desperately trying to solve the mystery of me—earnestly asked which came first, "the gags or the story". Indeed, some of my neighbours—many of whom never bothered to see the play anyway—took a curiously dim view of what I regarded as Comedy.

The most memorable example of this was my chance meeting with a rather supercilious lady whom, for simplicity and out of respect, I will call Mrs. Haughty. She had lived nearby for almost all of my life but, with her perennial air of superiority and entitlement, had always managed to ignore me. But on one particular day, shortly after the play opened, on a road in Glenageary, she not only engaged me in conversation, but even called me by my name! Our exchange went something like this:

MRS. HAUGHTY:	Bernard, I understand that you have written a play?
BF:	Yes I have, Mrs. Haughty.
MH:	And I understand that it is in the Abbey Theatre?
BF:	It is indeed.
MH:	And I believe that it is a comedy?
BF:	Yes it is.
MH:	And I understand that, in this comedy, there is a boy who throws a cat under a train?
BF:	Ehhh—yes, that is true, Mrs. Haughty.
MH:	And you think that is funny, do you?

With that, she disgustedly turned and walked away, never giving me a chance to reply. But if she had, what would I have said? Perhaps, if I had waited a few weeks, the reviewers would have told me that what I had written was a "black comedy". That might have helped in explaining its comedy to Mrs. Haughty. However, a few weeks later, when the play transferred to the Abbey Main Stage, it was then referred to as "a biting satire" and, in varying productions in the months and years that followed, I have seen it become "an absurd drama", "a rollicking send-up" and "a side-splitting night"!

So I could never have really explained the comedy to Mrs. Haughty or to anyone. To me, it was not a style or a title or a brand of comedy—it was simply a play that I had to write. At times, it became absurd, at times terrifying and sometimes frivolous—but, put together in the right, instinctive order, all these elements performed their functions of telling the story in its most powerful way and, mysteriously, it worked!

In the hiatus that followed the celebration of *Doctor Fell*, a fresh set of questions began to emerge, many of them harbouring thinly disguised challenges and others the dimly recognized traces of treachery.

The most common question was the harmless: "And what's next in the pipeline?" But, occasionally, came the warning, the shot-across-the-bow: "It's not going to be another comedy is it?" Probably the most threatening was one that was always asked in hushed tones, with a wink of the eye and the mischievous appearance of ill-will parading as undying support: "That *Doctor Fell* will be a hard act to follow, won't it?"

Each time I heard any of these questions, I was reminded of Brian Friel's masterpiece, *Faith Healer*, in which Francis Hardy, the faith healer of the title, performs a magical feat of healing and is at once commanded, by admirers and naysayers alike, to do it again and do it better! The play itself is written in a masterly blend of tragedy and comedy but, at its core, it is—I would suggest—Friel writing about the creative process: its mystery, its triumphs, its falterings, its recoveries and, principally, its unpredictability. Whether this is true or not, I do know that with each demand and question put to me, I had many a "Francis Hardy moment", and every time I prayed that what happened to him would not happen to me!

I know now, in hindsight, that what was critically expected of me at that time was another black comedy. However, in commissioning a new play the Abbey made no such stipulations—they just wanted a new work, on a story/theme of my choice, to be delivered in my own time, in no specific style and in no particular hurry.

This freedom, this openness-of-choice, had now become a feature of the Abbey's policy in commissioning new plays. Since early 1978, under the artistic directorship of Joe Dowling, new playwrights were openly welcomed, enthusiastically encouraged and, if showing signs of merit, offered the Peacock stage as a potential venue for a fully-rehearsed production of new work. I had the good fortune to be part of this policy, and to become, along with fellow newcomers such as Graham Reid, Neil Donnelly, Aodhan Madden and Frank McGuinness, part of the group popularly known as The Peacock Playwrights. From us were expected plays that showed a freshness, a knowledge of the restrictions and limitations of theatre, and an imaginative courage to break through these limitations and restrictions and, in doing so, to engage, inform and excite an audience. We joyfully accepted the challenge and, as part of this renaissance, we joined up with some established and truly gifted writers. Two of these have long stayed in my memory, as much for their influence as for how they are today so sadly missed.

The first is the great Stewart Parker, who, when I arrived at the Peacock in 1979, had already had two major successes to his credit: *Spokessong* (first seen at the Dublin Theatre Festival of 1975) and *Catchpenny Twist* (premiered at the Peacock in 1977). Both these plays, with differing theatrical brilliance, had courageously delved into political and sectarian no-go areas, and did so in an avalanche of creative comedy in a way that, since his departure, has never quite been equalled. In 1980, his *Nightshade* opened in the Peacock; this was an up-close opportunity for me to see him at work and, in my thirst for learning the trade, to try to uncover some of his magical comic secrets. However, it was his unreachably comic instinct that was at play—and to get an indication of that, we need look no further than the title of his much-praised 1981 radio drama *The Kamikaze Ground Staff Reunion Dinner*. His theatrical career continued in its brilliance until 1988 when, at the age of 47, far too soon, he left us. I miss the man and I miss the magic—but fortunately, the plays are there to be explored and admired, again and again.

The second playwright, who was supremely popular in the Peacock, with a following that I had often seen queuing from the box-office out into Abbey Street, was Pat Ingoldsby. Now a poet, he was then a brilliantly bizarre dramatist who had graduated from presenting television shows for children to (almost) exploding onto the Peacock stage in 1978 with his play *Hisself*. Like Stewart Parker, his humour was individual, almost beyond definition, but beyond doubt, he had the ability to immediately tap into a zeitgeist that was in itself hard to categorise, showing itself in his audiences of late-teen and early-twenties enthusiasts who saw him as playwright, prophet and peer—and who hailed him, unashamedly, as though he were a pop star. His *Rhyming Simon* came in the same year, followed by his equally comic but heartbreaking hospital play *When Am I Gettin' Me Clothes?* The typically titled *Yeukface the Yeuk and the Spotty Grousler* was seen in the Peacock in 1982, *The Full Shilling* at the Gaiety in 1986; and then Pat Ingoldsby disappeared from the world of theatre and moved towards new literary/entertainment horizons. Now a recluse who stands in the public eye—almost like a character from any of his groundbreaking plays—he sells his poetry in the streets of Dublin while shunning all publicity and refusing all interviews. With Stewart Parker, he remains one of the truly original players from the comic wing of The Peacock Playwrights.

So it was in this climate of theatrical openness, invention and style that I began to write my second play for Joe Dowling—and as *I Do Not Like Thee Doctor Fell* had graduated to the main stage of the Abbey, I felt that if I got this one right, there was just a possibility that it might premiere in the main auditorium. However, I was also pessimistically aware that I had a mountain to climb simply because I was writing a comedy and, as in the theatre of the Greeks and Romans, comedy continues to be regarded by many as a lower form of theatre and the poor cousin to tragedy. Moreover, even within the genre of comedy, there is a hierarchy of "types", against which each work is critically judged, identified and then neatly slotted into its box.

Black comedy—possibly because of its proximity to tension and tragedy—is probably the most respected form. Satire and parody remain highly regarded and the Commedia dell'arte style has enjoyed a revival (possibly because experts like to both explain it and pronounce it). After that, the status and appreciation levels drop sharply. Eventually, if a work is even suspected of being (or containing) "farce", "boulevard", "burlesque" or, worst of all, "pantomime", it moves into the danger zone of critical dismissal.

I would maintain, however, that far from being a lesser form of theatrical expression, pantomime is not only a worthy and specialized component of contemporary drama but also, when suitably used, can impact on an audience in a range that can spin from hilarious comedy to biting satire to the darkest of dark comedy. I have invoked it on occasions—when it suited the telling of the story—and I have always been grateful to my parents for exposing me to this historic form of theatre from a very early age.

For years, as a family, we never missed the Theatre Royal Christmas pantomime—and names like Mickser Reid, Jack Cruise (a magnificent dame), Danny Cummins, Cecil Sheridan, and Babs de Monte with Alice Dalgarno (two wonderful choreographers) were as familiar to me as the names of my friends and relations. But more than that, thanks to my father's interest in all things theatrical, I was taught (almost by osmosis) that pantomime was not all just laughter and hilarious interplay, but that it was rooted in centuries-old customs, culture and traditions and was bound by its own style and ritual. So, at the theatre, I would notice (or, disappointingly, not notice!) if the villain entered from stage-right (as, traditionally, he should) and if the hero first appeared from stage left. Equally, I always knew (a very pleasant expectation) that the Principal Boy would always be played by a leggy girl in a boy's costume and her romantic partner, the Principle Girl, was usually a popular female ingénue. The Dame, often the star of the show and usually the mother of the Principle Boy would, of course, be played by a man. The comedy—within such customs—always had a sense of knockabout abandon, a madcap hilarity that belied its allegiance to strict rituals that dated back to the harlequinade era of the eighteenth century but which, in time, allowed it to adjust to social changes in different times without ever betraying its beginnings.

But perhaps what appealed to me most about pantomime was that it so deliberately abandoned the fourth wall—thus inviting the audience to become part of the onstage cast and chaos. This always delighted me and, I like to think, influenced my own playwriting in that, unlike many playwrights, I take great heed of any audience at one of my plays, both in terms of capacity and reaction. Like Alan Ayckbourn (more of whom later) and Tom Stoppard, I would often go to a play of mine not to observe the play but to lurk at the back of the stalls and study the audience. In doing this, I always feel that I am paying homage to the great pantomime players and the gifted writers/manipulators, down the centuries, from the legendary George Robey and Les Dawson in England to Maureen Potter and Jimmy O'Dea in Ireland, who never lost contact with their audiences, forever inviting, engaging, coercing and controlling them into being part of the drama, but more importantly, being central to the comedic tension of the night.

In this, there is a refreshing theatrical faux-anarchism about pantomime, as generations of pantomime-goers—unlike the silent, well-dressed, well-drilled audiences of conventional theatre, or maybe in defiance of them!—are allowed to noisily respond to the characters onstage who have been endlessly teasing, tormenting, amusing and tantalizing them. In pantomime, the audience can give as good as it gets, assuming that it is in control, not realizing that it is forever, and understatedly, controlled from the stage. From there, the players can—and must—ensure that a richly satisfied audience will leave the theatre thinking that the night has belonged to them, and to them only. Thus is the magic created.

Equally understated, but in abundance in good and balanced pantomimes, and amid gales of laughter, is the threat of danger. In the anarchism of the medium, ridicule is never too distant—and the biting sarcasm that can often cross the footlights can equal some of the most cutting annihilations by contemporary stand-up comedians or the most scathing conclusions by ruthless satiric magazines. Young audiences may not—and need not—understand all or any of this, but as part of the historic general appeal of pantomime, adults excitedly await this moment when, traditionally, the most cutting remarks are smilingly delivered by the most amusing, most loved and most sympathetic characters onstage who have thus procured a licence to say the unsayable in the guise of harmless pantomime fun, to the uproarious joy of their knowing audience. In the past, I have sat at pantomimes and felt that the satire onstage was as scathingly accurate as anything I had seen on the BBC's *That Was The Week That Was* or RTÉ's *Hall's Pictorial Weekly*.

So, with this pantomime appreciation firmly implanted in my DNA, it is hardly surprising that, at times, it has winkled its way into my comedies. This was certainly true of *Canaries*, which became my second play, so called because it is set on the Canary Islands. It is, first and foremost, a satire, with serious undercurrents; and to contrast the light and shade I occasionally applied dollops of farce, while in a late scene of a fancy dress that goes wrong (which I could not resist) there was more than a little pantomime. Once again, this combination of many forms of theatre was dictated by nothing more than the demands of how best to tell the story.

Canaries opened at the Abbey for the 1980 Dublin Theatre Festival and was a popular success. Critically, however, there were murmurings that, after *Doctor Fell* (and presumably having got black comedy out of my system), I should have moved onwards and upwards, and closer to tragedy. Instead, in their view, I had dodged the challenge and gone for "easy laughs". And I thought—ah, if only that were possible.

Unfortunately, in theatre as in life, there are no easy laughs. Ask any poor devil who ever had to make a best man's speech, or any of us who ever tried to chat up an out-of-our-league stranger at a party, and prayed for laughs. We would be contented to see a smile, or half-smile. Now, put that same challenge to a playwright who sets out to extract laughter from a crowd of strangers, sitting in the darkness, probably in from the cold night, perhaps having spent twenty minutes trying to find a parking space and now angrily aware that, with the price of tickets and the cost of a baby-sitter, this night has cost them a lot of money and therefore, it had better be good! "Easy laughs" do not come easily.

Canaries, I would suggest, was a success, not because it had layers of farce, but because it was a stinging satire that hit its targets accurately and, in doing so, earned its laughter through an audience's recognition of what was onstage and their sheer relief that they were not in the same humiliating predicaments. In the glow of the play's success, I never tried to make these points, nor did I even try to defend the legitimacy of farce. Instead, when I was commissioned to write a new play for the Abbey, I wrote a full-blown, indisputable, unrepentant farce!

This was a theatrical area in which I enjoyed some comfort—because of my affection for the style—even if I always find it extremely difficult to write, and to get right. In later years, in plays that were regarded as my "darker" and "more serious" work, there is always more than a sprinkling of farce. My influences (those I blame!) are essentially the French masters—Molière, Labisch and Feydeau—and also our own Dion Boucicault. In Britain, I point the finger at Ben Travers, Pinero, Ayckbourn and Joe Orton—but, at the root of my appreciation for the relentless, logical lunacy that is the essence of good farce, I look no further than Stan Laurel and Oliver Hardy.

From my childhood, I—like many others who work in comedy—have regarded them, at their best, as the masterminds of everything perfect in this genre. This was perhaps never better demonstrated than in the thirty minutes of their 1932 film, "The Music Box", a simple story of them trying to deliver a crated piano up 131 concrete steps. Here we witness again their perpetual battle against an unsympathetic world, whether in human form (a nursemaid, a policeman, a postman, an outraged professor) or in inanimate objects (prams, pens, steps, a piano) which seem, in turn, to assume the personalities of their vexing human counterparts. Expertly woven into this comic extravagance is a verbal array of malapropisms, mispronunciations and witticisms, all underscoring their bewildered alienation in a society that they do not understand and that will never understand them.

So, it would not surprise me if there are elements of the comedy of Laurel and Hardy in my third play for the Abbey. However, *All In Favour Said No!* was not written as farce for the challenge, nor as an homage. Again, for me, it was the only style that suited a play about the ridiculousness of head-office hierarchies and the posturing of factory-floor unions when faced with the threat of a strike. Its success brought me great personal joy (as it got a lot out of my system)—and, I think, also granted me much comic confidence in having managed to write a full-blown farce where, throughout, when the comic buttons were pressed, the audience appropriately erupted.

Many of these "comic buttons", of course, do not come directly from the script but rather evolve from rehearsal room decisions—where the director, the playwright or an actor may occasionally make an assured declaration that if a particular word is stressed or a certain action is taken, the audience will certainly explode into laughter. It is a risky business and, at that early point in my career, I seldom attempted it, choosing rather to make quiet, tentative suggestions to the director in the coffee breaks. However, in the rehearsal for this play, I remember hearing myself confidently informing the entire room that, for better comic effect, a line should be directed to a different actor, in a different direction, at a lower tone. I then added that this would result in prolonged laughter before another line could be spoken. This was received in silence and then questioned by seasoned actors, but I remained adamant. At the first preview, before our first audience (the acid test of comedy), I waited in trepidation for the moment and, thankfully, when it came I was proven to be right. It was a small victory, probably long forgotten by everybody else involved, but for me it remains a turning point: the moment when, instinctively, I knew I was right and had the confidence to proclaim it.

However, with the passage of time and now away from the confidence-comfort of the rehearsal room, I sometimes think of that day and wonder if my words sounded like those of arrogant inexperience. The accuracy of my suggestions and corrections had not yet been tested before an audience and I seemed unaware that I was facing a veritable roll call of the most knowledgeable and experienced comic actors of that time, or maybe any time. The incomparable Tom Hickey was there, as were Bill Foley, Stephen Brennan, Maire O'Neill, Godfrey Quigley and Brid Ni Neachtain. And I, from my earliest play-going days, had always been in tongue-tied awe of the instinctive skill of such actors and their brilliant predecessors.

In 1964, I had been privileged to see both the renowned Harry Brogan (who, on his every exit line, could initiate a round of applause from even the coldest audience—often, it was rumoured, by clapping behind his back!) and the equally gifted Philip O'Flynn (whose droll delivery would make you believe that he was speaking to you and you alone) in *Juno and the Paycock* in the Queen's Theatre (the Abbey Theatre in exile). Brogan played Joxer Daly and O'Flynn was Captain Boyle and, if that wasn't enough, Maisie Madigan was played by the wonderful Eileen Crowe. As I remember, hers was a performance only matched, in the same role, by that great comedienne-turned-superstar Maureen Potter at the Gate Theatre in 1986. Now, would I have challenged these gifted performers about how they should deliver a comic line or portray a comic attitude? Or would I ever have interrupted the supreme Micheál Mac Liammóir—who, once again, I was privileged to see at The Gate Theatre in 1966, holding an audience enthralled as, with flawless comic precision, he allowed the silence to be held or the laughter to be released in his one-man show *I Must Be Talking To My Friends*? I think I would, most certainly, have held my tongue in check.

I did, however, actually work with a supreme master of comedy, David Kelly, in two of my own plays, *Canaries* and *Say Cheese*. So, in that Abbey rehearsal room, did I dare to interrupt or offer suggestions to this comic genius? Well, I did not need to because, with the famous humility of truly great artists, it was he who sometimes came to me for confirmation of his thoughts. Today I am humbled to remember quietly offering him my views and, even more amazingly, him accepting them. But then, I must also remember that all of this happened in rehearsal rooms where, traditionally, there is a created atmosphere of pretence and we all, like the actors themselves, are permitted to go into performance, to become other people and, sometimes, to become very brave people indeed.

In the years that followed, subsequent plays moved me through varied and different moods of comedy, from uproariously comic work to dark plays that provoke the kind of laughter that an audience will guiltily question themselves about on the way home. Moving from Dublin premieres of the plays at the Abbey and the Gate theatres to the Red Kettle Theatre in Waterford and the Laguna Playhouse in California brought different demands, new freedoms, changing styles and constant challenges, but always presented new opportunities to explore varying aspects of comedy and, occasionally, to encounter comedy in many unsuspected cultural flavours.

In various translations of the plays, I have sat in foreign auditoriums, not knowing a word of the language but hearing the laughter and the silences come at the right moments and knowing that this new audience was solidly in tune with the play. This, in itself, is wonderful evidence that internationally we have a broad comic alignment—that what is funny and ironic in one country, one culture, can find an exact replica of that reaction in another. However, there can be exceptions to this—and these are often comical in their own right.

I remember seeing the German premiere of *Doctor Fell*, which opens with a caretaker sweeping a room while idly singing a song. This sweeping continues until the second character arrives onstage and the play begins in earnest. In Ireland, audiences always delighted in the humour of how the caretaker, without supervision, haphazardly swept the room, pushing dust under rugs and hiding debris behind radiators. In Germany, however, the play began with the caretaker diligently sweeping the room, inch by inch, carefully collecting all the debris and putting it into small sacks. This continued for perhaps two minutes, then four minutes and, at six minutes, he was still sweeping. My fear, as I watched, was that very soon the audience would begin to leave, one by one, not having paid to see a man giving them a masterclass on how to sweep a room.

However, the audience stayed, the sweeping (eventually!) ended, the next character appeared and the dialogue began. At drinks after the play, the director asked me if I had any notes, comments or reactions. I said—truthfully—that it was an excellent production—but wondered at the length of time the caretaker took to sweep the room. The director was puzzled. "But," he said, "this caretaker is a sympathetic character and, for the play and for the comedy, we must ensure that the audience likes him, so we show that he works hard, is a trusted employee and does his tasks perfectly."

I, of course, agreed. But this was clearly a cultural difference where comedy clashed with comedy. In Ireland, we admired the caretaker for cutting corners; in Germany, doing the same, he would never have been a "sympathetic" character. He would have been a dosser, and immediately disliked; and the comedy would have suffered. Hence the sweeping marathon!

Years later, I told this story to Alan Ayckbourn—and he responded by reducing me to tears of laugher with even funnier cross-cultural experiences from his own career. The occasion of my meeting him was my visit to Scarborough where my play, *Happy Birthday Dear Alice,* was about to open at his Stephen Joseph Theatre. Over some days, I had the privilege of spending many hours and many meals in the company of this man who, for years, I had idolized as a master of comedy.

We talked about his wonderful play, *A Small Family Business,* which I had seen at the National—and which, to the best of my knowledge, has never been produced in Ireland. By Ayckbourn's own admission it is a play about organized crime, greed, sexual deviation, murder and drug-taking—and yet it is hilarious. Its gory murder scene, on the night I saw it (and I presume every night), had the audience in shrieks of the uncontrolled laughter of surprise, fear and relief.

Ayckbourn explained the process delightfully—quoting our need to laugh in the face of hopelessness and how, in the writing, it falls to the playwright to gently coax the audience to see the correct aspects from the correct angles and to firmly establish the comic context in both action and reaction. When I was not immersed in his theatrical experiences, his hospitality and his self-deprecation, we (as playwrights do) bemoaned the lack of appreciation for the art of comedy.

I used to regularly have these same conversations with Hugh Leonard (or "Jack" as he liked selectively to be known) and, almost as a game, we used to exchange examples of how comedy as an art form is so poorly regarded. I would cite how Molière was never admitted to the Académie Française in his lifetime, and Jack would trump that with how Laurel and Hardy, in over twenty-four years of great comedy, only got a Lifetime Achievement Academy Award when Hardy was already dead and Laurel was too ill to accept it. Ayckbourn tells the story of how a critic (in a clearly positive review of one of his plays) wrote that he had laughed shamelessly throughout. "Why 'shamelessly'?" Alan wryly wondered. And Hugh Leonard was forever amused at how producers, directors and actors all try desperately to forget that Chekhov was essentially a self-confessed comic writer and insisted that his major revered works were comedies. "But nobody believes him," Jack would say, with that knowing twinkle in his eye, "because they realise that there are no awards going for turning tragedy into comedy—it is the opposite that will have them applauded to the awards podium … even if their tragedy was a comedy in the first place!"

I have often regretted that, in the time since Jack died in 2009, he missed seeing at least two productions that would have pleased him greatly. He would certainly have revelled in the 2012 Sydney Theatre Company production of *Uncle Vanya* (with Cate Blanchett as Yelena) which, amid the tragedy of the play, did not ignore or dilute or diminish the comedy. In his review of the Broadway production in 2012, Ben Brantley of the *New York Times* wrote of the play's climax: "that scene is as rowdy and demented as anything out of a Marx Brothers movie and as utterly despairing as a choral lament from Sophocles". Jack would have felt vindicated!

I have also wished that he had lived to see The National Theatre's version of Goldini's often neglected *A Servant of Two Masters*, now in a sparkling new production and retitled *One Man, Two Guvnors*. This had wooed London audiences for months before transferring to Broadway in 2012 where I saw it with, once again, James Cordon in the lead. This was farce at its most brilliant, most assured, most accomplished, in a production that was fast-paced and ruthlessly pared down to its comic essentials—to the hysterical delight of New York audiences.

Jack would have loved that—and indeed, I know that he would have seen in it the essential comic truth of how hard work makes the art of comedy look easy. Even now, I can almost hear him repeating one of his favourite anecdotes, popularly attributed to the dying words of Edmund Kean. Visited by an acquaintance, the great actor was asked if his illness was very difficult to endure. "Dying is easy," he is reported to have said, "it is comedy that is difficult."

That difficulty, however, is often relieved by sheer good luck—the good fortune of being able to assemble a perfect cast, production team and director who recognize, understand and appreciate comedy. I have been fortunate in the premieres of my plays in being coupled with directors such as Patrick Mason, Joe Dowling, Ben Barnes, Paul Brennan, Pat Laffan, Mark Lambert, Jim Culleton and Andy Barnicle, who have nursed these first outings into existence with a firm appreciation of the seriousness of comedy and an understanding of its power, and in each case, taken the work to areas far beyond what I would have envisaged.

However, even with all these sure-fire precautions, there has always been a sober warning—and here, again, I draw on my many conversations and debates with Hugh Leonard—that comedies, once produced, have a shorter shelf-life than other forms of drama and that, in writing comedy, we should never expect much beyond the glittering fanfare of a first night and a run. Hugh's oft-repeated warning was always as succinct and sober as only he could be: "Theatrical graveyards are full of short-lived comedies that once packed houses and that the experts said would be enjoyed forever… but were never seen or heard of again".

I always argued against this pessimism, quoting age-old comedies that, hundreds of years later, are still with us, still giving us a context to their past, a relevance to our today and, in the best productions, a night of laughter that would surely have matched that of their glorious birth. I would reference Farquhar, Molière, Goldsmith, Congreve, Sheridan and Boucicault—giving both Molière and Boucicault special emphasis as, at the Abbey Theatre in the 1980s, I adapted both playwrights to a new setting and a modern audience, and both plays enjoyed a popular and critical reception.

When it came to the task of transposing and sharpening the work of these two ancient comedy writers, Molière was probably the most straightforward, and the play became an Irish-themed take on the ever-popular *Don Juan*. Boucicault, however, was more important to my case in defending the longevity of comedy because, after much research at the National Library, I had discovered a forgotten Boucicault farce titled *Forbidden Fruit*. This play had been a great success in the 1870s, but, according to Hugh Leonard's pessimistic prediction, was well beyond any hope of ever seeing the footlights of a theatre again, having already had its glorious moment over 110 years back.

However, on reading it, I could immediately see what had once made it successful, with its many hilarious sequences, some outlandish but contextually believable characters and a finale explosion of farce at its very best. I introduced the script to Joe Dowling, who also saw its value, and was commissioned to work on it. By the time it had taken its final form, I had developed some early scenes, rooted it in Dublin, given it the pomposity of a legal setting (ready for pricking), and endowed it with what I felt was a great title: *Wigs on the Green*. Joe enthusiastically approved the treatment (and the title) and the play was advertised as the Abbey Theatre's Christmas presentation of 1983. It was then that we received a letter from someone who said they also had written a play called *Wigs on the Green*, and that it had been performed locally. Initially, it was a shame—but I substituted the comic title *Petty Sessions* and the Boucicault play, risen from the dead, had a very successful Abbey Theatre run, and in 1996 was revived by Red Kettle Theatre Company in Waterford. To me, in my Hugh Leonard debates, this always became the closing speech in my defence of the longevity of comedy.

He (on taking the stand, so to speak) would look back no further than the last fifty or sixty years, to when the Abbey Theatre was in exile at the Queen's Theatre (1951–1966), and recall that, due to economic pressures and a bigger theatre to fill, comedy became almost a staple diet in the repertoire. The Abbey's comedy playwrights, who enjoyed great success and regularly packed the place, included John McCann, John O'Donovan, Louis D'Alton and George Shields. Their major successes included, respectively, *Put a Beggar on Horseback*, *The Less We Are Together*, *The Money Doesn't Matter* and *The Passing Day*... and having recited an even longer litany than this, Hugh would then rhetorically ask: "and do we hear of any of them, or their plays, now?" Occasionally, I might mention Lennox Robinson, an even earlier Abbey playwright whose name is still remembered and whose *Drama At Inish* and *The Whiteheaded Boy* are still, and rightly, enjoying revivals—and sometimes, if the moment was right, I might add two other playwrights of those later Queen's days: the eternally popular John B. Keane and Hugh Leonard himself, who started in that era of the Abbey. Hugh would, naturally, amusingly concede to the longevity of these "gifted" playwrights while still holding to his view that comedy, in itself and with its dependence on topicality, relevance and recognition, has a shorter shelf-life.

Of course, in fairness to the Abbey Theatre while at the Queen's and its quick turnover of playwrights, the theatre was on a survival course, having lost its own smaller theatre to the Abbey Street fire in 1951, so the choice of play had to almost guarantee a good box-office return. Added to that there was, in Dublin's social climate of the day, a great public appetite for comedy and light entertainment, and here the Abbey, intent on also offering realistic and serious drama, was competing with attractions such as the nearby Theatre Royal, a giant emporium of over 4000 seats. This dilemma for the Abbey was brilliantly captured in a cartoon from the *Dublin Opinion* (the satirical magazine of its day) which showed a crowd emerging from the Abbey at the Queen's, having been to see a fictitious three-act tragedy called *Every Each Is Both*; everyone in the crowd is guffawing in helpless laughter and a man is heartily telling his wife (with programme in hand) "Lawsie me. I nearly split my sides every time your man said that Me oul' Da is a bags". In other words, tragedy is wasted on any audience whose only wish is to see comedy in everything. Hence, perhaps, the plethora of forgotten comedies.

Taking all of that into consideration, I would—now that the great Hugh Leonard is no longer with us to continue this debate—concede that both viewpoints have value. I am now thinking of a play by Kevin Laffan that emerged in 1970 (when long titles were all the rage) called *It's a Two Foot Six Inches Above the Ground World*. It was a darkly humorous work that had long queues outside Dublin's Eblana Theatre for many weeks—and I remember it for two reasons: I liked it very much, and I was twice turned away from seeing it with House Full signs barring my way. Today, it is never spoken of—perhaps because, at the time, it was both topical and controversial—and the same can be said of Joe Orton's equally controversial comedies, whereas Harold Pinter's have survived and are still popular (and long may they remain so). And why on earth does nobody nowadays look to Herb Gardner's lovely, touching, 1962 American comedy *A Thousand Clowns* and set a course for its reappearance?

Clearly, the shorter shelf-life question of comedies is a complex one, one that is as hard to prove as it is to disprove—exceptions continue to get in the way of a final verdict. Perhaps Hugh Leonard, after such a splendid comedy-writing career, had moved on to realistic concerns about his "legacy" while he argued his pessimistic point of view—whereas I, starting out, was just grateful that I had arrived and had had some plays successfully produced, and knew that all I wanted to do was both enjoy and repeat the moment.

Indeed, in comedy, there is much to enjoy and nothing better than the exhilaration and self-satisfaction of hearing an audience respond, on cue, to created comic action in waves of laughter. The downside comes with the heart-breaking sense of confusion and mystery when the comedy doesn't work—when the sense of failure screams out in the silence of the audience. In tragedy, the silence of a bored audience can be excused as "rapt attention". In a comedy, there is nowhere to hide—and all escape routes are closed. The best we can do, in that nightmare silence, is to accept the mystery—and pray for less mystery and more hope in the next one.

For this, we rely again on our comic instincts—and those who write comedy are born to do that. How do they know they possess these mysterious instincts? They don't, until (and unless) they test them. Are there any signs that a comic instinct for storytelling lies within us? I expect that it is different in each of us.

For me, I remember my father having a wonderful sense of humour—not in the telling-of-jokes sense, but in his ability to observe both the peculiar and the mundane ordinariness of life and to reframe it in a comic way that managed to engage us, his children, as much in our childhood years as through our adolescence and into our adulthood. Thus, he was flexible in his humour—he could adjust—and he knew his audience.

If that was the source for me, I am very grateful. But how did this manifest itself in me in the days before I started writing publicly?

Well, perhaps a hint of my attitude to the world and my need to reframe it in a comic way was shown in a cartoon that I saw many years ago, and cut from the paper, pasted to cardboard and hung above my writing desk, maybe as a reminder or maybe as an encouragement. It is by Bill Tidy and was first published in *Punch* magazine in May 1968. As mysterious as comedy itself, it became my talisman, my influence, the manifestation of how (unbeknownst to many and maybe to me) I see the world.

The cartoon shows the headquarters of what I presumed to be The White Star Line just after news of the sinking of the *Titanic* had been announced. We see the crowds, now moving away, broken-hearted, lovingly comforting each other. The high-ranking official who imparted the news is still on the steps of the building and about to go inside. But his attention is drawn to a man who is approaching him, out of the departing crowd. This man is holding a rope that secures a polar bear, standing high on its hind legs. And the man—on behalf of the polar bear—is anxiously asking the official: "Yes, but is there any news of the iceberg?"

Now, why have I always thought that cartoon was so funny? I don't really know—but, without analysing the humour out of existence, is it perhaps because it tells us to see the alternative point of view, to comically flip the situation over, to dig deeper, and not to be afraid to be a little bit subversive. And maybe, for me, that is the root of comedy. Or maybe it's not. Maybe it's better not to ask, and just accept it as a joyful mystery... and then get on with it.

The Lambert Theatre and Puppetry Redefined

John McCormick

For the last three decades of the twentieth century the Lambert Puppet Theatre was effectively the national children's theatre of Ireland. Not tied to any specific educational programme (apart from the Safe Cross Code for crossing the road) it was able to offer quality entertainment to the young and the not so young. Emerging at a time when live puppet theatre was almost forgotten, Eugene Lambert (1928–2010) created a style of puppet theatre with a particular Irish flavour, frequently using techniques belonging to the more popular tradition of the Christmas pantomime.[1]

Shows at the Lambert theatre were close in style to much of the work of the large, heavily subsidized state theatres of Eastern Europe in the 1950s, where puppetry was seen as a significant factor in the imaginative development of the young and very much as part of everyday life. The Lamberts, working in the tradition of the private family company, did virtually everything themselves, repeatedly mounting shows marked by the quality of their design and lighting, sound and music, construction and dressing of the puppets, and other production values, despite limitations in finances and personnel.

There is a mistaken assumption that there was no history of puppetry in Ireland before the second half of the twentieth century. Surviving documentation is limited and travelling puppeteers, seldom chronicled, generally slipped under the radar of official permits. However, Randolph Stretch had a marionette theatre in Dublin's Capel Street that ran for some forty years in the eighteenth century. Puppet shows were a feature of Dublin life in the nineteenth century and travelling companies (often from England) toured widely. In the

J. McCormick (✉)
Trinity College Dublin, Dublin, Ireland
e-mail: JMCCRMCK@tcd.ie

E. Jordan, E. Weitz (eds.), *The Palgrave Handbook of Contemporary Irish Theatre and Performance*,
https://doi.org/10.1057/978-1-137-58588-2_19

1950s and 1960s companies with portable theatres, known as fit-ups, such as McCormick's, were still travelling throughout Ireland, and there were, and still are, a number of Punch "professors" (i.e., dedicated Punch and Judy show puppeteers).

"Modern" puppetry first came to Ireland in the 1940s with the Dublin Marionette Group of Nelson Paine, an amateur group that included such figures as the composer Brian Boydell. In the early 1950s Paine ran the short-lived travelling Puppet Opera Company. The arrival of television in 1965 heralded a new era for puppetry in Ireland, with the engagement of Eugene Lambert for an Irish-language programme *Murphy agus a chairde*. This was performed with string puppets by Eugene, his wife and their ten children.[2] As Irish television got into its stride, from 1968 to 1982 the Lamberts enjoyed enormous popularity with *Wanderly Wagon* in which puppets, operated by various Lamberts from underneath or behind pieces of furniture, were combined with live actors including Eugene Lambert himself as O'Brien, Norah O'Mahony as Godmother and Bill Golden as Forty Coats. *Wanderly Wagon* brought together a very distinguished team of actors, writers and designers. It was also the first programme in which RTÉ employed the technique of chroma key composition, which allowed the superimposition of action onto a separately filmed background. On the television screen the relative sizes of actor and puppet become blurred and the puppet itself, shown in close-up and apparently making eye-contact, becomes invested with a power that seems to oblige the spectator to suspend disbelief even while being confronted with a patently artificial figure.

When the Lamberts opened their own theatre some of the puppet characters, most notably Mr Crow, Sneaky the snake and the dog Judge, transferred happily to the live puppet stage, and indeed some of them continued with independent lives long after the axing of the programme. In 1972 the success of *Wanderly Wagon* allowed Eugene Lambert to buy an early nineteenth-century house in the residential suburb of Monkstown, County Dublin, where he felt that potential audiences might live. He converted the mews into a puppet theatre and the family formed the company, as had been the case with the travelling shows of the past. Eugene's wife Mai provided vital back-up, but retired from performing, whereupon she took care of the costumes as well as the shop that sold refreshments and other small items, all part of the economy of the theatre. Later it became possible for people to book a group of children into a regular Saturday afternoon show, after which a tea would be provided and there would be a visit to the small museum containing puppets from various Lambert shows together with an international collection. Some years later an adjacent mews was acquired, which enabled the theatre to be enlarged to a capacity of about 300 seats and provided it with much-needed workshop and storage space. The stage area was developed in a way that allowed for the setting or removal of a proscenium opening and the flying of scenic elements.

Television had allowed for actors to mingle with puppet figures without the more usual framing of a proscenium arch. When Eugene returned to live productions he reverted to the more traditional puppet stage with concealed manipulators and did not link in with what would become an increasing trend in puppet theatre, wherein the entire space of a normal theatre stage is opened up and shared by actors and puppets, and where the "puppet actor" would become a term replacing that of "puppeteer" or "manipulator". Much of the dynamic of this type of show lies precisely in the visible interchange between actor and puppet. Lambert's theatre showed how what might be regarded as a classical puppet theatre could make a transition into the modern world. For the most part the puppets and repertoire did not subscribe to any specific experimental trend, but the sense of design for both puppets and scenery was resolutely modern, as was the attention to lighting, sound and other technical aspects of the work.

The Lambert repertoire was mostly based on folk tales and fairy tales. In the 1970s a popular show was *Labhri Long Ears* (the king with donkey's ears—an Irish version of the Midas story). Another memorable early production was *Alice in Wonderland*, in which the recorded voices were provided by a number of major actors including Micheál Mac Liammóir. The most enduring shows included Oscar Wilde's *The Selfish Giant*, *The Happy Prince* and *The Fisherman and his Soul*. Productions of this nature were not possible without subsidy. Ireland cannot provide a regular adult audience for puppet shows and although a show for adults entails as much making, rehearsal and cost as one for children, it can give only a limited number of performances. Consequently the viability of the Lambert company has always depended on a repertoire of frequently revived productions for young audiences that can be presented hundreds of times. Shows including live speech have always proved the most popular in the repertoire, especially the comic pantomimes of *Aladdin* and *Cinderella* in which the verbal element, with space for improvisation, as in *Punch and Judy*, demands much audience involvement, or co-creation, with children being encouraged to call out to the puppets.

From the start the theatre in Monkstown was the base for the company and shows were generally given at weekends. During the week the company had an extensive touring schedule, travelling the length and breadth of Ireland. After some years the van was equipped with a duplicate set of equipment, puppets and staging which left the theatre itself ready for performance whenever necessary. The general practice was to rent a hall for a day and to offer two or three performances to audiences of up to 500. The 1970s and 1980s were a period when touring theatre was subsidized, but the unsubsidized Lambert Puppet Theatre, with its almost daily performances, reached many more people than the more official touring companies and was in real terms Ireland's most important popular theatre. By the 1990s some of the family were launched in their own careers and a new pattern began to emerge, which resulted in less touring and more shows given in the theatre to audiences consisting mainly of school groups brought there by bus.

The Lambert theatre reawakened an awareness of the possibilities of puppets at a time when this form of theatre was seldom seen in Ireland. Whist their own work was relatively classic, it related to practice in much of Eastern Europe, where the genre was taken far more seriously as a fundamental experience for younger audiences with an educational and cultural value as well as an entertainment one.

When the Lambert theatre first opened in 1972, the world of puppetry outside Ireland was in the throes of a fundamental change which would call into question the whole notion of what is or is not a puppet. The International Puppet Festival set up in Charleville-Mézières, France, in 1961 had become a place where it was possible to see puppet performance from many parts of the world, both of a traditional and, increasingly, more experimental nature. In 1991 the Irish branch of the Union Internationale de la Marionnette was set up with Eugene Lambert as its first president, and this was also the first year of an international puppet festival based on the Lambert theatre that would run for the next 20 years. Completely unsubsidized for the first ten years, and then partially subsidized by the Arts Council, it brought to Ireland a number of the world's top exponents of the art of puppetry, including Philippe Genty (2001), Philip Huber (2008), Karin Schäffer (2004), Frank Soehnle (2000), Enno Podehl (1998), Anton Anderle (1997), the Central (Obraztsov) Puppet Theatre of Moscow (2006), the Sicilian Opera dei Pupi (2004) and many others. It also made it possible for Irish audiences to see the amazing temple shadow puppets from Kerala (1997), which had never been abroad, and a performance from Mali (1995) in which a large animal puppet with an operator inside becomes in turn a stage for little puppets on its back.

Through the festival the Lamberts brought the best of international puppetry to Ireland, and in so doing frequently presented forms of visual theatre that stretched the limits of what is often thought of as puppet theatre. Audiences began to realize that a puppet need not be a surrogate human being but can be any object that may be endowed with human characteristics. This was demonstrated by Peter Ketturkat in 2005 with his ability to turn everyday kitchen equipment into characters with recognizably human modes of behaviour, or the Spanish company Tabola Rassa in 2009, which presented Molière's play *The Miser*, in which the "puppets" were taps and pieces of plumbing, and water replaced gold as a treasure to be stolen. Objects have a real or material function but can be endowed with a more figurative value. The idea of animating objects or materials which after the show would revert to their normal function was brilliantly displayed in 1996 by the Dutch puppeteer Feika Boschma, who could invest pieces of fabric with life. His show was wordless, reflecting the fact that in much contemporary puppet theatre the verbal element is at best secondary to the visual.

On today's puppet stage the puppeteer frequently appears onstage with the puppet and sometimes blends with it. In *The Gertrude Show* (2000) from Israel, parts of the body of the actor, such as the legs, become parts of the body of the almost life-sized puppet, and at a certain moment of the action it seems to the audience that the puppeteer has died whilst the puppet has taken over completely, an inversion of the usual situation where the puppeteer is alive whilst the puppet is dead material that has been animated. The Viennese marionettist Karin Schäffer presented this idea in the form of a conflict between the human manipulator and a marionette that is struggling to assert its independence. With the Polish company Teatr 3/4 in 1997 the "puppets" were the hands and feet of the performers, apparently detached from the body, whilst Claudio Cinelli, with only his two hands and a few feathers and eyes held between his fingers, gave a hilarious rendering of parts of *La Traviata* (*One More Kiss*) in 1998.

For some performers the staging and scenography can itself be a functional expressive element, as shown by FaultyOptic's remarkable *Snuffhouse Dustlouse* (1991), a Beckettian piece with semi-human figures in a complex set that takes on a life of its own. Stephen Mottram's wordless *The Seed Carriers* (1999), with a specially composed musical score, had a performance space that was neither a full open stage, nor a traditional puppet booth, but rather a set-up specially constructed for the show, as was the case with Sofie Krog's *Diva* (2008) with its incredibly complex rotating structure that had to evoke everything from an old theatre to a crazy scientist's lair in seven different scenes—everything managed by a single performer inside.

The mounting of a festival of this quality with so little money beggars the imagination, and much was due to the work of Eugene and Mai's daughter Miriam Lambert and her husband Trevor Scott, and later of Ronan Tully (a Lambert grandson). It was only after a number of years that the festival was finally recognized by the Arts Council, following a magical production of Hieronymus Bosch's *Garden of Earthly Delights* (1996) by the Spanish Company Bambalina. The last festival was in 2011, as rising costs subsequently meant that the budget was no longer adequate and the withdrawal of the Arts Council grant meant it had to be discontinued. The Irish situation was not unique, and a number of international puppet festivals failed to survive the years following the financial crisis of 2008.

The inspiration provided by the International Puppet Festival cannot be overemphasized, and it has been a major factor in helping define the direction in which contemporary puppetry is now moving in Ireland. Thanks to the Festival the Lamberts were able to make people in Ireland far more conscious of puppetry as one of the most interesting forms of alternative theatre today, and this has led to the setting up of a number of new puppet companies. The audiences for their own shows have remained faithful over three generations, and for many the name Lambert is thought of as synonymous with the word puppet.

Notes

1. In his earlier years Eugene Lambert (b. 1928), son of a Sligo librarian, although an electrician by training, was also a highly successful ventriloquist, frequently performing in workmen's halls and music halls in the UK. This undoubtedly honed his skills as a popular entertainer. Until his very last years, he would warm up audiences with the character of Judge from *Wanderly Wagon*.

2. Judy, Gene, Stephen, Miriam, David, Paula, Jonathan, Noel, Liam and Conor. Five of the Lambert children are still involved with puppets. Liam runs the theatre and Miriam gives solo performances, often for young children with stories such as *Goldilocks and the Three Bears*. In 1980 she took over the role of the popular RTÉ puppet Bosco, which then passed to her sister Paula. Bosco remains with Paula, who has her own travelling show with much audience interaction in the tradition of the Lambert theatre. Conor is a noted Punch "professor" with an interesting modern slant and is a talented scriptwriter, stand-up comedian and actor. Liam and his wife Eva have toured widely outside Ireland, including the Middle East.

Scenic Transitions: From Drama to Experimental Practices in Irish Theatre

Noelia Ruiz

Introduction

At first glance, one might be tempted to consider post-Celtic Tiger austerity to be innocuous for contemporary Irish theatre and performance. Certainly, subsequent to the government's official acknowledgement that the economy was in recession in September 2008, a proliferation of successful theatre makers emerged on the scene: THEATREclub (created 2008), which combines formal experimentation with socially engaged projects; ANU Productions (created 2009), a company internationally acclaimed for its multi-disciplinary, immersive site-specific work, often exploring historical events; Una McKevitt (created 2009), who delves into the possibilities of documentary theatre; and Dead Centre (created 2012), whose aesthetics are most definitely devoted to Lehmann's *Postdramatic Theatre* (2006) and European trends.

The full list is far more extensive and difficult to constrain to specific labels, particularly since most contemporary forms are interdisciplinary in nature. For instance, WillFredd Theatre (founded in 2010) seeks to create encounters that respond to and represent communities such as farmers, sign-language speakers or hospices, producing imaginative works that use live soundscape as a theatrical character. Collapsing Horse Theatre (founded in 2012) often blends theatre, puppetry and live music, while Dick Walsh Theatre (founded in 2012), which defines its work as "political art", might be located in the intersection between theatre and performance art.

All these practitioners depart from traditional dramatic conventions, experimenting to different degrees with theatrical form in terms of stage language,

N. Ruiz (✉)
University College Dublin, Dublin, Ireland
e-mail: noelia.ruiz@ucd.ie

E. Jordan, E. Weitz (eds.), *The Palgrave Handbook of Contemporary Irish Theatre and Performance*,
https://doi.org/10.1057/978-1-137-58588-2_20

acting style, the visual, spatial and scenographic dramaturgical possibilities, as well as new playwriting. They also have a common approach to the way in which they create, using devising strategies in a collaborative manner.

In effect, a new wave of Irish theatre makers has stemmed from a specific context in which different agents have played a role in the past three decades, namely political, economic, socio-cultural, institutional and artistic factors, as we shall see. In this context, enabled by the favourable economy of the Celtic Tiger, the 1990s saw the blossoming of an alternative scene to the predominant dramatic tradition of Irish theatre with the emergence of companies such as Pan Pan Theatre, Blue Raincoat, Corcadorca, Barabbas, Loose Canon and The Corn Exchange. In general these companies wanted to investigate form, and thus, theatricality. They wanted to break away from dramatic aesthetics and techniques, "the sort of text-based theatre that assumes psychological realism as its inevitable mode of performance".[1]

On a wider scale, in order to understand this blooming, we must contemplate a few epistemological shifts: both cultural and performative turns took place in the late twentieth century in Western humanities and social sciences, as Tracy Davis argues:

> Since the 1970s, we have marked the "linguistic turn" (emphasizing language's role in constructing perception), the "cultural turn" (tracking the everyday meanings of culture, and culture's formative effect on identities), and more recently the "performative turn" (acknowledging how individual behavior derives from collective, even unconscious, influences and is manifest as observable behavior, both overt and quotidian, individual and collective).[2]

In theatre and performance this meant, on the one hand, a turn towards intercultural practices, engaging predominantly with Eastern traditions that place the emphasis on the expressive, phenomenological body. Paradigmatic cases are Jerzy Grotowski,[3] who founded his Theatre Laboratory in 1959, Ariane Mnouchkine's Théâtre du Soleil, founded in 1964, and the work, especially in the latter part of the twentieth century, of Peter Brook. On the other hand, within the performative turn, there was a focus on context and process rather than product, as Erica Fischer-Lichte elucidates:

> In the 1990s, however, the focus of interest shifted to the processes of making, producing, creating, doing and to the actions, processes of exchange, negotiation and transformation as well as to the dynamics which constitute the agents of these processes, the materials they use and the cultural events they produce. (...) Thus, it seems that the discovery of the performative nowadays directs the humanities and cultural studies in particular.[4]

In practice, this shift manifested much earlier, especially in the ways in which practitioners adopted new methodologies, which in turn shaped content and form. Moreover, the departure from the dramatic text and its conventions implied not only formal experimentation but also a rupture with its power dynamics; thus, the hierarchy of the text, the playwright and the director as auteur was rejected, giving way to collaborative and interdisciplinary models of creation. These practices, in the many configurations they took, evolved from the experiments of the avant-garde and through the twentieth and twenty-first centuries into what was labelled "devised theatre", "post-modern theatre" and, more recently, "post-dramatic theatre". This originated contending arguments on the terminology to define these new forms, their aesthetics and their approaches to theatre-making. However, these different approaches are contingent to specific contexts and traditions. As Duška Radosavljević argues, the "power-dynamic between text and performance [...] has to be understood as being specifically characteristic of the English-speaking world and may not find easy equivalents in some of the other European cultures".[5]

Devised theatre's genesis can be traced back to post-war England. The first company to devise work was Joan Littlewood's Theatre Workshop, founded in 1953. It worked around dramatic texts or developed them, with Irish playwright Brendan Behan as a main collaborator—the legendary example being his play *The Hostage* (1958). The emphasis was on the way of generating the script: in a collaborative manner, through improvisations, within an interdisciplinary framework, with a focus on actor training, and with a strong sense of democratic ensemble in which all partakers had the same status (although under the direction of Littlewood). Besides, there was a general turn towards Eastern acting techniques, with a focus on physical training to gain theatrical expressivity. This new concept of the actor was central: no longer subsumed to the tyranny of the text, s/he was perceived as a creative artist, the "producer of theatricality and the channel through which it passes"[6] to the audience. This prominence of physicality was highly influenced by Antonin Artaud's *The Theatre and Its Double* (1938) and his then revolutionary and provocative discourse. Artaud's stance must be contextualized within the experiments of the European avant-garde, when a search for theatricality, or what makes theatre a unique art, took place:

> How is it Western theatre cannot conceive of theatre under any other aspect than dialogue form? Dialogue—something written and spoken—does not specifically belong to the stage but to books. [...] I maintain the stage is a tangible, physical place that needs to be filled and it ought to be allowed to speak its own concrete language.[7]

If in the UK a subversion of the processual aspects of theatre-making challenged the relationship and hierarchy of structural agents (which ultimately affected form), in continental Europe those experimentations focused on form per se. In this context, we might consider Bertolt Brecht's epic theatre[8] one of the first attempts to systematically formalize a body of theory and practice in which the dramatic form was challenged at its core. The advent of the post-modern stance penetrated these experimentations and, in parallel to the cultural turn, the performative aspects of theatre and performance came to the fore, exposing its liveness by means of self-referentiality or reflexivity, deconstruction, fragmentation and meta-theatricality, eventually blurring the lines between the fictive and the real. German dramatist Heiner Müller is probably the most iconic figure of this shift in the late 1950s.

As Deirdre Heddon and Jane Milling observe, scholarly discourses on post-structuralism, deconstructionism, hyperreality, post-colonialism and post-modernism in general "were, by the mid-1980s, circulating beyond the academy and informing not only critical responses to or engagements with performance practice, but also performance practices themselves".[9] These practices were initially labelled "post-modern theatre" until Lehmann's seminal *Postdramatisches Theater* was published in 1999 in German, and translated into English as *Postdramatic Theatre* in 2006 by Karen Jürs-Munby. At both practice and theoretical levels, the post-dramatic quickly became a paradigm, foregrounded by post-modernism in general, and deconstructionism in particular, as Lehmann states:

> To call theatre 'postdramatic' involves subjecting the traditional relationship of theatre to drama to deconstruction, and takes account of the numerous ways in which this relationship has been refigured in contemporary practice since the 1970s.[10]

Where the focus was on form, on process, or both, even if by symbiosis, contemporary theatre and performance practices became increasingly interdisciplinary and collaborative. However, the ideal egalitarian system that defined the initial *modus operandi* of devising theatre as an alternative to the predominant socio-political structures was to an extent, in the long term, a failure. Despite a few exceptions, in general some sort of structure or hierarchy proved to be necessary, thus positing the director as a leading figure who guides the decision-making process. A paradigmatic case is the Forced Entertainment company (which launched in 1984), which in its first couple of years explored a collective model with rotatory roles. Yet it soon realized that each member had different skills and preferences; consequently, Tim Etchells decided to step down as a performer to focus on directing. Conversely, along with other experimental models,[11] devised theatre, because of its collaborative and processual nature, allows all the participants to contribute creatively, and also allows for a democratic way of decision-making, even if the director makes the final choices. If this transition towards new models in the UK and other European countries blossomed in the 1970s, in Ireland it was adjourned to the 1980s.

The Irish Context: Ploughing the Soil

The establishment of the European Union (EU) as an economic power in the 1980s—culminating with the implementation of the euro in 2002—had a strong socio-economic impact, which in Ireland led to the so-called Celtic Tiger period in the 1990s. The opening of barriers facilitated mobility across

Europe, encouraged by the implementation of programmes like Erasmus (established in 1987), which fosters exchange among EU member countries and other Western states, along with increasingly affordable travel. On the other hand, European and national public funding provided new opportunities in the arts. For instance, the Arts Council of Ireland Travel and Training Award originated from a scheme called Artflight in 1991.

There was also a rise in international arts festivals across Europe and beyond, facilitated by the new open borders: no longer was a visa required to train or tour work in the EU. Internationalization, globalization and interculturalism became buzzwords, and despite the detrimental implications of these developments, such as cultural homogenization and the spread of neoliberalism and its ideologies beyond the Western world, they had a reinvigorating effect in countries like Ireland or Spain, which for decades had suffered from depressed economies and, consequently, from a certain isolation when it came to cultural exchange (among other things).

Within this context, 1991 was a vital year in contemporary Irish theatre, as three key companies emerged: Pan Pan Theatre in Dublin, Blue Raincoat in Sligo, and Corcadorca in Cork. They had the shared aim of offering an alternative to the traditional Irish dramatic realism that dominated institutional theatre. Hitherto, the experimental scene in Ireland played out mostly in the margins, with the exception of the physical and visual explorations of playwright Tom MacIntyre and director Patrick Mason at the Abbey Theatre in the 1980s, and the work of the Operating Theatre Company, founded in 1980 by theatre artist Olwen Fouéré and composer Roger Doyle.[12]

Corcadorca was born with the intention of exploring plays out of traditional venues, pioneering site-specific theatre in Ireland; Blue Raincoat had a focus on investigating play-texts through physical theatre, adopting the corporeal mime technique of Etienne Decroux; and Pan Pan, inspired by the avant-garde movement and European aesthetics, was committed to exploring the language of theatre itself, that is, theatricality.

These companies' initiatives quickly permeated the Irish theatre scene in the 1990s, chiefly in Dublin, demonstrated by the rise of other iconic companies that engaged with different theatrical forms, mainly European. The Corn Exchange (founded in 1995) developed a unique style inspired by Italy's commedia dell'arte and Chicago's improvisational theatre; Loose Canon (founded in 1996) occupied itself with Polish director Jerzy Grotowski's "poor theatre", while Barabbas (founded in 1993) examined the possibilities of the French "theatre of clown". They shared common ground in deviating from dramatic conventions in form, acting style and techniques, using a collaborative methodology, and drawing strongly on visual, spatial and compositional dramaturgy. In Belfast, Kabosh was founded in 1994 with the aim "to reinvent the ways in which stories are told, commissioning new writing and devising work for site-specific environments and installation".[13]

The cases of Blue Raincoat, Barabbas, Loose Canon and The Corn Exchange are representative of the turn towards physicality,[14] conceiving the actor's body and presence as theatricality's main vehicle. Annie Ryan (The Corn Exchange), coming from a solid training in commedia improvisation with the Piven Theater Workshop in Chicago, recalls being surprised at how disconnected Irish actors were from their bodies in the early 1990s Irish mainstream theatre. Subsequently, the focus of her work became

> to embody the moment, getting the actor to slow down enough to allow them to investigate how the body wants to respond to the now […] the idea of the body as the primary channel of performance, the idea of physical language coming first and then the text coming second.[15]

Jason Byrne (Loose Canon) recalls that during his institutional training he was still "locked" in traditional theatre in which "the word was still king".[16] He felt that there was something vital lacking in his education as an actor. He became fixated on Meyerhold, Grotowski and Stanislavsky:

> I felt that what these people seemed to be requiring or asking of their collaborators at the time were ensembles in terms of the physical training, the exercises and the preparation, the investigations they were going into. And I felt there was nothing I had touched on as a performer that required anything like the level of work that these people seemed to have done, and that mystified me. […] I remember Grotowski's work sounded the most accomplished. I had no idea what that work was, I hadn't seen it anywhere, all I had were the photographs in *Towards a Poor Theatre*, which kind of haunted me because of the viscerality of the physicality that was absolutely absent in anything that was happening around me here and even in the UK.[17]

In 1993 Mikel Murfi, a founding member of Barabbas who had trained at École Internationale de Théâtre Jacques Lecoq, Paris, organized a three-week workshop in Pearse Street, inviting actors who wanted physical theatre training. Ryan, Byrne, Michelle Reed (mask theatre), Cindy Cummings (choreographer), Veronica Coburn (youth theatre) and Raymond Keane (street theatre and puppetry) imparted training in their different areas of expertise. The workshop not only made it clear that there was an appetite among artists to pursue that type of training, but also fostered the formation of Barabbas and The Corn Exchange.

Ryan acknowledges that along with her desire to create an ensemble for physical, embodied theatre, there was another key factor in the formation of her company: the foundation of the Dublin Fringe Festival in 1995 by Jimmy Fay, which became a platform for those who had been honing their craft outside the limited mainstream channels. It coincided with a time when the underground cultural landscape in Dublin was thriving, especially the gay club scene as foregrounded by Tonie Walsh and his night events, Elevator, at the Ormond Multimedia Centre (currently the Morrison Hotel), where Fay and his company, Bedrock, started. Ryan also highlights the role of the Players (Trinity College Dublin's student drama society) as seminal in the formulation of the alternative scene in Ireland, acting as a pivotal hub for new artists. During her Erasmus year at Trinity (in 1989–1990) she met playwright and eventual partner Michael West, filmmaker Lenny Abrahamson, musician and film composer Stephen Rennicks and actor Dominic West. In the summer of 1990 she collaborated with West for the first time in a devised movement piece called *Scene Around Six* (1990), with Rennicks, Juliet Gruber, Amanda Hogan, Ryan, Jonathan Shankey and Dominic West. Since its inception, The Corn Exchange has created award-winning productions such as *Car Show* (Cultural Inspiration Award 1998, Special Judges' Award 1998), *Lolita* (Best Supporting Actress, Best Costume Design, Irish Times Theatre Awards 2002), *Mud* (Best Production, Irish Times Theatre Awards 2003), *Dublin by Lamplight* (Best Ensemble, Edinburgh 2005) and *Freefall* (Best New Play and Best Director, The Irish Times Theatre Awards 2009). Other companies that emerged from under the Players' wings were Rough Magic, Fishamble, Pan Pan and Loose Canon.

Raymond Keane recalls how after the Pearse Street workshop Coburn and Murfi approached him with the idea of creating a show together. He declined the invitation but stated he would be more interested in forming a company and the conversation started. Several weeks and cups of tea later, they decided to go ahead, spending a year exploring possibilities without presenting any work. For Keane, the most important aspect of that period was that it allowed them to discover who they were and the type of theatre they wanted to create—that is, formulate a vision. They initially framed themselves as influenced by the European traditions of clown, bouffon and commedia dell'arte, but eventually it became clear that the soul of the clown was their common bond.

By the end of 1993 they had the bones of a show and many ideas for others, which gave them the impetus to formalize the company and start the production process. Due to different factors, Keane recalls, "we launched ourselves with three shows back to back".[18] Their first devised show, *Come Down from the Mountain John Clown, John Clown* (1993), premiered at the Hawkswell, Sligo. It was followed in 1994 by *Half Eight Mass of a Tuesday* and a stripped-down production of *Macbeth* (1994) directed by Gerard Stembridge, as part of the inaugural "Barabbas... the Festival" at the Project Arts Centre. They applied for Arts Council funding and were awarded £10,000 in retrospect, after having spent £25,000 on the three shows, paying everybody except themselves.

Loose Canon was formed by Jason Byrne and Willie White, after graduating from Trinity College Dublin in 1996, as a showcase platform for themselves and other graduates. In Byrne's words, "it was pretty naïve but it turned into a full-scale, low-budget production".[19] Afterwards they mounted four Shakespeare productions and Jacobean tragedies, of which *The Spanish Tragedy* was nominated for Best Supporting Actor (Andrew Bennett) and Best Lighting Designer (Paul Keogan) in the Irish Times Theatre Awards 1997, and *Coriolanus* won the Spirit of Life Award in the Sunday Independent Awards 1998. Byrne, however, did not feel satisfied: "I was bored, I was really bored,

I was really frustrated and I didn't know how to break that cycle or what to do about it".[20] It was after his production of *Hamlet* (1999) that Byrne asked stunt choreographer Paul Burke if he could teach the company some exercises based on photographs from *Towards a Poor Theatre*. Originally, sixteen of them met twice a week for a couple of months which, in time, led to a core of actors: Deirdre Roycroft, Mark D'Aughton, Bryan Burroughs, Karl Quinn and Kevin Hely, joined at various stages by Bonnie McCormick and Lesley Conroy. Although Byrne admits he did not know at the time what the ultimate point of this process was, he could see that they were learning; the actors were changing, their physicality was developing and Byrne felt they were achieving a deeper line of work, so they kept training tenaciously. At that point, they were awarded some funding and they started working full time, dedicating their efforts towards a piece. After about five months they had twenty minutes of material that was deemed acceptable to present in public. The piece was completely silent, "because we couldn't even begin to speak, we were reinventing ourselves artistically".[21] Loose Canon members stopped working as freelancers for four years, training five hours per day and doing creative work in the afternoons. That phase came to an end when the company members started to have families.

In contrast, Pan Pan, founded by scenographer Aedín Cosgrove and director Gavin Quinn, aligned itself from its inception with the European avant-garde and its investigations in form and theatricality. As Quinn states:

> We were just interested in starting a company that would make theatre like the French model of theatre art, as opposed to the craft of making theatre, which was prevalent at the time. So the company started to explore those ideas of a more European aesthetic and the simple idea of theatre being conceptual, and very much a medium where you could use the kind of visual arts principles of line, form and colour.[22]

For Cosgrove, from the outset, they "had a very clear aim to be different, to be very distinct from what was happening in the other theatres, in the Gate, in the Abbey and even in the independent companies. We wanted to make our own identity, kind of like a band, we wanted our own sound".[23] Their first production, *Negative Act*, written and directed by Quinn, premiered at the Lombard Street Studio Theatre (now Green On Red Galleries) and toured later that year to the Lyon International Student Festival, France. It was inspired by "The Futurist Synthetic Theatre Manifesto", by F.T. Marinetti, Emilio Settimelli and Bruno Colla (1915), which urged a rupture of the Aristotelian unities: action, time and place, as well as text. Quinn recalls,

> it was a very abstract notion of four characters, in which one kept writing away from the other three. The title comes from the notion of doing nothing, the idea of nothingness, so the play itself was about nothing. Just using time onstage and being very much about building a language from nothing; so it was quite abstract

> and very conceptual. It had very [few] words in it and it was essentially what you could call an experimental piece.[24]

Since then, Pan Pan has created over thirty theatre and performance pieces and toured its work to festivals and venues worldwide. Its adaptations of the classics, such as *Mac-Beth 7* (2004), *Oedipus Loves You* (2005), *The Rehearsal, Playing the Dane* (2010), *The Seagull & Other Birds* (2014) and *The Good House of Happiness* (2017)—based on Brecht's parable play *The Good Person of Szechwan*—manifest a constant exploration of form and subject matter. Set in contemporary scenarios, often Irish, its adaptations investigate these works' possible meanings and how they might resonate with our society at large.

Pan Pan, unquestionably, has fostered European and post-dramatic aesthetics in Ireland. Touring internationally since its first production exposed it to different experimental approaches in different socio-cultural contexts with diverse theatrical traditions, shaping the company's aesthetics. Cosgrove recalls that period:

> We would go anywhere and do anything [...] I saw work over there [Poland], particularly, Leszek Madzik of Scena Plastyczna Kul.[25] That was very, very mind-blowing because he was doing everything with tin cans and bulbs in a very low-tech way, but it was incredible image making. And that was a course of possibility, because you did not need any money to do that, you just needed the ideas and the purpose, and to believe it was possible. So that was very inspiring and it definitely was a page-turner for me.[26]

Such was the drive behind Pan Pan's Dublin International Theatre Symposium (which ran from 1997 to 2002), conceived as a platform to present innovative international work. The biannual symposium featured companies such as Forced Entertainment, Ultima Vez, Big Art Group/Caden Manson, La Carnicería and Eugenio Barba's Odin Theatre. Victor Merriman's opening speech for the first symposium is a reflection of the spirit of the time in Ireland:

> May I assert that Irish theatre is indeed a European Theatre. This is a country in which the English language is spoken but it is not England. Neither is it imprisoned in the past of struggles of trying to define itself in opposition to England, a colonial power. But the country is finding its feet in a new Europe, a Europe of an expanding union, a European Union which is being challenged by the exclusions which at the moment, for historical reasons, it itself tolerates. Ireland has a role to play in that as evidenced by the recent European presidency successfully concluded. Irish theatre has a role to play in interrogating the kind of Europe and the kind of arts practice that we might wish to see developing.[27]

The symposium also hosted workshops and lectures, acting as a lab, and thus creating a space for the exchange of aesthetic approaches, new trends and methodologies. It also provided the opportunity to other Irish companies such as Corcadorca, Loose Canon, Bedrock, Cois Céim, Blue Raincoat, Fishamble,

Irish Modern Dance Theatre and The Corn Exchange to participate, collaborate and/or present work to international peers. Many Irish theatre makers recall the symposium's impact. Jo Mangan, another Trinity graduate who founded The Performance Corporation with Tom Swift in 2002, recalls her experience seeing a demonstration performance and open improvisation talk on "Theatre as an expression of rebellion" by Teatr Ósmego Dnia (Poland) during the second symposium (1998): "[I]t was joyous, because it was so different from anything I had seen in Ireland."[28] She joined a workshop with the Polish company the following year when they returned to the third symposium. Three years later The Performance Corporation's debut show, an adaptation of *Candide*, won awards both at the Dublin Fringe Festival and The Irish Times/ESB Irish Theatre Awards 2002. Since then the company has produced more than fifteen shows, "creating daring theatrical adventures in surprising places"[29] from site-specific pieces to flash mobs. In *Drive By* (2006), first performed at Cork Midsummer Festival in June, and subsequently at the Dublin Fringe Festival, the audience had to drive to a secret location on the outskirts of town and watch the show as in a drive-in theatre, turning on the radio to listen to the broadcast text, which blended live dialogue with recorded soundscapes. The plot revolved around boy-racers and was a response to road deaths in Ireland. The company's highly stylized scenography is juxtaposed with innovative technology. One of its latest adventures, *Expedition*, in collaboration with Vancouver's Boca del Lupo, is an evolving series of events involving artists, activists and scientists interested in exploring climate change. In 2002, the symposium was nominated for the Irish Times Theatre Awards Judge's Special Award. However, artistic choices led to the closure of the symposium in the same year, although Pan Pan continued formal and informal mentoring of artists such as Brokentalkers (founded in 2001), Dylan Tighe and Dead Centre.[30]

Loose Canon, Barabbas and The Corn Exchange were also key in nurturing a new generation of theatre makers, offering workshops in the respective techniques upon which, at least in part, they were founded. Keane believes many acting students were drawn to these workshops because, after attending shows, they realized there were other possibilities beyond the traditional, dramatic, text-based programmes. For Keane, this attraction had to do with the fact that they were breaking the rules and reinventing the notions of "what theatre is, the making of it and the presentation of it, something the big institutions are not allowed to do".[31] Their influence cannot be highlighted enough, as Ryan states:

> [P]eople that are now cast on the main stages are people who trained with Barabbas, who trained with Jason [Byrne], who trained with me. But now it's a whole other [situation] because all those teachers, me included, are now in The Lír [National Academy of Dramatic Art, Trinity] and we have a much more structured way of having that connection with the students, which is really great, and that's going to have a huge impact [on] the way people work here.[32]

In terms of fostering new aesthetics and experimental work in Ireland, the roles of the Dublin Theatre Festival (DTF; founded in 1957), Project Arts Centre (founded 1966), and, as stated by Ryan, the Dublin Fringe Festival (founded 1995), have been vital in encouraging the development of a healthy experimental scene in Irish theatre. Also, as Fintan Walsh emphasizes in *That Was Us* (2013),[33] other initiatives played an important role, particularly in the post-Celtic Tiger era. Examples include The Next Stage, an initiative launched in 2007 by the DTF and Theatre Forum and created "to promote artist development and participation during the duration of the festival" (4); and the establishment of the Lír Academy in 2011, in association with the Royal Academy of Dramatic Art (RADA), London. In *That Was Us*. contributors underline the impact of seeing international work at the DTF (which commissioned Walsh's book). For instance, Dylan Tighe recalls how Romeo Castellucci's *Genesi* (2000) "was the first time I had *experienced* a theatre performance rather than merely *watched* one [...] I had no theatrical compass with which to interpret the performance but it set my imagination free".[34]

There are, of course, other initiatives that must be acknowledged. Project Arts Centre launched an Associate Artist Scheme in 2005, under the direction of Willie White (2002–2011), with the objective of mentoring, co-producing and disseminating the work of thirty-four independent artists. In 2008 it was renamed Project Catalyst and then in 2013, under the direction of Cian O'Brien, Project Artists. It currently comprises three-year agreements with seven artists and companies: Brokentalkers, The Company, THEATREclub, Junk Ensemble, Louise White, Hilary O'Shaughnessy and Fearghus Ó Conchúir, as well as ongoing project-by-project relationships with a number of other artists. MAKE, an annual week-long residency organized by Cork Midsummer Festival, Dublin Fringe Festival, Theatre Forum and Project Arts Centre, came to inception in 2009, and since 2010 has been funded under the Arts Council Theatre Artists Development Scheme. Dublin Youth Theatre, founded in 1977 by educational psychologist Paddy O'Dwyer (who has remained an active influence ever since), has also played a vital part in fostering a new generation of theatre makers (e.g. THEATREClub and Shaun Dunne emerged from Dublin Youth Theatre), and under the artistic direction of Gary Keegan (2010–2014) and Willie White (2007–2010) a turn towards contemporary aesthetics was observable. The Irish Theatre Institute, under the Arts Council's 2010 Theatre Resource-Sharing Support scheme, set up Six in the Attic, providing artists with space, time and practical resources along with mentoring and advice services. Lime Tree Theatre in Limerick created a similar scheme in 2014, HatchLK, which was renamed this year as belltable:connect.

Apart from these institutions, independent companies such as The Performance Corporation and Pan Pan launched similar initiatives. The Performance Corporation's SPACE Programme (created 2008) is a residency offering creative practitioners an opportunity to collaborate, experiment and innovate without the pressures or expectations of creating finished products. Participants come from fields as diverse as theatre, science, video art, comedy, dance and contemporary music. Pan Pan's International Mentorship and Bursary Programme, launched in 2012 under the Theatre Artist Development Scheme, allows four to five artists to work with an international mentor for a period of nine to twelve months, developing an early-stage idea for performance.[35] It provides a creative and financial platform to explore practice without constraint. Some of the mentees so far have been Una McKevitt, Dick Walsh, Amy Conroy, Clodagh Deegan and Tom Creed. These artists, in their different capacities as directors, writers, designers, composers or performers, are prominent voices in contemporary Irish theatre, with a variety of styles and forms.[36]

Some of these programmes were a direct outcome of the devastating Arts Council cuts in 2010, when eleven companies in the Regular Funding Scheme (RFS) saw their subsidies withdrawn, among them Barabbas, Bedrock and Loose Canon, or faced major cuts that compromised their existence, such as The Corn Exchange and The Performance Corporation. The Arts Council's new funding model, following the report "Examining New Ways to Fund the Production and Presentation of Theatre", placed the emphasis on redistributing funding to achieve regional balance and "safeguarding funding for new and emerging artistic talent, [to] provide opportunities for artists within organizations no longer funded on a recurring basis".[37] Paradoxically, many of these RFS companies had a fundamental impact on the very development of this new generation of theatre makers; they had been pivotal in bringing new techniques, methodologies and forms to the Irish theatrical landscape, providing inspiration with their vision and something of vital importance: training.

Byrne, Keane and Ryan all agree that the cuts interrupted their careers at a delicate moment, when they felt a sense of growth and were about to take the next step forward. Furthermore, there was no prior indication or notice on this decision, provoking a high level of distress to individuals who were left literally unemployed overnight, with all the repercussions that implies. The Arts Council's decision to undermine the company model was sometimes justified by arguing that, rather than providing the necessary artistic output, some companies were running offices at a great expense. However, Keane argues that not only did the company model allow for artistic experimentation, but also

> a company cannot be managed without administrative help, from creative producers to administrators. Having a production company meant that we could pay people, we could afford holiday-pay, insurance, travel, training… We could make money and we could turn over at least three times what we were funded per year. Of course we were heavily funded but we were generating income and a place for people to work.[38]

Ryan highlights the danger this new model brings by focusing on audience numbers rather than on artistic integrity and experimentation. Like her, Keane and Byrne agree that, in the long term, project funding, which basically operates as a zero-hour contract, is not a viable way to sustain a healthy and solid arts scene. It risks a constant turnover of emerging companies that at some point might hit a funding glass ceiling, leaving them unable to develop and potentially eventually disappearing. The Arts Council, in what can be seen as an attempt to address some of these issues, launched in 2016 the Making Great Art Work Funding Framework, as part of a wider ten-year strategy. The framework included the introduction of the Strategic Funding scheme in 2018, to provide three years of consecutive funding to arts organizations, and the Artists' Support scheme, awarded to individuals to develop their practice, including travelling to learn or experience work abroad or availing of a residency.

This overall context is a reflection of Europe's socio-political climate and its turn towards neoliberal policies that heavily affect state funding of the arts and culture, along with health and other welfare and social protection policies. In the UK this process started in the 1970s, when Margaret Thatcher's Conservative government cuts made it impossible for many artists to continue their careers. In the case of theatre, like in Ireland in 2010, it meant the disappearance of many experimental companies and, with them, their critical stances. This phenomenon has been labelled by Aleks Sierz as "Thatcherite commercialisation",[39] denoting the conversion of theatre into a product, and its audiences into consumers. Although theatre has always had a commercial dimension, for Sierz non-mainstream theatre had been a commentator on "political, economical, social, personal and moral"[40] issues, and undermining the experimental scene compromises such an important role, necessary for a functional society.

In the case of Ireland, the increasing cuts in the arts since the early 2000s did not respond so neatly to the implementation of a government's specific ideology. The 2010 cuts were the direct outcome of the country's bailout-driven recession and the politics of austerity imposed by the EU. Conversely, the overall EU political position is clearly inclined towards neoliberal policies and related economical practices that jeopardize the arts, culture, education, workers' rights and healthcare. In the case of the arts, a dangerous narrative is gaining terrain, namely that they are inherently elitist, and have a tertiary role in the formation of citizenship. This narrative is particularly perilous in face of more pressing austerity issues, such as homelessness, in the case of Ireland. Thus, within this logic, the arts and culture are regarded as unnecessary, or as a luxury that should not rely on the taxpayer.

Therefore, within this context, the Arts Council of Ireland faced a dramatic reduction in its budget, which was addressed with a new funding scheme that redistributed funds. However, the decision to dismantle key theatre companies that had introduced new techniques and aesthetics to Ireland—thus changing its theatre landscape—and nurtured, via non-institutionalized training, a generation of theatre artists, seems more than unfortunate. Although some of these artists have managed in different ways to navigate the blizzard of post-Celtic Tiger hardships, it was a serious setback in their careers. In hindsight, the elimination of key Irish theatre makers lacked vision and forethought. On the other hand, in line with neoliberal ideologies and practices, it operated with the absence of an ethical human dimension, that is, the process was highly dehumanized. As Byrne argues, a more feasible and less invasive short-term plan to implement the new budget would have been desirable: for instance, a gradual two-year scheme to help these companies into the transition to more financially viable models, rather than being cut out overnight. In fact, the RFS still operates in such ways, in that companies have to apply yearly and wait for a letter to find out what their budget is, making it difficult to plan for the long term and basing those plans on a sort of trust that the system does not deliver back.

Although the new Arts Council framework seems like an attempt to tackle this situation, it remains to be seen if it will really create a more sustainable model for the healthy development of Irish arts, and nurture not only the promising new generation of experimental theatre artists, but also those who ploughed the field.

Notes

1. Jen Harvie and Andy Lavender, *Making Contemporary Theatre: International Rehearsal Processes* (Manchester: Manchester University Press, 2010), 2.
2. Tracy C. Davis, *The Cambridge Companion to Performance Studies* (New York: Cambridge University Press, 2008), 1.
3. The collaboration of Grotowski, Richard Schechner and Eugenio Barba in the 1960s initiated the discourse and development of intercultural theatre and performance.
4. Erika Fischer-Lichte, "From Text to Performance: The Rise of Theatre Studies as an Academic Discipline in Germany," *Theatre Research International* 24, no. 02 (1999): 168.
5. Duška Radosavljević, *Theatre-Making: Interplay Between Text and Performance in The 21st Century* (Basingstoke, Hampshire: Palgrave Macmillan, 2013), 65.
6. Josette Féral and Ronald P. Bermingham, "Theatricality: The Specificity of Theatrical Language," *SubStance* 31, no. 2 (2002): 94.
7. Antonin Artaud, *The Theatre and Its Double: Essays* (London: Calder & Boyars, 1970), 27.
8. Those were anticipated by Adolphe Appia, Edward Gordon Craig, Vsévolod Emílievich Meyerhold and Artaud.
9. Deirdre Heddon and Jane Milling, *Devising Performance: A Critical History* (Basingstoke: Palgrave Macmillan, 2006), 190.
10. Hans-Thies Lehmann and Karen Jürs-Munby, *Postdramatic Theatre* (London: Routledge, 2006), 3.
11. Among some practitioners there is a reluctance to use the term "devised" to define their work, even if the methodologies they apply are close to this model. This is partly explained by the political associations of the term and its association with non-text-based performance.
12. To a certain extent we might consider Rough Magic Theatre Company (founded in 1984), although its aim was not departure from the text but rather "commissioning new Irish work, presenting the best of contemporary international writing and innovative productions from the classical repertoire" ("http://www.roughmagic.ie/ | Rough Magic Theatre Company" 2017).

13. "Theatre Companies NI | Site Specific Theatre | Arts NI | Kabosh http://www.kabosh.net/" 2017.
14. It is worth noting that in the UK the turn to devised physical theatre in the 1980s and 1990s was a direct outcome of Thatcherism: because of financial pressures, non-funded companies could not afford to work full-time and the focus on actor training was not sustainable any longer. Hence, the actors needed to be already trained. Conversely, this implies a professionalization of acting through its public and private institutionalization, that is, the proliferation of acting courses, schools, and colleges and their correspondent qualifications. Heddon and Milling link this to the emergence of devising physical theatre companies across the UK, arguing that the heightened interest in physical training was an outcome of an increasing competitiveness among actors, where only the best prepared in all types of acting styles could access a wider range of working possibilities. Besides, Heddon and Milling identify "the dominance of television and film, with their overriding emphasis on naturalism" as further motivation for turning more towards physical theatre. Heddon & Milling, 159.
15. Interview with Annie Ryan, March 21, 2016.
16. Interview with Jason Byrne, April 15, 2016.
17. Ibid.
18. Interview with Raymond Keane, March 23, 2016.
19. Interview with Jason Byrne, April 15, 2016.
20. Ibid.
21. Ibid.
22. Interview with Gavin Quinn, July 6, 2011.
23. Interview with Aedín Cosgrove, August 1, 2013.
24. Interview with Gavin Quinn, July 6, 2011.
25. Polish director, scenographer and playwright, known for his expressive and unconventional staging; he is regarded as the representative of visual theatre in Poland. He founded the Visual Stage at the Catholic University of Lublin.
26. Interview with Aedín Cosgrove, August 1, 2013.
27. Original transcript, courtesy of Pan Pan Theatre Company.
28. Interview with Jo Mangan, May 20, 2017.
29. "About," The Performance Corporation, accessed September 7, 2017. http://www.theperformancecorporation.com/about/.
30. Dylan Tighe and Bush Mourkazel (co-founders of Dead Centre) have collaborated extensively with Pan Pan as performers and their work has been noticeably influenced by Pan Pan's aesthetics.
31. Interview with Raymond Keane, March 23, 2016.
32. Interview with Annie Ryan, March 21, 2016.
33. Fintan Walsh, "*That Was Us*": *Contemporary Irish Theatre and Performance* (London: Oberon Books, 2013).
34. Ibid., 93.
35. In the first mentorship the selected participants were Gina Moxley, Una McKevitt and the collaborative team of Tom Lane and Aoife Spillane-Hinks, mentored by Kirsten Dehlholm of Hotel Pro Forma, Denmark. In 2013, the mentor was Viviane De Muynck of Needcompany, Brussels, and the participants were Dick Walsh, Thomas Conway, Linnette Moran (Live Collision), Bush Mourkazel (Dead Centre) and Louise White. In 2014 they engaged Tim Crouch, UK, who mentored Amy Conroy, Paul Curley, Kate Heffernan, Hilary

O'Shaughnessy and Martin Sharry. And finally, in 2016, Stewart Laing from Untitled Projects worked with Tom Creed, Clodagh Deegan, Ruairí Donovan, Meadhbh Haicéid and Conor Hanratty.

36. In 2001 Rough Magic launched SEEDS; originally set up as a joint initiative of the Dublin Fringe Festival and Rough Magic to seek out, encourage, enable, develop and stage new Irish writing. The first edition included six emerging writers who worked to develop new plays, supported by both companies, and by six leading directors acting as mentors. In 2004 it extended the programme to include directors, and in 2006 to designers and producers.
37. Arts Council/An Chomhairle Ealaíon, *Examining New Ways to Fund the Production and Presentation of Theatre,* Dublin, May 2009, 6.
38. Interview with Raymond Keane, March 23, 2016.
39. Aleks Sierz and Martin Crimp, *The Theatre of Martin Crimp* (London: Methuen Drama, 2006), 8.
40. Ibid.

Bibliography

"About." The Performance Corporation. Accessed September 7, 2017. http://www.theperformancecorporation.com/about/

Artaud, Antonin. *The Theatre and Its Double: Essays.* London: Calder & Boyars, 1970.

Arts Council/An Chomhairle Ealaíon. *Examining New Ways to Fund the Production and Presentation of Theatre.* Dublin. May 2009.

Davis, Tracy C. *The Cambridge Companion to Performance Studies.* New York: Cambridge University Press, 2008.

Féral, Josette and Ronald P. Bermingham. "Theatricality: The Specificity of Theatrical Language." *SubStance* 31, no. 2 (2002).

Fischer-Lichte, Erika. "From Text to Performance: The Rise of Theatre Studies as an Academic Discipline in Germany." *Theatre Research International* 24, no. 2 (1999).

Harvie, Jen and Andy Lavender. *Making Contemporary Theatre: International Rehearsal Processes.* Manchester: Manchester University Press, 2010.

Heddon, Deirdre and Jane Milling. *Devising Performance: A Critical History.* Basingstoke: Palgrave Macmillan, 2006.

Lehmann, Hans-Thies and Karen Jürs-Munby. *Postdramatic Theatre.* London: Routledge, 2006.

Radosavljević, Duška. *Theatre-Making: Interplay Between Text and Performance in the 21st Century.* Basingstoke, Hampshire: Palgrave Macmillan, 2013.

Sierz, Aleks and Martin Crimp. *The Theatre of Martin Crimp.* London: Methuen Drama, 2006.

Walsh, Fintan. *"That Was Us": Contemporary Irish Theatre and Performance.* London: Oberon Books, 2013.

Key Moments and Relationships: Working with Pat Kinevane

Jim Culleton

Fishamble: The New Play Company (called Pigsback until 1996) had been producing new plays since 1990, when we presented a version of Molière's *Don Juan* by Michael West in the Project Arts Centre, Dublin. Many of the team (including Michael and I, as well as producer Fergus Linehan, and actors including Tom Murphy, Siobhan Miley, Kathy Downes and Clodagh O'Donoghue, with Dominic West in the title role) were students at the time. I remember fondly the sense of adventure and abandon we had with it, since we had no reputation yet to tarnish, and it was our first time receiving Arts Council funding in the form of a modest guarantee against loss, so we had nothing to lose.

Other new plays by first-time playwrights followed in the 1990s, including Gavin Kostick's first play *The Ash Fire* (1992) and Joseph O'Connor's first play *Red Roses and Petrol* (1995), both of which transferred to London, Deirdre Hines' first play *Howling Moons, Silent Sons* (1991), which won the Stewart Parker Trust Award and transferred into the Abbey, as well as early plays by our contemporaries, *This Love Thing* by Marina Carr (1991) and *Buffalo Bill Has Gone to Alaska* by Colin Teevan (1993). In 1996, Mark O'Rowe sent his first play *From Both Hips* to all the theatre companies listed in the Yellow Pages, including Fishamble, and we produced it the following year in the Project Arts Centre's temporary space at the Mint, off Henry Street (run at the time by Fiach Mac Conghail) and in Glasgow's Tron Theatre.

There was something exciting (and still is) about unleashing an original vision of the world from a first-time playwright. Fishamble has since produced

J. Culleton (✉)
Fishamble: The New Play Company, Dublin, Ireland
e-mail: jim@fishamble.com

E. Jordan, E. Weitz (eds.), *The Palgrave Handbook of Contemporary Irish Theatre and Performance*,
https://doi.org/10.1057/978-1-137-58588-2_21

a number of plays by first-time and emerging playwrights, including Gary Duggan, Ian Kilroy, Jim O'Hanlon, Abbie Spallen and Rosaleen McDonagh, as well as short plays by first-time playwrights Stella Feehily, Róisín Ingle and Belinda McKeon. Recently, we have produced plays by new writers Sonya Kelly and Margaret McAuliffe, whose plays have been developed through the *Show in a Bag* initiative run by Dublin Fringe Festival, the Irish Theatre Institute and Fishamble, as well as emerging writer Eva O'Connor, who won the Fishamble New Writing Award (http://fishamble.com/writing/fishamble-new-writing-award/). It is particularly special when one of these first-time playwrights continues to have an ongoing working relationship with Fishamble, as many writers have, including Pat Kinevane, whose relationship with Fishamble has created a body of work of which we are hugely proud.

Pat wrote his first play, *The Nun's Wood*, for Fishamble in 1998. Pat had already worked with us as an actor, and he came to me with an idea for a play he was thinking of writing. I asked him what he had in mind, and he said it was a story set in the grounds of a convent near where he grew up in Cobh, during the 1970s, also inspired by the Greek myth of Odysseus and Circe. I knew Pat had a vivid, theatrical imagination and a way with language, as well as a passion for his subject matter, so was delighted to encourage him and work with him on the development of the play.

The first draft arrived, with its characters Picus, Silvy, Jaso and Bellona, picking spuds in the field while their teenage hormones and pieces of broken crockery flew across the stage. As we read and listened to the youngsters arguing and flirting and fighting and seducing, it felt like a very new voice had arrived. Pat displayed a fearlessness and bravery in dealing with taboo subjects and wrote with a great sense of passion. It was clear that his work as an actor had informed *The Nun's Wood* with its great characterization and visceral dialogue.

As part of the development process, we staged a reading in the Project Arts Centre with Cillian Murphy and Olwen Fouéré as the Odysseus and Circe characters. It was electric, and I remember the actor, Marion O'Dwyer, who attended the event, saying that as soon as she heard the opening stage direction, she knew she was at something unique:

> The lights begin, in long lashes, to lace, lance and pair, like ropes of illumination, erratic, resembling the urgent flickers of emergency...An amethyst blanket covers [a body]. The bloodied hand of this corpse is framed in a cube of light...silvery beeches ... baked terracotta soil ('The Nun's Wood' by Pat Kinevane, in the anthology 'Fishamble/Pigsback: First Plays' edited by Jim Culleton, published by New Island Books, ISBN 1 902602 89 7).

Working on the first production in the Mint was a very collaborative experience, as we all tried to figure out how to create a swelteringly hot 1970s Cobh in a cold damp 1990s Dublin. Kieran McNulty created a beautiful forest of trees and a stream with real water, and it was stunningly lit by Paul Keogan, with gorgeous music by Laura Forrest-Hay.

The play was very well received in Dublin, so we decided to tour it, and I have great memories of discussing the touring logistics with Phelim Donlon in the Arts Council at the time. We brought the production around Ireland, a highlight of which was presenting the play at the Cork Opera House and coaches of people from Cobh coming to see their home town represented on stage. It struck such a chord with Irish audiences that it didn't seem possible for it to connect in the same way with audiences outside the country. However, the local does often reflect the universal, of course, and when the play won the BBC Stewart Parker Trust Award, we were invited to work with the Sibiu International Theatre Festival in Romania on a presentation of the play there, and it was astonishing to see how audiences felt that 1970s Cobh was remarkably similar to 1990s rural Romania. Audiences were also very taken aback when Pat attended a performance, followed by a post-show discussion during which a dozen top academics spoke from the audience (as is the custom there). He stood up to contribute to the discussion and addressed the audience in fluent Romanian, which he had learnt for the occasion.

Currently roles seem very fluid in theatre, with theatre artists and makers often moving effortlessly between writing, devising, directing and performing. We see this way of working first-hand through the *Show in a Bag* initiative, which is designed to support actors to create their own "light-footed" tourable show. It is refreshing to see actors and other theatre artists change and overlap roles as work is created in a new way. But back in the 1990s it was less frequent to see actors writing a play, even though there were notable exceptions, including Gina Moxley, Marie Jones, Donal O'Kelly, Billy Roche, Arthur Riordan, Hilary Fannin, Daniel Reardon, Eugene O'Brien and Pom Boyd. Pat was part of that group of actors who had an innate sense of how plays could work, in the same way that Shakespeare and Molière before him had, too.

The Nun's Wood began a collaboration with Pat which I am thrilled has continued to grow and change over the past two decades. It was followed by *The Plains of Enna*, another big, bold, ambitious work with an opera singer on stage among the actors, which we presented at the 1999 Dublin Theatre Festival.

Pat approached me in 2005 with a suggestion for a play about four elderly people at the end of their lives, whose stories are intertwined. When Pat had a first draft, we then spent a few weeks in the Neuroscience Building at Trinity College, Dublin, developing what would become *Forgotten*. Pat's trademark theatricality, his wicked sense of humour, his huge capacity for warmth and empathy, as well as his outrage at how some people are forgotten about at the end of their lives, fuelled the process. We were invited by the Irish Theatre Institute to present a showcase performance at the Dublin Theatre Festival in 2006 and we have been touring it ever since (for twelve years at the time of writing). We had no idea that the production of this play set in retirement homes across Ireland would go on to tour, not just across Ireland, but throughout Europe and to both coasts of the United States. There is something so truthful and full of love in Pat's writing (and performance) that makes a strong connection with people, no matter where they are from.

Pat came into the Fishamble office in 2009 with a few pages of text, spoken by a character called Tino McGoldrig, a homeless man tormented by the suicide of his brother. Gavin Kostick (Fishamble's literary manager), Orla

Flanagan (Fishamble's general manager at the time) and myself were blown away by the first few pages of the play, and by Pat's passion, his anger at the treatment of people with mental health issues, and his dark but hilarious sense of humour. *Silent* was commissioned with the support of the Arts Council and, on a train from the Irish Arts Center in New York to Washington DC as we toured *Forgotten*, Pat and myself began discussing the development of *Silent*. The sense of silence is central to the play, whether it's the silence when Tino did not speak out in support of his brother Pearse, or when life becomes silent for him on the streets, or the fact that Pearse looked like the silent movie star Rudolph Valentino. We started to explore how to stage some moments from Pearse's life as if they were scenes from silent movies. Pat thinks very physically about the plays so, in rehearsals, he would often suggest gestures and movements that could replace lines of dialogue. One day, we laid the play out on the floor and experimented with the order in which key events should be revealed to the audience; another time, we worked with choreographers on a residency in Edinburgh's Dance Base to develop the dance elements which Pat performs so wonderfully. Once again, a showcase performance at the 2010 Dublin Theatre Festival, supported by the Irish Theatre Institute and Culture Ireland, resulted in audience feedback and invitations from venues and festivals, and we started touring the production in 2011, with ongoing support from the Arts Council, Dublin City Council and Culture Ireland. *Silent* went on to win many awards, including an Olivier Award for Pat and Fishamble in 2016.

On the train from Brighton in May 2012, following a run there at the Brighton Festival, Pat read a few pages of a new script to me. The play was called *Underneath*, and it tells the story of a woman who speaks from her tomb after she has been murdered. She has been disfigured in a childhood accident, and suffered a lot of prejudice and bullying as a result. Once again, Pat's passion for exploring how we judge others based on outward appearance provided a backbone for the play, which is full of invention and fun. In the same way that *Forgotten* is inspired by Kabuki theatre and its production design uses a lot of the colour red, and *Silent* is inspired by silent movies and is full of silvery-grey, *Underneath* is inspired by the Egyptian pharaohs in their tombs, and the set is a collection of blood-splattered objects from the murder scene, represented by gold items. We had great fun in rehearsals for the play, working out what we could do with reams of gold fabric. Sometimes people refer to the plays as the "red one, the silver one and the gold one" instead of by their names, which I think is a reflection of how visual the productions are. Pat's scripts are not just spoken words, but ideas for a whole world, which demand a full investigation—aurally, physically and visually—in the rehearsal and design process.

When we were travelling to Los Angeles to present *Underneath* at the Odyssey Theatre, in association with Georganne Aldrich Heller, Pat showed me the lyrics to a half-dozen songs he had written. They will form part of a new play with songs that we are developing with Fishamble, working with composer Denis Clohessy, choreographer Emma O'Kane and producer Eva Scanlan. We felt that we needed one song more, to tell the full story of a man who is preparing to meet his estranged daughter. But we weren't sure what shape the song should take. In Los Angeles, Patricia Kelly (wife of Gene) saw *Underneath* and invited us to her house, where Pat was inspired by holding Cyd Charisse's dress from *Singin' in the Rain*, among other artefacts, and the final song became a tribute to Gene Kelly. Sometimes it is crucial to have well-laid plans, but sometimes, being open and allowing yourself to be spontaneous can suggest the way forward.

Irish Cinema and Theatre: Adapting to Change

Ruth Barton

Irish cinema and theatre have enjoyed a fluctuating relationship that has much to do with attitudes initially to modernity and subsequently to globalization. This relationship, further, is informed by discourses around cultural capital that have accompanied interactions between the two art forms since the invention of cinema.

The narrative of an upstart medium—film—disrupting and threatening the dominance of an older, established practice—theatre—is not specific to Ireland. It is a history that was replicated across the Western world as moving pictures exploded in popularity at the turn of the nineteenth century. In early cinema, actors from the legitimate theatre were happy to appear only anonymously on screen, for fear their reputations be compromised. That situation, of course, did not last any longer than the rise of celebrity discourse and the birth of the film star, yet professional movement between the two, in whatever direction, remains open to accusations of opportunism.

What is particular, although not unique, to the Irish context is the belated development of a national cinema and its struggle to legitimize itself in relation to literature and the theatre. There is no need to rehearse here the familiar story of the rise and fall of the Abbey Theatre during this time and its loss of critical favour in the post-revolutionary period, but it is important to remember that throughout the first half of the twentieth century the most compelling argument for the establishment of an Irish film industry was that it should model itself on the national theatre, re-make its best-known productions, and hire its leading actors, albeit in secondary roles. Behind this aspiration was an

R. Barton (✉)
Trinity College Dublin, Dublin, Ireland
e-mail: BARTONR@tcd.ie

E. Jordan, E. Weitz (eds.), *The Palgrave Handbook of Contemporary Irish Theatre and Performance*,
https://doi.org/10.1057/978-1-137-58588-2_22

insidious distrust of cinematic modernity, best expressed in a vigorous censorship regime. At least by tying film-making into the by-now conservative national theatre, the threat of the cinematic medium would be contained.

That moment culminated in a series of films, best known as the Abbey films, that have become bywords for cinematic stage-Irishness and a lack of medium specificity, but its resonances reach into the present day. The influence of these mid-century productions, films such as *Sally's Irish Rogue* (George Pollock 1958), *This Other Eden* (Muriel Box 1959) and *Broth of a Boy* (George Pollock 1959), on the evolution of Irish cinema has been negligible, or at least has only affected it in an inverse manner in so far as their model is one that present-day filmmakers are determined to avoid; yet certain of the critical issues they raise remain current. In particular, there are formal questions around the primacy of the word over the image and commercial considerations around audiences.

Another key concern is the movement of personnel—actors, writers and directors—between both media. And, inevitably, there is the issue of globalization. The address of the mid-century Abbey adaptations was to the global cinema audience, exposing these productions to the criticism that the local had become terminally diluted in the process. These same concerns remain today, although they are attenuated, as we shall see, by an alternative perspective that questions the assumptions of authenticity on which older arguments drew for their validity. My intention in this chapter, therefore, is not just to discuss adaptation, usually of theatre to film, in the Irish context, but also to consider how the two practices intersect and feed into each other, and why this might be considered liberating for both.

Analysing Adaptation

Outside of Barry Monahan's monograph *Ireland's Theatre on Film* (2009), and one or two specific case studies that I will shortly come to, very little critical attention has been paid to the movement between Irish stage and screen. This should not come as a surprise given the almost universal assumption that literary adaptations are book-to-screen, rather than play-to-screen. On a local level, the Irish novel's pre-eminence within cultural representations only serves to reinforce that premise. Nevertheless, there remains enough of value in the key texts on the subject to guide a discussion of the relationship. Recent developments in adaptation studies, particularly in key publications such as those by Linda Hutcheon (2012) and Robert Stam (2005), very usefully opens up the discipline to facilitate new critical approaches to it.[1] That the old cornerstones of analysis, notably fidelity to source material, have now largely been discarded in favour of theories of postmodern hybridity, intertextuality and eclecticism, is particularly helpful. No longer is the hierarchical privileging of one form over the other, nearly always the play or novel over the film, the starting point for analysis. Instead, questions of process and, to borrow a phrase from new-media discourse, remediation have more productively come to the fore as guidelines for consideration of the formal processes of change. As Robert Stam argues:

> one might easily imagine any number of positive tropes for adaptation, yet the standard rhetoric has often deployed an elegiac discourse of loss, lamenting what has been "lost" in the transition from novel to film, while ignoring what has been "gained".[2]

Linda Hutcheon, in turn, has argued that adaptation from stage to screen entails a less radical tonal shift than from novel to screen, citing Jonathan Miller's conclusion that

> most novels are irreversibly damaged by being dramatized as they were written without any sort of performance in mind at all, whereas for plays visible performance is a constitutive part of their identity and translation from stage to screen changes their identity without actually destroying it.[3]

Yet the differences between the two art forms, as Hutcheon readily acknowledges, remain significant. It also continues to be difficult, as I will shortly discuss, for adaptations to shake off the popular understanding of original versus copy. In an Irish context, where the pre-eminence of the word over the image has a strong imaginative grip, this is important in understanding the dominant critical approach to filmic adaptations of literary works. Conversely, as I wish to consider, it is this very particular relationship that frames much of the discourse around recent Irish film and Irish theatre.

Another significant difference between cinema and theatre is that theatre-going is more associated with the attainment of cultural capital. Of course, it is not just the preserve of the kind of educated individual that Bourdieu describes in "The Forms of Capital"[4]; the theatre embodies cultural capital, often through its building and location, through its performers and its audiences, as well as the texts it performs, in a way that the cinema, overall, does not. Tied to this is the uniqueness of each theatre performance and the impossibility of its true reproduction. Cinema-going may alter according to venue, and, with the increase in private, domestic viewing, differing modes of consumption of film, yet the image on the screen remains fundamentally the same for each viewer, however it is experienced.

Where Stam's and Hutcheon's work is useful in providing a wider analytic framework, we need to turn to local case studies to understand how issues of the national inflect these arguments, specifically in terms of discussing the relationship between Irish screen and stage. Here, too, the turn towards cultural studies in adaptation theory, and the recognition of the need to move beyond formalism, offer a way in to the debate for cultural theorists.

Hutcheon notes that

> General economic issues, such as the financing and distribution of different media and art forms, must be considered in any general theorizing of adaptation. To

> appeal to a global market or even a very particular one, a television series or a stage musical may have to alter the cultural, regional, or historical specifics of the text being adapted.[5]

This point is fundamental to most writing on adaptations of Irish plays, notably on two key texts, Jim Sheridan's 1990 adaptation of John B. Keane's *The Field* and Pat O'Connor's 1998 film of Brian Friel's *Dancing at Lughnasa*. The Sheridan adaptation was widely critiqued for substituting the identity of the stranger, whose bid to purchase the eponymous field sets in train the series of events that form the play's dramatic core, from returned British immigrant to returned American immigrant. The casting of the anodyne Tom Berenger as the "Yank" was read as further evidence of the compromises engendered by international financing and the pursuit of the American market. Similarly, the relocation of the time frame from the late 1950s or early 1960s to the 1930s was dismissed as a compromise by the film's detractors.[6] Sean Ryder writes of Sheridan's adaptation, specifically the mythic struggle of tradition (embodied by Bull McCabe, played by Richard Harris) versus modernity (the Yank), as a betrayal of the sense of the local embedded in Keane's writing:

> In an important sense, Keane's play is written from *within* the community life he dramatises, with a feeling for its nuances and complications; Sheridan, on the other hand, sees the same life from the schematic and often uncomprehending eye of the modern cosmopolitan.[7]

This kind of critique draws tellingly on a mode of discourse that favours the local originary text over what is perceived as a product that is fatally contaminated by commercial imperatives. However, an alternative reading of Sheridan's film sets it in productive tension, not with Keane's original play, but with the defining immigrant vision of Ireland, John Ford's *The Quiet Man* (1952). Thus, Maureen O'Hara's Mary-Kate Danaher becomes the landless Tinker Girl, the bucolic community of Ford's rural West is reimagined as the small-minded product of what Sheridan has referred to as the "incest culture", and the liberating "donnybrook" of the earlier film is restaged as the lethal blood-letting of a coward's fight.[8]

Aside from these thematic alterations, however you read them, there is a further issue with Sheridan's *The Field*, which is its staginess. It would be easy to ascribe that to its origins in a stage play; however, I would suggest that a better explanation lies in two key figures associated with the film. The first is Sheridan himself, who had only recently abandoned a career in theatre (at the Project Arts Centre) for film. His formal film training amounted to nothing more than a six-week course at New York University. Both his first film, *My Left Foot* (1989), and *The Field*, his second, reflect his lack of filmic experience. Both rely on strong scripts, narrative drive and well-turned performances for their impact. Neither exploits the visual or aural possibilities of the new medium, although certain sequences in *The Field*, notably the American wake, indicate that the new director was moving towards a greater confidence with camera-work. The other significant figure is the film's undoubted star, Richard Harris. Sheridan had planned to cast Ray McAnally in the role of the Bull McCabe, but McAnally died as the film was in pre-production, and Harris pushed hard for the part. Sheridan has been clear that he had difficulties with Harris on set and that the latter refused to take direction from him.[9] The result was a singular performance that can best be described as theatrical. Harris's Bull McCabe is highly performative; he booms out his lines as if he were projecting to the back of a filled auditorium, and every gesture is magnified. In part, this is consistent with Harris's personal performance style and the roots of it are evident in his early success in Lindsay Anderson's *This Sporting Life* (1963). However, one might guess too that Harris was seeking to guarantee his comeback through aligning himself with the more highly regarded stage tradition. In other words, he sought to accumulate cultural capital through being stagy.

In her study of *Dancing at Lughnasa*, Joan FitzPatrick Dean defends Pat O'Connor's 1998 production from critics who have found it lacking in comparison to Brian Friel's much-loved play. The film's ostensible conservatism, she argues, is undercut by its refusal to represent the Irish past in a nostalgic light. *Dancing at Lughnasa* (the film) "in fact challenges preconceptions about Ireland in the 1930s: some women did work outside the home; non-marital children and non-traditional family formations predate the 1990s; the threat of globalization beset rural Ireland decades ago".[10] As Dean discusses, although producer and impresario Noel Pearson had always envisaged *Dancing at Lughnasa* as a film, Friel immediately distanced himself from the enterprise: "Having cultivated non-naturalistic techniques unique to theatre throughout his career, he might well have suspected how rarely his dramatic strategies could survive the transition to film."[11]

In fact, much of Dean's short monograph bears out Friel's fears. As she discusses, a combination of alterations made by Frank McGuinness in his screenplay, and other changes introduced by Pat O'Connor, considerably diluted the energies of the original:

> Whereas Friel deployed a variety of theatrical strategies to subvert realism, O'Connor's film subordinated them to invisible editing and seamless, logical sequences. The cinematic space, especially the landscape, in O'Connor's film was so stable as to seem inert. And the film euphemized the women's suffering to provide a much happier ending.[12]

As well as altering the ending, the film re-imagined the iconic dance sequence so that "polite whoops replace roars. All of the sisters smile throughout the dance. With all their quarrels, secrets and unhappiness held in abeyance, the sequence provides a final happy moment in the film and in the life of the family".[13] Decorum replaces wildness, catharsis shame.

Dancing at Lughnasa, the film, in this reading, may have retained enough of Friel's original to challenge preconceptions of rural Ireland in the 1930s at the level of plot, but as a work of cinema, taking into account mise-en-scène, use of landscape, camerawork and performance, it is flawed. It remains fundamentally impossible, once again, to separate the original from the copy. Here again, casting needs to be considered, particularly the switch from Frances Tomelty in the role of the eldest sister, Kate, in the stage version, to Meryl Streep in the film version. Undoubtedly, this decision was driven by the need to appeal to an international audience, in particular those who could not be counted on to view the film because of their familiarity with the play. However, it raises further questions around adaptation and address. It is common practice in cinema to cast international actors in national productions and reviews of the film in the US suggest that the critical reception was enhanced by Streep's performance. Overseas, the cultural capital that the film drew upon for promotional purposes (Friel's award-winning play, real Irish locations, even Bill Whelan's Riverdance-style score) was unaffected by the loss of the original performers. Yet, one has to question whether Streep's casting did not end up as a distraction, her performance rather than her character taking centre stage.

Overall, *Dancing at Lughnasa* tests the defensive arguments around adaptation. "Perhaps one way to think about unsuccessful adaptations", Hutcheon reminds us, "is not in terms of infidelity to a prior text, but in terms of a lack of the creativity and skill to make the text one's own and thus autonomous".[14] Yet, Pat O'Connor had previously directed one of the most influential adaptations of the 1980s, *The Ballroom of Romance* (1982), a film that defined rural isolation, prejudice and the failure of romance just as acutely as Friel's play. The difference was evidently not lack of creativity and skill but the demands of financing and of pitching to a global market. *The Ballroom of Romance*, adapted from the William Trevor short story, was fully funded by RTÉ and made as a television film. It made no concessions to the overseas market, and indeed, remains commercially unavailable to this day.

The Word and the Image

Writing on adaptations and Irish cinema, Kevin Rockett has warned that

> In a society anchored in the culture of the word (whether oral tradition or the obsession with James Joyce's texts) recourse to the image is often deemed an unfortunate by-product of cinema. With very few exceptions, the failure to imagine visually a play, novel or even original script remains the most serious limitation to the development of a dynamic Irish cinema.[15]

In his list of failed productions, Rockett includes *Saltwater* (2000), directed by Conor McPherson from his own play, and *Disco Pigs* (Kirsten Sheridan 2001) from the play by Enda Walsh.[16] While few would disagree about *Saltwater*, it is more difficult to dismiss *Disco Pigs*. Sheridan's debut feature retained the casting of Cillian Murphy as Pig, replacing Eileen Walsh with Elaine Cassidy as Runt. Enda Walsh wrote the screenplay, adding in new scenes to bring the film to feature length. The claustrophobic effect of keeping to the limited range of settings inherited from the stage play worked well on film, heightening the sense that it was their oppressive closeness as much as any particular failure of the social order that was imprisoning the teenagers. The original stage play was performed with just two plastic chairs as props. Only once in the early sequences of the film does the camera open up to a vista of the beach, a shot that just serves to isolate the two figures further. The scenes in the Donegal reform school, to which Runt is sent, are not just the furthest from the original but the least consistent with the tone of the play. On the other hand, the final sequence on the beach is a masterful undercutting of the conventional Irish cinematic trope of escape from the corrupted city to the freedom of the coast.

Writers on both play and film commonly drew comparisons between this production and *A Clockwork Orange* (Stanley Kubrick 1971). It is easy to see why they might have, given the acting out of unfettered violence and teen resentment in *Disco Pigs*, not to mention the play's use of a private language (somewhat toned down in the film).[17] That Walsh invited such a reading is also in no doubt, and the Corcadorca website refers to the play as "Corcadorca's *A Clockwork Orange*". This appropriation of cinematic language in Irish drama is something to which I will shortly return. For the moment, it is worth pointing out that Walsh's use of language and the very particular associations that come with *A Clockwork Orange* allowed him to position his play outside of the Irish theatrical tradition and to address his generation on their terms, that is, through shared enjoyment of one of the cult films of global youth and anti-establishment culture. In this case, in a reversal of the flow of cultural capital discussed above, Walsh drew on the associations that had accumulated to Kubrick's film to enhance his play.

These examples provide a brief sample of recent stage-to-screen adaptations and, I hope, highlight the cultural assumptions around origins, commercialism and globalization that have accompanied critical discussions of this process. The other notable cycle of adaptations is the *Beckett on Film* (various directors 2002) series, a project that saw a selection of high-profile film directors take on the Beckett oeuvre. Because of the restrictions placed on the adaptations, they add little to the argument, and the critical response to them has been mixed. As Nicholas Johnson has pointed out, the availability of these films on YouTube has awarded them a high level of visibility and the platform for them to function as educational tools and productions of record.[18,19] Yet filmed versions of stage plays of this nature remain niche products with limited address.

Before moving on from adaptations, it is worth noting that this is not just a case of one-way traffic. The winning of an Academy Award in 2008 for best song was part of the global success story that was *Once* (John Carney 2007). In 2012, a stage musical scripted by Enda Walsh followed, and that soon too became a hit, playing on Broadway, the West End and further afield while winning eight Tony awards. Reviewing the musical's opening in Dublin in 2015, Mick Heaney wondered how this globalized product might play locally: "[A] fter all, what is a charmingly earthy portrayal of Irish urban life, at least for international audiences, runs the risk of appearing twee or hackneyed in local eyes."[20] His conclusion, that *Once* was as much about Dublin as *West Side Story* was about 1950s New York, resolved the issue. However, reviews of the musical in other territories lauded it for its un-globalized effect, notably its simplicity of staging and its emotional reach: "Instead of the usual industrial spectacle what we get is a musical about people and life's missed opportunities."[21] This suggests that the adaptation cannily reproduced exactly those qualities that won the film its awards and audiences—an almost homespun, spontaneous quality that capitalized, as Neasa Hardiman has argued in her article "Once Won't Happen Twice", on its peripherality as an Irish musical.[22] In other words, *Once* (the film and the musical) successfully played to its local strengths, rather than attempting to displace them, in a globalized marketplace.

Professional Intersections

The movement of writers, directors and actors between theatre and film provides a subtext to the narrative of adaptation. As I mentioned at the opening of this chapter, in the most sustained attempt to found an Irish national cinema, it was to Irish theatre that those involved, notably Louis Elliman and Emmet Dalton, turned. In *Ireland's Theatre on Film*, Barry Monahan creates a history of early to mid-twentieth century Irish cinema through the key adaptations and adaptors. These run from Alfred Hitchcock's *Juno and the Paycock* (1930), to John Ford's employment of the Abbey actors in *The Plough and the Stars* (1936), through to the so-called Abbey films already listed above and others. As his study documents, these adaptations were also accompanied by a sense of loss—of the original stage play, of the early, ideologically driven years of the national theatre, of the stage actor to the screen, and further of the stage actor as emigrant to Hollywood.

Yet this sense of loss was not universal. While some of the Abbey actors found life in Hollywood as jobbing character actors intolerable and returned home, others, such as Barry Fitzgerald, were liberated by the opportunities (and pay cheques) with which emigration rewarded them. Monahan has further argued for understanding the Abbey actors' communality as representing an ideal of national communality. On film, this translated into a way not just of representing national identity through narrative but also physically embodying it in performance, notably in sequences such as the pub brawl in *The Plough and the Stars*, a production that, typically, saw Hollywood stars (Barbara Stanwyck and Preston Foster) in the leads and the Abbey actors in the secondary parts.

All this has radically changed. Now Irish actors occupy lead roles in Irish and in Hollywood films equally (at least if they are male), and Irish screenwriters and directors commute comfortably between Dublin and Los Angeles. Certain high-profile Irish actors—Stephen Rea, the Cusack sisters, Ciarán Hinds, Cillian Murphy—move easily between screen and stage, and in 2015 a revival of Enda Walsh's *The Walworth Farce* played at the Olympia Theatre to sell-out houses, not least because it featured lead performances from father and sons Brendan, Domhnall and Brian Gleeson.

For the purposes of this chapter, what is of interest is the movement between Irish stage and screen not just of actors, but also of directors and writers. Alan Gilsenan, John Crowley, Martin McDonagh, Conor McPherson, Mark O'Halloran, Mark O'Rowe and Gerard Stembridge have all alternated between high-profile stage and screen productions. One answer to the question of why they have done so is, probably, because they could. The Ireland of the twenty-first century has a strong enough indigenous film industry to offer opportunities for such individuals to take on film projects without having to commit to relocation and to allow them to work with the kind of local narratives (or, in O'Halloran and O'Rowe's cases, to write them) that they might just as readily have worked with on stage. The other reason is, most certainly, because they want to. No longer is Irish film Irish theatre's dependent child; it now offers modes of expression of its own that are tempting to practitioners seeking to extend their range. Both forms can now equally claim cultural capital, if not equal cultural capital, particularly in the wake of Academy Awards and other high-profile wins for Irish cinema.

Another reason for this professional mobility can be found by considering how many contemporary film and theatre makers met through university drama societies. For most of the generation now at the forefront of film and theatre production, going to an internationally recognized film school or drama academy meant studying in the United Kingdom or further afield. Instead, they threw themselves into student drama productions. For instance, Stephen Rea and Stewart Parker started working together at the Queen's University Drama Society; Garry Hynes, Mick Lally and Maire Mullen co-founded the Druid Theatre company in 1975 after meeting at NUI Galway's Dramsoc. Another member of Dramsoc in the mid-1970s was Sean McGinley, who appeared with Druid while still a student, and then moved on to a lengthy career in film and television. Just a couple of years earlier at UCD, Neil Jordan met Jim and Peter Sheridan through UCD's Dramsoc and the three of them went on to form the Children's T Company. Two decades later, Conor McPherson was to meet actor Peter McDonald at Dramsoc, and the two subsequently launched the theatre company Fly By Night. McDonald then appeared in Paddy Breathnach's road movie *I Went Down* (1997), scripted by McPherson. He acted in a BBC Radio 4 production of McPherson's play, *This Lime Tree Bower*, and was then cast in *Saltwater*, the screen adaptation of *This Lime Tree Bower*. While a student at Trinity, Lenny Abrahamson successfully applied for funding from the Visual and Performing Arts Fund to make a short film, *3 Joes* (1991), featuring three fellow student actors, Gary Cooke, Mikel Murfi and Dominic West, written by Michael West, produced by Ed Guiney and scored by Stephen Rennicks. Murfi and Michael West went on to full-time theatre careers, while Dominic West has been a household name on television screens since starring in *The Wire* (2002–2008). Ed Guiney co-founded

Ireland's most successful film production company, Element Pictures, with another Trinity graduate, Andrew Lowe, and has produced all of Abrahamson's features to date. Rennicks's compositions remain crucial to Abrahamson's films. John Crowley became involved in theatre as a student at University College Cork and has moved between film and theatre since then.

The professional trajectories of these individuals suggest that few of them drew sharp distinctions between a career in cinema and in stage. Not having to decide between film and theatre training enabled them to move unproblematically between both, creating strong links and networks between the two art forms. Now Ireland has a National Film School, founded out of the Institute of Art, Design and Technology in 2003, and the Lír Academy, a dedicated training academy for theatre modelled in part on RADA, which opened in 2011. While this may not suggest the end of career mobility or of student drama societies, it will certainly produce a new brand of professional, and it remains to be seen whether earlier specialization will affect actors' future career moves.

This exchange between the two artforms has certainly brought them closer. Thematically, there are many overlaps between the central concerns of Irish drama and cinema. These include a focus on often-traumatized masculinity, urban and peripheral identities, and social isolation, as well as a critique of materialism. Others have argued that technology has broken down the barriers between all these modes of performance to the extent that none of them may have any separate identity in the future.[23] However, for the time being distinctions remain, certainly on a common-sense basis, in so far as most audiences for the productions discussed here can identify whether they are attending a play, a musical or a film.

Textual Game-Playing

The listing of college drama society graduates in the film and theatre worlds is far from a complete roll-call of practitioners. Obvious omissions include Marie Jones, Martin McDonagh, Mark O'Halloran, Mark O'Rowe and Enda Walsh, some of whose intersections between theatre and cinema have already been mentioned. Of these, the latter four all write for both screen and stage, and McDonagh has directed one short film (*Six Shooter* 2004) and two feature films: *In Bruges* (2008) *Seven Psychopaths* (2012) and *Three Billboards Outside Ebbing, Missouri* (2017). In this final section, I want to consider the intersections between theatre and cinema in the works of these writer-practitioners and the purpose of their textual game-playing. To spell it out, Marie Jones' best-known stage play remains *Stones in His Pockets* (1996), set during the filming of a Hollywood production in a small Kerry community. In Martin McDonagh's *The Beauty Queen of Leenane*, first performed in the same year as *Stones in His Pockets*, the village's bored inhabitants pass their time watching Australian soaps. In his *The Cripple of Inishmaan*, first performed the following year, a disabled boy is inspired by the filming of *Man of Aran* (Robert Flaherty 1934) to try his luck as a screen actor. The failed suicide attempt in *Six Shooter* references Beckett's *Waiting for Godot* (1953). *In Bruges* is an homage to Harold Pinter's *The Dumb Waiter* (1957) and contains an homage to *Don't Look Now* (Nicolas Roeg 1973) within its diegesis. Mark O'Rowe's stage productions are consistently referred to as Tarantino-esque and his screenplay for *Intermission* (John Crowley 2003) draws inevitable comparisons with the output of Guy Ritchie, notably *Lock, Stock and Two Smoking Barrels* (1998). Quentin Tarantino is also a common reference point for McDonagh's writing. Thus, film, television and theatre interweave throughout these writer/directors' works, setting what were once separate art forms into a dynamic process of mutual engagement.

Patrick Lonergan's comment on *In Bruges*—"the movie is both dazzled by the location and sceptical about its commodification"[24]—might equally apply to *Stones In His Pockets*, where the commodification of place at first appears to be an opportunity for its inhabitants but finally destroys them.[25] In both Jones's play and McDonagh's *Cripple*, Hollywood film-making suggests opportunities that will prove deceptive. Although the film in *Stones* is a fictional production, it bears some resemblance to Ron Howard's much critiqued *Far and Away* of 1992, a star vehicle for Tom Cruise and Nicole Kidman in which a woman of privilege is rescued by the farmhand in a way that plays on Irish "big house" fantasies of a new dawn in democratic relationships. *The Quiet Valley*, the fictional production at the heart of *Stones*, is as likely to be dismissed by the local community as *Man of Aran* is by McDonagh's islanders. Yet, while both plays reject the emancipatory potential of film as a harbinger of modernity, both writers, but particularly McDonagh, revel in the liberation from traditional stage versions of Irish dialogue that the Tarantino model offers. The relentless deployment of profanity and violence in *Cripple* removes it from its 1930s setting and relocates it in a contemporary model of performativity and irony. In this sense it has much in common with *I Went Down* and *Intermission*. It and *Stones* also reflect the moment of their creation, right at the beginning of the Celtic Tiger period, when the commodification of Ireland was becoming increasingly visible and discussed.

These tonal shifts, also found in the work of Enda Walsh, can be explained by a process of remediation, that is, the practice of one art form borrowing from the other and refashioning it. In the case in point, Irish theatre's borrowing from global cinema has a double impact. Thematically, it allows it to comment on the impact of the global on Irish culture, while artistically it allows for a new generation of playwrights to break with the traditional language of Irish theatre. Simultaneously, the movement of writers, directors and actors between theatre and cinema has brought the two art forms much closer together than had previously been the case. Strategically, it brings in new, younger audiences for Irish theatre.

It would be comforting, and provide a neat symmetry, to conclude that Irish cinema could similarly benefit from borrowing or incorporating theatrical practices. That this can happen was demonstrated by the collaboration between Lenny Abrahamson and Mark O'Halloran on Abrahamson's first feature,

Adam and Paul (2004). The film at once references Beckett (two latter-day tramps looking for "what's-his-name"), James Joyce's *Ulysses* (a day traversing Dublin) and early cinema (in its presentational form and music track). It looks theatrical, can sound theatrical and yet is fully cinematic. However, *Adam and Paul* is an individual auteur work. The pressing challenge for Irish cinema concerns the widely acknowledged scarcity of strong scripts as much as the primacy of the word over the image. It is no coincidence that the two 2016 Academy Award contenders for Best Picture—*Room* (Lenny Abrahamson 2015) and *Brooklyn* (John Crowley 2015)—were adaptations of well-regarded novels and one may venture that this lent the two films, despite their manifold individual merits, cultural capital in the eyes of the voters. No one is suggesting that the solution is for Irish cinema to break from the literary/theatrical tradition. However, as the case of *Once* demonstrates, Irish cinema can fruitfully negotiate itself a place within international circuits of entertainment by engaging with the language of global cinema (in this case the musical), just as Irish theatre has done, without compromising its identity or its address to local audiences. Again, no one model fits all, nor do all Irish plays draw from the language of cinema for their impact. Yet there are lessons to be learnt from each other's experiences, and the continuing exchange of personnel between both cinema and theatre suggests that this will indeed happen.

Notes

1. For a useful survey of the discipline, see Elliott (2014).
2. Robert Stam, "Introduction: The Theory and Practice of Adaptation," in *Literature and Film: A Guide to the Theory and Practice of Film Adaptation*, eds. Robert Stam and Alessandra Raengo, 1–52 (Malden, MA; Oxford: Blackwell Publishing, 2005), 3.
3. Linda Hutcheon, with Siobhan O'Flynn, *A Theory of Adaptation*, 2nd ed. (London: Routledge, 2012), 36.
4. Pierre Bourdieu, "The Forms of Capital," in *Handbook of Theory and Research for the Sociology of Education*, ed. John Richardson, 241–258, New York: Greenwood, 1986).
5. Linda Hutcheon with Siobhan O'Flynn, *A Theory of Adaptation*, 2nd ed. (London, New York: Routledge, 2012), 30.
6. See Rockett (1994: 126–39).
7. Seán Ryder, "Modernity's Other: *The Quiet Man*, *The Field* and *The Commitments*," in *The Quiet Man ... And Beyond. Reflections on a Classic Film, John Ford and Ireland*, ed. Sean Crosson and Rod Stoneman, 42–57 (Dublin: The Liffey Press, 2009), 51.
8. Ruth Barton, *Jim Sheridan: Framing the Nation* (Dublin: The Liffey Press, 2002), 151.
9. Ibid., 153–4.
10. Joan Fitzpatrick Dean, *Dancing at Lughnasa* (Cork: Cork University Press, 2003), 86.
11. Joan FitzPatrick Dean, *Dancing at Lughnasa* (Cork: Cork University Press in association with The Film Institute of Ireland, 2003), 21.

12. Ibid., 2–3.
13. Ibid., 35.
14. Hutcheon with O'Flynn, *A Theory of Adaptation*, 20.
15. Kevin Rockett, "Cinema and Irish Literature," in *The Cambridge History of Irish Literature, volume 2*, eds. Margaret Kelleher & Philip O'Leary, 531–561 (Cambridge, New York, Melbourne etc.: Cambridge University Press, 2006), 545.
16. Ibid.
17. For an interesting discussion of the contrasting reception of the stage play as it travelled to overseas festivals and performances, see Knowles (2004, 195–200).
18. Nicholas Johnson, "'The Neatness of Identifications': Transgressing Beckett's Genres in Ireland and Northern Ireland, 2000–2015," in *Staging Beckett in Ireland and Northern Ireland*, eds. Trish McTighe and David Tucker (London: Bloomsbury, 2016).
19. For a discussion of the reception of the *Beckett on Film* productions, see Kennedy (2009: 55–74). For previous television adaptations of Beckett's work, see Bignell (2009).
20. Mick Heaney, "Once more with feeling in Dublin," *The Irish Times*, July 16, 2015: 13.
21. Michael Billington, "Once—review," *The Guardian*, April 9, 2013, http://www.theguardian.com/stage/2013/apr/09/once-review-michael-billington
22. Neasa Hardiman, "Once Won't Happen Twice": Peripherality and Equality as Strategies for Success in a Low-Budget Irish Film.' in *Contemporary Irish Film, New Perspectives on a National Cinema*, eds. Werner Huber and Seán Crosson (Braumüller: Vienna, 2011).
23. Matthew Causey, "The Screen Test of the Double: The Uncanny Performer in the Space of Technology," *Theatre Journal* 51(4) (1999): 383–394.
24. Patrick Lonergan, *The Theatre and Films of Martin McDonagh* (London: Methuen, 2012), 14.5.
25. For an analysis of both films as commentaries on authenticity, see McGonigle (2008: 153–166). On the theme of the commodification of Irishness in *Stones in His Pockets*, see Sweeney (2004: 16).

Bibliography

3 Joes. Directed by Lenny Abrahamson. Ireland, 1991. Film.

Adam and Paul. Directed by Lenny Abrahamson. Ireland: Element Films, Speers Films, 2004. Film.

The Ballroom of Romance. Directed by Pat O'Connor. Ireland: RTÉ, 1982. Film.

Barton, Ruth. Jim Sheridan: Framing the Nation. Dublin: The Liffey Press, 2002.

Bignell, Jonathan. *Beckett on Screen: The Television Plays*. Manchester: Manchester University Press, 2009.

Billington, Michael. "Once—Review". *The Guardian*, April 9, 2013. http://www.theguardian.com/stage/2013/apr/09/once-review-michael-billington

Bourdieu, Pierre. "The Forms of Capital," in *Handbook of Theory and Research for the Sociology of Education*, ed. John Richardson, 241–258. New York: Greenwood, 1986.

Brooklyn. Directed by John Crowley. Ireland/UK/Canada: Wildgaze Films, Parallel Film Productions, 2015. Film.

Broth of a Boy. Directed by George Pollock. Ireland: Emmet Dalton Productions, 1959. Film.

Causey, Matthew. "The Screen Test of the Double: The Uncanny Performer in the Space of Technology." *Theatre Journal* 51(4) (1999): 383–394.

———. "Postdigital Performance", *Theatre Journal* 68 (2016): 427–441.

A Clockwork Orange. Directed by Stanley Kubrick. UK/USA: Warner Bros., Hawk Films, 1971. Film.

Corcadorca. "Disco Pigs". Available online. Accessed January 10, 2016. http://www.corcadorca.com/website/previous-productions/disco-pigs

Dancing at Lughnasa. Directed by Pat O'Connor. Ireland/UK/USA: Capitol Films, Channel 4 Films, Ferndale Films, Sony Pictures Classics, 1998. Film.

Dean, Joan Fitz Patrick. *Dancing at Lughnasa*. Cork: Cork University Press in Association with The Film Institute of Ireland, 2003.

Disco Pigs. Directed by Kirsten Sheridan. Ireland: Temple Film Productions, 2001. Film.

Don't Look Now. Directed by Nicolas Roeg. UK/Italy: Casey Productions, Eldorado Films, 1973. Film.

Elliott, Kamilla. "Rethinking Formal-Cultural and Textual-Contextual Divides in Adaptation Studies." *Literature Film Quarterly* 42, 4 (2014): 576–593.

Far and Away. Directed by Ron Howard. USA: Imagine Films Entertainment, Universal Pictures, 1992. Film.

The Field. Directed by Jim Sheridan. Ireland: Granada Television, Noel Pearson, Sovereign Pictures, 1990. Film.

Heaney, Mick. "Once More with Feeling in Dublin". *The Irish Times*, July 16, 2015: 13.

Hutcheon, Linda with Siobhan O'Flynn. *A Theory of Adaptation*, 2nd ed. London, New York: Routledge, 2012.

In Bruges. Directed by Martin McDonagh. UK/USA: Blueprint Pictures, Focus Features, Scion Films, 2008. Film.

Intermission. Directed by John Crowley. Ireland/UK: BBC/Brown Sauce Film Productions, 2003. Film.

I Went Down. Directed by Paddy Breathnach. Ireland/UK/USA: BBC, Easkel Media, 1997. Film.

Johnson, Nicholas. " 'The Neatness of Identifications': Transgressing Beckett's Genres in Ireland and Northern Ireland, 2000–2015," in *Staging Beckett in Ireland and Northern Ireland*, eds. Trish McTighe and David Tucker. London: Bloomsbury, 2016.

Juno and the Paycock. Directed by Alfred Hitchcock. UK: British International Pictures, 1930. Film.

Kennedy, Séan. "Samuel Beckett's Reception in Ireland," in *The International Reception of Samuel Beckett*, eds. Mark Nixon & Matthew Feldman, 55–74. London: Continuum, 2009.

Knowles, Ric. *Reading the Material Theatre*. Cambridge: Cambridge University Press, 2004.

Lock, Stock and Two Smoking Barrels. Directed by Guy Ritchie. UK: Summit Entertainment, The Steve Tisch Company, SKA Films, 1998. Film.

Lonergan, Patrick. *The Theatre and Films of Martin McDonagh*. London: Methuen, 2012.

Man of Aran. Directed by Robert Flaherty. UK: Gainsborough Pictures, 1934. Film.

McGonigle, Lisa. "Keeping It Reel: Hollywood and Authenticity in Two Recent Irish Plays," in *What Rough Beasts? Irish and Scottish Studies in the New Millennium,* ed. Shane Alcobia-Murphy, 153–166. Newcastle: Cambridge Scholars Publishing, 2008.

Monahan, Barry. *Ireland's Theatre on Film: Style, Stories and the National Stage on Screen.* Dublin: Irish Academic Press, 2009.

My Left Foot. Directed by Jim Sheridan. Ireland/UK: Ferndale Films, Granada Television, RTÉ, 1989. Film.

Once. Directed by John Carney. Ireland: Samson Films, 2007. Film.

The Plough and the Stars. Directed by John Ford. USA: RKO Radio Pictures, 1936. Film.

Rockett, Kevin. "Cinema and Irish Literature," in The Cambridge History of Irish Literature, Volume 2, eds. Margaret Kelleher & Philip O'Leary, 531–561. Cambridge, New York, Melbourne etc.: Cambridge University Press, 2006.

———. "Culture, Industry and Irish Cinema," in *Border Crossing, Film in Ireland, Britain and Europe,* eds. John Hill, Martin McLoone, and Paul Hainsworth, 126–139. London and Belfast: The Institute of Irish Studies/British Film Institute, 1994.

Room. Directed by Lenny Abrahamson. Ireland/Canada/UK/USA: Element Pictures/Film Four/FilmNation Entertainment, 2015. Film.

Ryder, Seán. "Modernity's Other: *The Quiet Man, The Field* and *The Commitments,*" in *The Quiet Man ... And Beyond. Reflections on a Classic Film, John Ford and Ireland,* eds. Sean Crosson and Rod Stoneman, 42–57. Dublin: The Liffey Press, 2009.

Sally's Irish Rogue. Directed by George Pollock. UK: Emmet Dalton Productions, 1958. Film.

Saltwater. Directed by Conor McPherson. Ireland: Alta Films, BBC Films, Treasure Films, 2000. Film.

Seven Psychopaths. Directed by Martin McDonagh. UK: CBS Films, Film Four, BFI, 2012. Film.

Six Shooter. Directed by Martin McDonagh. UK/Ireland: Missing in Action Films, Funny Farm Films, 2004. Film.

Stam, Robert. "Introduction: The Theory and Practice of Adaptation," in *Literature and Film: A Guide to the Theory and Practice of Film Adaptation,* eds. Robert Stam and Alessandra Raengo, 1–52. Malden, MA; Oxford Blackwell Publishing, 2005.

Sweeney, Bernadette. "Form and Comedy in Contemporary Irish Theatre," in *The Power of Laughter: Comedy and Contemporary Irish Theatre,* ed. Eric Weitz, 8–19. Dublin: Carysfort Press, 2004.

The Quiet Man. Directed by John Ford. USA: Republic Pictures, 1952. Film.

This Other Eden. Directed by Muriel Box. Ireland: Emmet Dalton Productions, 1959. Film.

This Sporting Life. Directed by Lindsay Anderson. UK: Independent Artists, Julian Wintle/Lesley Parkin Productions, 1963. Film.

Three Billboards Outside Ebbing, Missouri. Directed by Martin McDonagh. UK/USA: Blueprint Pictures/Film4/Fox Searchlight Pictures, 2017. Film.

West Side Story. Directed by Jerome Robbins, Robert Wise. USA: Mirisch Corporation, Seven Arts Pictures, Beta Productions, 1963. Film.

The Wire. HBO, 2002–2008. TV Programme.

Actor Training in Ireland Since 1965

Rhona Trench

This chapter examines actor training in Ireland over the past half-century. The task is difficult because of the incomplete and sometimes unreliable nature of the information available, but this study seeks to explore the kinds of training opportunities on offer, the mission statements of those training programmes, the course content and (where possible) the delivery methods of actor training. Added to this are the challenges involved in the diversified nature of theatre, the multiple approaches to actor training, the extent to which the repertoire of acting techniques is acquired and how these contribute to the industry-ready actor. There is difficulty with the word "training" itself and there are problems in examining the weighting given to the theoretical and the practical nature of acting; there is also a complete lack of published research on the area of actor training in Ireland.

Actor training programmes attract a wide spectrum of people from different professional and cultural backgrounds, including school leavers, artists (painters, sculptors and musicians for example), tradespeople, healthcare and other professionals, and working actors (seeking to widen and/or formalize their training).

I will offer key examples of training (with)in organizations in Ireland dedicated to actor training: institutions that have impacted greatly on theatre and performance in Ireland. A selection of interviews were carried out from practitioners working in third level institutions and/or theatre companies which offered insights into the current actor training situation.

R. Trench (✉)
Institute of Technology, Sligo, Ireland
e-mail: trench.rhona@itsligo.ie

E. Jordan, E. Weitz (eds.), *The Palgrave Handbook of Contemporary Irish Theatre and Performance*,
https://doi.org/10.1057/978-1-137-58588-2_23

Early Practices

In the 1960s, the lack of comprehensive professional acting training was evident.[1] People interested in the field might have come upon a small advertisement in the *Irish Times* for auditions for the Abbey Players; if they wished to respond, they simply arrived at the designated venue, auditioned, and if successful, they were accepted into the Abbey School of Acting. In the school they learned by observation and imitation from experienced actors. The School also provided evening classes for those who needed to earn a living during the day.[2]

In 1967, Frank Dermody revived the Abbey School of Acting. Its resources were limited, but included the likes of Joe Dowling, Veronica (Ronnie) Masterson, Ray McAnally, Stephen Rea, John Olohan and John Kavanagh. Teachers in the Abbey School were usually members of the company who were not working in a show for a particular duration, but who would take up acting roles at any point when the opportunity arose. Additionally, trainees were often called on to fill group scenes in plays at the Abbey and Peacock. However, in 1969, intervention by the Actors' Equity Association brought about changes regarding unpaid work for actors, and was one of the factors that led to the end of the School's apprenticeship-based learning approach in 1970. Following the closure, free workshops in voice, movement, improvisation and speech were offered by the Abbey to professional actors and former Abbey students, but by 1974 these activities could not continue because of cutbacks in spending.[3]

There were also part-time private courses in Dublin with an ad hoc, "on-the-job" approach to acting, such as the Brendan Smith Academy of Acting, founded in the 1960s, which was associated with theatre artists including Deirdre Donnelly, Owen Roe, Saoirse Bodley, Pauline Delaney and Pearse McCaughey; and the Irish Institute of Drama and the Allied Arts, founded in 1978, which offered courses in Dublin and weekend workshops in regional centres. In addition, the Oscar Theatre School, which ran in Dublin in the 1980s, had associations with performers like Alan Stanford, Kevin McHugh, Vincent O'Neill, Chloe Gibson, Liam Cunningham, Eugene O'Brien and Mary McEvoy, many of whom went on to establish sustainable careers in the industry. Acting in those schools was taught through individual tuition and group exercises.

The Focus

In 1963, Deirdre O'Connell, who attended the Stanislavski-based Actors' Studio in New York and studied with Lee Strasberg, took her vision to Dublin and opened an acting studio, which was to become the Stanislavski Acting Studio and Focus Theatre. Because of the influence of Stanislavski, the many interpretations of his system, the longevity of the Stanislavski school, and the legacy it left in Ireland, it is worth exploring the history of this theatre in further detail.

In 1967, O'Connell's collaborator Declan Burke-Kennedy finally found a small but permanent venue on Pembroke Place. The Stanislavski Acting Studio and Focus theatre was established there by O'Connell (from hereon in referred to as the Focus), Declan and Mary Elizabeth Burke-Kennedy, and Dick Callanan, and remained open until 2012.[4] In its first year it received a grant of IR£500 from the Arts Council to pay for publicity and production losses. Financial constraints prevented the company from paying the actors Equity rates, however, which impacted on the company's ability to transfer its shows to Equity theatres; an indication of the difficulties of sustaining a professional acting career.

In its forty years, however, the Focus staged over 250 productions: it trained and had associations with many actors and directors in Ireland, including Olwen Fouéré, Tom Hickey, Donal O'Kelly, Gabriel Byrne, Johnny Murphy, Gerard McSorley, Joan Bergin and Bosco Hogan. It also brought the work of international writers to Ireland, presenting plays not commonly performed in the country. In addition, it gave a platform to new work by writers such as Mary Elizabeth Burke-Kennedy, Michael Harding, Ena May and Barry McKinley.

For the Focus, reflecting its Stanislavski-based moorings, "[t]he philosophy of the studio was to emphasise the creative role of the actor while at the same time insisting on group or ensemble teamwork as the essence of good theatre".[5] The atmosphere of the ensemble works against competition, so that everyone in the training room understands that they share in the embodiment of the dramatic narrative. Smaller roles are as valued as larger ones, with each seen as offering a significant contribution to the overall performance.

The Stanislavski-based system of training, as used at the Focus Theatre's studio, draws upon an array of techniques rather than adhering to a rigid method. Each actor develops the skills necessary to inhabit the inner life of a character. The actor works on accessing emotional memories and sense memories, focusing on physical actions, motivations and objectives.

In 1971, improvisation-based performances at the Focus were held for the public on Sunday nights, with the audience sometimes proposing the issues presented. While those types of performances stopped in the 1970s—though they were briefly revived in the 1990s—they remained a significant part of the Stanislavski Studio's training practice throughout its existence.

As late as the 1980s, actor training in Ireland was a relatively small and specialized venture outside of formal institutions. These days training courses are run by organizations and theatre companies around the country for professional actors who want to retain a competitive edge, as well as for those who want to acquire new skills that might be needed for specific roles.

Company-Linked Training

Ireland produced many theatre companies during the 1990s, including Smashing Times (founded in 1991), Blue Raincoat (1991), Barabbas (1993), Corn Exchange (1995) and Loose Canon (1996), to name a few, and these provided specific kinds of training and development related to each company's vision. Those companies offering training to professional actors maintain the idea that actors should never stop training and should continue to evolve their techniques throughout their careers. For example, since 2011, every January, Blue Raincoat Theatre Academy in Sligo offers professional actors classes in the Étienne Decroux movement style and the Roy Hart voice technique.

Loose Canon, a company that worked with over seventy actors in its lifetime, was founded by Jason Byrne and Willie White, and "maintained a laboratory approach to its work".[6] From 2000 the company practiced physical and vocal training and improvisation every day until it wound down in 2014. That unrehearsed, spontaneous sense of a physical and vocal response to an aspect of a text or an idea was what Byrne wanted to retain. He then merged that sense of spontaneity back into the actual text the company was working on. Company performers were also mentored and guided by various international practitioners, including Eugenio Barba and his original students from the Odin Teatret, Kai Bredholt and Tage Larsen. Odin Teatret's training in movement and voice urged its actors to bring their training into their everyday lives, taking full responsibility for their own discipline.

Loose Canon was associated with productions of Elizabethan and Jacobean texts. Influenced by the training of Stanislavski, Jerzy Grotowski and Antonin Artaud, the company took ideas from each of those practitioners and adapted them according to the needs of its productions. The company wanted its performers to rely on acting skills before what it deemed were the externals, such as set, props and costume. It also sought to dissolve the fourth wall, so that no distinction was made between performers and audience. As the ensemble of actors became familiar with each other's work and process in the course of working together over a long period (sometimes up to a year on a performance), they also became more fluid in how they worked on the different projects they took on. Some actors who have worked with Loose Canon and who continue to work in the field include Lesley Conroy, Mark D'Aughton, Deirdre Roycroft, Karl Quinn, Bryan Boroughs and Kevin Hely.

Vocational Training

In today's conservatory-style programmes, trainee actors generally commit long hours to their timetables. Classes usually begin from 8:30 a.m. or 9:00 a.m. and run to 6:00 p.m., five days a week, with some evenings and weekends spent building and practising the skills learned in class and preparing for the coursework ahead. The majority of the actor training programmes included in this chapter engage with different theories and current interpretations of practical training, including the work of Stanislavski, Bertolt Brecht, Antonin Artaud, Jerzy Grotowski, Michael Chekhov, Jacques LeCoq and Étienne Decroux.

Founded in 1986 by Joe Dowling, the Gaiety School of Acting, The National Theatre School of Ireland, is a private school under the directorship of Patrick Sutton, and located in Dublin. When it started it provided a one-year, full-time course, eventually expanding to two years. The school emerged "as a response to the lack of actor training in Ireland at that time".[7] The Gaiety, then and now, views its responsibility as directly vocational, the word "vocation" suggesting that the actor aspires to a professional career in acting. It offers an intensive full-time, two-year programme, including training for stage, television and film. It offers comprehensive training without a specific academic accreditation.

Some of the modules currently taught in the Gaiety include Shakespeare and Stanislavski delivered by Liam Halligan, who trained at the Focus Theatre; the Chekhov technique taught by Paul Brennan; and the Theatre of Clown convened by Raymond Keane. Other modules teach Anne Bogart's Viewpoints approach, acting for camera, as well as modules in movement, voice and professional development. A pivotal module for the Gaiety is one called Manifesto, in which students devise and present their own work. Its former students include Colin Farrell, Olivia Wilde, Aidan Turner, Eva Birthistle, Sarah Greene and Colin O'Donoghue.

The Lír, National Academy of Dramatic Art, which opened in 2011, is still relatively young in institutional terms. Also located in Dublin, it offers a full-time, three-year, conservatory-style actor training programme which leads to a BA (Hons) in Acting, under the direction of Loughlin Deegan and validated by Trinity College Dublin. Its programme is developed in association with the Royal Academy of Dramatic Art (RADA) in London and Trinity College Dublin and was established "as a result of a recognised need for an academy of excellence within the island of Ireland".[8] The programme focuses on four key areas—acting technique, voice, movement and singing—whilst other classes in dramaturgy and text analysis complement the learning. Hilary Wood is the Head of Acting at the Lír and has worked with various institutions over a long career. Tutors Sue Mythen (movement) and Cathal Quinn (voice) are graduates of the Central School of Speech and Drama in London; many other theatre professionals are on the teaching staff, including playwright Gavin Kostick, director David Horan, actor Brian Burroughs and playwright/actor/director Paul Meade, each of whom has been associated with prominent theatre companies.

Other Third-Level Programmes

Actor training within academic contexts may have taken root in other countries long before, but in Ireland it began in 1987 with a two-year acting course at Trinity College Dublin, funded by the government as a third-level institution. Eventually, Trinity came to offer both a B.A. in Acting Studies (BAS), a three-year, Level 7 degree, which took in its last full cohort of students in 2006 and ended day-to-day operations at the end of the 2008–2009 academic year[9]; and a four-year B.A. (Hons) in Drama and Theatre Studies, an academically anchored programme that offers modules in all practical areas of theatre as a foundation for further work, study and/or training.

It should be noted that a number of third-level courses with strong practical components have emerged since the 1990s, based in Dublin, Galway, Sligo, Cork and Dundalk.[10] Most courses look to limit their intake to some degree, due to the specialized nature of the training, which favours smaller groups and which also enables one-to-one tuition. Admissions policies incorporate a range of combinations on an axis of academic grades and auditions.[11]

All of the courses have physical resources, with at the very least a "black box" type space and one other studio. Facilities in many of the institutions are being extended or upgraded (NUIG/IT Sligo), with a number of the courses operating in purpose-built accommodation (Lír/Gaiety). Most of the courses have associations with professional theatres and festivals and have specialists and/or adjunct professors connected with their programmes, which helps to raise the profile of the course. NUIG has partnerships with Druid, An Taibhdhearc and Decadent Theatre; UCD with Fishamble Theatre Company; IT Sligo with Blue Raincoat, the Hawk's Well Theatre and the Model[12]; DIT with the Project Arts Centre and the Mill in Dundrum; Bray with the Mermaid Arts Centre; and UCC with Corcadorca, the Cork Opera House and Everyman Theatre. Additionally, some have connections with adjunct professors, such as UCD's Sinead Cusack, Conor McPherson and Patrick Mason. This enables trainees to gain an insight into the working world of the industry across the broader area of performance.

It is through these links with the theatre sector that many programmes thrive. DIT's B.A. in Drama (Performance) is a case in point. Mary Moynihan comes from the Focus Theatre, having trained there for two years from 1990 to 1992; the legacy of Deirdre O'Connell's work in the 1960s continues with her. Following her training, she worked with the Focus as a professional actor and then as an associative artist and director from 2005 to 2014. In 2004, she took up a post in DIT, teaching acting, movement, drama facilitation and ensemble production. She continues to move between that work and her work in industry with Smashing Times Theatre Company.

Moynihan's approach to training stems from her own training under the Stanislavski system, but she also draws on the work of Michael Chekhov, Yoshi Oida, David Zinder and Viola Spolin. The work is about training the actor's body and voice and developing the actor before coming to a text. The aim "is for the actor to develop the creative skills through the senses which are necessary to recreate the conditions conducive to a creative state. The work includes the creative exploration of relaxation, imagination, sense memory, centres of energy and power, psychological gestures and improvisation work".[13]

The second example comes from the Institute of Technology Sligo, where Declan Drohan teaches on the B.A. in Performing Arts (Acting). Drohan trained as an actor at the Gaiety School of Acting, worked in the industry, then took a Masters in Drama, before going on to teach at DIT prior to his move to Sligo. Drohan is eclectic in his approach, so that students get to choose a style that suits them and the needs of the performance. He has a "body-centric idea central to his work, which seeks to make actors confident in their physicality, possessing an array of expressive possibility using the body while being content to be looked at".[14] Drohan draws on influences including (but not exclusively) Eugenio Barba, Tadeusz Kantor, Peter Brook and Michael Chekhov, and tends towards plays that are non-naturalistic in style, which arguably suit the work of those theorists. Barba was a former student of Jerzy Grotowski, who brought aspects of Eastern and Western performance styles together to the point where the performers negotiate stability and coherence, producing a contingency of meaning. Barba insists on the importance of choreographed physical and vocal scores and frees the actors to use improvisation in the rehearsal process. Peter Brook, a renowned theatre director who was influenced by Grotowski and Antonin Artaud, spent his life questioning the actor in the empty space as the founding principle of his theatre.[15]

A final example is Kellie Hughes, who is UCD's director in residence and the artistic director of the Ad Astra Academy, which offers talented students, regardless of their chosen degree, the opportunity to develop their artistic ambitions while in university. Hughes comes from a classical movement-trained background in Étienne Decroux's dramatic corporeal mime, which strives to develop the expressive potential of the body and place the actor at the centre of the creative process.[16] Until 2011 Hughes worked with Blue Raincoat Theatre Company in Sligo, a company which continues to use that training in its performances. Hughes is, of course, influenced by her own practices and experiences, privileging those movement techniques in her teaching within the context of UCD. This means that the UCD courses address the challenges of academic demands as well as the demands of the profession.

Those consulted during the interviews for this research practice as the dominant mode of learning, with intellectual engagement considered to be important if it is approached experientially first. This involves critical thinking about "ideas", "reflectiveness" and "problem-solving". Personal development and confidence are also considered an important part of the training process, and this works well on an individual basis where students who might need more physical or emotional training can receive tailor-made approaches to their specific needs.

Today's graduate of such academic institutions is expected to have an overall grasp and understanding of the components of theatre, so that they can work effectively as part of a team with an appreciation of the role of the other team members. Generally, the graduate of acting learns that the whole is greater than the sum of the parts and in most cases, the production is more important than the individual. Outside the rigorous comprehensive training for actors, which characteristically seeks to develop a variety of acting styles, improve vocal range, access the spectrum of emotional memory, analyse character, and enable students to become proficient in movement (e.g. mime and dance), be physically agile, learn accents and (in some courses) sing, trainees will obtain a broad programme of education. Along with learning about audition techniques and preparing for interviews, they also learn how to find collaborators, how to apply for funding, where to find funding opportunities, how to compile a CV and how to consider the challenges that might be encountered in their chosen career.

All of these skills are transferrable to other areas of life and necessarily include (but are not limited to) critical thinking, problem solving, communication skills, time management, interpersonal skills, leadership skills and organizational skills. Today, it is expected that the graduate of most actor training programmes in Ireland is capable of undertaking work in other spheres of employment or is positioned for further training. A high proportion of acting modules within third-level institutions have adapted to include an ongoing assessment approach, rather than relying solely upon the conventional, summative grading typical of third-level education. Ideally, the ambition is that the trained actor reaches their own potential, including a high level of physical and emotional intelligence.

Conclusion

Actor training in Ireland has come a long way since the Abbey Players, O'Connell's Stanislavski Studio and the short-lived acting academies that emerged in the 1970s. Despite their closure they still impacted greatly on acting and paved the way for future programmes by underlining the importance of actor training and the profession. The 1990s witnessed a consolidated number of third-level actor training courses. However, the Lír and the Gaiety are the only dedicated schools of acting in Ireland today, with the other courses offering acting classes and other support areas of practice and theory as part of a wider BA degree.

There is no one approach to training actors, any more than there is one kind of performance to work within. Student actors tend to be taught by current or former practitioners. There is no instruction manual for actor training because there is no single definitive interpretation of a method that works for all students, especially as the demands on the actor have expanded and varied in the age of post-modern, immersive, physical and devised theatre, as well as acting for camera.[17]

The overall intention is that trainees should learn that they are becoming members of the arts community, and that position comes with a responsibility that includes contributing to and embracing that community wholeheartedly, respectfully and diligently.

Notes

1. In Ireland, the concept of actor training co-existed with a vibrant amateur drama movement throughout the 1940s and the launch of the All Ireland Drama Festival in Athlone in 1953 brought matters to another level of dedication and expectation.
2. See Hugh Hunt, *The Abbey: Ireland's National Theatre 1904–1979* (Dublin: Gill and Macmillan, 1979), 235–238.
3. Ibid., 236.
4. See Mary Moynihan's insightful essay on the work of Focus Theatre in "Loving the Art in Yourself," in *Stanislavski in Ireland: Focus at 40*, eds. Steven Burch and Brian McAvera (Dublin. Carysfort Press, 2014).
5. Ibid., 8/9.
6. Interview with Jason Byrne, May 2016.
7. The mission of the school is "to provide excellence in the education and training of actors, delivering a comprehensive programme of study that nurtures the

physical, vocal, creative and intellectual development of each student". See www.gaeityschool.com (accessed 17/6/2017).

8. www.thelir.ie
9. The Irish National Framework of Qualifications (NFQ) offers measures to set out the level of qualification. Levels 5–9 are the only consideration here, Level 5 being a Leaving Certificate equivalent standard with Level 6 being Advanced and Higher Certification levels, Level 7 Ordinary Degree norms, and Level 8 matching international standards of depth and complexity for Honours degree programmes. Level 9 is a Masters standard qualification. See Irish National Framework Of Qualifications, http://www.nfq-qqi.com/ (accessed 18/6/2017).
10. In the Lír Academy, the B.A. in Acting runs for three years, and is dedicated solely to actor training as a vocation. The Lír also offers a Level 7 Foundation Diploma in Acting which runs for twenty-four weeks beginning in mid-September and ending in mid-April, and suggests that this one year might also help those students gain entry to its Level 8 degree.

    Additionally, NUIG (B.A. with Performing Arts Studies and B.A. in Drama, Theatre and Performance), UCC (Drama and Theatre Studies), IT Sligo (B.A. in Performing Arts) and Cork IT (Theatre and Drama Studies) offer undergraduate four-year Level 8 degree programmes of which actor training is a part; UCD (B.A. in English with Drama) and DIT Conservatory of Music & Drama (B.A. in Drama (Performance)) offers a three-year Level 8 degree, the latter of which also includes considerable practice in the programme.
11. Depending on the popularity and entry requirements of a programme, a select number of courses hold auditions on top of requiring particular scores in the Leaving Certificate exam; others have audition only (the Lír); and some have no audition but require a target number of points in the Leaving Certificate.
12. IT Sligo's Theatre Design strand is partnered with the Abbey and benefits actors, who get backstage tours and updates on relevant workshops.
13. (Interview with Moynihan, May 2016).
14. Drohan in an interview with the author, April 2016.
15. Agnes Pallai, the other IT Sligo acting teacher, comes with twenty-five years of experience of working in the conservatoire system in Hungary, which was solely Stanislavski-based and which is the central focus of her teaching. Marketa Formanova teaches the fundamentals of movement principles and a variety of dance methods in the field of performing arts. She engages with theories and methods from Rudolf Van Laban, Isadora Duncan and Jóse Limón.

    Influenced by Frankie Armstrong, Chloe Goodchild and Jasmin Martorelle, voice is taught by Bernie Meehan, whose work explores articulation, sound, rhythm, pitch, vocal anatomy and physiology, and breath work. IT Sligo training also benefits from inputs from Blue Raincoat actor Cíarán McCauley, and other current and former members of that troupe.
16. See Anne Dennis, "Étienne Decroux—An Actor, A Teacher of Actors; An Actor's Director," *Mime Journal*, Pomona College Theatre, Claremont Colleges, California, 1993/1994.
17. In 2015, Dundalk IT re-focused its three-year Level 7 degree in 2015 from a B.A. in Performing Arts to a B.A. in Theatre and Film Practice, to include acting for screen as part of the programme. The Gaiety too lists "Acting for Film and TV" as one of the options on its website. Bray Institute of Further Education

(BIFE) offers a Level 6 National Diploma award in Advanced Acting for Stage and Screen with the possibility of progressing to the final year of the B.A. degree in Performing Arts—Performance Theatre at the University of Swansea.

Bibliography

Arts Council. "Supporting the Production and Presentation of Theatre: A New Approach." Accessed August 6, 2010. http://www.artscouncil.ie

Bell, Lian. 2015. *An Overview of the Performing Arts Scene in Ireland*. IETM—International Network for Contemporary Performing Arts. 2015. Accessed September 9, 2016. https://www.ietm.org/sites/default/files/ireland-mapping_may2015.pdf

Cohen, Robert. *Acting Professionally*. California: Mayfield, 1998.

Chekhov, Michael. *To the Actor*. New York: Harper and Row, 1953.

Dennis, Anne. "Étienne Decroux—An Actor, A Teacher of Actors. An Actor's Director." *Mime Journal*. Pomona College Theatre, Claremont Colleges, California, 1993/1994

Hunt, Hugh. *The Abbey: Ireland's National Theatre 1904–1979*. Dublin: Gill and Macmillan, 1979.

Moynihan, Mary. "Loving the Art in Yourself." In *Stanislavski in Ireland: Focus at 40*. Edited by Steven Burch and Brian McAvera. Dublin. Carysfort Press, 2014.

Rideout, Nigel. *First Steps Towards an Acting Career*. London: A & C Black, 1995.

Stanford, Alan. *Arts in the Community: Presentations, Dublin*. Joint Committee on the Arts, Sport, Tourism, Community, Rural and the Gaeltacht, 2007.

Interviews

White, Willie. Artistic Director of the Dublin Theatre Festival. Interview with the author. April 2016.

Hughes, Kellie. Freelance director and actor. Interview with the author. March 2016.

Byrne, Jason. Interview with the author. May 2016.

Moynihan, Mary. DIT. Interview with the author. May 2016.

Drohan, Declan. IT Sligo. Interview with the author. April 2016.

Pete McDermott. DIT. Interview with the author. May 2016.

Website

www.irishplayography.com

Irish Theatre: A Designer's Theatre

Siobhán O'Gorman

Introduction

Reflecting on twentieth-century Irish theatre, questions of how and to what extent it might be considered "a designer's theatre" are complex ones. The contribution of design has certainly been obscured by the cultural and academic prominence of Irish theatre's literary traditions. Yet stage sets were central to the Irish Literary Theatre's efforts to conjure a distinctively Irish authenticity, for example with the placing of Douglas Hyde's *Casadh an tSúgáin* (1901) entirely within the one-room, domestic space of the rural peasant class. Following this, similar box sets portraying cottage interiors were regularly reused at the Abbey, both to depict the peasant settings prevalent in Irish drama and "with a minimum of adaptation to make up the one room on view in O'Casey's first two tenement plays".[1] Seaghan Barlow oversaw "the customary rearrangement of "basic" scenic elements" at the Abbey from 1911 until 1949[2]; by the mid-twentieth century the cottage kitchen set was "embarrassingly ubiquitous".[3] Yet the iconic nature of those stage images also reveals the extent to which design—however repetitious and recycled—helped to construct Ireland as lived on the stage. Indeed, those "designs" (which were not always envisioned by what we might conceive of today as professional theatre designers) were made iconic to a large extent through those very processes of repetition and recycling.

The establishment of icons also prompts iconoclastic approaches. Alongside the Abbey's scenographic renditions of cultural nationalism, approaches to design that drew on international trends also proliferated—for example Yeats commissioned a set of screens from Edward Gordon Craig, as well as collaborating with English visual artists including Charles Ricketts and Edmund Dulac

S. O'Gorman (✉)
University of Lincoln, Lincoln, UK

E. Jordan, E. Weitz (eds.), *The Palgrave Handbook of Contemporary Irish Theatre and Performance*,
https://doi.org/10.1057/978-1-137-58588-2_24

in the early twentieth century. During the 1920s, as Elaine Sisson discusses, the Peacock and the Gate experimented with design practices associated with German expressionism.[4] The Gate continued regularly to employ expressionist approaches, especially through the interplay of lighting effects on suggestively painted backcloths: Micheál MacLiammóir was a skilled draughtsperson, costume designer and scenic painter, and his artistic partnership at the Gate with director Hilton Edwards—a proponent of inventive stagecraft and lighting—made their company something of a designer's theatre.[5] In the 1960s, plans for a new Abbey Theatre (the original building had burnt down in 1951) signalled possibilities for change in design practices. Robin Walker designed a theatre that encompassed two back to back stages separated by a removable screen.[6] Had this been executed, it might have fostered more diverse design practices departing from those based on the dominant proscenium arch stage. Ernest Blythe, who was managing director of the Abbey Company from 1941 to 1967, opted for a more cost-effective plan by Michael Scott and Ronald Tallon. Still, the 1966 Abbey is a modernist cube, architecturally innovative for its time. Although the stage has a proscenium arch and fanned seating drawing the audience's attention in the direction of a facing stage, its spaciousness and technologies—such as flies, lifts and an extendable forestage— opened possibilities for more dynamic design offerings.[7] Moreover, following the opening of a new national theatre, a number of designers who had received specialist training in England joined the Abbey's team—including Bronwen Casson, Wendy Shea and Frank Conway—bringing with them new approaches to design.

Conway and Casson both trained under the innovative design team, Motley, at Sadler's Wells in London. There, designers were positioned as key collaborators in the theatre-making process. Conway went on to work on Druid's momentous productions of Tom Murphy's *Bailegangaire* and *Conversations on a Homecoming* in 1985. When Druid's founding director Garry Hynes took on artistic directorship of the Abbey in 1991, Conway worked that year with her on an inventively stark production of *The Plough and the Stars* and, in 1993, he collaborated with Hynes and actor Fiona Shaw on *The Hamlet Project*, a collaborative devising initiative characterised by a lack of hierarchy: "just the democracy of intense hard work, imagination and play".[8] These experiences, which authorised (rather than subordinated) the designer's contribution, may have aided Conway's confidence to offer such an iconoclastic design for Gary Duggan's *Shibari* in 2012, in which an upended traditional Irish kitchen hung over the stage throughout the duration of the actors' performances. As Ian Walsh points out regarding this production, Conway "literally turned the old design of the Abbey on its head".[9]

From the opening of the new Abbey theatre through to the 1980s, however—despite some inventive contributions by Casson and Shea (for example Casson's design for *The Sanctuary Lamp* in 1975 and Shea's design for *Waiting for Godot* in 1976)—more static approaches depicting Irish iconography endured. In 1964, the Abbey had hired Brian Collins as its resident designer;

he maintained standards in scenic painting there throughout 1960s and 1970s.[10] Scenographer Christopher Baugh, who contributed to the design of several Abbey productions from the late 1960s to the late 1970s, notes that cottage kitchens as well as painted backcloths depicting pseudo-impressionistic architecture or Connemara landscapes still seemed to prevail during the period in which he worked at Ireland's national theatre.[11] The longevity of practices—such as large-scale scenic painting, recycling stock materials and reproducing archetypal imagery—obscures advances in exploring further the imaginative, dynamic and sculptural possibilities of design in Irish theatre, in addition to the role of scenography in theatre-making processes and the roles of designers in collaboratively co-authoring productions. Departing from several existing published considerations of design in Irish theatre that have tended to examine the role of designers via work by particular directors or writers (often reinforcing the conventional positioning of designers as subservient to writers and directors),[12] this chapter seeks to foreground the specific contributions of designers. In addition, it seeks to trace genealogies of the designer's increasingly co-authorial input in contemporary Irish theatre practice. In order to offer depth as well as breadth, and to trace the genealogies of contemporary practice, I will home in on the work of two designers, focussing in particular on their activities during the 1980s: Bronwen Casson and Monica Frawley.

Scenography, Dramaturgy and Theatre-Making

Collaboration is paramount to the theatre designer's process, as Conway argues in his insightful essay, "The Sound of One Hand Clapping;" however, as he also points out, the specific role of theatre designers—who, he suggests, should be designated more aptly as "scenographers"—continues in the discourses of Irish theatre to be "undervalued, undermined even, a casualty of an outdated, unchallenged nineteenth-century perception [of 'doing the backgrounds' rather than theatre-making][13] that is still pervasive in the industry".[14] Conway's essay locates his own practice as a designer—with particular reference to his role in the Abbey's 2002 production of Marina Carr's *Ariel* (directed by Conall Morrison)—within wider histories and theories of scenography. A discussion of his process as a designer in an interview with John Kavanagh was published in 2001. In 2004, designer Joe Vaněk made a key contribution to the historiography of Irish scenography by designing the exhibition *Scene Change—100 Years of Theatre Design at the Abbey* for the Irish Museum of Modern Art to commemorate the centenary of Ireland's national theatre. Vaněk more recently has published *Irish Theatrescapes*, which provides visual documentation and textual accounts of his stage designs between 1984 and 2012, offering an alternative entry into Irish theatre history during that period.[15] Vaněk and Conway have gone some way toward documenting and exploring their own design practices within published works. The two main sections of this chapter seek to build on those important publications by focussing mainly on the work of Casson and Frawley. Select works by these artists offer illuminating case-studies on the increasing authority and generative contribution of designers in Irish theatre-making processes, which is central to the modernisation of design in Irish theatre.

The modernisation of design in Irish theatre can be linked to progressive movements towards Baugh's conception of "scenography as dramaturgy of performance", a phrase that forms the title of the final chapter in the second edition of his seminal monograph *Theatre, Performance and Technology* (2013). Baugh associates this concept with contemporary "post-dramatic culture[s] of performance"[16] in which "scenography is no longer primarily the servant of dramatic performance; it has floated free and may create from within its own practices and research".[17] In contemporary Ireland, such approaches are epitomised in the work of companies that centralise the collaborative work of designers and directors in theatre-making processes foregrounding scenography. Examples include: Blue Raincoat established in Sligo in 1991, which, though led by director Niall Henry, often collaboratively workshops existing play texts drawing on the skills of such directors as Kellie Hughes and designers including Jo Conway, Joseph Hunt and Michael Cummins; Pan Pan Theatre, founded in Dublin in 1991 by designer Aedín Cosgrove and director Gavin Quinn; and Dublin-based ANU Productions, established in 2009 and co-directed by visual artist Owen Boss and director Louise Lowe. The works of these companies have received considerable critical and scholarly attention within contexts such as scenography and corporal mime (Blue Raincoat), post-dramatic theatre (Pan Pan) and site-specific performance and community engagement (ANU).[18]

Yet twentieth-century Irish theatre history is punctuated by moments that indicate a gradual progression towards scenography as dramaturgy of performance. As Sisson points out, the work of the Dublin Drama League at the Abbey during the 1920s "represented a true ensemble company of artists, with designers, actors, writers and directors moving with ease between different responsibilities".[19] The cooperation of Edwards and MacLiammóir, from the late 1920s to the 1970s at the Gate, was characterised by a continually evolving quest for scenographic dramaturgies, drawing on a range of international influences and evidenced by the ways in which Edwards bemoaned "the lack of writers possessing an intimate knowledge of stagecraft".[20] In the early 1950s, Edwards and MacLiammóir tried to alleviate this problem by asking Maura Laverty to write a play without any stage directions, allowing for the artistic freedom of different theatre practitioners in the contexts of design, props and movement. That play was *Liffey Lane*, staged in March 1951 and, while Edwards admits that the Georgian door of Tony Inglis' set was probably too dominant, Edwards and MacLiammóir later found what they were looking for in the work of Bertolt Brecht, staging *Mother Courage* in 1959 and *Saint Joan of the Stockyards* in 1961.[21] At the Abbey, productions such as Alan Barlow's *The Playboy of the Western World* (1971), which placed actors on a circular stage backed with "a photo montage of newspapers showing the riots that accompanied [the play's] first performances",[22] revealed the extent to which designers might contribute to new interpretations of Irish classics. Each progression towards scenography as dramaturgy of performance helped to elevate the position of set and costume designers, in particular, who moved from manifesting received interpretations towards a more collaborative inclusion within processes of theatre-making, coalescing in the 1980s with the work of designers such as Casson and Frawley. Their contributions as designers to what might be considered dramaturgies of performance allow us to trace some of the national genealogies (which also have inevitably been influenced by international practices) of the most current approaches to scenography.

Bronwen Casson

Casson received undergraduate qualifications as a visual artist from the National College of Art and Design in Dublin. Due to a lack of specialist training for theatre designers in Ireland, she then built on her initial preparation by taking the postgraduate course in theatre design at Sadler's Wells. She joined the Abbey theatre in 1968, designing the set for a production of August Strindberg's *The Stronger* at the Peacock that year. She also took small acting roles and made props for the Abbey until 1970, when she designed a number of Peacock shows—gaining notice with a cycle of Yeats' plays between 1970 and 1971. She designed sets and costumes for Tom Murphy's *The Morning after Optimism* for the main Abbey stage in 1971 and later offered the memorable production design for Murphy's *The Sanctuary Lamp* (1975). By 1983 she had made her name, having designed a range of productions including over sixty for Ireland's national theatre. That year she joined a team of practitioners, including writer Tom MacIntyre, director Patrick Mason, and actor Tom Hickey, to work on the very physical, imagistic and linguistically-sparse *The Great Hunger*—a reimagining of Patrick Kavanagh's eponymous poem—on the Peacock stage. *The Great Hunger* was penned by MacIntyre on the basis of collaborative rehearsal room practices combining adaptation, improvisation, devising and design. As such, it made design a partner in the theatre-making process, foregrounding the visual, aural and material aspects of theatre. Cason worked on a series of productions encompassing the same key practitioners and embracing similar collaborative approaches to theatre-making, including *The Bearded Lady* (1984), *Rise Up Lovely Sweeney* (1985) and *Dance for your Daddy* (1987). Along with *Snow White* (1988)—for which Frawley was set and costume designer—these Peacock productions have come to be grouped under the appellation of Tom MacIntyre's "Theatre of Image".

Theatre that employs scenography as dramaturgy of performance is often characterised by collective creation within the production process, in which conventionally designated—and usually hierarchical—roles such as writer, director, designers and actors lose their rigidity and become less mutually exclusive. This was the case in the Peacock's productions of Tom MacIntyre's plays: rehearsals were also "a forum for discussion" in which everyone participated.[23] As Casson points out:

> Working on Tom MacIntyre's plays at the Peacock with the director Patrick Mason in this group or open situation gave me the opportunity to work as a designer in the manner in which I felt most comfortable theatrically. That is, I did not work in isolation or in some separate artistic limbo, but as part of a team, a cooperative.[24]

Casson explains that the set design for *The Great Hunger* emerged between the first and second week of rehearsals and that—having had some general discussions with Mason before rehearsals began—she joined the preparations with only a very general idea. Her design for *The Great Hunger* is notable for the way in which the "character" of Maguire's mother (The Mother) was reduced to a wooden effigy. The idea of representing The Mother as an object arose during rehearsals, when Casson discussed her ideas with the team. Together, it was decided that the effigy should be "a cross between a bog oak Madonna and a piece of kitchen furniture",[25] which would have to incorporate a drawer for additional props. After Casson did a rough sketch, the piece was realised by another designer, Frank Hallinan Flood, who also trained at Sadler's Wells and "had some experience of crafting such objects".[26] The published script (based on the 1986 revival of the production) reveals the ways in which meaningful scenography was created through the actors' haptic and affective engagements with The Mother, as well as other key props and objects. The setting described in the text is also based on Casson's work-shopped production design. It consists of three main areas: the outdoor area is placed centrally, marked by a wooded gate upstage; this is flanked by the kitchen area downstage left containing The Mother, a large black kettle and a bucket, and the chapel area downstage right signalled by a tabernacle resting on its pedestal.

In these 1980s productions of MacIntyre's plays at the Peacock, designers became partners in theatre-making in that their work not only fed back into textual development but was responsive to the rehearsal process. This was particularly evident in the approach to costume design, which Casson describes as follows:

> There was a general idea to begin with, then the cast tried on various found or bought garments until the right look was achieved. Some actors had a lot of input into their costume. Tom Hickey, for example, was happy to be left alone with a large heap of fairly suitable clothing and would build his own character's look by assembling various pieces together.[27]

With *The Bearded Lady*, the actors' movements (choreographed by Vincent O'Neill) informed Casson's approach to costume design. The play offers a loose adaptation of *Gulliver's Travels*—particularly focussing on Book IV—in which the conflict of reason and primitivism is mapped onto a male-female binary via the male Houyhnhnms and female Yahoos respectively. The presentation of this binary might be deemed problematic from a gender-conscious perspective, but these issues are beyond the scope of this chapter. In the production, the conflict between masculinity and femininity was embodied through contrasting movement. The male actors played the Houyhnhnms as horses; appearing authoritative and measured, they wore leotards, with hooved stilts elevating their bodies and further enforcing their poised and stylised movements, swishing their tails as they encircled Gulliver/Swift (played by Hickey wearing a frock coat and collar of the period). The female actors, playing the Yahoos as primitive monkeys, slunk about the stage grunting and gesturing rudely, scantily-clad with unruly mops of hair. Casson began with general costume designs that were adapted in rehearsals in response to the "movements and physique of [...] the Houyhnhnms and the Yahoos".[28] Despite the dynamic disparities between these groups of characters, the synergies between different roles during rehearsals led to a cohesive production, commended in *Theatre Ireland* by critic Joseph McMinn: "Everything about these sequences is well-combined, the movements, the costuming, the exchanges, the chess-like co-ordination of the horses, to produce an episode of really entertaining theatre."[29]

Like several productions by Pan Pan, from *Mac-Beth 7* (2004) to *The Tempest* (2017), many of these Peacock productions showcased scenography's potential to maximise the intermedial possibilities of adaptation by emphasising audiovisual elements, as well as the interconnected materialities of bodies, space and props. Although Pan Pan sees its influences as international, this company has inventively extended Irish approaches to stage adaptation by deliberately calling attention to the interpretative process: Pan Pan has incorporated lectures, rehearsals, auditions and active audience participation into its productions of very loosely adapted works, as well as using such meta-theatrical strategies as including Quinn directing as part of performances. During the 1980s, however, productions such as *The Great Hunger* and *The Bearded Lady* were innovative in their foregrounding of scenography as central to the adaptation process. This approach also is evident in the 1985 production of *Rise Up Lovely Sweeney*, which is based on the twelfth-century text *Buile Suibhne* (The Frenzy of Sweeney)—specifically using James G. O'Keefe's 1913 version of the text—and *Snow White*, which used Grimms' fairy tale as a point of departure, mediated by the Seventh Dwarf (Hickey) from the perspective of whom the story is told. The Sweeney of *Rise up Lovely Sweeney*, like the original character on which the play is based, resides in a military society. However, contemporary resonances—evoked in particular through design elements—allowed this stage adaptation to engage with the Troubles, which were during that time ongoing in Northern Ireland. The sound of helicopters introduced Jim Colgan's sound design and Casson's set included a TV presenting a range of images, evoking the contemporary "pervasive media consumerism" that surrounded such conflicts as the Troubles.[30] Bernadette Sweeney and Marie Kelly, in their individual contributions to their edited collection *The Theatre of Tom MacIntyre* (2010), both point to the organic development of the work, in which "Casson's design created a clinical but disjointed environment where Sweeney realized the ambiguous anxieties of the age in a contemporary, broken Ireland".[31] Kelly, drawing on prompt books for the production, argues that the notion of a multidimensional space for play "permeates everything from the casting of the actor to the use of text in rehearsal and performance, to the use of theatre space to the movement of the body on stage".[32] Indeed, the interaction of physicality and materiality were central to *Rise up Lovely Sweeney*. From the opening moments of the production video, we see a semblance of a derelict site covered with papers and waste, in which a seemingly abandoned television set depicts Elvis and there is an echoing of disjointed sounds, such as people barking and the phrase "tiocfaidh ár lá" (meaning "our day will come" and associated with the Provisional IRA's aspirations towards a united Ireland). Hickey—playing Sweeney—emerges from the wreckage and, after swirling in an increasingly fitful manner round a winding metal staircase centre stage to a recording of children's chants, begins slowly rummaging through the debris, his feet crunching amid it.

Building on the iconic mother figure in *The Great Hunger*, both *Rise Up Lovely Sweeney* and *Snow White* incorporate a dummy that is made in different ways to represent a human figure, showing continuity despite the fact that these productions were designed by Casson and Frawley respectively. The collaborative nature of production processes helps to explain this scenographic through-line: although Frawley replaced Casson as set and costume designer, much of the existing team remained. Each of these three productions capitalised on the uncanny qualities of inanimate figures anthropomorphised through live performance. Chantal Hurault, discussing the work of contemporary French theatre-maker Gisèle Vienne, points out that "in the realms of art and eroticism, dolls and mannequins are fetish objects, charged with a heavy history of contradictions, which, in their transgressive or immoral aspects, touch on religion as well as the marketplace".[33] Hurault suggests that the "incompleteness" of marionettes is intrinsic to their "plastic and dramatic charge" and that Vienne is interested in the "disturbance" released by manipulating such objects.[34] These thoughts can illuminate the ways in which dummies operated in the 1980s productions under discussion here. In one scene of *Rise Up Lovely Sweeney*, nurses roughly handle the dummy, making it writhe and spasm as part of an evocation of a wartime hospital; their prolonged interactions with the dummy progressively border on the sexual, adding to the sense of disturbance. Later, the dummy is placed on a chair to be examined by three men in bowler hats. In their engagement with it the lines between interrogation, torture and medical examination are blurred, combining images associated with a warzone in provocative, unsettling ways.

Monica Frawley

Frawley took over from Casson as part of the 1980s collaborations of Mason, MacIntyre and others at the Peacock for their final production: *Snow White*. She was in a key position to extend and build upon Casson's generative contribution to the production process, partly due to her background and experience, which will be discussed in this section. In *Snow White*, as in the earlier works penned by MacIntyre that Casson designed, Frawley's dress-maker's dummy becomes anthropomorphised through the central character's engagement with it. Sweeney highlights the design continuity, and the meaning of the dummy in *Snow White*: "Reminiscent of The Mother in *The Great Hunger* [...] the presence of a dressmaker's dummy, and Snow White's interaction with it, illustrates her perceived lack of physical affection."[35] Yet, as well as offering a sense of continuity, Frawley's design encapsulated the distinctive fairy-tale quality of Snow White's world: a swing dominated the sparse, pale grey expanse of the stage, which, when used by Snow White (Michèle Forbes) under Tony Wakefield's lighting, cast flickering, menacing shadows. Frawley saw working on *Snow White* as a key opportunity in that it was "about body, image, language, music, light—all combining to create a feeling" and, as such, bringing her closer to the kind of theatre that mattered to her.[36]

Like Casson, Frawley is partial to theatre-making practices that include designers in a process of collective creation, which—like the Peacock's earlier 1980s productions of MacIntyre's plays—*Snow White* offered. Frawley had "never been content to allow design to play second fiddle to any other aspect of theatrical production" and, in the first ten years of her career, she actively made and sought out work in which "the integrity of design [was] given due recognition".[37] Frawley was born in Dublin and studied there at the National College of Art and Design. Like Casson, she had to travel abroad to receive specialised training in theatre design but she was awarded an Irish Arts Council bursary for her final two years of study (1977 to 1979) at the Central School of Art and Design, London, where she was taught by Pamela Howard, author of the seminal *What is Scenography?* (2009). After Frawley graduated, she became a resident designer with the Irish Theatre Company (ICT) from 1979 to 1981, where her work included *John Bull's Other Island* and *Waiting for Godot*. Although she enjoyed her time with ICT, she felt that theatre could do something more. She also finds the very rigid, directive nature of Beckett's stage directions (which are continually imposed by the Beckett estate) restrictive to her creative capacities as a designer.[38,39] After a period of more challenging theatrical work as resident designer with the Contact Theatre in Manchester in 1982, she returned to Ireland to devise and produce *Forbidden Fruit* (1983) with designer and mask-maker Gabby Dowling.

Forbidden Fruit epitomised Baugh's concept of scenography as dramaturgy of performance in that, rather than serving dramatic performance, scenographic practices were the main modes of creation. Backed by an Arts Council Special Theatre Project grant, what Frawley and Dowling produced was an almost wordless, visual promenade piece that required spectators to move between seven performance spaces—each depicting one of the seven deadly sins. *Forbidden Fruit* was staged at Temple Bar Studios and, in fact, costumes and props here from the vast expanses of that venue's stock were used in the devising process. Initially mapped out by Frawley and Dowling, the performances were developed collaboratively with a range of visual artists and actors. The sins were depicted in a variety of ways; for example, performers became gurgling fish gorging themselves to play gluttony, a woman in a black plastic bag chased a woman dressed in white through a maze to depict envy, and a man sleeping at the seaside unaware of changing scenes about him depicted sloth. The phrase "the visual elements of theatre can generate a central excitement" appeared on the programme. Charles Hunter, writing for the *Irish Times*, referred to the production as "overtly polemical, arguing a position centre stage for the visual aspect of theatre".[40] *Forbidden Fruit* was well attended and largely well received, and it was nominated for a Harvey's Irish Theatre Award in the category of design. However, as another *Irish Times* critic, David Nowlan, pointed out, although this was "experimental theatre at its best", the various scenes appeared "as exercises for their own sake".[41] Yet *Forbidden Fruit* was a key intervention to promote the development of scenography in Irish theatre—the importance of which gained momentum in the Ireland of the 1980s with the proliferation of performance art and the establishment of such interdisciplinary companies as Olwen Fouéré and Roger Doyle's Operating Theatre.

Operating Theatre focussed on the cooperation between performance, the visual and music. Doyle, an actor and musician, also worked with Frawley on another landmark in her career: Frank McGuinness's adaptation of Bram Stoker's *Dracula* (1986), her first foray into directing. Druid, with whom Frawley had previously worked on *The Wood of the Whispering* (1983) and *Same Old Moon* (1984), premiered the play at its premises in Galway. Doyle created a chilling electronic soundscape encompassing music and effects—such as howling dogs to accompany the action—and Frawley designed a detailed, sculptural and multi-layered set in mottled off-whites, greys and charcoals (constructed by Flood). The multifaceted quality of the set promoted an appropriate Appian sense of depth and shadow when lit by Rupert Murray, who had joined the Project Arts Centre as resident designer in 1976 and, in 1978, co-formed an enterprise that would become Ireland's largest lighting sales and hire company. Critics largely lauded the production's design, with Nowlan eloquently describing the set as "a great Gothic wrap around setting that manages to be both English mansion and graveyard, in which there are more shapes and shadows than most could imagine, like a piece of crumbling masonry that becomes now a tree, now a giant bat".[42] The spine-chilling ambiance from the outset was established in the auditorium through sounds of thunder and lightning, as well a use of dry ice to convey fog, with a reviewer for *Galway City Tribune* advising attendees to "wear their woollies because it actually feels cold in the auditorium due to the atmosphere created".[43] Here, a strong design team contributed to the production of an atmosphere that was both appropriate for the play, and affective.

However, a scan through the reviews (assembled in the Druid Theatre Company Collection at the James Hardiman Library, NUI Galway) reveals that the actors' performances, in addition to McGuinness's script, were not so well received. There was a general sense that the design elements overshadowed the verbal and physical action. A juxtaposition of review titles points up this disjuncture: on the one hand, we have "Spine Chilling Fare" and "*Dracula* Gives Jitters"; on the other, we have "*Dracula* Actors Just Too Undead" and "Frawley Fangs Fail to Wake the Undead".[44] The failings of the performances were largely attributed to Frawley's inexperience as a director. Yet Frawley's conception of herself as an artist rather than a technician, and of design as significant in the process of theatre-making, seems linked to her desire to direct. Reflecting back on her career to date in 1989, she states: "I'm so amazed when I meet designers who have no desire to direct. Perhaps I'm different in terms of what I want and what my contribution might be. […] There's a political, diplomatic side to working as a designer and I'm not very good at it".[45] Frawley had already proven her diplomacy through working on such collaborative productions as *Snow White* and *Forbidden Fruit* so it appears that, here, the "political, diplomatic side" to which she refers relates instead to the conventional hierarchies of institutional theatre, in which design is often reduced to a mere servant of the director's and/or author's vision. Occupying the dual role of director and designer afforded Frawley the opportunity to contribute more thoroughly and meaningfully to the authorship of the production and, in spite of the ways in which that production pointed up her inexperience as a director, it deserves recognition for its scenographic accomplishment, achieved through the unified, collaborative work of the designers involved.

Frawley carried her innovative, authoritative approaches to design into her subsequent practice, which is characterised by a number of daring visual images. At Ireland's national theatre, these include her design for Michael Harding's *Una Pooka* (Peacock, 1989), as well as the world premiere of Marina Carr's *By the Bog of Cats …* (1998), the first play by a woman to reach the Abbey's main stage since Teresa Deevy's *The Wild Goose* (1936). Both productions were directed by Mason. *Una Pooka* offered a farcical take on the Pope's visit to Ireland in September 1979, probing on-going restrictions to Irish sexuality maintained through the enduring authority of the Church. Visually encapsulating themes of limitation and myopia, Frawley's set offered a distorted, tunnel perspective that squeezed the acting space and appeared to restrict the performers' movements. With Dave Nolan's sound setting the scene by juxtaposing a recording of the declaration of a new pope with frantic church bells at the beginning, and Wakefield's lighting casting obtrusive shadows throughout, the design team worked together to make palpable an appropriate claustrophobic atmosphere. Frawley, after explaining that the set came about through her experiments with perspective painting, discusses her self-assured process: "Even making the model I realised it was actually going to work and it only got better when you put people into it. I was extremely confident. I went at it with a kind of verve."[46] Almost ten years later, her approach to *By the Bog of Cats …* had quite the opposite effect to *Una Pooka*'s set. For Carr's blend of poetic naturalism and surrealism within a midlands' bog setting, Frawley's set extended towards the backdrop and sides in non-uniform horizontal strata that appeared to be covered in snow and that evoked a bog, sliced up and iced over; her design offered an edgeless quality that seemed to bleed into the audience space.

As *By the Bog of Cats* ... progressed to become Carr's most internationally-renowned play, Frawley's icy, contoured approach to the set became iconic—influencing many designers who worked on future productions, including Vaněk in his design for the San José Repertory Theatre production of the play in 2001, directed by Timothy Near.[47,48] Although Frawley returned to the text to conceptualise her design for a new Abbey production of the play in 2015, she again produced the appearance of frozen, horizontal layers—though perhaps subtler this time and supplemented with a use of video projections as well a caravan partially submerged in snow, which was absent in the original production.

Conclusion

1983 was a key year for the development of scenography in Ireland. That summer, Casson first worked with MacIntyre, Mason, Hickey and others on *The Great Hunger*, "a landmark in Irish theatre history".[49] Meanwhile Frawley and Dowling were working with their collaborators to create *Forbidden Fruit*, which premiered that December. Although there was less than the usual amount of commercial theatre on offer, experimentalism proliferated and, as Nowlan points out in an *Irish Times* retrospective of theatre in 1983, there was "a distinct consolidation during the year of what some like to call 'non-verbal' theatre".[50] Nowlan highlights the work of Vincent O'Neill with the newly established Oscar mime school, in particular *Kaleidoscope*, which premiered that February and *Pol*, produced as part of the Dublin Theatre Festival. He describes Polish theatre director Kazimierz Braun's production of *The Old Woman Broods* at the Project as one in which "the message was vastly more important than the medium and the images far more memorable than the words".[51] Nowlan also mentions works that now might be categorised as site-specific theatre in the devised work of Peter Sheridan, Maggie Byrne, Mick Egan and their colleagues in City Workshop, "a group almost indigenous to north central Dublin who wanted to say something, in theatrical terms, about the place they live in",[52] producing *Pledges and Promises* and *A Hape of Junk* in 1983. While Nowlan commends *Forbidden Fruit* as a production in which "the basic tools of visual dramatic communication [were] being fashioned", he sees such "un-literary theatre" as "by definition, a cul-de-sac" since theatre "is larger than the individual techniques used to stage a play". This statement illuminates an enduring critical block at the time with regard to scenography's dramaturgical possibilities. Ultimately, though, Nowlan highlights what he calls "emergent trends", in which aesthetics that he categorises as "non-verbal drama" really seemed to thrive, the pinnacle of which he identifies as *The Great Hunger*, which "[in] any year [...] would have been one of the best plays".[53]

Yet, while trends of theatre foregrounding—to varying degrees—visuals, sound, space and materiality coalesced in 1983 in ways that may have helped to advance the role of designers in Irish theatre, this was not—significantly—a period marked by a transformation of aesthetics and processes. In fact, the notion of transformation runs counter to the genealogical approach that I am seeking to offer here. Like Dan Rebellato, I use the Foucauldian sense of the term genealogy, to shed new light on history in ways that are productively revisionist, by stressing the far-reaching and intricate contingency of events.[54] By the time Casson and Frawley came to work on *The Great Hunger* and *Forbidden Fruit* respectively, both had already achieved recognition for their work at the Project, a venue that had espoused, from its inception in 1967, a visual arts philosophy that fostered collaboration and productive cross-pollinations between different arts practices, and—importantly—between Irish culture and its European and international counterparts.[55] Also known for cooperation between forms, Operating Theatre began as a music band in 1981, going on to tour their theatre production *Ignotum Per Ignotius* across Holland in 1982 and to premiere *The Diamond Body* at the Project in 1984. City Workshop's experiments began with *The Kips, The Digs, The Village* (1982) in which they engaged with the old Monto. Charlotte McIvor locates the work of ANU, which also has focussed on the old Monto, within this history of devised practices that draw on local places and communities. Moreover, Sheridan with his brother Jim had already been experimenting with form and space through their amateur group Slot Players as early as 1970. To further mine these histories, Edwards and MacLiammóir also experimented collaboratively with site-based work, for example in the first outing of the *The Pageant of St. Patrick* (1954), which represented fifteen-century scenes from the story of St. Patrick at several places significant to that story throughout the Boyne Valley in County Louth. As noted earlier, the work of Edwards and MacLiammóir sought continually to expand the dramaturgical potential of scenography. Companies such as Pan Pan and ANU do not acknowledge as influences the nationally proliferating practices that preceded their work; however, practices, such as those in which artists including Casson and Frawley were involved in the 1980s, helped to create an appetite for the work that these contemporary companies produce and, as such, have likely contributed to the positive academic and critical reception of their work nationally. A genealogical approach challenges the myth-making tendencies of dominant historical narratives, which often seek out moments of transformation or position certain individuals, groups or moments as originators of shifts within the historical landscape. Such myth-making can serve to reiterate and reproduce the privileging of certain people or moments over others by skating over the processual, interconnected ways in which the production and reception of artistic practices develop.

Frawley's career from *Forbidden Fruit* to *By the Bog of Cats ...* can be seen synecdochically to illuminate the ways in which approaches to designing for performance have developed in Ireland as a continual negotiation between iconoclastic approaches and the development of new icons. Within a wider western context, the progression broadly from *mise-en-scène* to stage design to scenography has coincided with an increasing appreciation for the dramaturgical potential of theatre's audio, visual and material elements since the nineteenth century. Baugh, in his seminal study, associates these developments with changing technologies of manufacture and control. In Ireland, an increasing professionalisation of design, with Irish artists such Casson and Frawley receiving specialised training abroad, has also contributed to an expansion of the authoritative role of designers within the collaborative process of theatre-making, be it through inclusion within devising processes or in contributing in highly creative, meaning-making ways to the staging of pre-written plays.

However, despite the increased authority of designers, the attribution of authorship in productions has largely remained hierarchical, and this has at times also served to skew the focus of theatre histories in the service of writers and, perhaps to a lesser extent, directors. This is an issue Conway laments as reinforced by much criticism and academic scholarship.[56] As McIvor and I state in our introduction to *Devised Performance in Irish Theatre*:

> The need to demarcate intellectual property by ascribing works to particular authors has led to a theatrical canon that, at times, forgets its own history. The anxiety to credit creative offerings to specific individuals within a hierarchical framework of author, director, and various other members of a production team (tiered on the basis of the perceived value of their inputs) is on-going.[57]

Morash and Swift, in 1994, were perceptive in revealing the lack of recognition for the immense contribution of designers in Irish theatre, using Casson's work on MacIntyre's plays as an example. Although these works, as these writers point out, drew on collaborative practice and pointed up the visual aspects of theatre, they were presented as the creation of a dramatist, a director and an actor (Hickey) "but not, significantly, a scenographer".[58] Subsequent histories of those MacIntyre productions at the Peacock during the 1980s, including the essays contained in Sweeney and Kelly's important collection, while acknowledging collective creation also have tended to trace the genealogies of these works to MacIntyre's—and to a lesser extent—Mason's backgrounds and experiences. Re-examining theatre practice of the past through the lens of scenography, in ways that account for its collaborative production and dramaturgical potential, allows us to acknowledge and explore the contributions of other collaborators, such as designers and actors, in ways that promote more holistic theatre and performance histories, as well as more complex genealogies of contemporary practice.

Notes

1. Nicholas Grene, *The Politics of Irish Drama* (Cambridge: Cambridge UP, 1999), 132.
2. Joe Vaněk and Helen O'Donoghue, *Scene Change: One Hundred Years of Theatre Design at the Abbey*, Exhibition Catalogue (Dublin: Irish Museum of Modern Art, 2005), 19.
3. Christopher Morash, *A History of Irish Theatre 1601–2000* (Cambridge: Cambridge UP, 2002), 121.

4. See Sisson, Elaine. "Experimentalism and the Irish Stage: Theatre and German Expressionism in the 1920s." in *Ireland, Design and Visual Culture: Negotiating Modernity, 1922–1992*, eds. Linda King and Elaine Sisson (Cork: Cork UP, 2011).
5. Thomas Madden's *The Making of an Artist: Creating the Irishman Micheál MacLiammóir* (2015) traces MacLiammóir's influences, dating back to his youth in London. More recently, Paige Reynolds examines the Gate Theatre in "Design and Direction to 1960," with a particular focus on the collaborations of Edwards and MacLiammóir during the late 1920s and early 1930s (pp. 207–211).
6. Morash, *A History of Irish Theatre 1601–2000*, 225.
7. See Christopher Morash's *A History of Irish Theatre 1601–2000* pp. 225–226 for more detail on the design of the 1966 Abbey theatre.
8. Frank Conway, "The Sound of One Hand Clapping", in *Staging Thought: Essays on Irish Theatre, Scholarship and Practice*, ed. Rhona Trench (Oxford and New York: Peter Lang, 2012), 20.
9. Ibid., 452.
10. Vaněk and O'Donoghue, *Scene Change*, 31.
11. Christopher Baugh, Interview by Siobhán O'Gorman in *Performing Scenographic Sense Memories*, prod. Siobhán O'Gorman and Noelia Ruiz. Dir. Steve O'Connor and Manus Corduff. Perf. Chris Baugh, Lian Bell, Denis Clohessy, Sabine Dargent, Joe Devlin, Emma Fisher, Kevin Smith, Joe Vaněk, Conleth White (Dublin: MART, 2015).
12. My own interview with designer Sabine Dargent, "Sculpting the Spaces of Enda Walsh's Theatre" (2015), is an example: by virtue its publication within a volume on playwright Enda Walsh, the published version focusses mainly on Dargent's relationship with that writer, and the production teams with which he has worked. Other examples include Cathy Leeney's "Patrick Mason: A Director's Festival Golden Fish" (2008) and Enrica Cerquoni's ""One bog, many bogs": Theatrical space, Visual Image and Meaning in Some Productions of Marina Carr's *By the Bog of Cats...*" (2003); these important essays examine the work of designers including Monica Frawley and Joe Vaněk via their relationships with a director and a writer respectively. More recently, in *The Oxford Handbook of Modern Irish Theatre* (2016), edited by Nicholas Grene and Chris Morash, direction and design are combined in surveys focussing mainly on the twentieth century before and after 1960 by Reynolds and Ian Walsh respectively. Although scenography is a collaborative process, I hope to redress hierarchies that have been difficult to avoid in existing scholarship by focussing here in more detail on scenography and the contributions of individual designers.
13. Conway, "The Sound of One Hand Clapping", 15.
14. Ibid., 34.
15. Joe Vaněk, *Irish Theatrescapes: New Irish Plays, Adapted European Plays and Irish Classics* (Cork: Gandon, 2015).
16. Christopher Baugh, *Theatre, Performance and Technology: The Development and Transformation of Scenography*, 2nd ed. (Houndmills, Basingstoke and Hampshire: Palgrave Macmillan, 2013), 224.
17. Ibid., 239.
18. Rhona Trench discusses the collaboration between Hughes, Conway, Hunt and Cummins in particular in "Staging Blue Raincoat's production of W.B. Yeats"

(2015). Trench is also author of the book *Blue Raincoat Theatre Company* (2015), in which she pays special attention to set, costume, sound and lighting design. Noelia Ruiz has published significant research on Pan Pan in essays such as "Mapping Contemporary European Theatres" (2015) and "Positive Acts" (2011). ANU has received attention from a range of scholars. See, for example, Brian Singleton's "ANU Productions and Site-Specific Performance" (2013), Miriam Haughton's "From Laundries to Labour Camps" (2014), and Charlotte McIvor's "A Portrait of the Citizen as Artist" (2015) in which McIvor also traces ANU's genealogies—in this case to earlier community arts practices.

19. Elaine Sisson, "Experimentalism and the Irish Stage: Theatre and German Expressionism in the 1920s", in *Ireland, Design and Visual Culture: Negotiating Modernity, 1922–1992*, eds. Linda King and Elaine Sisson (Cork: Cork UP, 2011), 41.
20. Hilton Edwards, *The Mantel of Harlequin* (Dublin: Progress House, 1958), 66.
21. A detailed examination of Edwards and MacLiammóir's engagement with Brecht, situated within its national and international contexts, will be offered in my monograph *Theatre, Performance and Design: Scenographies in a Modernizing Ireland* (Forthcoming).
22. Vaněk and O'Donoghue, *Scene Change*, 41.
23. Bronwen Casson, "'Environmental Design' and the Plays of Tom Mac Intyre", in *The Theatre of Tom Mac Intyre: "Strays from the Ether."* Eds. Bernadette Sweeney and Marie Kelly (Dublin: Carysfort, 2010), Kindle edition. n.p.
24. Ibid.
25. Ibid.
26. Ibid.
27. Ibid.
28. Ibid.
29. Joseph McMinn, "Theatre Review: *The Bearded Lady* by Tom Mac Intyre", in *The Theatre of Tom Mac Intyre: "Strays from the Ether."* Eds. Bernadette Sweeney and Marie Kelly (Dublin: Carysfort, 2010), Kindle edition. n.p.
30. Fintan O'Toole, "*Rise Up Lovely Sweeney*, by Tom Mac Intyre", in *Critical Moments*, ed. Julai Furay and Redmond O'Hanlon (Dublin: Carysfort, 2003).
31. Bernadette Sweeney, "A Vibrant Presence: A Biography of Tom Mac Intyre's Work", in *The Theatre of Tom Mac Intyre: "Strays from the Ether."* Eds. Bernadette Sweeney and Marie Kelly (Dublin: Carysfort, 2010), Kindle edition. n.p.
32. Ibid.
33. Chantal Hurault, "Gisèle Vienne: The Stage of Desire", trans. Michael West, in *No More Drama*, eds. by Peter Crawley and Willie White (Dublin: Carysfort / Project Arts Centre, 2011), 167.
34. Ibid., 164.
35. Sweeney, "A Vibrant Presence", n.p.
36. Monica Frawley, Interview by Derek West, *Theatre Ireland* 22 (1989): 36.
37. Ibid., 32.
38. Monica Frawley, Personal interview with Siobhán O'Gorman, September 25, 2014.
39. There is evidence to suggest that the powers of Beckett's Estate are waning, however, for example in relation to gender and casting as discussed in my essay "Beckett out of Focus" (2016), pp. 83–84.
40. Charles Hunter, "Making Theatre and Music Work in Tandem", *The Irish Times*, March 1, 1984, 12.

41. David Nowlan, "*Forbidden Fruit* in Temple Bar Studio", Review, *The Irish Times*, December 14, 1983, 10.
42. David Nowlan, "Curtain Down on a Year of Struggle and Achievement", *The Irish Times*, January 5, 1984, 10.
43. Druid Theatre Company. Special Collections at the James Hardiman Library, National University of Ireland Galway, T2 132–134.
44. Ibid.
45. Frawley, Interview by Derek West, 36.
46. Ibid.
47. Baugh, Interview by Siobhán O'Gorman.
48. Cerquoni explores different scenographies of *By the Bog of Cats…*, comparing the Abbey's original production, the San José Repertory Theatre's 2001 production, and the Irish Repertory production in Chicago (also 2001) directed by Kay Martinovich and designed by Michelle Habeck. The latter was characterised by "an utterly empty expanse of monochrome greyish flatness" in which shafts of "light partially infused the stage surface with the snowy and frozen appearance of a winter landscape" (194).
49. Bernadette Sweeney, *Performing the Body in Irish Theatre* (Basingstoke: Palgrave Macmillan, 2008), 50.
50. Nowlan, "Curtain Down", 10.
51. Ibid.
52. Ibid.
53. Ibid.
54. Dan Rebellato, *1956 and All That: The Making of Modern British Theatre* (London: Routledge, 1999), 13.
55. For further information on Casson's innovative engagements with materiality and space at the Project prior to the premiere of *The Great Hunger*, see John Barrett's "Environmental Design in the Dublin Theatre."
56. Conway, "The Sound of One Hand Clapping", 22.
57. Charlotte McIvor and Siobhán O'Gorman. "Devising Ireland: Genealogies and Contestations." in *Devised Performance in Irish Theatre: Histories and Contemporary Practice*, eds. Siobhán O'Gorman and Charlotte McIvor (Dublin: Carysfort: 2015), 25.
58. Christopher Morash and Carolyn Swift, "Ireland", in *The World Encyclopaedia of Contemporary Theatre: Volume 1, Europe*, eds. Don Rubin (London and New York: Routledge, 1998), 489.

Bibliography

Abbey Theatre. *Rise Up Lovely Sweeney*, 09 Sep 1985 [video]. Abbey Theatre Digital Archive at National University of Ireland, Galway, 2883_V_001.

———. *The Great Hunger*, 14 July 1986 [video]. Abbey Theatre Digital Archive at National University of Ireland, Galway, 2896_V_001.

———. *Snow White*, 22 June 1988 [video]. Abbey Theatre Digital Archive at National University of Ireland, Galway, 4651_V_001.

———. *Una Pooka*, 17 Apr 1989 [video]. Abbey Theatre Digital Archive at National University of Ireland, Galway, 826_V_001.

Barrett, John. "Environmental Design in the Dublin Theatre." In *The Theatre of Tom MacIntyre: "Strays from the Ether"*. Edited by Bernadette Sweeney and Marie Kelly. Dublin: Carysfort, 2010. N. pag. Kindle edition.

Baugh, Christopher. *Theatre, Performance and Technology: The Development and Transformation of Scenography*. 2nd ed. Houndmills, Basingstoke and Hampshire: Palgrave Macmillan, 2013.

———. Interview by Siobhán O'Gorman. *Performing Scenographic Sense Memories*. Prod. Siobhán O'Gorman and Noelia Ruiz. Dir. Steve O'Connor and Manus Corduff. Perf. Chris Baugh, Lian Bell, Denis Clohessy, Sabine Dargent, Joe Devlin, Emma Fisher, Kevin Smith, Joe Vaněk, Conleth White. Dublin: MART, 2015.

Casson, Bronwen. "'Environmental Design' and the Plays of Tom MacIntyre." In *The Theatre of Tom MacIntyre: "Strays from the Ether"* Edited by. Bernadette Sweeney and Marie Kelly. Dublin: Carysfort, 2010. N. pag. Kindle edition.

Cerquoni, Enrica. "'One Bog, Many Bogs': Theatrical Space, Visual Image, and Meaning in Some Productions of Marina Carr's *By the Bog of Cats*." In *The Theatre of Marina Carr: "Before Rules Was Made"*. Edited by Cathy Leeney and Anna McMullan. Dublin: Carysfort Press, 2003.

Conway, Frank. "Frank Conway in Conversation with John Kavanagh." Interview by John Kavanagh. In *Theatre Talk: Voices of Irish Theatre Practitioners*. Edited by Lilian Chambers, Ger Fitzgibbon and Eamonn Jordon. Dublin: Carysfort Press, 2001.

———. "The Sound of One Hand Clapping." In *Staging Thought: Essays on Irish Theatre, Scholarship and Practice*. Edited by Rhona Trench. Oxford and New York: Peter Lang, 2012.

Dargent, Sabine. "Sculpting the Spaces of Enda Walsh's Theatre: Sabine Dargent in Conversation." Interview by Siobhán O'Gorman. In *The Theatre of Enda Walsh*. Edited by Mary P. Caulfield and Ian R. Walsh. Dublin: Carysfort Press, 2015.

Druid Theatre Company. Special Collections at the James Hardiman Library, National University of Ireland Galway, T2 132-134.

Edwards, Hilton. *The Mantel of Harlequin*. Dublin: Progress House, 1958.

Frawley, Monica. Interview by Derek West. *Theatre Ireland* 22 (1989): 32–7.

———. Personal Interview with Siobhán O'Gorman, September 25, 2014.

Grene, Nicholas. *The Politics of Irish Drama*. Cambridge: Cambridge UP, 1999.

Haughton, Miriam. "From Laundries to Labour Camps: Staging Ireland's Rule of Silence in ANU Productions' *Laundry*." *Modern Drama* 57.1 (2014): 65–93.

Howard, Pamela. *What Is Scenography?* 2nd ed. London and New York: Routledge, 2009.

Hunter, Charles. "Making Theatre and Music Work in Tandem". *The Irish Times*, March 1, 1984: 12. *ProQuest Historical Newspapers*. Web. September 25, 2014.

Hurault, Chantal. "Gisèle Vienne: The Stage of Desire". Trans. Michael West. In *No More Drama*. Edited by Peter Crawley and Willie White. Dublin: Carysfort/Project Arts Centre, 2011.

Kelly, Marie. "New Dimensions: Spaces for Play in *Rise Up Lovely Sweeney*." In *The Theatre of Tom MacIntyre: "Strays from the Ether."* Edited by Bernadette Sweeney and Marie Kelly. Dublin: Carysfort, 2010. Kindle edition.

Leeney, Cathy. "Patrick Mason: A Director's Festival Golden Fish." In *Interactions: Dublin Theatre Festival 1957–2007*. Edited by Nicholas Grene and Patrick Lonergan with Lilian Chambers. Dublin: Carysfort, 2008.

MacIntyre, Tom. *The Great Hunger; The Gallant John-Joe*. Dublin: Lilliput, 2002.

Madden, Thomas. *The Making of an Artist: Creating the Irishman Micheál MacLiammóir.* Dublin: Liffey Press, 2015.

McIvor, Charlotte. "A Portrait of the Citizen as Artist: Community Arts, Devising and Contemporary Irish Theatre Practice." In *Devised Performance in Irish Theatre: Histories and Contemporary Practice.* Edited by Siobhán O'Gorman and Charlotte McIvor. Dublin: Carysfort, 2015.

McIvor, Charlotte and Siobhán O'Gorman. "Devising Ireland: Genealogies and Contestations." In *Devised Performance in Irish Theatre: Histories and Contemporary Practices.* Edited by Siobhán O'Gorman and Charlotte McIvor. Dublin: Carysfort, 2015.

"Memoranda: An Arts Notebook." *The Irish Times*, 10 Dec 1983: 16. *ProQuest Historical Newspapers.* Web. September 25, 2014.

McMinn, Joseph. "Theatre Review: *The Bearded Lady* by Tom MacIntyre." *The Theatre of Tom MacIntyre: "Strays from the Ether"* Edited by Bernadette Sweeney and Marie Kelly. Dublin: Carysfort, 2010. Kindle edition.

Morash, Christopher. *A History of Irish Theatre 1601–2000.* Cambridge: Cambridge University Press, 2002.

Morash, Christopher and Carolyn Swift. "Ireland." In *The World Encyclopaedia of Contemporary Theatre: Volume 1, Europe.* Edited by Don Rubin. London and New York: Routledge, 1998.

Nowlan, David. "Curtain Down on a Year of Struggle and Achievement." *The Irish Times*, January 5, 1984: 10. *ProQuest Historical Newspapers.* Web. September 25, 2014.

———. "*Forbidden Fruit* in Temple Bar Studio." Review. *The Irish Times*, December 14, 1983: 10. *ProQuest Historical Newspapers.* Web. September 25, 2014.

O'Gorman, Siobhán. "Beckett Out of Focus: *Happy Days* and *Waiting for Godot* at Dublin's Focus Theatre." In *Staging Beckett in Ireland and Northern Ireland.* Edited by Trish McTighe and David Tucker. London: Methuen, 2016.

———. *Theatre, Performance and Design: Scenographies in a Modernizing Ireland.* Basingstoke: Palgrave Macmillan, Forthcoming.

O'Toole, Fintan. "*Rise Up Lovely Sweeney*, by Tom MacIntyre." In *Critical Moments.* Edited by Julai Furay and Redmond O'Hanlon. Dublin: Carysfort, 2003.

Rebellato, Dan. *1956 and All That: The Making of Modern British Theatre.* London: Routledge, 1999.

Reynolds, Paige. Design and Direction to 1960. In *The Oxford Handbook of Modern Irish Theatre*, ed. Nicholas Grene and Chris Morash. Oxford: Oxford UP.

Ruiz, Noelia. "Positive Acts: The Evolution of Pan Pan Theatre Company." In *No More Drama.* Edited by Peter Crawley and Willie White. Dublin: Carysfort/Project Arts Centre, 2011.

———. "Mapping Contemporary European Theatre(s): Reconsidering Notions of Devised and Post-Dramatic Theatres." In *Devised Performance in Irish Theatre: Histories and Contemporary Practice.* Edited by Siobhán O'Gorman and Charlotte McIvor. Dublin: Carysfort, 2015.

Singleton, Brian. "ANU Production and Site-Specific Performance: The Politics of Space and Place." In "*That Was Us*": *Contemporary Irish Theatre and Performance.* Edited by Fintan Walsh. London: Oberon, 2013.

Sisson, Elaine. "Experimentalism and the Irish Stage: Theatre and German Expressionism in the 1920s." In *Ireland, Design and Visual Culture: Negotiating Modernity, 1922–1992.* Edited by Linda King and Elaine Sisson. Cork: Cork UP, 2011.

Sweeney, Bernadette. *Performing the Body in Irish Theatre*. Basingstoke: Palgrave Macmillan, 2008.

———. "A Vibrant Presence: A Biography of Tom MacIntyre's Work." In *The Theatre of Tom MacIntyre: "Strays from the Ether"* Edited by Bernadette Sweeney and Marie Kelly. Dublin: Carysfort, 2010. Kindle edition.

Trench, Rhona. *Blue Raincoat Theatre Company*. Dublin: Carysfort, 2015.

———. "Staging Blue Raincoat's production of W.B. Yeats's *The Cat and the Moon* (2009) and *At the Hawk's Well* (2010)." In *Devised Performance in Irish Theatre: Histories and Contemporary Practice*. Edited by Siobhán O'Gorman and Charlotte McIvor. Dublin: Carysfort, 2015.

Vaněk, Joe. *Irish Theatrescapes: New Irish Plays, Adapted European Plays and Irish Classics*. Cork: Gandon, 2015.

Vaněk, Joe and Helen O'Donoghue. *Scene Change: One Hundred Years of Theatre Design at the Abbey*. Exhibition Catalogue. Dublin: Irish Museum of Modern Art, 2005.

Walsh, Ian. "Directors and Designers Since 1960." In *The Oxford Handbook of Modern Irish Theatre*. Edited by Nicholas Grene and Chris Morash. Oxford: Oxford University Press.

Props to the Abbey Prop Man

Eimer Murphy

In *The Stage Life of Props* (2003) Andrew Sofer has described theatre as "a vast, self-reflexive recycling project",[1] a particularly accurate description when the theatre in question also happens to be the Abbey Theatre, Ireland's National Theatre (Fig. 1). Founded in 1904 at a time when, as John Harrington observes, "the focus was on national independence. To this national focus, drama was a significant contribution",[2] the fledgling Abbey Theatre placed great emphasis on the authenticity of its plays as depictions of real Irish people, in direct opposition to the caricatures usually seen on the English stage. Documents in the theatre's archive note: "It should be remembered […] that these plays are portions of Irish life, and are put on the stage with a care and accuracy of detail that has hardly been attempted before".[3] Such documents reveal that from those early days, enormous emphasis was placed on material authenticity as a prop to performance. The brochure further adds:

> The properties used by the company are all taken direct from the cottages of the peasantry. The spinning wheel, for instance, was in use near Gort for over a hundred years till it was bought by Lady Gregory. The little wooden vessels, like little barrels, were brought from the Aran Islands. The cowskin sandals, or "pampooties" worn by the people in *Riders to the Sea* come from Aran also […] In

E. Murphy (✉)
Abbey Theatre, Dublin, Ireland

E. Jordan, E. Weitz (eds.), *The Palgrave Handbook of Contemporary Irish Theatre and Performance*,
https://doi.org/10.1057/978-1-137-58588-2_25

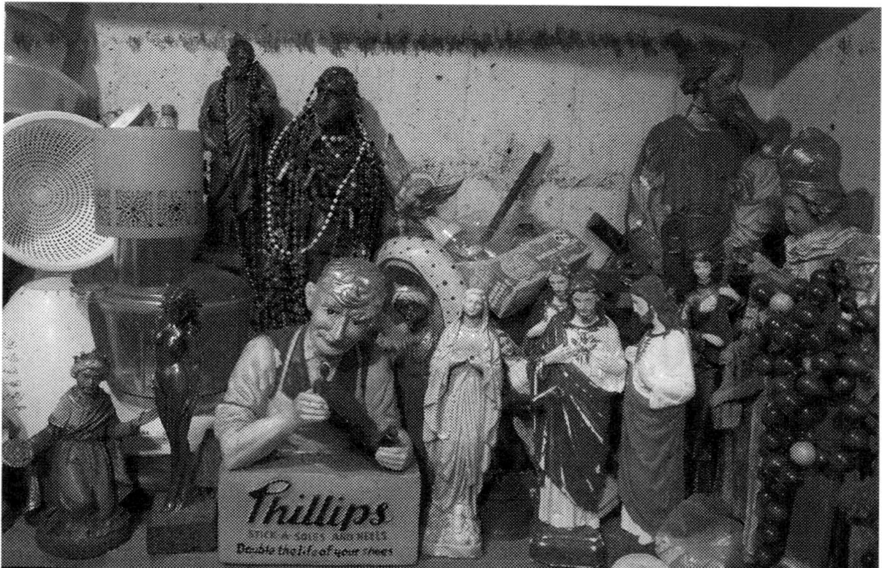

Fig. 1 Religious statues hung with rosary beads, alongside modern kitchen appliances and a vintage cobblers advertisement in an Abbey Theatre prop store, 2016. (Permission, Eimer Murphy)

> dressing this play a young man from the island was brought to the Abbey Theatre to revise all details, so that an exact reproduction of the Aran dress is now given. The turf baskets and panniers were brought from the extreme west of Kerry, and many other parts of Ireland contributed something.[4]

As a repertory company, the Abbey has always stored and reused its props, and today the prop rooms at the theatre contain a bewildering variety of unusual objects, the *things* of plays (Fig. 2). Among a stack of vintage farming tools in one corner lies the loy used by Christy Mahon to kill his father in J.M. Synge's *The Playboy of the Western World* (1907), while on a shelf the Marconi radio from Brian Friel's *Dancing at Lughnasa* (1990) sits alongside the dead black swan from Marina Carr's *By the Bog of Cats* (1998) and a realistic baby doll wearing toy glasses and a drawn-on beard, which played an unforgettable role in David Ireland's *Cyprus Avenue* (2016). One particular prop has had the longest career of all. Making its debut in the original production of Sean O'Casey's *The Plough and the Stars* (1926) this pram (Fig. 3) appeared in every subsequent revival of the play down the decades. In 1951, a fire broke out overnight in the backstage areas of the old Abbey Theatre. The prop rooms and scenic workshops were destroyed, taking most of the original props with them. Because *Plough* was the play running that week, the pram was onstage that night, and, although burnt to its chassis, as an essential prop for that play it was rescued from the smouldering ruins and hastily rebuilt by the Prop Master of the

KING'S THEATRE, GLASGOW,
JUNE 4th, for SIX NIGHTS.
Matinée, SATURDAY at 2 o'clock.

IRISH PLAYS,
By the NATIONAL THEATRE COMPANY,
from the Abbey Theatre Dublin.

FOUR PLAYS at each Performance.

On MONDAY, WEDNESDAY and THURSDAY at 7.30,
& SATURDAY at 2 o'clock.

"In the Shadow of the Glen" ... ... By J. M. SYNGE.
"Hyacinth Halvey" ... ... " LADY GREGORY.
"Kathleen ni Houlihan" ... ... " W. B. YEATS.
"Spreading the News" ... ... " LADY GREGORY.

On TUESDAY, FRIDAY, and SATURDAY at 7.30.

"A Pot of Broth" ... ... By W. B. YEATS.
"Riders to the Sea" ... ... " J. M. SYNGE.
"The Building Fund" ... ... " WM. BOYLE.
"Spreading the News" ... ... " LADY GREGORY.

Toured under the direction of ALFRED WAREING.

Fig. 2 Publicity brochure produced for a 1906 UK tour of the "new Irish plays" produced by the Abbey Theatre. (Permission, Abbey Theatre Archive)

day. The show famously didn't miss a performance, and went on in the undamaged Peacock Theatre the following night.

In his introduction to the *American Theatre Journal's* 2012 issue, editor Ric Knowles acknowledges: "Theatre practice has always and inevitably dealt with *stuff*, in all of its messiness", adding that the theatre "generates things in

Fig. 3 The original *Plough* pram, 1976. Bill Foley as Uncle Peter looks on while Siobhán McKenna as Bessie Burgess and Angela Newman as Jinny Gogan fight over the original pram in the 1976 production of *Plough*. The rough treatment of the pram in this scene lead to its eventual retirement from the stage in 1999. (Photo: Fergus Bourke, Permission, Abbey Theatre Archive)

abundance",[5] a knowing reference to the sheer amount of "things" prescribed by playwrights within the text of every script. In interview, playwright Frank McGuinness admitted that in writing a play "you just never realise how much there is in a single text [...] you just never realise that actually, and it always comes as a complete shock when you see the sheer size and scale of the demands you are making".[6]

To deal with all of this "abundance", the Abbey Theatre is unique in Ireland as it has always employed a Property Master. The current incumbent, Stephen Molloy, took up the role in 1978, giving him the distinction of being Ireland's longest serving theatre Prop Master.[7] My own background as an assistant stage manager revealed an aptitude for sourcing and making props, leading me to join the Abbey Theatre Prop Department in 2007. The role of the Property Master is a difficult one to define, as is, in fact, the very nature of the prop itself, and in writing this short piece I can offer only a glimpse into this largely intuitive, hugely experiential, ever-evolving role.

The Property Master

The document pictured in Fig. 4 is the official job description written for Stephen Molloy on commencement of his role in 1978. Although Molloy retains the traditional title, its use is often challenged by modern practitioners, many of whom prefer the title "Prop Manager". A *New York Times* article on Broadway Prop Master Abe Morrison notes that "such a title seems poorly chosen, considering how he sees his job". Morrison's own succinct definition of his role reads: "The director tells you what he needs, the designer says how it should look, and the actor tells you how it should feel. Then the producer tells you how much you can pay for it. The prop person tries to please all of them".[8] This definition touches on some of the peculiarities of the role.

Although prop people do not have a design title (the look of the prop officially falls under the remit of the set designer), we must have a good knowledge of design history. The definition also gives a nod to the fact that production budgets rarely live up to the scale and artistic vision of the creative team, necessitating lateral thinking and inventiveness. When designer Liam Doona wanted a Jacobean chaise longue for the 2014 production of *She Stoops to Conquer* (1773), naturally the budget would not stretch to such a valuable antique. A little creative sourcing (from me) and skilful craftsmanship (from Stephen) turned this sideboard into a convincing substitute (Figs. 5, 6, 7).

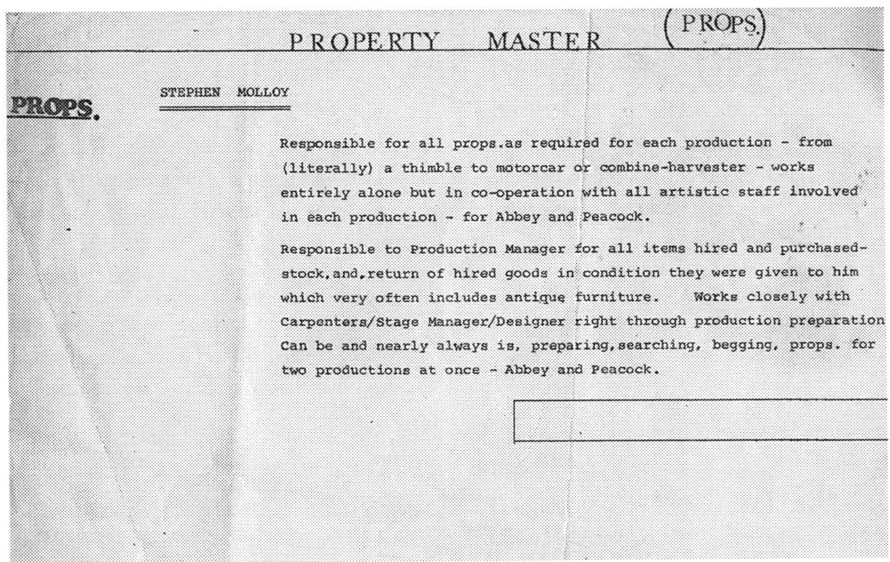

PROPERTY MASTER (PROPS)

PROPS.

STEPHEN MOLLOY

Responsible for all props.as required for each production - from (literally) a thimble to motorcar or combine-harvester - works entirely alone but in co-operation with all artistic staff involved in each production - for Abbey and Peacock.

Responsible to Production Manager for all items hired and purchased-stock,and,return of hired goods in condition they were given to him which very often includes antique furniture. Works closely with Carpenters/Stage Manager/Designer right through production preparation Can be and nearly always is, preparing,searching, begging, props. for two productions at once - Abbey and Peacock.

Fig. 4 The role of the Property Master, Abbey Theatre job description, 1978. (Permission, Stephen Molloy)

Fig. 5 Mid-century Jacobean style sideboard, 2014. When I found this oak sideboard in a second-hand shop, it was the potential of the "barley twist" base, a feature associated with Jacobean era furniture, and the panelled doors that caught my eye. (Permission, Eimer Murphy)

Although many objects in the Abbey prop rooms are now antiques in their own right, props are nonetheless working objects, earning their keep onstage where they are handled, thrown, dropped, or even painted, glued or screwed down to a surface. Prop managers are regularly torn between the desire to use an authentic object, and the knowledge that damage will inevitably occur onstage, whether by accident or by design. With his background in antique restoration, Stephen Molloy has an invaluable skill set, quickly repairing and restoring broken antiques such as a chair sourced by the author (Fig. 8) and managing, maintaining, and re-inventing the existing Abbey furniture stock by stripping back, re-upholstering and re-staining pieces to suit the overall design aesthetic of each production. In addition, Molloy combines the traditional crafts of wood restoration and upholstery work with an intuitive understanding of the particular demands routinely made on furniture when used onstage. Emotional outbursts in performance are often expressed through props, such as the violent throwing over of a chair. Molloy will invisibly reinforce an antique to enable it to withstand such treatment, ensuring that the prop performs consistently and reliably, performance after performance.

Almost anything can be classified as a prop, from tables to china tea sets, even mud, blood, fire, water or snow: if an actor handles it, it's the prop managers responsibility. The role often involves the invention and problem-solving inherent to building unique specialist props, such as the dead kitten with an inflatable belly from Carmel Winters *The Remains of Maisie Duggan* (2016), or this dandelion seed head (Figs. 9, 10) for the 2010 production of Thomas Kilroy's *Christ Deliver Us!*

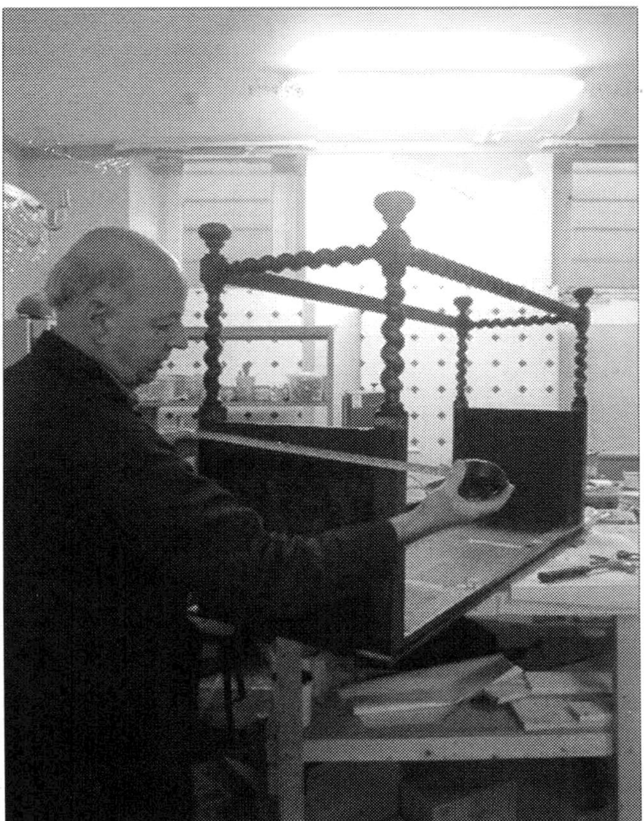

Fig. 6 Abbey Prop Master Stephen Molloy, 2014. Molloy began by dismantling the sideboard, and then skilfully reassembling the sections in a different order so that the barley twist base became the legs of the chaise, the top became the seat, and one of the carved doors became the back

For prop managers, finding the right thing is often as involved as making or inventing it. When writers write objects directly from their own life experience, often with deep significance attached, finding a real object that embodies all of that significance can be a complex process of eliminating the wrong thing, until we find the right one. Writer and director Philip McMahon describes the significance of one prop (Fig. 11), the teddy bear from his 2016 production *Town is Dead*:

> The bear is symbolic of William, the character who has died, so the bear is also symbolic of his youth and innocence and the cutting off of the possibility of his life [...] It was actually a bear that I remembered, and it didn't have to look like that bear exactly, but I just knew the texture of that bear, the feel of him.[9]

Fig. 7 The completed chaise, 2014. The finished prop as it appeared on the set of the 2014 production of Goldsmith's *She Stoops to Conquer* (1773). Set design by Liam Doona, directed by Conall Morrison

The "feel" of things refers not to a physical tactility, but is a more intangible, instinctual concept with which directors, designers and prop people must engage while manifesting these objects from the page into physical (and practical) reality.

The storytelling ability of the *right* object is inherently understood in theatre. Director Conall Morrison likened the prop managers role to that of a social archivist: "you're trying to find props which are true to the period of the play and the world of the play, but also are things which will resonate in the audience's

Fig. 8 Chair restoration, 2013. On the left is an Edwardian chair sourced by the author at the back of an antique dealers shed, and purchased for €20. On the right is the same chair after restoration and upholstery work by Stephen Molloy for the Abbey Theatre's 2013 production of Bernard Shaw's *Major Barbara* (1905). (Permission, Eimer Murphy)

imagination".[10] Designer Liam Doona spoke of being "opportunistic" with prop choices in order to "give you that extra bit of story or that extra bit of background".[11] When a suitably aged and worn object cannot be found, that extra background is added by prop people, who routinely manufacture evidence of an object's biography, such as the bag pictured in Figs. 12 and 13. This brand-new bag was artificially aged with paint, sandpaper and cheese graters to create wear and tear. Rips were added, and then mended with safety pins and rough stitching. The white tie cord was then replaced with baler twine to give it an object biography as the well-used and worn possession of Hester Swayne in Selina Cartmel's 2015 production of Marina Carr's *By the Bog of Cats* (1998).

Details such as these are generally appreciated by actors. In interview actor Aisling O' Sullivan said of props; "they help me to go deeper into the kind of hypnosis that's needed for acting".[12] Paradoxically however, much detail goes unnoticed by the audience, which is actually a testament to the authenticity of a well-researched or well-designed prop, as it is automatically accepted as belonging to the onstage world. However, props also have an uncanny ability to announce themselves, occasionally exposing the carefully crafted illusion of time and place.

Case in point: during my research I conducted a focus group with the Abbey Theatre Members Club, a group of devoted theatregoers who read the stage on a sophisticated level. In our discussion most admitted that they had not noticed the small details of the packaging in *The Wake* (Fig. 14) because it

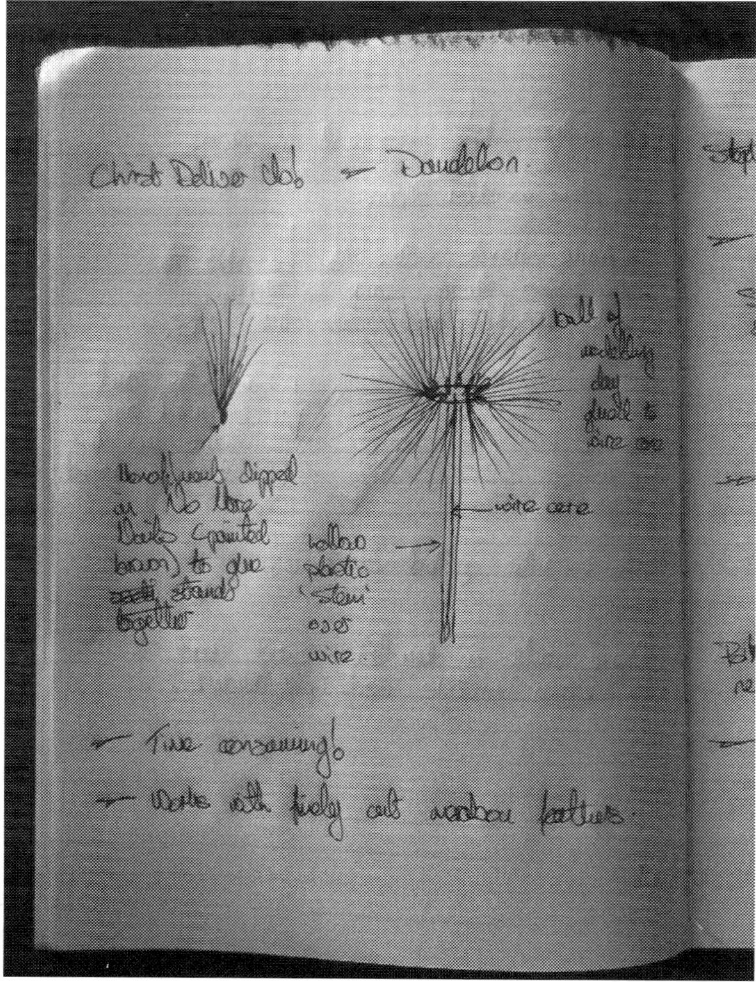

Fig. 9 Dandelion drawing, 2010. Director Wayne Jordan wanted a dandelion seed head that could be handled and then "blown" onstage during performance. This photograph shows my notes and drawings as I worked out the problem. 30 mm lengths of monofilament were glued together at one end making a cluster, and each cluster was then glued to a modelling clay ball mounted onto a wire stem. The monofilament was dipped into a container of finely cut ostrich feathers, which were trapped between the strands, to be blown free onstage. (Permission, Eimer Murphy)

"looked right". However they certainly notice a prop if its looks "wrong", such as this remarkable example from Abbey member Michéal McGuigan:

> Recently I was at an Arthur Miller, set in 1952 I think, or 1954 based in the New York docks, and they had a wooden crate with "Produce of Malawi" printed on it. And maybe I'm just a pedant or something, but it sent me to the phone to type in "when was Malawi established?" It was 1964.[13,14]

Fig. 10 The dandelion clock as it appeared onstage with Aoife Duffin as Winnie Butler in Thomas Kilroy's *Christ Deliver Us!* 2010. The build itself took about five days, however many more hours were spent in the "research and development" stage, where materials are gathered and tested, and prototypes made and discarded. Onstage, the effect lasted for approximately ten seconds. This prop remains one of my favourite prop challenges from The Abbey. (Permission Ross Kavanagh)

Fig. 11 Teddy bear prop from *Town is Dead* (2016) written and directed by Philip McMahon. This bear was difficult to find, McMahon rejected several before emphatically choosing this well-worn bear as coming closest to the "feel", if not the look, of the bear remembered from childhood. (Permission, Eimer Murphy)

My biggest piece of advice to anyone considering a role in theatre props is this: Always assume there is a Michéal McGuigan in every audience, and get the details right.

Fig. 12 Duffel bag before. Hester Swayne's bag for the 2015 production of Marina Carr's *By the Bog of Cats,* designed by Monica Frawley, directed by Selina Cartmell. (Permission, Eimer Murphy)

Fig. 13 Duffel bag, after breaking down, 2015. Hester Swayne's bag for the 2015 production of Marina Carr's *By the Bog of Cats,* designed by Monica Frawley, directed by Selina Cartmell. (Permission, Eimer Murphy)

Fig. 14 Making paper props for Tom Murphy's 1998 play, *The Wake*, 2016. Prop managers must also have a talent for counterfeiting and graphics work. Here, mid-1990s American cigarette packets, airline tickets, and Homestead bean labels were among the labels researched and reproduced for this production. Each packet of herbal cigarettes was repackaged in the "Winston" packaging pictured above, to appear in the play as duty-free brought home by returning emigrant Vera (played by Aisling O' Sullivan) in the 2016 production, directed by Annabelle Comyn and designed by Paul O' Mahony. (Permission, Eimer Murphy)

I leave the last word to playwright Frank McGuinness, a long time veteran of the Abbey Theatre, who gave this well-deserved tribute to our soon-to-retire Prop Master:

> I think the Abbey has a very honorable tradition of really minding what gets onto its stage, it always has done that. And we're spoiled in that way as well, definitely, we have somebody who can do it. We have the wonderful Stephen Molloy. He is brilliant. He's so inventive. There's no one else like him.[15]

Notes

1. Andrew Sofer (2003) *The Stage Life of Props*, page 3. Ann Arbor: University of Michigan Press.
2. John P. Harrington, J.P. (2009) *Modern and Contemporary Irish Drama*, introduction, page xi. New York: W.W. Norton & Co.
3. Abbey Theatre. (1906) *Irish Plays by The National Theatre Company, from the Abbey Theatre, Dublin*, page 2 [Publicity Brochure] (1906). Abbey Theatre Archive: ATA/MPG/1/A20.
4. Abbey Theatre. (1906) *Irish Plays by The National Theatre Company, from the Abbey Theatre, Dublin*, page 2 [Publicity Brochure] (1906). Abbey Theatre Archive: ATA/MPG/1/A20.

5. Ric Knowles,. (2012) "Editorial Comment: Theatre and Material Culture", page 1. In *Theatre Journal* 64.3 (2012).
6. Frank McGuinness, (2016) *Interview with Eimer Murphy, 15/05/2016.*
7. Frank McGuinness, a long-time veteran of the Abbey Theatre, gave me this lovely tribute to our soon-to-retire Prop Master: I think the Abbey has a very honorable tradition of really minding what gets onto its stage, it always has done that. And we're spoiled in that way as well, definitely, we have somebody who can do it. We have the wonderful Stephen Molloy. He is brilliant. He's so inventive. There's no one else like him. See Frank McGuinness, (2016) *Interview with Eimer Murphy,* 15 May 2016.
8. Jonathan Mandell, (2003) "THEATRE/The Tony Awards: Behind the Scene; Backstage at "Journey", a Diet Coke Distillery". *The New York Times,* 1 June. [online]Available at: http://www.nytimes.com/2003/06/01/theater/theater-tony-awards-behind-scene-backstage-journey-diet-coke-distillery.html.
9. Philip MacMahon, (2016) *Interview with Eimer Murphy,* 12 July 2016.
10. Liam Doona, (2016) *Interview with Eimer Murphy,* 7 June 2016.
11. Conall Morrison, (2016) *Interview with Eimer Murphy,* 2 May 2016.
12. Aisling O'Sullivan, (2016) *Interview with Eimer Murphy,* 8 July 2016.
13. McGUIGAN, M. (2016) *Interview with Eimer Murphy,* 15 June 2016.
14. Micheál McGuigan (2016) *Interview with Eimer Murphy,* 15 June 2016.
15. McGUINNESS, F. (2016) *Interview with Eimer Murphy,* 15 May 2016.

Bibliography

Abbey Theatre. (1906) *Irish Plays by The National Theatre Company, from the Abbey Theatre, Dublin,* page 2 [Publicity Brochure] (1906). Abbey Theatre Archive: ATA/MPG/1/A20.

Doona, Liam. (2016) *Interview with Eimer Murphy,* 06 July 2016.

Harrington, John. P. (2009) *Modern and Contemporary Irish Drama,* Introduction, page xi. New York: W.W. Norton & Co.

Knowles, Ric. (2012) "Editorial Comment: Theatre and Material Culture", page 1. In *Theatre Journal* 64.3 (2012).

Mandell, Jonathan. (2003) "THEATRE/The Tony Awards: Behind the Scene; Backstage at "Journey", a Diet Coke Distillery". *The New York Times,* 01 June. [online] Available at: http://www.nytimes.com/2003/06/01/theater/theater-tony-awards-behind-scene-backstage-journey-diet-coke-distillery.html [Accessed 03/09/2016]

McGuigan, Micheál. (2016) *Interview with Eimer Murphy,* 15/06/2016.

McGuinness, Frank. (2016) *Interview with Eimer Murphy,* 15/05/2016.

McMahon, Philip. (2016) *Interview with Eimer Murphy,* 12/07/2016.

Morrison, Conall. (2016) *Interview with Eimer Murphy,* 02/05/2016.

O'Sullivan, Aisling. (2016) *Interview with Eimer Murphy,* 08/07/2016.

Sofer, Andrew. (2003) *The Stage Life of Props,* page 3. Ann Arbor: University of Michigan Press

Irish Theatre: An Actor's Theatre

Bernadette Sweeney

In his performance notes the fifteenth-century Noh theatre practitioner Zeami offers us some ancient wisdom, found in generations of performance practice. As a description of the actor's process, it seems obvious: "The first thing to learn is how to become the character in question. After that, do what the character does", but it intrigues me that it comes from the Noh tradition, so far removed from recent Irish theatre practice.[1] Irrespective of time, form and culture, there are some irreducible elements to the work of the actor, and the work of the Irish actor is no exception.

Irish theatre is renowned for its playwrights, its politics and, to a lesser extent perhaps, its performers. It is widely considered a tradition of great literary wealth, of postcolonial significance, but what of the people who actually perform it? Who, night after night, take to our stages to sometimes almost empty houses in frustrating roles or substandard working conditions—what of the actors?[2]

The moment of performance has recently come under more academic scrutiny. It is an embodied phenomenon, it is elusive and evades documentation in any way that seems real—"all this is but a dream, too flattering-sweet to be substantial" (*Romeo & Juliet* II:2 line 140). The actors' work is for the most part unglamorous, it is draining and lacks financial stability. The costs of staying on the stage are high and some actors move into film (often moving over and back based on the availability of work), some move into production, directing, or move abroad to pursue other performance markets. Other actors expand their expertise and training into complementary areas such as yoga, pilates or other movement training, arts therapy or related fields. Some discover a niche role or form.[3] Sometimes the costs of staying on stage, as the recent *Waking the*

B. Sweeney (✉)
University of Montana, Missoula, MT, USA
e-mail: Bernadette.Sweeney@mso.umt.edu

E. Jordan, E. Weitz (eds.), *The Palgrave Handbook of Contemporary Irish Theatre and Performance*,
https://doi.org/10.1057/978-1-137-58588-2_26

Feminists movement has reminded us, are too high and our stages are ghosted by the unseen talent that has moved offstage for reasons of gender bias, career sustainability, lack of childcare, lack of roles or representation, and so on.[4]

My prompt has been to write on Irish theatre as an actors' theatre, but of course this is already problematic—how should I quantify Irish theatre? As mainstage work, community theatre, educational theatre, Irish-language theatre, theatre for social change, interdisciplinary work?—how should I represent the heft and scope of this widely divergent work, while trying to do justice to everyone? Well—I can't—but luckily these sectors are intimately linked and most practitioners have spent much of their career (often the most sustainable part) working in community or educational theatre (as an educator, and especially as a parent, I'm wondering if this is in fact the most important work we can have the privilege to make, although it's not always the most valued or well respected within the profession). As theatre makers, the smallest or least critically considered moment can be the one we remember best—when we introduce live theatre to a young audience, tell an especially powerful story, or connect with a particular audience or audience member. Some of the actors featured in this chapter are mentioned because they were responsible (at least in part) for founding a company, a movement, or a practice that has expanded Irish theatre in a new direction.

There are many theories on the work of the actor and I quote some here. But, mostly, this chapter is a historical perspective of the actor in Irish theatre, referencing some key actors from the past and present in an attempt to (re) place the work of the actor centre-stage in Irish theatre history. How to organise this material? I have opted to limit this chapter to the twentieth and early twenty-first century, and to look at a few key practitioners, representing moments and movements within that time frame. This is by necessity a sketch only. Featured actors have been chosen to provide a wide representation of performers, companies, time frames, as well as national and international experience, geography and gender. This chapter is informed by my experience as a practitioner as well as writer, as, like so many Irish actors, at home and abroad, my work in the theatre has been that of an actor, student, lecturer, dramaturg, writer, director and anything else related that will pay the bills. This has given me the opportunity to experience the privilege of making theatre and the magic that actors make and remake live every night before an audience, despite sickness, injury, and all the other real-life considerations that make their work all the more unlikely and more remarkable.

Polish theatre director and theorist Jerzy Grotowski describes the actor's work as one concerned with "discarding half measures, revealing, opening up, emerging [...] as opposed to closing up—is an invitation to the spectator".[5] What follows is a suggestion of a response to the task, illustrative rather than comprehensive—but it is, in Grotowski's words, half measures.

Many prominent Irish theatre companies were founded or co-founded by actors, and their roles in creating these stages merit our close consideration when considering Irish theatre as an actor's theatre. These companies have shaped the landscape of the profession: the Fay brothers at the Abbey; Micheál mac Liammóir and Hilton Edwards at the Gate and An Taibhdhearc; Marie Mullen and Mick Lally at the Druid; Stephen Rea at Field Day and so on. Christopher Morash and others have given us comprehensive histories of Irish theatre and readily identify that it did not begin with the founding of the Abbey—Dublin was a well-established centre for companies on their provincial tours from London. Traditional performances within communities—such as storytelling, mumming, performances by strawboys, wren boys and others—have ensured the presence of live theatre within our culture(s) for many years.[6] But the founding of the Abbey is often noted as a point of formalisation, a self-conscious moment of tradition-building, and accordingly I would like to begin by considering actor William Fay's contribution to Irish theatre.

William Fay and his brother Frank are well recognised figures in the history of the founding of the Abbey Theatre as Ireland's national theatre. Acting enthusiasts with hopes of a livelihood in the theatre, they trained with the Maud Ranford Dramatic School, Westland Row.[7] They were theatre makers in the way of so many actors—serving as performers, designers, set constructors, fund raisers and producers. They founded the Irish National Dramatic Society and, in this capacity, trained many young actors who would become founders of the professional theatre of Ireland, such as Sara Allgood and her sister Máire O'Neill. The Irish National Dramatic Society merged with Gregory and Yeats's Irish Literary Theatre to become The Irish National Theatre Society and opened the Abbey Theatre in 1904. William Fay gives us a wonderful insight into his work and life in the Irish Theatre in his book *Fays of the Abbey Theatre*:

> To-day, after giving much thought to the matter, I cannot make my mind up what was the real reason that induced me also to try and make a livelihood in the most precarious of all the arts. It may have been due to the fact that acting always seemed the most natural thing for me to do. Whether I did it well or ill it was always easy for me to impersonate other people. But, of course, Frank's influence counted, and if it hadn't been for Frank I daresay my acting would never have got beyond the back drawing-room stage.[8]

As builders or architects of Irish theatre, the Fays established the Abbey tradition in the moment of performance—and were previously overlooked because of this. Later scholarship has acknowledged the work of the Fay brothers, including for example Adrian Frazier's *Behind The Scenes: Yeats, Horniman and the Struggle for the Abbey Theatre* (1990) and again, Christopher Morash's *A History of Irish Theatre 1601–2000* (2002).

The founders of Dublin's Gate theatre and Galway's Irish language theatre An Taibhdhearc—Hilton Edwards and Micheál mac Liammóir—were not so overlooked as their visibility and output were extremely high. Their work is extensively documented by Christopher Fitz Simon's *The Boys* and other works as they, both English born, became giants of Irish theatre. Their work with the Gate, especially, brought international plays to the attention of Irish audiences.[9]

Like the Fay brothers they were actors who were also designers, directors, producers, and, as performers, constructed an Irish theatre by embodying characters every night from one season to the next. They also mentored many other young actors including Siobhán McKenna.

Born in Belfast in 1922, McKenna moved with her family to Galway in 1928. The family spoke Irish in the home and McKenna began her acting career in Irish-language drama while studying at University College Galway. She played a number of roles in Irish translations of canonical plays at An Taibhdhearc including Sean O'Casey's *Shadow of a Gunman* and *the Plough and The Stars* and O'Neill's *The Emperor Jones*. She joined the Abbey Players in 1944 and was tutored by actor F.J. McCormick during a tour of George Bernard Shaw's *Village Wooing*, thus honing her performer's craft in the model of master and apprentice. McKenna went on to perform in London and in a number of Hollywood film productions including *Daughter of Darkness* (1948) and *Dr. Zhivago* (1965).

In 1950 McKenna was commissioned by An Taibhdhearc to write an Irish-language translation of Shaw's *Saint Joan*, which she did, also taking the title role. When she later performed the role at the Phoenix Theatre, New York in 1956 *New York Times* critic Brooks Atkinson wrote: "Miss McKenna [...] fairly bursts into every scene, and usually at the top of her voice. She reads her lines with a sing-song rhythm that becomes rather hypnotic before the play is over. But the accent is Irish, which makes it particularly attractive to American ears, and the voice is extraordinarily powerful". As a consequence of this role, McKenna was the first Irish actor to win a Tony award.[10] This sing song quality to McKenna's voice contributed greatly to her last role as Mommo in Tom Murphy's *Bailegangaire* produced by Druid in 1985 where McKenna played the role of the bedridden *seanchaí* whose rhythmic storytelling carries the audience through hypnotic repetitions in the manner of the performance rituals of the *seanchaí* of old.

In including McKenna here, I think it is important to note that, in 1968 at the Abbey Theatre, she and Cyril Cusack starred in Anton Chekhov's *Cherry Orchard*, directed by Madame Knebal from the Moscow Art Theatre. McKenna, like Cusack and others in that production, was thus engaging in an internationally developed tradition of performing realism that reached back through the histories of the national theatres of Russia and Ireland.

McKenna was renowned throughout the 1970s for her touring production of *Here are Ladies*, performing Molly Bloom and Anna Livia Plurabelle from Joyce's *Ulysses*. However, McKenna's work was not just that of actor, translator and adapter, but of director too. Her directing credits included O'Neill's *Moon for the Misbegotten* in 1975 and Merriman's *Cúirt an Mheán Oíche* in 1984.

Kerryman Éamon Kelly and his wife Maura joined the Radio Éireann Repertory Company in 1952. From there he moved into stage acting and also developed an impressive career as a storyteller in the tradition of the *seanchaí*. Given his expertise as a storyteller, Kelly makes some wonderful observations on the work of the actor in his autobiography *The Journeyman:*

My first play on the stage of the new Abbey was *The Saint and Mary Kate*, adapted by Mary Manning from Frank O'Connor's novel of the same name. I played the part of a daft carpenter called Grog Mahon. I remember Patrick Murray's scenery had a towering contraption supporting a platform on which I did my work. Every night I had to climb up to it in a blackout. It was an unnerving experience. I dreaded missing my footing in the dark. The trick, I found, was to make a mental picture of the object and its direction from the wings while the light was on it. Then let your guardian angel take you by the hand when darkness fell.[11]

Kelly gives us an insight into the actor's process when he recounts how he created a habitual gesture for his character S.B. O'Donnell, as detailed in the script of Friel's *Philadelphia Here I Come*:

Here the script says that I take out my handkerchief, remove my upper denture, wrap it in the handkerchief and put it in my pocket. I had no false teeth to take out and I was in something of a quandary as to how I could make this piece of business look credible. Hilton [Edwards, director] unknowingly solved it for me. At the time he had put in a set of top dentures, which appeared to sit uncomfortably on his palate. He champed a little in the manner of a horse with an ill-fitting bit. He always had the denture in place, to enhance his smile, when he spoke to us on the floor, but when he went back to his directorial chair, he turned his head a little, holding a large handkerchief over the lower part of his face with his left hand, took out the offending denture with his right, folded the handkerchief over it quickly and put it in his pocket. An altogether slick operation. I practised this manoeuvre, taking out an imaginary denture behind the handkerchief, and it went well at rehearsal. As I have the knack of appearing gummy with my teeth in, when I did it on opening night it brought the house down.[12]

I feel it is worth quoting this excerpt in full as it gives us an insight into the process of an actor developing a character's mannerism.

This production of *Philadelphia Here I Come* opened at the Gaiety as part of the Dublin Theatre Festival on the 28 September 1964; it went on to tour internationally and had a long run on Broadway to great acclaim. Kelly was a fluent Irish speaker and so could move easily between languages. He was also fluent in the ways of rural Ireland, performing and disseminating the Irish storytelling tradition on stage and on radio and television with productions such as *The Rambling House* and *In My Father's Time*, continuing into his seventies.

American director Anne Bogart warns us against underestimating the work of the actor in rehearsal and performance: "[t]he assumption that a rehearsal is where the director tells the actors what to do while the actors store up that information is simply an avoidance of the actual crisis of effort and concentration needed to make art".[13] In any study of the career of an actor, what is often most astonishing is its intensity. Donal McCann is remembered by many as the finest Irish actor of his generation: from his role as Frank Hardy in Friel's *Faith Healer* (1980), to Captain Boyle in the Gate production of *Juno and the Paycock* (1986) to his final searing performance as Thomas Dunne in Sebastian

Barry's *The Steward of Christendom* (1995). He was the kind of actor who defied type, he could play the mean bravado of Boyle and the remote anguish of Gabriel in John Houston's film version of *The Dead*. He became synonymous with a kind of Irish performance style that is seemingly instinctive, honest and unrelenting. McCann's work was more poetic than mere realism; human, nuanced, intimate, and yet somehow larger than life. Playwright Hugh Leonard recalled watching McCann in a role Leonard himself had created:

> I remember [Donal McCann] came in, in the second act of *A Life* and he was playing the good-for-nothing Lar, the husband. He was wearing a watch-chain, sort of a fob, which went from his belt down in a loop and back up to his pocket. And I wondered why, because this character would never have a watch, he'd have pawned it. I said "What's he up to?" and then I forgot all about it. Then, later on, he asks somebody what they are going to drink and he reaches into his pocket and you see that there's a bottle opener on the end of the chain. I said, "Well I wish I'd thought of that."[14]

Marie Mullen founded the Druid Theatre Company in Galway in 1975, with Garry Hynes and the late Mick Lally. Druid has developed an international reputation for staging multiple works in a single production such as the *Leenane Trilogy* by Martin McDonagh (1997) and *Druid/Synge* (2005) when they staged the complete works of J.M. Synge. The company won four Tony awards for *The Beauty Queen of Leenane* in 1998, including best actress for Mullen in the role of Maureen Folan, and she plays the role of Maureen's mother Mag Folan in the 2016 Druid revival. For Druid/Murphy in 2012 she played Mother in *Famine* and Missus in *Conversations on a Homecoming*. For Druid/Shakespeare in 2015 she played Northumberland in *Richard II* and *Henry IV* parts one and two, and Exeter in *Henry V*. Mullen's stage work is largely associated with Druid, and Hynes as director, but she has also worked in film. Her credits include *The Butcher Boy* and the film version of Friel's *Dancing at Lughnasa*. She has been compared to Siobhán McKenna, with whom she performed in the first production of Murphy's *Bailgangaire* (1985) in the role of Mary. The comparisons became inevitable when Mullen played McKenna's role of Mommo in Druid's 2014 return to the play, staging it with its sister text *Brigit*. In an interview Mullen noted: "It's lovely that people are comparing me with Siobhán, but she was magnificent and it was a great gift to work with her. One thing I learned from Siobhán was that you must pay total attention to, and have absolute respect for the text. And for your audience. It's not about ego, it's not about you; in the end, it all comes down to being honest and true in relation to the play. You have to do the best service you can for the work itself." Mullen won the Special Tribute Award at the *Irish Times* Irish Theatre Awards in 2013. Her career is marked by her strong partnership with director and Druid co-founder Hynes, in one of the strongest and longest-lasting professional partnerships in Irish theatre history. Both women are ground-breakers, and Mullen's career success is a testament to the doggedness of the professional player, embodying her art night after night—as she moves faultlessly across roles—from Maureen to Mag in *The Beauty Queen of Leenane*, from Mary to Mommo in *Bailegangaire*—spanning generations within her life as a professional actor.

Tom Hickey trained with Deirdre O'Connell at the Stanislavsky Studio for actor training in Dublin, and honed his craft at the Focus Theatre, which he co-founded with O'Connell, playing roles in canonical plays such as *Miss Julie* and *Uncle Vanya*. He went on to develop an impressive career at the Abbey Theatre, playing in the premieres of many plays which have become key in the Irish canon, such as Frank McGuinness's *Observe The Sons of Ulster Marching Towards the Somme* (1985) and Tom Murphy's *The Gigli Concert* (1983). In the 1980s, Hickey was a core member of the group that brought Tom Mac Intyre's work centre stage at the Peacock, playing Tom Maguire in the controversial and since-lauded production of *The Great Hunger* (1983), adapted from the Patrick Kavanagh poem by Mac Intyre. Other plays by Mac Intyre in this sequence of work from 1983 to 1988 included *The Bearded Lady*, *Dance for your Daddy*, *Rise up Lovely Sweeney* and *Snow White*, but *The Great Hunger* is probably the most well recognised from this period as it was revived, performed in Paris, Edinburgh, as part of the Abbey tour to Russia, and elsewhere. This production is especially notable as it brought together a number of international influences to produce the work—actors Vincent O'Neill and Conal Kearney had trained in mime in Paris, Hickey in Stanislavski via the American Actor's studio with Deirdre O'Connell, while Mac Intyre was heavily influenced by Grotowski, Pina Bausch and others. Hickey remembered the rehearsal process for *The Great Hunger* as physically gruelling (personal interview), but said the resultant work was incredibly rewarding for him and the rest of the cast. This production confounded audiences expectations of how a revered Irish poem should be staged, and was in keeping with Kavanagh's gesture of writing such an uncompromising version of rural Ireland in the first place.

Tom Hickey's work with this sequence of Mac Intyre plays furthered his reputation as a physical actor ready to experiment and defy convention and his career since has lived up to his early innovation—he has performed in the first productions of a number of Marina Carr's plays, including *Portia Coughlan* (1996) *By the Bog of Cats* (1998) and *On Raftery's Hill* (2001). He worked again with Mac Intyre on *What Happened Bridgie Cleary* and the one-man show *The Gallant John Joe*, which has been revived on a number of occasions, including a recent tour in 2016 to highlight Parkinson's disease, on which Hickey has become a public figure as he continues to work while having the condition. He has performed in many productions in the UK, including a 2009 Complicité production of Beckett's *Endgame* directed by Simon McBurney.

His contribution to Irish theatre, like that of his fellow actors, is an entirely embodied one—he has lived his life before us on the Irish stage and brought his compelling, incredibly physical presence to many roles: Irish and otherwise. He has been instrumental in bringing an awareness of, and an ease with, international practices to the performance of Irish theatre.

Like Hickey, Jim Norton has developed a signature style informed by his training and early work. He trained for six months at the Royal Court, in a programme including mime, movement, mask work, comedy, text and improvisation with Keith Johnston. He also took movement classes with Litz Pisk. His early productions include *Juno and the Paycock* with Peter O'Toole and Siobhán McKenna. He has become associated with the work of Conor McPherson performing in *The Weir* (1997), *Port Authority* (2001), *Dublin Carol* (2000)—for which he won an Obie Award—and *The Night Alive* (2013). He won the 2008 Tony Award for his role as Richard Harkin in McPherson's *The Seafarer*—he also won the Olivier award for his performance in this role. He spoke eloquently on the challenge that faces every actor, with every role:

> you have had to, at some point, felt the emotion and sometimes that can be very frightening. I find it very frightening when I finally nail the essence of the character, of the black hole that you have to go into and I really experience it. It's very frightening but it's also a feeling of great power, you feel very powerful but then your job is to bring that on stage every night, it's like carrying something very precious in your hands on to the stage and saying here it is.[15]

Norton has worked extensively in the UK with the Royal Shakespeare Company (RSC) and at the National Theatre in London, and in US, and has often appeared with fellow Irish actor Ciarán Hinds, most recently in *The Crucible*, directed by Ivo van Hove on Broadway. Also on Broadway, he performed the role of Candy in *Of Mice and Men* (2014), his film credits include *Straw Dogs* (1971) and *Hidden Agenda* (1990). Norton suggests:

> The thing is to take the work seriously but not yourself because in the end we're just storytellers, strolling players, we're coming along for an hour or two of an evening to tell a story and to be as real as possible in that situation, and then you go off stage and check the football results.[16]

Like McCann before her, Olwen Fouéré is an Irish actor that defies type—she is as adept in Marina Carr's gothic realism as she is in the interdisciplinary performance explorations of her collaborations with Operating Theatre, co-founded with Roger Doyle in 1980, and her project TheEmergencyRoom (a necessary space), founded in 2009. She has often attributed her success across forms to her being raised in the west of Ireland by Breton parents and the consequent shift across language and culture.[17]

> I was so hungry for training when I started, but could only get full-time training abroad, and funding was a huge issue too. I was getting a lot of work at home, so that meant that I could learn through doing, but it was extremely hard and very,

> very painful at times because you're exposing yourself so much, and you're learning though doing and you're doing it in front of an audience and you're working with very experienced people. And sometimes it would take me weeks to discover something that I felt someone could have told me in a day.[18]

Fouéré identifies a 1978 production *The Fall of the House of Usher*, adapted by Berkoff, as directed by Peter Sheridan, as a key work of physical theatre. Workshopped over a number of months, it allowed her to experience the significant gain possible through an extended rehearsal period. Another role that shaped her subsequent career was Salomé in the eponymous play by Oscar Wilde, directed by Berkoff and staged at the Gate in 1988 before touring internationally.[19]

Although she has many mainstage roles to her credit—including Madame Pace in Pirandello's *Six Characters in Search of an Author* (1996), Hester Swayne in *By the Bog of Cats* by Marina Carr (1998) and Tamora in Shakespeare's *Titus Andronicus* (2005)—Fouéré is notable as an actor who moves smoothly across art forms, from the most realistic of realism, to interdisciplinary work, movement and towards performance art and installation. In many ways she is an actor before her time, as interdisciplinary work has become the norm only relatively recently in the Irish tradition.[20] Fouéré played Maeve in *The Bull* by Fabulous Beast/Michael Keegan Dolan in 2007 and in 2010 Fouéré's company TheEmergencyRoom paired with Rough Magic to produce *Sodome, My Love* by Laurent Gaudé, directed by Lynne Parker and translated by Fouéré herself. Here, Fouéré played a single survivor of the city of Sodom, the destruction of which is a cautionary bible story on the wages of sin. This one-person performance merged her talents with text and installation: according to Fintan Walsh, "Fouéré's voice is her most powerful instrument in imparting this tale: deeply textured, crystal clear, and resonant. She recites a monologue over the course of eighty minutes, her body dipping in and out of a series of awkward poses".[21,22] In 2013, like McKenna before her, Fouéré created an opportunity to develop a stream of consciousness style of performance by engaging with the work of Joyce: McKenna chose *Ulysses* and Fouéré chose *Finnegan's Wake*. *Riverrun* was first staged at the Galway International Arts Festival, co-directed by Fouéré and Kellie Hughes. She said of her process: "I still do not know how I know it. It has been a very different process in comparison to anything I have done before. It leads me. I dive in and hope only that I will not forget to swim".[23]

Fiona Shaw is another female Irish actor with an extraordinary body of work. Originally from Cork, she has worked nationally and internationally on stage and screen, and probably has one of the highest international profiles of any Irish actor. She has worked extensively with Shakespearean drama, at the RSC and elsewhere, and her long creative partnership with director Deborah Warner has resulted in a production history that reads like a who's who of women (and men) in the canon: *Electra* (1988), *Hedda Gabler* (1991), *Richard II* (1995), *Footfalls* (1994), *Medea* (2000), *Happy Days* (2007), *Mother Courage* (2009) and *The Testament of Mary* (2013).

She has often written and spoken about the phenomenon of performance, but I was especially struck by the following, which she wrote as part of a *Guardian* article on her work in a revival of *Electra* in the early 1990s. This is the conclusion of a searing article, where Shaw gives us a very personal insight into the challenges facing an actor when trying to work through personal tragedy, in Shaw's case, the death of her brother:

> Peter Stein said that tragedy was more necessary than comedy in a time of affluence. It puts you in touch with what needs to be faced—it cleans you, helps you. Electra made me realise that a play—with the right cast, in the right moment, in the right place—can be like sculpture and painting and literature all at once. As we flew out of Derry a few days later I wept for all sorts of reasons. I'd had a visionary time. People come to the theatre in the hope that it will have something to do with them—and when it touches them, it is both painful and brilliant.[24]

Stephen Rea is an internationally acclaimed actor of stage and screen, but one of his lasting legacies must be the founding of Field Day Theatre Company in Derry with Brian Friel, in 1980. This is another example of an Irish actor as an architect of Irish theatre, although neither Rea nor Friel could have realised the extent of their vision at that time. Field Day made a real contribution to the debate around the contemporaneous Troubles, with its extraordinary first play *Translations* (1980). Although Field Day's most consistent output was between 1980 and the mid-1990s, productions have continued intermittently since then, including the 2013 world premiere of Sam Shepard's *A Particle of Dread (Oedipus Variations)*. One of Field Day's greatest legacies, especially in their annual production period, was to bring productions on an extensive touring schedule around Ireland, revitalising audiences and introducing professional, live theatre to young people around the whole island. I have always felt that this is an under-appreciated aspect of the Field Day project, especially given the attention garnered by their publication projects. By bringing live theatre to under-served regions of the country, I believe that Field Day played a big part in shaping the subsequent generation of Irish theatre makers. Rea's more recent roles include playing 3 in Enda Walsh's *Ballyturk* in 2015 and paranoid loyalist Eric Miller in *Cypress Avenue* by David Ireland at the Abbey and later the Royal Court in 2016. Rea has an impressive film and television profile, from Neil Jordan's *The Crying Game* (1992) to Inspector Bucket in BBC One's *Dickensian* (2015).

Over the course of this chapter, I have a cited a number of international theatre directors and theorists in an attempt to put the work and processes of the Irish actor in a broader context of international practice. Over the course of his extraordinary career, Peter Brook has paid particular attention to the actor's journey, and poses some questions that are difficult to answer: "In the rehearsal process, one must take care not to go too far too soon. Actors who exhibit themselves emotionally too early on often become incapable of finding true relationships with one another […] How does one allow this intimate expression to grow until it can fill a vast space without betrayal? How does one raise the pitch of one's voice without it distorting the relationship? It is incredibly difficult: it is the paradox of acting."[25]

Lisa Dwan's work exemplifies Brook's "paradox of acting". Dwan originally trained as a dancer, but injury forced her to diversify. She had some early success in film and television, but came to prominence as a stage actor when she toured internationally with a Royal Court Trilogy of Beckett's work including *Not I*, *Footfalls* and *Rockaby*. This production was directed by Walter Asmus and premiered in 2012. Her descriptions of the experience of performance are very direct:

> my ears bleed, I pull my muscles, I'm up on my toes [...] I got a hernia from the physical effort of pushing the words out. I can taste my own stage fright; I can feel my stage manager's stage fright. There are moments when my internal voice is going, "When are you going to swallow? You're like a pelican!"[26]

The physical challenges of Beckett's later work are no secret, and many other Irish actors, including Fouéré and Shaw, have suffered through the challenge of following in Billie Whitelaw's footsteps. Dwan gives voice to the artistic rewards that come with such painful work:

> the restrictions that Beckett places on the body really are gifts to the actor, because they do liberate you in such a way that you become elemental. And it's not only the body that is restrained in these pieces—it's the voice as well. I've got a very kaleidoscopic voice, so I need to hone that, so not to allow the intention and the intent to leak away [...] In *Footfalls*, for example, I play the mother, I play the daughter, May—and the argument and the wounds in between them. The pain and the memories, and the ghosts, are coming under the bedroom door like wind.[27]

Although Dwan toured that production extensively, when it concluded in 2016 she had not yet had enough of meeting Beckett's exacting challenges. *No's Knife*, Dwan's own seventy-minute adaptation of Beckett's *Texts for Nothing*, co-directed by Joe Murphy, was produced by the Old Vic London in September 2016. She described the piece and its setting as

> the bog of our minds [...] When I enter into a landscape like this, so vast and various and raw and real and elemental, I don't feel like a human being, I don't feel like an idea of a woman any more. I'm child, I'm mother, I'm bird, I'm eagle, I'm air, I'm weapon, I'm wound, I'm water. When I commune in that way, and let my identity stretch, I feel really fulfilled. It feels like a very true space, and I feel full. And I feel that everything I have is enough.[28]

It strikes me the Dwan's descriptions of her experience of performance are not unlike those of Fouéré, doubtless there are more comparisons to be made between the innovative and viscerally inescapable work of these two women.[29] More recently, Dwan performed the title role in the Abbey production of

Marina Carr's version of Tolstoy's *Anna Karenina* in late 2016. Her film credits include *Oliver Twist* (1997), *the Tailor of Panama* (2001) and *Bhopal a Prayer for Rain* (2014); her television work includes *Mystic Knights* and *Fair City*.

Dwan is one of a newer generation of Irish actors who are shaping Irish theatre through their work across geographical and form boundaries. They often emerge from the professional training programmes and university theatre departments, such as those in Trinity College Dublin, The Gaiety School of Acting, and University College Cork's drama and theatre studies programme. Their careers are often fast-tracked by moving across stage, film and television platforms—and sometimes video gaming too. Their social media profiles keep them in the public eye and are perhaps helping to build a new audience, which responds to the slippage between forms as theatre becomes mediatised and boundaries dissolve between traditional performance categories of theatre, performance art, musical, dance and installation. Three young female actors are of particular note: Sarah Greene trained at the Gaiety School of Acting and has quickly developed her career on stage and screen. She was nominated for both a Tony and an Olivier award for her role as Helen McCormick in the 2013 London production of McDonagh's *The Cripple of Inishmaan*, which also starred Daniel Radcliffe. Her work with Druid Theatre Company includes roles in John B. Keane's *Big Maggie* and *Playboy of the Western World*. With Rough Magic she has performed in *Phaedre* and *Peer Gynt*. In 2012 Greene played Alice in *Alice in Funderland* a co-production with the Abbey and thisispopbaby (2012). This piece by Phillip McMahon and Raymond Scannell, directed by Wayne Jordan, brought the musical back to the national theatre. Greene played Alice, a Cork ingénue who gets lost in the underworld of the big city. *Alice in Funderland* stages queer culture, references high and low art and aims to heavily satirise mainstream social politics. This production brought an edgy, contemporary Dublin to the stage, and a new kind of audience to the seats. Greene also works in film; her credits include *Eden* (2008), *The Guard* (2011) and *Noble* (2014), and she has a growing television profile, including *Bachelor's Walk* and *Penny Dreadful*.

Ruth Negga trained as an actor at the Beckett Centre in Trinity College Dublin. She has an impressive range of theatre film and television credits, and roles have included Ophelia in *Hamlet* at the National Theatre, London, two seasons with the TV drama *Love/Hate*, and *Oedipus Loves You* with Pan Pan theatre company Dublin (2006). Negga, like Greene, is also developing an extensive film and television resume and audiences follow her work across stage and screen. She played Mildred Loving in *Loving* (2016), directed by Jeff Nichols, a film based a true story of interracial marriage in Virginia in the 1950s, which depicted how the couple were instrumental in challenging anti-miscegenation law in the US Supreme Court. This film received much critical attention at the Cannes and Toronto film festivals, and Negga was nominated for an Academy Award as best actress in a leading role in 2017. Negga plays Tulip O'Hare in the 2016–2017 season of television drama *Preacher*.

Charlie Murphy trained at the Gaiety School of Acting and has become well known to Irish audiences as Siobhan in five seasons of the gangland TV drama *Love/Hate*. On stage, she has appeared as Adele in *Our Few and Evil Days* by Mark O'Rowe (2014) with Sinead Cusack and Ciarán Hinds and she performed Isla in Enda Walsh's *Arlington* for the 2016 Galway Arts festival. She commented on the challenge of performing in such dystopian work: "Enda's worlds are quite harrowing and the play is quite dark but there are moments of pure comedy and fun to perform, so I haven't been dragging things home with me at night", she says.[30] Here, Murphy identifies the challenge to every actor, not to be "dragging things home at night". If an actor is to aim for Brook's "intimate expression", to be open, vulnerable, true to the moment and to the character, he or she must also find a way to be true to the self, and protect the emotional life of the actor while serving that of the character.

Jim Norton offers a pithy summation of the work of the actor: "I'm an actor for hire, that's what I am, I'm a strolling player."[31] For all its perceived glamour and the well-recognised rewards of being a high-profile actor, acting is a courageous and selfless act, and Irish theatre has benefitted from the work of actors in portraying characters, creating productions, companies, and shaping the emerging tradition. For every highly, even commercially, successful actor—such as Liam Neeson or Andrew Scott—there are countless others who drift away from the profession because of lack of job security and support. Recent Arts Council reports have chronicled the income of those in the acting profession, and actors like Owen Roe and Sharon Horgan have spoken out about the difficulties of making a living, even when appearing regularly on the main stages. Although the *Waking the Feminists* movement has refocussed some attention on this matter, it is not new, as evidenced by an *Irish Times* article from 1998, which opens with: "When their four-year-old daughter, Megan, was a baby, actors Owen Roe and Michele Forbes both appeared in Marina Carr's play, *The Mai*, at the Peacock. Finding reliable childcare for Megan every night was impossible. Their solution? They were not on stage at the same time, so they took turns holding the baby off-stage."[32]

Acting is a way of life, and although we have the occasion family dynasties, such as the Cusacks (Cyril, Sinéad, Sorcha, Niamh) or the Gleesons (Brendan, Domhnall, Brian), each actor has to find a way to pursue this way of life while managing to have a life, a viable career, relationships, perhaps a family. Is the current model unsustainable? Hopefully the current generation of actors will continue to speak out and help to make the necessary changes (David Kelly, Finnoula Flanagan, Anita Reeves, Micheál MacLíammóir, Barry McGovern, Sarah Jane Scaife, Donal O'Kelly, Des Nealon, Bríd Brennan, Eileen Walsh, Karl Shiels, Anna Manahan, Máire Nic Shiubhlaigh, Aaron Monaghan, Dermod Moore, Andrew Scott, Ali White, Aisling O'Sullivan, Mikel Murfi, Donal Donnelly, Tim Loane, Catherine Walsh, Brenda Scallon, Vincent O' Neill, Michael McElhatton, Barry Fitzgerald, Mary McEvoy, Ciarán Hinds, Andrea Irvine, Allen Leech, Karen Ardiff, Marie Jones, Garrett Lombard, Stephen Brennan, Sara Allgood, Rosaleen Lenihan, Bríd Ní Neachtain, Johnny Murphy,

Stephen Brennan, Rory Keenan, Nuala Hayes, Cillian Murphy, Aiden Gillen, Sinéad Cusack, Liam Cunningham, and so on) If I were to have used the space allowed here to simply list actors' names I would not have even begun to give an adequate representation of Irish actors' range of talents and achievements. I was tempted, nonetheless. Once again, if "all this is but a dream, too flattering-sweet to be substantial" (*Romeo & Juliet* II: 2), then to every Irish actor who will take the stage tonight, wherever that stage might be, to all who have before us and to all who will follow, thank you for giving substance to our dreams, and for allowing us to dream again.

Notes

1. Zeami, *Performance Notes*, translated by Tom Hare (New York: Columbia UP., 2008), 100.
2. See indicative list of names of actors towards the end of the chapter.
3. Such actors include Pat Kinevane and his work in the one-man show or solo-performance format *Forgotten* (2006), *Silent* (2011) and *Underneath* (2016). Pat Kinevane with Fishamble's artistic director Jim Culleton, won the Olivier Award for Outstanding Achievement in an Affiliate Theatre for *Silent*. See http://www.irishtimes.com/culture/stage/pat-kinevane-s-singular-vision-from-the-brink-of-the-world-1.2022636
4. http://www.wakingthefeminists.org/
5. Jerzy Grotowski, (ed. Eugenio Barba) *Towards a Poor Theatre* (London: Bloomsbury, 1991 (1968)), 212
6. See Morash's *A History of Irish Theatre 1601–2000*, Cambridge, 2002, Sweeney's *Performing the Body in Irish Theatre* Palgrave Macmillan 2008, and Pilkington's *Theatre and Ireland* Palgrave Macmillan 2010.
7. W.G Fay and Catherine Carswell, *The Fays of the Abbey Theatre*, https://archive.org/stream/faysoftheabbeyth006134mbp/faysoftheabbeyth006134mbp_djvu.txt, 34.
8. Ibid., 5.
9. See also Tom Madden's *The Making of an Artist: Creating the Irishman Micheál MacLiammóir* (Dublin: The Liffey Press, 2015).
10. Wolfgang Saxon, "Siobhan Mckenna Is Dead; Actress Known For St. Joan", *The New York Times*, November 17, 1986, http://www.nytimes.com/1986/11/17/obituaries/siobhan-mckenna-is-dead-actress-known-for-st-joan.html, par.8.
11. Éamon Kelly, *The Journeyman*, (Colorado: The Irish American Book Company, 1998), 127–8.
12. Ibid., 85–6.
13. Anne Bogart, *And then, you act* (London: Routledge, 2007), 39.
14. Hugh Leonard quoted in *Theatre Talk: Voices of Irish Theatre Practitioners*, eds. Lillian Chambers, Ger FitzGibbon and Eamonn Jordan (Dublin: Carysfort Press, 2001), 260.
15. Jim Norton quoted in Patrick O'Kane, *Actors' Voices: The People Behind the Performances* (London: Oberon Books, 2012), 293.
16. Ibid., 292.
17. Chambers et al., *Theatre Talk*, 155.

18. Ibid., 157.
19. See "Olwen Fouéré's corpus: the performer's body and her body of work" by Shonagh Hill in *Radical Contemporary Theatre practices by Women in Ireland*, eds. Miriam Haughton and Mária Kurdi (Carysfort, 2015).
20. I clearly remember, years ago, watching Fouéré participate in an open workshop on the Abbey stage conducted by Berlin's Schaubühne. As one of those in "the audience" I remember being struck by her honesty and her ability to remain open to learning while participating in what was essentially a performance. She was remarkable because of this—as probably the most experienced actor there she also seemed, to me at least, to be the most present, and the most humble.
21. Fintan Walsh, "Sodome: My Love", tmarchive.ie/web/Reviews/Current/Sodome--My-Love.html, par. 4.
22. See also Cathy Leeney's "Second skin: costume and body: power and desire", in *Radical Contemporary Theatre practices by Women in Ireland*, eds. Miriam Haughton and Mária Kurdi (Carysfort, 2015).
23. https://www.theguardian.com/stage/2014/feb/14/riverrun-joyce-finnegans-wake-olwen-fouere-national-theatre
24. https://www.theguardian.com/books/2012/jul/17/fiona-shaw-peace-camp-2012
25. Peter Brook, *There are no secrets: Thoughts on Acting and Theatre* (London: Methuen, 1993), 33.
26. Sarah Hemming, "Interview: Lisa Dwan", *The Financial Times*, https://www.ft.com/content/f0e27a1e-f8b9-11e4-be00-00144feab7de, par.4.
27. Michael Coffey, "Lisa Dwan and Walter Asmus", *BOMB Magazine*, April 12, 2016, http://bombmagazine.org/article/333746/lisa-dwan-walter-asmus, par. 10.
28. Belinda McKeon, "Lisa Dwan: 'Beckett Made These Wounds Universal'", *The Guardian*, September 17, 2016, https://www.theguardian.com/stage/2016/sep/17/lisa-dwan-samuel-beckett-nos-knife, par. 12.
29. See Fouéré entry.
30. Maria Rolston, "Charlie Murphy is drawn back into the darkness with new show Arlington", *Irish Examiner*, July 5, 2016, http://www.irishexaminer.com/lifestyle/artsfilmtv/charlie-murphy-is-drawn-back-into-the-darkness-with-new-show-arlington-408453.html, par.20.
31. Norton quoted in O'Kane, *Actors' Voices*, 302.
32. Anon, "Left Holding Baby Offstage", *The Irish Times*, November 12, 1998, http://www.irishtimes.com/culture/left-holding-baby-off-stage-1.213682, par.1.

Bibliography

http://www.wakingthefeminists.org/. Accessed 30 March, 2016.

Anon. "Left Holding Baby Offstage." *The Irish Times*, November 12, 1998. http://www.irishtimes.com/culture/left-holding-baby-off-stage-1.213682. Accessed 28 March, 2016.

Anon. "MacLiammóir's Magic Captivates an Innocent Galway." *Galway Advertiser*, March 13, 2014. http://www.advertiser.ie/galway/article/67950/macliammirs-magic-captivates-an-innocent-galway. Accessed 29 March, 2016a.

Anon. "Remembering Michael Mac Liammóir, an Irishman from London." *RTÉ Archives*, http://www.rte.ie/archives/2013/0306/374380-michael-mac-liammoire-an-irishman-from-london/. Accessed 29 March, 2016b.

Anon. "Siobhán McKenna -- A legend in Irish Theatre." *Galway Advertiser*, March 27, 2014. http://www.advertiser.ie/galway/article/68048/siobhn-mckenna-a-legend-in-irish-theatre. Accessed 28 March, 2016.

Armstrong, Maggie. "Stage - Mover and Shaker: The Solo comeback of Tom Hickey." *Irish Independent*, April 17, 2016. http://www.independent.ie/entertainment/theatre-arts/stage-mover-and-shaker-the-solo-comeback-of-tom-hickey-34628284.html. Accessed 20 April, 2017.

Auld, Tim. "Stephen Rea: 'I Never Wanted to be a Polite Actor.'" *The Telegraph*, March 25, 2016. http://www.telegraph.co.uk/theatre/actors/stephen-rea-interview-i-never-wanted-to-be-a-polite-actor/. Accessed 28 March, 2016.

Bogart, Anne. *And Then, You Act*. London: Routledge, 2007.

Brook, Peter. *There Are No Secrets: Thoughts on Acting and Theatre*. London: Methuen, 1993.

Chambers, Lillian, Ger FitzGibbon and Eamonn Jordan, eds. *Theatre Talk: Voices of Irish Theatre Practitioners*. Dublin: Carysfort Press, 2001.

Clayton-Lea, Tony. *All the Range*. https://issuu.com/caraaugust/docs/cara_july_2016. Accessed 10 July, 2016.

Coffey, Michael. "Lisa Dwan and Walter Asmus." *BOMB Magazine*, April 12, 2016. http://bombmagazine.org/article/333746/lisa-dwan-walter-asmus. Accessed 30 April, 2016.

Crawley, Peter. "Pat Kinevane's Singular Vision from the Brink of the World." *The Irish Times*, December 3, 2014. http://www.irishtimes.com/culture/stage/pat-kinevane-s-singular-vision-from-the-brink-of-the-world-1.2022636. Accessed 10 July, 2016.

http://www.dublincity.ie/sites/default/files/content//RecreationandCulture/libraries/Heritage%20and%20History/Dublin%20City%20Archives/Documents/Liammoir_collection.pdf. Accessed 30 March, 2016.

http://www.donalokellyproductions.com. Accessed 28 March, 2016.

Fay, W. G., and Catherine Carswell. *The Fays of the Abbey Theatre*. https://archive.org/stream/faysoftheabbeyth00613‍4mbp/faysoftheabbeyth006134mbp_djvu.txt. Accessed 21 March, 2016.

Fitz-Simon, Christopher. *The Boys: A Biography of Micheál MacLíammóir and Hilton Edwards*. London. Nick Hern Books. 1994.

Frazier, Adrian. *Behind The Scenes: Yeats, Horniman and the Struggle for the Abbey Theatre*. University of California Press, 1990.

Grotowski, Jerzy. *Towards a Poor Theatre*. London: Methuen, 1991 (1968).

Gussow, Mel. "Modify Beckett? Enter, Outrage." *The New York Times*, March 26, 1994. http://www.nytimes.com/1994/03/26/arts/modify-beckett-enter-outrage.html. Accessed 20 March, 2016.

Hemming, Sarah. "Interview: Lisa Dwan." *The Financial Times*. https://www.ft.com/content/f0e27a1e-f8b9-11e4-be00-00144feab7de. Accessed 17 July, 2017.

Haughton, Miriam and Mária Kurdi, eds. *Radical Contemporary Theatre Practices by Women in Ireland*. Dublin: Carysfort, 2015.

Kelly, Éamon. *The Journeyman*. Colorado: The Irish American Book Company, 1998.

Kennedy, Maev. "Olwen Fouéré's Riverrun, The Watery Voice of Joyce's Finnegan's Wake." *The Guardian*, February 14, 2004. https://www.theguardian.com/stage/2014/feb/14/riverrun-joyce-finnegans-wake-olwen-fouere-national-theatre. Accessed 28 March, 2016.

Laffan, Pat and Faith O'Grady. *Donal McCann Remembered: A Tribute*. Dublin: New Island Books, 2000.

Lane, Anthony. "Chatterbox."http://www.newyorker.com/magazine/2014/09/29/chatterbox. Accessed 30 June, 2017.

Leeney, Cathy. "Second Skin: Costume and Body: Power and Desire" in *Radical Contemporary Theatre Practices by Women in Ireland*, edited by Miriam Haughton and Mária Kurdi. Carysfort, 2015.

Madden, Tom. *The Making of an Artist: Creating the Irishman Micheál MacLíammóir*. Dublin: The Liffey Press, 2015.

Mikhail, E. H., ed. *The Abbey Theatre: Interviews and Recollections*. New Jersey: Barnes & Noble Books, 1988.

Morash, Christopher. *A History of Irish Theatre 1601–2000*. Cambridge University Press, 2002.

McKeon, Belinda. "Lisa Dwan: 'Beckett Made These Wounds Universal.'" *The Guardian*, September 17, 2016. https://www.theguardian.com/stage/2016/sep/17/lisa-dwan-samuel-beckett-nos-knife. Accessed 28 June, 2017.

O'Kane, Patrick. *Actors' Voices: The People Behind the Performances*. London: Oberon Books, 2012.

Pilkington, Lionel. *Theatre and Ireland*. Basingstoke: Palgrave Macmillan 2010.

Rolston, Maria. "Charlie Murphy is drawn back into the darkness with new show Arlington." *Irish Examiner*, July 5, 2016. http://www.irishexaminer.com/lifestyle/artsfilmtv/charlie-murphy-is-drawn-back-into-the-darkness-with-new-show-arlington-408453.html. Accessed 28 March, 2017.

Saxon, Wolfgang. Siobhan Mckenna Is Dead; Actress Known For St. Joan. *The New York Times*, November 17, 1986. http://www.nytimes.com/1986/11/17/obituaries/siobhan-mckenna-is-dead-actress-known-for-st-joan.html. Accessed 02 April, 2016.

Shaw, Fiona. "Playing Electra in Derry Helped Me see the Power of Tragedy." *The Guardian*, April 29, 2014. https://www.theguardian.com/stage/2014/apr/29/fiona-shaw-electra-northern-ireland-tragedy. Accessed 02 April, 2016.

Sweeney, Bernadette. *Performing the Body in Irish Theatre*. Basingstoke: Palgrave Macmillan, 2008.

Sweeney, Bernadette, and Marie Kelly. *The Theatre of Tom Mac Intyre: Strays from the Ether*. Dublin: Carysfort Press, 2010.

Walsh, Fintan. "Sodome: My Love." tmarchive.ie/web/Reviews/Current/Sodome--My-Love.html. Accessed 20 April, 2017.

Woddis, Carole. "Powerful Package Makes Electra a Gas." Herald Scotland, December 30, 1991. http://www.heraldscotland.com/news/12649839.Powerful_package_makes_Electra_a_gas/. Accessed 28 March, 2016.

Zeami. *Performance Notes*, translated by Tom Hare. New York: Columbia University Press, 2008.

The Figurative Artist & ÚNA'N'ANU

Úna Kavanagh

As I was working on a sculpture in 1991, during my Masters at the National College of Art and Design, there was a distinct moment of awareness and understanding of what kind of artist I was. I realized I was a figurative artist. The body was my metaphor. Some artists create only in a singular form, others in many. For example, Tracey Emin and Louise Bourgeois create sculptures, paintings, video, embroidery and installation. They use many and varied mediums with which to create. I felt that was the pathway I would also like to choose: let the concept choose the medium. At that time, to make one piece of sculpture or painting I would excavate and create; I would write, draw, compose. I would move and photograph myself and life models to see the three dimensional image in space. I would make maquettes, films and collages of photography. I was working on very large-scale pieces that took months to make. I had many ways of producing a final work. I had found my language and could express what I thought was the truth and a way of being in this world.

Today, particularly in my work with ANU, I still use the same artistic methodologies and language. They co-exist to help me create a live embodied performance with the company. The fifteen embodiments to date cross form from performance art, live art and film, to theatre, movement and dance.

I have used visual notebooks since I was a teenager as part of the making process. These are full of sketches, photos, miscellaneous objects and what I came to understand later as "internal monologues". I always knew I was a figurative artist. I felt that the connective metaphor for me as an artist was the body, in particular the female body. There were narratives I wanted to transmit through the sculptures and paintings; metaphors to communicate to an

Ú. Kavanagh (✉)
Actor, Theatre-Maker and Artist, Dublin, Ireland

E. Jordan, E. Weitz (eds.), *The Palgrave Handbook of Contemporary Irish Theatre and Performance*,
https://doi.org/10.1057/978-1-137-58588-2_27

audience, a witness, a viewer, an other. When I sat in the studio in those early days writing streams of thought and consciousness for sculptures, I remember observing "Why?". Why am I recording the fictional narrative, the psychological outlook, the trauma, the cause and effect, the geography of the female body? Why am I painting, drawing a score of emotional journeys for them, as well as making a final fragment held forever in a medium of clay or bronze? I realized only many years later that I was writing about my own body. I was using the body—the figure—as an artistic metaphor revealing political, social and cultural themes that stemmed from my own experience as a woman. I would later transfer the sculptural body to my own physical body and activate my work in a new way, as a performer and artist. It was a process: an artistic process that moved between image, word, sound, gesture, private and public, internal and external. It was a system of creative excavation and interrogation.

I engaged very quietly with this artistic practice for many years. In the 1990s and 2000s, I continued making large figurative pieces in ceramic. I was drawn to the nature of clay as it mirrored directly the fragility of humans. I navigated my way through performances in film, theatre, radio and television, while continuing a very quiet private arts practice at the kitchen table. Making, making, making. Sometimes in bronze, sometimes because of financial budgets and single parenting I could only have pencils, but that did not stop my engagement with an arts practice, or a way of making my art.

In 2007 I held a large solo exhibition with Amnesty International. It included sculpture, painting, film and animation. It was opened by Her Excellency Priscilla Jana—the South African Ambassador to Ireland—with an extraordinary speech about women, indigenous culture the body, humanity, war and poverty.

"I'm Only Human" has been the constant theme of my art works. It inspired my next solo public work, *Black Bessie*, produced in 2009. I had been writing this piece since 2000. I had long wanted to create a performative embodiment of an Irish woman. A nomadic, homeless Irish woman. A woman enslaved by a State, abused and thrown away by a patriarchal society, a metaphor for an Ireland that I saw everywhere. After the exhibition, I wanted to merge the worlds of my own personal art practice and place the body, the female body, the female Irish body, mine, at the core of this work. She came into being as *Black Bessie* in the 2009 Fringe Festival in Dublin, with Karl Shiels as director, Paul Walker and Semper Fi as co-producers. *Black Bessie* was nominated for the Fishamble New Writing Award, which was a delight, but more extraordinary was the fact that the performance had happened. I had borrowed from The Credit Union. I had hired Merrion Square Park. All the arts practices and disciplines I engaged with as an artist had run parallel to each other. Crossing art forms, the core of my practice is about using the metaphor of the female body to illuminate and address the potency of its (dis)placement within a patriarchal state.

The artistic crafts that I had quietly been working at for years had come together in a public expressionistic work of art that utilized Word, image, movement, sound, geography, environment and body as site. Sara Keating in the *Irish Times* wrote:

> The audience are gathered around a ring of votive candles as if in worship, the light barely illuminating the shape of a woman cowering under a blanket of leaves. This is Black Bessie, homeless and mad, who takes her name from the bike she rides.
>
> Úna Kavanagh's dense Beckettian text is a rush of words and thoughts and confessions. In under 30 minutes she shares her life story: a failed marriage, the death of her children, mental illness, and the strangling attitudes to sex that a repressed religious society engendered. Playing low to the ground, caressing the earth, Kavanagh—who also performs this short, impressionistic piece—embodies Black Bessie's own desperate desire to join her children in the grave.[1]

This was figurative nomadic art piece that was all about the presence and proximity of audience, witness and viewer. It was an ephemeral art piece that took place over seven days.

In early 2010, a few months later I walked into the Lab in Foley Street and met Louise Lowe and Owen Boss. The room was a bright white studio with images, portraits, histories, drawings, maps and photographs covering the walls. I felt instinctively that I had met with something very special: kindred thinkers and artists who were cross-pollinating art forms.

We were beginning at that time the development of *World's End Lane* in 2010. This was to become the first of four performances that make up "The Monto Cycle" (2010–2014), characterized by Brian Singleton in his book, *ANU Productions: The Monto Cycle*:

> Set within a quarter square mile of Dublin's north inner city these performances featured social concerns that have blighted the area over the past 100 years, including prostitution, trafficking, asylum-seeking, heroin addiction, and the scandal of the Magdalene laundries.[2]

These works combine site, history, archive, design, dance, image, sound, light, environment, community, local historians, performance, duration and an audience of one. For *Worlds End Lane* I was asked to respond to archives—to histories of real people—in this case "Honour Bright/Lizzie O'Neill". "I'm Only Human" rang out loudly in my head. This work, this excavation of histories, societies, injustices and humanity was incendiary. My figurative artistic journey continuing, I became a host-body. Part myself, part fictional artistic creation, part reality-inspired. This was a brand new way of making and the beginning of creating live-scores for live art performances.

In ANU, we work collectively and collaboratively as a group of artists. It reminds me of the shared studios I have worked in. Artists working solely, then collectively, provoking, creating, making, presenting new work and critiquing every day. This is at the heart of ANU's work. Provocations are set, artists make and respond through image, film, dance, scenes, music and sound composition, presenting back to each other and responding. As a company, we assimilate the language of visual art, of theatre, of dance, of design, of performance art and of durational performance. As a painting or a sculpture, creations such as *The ANU Triptych* (2016) or *The Monto Cycle* exist as works of art, born out of a studio practice and experienced by and communicated with audiences.

The creation of the scores for these embodiments have included looking at the histories of women and female bodies over the past hundred years. Honour/Úna, Magdalen/Úna, Alpha A/Úna, Bella/Úna, Linenopolis/Úna, Civilian/Úna: all inspired by real women, real histories. They emerge from the studio work. Everything is to be created. Every embodiment, every physical score, vocal score, durational presence begins with the artist delving into the source. That source is the company of artists, which includes designers, actors, dancers, artists, members of the community, academics, the archive, the research and the testimonies.

What is truly special to me is the audience. We, the company, make and create new work that goes live on a date for a certain duration and then ends. It is an ephemeral work shared with audiences, held in memory and body. I always feel like a physiological transformation of energy has taken place as each audience member is placed within the work. Their presence is a constant when creating the work. The audience ignite the work and are intrinsic to it. During the live performances, the audience become, as Peter Crawley put it, "the dramaturgs of their own experience". There really is an exchange between us. A communion of sorts. To me, it feels like a part in a musical score where—between the crotchets, the minims and the semi-breve—there is a note that only sounds when the audience creates it. A note echoed over and over in varying tones.

When I wrapped my arms around the audience in *World's End Lane* and asked them "Have you ever been loved?" that space appeared in the score for them. When I asked them to hold the bucket of breast milk in *Laundry* (2011), the space appeared. When I asked them to shoot the bell that was rung when the Magdalen escaped in *Vardo* (2014), the space was there. When I asked them to "Look At Me" in *Boys of Foley Street* (2012) it was there. Right up to today in *These Rooms* (2016) the moment when Ellen/Úna falls out of her standing after receiving news of her husband's death, an audience member is asked to "set her down". That space of communion, of holding, between me and the audience transcends into something unique and real. It is an exchange where we are both communing, both of us in full acknowledgement of each other. It is truly special to me. These, and many more, are some of the most precious moments I have experienced in any work of art. In that moment in time and space our presences co-exist and reality is forever changed. I feel privileged. I feel that we have both experienced a theatre or art that has transcended the form and held for a breath before the score continues. This is the extraordinary detail of ANU's work. I feel it. I remember it. I create the physical space for it. It only exists with an audience there. It is so exciting: everybody present.

Sometimes my artworks have existed within the ANU pieces. In my first film *Turbulence*, in *World's End Lane*. My figurative drawings were on the walls of "Bella's" room in *Vardo*, "Montopoly", a game I created, sitting in the window of the Oonagh Young Gallery, is in *Vardo*. "Alpha A thinks she is Cindy Sherman: Rage and Oblivion Selfies" is a new photographic work inspired by *Boys Of Foley Street* and "Magdalen" exists in film and photography. All these new artworks were inspired by my work with ANU.

As a figurative artist I continue to make work, sculptural and kinaesthetic, which includes using my own body as site and ANU continue to inspire me.

Notes

1. Sara Keating, "Fringe Reviews," *The Irish Times*, September 17, 2009.
2. Brian Singleton, *ANU Productions: The Monto Cycle* (Palgrave Macmillan, 2016), 1.

Bibliography

Keating, Sara. "Fringe Reviews." *The Irish Times*, September 17, 2009

Singleton, Brian. *ANU Productions: The Monto Cycle*. London: Palgrave Macmillan, 2016.

Irish Theatre: A Director's Theatre

Ian R. Walsh

Directors have been ill served by histories of Irish theatre. The dominant narrative of Contemporary Irish theatre is one that charts the development of playwrights and their contribution to a playwriting tradition in Ireland. The work of the director is at best name-checked in most theatre histories and at worst ignored entirely. In a programme note for a festival of his plays staged to celebrate his seventieth birthday, Brian Friel controversially expressed a view of the director as superfluous to the theatrical process. He wrote of directors as "interlopers" who "attempt to usurp the intrinsic power of the play itself".[1] For Friel, they contribute nothing and, although once deemed important, are now as "unnecessary as bus conductors".[2]

In this chapter, I wish to re-inscribe the important work of the director into the narrative of contemporary Irish theatre. To survey all the many directors that have worked in Ireland and their achievements would require a book length study, and so this chapter does not aim to offer a comprehensive survey.[3] My methodology here is revealed in my title, where I ask the reader to imagine Irish theatre not as privileging the playwright but as a director's theatre. I thus re-examine some productions that have been considered landmark achievements in contemporary Irish theatre, highlighting the contributions made by directors to their achievements. I take this position to acknowledge that the theatre is a collaborative artform created by a team of artists all contributing to the final production, and that spectators experience all aspects of a production at once rather than in sections and are therefore unable to isolate individual artists' contributions in moments of performance. The fact that three of the

I. R. Walsh (✉)
National University of Ireland Galway, Galway, Ireland
e-mail: IAN.WALSH@nuigalway.ie

E. Jordan, E. Weitz (eds.), *The Palgrave Handbook of Contemporary Irish Theatre and Performance*,
https://doi.org/10.1057/978-1-137-58588-2_28

productions discussed below are plays written by Brian Friel hopefully aids in countering his dismissal of the director.

I begin by placing the director at the accepted inaugurating moments of contemporary Irish theatre, which I identify as: Samuel Beckett's *Waiting for Godot* produced by the Pike Theatre in 1955 directed by Alan Simpson and Carolyn Swift and Brian Friel's *Philadelphia Here I Come!* (1964) produced by the Gate Theatre directed by Hilton Edwards.

Inaugurating Moments

In his influential *Contemporary Irish Drama*, Anthony Roche names Samuel Beckett as "the presiding genius of contemporary Irish drama".[4] He argues that Beckett's *Waiting for Godot* in particular had a "profound and far-reaching influence" in Ireland. It was the Pike Theatre's Irish premiere production of *Waiting for Godot* that toured for a year around Ireland in 1955 that was to introduce the work of Beckett to the island.

This production, directed by Alan Simpson and Carolyn Swift,[5] became a part of popular culture at the time:

> The pantomime actor, Jimmy O'Dea, introduced Godot into his variety routines, and a cartoon in one of the Irish daily papers showed a puzzled policeman explaining to his colleague that a suspicious-looking vagrant claimed to be "waiting for Godot".[6]

One of the reasons for the popularity of the Pike *Godot* in Ireland was that it was produced with a distinctly Irish flavour. The tramps were played by Austin Byrne and Dermot Kelly as two baggy-suited Dublin music-hall characters; Pozzo (Nigel Fitzgerald) was dressed as a "Somerville and Ross Anglo-Irish squire",[7] while Lucky (Dermot Donnelly) was styled as an Irish servant from a Boucicault play. This Irish setting was not created with the intention of reducing the work, as Christopher Morash points out "having sketched in a rough Irish framework, he [Simpson] left it at that, refusing to interpret the play any further".[8] For Simpson, the most important consideration for the director "is to achieve the atmosphere".[9] He writes: "I have found from working in the Pike, that my only true satisfaction in theatre comes from the creation of a complete involvement of emotion whether it be happy or sad, between an audience and cast".[10]

It was this that he wished to create in the Pike's *Godot* production. He writes: "In *Waiting for Godot* the objective of the producer should be to create the feeling that these four characters are isolated in eternity".[11] It was the physical space and limitations of the Pike theatre that developed Simpson's approach. The stage was only twelve feet by twelve feet. So small was the stage that Simpson claimed they were unable to mount a performance in English of Ionesco's *The Chairs* as they "simply did not have the room on the stage for the chairs themselves".[12] However, through a method of lighting that he had learnt from ballet, he was able to make the stage look bigger than it was. He writes: "In other words, I achieved something in the nature of a 3-D theatre, making the audience feel they were a part of the play and involving them in its action and atmosphere".[13] The legacy of Simpson and Swift as directors was this emphasis on atmosphere and communion with the audience. Indeed "a feeling of being isolated in eternity" is something that much of the most lauded of contemporary Irish theatre productions from Marina Carr's *By the Bog of Cats* (1998) to Enda Walsh's *Ballyturk* (2014) have engendered in audiences. For Roche "Contemporary Irish drama does not so much rely on a plot as on a central situation, whose implications are explored and unfolded in a process which is more likely to be circular and repetitious than straightforward".[14] In such drama, in which an audience is no longer following the unfurling of a simple narrative, it falls to the director to bring together all the resources of the stage—such as lighting, movement and use of space—to immerse an audience in a visually arresting and palpably atmospheric experience, what Simpson terms a "3D Theatre". Rebecca Schneider and Gabrielle Cody in their study of twentieth-century directing practices have identified this as key to the rise of the director. Schneider writes:

> The increasing polarization between the viewer and the viewed, a by-product of technologies of vision and "alienation" in industrialised urban society, contributed to a drive toward a director who could produce a "communal" experience [citing Cole and Chinoy 1976: 3] either through visual effects or ritual effects. The language of integration or of "primitive" communion became prevalent among artists.[15]

Interestingly the "inaugurating moments" of contemporary Irish theatre all date from the late 1950s and early 1960s. This was an unprecedented era in Ireland of increased industrialisation and the rapid growth of mass communications. T.K. Whitaker's expansionist programme for the opening up of the Irish economy gradually overtook Eamon De Valera's long-held policy of self-sufficiency—and television arrived in Ireland. The BBC was received from the late 1950s on the east coast and RTÉ began to broadcasting in 1961. It is thus not surprising that it is in this period that we see the emergence of the director as a more dominant force in Irish theatre.

The other most-cited production for ushering in a new type of theatre in Ireland is the 1964 production of *Philadelphia, Here I Come!* produced by the Gate Theatre for The Dublin Theatre Festival. Richard Pine claims that it is with this production that Brian Friel emerged as "the father of contemporary Irish drama".[16] But, on examination, the achievement of this production was also due in no small part to the influence and direct hand of two directors.

In 1963 Friel was invited to observe the celebrated director Sir Tyrone Guthrie at his theatre in Minneapolis. Friel wrote:

> [*Philadelphia*] would never have been written had I not been an apprentice there [Minneapolis] under the great Tyrone Guthrie. Indeed it was the first thing I wrote in a state of near giddiness when I came back to Ireland still on a Guthrie High.[17]

It is the direction of Shakespearean plays and classical drama that won Guthrie international renown. Samuel Leiter has argued in his survey of modern directors *From Belasco to Brook: Representative Directors of the English Speaking Stage* that few individuals have been as singularly responsible for the popular characterisation of the last century as "the age of the director" as William Tyrone Guthrie.[18] As a director, he is most associated with the contemporary use of an Elizabethan thrust stage in his productions. This was something he developed in the Ontario Festival and then institutionalised in his Guthrie Theatre in Minneapolis. The thrust stage, for Guthrie, greatly aided in the creation of a theatre that could never be reduced to naturalistic illusion. J.L. Styan writes of Guthrie as having "believed that the drama makes its effects, not by creating illusion, but by means of what he thought of as 'ritual', and he planned his stage upon the uncompromising theory that illusion was not the aim of performance".[19] This conception of the theatre in terms of ritual and make-believe proved inspirational to Friel. In *Philadelphia, Here I Come!* he discovered an inventive theatrical mode to depict the experience of emigrating from a rural community. It engineered a radical departure from the naturalistic staging of the past by creating the device of splitting Gar O'Donnell's consciousness between two characters: Gar Public and Gar Private. The play's structure is not dependent on the unfolding of a plot, but instead offers a series of remembered rituals enacted on Gar's last night in Ballybeg.

Although instrumental in its creation, Guthrie did not go on to direct *Philadelphia*. It was Hilton Edwards, a titan of the craft in Ireland, who directed the first production and indeed the subsequent productions in the West End and on Broadway. Edwards, along with Mícheal Mac Liammóir, was the co-founder of the Gate Theatre in Dublin. Counter to the Abbey theatre—which was considered a writer's theatre—the Gate set itself up as a theatre of the director, from its establishment in 1929 onwards. It aimed to experiment "in methods of presentation".[20] The leading director in the Gate was Edwards and he came to *Philadelphia* with nearly forty years of experience in staging innovative productions. Mac Liammóir wrote of him: "It was he who introduced to Dublin methods of production, décor, and lighting, handling of mass effects, experiments in choral speaking, in scenic continuity, in symphonic arrangements of incidental music, of mime and gesture hitherto barely understood".[21]

Edwards, like Guthrie, took inspiration in his approach to the stage from an earlier era in theatre history. His preferred style was that of the *commedia dell'arte*, as is evident from the title of his excellent book on stagecraft *The Mantle of Harlequin*. It is not hard to see why Edwards was attracted to *Philadelphia*, which has much in common with this theatrical style of presentation. The play takes as its main conflict the clash of generations, which was the basis of *Commedia* performances. Also in its dramaturgy of repeated enacted rituals, *Philadelphia* follows the structure of *commedia*, which was organised around a series of set pieces of comic business called *lazzi*. Gar Private, in his performativity and his mischievous servility to Gar Public, would seem to don the mask of Harlequin.

Roche tells us that Edwards consulted with Friel throughout the rehearsal process "in order to maximize the play's effectiveness as a piece of live theatre",[22] and Friel made alterations to the script in rehearsal as a result. The most significant change was made to the ending. The original script included an epilogue in which the two Gars sit on seats representing the airplane of the following day, bound for Philadelphia. Edwards cut this, incorporating the exchanges of the two in the airplane into the end of the piece. Friel conceded that the change worked better in performance. The short story writer Frank O'Connor wrote in his review of the play that he feared Friel had fallen "into the wicked clutches of the wicked magician, Hilton Edwards".[23] The playwright replied to O'Connor in *The Sunday Independent* defending his director, stating:

> I would like to point out that I was grateful to Mr. Edwards for the magic he worked with my play, that the magic was discreet and in tone, and flattered as I am by the epithet "innocent" I am afraid I cannot accept it in this context.[24]

Edwards, like Guthrie, conceived of theatre in terms of ritual communion with a live audience. He wrote, in a phrase that echoes Simpson: "the stage picture must step once more out of its frame and become three-dimensional; and it must live, not by its semblance of reality, but because it is reality—real actors speaking real words to real audiences.[25]

Christopher Murray has identified Yeats's remark "I always feel my work is not drama but the ritual of a lost faith" as a notion that is "embedded in much contemporary Irish drama".[26] After examining the work of Simpson, Guthrie and Edwards it would seem that such a notion has been embedded by directors whose common thread is a commitment to a theatrical experience that is not mimetic but immersive, aiming to create a temporary congregation of believers in artifice. The subsequent generation of directors would continue to act as masters of ceremonies to such strange rites.

Masters of Ceremonies

The effect of Edwards's production of *Philadelphia* on a generation of playwrights has been charted by Thomas Kilroy,[27] but less known is the lasting impression it had on the director Joe Dowling, who would come to have a significant influence on Irish theatre in subsequent years. Dowling, only 16 at the time, was so taken by the play that he attended almost every performance of the festival run. He writes:

> It wasn't just the theme of the play its brilliant technique or its compelling characters that changed my young life. No, it was the acting of that first company under Hilton Edwards' magnificent direction that really hit me in the solar plexus.[28]

Dowling's career in theatre did not, however, begin as a director at the Gate Theatre, but as an actor at the Abbey Theatre in the late 1960s. He trained at the Abbey School and then joined the company. Frustrated that the national theatre was losing younger audiences, he went to then Artistic Director Hugh Hunt and pleaded for something to be done. Hunt sent him to Manchester to see some of the theatre-in-education companies that were running effectively there. On his return, he set up the Young Abbey, which was a touring company that would bring productions to younger audiences.[29] It was with this company that he first began to direct, but he graduated to the Abbey main stage in 1975 after having served as an assistant director to Tomás Mac Anna, who remained a lifelong mentor. He was then made Director of the Peacock and subsequently became, at twenty-nine, the youngest-ever Artistic Director of the Abbey in 1978. While at the Abbey, he directed the premieres of a number of important Irish plays—including Brian Friel's *Living Quarters* (1975) and *Aristocrats* (1979). He also made a commercial and critical success of Friel's *Faith Healer* in the Abbey in 1980, after its disastrous premiere on Broadway.

This production is most often remembered for Donal McCann's stellar performance as the titular faith healer, Frank Hardy.[30] However, examining Dowling's rehearsal script of the play it is clear how much the director contributed to the performances.[31] The script shows a blank page for notes beside each typed page, just as in a stage manager's prompt copy. In the notes on these pages it is possible to chart how Dowling interprets and scores the performance as he marks movement (such as "slowly back"), gives suggestions on how a line should be said (such as "ironic"; "suddenly surprised") and offers criticism and encouragement (such as "a bit too staccato"; "enjoy it further").[32] The notes never invent new bits of stage business or radically change any part of the written script. There is no sense that the director wishes to impose his ideas on the play. Instead, he uses the text as a guide and mines it for inspiration. Dowling writes: "The directorial function is to draw the best from all the elements—actors, designers, technical crew, in order to fully realize the intentions of the text".[33]

In directing works by Friel,[34] Dowling learnt that "it is the minutiae of the work which provide its most important exploration".[35] For him, it is "the unspoken things, the silences, the misunderstandings, the deliberate confusions and the tricks of memory" in Friel's plays "which tell us the stories and maintain the narrative drive".[36] This attention to the minutiae is essential to *Faith Healer*. The play demands an almost bare stage, save for a few signature props and chairs, which has the effect of focussing the audience's attention on the body of the performer and their place on stage. In such a set-up, each movement and position on the stage become laden with meaning. Dowling first considered that the play should be staged in the smaller Peacock space due to the nature of the script, but then realised "that it can only work if it is this very compressed thing in a large space".[37] In the video of the 1990 revival production, Dowling's sense of compression is discernible: the figures on the large stage are lit in chiaroscuro with a strong contrast between light and dark.[38] The effect is one in which the lit figures present as a temporary illumination before an overwhelming darkness—a flame soon to be snuffed out. In the final moments of the piece the light grows dim and only a spotlight is left shining on Frank's/McCann's head as he raises his eyes to the heavens succumbing to an inevitable darkness that then falls. Murray writes of this moment of "compression" in the first production:

> In stepping towards the audience and into theatrical blackout, Frank Hardy establishes communion with the audience as a healer, and vice versa in the two-way traffic of the stage [...] So it was, on that glorious night at the Abbey premiere on 28 August 1980, when the audience sat stunned for a whole minute, it seemed, while registering the catharsis, pleasurable release after terrible, shared uncertainty.[39]

In 1985, Dowling had resigned his post at the Abbey, disgusted at the interferences of the Board in the management of the theatre. He went on a year later to exact revenge when he garnered worldwide acclaim directing O'Casey's *Juno and the Paycock*, a favourite of the Abbey repertoire, at the rival Gate Theatre. This eventually led Dowling into the directorship of the prestigious Guthrie Theatre in Minneapolis, a position he held until 2015. In gaining the position in Minneapolis, Dowling's career presents an extraordinary circularity, bringing him to the place that began the production that had inspired him all those years previously to dedicate himself to the theatre.

In 1998, Garry Hynes was honoured by Broadway with a Tony award for Best Director and has the distinction of being the first female to win that award. In a similarly circuitous journey to Dowling's, Hynes's success in New York represented a return rather than an arrival. It was in New York that she had first been inspired to work in the theatre. Hynes was the co-founder of Druid Theatre Company in 1975 and has been its Artistic Director from 1975–91 and from 1994 to the present. She was Artistic Director of the Abbey Theatre from 1991–94. She does not have any formal training in theatre, but instead learnt her trade through directing productions for the student drama society while attending University College Galway. As a student in the early 1970s, she spent her summers working in the USA, where she managed to see productions of the then vibrant theatrical avant-garde in New York City. She went to the Performance Garage, as well as seeing the work of Joseph Chaikin and Meredith Monk. These productions had a great impact on her and contrasted greatly with the work that was being produced in Ireland at the time. She writes:

> I saw theatre that was being made by young people, or people reasonably young and it was being made in small rooms, and it was immediate and it was accessible and it was available and it was tremendously exciting to me.[40]

Inspired by this experience, Hynes, the actor Marie Mullen—whom she met at university—and the actor Mick Lally formed Druid Theatre Company in Galway.

The intent of the company in its early years was to replicate in the west of Ireland what Hynes had seen in New York. In the early years, the company staged plays in "small rooms" in Galway city until they eventually secured rental of a building and created a small theatre there, which has become their permanent home.

The attraction and creation of work in "small rooms" formed Hynes as a director. She herself has spoken of trying to create an "intensification" of experience in her productions.[41] An important process for Druid is the use of the small theatre space in Galway. It has become common practice for the company to premiere their works in the Druid theatre and then bring them on tour. The theatre's limitations in terms of space have become one of the strengths of Hynes's productions, as the intimacy of the space leads to an intensification of experience for the audience.

This was made most apparent in one of Hynes's most legendary productions of Tom Murphy's *Bailegangaire*, which premiered in Druid in 1985. In the Druid Archives a letter from Ronan Wilmot (an actor and director of some note in his own right) details how affected he was by the performance of *Bailegangaire* at the Druid theatre. He writes of being "overcome and overwhelmed", saying "it was a joy to see it in Druid it was pure ecstasy". He finishes the letter with "never leave Galway".[42] When Druid productions go on tour, they generally try to replicate the feeling created by the Druid space for audiences in larger auditoriums. This is evident in the video of the same production of *Bailegangaire* at the Gaiety theatre in 1986.[43] The full expanse of the large Gaiety stage is reduced to a small playing area—through expert lighting by Roger Frith—of a small country kitchen set placed in the centre of the stage. This is a bold move in a static play where most of the action involves an old woman telling a story from a bed placed in the kitchen. Hynes showed great confidence in her actors, believing that through the strength of their performances they would capture and sustain the audience's involvement. Indeed, the performances from this production have also become the stuff of legend, in particular that of Siobhán McKenna.[44]

Unfortunately, the achievements of Hynes as director of this production have often been overlooked, replaced by a concentration on McKenna's performance and Murphy's writing. There is a moment in the 1986 production of *Bailegangaire* that serves as an example of Hynes's favoured "intensification" of experience already mentioned. At the end of Act One a distinct turning point is registered by the director when Mommo falls asleep; it is not as pointed or powerful in the printed text. The character, and the audience, are given a short reprieve from the incessant tale told by Mommo of "Bailegangaire and how it came by its appellation".[45] The stage direction in the script then states:

> She switches off the radio. She switches off the light. She goes to the table and idly starts lighting candles on the cake, using a new match to light each one. A car passes by outside. She blows out the candles, tires of them.[46]

In the video of the production filmed at the Gaiety theatre, Dublin in 1986 we see Marie Mullen as Mary follow the directions to switch off the radio and the lights.[47] She then goes to light the candles on the cake and does use a new match to light each one. However, she does not do this idly. After each match is struck and candle lit, she delivers a line. The act of lighting the candles is made overtly ritualistic in this moment and the lines become a type of transformative incantation. For, as the final candle is lit, Marie Mullen looks out to the audience and, instead of "tiring of the candles", she holds the lit match and shows in her face the dawning of a realisation, then blows out the candle with intent. This moment shows a change in her and anticipates her subsequent action, wherein she decides that the tale must be finished for her to gain freedom from the past and strength to face the future.

This moment thus doubles as both *anagnorisis* and an inciting moment of action. It is clearly communicated as such to the audience. Also, the symbolic power of the fragile flame of the birthday candle illuminating hope for these characters from the gloom of their lives is later picked up when Mary lights Mommo's cigarette, encouraging her valiantly to finish her tale. At this point, Mary repeats Dolly's complaint from earlier "Why doesn't she finish it and have done with it" but in this act of repetition she transforms the line to become a mission statement for heroic action—a prophecy fulfilled in the next Act. In Murphy's script, the lighting of the birthday candles is a ritual full of symbol and theatrical imagery, but it is not a significant moment for the inciting of action. The decision to get Mommo to complete her tale is made on Mary delivering the line "Why doesn't she finish it and have done with it" in the play text. Hynes plants the idea and the decision much earlier, giving the actor more to time to show her transformation and thus underscore this change for the audience. This is an example of how a director can not only enhance and communicate the intention of a script in performance, but also offer further clarity, spectacle and emotional depth.

Such interventions by directors can often become the element of the production that most resonates with audiences. For the director Peter Brook, the acid test for the ephemeral art of theatre is "what remains" once the performance has ended.[48] It is a "literal acid test" as what marks the "essence" of a performance is the "central image of the play" burnt into memory. Two such seminal productions of contemporary Irish theatre, with lasting theatrical images that were the creation of the directors rather than the playwrights, are *Dancing at Lughnasa* (1990) and *Woman and Scarecrow* (2006).

Sound and Vision

One of most controversial directorial interventions in Irish theatre is the staging of the dance sequence by Patrick Mason in the premiere production of Brian Friel's *Dancing at Lughnasa*. Mason trained at the Central School of Speech and Drama and subsequently taught there in 1972. That same year saw him arrive in Dublin to take up a position as voice coach in the Abbey. He then left Ireland to become a lecturer in Performance Studies at Manchester University in 1975, but returned to the Abbey as a resident director in 1978. After a long association with the national theatre, at which he directed seminal productions of plays by Friel, Leonard, Murphy, Kilroy, Mac Intyre, and, in particular, Frank McGuinness, he became Artistic Director from 1994–99.[49] Mason credits his collaborations with Mac Intyre and the actor Tom Hickey on a range of productions at the Peacock between 1982 and 1989 as influencing his development:

> I think it was the intensity and energy of that contact that really jolted me out of a more literal, realist kind of reading of text into a far more emblematic, symbolic reading of text and action. Since the work I did was trying to find some kind of synthesis between these two aspects of the work.[50]

Another influence on Mason's approach has been his extensive direction of opera. From opera he has learnt that "[t]heatre needs music, because music heightens energy. It is an irresistible force. With strict realism so much energy is concentrated on the introverted struggle to get an actor to project internal states. Music is extrovert".[51] With Friel's *Dancing at Lughnasa* (1990), a play that relies heavily on music and tableaux for its effects, Mason found the perfect piece in which to display the maturation of his style. This was most clear in the scene in which all the sisters temporarily forget themselves in a wild liberating dance. Under Mason's direction the five personalities of the women sound and signal individually, only to then harmonise and dissolve into each other, becoming ecstatic as they surrender to the tribal percussion of heavy bodhrán beats. The effect was one of a transcendent *coup de theatre*. The production became a theatrical phenomenon with long runs in the West End and on Broadway. Mason winning the Tony Award for Best Director in 1992. However, many academics have criticised how Mason had staged this dance, claiming its celebratory tone was contrary to the directions written by Friel in which the dance is described as "aggressive", "grotesque", erratic and "parodic".[52] Murray discusses this in a book on Friel:

> It became a "number", a display of ensemble dance. It is necessary to put all of this technical proficiency to one side if the strange and "parodic" dimension of the dance as conceived by Friel is to be entered.[53]

In this criticism the dance is viewed as mere entertainment ("a number") playing to please the crowd, robbed of some dark and dangerous performance potential. What is not taken on board is that, in his staging of the dance sequence as a display of virtuosity and celebration, Mason was allowing for the audience to share in the experience of the dance and thus enter the world of the play at a deeper level. In other words, in enjoying the dance the audience can experience the feelings of release and pleasure that the women on stage are feeling. Richard Dyer has written of such moments of escapism in musicals as offering "the image of 'something better' [...] that our day-to-day lives don't provide".[54] He identifies this utopianism of entertainment as being contained "in the feelings it embodies",[55] presenting the spectator with "what utopia would feel like rather than how it would be organized".[56] Thus, in experiencing the dance as "a number" under Mason's direction, the audience share in the liberation and abandon of the dance, which makes the subsequent tragic story of these sisters repressed and oppressed lives all the more poignant and heartfelt. The play would not have had the impact it did were it not for Mason's decision to stage this scene as he did.

A less controversial piece of staging that enhanced and captured the essence of an important contemporary Irish drama was the final Pietà-like image created by Selina Cartmell in the Irish premiere of Marina Carr's *Woman and Scarecrow* at the Peacock theatre (2007).

Cartmell has worked extensively in Ireland and was made Artistic Director of the Gate Theatre, Dublin in 2017. Her education in art history is very apparent in her work, which is characterised by captivating theatrical images.[57] When describing her process Cartmell resorts to the language of sculpture, describing rehearsals as "chipping away at this big piece of marble".[58] She brought this surreal visual sensibility to the Peacock production of *Woman and Scarecrow*, where the stage presented a surreal image of a bed and a wardrobe stuck in a barren snowy landscape. This contrasted with the mostly naturalistic staging by Ramin Grey in the premiere production at the Royal Court, London. The latter production presented the mythic aspects of the play as invading the natural space, whereas the Peacock production from the beginning placed the entirety of the action in an expressionistic psychic space. Carr has described the play as "a deathbed aria" and in her production Cartmell found an inventive piece of staging at the end of the play that managed to make the themes of the piece sing in one image.[59]

Instead of having Woman "throw herself on Scarecrow" and then die in her arms as the stage directions suggest, the Peacock production saw Olwen Fouéré's Woman carefully remove her nightdress and place herself in the lap of a seated Barbara Brennan as Scarecrow, falling into the same pose as Christ in Michelangelo's Pietà.[60] Shonagh Hill writes of this stage image as presenting two lasting impressions: it is a "beautiful monument to the silence of death" while also "highlighting Woman's control of the sculpting of her corpse and self-authored death".[61] The closing Pietà-like image in this production presented acceptance but also self-determination in its deliberate "constructedness" and theatricality. For Cartmell herself "[i]t captures everything in one image, without words, without anything".[62]

It should be clear from this short survey of landmark productions of contemporary Irish theatre that the achievement of the director cannot continue to be overlooked. That said, I am aware that, in making a claim here for the director in Irish theatre through some representative figures, I am guilty of overlooking the work of many important directors who have contributed to the rich landscape of Irish theatre and performance. The work of Lynne Parker,

Jason Byrne, Gavin Quinn, Conall Morrison, Annie Ryan, Sarah Jane Scaife and many more—particularly in their revivals of canonical work—continually challenge, invigorate and re-imagine what Irish theatre and performance is and can be. It also should be acknowledged that many contemporary Irish playwrights such as Enda Walsh, Conor McPherson and Mark O'Rowe regularly direct premieres and revivals of their own work, collaborating closely with designers and choreographers. Directors in Ireland are not as superfluous as "bus conductors" but are instead indispensable drivers in the creation of a production, steering audiences to share in a ritual of communion, intensifying the experience and making the essence of the piece visually immediate and arresting.

Notes

1. Anthony Roche, *Brian Friel: Theatre and Politics* (Basingstoke: Palgrave, 2012), 33.
2. Ibid.
3. For sample survey piece on Irish Directors see Walsh, Ian R. (2016), "Directors and Designers since 1960" in *The Oxford Handbook of Modern Irish Theatre* (Oxford: Oxford University Press), 443–458.
4. Anthony Roche, *Contemporary Irish Drama* (Basingstoke: Palgrave, 2009), 4.
5. Siobhán O'Gorman has cogently argued that Carolyn Swift contributed to the direction of the Pike shows along with her husband Alan Simpson, but her contribution has gone largely unacknowledged. See O'Gorman, Siobhan, "Hers and his: Carolyn Swift, Alan Simpson, and collective creation at the Pike Theatre" in *Women, Collective Creation and Devised Performance* (Basingstoke: Palgrave, 2016).
6. Christopher Morash, *A History of Irish Theatre 1601–2001* (Cambridge: Cambridge University Press, 2002), 207.
7. Alan Simpson, *Beckett and Behan and a Theatre in Dublin* (London: Routledge and Kegan Paul, 1962), 124.
8. Morash, *A History of Irish Theatre 1601–2001*, 203.
9. Simpson, *Beckett and Behan and a Theatre in Dublin*, 98.
10. Ibid., 8.
11. Ibid., 101.
12. Ibid., 6.
13. Ibid., 7
14. Roche, *Contemporary Irish Drama*, 4.
15. Rebecca Schneider and Gabrielle H. Cody, *Re: Direction: A Theoretical and Practical Guide* (London: Routledge, 2002), 5.
16. Richard Pine, *The Diviner: The Art of Brian Friel* (Dublin: University College Dublin Press, 1999), 190.
17. Quoted in Mike Wilcock, *Hamlet: The Shakespearean Director* (Dublin: Carysfort Press, 2002), 140.
18. Samuel Leiter, *From Belasco to Brook: Representative Directors of the English Speaking Stage* (New York: Praeger, 1991), 77.
19. J.L. Styan, *Modern Drama in Theory and Practice, 3 Vols.* (Cambridge: Cambridge University Press, 1983), 182.

20. Bulmer Hobson, *The Gate Theatre* (Dublin: Gate Theatre, 1934), 21.
21. Peter Luke, ed. *Enter Certain Players: Edwards, Mac Liammóir and the Gate, 1928–1978* (Dublin: Dolmen Press, 1978), 15.
22. Roche, *Brian Friel: Theatre and Politics*, 46.
23. Ibid., 47.
24. Quoted in Roche, *Brian Friel: Theatre and Politics*, 48.
25. Hobson, *The Gate Theatre, 45.*
26. Christopher Murray, *The Theatre of Brian Friel: Tradition and Modernity* (London: Methuen, 2014), 90.
27. Thomas, Kilroy (1992) "A Generation of Playwrights" *Irish University Review* 22: 1, 135–141.
28. Christopher Fitz-Simon, ed. *Players and Painted Stage: Aspects of the Twentieth Century Theatre in Ireland* (Dublin: New Island, 2004), 100.
29. Dowling has had a lifelong commitment to theatre education. He went on to set up the Gaiety School of Acting in Dublin and to found a theatre education programme in the Guthrie Theatre.
30. See Nicholas Grene "Defining Performers and Performances" in *The Oxford Handbook of Modern Irish Theatre* (Oxford: Oxford University Press, 2016), 459–477.
31. Abbey Digital Archive.
32. Abbey Digital Archive.
33. Alan J. Peacock, ed. *The Achievement of Brian Friel* (Gerrards Cross: Colin Smythe, 1992), 188.
34. Dowling also directed the premiere of *The Communication Chord* (1983) for Field Day Theatre Company and *Fathers and Sons* (Friel's adaptation of Turgenev's *A Month in the Country*) for the Gate in 1992.
35. Peacock, ed. *The Achievement of Brian Friel*, 180.
36. Ibid.
37. Lilian Chambers et al., eds., *Theatre Talk: Voices of Irish Theatre Practitioners* (Dublin: Carysfort Press, 2002), 135.
38. Abbey Digital archive.
39. Murray, *The Theatre of Brian Friel: Tradition and Modernity, 92.*
40. Garry Hynes, "Galway to Broadway and Back Again", *American Journal of Irish Studies* 9 (2012): 81.
41. Chambers et al., eds., *Theatre Talk: Voices of Irish Theatre Practitioners*, 200.
42. Druid Archive.
43. T2/1102A, VHS recording, *Bailegangaire*, 1986, Gaiety Theatre, Dublin. James Hardiman Library, NUI Galway.
44. McKenna was dying of cancer at the time and her creation of the role of Mommo in Bailegangaire has been celebrated as the final swansong of a remarkable Irish actress. See Nicholas Grene "Defining Performers and Performances' in *The Oxford Handbook of Modern Irish Theatre* (Oxford: Oxford University Press, 2016).
45. Patrick Lonergan, ed. *The Methuen Anthology of Irish Plays.* (London: Methuen, 2008), 111.
46. Ibid., 139.
47. T2/1102A, VHS recording, *Bailegangaire*, 1986, Gaiety Theatre, Dublin. James Hardiman Library, NUI Galway.
48. Peter Brook, *The Empty Space*, (London: MacGibbon and Kee, 1968), 136.

49. Mason is closely associated with the work of Frank McGuinness and directed the premieres of *The Factory Girls* (1982 Abbey), *Observe the Sons of Ulster Marching Towards the Somme* (1985 Abbey), *Dolly West's Kitchen* (1999 Abbey/Old Vic, London), *Gates of Gold* (2002 Gate Theatre, Dublin), and *The Hanging Gardens* (2013 Abbey).
50. Chambers et al., eds., *Theatre Talk: Voices of Irish Theatre Practitioners*, 320.
51. Frank McGuinness, "Mothers and Fathers", *Theatre Ireland* 4 (1983): 16.
52. Pine, *The Diviner: The Art of Brian Friel*, 35.
53. Murray, *The Theatre of Brian Friel: Tradition and Modernity, 137.*
54. Richard Dyer, *Only Entertainment*, 2nd ed. (New York: Routledge, 2002), 20.
55. Ibid.
56. Ibid.
57. Cartmell took a First in Drama and History of Art from Trinity College, Dublin and Glasgow University and graduated with an MA from Central School of Speech and Drama in Advanced Theatre Directing.
58. "Director with real bite and a bracing approach to the classics", *The Irish Times* March 4, 2013.
59. Rhona Trench *Staging Thought: Essays on Irish Theatre and Practice* (Bern: Peter Lang, 2012), 238.
60. Marina Carr, *Woman and Scarecrow* (Loughcrew: The Gallery Press, 2006), 68.
61. Trench, *Staging Thought: Essays on Irish Theatre and Practice*, 244.
62. *The Irish Times* March 4, 2013.

Bibliography

Brook, Peter. *The Empty Space*. London: MacGibbon and Kee, 1968.

Carr, Marina. *Woman and Scarecrow*. Loughcrew: The Gallery Press, 2006.

Chambers, Lillian, Ger FitzGibbon, Eamonn Jordan, Dan Farrelly, Cathy Leeney, Eds. *Theatre Talk: Voices of Irish Theatre Practitioners*. Dublin: Carysfort Press, 2002.

Dyer, Richard. *Only Entertainment*. 2nd ed. New York: Routledge, 2002.

Fitz-Simon, Christopher ed., *Players and Painted Stage: Aspects of Twentieth Century Theatre in Ireland*. Dublin: New Island, 2004.

Friel, Brian. *Plays Two*. London: Faber, 1999.

Hobson, Bulmer ed., *The Gate Theatre*. Dublin: Gate Theatre, 1934.

Hynes, Garry. "Galway to Broadway and Back Again" *American Journal of Irish Studies* 9 (2012): 79–96.

Leiter, Samuel. *From Belasco to Brook: Representative Directors of the English Speaking Stage*. New York: Praeger, 1991.

Lonergan, Patrick ed., *The Methuen Anthology of Irish Plays*. London: Methuen, 2008.

Luke, Peter ed., *Enter Certain Players: Edwards, Mac Liammóir and the Gate 1928–1978*. Dublin: Dolmen Press, 1978.

McGuinness, Frank. "Mothers and Fathers", *Theatre Ireland* 4 (1983): 14–16.

Morash, Christopher. *A History of Irish Theatre 1601–2001*. Cambridge: Cambridge University Press, 2002.

Murray, Christopher. *The Theatre of Brian Friel*, London: Methuen, 2014.

Nagy, Peter, Phillippe Rouyer and Don Rubin, eds., *World Encyclopedia of Contemporary Theatre*: Vol. 1, Europe. London: Routledge, 1994.

Peacock, Alan J. ed., *The Achievement of Brian Friel.* Gerrards Cross: Colin Smythe, 1992.

Pine, Richard. *The Diviner: The Art of Brian Friel.* Dublin: UCD Press, 1999.

Roche, Anthony. *Contemporary Irish Drama.* Basingstoke: Palgrave, 2009.

———. *Brian Friel: Theatre and Politics.* Basingstoke: Palgrave, 2011.

Schneider, Rebecca and Gabrielle Cody, eds., *Re: Direction: A Theoretical and Practical Guide.* New York: Routledge, 2002.

Simpson, Alan. *Beckett and Behan and a Theatre in Dublin.* London: Routledge & Kegan Paul, 1962.

Styan, J.L. *The Shakespeare Revolution: Criticism and Performance in the Twentieth Century.* Cambridge: Cambridge University Press, 1977.

———. *Modern Drama in Theory and Practice, 3 Vols.* Cambridge: Cambridge University Press, 1983.

Syssoyeva, Kathryn Mederos and Scott Proudfit eds., *Women, Collective Creation, and Devised Performance.* Basingstoke: Palgrave, 2016.

Trench, Rhona. *Staging Thought: Essays on Irish Theatre and Practice.* Bern: Peter Lang, 2012.

Wilcock, Mike. *Hamlet: The Shakespearean Director.* Dublin: Carysfort Press, 2002.

In the *Wake* of Olwen Fouéré's *riverrun*

Kellie Hughes

> *Here form is content, content is form. You complain that this stuff is not written in English. It is not written at all. It is not to be read—or rather it is not only to be read. It is to be looked at and listened to. His writing is not* about *something; it is* that something itself. (Samuel Beckett)

May 2016—the time of this writing—marks almost five years since the first spark of inspiration that led to Olwen Fouéré's *riverrun*, an adaptation of the voice of the river in James Joyce's *Finnegans Wake*. It has also been a year since Olwen last performed *riverrun*, her longest break from the piece since its premiere in Galway in 2013. We are preparing to fly to Washington with *riverrun* for the Ireland 100 at the Kennedy Center and have been finding days here and there in between other projects to prepare before our final week of rehearsals in The Lab. Jumping back into the river is always a delicate process. Olwen compares it to learning to swim again, diving off a cliff, hoping to find that her unquantifiable connection is still there. It always is.

I'm not sure where Olwen stops and *riverrun* begins. When Samuel Beckett described *Finnegans Wake* as being "not *about* something; it is *that something itself*", he could have been describing Olwen's relationship with *riverrun*. Just like the book itself, there is nothing to "get" in *riverrun*. Neither is it an explanation or a key, it is Olwen's embodiment of the journey of the river "Life" in Joyce's enigmatic book of the night.

My journey as co-director of *riverrun* began in late February 2013. At this point, Olwen had already completed her adaptation and performed a number

K. Hughes (✉)
UCD Ad Astra Academy–Performing Arts, University College Dublin, Dublin, Ireland

E. Jordan, E. Weitz (eds.), *The Palgrave Handbook of Contemporary Irish Theatre and Performance*,
https://doi.org/10.1057/978-1-137-58588-2_29

of rehearsed readings. I met with Olwen. Over coffee she invited me to join her, sound designer and composer Alma Kelliher—whom she had been collaborating with since August 2012—and consultant composer Susan Stenger for a long weekend to explore the sound world of *riverrun*. The work was exciting, energizing and inspiring. It still is.

It was that weekend, in Rough Magic Theatre Company's rehearsal space on South Great George's Street that I first truly experienced *Joyce's Wake*. Like many others, I had "read" *Finnegans Wake* in college. For me, that meant superficially skimming over the text until I found something that hooked me—usually something visual—reading until my attention waned then returning to skimming until a new section drew me in. I certainly couldn't claim to understand Joyce's infamously impenetrable text and stayed happily on the surface of *Finnegans Wake*, enjoying what T.S. Eliot described as its "merely beautiful nonsense".[1] Olwen's reading that day proved that Joyce's sound dance was so much more. Yes, it is a "collideorscape", replete with mixed metaphors, multilingual puns and bawdy humour, but underneath that exterior lies an elemental energy, a spiritual and metaphorical realm at work, a defiant rejection of logic that actively shuns our craving to solve its meaning.[2] As Olwen gave voice to these currents in the book in her reading of *riverrun*, I felt I was experiencing an expression of human existence and the universe, travelling to a space beyond rational thought. There were shards of elusive meaning, but ultimately Joyce's *Wake* read aloud felt like a challenge to us to embrace what we do not know or cannot understand, to come to terms with the fact that we will never have enough knowledge to decode the book, but that if we can surrender ourselves to a place of unknowing, its beauty beyond reason and intellect will reveal itself.

When I first came to work on *riverrun*, I was struck by the considerable responsibility I had taken on. Olwen had already conceived and constructed an incredibly beautiful piece of work and in collaborating on the staging of such a personal response to Joyce's work, I felt I ran the risk of polluting it. I had absolute trust in Olwen's vision for the work. However, co-directing any production is a delicate process. I am not sure that our collaboration would have worked as easily as it did without my background in performance.

Directing theatre came to me by chance rather than by design. During my time as an ensemble performer with the Blue Raincoat Theatre Company, I collaborated with the company on the creation of a number of new works from inside the performance, choreographed moments of movement for different productions and directed on occasion, most significantly the W.B. Yeats Project in 2009 and 2010. While working as an actor, I found myself always wanting, needing to step outside the performance and look in; I had an urge to be more actively involved in constructing and shaping the overall production. Gradually that urge guided me towards directing. As an actor involved in developing a new piece of theatre, you have a unique perspective on the work. It is important to trust that perspective, whether in the role of performer or director.

As a student, I was encouraged to think of myself as a creator, to be my own director and to maintain a third eye on the performance as a whole.[3] Olwen instinctively does this in her work and when working together we meet as artists in the world between the actor and the director. It is a blurry and not easily definable space, but it feels instinctively right and importantly negates any notion of hierarchy, control or creative domination. I step into the work to feel it from Olwen's perspective, she steps out to do the same. We both have our own jobs within the process. Inevitably, Olwen must surrender fully to her performance but, prior to this point, it is a negotiation: a meeting of individuals with an external and internal perspective on the work. Trust was and remains essential to our work, and this was built between us over time.

I can still discern the original underlying structure of *riverrun*'s vocal score in Olwen's performance today, an internal rhythm that was embedded in her engagement with the text, even during our first explorations. Olwen's instinctive vocal score provided our starting point in exploring the staging possibilities for the work. There was a clarity inside the obscurity of her vocal rhythm, an underlying organic logic that—though not definable—was there all the same, like in dreams. When you read Finnegans Wake, the beauty of the structure of its letters is arresting. As this aspect of Joyce's work is necessarily absent in live performance, the body and its sculptural quality, took on even more importance in staging *riverrun*. We expanded and contracted Olwen's vocal impulses into physical echoes. By witnessing what Olwen's inner landscape created in rehearsal and investigating a series of physical impulses inspired by individual sections, we developed a physical vocabulary, initially through improvisation. We then broke this vocabulary down further, exploring weight and working with or fighting against gravity, structure, rhythm, tempo, inter-corporeal and spatial articulation, instability, contradiction, energy and harmony. We gradually discovered how the body could express the shift from a tiny atom to an embodiment of the universe, a droplet of water to a vast ocean, all within the unceasing flow of the river, rising and falling, travelling from life to death to renewal.

New neural pathways—forged and strengthened in rehearsal—provided an inner structure, a core strength, like the postural muscles of the body invisibly supporting the performance. Olwen's performance needed to remain fluid, non-fixed, but with an underlying structure that would be ready to be called on at any moment, open to and welcoming change, always willing to deconstruct, expand or yield to a new impulse—should it occur. For *riverrun* to work, it must be unstable, unfixed, on the cusp of something rather than at its destination. This is why it has to remained a fluid engagement for Olwen, rather than a virtuosic demonstration of skill. The vital connection between performer and audience is paramount to the piece and, in order to serve that, Olwen's engagement with the performance must go beyond mere memory or reproduction to something hidden, yet essential.

Breath is central to the performance and structure of *riverrun*. A breath heralds the opening as Olwen approaches the microphone and breathes life into her instrument. The performance closes with an arrested breath mid-sentence. It is also written into the adaptation in the form "kneeplays", which form the joints between "meat" of each section of the performance.[4] At these moments, it is the breath that brings us deeper into the subconscious of the giant body of *Finnegans Wake*. The microphone provides a fixed point. It is a physical restriction to work around and a point of contact for the complex formation of language, light, music, sound and physicality that underlie the performance.

As work progressed, technical precision became incredibly important. Olwen's position at the microphone needs an exactness which is measured in millimetres. Her feet are constantly active, to maintain the feeling of progression and flow, and to support the body as a sculptural, three-dimensional entity. Precision had to become part of the larger portrait while supporting, and not blocking, the world of images and changing internal landscape that enables *riverrun* to flow through Olwen without censorship. Restriction, precision and exactitude all played out in rehearsal and worked to a point that then allowed for the possibility of freedom in performance.

The tension between precision and fluidity was present throughout the creative process of *riverrun*. Working with Olwen, Alma Kelliher and lighting designer Stephen Dodd, the technical development of *riverrun* was a collaborative process of discovery, trial and elimination. We worked to regain simplicity after exploring the myriad of ways to stage *riverrun*. Sound and light in *riverrun* work in harmony with Olwen to create an unstable and changing world, where the interaction between breath, movement, light and sound can shift universes. The essential interaction of sound and light with Olwen in performance begins from her live impulse. She is an instrument, composer, musician and conductor, accompanied by the supporting instruments of light and sound. I conduct this merging of elements from the outside to ensure a cohesive whole.

While we experimented with an array of ideas for a "set" for *riverrun*, anything other than the microphone and the scattering of salt that we eventually agreed upon felt out of place and situated the work too concretely, shutting down the potential for the audience to creatively engage and author their own journey down the river. Of course, when you strip away everything, whatever remains takes on huge significance. We experimented with seven different types of salt before finally settling on the natural sea salt that has toured with us around the world. Sound engineer Benny Lynch, in response to our concern that the microphone stand was visually problematic—cutting Olwen's body in half and interrupting the direct connection between Olwen and the audience—came to rehearsals a few days after we spoke with a bespoke stand: a thing of sculptural beauty that he created, inspired by the snaking microphone cable that also became an integral aspect of the visual world of *riverrun*.

To develop this detailed relationship between sound, light and live performance took time and space. We took time to get lost and not know, we took exploratory time, inventive, playful and sometimes frustrating time—and the space both physically and mentally to achieve it. This would have been impossible without producer Jen Coppinger and her unfailing support of the team's ongoing creative needs. She understood the value of investing time and money in technical exploration and still fights for us to have sufficient time and the right conditions to reconnect with *riverrun* when we tour to a new venue. As a site-responsive work, we use the unique aspects of each new place to frame *riverrun*, with traces of the sites *riverrun* has been performed in remaining, as each new venue makes its mark.

As we prepare to travel to Washington, I still find pleasure in the constant and subtle shifting nature or *riverrun*. Without it, the essence of what *riverrun* is would be lost. It is constantly evolving, like our process of rehearsal, which is extremely simple. We start each rehearsal day with a long warm up. This has developed into a mash-up of different physical techniques that Olwen and I use to access a place of stillness: an emptying out of the outside world and the creation of a concentrated space to work. We begin by reconnecting with the work and going back to a simple exploration of where Olwen and the material meet. There's a ritual and a sacred nature to the work that, though difficult to express, shouldn't be denied. But there is also a lightness, a joyous devilment that makes returning to *riverrun* a real gift. After a few days, we are joined by Benny Lynch and the duet between Olwen and the sonic world begins. Finally, lighting supervisor John Crudden joins us in tech and we begin the process of fully transporting *riverrun* to its new home.

riverrun has toured across three continents and the audience reaction continues to fascinate me. It asks a lot from the audience: patience and availability to the moment, a willingness to surrender and to let go of the natural desire to understand. In a world where information is one click away, the absence of readily accessible meaning is challenging, but when the audience begin to let go and you can feel the room transform, the living and dynamic exchange between actor and audience is palpable. It is at that moment that Olwen becomes "that *something* itself".

Notes

1. Jack P. Dalton, "A Letter from T. S. Eliot," *James Joyce Quarterly* 6.1 (1968): 80.
2. James Joyce, *Finnegans Wake* (Wordsworth Editions Ltd., Hertfordshire, 2012), 143.28.
3. I spent three years training with corporeal mime specialists Corinne Soum and Steven Wasson in London.
4. A term Fouéré borrowed from Robert Wilson to describe moments of transition.

Bibliography

Beckett, Samuel. *Dante... Bruno... Vico... Joyce...* in *Our Exagmination Round His Factification for Incamination of Work in Progress*. Faber & Faber, London: 1972.

Dalton, Jack P. "A Letter from T. S. Eliot." *James Joyce Quarterly* 6.1 (1968).

Joyce, James. *Finnegans Wake*. Wordsworth Editions Ltd., Hertfordshire, 2012.

Irish Theatre: A Writer's Theatre

Nicholas Grene

It was an Irish Literary Theatre (ILT) that W.B. Yeats, Augusta Gregory and Edward Martyn proclaimed in their 1897 manifesto, their aim to build up a "school of dramatic literature".[1] Comparable in many respects to other avant-garde theatre projects of the time—Antoine's Théâtre Libre (1887), the Moscow Art Theatre of Stanislakvski and Nemirovich-Danchenko (1898)—the ILT was distinctive in not being led by actors or directors. The objection of its founders to mainstream nineteenth-century theatre was not its emphasis on visual spectacle and its star-centred performance style but its lack of value for fine writing, whether Yeats's poetic drama or Martyn's Ibsenian allegories; Gregory would no doubt have shared that feeling, though she had not yet started on her prolific playwriting career. The ILT was so little theatrically based that, for their three seasons (1899–1901), they had to import a troupe of actors from England. The alliance of disparate elements that came together to form the Irish National Theatre Society (1903) included the theatre company led by W.G. and Frank Fay and many well-wishing cultural nationalists. But these latter fell away even before the Abbey Theatre opened in 1904, and with the three playwrights, Yeats, Gregory and J.M. Synge in control as directors, even the Fay brothers were to go by 1908. In 1909 the 22-year-old Lennox Robinson was made manager of the Abbey on the basis of six weeks observation in a London theatre arranged for him by Bernard Shaw. For all the eventual fame of some of its actors, the Abbey was from its beginnings a literary theatre, with writers at its centre.

It was not by any means the poetic theatre Yeats would have wanted. With the limited success of his mythological verse dramas, he turned towards the

N. Grene (✉)
Trinity College Dublin, Dublin, Ireland
e-mail: ngrene@tcd.ie

E. Jordan, E. Weitz (eds.), *The Palgrave Handbook of Contemporary Irish Theatre and Performance*,
https://doi.org/10.1057/978-1-137-58588-2_30

more rarefied form of plays for dancers based—very loosely—on Japanese Noh, and by 1919 was prepared to declare that, in defiance of the "People's Theatre" that the Abbey had become, he wanted "an unpopular theatre and an audience like a secret society where admission is by favour and never to many".[2] Still, there must have been a degree of chagrin in the failure of his plays to become mainstays of the theatre he had done so much to create. He was excited by the success of his version of *Oedipus the King* in 1926, and with plans for taking on the whole Theban trilogy of Sophocles, expressed his hopes in a letter to Gregory: "I feel that these three closely united plays put into simple speakable prose may be my contribution to the Abbey Repertory".[3] In fact, no plays of Yeats, not even the remarkable *Purgatory* (1938), have been regularly revived at the Abbey. The Yeats Festival, which staged seasons of his work from 1989 to 1993, proved merely an exception to the rule. Mary O'Malley's Lyric Players, set up in 1951, had the production of Yeats's work as a main objective, and no less than twenty three of his plays were staged at the Lyric over the years.[4] But, without the missionary zeal of O'Malley, the Belfast Lyric was to become as near a Yeats-free zone—like most other Irish theatres.[5]

The literary language for which Irish theatre became known from the early Abbey on was not Yeats's verse but the style advocated by Synge in the Preface to *The Playboy of the Western World* in which "every speech should be as fully flavoured as a nut or apple".[6] This colloquial high colour was a key dimension to the success of Sean O'Casey in the 1920s, though with a shift from peasant lyricism to urban demotic. Kenneth Tynan's famous review of Brendan Behan's *The Quare Fellow* in 1956 is expressive of what was by then an established stereotype: "The English hoard words like misers; the Irish spend them like sailors [...] It is Ireland's sacred duty to send over, every few years, a playwright to save the English theatre from inarticulate glumness".[7] For the rest of the twentieth century and into the twenty-first, there has continued to be a niche market abroad for Irish playwrights with this sort of unchecked flow of language. John Harrington has highlighted a contrary example in the New York tour of the Abbey with Tom Mac Intyre's *The Great Hunger* in 1988. This experimental production based on movement and image was cutting edge for Ireland, but it was old hat for American critics; it was not what they wanted and expected from Irish drama. Mel Gussow in his *New York Times* review complained that "the play seems to contradict the founding principles of the Abbey Theatre as a home for eloquence [...] the primary difficulty with *The Great Hunger* is not so much with its dearth of poetry as with the familiarity and ingenuousness of the performance techniques".[8]

The 1960s saw the emergence of a new generation of Irish playwrights, amounting to a second theatrical revival. Thomas Kilroy's "Groundwork for an Irish Theatre" is often taken as a key document in the imagination of that new movement, in which he himself was to be an important figure. Kilroy called for "a theatre deliberately geared to attract back the writer and provide a workshop for him".[9] Though Kilroy stresses the collaborative nature of the theatrical enterprise, citing the example of Joan Littlewood's Theatre Workshop with approval, the writer is for him at the heart of the matter. And so it proved in the next decade, as Tom Murphy, Brian Friel, Hugh Leonard, John B. Keane and Kilroy himself came to national and then international prominence. There was innovative dramaturgy in the production of their work, but it was the plays and the playwrights who were credited with the renewal of the Irish theatre after the doldrums of the 1940s and 1950s. Well into the twenty-first century, the international reputation of these dramatists—and successors such as Frank McGuinness, Conor McPherson, Marina Carr, Enda Walsh—has had the two main Dublin houses, the Abbey and the Gate, vying to put on their work.

The smaller independent companies that began to emerge in Ireland from the 1970s onward have also often been associated with individual Irish playwrights, even when that was not their original remit. Druid Theatre Company, founded in 1975, made its name with fresh revivals of the plays of Synge, but went on to stage two outstanding new plays by Tom Murphy in 1985, and (in collaboration with the Royal Court) produced *The Beauty Queen of Leenane*, Martin McDonagh's breakthrough success, in 1996. Rough Magic was established in 1984 primarily to produce work from outside Ireland—political plays from Britain and the USA—which was not otherwise being seen in Irish theatres. Yet within a few years they were bringing on new Irish writers, such as Donal O'Kelly, Declan Hughes, Gina Moxley and Arthur Riordan. Passion Machine, also founded in 1984, "was a project-based operation, staging only original Irish work, and was committed to a wholly indigenous populist theatre that depicted, challenged and celebrated the contemporary Irish experience".[10] But effectively it showcased the plays of its artistic director Paul Mercier. Red Kettle, set up in Waterford in 1985, staged many of the works of Jim Nolan, just as Corcadorca, founded in Cork in 1991, gave Enda Walsh his first productions. Even a company such as Corn Exchange, set up by director Annie Ryan in 1995 with a focus on ensemble-style production, has been closely associated with the writer Michael West.

A great deal of Irish theatre making over the last twenty-five years has been dedicated to resisting the hegemony of the playwright with site-specific, devised, collaborative, image or movement-based work. And yet text-centred plays continue to be highlighted and playwrights command most attention. A number of reasons can be advanced for this. There is the self-perpetuating dimension to the Irish theatrical tradition: the classic, often revived plays of Synge and O'Casey, in particular, provide the reference points in the expectations of international critics and audiences. Where those expectations for the "Irish play" are not met then the reception is one of disappointment, as in the case of Mac Intyre's *Great Hunger*. There is corresponding reward for talented writers who can deliver recognizable Irish plays, even if in parodic style, as in the case of McDonagh or Walsh. For the remainder of this essay, I want to look at three features that continue to make writerly drama so successful in contemporary Irish theatre both at home and abroad. The first is lyricism and musicality; established first by the example of Synge, this is a persistent element in the shaping of Irish drama, a poetic dimension to prose speech that strains towards music and often actually does use music itself as part of the play's effect. Secondly, there is the distinctive colouring of Irish English, whether rural dialect or urban patois. And, finally, there is a tolerance for, even an expectation of, narrative storytelling.

Lyricism, Music, Eloquence

"In Ireland", wrote Synge in 1907, "for a few years more, we have a popular imagination that is fiery and magnificent, and tender".[11] By the time of Friel's *Philadelphia Here I Come!* (1964) such a supposed popular imagination is no longer in evidence in the language. The characters in Friel's play express themselves in monosyllables, grunts, and a carapace of cliché. The subject of *Philadelphia* is the stultifying Irish small town that is driving Gar O'Donnell to emigrate, with its drunken schoolmaster, know-nothing priest, sexually repressed "boys", and inescapable class system that has doomed Gar's one attempt at a love affair. Above all, there is the inarticulateness that blights the relationship between himself and his elderly father/employer. But irradiating all this glum scene is Friel's ingenious theatrical device that gives to the mumbling Public Gar an unseen Private Gar who can voice all his unspeakable thoughts and feelings. This not only energizes the action with the comic brio of the cross-talk act between the two Gars, but allows for the lyrical recreation of a memory that could not be expressed any other way.

What Private Gar recalls, as the token of a lost love between himself and his father, is a childhood fishing expedition they took together:

> the boat was blue and the paint was peeling and there was an empty cigarette packet floating in the water at the bottom between two trout and the left rowlock kept slipping and you had given me your hat and had put your jacket round my shoulders because there had been a shower of rain. And you had the rod in your left hand—I can see the cork nibbled away from the butt of the rod—and maybe we had been chatting—I don't remember—it doesn't matter—but between us at that moment there was this great happiness, this great joy—you must have felt it too—although nothing was being said—just the two of us fishing on a lake on a showery day—and young as I was I felt, I knew, that this was precious, and your hat was soft on the top of my ears—I can feel it—and I shrank down into your coat—and then, then for no reason at all except that you were happy too, you began to sing.[12]

It's a beautiful passage and all the more poignant for the fact that, when Public Gar finally does decide hesitantly to ask his father whether he remembers it, he draws a complete blank. As a memory they fail to share, it apparently confirms their failure to be able to relate to one another emotionally. Yet the emotion is not lost on the audience, and in Private's recollection it is given full-throated theatrical expression.

Though Tom Murphy's characters often have flows of words, he seldom grants them the lyrical eloquence that Friel contrives for his. What Friel and

Murphy share is the use of music to express what words cannot. In *Philadelphia*, Gar feeds his sense of melancholy reflection as he prepares to leave Ballybeg by listening to Mendelssohn's Violin Concerto. In Friel's later play *Wonderful Tennessee* (1993), George, who is dying of throat cancer and unable to speak, is built into the play's architecture of meaning with the melodies he plays on the accordion. The most striking example of this substitution of the impact of music for the eloquence of language is Murphy's *The Gigli Concert* (1983). The Irish Man comes to the quack psychotherapist J.P.W. King in breakdown, one of the key symptoms of his depression the inability or unwillingness to communicate. This self-made man, a building developer who has constructed a thousand houses, "has come to a standstill":

> I was never a great one to talk much. Now I'd prefer to walk a mile in the other direction than say how yeh or fuck yeh to anyone.[13]

His obsession with wanting to sing like the Italian tenor Gigli is a yearning to transcend that stalled self. "Like, you can talk forever, but singing. Singing, d'yeh know? The only possible way to tell people. [...] Who you are?"[14] The play as a whole, with its integrated recordings of Gigli's songs and operatic arias, gives theatrical expression to the amplified, mythic dimensions of the Faustian drama. What we watch on stage may be little more than the drink-fuelled confessional interchange of two damaged men, with occasional appearances by Mona, J.P.W.'s marginalized lover, but what the music adumbrates is some other sublime order of things, and hearing is believing. The counterpoint between the speaking and the singing voices gives to the play an epic dimension of eloquence beyond what language alone could achieve.

By contrast with Friel and Murphy, Sebastian Barry is prepared to trust to words alone for poetic and dramatic impact. A writer who began his career as a poet and is now probably best known as a novelist, Barry has relied on a heightened, image-enriched style across genres Daringly, he opens his play *The Steward of Christendom* (1995), with the baby-talk monologue of the senile ex-policeman Thomas Dunne, remembering his childhood:

> Da Da, Ma Ma, Ba Ba, Ba Ba. Clover, clover in my mouth, clover honey-smelling, clover smelling of Ma Ma's neck, and Ma Ma's soft breast when she opens her floating blouse, and Da Da's bright boots in the grasses, amid the wild clover, and the clover again, and me the Ba Ba set in the waving grasses, and the smell of honey, and the farmhands going away like an army of redcoats but without the coats, up away up the headland with their scythes, and every bit of the sun likes to run along the scythes and laugh along the blades, now there are a score of shining scythes, dipping and signalling from the backs of the men.[15]

This acts as an overture to the play suggesting the Oedipal psychology of the protagonist, the colonial situation—the field workers on the estate like "an army of redcoats"—and the idyll of a lost pastoral. The structure of the play intercuts the present time 1932, where Thomas is incarcerated in a mental asylum in his native Wicklow village of Baltinglass, with flashback memories of family and his past life in the Dublin Metropolitan Police, including the trauma of the changed regime in 1922. But it is Thomas's monologue memories that take us most vividly into the mind of the Catholic loyalist he was, above all his paean to Queen Victoria, show-stopping in performance:

> When I was a young recruit it used to frighten me how much I loved her. Because she had built everything up and made it strong, and made it shipshape. The great world that she owned was shipshape as a ship. All the harbours of the earth were trim with their granite piers, the ships were shining and strong. The trains went sleekly through the fields, and her mark was everywhere, Ireland, Africa, the Canadas, every blessed place. And men like me were there to make everywhere peacable, to keep order in her kingdoms. She was our pride. Among her emblems was the gold harp, the same harp we wore on our helmets. We were secure, as if for eternity the orderly milk-drays would come up the streets in the morning, and her influence would reach everywhere, like the salt sea pouring up into the fresh waters of the Liffey. Ireland was hers for eternity, order was everywhere, if we could but honour her example. She loved her Prince. I loved my wife. The world was a wedding of loyalty, of steward to Queen, she was the very flower and perfecter of Christendom. Even as the simple man I was I could love her fiercely. Victoria.[16]

The Steward of Christendom was premiered at the Royal Court Theatre in London in the same year and the same venue as Sarah Kane's *Blasted*. Mark Ravenhill's *Shopping and Fucking*, the other landmark example of violently provocative "in yer face" theatre, was to follow the next year. Barry's unironized rhetoric is the more striking in such a context. The reviews quoted on the jacket of the Methuen collection of his plays, indicate how much the play's enormous success was conditioned by an awareness of Barry's Irish dramatic inheritance: "he is the new crown prince of Ireland's majestic theatrical tradition" said *Newsweek*; "I venture to suggest that not even O'Casey or Synge wrote better than this", wrote the *Guardian*.[17] Irish dramatists have a licence to speak out lyrically, beautifully; indeed it is expected of them. After all, the Abbey is "the home of eloquence", as Mel Gussow put it. This theatrical eloquence need not necessarily be Syngean mellifluousness or O'Casey's bravura Dublinese or even the well-wrought poetic language of a Sebastian Barry. Friel and Murphy could extend the expressiveness of their inarticulate characters when necessary with music. But the commitment within Irish theatre to large effects of sound and sense makes it possible for these playwrights to achieve the opulence of their dramatic texts.

Irish English

For Synge, it was the distinctive forms of Irish English dialect that made possible the lyricism he so admired in the speech of the country people. Language that had been the attribute of the comic stage Irishman with his bulls and blunders was transvalued into an admired poetry of the colloquial. Martin McDonagh was to put dialect speech to very different purposes in his plays of the 1990s set in Leenane and the Aran Islands.

McDonagh's language is a self-consciously adopted style, as he himself made clear: "In Connemara and Galway, the natural dialogue style is to invert sentences and use strange inflections. Of course, my stuff is a heightening of that, but there is a core strangeness of speech, especially in Galway".[18] Synge too, of course, worked with this "core strangeness of speech" derived from Irish-language syntax. Two features of Irish are particularly striking in Synge's Hiberno-English: the use of the copula to advance an important word or phrase to the head of a sentence, and the substitution of paratactic phrases for what in standard English would be subordinate clauses. One sentence from *Playboy* may be used to illustrate the effect. It is in Act II, when Pegeen has been frightening Christy with the prospect of hanging and at last reassures him he is safe. This is his relieved response: "It's making game of me you were [...] and I can stay so, working at your side, and I not lonesome from this mortal day".[19] The copula formation—"It's making game of me you were"—allows for inversion of normal word order, while the paratactic "and I not lonesome" makes for a smooth flowing full sentence running on to Synge's favourite resolving rhythmic chord "this mortal day".

A contrast to this style can be provided by some examples from McDonagh. The sly and manipulative mother Mag in *The Beauty Queen of Leenane* (1996) sidles into one of her endless demands on her middle-aged daughter and carer Maureen early in the first scene: "Me porridge, Maureen, I haven't had, will you be getting?"[20] This is a weirdly contorted version of "I haven't had my porridge: will you get it for me, Maureen?" that almost sounds like pidgin. McDonagh, like Synge, is using Irish-derived inversion but increasing the strangeness. The effect is to catch Mag's simultaneous insistence on the foregrounded "Me porridge", and her whining pseudo-tentativeness. But against the fluency of the Synge line, McDonagh contrives a halting ungainliness. It is even more striking in extended passages. This is the start of Maureen's confession of the circumstances that led to her mental breakdown:

> In England I was, this happened. Cleaning work. When I was twenty-five. Me first time over. Me only time over. Me sister had just got married, me other sister just about to. Over in Leeds I was, cleaning offices. Bogs. A whole group of us, only them were all English. 'Ya oul backward Paddy fecking ... The fecking pig's-backside face on ya.' The first time out of Connemara this was I'd been. 'Get back to that backward fecking pigsty of yours or whatever hole it was you drug yourself out of.'[21]

Again, McDonagh repeatedly uses the inverted word order—"In England I was, this happened", "Over in Leeds I was, cleaning offices". The racist abuse flung at Maureen by her English fellow workers is translated into crude Irish-sounding abuse: "The fecking pig's-backside face on ya". Insults in Synge's

Hiberno-English can be as colourful as his lyricism: not here. The pathos and pain of what Maureen suffered is rendered in staccato bursts of speech, distorted grammar and syntax, scraps of language as if torn from memory. McDonagh's harsh and discordant stage speech seems like a protest against exactly that tradition of lyricism that Synge had initiated, but it achieves its effect by a comparable highlighting of Irish English.

Marina Carr's use of regional language may also have an element of reaction against the Syngean inheritance. Carr comes from Offaly, one of the few counties in Ireland without a sea coast, part of the central plain often thought of as the least interesting part of the country: all flat fields and bogs. It has none of the picturesque reputation of the west coast, so attractive to writers and tourists alike. The Midlands accent also has generally been considered as flat and unattractive as the landscape. So, there was a certain local patriotism in Carr's setting of her plays in her native territory and in her use of the unlovely local dialect for her writing. *Portia Coughlan*, in fact, in its original orthographic rendering of the Midlands voice, appeared so impenetrable on the page that Carr revised it for a later edition. This is the protagonist Portia rejecting her role as wife and mother to her husband Raphael as it first appeared: "Ah never wanted sons nor daughters an' ah never pertended otherwise ta ya, toult ya fron tha start. Buh ya though' ya chould woo me inta motherhood. Well ud hasn't worched ouh has ud. Y'ave yar three sons now so ya behher mine thim acause ah chan't love thim Raphael, ah'm jus' noh able".[22] Revised/translated, this reads: "I never wanted sons nor daughters and I never pretended otherwise to ya; told ya from the start. But ya thought ya could woo me into motherhood. Well, it hasn't worked out, has it? You've your three sons now, so ya better mind them because I can't love them, Raphael. I'm just not able".[23] It seems there are limits to how non-standard English can be and still work on the page or stage.

However, the aggressive otherness of the local voice also features in *By the Bog of Cats* (1999), where it facilitates a use of folklore that reaches down to myth. In this modern re-creation of Euripides' *Medea*, the strange figure of the Catwoman—who lives off mice—is a choric prophet who dreams the destruction that the Traveller woman Hester Swane—Medea's counterpart—will bring upon her world: "Dreamt ya were a black train motorin' through the Bog of Cats and, oh, the scorch off of this train and it blastin' by and all the bog was dark in your wake, ya even quinched the jack-a'-lantern and I had to run from the burn. Hester Swane, you'll bring this place down by evenin'."[24] As a Traveller, Hester is marginalized like Medea, but she is unlike Euripides' foreign princess displaced to Thebes in being rooted in her own home territory of the Bog of Cats. "I was born on the Bog of Cats and on the Bog of Cats I'll end me days. I've as much right to this place as any of yees, more, for it holds me to it in ways it has never held yees. And as for me tinker blood, I'm proud of it. It gives me an edge over all of yees around her, allows me see yees for the inbred, underbred, bog-brained shower yees are."[25] This is no Syngean lilt, but the dialectal variation of the language lends authenticity to the sense of a dark chthonic force working through Hester's antagonistic energy.

The oddest case of all is Enda Walsh's *Disco Pigs*. For this play, Walsh invented a language, an idiolect shared only by the characters Pig and Runt. Walsh, coming from Dublin to live in Cork in the 1990s, has said that one stimulus for his writing was the sheer difference of Cork speech.[26] What he created in the play, however, was not merely a version of Cork dialect. It was Cork mixed with baby talk mixed with a layering of puns and onomatopoeia recalling the Joyce of *Finnegans Wake*. This is the play's opening sequence, in which the teenage Pig and Runt imagine/re-create the scene of their own (simultaneous) births:

> *Lights flick on.* PIG (*male) and* RUNT *(female). They mimic the sound of an ambulance like a child would, 'bee baa bee baa bee baa!!' They also mimic the sound a pregnant woman in labour makes. They say things like 'is all righ, miss', 'ya doin fine, luv', 'dis da furs is it?', 'is a very fast bee baa, al righ. Have a class a water!' Sound of door slamming. Sound of heartbeats throughout.*

RUNT. Out of the way!! Jesus out of the way!
PIG. Scream da fat nurse wid da gloopy face!
RUNT. Da two mams squealin on da trollies dat go speedin down da ward. Oud da fookin way!
PIG. My mam she own a liddle ting, look, an did da furs liddle baba! She heave an rip all insie!! Hol on Mam!!
RUNT. My mam she hol in da pain! She noel her pain too well! She been ta hell an bac my mam!
PIG. Day trips an all!
RUNT. Da stupid cow!!
PIG. Holy Jesus help me!!
RUNT. Scream da Pig Mam! Her face like a christmas pud all sweaty and steamy! Da two trollies like a big choo choo it clear all infron! Oudda da fookin way cant jaaaaa!![27]

Some of this is easy enough to understand when you know the forms. So, for instance, initial "th" consistently becomes "d": "da" for "the", "dis" for "this", "dat" for "that". This is no more than an orthographic rendering of common Irish pronunciation. So too is the erosion of terminal "d"—"hol" for "hold", "behine" for "behind". There are whole phrases that look odd on the page, but are clear enough on the ear: "Oudda fookin way cant jaaaaa!!" translates as "Out of the fucking way, can't you?" There are bits of standard baby talk like "big choo choo" for "train". But some of the most expressive words one would be hard pressed to translate. What does "gloopy" mean in "da fat nurse wid da gloopy face"? The sheer linguistic peculiarity of the text makes its huge international success more remarkable, particularly outside Ireland: there were no less than forty-two different productions of the play in German in one three-year period alone.[28] The play may well have appealed for its dramatization of the intense private world of the two adolescents and its psychotic conclusion for Pig. But the strange distinctiveness of Walsh's language took its place within a tradition of Irish English dramatic writing in the 1990s that included McDonagh and Carr, though each of them put their regional voices to such distinctive uses.

Storytelling

The Irish, of course, have no monopoly on narrative and monologue in the modern theatre, but the association of the oral storytelling tradition of the *seanchai* may have helped to naturalize narrative in Irish drama.[29] Two of the most innovative and influential plays in the contemporary period—Friel's *Faith Healer* (1979) and Murphy's *Bailegangaire* (1985)—are built around the telling of stories. The first monologue of *Faith Healer* is given by Frank Hardy, on a stage emptied of all but three rows of chairs and a banner reading "The Fantastic Francis Hardy/ Faith Healer/ One Night Only".[30] Frank introduces himself with wry self-irony as "The man on the tatty banner".[31] He tells his story with a seductive mocking charm and an audience has no reason to doubt its authenticity, until the second monologue, in which we hear a variant of the same story from Grace—Frank's wife, according to her, his mistress if you believe him. As we listen to the third version of events from Teddy, Frank's English manager, it is hard to know what to believe. Each performer in turn fills the theatre with his or her personality and style; we are made the confidants in turn of each of their confessional narratives. The drama consists not only in the tragic action itself but in the unbridgeable gaps between these three figures and the ways they have seen it.

At the centre of *Bailegangaire* is the literally endlessly repeated story of Mommo, the senile old crone sitting up in bed. Hers is the story of the grotesque laughing-contest of years ago, in which she was one of the unacknowledged protagonists. The clash depicted is between the unfinished business of that story, and its traumatic legacy for the grown-up granddaughters Mary and Dolly who are Mommo's carers. An additional opposition lies in the dramatic juxtaposition of the archaic old Ireland of Mommo's *seanchai* style with the realities of Mary and Dolly's 1980s modernity. Telling the story out to its end is a way of at last making a connection between the two.

Nothing could be less like *Bailegangaire* than the early plays of Conor McPherson. The monologues *Rum and Vodka* (1992), *The Good Thief* (1994) and *This Lime Tree Bower* (1995) are told by messed-up men in a world of drink-sodden urban grunge: by McPherson's own account, David Mamet was a major influence.[32] *The Weir* (1997), his first international success and still his most often revived play, used a rural setting and a more traditional subject matter: a group of men telling stories of the uncanny in a pub. The storytelling is grounded in a realistic situation: the ageing bachelors Jack and Jim, locals in the bar run by the (also unmarried) Brendan, are stirred by the arrival of Valerie, a woman from the city, who is brought in by Finbar, a neighbourhood man who has married and built a career as hotelier and estate agent in the nearby town. Partly to impress Valerie, each of the men—Jack, Finbar and Jim—tell a tale of the supernatural. While the first story, of the cottage Valerie has rented being disrupted by the fairies, is folklore remembered from generations back, the next two are uncomfortably closer to home and are based on the personal experience of the tellers. They precipitate the shocking revelation of Valerie's own story of the accidental death of her young daughter and the haunting of her that has followed. As much as *Bailegangaire*, *The Weir* is in its own way about the return of the repressed, in which the stories surface from below the level of ordinary social actuality, their telling an attempt to reach out to the shared community of an audience.

There is no such attempt at inclusion in Mark O'Rowe's play *Howie the Rookie* (1999). It consists of just two monologues, the story told first by the Howie Lee and then by the (unrelated) Rookie Lee, which between them conjure up an Irish underworld of casual violence and sordid sex. There is no specified setting and instead the language itself is used to create the scene in a cinematic style of self-narration. This is how Howie the Lee's monologue opens:

> Smoke.
> Black smoke ahead there, north end of the field.
> Thick, billowin', curlin' up.
> Somethin' burnin'.
> Me, The Howie, south end, amblin'.
> Approachin'.
> A figure.
> A man ahead, some fuck standin' there, stick in his hand, proddin' whatever's burnin'. Makin' sure it all goes up.
> Me, The Howie Lee, gettin' closer now.

The man turns out to be Ollie, burning his sleeping mat. Howie fills in the background:

> Ollie's flat befits a messy cunt like him.
> Kip the night, you kip on the guest mat under an oul' slumber-down. You're a bloke and you're game, you can kip in the bed *with* him. Game meaning gay, neither of which I am, furthest thing from, so I go the mat.[33]

We are indeed at some distance here from the ornate archaisms of Mommo's storytelling style. Written in a sort of telegraphese, its pointillist fragments of speech take over from hard-man movies the convention that the fewer words you use, the tougher you are. This style also involves playing off a received idea of Ireland. So, for example, in the country that only finally decriminalized homosexuality in 1993, the fact that some of the characters are "game", that is gay, is casually accepted. Any notion of a characteristically Irish sexual repression is challenged by scenes such as that in which the Howie Lee is propositioned in the pub lavatory by the aptly nicknamed Avalanche, the monstrous adolescent sister of his friend the Peaches. This is British "in-yer-face" theatre, Irish style: Ireland by the end of the twentieth century is modern enough to have its own urban criminal culture.

Conclusion

At the time of writing, I am serving as one of the *Irish Times* Theatre Awards judges for 2016. This has involved seeing some twenty five shows across the island in the first three months of the year. Setting aside productions of plays by non-Irish playwrights (Hannah Moscowitch, August Strindberg, Willie Russell, Eugene O'Neill, Patrick Marber, William Shakespeare), there have been revivals of plays by Sean O'Casey (two), Conor McPherson and Jimmy Murphy, and ten new Irish plays by named authors or co-authors. Only five productions have been devised or ensemble created, and one of those specifically for children. That may not be a representative example, but it is an indication that text-based writer's theatre is still dominant in Ireland. Performance styles have varied; several texts have been written by the actors themselves. However, the shaped script still seems to be central. This essay has sought to tease out some of the strands that have contributed to such a centrality: the inheritance from the author-dominated national theatre movement of the Abbey; the prestige of the classic works of Synge and O'Casey; the expectations of Irish drama generated in national and international audiences and critics for a lyrical flow of language, the high colour of Irish colloquial speech, narratives that illuminate the condition of Ireland. Whether we like it or not, such a writer's theatre has been normative, and we can only be grateful that so many extraordinarily creative dramatists have made it their own.

Notes

1. Lady Gregory, *Our Irish Theatre*, 3rd ed. (Gerrards Cross: Colin Smythe, 1972), 20.
2. W. B. Yeats, "A People's Theatre", *Explorations* (London: Macmillan, 1962), 254.
3. Quoted in W.B. Yeats, *The Writing of* Sophocles' King Oedipus, ed. David R. Clark and James B. McGuire (Philadelphia: American Philosophical Society, 1989), 36.
4. See Ian R. Walsh, 'Directors and Designers since 1950' in Nicholas Grene and Chris Morash (eds.), *Oxford Handbook of Modern Irish Theatre* (Oxford: Oxford University Press, 2016), 446–447.
5. Blue Raincoat in Sligo is a partial exception, having staged a number of innovative productions of Yeats.
6. J.M. Synge, *Collected Works*, IV, *Plays*: 2, ed. Ann Saddlemyer (London: Oxford University Press, 1968), 54.
7. Quoted in Michael O'Sullivan, *Brendan Behan: a Life* (Dublin: Blackwater Press, 1997), 208.

8. Quoted by John Harrington, 'The Abbey in America: the Real Thing' in Nicholas Grene and Chris Morash (eds.), *Irish Theatre on Tour* (Dublin: Carysfort Press, 2005), 46.
9. Thomas Kilroy, 'Groundwork for an Irish Theatre', *Studies*, 48, no. 190 (1959), 192–198 [193].
10. http://www.irishtheatre.ie/company-page.aspx?companyid=54. Accessed 16 March 2016.
11. Synge, *Collected Works*, IV, 54.
12. Brian Friel, *Selected Plays* (London: Faber, 1984), 83.
13. Tom Murphy, *Plays: Three* (London: Methuen Drama, 1994), 173.
14. Ibid.,179.
15. Sebastian Barry, *Plays: 1* (London: Methuen Drama, 1997), 239.
16. Ibid., 250.
17. Ibid., back cover.
18. Quoted in Joseph Feeny SJ, 'Martin McDonagh: Dramatist of the West', *Studies*, 87, no. 345 (1998), 24–32 [28].
19. Synge, *Collected Works*, IV, 113.
20. Martin McDonagh, *Plays: 1* (London: Methuen, 1999), 3.
21. Ibid., 31.
22. Marina Carr, *Portia Coughlan*, in *The Dazzling Dark New Irish Plays*, ed. Frank McGuinness (London: Faber, 1996), 269.
23. Marina Carr, *Portia Coughlan*, revised edition (Loughcrew: Gallery, 1998), 37.
24. Marina Carr, *By the Bog of Cats* (Loughcrew: Gallery, 1998), 20.
25. Ibid., 35.
26. Jesse Weaver, "'The Words Look After Themselves': the practice of Enda Walsh", in Nicholas Grene and Patrick Lonergan (eds.), *Irish Theatre Local and Global* (Dublin: Carysfort, 2012), 129–139 [130].
27. Enda Walsh, *Plays: One* (London: Nick Hern Books, 2011), 45.
28. See Werner Huber, "'What's the news from Kilcrobally?': Notes on the Reception of Contemporary Irish Theatre in German-Speaking Countries", in Grene and Lonergan, 81–91 [84].
29. On the international uses of the monologue see Clare Wallace (ed.), *Monologues: Theatre, Performance, Subjectivity* (Prague: Litteraria Pragensia, 2006).
30. Friel, *Selected Plays*, 331.
31. Ibid., 332.
32. See Gerald C. Wood, *Conor McPherson: Imagining Mischief* (Dublin: Liffey Press, 2003), 2, 10.
33. Mark O'Rowe, *Howie the Rookie* (London: Nick Hern Books, 1999), 7–8.

Bibliography

Barry, Sebastian. *Plays: 1*. London: Methuen Drama, 1997.

Carr, Marina. *Portia Coughlan*, in *The Dazzling Dark New Irish Plays*, ed. Frank McGuinness. London: Faber, 1996.

———. *By the Bog of Cats*. Loughcrew: Gallery, 1998.

———. *Portia Coughlan*, revised ed. Loughcrew: Gallery, 1998.

Feeny Joseph, S. J. "Martin McDonagh: Dramatist of the West." *Studies* 87, no. 345, 1998: 24–32.

Friel, Brian. *Selected Plays*. London: Faber, 1984.

Gregory, Lady. *Our Irish Theatre*, 3rd ed. Gerrards Cross: Colin Smythe, 1972.

Harrington, John. "The Abbey in America: The Real Thing," in Nicholas Grene and Chris Morash eds., *Irish Theatre on Tour*. Dublin: Carysfort Press, 2005, p. 35–50.

Huber, Werner. 'What's the news from Kilcrobally?': Notes on the Reception of Contemporary Irish Theatre in German-Speaking Countries' in Nicholas Grene and Patrick Lonergan eds., *Irish Theatre Local and Global* Dublin: Carysfort, 2012, 129–39.

Kilroy, Thomas. "Groundwork for an Irish Theatre," *Studies* 48, no. 190, 1959: 192–8.

McDonagh, Martin. *Plays: 1*. London: Methuen, 1999.

Murphy, Tom. *Plays: Three*. London: Methuen Drama, 1994.

O'Rowe, Mark. *Howie the Rookie*. London: Nick Hern Books, 1999.

O'Sullivan, Michael. *Brendan Behan: A Life*. Dublin: Blackwater Press, 1997.

Synge, J.M. *Collected Works*, IV, *Plays*: 2, ed. Ann Saddlemyer. London: Oxford University Press, 1968.

Wallace, Clare, ed. *Monologues: Theatre, Performance, Subjectivity*. Prague: Litteraria Pragensia, 2006.

Walsh, Enda. *Plays: One*. London: Nick Hern Books, 2011.

Walsh, Ian R. "Directors and Designers Since 1950," in Nicholas Grene and Chris Morash eds., *Oxford Handbook of Modern Irish Theatre*. Oxford: Oxford University Press, 2016, 446–7.

Weaver, Jesse, "'The Words Look After Themselves': The Practice of Enda Walsh", in Grene and Lonergan, 81–91.

Wood, Gerald C. *Conor McPherson: Imagining Mischief*. Dublin: Liffey Press, 2003.

Yeats, W. B. "A People's Theatre," *Explorations* London: Macmillan, 1962.

The Making of *Mainstream*

Rosaleen McDonagh

1. **Where did your initial idea for the recently produced play by Fishamble, *Mainstream* (2016) originate and how did it develop, in your opinion, from its original concept?**
   Mainstream is a comment on the state's process of assimilating and rehabilitating Travellers and people with impairments. Social policy in relation to Irish Travellers and Irish disabled people are similar. The entanglement between how we know each other, how we love each other, how we fight with each other, and how we are ashamed of one another was intriguing. *Mainstream* came from that place: my Traveller friends, my disabled friends. Conversations I have had with younger disabled women were fascinating, particularly their responses to an older generation of disabled women or girls who may have been institutionalized, or who may have received segregated education in the form of a "special school".
   A narrative from the perspective of a person with an impairment who has not experienced segregation or institutionalization is laden with all sorts of negative values about themselves and those who have experienced segregation. They are usually very frightened individuals. The tone, the texture, the intonation, and the intention carry a trace that manifests this stigma. They know it, they fear it, they imagine it. In some ways, they are contaminated by the legacy of that experience.
   That sense of jealousy, curiosity, anger, and betrayal fills all psyches with rage. This rage is compacted with arguments from a younger generation, such as "why didn't you finish the job of liberation?" The older people rage at such accusations, while trying to articulate the form of oppression and subversion that stole the energy from their lives. The pain, the hurt, the

R. McDonagh (✉)
Northumbria University, Northumbria, England

E. Jordan, E. Weitz (eds.), *The Palgrave Handbook of Contemporary Irish Theatre and Performance*,
https://doi.org/10.1057/978-1-137-58588-2_31

marking, the carrying, and the shaming of abuse is often masked by abstract conversations regarding politics and status. The public eloquence of activism often removes or denies the personal brokenness involved.

Sexuality is an intrinsic part of human identity. It would have been remiss, or at least odd, not to explore sexuality within the cultural context of Traveller identity and disabled identity. Pathologizing these characters and their relationships was of no interest to me. An old-fashioned romance is always interesting. In the scene of Jack and Mary-Ann's break-up, both people are fragmented. Their bodies and identities become secondary to their characters.

The cultural ephemera of documentaries—particularly *My Big Fat Gypsy Wedding* and *The Undateables*—shook me. My curiosity and interest was in asking the question, "why do people participate in such prurient, exploitative television?" And then "why is the mainstream, dominant, Settled, able-bodied gaze so interested in our lives, particularly in that format?" Continuously, in these documentaries, the material that is never aired is usually far more interesting. Editing is probably one of the most telling aspects of all areas of arts and entertainment—what gets left in, what gets left out, who gets asked, who does not—and that is why *Mainstream* was written and how it got staged.

2. **How did you become involved with Fishamble?**

   Many years ago, I applied to do their writing course with Gavin Kostic. At that time in my life, my writing and confidence were clumsy. It was a struggle for me to know how to be professional and creative in a Settled environment. Many years later, Fishamble did a call-out for disabled writers. They were proactive in giving people with impairments the opportunity to write and be part of an affirmative process where their work mattered. Writing was my only ambition.

   My short play, *RINGS*, was brought to America. The writer-director relationship is very important, not just in the rehearsal or the editing room. Watching Jim Culleton work with other writers and actors made me comfortable. Regardless of how a female character was written, Jim would always try to move it beyond a one-dimensional role. Attending a Fishamble play as a Traveller, the word "knacker" was never used. For me, that is when I really trusted Jim. It was not so much how he worked with me, it was more about how he worked with other artists. There is no suggestion that the word "knacker" is not part of the racist vocabulary of everyday Irish life. Fishamble had a way of depicting that racism in a more subtle way. Every Traveller hates that word. When we hear it, our attention gets drawn away from the play or the film or the book. All the explanations and rationale as to why writers and directors use it become redundant.

   As our professional relationship deepened, Jim from Fishamble Theatre Company helped me explore sensitive areas relating to Traveller identity. Part of me was not sure whether or not my family or a Traveller audience would applaud. This was very important and very challenging to me as a writer.

3. **What is the process of working with directors and the production team for your own writing like?**
My expertise is not so much in my writing, but in my editing skills. The idea of collaboration, whether big or small, is the best and most exciting way to work. However, the preface to this statement suggests collaboration only works when we all acknowledge our power, status and privilege in the rehearsal room. It does not have to be a big apology for being white, Settled, able-bodied, or male. No, this is about listening and acknowledging people's reality. It may mean working with people that have not had any opportunity to receieve professional theatre training. No writer, in my opinion, ever writes a piece on their own. Actors and directors play a huge part in my writing. It's not just about the performance or their aesthetic, but actors have an ability to deliver more than is written on the page.
The making of *Mainstream* had many dimensions. Working with a diverse cast was absolutely nerve-wracking and extraordinary, in a brilliant way. As a writer, being the only Traveller or disabled person in the room is not conducive to the artistic process. Work is much more enriching when you have two Travellers trying to figure out a piece of dialogue regarding Traveller heritage. Similarly, two disabled people from two very different disciplines attempting to find something in a particular piece of theatre can be stimulating.
Mary-Ann and Eleanor's scene in *Mainstream* was the hardest piece of dialogue for me to write. The scene was about them exposing each other's truths, lies and motivations. Mary-Ann's terror at being found out in helping her friend—Michael—to die; her anger towards Eleanor because of not being able to protect her friend, Eoin. Also the reality of Eleanor's motivation, the frustration of being found out and knowing that she can no longer evade what is happening to her own body. As women, writer or character, we have all paid the price of our prescribed gender. Within that, there is this compromise that is universal, dormant and awkward to articulate. The scene was as much about Traveller women and their relationship with Settled women as it was about women with impairments. It was an attempt to move beyond superficial representations of what women talk about. It was two women with impairments trying to get to grips with what is behind them and what is ahead of them. In my experience, conversations about sexuality with women, regardless of attraction or orientation—heterosexuality, gay sexuality, women's sexuality—are difficult, challenging and educational. Also, just the idea of two women with significant impairments talking about their bodies was, and will always be, important and relevant to me. Personally, this scene brought me tremendous emotional satisfaction due to the fact that on each of the ten nights in November 2016 that *Mainstream* ran in

Project, there were always women with disabilities in the audience. There were sniffles, people touching your arm or giving you a wink on the way out (or at least nodding). One audience member was bold enough to say, "thanks for not making it about the penis".

As a writer, it's important you know when to leave the room. It's also crucial that you respect the actors and other members of the production's talents and skills. Early in the rehearsal, you have to let go and realize it's about the piece—the play—and not about the writer. There is a responsibility on yourself as a writer to be able to work out in private; what is important, when you need to interject and when it's absolutely essential to be silent and let other people's voices be louder than yours. But, ultimately, for me the relationship is about the director and the writer. Respect, integrity, trust, generosity and being able to say, "Jim I'm tired now, will you carry this piece of work the rest of the way?"

4. **What is the process like for you as a writer? And do you find it challenging?**

Part of my struggle is learning to write in a Traveller voice or character. Historically, if all we have seen or read about ourselves has been written by a Settled writer, it's very difficult to build a new genre where we are confident in writing diverse Traveller narratives. This journey is painful.

Over the last twenty or thirty years, there's been a growing body of work by disabled writers and performers. This work influenced how I might envision a diverse or disabled aesthetic. It was a very positive way for me to strengthen and firm up my characters with impairments. There were references I could turn to, playwrights who have impairments, but this phenomenon has yet to happen for the Traveller community.

When someone like me speaks of diversity, we're usually talking, thinking or writing about the lived experience of intersectionality, where one or more identities are embodied. The fallout from this experience cannot be framed by labels such as sexism, racism, transphobia or homophobia. These appendices fail to apprehend the actuality of those of us who live our lives, or write their lives, intersectionally. In an Irish context, disablism or racism within the arts is experienced by a small minority—unlike sexism. The fact that the grouping is small does not lessen the impact of such discrimination. In a professional domain, it's tricky to name racism from a Traveller perspective, or indeed disablism. There is no Greek chorus or rallying cry from a substantial cohort. Relying on other disabled or diverse professionals to name racism often means you are compromised by putting their work and reputation in jeopardy. There's an in-joke that is almost silent, but active, between deaf, disabled, Traveller, black and ethnic minority groups about which one of us will be bold enough to name it and strong enough to live with the ramifications.

Yes, of course, writing is a challenge for everybody—and so it should be. My hope is that my writing can be part of a body of work whereby a Traveller canon is created. This canon can be generated and perpetuated by Travellers and other diverse categories of practitioners—directors, writers, technicians, actors, and so on.

In the current climate of Irish theatre, the conversation in the framework of Waking the Feminists has focussed on sexism and misogyny at all levels of the theatre industry in Ireland. If sexism is now being discussed and challenged, it is relevant to comment that racism has been (and is) very much embedded in all aspects of Irish theatre. Irish theatre is a microcosm of Irish life. It would be foolish to think that, for all it's self-perceived liberal ideas, Irish theatre has not been tarnished by racism—it has.

Racism in arts and entertainment has been universally criticised by black and ethnic minority groups. If we're talking about gender equality, racism and disablism need to be part of that conversation. It might be more conducive to suggest that people at all levels in the arts look at the sector and ask, "Where are my peers who identify as Travellers or disabled people positioned?" Collaborative processes and outreach programmes engaging with the category of under-represented groups are not fruitful for those involved if there is no parity of esteem for all parties. This means acknowledging diverse histories and also acknowledging a legacy of oppression and discriminatory practice often becomes institutionalised within the theatre sector.

It's important to point out that within oppressed groups, sexism and racism are very much at play externally. Within the community, gender roles are often rigid. This means there needs to be a two-pronged approach. Work internally within various communities including the Traveller community needs to be supported to encourage opportunities for women, disabled people and LGBTQ members. Raising ambition and opportunity within the Traveller community by ensuring affirmative programmes for Travellers are funded and resourced is of equal importance.

Now would be a good time to explain the biggest compromise in all my work, from the page to the stage—the lack of professional Traveller actors and actors with impairments. It's heart-breaking for a writer to create rounded characters, yet find there are no actors who are suitable for the part. Cripping up—the phenomenon where non-disabled actors play characters with impairments—is similar to the concept of blacking up. It's outdated and racist. Any director worth their salt, or writer, wants to have basic questions relating to the authenticity of the character answered in a straightforward way. This lack of diversity in Irish theatre is not just a point of political or sociological rhetoric; it leads to real dilemmas.

Lack of exposure, lack of opportunity, class, poverty and physical and attitudinal discrimination are some of the reasons why minority groups remain outside the realm of Irish theatre. While there are success stories of individual black actors or Traveller directors, these opportunities have yet to filter into the collective. Those of us who are in this space where decisions are made have a responsibility to reach out and pull our sisters and brothers up the ladder. Coming from an ethnic minority that has always been caricatured by Settled writers, the space within Irish theatre is often hostile. Building professional relationships is important. The compromise happens when your lived reality by way of stories or ideas do not match with the Settled version of what a Traveller play should be about. Conversations with colleagues are important—even if there is no production. Sometimes having a chat and up-skilling yourself are very useful ways for a writer to keep sane and keep loneliness at bay. Generosity, supporting other people's work and working outside your particular genre are some other ways to fortify oneself creatively. This is vital for inspiration, if nothing else. It's also important to be real and to accept that you are never going to be Marina Carr or Conor McPherson while, in the same breath, realizing that they might never have your audience.

5. **Do you think your play represents a contemporary Irish society; our national identity? And if so, how?**
National identity is much more subtle and nuanced than what we once thought it to be. More and more, I'm finding smaller theatres and venues with less well-known writers are speaking and writing with more genuine truth about Irish identity. There is a criticism that identity politics has no place in theatre. Following from this, there is also the belief that, within theatre, if you are going to be political, it must be with a small "p". For me, there is an appetite for all sorts of politics in Irish theatre.
There is no doubt that Irish theatre can be very insular; white, Settled people talking to themselves, about themselves. The trajectory of the white, Settled, dead male playwright is continually being echoed in Irish theatre, regardless of its content and contemporary value. Nostalgia and commerciality seem to be the cornerstone of Irish theatre. Diversity is spoken by way of gender. For me, diversity within Irish theatre needs to be understood in a much broader context. Often disabled artists are given secondary roles; similarly with Travellers. It's my dream that, some day, a Traveller director will not just direct one of my plays, but will direct plays that were written by Settled people that are unrelated to racism or Traveller identity.
To use the Bechdel test as a blueprint (which requires that two female characters in a film discuss something other than a man) my ambition as a writer is to find a way whereby characters with impairments can move beyond dialogue relating to their condition or body. In other words, their character is part of the story without any overt reference being made to their impairment or deafness. Similarly, for Traveller characters, I would like to pay deference to Traveller identity and the experience of racism, but to be able to move the characters beyond a fixed, one-dimensional identity.

6. **In relation to contemporary Irish theatre, how do you see it being represented in recent years, what do you think of the work people are putting out there and where do you see it going?**
Contemporary theatre is very subjective. Some pieces speak to and touch me in ways that I do not understand. For example, Amy Conroy's work is fascinating and always explores some aspect of human identity. Pat Kinevane's piece, *Silent*, wrenched the heart out of me. Dance pieces, such as the casement project by Fearghus ó Conchúir, excite me. Stacey Gregg's work is engaging. Annie Ryan's adaptation of Eimear McBride's book (*A Girl is a Half-Formed Thing*) left me very disturbed for almost a week. This is what's on, and we never know pieces that are not funded or never reach production. Obviously, the lack of diversity and the glaring omission of plays written by people from Traveller and other black and ethnic minority backgrounds is shameful. It's not just in the writing, but the representation of the Irish aesthetic in theatre is one-dimensional.

7. **Do you have any advice for people who are aspiring to work in the theatre, be it writers, directors, actors, and so on?**
Write, think, read, find connections or write really badly and then let that go and pick it up the following day. Accept that your skills, your ability, your experience, your knowledge and your strength cannot or should not be measured or compared to other writers.
People have different gifts to offer theatre. Skills and talent are there to be worked on, refining your craft means editing, reworking and reworking. It's a huge commitment. The writing lark may bring you up many cul-de-sacs before you find the path that is right for you. Read, write, hold on to your confidence, show people respect and work hard is probably old-fashioned advice, but it keeps you grounded.

Participatory Performance: Spaces of Creative Negotiation

Kate McCarthy and Úna Kealy

Introduction

Participatory forms of performance, as termed by Anna Harpin and Helen Nicholson, provide spaces of "creative negotiation between participation and performance". These spaces are those of imaginative invention, of conference and compromise, where challenging transfers involving participation and performance take place.[1] As Michael Rohd suggests, "[t]he act of expression is an act of connection—through it we become positive, active participants in our lives and in our communities".[2] This chapter explores the dynamic of creative negotiation from a practitioner perspective in order to consider how the work of two theatre organizations specializing in participatory performance use theatre as an act of engagement. The companies considered here occupy a very particular space in the narrative of theatre practice on the island, in which co-creation with participants is central to creating spaces of creative and collaborative negotiation.

This chapter considers and chronicles the work of Dublin-based Smashing Times Theatre Company, founded in 1990, and Kilkenny-based Equinox Theatre Company, founded in 2008, and their strategies of creative negotiation and participation. As a means of positioning these companies within the landscape of Irish social, economic and cultural development, the chapter charts the organic evolution of these companies from within wider social and political activism, which prioritized participation and action in the 1970s and

K. McCarthy (✉) • Ú. Kealy
Waterford Institute of Technology, Waterford, Ireland
e-mail: KMCCARTHY@wit.ie; UKEALY@wit.ie

E. Jordan, E. Weitz (eds.), *The Palgrave Handbook of Contemporary Irish Theatre and Performance*,
https://doi.org/10.1057/978-1-137-58588-2_32

1980s. The chapter also provides an example of how clusters of participatory-performance organizations impacted regionally by considering in detail the evolution of such practice in Waterford City during the 1970s and 1980s. The increase of participatory-performance theatre companies from the 1970s onwards challenged prevailing dichotomies of theatre-making, leading to new approaches and terminologies. The challenge of this subtly morphing practice continues to impact upon the discussion of practice and we create a reflective space within this chapter to consider how to write and talk about participatory forms of theatre.

An interpretivist theoretical framework informs this enquiry into the evolution and organization of participatory performance and its spaces of creative negotiation. The proposed study acknowledges Bruce McConachie's research,[3] which advances theatre historiography by advocating a rejection of the primary consideration of theatre aesthetics in favour of theatre histories that link to the societies from which they emanate. It adopts an approach which assumes "that the conditions of cultural production shape cultural content".[4] This approach proves useful in establishing an interpretation of not only *how* but *why* participatory performance emerged with such prominence during the timeframe considered. However, it is acknowledged from the outset that attempting to create a definitive history of participatory performance is not only impossible but unhelpful as a means of understanding the complex phenomenon under consideration; as such, we enthusiastically concede that the resulting narrative exists as one of a variety of possible interpretations of participatory performance on the island.

Methods utilized within the research include theatre historiography, observation, textual analysis, archival research and semi-structured interviews. Central to the analysis are interviews with Ollie Breslin of Waterford Youth Arts; Mary Moynihan and Freda Manweiler of Smashing Times; and Medb Lambert of Equinox. The interviews with Moynihan, Manweiler and Lambert were conducted specifically in preparation for this study in 2017, while the interview with Breslin was conducted in 2013 as part of the Performing the Region project within Waterford Institute of Technology. The use of semi-structured interviews with practitioners as a means of generating primary data incorporates analysis of these perspectives into the critical narrative and continues efforts to build an archival record of projects and practitioners, which often reside outside the critical domain.

Sandy Fitzgerald calls for the documentation and dissemination of how and why participatory performance happens, arguing that "validation works by building a history of record".[5] While *Theatre Talk* provides a valuable antidote to the problems of ephemerality in documenting theatre practice—offering an archival record of "the working conditions, the states of mind, the experiences and ideals of those at the front line"—the narratives captured there are predominantly those of practitioners working in non-participatory theatre practice.[6] Moynihan also articulates the importance of the documentation of practice as a means of challenging the loss of record caused by collective failings to secure the history, memory and impact of participatory performance. She states there is "a social duty to document this work at some point and make it available for the future". Thus, this chapter seeks to contribute to and help build a history of participatory performance throughout the island and comment on how the practice considered here engages with diverse communities.

The companies considered represent a selection of youth arts and theatre organizations with an established history of regional, national and international work. While participatory performance is documented in the northern part of the island in publications from David Grant, Mary Trotter, Matthew Jennings, and Alison Jeffers,[7] it is less well documented in the south and east, although Charlotte McIvor's "Community Theatre as Active Citizenship" in *Migration and Performance in Contemporary Ireland* offers a valuable contribution in this regard.[8] Gender featured as a selection factor, in that the interviewee gender balance reflects the gender balance of practitioners within the field. Waterford Youth Arts (WYA), a leading youth arts organization remains one of the longest established youth theatre groups on the island (Dunnett, 2009[9]); Smashing Times has worked throughout the island, while Equinox constitutes one of the few participatory performance companies working inclusively with people with and without disabilities on the island.

Slitting the Skylark's Throat: Problems of Terminology

The 1990s gave rise to a number of new and often contested terms to describe theatre practice that took place outside traditional theatre spaces and/or challenged or changed the typical arrangement of actor/performer and audience/spectator. These terms included, for example: applied drama, applied theatre and/or applied performance. Despite a lack of consensus in the discourse surrounding the early years of its emergence, the use of applied theatre as an umbrella term for forms of participatory performance became well established as evident, for example, in the publications of Philip Taylor,[10] and Tim Prentki and Sheila Preston.[11]

Monica Prendergast and Juliana Saxton identify what they term community-based theatre as one of the locations of practice in applied theatre.[12] Baz Kershaw identifies applied theatre as a term that has "generally displaced 'community theatre'",[13] a shift that requires reflection on the use of terminology in the field. Involving differently inflected but related terms and practices, such shifts in the terminology attempt to describe theatre practice within diverse educational and social settings. These terms, developed and popularized in the 1990s, have somewhat given way to a new array of terms such as socially engaged theatre,[14] or socially engaged art,[15] and descriptions used by the National Development Agency for Collaborative Arts (CREATE), such as collaborative arts,[16] or this chapter's preferred descriptor: participatory performance.[17] Arguably, therefore, the terminology used to describe the practice of concern to this chapter exists within a continual process of negotiation as the nomenclature shifts in response to diverse communities and changing contexts.

Before continuing, we reflect on our choice of language to describe the theatre practice under consideration. We have identified two phrases of particular importance: one relates to writing about performers with disabilities and the other relates to how to refer to theatre practice involving participatory elements. According to *Shift in Perspective: An Arts and Disability Resource Pack* the phrase, "people with disabilities", is the most widely used in Ireland, while the phrase, "disabled people", is more commonly used in Britain and Northern Ireland.[18] We avoid using the phrase disabled people in this chapter as the term "aligns disabled people with other minority groups […] and is rooted in identity politics".[19] Instead, we use the term people or artists with disabilities, where appropriate, placing the emphasis on the person ahead of any other descriptive term. We also resist the binary of actor/audience, often using the term participant instead. However, as practitioners in Equinox describe themselves as actors we use this term when describing their work.

The difficulties of definitions, labels and terms within the field of theatre practice—and particularly participatory performance—has caused much debate. There exists a significant body of literature relating to the conceptualization of terms such as applied theatre, socially engaged art, and participatory performance. In describing the oftentimes destructive challenges of imposing definitions on practice, Grant writes of the dangers of getting "bogged down" and refers to the Japanese metaphor of "slitting the skylark's throat to see what makes him sing".[20] We enter this debate trepidatiously, carefully and hopefully, using the descriptive phrase "participatory performance" when contextualizing the work of the companies considered here. We take our lead from Harpin and Nicholson, whose publication *Performance and Participation: Practices, Audiences, Politics* authoritatively interrogates the relationship between these concepts. While Harpin and Nicholson offer analyses of the negotiation between theatremakers and audiences, their edited collection frames perspectives on forms of participatory performance ranging from immersive theatre to community plays.

Fitzgerald describes the term 'community theatre' as laden with "political baggage",[21] contending that this baggage is signified by the word "community", as prefixing theatre practice in such a way makes it something other and less than theatre—the word "community" literally dominates and obscures the "theatre". The term community theatre, as Harpin and Nicholson also suggest, embeds dichotomies of amateur and professional; high aesthetics and low aesthetics; process and product; participatory and passive; and democratic and hierarchical. While the terms "community theatre" and "community drama" have served important functions in providing artists specializing in participatory practice space to validate their work and identity, particularly in terms of accessing funding structures and strands, they have also served to separate. Our challenge in writing this chapter was how to describe this practice while avoiding adding further tangles into a conversation already knotted with terminology debates. We recognize that labelling the practice of others with terms that they do not use contributes to and causes a further embedding of the dichotomies listed above and, as the practitioners we consulted identify their work, first and foremost, as theatre practice, the terminology we use to describe their particular practice follows their lead.

An Overview of Community Arts in Ireland

The emergence of community arts in Ireland shares its lineage with activist movements in 1960s Britain.[22] In the UK in the 1970s, theatre practice moved beyond the traditional theatre space, which, as Kershaw argues,[23] helped forge new relationships with audiences and communities. In this new relationship, participatory performance prompted a shift in how theatre was created and shared, which, Christopher Morash contends, led to a shifting "emphasis from the performance of the finished work before an audience to the production of the work by a community drawing on shared experiences".[24] The approaches used to engender a shared experience required a more fluid relationship between participants in order to create opportunities where they could "tell their story and [...] feel the power of these stories".[25] As Harpin and Nicholson suggest, there is an embodied and felt experience involved when stories are shared.[26] Thus, new models of practice were developed by companies using theatre in ways that challenged hierarchical structures and fostered collaborative working methods. These collaborative methods were recognized through policy and funding strategies by both the Arts Council of Northern Ireland and An Chomhairle Ealaíon, the Arts Council of the Republic.

Participatory practice emerged predominantly in Belfast and Dublin in the late 1970s and 1980s.[27] Performance art was simultaneously emerging, demonstrating a multidirectional shift in performance practice that aimed to connect and challenge audiences in new and diverse ways outside the typical black box of the theatre space.[28] Martin Lynch highlights the name change of the Turf Lodge Fellowship Theatre Company in 1976 to the Turf Lodge Fellowship Community Theatre Company as a reflection of an emerging determination amongst theatre practitioners to deal with social issues identified by and effecting the community.[29] At the same time that Lynch was informing the Arts Council of Northern Ireland of Turf Lodge's inclusion of "community" into its name, An Chomhairle Ealaíon was implementing policies that reflected a more artist- and community-centred approach to funding provision. An Chomhairle Ealaíon, influenced by the then Labour government, was moving towards greater representation of artists by increasing the number of Council members and including artists as appointees. Significantly, the Arts Act of 1973 "removed certain legal doubts and difficulties",[30] clarifying the responsibility of local authorities to fund arts practice and furthering what Patrick Cooke terms as the "democratisation of the arts" from the 1970s through the 1990s in particular.[31]

The emergence of socially engaged theatre—often departing from the literary and dramaturgical arrangements that dominated the Abbey, Peacock, Gate and Lyric stages—created by theatre companies and collectives that had developed audiences amongst working class and socio-economically disadvantaged communities was replicated by investments by both Arts Councils in infrastructure, artists and socially engaged practice. In its 1974 annual report, An Chomhairle Ealaíon asserts that the Council was "determined to pay particular attention to the educational aspect of its work".[32] Significantly, the William J.B. Macaulay Foundation Fellowship Award, a maximum award of £1,000IR offered annually to subsidize emerging creative workers to further their education was, in that year, awarded to Jim Sheridan. Of a total of fourteen previous recipients, the award had been offered to only one other theatre practitioner, Brian Friel, in 1963.[33] Sheridan's award signified recognition on the part of An Chomhairle Ealaíon of the changing nature of theatre practice on the island. Jim Sheridan's brother and theatre collaborator, Peter, wrote a vivid account of seminal moments and events of this time. In it, he conveys the mood and attitudes motivating him and his contemporaries to make theatre as a response to social, political and economic concerns. He captures the energy and intensity of these activists:

> [In 1972] I went to my first lecture: Professor Jim O'Malley on John Osborne, Harold Pinter and the angry generation of British dramatists. A student member of the Sinn Féin cumann stood up and led a walkout over Bloody Sunday. I met Shea [Jim Sheridan] with Neil Jordan on the concourse in front of the library. He'd abandoned auditions. There was a protest march to the British Embassy in Merrion Square. Sheila [Sheridan] joined me straight from school and we went together. The anger in the crowd was palpable. It was the first time I realised that a crowd has a mind, and when that mind fixes on something it is an unstoppable force. We weren't going home until our voice had been heard.[34]

Peter and Jim Sheridan used the Project Arts Centre as a laboratory for issue-based theatre productions from the mid-1970s, bringing Gay Sweatshop's *Mister X* and *Any Woman Can* to the Project in 1976, and premiering Peter Sheridan and Mannix Flynn's *The Liberty Suit* in the Olympia in 1977.[35]

A commitment to develop educational and participatory practice emerged as key concerns in arts provision in the late 1970s, with Ciarán Benson recommending to An Chomhairle Ealaíon the need to develop additional schemes "to involve writers, artists etc. in the community".[36] As the 1970s ended, Christopher Murray maintains, Irish theatre bridged two worlds: "the old or traditional and the new, in constant mutation".[37] Significantly, Murray also identifies the roles of Jim and Peter Sheridan as managers and writers for the Project Arts Centre as an important development stating:

> This is an altogether new situation in Irish theatre: that a young radical group should attain control of a state and municipally subsidized theatre.[38]

The "control" gained by Peter and Jim Sheridan, and others with whom they collaborated, marks an important hierarchical shift. The writer had begun to share esteem with theatremakers, programmers, creative collectives and participants who regarded theatre as a collaborative enterprise articulating specific local concerns.

Collaborative and participatory arts practice increased and developed throughout the 1980s. An increasing number of theatre companies engaged with the exclusions and political trauma of contemporary life on the island, using participatory performance as a means of excavating issues of economic malaise, emigration, abortion and the Troubles. Victor Merriman describes theatre practice at this time as replicating "models of theatre more familiar to audiences in Britain and the developing world".[39] The National Association of Youth Drama (formally re-named Youth Theatre Ireland in 2017) was established in 1980. Fitzgerald notes the importance of a meeting in 1983 in the North Star Hotel, Dublin, hosted by City Workshop—which saw fifteen organizations gather to discuss community arts—describing it as a seminal event in the history of community arts development on the island.[40] Meetings such as this led to the creation of Creative Activity for Everyone (CAFE) in 1983 and the ACE (Arts, Community, Education) Project in 1985. CAFE was founded "to promote community arts and to act as a network service for arts practitioners", and particularly those practitioners committed to cultural democracy.[41] The ACE Project was a joint initiative of An Chomhairle Ealaíon and the Calouste Gulbenkian Foundation to provide a formal "means for developing [an] understanding of the arts and education [and the] already existing category of community arts".[42]

The ACE report, entitled *Art and the Ordinary*, proposes that a central concern of artists during the 1980s was to use socially engaged cultural practice as a means of "changing society in the direction of greater equality and democracy".[43] Helen O'Donoghue's reflections on her work as an artist and co-founder and director of City Vision during that decade corroborates this orientation of focus and attitude:

> In retrospect, I feel that we were very cocky and believed that we could make an impact on the society that we were growing up in. The eighties was the period in Ireland when we wanted to work as artists in Ireland and connect with communities beyond the "closed" arts community offered to us at college.[44]

What emerges in O'Donoghue's reflection is the shared desire among practitioners in the 1980s to use aesthetic means to engage with participants and use arts practice as a means of social and cultural development. Evident in her remarks is the desire to negotiate increased access to participatory arts opportunities for theatremakers and participants alike.

Negotiating Participatory Performance in Waterford

This urge to create participatory performance and implement social change extended nationwide and had important impacts regionally. One example of regional cultural development dominated by organizations specializing in participatory performance took place in Waterford. In the late 1970s, the Combat Poverty Agency facilitated a meeting in Waterford city inviting groups and individuals to consider how they might collaborate to combat social exclusion and improve the social and cultural fabric of the city. Ollie Breslin characterizes this collaboration as "a left-wing, agitating set-up, about people getting organised and fighting for their rights", reflecting on the 1970s as "kind of a radical time, not necessarily in politics, but amongst ordinary people involved in these things".[45] Breslin's comments reveal a deliberate collective effort to negotiate creative spaces, where those who described themselves as artists and those who did not could collaborate within participatory arts practice.

In 1980, in an effort to establish an arts centre in the city, the Waterford Resource Centre established a sub-committee to propel this objective, and Waterford Arts for All (WAFA) was founded. WAFA was a "democratic organisation", which used the arts to address unemployment amongst young people.[46] In November 1980, WAFA organized an Arts for All Festival which programmed events throughout the city in pubs and community centres to "highlight the idea that the arts was not elitist" (Breslin).[47] A further key development in Waterford City was the founding of the Ciotóg drama group. Although Fitzgerald states that Ciotóg was established in 1970,[48] Breslin states that it grew out of WAFA under Ted O'Regan's direction. As a pioneer of youth drama in Ireland, O'Regan, and his wife Mary, had facilitated drama and visual art workshops from the 1970s onwards. Breslin recalls O'Regan inviting eight actor/facilitators to form Ciotóg, deliberately selecting a gender-equal ensemble, an ethos which continues to underpin the work of WYA.

O'Regan trained the members of Ciotóg in performance and facilitation, using theatre-based exercises and role-play to explore topics such as mental health. O'Regan was influenced by Dorothy Heathcote's work and adopted her praxis in the creation of a drama in education model.[49] This ethos saw the company touring community centres, hospitals and women's organizations, where they "presented plays as a stimulus for discussion", Breslin says. At the same time as Ciotóg formed, the Arts For All Theatre Company came into being and Breslin acknowledges the "interesting dynamic" that existed between Ciotóg, and the Arts For All Theatre Company actors, reflecting on the frisson of tension developing between so-called "community" and "professional" theatre collectives.

Ciotóg disbanded after two years, when the company was unsuccessful in gaining support from An Chomhairle Ealaíon or Waterford City Council, but in 1985, in consultation with O'Regan, Claire Hayes (member of Ciotóg) and Breslin established Waterford Youth Drama (now Waterford Youth Arts 1985–present). Although Hayes emigrated a few months later, the company, led by Breslin, remained. Around this time in 1988 another Waterford practitioner, Miriam Gallagher, was pioneering participatory performance in prisons and other participant groups. Gallagher's philosophy was to "aim for the highest quality of work [and to] focus artistically, socially and culturally on the community".[50] Common among these Waterford practitioners was their commitment to accessing and creating new spaces in which shared social concerns could be negotiated.

Throughout this time a central shared concern of all arts organizations within Waterford city was the campaign for a dedicated arts space. In 1984, Garter Lane Arts Centre opened and, the following year, Red Kettle Theatre Company (1985–2014) was formed. In 1993, key members of these organizations created Waterford Spraoi (1993–present). While not all of the organizations created during that time continue to exist, the key personnel, and others who came to and stayed in the city to work as cultural activists, continue to make significant contributions to the cultural life of the city. This documentation of participatory performance in Waterford contextualizes the development of practice up to, and including, the early 1990s. The following section continues the narrative by exploring the work of two companies with expertise in the field of participatory performance.

Smashing Times Theatre Company: "A daring adventure"

Established in 1991, Smashing Times Theatre Company is "a professional theatre and film company involved in performance, training and participation".[51] The company's mission statement describes the work as "underpinned by a rights-based approach and a commitment to artistic excellence and social engagement".[52] Learning about theatre as an art form during her training at the Focus Theatre in Dublin, Moynihan, co-founder and current artistic director, recognized the potential of theatre as a tool of empowerment. She cites a desire to improve access to theatre and to create opportunities for women theatremakers as primary motivations in her establishment of the company. Moynihan, and manager, facilitator and project co-ordinator, Freda Manweiler, offer insights into the company's origins and development, and their creative strategies in negotiations with the diverse communities with which they work. In the late 1990s, Manweiler joined Smashing Times; her background in refugee resettlement and integration, community relations, and education and training for immigrant and refugee women corresponded with the company's ethos of social engagement. From the outset Manweiler's recognition of the power of the processes of "community development and community education, particularly in post-conflict work" harmonized with and developed participatory performance practice within the company.[53]

Moynihan acknowledges Italian actor, activist and playwright, Franca Rame as a key influence on the company's early work. Speaking at a theatre conference in Dublin in 1985, Rame noted "the absence of women speakers" asking: "Where are the women? They are around. It's just that the men can't see them".[54] Steve Wilmer argues that to secure directing work on the island during this period, women created their own organizations and Smashing Times' formation in this year supports this theory.[55] In the early 1990s Smashing Times produced the work of Rame, Dario Fo and Trouble and Strife. As a theatre collective, Trouble and Strife collaboratively devised work based on research, dialogue and workshops,[56] a model which Smashing Times adopted and continues to practice. Moynihan performed Rame's work during a women's health week and the company used post-show discussions to engage and involve audiences. The positive levels of engagement within these post-show discussions evidenced an opportunity to develop forms of participatory activity and the company found a model to support this intention with the work of Augusto Boal.

Creative Negotiations

Smashing Times uses theatre and storytelling "to explore issues, promote peace-building, [and] mental health", and Moynihan characterizes this work as "provocative … and challenging at times". The company uses a range of drama-based models for anti-racism and anti-sectarianism projects, and for projects exploring gender equality and human rights. In describing how the company develops its participatory performances, Moynihan explains that the process uses both script-based and devising approaches. The company gathers stories from participants, a process which is then followed by "a long process with communities where those stories are given to writers and productions are created". Although the facilitators and practitioners are often called to dramaturgically shape the work, Moynihan reflects that in some projects "the work itself and the people you engage with give you the form that's needed to bring the project alive". In this way, the company's work negotiates a key binary inherent in participatory performance—that between the participant and the practitioner. The company addresses this binary by "always remembering that this is an art form," thus foregrounding, as Alistair Martin-Smith theorizes,[57] the aesthetic intention of the work.

In making such work, the dyadic model of performance and post-show discussion, as developed in the early years of the company, endures as a core feature of Smashing Times' practice. Philip Taylor proposes the intentionality of the work and participation as key characteristics of participatory performance and argues for "the artfulness of the theatre form" as crucial in bringing about social change.[58] It is through participation in the art form that the company's work challenges, provokes and explores issues of relevance to participants. Smashing Times' commitment to social engagement creates a space in which to engage participants, however, Moynihan and Manweiler emphasize that the performances created must "stand up" as theatre.

The relationship between the aesthetic and the instrumental is a central concern in participatory performance theory and practice,[59] and constitutes a significant negotiation taking place in the space between performance and participation. Manweiler succinctly articulates how the balance between the aesthetic and the instrumental intention is achieved:

> One of the things that's really important is the fact that it is an artistic process and creative and theatre principles underpin the work. The by-product is community development and community education, but that can only happen with a very high quality theatrical production and workshop process.

Creating an "'aesthetic space'" or a "'creative gap'", as Anthony Jackson argues, offers opportunities for "participants [to] forge, negotiate, and own, meaning".[60] Smashing Times enters this negotiation with participants by remaining truthful to the participants' voices "and using that voice to make theatre". This incorporation of participants' voices constitutes an empowering creative negotiation between participant engagement, authorship, performance practice and the instrumental intention that makes this type of practice distinct.

Referring to Paul Kennedy, an artist collaborating with Smashing Times, Moynihan recounts his maxim that "half the circle is the performance, and the other half is audience feedback and engagement". This philosophy reflects the aesthetic–instrumental balance sought within the company's practice. In order to optimize the integration between the aesthetic and instrumental within the circle of participation and performance, Manweiler highlights the importance of the company's support structures around facilitator training:

> There's a lot of work that goes into prepping, we train our facilitators, there's a lot of support projects in place [...] we're not ticking boxes, but there's a whole load of processes have to happen before the work happens and that has to happen after the work happens. So there is a whole invisible thing that goes on around it. Even with facilitators or artists, they have to have that structure as well when they come in to engage in this type of work.

This highlighting of the importance of "very skilled facilitation" in the company's engagement with participants is an approach that also "trust[s] the participant that the work is resonating with them". It further demonstrates the empowering ethos of this practice, which invests in the facilitator and validates the participant's perspective.

Recent scholarship argues for the value of assessing and evaluating "both intended and unintended" impacts of practice.[61] Smashing Times articulates a commitment to documenting the impact of their work. As such, the company gathers post-project testimonials, which they view as very valuable in monitoring and supporting the participants. In this respect, Manweiler raises the importance of reflection in and on action, emphasizing the need for facilitators to remain flexible and "to keep the creative process going". Moynihan describes the work "as a two-way process where, artistically, the artists benefit as much as the communities benefit". In this way, facilitation acknowledges that iterative moments of reflection within the aesthetic process constitute an effective strategy of negotiation within what Moynihan describes above as the circle of engagement. In recommending developments for future participatory performance in the sector, Moynihan advocates for participatory performance to become "a normal part of your work to engage in education, [and] to engage in the community". She argues that using performance in this way creates "new frontiers" and reflects on the journey of Smashing Times as "a daring adventure".

Equinox Theatre Company: "Our adventures together"

Equinox Theatre Company—based in Callan, Co. Kilkenny, and partnered with the Kilkenny Collective for Arts Talent (KCAT)—facilitates a collaboration between artists with different backgrounds and abilities.[62] A number of Equinox company members graduated from a KCAT FETAC Level 5 programme in theatre. Currently, there are eight actors in the company working two days a week: the majority of these have second jobs working in local businesses. Since 2008, when the company formed, devised productions include: *Footballhead*; *The Lost Prince*; *(The Making of) The Frogs After Aristophanes*; *Bridge Street*; *Memory Box*; and *The M House*. Established in 1999, KCAT operates as an art and study centre under the umbrella of the Camphill Communities Arts and Life-Long Learning initiative. Medb Lambert, artistic co-ordinator with Equinox, describes how Equinox offers opportunities to consider the challenges of creative negotiation, in partnership with KCAT. Artist George McCutcheon was the inspiration behind the collective. According to Lambert, McCutcheon was a man making "incredible constructions" in his bedroom; he was also a man with Down syndrome. A collective formed within Kilkenny to support McCutcheon in his work, which led to an EU grant in the mid-1990s. This subsequently led to what Lambert describes as the "discovery of a lot of artists working away in their bedrooms making art that didn't have access to training or anything". Thus, McCutcheon is acknowledged as the father of KCAT, which currently provides a creative space for artists to meet and collaborate and houses a number of working studio spaces—including Equinox Theatre Company.

Equinox state an intention to create unique and inclusive theatre practice that reflects the lived experience of the participants: "we want to say things like we see them. We want to tell the truth".[63] This mission statement reflects what Fitzgerald asserts as a core value within participatory performance, which he articulates as "the right of people to contribute to and participate fully in culture, the right to have a voice and the right to give a voice".[64] This ethos also responds to what Peter Kearns asserts as "a call for emancipatory arts processes … [that] show the means of carrying out aesthetic expression with social and cultural transformation".[65] Equinox present themselves as an ensemble that consciously demonstrates the interplay between the aesthetic and the instrumental. By identifying as actors "we have chosen to become actors", thus reflecting the validation that participation in Equinox's performances provides.[66]

Creative Negotiations

The only qualification required to join Equinox is "a need to make theatre" (Lambert). Lambert acknowledges her creative role in the process, but emphasizes that the ensemble led the way in terms of ideas and content. The dramaturgical structuring of the content is supported by Lambert in her role as a guide or facilitator who "knows how to navigate" the dramaturgical space. Although she directs, facilitates, performs, and produces, Lambert describes herself as a set designer. This training reveals itself as an important feature of the devised work. It is evident in *Memory Box*, produced in 2015, and *The M House*, produced in 2017, where "the physical environment informs the narrative" (Lambert). This is expressed in the company's mission statement, which recognizes that "some of us choose not to communicate verbally and so we understand that some of our audience probably choose not to engage with the world aurally".[67] This recognition of participants' diverse ways of perceiving, experiencing and communicating demonstrates the company's commitment to equality of participation and access, validating the participants' experience and means of expression. By providing opportunities for people with disabilities to engage on a professional level with theatre as an art form, Equinox also supports participants in their training, experience and development as artists.

While physical and visual dramaturgical elements are important to the company, narrative-driven work is of equal interest. In terms of script development, each scene is first created non-verbally and explored in different ways with "different energies". Participants then negotiate a summary of the scripted work using a variety of expressive strategies. In order to create meaningful connections between participants, Lambert stresses the importance of long-lasting collaborations emphasizing that "it [the work] needs time, time, time". She asserts a commitment to developing participatory performance over periods of time of up to two years, describing the company's timeline for devised projects as nine months in development, three months "digesting" the work, and between six and nine months in rehearsal. She acknowledges that, although time is the company's most valuable resource, these long development phases create challenges as not all of the participants can work over these timeframes. Therefore, the negotiations Lambert undertakes during each project are those of dramaturgical space, dramatic and theatrical text development, and the interchange of participants over extended timeframes.

Equinox's current production, *The M House*, a play about the "ridiculous nature of our one-size-fits-all culture" has been in development since September 2016, during which time a work-in-progress was also performed.[68] Multiple aspects of the production demonstrate how participatory performance, as designed and facilitated by Equinox, responds to guidelines offered by Arts and Disability Ireland. These recommend that "projects should be based around the self-identified interests/needs of the participants, who should be involved as fully as possible in the planning, management and evaluation of a project".[69] The programme note to *Memory Box* reflects this ethos in stating that the company works "together to make great art ... making decisions together and sharing experiences".[70] One of the founding members of Equinox, Belinda Henzey, shares her experience in describing the inciting incident for *The M House* as the decision by a local bus company to discontinue the route enabling her travel to Callan and participation with Equinox. Henzey's experience led the company to consider how policy decisions directly impact on people. The production encourages participants to consider "what attitudinal changes need to be made in order to improve access for people with disabilities".[71]

Prior to the interview with Lambert for this chapter, a rehearsal of the company's production of *The M House* was observed, which demonstrated how the negotiation between the participants and the dramaturgy supported the performance. In the rehearsal it was evident that each participant shared the creative space, equally reflecting the ethos of mutuality recommended by Arts and Disability, Ireland.[72] In navigating the dramaturgical space, the script is crafted so that the actors can help each other out, if difficulties arise, while remaining in character, thus evidencing and further building a strong ensemble. Lambert's set designs also function as a supporting structure for the actors, both spatially and figuratively. Act One uses a large box containing the actors in a confined space. In conversation with the company, the actors discussed the practicalities of Lambert's design. They explained how "the box binds" the ensemble in a helpful way, and reflected that the box also functions as a character, shaping their use of the physical space while providing a powerful visual metaphor of the ways in which people of mixed abilities are often all subjected to the same policies, regardless of the challenges these policies create for individuals. *The M House*, therefore, provides another space in which participants are invited to consider the impacts of policy decisions through a variety of creative negotiations, which Lambert describes as "our adventures together".

Conclusion

Harpin and Nicholson argue that participatory performance allows for theatre practice in which decisions are approached from the "bottom-up".[73] This reflects the seemingly inescapable situation in which any analysis of theatre practice, and particularly participatory performance, must constantly refer to the established hierarchical arrangements that continue to dominate theatre. This chapter has sought to demonstrate that participatory performance is built upon, and characterized by: a dedication amongst participants towards the creative negotiation of spaces of dramaturgy; inclusivity; and democratic discussion and decision making, which extend beyond the physical spaces of practice and performance into shared geographical, social and psychological spaces. The chapter also interrogates these spaces of creative negotiation, using practitioners as guides in this task so as to document, reflect and capture the ephemeral nature of participatory performance as it currently exists on the island. We have exercised care in our use of terminology and language, avoiding definitions and labels in an attempt to reflect the complexity of the field of practice and in recognition of existing and unresolved debates within the critical sphere. This confusion and debate is arguably of little or no importance to participants; however, language is a powerful construct and the discussion here evidences that such debates are most effectively negotiated when informed by practice. This chapter documents the ways in which participants, who collectively make and shape the spaces in which they work, demonstrate the "adventure" of a creative process that is inclusive, democratic, supportive and critical.

Notes

1. Anna Harpin and Helen Nicholson, eds., *Performance and Participation: Practices, Audiences, Politics* (Hampshire: Palgrave, 2017), 4.
2. Michael Rohd, *Theatre for Community, Conflict and Dialogue: The Hope is Vital Training Manual* (Portsmouth: Heinemann, 1998), xix.
3. Bruce A. McConachie, "Towards a Postpositivist Theatre History". *Theatre Journal* 37, no. 4 (1985): 465–86.
4. Aeron Davis, "Investigating cultural producers", in *Research Methods for Cultural Studies*, ed. Michael Pickering (Edinburgh: Edinburgh University Press, 2008), 53.
5. "Community Arts: Ten Texts to Get You Started", Sandy Fitzgerald. Accessed 11 May, 2017, http://www.bluedrum.ie/SandyFitzgeraldSelects.htm.
6. Lillian Chambers, Ger Fitzgibbon, and Éamonn Jordan, *Theatre Talk: Voices of Irish Theatre Practitioners* (Dublin: Carysfort Press, 2001), ix.
7. David Grant, *Playing the Wild Card: Community Drama and Smaller-Scale Professional Theatre – A Community Relations Perspective* (Belfast: Community Relations Council, 1993); Mary Trotter, *Modern Irish Theatre* (Cambridge: Polity Press, 2008); Matthew Jennings, "Aesthetics and Efficacy in Community Theatre in Contemporary Northern Ireland", *Research in Drama Education: The Journal of Applied Theatre and Performance*, 15, no. 1 (2010): 111–117; and, Alison Jeffers, "Authority, Authorization and Authorship: Participation in Community Plays in Belfast", in *Performance and Participation: Practices, Audiences and Politics*, eds. Anna Harpin and Helen Nicholson (Hampshire: Palgrave, 2017).
8. Charlotte McIvor, *Migration and Performance in Contemporary Ireland: Towards a New Interculturalism* (London: Palgrave Macmillan, 2016).
9. Rhona Dunnett, "Centrestage+10: A report on Youth Theatre in Ireland". accessed 10 January, 2017, http://www.youththeatre.ie/content/files/merged.pdf.
10. Philip Taylor, *Applied Theatre: Creating Transformative Encounters in the Community* (Portsmouth: Heinemann, 2003).
11. Tim Prentki and Sheila Preston, eds., *The Applied Theatre Reader* (London: Routledge, 2009).
12. Monica Prendergast and Juliana Saxton, eds., *Applied Theatre: International Case Studies and Challenges for Practice* (Bristol: Intellect, 2009).
13. Baz Kershaw, "Towards a Historiography of the Absent: On the Late Pasts of Applied Theatre and Community Performance", in *Critical Perspectives on Applied Theatre*, eds. Jenny Hughes and Helen Nicholson (Cambridge: Cambridge University Press, 2016), 16.
14. Nicola Shaughnessy, *Applying Performance: Live Art, Socially Engaged Theatre and Affective Practice* (Hampshire: Palgrave, 2015).

15. Jenny Hughes, and Helen Nicholson, eds., *Critical Perspectives on Applied Theatre* (Cambridge: Cambridge University Press, 2016).
16. "History of CREATE", CREATE. Accessed 11 May 2017, http://www.create-ireland.ie.
17. Harpin and Nicholson, *Performance and Participation.*
18. Arts and Disability Ireland, "Shift in Perspective: An Arts and Disability Resource Pack". Accessed 11 May, 2017, http://adiarts.ie/assets/uploads/2016/02/Shift_In_Perspective.pdf.
19. Arts and Disability Ireland, "Shift in Perspective."
20. Grant, *Playing the Wild Card*, 5.
21. Sandy Fitzgerald, *An Outburst of Frankness: Community Arts in Ireland –A Reader* (Dublin: TASC at New Island, 2004), 76.
22. See Ciarán Benson, *The Place of the Arts in Irish Education* (Dublin: An Chomhairle Ealaíon, 1979). Accessed 11 May 2017, http://artsineducation.ie/en/reading-room/ and Fitzgerald's, *An Outburst of Frankness.*
23. Baz Kershaw, *The Politics of Performance: Radical Theatre as Cultural Intervention* (London: Routledge, 1992).
24. Christopher Morash, *A History of Irish Theatre 1601*-2000 (Cambridge: Cambridge University Press, 2002), 262.
25. Fitzgerald, *An Outburst of Frankness*, 79.
26. Harpin and Nicholson, *Performance and Participation.*
27. See Morash, *A History of Irish Theatre 1601*-2000; Fitzgerald, *An Outburst of Frankness*; Victor Merriman, *Because We Are Poor: Irish Theatre in the 1990s* (Dublin: Carysfort Press, 2011); and, Patrick Cooke, "Cultural Policy in Ireland", in *Art and Architecture of Ireland, Volume V: Twentieth Century*, eds. Catherine Marshall and Peter Murray (Dublin: Royal Irish Academy, 2014), 107–114 for further discussion.
28. Áine Phillips, *Performance Art in Ireland: A History* (Bristol: Intellect, 2015).
29. Martin Lynch in Fitzgerald, *An Outburst of Frankness.*
30. An Chomhairle Ealaíon, *An Dara Tuarascáil Bhliantúil is Fiche, maille le Cuntais ó lú Aibreán, 1973 go 31ú Márta, 1974* (Dublin: An Chomhairle Ealaíon, 1974) 8. Accessed 11 May 2017, http://www.artscouncil.ie/publications.
31. Cooke, "Cultural Policy in Ireland", 113.
32. An Chomhairle Ealaíon, *An Dara Tuarascáil Bhliantúil is Fiche, maille le Cuntais ó lú Aibreán, 1973 go 31ú Márta, 1974*, 5.
33. Ibid., 9.
34. Peter Sheridan, *Break a Leg: A Memoir*, (Dublin: New Island, 2012), 93.
35. Ibid.
36. Ciarán Benson, *The Place of the Arts in Irish Education*, 136.
37. Christopher Murray, "Irish Drama in Transition 1966–1978", *Études Irelandaises*, 4, (1979): 301. Accessed 11 May 2017, http://www.persee.fr/doc/irlan_0183-973x_1979_num_4_1_2605.
38. Ibid., 300.
39. Merriman, *Because We Are Poor: Irish Theatre in the 1990s*, 55.
40. Fitzgerald, *An Outburst of Frankness.*
41. "History of CREATE", CREATE.

42. Ciarán Benson, *Art and the Ordinary: The report of the Arts Community Education Committee* (Dublin: Arts Community Education Committee, Arts Council of Ireland, 1989), 9.
43. Ibid., 22.
44. Fitzgerald, *An Outburst of Frankness*, 14.
45. Quotations attributed to Ollie Breslin in this chapter are taken from an interview conducted by Kate McCarthy, Úna Kealy, Síle Penkert and Waterford Institute of Technology Humanities Research Summer School, 5 June 2013.
46. Fitzgerald, *An Outburst of Frankness*, 258.
47. Merriman, *Because We Are Poor: Irish Theatre in the 1990s*, 156.
48. Fitzgerald, *An Outburst of Frankness*.
49. Ted O'Regan, *A Sense of Wonder: An Introduction to Drama Education* (Dublin: Liffey Press, 2004), 31.
50. Miriam Gallagher, *The Gold of Tandragee and Other Plays* (Dublin: Mirage, 2008), x.
51. "About us", Smashing Times Theatre Company. Accessed 11 May 2017, http://www.smashingtimes.ie/aboutus/.
52. Ibid.
53. Henceforth, quotations from the interview with Mary Moynihan and Freda Manweiler conducted by Kate McCarthy on 9 January 2017 will be attributed to the interviewee surname only. This convention is also adopted in attributing quotes by Medb Lambert and the Equinox ensemble. Two interviews with members of Equinox Theatre Company were conducted by Kate McCarthy on 10 January 2017. Equinox Theatre Company members include: Shane Byrne, Janice de Bróithe, Gary Comerford, Sighile Hennessy, Belinda Henzey, Susie Lamb, Mairéad Maguire and Jim Rohan.
54. Steve Wilmer, "Women's Theatre in Ireland: An Exciting Past, Dispiriting Present, and Hopeful Future", *New Theatre Quarterly* 28. no. 7 (1991): 360.
55. Ibid.
56. Lizbeth Goodman, *Contemporary Feminist Theatres: To Each Her Own* (London: Routledge, 2003).
57. Alistair Martin-Smith, "Setting the Stage for a Dialogue: Aesthetics in Drama and Theatre Education". *Journal of Aesthetic Education* 39, no. 4 (2005): 3–11.
58. Taylor, *Applied Theatre*, 101.
59. Helen Nicholson, *Applied Drama: The Gift of Theatre* 2nd ed. (Basingstoke: Macmillan, 2014).
60. Anthony Jackson, *Theatre, Education and the Making of Meanings: Art or Instrument* (Manchester: Manchester University Press, 2007), 271.
61. Michael Etherton and Tim Prentki, "Drama for change? Prove it! Impact assessment in applied theatre", *Research in Drama Education: The Journal of Applied Theatre and Performance* 11. no. 2 (2006): 139.
62. "About Us", KCAT. Accessed 11 May 2017, http://www.kcat.ie/WP/.
63. "KCAT Art and Study Centre", Equinox Theatre Company. Accessed 11 May 2017, http://kcat.ie/equinox-theatre/.
64. Fitzgerald, *An Outburst of Frankness*, 79.
65. Peter Kearns, "Emancipatory Arts Processes", in *Face On: Disability Arts in Ireland and Beyond*, ed. Katie O'Reilly (Dublin: Arts & Disability Ireland, 2007), 142.

66. "KCAT Art and Study Centre", Equinox Theatre Company.
67. Ibid.
68. "April 2017 *The M House*, Equinox Theatre Company", Watergate Theatre, Kilkenny, accessed 11 May 2017, http://watergatetheatre.com/events/the-m-house/.
69. Arts and Disability Ireland, "Shift in Perspective".
70. Equinox Theatre Company, *Memory Box* (Callan: Equinox Theatre Company, 2017).
71. Arts and Disability Ireland, "Shift in Perspective".
72. Ibid.
73. Harpin and Nicholson, *Performance and Participation*, 2.

Bibliography

Arts and Disability Ireland. "Shift in Perspective: An Arts and Disability Resource Pack." Accessed May 11, 2017. http://adiarts.ie/assets/uploads/2016/02/Shift_In_Perspective.pdf.

An Chomhairle Ealaíon. "An Dara Tuarascáil Bhliantúil is Fiche, maille le Cuntais ó lú Aibreán, 1973 go 31ú Márta, 1974." Accessed May 11, 2017. www.artscouncil.ie/publications.

Benson, Ciarán. "The Place of the Arts in Irish Education." Accessed May 11, 2017. http://artsineducation.ie/en/reading-room/The_Place_of_the_Arts_in_Irish_Education.pdf.

Benson, Ciarán. *Art and the Ordinary: The Report of the Arts Community Education Committee*. Dublin: Arts Community Education Committee, Arts Council of Ireland, 1989.

Chambers, Lillian, Ger Fitzgibbon, and Éamonn Jordan, eds. *Theatre Talk: Voices of Irish Theatre Practitioners*. Dublin: Carysfort Press, 2001.

Cooke, Patrick. "Cultural policy in Ireland." In *Art and Architecture of Ireland, Volume V: Twentieth Century*, edited by Catherine Marshall and Peter Murray, 107–114. Dublin: Royal Irish Academy, 2014.

CREATE. "History of CREATE." Accessed May 11, 2017. http://www.create-ireland.ie.

Davis, Aeron. "Investigating Cultural Producers." In *Research Methods for Cultural Studies*, edited by Michael Pickering, 53–67. Edinburgh: Edinburgh University Press, 2008.

Dunnett, Rhona. Centrestage+10: A Report on Youth Theatre in Ireland Accessed January 10, 2017. http://www.youththeatre.ie/content/files/merged.pdf.

Equinox Theatre Company. *Memory Box*. Callan: Equinox Theatre Company, 2016.

Equinox Theatre Company. "KCAT Art and Study Centre." Accessed May 11, 2017. http://kcat.ie/equinox-theatre/.

Etherton, Michael, and Tim Prentki, eds. "Impact assessment and applied drama." *Research in Drama Education: The Journal of Applied Theatre and Performance* 11, no. 2 (2006): 139–269.

Fitzgerald, Sandy ed., *An Outburst of Frankness: Community Arts in Ireland –A Reader*. Dublin: TASC at New Island, 2004.

Fitzgerald, Sandy. "Community Arts: Ten Texts to Get You Started." Accessed May 11, 2016. http://www.bluedrum.ie/SandyFitzgeraldSelects.htm.

Gallagher, Miriam. *The Gold of Tradagee and Other Plays*. Dublin: Mirage, 2008.

Goodman, Lizbeth. *Contemporary Feminist Theatres: To Each Her Own*. London: Routledge, 2003.

Grant, David. *Playing the Wild Card: Community Drama and Smaller-Scale Professional Theatre – A Community Relations Perspective*. Belfast: Community Relations Council, 1993.

Harpin, Anna, and Helen Nicholson, eds. *Performance and Participation: Practices, Audiences, Politics*. Hampshire: Palgrave, 2017.

Hughes, Jenny, and Helen Nicholson, eds. *Critical Perspectives on Applied Theatre*. Cambridge: Cambridge University Press, 2016.

Jackson, Anthony. *Theatre, Education and the Making of Meanings: Art or Instrument*. Manchester: Manchester University Press, 2007.

Jennings, Matthew. "Aesthetics and Efficacy in Community Theatre in Contemporary Northern Ireland." *Research in Drama Education: The Journal of Applied Theatre and Performance* 15, no. 1 (2010): 111–117.

Jeffers, Alison. "Authority, Authorization and Authorship: Participation in Community Plays in Belfast." In *Performance and Participation: Practices, Audiences and Politics*, edited by Anna Harpin, and Helen Nicholson, 209–229. Basingstoke: Palgrave Macmillan, 2017.

KCAT. "About Us." Accessed May 11, 2017. http://kcat.ie/.

Kershaw, Baz. "Towards a historiography of the Absent: On the Late Pasts of Applied Theatre and Community Performance." In *Critical Perspectives on Applied Theatre*, edited by Jenny Hughes, and Helen Nicholson, 15–39. Cambridge: Cambridge University Press, 2016.

Kershaw, Baz. *The Politics of Performance: Radical Theatre as Cultural Intervention*. London: Routledge, 1992.

Kearns, Peter. "Emancipatory Arts Processes." In *Face On: Disability Arts in Ireland and Beyond*, edited by Katie O'Reilly, 138–146. Dublin: Arts & Disability Ireland, 2007.

Lynch, Martin. "The History of Community Arts in Ireland According to Martin Lynch." In *An Outburst of Frankness: Community Arts in Ireland –A Reader*, edited by Sandy Fitzgerald, 56–79. Dublin: TASC at New Island, 2004.

Martin-Smith, Alistair. "'Setting the Stage for Dialogue': Aesthetics in Drama and Theatre Education." *Journal of Aesthetic Education* 39, no. 4 (2005): 3–11. Accessed October 27, 2010.

McConachie, Bruce A. "Towards a Postpositivist Theatre History." *Theatre Journal* 37, no. 4 (December 1985): 465–486.

McIvor, Charlotte. *Migration and Performance in Contemporary Ireland: Towards a New Interculturalism*. London: Palgrave Macmillan, 2016.

Merriman, Victor. *Because We Are Poor: Irish theatre in the 1990s*, Dublin: Carysfort Press, 2011.

Morash, Christopher. *A History of Irish Theatre 1601-2000*, Cambridge: Cambridge University Press, 2002.

Murray, Christopher. "Irish drama in transition 1966-1978." *Études Irlandaises* 4 (1979): 287–308. Accessed May 11, 2017. http://www.persee.fr/doc/irlan_0183-973x_1979_num_4_1_2605.

Nicholson, Helen. *Applied Drama: The Gift of Theatre*. 2nd ed. Basingstoke: Macmillan, 2014.

O'Regan, Ted. *A Sense of Wonder: An Introduction to Drama Education*. Dublin: Liffey Press, 2004.

Phillips, Áine. *Performance Art in Ireland: A History*, Bristol: Intellect, 2015.

Prendergast, Monica, and Juliana Saxton, eds. *Applied Theatre: International Case Studies and Challenges for Practice*. Bristol: Intellect, 2009.

Prentki, Tim, and Sheila Preston, eds. *The Applied Theatre Reader*. London: Routledge, 2009.

Rohd, Michael. *Theatre for Community, Conflict and Dialogue: The Hope is Vital Training Manual*. Portsmouth: Heinemann, 1998.

Shaughnessy, Nicola. *Applying Performance: Live Art, Socially Engaged Theatre and Affective Practice*. Basingstoke: Palgrave Macmillan, 2015.

Sheridan, Peter. *Break a Leg: A Memoir*. Dublin: New Island, 2012.

Smashing Times. "About us." Accessed May 11, 2017. http://www.smashingtimes.ie/.

Taylor, Philip. *Applied Theatre: Creating Transformative Encounters in the Community*. Portsmouth: Heinemann, 2003.

Trotter, Mary. *Modern Irish Theatre*. Cambridge: Polity Press, 2008.

Watergate Theatre. "The M House." Accessed May 11, 2017. http://watergatetheatre.com/events/the-m-house/.

Wilmer, Steve. "Women's Theatre in Ireland: An Exciting Past, Dispiriting Present, and Hopeful Future." *New Theatre Quarterly* 28, no. 7 (1991): 353–360.

PART III

Interfaces

Other Spaces (Non-theatre Spaces)

Charlotte McIvor

This chapter investigates Irish theatre and performance staged in non-theatre spaces from the mid-late twentieth to early twenty-first century. For the purposes of this chapter, non-theatre spaces are defined broadly as locations outside either a theatre building or any space intended for live performances. My broad categorization of non-theatre spaces encompasses privately and publicly owned architectural spaces and public (or semi-public) environments, such as streets, when appropriated for theatrical projects and used to stage work with a varying level of spectacle (with or without the proper permits).

In this chapter, I focus on two major strands of contemporary Irish performance work: (1) street arts, and (2) site-specific theatre and performance. Both strands have affected the evolution of Irish theatrical practices in non-theatre spaces since the mid to late 1970s. This chapter is necessarily non-comprehensive but attempts to reference the broadest range of practice possible, while engaging with key selected companies and artists. The chapter ultimately argues that the move of Irish artists, companies and festivals into non-theatre spaces—from the early twentieth century to the present—constitutes varying but directed political manoeuvres that call into question the meaning and political efficacy of theatre as a communal act in Irish society, as well as in the inter/transnational networks through which Irish theatre and performance circulate.

The modern early twentieth-century staging of Irish theatre and performance in non-theatre spaces could be traced back to William Butler Yeats's initial 1916 staging of his Nôh plays for dancers in the private home of Lady Cunard in London weeks before the Easter Rising and to Inghinidhe na hÉireann's staging

C. McIvor (✉)
National University of Ireland Galway, Galway, Ireland
e-mail: charlotte.mcivor@nuigalway.ie

E. Jordan, E. Weitz (eds.), *The Palgrave Handbook of Contemporary Irish Theatre and Performance*,
https://doi.org/10.1057/978-1-137-58588-2_33

of street spectacles, pageants and tableaux vivant as part of their nationalist endeavours.[1] The early twentieth-century history of Irish theatre indeed centrally involves the transfer (or exile) of experimental and political theatre practices outside traditional theatre spaces. This either followed on from aristocratic and monarchical practices of staging theatre in the private home, as in Yeats's experiments with Nôh drama, or reflected the alliance between artists and activist organizations, such as Maud Gonne and Inghinidhe na hÉireann, which led to an explosion of attendance across Irish society at diverse artistic and cultural events staged in a variety of spaces and formats. As Paige Reynolds notes of the relationship between cultural nationalism, theatre and early twentieth-century Ireland:

> Audiences assembled across Ireland in wildly different venues for dramatic productions, as well as literary readings, sporting events, musical concerts, political oratory, and other performances staged by organizations like the nationalist Gaelic League.[2]

Joan Dean's comprehensive study of Irish historical pageants from the early twentieth century to the present day (a significant subgenre of the wider activity traced by Reynolds) details the performative and political stakes involved in moving outside the theatre and including larger collectives of performers and audience members. Dean mentions the early twentieth century activities of the Gaelic League or, more recently, Galway's Macnas, also discussed in this chapter. She explores the creation and consumption of historical pageants, which "mobilized a large number of amateurs to create impressive spectacles that could attract publicity, enlarge participation and channel enthusiasm".[3] Dean observes that

> Irish historical pageants appropriated spaces, typically public and occasionally site-specific ones. Against a natural landscape, in sporting arenas, or even in school halls, pageants could attract spectators who might never attend a play in a conventional theatre, let alone Ireland's national theatre, the Abbey.[4]

She elaborates: "Historical pageants create a dynamic between spectator and spectacle quite unlike the relationship between audience and drama in purpose-built theatres." Ultimately, Dean argues that "[h]istorical pageants did more than efface the distinction between spectator and spectacle: their reenactment of the past manipulated the audience's sense of time and place",[5] a key aim of many of the contemporary late twentieth and early twenty-first century Irish artists and companies profiled in this chapter.

This chapter draws together the interrelated contemporary genealogies of street theatre and site-specific theatre and performance. In doing so, it links the earlier twentieth-century history of Irish theatre and performance in spaces outside the theatre with an ongoing multiplication in performances that engage with both non-theatre spaces and use interdisciplinary arts techniques for their creation and dissemination. At the beginning of the twentieth century, and now at the start of the twenty-first, Irish artists, activists and activist-artists have repeatedly used a dialectic between audience, performance and space to call into question the meaning and efficacy of performance as a shared social and political event. This chapter traces that use in a contemporary context.

I work from a broad understanding of performance in order to trace the genealogy of interdisciplinary performance, which draws on visual art, dance, performance art, and music. I argue that such performances have informed the development of, and interplay between, a wide range of Irish theatre and performance practices in non-theatre spaces. Work classified broadly within Irish theatre (as determined by the funding streams accessed by artists and companies, as well as their own advertising and self-identification) has become increasingly interdisciplinary since the late-1990s and early 2000s.[6] This means that tracing the tangled (and often submerged) formal influences revealed by a dialogue between contemporary street arts and site-specific theatre has become an increasingly urgent practice within the broader field of Irish theatre and performance historiography.

Anxiety over the dilution of site-specific theatre as a term led the *Guardian*'s Andy Field to acidly term the "suffocating umbrella of 'site-specific'" as a "piece of shorthand that crudely shackles together artists whose works couldn't be more different". Field fears that "by labelling them thus, they become merely another new-fangled and eminently bracketable novelty act, cast in opposition (or as a diverting supplement) to 'straight' theatre".[7] This chapter's broad classification of the roots, influences and practices of Irish theatre and performance in non-theatre spaces does not intend to replicate this dilution, but rather map the complex and materially-situated genealogies activated by individual Irish artists' conscious moves outside of theatre buildings and purpose-built auditorium spaces—and away from other hallmarks of modern Irish theatrical form, like playwright-driven work. Importantly, I do not conflate "site-specific" and "immersive" theatre practices, although I deal finally with the work of ANU Productions, which is both site-specific and immersive.[8] A huge range of practice that is profiled (briefly) here uses the creative value of non-theatre spaces and landscapes to facilitate new kinds of engagement with audience members and formal theatrical techniques, as well as with local political, social and cultural economics. Looking at contemporary Irish work outside traditional theatre spaces provides a crucial network of references and unexpected influences. These aid in conceptualizing the necessary theoretical and interdisciplinary tools or "ways of seeing" that should characterize a robust Irish theatre and performance historiography of the present.[9]

Street Theatre, Community Arts and Other Related Genealogies

Contemporary street arts (which I define as encompassing street theatre, spectacle, circus and performance art staged on the street) emerged in Ireland in the late 1970s and early 1980s. It was developed largely in relation to community arts, although this area of practice also builds on a long history of Irish pageantry and political spectacle. In the 1970s and 1980s in Northern and Southern Ireland there was a proliferation of alternative and radical theatre and performance activity that produced work intended for non-theatre spaces and venues, whether the street or community centres.[10] The Arts Council in the Republic currently disburses funding for this genre of work under "street arts and spectacle" and highlights its ability to "engage with large audiences in unique and distinctive settings". Additionally, the Arts Council highlights "the opportunities provided through this artform to create experimental partnerships, especially with festivals, and to work with other artform professionals to create new and original work",[11] a cross-art-form pollination that this section of the chapter maps in part.

The growth of regional companies and festivals incorporating street arts as a central mode of community engagement include Macnas (Galway), Spraoi (Waterford) and Buí Bolg Productions (Wexford) in the 1980s and 1990s.[12] These festivals sought to animate not only these locations as centres of art-making within a national context, but also to empower local residents (particularly those identifying as non-artists) as co-creators of the work. As Paula Clancy traces, the regional creation of these companies and festivals and their commitment to access and inclusivity matched the changing priorities of the Arts Council from the 1970s onward. The Arts Council has "constantly renewed its commitment to developing and implementing policies concerned with making the arts accessible to all sections of Irish society, and in particular to those who have been 'culturally disenfranchised'".[13]

A definitive figure in this body of work whose legacy has only recently begun to be interrogated is Thom McGinty, or the "Diceman", who moved to Ireland from Scotland in 1976. His eclectic brand of solo street performance made central use of durational stillness and movement as well as drag. He arguably pioneered contemporary street arts in Ireland. McGinty was based primarily on Grafton Street in Dublin, as he got his start working for The Diceman games shop on this street, but he also performed his material internationally.[14] In addition, he worked with theatre companies—including the Grapevine Theatre Company in Dublin and Dandelion Theatre Company in Galway (which he founded)—famously played the executioner in the Gate Theatre's 1989 production of Oscar Wilde's *Salomé* and appeared in Frank McGuinness's first play, *The Glass God* (1982). McGinty's work was political in nature and he explicitly supported causes including "gay rights, the Birmingham Six and the plight of the Tibetans".[15] He is credited with being "one of the first public figures in Ireland to announce himself as HIV-positive".[16] His disclosure of his HIV status on the *Late Late Show* in November 1994 has been cited as a landmark event. After his death on 20 February 1995, his coffin was carried through the streets of Dublin and more than 2000 silent onlookers are reported to have assembled to mark the event.

McGinty's influence has been subtle but far-reaching. As Fintan Walsh argues, "The influence of his approach in terms of characters and costumes can be seen running throughout the Alternative Miss Ireland competition from the very first year".[17] Alternative Miss Ireland, a "queer beauty pageant" (running first in 1987 and then between 1996 and 2012) was a major venue for the development of the mainstream (as opposed to subcultural) persona of Panti: an Irish drag queen, performance artist, and social activist. More broadly, it was "instrumental in cultivating a queer performance scene that bridged both social and theatrical contexts".[18]

Traces of the Diceman's influence vis-à-vis Alternative Miss Ireland can be traced through to THISISPOPBABY, "a theatre and events production company" led by Jennifer Jennings and Phillip McMahon "that rips up the space between popular culture, counter culture, queer culture and high art".[19] Their work has ranged from bringing queer artists—including, most significantly, Panti—from the fringes of club spaces onto the mainstream space of the Abbey stage, to running a "performance, art and electropop space" at the Irish summer music and arts festival Electric Picnic, to mounting their performance art club WERK at the Abbey (2010, 2012) and in situ at the Melbourne Festival (2013). THISISPOPBABY's output focusses on the production of new dramatic works (such as Mark O'Halloran's play *Trade* staged in a Northside B&B for the 2011 Dublin Theatre Festival); the transfer of club and performance art practices of engagement into mainstream theatre spaces (such as through the mounting of WERK'S first six incarnations in the "belly of the Abbey Theatre");[20] and on the transmission of theatrical and performance art practices within typically non-theatrical festival events. Their work crystallizes the increased permeability of boundaries between theatre and non-theatre spaces in contemporary Irish theatre and performance culture. The genealogical line that can be traced from the Diceman to Alternative Miss Ireland to Panti to THISISPOPBABY also makes evident the explicitly politicized (and queer) nature of bringing performance into non-theatre spaces.

Moving west, Macnas was founded in 1986 by Ollie Jennings, Páraic Breathnach, Pete Sammon and Tom Conroy with their first work *The Big Game*, which was created for "the Connacht senior football final in 1987". As Christie Fox describes, "The performances are nonnaturalistic: Macnas freely incorporates puppets, multiple casting, music, shadow play, and mime to suggest a mood, emotion, or even the outline of a narrative, marking its work as distinctly postdramatic".[21] The company narrates its beginnings as heavily influenced by "a depleted economy with high levels of unemployment and little in the way of theatre outside Dublin".[22] It records support not only from the Arts Council but "community employment schemes administered by FÁS" as integral to its early and ongoing sustainability.[23] The working model of "professional artists training voluntary participants to help create large-scale community celebrations" was characteristic of the company's work from its beginnings.

The development of Macnas within a regional context testifies strongly to the relationship between theatre staged in non-theatre spaces and the commitment of its artists to using performance to activate audiences' relationship to the local, often in explicitly politicized ways. As Brian Singleton observes of site-specific performance in general:

> Moving away from a theatrical structure of active artists and passive spectators was a very political challenge to the hierarchies of consumption of culture, and imbued the spectators with a sense of agency that they might take from art and engage politically in their own worlds.[24]

The extremely politicized modern genealogical roots of, and contemporary modes of engagement with, non-theatre spaces within an Irish context bear out Singleton's claim. John Arden and Margaretta D'Arcy's 1975 production of their twenty-four hour play *The Non-Stop Connolly Show* at Liberty Hall is another important point of reference.[25] Yet, the imbrication of street arts with local and national tourist economies (such as Spraoi's staging of its annual festival over the August Bank Holiday weekend, a strategy estimated to bring "in excess of 80,000 people to the city"),[26] raises questions about the entanglement of aesthetic and economic agendas. Does widening access through participation in street arts projects designed to generate large crowds create what Michael McKinnie terms "monopolistic performances"? Such performances "produce their value by appropriating and trading self-consciously on the non-replicable qualities of places according to a logic that is substantially economic". McKinnie goes on to observe that performance sited in non-theatre and particularly urban spaces appear

> to achieve greater spatial efficacy than is often the case with performance events; it seemingly cultivates ideal economic subjects; and it apparently creates new productive spaces within the urban environment. These things are particularly important at a time when cities are competing aggressively with each other to attract transnational capital, and they illustrate distinctive, and rarely acknowledged, ways in which site-specific performance is tied up with contemporary urban development.[27]

Macnas, for example, records that the "combined effect of Druid, The Galway Arts Festival and Macnas identified Galway as the city of creativity, imagination and culture—a place where anything could happen".[28] This identity is marketable as well as creatively generative, as Galway's recent successful bid to become the 2020 European capital of culture made evident.

While working primarily with parade and street spectacle, Macnas has also made works for theatre spaces including *Táin* (1992), *Buile Shuibhne/Sweeny* (1994), *Balor* (1995), *Rhymes from the Ancient Mariner* (1996), *The Dead School* (1998), *Diamonds in the Soil* (1998) and *The Lost Days of Ollie Deasy* (2000). It has also experimented with the use of "unusual venues such as disused garages, deserted warehouses and old cinemas with shows like *Alice in Wonderland* (1989), *Treasure Ireland* (1990) and *Circus Story* (1991)", in a series of works they describe as "unashamedly aimed at a family audience and at making the theatrical experience exciting, inspiring and accessible".[29] As

Macnas themselves imply here, the populist appeal of their work has led to a paucity of critical recognition, at least in scholarship—with Christie Fox and Joan Dean's substantial treatment of the company in their monographs vital exceptions.[30]

Macnas represents a crucial catalyst in the evolution of theatre for non-theatre spaces in Ireland. Macnas's parades exist within a "*theatrical* genre [emphasis mine]" and "rely on communicative devices found in other theatrical forms".[31] As Fox argues, the company constantly interrogates "theatrical definitions, including 'actor' and 'spectator'", often coming up with "a surprising answer to the question of what conditions may best serve a theatrical event".[32] Macnas's early and central dependence on collaboration with non-professional participants anticipated the use of non-professional collaborators in much contemporary Irish post-dramatic and devised theatre work, including that of companies ANU Productions, Brokentalkers, junk ensemble and THEATREclub. This evolving body of practice, like Macnas, is also highly visual in its use of theatrical form. It also experiments with its use of sites—both occasionally and as a central element. Fox summarizes the ripple effects of Macnas (and other Irish companies working with parade and street spectacle) thus:

> the theatrical parade has influenced indoor Irish theatre, in that the genre experiments with theatrical elements in a low-risk situation. The parade can "audition" methods and techniques that are later brought indoors (or not) by Macnas or other theater companies.[33]

Fox places Macnas centrally within a paradigm shift in Irish theatre, beginning in the 1970s but solidifying in the 1990s, that she terms "the Irish theatre of movement".[34] This movement, according to Fox, also included companies such as Barabbas Blue Raincoat, Corn Exchange, CoisCéim and Fabulous Beast Dance Theatre, as well as the movement-influenced work of playwrights including Thomas Kilroy and Tom Mac Intyre. She details that:

> This new theater de-privileged text and emphasized physical performance. Much of it was in search of a distinctly Irish type of physicality or gesture, created from a synthesis of ancient Irish performance forms such as mumming and European performance forms such as the commedia dell'arte and French mime. Physical theatre practitioners sought to define a new style of movement and of theatre that reflected Irish society more fully.[35]

This fuller reflection, according to Fox, was attempted formally through a common adoption of a "collaborative method which combined with devised theatre and a decentering of the text, mirrored the disintegration of Ireland as a shared place or communally recognizable society".[36] The individuals, events and companies briefly profiled in this section—Thom McGinty, Alternative Miss Ireland, THISISPOPBABY and Macnas—epitomize the broad and multi-rooted influences and legacies of what Fox identifies as the Irish theatre of movement, as well as the crucial connection between this paradigm shift and an explosion in contemporary performance staged outside traditional theatre spaces. Those profiled in this section do not fit easily into modern genealogies of Irish theatre and performance if conventionally understood as the histories of playwrights, productions, actors and directors from the early twentieth century onwards. But the performance interventions outside of theatre spaces from the 1970s onwards detailed here have fundamentally expanded the visual grammar, spatial orientations and participatory possibilities of contemporary theatre and performance in Ireland today.[37]

Site-specific Theatre and Performance in Contemporary Ireland: An Overview

This section discusses practices in non-theatre spaces more firmly grounded in interrogating "site". Site-specific theatre and performance approaches have resulted in a wide range of theatrical practice in the Irish context, and often draw on similar aesthetics and collaborative approaches as those outlined for street arts.

My discussion of contemporary Irish site-specific practice focuses on two major areas in this genre of work: (1) the use of site-responsive staging to challenge audience's relationships to canonical texts and authors (Corcadorca's Shakespeare productions, Company SJ's body of work on Beckett) and (2) the production of new work in response to non-theatre spaces (The Performance Corporation, ANU Productions). These companies make visible a wide range of Irish approaches to site-specificity. Their approaches range from productions of canonical works in response to site, to new plays written by playwrights or devised by ensembles (such as most of Performance Corporation's dramatic output to date, authored by co-founder Tom Swift), to immersive and non-narrative work made for small-scale audiences that draws on interdisciplinary arts practices, particularly borrowing from visual art. ANU's non-narratively driven works in this latter genre, which centralize minoritarian voices and challenge narratives of the nation and commemoration, have rapidly attracted significant critical attention for being staged in anticipation of, and then frequently under commission for, Ireland's Decade of Centenaries.[38]

Inherent in this range of Irish practice, of which Corcadorca, Company SJ, Performance Corporation and ANU are only partly representative, are the tensions that have continued to characterize debates around the definition and politics of site-specific theatre and performance in the wider field of theatre and performance studies. Mike Pearson and Michael Shank's landmark 2001 definition of site-specific theatre outlines that, "Site-specific performances are conceived for, mounted within, and conditioned by the particulars of found spaces, existing social situations or locations, both used and disused". They continue, alleging that these performances "rely, for their conception and their interpretation, upon the complex co-existence of, superimposition and interpenetration of a number of narratives and architectures, historical and contemporary".[39] But, as Joanne Tompkins observes, "the genre of site-specific performance is increasingly being ascribed simply to a production that takes place outside a conventional theatre venue, rather than to performances that have been developed in the context of a particular location".[40] Writing about 2011, a year that saw landmark site-specific work—including the premiere of ANU Productions' *Laundry*, THISISPOPBABY'S production of Mark O'Halloran's *Trade*, and Corcadorca's production of Franz Xaver Kroetz's *Request Concert* (which played in different sites in Cork, Kilkenny, Galway and Dublin)—Kathryn Rebecca Von Winkle situated practices of Irish site-specific theatre as occurring on a spectrum between "'environmental' theatre which abolishes the distinction between the space of the performer and that of the audience, and 'promenade' theatre, in which the audience moves throughout the space, following the action or viewing it from different vantage points".[41] Van Winkle emphasizes the relationship between performance, audience and mobility as a key factor in the experience and aesthetic of various site-specific theatre approaches. I wish to turn next to the relationship between text, canonicity and site.

Corcadorca and Company SJ directly interrogate the relationship between site, key dramatic canons (William Shakespeare and Samuel Beckett) and the urban geographies of Cork and Dublin as a major aspect of their work. These companies' interrogations of key dramatic canons through engagement with site query the relationship between textuality and site in Ireland today. This is a particularly fertile engagement considering the over-determination of Ireland's landscape by its tourist industry, which in turn trades centrally on images of literary and dramatic masters such as Beckett and W.B. Yeats (another key artistic interlocutor for Sarah Jane Scaife, artistic director and founder of Company SJ). Shakespeare, of course, is not Irish (despite more than 4700 documented productions of Shakespeare between 1660 and 1904 and a more recent revitalization of Shakespeare in Ireland, including through the work of Second Age Theatre Company between 1989 and 2013 and Druid Theatre Company's 2015 *DruidShakespeare*).[42] But the importation of Shakespeare and the exportation of Company SJ's site-specific Beckett work to Japan, the UK and, most recently, the USA raises important questions about the relationship between Irishness, site and the Irish use of grammars of site-specific theatre and performance today.

Corcadorca was formed in 1991 and the company describes itself as pioneers of "the art of theatre performance in unusual venues",[43] and, indeed, it is the first-formed and longest-running Irish company devoted to this work. Their work is extremely wide-ranging, encompassing the premiere of original Irish dramatic works (most notably that of playwright Enda Walsh and playwright/novelist Pat McCabe), the staging of international classics including Eugene O'Neill's *The Hairy Ape* and Georg Büchner's *Woyzeck*, as well as a long-term engagement with new stagings of Shakespeare including to date: *Romeo and Juliet* (2012), *The Winter's Tale* (2011), *The Tempest* (2006), *The Merchant of Venice* (2005) and *A Midsummer Night's Dream* (2001).[44]

For the purposes of this section, I will focus on their production of *The Merchant of Venice*, which was presented during Cork's year as a European Capital of Culture in 2005, as part of a larger Corcadorca-led project entitled "Relocation", which involved partnership with three other European site-specific theatre companies. Corcadorca's *The Merchant of Venice* interrogated Corkonian and Irish identity in the context of Europe, during a period where Corcadorca as an Irish company described themselves as "suddenly exposed to different resident cultures and colours",[45] due to an increased inward-migration to Ireland that began in the mid-1990s.[46] Corcadorca's *The Merchant of Venice* featured professional and community actors and musicians, with Polish actors playing the Jewish roles and thus standing in for the increased number of racial and ethnic identities in contemporary Ireland.[47] Lisa Fitzpatrick writes that, "Although this production foregrounded the persecution of Shylock, it also offered an experience in which various races and nationalities gathered in the same space and engaged with a living performance as a unified community of spectators".[48] As Fitzpatrick describes:

> The scenes were performed in a number of spaces in Cork, the production travelling through the streets and over the bridges of the city to map the streets of Venice, blurring the relationship between the real and performed one, and creating, from the real city, an iconic map of the fictional one. Cork's history as a merchant trading port and its watery landscape (the rivers Lee and Blackwater wind through its centre) facilitated the relationship between real and the performed, and creating, from the real city, a map of the fictional one.[49]

Corcadorca's *The Merchant of Venice* animated many of the key debates around site-specific performance and its power to transform spaces through theatrical interventions. As Cathy Turner writes, "each occupation, or transversal, or transgression of space offers a reinterpretation of it, even a rewriting".[50]

In the case of Corcadorca's *The Merchant of Venice*, this reinterpretation took place on several levels. The production asserted Cork's placement within a wider network of European identity, merging the work of an English playwright with an explicit focus on Italian, Irish and Polish national identities. The play's original setting was built on by its Irish intercultural reimagining, achieved by casting and thematic emphasis in production. Furthermore, *The Merchant of Venice* was one of four site-specific productions by Corcadorca's "Relocations" project, which involved "four international theatre companies transforming Cork City over Summer 2005 with a series of premiere productions in unexpected places".[51] The other partner companies included Poland's Teatr Biuro Podrozy (*What Bloodied Man is That*), France's Compagnie Jo Bithume (*Victor Frankenstein*) and Scotland's Grid Iron Theatre (*The Devil's Larder*).

The aim of bringing these companies to Ireland was motivated by Corcadorca's own desire to explore "the strong tradition of off-site theatre (theatre which is not in a theatre venue) which exists across Europe" because, as they wrote at the time, "off-site theatre was relatively new to Ireland".[52] "Relocations" was therefore pedagogical for Corcadorca itself as well as for its audiences. All three invited companies responded specifically to Cork as a site and/or artistic community, and all three companies premiered new works for Relocations. Teatr Biuro's *What Bloodied Man is That* was inspired by Cork's Elizabeth Fort, Compagnie Jo Bithume responded to Cork's Grand Parade with *Victor Frankenstein* and Grid Iron developed *The Pig's Larder* with Scottish and Cork-based collaborators.[53] As part of the Cork Capital of Culture programme, access to all the performances was free and tickets were "distributed by a lottery run by a local newspaper".[54]

Company SJ's recent reimaginings of Samuel Beckett's work (both drama and prose) in urban spaces originally sited in Dublin (and then often transplanted worldwide) explicitly take up the theme of site-specific theatre and performance as a form that can expose the relationship between artistic innovation and economic inequalities, particularly within urban geographies. Company SJ was officially founded in 2009 by director Sarah Jane Scaife with producer Polly O'Loughlin and seeks to "fuse performance and research as an active artistic engagement between the two, presenting the work of Irish playwrights and in particular Beckett from and for a 21st century Ireland", resulting in a series of works known collectively as "Beckett in the City".[55] The seeds for this company were sown in the 1990s with Scaife's previous company "Throwin' Shapes" which "specialized in the work of W.B. Yeats and Samuel Beckett".[56]

Scaife's engagement with Beckett in particular raises key questions about the relationship between textual canonicity and the director/actor/designer as co-author of the performance text. This context arises specifically from the Beckett Estate's notoriously stringent control of production of the author's work that, as S.E. Gontarski argues, "remains committed to the decidedly untheatrical ideology of invariant texts in the face of overwhelming evidence to the contrary".[57] Company SJ's work on Beckett uses site as the mediating landscape through which to examine the limits of artistic license for artists investigating Beckett in productions, including *Rough for Theatre I* (2013), *Act Without Words II* (2013), *Fizzles* (2014) and *The Women Speak* (*Footfalls*, *Rockaby* and *Come and Go*) (2015). In emphasizing site, these productions also illuminate the material and political economies that make art-making possible and make Beckett's work continue to resonate for contemporary audiences. Scaife explicitly addresses themes including class and gender in the visual aesthetics and staging locations of the works.

In his September 2013 review of Company SJ's productions of *Rough for Theatre* and *Act Without Words II*—both staged in a car park hemmed in one side by the Ulster Bank headquarters—Fintan O'Toole speaks of the challenge of context in staging Beckett's work. Beckett was writing directly in response to "the second World War and the Holocaust, the threat of nuclear apocalypse, enslavement and oppression, real, observed human miseries". But O'Toole argues that their

> aesthetic depends on these contexts remaining almost entirely unstated. They work negatively: we apprehend them because they are almost (but crucially, not completely) absent [...] Put them in and the plays' immense tact is overwhelmed and reduced to crude pieties.[58]

For O'Toole, Scaife's production succeeds because "the plays are vividly and immediately rooted in a place, but not at all confined by it".[59] The themes and contexts most immediately interrogated by Company SJ's Beckettian engagements are class (particularly homelessness) and gender, in both historical and contemporary Irish contexts. *The Women Speak*'s production note explicitly asks:

> The 'unruly' female body has been hidden and controlled behind walls: walls of the laundries, the mother and baby homes, even the domestic home itself. How is it possible for Beckett's abstract, modernist works to speak to this trauma?[60]

The sites for Company SJ's Beckett in the City so far include: a Dublin city centre car park (*Rough for Theatre I, Act Without Words II*), 14 Henrietta Street—an upper-class residence turned legal offices turned tenement, which has now been designated for artists' use—(*Fizzles*) and the City Library at Parnell Square Cultural Quarter (*The Women Speak*). The Dublin city centre car park and 14 Henrietta Street index the limited mobility of financial resources between the upper and lower echelons of society. One upper-class gentleman's home at 14 Henrietta would eventually house hundreds of individuals living in tenement arrangements, before being designated as an artists' space.[61] This latest use activates the site as both a location that can house resistant representations, as in Company SJ's work, but also indirectly raises the question of whether designating spaces for artists in impoverished neighbourhoods leads to gentrification. The setting of the City Library makes use of a public space that houses a service meant to be accessible to all in order to serve as a "window on the world of knowledge and culture, a centre of learning and literature, a commune of research and reading and a hub of ideas and creativity".[62] Company SJ's intervention makes this space of the library a critical as well as a communal window, through its animation of unsettled and seething histories of women's marginalization and degradation.

These works push at the limits of Beckett (and the Beckett Estate's) directives on how these works can and should be staged. They invoke the figure of Beckett, who typifies the canonical power of theatre as an institution of prestige and legality, to question who actually has access to social and theatrical narratives in Ireland today. Similar to Corcadorca's *The Merchant of Venice*, Company SJ's Beckett in the City series transposes canonical works into the present through a confrontation not only with site, but also with the bodies that people their productions, in role as characters and in the audience. By breaking down barriers between audience and performance, and moving their theatrical events outside of theatre spaces, Corcadorca and Company SJ draw attention to theatre's power to interrogate the limits of social inclusion within the frame of live performance. Their work provocatively marries site with canonical texts in order to expose how text and site are mutually and continually transformed by the political economies of space, place and privilege.

Established in 2002 by Jo Mangan and Tom Swift, the Performance Corporation describes their mission as "to create daring theatrical adventures in surprising places".[63] While they have worked with a wide range of collaborators Mangan, in the role of director, and Swift, in the role of playwright, have largely shaped the direction of the company. While based in County Kildare, through their projects, the Performance Corporation has:

> jumped off the towering sand dunes on Ireland's Atlantic coast, tip-toed through the gothic halls of Edinburgh's Old Medical School, electrified a crumbling sports arena in Washington DC, driven at top-speed through Dublin's dangerous docklands, and danced a dance in the shadow of a tree in a Kenyan fishing village.[64]

Their work frequently arises through commission by different sites or organizations and/or is purpose-made for specific festivals or events. As a result, the creation of Performance Corporation's work attends to, as Mike Pearson outlines, "what is operational, what under control, what an intended feature of intelligibility, what to be actively disattended, and what clearly apparent in a situation of excess" in the sites they are interacting with, rather than their work (although playwright-driven) simply being transferred to different locations with site as backdrop.[65] In other words, unlike Corcadorca and Company SJ, who used the texts to lead the confrontations with the sites they chose to work in, it is the site that determines the direction and content of Performance Corporation's work. As Pearson continues, "Although the stage is a site of imagination and site always inescapably itself, site may be transformed by the disruptive presence of performance seeking a relationship other than that of a ready-made scene backdrop against which to place its figures".[66]

One of Performance Corporation's strongest partnerships has been with Washington, D.C.-based organization, Solas Nua, the "only organization in the United States devoted exclusively to contemporary Irish arts",[67] with whom they have produced *Kiss USA* and *GAA!* (2010) and *Swampoodle* at the Uline Arena (2011). *Swampoodle* and *GAA!* engaged the relationship between the Irish diaspora and contemporary Irish theatre-making, while *Kiss USA* and *GAA!* were occupied more broadly with theatre's ability to disrupt and transform public space in a mode similar to (but somewhat less politicized than) Augusto Boal's invisible theatre and a more recent fad for flash mobs. *Swampoodle* used a company of Washington, DC-based and Irish actors to resurrect the history of a former Irish ghetto neighbourhood of the same name that had been replaced by Union Station and the Uline Arena. It layered events from the history of the neighbourhood with subsequent occurrences like appearances by the Beatles and Malcolm X in the arena.[68] *Kiss USA* (a US transplant of a similar performance staged for the Dublin Theatre Festival in 2008) and *GAA!* were described by Performance Corporation and Solas Nua as "theatrical espressos" due to their staging as flash mobs in front of the White House and at lunchtime in Farragut Square, a business district in downtown

Washington, D.C.[69] Performance Corporation also dabbled in flash mobs with *Jig!* (2009), "the world's first 'Flash Céilidh'" staged "outside the Central Bank in Dublin" on St Patrick's Day, 17 March.[70] The "flash" nature of these projects communicate Performance Corporation's interest in site-specific performance as a disruptive, temporally limited and publicly accessible form, capable of bringing theatre into the everyday for gathered people not necessarily intending to become a theatre audience.

Apart from their engagement with site, Performance Corporation's visual and physical aesthetic shares much with the Irish theatre of movement, as identified by Christie Fox. They foreground a spectacular physical theatre approach under Mangan's direction in many of the works they have staged, with their actors' performances often verging on clown. This is notable in productions including *Lizzie Lavelle and the Vanishing of Emlyclough* (2007), *The Nose* (2008) and *Slattery's Sago Saga* (2010) among others. Over the years, they have also engaged in a sustained critique of the neoliberal and corporate business practices that shaped the rise and fall of the Celtic Tiger (a history that their company's work straddles) in works including *The Yokohama Delegation* (2005) and *PowerPoint* (2009), performed in a hotel in a meeting room used by businesses.

Founded in 2009, ANU Productions is fronted by co-artistic directors, Louise Lowe and Owen Boss, with Lowe identifying individually as a theatre director and Boss as a visual artist. ANU's works are created with a rotating ensemble of often recurring collaborators and have been mostly based in Dublin city centre, with the exception of *Beautiful Dreamers* (2014, Limerick, a co-production with Performance Corporation) and *Angel Meadow* and *On Corporation Street* (2014 and 2016, Manchester, a partnership with HOME). ANU divides their work into the following categories: theatre, gallery installation, and museum interpretation/commemoration.[71] Deep excavations of local sites and histories that blend the past and the present have consistently driven ANU's work since their inception from a multidisciplinary and site-specific artistic approach. They state that: "[b]ringing the voices of the past to the fore, we aim to blur the lines between interactive, participative, site specific and installation art, challenging accepted conventions of theatre and visual art".[72]

It was their Monto Cycle staged between 2010 and 2014 that arguably catapulted ANU to national and international recognition. This cycle included *World's End Lane* (2010), *Laundry* (2011), *Boys of Foley Street* (2012) and *Vardo* (2014). It explored the history of a quarter-mile area in north city centre Dublin known as the Monto, formerly the largest red light district in Europe. The Monto Cycle not only unfolded this history of prostitution in the area with *World's End Lane*, but also delved into the incarceration of women by religious orders in the neighbourhood's Magdalene Laundry until 1996 (*Laundry*). It examined the origins and persistence of the heroin epidemic in this community (*Boys of Foley Street*), and considered the relationship between the growth of new communities post-1990s and a once-again thriving sex trade practiced by both white Irish-born and migrant sex workers in the area (*Vardo*). Through animating minority histories (such as the various interconnected groups of those marginalized in the Monto), ANU comments on exclusions of individuals and communities from Irish national narratives and the unfinished projects for justice revealed by each separate work.

ANU typically caters to small audiences for each performance rotation of their work, but may stage the work 8–10 times in a single day during each run. The intake for the Monto Cycle, as well as the recent works *Thirteen* (2013) and *Sunder* (2016), was as few as three to four audience members per performance rotation, with many pivotal moments in the performance happening one-on-one between audience member and performer. Miriam Haughton argues that the immersive nature of their work, combined with the scale of encounter between audience member and performer(s), results in communion as a central experience and landmark of what ANU does, leading to a critical engagement not only with the performance but the wider world and Irish society in particular. She elaborates:

> This "communion" occurs as moments of sharp, tense and interior reflection for the individual, without the security of an audience or a theatre building. One is guided into alien places, where the histories of the sites explode with such powerful energy that one no longer seeks to distinguish between performers and community, but the ghosts and the living. One is shell-shocked by what they see, and shell-shocked that they had not noticed it before.[73]

Emerging scholarship on ANU's work, such as that of Haughton and Brian Singleton, has emphasized spectatorial reception and its relationship to political agency as possible, foreclosed within or catalyzed by performance as a live encounter. Singleton offers of *Laundry* that "at the moments of seeming acts of agency by spectators, such as helping a woman to escape, spectators' agency with the ghosts of a shameful past was seen to be too little too late".[74] Crucially, ANU's thematic focus on the ethics of memory as a lived experience of the present has collided with the most sustained period of official state-level reflection in modern and contemporary Irish history on Irish history itself: the Decade of Centenaries.

ANU's dramaturgical insistence on the seething presence of the past (shameful or otherwise, but usually so) in the now has led to them becoming Ireland's most commissioned theatre company during the Decade of Centenaries. This period of state commemoration encompasses:

> the Centenary of the Ulster Covenant, the foundation of the Irish Volunteers, the Home Rule and Land Bills, the 1913 Lockout, the 1916 Rising and many anniversaries relating to World War One, including the Gallipoli landings, the Somme offensive and the battle of Messines Ridge. Also of note will be the Literary Revival, the suffrage movement, the struggle for workers' rights and many other key events and themes of the period.[75]

They have worked on commemorative projects with a range of state and non-state actors including Dublin City Council, Dublin Bus, the Irish Congress of Trade Unions and Irish Heritage Trust, Fáilte Ireland, the National Museum of Ireland, the Department for Culture, Heritage and the Gaeltacht, and the National Archives of Ireland. The rise of ANU immediately prior to the Decade of Centenaries (which officially began in 2012) has given them an incredible range of opportunities, as well as illustrating once again the wide web of material entanglements that site-specific performance tactics engender.

While all theatre and performance practices are rooted in material economies and infrastructures, the partnerships between ANU and stakeholders from the non-arts sectors (particularly public agencies) provide a range of case studies that may help us probe deeper into the evolving relationship between theatre and performance staged in non-theatre spaces, and the role of both the state and private industries in defining the future limits and possibilities of this work in Ireland and beyond. ANU's division of its practice into theatre, gallery installation and museum interpretation/commemoration emerged around the time of the *Pals* (2015) premiere. It is the last category, of museum interpretation/commemoration, under which the outcomes of most of the above partnerships are listed, such as the Fáilte Ireland Commission *Glorious Madness* (2015), *Beyond Barricades: A Journey Through Time* (Dublin Bus, 2016) and state national commemorations including appearances at the 2013 commemoration of the 1913 Lockout and the 2014 commemorations of both the Irish Citizen Army and Cumann na Ban.

The implications of ANU's semantics regarding this last category lay outside this chapter's scope, but in a way, ANU's work brings this chapter full circle while pointing us towards possible directions for the future of Irish work staged in non-theatre spaces. Like many early twentieth century Irish nationalists and/or artists who used the power of spectacle to solicit public reflection on the necessity and pragmatics of Irish nationalist struggles (as outlined by Paige Reynolds and Joan Dean), ANU engages with spectacle as a vehicle for expressing current struggles, as well as operating explicitly in a commemorative mode as I have outlined. Their use of interdisciplinary arts techniques in their "theatre" practice—such as visual art, dance, performance art and film—extends early twentieth-century strategies. Their own work is linked explicitly to the Irish genealogy of street arts and community arts identified in the middle of this chapter, particularly through their consistent engagement with community partners and performers in making their work.[76]

ANU are unmistakable enmeshed at the centre of this Decade of Centenaries as a theatre company commissioned to commemorate. But they remain eager to stay critical in their politics, even of the links that make their work possible, and have perhaps given us a new model for an Irish "national" theatre. Notably, they are not tied to any one space, but rather to a dramaturgical commitment to illuminating interconnections between the past and present from the perspective of those frequently written out of history. They ultimately do so through using site as a space of encounter that enhances and intensifies these perspectives, even while being beholden as a company to what may be pointedly competing agendas between themselves and their sponsors. Across their programme of commemorative partnerships, they do not emphasize a glorious history of the Irish nationalist struggle and resultant state, but rather its collateral damage—such as women and children, a focus seen across two of their most recent works, *Glorious Madness* and *Sunder*, the former under commission from Fáilte Ireland, the second their own independent theatre work.

ANU's exposure of the instability of not only memory and site, but the collaborations necessary or useful in staging work in non-theatre spaces as part of programmes of public engagement (or commemoration), question the efficacy (and ethics) of theatre itself as a mode of encounter, inside or outside established theatre spaces. ANU insists that measured consideration of the entanglement of past and present is the dramaturgical formula for making work in the now, whether or not one is working in an explicitly commemorative mode. By working outside of designated theatre spaces at the intersection of past, present and future through a combination of artistic forms and modes of presentation that they nonetheless designate "theatre", ANU challenge Irish audiences to define and redefine theatre's use, ethics, and aesthetics for a new century. In doing so, they build on the work of their predecessors (only a very few of which have been profiled here) on pushing the possibilities of site as a scenographic and experiential tool of the Irish theatre. Further work is needed in this area, particularly to connect this most recent phase of work as represented by ANU and others back to even earlier modern and pre-modern genealogies of Irish performance. But as we move further into the twenty-first century, the use of non-purpose built spaces for theatre making in Ireland is unquestionably at the forefront of our continually evolving innovatory practices.

Notes

1. See Marjorie Howe, *Yeats's Nations: Gender, Class and Irishness* (Cambridge: Cambridge University Press, 1998), Paige Reynolds, *Modernism, Drama and the Audience for Irish Spectacle* (Cambridge: Cambridge University Press, 2007), and Joan Dean, *All Dressed Up: Modern Irish Historical Pageantry* (Syracuse: Syracuse University Press, 2014).
2. Paige Reynolds, *Modernism, Drama and the Audience for Irish Spectacle*, 21.
3. Joan Dean, *All Dressed Up*, 4.
4. Ibid., 4.
5. Ibid., 5–6.
6. For further discussion of the implications of "Irish theatre" as a term, see Charlotte McIvor and Siobhán O'Gorman, "Devising Ireland: Genealogies and Contestations", in *Devised Performance in Irish Theatre: Histories and Contemporary Practice*, (Dublin: Carysfort Press, 2015), 2–3.
7. Andy Field, "'Site-specific theatre'? Please be more specific", *The Guardian*, 6 February, 2008. Accessed 28 April 2016, http://www.theguardian.com/stage/theatreblog/2008/feb/06/sitespecifictheatrepleasebe.
8. See Ciara L. Murphy elsewhere in this volume for a fuller discussion of the key differences between immersive and site-specific performance.
9. I reference here the title of John Berger's seminal 1972 four-part BBC television series, *Ways of Seeing*, on visual culture and ideology.

10. See David Grant, "Chapter 10: Framing Reality: A Case Study in Prison Theatre in Northern Ireland", in *Performing Violence in Contemporary Ireland*, ed. Lisa Fitzpatrick (Dublin: Carysfort Press, 2009), Kindle edition.
11. Arts Council/ An Chomhairle Ealaíon, "Street Arts and Spectacle-Overview". Accessed 2 May 2016, http://www.artscouncil.ie/Arts-in-Ireland/Street-arts-and-spectacle/Overview/.
12. In operation since 1993, Spraoi is both an annual festival that "concentrates on showcasing top quality national and international street arts and world music" and a street arts company producing original work under commission from other national and international festival and events. Spraoi, "History & Timeline". Accessed 2 May 2016, http://www.spraoi.com/history-timeline/.
13. Paula Clancy, "Rhetoric and reality: A review of the position of community arts in state cultural policy in the Irish Republic", in *An Outburst of Frankness-Community Arts in Ireland- A Reader*, edited by Sandy Fitzgerald (Dublin: tasc at New Island, 2004), 87.
14. Lawrence William, "The Diceman", *History Ireland.* Accessed 1 May 2016, http://www.historyireland.com/20th-century-contemporary-history/the-diceman-by-lawrence-william-white/.
15. Brendan Kennelly, "the diceman". Accessed 27 April 2016, http://www.diceman.ie/about/diceman.html.
16. Lawrence William, "The Diceman".
17. Fintan Walsh, *Queer Performance and Contemporary Ireland: Dissent and Disorientation*, (Basingstoke, Hampshire: Palgrave Macmillan, 2016), 153.
18. Ibid., 25.
19. THISISPOPBABY, "About". Accessed 1 May 2016, http://www.thisispopbaby.com/about.
20. THISISPOPBABY, "WERK//Issue 6//The Ecstasy of Tomorrow". Accessed 1 May 2016, http://www.thisispópbaby.com/past/werk-ecstasy.
21. Christie Fox, *Breaking Forms: The Shift to Performance in Late-Twentieth Century Irish Drama* (Newcastle: Cambridge Scholars Publishing, 2008), 62.
22. Macnas, "Introduction", *Joyful Abandonment*, 11.
23. Macnas, "Introduction", *Joyful Abandonment*, 11. FÁS is the Irish National Training and Employment Agency.
24. Brian Singleton, "ANU Productions and Site-Specific Performance: The Politics of Space and Place", in *"That Was Us": Contemporary Irish Theatre and Performance*, edited by Fintan Walsh (London: Oberon Books, 2015), 22.
25. See Michael Jaros, "Spectres of Connolly: *The Non-Stop Connolly Show* Reconsidered", in *Devised Performance in Irish Theatre: Histories and Contemporary Practice*, eds. Siobhán O'Gorman and Charlotte McIvor (Dublin: Carysfort Press, 2015), 33–46.
26. Spraoi, "History & Timeline".
27. Michael McKinnie, "Rethinking Site-Specificity: Monopoly, Urban Space, and the Cultural Economics of Site-Specific Performance", in *Performing Site-Specific Theatre: Politics, Place, Practice*, edited by Anna Birch and Joanne Tompkins (Houndsmill, Basingstoke, Hampshire: Palgrave Macmillan, 2012), 24.
28. Macnas, "Introduction", *Macnas: Joyful Abandonment*, 11.
29. Macnas, "History". Accessed 3 May, 2016, http://macnas.com/about/history/.

30. See Fox, *Breaking Forms*, 113–139, and Dean, *All Dressed Up*, 223–256.
31. Fox, *Breaking Forms*, 67.
32. Ibid., 67.
33. Fox, *Breaking Forms*, 67.
34. Ibid., 3.
35. Ibid., 5.
36. Ibid., 7.
37. They also draw on earlier Gaelic pre-modern traditions of performance as detailed by Lionel Pilkington in *Theatre & Ireland*, drawing on the work of Alan J. Fletcher, 26–27, but a full discussion of this area lies outside the scope of this chapter.
38. While this chapter will deal in passing with the immersive aspects of site-specific theatre and performance in an Irish context, a full consideration lies outside the scope of this present chapter. For more explicit discussion in an Irish context, see Ciara L. Murphy, "Audience: Immersive and Participatory" in this volume and Miriam Haughton, "From Laundries to Labour Camps: Staging Ireland's "Rule of Silence" in ANU Productions' *Laundry*", *Modern Drama* 57.1 (Spring 2014): 65–93.
39. Mike Pearson and Michael Shanks, *Theatre/Archaeology* (London and New York: Routledge, 2001), 243.
40. Joanne Tompkins, "The 'Place' and Practice of Site-Specific Theatre and Performance", in *Performing Site-Specific Theatre: Politics, Place, Practice*, edited by Anna Birch and Joanne Tompkins (Houndsmill, Basingstoke, Hampshire: Palgrave Macmillan, 2012), 3.
41. Kathryn Rebecca Von Winkle, "You Had To Be There: Irish Theatre in 2011", *New Hibernia Review/Iris Éireannach Nua* 16.4 (Fómhar/Autumn 2014): 133–134.
42. Patrick Lonergan, editor, "Shakespeare's Plays in Dublin, 1660-1904", National University of Ireland, Galway. Accessed 31 May 2016, http://www.nuigalway.ie/drama/shakespeare/.
43. Corcadorca, "About Corcadorca". Accessed 15 May 2016, http://www.corcadorca.com/website/about-corcadorca.
44. Corcadorca, "Previous Productions". Accessed 15 May 2016, http://www.corcadorca.com/website/previous-productions-2.
45. Corcadorca, "*The Merchant of Venice*". Accessed 16 May 2016, http://www.corcadorca.com/relocationshow3.html.
46. See Charlotte McIvor, *Migration and Performance in Contemporary Ireland: Towards a New Interculturalism* (Basingstoke: Palgrave Macmillan, 2016).
47. Polish residents were verified as the largest Irish minority ethnic group by the 2011 Census, with the "largest increase between 2006 and 2011" as numbers almost doubled from "63,276 persons in 2006 to 122,585 in 2011". See Central Statistics Office, *Profile 6: Migration and Diversity* (Dublin: Central Statistics Office, 2012), 7.
48. Lisa Fitzpatrick, "Staging *The Merchant of Venice* in Cork: The Concretization of a Shakespearean Play for a New Society", *Modern Drama* 50.2 (Summer 2007): 169.
49. Ibid., 171.
50. Cathy Turner, "Palimpsest or Potential Space? Finding a Vocabulary for Site-Specific Performance", *New Theatre Quarterly* 20.4 (2004): 373.

51. Corcadorca's Relocation, "Relocation Home". Accessed 17 May 2016, http://www.corcadorca.com/relocation.html.
52. Ibid.
53. Ibid.
54. Fitzpatrick, "Staging *The Merchant of Venice in Cork*", 171.
55. Company SJ, "About Company SJ". Accessed 15 May 2016, http://company-sj.com/about.html.
56. Irish Theatre Institute, "Companies: Company SJ". Accessed 16 May 2016, http://www.irishtheatre.ie/company-page.aspx?companyid=553.
57. S.E. Gontarski, "Reinventing Beckett", *Modern Drama* 49.4 (Winter 2006): 430.
58. Fintan O'Toole, "Two Samuel Beckett plays in a car park? Unmissable", *The Irish Times*, 21 September 2013. Accessed 17 May 2013, http://www.irishtimes.com/culture/culture-shock-two-samuel-beckett-plays-in-a-car-park-unmissable-1.1533672.
59. O'Toole, "Two Samuel Beckett plays in a car park?"
60. Company SJ, "Productions: *The Women Speak*". Accessed 17 May 2016, http://company-sj.com/women_speak.html.
61. For more information, see Previously Grant-Aided Projects, "14 Henrietta Street", The Heritage Council. Accessed 27 May 2016, http://www.heritagecouncil.ie/architecture/previously-grant-aided-projects/14-henrietta-street/.
62. City Library and Services, "A New City Library for Dublin at Parnell Square". Accessed 21 March 2017, http://parnellsquare.ie/about-the-project/city-library-services/.
63. The Performance Corporation, "About Us". Accessed 22 May 2016, http://www.theperformancecorporation.com/about/.
64. The Performance Corporation, "About Us".
65. Mike Pearson, *Site-Specific Performance* (Houndsmill, Basingstoke, Hampshire: Palgrave Macmillan, 2010), 2.
66. Ibid., 2.
67. Solas Nua, "Home". Accessed 22 May 2016, http://www.solasnua.org/.
68. Nelson Pressley, "Theatre Review: 'Swampoodle' at Uline Arena", *The Washington Post*, 25 May 2011. Accessed 22 May 2016, https://www.washingtonpost.com/lifestyle/style/theater-review-swampoodle-at-uline-arena/2011/05/25/AGQRBXBH_story.html.
69. The Performance Corporation, "*GAA!*" Accessed 22 May 2016, http://www.theperformancecorporation.com/portfolio-item/gaa/.
70. The Performance Corporation, "*Jig*!" Accessed 22 May 2016, http://www.theperformancecorporation.com/portfolio-item/jig/.
71. ANU Productions, "About ANU". Accessed 31 May 2016, http://anuproductions.ie/about-anu/.
72. Ibid.
73. Miriam Haughton, "Mirror, Mirror on the Wall: Unwanted Reflections in ANU Productions' *The Boys of Foley Street* (2012)", in *Masculinity and Irish Popular Culture: Tiger's Tales*, eds. Conn Holohan and Tony Tracy (Houndsmill, Basingstoke, Hampshire: Palgrave Macmillan, 2014), 154.
74. Singleton, "ANU Productions and Site-Specific Performance", 31.

75. Decade of Centenaries, "About". Accessed 21 March 2017, http://www.decadeofcentenaries.com/about/.
76. See Charlotte McIvor, "A Portrait of the Citizen as Artist".

Bibliography

Central Statistics Office. *Profile 6: Migration and Diversity*. Dublin: Central Statistics Office, 2012.

Clancy, Paula. "Rhetoric and reality: A review of the position of community arts in state cultural policy in the Irish Republic." In *An Outburst of Frankness – Community Arts in Ireland – A Reader*, edited by Sandy Fitzgerald, 83–114. Dublin: TASC at New Island, 2004.

Dean, Joan. *All Dressed Up: Modern Irish Historical Pageantry*. Syracuse: Syracuse University Press, 2014.

Field, Andy. "Site-specific theatre? Please be more specific." *The Guardian*. February 6, 2008. Accessed April 28, 2016. http://www.theguardian.com/stage/theatreblog/2008/feb/06/sitespecifictheatrepleasebe.

Fitzpatrick, Lisa. "Staging *The Merchant of Venice* in Cork: The Concretization of a Shakespearean Play for a New Society." *Modern Drama* 50.2 (Summer 2007): 168–183.

Fox, Christie. *Breaking Forms: The Shift to Performance in Late Twentieth-Century Irish Drama*. Newcastle: Cambridge Scholars Publishing, 2008.

Gontarski, S.E. "Reinventing Beckett." *Modern Drama* 49.4 (Winter 2006): 428–451.

Haughton, Miriam. "Mirror, Mirror on the Wall: Unwanted Reflections in ANU Productions' *The Boys of Foley Street* (2012)." In *Masculinity and Irish Popular Culture: Tiger's Tales*, eds. Conn Holohan and Tony Tracy, 142–158. Houndsmill, Basingstoke, Hampshire: Palgrave Macmillan, 2014.

———. "From Laundries to Labour Camps: Staging Ireland's 'Rule of Silence' in ANU Productions' *Laundry*." *Modern Drama* 57.1 (Spring 2014): 65–93.

Howe, Marjorie. *Yeats's Nations: Gender, Class, and Irishness*. Cambridge: Cambridge University Press, 2008

Macnas. *Joyful Abandonment*. Dublin: Liffey Press, 2007.

McIvor, Charlotte and O'Gorman, Siobhán. Devising Ireland: Genealogies and Contestations In *Devised Performance in Irish Theatre: Histories and Contemporary Practice*, eds. Charlotte McIvor and Siobhán O'Gorman, 1–32. Dublin: Carysfort Press, 2015.

McIvor, Charlotte. *Migration and Performance in Contemporary Ireland: Towards A New Interculturalism*. London: Palgrave Macmillan, 2016.

———. A Portrait of the Citizen as Artist: Community Arts, Devising and Contemporary Irish Theatre Practice In *Devised Performance in Irish Theatre: Histories and Contemporary Practice*, edited by Siobhán O'Gorman and Charlotte McIvor, 47–66. Dublin: Carysfort Press, 2015.

———. "Witnessing the (Broken) Nation: Theatre of the Real and Social Fragmentation in Brokentalkers' *Silver Stars, The Blue Boy* and *Have I No Mouth*," in *"That Was Us": Contemporary Irish Theatre and Performance*, edited by Fintan Walsh, 37–56. London: Oberon Books, 2013.

McKinnie, Michael. "Rethinking Site-Specificity: Monopoly, Urban Space, and the Cultural Economics of Site-Specific Performance." In *Performing Site-Specific*

Theatre: Politics, Place, Practice, edited by Anna Birch and Joanne Tompkins, 21–36. Houndsmill, Basingstoke, Hampshire: Palgrave Macmillan, 2012.

Pearson, Mike. *Site-Specific Performance.* Houndsmill, Basingstoke, Hampshire: Palgrave Macmillan, 2010.

Pearson, Mike and Shanks, Michael. *Theatre/Archaeology*. London and New York: Routledge, 2001.

Pilkington, Lionel. *Theatre & Ireland.* Houndsmill, Basingstoke, Hampshire: Palgrave Macmillan, 2010.

Reynolds, Paige. *Modernism, Drama and the Audience for Irish Spectacle.* Cambridge: Cambridge University Press, 2007.

Singleton, Brian. "ANU Productions and Site-Specific Performance: The Politics of Space and Place." In *"That Was Us": Contemporary Irish Theatre and Performance*, edited by Fintan Walsh, 21–36. London: Oberon Books, 2015.

Tompkins, Joanne. "The 'Place' and Practice of Site-Specific Theatre and Performance," in *Performing Site-Specific Theatre: Politics, Place, Practice*, edited by Anna Birch and Joanne Tompkins, 1–20. Houndsmill, Basingstoke, Hampshire: Palgrave Macmillan, 2012.

Turner, Cathy. "Palimpsest or Potential Space? Finding a Vocabulary for Site-Specific Performance." *New Theatre Quarterly* 20.4 (2004): 373–390.

Von Winkle, Kathryn Rebecca. "You Had To Be There: Irish Theatre in 2011." *New Hibernia Review/Iris Éireannach Nua* 16.4 (Fómhar/Autumn 2014): 133–146.

Walsh, Fintan. *Queer Performance and Contemporary Ireland: Dissent and Disorientation.* Basingstoke, Hampshire: Palgrave Macmillan, 2016.

William, Lawrence. "The Diceman." *History Ireland.* Accessed May 1, 2016. http://www.historyireland.com/20th-century-contemporary-history/the-diceman-by-lawrence-william-white/.

Irish Plays in Other Places: Royal Court, RSC, Washington and Berlin

Kevin Wallace

Ireland has gone through at least two seismic shifts since the beginning of the twenty-first century. The economic boom of the late 1990s and early 2000s brought with it great prosperity, social mobility and the nagging question "What does it mean to be Irish?" The missing element in that question being "now that we are rich". Ireland became known as a globalized, largely secular society—no longer exclusively Catholic, rural or anti-British. In addition, the facts that there was relative peace in Northern Ireland and that net emigration had been replaced by immigration, this meant that the calcified certainties of Irish identity, and the image of Ireland and the Irish, were beginning to give way. Within a decade, however, that question about identity was no longer being asked. Ireland was poor again, the economy had collapsed, there was once more massive emigration and unemployment. And yet, the cultural iconoclasm of the Celtic Tiger and its attendant social change had not been reversed. In the theatre, this can be seen in the evolution of the aesthetics in work from the early 2000s to the present.

This chapter will examine how the first productions of Irish theatre abroad altered or reinforced notions of the "Irish play". It will focus specifically on the work of Marina Carr, Martin McDonagh and Enda Walsh during the period 2000–2015, in productions with the Royal Shakespeare Company (RSC), the Royal Court theatre, some Broadway productions, and Walsh's work in Germany—at the Munich Kammerspiele and the *Theater Oberhausen* in Berlin. The argument will focus on the later work of Carr, McDonagh and Walsh, paying special attention to Carr's *On Raftery's Hill* (2001), *Woman and Scarecrow*

K. Wallace (✉)
Dún Laoghaire Institute of Art, Design and Technology, Dublin, Ireland

E. Jordan, E. Weitz (eds.), *The Palgrave Handbook of Contemporary Irish Theatre and Performance*,
https://doi.org/10.1057/978-1-137-58588-2_34

(2006) and *The Cordelia Dream* (2008); McDonagh's *The Lieutenant of Inishmore* (2001) and *The Pillowman* (2003); and Enda Walsh's *The New Electric Ballroom* (2008) and *Penelope* (2010). The chapter will first examine what is an "Irish play", then how British and American productions have related to that concept and finally how the plays discussed herein have dealt with these discourses. In particular, this chapter will examine what happens when this type of Irish play is premiered abroad.

In Irish drama, the question of the relationship between the nation and the stage has been explored extensively. Nicholas Grene's work clearly identifies the connection between the theatre and the "Irish Question".[1] He argues that

> Irish drama since the time of the early Abbey has remained self-consciously aware of its relation to the life of the nation and the state [... and as] long as there has been a distinct Irish drama it has been so closely bound up with national politics that the one has often been considered more or less a reflection of the other.[2]

For Grene, Irish drama from the late nineteenth through the late twentieth century sets out to "reformulate the Irish Question".[3] Victor Merriman also argues that Irish theatre is unique due to its "social significance [resting] on the pledge that acts in the theatre [are] ... part of a broader cultural conversation about who we are, how we are in the world and who we would like to be".[4] Parsing these points, the argument is made that the mission of Irish drama is to ask who the Irish are and what Ireland is. From this point of view, Irish dramas continue the process of internal nation building both through national conversations and by working out Ireland's relationship with the world and, in Grene's view, especially Britain. Indeed, Grene's point is not only a postcolonial one, Irish drama's relationship with Britain remains complex in the late twentieth and early twenty-first century. England was often the location of the premiere and sometimes the only staging of Irish plays, and the RSC and Royal Court were producers and co-producers of a significant number of theatre works. The postcolonial matrix of symbols, biases and ideas about Ireland and Britain,[5] thus remains a frame of reference for some for these plays. What remains interesting, nevertheless, is how that came to be and how the plays themselves enable or circumvent it.

Moving beyond these islands, the chapter will use the work of Claudia Harris to examine the complex reactions to Carr's American production of *On Raftery's Hill* in 2001 and how its unintended signification of naturalism overdetermined the play. Finally, and in stark contrast, the chapter will examine the German productions of Walsh's *Penelope* and *The New Electric Ballroom*. Clare Wallace rightly notes that European productions of Carr's work have "stressed" the Irishness in the plays to authenticate the productions.[6] However, it will be argued that by the time of Walsh's German performances these European (both in the UK and in German) productions helped facilitate a reconsideration of the dominant theatrical forms and/or aesthetics in Irish plays. It will be argued that the influences of these foreign productions have enabled Irish playwrights' work to grow and develop in relation to the category of "Irish drama" (with its attendant national issues elements) and beyond it.

The Royal Court Theatre has a long history with Irish playwriting. It produced versions of Yeats and Beckett and O'Casey's work in the 1950s. By the 1990s it was producing and later premiering the work of Irish playwrights including Billy Roche, Tom Murphy, Marina Carr, Enda Walsh, Conor McPherson and Stella Feehily. Part of the raison d'être of the Royal Court is as a writers' theatre,[7] it has been the home to controversy and experiment from the 1950s to present. Its productions of McDonagh and Carr's earlier work (McDonagh's *The Beauty Queen of Leenane*, *A Skull in Connemara* and *The Lonesome West* and Carr's *Portia Coughlan*, *On Raftery's Hill*, and *Woman and Scarecrow*), and also McPherson's *Dublin Carol* (1999), *The Weir* (1997) and *Shining City* (2004), clearly fulfil this remit. Strikingly, it productions also chart a shift in the approach and aesthetic of the playwrights to their work from 2000 to the present.[8] Carr and McDonagh's earlier plays reflected on the aesthetic of the Abbey and the archetypal image of the Irish play. The reactions to this will be discussed below, but one of the paradoxes of that initial aesthetic was that it was an uncomfortable reflection of colonial tropes.

Marina Carr's *On Raftery's Hill*, a Druid-Royal Court co-production, laden with tropes of Irishness (the farmhouse and the Midland dialect Carr used in her plays from 1995–2003) had its American premiere in Washington, D.C. at the John F. Kennedy Center for Performing Arts, as part of the "Island: Arts from Ireland" festival. The reaction to it, according to Carr herself, led to censure from the Irish establishment. In an RTÉ *Arts Lives* documentary she told Fintan O'Toole that "I got wrapped over the knuckles [... for] disgracing everyone, letting the side down [...] here we are in Washington, aren't we a great little nation and here's this black ugly in the middle of it".[9] In that documentary, O'Toole argues that this may have been due to the audience's shock that the same nation that produced Riverdance produced *On Raftery's Hill*. This play is a tortured, intimate exploration of the complex and contradictory emotional turmoil of victims of familial incest in rural Ireland. Its structure is not straight-forward or conventional. Comprising two acts, the play's plot is foreclosed, and its narrative is shut down in the second act, or rather at the end of the first act. There is no resolution to the moral dilemma posed by the play. The protagonist Sorrel Raftery is effectively bought-off at the end by her father/grandfather/abuser, Red Raftery. Rejecting her fiancé, Sorrel entrenches herself further within the familial, or tribal, identity. There is no punishment for Red, the sadistic rapist, in fact the denouement of the play (if it can truly be said to have one) is Sorrel's rejection of escape.

The image of the Irish in both cases (and as we will see in McDonagh's early work) is at once too close and too far from the archetype of Irish theatre. It could be argued that nearly nine decades after the Abbey first opened, the shadow of kitchen sink drama and Syngian comedy still colours reactions to Irish plays. Indeed, the experience of watching *On Raftery's Hill* is thoroughly unsatisfying due to it being an uncomfortably heightened depiction of abuse without a resolution, without justice for Sorrel and without punishment for Red. In the early 2000s Ireland was coming to terms with clerical sexual abuse, but the issue of incestuous and domestic familial abuse was still only beginning to be worked-through. Up until the time of the Thirty-First Amendment of the Irish Constitution, the children's rights referendum in 2012, the family took precedence over the state and children were effectively the property of the family unit. At its time of premier, *On Raftery's Hill* was breaking a significant taboo. Moreover, it was doing so in the middle of Irish America.

Harris's dissection of the critical reaction to the Washington opening of the play throws up some interesting paradoxes. She notes that Lloyd Rose, who reviewed the play for the *Washington Post*, misunderstood it. She contends "that Rose could find any humanness in the characters implies a misunderstanding … instead of human qualities the characters display animal characteristics; in fact animalism saturates the play's metaphors, pervasively undercutting every character and action". Harris underlines how the context of the performance encouraged audiences to see "performances of Irish cultural truths". She refers too to Enrica Cerquoni's review of the Irish Repertory of Chicago's production of *By the Bog of Cats*… in 2001, whose audience were "'admittedly baffled' […] and anxious to ask questions after the show."[10]

The later Royal Court production of Carr's *Woman and Scarecrow* had a Beckettian tone and broke away from her Midland plays and their aesthetic (which was used in *On Raftery's Hill*), in so doing it courted a completely different set of reactions and receptions. Its aesthetic and narrative effectively distanced it from the above preconceptions about "Irish Drama". Similarly, McDonagh, McPherson and Walsh's work all underwent a shift from the iconic or stereotypical ideas of Irish plays towards something else. McPherson's *Shining City* moved his oeuvre from monologues to dramatic action. While the play still relies heavily on storytelling—like *The Weir*—*Shining City* began to take McPherson in a different direction.

McDonagh's Aran Islands "Trilogy" (so-called despite only two of the three plays being produced) was greeted with mixed reactions. His earlier three plays, *The Beauty Queen of Leenane* (1996), *A Skull in Connemara* (1997) and *The Lonesome West* (1997)—the Leenane Trilogy—had been controversial but had also received significant critical plaudits. Key to the controversy is the dissonance the plays produce: at once comedy, parody and re-presentation of stereotyped Irish drama. The plays create a double image of Irishness superimposed with a clichéd and stereotyped image of western Ireland. Indeed, Eamonn Jordan has noted, in *Dissident Dramaturgies*, how critical responses to McDonagh are stultified by their concerns with some kind of realism.[11] However, he also notes that McDonagh, in the five plays of the Leenane and Aran sequences, "simplifies character motivation and de-privileges a depth model".[12] Jordan astutely notes that some of the critical reactions to this work "because of the apparent roughness, inappropriateness, tactlessness and incompleteness of the plays … [looses] no opportunity to confront them, but it is a bit like taking Pablo Picasso's later works to task because they are not especially accurate".[13]

> Yet he notes too, echoing Declan Kiberd, that international audiences "may hanker after that 'frisson', either unaware or uninterested in the fact that in McDonagh's work the west is a fiction, bled of its emblematic resonances."[14]

This resonance and the attendant symbolism of rural Ireland and its pastoral connotations is an issue that Jordan highlights as being played with by multiple playwrights,[15] however it is McDonagh who is perhaps the most irreverent of them all. This irreverence however has been noted by Merriman as creating "gross caricatures with no purchase on the new consumer-Irish consensus [and] lies in their appearance as ludicrous Manichean opposites—the colonized simian reborn."[16] While Jordan is correct to point out the limitations of this kind of critique, there is something to Merriman's concern regarding colonial tropes. McDonagh and Carr's work was being premiered abroad. Specifically, *The Lieutenant of Inishmore* and *On Raftery's Hill* were premiering in post-colonial spaces. McDonagh's in England with the RSC and Carr's in Washington. *On Raftery's Hill*'s first run was a co-production between the Royal Court and the Druid theatre company. While its first performances were in Galway's Town Hall Theatre, on 9 May it moved to an infamous show-case at the "Island: Arts from Ireland" festival, followed by a run in Dublin's Gate theatre and at the Royal Court Theatre, London in July.

This "Island: Arts from Ireland" festival was the idea of former American ambassador to Ireland, Jean Kennedy Smith and was opened on 14 May 2000 by President Mary McAleese.[17] This was an official re-presentation of Irish arts to Irish-America, and the grotesque images of incest and abuse in the performance were shocking to the audience and the hosts. Claudia Harris points out the contextual frames for the play were the Clinton administration, the peace process in Northern Ireland and the marketing of Ireland and Irish culture in the United States.[18] Yet, after noting this, she sets it aside and makes a crucial point: Garry Hynes in the Druid co-production's programme notes states that "[Carr] is creating an extraordinary imaginative world in her plays—she's not bound by naturalism or spurious authenticity. She has a poetic world of her own".[19] Harris claims that the staging of the production used a "realistic farmhouse boxset", inscribing naturalism on Tony Walton's design. She notes that the critical reception of the work tended to miss the "opportunity to explain the classical underpinnings of Carr's work", which was "obscured by the miasmal mists" of romanticized stereotypes of Ireland and Irishness.[20] This she relates to the marketability of Irishness and stereotypes of the "Irish play" to American audiences.

Unlike McDonagh's Leenane and Aran sequences, this troping of Irishness is not in *On Raftery's Hill* itself, it is an effect of the discursive landscape into which it was placed. However, those discourses were activating what

Harris noted about the play's apparent naturalism, a point echoed in Jordan's above consideration of McDonagh's work.[21] The case of *The Lieutenant of Inishmore* is compounded by the Republican elements in the text. Jordan argues that in this play McDonagh has removed all maturity and depth from the actions of terrorists, in contrast to some other playwrights who had depicted the Irish Republican movement as having "resonance and depth to [its] motivation".[22]

Plays in the vein of the *The Lieutenant of Inishmore* and *On Raftery's Hill* are available for the kind of criticism obsessed with politics, mimesis and authenticity that Jordan notes above, due to their production of dissonance in their parodic re-presentation of Ireland, especially in productions abroad. As Harris notes, marketing the dramas within the sphere of Ireland and Irishness delimits what is received by the audience. She states the "Raftery's show no similarity to the picture-perfect Irish farm family Americans romanticize".

> Harris asks the questions: But what is the possible danger in staging these violent and taboo interactions? Does explicit abuse on stage shock enough to make audiences question the wide-spread practice, or do Carr's well-written, disturbingly funny plays aptly referred to by Grene as 'black-pastorals' … simply make abuse seem a natural even tolerable part of Irish life?[23] To answer this, Harris notes Jill Dolan's argument that theatre that is "'still caught in representational systems' to which they refer offer little possibility for radical change".[24]

The more that the plays appear to reflect some kind of relationship with the style of the Abbey's kitchen-sink dramas, or with Syngian comedy, the more over-determined they are by the power of these ideas. As a result, they appeal to Grene's description of Ireland as "a marketable phenomenon, a space, a place which *needed* to be represented and represented truly".[25] This urge towards, or appeal to, the authentic is precipitated by the shadow of the semiotics of the Irish pastoral. In both cases this sign system was made up of confined spaces, accents and archetypal characters. The staging of these dramas abroad redoubles this effect, because the images of Irishness became detached from mimesis and instead become a series of authorizing truisms that contained and delimited representation, rather than facilitating expression.

By 2006, however, something equally fascinating was happening in productions that did not facilitate this kind of easy over-determination of a play and its association with Ireland. *Woman and Scarecrow* and *The Cordelia Dream* were a return for Carr to a more overtly Beckettian aesthetic, not seen since her first play *Ulaloo* in 1989. While there are thematic parallels and resemblances to the Midland plays, *Woman and Scarecrow* notably drops the use of the Midland dialect used in Carr's work from *The Mai* (1995) to *Ariel* (2002) and returns to an absurdist naming of the character, in this case: Woman, Scarecrow and Him. The play premiered at the Royal Court in July 2006, followed over a year later by an October 2007 Abbey Theatre production in Ireland during the Dublin Theatre Festival. *Woman and Scarecrow*, like Carr's other absurdist plays (and to an extent like her Midland plays), is about failure. In this case, the title character Woman has failed herself. Scarecrow represents something akin to her Freudian death drive (both a creative force and the harbinger of her demise) or a spirit guide of some sort. Woman's husband, Him, has also failed her but there was another man, other than Him, whom Scarecrow calls "[t]he him that should've been *the him*".[26] Scarecrow tells Woman, whom she describes as "surface bitch", that the other man loved her, and more than that, he loved Scarecrow—Woman's inner being—but that Woman had failed her (and herself) in not pursuing that relationship, and not pursuing happiness.[27] This play, like Walsh's discussed below, works with confinement, self-imprisonment and failure, but unlike Walsh's work it hints at transformation. Dvořák's *Rusalka* is introduced with a reference to "The Song to the Moon" in the dialogue, but also as a score at the end of the play.[28] *Rusalka* is the story of a nymph reminiscent of Hans Christian Andersen's "A Little Mermaid", who dies wishing to be made human because she loves a human, so that her soul would live forever with his in the afterlife: "Make me human. Make me Human. And then divine".[29]

The Beckettian trend in Carr's work continued with *The Cordelia Dream*, produced by the RSC in 2008. This play departed completely from the Midland ethos. The dialect is gone and, like *Woman and Scarecrow*, the action moves into an absurdist purgatorial space, empty but for a piano and inhabited only by two characters named man and woman. The play was critically panned and at the time of writing is yet to be produced in Ireland. That aside, what it shows is a culmination of an aesthetic shift away from theatre laden with markers of Irishness. Symbols of identity that over-determine a play in the eyes of the audience, like dialects, were absent.

Like Carr, after the Aran Islands plays McDonagh's style and focus began to shift. *The Pillowman* (2003), which premiered in London at the Cottesloe Theatre, has no apparent connection to Ireland in its plot or its aesthetic. The claustral effect of images of Ireland does not carry over into this work. In fact, removing iconic Irish signifiers freed it completely to work in another aesthetic mode.

Walsh's *The New Electric Ballroom* was first produced at the Munich Kammerspiele in 2004. Like *Penelope* and *The Walworth Farce*, this play is based on a sequence of re-enactments, and characters stuck in their own stories.[30] This play is set in a rural Irish town with two spinster sisters in their sixties, Clara and Breda, "replaying the frustrating story of trying to [lose their virginity] in their late teens. The object of their attention was a showband frontman, one Roller Royle".[31] For Ondřej Pilný the characters in the play are caught in an endless "repetition of the same … double-bind situations … Moreover, the sudden, shocking outbursts of violence are expressive of the frustrated desire of the characters to step outside" these patterns.[32] While *The New Electric Ballroom* treats an issue very similar in terms of plot to *The Beauty Queen of Leenane*—Irish spinsters caught in a repetitive cycle that forecloses or foreclosed their sexuality—it also echoes Beckett's *Endgame* and *Waiting for Godot*. As Pilný suggests in *The New Electric Ballroom* "the re-enactment of the stories of the past is ostentatiously presented … as protection from the hostile world outside". Just as the recitation of Hamm's chronicle in *Endgame* or Vladimir and Estragon's wait in *Godot* is all that remains of agency for these characters in their devastated worlds, the sisters' story, no matter how tedious, must continue.

Something similar can be seen in *Penelope*. However this play, commissioned by and performed for the first time in the *Theater Oberhausen* in Berlin, used the conceit of the Greek myth of Penelope (Odysseus's loyal wife who was beset by suitors while her husband was lost for seven years) and comprised dramatis personae loosely based on key figures in Ireland's financial collapse of 2008–2009. *Penelope* is arguably more of a national issue play than any other mentioned in this chapter, but at the same time it is also the most abstract.

Pilný argues that *Penelope* reflects

> prominent aspects of the post-Celtic Tiger atmosphere: the protagonists are ex-businessmen surrounded by the debris of former prosperity, while their names are based on those of prominent Irish business moguls, bankers and developers who were directly involved in the downfall of the Irish economy. Moreover, the play includes a satirical interpretation of the fairy tale about the Magic Porridge Pot, in which an entire town is seen as having "ground to a standstill when it became awash with porridge" since its inhabitants "took with no notion of responsibility or future".[33]

The characters' names, Quinn, Fitz, Dunne and Burns, echo the names of Irish businessmen and bankers who figured prominently in the media after the collapse of the Celtic Tiger. Like the other plays discussed here—*Woman and Scarecrow*, *The Pillowman* and *The Cordelia Dream* flies—*Penelope* flies from any sense of providing a mimetic representation of Ireland. And yet the fixed space remains. For *Woman and Scarecrow* it is Woman's bedroom; in *The Cordelia Dream* it is a "space with a piano"[34]; in *The Pillowman* there are two literally carceral spaces (an interrogation room and a cell); but in Penelope it is a "*dilapidated swimming pool, drained of water. There are two ladders at the back of the pool where the actors enter. … The pool's been turned into a living space* … [with] *a CCTV camera in the pool looking down at the men*".[35] While each of these plays is using fixed spaces, *Penelope*'s is unique. Having as much in common with Sarah Kane's *Cleansed* (1998) as it does with Walsh's other work, the swimming pool is repurposed as a living space by the suitors, repurposed again as space of surveillance by *Penelope* herself and then finally used by the suitors as a performance space for their meta-theatricality. Walsh takes his trilogy of plays about people caught in the trap of re-enacting their own stories to a new level in *Penelope*. While Pilný notes that the men in the play "are locked in the endless routine of courting, just as the characters in *The New Electric Ballroom* and *The Walworth Farce* are stuck in their reenactments",[36] their meta-theatrical performances go beyond the personal traumas of *The New Electric Ballroom* and *The Walworth Farce*, becoming a grotesque globalized parade of kitsch.

The productions of plays by Irish playwrights in British theatres drove the development of new styles and forms of Irish theatre. Re-envisioning and out-growing the shadow of the "Irish play" and its concomitant mimetic trap. Walsh's plays premiering in Germany furthered this trend in a number of ways. *Penelope* extends the globalized and interconnected ethos that began to be seen in Carr's, McDonagh's and McPherson's work after 2003. Walsh's two plays enacted and produced a globalized discourse and aesthetic for Irish theatre. They reimagined the system that produced the images of Ireland and Irishness in myriad ways. During the 1990s, numerous Irish plays (especially but not only Marina Carr's) utilized a Greek mythological schema (Ovid's *Metamorphosis* for *Portia Coughlan*, Medea for *By the Bog of Cats*, Elektra and Orestes for *Ariel*) but *Penelope* inverts this. Rather than using characters and scenarios from the twenty-first century to play out a Greek inspired tragic plotline, it uses the Greek elements as a surface conceit and repurposes and re-actualizes them in order to speak to the Irish and European financial crisis of the early twenty-first century. At the same time, *Penelope* has echoes of Murphy's *A Whistle in the Dark* (1961). Murphy's play presented an image of Ireland unacceptable to the establishment (specifically the former politician Ernest Blythe, then the Abbey's Artistic Director) but Penelope produces an image of dissent. At the date of this writing, six years after its premier, *Penelope*, although subsequently produced by Druid and a winner of the Fringe First in 2010,[37] has not yet been performed in the Abbey. The play deals directly with the European financial crisis and speaks to the fallout from the Celtic Tiger in Ireland, and yet the Irish national theatre has not yet seen fit to consider it for its main stage. *Penelope* speaks truth to power, not just with its narrative but also with its aesthetic. A curious, sometimes frenetic, postmodern pastiche and satire, *Penelope* looks nothing like an "Irish play" and yet at this point it identifies a kind of double bind. Perhaps *Penelope* is too far adrift aesthetically to be recognized as "Irish enough"?

Penelope's comparison to *A Whistle in the Dark* however is not merely about uncomfortable or taboo discourses. Both plays were premiered abroad, but, whereas *A Whistle in the Dark* was an exile, a forced emigrant, *Penelope* chose to go abroad, like a citizen of Europe. The work of the playwrights discussed here, from McPherson and McDonagh to Carr and Walsh, were not staged abroad to circumvent censorship or to find a safe space to break convention or taboo (in fact the reaction to *On Raftery's Hill* in Washington shows quite the opposite), these plays are mobile and were produced or co-produced by foreign theatres or theatre companies (*The Lieutenant Of Inishmore* and *The Cordelia Dream* for the RSC, *Woman and Scarecrow* for the Royal Court and Walsh's plays for German companies). This internationalization brought with it freedom. Contrary to traditional postcolonial theories, the performances in the British theatres in the 1990s and early 2000s drove the development of Irish drama in new directions: first with McPherson and O'Rowe and their monologues; then with McDonagh and Carr and their sometimes grotesque, sometimes absurd parodies and tragedies. While at times this led to controversy, it also led to a creative catharsis and multiple new directions for Irish dramas. So much so, arguments around an imaginary tradition of Irish playwrights as quoted by Merriman,[38] and by Fintan O'Toole,[39] cease to have purchase. Not merely, as O'Toole suggests, because of the changing landscape of theatre production (with the emergence of theatremakers and Irish devised theatre) but because the work of the playwrights, the plays themselves, do not fit that model.[40] The plays do not match the ideal due to their aesthetic and due to the fact that they are being made in a globalized way. Rather than the plays resisting anything, *Woman and Scarecrow*, *The Cordelia Dream* and *Penelope* show the collapse of apparently naturalistic settings and the reduction of markers and symbols of Irishness—such as Carr's Midland dialect or McDonagh's scrupulously accurate props (e.g. complan). All of these markers are what Grene calls Ireland's need "to be represented and represented truly".[41] The dissonance produced by Royal Court productions and co-productions of Carr and McDonagh's earlier work is not then caused by the plays refusing anything or neglecting anything, but rather by a mixed aesthetic. The uses of the grotesque and its excessive signification mixed uncomfortably with what critics and audiences saw as markers of naturalism (accents and dialects, props, interior domestic spaces and especially kitchens). The excessive was confused for, and conflated with, the realistic a tendency Eamonn Jordan noted in relation to McDonagh's work—like demanding a cubistic painting present an image like a figurative one.[42]

This chapter began with a discussion of the overtly postcolonial nature of Irish national theatre. However, rather than confining the work to traditional genres or expectations, the influence of foreign productions on the plays and their playwrights liberated them. Yes, the grotesque and excessive productions of Carr and McDonagh's earlier works do walk a tight rope, but by the end of the first decade of the twenty-first century, the tropes of Irishness and its signifiers of authenticity had begun to fall away. It could be argued that Grene and Merriman's mission for Irish drama still holds true, asking who the Irish are and what Ireland is. Nonetheless, this is no longer the Irish Question as it was formulated in relation to the United Kingdom but rather a global question, and while that has its own dangers, the postcolonial paradox may at last have been circumvented.

Notes

1. Nicholas Grene, *Politics of Irish Drama: Plays in Context from Boucicault to Friel* (Cambridge: Cambridge University Press, 1999), 1–7.
2. Grene, *Politics of Irish Drama*, 1.
3. Grene, *Politics of Irish Drama*, 6–7.
4. Victor Merriman, "Settling for More: Excess and Success in Contemporary Irish Drama", In *Druids, Dudes and Beauty Queens: The Changing Face of Irish Theatre*, ed. Dermot Bolger (Dublin: New Island, 2001) 55–71 (55).

5. See David Lloyd's *Anomalous States: Irish Writing and the Post-colonial Moment* (Durham: Duke University Press, 1993).
6. Clare Wallace, "Authentic Reproductions: Marina Carr and the Inevitable", in *The Theatre of Marina Carr: "before rules was made"*, ed. Cathy Leeney and Anna McMullan (Dublin: Carysfort Press, 2003) 43–64 (43–45).
7. Philip Roberts, *The Royal Court Theatre and the Modern Stage* (Cambridge: Cambridge University Press, 1999), 45, 76, 178, 228.
8. For more on this see Peter Harris's *From Stage to Page: Critical Reception of Irish Plays in the London Theatre, 1925–1996.*
9. "Fintan O'Toole: Power Plays".
10. Claudia W. Harris, "Rising Out of the Miasmal Mists: Marina Carr's Ireland", in *The Theatre of Marina Carr: "before the rules was made"* ed. Cathy Leeney and Anna McMullan (Dublin: Carysfort Press, 2003) 216–232 (231).
11. Eamonn Jordan, *Dissident Dramaturgies: Contemporary Irish Theatre* (Dublin: Irish Academic Press, 2010), 134–149.
12. Ibid., 134.
13. Ibid., 149.
14. Ibid., 148.
15. Ibid., 40–155.
16. Merriman, "Settling for More", 60.
17. "Kennedy Centre Is Filled With The Sounds of Ireland 2000".
18. Harris, "Rising Out of the Miasmal Mists", 218–219.
19. Ibid., 222.
20. Ibid., 222–229.
21. Jordan, *Dissident Dramaturgies*, 149.
22. Ibid., 143.
23. Harris, "Rising Out of the Miasmal Mists", 228.
24. Ibid., 229.
25. Grene, *Politics of Irish Drama*, 2.
26. Marina Carr, *Woman and Scarecrow* (Oldcastle: Gallery Press, 2006), 29.
27. Ibid., 30.
28. Ibid., 75.
29. Ibid., 76.
30. Ondřej Pilný, "The Grotesque in the Plays of Enda Walsh", *Irish Studies Review* 21 (2013): 218.
31. Ibid.
32. Ibid., 219.
33. Ibid., 220.
34. Marina Carr, *The Cordelia Dream* (Oldcastle: Gallery Press, 2008), 8.
35. Walsh, *Penelope* (London: Nick Hern Books, 2010), 3.
36. Pilný, "The Grotesque in the Plays of Enda Walsh", 222.
37. "Press Release: Third Fringe First for Druid and Enda Walsh".
38. Merriman, "Settling for More," 61–63.
39. "Fintan O'Toole: Power Plays", *Arts Lives.* RTE One. Dublin, Ireland: RTE, 7 June, 2012.
40. Ibid.
41. Grene, *Politics of Irish Drama*, 2.
42. Jordan, *Dissident Dramaturgies*, 149.

Bibliography

Carr, Marina. *Marina Carr: Plays 1*. London: Faber and Faber, 1999.
———. *On Raftery's Hill*. Oldcastle: Gallery Press, 2000.
———. *Woman and Scarecrow*. Oldcastle: Gallery Press, 2006.
———. *The Cordelia Dream*. Oldcastle: Gallery Press, 2008.
Cerquoni, Enrica. "Review of *By the Bog of Cats*...." Irish Theatre Magazine 2: 70.
Druid Theatre Company. "Press Release: Third Fringe First for Druid and Enda Walsh". Accessed 1 March, 2016. http://www.druid.ie/news/press-release-third-fringe-first-for-druid-and-enda-walsh.
"Fintan O'Toole: Power Plays." *Arts Lives*. RTE One. Dublin, Ireland: RTE, 7 June, 2012.
Grene, Nicholas. *The Politics of Irish Drama: Plays in Context from Boucicault to Friel*. Cambridge: Cambridge University Press, 1999.
Harris, Claudia W. "Rising Out of the Miasmal Mists: Marina Carr's Ireland." In *The Theatre of Marina Carr: "Before the Rules Was Made"*, edited by Cathy Leeney and Anna McMullan, 216–232. Dublin: Carysfort Press, 2003.
Harris, Peter. *From Stage to Page: Critical Reception of Irish Plays in the London Theatre, 1925–1996*, Oxford: Peter Lang, 2011.
Haughey, Paul, Cormac O'Brien, and Josh Tobiessen. 2001. "Struggling Toward a Future: Irish Theatre Today." *New Hibernia Review* 5:126–133. doi: https://doi.org/10.1353/nhr.2001.0028.
Jordan, Eamonn. *Dissident Dramaturgies: Contemporary Irish Theatre*. Dublin: Irish Academic Press, 2010.
Kiberd, Declan. *Inventing Ireland: The Literature of the Modern Nation*. London: Vintage, 1996.
Little, Ruth, and Emilie McLaughlin. *The Royal Court Theatre: Inside Out*. London: Oberon Books, 2007.
Luckhurst, Mary. "Martin McDonagh's Lieutenant of Inishmore: Selling (-Out) to the English." *Contemporary Theatre Review* 14:34–41. doi: https://doi.org/10.1080/10486800412331296309.
Lloyd, David. *Anomalous States: Irish Writing and the Post-colonial Moment*. Durham: Duke University Press, 1993.
McDonagh, Martin. *Martin McDonagh: Plays 1*. London: Methuen, 1999.
———. *The Pillowman*. London: Faber and Faber, 2003.
———. *The Cripple of Inishmaan*. London: Methuen, 2013.
———. *The Lieutenant of Inishmore*. London: Methuen, 2014.
McPherson, Conor. *Shining City*. London: Nick Hern Books, 2010.
Merriman, Vic. "Settling for More: Excess and Success in Contemporary Irish Drama." In *Druids, Dudes and Beauty Queens: The Changing Face of Irish Theatre*, edited by Dermot Bolger, 55–71. Dublin: New Island, 2001.
Pilný, Ondřej. 2013. "The Grotesque in the Plays of Enda Walsh." *Irish Studies Review* 21:217–225.
Roberts, Philip. *The Royal Court Theatre and the Modern Stage*. Cambridge: Cambridge University Press, 1999.
Royal Court Theatre. "Ireland at The Royal Court Theatre". Accessed 2 November, 2015. http://www.royalcourttheatre.com/project/ireland.

RTE. "Kennedy Centre Is Filled With The Sounds of Ireland 2000". Accessed 10 February, 2016. http://www.rte.ie/archives/2015/0514/701002-irish-arts-festival-in-the-us/.

Wallace, Clare. "Authentic Reproductions: Marina Carr and the Inevitable." In *The Theatre of Marina Carr: "Before Rules Was Made"*, edited by Cathy Leeney and Anna McMullan, 43–64. Dublin: Carysfort Press, 2003.

Walsh, Enda. *Enda Walsh: Plays 1*. London: Nick Hern Books, 2010.

———. *Penelope*. London: Nick Hern Books, 2010.

———. *The New Electric Ballroom*. London: Nick Hern Books, 2014.

Ripping Up the Original?: Fictional Adaptations in Contemporary Irish Theatre

Anne Fogarty

Literary adaptation is a fickle art, simultaneously beholden to the original work and yet compelled to reinvent it. Loyalty and infidelity are the dual opposing forces that fuel any endeavour to reconceive a pre-existing text.[1] In adaptation, any homage to an acknowledged masterwork is always accompanied by the need to oust it and estrange it from itself. At once acolytes and mediators, those who adapt literary texts seek to create them anew. Increasingly, adaptation studies emphasize the autonomy of play scripts devised from original sources and view them as independent works in their own right.[2] Adaptation seen in this manner forces us to rethink sacrosanct notions of originality and narrow views of authorship as delimited and watertight, and to question the proprietary boundaries of literary icons.

Transpositions of the novels of James Joyce, Samuel Beckett, Flann O'Brien and key contemporary Irish fictions—including Patrick McCabe's *The Butcher Boy* (1992) and *The Dead School* (1995), Eimear McBride's *A Girl is a Half-Formed Thing* (2015) and Emma Donoghue's *Room* (2010)—have been a fertile field in recent Irish theatre.[3] Their experimental aspects notwithstanding, this proliferation of literary adaptations could awaken suspicions of opportunistic recycling. Viewed cynically, such work seems to exploit the undeniable aura held by the mainstays of the Irish literary canon and the small number of contemporary texts that have been embraced as instant classics. Trading on the cultural capital of the fiction of Joyce, Beckett and O'Brien could be construed as an unimaginative endorsement of works long since considered to be cornerstones of international modernism and world literature. Meanwhile,

A. Fogarty (✉)
University College Dublin, Dublin, Ireland
e-mail: anne.fogarty@ucd.ie

E. Jordan, E. Weitz (eds.), *The Palgrave Handbook of Contemporary Irish Theatre and Performance*,
https://doi.org/10.1057/978-1-137-58588-2_35

dramatizations of recent, award-winning fiction could similarly stand accused of profiting from lauded texts for their cachet and accessibility.

Using the widespread recognition of well-known, acclaimed novels could appear to be a canny marketing strategy, an effective method for ensuring a guaranteed audience and for cushioning against uncertain box office returns. Plying pre-existing works that already possess a cast-iron cultural status avoids the risks of having to break new ground and introduce audiences to texts that are unknown or unfamiliar. Additionally, the staging of work by Joyce, Beckett and Flann O'Brien seems to align with the conservative tenets of Irish cultural tourism, which habitually invokes these talismanic authors with little real concern for the dense material contexts and underpinnings of their writings—or for their radicalism, complexity and waywardness. Likewise, staging novels with an international purchase such as *The Butcher Boy* or *Room* seems merely to capitalize on the global reach of Irish culture and to retool texts whose potency and appeal have also been enhanced by successful cinema versions.[4]

However, if adaptations are above all motivated by a compulsion to repeat, then it must also be recognized that recent dramatizations of Irish novels evince a nostalgia for originals that can never, in the final reckoning, be reconstituted.[5] Adaptations, it will become apparent, invariably involve daunting imaginative leaps and are much more acts of creative hubris than pious expressions of homage. Moreover, close analysis reveals that the aesthetic principles, conceptual structures and dramaturgy of fictional adaptations on the Irish stage decidedly refute any accusations of derivativeness, empty appropriation or inauthenticity. Rather, these reworkings call the bluff of those who wish to preserve a static canon of great Irish writers or to reduce them to formulaic points of reference. Paradoxically, given their symbiotic connection with classical works, these adaptations take issue with the cult of the author and seek to move beyond writer-driven and text-based theatre. Taking their brief from the experimentalism of modernism and a certain tranche of avant-garde contemporary fiction, they animate and revivify the novels that act as their starting points by searching for new modes of performativity and theatrical experience that invite their audiences actively to imagine scenarios that are not mimetically represented.

All of the adaptations discussed in this essay play with notions of character and the possibilities of narration and utilize the ability of actors to move rapidly between multiple different personae and the facility of the stage to represent numerous parallel spaces, thereby eschewing the fixities of a naturalistic dramatis personae or mise-en-scène. The signature styles of the original author are retained in part, but also deconstructed to allow for embodied modes of performance and for a questioning of verities about the nature of the subject, the operations of empathy and the illusion-making propensities of theatre. By variously foregrounding the potency of dramatic voices, monologues and duologues, and the charisma of the solitary performer, these productions invite audience engagement while exposing the limits of humanistic notions of bounded personae.

Overall, an oscillation between immersion and disengagement is a defining aspect of these very diverse adaptations. While an emphasis on the physical dimensions of performance propels them, they are also driven by a scepticism, which prevents spectators investing wholly in the illusionary forces of characters as quintessential properties of the stage or in theatre's ability to sustain cohesive narratives and reliably hold a mirror up to our world. The cultivation of varying types of estrangement—Brechtian-style alienation effects—is a marked feature of all these texts.[6] Inner division is prominently dwelt on and graphically rendered in these works, which harness the dramatic potential of fissures, divisions and spatial disjunctions and aim at chaotic multiform structures, rapid contrasts, dissonance and dispersion more than cohesion or resolution.

Ulysses, Dermot Bolger's adaptation of Joyce's modernist epic, was first staged in the Zellerbach Theatre, Philadelphia, in 1994 to coincide with the ninetieth anniversary of Bloomsday. Due to issues with copyright, a long interval took place before it premiered in the Tron Theatre, Glasgow, and the Project Arts Centre, Dublin—in 2012. Even though Bolger's text was legally recognized at the time as a discrete entity, it could only be staged in Europe after the release of Joyce's works in that year from copyright. A revised version was performed in the Abbey Theatre, Dublin, in October 2017, directed by Graham McLaren, as part of the Dublin Theatre Festival. Bolger was commissioned to undertake the adaptation by Greg Doran from the Royal Shakespearean Company, who directed it. In interview, he has commented on his reluctance to assume the task. It is notable that it is the iconicity of Joyce's work that daunted him, not its complexity or encyclopaedism.[7] Structurally, his text pits the complex against the simple: originally titled, *A Dublin Bloom*, the cast consists of ten actors, three of whom play the central roles of Leopold Bloom, Molly Bloom and Stephen Dedalus, the other seven taking on a variable, ever-changing array of over seventy parts.[8] In this manner, the fetishization of the principal characters and the seeming clarity of elements of the plot—such as Molly's affair and Bloom's quest for a son—are undermined by the rapid-fire appearance of minor roles, and shifts of scene.

Bolger draws out the chaotic verve of Dublin life, thereby unsettling any assumptions we might have about the trajectory of Joyce's novel. A further disruption of inherited structures is achieved by the constant intercutting of the ongoing action with interjections by Molly Bloom, who occupies one of the key spaces on the stage. Her reflections are thus no longer self-enclosed and set apart, but rather serve as a dialectical commentary on the action as well as a perpetual reminder of the otherness of the private female world to which she is consigned. Bolger's text ultimately makes No. 7 Eccles Street, the home of the Blooms, less of an ambiguous destination than it is in Joyce. It also imparts even greater mythical force to the potential friendship between Bloom and Stephen than *Ulysses* allows for. Molly's parting ruminations, however, with their lightning-quick transitions between querulousness and acceptance, stress the unfixed and unresolved nature of the action, urging us to reconsider it from a very different point of view.

Frank McGuinness's adaptation of Joyce's "The Dead" staged in the Abbey Theatre in Dublin in December 2012 and directed by Joe Dowling, also uses the symbolic disposition of stage space, a recalibration of the principal and minor characters and an unsettling structure to urge his audience to rethink the closing story of *Dubliners*. Above all, McGuinness knowingly plays with spectators' foreknowledge of the text and works to shake the nostalgia for Edwardian Dublin with which it has become associated, especially in the wake of John Huston's 1987 cinematic adaptation.[9] McGuinness in his prefatory observations declares that he conceives of the figures in the play as caught between historical eras, scarred by the memory of the Famine on the one hand but also poised, on the other, for the revolutionary changes in the future set in motion by the 1916 Rising.[10] At the beginning of the Abbey production, the entire cast sing Thomas Moore's "Oh Ye Dead" on a bare stage; the characters are thus suggestively profiled not only as melancholic spectres but also as revenants capable of mobilizing restless social forces and emotions.

In a radical alteration to Joyce's plot, McGuinness proleptically foregrounds Michael Furey. He is part of the initial assembly of characters on stage: they melt away, leaving him alone to sing the final stanza of Moore's song. It is thus intimated that Furey is part of a collective unconscious and that he has an independent existence outside of his thwarted devotion to Gretta Conroy, the central female protagonist. Indeed, McGuinness's text places an even greater emphasis on the collective at the New Year's party held by the Misses Morkan than Joyce's story does, undoing in the process its concentration on the interiority of Gabriel Conroy, the principal male figure. Scenes highlighting the viewpoints of several of the female characters—Gabriel's aunts, the hosts of the party, Lily, the maid, Gretta Conroy and Molly Ivors—are given an even more decided prominence than in the original story, highlighting the uneasy balance of power between the sexes in this social milieu. Gender conflict and familial tension are accorded greater weight too due to McGuinness's re-envisaging of Mrs Malins, the mother of Freddy Malins, the hapless drunkard at the party who all too readily occupies the role of the inebriated stage Irishman. In Joyce's text Mrs. Malins is depicted as a loquacious and endearing bore; in McGuinness's hands she is transformed into a Wildean figure: acerbic, wittily needling and overbearing, who simultaneously dominates her son and laments his failings.

Above all, McGuinness purposefully remoulds the ambiguities that accrue at the end of Joyce's story. In the final scenes, two triads of figures are counterpointed: Freddy Malins, ominously singing "Let Me Like a Soldier Fall", Mrs Malins and Mr. Browne who convivially like "three brave comrades" (66) depart into the snowy nocturnal landscape; Gretta Conroy, Gabriel Conroy and Michael Furey, who are in the bedroom of the Gresham hotel. In each case, the interlinking suggests a queering of relations and a crossing of gender roles. Michael Furey, albeit spectrally, is commuted from a romantic absence to a participatory presence who sings "The Lass of Aughrim" after Gretta has made her confessional divulgence about their friendship and his early death. His performance is intertwined with Gretta's convulsive grief and Gabriel's pained discomfiture. The repeated refrain, "Lord Gregory let me in" (79), evinces his unrequited love for Gretta and points up the couple's own overwhelming emotions. An uncanny but palpable presence, Furey is anything other than a closed-off memory. Rather, he acts as instigator of a three-way desire. McGuinness renders him firmly part of the queer alliance between husband and wife depicted in the final moments of his play.

Further, he daringly alters the sculpted, poetic ending of Joyce's "The Dead" by breaking up the final paragraphs and partially rewriting them. Instead of impersonal monologue, Gabriel directs his words towards the sleeping Gretta. His pronouncements are tentative and transactional; his overall endeavour is co-operatively to accommodate both her point of view and that of Michael Furey. If his struggle to comprehend and arrive at empathy sacrifices some of the musicality of Joyce's well-known and oft-rehearsed ending, it does so in the interest of injecting a fresh affirmativeness into the closing lines.

Corn Exchange's inventive and deliberately estranging adaptation of Joyce's *Dubliners* premiered in the Gaiety Theatre, Dublin in October 2012. It was jointly adapted by Michael West and Annie Ryan and directed by the latter. As with the company's other productions, *commedia dell'arte* techniques were deployed to reinterpret nine of the stories in Joyce's volume.[11] Grotesque, mask-like make-up, the playing up of stereotypical roles and emotions—such as anger, frustration, fear and malice—and an exaggerated gestural language proved to be an enlightening route into these tales with their lurid emphasis on human failure and violent, conflict-ridden social interactions. Paradoxically, an anti-naturalistic acting style heightened the realist vein of these narratives, that are saturated with detailed geographical and social knowledge of Dublin. In performance, precise allusions to districts of Dublin (laden with implicit presumptions about class and social stratification) aroused as much laughter in the Gaiety Theatre as the re-interpretation of the visceral conflicts in the stories.

Commedia dell'arte has been described as the "comedy of a known character reacting to an unknown situation".[12] The depiction of the figures in the stories as stock types, innocents, fools, viragoes and drunkards, who are yet faced with the prospect of failure and searing visions of their personal ignominy allowed for painful and often jagged shifts between comedy and tragedy throughout. Indeed, the unearthing of the macabre comedy of *Dubliners* was one of the startling aspects of the production overall. As in *commedia dell'arte*, laughter acted not just as an emotional safety valve for these dark narratives about moral deadlock, but also served to implicate and involve the audience in the bleak insights conveyed.

Memorably, in his stern pronouncements about *Dubliners* Joyce stressed that his fellow citizens needed to see themselves in his "nicely polished looking glass".[13] Corn Exchange's production did not shirk this satirical intent as it pointed to the contemporary relevance of these moments of breakdown in the lives of an array of Dubliners of different ages. In the opening scene, the ensemble wanders onto the stage one by one and pace about against a backdrop of the city, thereby blurring the lines of division between Dublin in the past and the present, and between the city imagined by Joyce and the reinvented space projected by this contemporary dramatization. An oscillation between immersion and distance characterized the succession of stories, which move from the young boy's first-person narration in "The Sisters" and "An Encounter" to the third-person perspective in "Eveline", "A Mother", "The Boarding House", "Counterparts" and "A Painful Case", to Gabriel Conroy's final stark realizations about his failure as husband and lover in "The Dead".

The preservation of a gap between character and actor is, as Lenny Abrahamson noted, an abiding feature of Corn Exchange's productions.[14] This gap is especially conveyed by unanticipated shifts of mood—startlingly, the paedophile who menaces the boys in "An Encounter" is revealed to be comic in part—and the increasingly histrionic performance style, especially in the depiction of the sordid squabbles in "A Mother" and "The Boarding House". The deliberately excessive enactment of the mother as a hilariously comic virago in the latter narratives wrenches them completely away from any naturalist pretensions without, however, forfeiting sympathy for her scheming designs. The manic, grotesque routines of *commedia dell'arte* are ultimately offset by the melancholy and introspection of "The Dead", the closing story. This adaptation of *Dubliners* by Michael West and Anne Ryan revivified it by working against Joyce's realist designs and also bore out that iconoclasm and reverence can be mutually compatible aims in the reinvention of a twentieth-century classic.

Riverrun, Olwen Fouéré's adaptation of Book IV of Joyce's *Finnegans Wake*, co-directed by Kellie Hughes for The Emergency Room, first opened at the Galway Arts Festival in 2013. It thereafter travelled to Dublin, London, Sydney, Adelaide and New York. Fouéré sinuously enacts the movements of Anna Livia on a bare stage in front of a microphone, immersing her audience simultaneously in the flowing but mystifying torrents of Wakean language, in which words are overlaid and swim in and out of focus. Book IV of the *Wake*—predicated on Giambattista Vico's principle of the *ricorso* or return, an era in which life is regenerated out of chaos—looks forwards and backwards in time and follows the fluctuations of the river Liffey as life-force, post-human icon, flesh-and-blood woman, archetypal symbol and distillation of the feminine and the maternal.

Through the alchemy of her rhythmical, balletic performance and incantatory, susurrating delivery, Fouéré at once becomes Joyce's protean figure and transforms herself in hallucinatory fashion, caught as she is in an intense spotlight, into a physical medium for his language. Her muscular but ecstatic swimming movements enact Anna Livia's travails and the efforts required by spectators to cast aside rationalist and pragmatic views of language: a preliminary to taking on board and becoming attuned to the playful, fusional neologisms of the *Wake*. Choreography, sound and lighting design are deployed to capture the shadow-play of a fluvial landscape and the ebb and flow of the river and of the narrative arcs of Book IV, which look back on Anna Livia's life and primal phases of history, herald a new dawn and represent the rebirth through entry into Dublin bay as conjointly a strenuous reawakening and a prolonged and exhausting journey towards death. Moving beyond the conventions of monologue, Fouéré in her avant-garde adaptation of the *Wake*, chimes with the experimentalism of Joyce's text, by creating a "bodied space", a visual, acoustic and corporeal field of play in which elements of Book IV can be conjured up and rhythmically re-ordered but permitted to retain their fluidity, open-endedness and mystery.[15]

Strikingly, adaptations of Beckett's fictional works have become the preserve of the solo performer: Barry McGovern, Conor Lovett and Lisa Dwan have staged distinctive and acclaimed versions of his texts, which have powerfully resonated with audiences. Notwithstanding numerous other theatrical involvements, it is telling that an exclusive focus on Beckett is assumed to be the sole calling of all these actors, in keeping with the purist devotion and single-minded discipline required of a performer of his work. To adapt Beckett, it would appear, is an all-consuming *métier*. Barry McGovern's one-man show, *I'll Go On*, based on the trilogy of novels, *Molloy*, *Malone Dies* and *The Unnamable*, pioneered the adaptation of Beckett's fictional texts for the contemporary stage in Ireland and significantly widened the audiences for his work nationally and internationally. In a text devised by McGovern and Gerry Dukes, it was first staged in the Gate Theatre, Dublin in 1985, toured for some eight years to nine different countries and was revived in 2013–14 for shows at the Edinburgh Theatre Festival and the Kirk Douglas Theatre, Los Angeles. McGovern gained permission from Beckett, who usually vetoed any interference with his texts, to mount the show. The author's imprimatur thus lent aura and authority to this remoulding and interpretation of his novels.[16] The adaptation, even though free-wheeling in its stripping away of much of the text, is fastidious and exacting because of the precision of McGovern's delivery and his haunting physical embodiment of Beckett's characters and de-individuated non-personae.

A preamble in which McGovern mocks the audience for their pretensions in coming to a performance of Beckett's trilogy was added to recent productions, nicely capturing the dual nature of his interpretation which aims, on the one hand, to mediate these difficult texts and, on the other, unflinchingly to live up to their assault on narrative and on metaphysical first principles. McGovern initially draws out the entertainingly absurdist facets of the novels—such as Molloy's mathematical dilemma about how to rotate his sucking stones, his abusive non-relationship with his mother or his difficulty in establishing an alibi when apprehended by policemen—but uses these comic routines as a pathway into the tortured philosophical meditations on identity and the nature of knowledge that are the central preoccupations of the trilogy. The *clochard*-like Molloy cedes to the ascetic and chilling figures of Malone and the Unnamable. The rigorous physicality of McGovern's performance creates a mesmerising spatial field in which to engage with what Dirk van Hulle has dubbed Beckett's texts "in regress".[17] A hypnotic concentration on the spot-lit body of the performer, torso stripped bare, devoid of props, or dressed in a shroud, allows for a full encounter with Beckett's portrayal of voided and negated states and his decomposition of characters and plots. McGovern's ability to counterbalance the humanist concerns of Beckett's work, its comic propensities, its reliance on the performativity of the voice and its ineluctable movement towards nothingness, abstraction and diminution is also evident in his adaptation of *Watt*, performed at the Gate Theatre, Dublin in 2010 and of *First Love*, staged in the O'Reilly Theatre, Dublin in 2016.

Following in the wake of McGovern, but with a distinctive aesthetic of their own, Conor Lovett and Judy Hegarty-Lovett, founders of Gare St Lazare Players, have jointly adapted over ten of Beckett's fictional works, including *Molloy*, which premiered at the Battersea Arts Centre in 1996, and *Malone Dies* and *The Beckett Trilogy*, which opened at the Kilkenny Arts Festival in 2000 and 2001. Like McGovern, too, they have adapted some of Beckett's short early fiction: *First Love*, which premiered in Siamsa Tíre, Tralee in 2008; *The End*, staged at the Kilkenny Arts Festival in 2008; and *The Calmative*, which was performed in the Cork Opera House in 2010. Beckett's late fiction is also part of their repertoire: they have produced *Lessness* at the Kilkenny Arts Festival in 2002; *Worstward Ho* at the Cork Public Museum; and *Texts for Nothing* at the Masonic Lodge, Cork in 2005. They have collaborated on almost all of their Beckett productions, with Judy Hegarty-Lovett acting as director and Conor Lovett as the solo performer.

Lovett studied in Paris with Jacques Lecoq and trained in the forms of mime and physical theatre that he champions. Lecoq's methodology involved educating actors in the natural dynamics of the body and in the spatial territories of emotions and social interactions. His precepts were rooted in what he saw as the central modes of European theatre: tragedy, clowning and *commedia dell'arte*. A key tenet was that emotions and actions should be rendered externally not internally.[18] Lovett's training in the communicative openness and pared-back aesthetic advocated by Lecoq is evident in his performances of Beckett. In *The Beckett Trilogy* and *First Love*, a focus is maintained throughout on the body of the actor standing centre stage, using an economic array of gestures to relay his story directly and without unnecessary distractions to the audience. Lovett's retention of his Cork accent further reinforces the sense of a performer using every aspect of his body without impediment as part of his theatrical toolkit. Yet the performances go beyond mere acts of story-telling or communication; the illusion of ease always remains in tension with the insistent voicing of these Beckettian anti-narratives and their complex, discomfiting meditations on existence and nullity.[19] Overall, Lovett's interpretations of Beckett are more muted and sombre than those of McGovern. Both actors, however, exploit the degree to which Beckett's work provides latitude for play with theatrical and narratorial voices and severs them from links with concepts of a fixed self or stage persona.

The technically proficient but emotionally disturbing free play of the voice is likewise a prominent feature of Lisa Dwan's recent adaptation of Beckett. Building on her acclaimed performances in *Not I*, *Rockaby* and *Footfalls*, Dwan, strategically moved into a terrain which has hitherto been dominated by male performers. She adapted several of Beckett's late pieces of fiction in *Texts for Nothing* for a show titled, *No's Knife*, which premiered at the Lincoln Centre, New York in 2015 and toured to the Old Vic, London in 2016 and the Abbey Theatre, Dublin in 2017.[20] In *Texts for Nothing* an anguished, non-corporeal voice speaks in a void and is seemingly trapped between life and death. Initially bound in the manner of Prometheus to a rocky cleft in a stage set depicting a ravaged post-apocalyptic natural scene devoid of any other signs of human life, Dwan gives voice to the frenzied thoughts and emotions of the disembodied, voided personae in these texts.[21] Her writhing body and wanderings through the waterlogged scene and gradual advance to front stage to come close to the audience act as a devastatingly ironic counterpoint to the painful, beseeching but fragmentary statements that she violently spits out. In this radical exercise in post-dramatic theatre, the audience is compelled to fixate on a female figure who, while functioning as an embodiment of non-being, exercises designs on their attention. In her adaptation, Dwan at once feminizes the creaturely, post-human voices in Beckett's texts and adopts their shattered and placeless perspective on things. Performativity in her anguished monologues is linked not to a reliable narrative or the projection of character but to an affective, vocal and gestural vocabulary that is articulated by language, the senses and the body but also transcends them and lays them waste.

Anthony Cronin has bitingly observed that many aficionados of Flann O'Brien esteem his work because it brings them into contact with the disappointed life.[22] Amongst the many ironies of the reception of his oeuvre is that the stage success he courted in his lifetime has been achieved posthumously. His principal novels have been winningly adapted by the experimental Sligo-based Blue Raincoat Theatre Company that specializes particularly in staging the plays of Yeats, but has also performed several dramas by Beckett and Ionesco. The company premiered adaptations by Jocelyn Clarke in the Factory Performance Space, Sligo of *The Third Policeman* in 2006, *At Swim-Two-Birds* in 2009 and *The Poor Mouth* in 2011. The shows were directed by Niall Henry, one of the original founders of the company, and have remained in their repertoire, touring in later revivals to Dublin, Glasgow and Edinburgh. Blue Raincoat Company was set up as a tightly knit regional collective; it eschews traditional text-based modes of acting and favours stagings that foreground the body and make use of movement and experimental visual and auditory techniques derived eclectically from cabaret, mime, circus and European avant-garde and post-dramatic theatre movements.[23] Simultaneously, they are driven by their desire to put on shows that will appeal to audiences.

Their productions of O'Brien's novels were played by a small ensemble of five or six actors, which necessitated the doubling up and reconfiguration of parts. Additionally, his experimentation with narrative form, questioning of conventional plots, watertight novelistic characters and courting of absurdity and improbability are further heightened in performance. Jocelyn Clarke's scripts, however, also drastically curtail certain aspects of O'Brien's texts, making them taut on stage and dislocating some of their well-known embellishments.

To this end, Finn Mc Cool is largely absent from *At Swim-Two-Birds* and the self-reflexive scholarly discussion of de Selby's masterpieces is missing from *The Third Policeman*.

By and large, Clarke's adaptations under Niall Henry's direction recast O'Brien's metafictions as meta-theatre, while keeping faith with his radical and mischievous disturbance of all literary proprieties. Hence, the multi-layered probing of novel writing in *At Swim* becomes a manic exploration of the art of the playwright. The set depicts a miniature nineteenth-century music hall, thus confronting the audience with a theatre within a theatre. The narrator is transformed into a beset playwright/ ringmaster trying to tame the rambunctious energies of his actors and characters who frantically change roles and costumes. While some of the surprising quietism of the reconciliation of the student with his uncle is retained, the ending pointedly overlaid several different conclusions and underscored the arbitrary and beguiling plurality of theatrical stories, which can never be contained or even properly brought to a halt. In similar fashion, the adaptation of *The Third Policeman* emphasizes the macabre and surreal qualities of a world devoid of any stable sense of reality, moral rectitude or cause and effect. The production exploits the bizarre preoccupations of O'Brien's policemen with the effect of bicycles on the human body and the dislocating nature of a vertiginously structured imagined, theatrical reality, which keeps shifting boundaries.

It is notable that many of the novels currently adapted for the contemporary Irish stage are by writers who have been involved in the theatre and have an intimate understanding of its workings. This is the case with the novelist Patrick McCabe, who is an actor and a gifted performer of his own work. He adapted his most successful novel, *The Butcher Boy*, for the stage in 1992, unusually almost simultaneously with its publication.[24] Titled *Frank Pig Says Hello*, the adaptation was performed in Lombard Street Studio, Dublin, directed by Joe O'Byrne and revived in 2002. A revised version was performed in 2017 at the Dublin Theatre Festival.[25] Conspicuously, it shies away from monologue and the unabashed intimacy of the first-person narrator that had endeared itself to readers of the novel and instead deploys a split persona to render its central protagonist. Frank Pig is divided into Piglet and Frank, and is thus permanently split between youthful innocence and a cynical, disabused adult self. There were only two actors in the original cast, one of whom, David Gorry, played Piglet and the other, Sean Rocks, everyone else. Primacy was given in this way to Piglet, while all the adult roles were folded into and elided with each other.

Simultaneously, the rhythmic stream of consciousness of Francie Brady in *The Butcher Boy* is turned into self-interrogation, dialogue and social altercation. His internal world is externalized and theatricalized in McCabe's adaptation and transmuted into the distinctive gestural and physical language of the actors, who, under Joe O'Byrne's direction, particularly drew on the vocabulary of movement used in silent cinema.[26] If the novel shows Frankie's poverty, social ostracism and neglect to be the cause of his descent into madness, the play concentrates more on the conflicted social scene and his self-division, with the ending holding out the flickering hope that his peculiar powers of imagination will allow him to transform the malignant world in which he lives.

McCabe's adaptation of his 1996 novel *The Dead School* in 1998, which opened in the Black Box Theatre, Galway, directed by Joe O'Byrne for Macnas Theatre Company also lent itself to a non-naturalistic staging.[27] McCabe's febrile story of the clash of values between two school teachers, the authoritarian, unyieldingly Catholic traditionalist, Raphael Byrne, and his more liberated and secular younger colleague, Malachy Dudgeon, was turned into a madcap, frenzied performance that particularly revelled in chaotic classroom scenes, with adult actors transmogrifying into unruly children—in which the teachers tried to impose discipline and their distinctive but distorted worldviews. A reworking of *The Dead School*, written and directed by Andrew Flynn, was staged by Decadent Theatre Company in Galway Town Hall in February 2016 and subsequently went on a nationwide tour. In an indication that adaptations, like translations, warrant frequent reinvention, Flynn's altered version allowed for a more even-handed concentration on the younger of the teachers. The production foregrounded the pathos of his decline into madness more fully, while depicting the dysfunctional primary school in which he works to be a site of unruly energies and clashing ideologies.

The recent persuasively realized adaptations of Eimear McBride's award-winning and much-lauded 2013 novel, *A Girl is a Half-Formed Thing*, and of Emma Donoghue's acclaimed 2010 fiction, *Room*, both of which are concerned with sexual abuse, indicate the appetite for innovative plays that resonate with current concerns. *Girl* was adapted and directed by Annie Ryan and premiered in September 2014 at the Samuel Beckett Centre, Dublin.[28] The intense, searing monologue performed by Aoife Duffin on a bare stage streamlined McBride's text, which uses a re-fashioned, opaque English, reminiscent of Joyce's stylistic experiments in *Ulysses*, with melded words, broken syntax and tangled expression, but preserved its affective core. In the novel, the struggle of the unnamed girl to find a language to express the lasting emotional damage resultant on being raped by an uncle when she is a young teenager is paramount. Ryan draws on McBride's shattered English, but her rendering of the girl uncovers the degree to which she ventriloquizes and is scripted by the voices of others, her berating mother, her moralizing grandfather, her beloved brother and the succession of men whom she violently seduces or allows to sexually abuse her. The audience was brought on a multi-voiced, visceral journey with Girl and physically immersed in her ever-changing and inchoate emotions about her identity, which lead ultimately to her suicide, a tragic ending represented as a non-cathartic obliteration.[29]

The muddying of expectations about closure and the consolatory endings of fairy tales are also facets of Emma Donoghue's adaptation of *Room*.[30] Premiered at Theatre Royal Stratford East in May 2017, directed by Cora Bissett, before transferring to Dundee Rep Theatre and the Abbey Theatre, Dublin, the stage version splits Jack (in a manner recalling McCabe's bipartite hero in *Frank Pig Says Hello*) into a child and adult self, dividing his layered, witty and sharp-eyed apprehensions of the oppressive world in which he grows up between these aspects of himself. The casting of black actors in most of the main roles, except for the abusive Old Nick, also subtly shifted the social milieu of the text and the unspoken assumptions that it challenged. Furthermore, the play radically augmented the novel and Donoghue's film script by the addition of music composed by Cora Bissett. The objective was not to transform the text into a musical but to use the songs as parallel dimensions and alternative bodied spaces in which the unvoiced emotions of Jack and Ma could be articulated and communicated. While the actuality of the persistent assaults on Ma were rendered more palpable than in the novel, so too were the contours of Jack's innocent world, revealed by a revolving set as he hides in a wardrobe and blocks out what is happening.

The novel allows Ma's perspective to dominate in the second half after Jack and she escape from Room and intimates that, although mother and son remain together, they are lastingly damaged and will never integrate into social life. The play, by contrast, was more hopeful, partly because it gave credence to Jack's perspective throughout. Where in the novel his grandfather rejects Jack as misfit because he is produced by rape, he is won over and reconciled to him in the play. The joint visit by Ma and Jack to Room, which was due to be bulldozed, concludes the stage adaptation. It is a reprise that bears out that Jack has been ineradicably marked by his upbringing in confinement. But it is also suggested that Ma and Jack can turn their back on the sexual abuse to which they have been subjected and that their intimate bonds will carry them into an uncertain future. While they walk away towards freedom in the closing moments, a qualifying ambiguity is retained by the insights into the omnipresence of the sexual abuse of children and women conveyed throughout the play.

Gérard Genette has postulated that all texts are palimpsests and that adaptations only differ in the degree to which this is made manifest.[31] Literary adaptations on the contemporary Irish stage betray, in part, a conservative wish to cleave to classical works that are well known and trade on the cultural capital they represent. But, by and large, recent fictional adaptations have enabled writers, directors, designers and actors to make free with stage conventions and create physically engaging, affectively immersive and innovative performances. Notably, the texts that have been adapted are modernist and experimental and provide leeway for play with ideas of performativity and fictionality and notions of voice, character and the confessional self. Paradoxically, in many instances, given that many novels must necessarily be substantially cut and rearranged to be transposed onto the stage, the existence of originals—even ones as weighty as those by Joyce, Beckett and Flann O'Brien—have furthered the development of post-dramatic shows, freed of their text-based starting points. The readiness to adapt contemporary fictions by Patrick McCabe, Eimear McBride and Emma Donoghue, moreover, is testament to an increased confidence in the purchase, relevance and longevity of new work and of the value of persuading audiences of its resonance.

Notes

1. On debates about fidelity and infidelity in adaptations, see Rachel Carroll, ed., *Adaptation in Contemporary Culture: Textual Infidelities* (London: Continuum, 2009), 1–57 and David T. Johnson, "Adaptation and Fidelity", in *The Oxford Handbook of Adaptation Studies*, ed. Thomas Leitch (Oxford: Oxford University Press, 2017), 87–100.
2. On varying concepts of adaptation, see Timothy Corrigan, "Defining Adaptation", *The Oxford Handbook of Adaptation Studies*, 23–25.
3. Patrick McCabe, *The Butcher Boy* (London: Picador, 1992) and *The Dead School* (London: Picador, 1995); Emma Donoghue, *Room* (London: Picador, 2010).
4. *The Butcher Boy*, directed by Neil Jordan (1997, Warner Brothers); *Room*, directed by Lenny Abrahamson (2015, Element Pictures/Film4).
5. On adaptation as a form of repetition or return, see Margherita Laera, ed., *Theatre and Adaptation: Return, Rewrite, Repeat* (London: Bloomsbury, 2014), 1–10.
6. For a discussion of the underlying principles of Bertolt Brecht's drama, see Fredric Jameson, *Brecht and Method* (London: Verso, 1998).
7. Dermot Bolger, "Staging *Ulysses*: What impressed me most was also what scared me most", *The Irish Times*, October 27, 2012.
8. Dermot Bolger, *A Dublin Bloom* (Dublin: New Island Books, 1995).
9. *The Dead*, directed by John Huston (1987, Vestron).
10. Frank McGuinness, "Notes", James Joyce, *The Dead, A Dramatization by Frank McGuinness* (London: Faber, 2012), 7. All further references will be cited in parentheses.
11. For an account of the non-mimetic aesthetic principles informing Corn Exchange's productions, see "Annie Ryan and Michael West in Conversation with Luke Clancy", *Theatre Talk: Voices of Irish Theatre Practitioners*, ed. Lilian Chambers, Ger Fitzgibbon and Eamonn Jordan (Dublin: Carysfort Press, 2001), 424–31.
12. Carlo Mazzone-Clementi quoted by Avner Eisenberg, "Foreword", in *The Routledge Companion to Commedia dell'Arte*, ed. Judith Chaffee and Olly Crick (Abingdon: Routledge, 2015), xiii.
13. James Joyce to Grant Richards, 23 June 1906, *James Joyce, Letters, Volume 1*, ed. Stuart Gilbert (New York: Viking Press), 64.
14. Lenny Abrahamson, Programme, *Dubliners by James Joyce*, 5.
15. For an account of drama as scenic, corporeal and experiential, see Stanton B. Garner, Jr., *Bodied Spaces: Phenomenology and Performance in Contemporary Drama* (Ithaca: Cornell University Press, 1994).
16. On the genesis of *I'll Go On*, see Barry McGovern, "Practice in Focus: 'That's how it was and them were the days'", in *Staging Beckett in Ireland and Northern Ireland*, ed. Trish McTighe and David Tucker (London: Bloomsbury Methuen Drama, 2016), 23–38.
17. Dirk van Hulle, *Manuscript Genetics, Joyce's Know-How, Beckett's Nohow* (Gainesville: University of Florida Press, 2008), 117–23.
18. For an outline of Lecoq's philosophy of theatre, see Jacques Lecoq with Jean-Gabriel Carasso and Jean-Claude Lallias, *The Moving Body: Teaching Creative Theatre*, trans. David Bradby (London: Methuen, 2002).

19. For a counter-perspective, see Fintan O'Toole who argues that Conor Lovett is a "seanchaí unplugged", in "*The Beckett Trilogy*", *The Irish Times*, 18 May 2002.
20. Beckett wrote *Texts for Nothing* in the 1950s. See Samuel Beckett, *Texts for Nothing and Other Shorter Prose* (London: Faber and Faber, 2010).
21. For an analysis of nullity and the imaginary in *Texts for Nothing*, see Fintan O'Toole, "Given Up For Dead", Programme, *No's Knife*, 6–8. See Michael Billington's contrasting assessment of the painterly, non-theatrical nature of Dwan's adaptation, "*No's Knife* Review", *The Guardian*, 4 October 2016.
22. Anthony Cronin, *No Laughing Matter: The Life and Times of Flann O'Brien* (New York: Fromm International Publishing Company, 1998), vii–x.
23. For a history of the company and analysis of its performance principles, see Rhona Trench, *Blue Raincoat Theatre Company* (Dublin: Carysfort Press, 2015).
24. The novel was also adapted for cinema: *The Butcher Boy*, dir. by Neil Jordan (1997, Geffen Pictures, 1997).
25. *Frank Pig Says Hello* was published in *Far From the Land: Contemporary Irish Plays*, ed. John Fairleigh (London: Methuen, 1998), 238–307.
26. For a review of the 2002 revival of the play, see Fintan O'Toole, "*Frank Pig Says Hello*", *The Irish Times*, 1 November 2002.
27. Patrick McCabe, *The Dead School* (London: Picador, 2002).
28. Eimear McBride, *A Girl is a Half-Formed Thing, Adapted for the Stage by Annie Ryan* (London: Faber and Faber, 2015).
29. For an illuminating discussion of the dominance of monologue in contemporary Irish theatre and its connection to the demise of metanarratives and a new-found faith in the personal and confessional, see Eamonn Jordan, *Dissident Dramaturgies: Contemporary Irish Theatre* (Dublin: Irish Academic Press, 2010).
30. Emma Donoghue, *Room, Adapted for the Stage by Emma Donoghue* (London: Oberon Books, 2017).
31. Gérard Genette, *Palimpsests: Literature in the Second Degree*, trans. Channa Newman and Claude Doubinsky (Lincoln: University of Nebraska Press, 1997).

Bibliography

Beckett, Samuel. *Texts for Nothing and Other Shorter Prose*. London: Faber and Faber, 2010.

Billington, Michael. "*No's Knife* Review." *The Guardian*, October 4, 2016.

Bolger, Dermot. "Staging *Ulysses*: What Impressed Me Most Was Also What Scared Me Most." *The Irish Times*, October 27, 2012.

Carroll, Rachel, ed. *Adaptation in Contemporary Culture: Textual Infidelities*. London: Continuum, 2009.

Chaffee, Judith and Olly Crick, eds. *The Routledge Companion to Commedia dell'Arte*. Abingdon: Routledge, 2015.

Chambers, Lilian, Ger Fitzgibbon and Eamonn Jordan, eds. *Theatre Talk: Voices of Irish Theatre Practitioners*. Dublin: Carysfort Press, 2001.

Cronin, Anthony. *No Laughing Matter: The Life and Times of Flann O'Brien*. New York: Fromm International Publishing Company, 1998.

Donoghue, Emma. *Room*. London: Picador, 2010.

Fairleigh, John, ed. *Far From the Land: Contemporary Irish Plays*. London: Methuen, 1998.

Garner Jr Stanton B., *Bodied Spaces: Phenomenology and Performance in Contemporary Drama*. Ithaca: Cornell University Press, 1994.

Genette, Gérard. *Palimpsests: Literature in the Second Degree*. Translated by Channa Newman and Claude Doubinsky. Lincoln: University of Nebraska Press, 1997.

Gilbert, Stuart. *James Joyce, Letters, Volume 1*. New York: Viking Press.

Jameson, Fredric. *Brecht and Method*. London: Verso, 1998.

Jordan, Eamonn. *Dissident Dramaturgies: Contemporary Irish Theatre*. Dublin: Irish Academic Press, 2010.

Laera, Margherita, ed. *Theatre and Adaptation: Return, Rewrite, Repeat*. London: Bloomsbury, 2014.

Lecoq, Jacques with Jean-Gabriel Carasso and Jean-Claude Lallias. *The Moving Body: Teaching Creative Theatre*. Translated by David Bradby. London: Methuen, 2002.

Leitch, Thomas. *The Oxford Handbook of Adaptation Studies*. Oxford: Oxford University Press, 2017.

McCabe, Patrick. *The Butcher Boy*. London: Picador, 1992.

———. *The Dead School*. London: Picador, 1995.

McTighe, Trish and David Tucker, eds. *Staging Beckett in Ireland and Northern Ireland*. London: Bloomsbury Methuen Drama, 2016.

O'Toole, Fintan. "*Frank Pig Says Hello*." *The Irish Times*, November 1, 2002.

———. "Given Up For Dead", Programme, *No's Knife*.

———. "*The Beckett Trilogy*." *The Irish Times*, May 18, 2002.

Trench, Rhona. *Blue Raincoat Theatre Company*. Dublin: Carysfort Press, 2015.

van Hulle, Dirk. *Manuscript Genetics, Joyce's Know-How, Beckett's Nohow*. Gainesville: University of Florida Press, 2008.

Circuitous Pathways: Marina Carr's Labyrinth of Feminist Form in the US World Premiere of *Phaedra Backwards*

Melissa Sihra

Marina Carr's adaptation of the Phaedra/Hippolytus myth offers circuitous pathways which, like the legend of the Minotaur's labyrinth, open up a maze of feminist possibilities. *Phaedra Backwards* premiered at the McCarter Theatre, Princeton, on 18 October 2011 with a predominantly female production team. The multiple-frames of female *auteurship* offered an important act of resistance to the performance conditions of the originals. Emily Mann directed Carr's script with set-design by Rachel Hauck and costume by Anita Yavich and Stephanie Roth Haberle played the role of Phaedra. Carr's earlier Greek adaptations *Ariel* (Aeschylus' *Oresteia* 2002, Abbey Theatre) and *By the Bog of Cats*... (Euripides' *Medea* 1998, Abbey Theatre) pulsate with the rough intimacy of the rural Irish Midlands, while her more recent *Hecuba* (Swan Theatre, RSC, 2015) is situated in "the fragile Greek state circa 500 BC".[1]

The original Greek myth(s) tell the story of Queen Pasiphae who, married to King Minos of Knossos and mother to Phaedra and Ariadne, becomes infatuated with the White Bull. She seduces the White Bull by climbing inside a hollow wooden cow and becomes pregnant with the Minotaur—a half-bull, half-human child. The Minotaur is a kindly infant, but grows up with the untameable animalistic urge to eat humans and is banished to an elaborate underground maze called the Labyrinth at the palace at Crete. Ariadne marries Theseus but dies when he abandons her. Phaedra then marries Theseus, who slays the Minotaur and who already has a son called Hippolytus.

M. Sihra (✉)
Trinity College Dublin, Dublin, Ireland
e-mail: MSIHRA@tcd.ie

E. Jordan, E. Weitz (eds.), *The Palgrave Handbook of Contemporary Irish Theatre and Performance*,
https://doi.org/10.1057/978-1-137-58588-2_36

In the source-texts, such as Euripides' *Hippolytus* (Athens, *c.* 428 BC), Phaedra lustfully falls in love with her step-son Hippolytus, who rejects her and she kills herself. Carr inverts the Euripidean sexual politics in *Phaedra Backwards*, the idea of going backwards resonates through both the form and the content. *Phaedra Backwards* takes place in eternal time, poised somewhere on the brink of infinity; "*Now and Then. Then and Now. Always*".[2] In Carr's reimagined antiquity the ever-changing light is "*magical, from some dark fairy tale*" and an effect of epic distance is captured upon "*A stone terrace. A stone floor. The bay and the mountains surround this terrace*".[3] Carr modernizes the story with deliberate anachronism. Time-periods, costumes and props are mismatched to capture a faded decadence and austere grandiosity which includes champagne, mobile-phones, mechanical cows and a "*formerly good dining table, now a battered vestige of itself. Destroyed chairs. A lonely chaise longue*".[4]

Like Harold Pinter's *Betrayal*, Carr begins the story at the end and moves back in time to the beginning, presenting a fluid matrix of space and time.[5] The play opens with the announcement of Hippolytus' death and continues through past and present events up to the moments before Phaedra's death. A realignment of Aristotelian unities enables liberation from the constrictions of the "well-made play" and is central to Carr's dramaturgy in *The Mai* (1994) and *Portia Coughlan* (1996), where the deaths of the protagonists are revealed in the middle. Stephanie Roth Haberle observes how the effect of having the first scene as the end of the play "puts the dramatic tension into how the characters get there, and how the inevitable future changes them and their relationships".[6] Emily Mann develops the point: "The play is, of course, backwards in a variety of ways. For one, it starts at the end. But also, when one thinks about the Phaedra myth, one often thinks, 'Oh, that's about an older woman falling madly in love with a younger man.' And Marina turns that on its head. In *Phaedra Backwards*, it's the young man obsessed with the older woman."[7]

The stage-directions at the beginning reveal the centrality of "Time" to the meaning of the story, echoing the metaphysical concerns of Carr's earlier works where circularity, repetition and the presence of the past are key. Carr observes an awareness of lateral temporalities: "I believe we are of time, but also beyond it. [...] that [we] are both within it *and* outside of it";[8] "I have never believed that time is linear".[9] In Mann's production, the time-title "*Now and Then. Then and Now. Always*" was projected onto a screen at the beginning of the show, fading and rapidly followed by the words "*Once Upon a Time. The End*".[10] Phaedra then enters for the Prologue as evocative film footage from her childhood is played out on the screen behind her. Shot on location, the footage showed the child Phaedra, her sister Ariadne and her half-brother the horned infant Minotaur (these children later appear onstage). Moving perspex lines crossed over the cinematographic images enabling a shifting, sliding effect, which Jill Dolan observed as "multiplicit perceptual fields".[11]

Along with the fluid "*sound of the sea a constant score*", Carr breaks the boundaries of realism with the dual-protagonists Phaedra and the Minotaur.[12] We are told that, "*Two other scores inhabit the place. Phaedra's score and the Minotaur's*".[13] The double "score" manifests on stage through Phaedra's sensual awareness of the Minotaur's physical presence as he moves around her, though he is not seen by any other character. The Minotaur traverses through time and space, expressing an uncanny transhistoricity in his first line: "The Druids align. Dinosaurs in St. Paul's again. It is time. It is way past time."[14] Notions of plurality are embodied in this half-human half-bull who resembles the strangely aligned "*Picasso Minotaur drawings*".[15] He bursts forth onto the stage with bestial power: "*From a great distance. Ripping through a dimension.*"[16] In a highly physicalized performance, actor and choreographer Julio Monge's hybrid Minotaur oscillated between predatory animalistic urge and tenderness. His home, the Labyrinth, is a network of radical possibilities which poses a threat to the authority of Theseus. As a counter-patriarchal locus, the labyrinth embodies Sue Ellen Case's definition of feminist theatre as,

> elliptical rather than illustrative, fragmentary rather than whole, ambiguous rather than clear and interrupted rather than complete. This exists within the text and at its borders; the feminine form seems to be without a sense of formal closure—in fact it operates as anti-closure.[17]

This notion of "elliptical", incomplete sites without "formal closure" expresses the essence of both the labyrinth and the "feminine form" of Carr's adaptation.

Dominant interpretations of the Phaedra/Hippolytus legend have determined Theseus' slaying of the Minotaur as the birth of Western Civilization with the annihilation of barbarism. Carr's adaptation counter-proposes that Patriarchy is in fact the savage beast, where the death of the Minotaur is seen as "the beginning of the end".[18] "Yes, this is how I was sent into the world", laments the Minotaur, "All the nobility of the white bull. But unfortunately too in my mix, all the shadowy faculties of your race".[19] Monge observes, "The original myths and tales always look at the Minotaur from a dark perspective, the monster, the eater of people. But you see him here sort of being a guide on the path to light [...] he seems to me like a character full of light and truth".[20] The Minotaur embodies the infinite potential of the imagination. He is the soul-figure and enlightenment. Carr says, "*Phaedra Backwards* is about death. And it is also about dealing with mystery. It's about encountering things that are not comprehensible, and allowing them entry into your life".[21]

As an American world-premiere, *Phaedra Backwards* opens up issues regarding the signification of Irish theatre in international and intercultural contexts. *Phaedra Backwards* is the fourth of Carr's plays to premiere internationally and her first American world-premiere. *Woman and Scarecrow* first opened at the Royal Court, Jerwood Theatre (2006), with *The Cordelia Dream* (RSC, Wilton's

Theatre) and *Hecuba* in 2015 (RSC, Swan Theatre Stratford). Originating abroad with non-Irish artists, *Phaedra Backwards* does not address Irish cultural or political issues (this has been the only production of the text to date). The most "Irish" characteristic of this production was perhaps the framing of the playwright herself as an "authentic" embodiment of Hiberno-cultural-capital. Whilst *Phaedra Backwards* does not explore aspects of Irish life per se, the iconic presence of Marina Carr in Princeton offered a consolation of "Irishness" that was absent within the play. Tall, slender and soft-spoken with long black hair, white-skin and green eyes, Carr epitomizes the image of Dark Rosaleen—the *Roisin Dubh* who immortalizes ideal of Irish womanhood. This iconicity worked within and against the text, being in contrast to the explicit violence and sexuality of the production. Carr's "Irishness" was contextualized during the run within the location of Princeton University as a renowned international Centre for Irish Studies. Emily Mann writes in her Program Note:

> Dear Patrons,
>
> It brings me great joy to welcome you to the world premiere of Marina Carr's latest work, *Phaedra Backwards*. A storyteller cut from the same cloth as those poets who told the Phaedra myth thousands of years ago, Marina Carr has been dubbed by the Abbey Theatre (the national theatre of Ireland) as one of "Ireland's greats." Her plays have ignited imaginations on both sides of the Atlantic for their bold, theatrical and modern renderings of ancient tales.[22]

The predominantly white middle-class Princeton theatregoers were at times shocked by the graphic sexual and violent content of the piece, which was in contradistinction to the dreamy feminine artwork of the Program and the romantic framing of Carr as "one of Ireland's greats".[23] Along with the cultural validation of The Abbey Theatre, Mann's reference to "both sides of the Atlantic" situates Carr as an innate link between America and literary Ireland.[24] This resonates with the way in which Colin Graham describes Ireland as a signifier, "a floating, Atlantic Ireland [which is] more than an act of desperate exilic imagination. Detaching Ireland from its real place [enables] Ireland's dissipation into a plethora of images and its formation of itself as a fantasy island".[25] In *Phaedra Backwards*, Carr brings us to a place that is at once familiar and distant; past and present, and which, as a site of abstraction and fantasy, is much like anachronistic constructions of "Ireland" itself. Declan Kiberd denotes a similar, "Ireland of the *The Wizard of Oz* where 'there's no place like home,' an 'Ireland' which is a no-place utopia".[26] Even though *Phaedra Backwards* ostensibly has nothing to do with Ireland, it will always-already be "Irish" by virtue of the situatedness of the playwright. Kiberd observes how, "Even when Irish writers are writing about non-Irish themes, their work is re-nationalised abroad".[27] The ability, according to Mann, of Carr to "ignite imaginations" on both sides of the Atlantic makes for a valuable globalized exchange, where the cultural capital of Irishness becomes a way to promote and fund the production. Over the course of the eighteen months prior to opening, Carr participated in script workshops, artist and donor invitation-only rehearsed readings, post-show discussions, online interviews, "talk-back" discussions with Theatre and Performance Studies students at Princeton University and (unusually) gave a pre-show speech in the foyer of the theatre on the opening night in front of patrons, sponsors, donors and the press, accompanied by Leonard Milberg (the key benefactor of The Princeton University Fund for Irish Studies).

This was the first time that Carr's theatre had multicultural actors and accents in a premiere of one of her plays (as opposed to her "Irish" plays being produced in diverse accents). This diversity internationalized Carr's dramatic voice and opened up new political resonances, which facilitated the layering of realities inherent to the text. In *Phaedra Backwards* the Minotaur—bull-man and "monster" figure—is a visceral embodiment of intrinsic otherness; the familiar and the unknowable. As a Puerto Rican actor and choreographer, Julio Monge's ethnicity enabled a politicization of otherness and oppression within the context of the play. The degraded status of the outsider is central to Carr's work and the Minotaur expresses a key re-evaluation of the source text(s). Nanny, the Sappho-reciting old crone, senses the Minotaur's hovering presence as she brings coffee and bread rolls to the table:

Nanny:	I can't see you but I know you're near. *Minotaur sniffs her, circles her.*
Minotaur:	I bet you dream about me.
Nanny:	All women dream of the bull. [...] I said away with you. There is no place for you here.
Minotaur:	No and never was.[28]

Monge's Caribbean identity was a powerful politicization of the exilic figure. His sustained muscular tension between bull-like impulse and human restraint conveyed an enslaved, colonized or immigrant Other. Minos—brash American despot and patriarch—banishes him to the unfathomable recesses of the labyrinth; "He belongs in a shed or the open meadow or the last stall in some abattoir. [...] He's some evil growth from some horrific urn".[29] Ariadne assists Theseus in the slaying of the Minotaur: "It had to be done, no place here for that sort of manifestation".[30] It is Phaedra who cannot bear his annihilation: "Ever occur to you it's here is all wrong? Not him! No place for the impossible, the unreal, the unbelievable, just take a knife and cut out what lies under the maggoty stones no one dares turn".[31] With his marked difference, Monge's Minotaur brought the oppressed figure beyond the context of Irish culture more so than has occurred in any other productions of Carr's work.

Phaedra Backwards is written predominantly in Standard English and is epic in tone, but Carr's syntax and subtle use of Irish phrases lends a sedimented layer of Irishness to it. While the diversity of the actors' accents offered a new politicization to Carr's writing, undercurrents of Irishisms could be felt operating in traction with actors' accents during the production. While the syntax would be difficult to discern on a first viewing, the accents were at times at odds with the rhythm of language which metatheatrically underscored the sense of strategic anachronism. For example, when Pasiphae is waiting for the wooden cow to be built, she says to the Inventor, "You've me driven mad with the waiting", clearly displaying roots in Hiberno-English.[32] One of the few Irishisms can be identified when Aricia, Hippolytus' girlfriend, is complaining about Phaedra, "It's not fair such a wagon gets to live in such a place".[33] In the same scene, Phaedra says of Theseus, "My husband would like me to behave like an auld biddy at a tea party".[34] Phaedra later says to Aricia, "There isn't one square inch of earth or ocean floor that has not been flowered by corpses. That cedar perfume you're wearing this evening was decanted from your great-grandfather's arse".[35]

Re-nationalizing *Phaedra Backwards* is perhaps a forgone conclusion when presented within the environs of Princeton University. As a Centre for Irish Studies, Princeton reverberates with an awareness of the legacies of Irish emigration, colonization, the Great Famine, diasporic displacement, the painful processes of decolonization and the anxieties of the post-colonial condition. Palpitating beneath the Classical Greek frame of the play are further possible Irish nodal points, particularly in the idea of the eternal return of the dead. In Carr's plays, as in Irish theatre and culture, the dead are a barely suppressed energy simmering beneath mundane reality, embodying an unresolved history. *Phaedra Backwards* begins at the end of the tale and sifts through Phaedra's memory and experience, confronting a violent past in order to make sense of what Mann calls "the crumbling present".[36] The fractured and subjective operation of memory is central to the work, and is also a key theme in modern Irish drama, such as the work of Brian Friel, where an exploration of memory's inability to restore and recuperate is ever-present. The fissured screen of perceptual fields marks the aporia inherent to the always unresolved act of remembering. Loss, of course, is central to the act of remembering and resonances of death and violence serve as metaphors for the effects of loss that are central to Irish history.

As a treatment of the shaping of our histories through the fractured lenses of the past, *Phaedra Backwards* is nostalgic in terms of *nostos*—the desire to "return home"—and *algos*—"pain". Kiberd observes how "Ireland is a Revival-myth and a discursive entity which is always about to disappear".[37] The play resonates interculturally as a symbolic enactment of the displaced diasporic subject who is always already "at a loss"—painfully negotiating an irretrievable notion of "homeland". Perhaps "Ireland" itself is a labyrinth, a projected locus of fantasy whose network of infinite signification is "without a sense of formal closure".[38] Many of Carr's plays express the need for female subjectivity, where a quest for the literal and figurative consolation of home is articulated. In scene 4 Phaedra says to Minotaur:

> We wanted to see our one-time home, this bay, these cliffs, so we climbed a hill of stone, searching the horizon as night came on. Then, there it was, the sweetest

orb and we longed to return until we realised we were looking at the sun and would never see the earth again.[39]

Centring upon Phaedra's attempts to resolve the violence of her past and to access self-determinacy, the play can be seen as a new mode of feminist storytelling through which to claim a site of origins and mythology for women and the Other in Classical Greek mythology through Irish and intercultural contexts.

Notes

1. Marina Carr, *Marina Carr: Plays Three* (London: Faber & Faber, 2015), x.
2. *Phaedra Backwards*, in *Marina Carr: Plays Three*, 75.
3. Ibid.
4. Ibid.
5. Carr referred to *Phaedra Backwards* as "feminist" in her "John McGahern Annual Lecture", St. Patrick's College, Drumcondra, June 2014. Unpublished.
6. Stephanie Roth Haberle, 'Why Phaedra Backwards?' Program Notes, *Phaedra Backwards*, Matthews Theatre, McCarter Theatre Center, Princeton, 18 October–6 November, 2011.
7. Emily Mann, "Why Phaedra Backwards?" Program Notes, *Phaedra Backwards*, Matthews Theatre, McCarter Theatre Center, Princeton, 18 October–6 November, 2011.
8. "Marina Carr in Conversation with Melissa Sihra", in *Theatre Talk: Voices of Irish Theatre Practitioners*, eds. Eamonn Jordan, Lilian Chambers and Ger Fitzgibbon (Dublin: Carysfort Press, 2001), 57.
9. Ibid.
10. Projected onto back screen in Production. *Phaedra Backwards*, in *Marina Carr: Plays Three*, 75.
11. Jill Dolan in Conversation with Melissa Sihra, Unpublished, McCarter Theatre, Princeton 15 October 2011. Dolan is the Annan Professor in English and Professor of Theater in the Lewis Center for the Arts at Princeton University.
12. *Phaedra Backwards*, in *Marina Carr: Plays Three*, 75.
13. Ibid.
14. Ibid., 97.
15. Ibid., 84.
16. Ibid.
17. Sue-Ellen Case, *Feminism and Theatre* (New York: Palgrave Macmillan, 1988), 129.
18. "The Beginning of the End", was projected onto the back screen at the beginning of Scene Three which is the first entrance of the Minotaur.
19. Marina Carr, *Phaedra Backwards* (Princeton: *In an Hour Book*, 2011), 38.
20. Julio Monge, "Why Phaedra Backwards?" Program Notes, *Phaedra Backwards*, Matthews Theatre, McCarter Theatre Center, Princeton, 18 October–6 November, 2011.
21. Marina Carr, "Why Phaedra Backwards?" Program Notes, *Phaedra Backwards*, Matthews Theatre, McCarter Theatre Center, Princeton, 18 October–6 November, 2011.

22. Emily Mann, "Note from the Artistic Director", Program, *Phaedra Backwards*, Matthews Theatre, McCarter Theatre Center, Princeton, 18 October–6 November, 2011.
23. Ibid.
24. Ibid.
25. Colin Graham, *Deconstructing Ireland: Identity, Theory, Culture* (Edinburgh: Edinburgh University Press, 2001), 4–5.
26. Declan Kiberd, "Towards a New Irish Studies", Panel Discussion, Making Ireland Research Theme, The Long Room Hub, Trinity College Dublin, 18 April 2017. Unpublished.
27. Ibid.
28. Carr, *Phaedra Backwards*, 38–39. The poetry of Sappho is not written into Carr's play, but in the production the Nanny recited Sappho as she went about her household chores.
29. Ibid., 52–53.
30. Ibid.
31. Ibid.
32. Ibid, 8.
33. Ibid., 14.
34. Ibid., 22.
35. Ibid., 24.
36. Mann, "Why Phaedra Backwards?"
37. Kiberd, "Towards a New Irish Studies".
38. Sue-Ellen Case, *Feminism and Theatre* (New York: Palgrave Macmillan, 1988), 129.
39. Carr, *Phaedra Backwards*, 31.

Bibliography

Carr, Marina. *Phaedra Backwards*. Princeton: *In an Hour Book*, 2011.

———. "Why Phaedra Backwards?" Program Notes, *Phaedra Backwards*. Matthews Theatre, McCarter Theatre Center, Princeton. October 18–November 6, 2011.

———. "John McGahern Annual Lecture." St. Patrick's College, Drumcondra, June 2014. Unpublished.

———. *Marina Carr: Plays Three*. London: Faber & Faber, 2015.

Case, Sue-Ellen. *Feminism and Theatre*. New York: Palgrave Macmillan, 1988.

Dolan, Jill in Conversation with Melissa Sihra. Unpublished. McCarter Theatre, Princeton 15 October 2011.

Graham, Colin. *Deconstructing Ireland: Identity, Theory, Culture*. Edinburgh: Edinburgh University Press, 2001.

Kiberd, Declan. "Towards a New Irish Studies." Panel Discussion. Making Ireland Research Theme. The Long Room Hub, Trinity College Dublin. 18 April 2017. Unpublished.

Mann, Emily. "Note from the Artistic Director." Program, *Phaedra Backwards*. Matthews Theatre, McCarter Theatre Center, Princeton. October 18–November 6, 2011.

Mann, Emily. "Why Phaedra Backwards?" Program Notes, *Phaedra Backwards*. Matthews Theatre, McCarter Theatre Center, Princeton. October 18–November 6, 2011.

Monge, Julio. "Why Phaedra Backwards?" Program Notes, *Phaedra Backwards*. Matthews Theatre, McCarter Theatre Center, Princeton. October 18–November 6, 2011.

Roth Haberle, Stephanie. "Why Phaedra Backwards?" Program Notes, *Phaedra Backwards*. Matthews Theatre, McCarter Theatre Center, Princeton. October 18–November 6, 2011.

Sihra, Melissa. "Marina Carr in Conversation with Melissa Sihra." in *Theatre Talk: Voices of Irish Theatre Practitioners*, edited by Eamonn Jordan, Lilian Chambers & Ger Fitzgibbon. Dublin: Carysfort Press, 2001.

Being Intercultural in Irish Theatre and Performance

Cathy Leeney

In 1994, a co-operatively written performance entitled *True Lines* was produced by Bickerstaffe (the Kilkenny theatre company) and was later staged as part of the Dublin Theatre Festival. Its representation of Irish people abroad in the world and moving foot loosely through it surprised many reviewers, and this spectator. For the first time, I saw on stage a different experience of Irish migrants, a way of living beyond national identity identifiable to many young Irish, who entered into a situation of global liberty and risk just as a period of economic boom and social change was gathering momentum at home. What was not fully anticipated at the time was that Ireland would not, for much longer, be a country characterized by emigration—whether for economic or lifestyle reasons—but one of immigration, receiving new populations from Europe, Africa and Asia at unprecedented levels. Between the identity refuge of nation and ethnic solidarity, and the globalized, post-modern demands of neo-liberal fluidity and precarity, migrants, in hope, look for better lives. And some want to make theatre. What follows is a survey of some ways that this change has influenced Irish theatre and performance practices, and how selected dedicated individuals have worked to break open the artistic and thematic isolation of Irish theatre.

This chapter owes a significant debt to Charlotte McIvor and Matthew Spanglers' *Staging Intercultural Ireland*, an enterprising and inspiring book of essays, interviews and plays about intercultural Ireland and its theatre. I will try here, however, to use a different perspective. Although including some of the companies and practitioners that McIvor and Spangler deal with, I aim to con-

C. Leeney (✉)
University College Dublin, Dublin, Ireland
e-mail: catherine.leeney@ucd.ie

E. Jordan, E. Weitz (eds.), *The Palgrave Handbook of Contemporary Irish Theatre and Performance*,
https://doi.org/10.1057/978-1-137-58588-2_37

sider the processes of preparing performance as a potentially key site of interculturality, to argue that collaborative process and participation in performance defines intercultural value. I will, briefly, link this notion of process with examples of non-theatrical performances. I am looking at three aspects of how theatre has changed due to newly diverse residents in Ireland: how the theme of interculturalism has been staged in a range of examples, and how inward migration has been linked with issues of social justice in theatre; how theatrical and performance modes and traditions from other countries may have impacted on the aesthetic of Irish theatre; and finally the question: what might be the most intercultural practices in making theatre and performance, practices that may benefit social and theatrical pluralism for individuals and society in general? Put simply, does interculturalism illustrate that culture is something we do, not something we have?

Culture and Interculture: The Irish Context

When indigenous professional theatre in Ireland took off in the early years of the twentieth century, playwrights and theatremakers sought inspiration in plays and practices in Europe and beyond. Augusta Gregory translated commedia dell'arte plays by Goldoni and Molière for the Abbey stage. With the aim of engaging audiences through a to-and-fro movement between empathy, and meditative distanced trance, W.B. Yeats explored Japanese Nôh Theatre conventions, employing selected staging elements from Nôh tradition to frame Irish mythic narratives. Both Yeats and Gregory were attracted, whether in commedia dell'arte or in Nôh traditions, to an emphasis on the body and choreographic movement working alongside dialogue to foreground archetypal narratives and characters in preference to realist psychology and materialism.

But can these influences be described as intercultural? Arguably they are better categorized as cultural appropriations, which are an integral part of artistic practice, and which won wider and enhanced cultural status for the Irish myths of Yeats's plays, and for the Hiberno-English idiom of Gregory's. Critic Michael Cronin asserts that such translations "would radically alter the destiny of Irish literature in the English language in the twentieth century".[1] Yeats's adaptations of Nôh theatre elements, and his collaboration in London with Michio Ito, whose dance style inspired the poet to write *At the Hawk's Well* (1916), was actually more connected with the European dance avant garde at the time. Ito had trained at the Dalcroze Institute, and had been inspired by Isadora Duncan, Edward Gordon Craig and Adolphe Appia. Notwithstanding Cronin's argument, that translation of classic plays brought kudos to the cultural status of Irish theatre, Yeats's fascination with the theatre spaces of Craig, and the dance practices of Ito and Ninette de Valois satisfied his instinct that the moving body in space is a key generator of theatrical meaning that superseded realist theatrical styles.

"Magpie" modes of intercultural reference enlivened the developing Irish stage, but in the early period of the Irish cultural renaissance, nation and theatrical performance were directly linked. The stage was a laboratory for the creation of a distinct Irish identity. Influences from abroad, whether literary, stylistic or performative were, in general, firmly brought into service as they added value to the main aim: exploration, celebration, elaboration and interrogation of Irishness.

The playwright most controversially positioned in relation to theatre's mirror function in creating identities, is J.M. Synge. His plays for the Irish National Dramatic Company and then at the Abbey Theatre are, at one level, profoundly local in their representations of situations and idiom drawn from Irish cultural practices and social conditions. Yet, these same plays have taken on a new life in relation to intercultural Ireland, and in post-colonial and postmodern stagings, they have yielded up intercultural possibilities that illustrate the paradoxical link between the local and the global.

Ireland's post-colonial history provides a meaningful link with other parts of the world that are engaged in the complex process of throwing off oppression and negotiating the trap of repeating colonial hierarchies under a new flag, not to mention idealizing the trappings of new nationhood. Several productions of *The Playboy of the Western World* (1907) that will be examined here, illustrate the play's openness as a site for intercultural representation, tested through translation in the broadest sense, against intercultural social realities, within Ireland and internationally. *Riders to the Sea* (1904), Synge's threnodic ritual one act, has, too, revealed itself as richly enabling of intercultural collaborative process.[2]

Theory of Making Intercultural Performance

Patrice Pavis has examined issues of theatrical practices across cultures. He describes how a source culture is modelled, both culturally and artistically, for presentation to a target audience. How Peter Brook and his collaborators re-sculpted the classic Indian epic poem *The Mahabharata* for presentation to a West European audience is one controversial example.[3] Pavis's analytical model for intercultural mise-en-scène takes the shape of an hour-glass, made up of a "cascade of interventions", through which the source (text, narrative) is processed, and then received by the target spectators.[4] At the top of the hour-glass is the beginning of the production process, and as the form takes shape, each stage of cultural intervention is noted in intercultural terms. Stages of cultural modelling include, for example, the interventions of author(s), translator, director, designer, performer, choreographer, and finally, audience. The pressures exerted in the process itself are eloquently expressed through the narrowing central passage of the hour-glass, opening out towards performance for a live audience.

Pavis recognizes at each point how cultural power validates the artistic modelling of the resultant staging and reception. In this way, the history of cultural power between nations, cultures or regions impacts on how the performance represents the source culture, and how audiences (the "target") receive and accept the performance. As a post-colonized society, Ireland occupies an historically subordinate cultural position, which is potentially a "salutary reminder of the persistent neo-colonial relations with the 'new' world order".[5] However, Ireland's aspirational first-world status is signalled by its membership of the EU, its economic success over the years between the twentieth century and the twenty-first, and its new role as a destination for migrants. This complicates the country's attitudes to cultural plurality. Increasingly globalized, Irish national culture is challenged to investigate "who are the new historical subjects that remain unrepresented?"[6]

Changes in population through migration into Ireland brought interculturality into relative prominence in theatre and performance.[7] Irish society in general is being renewed in fundamental ways due to significant displacement of people through war, inequality and climate change. These changes are likely to continue and grow. How theatre has kept up with, reflected, and impacted on these societal changes is an open question nested in the wider question of how theatre and performance, in general, catalyzes change in social behaviours and values. The modest flourishing of intercultural collaborative work in the period known as the Celtic Tiger was followed by a collapse of arts and culture funding after 2008. This decimated the intercultural theatre scene. The productions and companies discussed here comprise, necessarily, a severely limited sample, are largely Dublin centred, but serve to illustrate ways of assessing interculturality in performance that may connect with experiences elsewhere in Ireland.

The extent to which Irish theatre has ceased interrogating its post-colonial condition, and switched to a focus on a first-world, postmodern condition is reflected in the marginal positioning of much intercultural practice that confronts the identity and value issues arising from inward migration. Calling the Irish "the blacks of Europe" is no longer a convincing identifier of shared oppression, if it ever was. This chapter explores and critiques how theatre and, to a lesser extent, performance outside theatres, may be intercultural in its themes, in its modes of theatricality, and in its processes of creation, including the final collaborator, the audience.

Intercultural Performance: Social Aims

Definitions of interculturalism are many and contested. I have chosen to distinguish a number of ways of thinking about defining its presence in theatre and performance since the impact of global mobility on Ireland. Do we identify intercultural performance through its theme, its aesthetic, its process? Intercultural theatre is often an aspect of theatre that pushes for social change more broadly, it highlights where racial and ethnic division is intertwined with class, gender and economic division and where these become manifest in access to power, and social justice. How does interculturality crisscross with categories of economic class?[8] Companies such as Calypso Theatre Company

(1993–2008), Arambe Productions (2003–present) and Camino de Arula (2007–2016) have created performances that challenge audiences to reflect on their own attitudes to racial and cultural otherness, often contextualizing representations in social and economic reality. This approach recognizes the commonality of interests between, for example, Travellers and immigrants through their shared "outsider" status and consequent disempowerment. Camino de Arula's staging of Athol Fugard's *Sizwe Bansi is Dead* (1972) was "a complex combination of Fugard's [South African apartheid] play and visual references to the experiences of Travellers and poor Irish people, and the racialization of migrants and asylum seekers".[9] The mission of Camino de Arula was explicitly to showcase African theatre, while addressing Irish social issues. Both Camino de Arula and Arambe were established by Nigerian-Irish theatre makers: Kunle Animashaun and Bisi Adigun respectively. Arambe initiated performance opportunities for African-Irish theatre practitioners; from 2003 the company produced work by West African playwrights (including Adigun) and Irish plays featuring black performers.[10] Characterized by Nigerian performance conventions and their re-invention by internationally renowned playwrights—such as Wole Soyinka, Ama Ata Aidoo and Ola Rotimi—this theatre serves ritual, religious, and social purposes, making it inherently political in its relation of discourses on society and the circulation of power.[11] Bisi Adigun directed Rotimi's *The Gods Are Not to Blame* (1968) in 2004, and went on to write, amongst many plays, *Once Upon a Time* and *Not So Long Ago* (2006), which feature unfamiliar (to Irish audiences) stagings centred on ensemble, music, singing and rhythmic language, with elements of Brechtian Lerhstücke. Each "sketch" unpacks a specific experience of racialization, or conflict of cultural values. The play interrogates integration, power and interculturalism across categories such as gender, class and hybrid identity. This style of theatre has long been undervalued in the Irish context, which foregrounds literary quality. The power of performance to raise consciousness about conflicts of social interest and to critique material, everyday issues is widely dismissed as not being the function of theatre. Arambe is perhaps best known for its co-production with the Abbey Theatre of a version of Synge's *Playboy of the Western World* in 2008; this will be discussed later. According to critic Jason King, the "most successful intercultural production" is not Adigun and Doyle's *Playboy*, but *The Paddies of Parnell Street* (2013), Adigun's transposed version of Jimmy Murphy's *The Kings of the Kilburn High Road*. King argues in favour of *Paddies* as a winning re-appropriation of Murphy's vivid drama of Irish migrant labour in London, tellingly transferred to contemporary Dublin's inner city. Adigun began in 2006 by staging "an interpretation of Murphy's play with an all-West African cast, and then went on to adapt the storyline for a Lagos production in 2010, entitled *Home, Sweet Home*, set in present-day London".[12] These initiatives place Adigun and Arambe Productions at the forefront of a sustained challenge to parochialism in Irish theatre, and its cultural self-absorption, and racially limited casting practices.

Participation and Collaboration: Intercultural Processes

From its founding in 1993, until 2008 when it lost its Arts Council funding, Calypso Theatre Company's work has been influential in changing the aesthetic of theatre that has a socio-political role, and finding stimulating, entertaining and engaging ways to make work and involve audiences. With *Asylum! Asylum!* (1994) Donal O'Kelly predicted how enforcement of an EU "fortress Europe" policy might play out in the lives of an Irish family when they encounter Joseph Omara, an asylum seeker from Uganda. The family is divided in their attitudes towards Joseph's situation. In Fintan O'Toole's *Irish Times* review, he sees the play as caught between the tendency "to equate 'issues' with naturalism" and the "moments of strangeness when deep memories of home, of torture and of alienation are expressed to powerful effect".[13] A revival of the play in Cork in 1997, directed by Victor Merriman, was criticized by critic Mary Leland as tilted towards polemic. Leland overlooked the formal complexity of O'Kelly's text. Brian Singleton, although acknowledging the form of the play as realist, unpacks how it is also metaphorical: the Irish family serves as an image of conflicting attitudes to inward migration, and how assumptions about Irishness will be disrupted and inevitably changed.[14] Many critical responses to the production revealed a negative sensitivity to "issues" in Irish theatre, however they are presented.

Calypso's participation in the Féile Fáilte parade in 1997, *Farawayan* (1998), and ongoing seminars, debates and workshops, illustrates their awareness that engagement with audiences needs to go far beyond the limits of performances in theatres. Roddy Doyle's *Guess Who's Coming for the Dinner?* (2001) succeeded in widening Calypso's audience beyond "the converted". The predominantly televisual style of the piece featured a family typical of the sitcom genre, headed by a stereotypical patriarch, Larry Linnane (expertly played by Gary Cooke). Theatrical elements in Bairbre Ní Chaoimh's direction were overwhelmed by the play's easy humour. To reassure those worried by a no less than saintly Nigerian immigrant's threat to Larry's sense of his authority over the family (read nation), Ben, the asylum seeker, finally makes a definitive exit from the play and from Larry's life. Larry has, as it were, the last word, and the "other", or stranger, is theatrically erased.

As inward migration became more visible in Irish society, Calypso had a growing awareness of all the artistic talent within the new minority ethnic communities for which there was no suitable outlet.[15] The Tower of Babel (2002) programme integrated members of new communities and separated minors who were living in Dublin hostels into a range of creative activities. Workshops, film-making, and devised performances led to its showcase production *Mixing It on the Mountain*, written by Maeve Ingoldsby.[16] With its base in participative and collaborative actions, projects and networks, the production moved the work of Calypso to a new level of sophistication in intercultural terms. The company's explorations of experiences of migration, exile and disempowerment were no longer merely the theme of the production; the process itself functioned as an active interrogation and undoing of segregation and conflict. Music and dance were central to the aesthetic of the mise-en-scène. Dialogue was in numerous languages, untranslated. The aesthetic of performance was collaborative, festive, and emphasized the empowerment of the participants, including audiences. In her analysis of the work of the company, Julie Shearer judged *Mixing It on the Mountain* to have had "the most dramatic social impact in practical terms" due to its participative making and performative style.[17]

Over the life of the company, Calypso's concern with power in society, through its investigation of an international range of writing for the stage, developed into cultural and theatre practices that empowered those involved. Their awareness of cultural modelling—reminding Irish audiences of their inheritance of migration in the (ongoing) Irish diaspora—developed to connect experiences of powerlessness across national, cultural and historical boundaries. Through crisscrossing Patrice Pavis's ideas of source and target cultures, Calypso achieved a coherent investigation of performance for a live audience as an integrative process.[18]

A significant strand of intercultural awareness has developed through participatory events that are cultural and performative in broad terms, and are organized by individuals or groups with a shared national identity. One example, "Experience Japan", takes place at Farmleigh House in North West Dublin and is supported by the Integration Office of Dublin City Council, the Office of Public Works and the Japanese Embassy. The artistic and performance components of this event are curated and co-ordinated by Nobuko Ijichi. Since its initiation in 2011, the day-long event has been modelled on Japanese Matsuri, local festivals that are often collaboratively organized and that include food, entertainment, games, music and dance.[19] Many Matsuri in Japan take place in late summer or autumn, marking the rice harvest. "Experience Japan" attracts large numbers of visitors, and the emphasis is on participation in activities such as martial arts, animé film-making, traditional crafts, eating, drumming, calligraphy and so on. Ijichi believes that the participatory activities are the most valuable in intercultural terms, and are the most popular.[20] She aims to include, each year, images and practices that reflect Irish/Japanese cultural integration, leading non-Japanese visitors to connect Japanese with familiar forms. The Polish, African and Chinese communities in Ireland also hold annual festival events. The Irish Refugee Council's "Our Table" programme "creates a space where food breaks down barriers, and people feel connected" (www.ourtable.ie). In 2016, "Our Table" took place at Dublin's Project Arts Centre, where participants presented dishes from a range of countries and culinary traditions. The issue of food and cultural identity is acute in the Irish context, as residents in Direct Provision Centres are not allowed to cook for themselves. This impacts deeply on family and cultural life and a rich resource of food knowledge and cooking skills, usually passed from parent to child, is lost (www.irishrefugeecouncil.ie). Such performative celebrations of identity, drawing active participation and blurring the boundary between creators and audiences, are an intercultural challenge to the passivity of more mainstream theatrical performance.

Venues and Target Audiences

The location of intercultural performance speaks of tendencies to marginalize what is not familiar and validated as "Irish". Calypso's venue record varies, for example, from the mainstream Abbey, Ireland's national theatre (*Asylum, Asylum!*, albeit in the smaller Peacock Theatre), Andrew's Lane (closed in 2007) and the Samuel Beckett Theatre, to unconventional spaces such as the Olympic Ballroom. This move towards alternative spaces reflects the company's developing strategies in reaching different audiences. Project Arts Centre has had a significant role in staging the work of companies founded by new Irish practitioners. As venues often define audiences and cultural kudos, it is worth noting that performances involving non-Irish casts or theatrical styles have a history of being on the margins. Outside of the exceptional cases of touring productions in Festivals (Dublin Theatre Festival and Fringe Festival), access to main stages has been rare. In 2006, Dublin playwright Paul Mercier wrote and directed *Homeland* on the Abbey Theatre stage. It was ambitious in its attempt to capture the ethnically changing face of the capital's streets; the cast and production teams nonetheless were Irish, and, while Mercier's dynamic staging communicated the alienation of "new Irish", its point of view remained firmly at home base, with mythical Oisín transposed into an Irish entrepreneur, Niamh as a phoney in a blonde wig, and Tír na nÓg as an advertising falsehood.[21]

The failure of the Abbey Theatre up to 2007 to recognize inward migration as a challenge to its role as a national cultural institution, was retrieved when Bisi Adigun and Roddy Doyle collaborated in re-writing J.M. Synge's *The Playboy of the Western World*, staged with huge success in 2007 and 2008/9. This playboy, Christopher Malomo, was a Nigerian asylum seeker in West Dublin. The premise was drawn from Adigun's idea that asylum seekers, like Synge's anti-hero, arrive bearing a story to justify, and ideally enhance, their reception. Synge's ironic analysis of attraction towards otherness, that ends in bitter rejection, was presented in contemporary societal terms. The version grew from the question of "how the relations between a refugee and a host community could hinge upon conflicting interpretations of heroism and victimhood".[22] In Synge's original, father and son leave the stage to live "a romping lifetime";[23] Adigun and Doyle's father and son exit surely with far more precarity, into a tenuous image of global patriarchal adventure. The co-writers replaced Pegeen's final famous lament at her loss, with the expletive "F*** off". Such was the comic and emotional momentum of the performance at that point however, that the target of her violence, so directly expressed, was ambiguous, and scarcely allowed to resonate fully in racial terms: is Pegeen addressing her disdain towards Christopher (and his undead father) or the dysfunctional family and community structures that confine her, or both? The performance held in suspension possible racist meanings with Pegeen's critique of gender oppression in Irish communities.

At the stage of transposing Synge' play, Adigun asserts that "the process of writing" with Doyle was a "genuinely intercultural collaboration".[24] To link this comment with Pavis's terms—cultural and artistic modelling of two source cultures—the Nigerian and Irish elements were brought into relation through Christy's metamorphosis into Christopher Malomo.[25] How later phases of production however, projected "ways of thinking, schemas and categories onto the [Irish] target culture" shifted the emphasis.[26] The National Theatre staging of the production positioned it powerfully in cultural terms. Its attraction for sell-out audiences was significantly enhanced by Doyle's involvement, as a popular chronicler of working class Dublin life. Both the dramatic space of the production (West Dublin) and the theatrical space, the Abbey main stage, supported the weighting of the values of the target culture. How the project failed to capitalize fully on its initial success, and its potential to present, internationally, a contemporary image of race issues and immigration in Ireland, arose through a dispute between Adigun and the Abbey's handling of his rights as co-author, a lose-lose intercultural result.[27] In its reading of Christy's "gallous story" as a migrant's strategy to gain asylum,[28] Adigun's concept for his and Doyle's transposition is brilliant, even as it works to entertain Irish audiences with the dark comedy of their own power to mythologize or reject.

More Synge and Intercultural Performance

Synge's plays have attracted attention as sites for intercultural transfer and exchange, seeming to exemplify the paradox of the local as a ground for global connection. Angela Bourke notes "the meticulousness of his [Synge's] ethnographic scholarship" in his observations of human behaviour and ritual,[29] while his use of Hiberno-English in the mouths of his characters is simultaneously an artifice and an echo of heard speech.[30] Synge's dramas have been transposed into West Indian and Ugandan contexts, and into a contemporary Chinese environment as a project of Pan Pan Theatre. The role of the translator across cultures is described by David Johnston as "cultural enablement".[31] Related to performance (as opposed to text solely) the phrase resonates with the complexity of cultural modelling that Patrice Pavis theorizes.[32] Johnston demands that "all necessary extratextual information or informing intratextual assumptions" are attended to, in order that the play be "experienced organically".[33] But even allowing for such a process of linguistic mediation, the collaborative processes of casting, rehearsal, production and reception may at least modify, if not overtake, textual transposition. Pavis's "hour-glass" model of intercultural mise-en-scène suggests up to eight distinct processes of cultural intervention or modelling occur between sources and targets—that is to say between text and translator/designer/director—before that between performer and audience, emphasizing how contests of cultural power are activated in each process.

Pan Pan's *Playboy* premiered in Beijing in 2006 as one half of an intercultural Sino-Irish project that was funded in part by Culture Ireland. Less commented on by Irish critics was the part of the project comprising a play authored by Sun Yue and Wang Zhaohui. *Fight the Landlord* concerned the issue of housing in contemporary China, a topic hugely relevant to Ireland. As a two-part project, Pan Pan's approach was contiguous with the company's record in artistic liaison and collaboration with European and world theatremakers over several decades; Pan Pan's Irish-based work evidences awareness of post-national, postmodern performance aims and styles. However, by isolating the *Playboy* performance, several interesting issues of cultural power arise. Subsequent to the Beijing staging, later in 2006, the production travelled home (in Syngian terms) and away (for the all-Chinese cast) to Project Arts Centre in Dublin.

Textual, mise-en-scène and reception processes in the performance showed how this *Playboy* exemplified the problematics of interculturalism. Was this amongst the aims of Pan Pan and director Gavin Quinn? If so, then Sara Keating's analysis is insightful: the critic evaluates how the Dublin staging "created a sort of double vision in which the text and performance competed with each other rather than acting as complementary forces". The performance, then, was a significant cross-cultural achievement. Keating goes on to describe its "suspended duality", which points towards a consciousness of intercultural impossibility.[34]

The willingness of the production to refuse an appearance of theatrical/cultural integration was compromised though, where Quinn's defining role as Irish director, arguably, threw the power dynamics out of kilter. Quinn adapted Synge's text; this was then translated by Sun Yue into Mandarin urban argot. Quinn chose to situate the action in a "whore dressers", a hair salon that acts as a front for the purchase of sex. The translator Sun felt that the production expressed China as seen from a Western point of view,[35] emphasizing the outsider's perception of otherness as commodity. Through his choices, Quinn collapsed the meaning of Pegeen's and the Widow Quin's desire, into an objectification of the body in commercial exchange. Critic Shaun Richards remarks that "[A]n issue which clearly engaged Synge is the denial of desire"; it is interesting that, to different degrees, neither Adigun/Doyle's nor Pan Pan's versions of Pegeen and the Widow Quin risk female embodiments of frank sexual desire that resists market evaluation. Synge's vision of a possible counter-femininity, visible as jouissance or joy in the body,[36] in the text of the play, which dogged *The Playboy*'s first production, still seems to be a source of anxiety in the twenty-first century. In the context of intercultural performance, however, the issue of the sexualization of the racially "other" body, regardless of gender, is a recognized node in the arsenal of racism's fearful depersonalization.[37] In a historical switchback of *Playboy*'s record, Chinese audiences had concerns with the context of the action and with the costuming of some of the performers. Police from the cultural ministry attended, but no official censorship was imposed.[38] This situates the Chinese view as stuck in the past, since it parallels the well-known Abbey audience response to the premiere of the play in 1907. In interview with Sara Keating, Quinn, the director, explained that he was careful to avoid invoking religious controversy; references to Christy's Islamic identity were removed, as it was thought too controversial that Christy (Cheng Junnian), played by Ma Shang, came from north-East China and was half Chinese, half Russian.[39]

In terms of its mise-en-scène and reception in Ireland, the Pan Pan *Playboy* was a prestigious success for the company. Aedín Cosgrove's design incorporated self-conscious elements in the staging, including live video images on stage of performers preparing in their dressing rooms, mirrored reflections of the audience, and use of direct address. These moved the audience's experience towards self-aware participation. But these impacts may have been masked by an imbalance in what Emer O'Toole describes as Pan Pan's gain in cultural capital in the project, a gain that was not equally shared by their Chinese partners.[40] Translator Sun Yue and Wang Zhaohui earned more creative agency in *Fight the Landlord*, the follow-up play in the partnership, but this did not travel to Ireland, and saved Irish audiences from the challenge of extending their theatrical interest beyond recognizing the appeal of Synge. Rustom Bharucha has identified how nationalism is implicit in interculturalism; even as intercultural performers and performances work to disrupt redundant definitions of national narcissism, they refer to separate cultural identities as the felt roots of meaning. As Bharucha expresses it, "my interculturalism has brought me home".[41] The tension between the local and the global regenerates itself, is never static, and, as arises later, changes from one generation of inward migration, to the next, first generation, hyphenated Irish.

Synge's *Riders to the Sea* (1904), the ritual masterpiece of his oeuvre, is the starting point of Nervousystem's extraordinary staging, entitled *Weaving the Cry* (2010 at The Back loft, Dublin, and 2011 at Project Arts Centre). The cultural common grounds between the west of Ireland and the north-west corner of Spain, Galicia (remote communities, livelihood reliant on fishing, an implacable sea and fateful loss and grief) underpinned the company's crisscrossing of Synge's text and characters with Galician music and chant, and a free intertextuality that offered both estrangement and absorption.

Collaborative composition is Nervousystem's creative practice. Marián Araújo, who played Maurya, describes how "we [the actors] have a desire and we have an objective but we never really know how we are going to get there".[42] Actor-centred work, based on Grotowskian training and intense physicality and rhythmic control, led to a deep collaboration based on "the spine of Synge's text. This was used to structure and relate to new [interpolated] material generated by the group", including dramaturg Jeffrey Gormly and director Aiden Condron. As Araújo's Galician song and ritual actions powerfully transposed the final stages of Maurya's descent into grief and loss, distance from the familiar text was counterpointed by recognition of the emotions evoked by the bodies and the space. Gormly's task as dramaturg was as a kind of plumber; he "plumbs" the text, "making sure all the pipes connect up, [...] that, with all the associative movements away from the traditional narrative [of Riders], there is still a true, through line of simple action and speech to carry the audience".[43] For Nervousystem, estrangement emerges as an aesthetic, favouring no cultural source as definitive. The production reached to the core of ritualized loss, freeing an Irish audience from the cultural baggage borne by such a canonical play; it brought Maurya convincingly to exhausted acceptance, to the end of relentless pain, and rest "in the long nights after Samhain".[44] Gormly believes that Nervousystem's method of "actors generating physical and textual material in relation to the text is, of itself, an intercultural practice".[45] The company's way of working exemplifies how the "cascade of interventions" in bringing a staging into being, which Pavis explores,[46] is finely balanced to maintain an open structure into which the audience finally enters, where source and target cultures intersect and exchange.

In *Weaving the Cry*, the rectangular performance space was presented in an open configuration, the audience scattered about in small groups, isolating each spectator, while also integrating each presence into the mise-en-scène. No one viewpoint was privileged. In Gormly's opening line, arising from his textual response to the "scores" of the actors in rehearsal, the question of "who is shaping whom" haunts the audience's part-voyeuristic, part-participative positioning: "CATHLEEN: does wave shape land, or island cage the sea?"[47]

A parallel sense of the reciprocal shaping of person by space, and space by person is given an urban meaning in desperate optimists' [sic] *Moore Street*, part of their film sequence *Civic Life* (2006). desperate optimists was founded in 1992 in the UK by Christine Molloy and Joe Lawlor (both Irish by birth). Their work includes award-winning theatre, internet and film productions. In *Moore Street*, a young woman, played by Caroline Lambe, walks at night in Dublin's city centre. Moore Street, on the north side of the city, resonates with associations: it was a scene of revolutionary resistance in 1916, a vigorous street market over many decades, and more recently, a location of significant presences of inward migration from Eastern Europe, Asia and Africa. The woman whispers her thoughts to a distant loved-one, speaking in English and Swahili as she walks, reflecting on her migrant condition. She describes her ambivalent feelings towards her new location, while she imprints the city's somewhat sinister spaces with her presence. She sees that "there are advantages to being an outsider … I don't want to belong". With remarkable economy, the film captures the contradictory emotions of the immigrant, the freedom of exile, the longing for home; strategies for survival of her sense of self include her suspicion of "belonging", as she says, "some crazy ideas are wrapped up in that one word".

A group of migrant friends join her silently, and walk away from the camera up the centre of the deserted street. She is torn between the past and the present, and between places: "Will I ever see you again?" She is engaged in a spatial process, a transaction, as she walks the city with her friends. In his commentary on the film, Chris Darke identifies the setting as, "this space that is not yet her place".[48] She considers how "I will give this city the parts of me it needs, and protect the rest". A reciprocal relationship between space, identity and place/time is suggested with deceptive simplicity; residency in a place is a process through which change happens in both directions, to the place and to the person. The film is a "meditation" on the question "do we live in the city or does the city live through us?"[49] Identity, place and culture are things we do, the film suggests, not things we have.

Form, Language and Performance: Eastern European Collaboration

The aesthetic influence of Eastern European theatre on Irish practices is an under-examined field. While Stanislavski and his US interpreters have been influential in actor training in Ireland, more recently visiting festival productions and study visits to Europe have impacted on anti-realist performance styles. Spatial and scenographic innovation has followed from figures such as Jacques Lecoq, Eugenio Barba and Jerzy Grotowski, while the work of Kazimierz Braun, Yuri Lyubimov, Silviu Purcharete and Árpád Schilling, all Dublin Theatre Festival invitees, have shown different styles of mise-en-scène.[50]

Polish migration to Ireland has been significant since the early years of the twenty-first century, and has brought passionate and skilled theatre practitioners and researchers. Cultural overlapping between Ireland and Poland (Roman Catholic traditions, a history of colonization and both military and cultural conflict) creates a firm base of historical and religious commonality, but theatrically the countries' traditions are widely different. For much of the twentieth century, theatre in Poland, under Communist censorship, necessarily adopted symbolic, metaphorical and coding strategies; state control was less equipped to deal with non-verbal elements of performance. The actor's body was, in contrasting ways, central to the practices of Grotowski and Tadeusz Kantor, for example. Polish Theatre Ireland was founded in 2008 by Kasia Lech, Anna Wolf and Helen McNulty, and aims to represent the Polish diaspora in Ireland, and to create sites of intercultural exchange.[51] Lech believes that those productions that grew out of close collaboration between actors from a variety of cultural backgrounds, were most successfully intercultural. *Scent of Chocolate* (2008) by Radosław Paczocha, for example, performed alternately in Polish and English, tackled what Johnston calls "the rich connotative functions of language": the challenge of translation in enabling the "inter-animation of words" in I.A. Richard's phrase.[52] With this production, the challenge went beyond the languages themselves, into actors' concerns with orality in performance, in other words, speech and its connections with body, character and audience. As a Polish-trained actor, Lech describes her experience of performing in English as like her, as a right-handed person, "using my left hand", and out of this awareness came the company's aim to begin to create a collision of character, accented speech and audience: "an aesthetic of interculturalism".[53]

It is worth noting that rehearsal is more complex and extended when intercultural collaborations are involved. Even more ambitiously, *Chesslaugh* Mewash (2011) brought together performers and their languages—Irish, Lithuanian, English, Polish, Slovakian and French—to stage the issue of language itself against a background of projected backdrops of poetic texts by Czesław Miłosz, the Nobel prize-winning Polish poet. Miłosz's writing, appropriately, is seen by many as a witness to history and the individual life in it. From the perspective of interculturality, the process of devising and rehearsal was intense. John Currivan, an Irish cast member, posed himself the question "What is my language and what's my origin?"[54] expressing a sense of borders dissolving. Lech identifies this question as relevant to Irish theatre generally, exposing the tension and uncertainty in opening an inward focus outwards, and shedding expectations of familiarity in favour of the "estrangement, glitches, mistakes and confusions which fuel movement and change".[55] Homi Bhabha captures this sense of a way of being through hybrid identity, what he calls "new historical subjects", and a return "to that act of living in the midst of the 'incomprehensible'".[56]

Bubble Revolution (Julia Holewińska 2013) met the hunger for Polish plays amongst the Irish-Polish diaspora, most of whom are in their thirties. This cohort's childhood experience of the collapse of Communism and the disillusionment with liberal capitalism that ensued, reflected their direct experience. When the production travelled to the Edinburgh International Festival in 2016, the audience changed in Lech's view. As the sole performer, she was approached afterwards by first-generation British Poles, keen to learn more about their parents' lives in Poland before migrating to the UK. She flags this as predictive of changes in future Irish audiences made up of first generation migrant communities—the children of immigrants—who will be caught betwixt and between their inherited values and their lived experiences of growing up in Ireland. This interculturalism is constantly in flux, reforming to reflect history, whether environmental, economic or political, in human terms.

Amongst several companies and projects throughout Ireland that explore the rich playwriting and theatrical traditions of Polish culture, Enigma Theatre (2013–present) produced Stanislaw Ignacy Witkiewicz's 1923 canonical avant-garde drama *The Madman and the Nun* (2014). The play's symbolic and absurdist qualities famously attracted Polish director Tadeusz Kantor, who re-invented the piece in 1963. Enigma Theatre staged a new version by Karolina Szemerda, who also co-directed, setting out with an intercultural agenda and working collaboratively with Irish and French performers, musicians and designers. As the play explored the individual's fight for independence from societal demands, the aim was to relate this personal struggle to cultural alienation, unremitting change in the contemporary world, and conflicting desires to belong. Szemerda used Beckett's theatre as "a bridge for our creative rehearsal process" to connect non-Polish participants into an engagement with Witkiewicz's work. Quoting Ann Bogart's view that "culture is shared experience", Szemerda came to see how "creativity can cultivate a sense of home".

This ideal of intercultural practice is deeply collaborative and interrogates identity and culture as actions and processes that are open to change.

In Ireland, the marginal position of non-Irish theatremakers illustrates how mainstream theatre effectively maintains conservative ties with issues of national exclusivity, and with the social control of representations of identity. The non-Irish or Traveller performer, in particular, experiences incomprehension and miscomprehension of their training, experience and potential to perform a variety of roles. Skin colour is a key issue, leading to type-casting in a very limited range of parts, and accented speech is a definitive barrier to many agents and directors. These findings are part of a 2013 report by Richard Wakely, commissioned by local authorities, including South Dublin County Council Arts Office. Amongst artists in general, and theatre makers too, the responses of those interviewed measure the dislocation that persists between the intercultural society outside the theatre, and the representations on its stages.

Intercultural theatre and performance, vulnerable and often marginalized as it has been, has impacted in formative ways on Irish performance practices, and has challenged theatremakers in Ireland to look outwards, to diversify their theatre aesthetics, and to be more aware of multiple audiences and values. Through intercultural collaborative processes, and a heightened awareness of the exchange of cultural power in making performances, theatre and performance has significant potential to explore and address the estrangement experienced by minority identities. It is clear from the strategies and achievements of companies and individuals surveyed in this chapter that creative activity, including the creative role of the audience in participating in the live event, has the power to affirm a sense of home that is beyond nation or race. Homi Bhabha imagines a search for "a world of reciprocal recognition",[57] in a global context haunted by the question: "who are the new historical subjects who remain unrepresented"?[58] where Raymond Williams's idea of a cultural "knowable community" is in an intense process of confusion and change. In conclusion, and in a utopian spirit, Irish theatre must necessarily embark on a theatrical search to "initiate new signs of identity and innovative sites of collaboration, and contestation, in the act of defining the idea of society itself".[59] I wish to thank Bisi Adigun, Jeffrey Gormly, Nobuko Ijichi, Kasia Lech, and Karolina Szemerda for generously giving of their time in responding to questions in person, by phone, and/or by e-mail.

Notes

1. Michael Cronin, "Lady Augusta Gregory 1852–1932", in *Encyclopedia of Literary Translation Into English, vol. A - L*, ed. Olive Classe (London, Taylor & Francis, 2000), 582–583.
2. See also Melissa Sihra, "Re-location and Re-locution: Adapting Synge", in *Synge and His Influences* ed. by Patrick Lonergan (Dublin: Carysfort Press, 2011), 225–243.
3. *The Mahabharata* was first produced in 1985 by Peter Brook's CIRT at the Avignon Festival in France. See Rustom Bharucha, "Peter Brook's *Mahabharata*:

A View from India", *Economic and Political Weekly*, vol. 23, (32) (Aug.6, 1988), 1642–1647.

4. Patrice Pavis, *Theatre at the Crossroads of Culture,* trans. Loren Kruger (London: Routledge, 1992), 183–185.
5. Homi Bhabha, *The Location of Culture* (London: Routledge, 1994), 9.
6. Ibid., 316.
7. Charlotte McIvor and Matthew Spangler, eds., *Staging Intercultural Ireland: New Plays and Practitioners' Perspectives* (Cork: Cork University Press, 2014), 4–6.
8. Karen Fricker and Ronit Lentin, eds., *Performing Global Networks* (Newcastle: Cambridge Scholars, 2007).
9. Ronit Lentin and Elena Moreo, eds., *Migrant Activism and Integration from Below in Ireland* (London: Palgrave Macmillan, 2012), 182–200.
10. McIvor and Spangler, eds., *Staging Intercultural Ireland: New Plays and Practitioners' Perspectives*, 197–198.
11. See McIvor and Spangler, *Staging Intercultural Ireland: New Plays and Practitioners' Perspectives*, 198 and Jane Plastow "Background" in Wole Soyinka, *Death and the King's Horseman* (London: Methuen, 1998), xvii-xxiii, xviii-xix.
12. McIvor and Spangler, eds., *Staging Intercultural Ireland: New Plays and Practitioners' Perspectives*, 198.
13. Fintan O'Toole, *Critical Moments: Fintan O'Toole on Modern Irish Theatre*, ed. Julia Furey and Redmond O'Hanlon (Dublin: Carysfort Press, 2003), 126–128.
14. Brian Singleton, *Masculinities and the Contemporary Irish Theatre* (Basingstoke: Palgrave, 2011), 141–3.
15. McIvor and Spangler, eds., *Staging Intercultural Ireland: New Plays and Practitioners' Perspectives*, 345.
16. Ibid., 346–347.
17. Julie Shearer, *Others Amongst Us: Representation of Refugees on the Contemporary Irish Stage* Unpublished M.A. Thesis (University College Dublin, 2003), 55.
18. Pavis, *Theatre at the Crossroads of Culture,* 183–186.
19. Nobuko Ijichi, Personal Interview, 23 November, 2016.
20. Ibid.
21. Mercier's *Native City* in 1998 included, amongst a cast of over thirty, two Eastern European performers in the roles of Bosnian refugees.
22. Bisi Adigun, "Re-Writing Synge's *Playboy* - Christy's Metamorphosis a Hundred Years On", in *Synge and His Influences* ed. by Patrick Lonergan (Dublin: Carysfort Press, 2011), 259–268.
23. J. M. Synge, *Collected Works, IV: Plays, Book 2*, ed. Ann Saddlemyer (Gerrards Cross: Colin Smythe, 1982), 173.
24. McIvor and Spangler, eds., *Staging Intercultural Ireland: New Plays and Practitioners' Perspectives*, 266.
25. Pavis, *Theatre at the Crossroads of Culture,* 185.
26. Ibid., 186.
27. McIvor and Spangler, eds., *Staging Intercultural Ireland: New Plays and Practitioners' Perspectives*, 1.
28. Synge, *Collected Works, IV: Plays, Book 2*, 169.
29. Nicholas Grene, ed., *Interpreting Synge: Essays from the Synge Summer School 1991–2000* (Dublin: Lilliput Press, 2000), 68.

30. See also Élís Ní Dhuibhne, "The Best Field Worker: Synge and Irish Folklore", in *Synge and His Influences* ed. Patrick Lonergan (Dublin: Carysfort Press, 2011), 93–110.
31. David Johnston quoted by Melissa Sihra in "Re-location and Re-locution: Adapting Synge", in *Synge and His Influences* ed. by Patrick Lonergan (Dublin: Carysfort Press, 2011), 225–243, (230). See David Johnston, "En Otras Palabras: Frank McGuinness and Spanish Drama', in *The Dreaming Body* ed. by Melissa Sihra and Paul Murphy (Gerrards Cross: Colin Smythe and Oxford University Press, 2009), 184.
32. Pavis, *Theatre at the Crossroads of Culture,* 183–185.
33. David Johnston, *Translation for the Stage: Product and Process* (Maynooth: NUI Maynooth, 2002), 184.
34. Sara Keating, 'Evolving Playboys for the Global World' in *Synge and His Influences* ed. by Patrick Lonergan (Dublin" Carysfort Press, 2011), 245–257.
35. Emer O'Toole, *Rights of Representation: The Ethics of Intercultural Theatre Practice* (Unpublished Ph.D. Thesis, University of London, Royal Holloway, 2012), 139.
36. Jouissance, in Hélène Cixous's definition. See Cixous and Catherine Clément, *The Newly Born Woman*, translation by Betsy Wing (London: I.B. Tauris, 1996).
37. Frantz Fanon, *Black Skin, White Masks* (New York: Grove Press, 2008) and Homi Bhabha, "The Other Question: Difference, Discrimination and the Discourses of Colonialism", in *Out There*, ed. by Russell Ferguson [et al.] (New York: New Museum of Contemporary Art, 1990).
38. O'Toole, *Rights of Representation: The Ethics of Intercultural Theatre Practice,* 145.
39. Ibid., 158, and Patrick Lonergan, ed., *Synge and His Influences* (Dublin: Carysfort Press, 2011), 252, 257.
40. O'Toole, *Rights of Representation: The Ethics of Intercultural Theatre Practice,* 144–146.
41. Rustom Bharucha, *Theatre and the World* (London: Routledge, 1993), p.13
42. Lauren O'Toole, In Conversation with Nervoussystem: Weaving the Cry, entertainment.ie. Accessed 21 Oct. 2016.
43. Jeffrey Gormly, E-mails to the author 21 June 2016 and 22 April 2017. Gormly describes how his dramaturgical "plumbing" carries the audience "from [the] beginning to [the] end of the piece, joining the moments of exploration or reverie".
44. J. M. Synge, *Collected Works, III: Plays, Book 1*, ed. Ann Saddlemyer (Gerrards Cross: Colin Smythe, 1982), 25.
45. Telephone interview.
46. Pavis, *Theatre at the Crossroads of Culture,* 189.
47. Jeffrey Gormly, *Weaving the Cry*, Unpublished manuscript (2010)
48. Chris Darke, "The Long and the Short of *Civic Life* Films", in desperate optimists, *Civic Life* [Booklet] (desperate optimists, 2006), 32–42 (32).
49. Ibid., 33.
50. See Ros Dixon, "West Meets East: Russian Productions at the Dublin Theatre Festival, 1957–2006", in *Interactions: Dublin Theatre Festival 1957–2007,* eds. Nicholas Grene, Patrick Lonergan and Lilian Chambers (Irish Theatrical Diaspora Series, 3) (Dublin: Carysfort Press, 2008)
51. Charlotte McIvor, *Migration and Performance in Contemporary Ireland* (Basingstoke: Palgrave, 2017), 367–72.

52. David Johnston, quoting I.A. Richards, in *Translation for the Stage: Product and Process* (Maynooth: NUI Maynooth, 2002), 1.
53. Kasia Lech, Telephone Interview, 2 December, 2016.
54. McIvor and Spangler, eds., *Staging Intercultural Ireland: New Plays and Practitioners' Perspectives*, 369.
55. Lech, Telephone Interview.
56. Bhabha, *The Location of Culture* (London: Routledge, 1994), 316.
57. Ibid., 12.
58. Ibid., 316.
59. Ibid., 316.

Bibliography

Bhabha, Homi. *The Location of Culture*. London: Routledge, 1994.
Bharucha, Rustom. *Theatre and the World*. London: Routledge, 1993.
———."Peter Brook's *Mahabharata*: A View from India," Economic and Political Weekly 23, (32) (Aug.6, 1988), 1642–7.
Cixous, Hélène and Catherine Clément. *The Newly Born Woman*. Translated by Betsy Wing. London: I.B. Tauris, 1996.
desperate optimists. *Moore Street*, in *Civic Life* [DVD and Booklet]. desperate optimists, 2006.
Classe, Olive, ed. *Encyclopedia of Literary Translation Into English, vol. A–L*. London, Taylor & Francis, 2000.
Fanon, Frantz. *Black Skin, White Masks*. Translated by Richard Philcox. New York: Grove Press, 2008 [First published 1952].
Ferguson, Russell et al., eds. *Out There*. New York: New Museum of Contemporary Art, 1990.
Fricker, Karen and Ronit Lentin, eds. *Performing Global Networks*. Newcastle: Cambridge Scholars, 2007.
Gormly, Jeffrey and Nervousystem. *Weaving the Cry*. Unpublished Manuscript, 2010.
Gormley, Jeffrey. Telephone Interview. June 1, 2016 and e-mails 21 June 2016 and 22 April 2017.
Grene, Nicholas, Patrick Lonergan and Lilian Chambers, eds. *Interactions: Dublin Theatre Festival 1957–2007*. Dublin: Carysfort Press, 2008.
Grene, Nicholas, ed. *Interpreting Synge: Essays from the Synge Summer School 1991–2000*. Dublin: Lilliput Press, 2000.
Ijichi, Nobuko. Personal Interview. Nov. 23, 2016.
Lentin, Ronit and Elena Moreo, eds. *Migrant Activism and Integration from Below in Ireland*. London: Palgrave Macmillan, 2012.
Lentin, Ronit and Gavan Titley, eds. *The Crises of Multiculturalism: Racism in a Neoliberal Age*. London: Zed Books, 2011.
Johnston, David. *Translation for the Stage: Product and Process*. Maynooth: NUI Maynooth, 2002.
King, Jason. "Contemporary Irish Theatre, The New *Playboy* Controversy and the Economic Crisis." Irish Studies Review 24, 1 (2016).
Knowles, Ric. *Theatre & Interculturalism*. Basingstoke: Palgrave, 2010.
Lech, Kasia. Telephone Interview. Dec. 2, 2016.

Leland, Mary. [Review of] *Asylum! Asylum*! by Donal O'Kelly. *The Irish Times*, September 24, 1997.
Lentin, Ronit and Robbie McVeigh, eds. *Racism and Anti-Racism in Ireland*. Belfast: Beyond the Pale, 2002.
Lonergan, Patrick, ed. *Synge and His Influences*. Dublin: Carysfort Press, 2011.
McIvor, Charlotte. *Migration and Performance in Contemporary Ireland*. Basingstoke: Palgrave, 2017.
McIvor, Charlotte and Matthew Spangler, eds. *Staging Intercultural Ireland: New Plays and Practitioners' Perspectives*. Cork: Cork University Press, 2014.
O'Kelly, Donal. *Asylum! Asylum!* in *New Plays from the Abbey Theatre 1993–1995*. ed. Judy Friel (Syracuse University Press, 1996).
O'Toole, Emer. *Rights of Representation: The Ethics of Intercultural Theatre Practice*. Unpublished Ph.D. Thesis (University of London, Royal Holloway, 2012).
O'Toole, Fintan. *Critical Moments: Fintan O'Toole on Modern Irish Theatre*. Ed. by Julia Furey and Redmond O'Hanlon. Dublin: Carysfort Press, 2003.
O'Toole, Lauren. "In Conversation with Nervousystem: *Weaving the Cry*." entertainment.ie.
Pavis, Patrice. *Theatre at the Crossroads of Culture*. Translated by Loren Kruger. London: Routledge, 1992.
Shearer, Julie. *Others Amongst Us: Representation of Refugees on the Contemporary Irish Stage*. Unpublished M.A. Thesis, University College Dublin, 2003.
Sihra, Melissa and Paul Murphy, eds.*The Dreaming Body: Contemporary Irish Theatre*. Gerrards Cross: Colin Smythe and Oxford University Press, 2009.
Singleton, Brian. *Masculinities and the Contemporary Irish Theatre*. Basingstoke: Palgrave, 2011.
Synge, J. M. *Collected Works, III: Plays, Book 1*. Ed. by Ann Saddlemyer. Gerrards Cross: Colin Smythe, 1982.
———. *Collected Works, IV: Plays, Book 2*. Ed. by Ann Saddlemyer. Gerrards Cross: Colin Smythe, 1982.
Szemerda, Karolina. E-mails to Author. March 4 and 9, 2017.
Wakely, Richard. *Research Report into the Practices of Professional Artists from Immigrant, New Communities and Traveller Backgrounds*. Commissioned by South Dublin County Council Arts Office et al. Dublin, 2013.
www.irishplayography.ie
www.irishrefugeecouncil.ie
www.ourtable.ie

Once Upon a Time in the Life of Arambe: A Personal Reflection

Bisi Adigun

> My kind of storytelling has to add its voice to this universal storytelling before we can say, "Now we've heard it all". I worry when somebody from one particular tradition stands up and says, "the novel is dead, the story is dead". I find this to be unfair, to put it mildly. You told your own story, and now you're announcing the novel is dead. Well, I haven't told mine yet.[1]

Arambe Productions (Arambe) is Ireland's first African theatre company. It was founded in 2003 to achieve a dual aim: to diversify Irish theatre by introducing Irish audiences to the tradition of African theatre and to provide a platform for African immigrants living in Ireland to present, re-present and express themselves through the art of theatre. It was with a view to achieving these two aims that Arambe has made it its business, since its humble inception, to present a text-based or devised African play and/or a reinterpretation of a relevant play in the Irish canon, on a yearly basis. Of all the projects that Arambe has embarked upon to date, *Once Upon A Time*, a developmental project, is undoubtedly the show that would come to mind were the company to be challenged to prove that "it does what it says on the tin". The project not only highlighted the dynamism and rich tapestry of African theatrical and oral traditions on a mainstream Irish stage, it also, more significantly, enabled Arambe to identify, nurture and showcase the performance skills of many of Ireland's

B. Adigun (✉)
Trinity College Dublin, Dublin, Ireland
e-mail: ADIGUNO@tcd.ie

E. Jordan, E. Weitz (eds.), *The Palgrave Handbook of Contemporary Irish Theatre and Performance*,
https://doi.org/10.1057/978-1-137-58588-2_38

African immigrants, a majority of whom have subsequently gone on to become professional thespians in their own rights. This chapter is a personal reflection on how the idea for *Once Upon A Time* came about, the process that was involved in making the show and how the project has become the most seminal in the life of Arambe.

The first major theatre production by Arambe was Ola Rotimi's *The Gods Are Not To Blame*, a Nigerian adaptation of Sophocles' *Oedipus the King* at the Dublin Fringe Festival in 2003. While the cast of the production comprised over twenty performers, all Africans living in Ireland, only three were trained actors: me, who played the part of the protagonist, Odewale; Mojisola Adebayo, who played the part of Queen Ojuola, Odewale's wife; and Kunle Animashaun, who played the part of Alaka, Odewale's childhood friend.

Ironically, it was on the opening night of *The Gods* at the Fringe that it became apparent that the rest of the company did not know what was entailed in mounting a play professionally. So, it was with a view to giving the performers who had worked on Arambe's first major production a crash course in the art of theatre making—from an idea to performance—that the seed for the idea of *Once Upon A Time* as a developmental project was sown. The idea, which was predicated upon the simple notion that theatre makers, particularly playwrights, directors and actors, are in the business of telling stories, was to go back to the basics. Africa has a rich tradition of storytelling, so there was no better way to ground budding African actors in the art of theatre making than to initiate a project that would necessitate suggestions of and research into interesting folk tales and moonlit stories from different parts of Africa to adapt for a final performance showcase. With this in mind, Arambe made its first project grant application to the Arts Council. The application was successful and we swung into action immediately.

The project, which was scheduled to run over twelve weekends, was implemented in three stages—research/development, expert theatre workshops series and rehearsal/performance. The first stage began in earnest on Sunday, 13 March 2005 with an open audition. A dozen interested participants, originally from various African countries (including Angola, Cameroon, Nigeria and Uganda) turned up in response to the advertisement that had been placed in the multicultural newspaper, *Metro Eireann*. This had invited any interested Africans living in Ireland who wished to participate in a theatre developmental project that would culminate in a once-off performance showcase. Again, it was very apparent that, aside from a few people who had performed in the *The Gods*, most of the African brothers and sisters who turned up at the open audition had little or no experience of being on stage. The open audition session was used to introduce the project to everyone, while reiterating what had been stated in the advertisement: that no experience was required to partake in the project but enthusiasm was. The group was also reassured that, being a developmental project, the process of suggesting, selecting and turning relevant stories into stage plays would be privileged over and above the planned performance showcase at the end. Finally, auditionees were also apprised of the fact that, in an effort to expose them to a variety of performance techniques, a number of well-known theatre directors/practitioners within and outside Ireland had been contacted and they had agreed to facilitate theatre workshops with them.

After the first three weeks of working with the group, during which we researched, brainstormed and agreed on a selection of stories that would be adapted to stage, the series of workshops with invited practitioners commenced. The first facilitator who was invited to work with the group was theatre director/actor Raymond Keane, of the then Dublin-based Barabbas Theatre Company. Although Keane's focus was on clowning and miming, his workshop was geared towards exposing participants to the importance of mime in a storytelling performance and on teaching them how to concentrate and be alert at all times on stage, even when the focus of attention is on another actor. After Keane's session, the group had the privilege of working with Jimmy Fay, then director of Dublin's Bedrock Theatre Company. Through an intensive theatre workshop, consisting of various theatre games and exercises, Fay emphasized the importance of group work, trust and stage concentration for a good ensemble performance. Then John Martin, the director of the London-based Pan Centre for Intercultural Arts was invited to work with the group. Martin is a director of many international storytelling performances, so his workshop was aimed at introducing the group to the importance of storytelling and exposing participants to various storytelling, improvisational and role-playing techniques. By the time we met in the ninth week into the project, all the stories selected for performance had been written, adapted and bound as scripts. The sense of joy and relief in all the participants when the script was presented to each of them was palpable. With that, the casting of the roles in each of the stories was done, ensuring that each participant featured in at least two stories. Soon thereafter, rehearsals commenced. While I was charged with the responsibility of co-ordinating the participants and directing the showcase, Chrissie Poulter, a theatre practitioner and lecturer at the Samuel Beckett Centre at Trinity College Dublin, who served as a consultant during the project, worked with the cast maintaining a particular focus on working as a group, staying in character, and relaxing on stage.

To highlight the vastness and cultural diversity of the continent of Africa, eight stories were selected from various parts of sub-Saharan Africa, namely, "Why do we tell Stories" and "Moremi" from Nigeria; "Talk" and "Bitter Pill" from Ghana; "Truth and Falsehood" from Senegal; "The Jackal's Lawsuit", "Justice" and "How a Woman Tamed Her Husband" from Ethiopia; and the South African story, "Where do stories come from?" Each of the stories was narrated as actors reenacted relevant characters. To retain the storytelling essence of the show, each of the dramatized stories was linked by a narrator and to make the showcase a piece of "total theatre", the whole performance was appropriately interspersed with music, song, dance and mime. It is worth noting that the process was documented on video as much as possible from the beginning to the end. To put the performance showcase into proper perspective for our invited audience, a short documentary chronicling the whole process was shown at the beginning. The performance showcase itself can be described as multimedia, it began with all the actors on stage watching the documentary with the audience. As soon as the documentary was over, the lights went down and performers took their positions as the call, "Story! Story!" and the refrain: "Storyyyyy!" began in various African languages. This was followed by an African song about stories, and with that the storytelling performance, which lasted about an hour, began.

Whereas all eight stories that were performed are from the continent of Africa, each one of them explored a theme or themes that are universal. Due to the constraint of space, I will briefly discuss two stories, namely "Justice" and "The Jackal's Lawsuit", because they explore the issue of justice from divergent perspectives. "Justice" tells the story of a woman who looking for her goats that had wandered from the herd. In the course of her search, she comes upon a man sitting by the side of the road brewing himself a cup of coffee. Not knowing that the man is deaf, the woman asks him if he has seen her goats "come this way".[2] The man presumes the woman is asking for the water hole, so he vaguely points to the river. The woman thanks him and heads in the direction of the water hole. By sheer coincidence, she finds her goats close to the river, but a young kid has broken its leg while playing on the rocks. The woman picks the kid up and on her way back home, once again, she comes to the spot where the man is sitting, now drinking his coffee; in gratitude she offers the kid with the broken leg to the man, saying: "Would you take this injured kid? Perhaps you can look after it better than I can". The man thinks the woman is accusing him of injuring the kid and in no time they start shouting on each other:

DEAF MAN: No, no it wasn't me.
WOMAN: Of course, it was you. Here take the kid.
DEAF MAN: Leave me alone. I had nothing to do with it!
WOMAN: Still you knew the kids were there.
DEAF MAN: Leave me alone. I had nothing to do with it!
WOMAN: But you pointed the way.
DEAF MAN: It happens all the time with goats!
WOMAN: I found them right where you said they would be.
DEAF MAN: Go away and leave me alone, I never saw him before in my life![3]

The more passersby gather, wondering what is going on, the more the misunderstanding between the woman and the deaf man escalates. After a few more exchanges of harsh words, the man in anger strikes the woman on the cheek. As a result, the woman with the help of all the bystanders who witness the assault, drags the man to the village judge. Before the judge, the woman, still with the kid in her arms, narrates her side of the story; then the deaf man gives his own account, before the passersby tell the judge what they witnessed.

"The judge kept nodding his head, but that meant very little", in the words of the Narrator of the story, "for the judge, like the man before him, was very deaf. Moreover, he was also very near-sighted".[4] It is hardly surprising then that the judgment rendered by the judge is as follows:

JUDGE: Such family rows are a disgrace in our community. (*To the DEAF MAN*) From this time forward stop maltreating your wife. (*To the WOMAN*) As for you, do not be lazy. Hereafter, do not be late with your husband's meals. (*Looking at the baby goat*) And as for the beautiful infant, may she have a long life and grow to be joy to you both.[5]

Obviously, the story of *Justice* is a slapstick comedy meant for high entertainment. But as the Yoruba people of western Nigeria would say: it is through jests that serious issues are foregrounded. In other words, justice is a fundamental human right that concerns every human being all over the world. People are bound to misunderstand one another for all sorts of reasons: differences in opinion, ideology, worldview, class, cultural background, social status, sexual orientation and so on. It is thus the role of the judiciary in every civilized nation in the world to independently and without fear or favour resolve any misunderstanding or dispute between two or more rowing parties.

In "The Jackal's Lawsuit", the Jackal and the Leopard went out on a hunting expedition. The former captured a cow while the latter could only capture a goat. They brought their respective prizes home, leaving them in the fields to pasture. Leopard was not happy that his hunting partner had captured a bigger animal than his. Thus, out of jealousy he could not sleep. So, he came out in the middle of the night to take a look at both animals only to discover that Jackal's cow had given birth to a calf. He was overcome with so much envy that he decided to tether the new-born calf with the goat. The following morning, Leopard announced to Jackal that overnight he had been lucky as his goat had given birth to a calf. "That can't be," Jackal responded in amazement, "For a goat can only give birth to a kid." To prove his point, Leopard brought Jackal to the field and showed him the calf tethered with the goat:

LEOPARD: Now you can see for yourself. I have spoken the truth.
JACKAL: Since only a cow can give birth to a calf, the calf is mine.
LEOPARD: Do you see the proof and continue to argue? Can't you see the calf with my goat?
JACKAL: Yes, I see her. But even if I saw her standing with an elephant, still she would be mine.
LEOPARD: Let us be judged! Others will recognise that justice is on my side.[6]

Leopard is right. When they meet and narrate their case to other animals, namely Gazelle, Hyena and Klipspringer, it is clear that they are all afraid of the

Leopard. Consequently, they give the judgment they think the leopard will be happy with against a reasoned and unbiased judgement as evidenced by the following:

GAZELLE:	Well when I was young, it was true that only cows had calves. But times have changed. The world moves on. Now, as you can see, it is possible for goats to have calves. This is my judgement, as Heaven is my witness!
NARRATOR:	Then the Hyena came forward.
HYENA:	I have given this a serious thought, and I have come to the conclusion that ordinary goats cannot have calves but goats that are owned by Leopards can. That is my judgement, as Heaven is my witness!
NARRATOR:	And at last the Klipspringer gave his view.
KLIPSPRINGER:	Once it was the law of the living things that each one should bear only his own kind. Lions bore lions, goats bore goats, and camels bore camels. But the law has been changed. It is now permitted for goats to bear calves. That is the truth, as heaven is my witness![7]

But, is this really the truth? Has the law of nature changed to the extent that it is now permitted for a goat to beget a calf, simply because the goat belongs to the Leopard? It is the Baboon to whom Jackal insists they should take their case who finally and cleverly resolves the conundrum. When Jackal and Leopard get "to the rocky place where Baboon lived", according to the Narrator, "they found him turning over stones to get at the ants and grubs that lived there". Then:

NARRATOR:	Both Leopard and Jackal told their stories. Baboon listened with a far-off look in his eyes. When they were through, they waited for his judgement. But he said nothing. (*Silence*) He held a small stone in his hand and plucked at it with his fingers.
LEOPARD:	(*Impatiently*) Well? You see how it is. What is your verdict?
BABOON:	Can't you see I'm busy?
LEOPARD:	What are you doing?
BABOON:	I have eaten my meal and now I must play a little music before I judge.
LEOPARD:	Music? What music?
BABOON:	(*With irritation*) The music I am playing on this instrument!
LEOPARD:	Ha! What instrument? A stone! What a stupid person we have asked to judge for us! No music can come from a stone?

BABOON: (*Looking at LEOPARD*) If a calf can come from a goat, surely sweet music can come from a stone.

LEOPARD: Wait! I can hear it now. Hmm! What a lovely music![8]

What this story clearly demonstrates is that it takes courage and, more importantly, wisdom to be a just judge. But aside from the lessons and morality contained in the story, it is perhaps one of the most entertaining of all the stories performed on that evening of 25 May 2005. I recall that as the lights went down on the story, the audience roared in laughter, accompanied by a thunderous applause. Looking back now, I cannot say precisely what aspect of the ending of the story the audience clapped for and what aspect made them laugh. But I remember vividly that it was one of the stories that was spectacularly well acted, as it was accompanied with animal-like costumes, and masks, as well as appropriate make-up and props. But, more importantly, the actors Biola Tubi, Gabriel Akujobi, and Larry Ojelade who respectively played the parts of the Jackal, Leopard and Baboon were exceptionally compelling. It is noteworthy that Akujobi, in particular, has gone on to become a professional actor in his own right.

Kunle Animashaun, who played the storyteller in the very first story, "Why Do We Tell Stories", as well as the part of the king in the story of "The Bitter Pill", has also gone on to form his own theatre company, Camino Productions, after working with Arambe for many years. Animashaun produced the Nigerian play, *Wedlock of the Gods* in 2007 and the South African play, *Sizwe Bansi is Dead* in 2008. As part of the Arts Council's Theatre Artist in Residency Scheme 2013/2014, Animashaun was appointed artistic director in residence at Tallaght Community Arts, which afforded him the opportunity to work extensively with diverse people living in and around the area of South Dublin County Council. For many other participants, who have since gone into other enterprises that have nothing to do with the performing arts, there is no doubt that they too gained one or two things from participating in Arambe's *Once Upon A Time* developmental project.

For me, the founder and artistic director of Arambe, I can never underestimate the importance of being in a position to initiate and successfully implement the *Once Upon A Time* project. It was a unique and once-in-a-life-time experience that not only afforded me the opportunity to achieve my aim of founding Arambe, but also to improve upon my people-management skills, which are crucial for any theatre director/producer worth his or her salt. In fact, I would go as far as stating unequivocally that it was the experience of knowing that all will be well in the end, which I gained while co-ordinating and directing *Once Upon A Time*, that has stood me in a good stead whenever I have had doubts about any of the subsequent productions I had initiated, produced and directed for Arambe. It was a major milestone in the history of Arambe by virtue of the fact that it not only enabled us to achieve our main aim of identifying, nurturing and showcasing the artistic talents of Ireland's African immigrants, but also culminated in our second developmental project, *Not So*

Long Ago. Beginning where *Once Upon A Time* ends, *Not So Long Ago* is a dramatization of a series of the real-life contemporary experiences of African immigrants living in Ireland. We felt that in an increasingly diverse Ireland, there are bound to be cross-cultural misunderstandings. So, our aim was to use the artform of theatre to highlight some of the cultural differences between African immigrants and Irish people, with a view to fostering cross-cultural understanding and a harmonious existence between Africans and their Irish hosts, for, as the saying goes: "a problem defined is a problem half-solved". In 2006, Arambe presented *Once Upon A Time* and *Not So Long Ago* as a double bill for a ten-day run at the O'Reilly Theatre, in Dublin, to a critical acclaim. From that humble beginning, Arambe went from the fringe of the Irish theatre to the mainstream, representing and dramatizing the stories of Africa and Africans on the Irish stage.

Notes

1. Chinua Achebe, *There Was A Country: A Personal History of Biafra*, London: Penguin Books, 2012.
2. Bisi Adigun, "Upon A Time and Not So Long Ago", in *Staging Intercultural Ireland: New Plays and Practitioners Perspectives,* eds Charlotte McIvor and Matthew Spangler (Cork University Press: 2014), 205.
3. Ibid.
4. Ibid., 206.
5. Ibid.
6. Ibid., 207.
7. Ibid., 207–208.
8. Ibid.

Bibliography

Achebe, Chinua. *There Was A Country: A Personal History of Biafra*. London: Penguin, 2012.

Adigun, Bisi. "Upon A Time & Not So Long." in *Staging Intercultural Ireland: New Plays and Practitioners Perspectives,* edited by Charlotte McIvor and Matthew Spangler. Cork University Press: 2014, 201–244.

Intercultural Arrivals and Encounters with Trauma in Contemporary Irish Drama

Eva Urban

This chapter will explore a range of contemporary Irish plays that dramatize and interrogate tropes of traumatic immigration and intercultural relations within the context of the politics of representation. Not only do these plays have in common a focus on the experiences of newcomers in Ireland; but they also both dramatize and disrupt concepts of immigration, community, diasporic trauma, victimhood, social divisions, civilization and the artistic representation of pain and suffering. In this manner, the plays share a focus on the humanity and the individual complexity of their protagonists and on their distinctive human experiences. This emphasis eschews any reductive, divisive and dehumanizing notions of community and identity. The plays also render the experiences of immigrants to Ireland while employing familiar Irish dramaturgical devices, such as tropes of home versus emigration, disrupted realism, expressionist elements or traditional monologue formats.

In spite of Ireland's rapid development towards an intercultural society in the last twenty years, only few plays and theatre productions in mainstream theatres have since included the "New Irish" as either characters or professional actors cast in productions.[1] However, in an article published in 2005, Jason King argues that a number of intercultural plays function "to at least widen an imaginative space of intercultural contact that seems largely absent from other areas of the Irish public sphere".[2] Most of these types of plays have remained unpublished until very recently. The handful of earlier published plays listed in a footnote by Charlotte McIvor and Matthew Spangler are exclusively by male Irish playwrights.[3] Therefore, the often bemoaned lack of attention paid to Irish women playwrights could be extended towards an

E. Urban (✉)
The Senator George J. Mitchell Institute for Global Peace, Security and Justice, Queen's University, Belfast, UK

E. Jordan, E. Weitz (eds.), *The Palgrave Handbook of Contemporary Irish Theatre and Performance*,
https://doi.org/10.1057/978-1-137-58588-2_39

intersectional feminist critique. However, in her pioneering book *Stage Migrants: Representations of the Migrant Other in Modern Irish Drama* (2010), Loredana Salis draws attention to plays by women that deal with issues of migration in the context of Northern Ireland. She argues that "there is also a type of theatre which confirms that, in the longer term, Northern Irish theatre will produce works where migrants play an active role—as writers, producers, and actors, for instance—and where plays are performed or composed by migrants or they are about migrants living in the region".[4] She goes on to analyze a number of recent examples from both North and South, including multilingual works. McIvor and Spangler's recent collection shifts the balance of published plays and academic analysis in the Republic of Ireland towards a closer consideration of a wider range of new intercultural plays from the Fringe theatre scene. In its important interview section, it also gives a voice to emerging "New Irish" theatre directors and performers.

Plays examined here will include Mirjana Rendulic's *Broken Promise Land* (2013); Owen McCafferty's *Quietly* (2009); Donal O'Kelly's *Asylum! Asylum!* (1994); Gavin Kostick's *This Is What We Sang* (2009); Elizabeth Kuti's *The Sugar Wife* (2005); Gianina Cărbunario's *Kebab* (2007); Paul Meade's *Mushroom* (2007); and Stacey Gregg's *Shibboleth* (2015). *Asylum! Asylum!* (1994), more topical than ever during the current refugee crisis (at the time of writing, 2017/2018), documents the traumatic journey of a recently arrived asylum seeker in Ireland. In *Shibboleth* (2015), *Quietly* (2009), and *This Is What We Sang* (2009), immigrants from the European continent shed new light on the collective trauma of the Northern Irish Troubles and the Peace Process by offering outside perspectives, which sometimes come with their own experiences of traumatic encounters. *Shibboleth* documents both the experiences and views of native Northern Irish workers and those of Polish workers at a time of rising sectarian tensions, xenophobia, and violence. While *This Is What We Sang* stages the historical experiences of Jewish immigrants who find themselves caught between the sectarian divisions in Northern Ireland. *Quietly* quietly reveals the suffering of a young Polish man who manages a pub in Northern Ireland. He at first appears to act as a mere outside observer and witness to sectarian divisions between Loyalists and Republican factions, before it is gradually revealed that he himself is threatened by xenophobic violence. *Mushroom* (2007) exposes and subverts the limiting notion of reducing the experience of international workers to a one-dimensional representation of economic migration. The play instead emphasizes their agency, human complexity, and the richness of their often cosmopolitan attitude and life experience. *Mushroom* dramatizes the working lives of Eastern Europeans in Ireland and offers a glimpse into both their positive visions and their critical views of Ireland and the Irish to Irish audiences. In contrast, *The Sugar Wife* (2005) and *Kebab* (2007) turn the concept of the outside observer within the Irish community on its head by dramatizing an awakening awareness of Ireland's troubled relationship with historical and contemporary forms of international slavery. In *The Sugar Wife*, set within Dublin's nineteenth-century Quaker community, a philanthropic wife who sees herself as someone who charitably helps to alleviate misery, is suddenly confronted with the role of her husband's tea business in the American slave trade. She encounters not only her husband's morally dubious actions, but also the exploitation of the suffering of a visiting former slave by an anti-slavery activist and artistic photographer. She is thus made painfully aware of the photographer's artistic attraction to her own psychological suffering. This experience also makes her realize her own abuse of the suffering of the Irish poor for personal gratification in her own philanthropic work in the Dublin slums. The recent play *Kebab,* which dramatizes the exploitation of a young Romanian sex worker in Ireland, in somewhat the same manner it compels Irish middle class audiences to uncomfortably recognize Ireland's role in the contemporary global sex trade. However, the complex critical interrogation of different forms of slavery and violent abuse is further complicated in both plays: they highlight connections between art and altruism and their relationship with lust for pornographies of pain and suffering. In this sense, the plays could also be seen to encapsulate the moral ambiguities of the politics of victimhood and pain in artistic creation and spectatorship. *Broken Promise Land* (2013) proposes a somewhat more liberating narrative. This monologue play empowers its Croatian lap-dancing heroine by allowing her to self-consciously tell and shape her own narrative. She subverts notions of victimhood by controversially painting a picture of an international lap-dancing culture that allows young women to gain the financial means necessary for a self-determined life in a capitalist world.

I will begin my analysis with Donal O'Kelly's now classic *play Asylum! Asylum!* (first performed at the Peacock in Dublin in 1994) and relate it to more recent works by both Irish and immigrant playwrights. A traditional trope in Irish plays is the traumatic departure or return of Irish emigrants to or from the UK or the USA. In the plays selected here, a common trope of the arrival of non-Irish immigrants to Ireland operates. In *Asylum! Asylum!* we gradually learn of the repressed trauma of a Ugandan asylum seeker who was subjected to torture in his home country, and we are confronted with his experiences with the immigration authorities in Ireland. In a counter-trope reflecting the traditional Irish emigrant plot, an Irish immigration officer seeks a new life and job on the European continent. The play features the first black protagonist in Irish Drama at the advancing of the Celtic Tiger economic boom in Ireland, and is significant as the first play to address new immigration to Ireland.[5] However, according to Victor Merriman, the play is an example of "the deployment of a postcolonial aesthetic of disrupted realism", which in its dramaturgical structure was already anticipated by M.J. Molloy's 1950s play *The Wood of the Whispering*: "If the persistence of realism is an analogue for attempts to posit a stable social reality as imagined by a comfortable elite, disrupted realism manifests the urgency of postcolonial desires."[6] Such a "postcolonial aesthetic of disrupted realism" is a feature common to many of the intercultural Irish plays examined here. In *Asylum! Asylum!* the Ugandan Joseph Omara is seeking asylum in Ireland, having survived a massacre and torture in Bucoro, Bulu District, Northern Uganda. At the end of the play he is violently deported by the immigration authorities as his asylum case is defeated in court. In the course of the play we learn that the well-educated young man has lost his father, who was the local schoolteacher in his home village, in a horrifying act of torture carried out by Ugandan military. Joseph tells the characters Bill, Mary and Leo Gaughran how he disowned his father out of fear, and watched him die in the fire. As a result of this trauma, Joseph has an obsession with his happy childhood memories of his father that he repeats over and over again in a trance-like performative way. The members of the Irish Gaughran family in this play also lack a sense of belonging, because of tragic family circumstances over generations. Beyond the effects of an early loss of the wife and mother of the family, experiences of wartime trauma are revealed when reference is made to the fact that this matriarch's own family were German immigrants, and possibly refugees from either the Second or First World War. The father of the family, Bill Gaughran has also been affected by his experience of the bombing of the Shortstrand in Dublin in the Second World War.

Gavin Kostick's 2009 play *This Is What We Sang* focusses on one such earlier wave of immigration—it tells the story of the Irish-Jewish community's arrival in Northern Ireland and of its successful integration into Northern Irish society and business life.[7] In this play, the character of Bill directly compares nineteenth century Jewish immigrants fleeing persecution in Eastern Europe to contemporary refugees and asylum seekers, thereby asking for empathy with their plight. He offers a justification for the possibility that some immigrants may have to invent "stories" just to survive—a possible survival mechanism that Joseph in *Asylum! Asylum!* is directly accused of by Leo who calls him a "sharp operator".[8]

BILL. […] I suppose it's just, when people tell you stories about this or that, well, it's rarely perhaps quite as simple as is made out. […] What I think was this—it was greyer. They were trying to get to New York, or Canada or South Africa, but a lot of the countries they came out of wouldn't let them out with more than a certain amount of money, and they were scared that when they got to the other end, they wouldn't be let in. Because they were too poor. Or maybe they were smuggling a bit. Or maybe their paperwork wasn't in order, a lot of the places these people were coming from wouldn't even give them a passport. Latvia, Lithuania, Poland. So in a way, they were the illegal immigrants of their day and only too ready to jump ship if it got them through.[9]

Bill maintains that he is "not in the slightest bit blaming them" for trying to survive, and that as far as he is concerned "they did absolutely the right thing", characterizing them as "brave and adventurous people".[10]

Issues around the traumatic experiences of immigrants are examined within a wider European context in *Asylum! Asylum!* as Joseph's account of the burning in Bucoro is paralleled with a fictionalized rendition of a historical act of arson by neo-Nazis in Rostock, Germany in 1992. In the fictional version of this event in the play, Leo witnesses the burning of an asylum seeker's hostel in Berlin in his professional role as a member of Europol (Europol had nothing whatsoever to do with the actual 1992 event in Rostock, which involved only local police forces). Taking slight liberty with the details, O'Kelly integrates this real life event as recounted by Leo into *Asylum! Asylum!*, which becomes an independent piece of strong agitprop drama within the magic-realist frame of the play. Leo enacts his own memory of witnessing the atrocity through vivid and highly visual language communicated in short forceful sentences. The performance of his speech is designed to recreate the horror witnessed by Leo both for his audience within the play and for the actual audience of the play's production, and to strengthen Leo's new political message against the mistreatment of asylum seekers. Doubt about the factual accuracy of his storytelling performance is introduced through the magic symbolist dramaturgical element of a ghostly appearance by Joseph's father at the end of his "play within the play".[11] This magic-realist device of a haunting ghost is a common appearance in Irish drama such as, for example, the ghost of Lily Mathews in Stewart Parker's *Pentecost* (1987). It usually symbolizes trauma and remorse related to violent incidents that have occurred in the past. For Leo, the ghost symbolizes his profound guilt and remorse at having been a witness and bystander of the atrocity without taking any action to help the victims. It parallels Joseph's traumatic guilt expressed in a similar previous performance, in which he recounts how he watched his father being tortured and killed without intervening.

Leo is deeply traumatized by this event, which destroys his trust in European civilization and prompts him to quit his job as an enforcer of European border control. In a way, he reacts like the people about whom sociologist Norbert Elias wrote when he argued that "brought up in the idea that their own, higher civilization was a part of their 'nature' or their 'race', might very well have fallen into despair and been driven to the opposite extreme, when, as adults, they noticed that this flattering belief was contradicted by events".[12] In his essay "The Breakdown of Civilization" Elias argued that "it was partly due to the idea of civilization as a natural inheritance of the European nations that many people reacted to events such as the open relapse of the National Socialists into barbarism at first with incredulity—'that cannot happen in Europe'—and then with stunned surprise and dejection—'how was it possible in a civilized country?'"[13] Flawed notions of what constitutes civilization are also critically explored at various levels throughout the play: from a postcolonial angle and in what could be described as a critique of neo-colonialism in Ireland.[14] Before taking up the Europol job, Leo had contrasted his idealistic vision of European civilization with an image of a jungle to encapsulate his situation and life in Ireland. He had plotted to escape out of this "jungle" and enter Europe. Leo describes the Irish jungle as a stifling atmosphere of oppressive parochialism and nepotism: "Nobody gives you credit here. It's small, it's parochial, nothing is decided on merit, […] back biting and back stabbing, I can't stick it anymore."[15] This reference to neo-colonial corruption might link Leo's concept of the jungle to an idea of a formerly colonized nation that has failed to complete a process of de-colonization. As Mária Kurdi argues "Leo's hostile treatment of Joseph is fuelled by the suppression of his own share of the third-world memory as a corollary to his determination to emigrate and rise in the first world of the continent, working for Europol".[16] Leo's ideal vision of "European civilization" as opposed to the "jungle" not only has obvious imperialist undertones, but it could also be said to correspond to Merriman's interpretation of the aspirations of the economic development of Celtic Tiger Ireland:

> Tiger Ireland reached its zenith in the years 1998 – 2000 and was marked by deep divisions within the society and between a reified version of Ireland successful and Europe's others, "the wretched of the earth," to borrow from Fanon.[17]

Celtic Tiger Ireland positioned the country as a successful leading European nation that had left its colonial past safely behind and opposed it to poorer nations ("the wretched of the earth") with a new national confidence. However, Leo's binary notion of civilization and jungle is undermined after he witnesses the barbaric incident in Berlin and returns to Ireland: His former colleague Pillar, when arresting and deporting Joseph, tries to avoid following all of the new immigration rules and asserts that he wants to behave "civilized". To him the new regulations involving excessive brutality are rules of the "jungle": "*Pillar violently clasps handcuffs on Joseph's wrists and exclaims:* Nothing compared to what I'm saving him from. He should be on his knees thanking me! (shouts) For fuck's sake! I'm trying to be civilised!"[18] Ironically, to him, "civilized" here means the lack of asylum rules and regulations in Ireland at the time when the play was written, when Ireland was still "without a clearly defined immigration policy".[19] The play imagines what will happen once strict standardized immigration rules come into place and prompts the question of whether a system based on "nod and wink"[20] policies might in fact be more humane. In opposition to these cruel "rules of the jungle", Leo's father Bill, a retired Sacristan and his human rights activist lawyer sister, Mary, believe real civilization to mean humane behaviour and conditions among people, love and compassion. They can therefore be said to follow a Christian (Bill) and a humanist enlightenment model of civilization (Mary) rather than an imperialist colonial one that stresses modern rationalization/mechanization. However, while Mary is directly described as a follower of Europe's "long liberal tradition",[21] and of enlightenment thinker Rousseau, there is also a hint at the fact that her romantic feelings for Joseph appear partly aroused by his suffering and Joseph points out their patronizing nature: "JOSEPH. Joseph the Innocent. Joseph the Noble Savage. That's what you want, Mary. You don't want Joseph Omara the small-time smuggler who made his living out of what the fucking department calls crime."[22] At the other end of the spectrum, the Darwinism of "the rules of the jungle", as followed by Leo before his remorseful change of heart, includes the cynical use of the trauma and suffering of others for his own personal advancement. When asked to "perform" the role of an asylum seeker at the interview for the Europol job, he tells Joseph's story of the murder of his father. He thus calculatingly uses Joseph's trauma as creative inspiration to demonstrate his insight for the job.

The use and abuse of the traumatic experiences of others is a trope common to several other plays examined in this chapter, such as Kuti's *The Sugar Wife* and Carbunario's *Kebab*. In both plays, the victims of a parasitic and sadistic abuse of their suffering are women. In *The Sugar Wife*, the complexities of altruism are critically examined as the protagonist Hannah Tewkley—the philanthropic and idealist wife of a Quaker tea merchant in an 1850s Dublin traumatized by the famine—thrives upon her idea of helping the poor and oppressed. She gains self-satisfaction from the suffering of a syphilitic prostitute, whom she seeks to help on her own self-righteous terms. However, when the former African-American slave Sarah stays at her house to give an anti-slavery lecture series in Ireland, Hannah is confronted with the involvement of her husband's tea business in American slavery, as well as with his infidelity. Repulsed, she begins an affair with Sarah's rescuer, Alfred, an art photographer and abolitionist activist who took sexualized photographs of Sarah, pornographically highlighting the physical wounds she received as a victim of the slave trade's violence. Sarah plays a double role as a lecturer and witness endowed with agency for the political abolitionist cause on the one hand and a passive "mutilated black body" on the other. Sarah's double role corresponds exactly to the manner in which, as Alan Feldman describes, "the slave's authentification of his/her spoken biography through the exposed and mutilated black body" is witnessed by "the nineteenth century abolitionist audience, ensconced in bourgeois rectitude, clothed and relatively insulated from day to day personal violence": "The ex-slave is endowed with the status of speaking subject, but his/her logos both originates in and requires the supplement and the archive of the subjugated body."[23] Alfred's photographer's gaze and that of his nineteenth century abolitionist bourgeois audience thus function as a metaphorical critique of what Feldman problematizes as the voyeuristic spectatorship provoked by "museums of suffering" in his article "Memory Theaters, Virtual Witnessing, and The Trauma-Aesthetic": "The museum format freezes the past, transforming it into discrete units of time, and petrifying it within classificatory labels, all of which situate the past as an object of spectatorship, no matter how empathic this gaze may be."[24] This act of freezing past events of violent abuse for public "viewing" implies the objectification not only of classified "units of time," but also the objectification and categorization of victims who are thus dehumanized again as objects of spectatorship. Feldman argues further that "an opening of not only the speech, but also the body of the political victim, in the form of accounts of terror and pain inflects" the "collation and public archiving of these accounts 'with a postmortem aesthetic akin to the public anatomic dissection theaters of the seventeenth and eighteenth centuries'".[25] This kind of public archiving of physical suffering was hotly debated in relation to an artistic event: Brett Bailey's *Exhibit B* at the Barbican in London in 2014. This live human exhibition, which featured "black actors chained and in cages to depict the horror of slavery" and which was critically described as a "human zoo" was eventually closed down after sustained protests.[26]

In *The Sugar Wife*, the "aesthetic" exposed for spectatorship concerns the body of a living human person whose suffering, however empathically gazed at, serves artistic creation. When Alfred shows the pictures that bear witness to Sarah's trauma to Hannah's husband, it becomes clear that Sarah is his artistic muse:

SAMUEL. And here. But so thin. So sickly. And the metal collar. And these scars.
ALFRED. Yes, she bears them still. Though now at least she has clothes to cover them.
SAMUEL. *looks through the plates, examining them.*
SAMUEL. So. She is thy – muse. Would that be right? Thy muse?
ALFRED. Yes, perhaps. She is my muse, among other things.
[…]
SAMUEL. This is not cold science. To capture her mystery, to convey her – vulnerability. That is all I aspire to. As a broken bird. A captive creature, as she once was.[27]

A sinister sense of sadistic sexual pleasure gained from these photographs complicates her rescuer's relationship with Sarah, which turns out to have been based on sexual attraction from the moment he spotted her in chains and decided to buy her freedom. In fact, Sarah seems to have been aware of this dimension from the start and plays up to Alfred's attraction to make him rescue her. Only when the Quaker wife finds out about this does she realize that she is merely the photographer's next artistic muse, embodying pleasurable female human suffering for him to draw inspiration from. However, while Hannah is shocked at Sarah's revelation, Sarah pragmatically points out that desire is at the heart of all human motivation and that nothing would ever get done without it:

SARAH. He loved my scars. He took pictures of all of them, one by one.
HANNAH. To be motivated by lust, by the basest – an abomination –[28]
[…]
SARAH. Nothing gets done without desire. You of all people must see that now. We are greedy creatures. Desire. Flesh. Money.[29]

In this manner, Sarah reminds Hannah of the role of desire and the ambiguous motivations for her work towards alleviating the suffering of others. This makes Hannah embark on a deeper questioning of her own moral principles and a self-reflexive re-evaluation of what constitutes morality in others.

In Gianina Cărbunario's play *Kebab*, translated by Philip Osment and first performed at the Project Cube in Dublin during the Dublin Theatre Festival in 2007, greed, "Desire. Flesh. Money" and artistic ambition are the major themes. Mădălina, a fifteen-year-old girl recently arrived in Ireland from Romania, is exploited by two young Romanian men in the Irish sex industry. Lured to Ireland by her "boyfriend" Voicu with the promise of a regular job, Mădălina is soon told to give up her first Irish job in a Kebab shop and instead is "trained" to become a sex worker by the ruthless Voicu. When this proves too dangerous however, Voicu develops a new "business" idea together with Bogdan, a Visual Arts student: Bogdan films Voicu and Mădălina having sex while clients pay to watch them online. The boundaries in the ménage-a-trois relationship that develops are blurred. However, despite the mutual friendship and sexual relationship between the three young people, it is clear that Mădălina is considered an object and property by both young men as they disrespect and violently abuse her:

VOICU. That's enough pissing about. Our *public* awaits!!
MADALINA. I am sexy! I am sexy!

Another beep from the computer. Voicu slaps her.
You are wicked nice.
Voicu strikes her again. Her nose bleeds. Mădălina covers her face with her hands.

VOICU. Go to the bathroom and clean yourself up. Now!
BOGDAN. (*Sitting down with the camera behind the laptop.*) Let her stay like that. (*To Madalina.*) Take your hands away from your face. Look at me.[30]

It is unclear who abuses her most: Voicu who sells her body and services for his own financial profit; or Bogdan, who, like Alfred in *The Sugar Wife*, uses her suffering as artistic inspiration for his research film project to obtain a Masters in Visual Arts. Once Bogdan has obtained his Master's Degree, he drops the newly pregnant girl and refuses to honour his original promise to her to start a new life with her. He declares that he wants a normal life away from the dirt associated with a sex worker.[31]

In Cărbunariu's *Kebab,* symbolism also operates on a dramaturgical level as the "in-yer-face" theatricality of sex, violence, and objectivization (reminiscent of Mark Ravenhill's *Shopping and Fucking*) is counterpointed with a number of alienation devices and scenes dramatized in expressionistic, nightmarish stylization. For example, the realistic dialogue between Bogdan and Mădălina in Scene 5 is followed by a scene that breaks the realist framework with the parody of a Brechtian episode title, suggesting a display of "horror cartoons—Gymnastics: Our girls take Gold". This dramaturgical rupture highlights Mădălina's ruptured self as she appears to create a fantasy world in her mind of "horror cartoons" designed to detach herself from reality. This desire for distance arises from the forced physical intimacy vividly described by Sara Keating in her *Irish Times* review of Orla O'Loughlin's production in Dublin as "all overlapping limbs and intermingling bodies, forcing the characters, sandwiched together on a tiny couch, into an uncomfortable, inescapable intimacy".[32] Bernard McKenna, in his emphasis on "the theatrical representation of the traumatic event" describes "'distancing', a psychic construction of a fantasy life designed to protect an individual from further damage" as a common "symptom of traumatic rupture".[33] As we learn in the following ironically subtitled paragraphs of Mădălina's abstract monologue, "Gymnastics" and "Our girls take gold" here refer to painful sex acts, such as anal sex, which are demanded by many of Mădălina's customers and which her pimp Voicu "trained" her for as these "Compulsory Routines" presumably pay particularly well.[34] In the last paragraph of her monologue in Scene 6, subtitled *On the Podium*, the reason why Mădălina finds herself in this situation in Ireland is explained by an unspecified, repressed, even greater unhomely horror awaiting her "at home": "Home? This isn't my home, but then home's not home either. Because home is worse than anywhere that's not home. Never going back home. Never going back. No."[35] In Scene 10 *Horror Cartoons—Fairystories from Childhood*, in a manner reminiscent of the role of fairytales in psychoanalysis, Mădălina directly compares herself to a fairytale character who ran away from home: "I'm not Maddy any more. No, I'm not Maddy any more. I'm little Red Riding Hood—running like mad through the forest."[36] In an expressionistic telling of a version of *Little Red Riding Hood* Bogdan and Voicu take on the roles of "the boy who cries wolf and makes the townsfolk think he's coming to eat them up" and "the eldest of the three little billy-goats—the naughty one who opens the door to the wolf".[37] In the macabre Scene 14 *HORROR CARTOON—ABRAKEDABRA* the victimization of Mădălina at the hands of Bogdan and Voicu is nightmarishly brought to a climax as she is described by all in their sleep as "kebab meat", "fresh kebab meat", "sliced kebab meat", "grilled kebab meat",[38] with Mădălina herself concluding that "every night I dream that I'm a doner kebab", imagining herself as dead flesh.[39] In the next abstract scene it is implied that they kill her. While *The Sugar Wife* unambiguously critiques voyeurism and the artistic exploitation of the suffering of others, *Kebab* has been attacked for the play's own pornographic nature. For example, Charles Spenser, in his review of the 2007 Royal Court performance expressed a wish for "fewer in-yer-face dramas offering voyeuristic voyages round the underclass", regretting that "here we are, yet again, in some grotty flat where a ménage-à-trois of desperate kids indulge in lashings of loveless sex and graphic violence for the titillation of the audience".[40]

While its title suggests a similarly traumatic immigrant experience in the sex industry as that of Mădălina in *Kebab*, Mirjana Rendulic's partly autobiographical one-woman monologue play *Broken Promise Land* tells a very different story. The protagonist, Tea/Stefica, performs her own experience as an empowering one: as a young woman she escapes the limitations of poverty in post-war

Croatia and, if not fulfilling her initial American College dreams, succeeds in gaining access to higher education in Ireland after working and earning well as a lap dancer in several countries, including Ireland. In McIvor's words, "the play challenges stereotypes of dancers and sex workers as victims through relating a fictionalised version of Rendulic's experience",[41] and "perhaps controversially, does not represent scenarios of exploitation and violence in the sex industry apart from Stefica falling victim to a scammer who promises to transport her to the US for Euro 6000, but instead takes her money and leaves her behind".[42] McIvor quotes Rendulic's assertion quoted in an *Irish Examiner* review by Caomhán Keane that her protagonist is "not a tragic martyr, she's just a girl with a mission".[43] This concept of refusing victimhood, at the centre of Rendulic's play, challenges not only "the habitually marginalised typecasting of Eastern European actresses in Ireland"[44]; but it also challenges the politics of trauma around conceptions of damaged selfhood and identity in academic discourse. "This defiant portrayal of a woman's life remaining whole" in the face of great adversity is in fact a critique of a concept of trauma that habitually insists on the inevitability of brokenness after trauma.[45] Instead, it posits another possible way forward: the transcending of traumatic experiences that, in the case of Rendulic herself and her protagonist, are likely to have occurred, but that are—rather than simply repressed—consciously overcome through the creative "defiance" of this play and its fully rounded central character.[46] This resonates with Irene Visser's argument in her essay "Trauma and Power in Postcolonial Literary Studies", in which she underlines the power of human resilience in the face of trauma with a quotation from Chinua Achebe on colonial trauma:

> In this respect, resistance and resilience are to be seen not merely as responses of individuals but more importantly, as part of a communal process of living and working through trauma. This resonates with Chinua Achebe's remark in a recent essay, published in 2010, that while colonialism "was essentially a denial of human worth and dignity" it is important to understand that "the great thing about being human is our ability to face adversity down by refusing to be defined by it, refusing to be no more than its agent or its victim."[47]

A similarly defiant, fully rounded central character who immigrated to Ireland not for economic reasons, but out of cultural curiosity, a sense of adventure, and to fulfil his spiritual dreams, is the cosmopolitan Polish man Andrzej in Paul Meade's play *Mushroom*. He expresses an important characteristic that appears entirely ignored in contemporary dehumanizing discussions about "economic migrants": Andrzej reclaims his humanity by highlighting the wealth of his international experience, obstinately refusing to be reduced to a cardboard cut-out stereotype and to be patronized by people who have never experienced even a fraction of his vastly rich experience:

ANDRZEJ. [...] They look at me they see a Polishman. I look at them and I think, I have worked all over the world, I fixed roofs in Italy, I built saunas in Germany, I sold kebabs by the Black Sea, I saw the Pyramids, I spoke to the oracle at Delphi, I. ... and you say...'Good man yourself'. What do you think I am doing here? A job? Ha, Ha. A job? I can get a job anywhere. I came because... but they don't understand. I came...I came because of Newgrange.[48]

This insistence on self-expression and on a depth of insight and experience conveys a strong sense of personhood, agency and self-determination instead of passive objectified victimhood. It suggests that the character of Andrzej would, similarly to Tea/Stefica in Rendulic's *Broken Promise Land*, reject the limitations of a concept of traumatic immigration by insisting on his own unbroken strength and vigour, which he has actually gained from his international experience. When things don't work out as imagined, Andrzej open-mindedly looks for "a different perspective".[49] Rather than merely performing immigrant workers on mushroom farms for Irish audiences, Meade's *Mushroom* performs active immigrant workers' minds and dramatizes critical immigrant perceptions of Ireland. According to Jason King, the play, which "portrays the mushroom tents and chicken farms of rural Monaghan to be grim settings",[50] provides "a defamiliarised vantage point from which members of the audience can imagine how they must appear to immigrant agricultural labourers and mushroom pickers whom they would otherwise never encounter".[51] I would add to King's analysis that the play allows audiences to encounter immigrant workers as independent thinkers in a way that they might not be open to encounter within society, which, as the play highlights, often fails to integrate newcomers and outsiders as full members. However, the thoughts of immigrants as represented in the play are not always insightful and are at times offensive, especially when dealing with the hurt of rejection. They sometimes portray an immaturity, cultural prejudice and racist contempt for the Irish that is every bit as nasty as that of anti-immigrant xenophobes: "They (Irish people) are all fat in the face and they have big ears. Like this... (*she demonstrates*). Their food is so bad".[52] The racism of anti-immigrant xenophobes is forcefully critiqued in an earlier play dealing with exploited Bosnian immigrant workers on a mushroom farm in Northern Ireland, Damian Gorman's significantly-named *Darkie* (2005).[53] By allowing immigrant characters to express a variety of opinions freely, Meade's *Mushroom* more fully humanizes them with strengths and weaknesses, far from creating mere one-dimensional or idealized victims against the backdrop of a critical representation of Irish society. The alienation experienced by immigrants is dramatized through the expressionist technique of two dialogues in two different countries (Ireland and Romania) running on a parallel level. These dialogues intercept each other, thereby suggesting rupture as a fundamental experience of the characters. However, according to Loredana Salis "the play follows the parallel lives of the protagonists to show how, regardless of their backgrounds and cultural differences, these people share more than it may at first seem",[54] thus emphasizing universal human experiences through a dramaturgy of rupture. This expressionistic dramaturgy of cross-dialogues is a device commonly used in Irish Drama, such as for example in *The Silver Tassie* (1927) by Sean O'Casey and in Frank McGuinness's *Observe the Sons of Ulster Marching towards the Somme* (1985). Consequently, I argue that, by employing a defamiliarization device familiar to Irish audiences, Meade's *Mushroom* makes "the other" more familiar.

Gavin Kostick's *This is what we sang*—based on a collection of interviews with the Belfast Jewish community—also applies a common feature of Irish dramatic structure in order to effect a sense of familiarity. In contrast to *Mushroom's* defamiliarization devices, this play is composed in a traditional Irish monologue structure. Several characters of one immigrant Jewish family alternate in telling the story of their lives. It has this structure in common with some of the most well-known modern Irish plays, such as, for example, Brian Friel's *Faith Healer* (1979). Eamonn Jordan distinguishes three different main types of monologue clusters in Irish drama, "single character interior monologues", monologues performed by a single actor "impersonating a range of characters", and monologues that "consist of two or more characters narrating a sequence of events from their own perspectives".[55] This formal structure also, in some sense, engages with the dialectical concept of traditional study of the Talmud, which is based on the idea of a series of arguments between different voices with a focus on the continuous dynamic of the argument rather than the conclusion. In the words of Steven Jaffe in an interview with Jo Egan: "The way of studying the Talmud is by argument. The Talmud itself is a series of arguments between Rabbis who lived in the first century onwards and they are constantly arguing and therefore it's a dialectic. The essence of it is in the argument rather than the conclusion. It's a thinking thing rather than a clear yes or no."[56] The play was staged site-specifically in Belfast's Synagogue, and the monologues were symbolically framed with an enactment of the Jewish religious ritual of Yom Kippur:

> *Enter* LEV, HANNAH, SISS, *to the edge of the playing area, predominantly in white (but not obsessively so). Enter* BILL *in a suit, separate. They are barefoot. They stand waiting. They don't engage with each other. Enter Saul singing the Kol Nidre (the prayer before evening service).*
>
> The story is told through the stages of:
>
> *Repentance.*
> *Sacrifice.*
> *Forgiveness.*
>
> All these are both in relation to God and man. The characters are speaking to God (or to their own sense of the divine) and man.
>
> The characters all understand what they are being asked for, but don't necessarily agree with it.[57]

Occasionally, in the individual monologues and in quotations from interviews collected in the epigraph, references to anti-Semitism and discrimination against the Jewish people caught up between the Protestant–Catholic division in Northern Ireland are made. For example, in the Section 1 Repentance, the character of Siss reflects on her personal experience growing up as a Jewish child in Belfast in the 1930s and 40s, asking herself whether her life "was limited by anti-Semitism" and concluding "that's too much to say. I don't know" and "But no, anti-Semitism wasn't a big thing in my life".[58] According to Siss, it was quite simply the same bigotry that prevented Catholics from joining the Protestant Tennis clubs that was applied to Jews, but she insists that "rather than cry about it, we formed our own".[59] However, she also recalls an episode playing with children in the street who sang two different versions of a song about King Billy and how she got caught up in between the resulting Unionist–Nationalist confrontation, being called "yid": "I tried to say it was only a game that had gone wrong, and one of the boys said, 'what's it to you yid?'"[60]

This experience of an outsider caught between the sectarian divisions in Northern Ireland is mirrored in the more immediately threatening experience of a Polish bar worker in contemporary Belfast in Owen McCafferty's *Quietly*. The play is set on a quiet evening that Polish barman Robert spends chatting to a customer, Jimmy, in his pub. As they discuss the football game of the day between Northern Ireland and Poland, violent clashes between Northern Irish and Polish football hooligans are reported. When Loyalist Ian arrives in the pub, Robert witnesses a tense "truth and reconciliation" meeting between a Loyalist perpetrator of sectarian violence and the son of one of his Catholic victims. It is revealed that Catholic Jimmy's father was killed by a bomb thrown into an innocent group of men watching a football game in a local pub by Ian when both men were sixteen-year-old teenagers in 1974. Their dialogue expresses the traumatic memories of both men. Helen Meany, in her review of the 2012 Abbey Theatre production, argues that "rather than staging a 'truth and reconciliation' process in microcosm", McCafferty "shows how these two men have been moulded by their backgrounds, each steeped in prejudice against the other's traditions and beliefs". Meany goes on to maintain that "even now, they find that hard to shake off; through the character of Robert, it is suggested that the sectarianism with which Ian and Jimmy grew up has found a new outlet in racist intolerance".[61] Later at night, after Ian and Jimmy have left the pub, Robert is afraid to leave for fear of being attacked by a group of drunken teenagers shouting xenophobic abuse at him from the outside. As he prepares to protect himself with a baseball bat positioning himself behind the door, we get a sense that he has already experienced the trauma of being the target of xenophobic violence and that standing behind the door with a baseball bat might well be his evening routine. The play thus concludes with what seems like a routine threat of violence that recalls the sectarian violence that killed the victims of the Loyalist bomb attack on the day of an important football game in a pub similar to Robert's workplace.

Robert starts to clear up. The kids in the street start beating on the window shutters. They shout abuse:

VOICES. Three-two – three-two – fucking Polish bastard – go back to where you come from and shite in the street you fucker – polish wanker – three-two – three-two – three-two.

Robert gets a baseball bat from behind the bar and stands waiting. Lights fade to dark.[62]

Similarly, in Stacey Gregg's 2015 play *Shibboleth*, which also dramatizes the difficult situation of Polish workers in a society already divided by sectarian lines, an undercurrent threat of violence is always present underneath the minimalist colloquial dialogue. In her "Afterword" Gregg describes the title as symbolizing not only the play's dramaturgical representation of the continuous divisions in Northern Irish society, but also the complex linguistic divisions that keep people apart: "I called it Shibboleth, a Hebrew word for words or customs one tribe uses to mark itself apart from others. A linguistic wall, of sorts."[63] In *Shibboleth* the conversation of a group of construction workers who are building a "peace wall" to prevent violence between Republicans and Loyalists in Belfast is ironically peppered with a singing wall as "almost every scene is divided by one of James Fortune's genre-hopping musical interludes".[64] The Northern Irish workers' expressions of xenophobic hatred against Eastern European immigrant workers are counterpointed with expressions of solidarity and support for each other as "on site, the workers' conversations slip frequently into a poetic unified consciousness, or a mantra of groupthink".[65] This "mantra of groupthink" is expressed in the frequent repetition of the colloquial linguistic turn of phrase: "Looking out for the Lads":

STUARTY Look what the European Union brought in.
MO Flip who's that?
BRICKIES Who?
STUARTY Pole.
MO A pole?
STUARTY He's the Pole.
COREY A telegraph?
ALAN Right enough?
MO Job thief, give him a slap.
STUARTY Look out for the Lads.
BRICKIES Look out for the Lads.[66]

Ironically, the Lads turn out not to look out for the Lads at all as in the end their aggression turns against one of their own group, when Mo is beaten to death by Corey after he made advances to Corey's Polish girlfriend, Agnieska, whose father Yuri also works on the site. This violent outcome undermines the fictive notion of solidarity within sectarian or right-wing nationalist groups.

Such collective loyalties are exposed as arbitrary, temporary, self-interested, and as based on the manipulation of particular circumstances of competition by the powerful. In the case of Northern Ireland (as elsewhere in the UK, Europe and beyond), the analysis that "the various sections of a polarized proletariat are apparently more willing to ally with their bourgeois co-religionists so as to engage in sectarian warfare, rather than co-opting in a united struggle to improve their living conditions as a class" still applies and can be extended: time and time again national and ethnic identity politics is used to create a false sense of collectivity, and foreigners and immigrants are used as convenient scapegoats for the exploitation of the working classes by those in positions of power.[67] In the words of Peter Crawley in his review of *Shibboleth* in the *Irish Times*, "There is an acrid wit in Stacey Gregg's new play, centred around the extension of such a wall, that 'Themens' and 'Usens' are never explicitly named, as though belief in division itself had eclipsed actual identity".[68] Crawley wittily concludes: "Perhaps that's why the wall in Gregg's play has its own voice, supplied by the versatile singer Cara Robinson, as insatiable and insistent as the plant in *Little Shop of Horrors*: 'Build me'".[69] Through the use of familiar Irish dramaturgical devices, plays staging intercultural arrivals and encounters—as do all the examples explored in this chapter—make "the New Irish" more familiar to Irish audiences. This emphasis on a shared humanity thus reveals the senselessness of divisions or "walls" between people from different religious, national, political or ethnic origins that are built on superficial ideas of exclusive communities and limited notions of identity.

Notes

1. Brian Singleton has drawn attention to the fact that in Irish mainstream theatre productions "the notion of colour-blind casting remains an alien practice". Brian Singleton, *Masculinities and the Contemporary Irish Theatre* (Basingstoke: Palgrave Macmillan, 2011), 20. Quoted in *Staging Intercultural Theatre: New Plays and Practitioner Perspectives*, edited by Charlotte McIvor and Matthew Spangler (Cork University Press, 2014), 2. I would extend this to the notion of nationality-blind/ethnicity-blind casting also. This does not mean that works including either international characters or international actors or both are not written or produced, but they rarely make it from the vibrantly cosmopolitan young Fringe scene into the mainstream theatre sector. An important example of international and colour-blind casting was the 2013 international co-production, *The Conquest of Happiness*. See Eva Urban, "'Actors in the same tragedy': Bertrand Russell, Humanism, and 'The Conquest of Happiness'", *New Theatre Quarterly* 31, Issue 04 (November 2015): 343–358.
2. Jason King, "Interculturalism and Irish Theatre", *Irish Review* 33, Global Ireland (Spring, 2005), 23–39.
3. Charlotte McIvor and Matthew Spangler, eds., *Staging Intercultural Ireland: New Plays and Practitioner Perspectives* (Cork University Press, 2014), 2.
4. Loredana Salis, *Stage Migrants: Representations of the Migrant Other in Modern Irish Drama* (Newcastle: Cambridge Scholars Publishing, 2010), 10.

5. For an account of the play's production and reception history see Victor Merriman, *Because We Are Poor: Irish Theatre in the 1990s* (Dublin: Carysfort Press, 2010).
6. Merriman, *Because We Are Poor*, 55.
7. Please see Loredana Salis, *Stage Migrants: Representations of the Migrant Other in Modern Irish Drama* (Newcastle: Cambridge Scholars Publishing, 2010) for a detailed account of an earlier play with a similar theme: Rebecca Bartlett's *Shalom Belfast!* (2000), 10–11.
8. Donal O'Kelly, *Asylum! Asylum!* In *New Plays from the Abbey Theatre*, edited and with an Introduction by Christopher Fitz-Simon and Sanford Sternlicht, 119.
9. Ibid., 46.
10. Ibid., 46–47.
11. Ibid., 166.
12. Norbert Elias, "The Breakdown of Civilization", in *The Norbert Elias Reader*, 1998, 119.
13. Ibid., 114.
14. "The nationalist bourgeoisie, to use Frantz Fanon's term, inaugurated and maintained a neo-colonial social order in Independent Ireland, in which, broadly speaking, relations of domination established during the colonial period persist." Victor Merriman, "Postcolonial Criticism, Drama, and Civil Society", *Modern Drama* (2004): 626.
15. Ibid., 134.
16. Kurdi, *Codes and Masks: Aspects of Identity in Contemporary Irish Plays in an Intercultural Context*, Peter Lang, 2000, 93.
17. Merriman, *Because We Are Poor*, 629.
18. O'Kelly, *Asylum! Asylum!*, 163.
19. Ibid., 90.
20. Ibid., 34.
21. Ibid., 147.
22. Ibid., 151.
23. Alan Feldman, "Memory Theaters, Virtual Witnessing, and The Trauma-Aesthetic", *Biography*, Volume 27, Number 1, Winter (2004): 188.
24. Ibid., 165.
25. Ibid., 167.
26. Hugh Muir, "Slavery Exhibition featuring black actors chained in cages shut down", *Guardian*, 24 September 2014.
27. Elizabeth Kuti, *The Sugar Wife* (Nick Hern Books, 2005), 31.
28. Ibid., 70–71.
29. Ibid., 71.
30. Gianina Cărbunario, *Kebab*, translated by Philip Osment (Royal Court, Oberon Modern Plays, 2007), 49.
31. For a detailed analysis of the representation of the prostitute's body as dirt in *Kebab* within a biopolitical framework see Sarah Heinz, "The Shite of Dublin: Body Metaphors, Biopolitics, and the Functions of Disgust in Sebastian Barry's *The Pride of Parnell Street* and Gianina Carbunariu's *Kebab*", *JCDE: Journal for Contemporary Drama in English*. 1.1 (2013): 80–91.
32. Sarah Keating, Review of *Kebab*, *The Irish Times*, 1 October 2007.

33. Bernard McKenna, *Rupture, Representation, and the Refashioning of Identity in Drama from the North of Ireland, 1969–1994*, (Praeger: Westport, Connecticut, 2003), 2.
34. Kuti, *The Sugar Wife*, 33.
35. Ibid., 34.
36. Ibid., 44.
37. Ibid.
38. Ibid., 53.
39. Ibid., 54.
40. Charles Spenser, "Kebab: A pile of rancid clichés", *Telegraph*, 25 October 2007.
41. Charlotte McIvor, "Introduction to Mirjana Rendulic's *Broken Promise Land* (2013)", in *Staging Intercultural Ireland: New Plays and Practitioner Perspectives*, edited by Charlotte McIvor and Matthew Spangler, 319.
42. Ibid., 320.
43. Caomhán Keane, "New play captures life as a lapdancer in Celtic Tiger Ireland", *Irish Examiner*, 11 March 2013, cited in McIvor, "Introduction to Mirjana Rendulic's *Broken Promise Land* (2013)", 319.
44. McIvor, "Introduction to Mirjana Rendulic's *Broken Promise Land* (2013)", 322.
45. Ibid.
46. Ibid.
47. Irene Visser, "Trauma and Power in Postcolonial Literary Studies", in *Contemporary Approaches in Literary Trauma Theory*, edited by Michelle Balaev, 106–129, 108.
48. Paul Meade, *Mushroom*, in *Staging Intercultural Ireland*, edited by Charlotte McIvor and Matthew Spangler (Cork: Cork University Press, 2014), 249–300 (251).
49. Ibid., 250.
50. Jason King, "Introduction to Paul Meade's *Mushroom*," In *Staging Intercultural Ireland*, 245.
51. Ibid., 247.
52. Meade, *Mushroom, 268.*
53. See Salis for a detailed analysis of *Darkie*.
54. Loredana Salis, "Immigrant games: sports as a metaphor for social encounter in contemporary Irish drama", *Irish Studies Review*, 18,.1, February 2010, 57–68 (62).
55. Eamonn Jordan, *Dissident Dramaturgies*, (Irish Academic Press, 2010), 219.
56. Steven Jaffe, in an interview with Jo Egan, quoted in Jo Egan, "The Lamplighters", in Gavin Kostick, *This Is What We Sang*, Belfast: Kabosh, Lagan Press, 2009.
57. Gavin Kostick, *This is What We Sang* (Kabosh, Lagan Press, 2009), 26.
58. Ibid. 40.
59. Ibid., 39–40.
60. Ibid.
61. Helen Meany, "Review of *Quietly*", *Guardian*, 28 November 2012.
62. Owen McCafferty, *Quietly* (Faber and Faber, 2012), 32.
63. Stacey Gregg, *Shibboleth*, London: Nick Hern Books, 101.
64. Peter Crawley, "*Shibboleth:* Examining the Walls than run through Northern Irish heads", *Irish Times*, 8 October 2015.

65. Ibid.
66. Gregg, *Shibboleth*, 28.
67. John Martin, "The Conflict in Northern Ireland: Marxist Interpretations", *Capital and Class*, 1982, 6, 56–71 (60). Quoted and applied to an analysis of Northern Irish Drama in Eva Urban, *Community Politics and the Peace Process in Contemporary Northern Irish Drama* (Oxford: Peter Lang, 2011), 27.
68. Peter Crawley, "*Shibboleth*: Examining the walls that run through Northern Irish heads", *Irish Times*, 8 October 2015.
69. Ibid.

Bibliography

Cărbunario, Gianina. *Kebab*, translated by Philip Osment. Royal Court, Oberon Modern Plays, 2007.

Crawley, Peter. "*Shibboleth*: Examining the Walls That Run Through Northern Irish heads." *The Irish Times*, October 8, 2015.

Feldman, Alan. "Memory Theaters, Virtual Witnessing, and The Trauma-Aesthetic." *Biography* 27, Number 1, Winter (2004): 165.

Goudsblom, Johan and Stephen Mennell, eds. *The Norbert Elias Reader: A Biographical Selection*. Oxford: Blackwell, 1998.

Heinz, Sarah. "The Shite of Dublin: Body Metaphors, Biopolitics, and the Functions of Disgust in Sebastian Barry's *The Pride of Parnell Street* and Gianina Carbunariu's *Kebab*." *JCDE: Journal for Contemporary Drama in English* 1.1 (2013): 80–91.

King, Jason. "Interculturalism and Irish Theatre." *Irish Review* 33, Global Ireland (Spring, 2005): 23–39.

Kurdi, Maria. *Codes and Masks: Aspects of Identity in Contemporary Irish Plays in an Intercultural Context*. Peter Lang, 2000.

Kuti, Elizabeth. *The Sugar Wife*. Nick Hern Books, 2005.

McCafferty, Owen. *Quietly*. Faber and Faber, 2012.

McIvor, Charlotte and Matthew Spangler, eds. *Staging Intercultural Ireland: New Plays and Practitioner Perspectives*. Cork University Press, 2014.

McKenna, Bernard. *Rupture, Representation, and the Refashioning of Identity in Drama from the North of Ireland, 1969–1994*. Westport, Connecticut: Praeger, 2003.

Meade, Paul. *Mushroom*. In *Staging Intercultural Ireland*, edited by Charlotte McIvor and Matthew Spangler. Cork University Press, 2014.

Merriman, Victor. *Because We Are Poor: Irish Theatre in the 1990s*. Dublin: Carysfort Press, 2010.

Muir, Hugh. "Slavery Exhibition Featuring Black Actors Chained in Cages Shut Down." *Guardian*, September 24, 2014.

O'Kelly, Donal. *Asylum! Asylum!* In *New Plays from the Abbey Theatre 1993–1995*, edited and with an Introduction by Christopher Fitz-Simon and Sanford Sternlicht. Syracuse, New York: Syracuse Univeristy Press, 1996.

Salis, Loredana. *Stage Migrants: Representations of the Migrant Other in Modern Irish Drama*. Newcastle: Cambridge Scholars Publishing, 2010.

Singleton, Brian. *Masculinities and the Contemporary Irish Theatre*. Basingstoke: Palgrave Macmillan, 2011.

Urban, Eva. *Community Politics and the Peace Process in Contemporary Northern Irish Drama*. Oxford: Peter Lang, 2011.

Dramaturgical Complicity: Representing Trauma in Brokentalkers' *The Blue Boy*

Kate Donoghue

Brokentalkers' *The Blue Boy* takes as its subject the abuses perpetrated within Dublin's Artane Industrial School, and approaches the worrisome task of representing those abuses from a unique dramaturgical standpoint.[1] Charlotte McIvor has stated that "only by working from a state of formal as well as thematic brokenness can the art of theatre prove capable of mourning the violence 'collectives' have done to individuals within the Irish nation".[2] The state of formal brokenness from which *The Blue Boy* springs is so effective (and affective) because it dramaturgically mimics the trauma-symptom—the bodily sensations experienced by trauma sufferers after the fact, such as flashbacks, hallucinations or unbidden psychosomatic responses. In this sense *The Blue Boy*, as a piece of performance work, provides a unique apparatus for the consideration and collectivization of the trauma of institutional abuse; one which is urgently mandated by a contemporary Irish culture that continues to produce works like this one. Unlike other representations of industrial schools, which might tangentially absolve the community by ascribing institutional abuse exclusively to the past, *The Blue Boy* testifies to the perpetuity of the trauma resulting from those abuses. It is thus as much an indictment of the wider society, of which Artane Industrial School was a part, as it is of the institution itself.

The Blue Boy is framed metaphorically by the walls of Artane Industrial School, the structures that concealed the abuses within from public view, and symbolically prevented the community's outrage and intervention. These walls are corporealized on stage by a scrim, which bisects the stage space horizontally, creating a foreground that is open to the spectator, and a background into

K. Donoghue (✉)
University of Manchester, Manchester, UK

E. Jordan, E. Weitz (eds.), *The Palgrave Handbook of Contemporary Irish Theatre and Performance*,
https://doi.org/10.1057/978-1-137-58588-2_40

which the lighting design selectively either affords or denies a view. At the top of the play, Gary Keegan, co-artistic director of Brokentalkers, stands in front of the scrim and addresses the audience, producing an old measuring ruler, and telling us that he used to play with it as a child. Clicking the ruler's joints into different combinations, Keegan shows us how the ruler can transform into a horse, a television screen, a dinosaur, and an electric guitar (to name a few). With each successive evolution of the ruler, Keegan pauses, waiting for the audience to supply him with the answer to the implied question: "what is it now?" During the performance I attended, the audience obliged him, laughing along with Keegan's "playing". He tells us that the ruler used to belong to his grandfather, who was an undertaker in the area surrounding Artane. When a child in the school died, it was Keegan's grandfather's job to travel to where the body lay, and measure the corpse with this ruler, to build a coffin to size. He says the sight of the children's bodies, which were never without significant bruising, haunted his grandfather because "he didn't know where [the bruises] came from".[3]

At this point, interviews with Keegan's mother begin to play over the theatre's audio speakers. In the audience, we hear her voice, but we do not see a representation of her image. In this recording, Keegan's mother details what her life has been like, living a stone's throw from the School. The audience sees key phrases from her speech projected in text on the scrim. This technique is employed for all the subsequent recorded interviews we hear: recordings of Keegan's mother, and, chiefly, recorded testimonies from survivors of industrial schools.

As the play begins, lights flash intermittently behind the scrim. We see glimpses of masked figures appear and disappear during these brief blackouts, which seem too short to allow them to traverse the stage: it is as though they have materialized out of thin air. The lights are brought up in full when we hear the voice of an old man begin to describe his life as an inmate of Artane. As the voice speaks, it becomes apparent that one of these "dancers" is actually a boy-sized puppet.

The strobe lighting effect, which illuminates the "back" stage like lightning, as well as the disorienting repositioning of the dancers during the blackout, prompt the audience to respond physically as one would to a scare in a horror film. Unlike those in horror films, however, the bodies appearing unexpectedly from the darkness in *The Blue Boy* are real. Each subsequent cycle of blackout/illumination, the duration of which is wholly outside the audience's control, carries with it the threat that something both unbearable and inescapable will become visible on stage. When that something does not appear, the dreadful anticipation begins building for "the next time".

Patrick Duggan, a performance theorist primarily focused on trauma, notes that this anxious vacillation between dread and seeming relief constitutes a "presence-in-torture effect", wherein the difference between "real" torture and the anticipation of it is elided: it does not matter whether a blow actually makes contact with one's body—severe enough anticipation of one can have the same physiological effect on the individual "being" tortured.[4] In *The Blue Boy*, there is a moment when a survivor's voice begins rattling off a list of objects, and it is not immediately apparent what the objects have in common with one another: "a piece of chalk, a wooden stick, a rosary bead".[5] As the list continues, a dancer begins pelting the floor with snapdragon fireworks, and the implied meaning is made clear: these everyday objects have become weaponized. This is a transformation that is common in torture scenarios: Elaine Scarry attests that the use of everyday objects (pieces of furniture, soft drink bottles) as instruments of torture "[annihilates the meanings of] the objects themselves and with them the fact of civilisation".[6] The semiological disturbance created dramaturgically by *The Blue Boy* engenders this type of environment within the theatre: we need only hear the names of these objects in order to wince as though we ourselves have been struck.

Because *The Blue Boy*'s dramaturgical potency is based on the audience's inability to identify what is being seen, the "presence-in-torture" effect evoked during the performance is really a "presence-in-trauma". Like the trauma sufferer, whose initial experience of the event is too horrific to put into words,[7] the audience bearing witness to this mode of performance might experience a symbolic tear——or brief collapse—in which what is perceived registers only belatedly (as was the case with me, and the puppet I initially mistook for a live body). This representational strategy can allow the audience to come to know a presence-in-trauma in a physical, embodied way, like the Artane inmates. Simultaneously, the scrim's presence casts audience members as complicit onlookers—those who watch and understand, but do nothing to stop what is happening, much like the wider Irish community whose collective silence enabled abuses in care institutions like Artane to continue.

The movement vocabulary employed in *The Blue Boy* is grotesque: the dancers often mime acts of self-harm, such as slamming their heads or bodies into the walls. There is a moment when a dancer places a mask on the back of her head, so that her limbs appear to bend backward. Even though we can perceive that this dancer's movements appear contorted because she is facing backward, and even though, when the dancers crash their foreheads into the table, we can see their palms on the tabletop, waiting to mitigate the impact, we respond physically, as we would to real horrors. I felt the hair on the back on my neck stand on end; audience members beside me squirmed in their seats. These moments override the distinction within our bodies between what is real and what is representational. Theodor Adorno suggests that "art makes a gesture-like grab for reality only to draw back violently as it touches that reality".[8] The indicators of mimesis within *The Blue Boy* (the palms on the tabletop, for example) should be enough to ensure that the audience perceives the representation of abuse and pain "recoiling" from the reality of it, but they are not; the audience is touched physically and symbolically by the very real threat of harm constructed within the mimetic frame of the play. It is an irruption of the abject into the world of the theatre, which creates an "unease cognate with traumatic repetition".[9] In this way, *The Blue Boy* hijacks our perceptive capabilities, causing us to enter into the same state of symbolic uncertainty that trauma occupies, and forcing us to confront "the ultimate formlessness" within the bodies of the dancers and, by extension, ourselves.

The coarse grey uniforms the dancers wear drown the bodies within them. It becomes difficult to tell the figures apart. In unifying the dancers aesthetically, Brokentalkers have "marked the victims":[10] a phrase Anne Goarzin invokes to describe the yellow stars worn by Jews during the Holocaust. Presenting an undifferentiated series of bodies marked in this way collapses the distinction between the sign (inmate of Artane, abuse victim, little boy, trauma sufferer) and the real body (that of the actual individual boy each dancer might represent, that of the dancer him or herself). This is a traumatic denial of subjectivity within the performance frame that is directly mimetic of the assault on the identities of the inmates perpetrated by the Christian Brothers in Artane.

We do not see any abusers represented onstage (with one notable exception, unpacked below); rather, dancers throw themselves around the space as though moved by an invisible outside force. Nor do we see of any of the survivors whose testimony forms the backbone of the play. Despite the dancers' frenzied embodiment of presence-in-trauma, it is these absent bodies that nonetheless demand to be considered. Jack Santino argues that shrines "insist upon the presence of absent people".[11] In this sense, *The Blue Boy* is certainly a "shrine" to what happened within Artane, and, by extension, within the entire institutional care system in Ireland. That we only hear and do not see actual survivors in this piece complicates our ability as audience members to witness their trauma, and commemorates the community's collusion in the abuses as much as it does the abused individuals themselves.

One of the most physically affecting sequences of the play involves a video clip in which a cartoon lamb has been captured by two hungry wolves. The lamb cries out for help, and tries to run from the wolves who recapture it at once, and physically fight over its small body, tossing it back and forth between them until all three are sent hurtling over a cliff (as so often happens in cartoons). The wolves fall out of the frame, and we are left to focus only on the lamb, tumbling over and over through an endless blue void, crying out for help that does not come. While this footage plays, the dancers whirl violently through the space, ending in complete stillness as the lamb continues to careen through the air. Brokentalkers' metaphor here is obvious: the lamb-as-innocent/lamb-as-sacrifice trope which saturates Christian scripture. That this lamb is framed by its source, a popular cartoon, ironically recalls the safe atmosphere of children watching television at home. The video, edited to prolong the lamb's fall indefinitely, denies the audience (in a way that is, again, mimetic of the real experiences of Artane inmates) the *deus ex machina* trope, which also features inevitably in cartoons: the fall should be broken. The lamb should be caught.

As audience members, the affective sensation is one which makes us feel impelled to come to the aid of the victims. We want to help—we feel physically moved to do so—but we do not. The performance frame prevents the (western-inscribed) audience from stopping the show. We cannot return the reach of the dancers because of the physical barrier presented by the scrim. We cannot help in this situation because what we really desire is impossible: to step into history and retroactively intervene on behalf of the abused children. Of course, the performance frame is a construct, and the scrim is a piece of netting. Neither of these are truly substantial enough barriers to prevent an audience member from intervening if they so wished. By generating this feeling—an urgent desire to help—within spectators, and subsequently relying on their social conditioning to make intervention impossible, *The Blue Boy*, in an affective and embodied way, recreates precisely within us the complicity of the state and society that allowed abuses like those in Artane to go unpunished.

That complicity is further exacerbated by another video: the noted exception, and only visual representation of an abuser in the entire play. It is a celebration of Brother Joseph O'Connor and his work with the Artane Boys' Band, filmed for RTÉ in 1976.[12] By the time this footage is shown, O'Connor has been outed by survivors' testimony within the performance as one of the most notorious perpetrators of physical and sexual abuse against inmates. In the interview, O'Connor describes himself as a "strict disciplinarian", and the camera frequently pans over the pale faces of boys in the band. O'Connor is cheered on by a live audience—his sickening persona is woven into the fabric of daily life in mid-century Ireland.

The order in which the images in the videos are dramaturgically meted out to the audience guarantees that they are issued with a witness's imperative: to know the truth through presence, in both the theatre building and in the wider community. This imperative is underscored in the play's final moments: a survivor's confession, "I will never get over it," is followed by a song, sung by Keegan and the dancers, which eerily and endlessly asks, "What do you do, you do, you do?"[12] The mandate to remember ethically and to actively witness has been crucially woven into *The Blue Boy*'s performance dramaturgy. The play's closing atmosphere brings us to the realisation that the scenographic world of the production comprises of not only the stage, but also the "real" world into which this mandate has now been explicitly issued.

Notes

1. This essay is written in response to a performance attended during *The Blue Boy*'s 2016 run in the Project Arts Centre Dublin. It was part of a revival tour of the Dublin Theatre Festival production and featured several changes made since the 2011 premiere. "Interview with Gary Keegan—Brokentalkers—The Blue Boy", *No More Workhorse*, 22 Mar 2016. http://nomoreworkhorse.com/2016/03/22/interview-with-gary-keegan-brokentalkers-blue-boy. Accessed 4 Aug 2016.
2. Charlotte McIvor, "Witnessing the (Broken) Nation: Theatre of the Real and Social Fragmentation in Brokentalkers' Silver Stars, The Blue Boy, and Have I

No Mouth", in *That Was Us: Contemporary Irish Theatre and Performance*, ed. Fintan Walsh (London: Oberon Books, 2013), 41.
3. Patrick Duggan, *Trauma-Tragedy: Symptoms of Contemporary Performance* (Manchester: University of Manchester Press, 2012), 161.
4. Brokentalkers, *The Blue Boy*, dir. Gary Keegan and Feidlim Cannon, Project Arts Centre, Dublin, Ireland. Accessed 8 Apr 2016.
5. Elaine Scarry, "The Structure of Torture: The Conversion of Real Pain into the Fiction of Power", in *The Body: Critical Concepts in Sociology, Vol IV: Living and Dying Bodies*, ed. The Aberdeen Body Group (London: Routledge, 2004), 323.
6. Bessel Van der Kolk, *The Body Keeps the Score* (London: Routledge, 2015), 176.
7. Qtd. in Duggan, *Trauma-Tragedy*, 68.
8. Duggan, *Trauma-Tragedy*, 64.
9. Anne Goarzin, "Articulating Trauma", in *Études Irlandaises* 36.1 (2011). etudesirlandaises.revues.org/2116. Accessed 1 Aug 2016.
10. Jack Santino, "Performative Commemoratives, the Personal, and the Public: Spontaneous Shrines, Emergent Ritual", in *The Performance Studies Reader*, ed. Henry Bial, 2nd ed. (London: Routledge, 2007), 130.
11. Brokentalkers, *The Blue Boy*.
12. Ibid.

Bibliography

Brokentalkers. *The Blue Boy*. Directed by Gary Keegan and Feidlim Cannon. Project Arts Centre, Space Upstairs, Dublin. April 8, 2016.

Duggan, Patrick. *Trauma-Tragedy: Symptoms of Contemporary Performance*. Manchester: University of Manchester Press, 2012.

Goarzin, Anne. "Articulating Trauma." *Études Irlandaises 36. 1*, 2011. Accessed August 1, 2016. etudesirlandaises.revues.org/2116.

"Interview with Gary Keegan—Brokentalkers—The Blue Boy." No More Workhorse, March 22, 2016. Accessed August 4, 2016. http://nomoreworkhorse.com/2016/03/22/interview-with-gary-keegan-brokentalkers-blue-boy.

Kristeva, Julia. *Powers of Horror: An Essay on Abjection*. New York: Columbia University Press, 1981.

Lacan, Jacques. "The Essence of Tragedy: A Commentary on Sophocles's ANTIGONE." In *Seminar VII: The Ethics of Psychoanalysis*. Edited by Jacques-Alain Miller and Dennis Porter, London, Routledge, 1992.

McIvor, Charlotte. "Witnessing the (Broken) Nation: Theatre of the Real and Social Fragmentation in Brokentalkers' Silver Stars, The Blue Boy, and Have I No Mouth." In *That Was Us: Contemporary Irish Theatre and Performance*. Edited by Fintan Walsh, London, Oberon Books, 2013.

Santino, Jack. "Performative Commemoratives, the Personal, and the Public: Spontaneous Shrines, Emergent Ritual." In *The Performance Studies Reader*. Edited by Henry Bial, 2nd ed., London, Routledge, 2007.

Scarry, Elaine. "The Structure of Torture: The Conversion of Real Pain into the Fiction of Power." In *The Body: Critical Concepts in Sociology, Vol IV: Living and Dying Bodies*. Edited by The Aberdeen Body Group, London, Routledge, 2004.

Between the City and the Village: Liminal Spaces and Ambivalent Identities in Contemporary Irish Theatre

Brian Devaney

Introduction

The interaction of the urban and the rural may be found in multiple Irish cultural forms such as, but not limited to: literature, cinema, television, art, current affairs and, of course, drama. Cultural forms are often reflective of the society from which they have emerged and so, by examining cultural representations in these forms, some insight into the social dynamic may be garnered. Furthermore, such representations are arguably performative, in that they add to the construction of identities on multiple levels.

Maria Edgeworth's 1800 work *Castle Rackrent*, which is considered to be "the first Anglo-Irish novel",[1] attempts to appropriate Irish peasant life and deliver it to an educated urban class. The novel's narrator, Thady Quirke, is described as "an illiterate old steward" who relates the tale "in his vernacular idiom" and a glossary is provided to assist "the *ignorant* English reader (emphasis in original)".[2] Despite speaking in a local dialect, Thady still speaks in English and not his native Gaelic, and therefore Edgeworth's representation of peasant life in Ireland presents an appropriable image of the Irish. So much so, that it is reported in Kathryn J. Kirkpatrick's introduction to the novel that King George III "was much pleased with *Castle Rackrent*—he rubbed his hands and said [...] I know something now of my Irish subjects".[3] This is not to ignore Edgeworth's subversive work in depicting an estate ultimately passing from the landlord to its tenant, and the social commentary inherent to that aspect of the

B. Devaney (✉)
Independent Researcher, Kerry, Ireland

E. Jordan, E. Weitz (eds.), *The Palgrave Handbook of Contemporary Irish Theatre and Performance*,
https://doi.org/10.1057/978-1-137-58588-2_41

novel, rather, the example of *Castle Rackrent* highlights the long-standing nature of urban/rural dialogue in relation to the concept of representation.

In a contemporary context, urban and rural representation has been similarly reflective of changes in national identity. In film, images of rural Ireland have developed from the stereotypical, Bord Fáilte-esque "Irishness" seen in the *The Quiet Man*, 1952, to the more alienated, and existentially introspective landscape in Lenny Abrahamson's 2007 work, *Garage*. Similarly, the locus of identity that is the national television soap opera has reflected changes in Ireland's relationship with itself, moving initially from urban based drama *Tolka Row* (1964–1968), to a rural setting in *The Riordans* (1965–1979), *Bracken* (1978–1982), *Glenroe* (1983–2001), and back again in *Fair City* (1989–present).

These examples provide snapshots of the merits of examining the urban/rural dialogue across various media as a means of interrogating the nation, and also illustrate the persistence and relevance of this discourse across culture and time. In the context of Irish drama, there has been a shift from the retrospective representations of rural peasant life of the Irish Literary Revival, where "The poor Irish peasant perpetuates national and racial identity and becomes the symbol of Ireland",[4] to Celtic Tiger Ireland, where, as argued by Victor Merriman: "the cultural tone [...] is structured around a notion that the past is best forgotten, as its hopes and struggles have lost their relevance now that the appearance of success is everywhere evident".[5]

This statement also raises a question that must be addressed: in a post-Celtic Tiger society, where the appearance of success is no longer everywhere evident, is the past still "best forgotten" or has that dynamic changed over time in what is now a liminal space that is neither entirely rural nor completely urban? To answer this, this chapter looks at issues of urban and rural representation in contemporary Irish theatre, and interrogates the relationship of both spaces to each other.

Representations of the Rural

The interaction between the urban and the rural in Irish theatre is long-standing, with the riots that accompanied the premiere of J.M. Synge's *The Playboy of the Western World* at the Abbey Theatre in 1907 exemplifying the performative nature of that interaction. Synge's representation of a savage peasantry challenged the pastoral and idealistic imagery associated with peasant life presented by the Nationalist movement in their attempt to forge an idealized national identity. As asserted by Declan Kiberd, the Nationalist movement was a group "committed to the social construction of precisely the kind of Cuchulanoid heroism which the playwright [Synge] was so mischievously debunking".[6] Thus, representation in art may be seen to be an ambivalent entity: a marker of identity on the one hand, and a challenge to such static notions, as seen in *The Playboy of the Western World*, on the other.

More recently, the works of John B. Keane, a playwright synonymous with rural Ireland, examine the interaction of rural communities with external forces, and the tensions inherent to that interaction. The character of Mena Glavin in *Sive* (1959) is trapped between a traditional rural mode of living and a far more progressive and modern interpretation of it, which rejects the traditional extended family household in favour of a household akin to the modern nuclear family. Mena's ambivalent position is reinforced through her matchmaking, a representation of traditional values, to show her own interpretation of modernity. This makes her as much of a tragic figure as the eponymous Sive, who, unable to locate herself in the intersection of these two worlds, performs the ultimate rejection of her surroundings and takes her own life.

In Keane's *The Field* (1965), the interaction between traditional rural life and an encroaching modernity, and the reappraisal of identity on both personal and national levels involved in that realignment, is far more explicit. Tradition and modernization trade blows through the characters of the Bull McCabe and William Dee. Jacqueline Genet argues that "Over the years the rural countryside had changed from a place which preserved the riches of an ancient culture to an industrial resource to be exploited economically",[7] it is precisely this change that is dramatized in *The Field*.

Though Keane's dramas focus on rural communities and the tensions contained therein, his works address much broader concerns. Keane's plays animate common human anxieties within a rural framework; anxieties that transcend any urban/rural divide. The rural setting of Keane's works allows the examination of a community pared back to its essentials, in which the interaction between the individual and a changing society that seeks to redefine is laid bare. To quote from the theatre critic Michael Sheridan, it is through "the claustrophobia of the provincial setting" that the "truths about people can oftentimes be more clearly expressed".[8]

Conor McPherson's *The Weir*, first performed in London in 1997, is set in a small bar in rural Ireland and, like Keane's works, it presents an interaction between a traditional rural order and modernizing version of it. This finds expression in the opposing characters of Brendan and Finbar. Brendan, the bar owner, informs regular customer Jack that his sisters have been putting pressure on him to sell some land, so they can buy "new cars for the hubbies, you know?"[9] Brendan voices his opposition to the idea through a number of compound and unfinished sentences: "I'm just. It's a grand spot up there. Ah, I don't know. Just...".[10] His empty verbal spaces signify the unspoken traditional values shared by Brendan and Jack. The character of Finbar, a local businessman, is directly contrasted with such a value system. As stated by Andrew Hazucha, Finbar may be seen to be "the voice of New Ireland: unwaveringly self-confident, full of capitalist bravado, and a staunch advocate for land development and tourism".[11]

Three old black-and-white photographs, "a ruined abbey; people posing near a newly erected ESB [Electricity Supply Board] weir; a town in a cove with mountains around it" are permanent fixtures in the bar, and are themselves reflective of a sequence of tradition succumbing to progress.[12] The titular weir was built in 1951 “to regulate the water for generating power for the area and for Carrick as well” and is symbolic of the intrusion of modernity onto the rural Irish landscape.[13] To echo Jacqueline Genet’s point, the three photographs document the process of the rural Irish landscape transforming from “a place which preserved the riches of an ancient culture”, represented by the ruined abbey, “to an industrial resource to be exploited economically” as depicted in the photograph of the weir that also powers the nearest urban centre, Carrick, which is the final photograph of the trio.[14] A further example of this modernizing and globalizing world is hinted at by the reference to the summer tourists as the Germans, despite their nationality being unknown and irrelevant: “Where are they from. Is it Denmark, or Norway? It’s somewhere like that… Ah I don’t know where the fuck they’re from”.[15] However, it must be noted that, despite the tourists personifying an anonymous exteriority, the local community has also learned to capitalize on their regular annual arrival in terms of seasonal income.

In relation to the figurative nature of the weir itself, McPherson has been quoted as saying that: “On one side it is quite calm, and on the other side water is being squeezed through. Metaphorically the play is about a breakthrough. Lots under the surface is coming out”.[16] The supernatural stories that are told by the occupants of the bar replicate that “breakthrough” and grow darker and more revealing as the play progresses. These stories facilitate, as asserted by Nicholas Grene, a collapse of “the distinction between the world of the archaic country pub and the modern city milieu from which Valerie comes”.[17] They address issues of “loneliness, desolation, sexual perversion, mortality”, issues common to both urban and rural life, thereby exposing a “universal humanism” in operation in the play.[18]

Thus, in *The Weir*, rural Ireland is not depicted as a remote idyll. It is subject to the external influence of a modernizing and globalizing world, and the depictions of desolation, loneliness, and isolation in the village mark it as a place of imperfection. Similarly, urban Ireland, as seen through the character of Valerie who is seeking refuge in the countryside following traumatic events in Dublin, is also depicted as a place of dysfunction. The play explores the common ground between both realms through the medium of storytelling, and examines the ambiguous relationship between the community, tradition, and an imposing modernity. The work also dissolves the urban/rural divide through its presentation of what Nicholas Grene terms “universal humanism”. In terms of an increasing sense of globalization, the Germans, who remain anonymous and without nationality in the text, are located as eternal outsiders, but then again, we have not yet heard their stories.

Rural Ireland’s interaction with a globalizing world is further documented in Marie Jones’s *Stones in His Pockets*. First performed in Belfast in 1999, the play is set in a “scenic spot near a small village in Co. Kerry”.[19] The work centres on the appropriation of an image of rural Ireland by a Hollywood film crew for a global market, and highlights the discrepancies that lie between this image and the reality behind it. The image of rural Ireland being created and disseminated by the Hollywood crew is shown to be an inherently constructed one; the film's director is said to be "not happy with the cows [...] He says they're not Irish enough".[20] This inauthenticity is further highlighted by the Hollywood star, Caroline Giovanni's, attempts to improve her Irish accent (It is worth remembering, though not directly part of this examination, that Caroline is embodied by a male actor). Her dialect coach, John, tells her not to worry about it as: "Ireland is only one per cent of the market".[21] Furthermore, she is told to "be careful Caroline, you can't be too exact, you won't get away with it in Hollywood, they won't understand".[22] Thus, to draw from postmodern theory, the representation of rural Ireland by Hollywood in the play is a simulacrum, that is, an "identical copy for which no original has ever existed".[23]

The entire play is performed by just two actors, "who between them play 14 roles, signalling character changes with minor alterations in costume, movement, or lighting".[24] Such versatility in performance by the actors in the work carries a comic charge in what is a very humorous play, but also hints at possible further layers of interpretation and representation. Thematically, the play examines the dissemination of homogenized images within mass culture, and explores the gulf between such images and the reality they purport to represent. Similarly, the fact that all the characters are played by just two actors hints a homogenizing process at play between the work, which itself has become a constituent part of mass culture, and the audience's reception of the characters portrayed in broad stereotypical brushstrokes for comic and satirical effect. However, the inauthenticity of this homogenizing process is also highlighted in the play, through the physical performance of the actors, who, as put forward by Patrick Lonergan, "by showing how one body can be used to perform multiple identities [...] counteract the tendency within mass culture to present homogenized versions of identity as if they are authentic".[25]

The film being produced in the play is about the nineteenth century Irish Land War. In this context, Lonergan makes the astute observation that "The Hollywood film shows how the Irish responded to being 'dispossessed' of their land in the past; the irony that Jones reinforces is that the company making this movie is dispossessing the Irish of their entitlement to define their own identity in the present".[26] The character of Sean is dispossessed of his own place in the community, being thrown "out of the pub in his own town" after approaching the film's star Caroline.[27] Ultimately, perhaps arising from his inability to reconcile lived reality with an inauthentic culturally projected image of it, Sean commits suicide by drowning with stones in his pockets. Sean's drug-fuelled negotiation of lived reality, set against the projected image of it, is highlighted by his friend Fin's account of his social withdrawal: "everything he wanted was somewhere else [...] he stopped going out he just got his gear and stayed in his room with his movies... virtual reality".[28]

Lonergan makes the point that Sean's death "is also intended to pose a question to the audience: if Irish identity is created for global consumption, how does that affect the identities of real Irish people?"[29] Rural Ireland in the work has an ambivalent relationship with such globalizing processes, being dispossessed of identity by them while simultaneously capitalizing on them and erecting signs proclaiming "Caroline Giovanni dined here" on the other.[30]

Stones In His Pockets presents rural Ireland as forming a part of a larger global network, and as not immune to idealized, culturally inauthentic images, as evidenced in Sean's demise. Such idealizations ignore dysfunction, and the play explores the gulf that lies between them and reality itself. These discrepancies are not limited to the rural environment, and the themes explored hold relevance for both urban and rural audiences alike.

Dysfunction in both rural and urban environments is evident in Ursula Rani Sarma's work *...touched...*. First performed in Edinburgh in 1999, *...touched...* employs a shifting non-linear narrative that vacillates between the urban "sluggy city"[31] and the rural "crotch of the country".[32] Similar to *Stones in his Pockets*, naturalistic representation is eschewed by the work, and all of the characters in the play are embodied by just three actors, thus raising issues of subjectivity, interpretation, and representation in the piece. The play traces the childhood and teenage years of its two main characters: Cora and her younger brother Mikey. Following the death of their mother, the two siblings are relocated from the city to Uncle Dan and Auntie Mary's small pub in the countryside. In their new environment, Cora and Mikey spend their time dreaming up a plan "about getting away, coming up to the city".[33] From Uncle Dan's ignored alcoholism, to the secrecy surrounding the abuse experienced by Cora at the hands of Dr Cloughasy, rural Ireland is portrayed as a place of unspoken dysfunction. Cora's Auntie Mary, voiced by the character that plays Mikey, insists on Cora's going for ice cream with Dr Cloughasy, due to her interpretation of him as a man of importance in the local community. She berates Cora for initially refusing the offer: "the kind Doctor is being very generous with his time, Cora, and all you can be is ungrateful",[34] thereby inscribing her own narrow view of social hierarchy on Cora.

Ultimately, the nine-year-old Cora goes with Dr Cloughasy, who molests her, and a repeating pattern of sexual abuse begins, continuing until she is in her "late teens".[35] Finally, following Dr Cloughasy's aggressive attack on Cora's American suitor, and his subsequent attempt to assault her, she reveals her secret to her brother Mikey. She admits that she does not "tell him the whole story" but still tells him "where I left him down on the strand" and Mikey murders her abuser.[36] Mikey's representation of Mrs. Smith's praise of Dr Cloughasy following the news of his death highlights the discrepancy between perceived social stature and experienced reality in the rural community. Despite his heinous actions against Cora, Mrs. Smith, as voiced by Mikey, speaks of Dr Cloughasy as being "good [...] decent [...] honourable [...] hard working [and] educated".[37] Cora and her brother then escape from this "crotch of the country" to Dublin.[38]

However, what they find there is a far from the idealized vision that they had created. Having robbed a shop, the pair encounter Macca, a character played by the actor who portrays Dr Cloughasy, who assists them in their escape, albeit for a fee. Urban loyalty and the disconnecting anonymity of the urban environment are then highlighted through Macca's turning informer to the police in order to save himself. This sense of anonymity is reinforced by Macca's final line of the play. Having squandered the five hundred euro given to him by Mikey on drink, and having unintentionally led the Guards on a wild goose chase for Cora and Mikey, his final words "Anyway... you coming for a pint?"[39] hint at the fleeting and impermanent nature of anonymous existence in the urban environment. It is presumed that Cora and Mikey have gone to London at the end of the play, having escaped from one hell "to another kind of hell, carrying their own dangers with them".[40]

Dysfunction is a commonality between both rural and urban environments in *...touched...*, ranging from the alcoholism, sexual abuse, and the blinding social hierarchy of Cora and Mikey's childhood, to the violence, isolation, disloyalty and disconnect both found and embodied by them in Dublin.

Urban Ireland on Stage

Having looked at a selection of works set in rural Ireland, and *...touched...*, which is set in both urban and rural environments, this chapter now examines representation and the distinctions and commonalities between the two settings. This begins with two of Declan Hughes' plays—*Digging for Fire* (1991) and *Shiver* (2003)—that are separated by over a decade and illustrate a development in the narrative of Irish identity from an urban perspective.

First performed by Rough Magic in October 1991, Hughes' *Digging For Fire* documents a reunion between college friends in "the southside of Dublin".[41] However, as the alcohol flows, fractures within the group present themselves, and the tensions between lived experience and the idealism of the past come to the fore. Hughes, in his introduction to *Plays: 1*, predicts that "plays about groups of friends [...] will increasingly come to replace the family drama [...] for obvious sociological reasons",[42] thus further delineating a difference between his work and the traditional family-based plays of the past. Over the course of the reunion, secrets are uncovered that result in the dissolution of friendships and the disintegration of the suburban married life of Brendan and Clare.

Questions of identity and the collapse of static notions of self are central to the play, a fact that is emphasized in Hughes' introduction to this collection of his work, where he offers a description of the increasingly global culture of his youth. He describes the similarities of growing up in Dublin, or Manchester, or Seattle as "The cultural influences were the same: British and American TV, films and music. You read Irish literature, but mostly for the past; to discover the present you looked to America".[43]

This sense of a fluid and global personal identity is echoed in the play by the character of Danny, who has moved to New York to pursue a career as a writer. He describes growing up "with the TV on (and I'm not unique in this), with England and America beaming into my brain; I never had a single moment of,

I don't know, 'cultural purity'. I didn't know where I was from".[44] This in turn leads to Danny's rejection of static notions of national identity, and his realization "that *there* is as much *here* as *here* is",[45] a statement that simultaneously denies simplistic definitions of the self and highlights the effects of an increasingly globalized world on processes of identification.

Ultimately, Danny's boast of having an article published in the *New Yorker* is shown to be untrue, and his time in New York is revealed to have been "pretty meaningless" as he spends his days "not writing a word and deluding" himself that he is "in the thick of a modern maelstrom".[46] Despite his previous rejection of a simplistic identification with nation, Danny admits to the inescapable nature of it, stating that home was "all I ever thought about while I was away. I brought my village with me".[47]

It may then be surmised that there is an incongruence between Danny's ideals and his experience of lived reality. This tension between the ideal and reality is comically foreshadowed in the play by the account of "Bolshevik Brian [...] the Students' Union guy [who] got his *glasnost* out of the way early" and is now a radio DJ who boosts ratings, and therefore revenue, through scandal and controversy.[48] The break-up of the marriage between Clare and Brendan may also be viewed as symptomatic of the isolation of the self that is involved in a submission to oppressive social codes. Clare once shared Danny's idealism, a point reinforced by Breda's assertion to her that "you and Danny, you were the ones that were gonna do it all".[49] Clare admits to Brendan that she settled for a more mundane life with him. She got scared by Danny's freedom, met Brendan and did "exactly what I swore I wouldn't do, what my mother and nuns prayed I would do—the H fucking Dip".[50] Following the reunion, Clare's sense of self is reignited. She explains to Brendan: "This is what I'm truly like. I tried to be someone else, the one who was married to you. But I'm not her".[51]

Thus, though the play ends with a marriage in tatters and the dissolution of a group of friends, it is not an overly negative ending. Having become aware of her own self-isolation from her true feelings due to her submission to social conformity, the play closes on Clare dancing in a sunlit room to a song called "True Faith". Indeed, as Jason Buchanan asserts:

> Hughes's narrative frames the break-up as an escape from the historical nostalgia and village mentality that keep individuality locked into the same historical patterns [...] her dancing is a self-contained unfurling of her identity as an unfettered identity [...] finally separated from Irish history and tradition, in a rebirth into the new.[52]

There is an interesting counterpoint to Clare's "unfettered identity" being reborn "into the new" in Hughes' *Shiver*, a work that premiered over ten years after *Digging For Fire*. First performed in Dublin in 2003, *Shiver* documents the influence of "the new" referenced in *Digging For Fire* on two suburban couples. We encounter Jenny and Richard, who are returned emigrants attempting to exploit the trend of internet start-up companies with their dot. com enterprise named "51st State". We also meet Marion, an executive in a large multi-national company, and her husband Kevin, a stay at home father, teacher on a career break, and reluctant writer. Jenny, Richard, and Marion fully embrace the "unfettered identity [...] separated from Irish history and tradition" hinted at in Buchanan's analysis of *Digging For Fire*. According to Buchanan they "are representative of the Celtic Tiger's ideological and cultural impact as they recklessly chase the idol of the new" while Kevin "voices a counter-narrative [...] and reacts with disgust at their consumerist and reckless attitudes".[53]

Richard and Jenny's enterprise, "51st State", seeks to create a new globalized form of Irish identity that dismisses traditional markers of Irishness, such as the poet Seamus Heaney, as constituting part of a "Celtic souvenir shop".[54] However, by attempting to disseminate a form of Irish identity without history to a global virtual world, it may be argued that the image being represented is one that is heavily homogenized and similar to that seen in Marie Jones' *Stones in his Pockets*, that is, a simulacrum, an "identical copy for which no original has ever existed".[55]

In essence, the play dramatizes the increasing alienation that arises from the conflict between a virtual reality embodied in continual redefinition in the quest for the new, and reality as experienced by the characters in the play. This is mirrored in Kevin's quasi-religious, allegorical gold-rush story, where multitudes abandoned their everyday lives in an unsuccessful quest for foreign buried treasure following one stoneworker's initial discovery of "old Viking coins".[56] At the conclusion of the play, we find all of the characters in a worse state than when we first met them. Jenny and Richard's "51st State" has bankrupted them and they are now running a small catering company. Kevin has died somewhat ambiguously, we are never sure if it was an accident or a suicide, and Marion has been left widowed and jobless following the collapse of her large multi-national employer.

Thus, all characters have fallen victim to the abandonment of identity in some form: national identity in the case of Jenny and Richard; personal identity in the case of Marion's sacrifice for career progression; and masculine identity in a world that measures masculinity through performance in the case of Kevin. Jason Buchanan's assertion that "While Clare's dancing [in *Digging For Fire*] offered the hope of moving beyond a claustrophobic history, Marion and Jenny represent the damage that is done when the drive for newness is completely unhinged from any sense of history or place" is an astute one.[57] It highlights Hughes's interrogation of the constructed nature of identity on both personal and national levels.

Another work that deals with the representation of the urban in contemporary Irish theatre—Daragh Carville's *Language Roulette* (1996), set in 1994 during a ceasefire Belfast—is similar to Hughes' *Digging For Fire* in that it dramatizes the reunion, and subsequent dissolution, of a group of friends. Like *Digging For Fire*, the play is punctuated with alternative music, ranging from the Beastie Boys to Nirvana to Oasis to Stereolab, thus situating the characters in a contemporary counter-cultural context, one many audience members may find relevant. This context is further added to by the use and abuse of drugs and alcohol in the piece as joints are smoked, mysterious pills ingested, and the concept of "Pound-for-a-Pint" night in the Belfast bar is taken to excess by Ollie. In the work, the alcohol and drug fuelled urban environment acts as a catalyst in exposing past relationships between characters, a past that ultimately isolates them from each other.

The above works are some examples of urban representation in contemporary Irish theatre: by no means an exhaustive list. Further plays that the reader may find of note in this context include, but are not limited to: Enda Walsh's *Disco Pigs* (1996); Jimmy Murphy's *A Picture of Paradise* (1997); Pom Boyd, Declan Hughes and Arthur Riordan's *Boomtown—A City Comedy* (1999); Dermot Bolger's *The Passion of Jerome* (1999) and Mark O'Rowe's *Howie the Rookie* (1999).

Liminal Spaces

Having explored the representation of both the urban and the rural on stage in contemporary Irish theatre, a more liminal space will now be examined, an ambiguous space that is neither the city nor the village. Billy Roche's *The Wexford Trilogy* of plays is set in small town Ireland and features elements of both rural and urban living, while never being fully set in either. In this ambivalent setting, Roche explores the influence of modernized society on lives lived in a small town, and the interaction of traditional values with that development. This interaction will be explored in two plays from the trilogy: *A Handful of Stars* and *Poor Beast in the Rain*.

The first play of the trilogy, *A Handful of Stars*, was first performed in London in 1988, and is set in "a scruffy pool hall [...] in a small town somewhere in Ireland".[58] The action follows the misadventures of Jimmy Brady, a "tough boy of seventeen or so" and his struggle to locate himself within his surroundings.[59] From the outset, the concept of hierarchy is presented by the back room off the main pool hall, which is an exclusive space for those Jimmy terms "the élite",[60] a space that Jimmy also recognizes as one where he doesn't "belong".[61] In this way, issues of place, power, agency and authority are foregrounded in the work. The small town presented to us in *A Handful of Stars*, and the social anxieties contained therein, provides a generic blueprint for the operation of social structures within any community, large or small. In support of this, Roche is quoted in an essay by Christopher Murray as stating that "the setting is a metaphor for the world".[62] It is, as asserted by Murray, "social criticism by astute manipulation of the synecdoche: the setting within the setting, the part for the whole, the pool hall for the town, and the town for the nation".[63]

The setting of the play has both urban and rural influences, while never existing solely in either realm. Some of the characters we meet are employed in a local factory, itself a marker of industrialization and urban life. It is also a location that marks Jimmy's alienation from his environment as he is refused a job there, while the man interviewing him keeps his position despite being caught stealing from the job. There is also a sense of claustrophobia in the piece, one that, to quote from Michael Sheridan's assertion referenced at the beginning of this chapter, is reflective of that of the rural environment and reveals certain "truths about people".[64]

It is in this atmosphere of stifling claustrophobia that we find Jimmy, who rebels in an effort to create an identity for himself within the confines of the community. The constricting nature of the world Jimmy finds himself in is highlighted by his attributing his failure at a job interview to being asked about his father, a man of ill-repute within the community. Due to the dominant position of parochial attitudes within the community's hierarchy, Jimmy states: "fellas like meself and me Da don't have a ghost of a chance".[65] The influence of a parochial mentality in a quasi-urban space is also reflected in the character of Stapler, recognizable by his "scruffy pair of Beatle boots. Who else wears them in this town any more, only Stapler".[66] Similarly, Jimmy's love interest Linda hears about his being with another woman in the pub where "the whole feckin' place was laughin' at me [Linda] down there",[67] further highlighting the invasively insular nature of the community.

It is also significant that, as part of Jimmy's final rebellion, he scrawls his name in chalk on the door to the exclusive back room of the pool hall, thereby drawing attention to the barriers he has encountered in the community, while also attempting to "find his identity in a society which has branded him an outcast".[68] The cyclical nature of rebellion against an alienating society is also hinted at through the character of Stapler, who is a few years older than Jimmy, and someone that he looks up to. Jimmy and Tony have been climbing in through a broken window and taking refuge in the pool hall at night. However, it comes as a surprise to Jimmy that Stapler did the same thing as a youth. When asked how he got in to the pool hall at the end of the play, Stapler informs Jimmy "that window has been broken for fifteen years. Why, did you think you were the first to discover it or somethin'?"[69] However, Stapler has learned to adapt to his environment in order to survive, unlike Jimmy, who Stapler describes as waging "war on everybody".[70]

Ultimately, Jimmy's "war on everybody" is about the social constructs Jimmy feels imprisoned by. He is cast as an outsider by the community and he assumes the role of rebel, refusing to be assimilated by a society that is hypocritical and imbalanced in his eyes. He states: "nobody's goin' to wrap me up in a neat little parcel" and that "that's the difference between me and Conway. He tiptoes around. I'm screamin'".[71] Jimmy is also a product of his own past, and the broken marriage between his parents is an influence on him. Earlier in the play Jimmy describes a loving and tender moment he witnessed between them, and at the conclusion of the piece it is suggested that his erratic behaviour may actually have its roots in an attempt to "get them talking again if nothing else".[72] Thus, in *A Handful of Stars*, Roche provides a social critique of life in a small town, an urbanized space that is still subject to traditional hierarchies and value systems, and Jimmy's fate, in the words of Christopher Murray, "proposes a strong attack on Irish social structures" both urban and rural.[73]

The second work in Roche's trilogy of plays, 1989's *Poor Beast in the Rain*, is also set in the quasi-urban, semi-rural setting of "Wexford, a small town in Ireland".[74] Similar to *A Handful of Stars*, the traditional familial setting is eschewed in favour of a public and primarily masculine den of iniquity, or as Christopher Murray puts it: "a betting shop, once more a metaphor for play, gaming, or chance, [...] a public resort of somewhat dubious relation to domestic norms".[75] The action of the play takes place over one weekend, the all-Ireland hurling final weekend, in which Wexford is competing. We meet Steven, the overly mild-mannered betting shop owner, his daughter Eileen, the older Molly, a straight talking and somewhat bitter employee of the shop, and two regular customers, Joe who appears to operate on some level of celebratory nostalgia, and the naïve Georgie who is in love with Eileen. As the story unfolds we discover that Steven's wife, and Eileen's mother, abandoned the family to escape to England with a new lover, Danger Doyle, and it is his return that drives the dramatic action of the latter part of the play.

As in *A Handful of Stars*, the claustrophobic nature of living in small town Ireland is represented in the play. This may be seen in the graffiti describing Steven as a eunuch following his wife's leaving him,[76] Joe repeating the rumour of Johnny Doran's bedding of Eileen,[77] and Danger's account of Eileen's mother's fears of ostracism if she returned as "they'd turn the poor crator to dust so they would".[78] It is also a place that appears to be mired in the past, and archaic traditional values are illustrated in the large numbers of women travelling on the bus to the hurling match being described by Joe as "auld codoligy".[79] Eileen foregrounds the isolation from the modern world in what is still an urban centre, albeit a small one, in her discussion with Georgie at the beginning of the play: "we might as well be livin' in the back of beyond as livin' here [...] Stylewise. Music-wise. Sure by the time somethin' reaches us here it's already got out of date everywhere else".[80] In the play, Wexford is a town that is still subject to traditional values and hierarchies, much the same as the nameless town portrayed in *A Handful of Stars.*

Much of the action of the play develops from the return of Danger Doyle, a character raised to mythological status in the nostalgic eyes of his one-time friend Joe. This is a point echoed by Roche in his afterword to the trilogy of plays. He describes *Poor Beast in the Rain* as "a rainy day sort of a play which is held together by an ancient Irish myth as Danger Doyle returns like Oisín to the place of his birth".[81] There is also a myth-making process in operation in the community, with the hurler Red O'Neill being celebrated in song and wearing a jersey so huge that "you'd want to be Charles Atlas to lift it nearly".[82]

However, such hero worship may also be a form of escapism as the town's men appropriate the deeds of the hero, in a similar way to Joe living vicariously through his nostalgic stories about Danger. Molly deconstructs such displaced identificatory processes and highlights their fallacious and parasitic nature, telling chief mythmaker Joe that he "had nothin' to do with it boy. Big Red O'Neill scored the goal all by himself".[83] She continues: "Big Red O'Neill must be browned off carryin' you crowd of ejits on his back everywhere he goes. It's a wonder some of yeh wouldn't get down and walk a bit of the way once in a while."[84]

Danger himself deconstructs Joe's version of the past throughout the play, constantly correcting him on his embellished stories. Danger is also conscious of the limiting nature of myth and his own confinement by an embellished past, having returned "to kiss the cross they hung me on".[85] Following Georgie's maniacal shouting about "Danger Doyle, the big hard man cryin' his eyes out up in the courtroom",[86] Danger tells Eileen that "with a bit of luck he [Georgie] might wind up washin' my name away for once and for all".[87]

Roche presents the falsities of myth and myth-making within a community on stage, and blind loyalty to such myths is interrogated by the work. Danger, having returned to the small town from the metropolis of London, examines the community with a new sense of freedom, a freedom previously denied to him on account of the limiting nature of his existence within an insular myth-making society. As noted by Christopher Murray, with *Poor Beast in the Rain*, "Roche reveals the pride and the folly of local heroism and easy loyalty",[88] an inquiry equally relevant to both urban and rural societies, and one that is examined by the work in a liminal space that is neither one nor the other.

Conclusion

Having analyzed the influence of a modernizing and globalizing world on rural Ireland, examined the influence of the past in a selection of urban-set works, and highlighted the existence of a liminal space that is neither the city nor the village in the works of Billy Roche, a question posed at the beginning of this chapter may now be returned to. That is, in present-day post-Celtic tiger Ireland, in terms of Irish theatre, is the past still "best forgotten" or has that dynamic developed over time, leading to an ambivalent moment where the past and the present co-exist in a liminal space that is neither entirely rural nor completely urban?

As demonstrated in the works of John B. Keane, Conor McPherson and Marie Jones, rural Ireland on-stage does not exist within a vacuum, rather it is subject to the external pressures of a modernizing and globalizing world. Both *The Weir* and Ursula Rani Sarma's *...touched...* highlight an element of dysfunction common to both urban and rural worlds. Similarly, just as the rural-set plays studied here are subject to the influences of modernity, the urban-set plays of Declan Hughes and Daragh Carville have been shown to highlight the imperfections of urban life, and the inescapable influence of the past upon the present. Finally, two of Billy Roche's plays have been looked at in terms of their representation of an ambivalent space, a space that is neither completely rural nor fully urban, but one that contains influences from both sides of that increasingly irrelevant divide.

The characters of the plays considered here, and their shifting and fluid identities, also reflect that ambivalence. In *The Weir*, Brendan moves between maintaining traditional values in terms of land, to taking advantage of the regular visits of the "Germans". The locals of *Stones in His Pockets* are dispossessed of identity by globalizing forces, while also capitalizing on that very process. Both Cora and Mikey in *...touched...* idealize the urban world from their rural setting, but on their arrival in Dublin realize the falsehood of that idealization. Danny in *Digging For Fire* seeks an escape from tradition but also admits that home was "all I ever thought about while I was away. I brought my village with me".[89] In *Shiver* there is a blatant rejection of the past in Richard and Jenny's "51st State", however, the fates of the characters in the work also suggest "the damage that is done when the drive for newness is completely unhinged from any sense of history or place".[90] In *Language Roulette* the past is a force that, when denied, tears friendships and relationships apart. In *A Handful of Stars* Jimmy is an ambivalent character in that he, perhaps on an unconscious level, seeks the acceptance of a society he is not willing to accept himself. Similarly, in *Poor Beast in the Rain* Danger Doyle deconstructs the myth-making processes of the small town, despite occupying a mythological space in the community.

From the analysis outlined here, it may be argued that post-Celtic tiger Ireland is indeed at an ambivalent moment, one where the past cannot be denied, and where the distinction between the urban and the rural is growing increasingly vague. The blurring of the distinction between the urban and the rural and the past and the present is evident in contemporary Irish theatre, and may indeed indicate a future direction for it. The work of Martin McDonagh, a writer more influenced by Australian soap-opera and Quentin Tarantino than the Irish dramatic tradition of Synge,[91] demonstrates this cultural fluidity. In his *Leenane Trilogy* of plays McDonagh inflects the kitsch notion of the rural Irish play to challenge and subvert traditional perceptions of Irish theatre, and, as Nicholas Grene notes, in them "the cult of Connemara and the culture of weepy Irish nostalgia are treated to a savagely sardonic iconoclasm".[92]

The blurring of static and increasingly irrelevant distinctions is similarly evident in Roddy Doyle and Bisi Adigun's 2007 adaptation of what may be deemed the quintessential rural Irish play, Synge's *The Playboy of the Western World*. In this work, the setting of the play is shifted from the early 1900s to the present, and also from the west of Ireland to a bar in west Dublin, with Christy Mahon represented as a Nigerian immigrant. As Mary Trotter observes, "placing the production in the context of *The Playboy* permits this new adaptation to claim its lineage among national plays seeking to, in Christopher Murray's terms, hold the 'mirror up to nation' in a moment of cultural crisis".[93] She continues by asserting that both McDonagh's *Leenane Trilogy* and the adaptation of *The Playboy* by Doyle and Adigun are reflective of how "contemporary theatre seeks to break away from the tropes of the classic Irish play by commenting ironically upon them",[94] revealing an ambivalence at the heart of Irish theatre's relationship with its past. Similarly, urban-set plays, such as the adaptation of *The Playboy* mentioned here, locate a form of the village within the city, a form of community within the anonymous urban environment.

As argued by Declan Hughes, it is no longer a case of "Either/or" but of "Not only but also".[95] The liminal spaces presented by Billy Roche's works dialectically synthesize the rural setting and its inescapable encroaching modernity with the urban setting that is still subject to the past, and dramatize what Hughes deems to be the "objective correlative for Ireland", the space "*between* cities".[96] This in-between and liminal space is one where past and present exist in symbiosis, forging a new future that, while conscious of the past, is not mired in it, and is reflective of fluid and ambivalent identities on cultural, national, and personal levels.

Notes

1. R.F. Foster, *Modern Ireland: 1600–1972* (London: Penguin, 1988), 181.
2. Maria Edgeworth, *Castle Rackrent* (Oxford: Oxford University Press, 2008), 3–4.
3. Kathryn J. Kirkpatrick in Edgeworth, *Castle Rackrent*, ix.
4. Jacqueline Genet, ed., *Rural Ireland, Real Ireland?* (Gerrards Cross: Colin Smythe, 1996), 13.
5. Victor Merriman, *Because We Are Poor: Irish Theatre in the 1990s* (Dublin: Carysfort Press, 2011), 201.
6. Declan Kiberd, *Inventing Ireland: The Literature of the Modern Nation* (London: Vintage, 1996), 183.
7. Genet, *Rural Ireland, Real Ireland?*, 15.
8. Michael Sheridan, "John B. tills a fertile field", *The Irish Press*, 24 February 1987, 9.
9. Conor McPherson, *The Weir* (London: Nick Hern Books, 1997), 4.
10. Ibid., 4.
11. Andrew Hazucha, "The Shannon Scheme, Rural Electrification, and Veiled History in Conor McPherson's *The Weir*", *New Hibernia Review* 17, Number 1, (Spring 2013): 75.
12. McPherson, *The Weir*, 3.
13. Ibid., 18.
14. Genet, *Rural Ireland, Real Ireland?*, 15.
15. McPherson, *The Weir*, 50.
16. Conor McPherson quoted in Hazucha, "The Shannon Scheme, Rural Electrification, and Veiled History in Conor McPherson's *The Weir*", 70.
17. Nicholas Grene, "Ireland in Two Minds: Martin McDonagh and Conor McPherson", *The Yearbook of English Studies* 35, (2005): 308.
18. Ibid.
19. Marie Jones, *Two Plays: Stones In His Pockets, A Night In November* (London: Nick Hern Books, 2000), 8.
20. Ibid., 28.
21. Ibid., 13.
22. Ibid., 15.
23. Frederic Jameson, *Postmodernism or, The Cultural Logic of Late Capitalism* (London: Verso, 1991), 18.
24. Patrick Lonergan, *Theatre and Globalization: Irish Drama in the Celtic Tiger Era* (London: Palgrave Macmillan, 2010), 10.
25. Ibid.

26. Ibid., 11.
27. Jones, *Two Plays: Stones In His Pockets, A Night In November*, 47.
28. Ibid., 46.
29. Lonergan, *Theatre and Globalization*, 12.
30. Jones, *Two Plays: Stones In His Pockets, A Night In November*, 21.
31. Ursula Rani Sarma, *...touched...*, *BLUE* (London: Oberon Books, 2002), 17.
32. Ibid., 21.
33. Ibid., 22.
34. Ibid., 24.
35. Ibid., 15.
36. Ibid., 31.
37. Ibid., 32.
38. Ibid., 21.
39. Ibid., 39.
40. Mary Leland, "Touched", *The Irish Times*, 8 October 1999.
41. Declan Hughes, *Plays: 1—Digging For Fire, New Morning, Halloween Night, Love and a Bottle* (London: Methuen, 1998), 3.
42. Ibid., x.
43. Ibid., ix.
44. Ibid., 35.
45. Ibid., 38.
46. Ibid., 74.
47. Ibid.
48. Ibid., 9.
49. Ibid., 29.
50. Ibid., 49.
51. Ibid., 50.
52. Jason Buchanan, "Living at the End of the Irish Century: Globalization and Identity in Declan Hughes's *Shiver*", *Modern Drama* 52, Number 3, (Fall 2009): 308–309.
53. Ibid., 310.
54. Declan Hughes, *Shiver* (London: Methuen, 2003), 26.
55. Jameson, *Postmodernism or, The Cultural Logic of Late Capitalism*, 18.
56. Hughes, *Shiver*, 70.
57. Buchanan, "Living at the End of the Irish Century", 320.
58. Billy Roche, *The Wexford Trilogy: A Handful of Stars, Poor Beast in the Rain, Belfry* (London: Nick Hern Books, 2000), 2.
59. Ibid.
60. Ibid., 33.
61. Ibid., 34.
62. Christopher Murray in *Theatre Stuff: Critical Essays on Contemporary Irish Theatre*, ed. Eamonn Jordan (Dublin: Carysfort Press, 2000), 209.
63. Ibid., 210.
64. Sheridan, "John B. tills a fertile field", 9.
65. Roche, *The Wexford Trilogy*, 37.
66. Ibid., 20.
67. Ibid., 47.
68. Murray in Murray in *Theatre Stuff: Critical Essays on Contemporary Irish Theatre*, 213.

69. Roche, *The Wexford Trilogy*, 61.
70. Ibid., 64.
71. Ibid., 60.
72. Ibid., 65.
73. Murray in *Theatre Stuff: Critical Essays on Contemporary Irish Theatre*, 214.
74. Roche, *The Wexford Trilogy*, 68.
75. Murray in *Theatre Stuff: Critical Essays on Contemporary Irish Theatre*, 214.
76. Roche, *The Wexford Trilogy*, 109.
77. Ibid., 91.
78. Ibid., 99.
79. Ibid., 72.
80. Ibid., 70.
81. Ibid., 188.
82. Ibid., 93.
83. Ibid., 107.
84. Ibid., 108.
85. Ibid., 121.
86. Ibid., 120.
87. Ibid., 122.
88. Murray in *Theatre Stuff: Critical Essays on Contemporary Irish Theatre*, 216.
89. Hughes, *Plays: 1*, 74.
90. Buchanan, "Living at the End of the Irish Century", 320.
91. Lonergan, *Theatre and Globalization*, 104–107.
92. Grene, "Ireland in Two Minds", 301.
93. Mary Trotter, *Modern Irish Theatre* (Cambridge: Polity, 2008), 195.
94. Ibid., 196.
95. Declan Hughes in *Theatre Stuff: Critical Essays on Contemporary Irish Theatre*, 9.
96. Ibid., 12.

Bibliography

Buchanan, Jason. "Living at the End of the Irish Century: Globalization and Identity in Declan Hughes's *Shiver*." *Modern Drama* 52, Number 3, Fall (2009): 300–324.

Edgeworth, Maria. *Castle Rackrent*. Oxford: Oxford University Press, 2008.

Foster, R.F. *Modern Ireland: 1600–1972*. London: Penguin, 1988.

Genet, Jacqueline, ed. *Rural Ireland, Real Ireland?* Gerrards Cross: Colin Smythe, 1996.

Grene, Nicholas. "Ireland in Two Minds: Martin McDonagh and Conor McPherson." *The Yearbook of English Studies* 35, (2005): 298–311.

Hazucha, Andrew. "The Shannon Scheme, Rural Electrification, and Veiled History in Conor McPherson's *The Weir*." *New Hibernia Review* 17, Number 1, Spring (2013): 67–80.

Hughes, Declan. *Plays: 1—Digging for Fire, New Morning, Halloween Night, Love and a Bottle*. London: Methuen, 1998.

———. *Shiver*. London: Methuen, 2003.

Jameson, Frederic. *Postmodernism or, The Cultural Logic of Late Capitalism*. London: Verso, 1991.

Jones, Marie. *Two Plays: Stones in His Pockets, A Night in November*. London: Nick Hern Books, 2000.

Jordan, Eamonn, ed. *Theatre Stuff: Critical Essays on Contemporary Irish Theatre.* Dublin: Carysfort Press, 2000.
Keane, John B. *Sive.* Dublin: Progress House, 1959.
———. *The Field.* Cork: Mercier Press, 1966.
Kiberd, Declan. *Inventing Ireland: The Literature of the Modern Nation.* London: Vintage, 1996.
Leland, Mary. "Touched." *The Irish Times*, October 8, 1999.
Lonergan, Patrick. *Theatre and Globalization: Irish Drama in the Celtic Tiger Era.* London: Palgrave Macmillan, 2010.
McPherson, Conor. *The Weir.* London: Nick Hern Books, 1997.
Merriman, Victor. *Because We Are Poor: Irish Theatre in the 1990s.* Dublin: Carysfort Press, 2011.
Morin, Emilie. "The Celtic Tiger, Its Phantoms and Conor McPherson's Haunted Rooms." *Textual Practice* 28, Number 6, (2014).
Rani Sarma, Ursula. …*Touched… BLUE.* London: Oberon Books, 2002.
Roche, Billy. *The Wexford Trilogy: A Handful of Stars, Poor Beast in the Rain, Belfry.* London: Nick Hern Books, 2000.
Sheridan, Michael. "John B. Tills a Fertile Field," *The Irish Press*, February 24, 1987.
Trotter, Mary. *Modern Irish Theatre* Cambridge: Polity, 2008.

Verse in Twenty-First Century Irish Theatre

Kasia Lech

The new millennium has brought a renewed interest in verse as a theatrical language through which to engage with contemporary audiences in Ireland. This chapter aims to document how theatremakers in Ireland have explored the potential of verse, and forms of communication that approximate the linguistic energy of verse, in a wide selection of dramatic texts and theatrical performances: new writings, musicals, devised performances, and innovative stagings and translations of classics. Dublin rapper Lethal Dialect provided a fitting metaphor for the diversity within these new works. Speaking in 2012 at the Abbey Theatre about the value of expressing oneself through the rhythm of verse, he said that using rhythmical language to talk about everyday issues allowed him to speak about these issues in his own way; the people, who listen do not have to agree with him, but can still appreciate the rhythm and, in turn, can appreciate his work.[1] More recently, he observed that "Hip-Hop is something which allows you to be a thinker".[2] In short, using rhythmical language facilitates and connects his critical engagement and point of view with different audiences.

Lethal Dialect's comment, made within the walls of the Abbey, creates a link between the popularity of highly rhythmic music like rap and hip-hop amongst artists and audiences and its increasing appeal for theatremakers. As the comment was made at the national theatre of Ireland, co-founded by W.B. Yeats, it also carries a symbolic significance. On the one hand, it may be a harbinger of a verse drama revival in Ireland. On the other—as it was made by a rapper and hip-hop performer rather than a poet, a playwright, or even a director—it proclaims the search for new forms and aesthetics of verse in contemporary theatre,

K. Lech (✉)
Canterbury Christ Church University, Canterbury, UK
e-mail: kasia.lech@canterbury.ac.uk

E. Jordan, E. Weitz (eds.), *The Palgrave Handbook of Contemporary Irish Theatre and Performance*,
https://doi.org/10.1057/978-1-137-58588-2_42

challenges traditional models of creative ownership, and promises a dialogue between the past and present. The appearance of Lethal Dialect in the Abbey is also a fitting metaphor of the Abbey's unique position within the city of Dublin and the tensions between low and high cultures this position brings about. The national theatre lies in the middle of one of the city's most notorious streets, with the sound of Dublin's street rappers often heard in its area and the poets like Pat Ingoldsby selling their works on nearby Westmoreland Street. All these will resonate throughout the upcoming survey.

Revisiting the Past

One reason to use rhythmical language on the stage is to re-energize classical repertoire and re-examine the relationship between the present and the past. The Abbey's decision to commission Seamus Heaney's new translation of Sophocles' *Antigone* as part of the theatre's centenary celebration in 2004 and "The Abbey and Europe" season is the most obvious example. Heaney's choice of verse rhythms for *The Burial at Thebes* arose from his multi- and transcultural inspirations, including Greek tragedy, Irish lament *Caoineadh Airt Uí Laoghaire* by Eibhlín Dubh Ní Chonaill, Anglo-Saxon poetry, and George W. Bush. The latter unlikely inspiration came from Heaney noticing that Creon's points against Antigone were similar to those used by George W. Bush to forward his argument for war in Iraq. Heaney then decided that Creon should speak in iambic pentameter as a conventional rhythm and the medium "to honour the patriots in life and death".[3] Taking into account that the Republicans' traditions emphasize commemoration, one "hears" a touch of sarcasm in this sentence and sees a clear link between these two comments.

Heaney used verse to re-translate *Antigone*—that "had become an accumulation of [political, social, and philosophical] issues" and "a work that was as much if not more at home in the seminar room than on the stage"—back into theatre language.[4] The play gained interest from a variety of theatre artists. For example, Lorraine Pintal and Patrick Mason directed it for the Abbey in 2004 and 2008, Marcela Lorca staged it for the Guthrie Theatre in Minneapolis in 2011 and Dominique Le Gendre collaborated with Heaney and Derek Walcott on an opera version of the play presented in 2008 at London's Globe.

Heaney's *The Burial at Thebes* has been discussed extensively by scholars; however, the less internationally recognized interpretations of classical texts by Corcadorca and Rough Magic, with their Artistic Directors Pat Kiernan and Lynne Parker respectively, also deserve attention. Corcadorca's 2005 staging of Shakespeare's *The Merchant of Venice*, directed by Kiernan, was a promenade production, featured international actors, and explored Irish tolerance just one year after Ireland opened its borders to citizens of the new countries that had joined the European Union. In 2018, this is still one of very few examples of a major Irish theatre company recognizing the presence of migrant voices.[5]

Rough Magic, committed to presenting "new Irish work for the stage" and "innovative productions from the classical repertoire",[6] engaged with the European canon and, in some cases, introduced it to Ireland as well as commissioning new translations. In 2006 their take on the central conflict in Shakespeare's *The Taming of the Shrew*, directed by Lynne Parker, was embodied through tango. It was followed in 2007 by Parker's staging of Friedrich Schiller's *Don Carlos* (in a version by Mike Poulton) that explored the performance of power in the play as the point of tangency between the source and the contemporary audiences of Ireland. The two shows received multiple *Irish Times* Theatre Awards, including Best Production awards.

Tom Creed's 2008 staging of *Life is a Dream* (Jo Clifford's translation of Calderón's *La vida es sueño*) used verse structure to bring Calderón's *Polonia* closer to Ireland, by highlighting the live presence of Irish actors and spectators. The audiences of Creed's show sat together on two sides of the stage, constantly reminded they were watching and being watched, which linked with the formal mode of the language to highlight that what the audience saw was actors performing. The irregular verse pattern (lines varied from one syllable to seventeen syllables long), closer to contemporary verse than to the seventeenth century's regular structures, linked with contemporary references in Clifford's translation. For example, Clarín bemoaned being hungry and called his diet an "anorexic school of thought".[7] The production started with verse spoken by Corkonian Hilary O'Shaughnessy as Rosaura; the audience saw her just seconds later climbing down on a rope hanging from an unidentifiable place above the stage. The actors' delivery of Clifford's verse in their Irish accents functioned as a further reminder that the theatre space was shared by Irish audiences and actors. This, in turn, encouraged the audiences' collective response, mobilized metatheatrical aspects of the play, and supported Creed's and Clifford's deconstruction of the dichotomy between the powerful and the powerless.

Rough Magic presented all three productions in the Project Arts Centre (Dublin), a space equated with new, cutting edge art. *Life is a Dream* and *Don Carlos* were professional Irish debuts of the two plays. During the 2011 Ulster Bank Dublin Theatre Festival, Rough Magic's actors (directed by Lynne Parker) rapped Arthur Riordan's new version of Henrik Ibsen's *Peer Gynt*. The production also featured Riordan performing. Riordan is a co-founder and a regular collaborator of Rough Magic and his works often explore aspects of Irish history that are highly charged with emotions. For example, in 2004 Rough Magic produced *Improbable Frequency*. This musical in verse explores Irish neutrality during World War II and its relationship with both the UK and Germany. The play features the Red Bank Restaurant on D'Olier Street in Dublin that during World War II became a meeting point for groups associated with Nazi Germany;[8] or, as Riordan described it:

> There's a place where the barman will smile
> If you drink yellow beer and you whisper "*Seig Heil*"! –
> Not that we're Nazis, we just like the style,
> Down at the Red Bank Restaurant.[9]

In the play, the dual function of formal language mirror an Ireland being torn between its neutrality, its commitment to keep the newly won independence from Britain, and its continuous fight for a united Ireland. On the one hand, the heightened rhythm helps to establish the playful atmosphere of the piece and Dublin in 1941 as a city that does not seem to notice,

> That something rather untoward
> Is happening over there.[10]

On the other hand, Riordan's rhyming structures draw attention to the uneasy choices facing Ireland. For example, one of the songs featured lines:

> You may say the Aryans
> Are only barbarians.[11]

The word barbarian echoes the views of English colonizers in Ireland, claiming they were bringing civilization to Irish "barbarians",[12] which provided historical context for Irish neutrality; at the same time, it questions these views by linking the term with one that connoted Nazism. Later in the play, "drink" rhymes with "think" in lines that explain "the right" of a man to forget about any troubles.[13] When a British spy interrogates an Irish civil servant, "views" rhymes with "choose", highlighting the instability of Ireland's neutrality.[14]

Improbable Frequency, again directed by Lynne Parker, became highly popular in Ireland and was brought to the Abbey stage in 2005 and revived for another run at the Gaiety Theatre in 2012. More recently, in 2015, Rough Magic produced and Parker directed another of Riordan's verse-musicals: *The Train*. The title refers to the 1971 Contraceptive Train, a protest by forty-seven women, who embarked on a journey from Dublin to Belfast to buy contraceptives, not fully legal in Ireland until 1993.[15] The production made references to the Equality Marriage Referendum that happened just a few months before *The Train* premiered, highlighting the fight for rights and equality as an ongoing process in Ireland.

Arthur Riordan's works also facilitate the dialogue between past and present on another level. In 2001, he co-wrote (with Des Bishop) and performed in *Rap Éire*. The play, produced by the Kilkenny Bickerstaffe Theatre Company, premiered in Limerick's Belltable. *Rap Éire* features hip-hop to tell a story of a New York rapper coming to Ireland in the 1990s and encountering Irish society in the early years of the Celtic Tiger. A decade later, the millennial actor and playwright Stefanie Preissner wrote her plays *Our Father* and *Solpadeine is My Boyfriend* about post-Celtic Tiger Ireland using a hip-hop and rap-derived verse. She referred to Riordan's work as her direct source inspiration as a writer.[16]

New Voices of Ireland

Corkonian Stefanie Preissner's work first gained attention at Dublin's 2011 ABSOLUT Fringe Festival, an annual event during which emerging multidisciplinary artists present their work. During this particular edition of Fringe, audiences encountered three different shows that featured new voices of Ireland speaking in verse about their identity and negotiating their artistic response to global, national and local politics: Polish Theatre Ireland's *Chesslaugh Mewash*, Neil Watkins's *The Year of Magical Wanking* and Preissner's *Our Father*.

Polish Theatre Ireland, formed in 2008 to intertwine Polish and Irish theatre traditions, used the poetry of the Nobel poet Czesław Miłosz to devise *Chesslaugh Mewash*. Under the direction of Anna Wolf, the company spoke verse in Polish, English, Lithuanian, French, Irish, and Slovak to explore their own precarious and transnational identities in relation to globalization and social networks. There is a link here to Corcadorca's *The Merchant of Venice* and to an experiment by Gúna Nua theatre company. In 2007, the company worked with Irish-based actors from Nigeria, Slovakia, India, Moldova, France, and Ireland to devise the verse drama *Urban Poems* and give voice to "the new generation of immigrants who have decided to make Ireland their home".[17] These examples suggest that verse is a suitable form with which to explore changes within the cultural and linguistic landscape of Ireland. Currently, the inhabitants of Ireland speak at least 182 different languages,[18] and 13% speak a language other than English or Irish at home with their family; this links with ethnic diversity: 18% of people in Ireland do not identify themselves as White Irish.[19]

Neil Watkins wrote and performed rhymed slam-poems of his *The Year of Magical Wanking*. His self-interrogation and performative confession, directed by Philip McMahon, featured a year in Watkins's life and started with a rhythm of verse highlighting the convention of the prayer and Watkins' play on it:

> Great spirit and Great Mystery hear my prayer.
> Bless all the beings gathered in this room.
> I bid your tastebuds welcome to my womb.
> This is my fruit I bare my fruit. Let's share.
> (…)
> I am Neil Martin Watkins and I am
> A sex and love addicted innocent.
> There's pattern I've adopted that would taint the
> Love Saints. I wank, therefore I slam.[20]

The opening sequence set the scene for a performative exploration of Watkins' identity in relation to sexual abuse, rape, the Catholic Church, drug addiction and HIV.

Our Father, directed by Tara Derrington and featuring Preissner in a leading role, focused on a young woman, Ellie, dealing with the death of her mother. It was written in a rap-inspired rhymed verse and performed with the addition of live drumming by Josephine Linehan intensifying the beats. The rhythm and rhymes facilitated Preissner's performance of pain,[21] which was particularly visible in the finale:

> Because then I can breathe and it's not so chaotic... something something anti-biotic.
> I miss my mother, and I want to go back, to be more understanding and cut her some slack.
> But I don't have that option, no matter how much I pray, I rhyme to fill the silence and then I'm ok.
> There's nothing wrong, I'm fine, I'm fine, I'm going to .... have a glass of wine.
> I do not like the red wine here... Maybe I will have a beer.
> And as I start to speak in rhyme, my mind stops racing and I slow down time.
> I cannot think of anything else except what word will rhyme with else.
> And keeping busy is always best, rest, chest,[22]

The line and the play broke off suddenly and the audience was left with an impression that Ellie would need many more rhymes to finally move on. One year later, Preissner wrote and performed a one-woman show *Solpadeine is My Boyfriend* (directed by Gina Moxley). This continuation of *Our Father*, in a mixture of rhymed verse and rhymed and unrhymed prose, focussed on Ellie's responses to the drastic social and personal changes caused by the economic crisis and emigration in post-Celtic Tiger Ireland.

Watkins's and Preissner's shows, nominated for the ABSOLUT Fringe Awards, suggest that some contemporary artists find verse appropriate for performances that have elements of autobiography. The productions, performed by their playwrights either under their own name (as in the case of Watkins) or under a fictional character name (in the case of Preissner), also show how actors use verse to take control of their creative destiny and highlight their authorship of the theatre event. Moreover, Watkins and Preissner's writings embrace the vernacular through formal language, which brings about an interesting tension between high and low cultures and shows that contemporary verse-drama can no longer be exclusively associated with the "language of the Gods", to recall Ibsen's argument to ban verse from the stage;[23] or, as Preissner puts it, "It's not all mountains and sheep and Emily Dickinson".[24]

This is not unique in contemporary Irish theatre and the works of Emmet Kirwan (another actor-writer) are a good example. Kirwan writes in Dublin slang in rap and spoken-word form, and arranges his words into lines that remind one of verse lines; as he says, the format of lines is to "help the actor or reader, reproduce the prosody and performance style of the play's spoken-word and rap elements".[25] These, in turn, serve as a platform for shared experiences of Dublin as a city, its stories, and soundscape.

Urban Rhythms

Dublin Oldschool by Emmet Kirwan is a two-hander play focussed on two brothers from Tallaght, an area commonly associated with one of the highest crime rates in Dublin. It premiered in 2014 at Dublin Fringe Festival and was developed in collaboration with Fishamble: The New Play Company. The play received multiple awards, including the Stewart Parker Trust Major Bursary for Kirwan, the Best Performers Award at Dublin Fringe for Ian Lloyd Anderson and Kirwan, and in 2017 was invited to the National Theatre in London.

Anderson and Kirwan performed heroin-addict Daniel (in his early thirties) and wannabe DJ Jason (in his late twenties) respectively, and also took on multiple characters encountered by Jason on his drug-fuelled weekend (Thursday to Monday) in Dublin. Throughout the performance, the intensity of the rap rhythm changed in relation to Jason's experiences. The more heightened they became (either through sex, drugs or music), the shorter the verse lines were and the more intense the beat was; the quote below came after Jason took methoxetamine (rhino):

> Rhino takes me to catch,
> with the cardio skills to match.
> Soooooooooooooooooooo
> Quick as a breeze
> I leave him to wheeze
> the side of the road
> all be told,
> I stop, with a cheeky little wave
> and him looking back to me.
> Don't mistake this move for alacrity.
> It's perspicacity.
> It's tenacity!
> Is it termerity?
> More like focused serenity,
> to eye the angles of escape,
> and give a little hope.[26]

In the performance, Kirwan played with the onomatopoeic rhyme between "wheeze" and "breeze" and the prolonged vowel in "so" to highlight the energy and thrill Jason gets from the drug. As the play unravelled, the audience learned that these moments of heightened experiences were Jason's escape from seeing himself as just one of the "fucking ejits" with "nothing going for [them]".[27] This element brings Kirwan's work close to Preissner's plays, in which rhythm is also connected with escapism.[28]

However, Jason's subtext was not the only role that verse had in *Dublin Oldschool.* Kirwan and Anderson performed on a bare, black stage with microphones as their only "props"; and it was the characters that Jason encountered, the references to specific Dublin locations (for example "Thomas Street, corner Francis", Merchants Quay, the River Liffey), and most importantly the rap-verse delivered in Dublin accents that evoked the spaces and soundscape of Dublin. From the start, Kirwan and Anderson's performance made reference to Dublin street rappers through the rhythm, the actors' accents, and their movements and manner of "rapping". At the start of the performance, instead of checking sound, they decided to "check the vernacular" and their "Dublin diction", testing the audience's ability to understand and tuning them into Dublin accent and slang.

Dublin Oldschool was directed by Philip McMahon (also the director of Watkins's *The Year of Magical Wanking*), who played with verse as a way to evoke Dublin's geography in his other production: *Alice in Funderland*. This musical, developed by THISISPOPBABY and presented by the Abbey in 2012, also featured Kirwan and Anderson. *Alice in Funderland* had only a few lines spoken in verse; a nursery rhyme visualized and commented on the River Liffey dividing Dublin into south and north and the social divisions, antagonisms, and stereotypes it created. It is in response to some of these divisions that Kirwan decided to write *Dublin Oldschool* and give voice to the working-class areas of Tallaght and Dublin working class in general, because, as he says:

> That voice is rarely seen, the dispossessed or the voiceless, and often if it is that voice or working class, it's a working class voice from 100 years ago and that can see[m] as too distant in the past.[29]

If one contextualizes Kirwan's words with works like those of Corcadorca, Gúna Nua, Watkins and Polish Theatre Ireland, it seems that verse appeals to the artists whose voices are underrepresented on the theatrical, and arguably public, stages of contemporary Ireland. One could, of course, argue that the artists choose verse as a mode of expression because of their exposure to rap and spoken-word culture. However, I would argue that there is more to it.

Verse, as a mode of language, is organized not only by rules of grammar or syntax, but also by the use of the line. These lines organize the thoughts, but also create a pattern that heightens the rhythm. In a live performance, rhythmical and lexical levels of verse interact and these interactions are emphasized by the heightened rhythm of verse. In addition, heightened speech brings issues of performativity and performance to the fore, including issues of language and identity. This, in turn, highlights the layers of meaning and tensions inherent in performing a working-class Dublin vernacular to the rhythm of hip-hop, which is associated with American Black culture, or delivering an English-language translation of Polish poetry with a Slovak accent (*Chesslaugh Mewash*). Therefore, it may be that the heteroglossic quality of verse is what appeals to the artists whose identities escape simple geographical or cultural boundaries. With that in mind, it is an exciting perspective, and looks forward to more underrepresented groups appearing on Irish stages.

In Search of New Forms

Verse also underlines some exciting quests for new theatre forms and for new ways of creating theatre. Mark O'Rowe's *Terminus*—a play written in prose, but enriched with superimposed internal rhymes—pushes theatrical form and verse beyond verse drama. This play of interlocking monologues by the three characters (a young woman, her mother, and a serial killer) was directed by the author and premiered in 2007 at the Peacock Theatre. The presence of rhymes in the live performance helped to interlock the stories of the three characters; the speed with which the actors delivered their lines and the fact that these lines were the main carrier of meaning, meant that the audience needed great focus to follow the story; by connecting words, rhymes helped the audience to connect meanings. For example, at the start of the performance Andrea Irvine as A described her shift at the Samaritans:

> The first I **answer**'s a woman with **cancer**; number two, a newly widowed father; both of them looking for ***counsel***, compassion; neither receiving much of either. Nor does the next in line, whose voice I'm trying now to **place**, whose **face**, but can't; I'm **blocked**, then **shocked** when she says she's pregnant – four weeks until her delivery **date** – but that she wants to **terminate**. 'That's way too **late**,' I shout.[30]

I highlighted all the rhymes in bold and marked a pararhyme with italics to show how these words carry the key information about the callers, their issues, and A's reaction to them. In performance, the soundscape created by these rhymes also enriched the space that was occupied only by three actors. After winning a Scotsman Fringe First Award at the 2008 Edinburgh Fringe Festival, and following its international tour, *Terminus* was brought back to the Peacock stage in 2009.

Another example is a collaboration between Australian artist Paul Kelly and Irish singer-actress Camille O'Sullivan. Their *Ancient Rain*, directed by Chris Drummond, premiered at the 2016 Dublin Theatre Festival and Melbourne Art Centre. The artists combined Irish poetry in verse—including works by recognized poets like W.B. Yeats or Seamus Heaney and up-and-coming ones like Enda Wyley—with their Irish and Australian accents and music to perform multiple characters. The value of this experiment should not be undermined by the chilly reception it receives from Irish reviewers.[31] It was received much better in Australia, where the critics found the results of the experiment puzzling and challenging but also momentarily inspiring and aesthetically very pleasing.[32]

The appetite for verse and verse-like forms in Irish theatre is growing. Some contemporary practitioners clearly find rhythmical language not only appropriate as a means of dealing with difficult issues, but also able to provide a platform for experimentation. It is a source of revitalizing energy that appeals to these artists and, arguably, their audiences—as its recognition through awards and growing interest indicate. This recognition goes beyond the theatre. For example, Preissner was commissioned to write *Can't Cope, Won't Cope,* an RTÉ TV Drama about two female millennials living in Dublin. Kirwan has recently developed another theatrical project into a short movie, *Heartbreak*, that uses spoken word to tell the story of a pregnant teenager growing up and raising her son in contemporary Ireland. *Heartbreak* was released on YouTube and two days later had almost a million views;[33] it received the Irish Film and Television Academy 2017 Best Short Film Award. In June 2018, a movie adaptation of *Dublin Oldschool* will premiere in Irish cinemas.

These new practices also have a unique opportunity to connect with Irish traditions of verse drama and, by doing so, to strike and lengthen their roots on Irish stages. In this context, it is important to once again recall *Ancient Rain* by Kelly and O'Sullivan and mention Eamonn Carr's *Dusk*, directed by Denis Conway at Dublin's New Theatre in October 2016. Carr's verse play, inspired by the works of W.B. Yeats, features Japanese dances, elements of Nôh theatre, and, in the words of its creators, "super-hero" Cú Chulainn talking to a young contemporary woman on the eve of her wedding.[34] And, although it seems that the other artists discussed here have rarely engaged directly with Irish traditions of verse drama, best exemplified by the works of W.B. Yeats and Austin Clarke, they arguably prepare the ground for these traditions to be rediscovered. The theatremakers featured here embrace the enhanced musicality of verse and engage with inter-, trans- and multicultural contexts; this cultural curiosity, experimentation, and musicality were central in the theatre of Yeats.[35] While the new works do not seem to search for a "truly" Anglo-Irish mode of verse, like Austin Clarke did,[36] they use the rhythm of verse to explore interactions between the local and the global. Perhaps, paradoxically, looking outwards and into the future is the best way for Irish theatre to discover new ways of re-engaging with its verse drama tradition.

Notes

1. Lethal Dialect, "Streets to the Stage: Dublin Stories as Poetry" (talk, Abbey Theatre, Dublin, Ireland, April 17, 2012).
2. Lethal Dialect, interview by Brian Cunningham, *Babylon Radio*, last modified February 24, 2016. Accessed 22 April 2017, http://babylonradio.com/dublins-dialect-interview-paul-alwright-k-lethal-dialect/.
3. Seamus Heaney, "'Me' as in 'Metre': On Translating *Antigone*", in *Rebel Women: Staging Ancient Greek Drama Today*, ed. John Dillon and Steve E. Wilmer (London: Methuen, 2005), 170–173. Seamus Heaney, "A Note by Seamus Heaney", in *The Burial at Thebes. Theatre Programme* (Dublin: The Abbey Theatre, 2004).
4. Seamus Heaney, "The Jayne Lecture: Title Deeds: Translating a Classic", *Proceedings of the American Philosophical Society* 148, no. 4 (2004): 411–426.
5. See for example: Charlotte McIvor and Matthew Spangler, *Staging Intercultural Ireland: New Plays and Practitioner Perspectives* (Cork: Cork University Press, 2014) or Kasia Lech, "Difficult Encounter: Polish Theatre on the Irish Stage between 2004 and 2015", *Litteraria Pragensia* 25, no. 50 (2015): 32–46.
6. Lynne Parker, "About Rough Magic", *Rough Magic*, accessed 22 May 2017, http://www.roughmagic.ie/about-rough-magic.
7. Pedro Calderón de la Barca, *Life is a Dream*, trans. Jo Clifford (London: Nick Hern Books, 1998), iii, 68.
8. Eunan O'Halpin, *Spying on Ireland: British Intelligence and Irish Neutrality During the Second World War* (Oxford: Oxford University Press, 2008), 32.
9. Arthur Riordan, *Improbable Frequency* (London: Nick Hern Books, 2005), 16.
10. Ibid., 7.
11. Ibid., 17.

12. John Patrick Montaño, *The Roots of English Colonialism in Ireland* (Cambridge University Press, 2011), 26.
13. Riordan, 19.
14. Ibid., 21.
15. John O'Beirne Ranelagh, *A Short History of Ireland.* (Cambridge: Cambridge University Press, 2012), 296.
16. Kasia Lech, "Pain, Rain, and Rhyme: the Role of Rhythm in Stefanie Preissner's Work", in *Radical Contemporary Theatre Practices by Women in Ireland*, ed. Miriam Haughton and Mária Kurdi (Dublin: Carysfort Press), 163.
17. David Parnell, "Changing the Rhythm", *Irish Theatre Magazine* 7, no 32 (2007): 48.
18. Kathleen Shields, "Translation and Society in Ireland, 1900-Present", in *Sociolinguistics in Ireland*, ed. Raymond Hickey (Basingstoke: Palgrave, 2016), 359.
19. Central Statistics Office, "Census 2016 Summary Results – Part 1", *Central Statistics Office*, last modified April 6, 2017, accessed 22 April 2017, http://www.cso.ie/en/media/csoie/census/documents/census2011pdr/Census_2011_Highlights_Part_1_web_72dpi.pdf, 54 and 60.
20. Neil Watkins, "The Year of Magical Wanking", in *The Oberon Anthology of Contemporary Irish Plays*, ed. Thomas Conway. (London: Oberon Books, 2012), 293.
21. Lech, "Pain, Rain, and Rhyme", 161.
22. Stefanie Preissner, *Our Father* (theatre script, Author's private collection, 2011).
23. Henrik Ibsen, "To Edmund Gosse", January 15, 1874, in *The correspondence of Henrik Ibsen*, ed. Mary Morison (New York: Haskell House, 1905), 269.
24. Quoted in Lech, "Pain, Rain, and Rhyme", 163.
25. Emmet Kirwan, "Writer's Note", in *Dublin Oldschool*, Emmet Kirwan (London: Methuen, 2016), 4.
26. Emmet Kirwan, *Dublin Oldschool*,13–14.
27. Ibid., 61.
28. Lech, "Pain, Rain, and Rhyme", 161.
29. Quoted in Aoife Barry, "When a working class person writes, you're asked: Is it like Roddy Doyle?", *TheJournal.ie*, last modified 31 January 2016. Accessed 22 May 2017, http://www.thejournal.ie/emmett-kirwan-interview-2574261-Jan2016/.
30. Mark O'Rowe, *Terminus* (London: Nick Hern Books, 2007), 5.
31. Fintan O'Toole, "*Ancient Rain* review", *Irish Times*, last modified 30 September 2016. Accessed 22 April 2017, http://www.irishtimes.com/culture/stage/ancient-rain-review-seems-designed-to-tantalise-us-with-what-might-have-been-1.2811901.
32. Jane Howard, "*Ancient Rain* review", *The Guardian*, last modified 13 October 2016. Accessed 22 April 2017, https://www.theguardian.com/stage/2016/oct/13/ancient-rain-review-an-emotive-fusion-of-poetry-and-cabaret. Christopher Wallace-Crabbe, "Death, beauty and poetry come together in *Ancient Rain*", *The Conversation*, last modified 13 October 2016. Accessed 22 April 2017, http://theconversation.com/death-beauty-and-poetry-come-together-in-ancient-rain-66986.
33. Katie McNeice, "'In Awe of All Mná' – IFTA 2017 Best Short Film goes to viral 'Heartbreak'", *IFTN*, last modified 10 April 2017. Accessed 22 April 2017,

http://www.iftn.ie/news/?act1=record&only=1&aid=73&rid=4290477&tpl=archnews&force=1.

34. Red Iron Productions, "*DUSK*", *Red Iron Productions*. Accessed 22 May 2017, http://www.redironproductions.com/current-productions.html.
35. Barry Sheils, *W.B. Yeats and World Literature: The Subject of Poetry* (London: Routledge, 2016), 3. James W. Flannery, *W.B. Yeats and the idea of a theatre* (London: Yale University Press, 1976), 192–193.
36. Robert F. Garratt, *Modern Irish Poetry: Tradition and Continuity from Yeats to Heaney* (London: University of California Press, 1986), 110.

Bibliography

Barry, Aoife. "When a Working Class Person Writes, You're Asked: Is It Like Roddy Doyle?" *TheJournal.ie*. Last modified 31 January 2016. Accessed 22 May 2017. http://www.thejournal.ie/emmett-kirwan-interview-2574261-Jan2016/.

Calderón de la Barca, Pedro. *Life Is a Dream*. Translated by Jo Clifford. London: Nick Hern Books, 1998.

———. *Life Is a Dream*. Translated by Jo Clifford. Directed by Tom Creed. Performed by Mark Lambert, Paul Reid, et al. Dublin: Rough Magic, April 11, 2008. Project Arts Centre. Live Performance.

Carr, Eamonn. *Dusk*. Directed by Denic Conway. Performed by Garrett Lombard, Denis Conway, Caoimhe Mulcahy, et al. Dublin: Red Iron Productions, October 10, 2016. New Town Theatre. Live Performance.

Central Statistics Office. "Census 2016 Summary Results – Part 1." *Central Statistics Office*. Last modified 6 April 2017. Accessed 22 May 2017. http://www.cso.ie/en/media/csoie/census/documents/census2011pdr/Census_2011_Highlights_Part_1_web_72dpi.pdf.

Dialect, Lethal. *Babylon Radio*. By Brian Cunningham. Last modified 24 February 2016. Accessed 22 May 2017. http://babylonradio.com/dublins-dialect-interview-paul-alwright-k-lethal-dialect/.

———. "Streets to the Stage: Dublin Stories as Poetry." Talk, Abbey Theatre, Dublin, Ireland, 17 April 2012.

Flannery, James W. *W.B. Yeats and the Idea of a Theatre*. London: Yale University Press, 1976.

Garratt, Robert F. *Modern Irish Poetry: Tradition and Continuity from Yeats to Heaney*. London: University of California Press, 1986.

Heaney, Seamus, and Dominique Le Gendre. *Burial at Thebes*. Directed by Derek Walcott. Performed by Idit Arad, Brian Green, et al. London: Manning Camerata, October, 2008. Globe Theatre. Live Performance.

Heaney, Seamus. "'Me' as in 'Metre': On Translating Antigone." In *Rebel Women: Staging Ancient Greek Drama Today*, edited by John Dillon and Steve E. Wilmer, 169–173. London: Methuen, 2005.

———. "The Jayne Lecture: Title Deeds: Translating a Classic." *Proceedings of the American Philosophical Society* 148, no. 4 (2004): 411–426.

———. *The Burial at Thebes: Sophocles' Antigone*. Directed by Patrick Mason. Performed by Gemma Reeves, Declan Conlon, et al. Dublin: Abbey Theatre, 3 May 2008, Abbey Theatre. Live Performance.

———. *The Burial at Thebes: Sophocles' Antigone*. Directed by Marcela Lorca. Performed by Sun Mee Chomet, Stephen Yoakam, et al. Minneapolis: The Guthrie Theater, 19, 21, 22 October 2011. The Guthrie Theater. Live Performance.

———. *The Burial at Thebes: Sophocles' Antigone*. Directed by Lorraine Pintal. Performed by Ruth Negga, Lorcan Cranitch, et al. Dublin: Abbey Theatre, 2004. The Abbey Theatre Archive. Video Recording.

———. *The Burial at Thebes: Sophocles' Antigone*. London: Faber&Faber, 2004.

Howard, Jane. "*Ancient Rain* Review." *The Guardian*. Last modified 13 October 2016. Accessed 22 May 2017. https://www.theguardian.com/stage/2016/oct/13/ancient-rain-review-an-emotive-fusion-of-poetry-and-cabaret.

Ibsen, Henrik. "To Edmund Gosse." 15 January 1874. In *The Correspondence of Henrik Ibsen*, edited by Mary Morison, 268–269. New York: Haskell House, 1905.

———. *Peer Gynt*. Translated by Arthur Riordan. Directed by Lynne Parker. Performed by Rory Nolan, Peter Daly, Arthur Riordan, et al. Dublin: Rough Magic, 27 September 2011. O'Reilly Theatre. Live Performance.

Kelly, Paul, and Camille O'Sullivan. *Ancient Rain*. Directed by Chris Drummond. Performed by Paul Kelly, Feargal Murray, Camille O'Sullivan, et al. Dublin: Far and Away productions and Brink Productions, 29 September 2016. Olympia Theatre. Live Performance.

Kirwan, Emmet. *Heartbreak*. Short movie. Directed by Dave Tynan. Performed by Emmet Kirwan, Jordanne Jones, Deirdre Molloy, et al. Produced by Liam Ryan et al. 2017. Accessed 22 April 2017, https://www.youtube.com/watch?v=uv9oax2N160.

———. "Writer's Note." In *Dublin Oldschool*, by Emmet Kirwan, 4. London: Methuen, 2016.

———. *Dublin Oldschool*. Directed by Philp Mc Mahon. Performed by Emmet Kirwan and Ian Lloyd Anderson, Dublin: Project Arts Centre, 2014. Video Recording, Author's private collection.

———. *Dublin Oldschool*. London: Methuen, 2016.

Lech, Kasia. "Difficult Encounter: Polish Theatre on the Irish Stage Between 2004 and 2015." *Litteraria Pragensia* 25, no. 50 (2015): 32–46.

———. "Pain, Rain, and Rhyme: The Role of Rhythm in Stefanie Preissner's Work." In *Radical Contemporary Theatre Practices by Women in Ireland*, edited by Miriam Haughton and Mária Kurdi, 151–166. Dublin: Carysfort Press.

McIvor, Charlotte and Matthew Spangler. *Staging Intercultural Ireland: New Plays and Practitioner Perspectives*. Cork: Cork University Press, 2014.

McNeice, Katie. "'In Awe of All Mná' – IFTA 2017 Best Short Film goes to viral 'Heartbreak,'." *IFTN*. Last modified 10 April 2017. Accessed 22 April 2017. http://www.iftn.ie/news/?act1=record&only=1&aid=73&rid=4290477&tpl=archnews&force=1.

Montaño, John Patrick. *The Roots of English Colonialism in Ireland*. Cambridge University Press, 2011.

O'Toole, Fintan. "*Ancient Rain* Review." *Irish Times*. Last modified 30 September 2016. Accessed 22 May 2017. http://www.irishtimes.com/culture/stage/ancient-rain-review-seems-designed-to-tantalise-us-with-what-might-have-been-1.2811901.

O'Halpin, Eunan. *Spying on Ireland: British Intelligence and Irish Neutrality During the Second World War*. Oxford: Oxford University Press, 2008

O'Rowe, Mark. *Terminus*. Directed by Mark O'Rowe. Performed by Kate Brennan, Andrea Irvine, Karl Shiels. Dublin: Abbey Theatre, 19 November 2009. The Peacock. Live Performance.

———. *Terminus*. London: Nick Hern Books, 2007.

Parker, Lynne. "About Rough Magic." *Rough Magic*. Accessed 22 May 2017. http://www.roughmagic.ie/about-rough-magic.

Parnell, David. "Changing the Rhythm." *Irish Theatre Magazine* 7, no. 32 (2007): 48–53.

Polish Theatre Ireland. *Chesslaugh Mewash*. Directed by Anna Wolf. Performed by Alicja Ayres, Oscar Mienadi, Eva Docolomanska, et al. Dublin: Polish Theatre Ireland, 20 September 2011, The Lir, Live Performance.

Preissner, Stefanie. *Can't Cope, Won't Cope*. TV series. Directed by Cathy Brady. Dublin: Deadpan Pictures, 2016. Television.

———. *Our Father.* 2011. TS. Author's private collection.

———. *Our Father.* Directed by Tara Derrington. Performed by Stefanie Preissner, Gene Rooney, and Pat Nolan. 2011. Dublin: With an "F" Productions, April, 19, 2012. The Civic Theatre. Live Performance.

———. *Solpadeine Is My Boyfriend*. Directed by Gina Moxley. Performed by Stefanie Preissner. Dublin: With an "F" Productions, 15 September 2012. Project Arts Centre. Live Performance.

Ranelagh, John O'Beirne. *A Short History of Ireland*. Cambridge: Cambridge University Press, 2012.

Red Iron Productions. "*DUSK*." *Red Iron Productions*. Accessed 22 May 2017. http://www.redironproductions.com/current-productions.html.

Riordan, Arthur. *Improbable Frequency*. London: Nick Hern Books, 2005.

——— and Des Bishop. *Rap Éire*. Directed by Jimmy Fay. Performed by Arthur Riordan, Des Bishop, Fiona Condon, et al. Limerick: Bickerstaffe Theatre Company, September, 2001. Belltable. Live performance.

——— and Bell Helicopter. *Improbable Frequency*. Directed by Lynne Parker. Performed by Cathy White, Rory Nolan, et al. Dublin: Rough Magic, 27 September 2004. O'Reilly Theatre. Live Performance.

——— and Bill Whelan. *The Train*. Directed by Lynne Parker. Performed by Kate Gilmore, Emmet Kirwan, et al. Limerick: Rough Magic, 29 September 2015. Lime Tree Theatre. Live Performance.

Scannell, Robert, and Phillip McMahon. *Alice in Funderland*. Directed by Philip McMahon. Performed by Ian Lloyd Anderson, Emmet Kirwan, et al. Dublin: THISISPOPBABY and Abbey Theatre, 17 April 2012. Abbey Theatre. Live Performance.

Schiller, Friedrich. *Don Carlos*. Translated by Mike Poulton. Directed by Lynne Parker. Performed by Kathy Kiera Clarke, Eleanor Methven, et al., Dublon: Rough Magic, 8 March 2007. Project Arts Centre. Live Performance.

Shakespeare, William. *The Merchant of Venice*. Directed by Pat Kiernan. Performed by Mark D'Aughton, Ewa Szumska, David Ugo, et al. Cork: Corcadorca, 14 June 2005. Old Irish Distillery, City Courthouse, and Liberty Street. Live Performance.

———. *The Taming of the Shrew*. Directed by Lynne Parker. Performed by Tadhg Murphy, Rory Keenan, et al. Dublin: Rough Magic, 6 March 2006. Project Arts Centre. Live Performance.

Sheils, Barry. *W.B. Yeats and World Literature: The Subject of Poetry*. London: Routledge, 2016.

Shields, Kathleen. "Translation and Society in Ireland, 1900-Present." In *Sociolinguistics in Ireland*, edited by Raymond Hickey, 344–364. Basingstoke: Palgrave, 2016.

Wallace-Crabbe, Christopher. "Death, beauty and poetry come together in *Ancient Rain*." *The Conversation*. Last modified 13 October 2016. Accessed May 22, 2017.

http://theconversation.com/death-beauty-and-poetry-come-together-in-ancient-rain-66986.

Watkins, Neil. "The Year of Magical Wanking." In *The Oberon Anthology of Contemporary Irish Plays*, edited by Thomas Conway, 291–326. London: Oberon Books, 2012.

———. *The Year of Magical Wanking*. Directed by Philip McMahon. Performed by Neil Watkins. Dublin: THISISPOPBABY, 9 September 2011. Project Arts Centre. Live Performance.

The Gate Theatre on the Road: O'Casey, Pinter and Friel

Mária Kurdi

Irish theatre, emerging in the early twentieth century as a seminal cultural formation that participated in the anticolonial movement by its own experimental and innovative means, has never been an isolated, inward-looking project. On the one hand, as is well documented by a number of researchers, it has been sensitive to continental influences from the start. On the other, a few years after their foundation the major Irish theatres and companies, beginning with the Abbey, became eager to take selected performances of their repertoire on tour in Ireland and abroad. In this way, a tradition of touring productions developed that was rooted in the need of Ireland's theatres to elicit responses from a variety of audiences and provoke reflections from non-Irish theatre-goers and critics. In Christopher Morash's words, "as much as Irish theatre imagined itself as national, it has always been at its most vibrant when it has become most international".[1] The most widely known theatres and companies established in Ireland across the last century, the Abbey (1904–present), the Gate (1928–present), Druid (1975–present), Field Day (1980–present), Rough Magic (1984–present) and Charabanc (1984–1995), not to mention more recent companies, have toured a great number of solo or joint performances. Several of their toured productions are discussed by contributors to the books published in the Irish Theatrical Diaspora Series, which was launched in 2005 to

M. Kurdi (✉)
University of Pécs, Pécs, Hungary
e-mail: mkurdi@dravanet.hu

E. Jordan, E. Weitz (eds.), *The Palgrave Handbook of Contemporary Irish Theatre and Performance*,
https://doi.org/10.1057/978-1-137-58588-2_43

investigate the international journeys of Irish theatre. This chapter will look specifically at the touring history of the Gate Theatre.

The founders of the Gate Theatre, Hilton Edwards and Micheál MacLiammóir, consciously created a "director's theatre",[2] which embraced its mission to run a repertoire of modern drama, Irish and non-Irish plays. Evaluating their approach, Richard Pine and Richard Cave state that "[t]he achievement of the Edwards-MacLiammóir partnership is that they succeeded in fusing their individual talents into a comprehensive stage-craft which married the techniques of staging (lighting, choreography, diction) with those of décor (colours, shapes and textures)".[3] Given that the presence of avant-garde trends had inspired many European theatres to become open to the new and less travelled, it is not surprising that invitations for guest performances came early in the Gate's history. Richard Pine assesses the importance of touring their work in those years as follows: "For Edwards and MacLiammóir, the challenge was to present their work outside the confines of the Irish theatrical context, both for the experience of playing abroad and to test their work on foreign audiences".[4] The Gate's first tours abroad date back to the mid-1930s. As Christopher Fitz-Simon writes, in 1934

> There was a genuine invitation to the Gate from Anmer Hall to play at the Westminster Theatre in London. Hall was a wealthy impresario, whose policy was to provide a London venue for plays which would not otherwise be seen except in "art" theatres like the London Gate. He had read *The Times* review of 23 September 1933, in which [Lord] Longford's *Yahoo* was praised, and had been interested in the work of the Dublin Gate ever since. It appears, among the board tensions, that there was a shared desire for the Gate's work to be exposed elsewhere.[5]

The invitation was accepted and the Gate's productions of *Yahoo*, a revival of *Hamlet* and Denis Johnston's new play *A Bride for the Unicorn* travelled to England and gained considerable success there. Next an invitation came from Egypt, where the Gate's programme was to represent a larger cross-section of their productions, including *Heartbreak House* and *The Taming of the Shrew*.[6] Despite some debates among the leaders of the company, the purpose, Pine and Cave note, was clear: "[t]hese first tours were undertaken partly because of the prestige bringing an Irish company to continental and transatlantic centres where they were acclaimed, partly to accustom the company to the appreciation of new audiences, and also to earn revenue which at times was badly needed".[7]

In a ground-breaking enterprise in 1991 the Gate—the first theatre in the world to do so—presented all the stage plays by Samuel Beckett and subsequently toured these performances to London, New York and Sydney. Thanks to its Beckett Festival, half the number of the Irish productions that toured to Britain in the period 1990–2006 were produced by the Gate, Cave notes.[8] Their touring of Beckett's plays is discussed in considerable detail by numerous articles.[9] Therefore in the present chapter I shall examine another slice of their vivid touring activities after Michael Colgan became artistic director of the theatre in 1983. Surveying the period from the mid-1980s onwards, my focus will be on the touring of the Gate's eminent productions of plays by Sean O'Casey, Harold Pinter and Brian Friel, relying primarily on a selection of relevant theatre reviews.

Under Colgan's stewardship, O'Casey's *Juno and the Paycock* was mounted in July 1986 by the Gate under the direction of Joe Dowling, with set design by Frank Hallinan Flood. The cast included Donal McCann (Boyle), Geraldine Plunkett (Juno), John Kavanagh (Joxer), Rosemary Fine (Mary), Maureen Potter (Maisie Madigan), Pauline Delany (Mrs. Tancred), Joe Savino (Johnny), Gerald McSorley (Bentham), Seamus Forde (Nugent) and David Herlihy (Jerry Devine). The production gained legendary status, characterized by Bernice Schrank: "This was the first time that the Gate presented a professional production of an O'Casey play. The location was new, and the approach, fresh. Dowling handled the play not like the museum piece it was in danger of becoming, but [...] like the work of a new playwright."[10] Morash also considers the Gate's 1986 *Juno* as a production that marked a new era in the history of its staging because, "Dowling broke with the comic sentimentalism which had traditionally characterized productions of the play, instead emphasizing stylistic contrasts within the text, playing some scenes to bring out music hall influences, and others with a graphic realism which contradicted the myth of picturesque poverty that the play is often made to support".[11]

Colgan's recollections of his early years at the Gate include the international tour of this production, he notes that it was a milestone in their history: "We had our first big success in New York with *Juno and the Paycock* which was also non-traditional Gate fare. They [the old Gate] went around the world and were the first Irish company to go to Egypt; we were the first to go to Jerusalem."[12] Indeed, the 1986 Gate production of *Juno* toured to Jerusalem, Edinburgh, New York and then London. In June 1988 it was one of the plays to represent Ireland at the First New York International Festival of the Arts, where it proved hugely popular with both critics and audience. Leslie Bennetts's feature in the *New York Times* notes that the Gate's *Juno* played "to standing ovations every night at the Golden Theater". She complicates the view that this drama is merely tragicomic, while focussing on the acting of Joxer Daly's figure—not central, yet here somehow emblematic—maintaining that

> Although Joxer Daly is generally regarded as a supporting character in Sean O'Casey's *Juno and the Paycock*, as portrayed by John Kavanagh in the Gate Theater Dublin's current production, he is the riveting personification of human degradation. [...] Not for a moment can one dismiss him as a harmless fool, and in the chilling images of the play's closing moments he achieves an unforgettable stature as an emblematic figure of evil, leaving one with goose-bumps as the curtain comes down.

Bennetts also quotes Kavanagh himself, who told her that in his understanding Joxer is "a rogue, but he's a beggar. He really has absolutely nothing. When you're starving to death, there are very few principles".[13]

Notably, it was while touring abroad and earning positive critical comments that the potential broader significance of the Gate's *Juno* for Irish modernism and the modern world theatre really showed itself. In the *New York Times*, Mel Gussow sums up this new achievement by claiming that "there are indications here and in England, as well as in Ireland, that [O'Casey] is finally being accepted as a 20th-century master".[14] Regarding O'Casey's relation to the Irish dramatic tradition, John P. Harrington makes the point that in the Gate production a noteworthy theatrical feature of the play was coming to the surface, namely "a strong influence from the work of Samuel Beckett. [...] In the retroactive influence of Beckett on O'Casey, Irish drama was revitalized by non-Irish Irish drama, and the result of cross-fertilization was a localized drama that was not parochial".[15] Also, the success of the production affected the career of its director, Joe Dowling, who says in an interview that "Sean O'Casey changed my life! Once I did that production of *Juno and the Paycock* in the Gate in 1986 and it went to Broadway in 1988—that was really what launched me on an American career". Praising the original cast as "phenomenal", he mentions that "Frank Hallinan Flood's great set" contributed considerably to the production as it "really redefined the idea of what that house was like and how those people lived, so closely on top of each other".[16]

Playing for forty performances at the Albery Theatre in London in 1993, the Gate's *Juno* had a somewhat changed cast but was still directed by Dowling. One of the critics, Irving Wardle, was inspired to recall the production's tour to Edinburgh in 1987 for the sake of comparing the potential effects of this theatrical realization in different contexts and historical moments. Back then, Wardle ponders, the revival of the play could have been interpreted as "a heart-breaking commentary on the futile self-destruction of Beirut". When the play finally reached London in 1993, Wardle continues,

> it applies with equal force to the former Yugoslavia. Everybody loves this play, but Dowling's version (nothing lost in the recasting) is one of the revelatory events of the past 20 years. Its innovations are easily described: it amplifies O'Casey's stage directions; acknowledges the worthlessness of Joxer and Captain Boyle; and gives the grieving Mrs Tancred her full due. The effect is to convert an uproarious national classic into a devastating international masterpiece.[17]

Tellingly, Wardle's article is titled "A Giant among Kings", which implies the vital importance of rediscovering and staging O'Casey's drama as an integral part of modern theatre. Moreover, Wardle admires the Gate production because it convincingly shows the play's ability to speak to audiences of all times and any location, reconfirming the writer's place among the classics of world theatre. Thanks to the Gate's 1986 innovative production and its tour to other parts of the English-speaking world and, of course, to the re-evaluation of the playwright's oeuvre by dedicated scholars like Christopher Murray, it seems that O'Casey and his *Juno* have secured inclusion in the canon of modern western theatre.[18]

* * *

The Dublin Gate developed a unique and mutually beneficial relationship with British playwright Harold Pinter (1930–2008). Pinter was by no means alien to Ireland: in the early 1950s his career as actor began there with the renowned Anew McMaster and his travelling theatre troupe.[19] The influence of Irish modernist writers proved a catalytic force in shaping Pinter's texts; including Beckett's theatre style and Augusta Gregory's treatment of language as theme. Also, literary allusions in Pinter's works demonstrate that he became a dedicated admirer of Yeats and Joyce, who keep ghosting his texts, not to speak of his direction of the world première of Joyce's *Exiles* at the Mermaid Theatre, London in 1970.

The Gate organized four major festivals of Pinter's work, the first two in 1994 and 1997, with the author participating as both actor and director. Anthony Roche quotes Colgan, who "rightly argued that he regarded Pinter as one of the greatest living playwrights and one he wished to honour, by mounting productions of plays of classic status that had rarely received professional Irish productions".[20] The May 1994 event, theatre critic Michael Billington states, was the first-ever Pinter Festival in the world. It was welcomed by Billington with due enthusiasm: "Colgan's bold idea was to acknowledge a living writer, to introduce Dublin audiences to some of the less familiar plays, and to put long and short pieces together in illuminating juxtaposition [...] and the mixture of British and Irish actors yielded fascinating dividends".[21] In intriguing arrangements, *The Dumb Waiter* was paired with *Betrayal*; *Old Times* with *One for the Road*; and *Landscape* (directed by Pinter himself) with *Moonlight*. Roche comments that the festival proved to be "invaluable for the exposure it afforded both Irish actors and audiences to the shock of Pinter's theatrical language".[22] A shock, yet perhaps also an experience of recognizing some resemblance in style to the language-driven heritage of Irish drama. From the 1994 festival, *Landscape* was transferred to the National Theatre, London.

In 2001, to celebrate Pinter's seventieth birthday, the Gate staged a number of his plays again, including *A Kind of Alaska*, *One for the Road*, *The Homecoming* and *Landscape*. Among these, the production of *The Homecoming* attracted the most critical attention and, together with the other three plays above, it was taken on tour to New York as part of the Harold Pinter Festival there in the same year. In Billington's view, it is precisely the continuing and fruitful connection with the Gate that helped Pinter achieve an "iconic status" on the contemporary stage. About the two-week festival in New York's Lincoln Center in July 2001, devoted to the playwright's work, Billington says: "If the event was the brainchild of the Lincoln Centres' Nigel Redden, it was Michael Colgan of Dublin's Gate Theatre who supplied the bulk of the material: the Almeida's double bill of *The Room* and *Celebration* were complemented by new Dublin productions by Robin Lefévre of *One for the Road*, starring Pinter himself, and of *The Homecoming*, with Ian Holm as a Lear-like Max".[23] The tour in New York was a huge success in terms of both audience admiration and critical appreciation. The commendatory review by Les Gutman and David Lohrey in *Curtain Up*, which surveys all of Pinter's work at the Lincoln Festival, treats *The Homecoming* as special. In recognition of the exceptional merits of the production, the authors write that "there is no indication that the organizers intended a 'centrepiece' for the Pinter Festival, but it certainly appears that in *The Homecoming*, they have one. [...] On virtually every level, this shimmering staging pays homage to its playwright [...] a production as finely tuned in its detail as an expensive Swiss chronograph".[24] The unorthodox simile the critics use calls to mind the best of avant-garde art, mesmerizing with its mysteriously adroit re-assemblage and re-polishing of familiar details.

Shortly after its tour in New York, the 2001 Gate production of *The Homecoming* transferred to London. In the home country of the playwright, the comments were illuminating in yet other ways. Discussing the masterful realization of the Pinteresque (and through it, also the Beckettian) role of silences, Emer O'Kelly enthuses over how deeply "the silence is palpable in the play, as it is in this production, and it reeks with the nauseating stench of humanity in decay".[25] Other critics focus more on the acting, primarily on Ian Holm's memorable playing of the father, Max. Billington in the *Guardian* writes that the celebrated English actor, so familiar to the London audience, "initially makes Max a little big-shot: a stick wielding, Cockney cock-of-the-walk". He adds, "Holm makes brilliantly clear that all this is a front, that Max is rattled by his sons' insubordination, his brother's domestic competence, his own declining virility".[26] For the English (and Irish) audiences, Holm's impersonation of Max—the patriarch losing his once tight power over his family but still obstinately sticking to a ghostly semblance of it—might have had resonances with Tom Murphy's father of the Carney family in *A Whistle in the Dark*, which premiered in London in 1961.

The other production of Pinter by the Gate that earned acclaim in England was *One for the Road*, mostly because it starred Pinter himself in the role of the strangely unpredictable torturer, called Nicholas. Alastair Macaulay offers a glimpse of Pinter as a Pinter actor, observing that his "interpretation is full of compelling self-contradictions; [...] Moment by moment, your understanding of the scene before you keeps being mysteriously and drastically changed, as if by sudden shafts of light from unexpected angles".[27] Coming from Ireland, where dozens of plays had been written and staged that established dualities that defy black-and-white solutions, the production demonstrated the centrality of ambiguities and contradictions as a hallmark of Pinter's dramatic style.

Surprisingly, the year Pinter received the Noble Prize (2005) and turned seventy-five "went conspicuously unmarked in his native land. It was, once again, the Gate Theatre, Dublin that staged a weekend hooley", called the Pinter 75—A Celebration, as Billington notes.[28] The international event included the staging of *Old Times* and *Betrayal*, and "[t]he whole weekend was a star encrusted affair featuring Michael Gambon and Jeremy Irons, [...] as well as Derek Jacobi, Sinead Cusack, Janie Dee and Stephen Rea".[29] *Betrayal* and *The Homecoming* transferred to London's Comedy Theatre and *Celebrations* had a reading in London at the Noël Coward Theatre (Albery) directed by Alan Stanford, the Dublin Gate Theatre's partner in this venture was Sonia Friedman Productions. In 2006 Pinter received the tenth Europe Theatre Prize award in Turin, to join a line of recipients including Ariane Mnouchkine, Peter Brook and Heiner Müller, among others. Eager to take part in the celebratory programme organized in honour of the new prize-winner, the Gate Theatre offered a performance, titled *Pinter Plays, Poetry & Prose*, in which passages from the playwright's works were read by Charles Dance, Michael Gambon, Jeremy Irons and Penelope Wilton.[30] In 2008, the year of Pinter's death, the Gate's production of *No Man's Land* starring David Bradley, Nick Dunning, Michael Gambon and David Walliams, opened in Dublin and then transferred to London, where it won three Olivier award nominations.

The above survey of the Gate Theatre's productions and touring of Pinter's work demonstrates an unparalleled collaboration between Irish and English directors, actors and theatremakers in bringing great art to international audiences. Michael Colgan received an OBE from Queen Elizabeth II in 2010 for services to strengthening cultural links between Ireland and the UK.

* * *

A long and fruitful association between Brian Friel and the Gate started when Friel's *Philadelphia, Here I Come!* premiered, directed by Hilton Edwards in 1964. From the 1990s onwards, the Gate has ventured to stage and tour several of the playwright's works, becoming the prominent Irish theatre to publicize them at home and abroad. In 1994 *Molly Sweeney* premiered at the Gate directed by Brian Friel himself, starring Catherine Byrne, Mark Lambert and T.P. McKenna. Anthony Roche remarks that the performance coincided with a major political event, presumably important for Friel, born and bred in the North, as 1994 was "the year of the first Northern Ireland ceasefire".[31] The production transferred to the Almeida Theatre in London for the 1994–1995 season, where the programme note for the first performance, titled "The End of the World", was written by the Irish theatre critic Fintan O'Toole. Introducing the playwright and his work, O'Toole pointed out that Friel "comes from Northern Ireland but lives across the border in the Republic. Borders and boundaries, exile, shifting between states—these are consistent keynotes in his work, and they recur in *Molly Sweeney*".[32] Indeed, the play depicts shifting borders—like the ones between reality and fiction, seen and unseen—offering a metaphysical view of existence between these.

Having been located in its time and in Friel's oeuvre so firmly by O'Toole, the critical reception of the production in London turned out to be somewhat uneven. The repeated use of the monologue form, not yet so widely used in world theatre as it would be ten or twenty years later, seems to have puzzled the first reviewers of the London premiere. In the *New York Times* Sheridan Morley's comments introduced the play as a weaker version of the form that had been so successful with *Faith Healer*, calling *Molly* a "touching and haunting chamber piece [which] never quite comes to the point of dramatic energy". While the play has a "bleak, interior-monologue poetry", it lacks dramatic development for Morley.[33] In contrast, Richard Christiansen in the *Chicago Tribune* praises the play's lyricism, along with the dramatic power the production achieved: "the emotional firestorm set off in the calm, measured, beautifully written monologues of the play is incredible. As Molly stands there, through the luminous presence of the actress Catherine Byrne, speaking of the strange and awesome world she now inhabits, this simple young woman from a tiny Northern Ireland town becomes a great tragic heroine."[34] Pointing to local groundedness as the basis for this tragic height, Christiansen identifies a potential carried by the best of Friel.

Because American papers had already introduced *Molly* by reporting about its London debut, it was predictable that the production would go to New York. It was produced in 1996 at the Roundabout Theatre Company in conjunction with the Gate, again under the directorship of Friel. Catherine Byrne continued to play the role of Molly, while the male actors changed: Frank was played by Alfred Molina, and Doctor Rice by Jason Robards. Some of the reviewers' comments repeat the above opinions about the play's lack of theatricality, while they strive to show due reverence to the playwright by stressing the lyrical dimension of the work and the outstanding performance of the protagonist. According to Vincent Canby *Molly* is "a melancholy tale", the form of which is undramatic, enjoyable mostly in reading. Ms Byrne as Molly, the reviewer continues, "speaks the lines with passion but also with simplicity. It's an unusual performance in that the actress must simultaneously stand outside the character and interpret it, something not easily done. Even as she is reliving Molly's confusion, and eventual withdrawal from the world, she has to be a kind of informed commentator".[35] Underscoring this double movement of Byrne's performance, Canby actually confirms how dramatic the play is, albeit in a less conventional way: the audience are constantly reminded that the character on stage is performatively constructed. Other reviewers of *Molly* in New York also primarily appreciate Byrne's acting. To contextualize the play in theatre history, Greg Evans reminds his readers that the actress is known to Broadway audiences from playing in *Dancing at Lughnasa* and *Wonderful Tennessee*, and she "gives the play its foundation with her delicately nuanced performance" this time too.[36] John Simon in *New York Magazine* captures the beauty of Byrne's use of language: "Her words, coming from far deeper than her throat, are eager to erupt but too modest to explode. And all this with an Irish lilt as delicate as the fuzz on a peach. And when the mouth falls silent, how the face goes on speaking."[37] While it is emotionally overcharged, if not verging on the sentimental, this characterization implies something essential about the intimate nature of monologue theatre, in which both words and silences tend to be conveyed with heightened expressiveness.

Over a decade after his version of Chekhov's *Three Sisters* (premiered by Field Day in 1981), in the 1990s Friel returned to writing adaptations of Chekhov. His *Uncle Vanya* was produced at the Gate in 1998 as part of the Dublin Theatre Festival, directed by Ben Barnes. The next Friel production at the Gate, in 1999, was *Aristocrats*, widely thought of as a Chekhovian play despite not being an adaptation, also directed by Barnes. In the same year, as Friel turned seventy, the Lincoln Center Festival of New York hosted a Brian Friel Festival, to which the above two productions were invited. A third Friel play, *The Freedom of the City* was on the programme as well, performed by the Abbey Theatre's company, the order placed it between *Uncle Vanya* and *Aristocrats*. Reviewers of the Gate's performances are eager to identify for their American readers what they regard as characteristically Frielean aspects in conjunction with Irish cultural resonances, while also implying that the plays' cross-cultural nature is inevitable. The choice of this particular group of three plays is tellingly commented on by Les Gutman in *CurtainUp*, for whom they signal different paths in the writer's oeuvre: "Instead of opting for his best known plays, the festival focuses on plays which illuminate the varied dimensions of Friel's playwriting interests."

Further on, Gutman points to the Hibernicized elements of Friel's *Uncle Vanya*, which "now has the overlay of a distinctly Irish sensibility" enhanced by the acting. As a notable example, he highlights Eamon Morrissey, whose artistic impersonation of Telegin contributes an "unabashedly Celtic flavor as the genetically sudoriferous gentleman who long ago fell on hard times". However, Gutman finds fault with the Gate's *Aristocrats*, missing from it the characteristic hovering of Frielean suggestion: "[D]espite several notable performances (Mark Lambert's Casimir is an idiosyncratic pleasure to watch most of the time, Donna Dent's Alice is as rough and fragile as a cracking piece of glass and Catherine Byrne's Judith is an understated gem) [...] there is a slightly cynical, matter-of-fact tone to the presentation that would be better left to the audience's imagination."[38]

In stark contrast to Gutman's reservations about *Aristocrats*, Ben Brantley in *The New York Times* calls the production "infinitely touching [...] directed with precision and delicacy by Ben Barnes", and writes that it captures the Frielean habit of intertwining fact and fiction in nuanced ways. Brantley also contends that the play, in this interpretation, shows parallels with other contemporary classics, with adjectives like "cryptic" and "opaque" evoking a similarity to Pinter's *The Homecoming* and Sam Shepard's *Buried Child*. Yet the subject of *Aristocrats*, according to Brantley, is uniquely national since "[i] mages of dislocation and disembodiment" in the play highlight the illusory nature of the reunion of an Irish Catholic Big House family, a historically grounded, often explored social issue in Irish literature.

Friel's *The Home Place*, which is close to *Aristocrats* in representing loss and the fading away of a culture—late nineteenth century Anglo-Irish in this case—also premiered at the Gate in February 2005, directed by Adrian Noble. Soon the production transferred to the Comedy Theatre in the West End for a three-month run. Reviews by English critics alternate between regarding it as a less significant work of the famous playwright, unevenly acted, and praising its tone and masterly details in text, dramaturgy and staging. Lyn Gardner in the *Guardian* discovers echoes of history, nostalgia and hauntedness in the work, which make it Frielean, yet finds it without the vitality of his earlier, historically rooted masterpieces like *Translations* or *Aristocrats.* Moreover, she argues that Tom Courtenay does not quite capture the anguish and tragedy of Christopher, the benign and paternalistic Anglo-Irish landlord of Bellybeg, "a kindly dinosaur on the verge of extinction" in Gardner's wording.[39] To set some balance, the reviewer adds that Margaret, the local Irish housekeeper of the Big House, is performed sensitively by the renowned actress Derbhle Crotty. In contrast, Charlotte Loveridge in *Curtain Up* is convinced that "For many, Tom Courtenay's thoroughly sympathetic portrayal of a flawed man will be the pivotal success of the evening".[40] Kate Bassett in the *Independent* reports feeling mesmerized by Courtenay's acting of Christopher: "At first you think his slow, sing-song way of speaking [...] is going to become an irritating mannerism. But is actually intriguing, conveying gentleness and even weakness and subtly suggesting assumed superiority [...]. His collapse into despair and near-madness is, in turn, charted very swiftly but entirely convincingly."[41]

With Ralph Fiennes in the title role, Ian McDiarmid playing Freddy and Ingrid Craigie playing Grace, *Faith Healer*, directed by Jonathan Kent, was put on by the Gate in early 2006, enjoying a sell-out run of six weeks in Dublin. It then transferred to the Booth Theater in New York, where the play had its world premiere in 1979 at the Longacre Theater—proving a box-office failure. The 2006 transfer featured the same male actors as performed at the Gate, with American actress Cherry Jones as Grace. It ran for several months and received four Tony nominations, including Ralph Fiennes for leading actor, Mark Henderson for lighting and Best Revival of a Play—Ian McDiarmid received the Tony for best featured actor. In the *New York Times* Ben Brantley assesses the set (designed by Jonathan Fensom) which "remains subtle and austere, with extraordinary, crepuscular lighting (by Mark Henderson) that slyly seems to be generated by the characters' changing moods".[42]

In 2009, when Friel turned eighty, the Gate brought three productions to the Parade Theatre in Sidney, advertised as "The Sydney Festival 2009: the Gate Friel Season". Under the direction of Fergus Linehan, the Festival included the likes of Canadian theatremaker Robert Lepage's work, as well as other theatre, film, dance and music. The Friel plays were revivals of recent hits from the Gate: *Faith Healer*, *The Yalta Game* and *Afterplay.* The occasion became a celebration of Friel as one of the world's greatest living playwrights at the time; in the reviews, the plays and their author enjoyed joint emphasis along with the performance dimension of the productions.

Faith Healer was directed by Robin Lefévre, and starred Owen Roe as Frank, Kim Durham as Freddy and Ingrid Craigie as Grace again—as in the original 2006 Dublin production. In *Australian Stage* Aleksei Wechter argues that, although dramatic action is missing from *Faith Healer*, it is "a delicate web of memory and myth" giving a taste of "the majesty of Friel's writing which is wonderfully realised in the Gate's production".[43] Of the three characters, Wechter finds Teddy the most likeable, because "Durham revels in the idiosyncrasies of Teddy and the tales of the talent he has managed over the years".[44] In his Theatre Diary, Kevin Jackson comments on the theatrical effects saying that the whole production impresses as, "Wonderful to hear and watch. There is something tribally basic about the writing and the playing—a simple relatively unadorned trust in the power of using words to tell a story. Just that and us".[45] Bryce Hallett's review in the *Sydney Morning Herald* also praises the style and the creation of intimacy with the audience, adding that the storytelling "as to be expected of the Gate Theatre, is highly accomplished and the play's intricate layers and darkening vision works its magic in the most natural and unforced of ways".[46]

Later in 2009, the three Gate productions went to the Edinburgh International Theatre Festival. "The Gate Friel Season" earned a Herald Angel Award, which is usually given to the best performers and backstage work. *The Yalta Game* and *Afterplay* originally premiered at the Dublin Gate in 2001 and 2002, directed by Karel Reisz and Robin Lefévre respectively. Of the two, *Afterplay* transferred to the Gielgud Theatre in London, earning praise from Michael Billington in the *Guardian*, as remaining true "to the spirit of Chekhov's own plays, in which an elegiac sense of death and failure is always accompanied by an intense awareness of the possibilities of life".[47] It is also true to Friel's own oeuvre, one must add, which abounds in the expression of ranges of emotion and, thus, *Afterplay* retains a Chekovian tone that was brought to life in the skilful and evocative performance of the Gate production. *The Yalta Game* (directed by Patrick Mason, starring Risteár Cooper and Rebecca O'Mara), part of the 2009 tours of Friel's work by the Gate, was reviewed very favourably after its Australian show by theatre director and critic Augusta Supple; for her it is "a beautifully sparse script deftly performed by O'Mara and Cooper. The focus is truly on the quality of the performance".[48] In this revival, *Afterplay* starred Francesca Annis and Niall Buggy under the direction of Garry Hynes. The two Chekovian shorts featuring in the Edinburgh Festival after the Sydney tour were reviewed together by Peter Geoghegan, who calls attention to Hynes's "unfussy direction", which "complements Friel's exquisite writing by drawing out its emotional depth without suppressing its lighter moments. Such intricate intermingling of light and shade, fantasy and reality, marks *Afterplay* out as so much more than a clever theatrical conceit well executed".[49] *The Yalta Game*, Geoghegan continues, has a Spartan set (Liz Ashcroft's work) to focus attention on the two characters' "razor-sharp exchanges [which] are delivered almost without skipping a breath".[50]

In sum, the Gate's productions presented new aspects of Friel's work to audiences across borders of the English-speaking world, leading to celebration of his work as a contemporary playwright on an international stage.

* * *

The above survey aims to document that since the 1980s, the Gate Theatre of Dublin has taken productions of several plays, Irish and non-Irish on tours abroad, often to stage them in noteworthy international festivals. Their capacity to translate the issues in the playwrights' texts, and their culture or specific worldview, has seen validation through awards, nominations, reviews and box-office popularity. It is fair to say that the Gate's company and artistic team have served as ambassadors of Irish theatrical culture throughout the last few decades, shaping and reshaping awareness of and attitudes to it among a wide range of audiences on three continents. Grene and Morash, in their introduction to *Irish Theatre on Tour*, say that "the study of Ireland's theatrical diaspora now looks less like an interesting byroad leading away from the main street of theatre history, and more like a path to the heart of some of the most pressing issues facing Irish culture in the twenty-first century".[51] The most significant issue seems to be the need for constant renewal of the perspectives and techniques with which Ireland can speak from the stage about itself and the global concerns it shares with other nations, social groups and individuals.

Notes

1. Christopher Morash, *A History of Irish Theatre 1601–2000* (Cambridge: Cambridge University Press, 2002), 275.
2. Ibid., 182.
3. Richard Pine and Richard Cave, *Theatre in Focus: The Dublin Gate Theatre 1928–1978* (Cambridge and Teaneck, N. J.: Chadwyck-Healey, 1984), 22.
4. Richard Pine, "The Gate—Home and Away", In *Irish Theatre on Tour*, ed. Nicholas Grene and Chris Morash (Dublin: Carysfort Press, 2005), 162.
5. Christopher Fitz-Simon, *The Boys: A Biography of Micheál MacLíammoír and Hilton Edwards* (London: Nick Hern Books, 1994), 84–85.
6. Ibid., 89.
7. Pine and Cave, *Theatre in Focus: The Dublin Gate Theatre 1928–1978*, 59.
8. Richard Cave, "Abbey Tours to London after 1990", in *Irish Drama: Local and Global Perspectives*, ed. Nicholas Grene and Patrick Lonergan (Dublin: Carysfort Press, 2015), 49.
9. For instance in "Samuel Beckett, the Gate Theatre Dublin, and the Contemporary Theatre Sector: Fragments of Performance History", by Anna McMullan and Trish McTighe (*Breac*, issue 2, 2014), in some chapters of the book *The International Reception of Samuel Beckett* edited by Mark Nixon and Matthew Feldman (London: Bloomsbury Publishing, 2011), in "The Gate Theatre's Beckett Festivals: Tensions between the Local and the Global", by David Clare, 39–50 in *Staging Beckett in Ireland and Northern Ireland* (edited by Trish McTighe, London: Bloomsbury Publishing, 2016), in "Beckett at the Gate" by Julie Bates, 478–488 in *The Oxford Handbook of Modern Irish Theatre* edited by Nicholas Grene and Chris Morash (Oxford: Oxford University Press, 2016), etc.
10. Bernice Schrank, *Sean O'Casey: A Research and Production Sourcebook* (Westport, Co.: Greenwood Press, 1996), 41.
11. Christopher Morash, "Ireland", in *The World Encyclopaedia of Contemporary Theatre: Volume I: Europe*, ed. Don Rubin. (London and New York: Routledge, 1994), 481.
12. Michael Colgan, "Michael Colgan in Conversation with Jeananne Crowley", in *Theatre Talk: Voices of Irish Theatre Practitioners*, ed. Lillian Chambers, Ger FitzGibbon and Eamonn Jordan (Dublin: Carysfort Press, 2001), 79.

13. Leslie Bennetts, "The Arts Festival; How a Dublin Actor Metamorphoses into Cringing, Drooling, Evil Joxer", *The New York Times*, 28 June 1988.
14. Mel Gussow quoted in Schrank, *Sean O'Casey: A Research and Production Sourcebook*, 211.
15. John P. Harrington, *The Irish Play on the New York Stage, 1874–1966* (Lexington, Kentucky: The University Press of Kentucky, 1997), 121.
16. Joe Dowling, "Joe Dowling in Conversation with Tony Ó Dálaigh" in *Theatre Talk: Voices of Irish Theatre Practitioners*, 131–132.
17. Irving Wardle, "A Giant among Kings", *The Independent*, 23 May 1993.
18. See, in addition to his essays on the playwright, Christopher Murray's substantial biography, *Sean O'Casey: The Writer at Work* (Montreal: McGill-Queen's University Press, 2004).
19. Anthony Roche, "Pinter and Ireland", in *The Cambridge Companion to Harold Pinter*, ed. Peter Raby (Cambridge: Cambridge UP, 2001), 175.
20. Ibid., 175.
21. Michael Billington, *Harold Pinter*, (London: Faber and Faber, 2009), 614–615.
22. Roche, "Pinter and Ireland", 176.
23. Billington, *Harold Pinter*, 711.
24. Les Gutman and David Lohrey, "Harold Pinter Festival: A part of Lincoln Center Festival 2001", *CurtainUp*, 2001.
25. Emer O'Kelly, "Awesome Theatre", *Sunday Independent*, 17 June 2001.
26. Billington, "The King of the Jungle", *The Guardian*, 16th June 2001.
27. Alastair Macaulay, "Pinter shows off his talent for menace", www.haroldpinter.org.
28. Billington, *Harold Pinter*, 727.
29. Ibid., 727.
30. Morash, *A History of Irish Theatre 1601–2000*.
31. Anthony Roche, "Friel and Synge: Towards a Theatrical Language", *Irish University Review* 29.1 (Spring/Summer 1999): 160.
32. Ibid.
33. Sheridan Morley, "London Theatre: Friel's *Molly Sweeney*: Of Blindness and Vision", *The New York Times*, November 1994.
34. Richard Christiansen, "Friel's Gift to Theater's Soul", *Chicago Tribune*, 16 December 1994.
35. Vincent Canby, "Theater Review: Seeing, in Brian Friel's Bellybeg", *New York Times*, 8 January 1996.
36. Greg Evans, "Review: "Molly Sweeney", *Variety*, 7 January 1996.
37. John Simon, "Out of Sight", *New York Magazine*, 22 January 1996.
38. Les Gutman, "Brian Friel Festival, Lincoln Center Festival 99", *CurtainUp* 1999.
39. Lyn Gardner, "*The Home Place*. Comedy, London", *Guardian*, 27 May 2005.
40. Charlotte Loveridge, "A *CurtainUp* London Review of *The Home Place*", *CurtainUp*, 2005.
41. Kate Bassett, "The Home Place, Comedy, London", *Independent*, 29 May 2005.
42. Ben Brantley, "Lincoln Center Festival Review; Lyrical Lapses in Old Truths in a Crumbling Irish Family", *New York Times*, 23 July 1999.

43. Alexei Wechter, "*Faith Healer*, Gate Theatre", *Australian Stage*, 20 January 2009.
44. Ibid.
45. Kevin Jackson, *Theatre Diary*, 21 January 2009.
46. Bryce Hallett, "Mosaic of intimate narratives tells tale of fateful homecoming", *Sydney Morning Herald*, 20 January 2009.
47. Michael Billington, "*Afterplay*." Gielgud Theatre, London, *Guardian*, 20 September 2002.
48. Augusta Supple, "The Yalta Game: Gate/Friel", www.augustasupple.com, 29 January 2009.
49. Peter Geoghegan, "Friel's trilogy a triumph", *Sunday Business Post*, 7 September 2009.
50. Ibid.
51. Grene and Morash, *Irish Theatre on Tour*, xviii.

Bibliography

Bassett, Kate. "The Home Place, Comedy, London." *The Independent*, May 29, 2005.

Bennetts, Leslie. "The Arts Festival; How a Dublin Actor Metamorphoses into Cringing, Drooling, Evil Joxer." *The New York Times*, June 28, 1988.

Billington, Michael. "The King of the Jungle." *The Guardian*, June 16, 2001.

———. "*Afterplay*." Gielgud Theatre, London. *The Guardian*, September 20, 2002.

———. *Harold Pinter*. London: Faber and Faber, 2009.

Bishop, Caroline. "Gambon Leads Quartet into No Man's Land." *Official London Theatre*, July 8, 2008.

Brantley, Ben. "Lincoln Center Festival Review; Lyrical Lapses in Old Truths in a Crumbling Irish Family." *The New York Times*, July 23, 1999.

———. "Ralph Fiennes, Portraying the Gaunt Genius in 'Faith Healer'." *The New York Times*, May 5, 2006.

Canby, Vincent. "Theater Review: Seeing, in Brian Friel's Ballybeg." *The New York Times*, January 8, 1996.

Cave, Richard. "Abbey Tours to London after 1990." Irish Drama: Local and Global Perspectives. Ed. Nicholas Grene and Patrick Lonergan. Dublin: Carysfort Press, 2015. 49–64.

Chambers, Lillian, Ger FitzGibbon and Eamonn Jordan, eds. *Theatre Talk: Voices of Irish Theatre Practitioners*. Dublin: Carysfort Press, 2001.

Christiansen, Richard. "Friel's Gift to Theater's Soul." *Chicago Tribune*, December 16, 1994.

Colgan, Michael. "Michael Colgan in Conversation with Jeananne Crowley." Theatre Talk: Voices of Irish Theatre Practitioners. Ed. Lillian Chambers, Ger FitzGibbon and Eamonn Jordan. Dublin: Carysfort Press, 2001. 76–89.

Dowling, Joe. "Joe Dowling in Conversation with Tony Ó Dálaigh." Lillian Chambers et al. 124–139.

Evans, Greg. "Review: "Molly Sweeney."" *Variety*, January 7, 1996.

Fitz-Simon, Christopher. *The Boys: A Biography of Micheál MacLíammoír and Hilton Edwards*. London: Nick Hern Books, 1994.

Gardner, Lyn. "*The Home Place*." Comedy, London. *The Guardian*, May 27, 2005.

Geoghegan, Peter. "Friel's Trilogy a Triumph." *Sunday Business Post*, September 7, 2009.

Grene, Nicholas and Chris Morash, eds. *Irish Theatre on Tour.* Dublin: Carysfort Press, 2005.

Grene, Nicholas and Patrick Lonergan, eds. *Irish Drama: Local and Global Perspectives.* Dublin: Carysfort Press, 2015.

Gutman, Les. "Brian Friel Festival, Lincoln Center Festival 99." *CurtainUp* 1999.

———. and David Lohrey. "Harold Pinter Festival: A Part of Lincoln Center Festival 2001." *CurtainUp* 2001.

Hallett, Bryce. "Mosaic of Intimate Narratives Tells Tale of Fateful Homecoming." *The Sydney Morning Herald*, January 20, 2009.

Harrington, John P. *The Irish Play on the New York Stage, 1874–1966.* Lexington, Kentucky: The University Press of Kentucky, 1997.

Jackson, Kevin. *Theatre Diary*, January 21, 2009.

Loveridge, Charlotte. "A *CurtainUp* London Review of *The Home Place*." *CurtainUp*, 2005.

Macaulay, Alastair. "Pinter Shows Off His Talent for Menace." www.haroldpinter.org

Morash, Christopher. *A History of Irish Theatre 1601–2000.* Cambridge. Cambridge UP, 2002.

———. "Ireland." In *The World Encyclopaedia of Contemporary Theatre: Volume I: Europe*, ed. Don Rubin. London and New York: Routledge, 1994, 467–482.

Morley, Sheridan. "London Theatre: Friel's *Molly Sweeney*: Of Blindness and Vision." *The New York Times*, November 9, 1994.

O'Kelly, Emer. "Awesome Theatre." *Sunday Independent*, June 17, 2001.

Pine, Richard, and Richard Cave. *Theatre in Focus: The Dublin Gate Theatre 1928–1978.* Cambridge and Teaneck, N. J.: Chadwyck-Healey, 1984.

Pine, Richard. "The Gate – Home and Away." Grene and Morash 161–177.

Roche, Anthony. "Friel and Synge: Towards a Theatrical Language." *Irish University Review* 29.1 (Spring/Summer 1999): 145–161.

———. Pinter and Ireland. In *The Cambridge Companion to Harold Pinter*, ed. Peter Raby. Cambridge: Cambridge UP, 2001, 175–191.

Schrank, Bernice. *Sean O'Casey: A Research and Production Sourcebook.* Westport, CO: Greenwood Press, 1996.

Simon, John. "Out of Sight." *New York Magazine*, January 22, 1996. 48–50.

Sommer, Elise. "A *CurtainUp* Review: The Faith Healer." *CurtainUp*, 2006.

Supple, Augusta. "The Yalta Game: Gate/Friel." www.AugustaSupple.com, January 29, 2009.

Wardle, Irving. "A Giant among Kings." *The Independent*, May 23, 1993.

Wechter, Alexei. "*Faith Healer*, Gate Theatre." *Australian Stage*, January 20, 2009.

Festivals and Curation: What Is a Festival For?

Willie White

> *As a rule (except for a few big cities), it is a single venue or a single festival that alone defines the horizon of the audience (as well as that of the local professional critics). The terrain of its judgement is paradoxically demarcated by the curator himself—only the art that he is showing actually exists.* (Florian Malzacher)[1]

The 2014 edition of Dublin Theatre Festival opened ambitiously with the Schaubühne am Lehniner Platz, Berlin's production of *Hamlet*, directed by its leader, Thomas Ostermeier, at the Bord Gáis Energy Theatre (BGET), which played for three performances in the 2,111-seat venue. *Hamlet* was the type of production one might expect to be presented by a festival that styles itself as bringing the best theatre in the world to Dublin. The Schaubühne had previously enjoyed acclaimed, sold-out performances of Ostermeier's *Hedda Gabler* at the Abbey Theatre during the 2006 festival. Anchored by Lars Eidinger's extravagant, powerful performance in the title role, *Hamlet* was well travelled, having visited many major cities and festivals since its premiere in 2008. Its six actors were supported by a further company of more than thirty to achieve Jan Papplebaum's scenography, video by Sébastien Dupouey and lighting by Erich Schneider in a performance that ran for two hours and thirty minutes without an interval. This was a major undertaking for an organisation on the scale of Dublin Theatre Festival. It also marked a break with the long-established practice of using the Gaiety Theatre, roughly half the capacity of the BGET, to host the opening performance, due to the venue's unavailability that year. The exceptional

W. White (✉)
Dublin Theatre Festival, Dublin, Ireland
e-mail: willie@dublintheatrefestival.com

E. Jordan, E. Weitz (eds.), *The Palgrave Handbook of Contemporary Irish Theatre and Performance*,
https://doi.org/10.1057/978-1-137-58588-2_44

circumstances effectively meant that the festival was presenting three performances at the BGET when it might otherwise have presented a two or three-week season at the Gaiety. Nonetheless, opening night saw the largest attendance in many years, with over one thousand people watching the first performance of *Hamlet*.

The production elicited a five-star review from Peter Crawley, the lead theatre critic of *The Irish Times*, a reprimand from his former university teacher—"Come on, Peter"—in the letters page of the same newspaper, and a mention on the most listened-to national morning radio show, more associated with its coverage of current affairs, due to a chicken carcass being thrown in the direction of the stalls during the banquet scene. Anecdotally, the post-show discussion following the second performance was ill-tempered with attendees exercised by the production's indifference to the fourth wall and the company's non-combative response to accusations of disrespecting the audience.

Though it is not uncommon that a work of art should prompt differing reactions on the basis of taste, some of the negative reaction to *Hamlet* was greater than this. It sought to disqualify Ostermeier's production as art, *a priori*. There was an insistence by some that Shakespeare should not, or could not, be done like this; audiences should not, and could not, be engaged with in this manner—a view that seems unaware of the raucous atmosphere in which Shakespeare's plays originated four hundred years earlier.

While festival organisers must take due care to advise patrons of content liable to shock or disturb, they also try to make space for the provocations of art. The reactions of some amongst the Dublin audience contrast with those of others who encountered the production. In London, where *Hamlet* enjoyed a successful run at the Barbican Centre, it offered a welcome and radical contrast to more familiar, often more reverent approaches to Shakespeare in his country of origin. In Berlin, while critically lauded, it attracted less notice, arguably due to its familiar aesthetic for German audiences. In Australia, the Sydney Morning Herald pronounced it the highlight of the city's international festival that year.[2]

This case history is rehearsed to animate some of the many factors that influence the decision-making process for a festival programme, though decisions are popularly assessed as, and distilled to, an "artistic" choice; it embodies the "demarcated terrain of judgement" referred to by Florian Malzacher above. It also sketches an enduring fault line between a set of expectations for theatre programming that have been established in Ireland over many years and those of other traditions of European and world theatre. What, then, is a festival for in a given context and how can programming decisions be both pragmatic and have artistic integrity?

Taking a cue from developments in the field of visual arts in the second half of the twentieth century, which has produced celebrated figures such as Harald Szeeman (and, more recently, the hyperactive Hans Ulrich Obrist), the performing arts, in addition to a multitude of other activities of editing and selection, have increasingly begun to annex the curatorial identity. However, it remains to be seen whether this term is adequate within the Irish context.

Curation implies an institutional setting—or at least an institutional attitude. Regardless of the admixture of advocacy, co-production, curation, presentation and programming that the post adopts, the role of the Artistic Director frequently combines with that of Chief Executive. Artistic directorship is more than an exercise of judgement inflected by taste; it also seeks to create the conditions in which the work of art is received.

"What's the theme?" is a frequent question of artistic directors, anticipating that there must be an organising principle to a programme, expressing an idea that has been conceived by a curator or a link that has been established between a number of works. Of course, unless said curator has considerable financial resources, accommodating infrastructure and abundant negotiating skills, as well as some luck, it will be very challenging to arrange a programme composed of others' works that can be orchestrated to express a coherent whole. A theme manifests deliberation in the selection of works or a diagnosis of the preoccupations of a group of works. Nonetheless, on a smaller scale, it can be possible to present clusters of works that resonate with each other, or to make a geographic link. The reality is that a programme is often guided by artistic enquiry, but governed by expediency. One can look enviously at a festival such as the multidisciplinary steirischer herbst in Graz, Austria whose leitmotifs were *Les Liaisons Dangereuses* in 2015 and *Where Are We Now?* in 2017 and whose multidisciplinary programmes were composed accordingly.

Even when a themed festival is not practically or financially viable, certain topics can assert themselves. This might be the result of one-off funding call-outs, for example when an additional subsidy was made available in Ireland to mark the centenary of the 1916 Easter Rising, or at the fruition of the relationship with an international cultural agency, often also marking an anniversary. Sometimes, activism at a grassroots level can influence a programme. One recent example of this is the movement provoked by the exclusion of female theatre artists from the centenary celebrations of the Abbey Theatre in 2015. #WakingTheFeminists prompted artistic decision makers to urgently reassess the gender balance of their programmes, both historically and for the future. Parenthetically, the 2017 edition of the Festival Theaterformen in Hannover, Germany, directed by Martine Dennewald, presented a programme led entirely by female artists and it underscored this bold decision by not referring its exceptionalism in marketing and publicity materials. Achieving such a programme required Dennewald to go about her research in a different way, often seeking out artists that lay outside the established festival circuit. So the process of creating a programme is rarely reducible to simple thematising, or selecting according to what one "likes" or "dislikes".

Even in a globalised world, with cheap air travel and widely circulating video documentation, it is necessary to mobilise the heavy infrastructure of performance in order for projects to materialise in your home city. While work can be spoken about and taught, there really is no complete substitute for the immediate and complex experience of live performance. Otherwise, we might have resigned ourselves to the convenience of live performances broadcast on cinema screens.

In the light of asymmetric funding systems between Ireland and many strong European theatre cultures, the difficulty of maintaining an active dialogue with contemporary performance (and contemporary audiences) is exacerbated by the physics of moving people and things from one place to another. Bringing international work of scale to Dublin is an further-logistical undertaking—it is not simply another few hundred kilometres along the motorway for the freight trucks. At the end of that road is an audience starved of regular opportunities to see international projects, which are often received as formally challenging, provocative or pretentious due to their unfamiliar aesthetic.

The purpose of a festival with a progressive sensibility is to get as close as possible to showcasing the state of the art—or as close as its audience can tolerate. A particular challenge for a small performing-arts community such as Ireland's is the lack of contemporary performing-arts projects that can be seen outside of festival contexts. Dublin Theatre Festival, along with Dublin Dance Festival and Dublin Fringe Festival, accounts for most of the international work that is presented in the city in any given year. Even a much larger, wealthier and more cosmopolitan city like London, which is an important reference for Irish spectators, can be characterised by a "narrowness of taste and timidness amongst audiences".[3] Ruth Mackenzie knows this audience well as former director of the London 2012 Cultural Olympiad and now leads the Holland Festival. She believes that (compared to a London audience), "One of the reasons that the Amsterdam audience is adventurous is because they routinely see innovative work from great international artists."

It is an assumption that the programme of a festival is the result of a type of Olympic process, and that what is presented is simply the best available or existing work. Yet in the field of international contemporary performing arts of the past fifty years, there are many significant artists whose works have never been seen by Dublin audiences, or else who have been represented by their later work, rather than the pieces with which they established their reputations. Dublin has never seen Pina Bausch, or Ariane Mnouchkine; Peter Brook's *Le Costume* was presented, but not *The Mahabharata*; the Wooster Group made its first Irish appearance in 2012, a full thirty-seven years into the company's career. Even notable companies closer to home don't necessarily bring their best-known, or their larger-scale productions: The Royal Shakespeare Company has not toured a production of a play by the writer after whom they were named, as opposed to a staging of one of his poems or a play by a contemporary author, since 1996. Potential game-changers have not featured in artists' and audience's curricula; the inclusion, or omission, of significant productions shapes the artistic development of a small community such as Irish theatre and determines the possibilities for the art form. It can often mean that the introduction of well-established aesthetic trends are received as novelty. Festivals, due to their relative durability and the visibility they can enjoy, play an important role in the development of the artform, giving it an opportunity to hold on to relevance and resources by continuing to expose audiences and artists to international work.

However, presenting contemporary art is an intrinsically risky and uncertain undertaking and in festivals in Ireland, income earned through ticket sales is a significant and unpredictable component to the budget. If a particular project with a large capacity falls short of its sales target, this is likely to have a debilitating impact on the programming capacity for future years. Add to this the fact that few arts organisations can afford to build up substantial reserves and this means that one year's underperformance effectively ends up borrowing money from the programming budget of subsequent years. This can lead to a culture that militates against risk on a large scale, where the first indicator of success is the avoidance of loss. This pressure does not rule out artistic risk but it does narrow its scope when the financial outcome of the festival can hang in the balance.

Long accustomed to presenting rather than producing or coproducing projects, Dublin Theatre Festival has become more invested in Irish work since 2010. The Irish Theatre Trust, originally established by the organisation's board in the early 2000s, has supported nine festival projects and co-productions since its revival in 2011. Three further projects have been co-produced through the EU-funded NXTSTP network from 2012 to 2017, where Dublin Theatre Festival is partner in a €2.4 million project with leading festivals in Austria, Belgium, Estonia, France, the Netherlands, Portugal and Sweden. Dublin Theatre Festival also initiated a co-production with the Lyric Theatre, Belfast in 2015 for the Irish premiere of Conor McPherson's *The Night Alive*.

A festival presentation is attractive to many artists, as it offers a guaranteed income and a high profile, and can lead to further opportunities. Certainly, Irish artists have become much more prominent in programmes over the last decade and visits by international presenters, supported by the Irish Theatre Institute and Culture Ireland, have raised their international profile. Recent years have seen a generation of independent, Irish-bred companies such as Brokentalkers, Corn Exchange, Dead Centre, Gare St Lazare Players, Pan Pan, Teac Damsa and THEATREclub tour Dublin Theatre Festival premieres to Europe, North America, Asia and Australia, with the festival platform acknowledged as a factor in this success. This international mobility has contributed to the transformation of Irish theatre, and it can be argued that its Irish companies that are now becoming important conduits of international aesthetics for a local audience as their practice expands beyond the playwriting for which the festival was once best known.

In the development of the performing arts in Ireland, festivals presenting international work are key to introducing new aesthetic perspectives to the conversation about the contemporary state of the art. Artists and indeed audiences rely on this to stay connected with the contemporary artform. The key task of the Artistic Director of Dublin Theatre Festival is to overcome the constraints of limited resources and as far as possible to ensure that audiences and artists are exposed to work that challenges the form, and the Irish perception of how theatre is "meant" to look and function. At the same time the festival should be supporting and encouraging Irish artists to create excellent theatre and to take their place on world stages. That's what I think a festival is for.[4]

Notes

1. Florian Malzacher in *No More Drama*, eds. Peter Crawley and Willie White (Dublin: Project Arts Centre, 2011), 106.
2. http://www.smh.com.au/entertainment/theatre/performances-seared-into-the-memory-20101228-1997f.html
3. "There's an awful lot of British theatre I couldn't programme" Ruth Mackenzie, Artistic Director Holland Festival interviewed by Lyn Gardner https://theatre-anddance.britishcouncil.org/blog/2017/08/ruthmackenzie/
4. Thanks to Briony Morgan for editorial assistance with this article.

Bibliography

Crawley, Peter and Willie White, eds. No More Drama. Dublin: Project Arts Centre, 2011.

Interart Relations and Self-Reflexivity in Contemporary Irish Drama

Csilla Bertha

Self-reflexivity has always been encoded in the arts, but as a critical mode of reading and interpretation it became favoured only in recent decades. One of the privileged strategies of introducing self-referentiality into a work of art is integrating other artforms, with the function of mirroring. In the interart relationships—the interaction between the different art forms within a work of art—art calls "attention to its own prerequisites and qualifications as construction".[1] Such relationships enhance the possibilities of the representation of issues, problems, dilemmas in individual arts, and in their togetherness multiply art's potentials.

An examination of a few contemporary Irish plays dramatizing artist-protagonists and/or presenting artworks on the stage will hopefully illuminate a few ways in which the artist and art itself in their different manifestations are integrated into theatrical performance, how those art forms interact with one another, and how such interactions enhance the self-reflexivity of drama and theatre. I prefer to use the term *interart*, although remain aware that today intermedial(ity) is more frequently applied to much the same phenomena. But the latter includes new technical, electronical, digital media, whereas I wish to focus on the traditional art forms in the theatre. *Künstlerdrama*—a would-be literary term offering a theatrical parallel to the German *künstlerroman* (meaning "artist novel")—would help to denote plays that foreground the artist's existence and art's values and potentials. This type of drama multiplies the layers of self-reflexivity with more immediacy and power than the artist novel, since the artwork, when staged, exerts its own impact directly.

C. Bertha (✉)
University of Debrecen, Debrecen, Hungary

E. Jordan, E. Weitz (eds.), *The Palgrave Handbook of Contemporary Irish Theatre and Performance*,
https://doi.org/10.1057/978-1-137-58588-2_45

Theatre as a composite genre has always incorporated various forms of art—verbal, visual, audial, kinetic—in differing proportions, allowing them to amplify each other's voices. This phenomenon has been remarked upon since the ancient Greeks: already Aristotle in his *Poetics* talks about the multiplicity of arts involved in tragedy. Evidently, however, the proportion of non-verbal components has increased in the last decades. The contest between art forms (comparing and contrasting words and music, poetry and painting, music and visual arts, to establish the superiority of one over another) looks back at centuries-long debates. Theatre, however, allows the different arts to coexist without contest—even when the rivalry itself is thematized, as, for instance, in Brian Friel's *Performances* (2003).

Still, in some periods the fear of the dominance (indeed, what sometimes is called the "imperialism") of language, which, paradoxically, is accompanied by the distrust in language's power, led to the emphasis on other means of presentation. Ulla-Britta Lagerroth asserts that the "interart turn" is "related to a total distrust of traditional languages" in Romanticism, then in Symbolism, and later again in Modernism. Discussing theatre, she quotes Marianne Kesting as demonstrating how that distrust "gave rise to 'the theatre of silence'",[2] which happened, she contends, simultaneously with the establishment of the modern theatre language, the language of the re-theatricalized theatre, a language not of words spoken on stage, but a language of space and scenography, of body and choreography, of light and music. This re-theatricalized language invades the dramatic text, where it takes over the function of dialogue and monologue.

In the Irish intellectual tradition, where, in contradistinction to the classical dualist "*either/or*" logic, the "more dialectical logic of *both/and*" is intrinsic,[3] the destabilization of language's dominance does not necessarily lead to its replacement by other forms of art. "Words" may no longer be "alone [...] certain good" (as Yeats believed in his early career[4]) but the art of words, together with other art forms, may all participate in interart relationships on the stage. And they do, in a great number of contemporary Irish plays, which, in contrast with the general complaint that Irish drama is too verbal, employ powerful visual imagery and audial effects (if not always as art forms) to complement the words. Many of them go further: they frame artists and/or artworks in the stage space to implement interart self-reflexivity. The critical approach focusing on interart relationships helps to highlight how the collaboration of different arts, *including* and not substituting verbal language, enhances theatricality.

Erika Fischer-Lichte offers two theoretical models to describe "the increasing dissolution of boundaries between different art forms": the first compares individual art forms "with regard to their specific achievements and effects [exploring] the possibilities and limitations of transferring the potential of one artistic practice to another in order to transcend the boundaries between them" (Lessing's model). The second (Goethe's and Wagner's) focuses "on the interaction and interplay between the arts", Wagner demanding "a union of all the arts by fusing the different art forms" in a way that "they can no longer be demarcated or identified separately".[5] In the theatre both practices may be detected: in some cases the differences become dissolved by one art form taking over the potentials of another while in others, the specificity of each highlights their interplay. Irina Rajewsky's terms for the types of interaction in intermedial studies, "media combination" and "intermedial references",[6] are also helpful in describing the presence and interaction of different artistic practices combined in the theatre, either in their own materiality or, in the second case, present only through references in another medium (for example, evoking paintings through ekphrasis, a literary description of visual art).

The Artist

At least from Synge and Yeats on, a high number of Irish playwrights dramatize artists and their plight, difficulties, failures and tragic victories. Among Yeats's plays that more directly feature artists per se rather than Cuchulain- or Deirdre-like heroes as equivalents of the artistic value-system and behaviour, *The King's Threshold* (1904) and, much later, *The King of the Great Clock-Tower* (1934), together with its twin-piece, *A Full Moon in March* (1935), centre on artists empowered by a superior gift, threatened by a worldly power and triumphing—at the price of their lives.

Yeats's artists, taking symbolic, mythic or folktale-like shapes (such as the poet as Stroller or Swineherd), are clearly distinguished on the stage from figures of the world's hierarchy. In his symbolic theatre the distinctions become visibly staged (the severed head singing a triumphant love-song, the mute and for long, almost motionless, statue-like Queen dancing in acceptance and glorification of self-sacrificial adoration as opposed to the physical violence of the King's men). "Words alone are certain good", but from his early plays on, Yeats also inscribed, in interaction with his poetic language, carefully designed stage-images, colours, lights, masks, movements, gestures, shapes, singing, music and dance—the whole scenography (partly thanks to the inspiration of the Japanese Noh, innovative directors such as Gordon Craig and collaboration with dancers). The different art forms do not amalgamate but rather strengthen each other's effect in their own particularities. It is true that what comes through in the words of the poet-playwright's written text is what survives to posterity, unlike ephemeral performances—but through the words, all the images can come to life again and again in their rich theatrical variety. In modernist and sometimes even in postmodern theatre words are still the points of departure for the theatrical imagination.[7]

In contemporary drama, artist figures receive much less heroic but rather more ironic dramatizations than in Yeats's works, yet the idea of triumphing through self-sacrifice survives. Probably the most emblematic artist figure is Frank Hardy in Brian Friel's *Faith Healer* (1979), a play that most directly thematizes the artist's uncertainties, anxieties, the contradictions of being gifted and cursed by unusual talent, and the danger of slipping into seeking the audience's favour as "con-man" instead of following one's own "standard of excellence".

Curiously, in this play the artist's passion, ambition, anguish and achievement all come through to the audience—apart from the body of the performer in the stage space—almost entirely via words, given that it is a monologue play. And yet, this most extensively verbal drama displays also a metatheatrical depth since it performs performance: performs theatrical art itself. The boundaries between life and death are transgressed in several ways: not only does the dead Frank come on stage in the last act to talk to the audience about his own death, but he also crumples up the newspaper clipping about his miraculous healing on the stage that—as he explains—he "crumpled [...] up and threw [...] away" in his last night of life.[8] And the boundaries between stage and auditorium, between art and life also dissolve as Frank, the dead dramatic character, re-enacts his last action in the presence of the audience: the living actor acts out a dead person acting as if alive, performing both his own living and dead selves. And so the mirroring goes on and on. Consisting only of four monologues—the most consciously theatrical form of communication—the play self-reflexively calls attention to its own performativity that is due in part to the almost bare stage featuring only a poster and rows of chairs in front of which the monologues are delivered. This setting, as Anthony Roche observes, "makes the audience itself a crucial participant in the faith-healing ritual, extending the drama from the confines of the stage to embrace the entire auditorium".[9]

Jim Nolan's *Blackwater Angel* (2001) echoes similar issues and dilemmas, and uses *Faith Healer* as intertext. Nolan's artist-healer protagonist, based on the historical figure of Valentine Greatrakes, wrestles with the same sort of "agonizing questions", uncertainties, self-doubts as Frank Hardy. Both healers suffer from the lack of control over their miraculous gift and their helplessness when it is ebbing. And both gain a sort of redemption through accepting their own impotence and through their self-sacrifice. Frank Hardy, in his last performance, describing the ritualized space where he meets his murderers, ritualizes his own death and—as Richard Rankin Russell analyses in detail—the audience becomes "enveloped in Frank's profound sense of spirituality" as he "steps into community with both his murderers and the audience members", transforming and extending the stage into a sacred space.[10]

Theatre

Blackwater Angel also reflects theatre-art in its plot and structure. Nolan deploys play-within-a-play, multiplication of angles and reduplication of situations through a combination of the internal play-within-a-play and the framing play as *theatrum mundi*. The actors of the inset play provide inspiration, set examples of perseverance and of respect for the vocation to the protagonist and, mirroring life, help their audience—other characters—in gaining self-esteem.[11]

The broken, failed but repentant healer at the end of the play reluctantly makes what feels to him the biggest sacrifice: to try to heal without faith in his own capability and worthiness. He has learned from the actors that instead of seeking explanations for everything, he should embrace the mystery of the gift and, like Frank Hardy, he also understands his responsibility to serve. Given that realization, Greatrakes regains the inner voice that earlier inspired and guided him—the celestial singing of the mysterious child, Angel—and that closing takes this drama also back to the sacred.

Nolan utilizes the play-within-a-play in other artist-plays, too. Revisiting Shakespearean characters and situations, *Moonshine* (1991) has almost as many layers as Tom Stoppard's *Rosencrantz and Guildenstern Are Dead* (1966), with its local artisans attempting to perform the artisans in *A Midsummer Night's Dream* performing the inset play, *Pyramis and Thysbe* to entertain Theseus and Hyppolita in the framing play. The whole performance then folds back on itself, and becomes the inset play around which the local people act out their own grievances and conflicts. *The Salvage Shop* (1998), while "not directly employ[ing] metatheatre", uses "the visually emphatic conceit of a second-hand shop to promote the dramatic idea of salvaging damaged relationships".[12]

Theatre-art becomes thematized and acted out frequently through plays- and play-acting-within-a-play, in such different works as, for instance, Frank McGuinness' *Carthaginians* (1988) and *Mutabilitie* (1997), Brian Friel's *Crystal and Fox* (1968), *The Freedom of the City* (1973), Thomas Kilroy's *The Madam McAdam Travelling Theatre* (1992), *The Secret Fall of Constance Wilde* (with puppets and a stage-within-the-stage, 1997) and *Blake* (as guests watch the lunatics in the madhouse as entertainment, 2001, published 2015, currently unperformed) and Stewart Parker's *Heavenly Bodies* (1986). The latter is a fantastic biography of Dion Boucicault—and, through that, a pronounced self-portrait of playwright Stewart Parker—which, when performed in the Peacock in 2004, gained more immediacy and weight through the parallelism between its performances and the simultaneous run of *The Shaughraun* (1874) on the main stage of the Abbey. The inbuilt references to and excerpts from Boucicault's work in Parker's play further expand the layering and self-reflection through this brilliant gesture of the theatre (moreover, on the hundredth anniversary of the opening of the Abbey). In this theatre-wide *mise-en-abyme*, the two plays in such close proximity keep reflecting back on each other.

In several plays of the younger generation metatheatricality works in more overt forms. In particular, Enda Walsh's plays "about performance and performativity *vis á vis* creativity and death"[13] abound in play-acting, clowning, shifts of roles. In *The Walworth Farce* (2006), reality and theatre, life and art blend into each other, as a director father insists that his two sons enact his script, rigorously observing every detail. As it transpires, play-acting serves to repress real memories of a murder while re-enacting the falsified version of their own past. All this is disrupted when an uninitiated person, a young woman, enters, whereupon unrehearsed violent forms of behaviour destroy both the "performance" within the play and the lives of the play's characters. In *Ballyturk* (2014), portraits on the wall indicate the figures that the characters in the play impersonate in turns, thus the mirroring goes from images to the invisible fictional characters they depict to actors impersonating them, acting out their roles as actors. Unexpectedly, a third person (an allegorical figure of death) appears who changes the atmosphere and prompts the characters to enact their own selves, fears and anxieties. This third figure walks in when the back wall opens "onto a small hill of green perfect grass... [and] falls onto this grass".[14] With that this "abstract, surreal, and postmodern" play moves away from the frenetic farce of Walsh's previous plays towards the metaphysical, as the playwright is "seeking a contemporary form for absurdist tragedy".[15]

Music

In many other plays self-reflexivity is enhanced through staging other, specific forms of art. Music—as paradigmatic for all other arts, often considered an "absolute" art because it is spiritual and non-representational, with no conceptual content, offering the purity to which other arts aspire[16]—seems to be the most frequently recurring art form on stage. Not only as a background or mood- and atmosphere-creating agent, but also often as a thematic part of the play. Brian Friel's *Philadelphia, Here I Come!* (1964), *Dancing at Lughnasa* (1990), *Give Me Your Answer, Do!* (1998) and others famously deploy music as an organic element of the composition, his *Aristocrats* (1979), *Wonderful Tennessee* (1993), *The Home Place* (2005) make music and musicians even more central while *Performances* features a composer for its protagonist.

Tom Murphy no less importantly uses music as a thematic and structural element, although so far he has not worked with a musician protagonist. The use of singing in *Conversations on a Homecoming* (1985), *The Wake* (1997) and *The House* (2000), among others, offers redeeming moments and articulates feelings beyond verbalization. Most elaborately so in *The Gigli Concert* (1983) it offers an embodiment of beauty and spiritual desire, becoming an obsession that leads to reaching the impossible in a magical—spiritual and theatrical—transformation.[17]

The allure of music lingers in Marina Carr's *The Mai* (1994) through the cellist Robert and the Mai herself, in *Portia Coughlan* (1996) through the angelic-demonic voiced Gabriel, and the same writer also has a whole play that revolves around two musician protagonists: *The Cordelia Dream* (2008). Even a very different kind of play, Mark O'Rowe's *Terminus* (2007), full of the most savage brutality of the Dublin underworld, but also of supernatural experiences, demons, angels and pacts with the devil, culminates in an unexpected scene of the fulfilment of the serial-killer protagonist's lifelong desire to sing, something for which he had sold his soul. In a humiliating position: naked, hanging by his intestine on a crane, his triumphant singing mesmerizes the crowd below and he knows that this will "ease whatever suffering is in store" for him in Hell.[18] The monologue-play's rhythmic, rhyming prose itself provides a heightened musicality.

In Friel's *Performances* a *paragone*—a contest between words and music—develops through Leoš Janáček's encounter with the PhD student Anezka, writing her dissertation on the composer. All this happens seventy years after his death, when Janáček talks, plays the piano and mentions angrily the publication date of one of his works long after he was buried—not as a gratuitous theatrical game but as a representation of the artist's confrontation with the afterlife of his work; an investigation into what happens to the work, how valuable life experiences are vis-à-vis the accomplished work, after the death of the author. Janáček insists that nothing matters, only the work, everything else is "ancillary", while Anezka, repeatedly quoting the composer's own words in his love-letters as evidence of his indebtedness to a young woman for inspiring his last composition, maintains that experienced passion becomes a significant part of the created work. The play keeps "hesitancies" vivid, balancing between the two truths.

Questioning the power of words versus other forms of expression is a well-known recurring theme in Friel's oeuvre. He sometimes uses music at points where emotion is heightened "beyond the boundaries of language", when music "can hit straight and unmediated into the vein of deep emotion", as he confessed in 1999.[19] In *Wonderful Tennessee*, words are often silenced or counterpointed by music; a writer-figure suggests that the most perfect book might have been written without words, and a terminally ill musician's accordion-playing suddenly stops in mid-phrase, more potently conveying his whole life story than words ever could. In *Give Me Your Answer, Do!*, Tom, the dried-up writer silenced by the tragedy in his family, is continuously juxtaposed with his wife, whose musical talent is wasted due to circumstances. And the famous closing sentences of *Dancing at Lughnasa* assert the superiority of dance to words in its potency "to be in touch with some otherness".[20] In *Performances*, Janáček derides writers as "people who huckster in words merely report[ing] on feeling" while "we"—that is, musicians, composers, singers—"*speak* feeling".[21] But, as Nicholas Grene helpfully observes (speaking about *Lughnasa*), "it is with the hypnotic suggestiveness of language itself that language is renounced".[22]

The contest between words and music in *Performances* is somewhat disingenuous, however, since words juxtaposed to the music are not words of poetry or fiction but those of the composer's letters and the prosaic arguments of the non-artist scholar. Friel very daringly gives music centre stage, letting it occupy a huge part of performance time—the first two movements of Janáček's *Second String Quartet* or *Intimate Letters* are played off-stage, the last two on-stage—and letting it speak for itself and directly to the audience. The words, communicating conflicting views, truths, arguments, are all counterpointed by the music in its own mediality, without blurring the boundaries. In this "media combination" words do not aspire to the condition of music, and the music does not convey a narrative. In the totality of the theatrical experience, the art forms interact to enrich each other's effect in the Lessing model. The dominant feeling created is complementarity and balance. The framing—the arguments about the inspiration, influence, emotions, life experience carried in the music—necessarily modifies the listener's experience of the music itself. So, eventually, not so much the different forms of art themselves as their reception will be changed when artworks appear in a new framing environment.

Nevertheless, not all artist-plays focus on artistic problems. Marina Carr's *The Cordelia Dream*, another *künstlerdrama*, resembles *Performances* in that it features composers and compositions with live music as the central part of the performance. Both plays transgress borders between life and death as they bring a protagonist back from death in a way that for a while s/he looks, behaves, speaks like a living being. Yet the emphasis and the presentation of art on stage differs because Carr's play concentrates on the psychological problems of the artists as hypersensitive, unconventional figures and much less on art itself. While *Performances* explores the potential of music and words, *The Cordelia Dream* delves into the bond between artist father and daughter and their jealousies and ambitions in a love–hate relationship that must destroy the other.

Music obviously is an integral part of each play but in Friel's, Janáček's music is played by real musicians: a string quartet as part of the performance of *Performances*—reversing the theatrical practice of actors acting other artists. In *The Cordelia Dream* the playtext only suggests the kind of music, if at all, that is played by musicians situated on the side of the stage, hardly noticeable by the audience. The music for the premiere was composed by Conor Linehan, described by a reviewer as "a sort of plangent, hysterical modernist mish-mash [...] played spiritedly [...] on a string trio against a piano recording".[23] Clearly, Carr's play is more preoccupied with the correspondences of the characters to *King Lear* than artistic dilemmas, so the examination of intertextual aspects would lead more to its core.

In Friel's *The Home Place*, differently from *Performances*, poetry and music do blend together in a Wagnerian fusion in the musicalization of poetry, or, more exactly, in poetry set to music. The schoolmaster Clement, another artist-figure (with all the conventional attributes of being dishevelled, drunk yet devoting his life and energies to creating), performs with his choir the Thomas Moore songs that he has set to three-part harmony. Moore's words and Clement's music become combined and merged also in their emotional and psychological effect as they evoke powerful memories (personal and cultural) in the protagonist Margaret, and help her to decide about returning to her home rather than becoming an esteemed adornment (the landlord's wife) of the English landlord's family.[24]

Visual Arts: Painting and Sculpture

Visual arts have also been declared superior to literature (poetry) since at least the time of Leonardo da Vinci, on the basis of their spatiality, offering an instant absorption as opposed to poetry's linearity in time.[25] The heterotopic space of the theatre and the expansion in physical time of the performance, can bring together spatial and temporal arts without rivalry in its "total" art as Wagner understood it. McGuinness' *Innocence* (1986) and *The Bird Sanctuary* (1994) feature painters, while Thomas Kilroy's *The Shape of Metal* (2003) and McGuinness's *Observe the Sons of Ulster Marching towards the Somme* (1985), present sculptors and sculpture with intriguing solutions for the stage presence of art and artist.

In *Innocence*, a play about the life and art of Michelangelo Merisi da Caravaggio, painting is transformed with the most theatrical means and is brought to life in ephemeral performance. No physical artwork is placed on stage, and nor does the artist appear with canvas and brush in hand. McGuinness's strategies to re-create Caravaggio's paintings on stage include "intermedial references", such as *charade*, *tableau vivant*, colours, lights, movements and metonymy (for instance, emblematic objects and images). Ekphrasis is also deployed, but not only in its original meaning—in W.J.T. Mitchell's definition, the "verbal representation of visual representation"[26]—but also in what I would call gestural ekphrasis: visual images re-presented with gestures, movements, the performers' bodies. Boundaries between solid, unchanging artworks and the ever-changing theatre presence are dissolved, with scenes becoming painterly and paintings transforming into the living figures' performances.

Caravaggio's famous "chiaroscuro" effects are themselves very theatrical: the coexistence of sharp light and deep darkness, often without transitory shades in-between, replacing the dominance of the line, with which he renewed contemporary (late-Renaissance) painting and introduced Baroque techniques. He also followed the painterly tradition that condenses whole narratives into paintings. On the stage the reverse process takes place: the narratives of paintings become opened up and spread out to the viewers. One of the several examples of providing the audience with a picture's genesis is when Caravaggio's model, Antonio, offers him a bowl of fruit with the painter watching him, "*rearranging his hand and pulling Antonio's shirt from his shoulder to expose the flesh*".[27] Here the artist prepares his model for painting, while in a *tableau vivant* the picture *Boy with a Basket of Fruit* itself formulates in front of the spectators' eyes. Yet all of it operates as part of the stage action. Or, in one of the most elaborate tableaux vivants close to the end of the play and following the painter's death, Lena, Caravaggio's friend/lover, orders Antonio to strip and then arranges the red cloak around him and puts the cross into his hand so he transforms into Caravaggio's John the Baptist. The transgression of the boundaries between word and image through movement results in the transparency of the figure: the model of the original picture, this lowest of the low, a "rent-boy", transubstantiates in front of the audience's eyes into John the Baptist, the herald of the Saviour. In Eamonn Jordan's succinct phrasing, "[b]y using the lowly, Caravaggio was in fact painting their potential salvation".[28] In a similar fashion, McGuinness turns the prostitute Lena into Mary Magdalena of the painting *The Penitent Magdalena*, cradling an imaginary child that was never born but which now she pronounces dead. Moreover, Hiroko Mikami, further elevating Lena, expands the reference to a Virgin Mary image, cradling the infant Jesus.[29] Such gestural ekphrases on stage lend a sort of stillness, silence, stasis to the scenes: this is similar to ekphrastic narration, where "the verbal representation of the visual representation" desires to "still the movement of linguistic temporality into a spatial, formal array".[30] Other scenes, by contrast, spread out Caravaggio's pictorial world in time, through dynamic movement and gestural metonymy (emblematic figures, objects of his paintings), as in the opening sequence.

McGuinness's protagonist himself asserts: "I take ordinary flesh and blood and bone and with my two hands transform it into eternal light, eternal dark. [...] For my art balances the beautiful and the ugly, the saved and the sinning."[31] And so seems to do also McGuinness, in whose theatre the "beautiful and the ugly, the saved and the sinning" are blended into the same entities, in the process of their transformation back into "flesh and bone" in the dramatic reality of his play, while holding together the "eternal light, eternal dark".

Mikami and Jordan each identifies in detail Caravaggio's paintings evoked in the play in their illuminating analyses, so here I only call up one beautifully composed stage manifestation of the artist's transformation of reality into art. His dead or suffering models, his "victims" haunt him and he, raising a knife, says:

CARAVAGGIO [...] This is how I die. How I kill myself. This is how I paint. Living things. In their life I see my death. I can't stop my hand. I can't stop my dying. But I can bring peace to what I'm painting.

SISTER Then raise your hand in peace. Paint.
(SISTER *takes the knife from* CARAVAGGIO. *He raises his hands. Light rises from his raised hands, drawing* WHORE, ANTONIO *and* LUCIO *from the darkness.* [...])[32]

As in Caravaggio's paintings light often seems to radiate from the figures themselves, so McGuinness' artist-protagonist, with the purgative power emanating from himself, is now able to give love, life and health as he consoles and heals his models in a series of ritual gestures—even though only in a dream.

Caravaggio, along with other artist-figures in McGuinness's plays—the trickster-like mock-artist in *Carthaginians*, the sculptor Pyper in *Sons of Ulster*, the art historian in *Dolly West's Kitchen* (1999), actors in *Gates of Gold* (2002), poets, playwrights, writers in *Mutabilitie* and in *The Hanging Gardens* (2013)—is the agent of turning the established (social, political or aesthetic) order upside down, transgressing boundaries of genres and dramatic styles, as well as those between different concepts of space and ontological states. Most of his artists are endowed with some kind of superhuman ability, a few of them are presented even as witch-like, including the File, the Irish poet in *Mutabilitie* and Eleanor Henryson, a painter in *The Bird Sanctuary*. The latter is a less violent, somewhat more domesticated artist than Caravaggio, who is presented in relation to her family, in a domestic space and the realistic milieu of contemporary Ireland. The whole play seems to be more embedded in traditional realism of dramatic style, character and setting—which makes the manner in which art and the artist-protagonist lift it out of realism all the more puzzling.

Eleanor's creative force is closely connected to magic. The plot reveals the effectiveness of her black magic practised on stage, raising the crucial question of whether witchcraft can be accepted as associated with art and the artist's sensitivity. Christopher Murray interprets the artist as "both seer and destroyer", evoking "chthonic forces".[33] Theatrically, it is also intriguing how and to what effect can witchcraft coexist with dramatic realism. Language and painting here again interact to amplify each other's voices, sometimes contradicting, other times empowering each other in broadening the theatre space to include the invisible.

Of the three moments of witchcraft, the third, which occurs at the end of the play, provides a revelation that remains full of ambiguity yet testifies to art's capacity to turn the evil forces into something creative and thus healing.[34] Three realistic family portraits, part of Eleanor's self-imposed task to preserve the family, gain special significance in the spatial arrangement. These paintings of Eleanor's dead parents and living siblings come alive when the subjects of the paintings or their descendants inadvertently adopt the poses of those in the pictures, the drama at this point playfully enacting Wilde's idea of life imitating art. The earlier warring family members reconcile in this (unconscious) imitation of peaceful scenes. The reduplication of the two-dimensional paintings by the three-dimensional actor figures onstage self-reflexively demonstrates some of the methods applied in *Innocence* to evoke paintings in gestures while also draws attention to the similarities and differences between life and created art—with the understanding that what is "life" onstage is itself art, artistically arranged and transformed.

The huge bird sanctuary image revealed in the final tableau behind those paintings and living characters is of a different nature. This culmination of the artist's oeuvre, while constructing a theatrical moment of the summation of the whole play, remains enigmatic in its very mode of existence. The stage directions leave it unclear if it is a painted wall, a painting framed in the wall or solely the magic work of the imagination that conjures up the vision so strongly that others can see it as well: "*the back wall magically reveals the bird sanctuary*".[35]

Its function of bridging the inside and the outside through dissolving borderlines makes the bird sanctuary image reflect, in a metatheatrical manner, on what is crucial in theatre: the manifold interplay between the physical and the fictional. Gay McAuley regards the two related issues of the "onstage/offstage dialectic" on the one hand, and, on the other, that of "the complex relationship between the physical or material reality and the fictional, illusory world created in and by" it, lying at the "very heart of theatrical semiosis".[36] McGuinness's play answers the on-stage/off-stage dilemma by offering the experience of simultaneous inside and outside views in a manner entirely integral to the medium of theatre as words and painting in their interart relationship bring forth the union of the physical and the fictional within the dramatic space of the theatre.

The indeterminacy of the bird sanctuary painting's/evocation's materiality also reflects on the "heightened awareness of the materiality and mediality of artistic practices" in studies of intermediality.[37] The theatrical magic of its appearance and the characters' words draw attention not only to the materiality, but also to the possibility of its total *immateriality*. The issue of the "mediality of artistic practices" is highlighted through the presentation of the artist as *both* physically engaged in painting (in stage images of paints, brushes, even seaweeds that will appear in the image, and in the words of family members about the artist working on this one painting for three years) *and* also (only?) mentally conjuring it up. Moreover, the image involves the audience in the action of bringing it forth. As Helen Heusner Lojek suggests: the "audience in effect joins Eleanor in a creative collaboration that ends with the dissolving backdrop at the end. If the final dissolve works, it is a brief stage incarnation of an imaginative reality that author, actors, and audience have already created."[38]

All this problematizes the ontology of art itself. Can a strong imagination alone be regarded as art? A hypnotic power to persuade others to see something which is not there? Is it witchcraft that makes the back wall disappear and the stage characters see it as painting? Or is it a view of the outside? The intriguing feature is that McGuinness keeps the ambiguities alive through the combined effect of words and images. Eleanor's very words to her sister as she conjures up the painting, question its material existence: "If you look, you'll see. The bird sanctuary. Believe me, you'll see it. Pretend, pretend. Keep the faith, dear sister."[39] Each word—"believe", "keep the faith", "pretend"—contributes to the uncertainty. Does the reception of art depend entirely on belief, faith, pretension? The playtext makes it clear that the undecidability of the substance of this painting or vision must lift the presentation's seeming realism to surrealism and transcend the borders between nature and art.

In the process of the disappearance of the wall, petty human hostilities also become annulled. Eleanor's offer to walk with her sister—with whom she has been shown to share a love-hate relationship—into the bird sanctuary, "into eternity", verbally opens up the space to another dimension, just as the bird sanctuary image does visually. In that transformation the extraordinary enters the ordinary, the house has become what Eleanor always wanted it to be: a sanctuary and the sanctuary itself turned into an "artifice of eternity".

The artist and witch Eleanor in her liminal position—between living in this world and communicating with the other—succeeds in uniting matter and imagination, nature and art. The closing scene could be read both as a mirror up to nature and as the wall becoming transparent to allow nature to enter the house. In the final tableau, blending the Aristotelean "*natura naturans*" (creative principle) and "*natura naturata*" (created form), nature is being interiorized, although less in the picture itself (which, obviously, varies from one theatre, director, performance to another) than embodied in the theatrical moment of the transformation.[40]

Sculpture, another form of visual art, seems to keep its identity more clearly than painting. At least it behaves in a rather different way in Thomas Kilroy's *The Shape of Metal.* Here the autonomy of art—sculpture and language—is more emphasized: sculptures appear on the stage very much in their materiality. The boundaries between art and life, on the other hand, become destabilized from the beginning.

The eighty-two-year-old protagonist Nell Jeffrey's story and ruminations raise as many questions about art and the artist as they do about life and human relationships. Failure is very much in the centre of her meditations. Presenting a few of her works on the stage, and letting the audience hear about her critical success (a whole room is devoted to her works in the Irish Museum of Modern Art), Kilroy complicates and deepens her concerns about artistic failure, incompleteness, the drive to, and the impossibility of, achieving perfection.

Her failure may be, at least in part, associated with her ability to create and destroy magnificently. An artist and a powerful mother—a creator in a double sense—she tends to intrude into others' lives in a goddess-like manner; to shape lives as she shapes metal. The parallel is drawn early on when Grace, Nell's long-dead daughter enters first as a "mounted head", shaped by her mother. A bronze head that speaks—evoking the old Irish myth of the speaking head and at the same time asserting the vitality of art. Grace's monologue verbally reinforces the ambiguity between life and art when she talks about her mother transforming "stone or metal [...] into Grace finally at peace. [...] Grace inside the silence. Safe."[41] Which is turned into the other? Metal into Grace or Grace into metal? At its second appearance, the bronze head tells more unequivocally her tragic story, with the frightening aspect of being silenced, becoming an artwork instead of a living being. As it transpires, Nell's motherly love and over-protectiveness, complemented by the artist's impulse to act and intrude omnipotently, emotionally crushed and chased away the daughter.

While the bronze head closely relates to Nell's private life and feelings, the other prominent sculpture onstage, her masterpiece, *Woman Rising from Water*, visually mediates her artistic dilemmas. Those that she articulates verbally are the overriding Beckettian notion of failure as the condition of art, counterbalancing the Yeatsean desire for perfection. Incompletion and unfinishedness—which Nell deems more human—becomes juxtaposed to completion, the finished quality of work. *Woman Rising from Water*, expresses a process rather than a fixed state, and becomes a metaphor for life, personality and art, all being in the making, never reaching perfection, alive with birth, change, and movement incorporating time in a modernist way. Emerging from "rubble"—according to the stage directions[42]—it is a portrait of the modernist artist, trying to bring order and harmony into the chaos of the world. The image reinforces the parallel between biological and artistic creation and their mutual reflection of each other. But in contrast with one of her inspirations,

Brancusi's *Sleeping Muse* with its male idealization of the female muse, Nell's woman, arising out of the feminine element: water, is an image of the new woman who wants to tell her own story and so has an unidealized, "far less benign, more witchlike" face.

The title of the play contains metal, but the masterpiece is carved out of white marble. The bronze head and the marble statue embody two different attitudes to art and to life. Kilroy said in an interview that, "I believe form is discovered within the material",[43] and similarly his protagonist has brought out the shape hidden in the beautiful white marble whereas she has imposed her will onto the cast of metal. Her desperate action of smashing the marble into pieces towards the play's end becomes a violent act against both art and life (since this sculpture was intimately related to Grace), again blurring (or rather, smashing) borders between art and life, raising questions of whether an artist has the right to destroy his/her work any more than a mother her child.

The Shape of Metal's focal issues of giving "shape" to matter, giving form to life and life to art, self-reflexively comment on the playwright's art and of any art's form, including theatre's nature and possibilities. The paradox of artwork being finished, polished and yet remaining forever unfinished, changing, transpires also through the coexistence of the tangible object onstage and the uniqueness and changeability of each theatrical performance, where statues are crushed, yet each time reintegrated. The art of failure, in the last analysis, does not become the failure of art. The artist can still show images of wholeness in the theatre, even in their incompleteness.

Writers, Poets, Playwrights

The "interart aspect of the artist-hero is of course evident when he (or she) is not a writer but a musician (or […] a painter or a person of any other artistic profession)", maintains Lagerroth.[44] But writers, poets, playwrights *per se* as artist-protagonists, obviously also raise self-reflexive dilemmas and may enter into interart relation with the theatre-art that they become a part of, as, for example those in Friel's *Give Me Your Answer, Do!*, McGuinness' *Mutabilitie* and *The Hanging Gardens* (2013), Kilroy's *Tea and Sex and Shakespeare* (1968) and *Blake*.

To present writing or the written work, however, must be most difficult, so it mostly remains outside the stage space, and appears through references to and consequences of the writer figure's work—again primarily in words. William Blake offers an especially valuable model: being both poet *and* visual artist. His passionate visionary, prophetic truth-seeking shapes his stage rendering. His incarceration in a madhouse sharpens questions of how madness and artistic passion are related. Similarly to the questions raised in McGuinness' *The Bird Sanctuary* about the relation between art and witchcraft, here, too, it remains undecided, whether Blake's magic-mystic visions and prophetic art were madness or if madness provides deeper understanding of what lies beyond the visible. Kilroy draws a delicate line between the prophetic and the lunatic, the messianic and the childishly naïve, the self-righteous moral judge and the humble repentant. He both reinforces and denies equations (for instance, the lunatics are not necessarily artists), but the artist going down to hell does bring back deeper understanding, which enables him to exercise mercy and forgiveness.

Blake's uneducated, yet deeply sensitive wife, Catherine, the reality-principle in his life and in the play, complements his figure beautifully. She herself is common sense impersonate, yet is "mad" enough to follow and accompany him everywhere and share his visions without rationally understanding them. Directly opposed to her is Dr. Hibbel, the madhouse doctor who is entirely deaf and blind to Blake's visionary talent and whose aim is to bring him back to "reason" at all costs. This underlines the classical divisions between rationality and artistic sensitivity, reason and madness, order and chaos, the ordinary and the supernatural. In what Thierry Dubost calls Kilroy's "symphonic theatre",[45] the poet's lines are referenced or quoted throughout and scenic images echo his paintings. The closing scene of *Gesamtkunstwerk* brings together vividly the Blakean contrasts into a theatrical vision: Blake's plates of illumination projected on a white sheet as if coming out of the printing press, appear "drift[ing] upwards [...] into the atmosphere",[46] while the lunatics' chorus—now rid of their white asylum shifts, emerging in "gold coloured robes"—sing lines of *Jerusalem*, with the leading of an individual male voice. Images and words (with music) illuminate each other, just as Blake's etchings illuminated his visionary words. All this envelopes the artist couple, abandoned in their work in a small workshop suspended above the stage. Yet the ambiguities do not disappear, "the transformation of the asylum into a New Jerusalem is not temporally defined, and the ultimate metamorphosis remains open to interpretation, thanks in particular to the ephemeral visual presentation of Blake's plates".[47]

Conclusion

These few examples of *künstlerdrama* feature artists who, despite their very different orientations, qualities, interests and presentations, seem to share deep concerns that their creators as artists share. They all preserve some of the ancient Irish artist-file-seer-poet's self-destructive, self-sacrificing, most unselfish and most selfish, obsession with their art and their necessary devotions, the combination of creation and destruction, the desire to heal and the dark abyss of failure. All those dilemmas, profound contradictions, uncertainties, their hell-bound journeys and resurfacing with some revelation or just deepened sensitivity to suffering become more pointedly theatrical through the presence or emergence of artworks as parts of the performances. In all these examples the audience also, directly or indirectly, becomes involved in constructing meaning, and is offered a significant role to play in the moral or aesthetic judgement and so in completing the theatrical process. The interaction of verbal utterances—the playtext—with the extra-textual elements of scenography and the artworks of music, painting, sculpture, either in their own materiality or evoked through other forms of art and in the imagination through words, infinitely enriches and broadens meanings and reflects back on theatre itself through a million prisms.

Interart relations are often defined as meaning created in the interstitial places, in-between the different forms of art. But I believe it would be more true to say that meaning is formed in the conjoint effect of all the arts involved. That is what theatre is capable of doing by uniting the heterogeneous components into a new complexity.

Notes

1. Ulla-Britta Lagerroth, "Reading Musicalized Texts as Self-Reflexive Texts. Some Aspects of Interart Discourse," in *Word and Music Studies. Defining the Field*. ed. Walter Bernhart et al. (Amsterdam: Rodopi, 1999), 206.
2. Lagerroth, "Reading," 211–12.
3. Richard Kearney, "Introduction: An Irish Intellectual Tradition," in *The Irish Mind*, ed. Richard Kearney (Dublin: Wolfhound, 1985), 9.
4. As he proclaimed in "The Song of the Happy Shepherd," in W.B. Yeats, *Collected Poems* (London: Macmillan, 1971), 7–8.
5. Erika-Fischer Lichte, "Introduction: From Comparative Arts to Interart Studies," *Paragrana* 25:2 (2016): 12–13.
6. Irina O. Rajewsky, "Intermediality, Intertextuality, and Remediation: A Literary Perspective on Intermediality," *Intermedialities* 6 (Automne, 2005): 51–52.
7. Which, of course, does not deny the existence and relevance of dominantly visual theatre, for instance the spectacular performance of the dance-play, *Loch na hEala*, dir. by Michael Keegan-Dolan at the 2016 Dublin Theatre Festival.
8. Brian Friel, *Faith Healer*, in *Selected Plays* (London: Faber, 1984), 371.
9. Anthony Roche, *Brian Friel. Theatre and Politics* (Houndmills, Basingstoke: Palgrave Macmillan, 2011), 158.
10. Richard Rankin Russell, *Modernity, Community, and Place in Brian Friel's Drama* (Syracuse, NY: Syracuse University Press, 2014), 135–38.
11. For a more extended discussion of the play-within-the-play see my essay "Theatricality and Self-Reflexivity: The Play-within-the-Play," in *Irish Theatre in Transition*, ed. Donald E. Morse (Basingstoke: Palgrave Macmillan, 2015), 99–121.
12. Christopher Murray, "Triumph of the Literary Play? Jim Nolan's *Blackwater Angel*," *Irish Literary Supplement*, March 22, 2002, 16.
13. Clare Wallace, "'… ultimately alone and walking around in your own private universe.' Metatheatre and Metaphysics in Three Plays by Enda Walsh," *Hungarian Journal of English and American Studies* 23:1 (2017): 36.
14. Enda Walsh, *Ballyturk* (London: Nick Hern Books, 2014), 36.
15. Christopher Murray, "The Plays of Enda Walsh: An Interim Report," *Hungarian Journal of English and American Studies* 23:1 (2017): 26, 31.
16. Lagerroth, "Reading," 209.
17. Since several excellent analyses have been written about the relationsip between words and music in *The Gigli Concert*, its opera-like quality, the function and

transformative power of music (among others, by Alexandra Pulain, Fintan O'Toole, Declan Kiberd, Nicholas Grene), here I do not discuss this play.

18. Mark O'Rowe, *Terminus* (London: Nick Hern Books, 2007), 48.
19. Brian Friel, "Seven Notes for a Festival Programme," in *Brian Friel: Essays, Diaries, Interviews, 1964–1999*, ed. Christopher Murray (London: Faber, 1999), 177.
20. Brian Friel, *Dancing at Lughnasa* (London: Faber, 1990), 71.
21. Brian Friel, *Performances* (Loughcrew: Gallery, 2003), 31.
22. Nicholas Grene, "Friel and Transparency," *Irish University Review* 29:1 (Spring/Summer 1999): 142.
23. Michael Coveney, "The Cordelia Dream in Wilton's Music Hall, London." *Independent*, Januay 1, 2009. Accessed April 15, 2017. http://www.independent.co.uk/arts-entertainment/theatre-dance/reviews/the-cordelia-dream-wiltions-music-hall-london-1219767.html
24. See my more detailed discussion of *The Home Place* in "Memory, Art, *Lieux de Mémoire* in Brian Friel's *The Home Place*," in Christopher Murray, *The Theatre of Brian Friel: Tradition and Modernity* (London: Bloomsbury Methuen, 2015). 230–45.
25. In his famous *Paragone*, Leonardo da Vinci claims that in painting the proportions of objects that appeal to the harmony of the soul, can be perceived all at once while poetry makes them manifest stretched out in time. He asked the Hungarian King Matthias to decide which is superior: a poem celebrating his birthday or the portrait of his beloved, and felt triumphant to hear the obvious choice the king made. Leonardo da Vinci, *Tudomány és művészet* (Budapest: Magyar Helikon, 1960), 86.
26. W.J.T. Mitchell; *Picture Theory* (Chicago: University of Chicago Press, 1994), 152.
27. Frank McGuinness, *Innocence* (London: Faber, 1987), 17.
28. Eamonn Jordan, "The Masquerade of the Damned and the Deprivileging of Innocence: Frank McGuinness's *Innocence*," in *The Theatre of Frank McGuinness. Stages of Mutability*, ed. Helen Heusner Lojek (Dublin: Carysfort, 2002), 58.
29. Hiroko Mikami, *Frank McGuinness and his Theatre of Paradox* (Gerrards Cross, UK: Colin Smythe, 2002), 60.
30. Mitchell, *Picture*, 154.
31. McGuinness, *Innocence*, 3.
32. Ibid., 55.
33. Christopher Murray, "Joyce, Yeats and *The Bird Sanctuary*," *Irish University Review* 40:1 (Spring/Summer, 2010), 77, 75.
34. See more about McGuinness and witchcraft in my "Borderlines Destabilized—Witches and Witchcraft in Frank McGuinness's Plays," *Hungarian Journal of English and American Studies* 20:2 (Fall 2014): 33–49.
35. McGuinness, *The Bird Sanctuary*, in *Plays 2*. (London: Faber, 2002), 342.
36. Gay McAuley, *Space in Performance: Making Meaning in the Theatre* (Ann Arbor, MI: University of Michigan, 1999), 23.
37. Rajewsky, "Intermediality," 43–4.
38. Lojek, *Contexts*, 243.
39. McGuinness, *The Bird*, 342.
40. It is a different matter, and its solution is left to the directors, how to present this ambiguity. If a vision becomes visible in some material form, is it still a vision? Or through its very existence onstage, becomes an artifact?

41. Thomas Kilroy, *The Shape of Metal* (Loughcrew: Gallery, 2003), 11.
42. Kilroy, *Shape*, 27.
43. Mária Kurdi, "'The Whole Idea of Writing Historical Fiction is Paradoxical.' Talk with Irish Playwright Thomas Kilroy." *Hungarian Journal of English and American Studies* 8:1 (Spring 2002): 261.
44. Lagerroth, "Reading," 212.
45. Thierry Dubost, *The Plays of Thomas Kilroy* (Jefferson, NC: McFarland, 2007), 81.
46. Thomas Kilroy, *Blake* (Loughcrew: Gallery, 2015), 64.
47. Dubost, *The Plays*, 96.

Bibliography

Bertha, Csilla. "Borderlines Destabilized--Witches and Witchcraft in Frank McGuinness's Plays." *Hungarian Journal of English and American Studies* 20:2 (Fall 2014): 33–49.

———. "Memory, Art, *Lieux de Mémoire* in Brian Friel's *The Home Place*." In Christopher Murray. *The Theatre of Brian Friel: Tradition and Modernity*, 230–45. London: Bloomsbury Methuen, 2015.

———. "Theatricality and Self-Reflexivity: The Play-Within-the-Play in Select Contemporary Irish Plays." In *Irish Theatre in Transition*, edited by Donald E. Morse, 99–121. Houndsmills, Basingstoke: Palgrave Macmillan, 2015.

Coveney, Michael. "The Cordelia Dream in Wilton's Music Hall, London." *Independent*, 1 Jan (2009). Accessed April 15, 2017. http://www.independent.co.uk/arts-entertainment/theatre-dance/reviews/the-cordelia-dream-wiltions-music-hall-london-1219767.html

Dubost, Thierry. *The Plays of Thomas Kilroy*. Jefferson, North Carolina: McFarland, 2007.

Fischer-Lichte, Erika. "Introduction: From Comparative Arts to Interart Studies." *Paragrana* 25:2 (2016): 12–26.

Friel, Brian. Faith Healer. In *Selected Plays*. London: Faber, 1984. 327–76.

———. *Dancing at Lughnasa*. London: Faber, 1990.

———. *Wonderful Tennessee*. London: Faber, 1993.

———. "Seven Notes for a Festival Programme." In *Brian Friel: Essays, Diaries, Interviews, 1964–1999*, edited by Christopher Murray, 173–80. London: Faber, 1999.

———. *Performances*. Loughcrew: Gallery, 2003.

Grene, Nicholas. "Friel and Transparency." *Irish University Review* 29:1 (Spring/Summer 1999): 136–44.

Jordan, Eamonn. "The Masquerade of the Damned and the Deprivileging of Innocence: Frank McGuinness's *Innocence*." In *The Theatre of Frank McGuinness. Stages of Mutability*, edited by Helen Heusner Lojek, 50–78. Dublin: Carysfort, 2002.

Kearney, Richard. "Introduction: An Irish Intellectual Tradition." In *The Irish Mind*, edited by Richard Kearney, 7–14. Dublin: Wolfhound, 1985.

Kilroy, Thomas. *Blake*. Loughcrew: Gallery, 2015.

———. *The Shape of Metal*. Loughcrew: Gallery, 2003.

Kurdi, Mária. "'The Whole Idea of Writing Historical Fiction Is Paradoxical.' Talk with Irish Playwright Thomas Kilroy." *Hungarian Journal of English and American Studies* 8:1 (Spring 2002): 259–67.

Lagerroth, Ulla-Britta. "Reading Musicalized Texts as Self-Reflexive Texts. Some Aspects of Interart Discourse." In *Word and Music Studies. Defining the Field*, edited by Walter Bernhart, Steven Paul Scher, and Werner Wolf, 205–20. Amsterdam: Rodopi, 1999.

Lojek, Helen Heusner. *Contexts for McGuinness' Drama*. Washington, D.C.: The Catholic University of America Press, 2004.

McAuley, Gay. *Space in Performance: Making Meaning in the Theatre*. Ann Arbor, MI: University of Michigan, 1999.

McGuinness, Frank. *Innocence*. London: Faber, 1987.

———. The Bird Sanctuary. In *Plays 2*. London: Faber, 2002. 265–342.

Mikami, Hiroko. *Frank McGuinness and His Theatre of Paradox*. Gerrards Cross, Bucks.: Colin Smythe, 2002.

Mitchell, W.J.T. *Picture Theory*. Chicago: University of Chicago Press, 1994.

Murray, Christopher. "Triumph of the Literary Play? Jim Nolan's *Blackwater Angel*." *Irish Literary Supplement*, March 22 (2002): 16.

———. "Joyce, Yeats and *The Bird Sanctuary*." *Irish University Review* 40:1 (Spring/ Summer, 2010), 69–80.

———. "The Plays of Enda Walsh: An Interim Report." *Hungarian Journal of English and American Studies* 23:1 (Spring 2017): 13–33.

Nolan, Jim. *Blackwater Angel*. Loughcrew: Gallery, 2001.

O'Rowe, Mark. *Terminus*. London: Nick Hern Books, 2007.

Rajewsky, Irina O. "Intermediality, Intertextuality, and Remediation: A Literary Perspective on Intermediality." *Intermedialities* 6 (Automne, 2005): 43–64.

Roche, Anthony. *Brian Friel. Theatre and Politics*. Houndmills, Basingstoke: Palgrave Macmillan, 2011.

Russell, Richard Rankin. *Modernity, Community, and Place in Brian Friel's Drama*. Syracuse, NY: Syracuse University Press, 2014.

Wallace, Claire. "'… Ultimately Alone and Walking Around in Your Own Private Universe.' Metatheatre and Metaphysics in Three Plays by Enda Walsh." *Hungarian Journal of English and American Studies* 23:1 (2017): 35–50.

Walsh, Enda. *Ballyturk*. London, Nick Hern Books, 2014.

Yeats, William Butler. *Collected Poems*. London: Macmillan, 1971.

da Vinci, Leonardo. *Tudomány és művészet* [Science and Art], edited and translated by Tibor Kardos. Budapest: Magyar Helikon, 1960. [Selection of essays on art in Hungarian]

"Contempt of Flesh": Adventures in the Uncanny Valley—Stacey Gregg's *Override*

Ashley Taggart

Stacy Gregg makes it very clear in the "author's notes" to *Override* (2013) that, despite her exploration of trans- and even posthuman themes, despite her second-act title of *Techgnosis*, despite the epigraph from *Bladerunner*, we are not here entering the realm of science fiction. Far from it, in fact, "the style might feel retro or bricolage, as though we could be in the 1960s or 1990s, or an unplaceable contemporary space". Stylistically, the piece foregrounds its own anti-naturalistic credentials: a two-act, two-hander set in an "unplaceable space" in a pointedly indeterminate time. In it, Mark and Violet have run away from technological society to raise their future child closer to nature. No augmentations, no bionic limbs, no embryo selection. They want everything, from their flesh to their love, to be real—but this comes at a cost.

Throughout the play, it is evident that Gregg's focus is very much the present, the play's moral leverage exerted on the way we live now, the blurry compromises and muddied thinking around our current attitude to technological "enhancement", "augmentation" and even replication. As she pointed out in an interview,

> There are cyborgs among us now—it just depends on what language you use. There'll be people in the audience with cochlear implants, hip replacements and pacemakers.[1]

So, for every reference in the play to nascent scientific developments, such as android sex "companions", nanotech upgrades, and prosthetic skin, she includes counterbalancing pointers to the mundane technologies of our current, and past, lives.[2]

A. Taggart (✉)
University College Dublin, Dublin, Ireland

E. Jordan, E. Weitz (eds.), *The Palgrave Handbook of Contemporary Irish Theatre and Performance*,
https://doi.org/10.1057/978-1-137-58588-2_46

After Vi reveals to her partner, Mark (a radical campaigner against biotech, especially "companions") that she herself has undergone bio-upgrades, she attacks him, exposing his high-minded disgust, his protective absolutism, by pretending to be one of these tech-sex creations herself.

> …I'm a companion: I am a lump of tech. I'm a flipping glorified toaster…
> An enhanced human is still *human*. NOTHING LIKE a machine.[3]

Later, she uses the same (very) domestic appliance to confront him "in the flesh". Significantly, it is this conflict which leads to the first suggestion that he might perform a lethal "override" to inactivate all her enhancements—in the process jeopardizing her life and their happiness.

> MARK: Vi
> *She goes to the kitchen.*
> Violet?
> *He watches.*
> *She picks up a toaster. It has features that kind of make it look like it has a face.*
> *She returns with it.*
> *She brings it, up close to his face.*
> *He eyes her, uncertain.*
> VI: Kiss it.
> MARK: Kiss it.
> Kiss the toaster.
> Tongue it.
> Finger its little wires.
> Look at its little face.
> MARK: Stop being.
> VI: How do you know it doesn't love you?[4]

In the moments leading up to Mark's climactic decision, when it becomes obvious he cannot overcome his revulsion at her augmentations, she reverts to goading him with the same humble, lo-tech appliance, but this time drives the analogy further, challenging his psychological boundaries, as hers have been challenged physically.

> *He cups her face.*
> *But he can't kiss her.*
> *She looks sad.*
> VI: You could be kissing a toaster. Would it matter? If it told you it loved you?
> *They stare at one another.*
> Who are you to say it doesn't?[5]

She assumes the role of "glorified toaster" to point up Mark's desperate need for rigid boundaries, driven by his own profound ambivalence (he has just disclosed a recurring dream of being screwed by a robot, and will later find out he was, in fact, "selected" as an embryo before birth). But this sardonic invocation of his own fears is more than Mark can tolerate,

He waits until she has gone.
He stamps on her plants.
He twists his engagement ring.
He gestures impulsively.
MARK: *(A command.)* Override.[6]

It is one of many ironies in the play that it is Vi (Violet) who comes across as closer to the living world. She is, indeed, "a force of nature"[7] and is first seen coming in from the garden, planting a window-box and a hanging basket. Gregg describes her in typically playful fashion. "*She is slapdash. Sensual. She opens things in shops to smell them, even when they aren't testers. She guestimates ingredients when cooking*. He, on the contrary, "*doesn't slouch. He likes his cutlery clean and his underwear folded.*"[8]

Later, after the secret of her own extensive "implants" has been revealed, she is seen destroying these very flower boxes, questioning the veracity of the world they have retreated to, and, by implication, the fundamental basis of their entire relationship.

> None of this is "real", is it? Rubbish synthetic crap. I hate this place it's a coffin!... *Little cottage little cottage*. CRAP. Smell these? Nice? Organic? O LOVELY – "they're as good as real" you said. Astroturf and Easigrass.
> *She rips up a plant and holds it to him.*
> That's a begonia!
> *She shakes it wrathfully in his face.*
> Looks like a nasturtium.
> It's a BEGONIA.
> Mixed up the bloody -
> What's the point of being here if they can't even get the artificial flowers right![9]

So—the rural idyll they have created, supposedly in defiance of invasive technology, and as a statement of radical resistance—turns out to be a product of that same process. Their Eden is blighted from the inside, itself a result of genetic and nanotech innovations. The garden is no more "unsullied" and "pure" than Vi herself (or indeed Mark). As she repeatedly points out, "We're just a splat of neurons, Mark, we're not special... We're juice and carbon."[10] But this is the point. There are no Platonic absolutes in nature: chasing perfection we lose ourselves. This is one the play's key dynamics.

Besides, the annexation of the natural by the manufactured is already so far advanced that it is almost impossible to lay down clear lines of demarcation. Humankind has used selective breeding of animals and plants for many thousands of years—is this "unnatural"? What about deliberate hybridization? And GM crops?

In us (and in Vi) similar conceptual gradients need to be acknowledged. Is autotransplantation (from one body part to another) somehow natural but xenotransplantation (from a donor) not? And this before we even confront the complexities of augmentation, A.I., and the elective "upgrading" of organs, limbs, and indeed the brain. Faced with all this—Mark's plaintive response,

"We're supposed to be evolving as a species",[11] is both feeble, and an abnegation of responsibility—handing it back to natural selection.

We cannot ring-fence ourselves from the incursions of technology. At one point, Vi lays out the incremental changes in her mother.

> VI: You know Mum was on a stick, when I was little?
> MARK: *(Controlled.)* mmhm?
> VI: Yeah. Then it went away. *(Does a magic gesture.)*
> Pacemaker too. Then the works. Just a plastic pump for a heart, Mark.
> Yep.
> Had her eyes lasered.
> Cochlear implant.
> Dentures.
> Prosthesis, the last few years God bless her, a beautiful bionic leg.
> Lovely new hips.
> A white. Shiny. Plastic. Pump for a heart.
> Yep.
> Truckloads of drugs. Statins. Warfarin you name it, she munched it.
> Therapeutic to a point, but think she got carried away. Got the bug.
> ... Always after the latest gizmo—and you wonder why I never said "pop around Mark, meet my Ma." She made a killer raspberry sponge.[12]

The staccato build of the sentences, their considered roughness, leading to a final bathetic puncturing, is typical of her writing here and elsewhere. Gregg enjoys working with fractured ideas, overlayered dialogue, the unfinished thoughts, aborted gestures and punctuating grunts of "normal non-fluency". By her own admission she struggles with "logic and lucidity" in her writing. But then,

> That's what consciousness feels like. Life is not formulaic: where's my fifth act? I have no other mode to set about writing characters than one that is naturally fragmented and self-contradictory. That is how I am in the world, and I'm not interested in—and truthfully I'm not capable of—writing in another way.[13]

Within the play, it is precisely Mark's anxious need for "logic and coherence", his inability to accept the stark contingency that we may be nothing more than a "splat of neurons", and that, on the tech side, "an enhanced human is still human", which leads to the loss of their joint future, their unborn child, and all the human aspects of Vi.

When she first declares her enhanced status, as audience, we witness his mind lurching from thought to thought in an attempt to reconcile himself to this information. At pivotal moments like these, Gregg's "broken" dialogue is most effective. His initial reaction is visceral disgust, then he spirals down into the implications for their child—his sense of alienation extending to the unborn.

MARK: "a" baby
VI: *(Shocked)* our baby
MARK: "a" baby
VI: Don't. Mark
MARK: "a" baby that might be
VI: it's not
MARK: Hybrid.
Fucking.
Anything.
Hybrid.
Born to something with *that* in it.
Tech bits. Machine. Dead stuff.
Creepy.[14]

At this point, Mark has fallen into the "Uncanny valley". This term, coined by the robotics engineer Masahiro Mori in 1970, describes our strange revulsion towards things that appear nearly human, but are *not quite right*. This revulsion usually involves robots, but can also include computer animations and medical conditions (the "valley" being the "region of negative emotional response"). One theory is that this reaction stems from an evolutionary tendency to be repulsed by anyone who looks sick or unhealthy or *wrong*. In other words, "pathogen avoidance". But another theory is perhaps more telling, with researchers speculating that the uncanny valley, particularly in regards to humanoid robots, triggers an innate fear of death, as they often seem to move like lifeless puppets, reminding us of our own mortality.

The overarching irony is that Mark's fear of death is what brings it upon them. His repeated question, "Would you want to live for ever? If you could?"[15] seeming less and less relevant, when (in the aftermath of his "override" command) his child dies and his partner (literally) falls apart before his eyes. Desperate for purity, he corrupts those around him. He casts around for secure definitions, trying to ascertain whether the extent of her implants has compromised her.

VI: ...We'd know. We'd just know if I was like that.
MARK: *(Shouting.)* You WOULDN'T. How do we find out without—we need to get you scanned so I know what you are. I'm not with a.[16]

In doing so, it entirely escapes him that, in his revulsion at technology, he turns to further technology for reassurance.

In his fear and confusion, he is no longer open to such contradictions—instead turning his fury on Vi, accusing her of a serious crime, "You'll be done for Contempt of Flesh."[17] We are reminded that, in the world of the play, all biotech has been banned, the rule being "No hard tech in a soft body", and that Vi is now in breach of that. Her response is consistent, and consistently nuanced: "Getting your teeth straightened, glasses, vaccines—we've always been enhanced."[18] Yet he is implacable: "Enough work done, and you're halfway to being a sex bot."[19]

By the end of the play, due to his unilateral decision to override her implants, she has degenerated, or "degraded", to the point where she not only loses her replacement arm, but is reduced to a grotesque assemblage of parts (a glorified toaster). Ultimately, Vi

> *is just a cube-like hub with a voice transmitter. Her bionic, non-degrading components, wires and internal hardware are still connected, laid out how they would have been if still her body. Her housecoat is laid out too.*[20]

In a bizarre coda, Mark, faced with the enormity of what he has done, still cannot accept her loss. His need to "build these perfect worlds in [his] head"[21] has now blasted and ruined their shared vision, leaving behind only a "cube-like hub"—which, in an act of darkly comic desperation, he tries to have sex with. When this is unsuccessful, he resorts to the very act he has decried all along, and has an "augmented reality lens" fitted to his brain, so that he can "see" Vi once again. There is something eerily appropriate in the new "virtualised" Violet's observation that "I'm in your head?", while his final response strongly suggests that's where she's been all along: "Everything's perfect now, isn't it?"[22]

Notes

1. matttrueman.co.uk, published 6 October 2013, accessed 15 June 2017.
2. Again--Gregg is not straying far from contemporary reality. The first commercially-available sex-bot is being marketed later this year (2017) by a firm in California, at over $11,000. Her name is "Harmony."
3. Stacey Gregg, *Override* (London: Nick Hern Books, 2013), 29.
4. Ibid., 36.
5. Ibid., 40.
6. Ibid.
7. Ibid., 16.
8. Ibid., 9.
9. Ibid., 23.
10. Ibid., 27.
11. Ibid., 33.
12. Ibid., 30.
13. Peter Crawley, "Stacey Gregg on Gender, Identity and the Theatre's 'Gutting Lack of Women'," *The Irish Times*, 12 November 2015, http://www.irishtimes.com/culture/stage/stacey-gregg-on-gender-identity-and-the-theatre-s-gutting-lack-of-women-1.2424367.
14. Gregg, *Override*, 26.
15. Ibid., 44.
16. Ibid., 26.
17. Ibid.
18. Ibid.
19. Ibid.
20. Ibid., 60.
21. Ibid., 35.
22. Ibid., 66.

Bibliography

Gregg, Stacey. *Override*. London: Nick Hern Books, 2013.

Crawley, Peter. "Stacey Gregg on Gender, Identity and the Theatre's 'Gutting Lack of Women'." *The Irish Times*, November 12, 2015. http://www.irishtimes.com/culture/stage/stacey-gregg-on-gender-identity-and-the-theatre-s-gutting-lack-of-women-1.2424367.

matttrueman.co.uk. Interview with Stacey Gregg. Published October 6, 2013. Accessed June 15, 2017.

Mori, Masahito. "The Uncanny Valley." Translated by Karl F. MacDorman and Takashi Minato *Energy* 7, no. 4 (1970): 33–35.

http://www.comp.dit.ie/dgordon/Courses/CaseStudies/CaseStudy3d.pdf

PART IV

Reflections

The Dance of Affect in Contemporary Irish Dance Theatre

Aoife McGrath

This chapter discusses developments in contemporary dance theatre in Ireland. In particular, I will look at how dance theatre choreographers are engaging with a "terrible inheritance" of corporeal oppression in Ireland, through an investigation of my experience of the choreography of affective encounters in their work.[1] Dance scholar André Lepecki speaks of how certain contemporary European choreographies work to "unveil" bodies "as critical mass, as a terrible inheritance", in which the choreographers and dancers are "fully aware of the fact that they are inhabited by regimentation and control".[2] In each of the works discussed, the choreographers highlight the control and policing of corporealities in Ireland, making visible the resultant oppression of those deviant to desired norms. Yet, within the confinements of this regimentation, the interactions and affective encounters of dancers with each other, and with the objects and spaces containing their movements, cause transformations in the affective environment to materialise for the spectator.

Almost a century after the founding of the Irish state, the oppressive church and state structures that have provided the foundations for Ireland's social fabric, and the accompanying societal blindness to their failures, are in urgent need of questioning, dismantling and refiguring. Need for an acknowledgment of these failures has become acute following a series of pivotal changes in Irish society over the past decade: the spectacular crash of the Irish economy with the onset of the global recession in 2008; the resulting collapse of the leading political party in 2010; and the disintegration of the (already weakening) moral authority of the Catholic Church in the wake of

A. McGrath (✉)
Queen's University Belfast, Belfast, Northern Ireland
e-mail: aoife.mcgrath@qub.ac.uk

E. Jordan, E. Weitz (eds.), *The Palgrave Handbook of Contemporary Irish Theatre and Performance*,
https://doi.org/10.1057/978-1-137-58588-2_47

the publication of reports enquiring into the many decades of abuse of some of the most vulnerable in society—babies, children and women—in state- and church-run institutions.[3] I am interested in interrogating how, in the wake of this period of economic and social collapse and its attendant danger of a petrification of movement for change, the choreography of affective encounters in dance performance can highlight both the experience of oppression for certain marginalised corporealities, but also a space for imagining possible future, collaborative and emancipatory moves.

Dance and Affect

In his *Ethics*, Benedict de Spinoza is interested in understanding what an individual can do to increase their agency and freedom to act in the world. He argues that the work of affects—how we are affected by "passions" (feelings and desires) that are experienced in the encounter with other bodies—is related to the power of agency for action: "by [affectus] I understand affections of the body by which the body's power of activity is increased or diminished, assisted or checked".[4] For this chapter, my reading of affective encounters in dance performance originates from my position as spectator. This necessarily brings a heightened focus to the aesthetic-political dimension of affect. Paying attention to affect is, as Brian Massumi argues, inherently political, as it involves "understanding the world as an ongoing process in continual transformation [...] [which] takes change as primary, and sees the regularities of life as temporary barrier islands of stability in stormy seas".[5] However, the processual nature of affect seems to make its socio-political impact difficult to "pin down" when considering its effects on events, and capacity for political movement in the sense of social change.[6] Although for many thinkers the virtual aspects of affect's processual nature is of primary interest,[7] there is an acknowledgement that the "passage of intensities" caused by affective encounters can result in bodily accumulations. Megan Watkins, for example, highlights the difference between Spinoza's terms "affectus" (the capacity for a body to affect and be affected) and affectio (the impact the affecting body leaves on the affected) in the context of pedagogical encounters, and argues for the material impact of affect, suggesting that affective encounters leave a "residue" which accumulates over time to create change.[8,9] Similarly, Massumi suggests that "the experience of a change, an affecting-being affected, is redoubled by an experience of the experience. This gives the body's movements a kind of depth that stays with it across all its transitions—accumulating in memory, in habit, in reflex, in desire, in tendency."[10] I propose that in dance performance we can experience a choreography of these affective accumulations. Through the residues and imprints created through affective encounters in dance performance, we can experience the ability of affect to transform relationships, both between individual dancing bodies, and between individual bodies and their relationship with social constructs of the body politic. The spectator of these danced encounters also has an affective experience of their movements, and so the transformations engendered by their danced repetitions signals the capacity for future social and political change, as the imprint on the spectator is carried beyond the performance.

Dance and Politics in Ireland

The intertwining of dance and politics in Ireland can be traced back to the founding of the state. The imagining and moulding of a post-colonial "Irish" corporeality and an "Irish" way of moving during the Gaelic Revival period in the late nineteenth and early twentieth centuries, placed dance politically, as Helen Brennan notes, in an "arena for combat".[11] In creating a decolonized national identity, it was important that an "Irish" body combatted the coloniser's projections of a "degrading" femininity.[12] The close interconnections of church and state in Ireland resulted in the imposition of strict moral codes and limitations on the expression of sexualities, fostering a culture of shame and taboo in relation to corporeal matters. In addition, any foreign influences in the expression of national identity through dance were shunned.[13] In the attempts of cultural organizations to liberate Ireland from its colonization, the corporeal was recolonized in a restrictive and oppressive fashion by the nationalist campaign. Corporealities that did not fit the nationalist and church visions of social acceptablility suffered oppression and containment, with those judged to be deviant from state and church ideals often being incarcerated, abused and tortured; examples include the women imprisoned in the Magdalene Laundries, the babies and children abused in mother and child homes and Industrial Schools, and the discriminatory treatment of anyone of a different sexual orientation to the heterosexual norm.

In this sociocultural and political context of corporeal oppression, dance in Ireland can be seen to have operated at the extreme ends of a corporeal continuum. On the one hand, it functioned as an important, and strictly regulated, performance of national identity in the example of traditional Irish step dance, and on the other, it constituted a site of creative, experimental resistance to corporeal conformity in the examples of some modern and contemporary theatre dance. Instances of the latter range from Yeats's dance theatre experiments dedicated to decolonization in collaboration with choreographers Michio Ito and Ninette de Valois in the early twentieth century, through to Erina Brady's expressionist modern dance and dance theatre works for the Irish School of Dance Art in the 1930s and 40s that tackled subjects such as Ireland's tuberculosis epidemic, and on to the seminal works of Joan Davis' Dublin Contemporary Dance Theatre (DCDT) in the 1970s and 80s.[14] DCDT's works encompassed many choreographic genres, reflecting the different dance training backgrounds of both its homegrown and its international choreographers and dancers, and ranged from postmodern pieces in the mode of Judson Dance Theatre, to more narrative-based works. There were also pieces that engaged in explicit sociopolitical critique, such as

Acid Rain (1982), choreographed by Sara and Jerry Pearson with music by Meredith Monk, which saw the company, "wilting from pollution, while the self-deception of mankind refuses to recognise how terminal is the menace from above",[15] and *Anna Livia* (1981), choreographed by Davis, which danced the "squabbles and confusions" of Dublin politics to a soundtrack of "press cuttings and radio news".[16] As Emma Meehan suggests, DCDT's work also reflected the increasing influence of globalisation on Irish society, "[b]ringing together [an] increased mobility and [the] shifting nature of identities within an Irish landscape".[17]

The mid-1990s then saw the founding of a profusion of contemporary dance companies that, following in the footsteps of DCDT, address Irish cultural and political issues explicitly in their works. Examples include David Bolger's CoisCéim Dance Theatre, which has produced pieces on subjects such as the Great Irish Famine (*Ballads* [1997]), immigration, racism, and citizenship (*Dodgems* [2008]), and, most recently, an exploration of the 1916 rebellion from the perspective of civilians during a raid of their home (*These Rooms* [2016], in collaboration with ANU Productions). Similarly, Michael Keegan-Dolan's works for Fabulous Beast Dance Theatre engaged explicitly with some of the most difficult issues facing Irish society: the internationally acclaimed *Midlands Trilogy* includes *Giselle* (2003), his reworking of the romantic ballet inspired by the death of fifteen-year-old Ann Lovett and her newborn baby in 1984, which tackles the silencing and oppression of the feminine in Irish society;[18] *The Bull* (2005), based on the ancient Irish myth *An Táin Bó Cúailnge*, which delivered a riotous and excoriating critique of Celtic Tiger greed; and *James Son of James* (2008), which explored the dangers of "hero worship", political corruption and societal fear of change. John Scott's work with the Centre for Care for Survivors of Torture in Dublin resulted in the piece *Fall and Recover* (2004) for his company, Irish Modern Dance Theatre, which gave an insight into the lives of refugees and asylum seekers in Ireland through the performances of eleven torture survivors from nine different countries. Dublin's Liz Roche Dance Company's cross-border collaboration with Belfast's Maiden Voyage Dance Company, *Neither Either* (2014), examined themes of conflict and the difficulties of living with opposing states of mind, through a danced exploration of Seamus Heaney's poetry. A collaboration with spoken word poet Elaine Feeney and screendance artist Mary Wycherley then formed the basis for Liz Roche's important and timely work on women's lack of bodily autonomy in Ireland, *Wrongheaded* (2016).

A new wave of choreographers and companies has emerged in the last decade that is continuing to develop dance theatre in innovative ways, while extending the interrogation of the relationship between the corporeal and the body politic in Ireland. Examples include the dance theatre of Emma Fitzgerald and Áine Stapleton (of Fitzgerald and Stapleton), which interrogates gender oppression in Ireland through an improvisatory dance practice that often utilizes nudity, and is inspired by seminal American postmodern choreographer, Deborah Hay. Dancer and choreographer Oona Doherty's work also grapples with gender stereotyping. In her recent piece, *Hope Hunt* (2016), she examines the embodiment of masculinities in "an attempt to deconstruct the stereotype of the concrete disadvantaged male, and raise it up into a Caravaggio bright white limbo".[19] The cross-border dance theatre company Ponydance specializes in irreverent, circus-infused dance comedy, and their annual *Pony Panto* has become a Christmas-time institution in Belfast. For the remainder of the chapter I will discuss specific works by dance theatre choreographers who are at the forefront of this latest wave: *The Falling Song* (2012) by Megan and Jessica Kennedy of Junk Ensemble; *Tabernacle* (2011) by Fearghus Ó Conchúir; and *Dancehall* (2016) by Emma Martin. In examining how these choreographers and dancers engage in an interrogation of the moulding of corporealities in Ireland, I will pay particular attention to the choreography of affective encounters in their work; how, through lending an embodied "visibility" to the affective experience of oppressive social constructs, and how individuals engage with them and move through them, the dance negotiates, and brings awareness to, the "terrible inheritance" of corporeal oppression in Ireland, while also signalling possibilities for future moves.

The Falling Song (2012)

In *The Falling Song*, choreographers Jessica Kennedy and Megan Kennedy of dance theatre company Junk Ensemble sought to create a piece in which "male physicality is pushed to the extremities to explore self-destruction, invincibility and failure".[20] The piece, performed by four male dancers, features the integration of performances by a children's choir and live percussion by George Higgs. One of the Kennedys's motivations for creating the work was the increased rate of suicide in the male population in Ireland during the economic recession.[21] The National Suicide Research Foundation showed a "spike" in suicides in Ireland during the height of the recession in which "almost 500 additional deaths between 2008 and 2012 were linked to the economic downturn".[22] Suicide is never explicitly referenced in *The Falling Song*. Instead we witness a multitude of encounters between the dancers, and the dancers and the children, playing with the theme of falling, and the repetition of these encounters builds an affective environment of foreboding. The danger of falling underscores even the more comic and lighthearted scenes, as, for example, when one of the dancers puts on a sparkling blue shirt and boot slippers and performs a fantasy, figure-skating routine, complete with daring jumps and risky turns to 80s synthesizer sounds, or when the four dancers take turns to manipulate large, cardboard, cut-out clouds to cover up the behind-the-scenes machinations needed to create the illusion that they are flying. The ever-present fear of falling that builds throughout the work connects with the economic and social precarity of Ireland's post-recessionary, neoliberal realities. In particular, it lends visibility to the growing awareness of the pressures exerted on men and boys by the patriarchal construction of masculinities in Ireland. Fintan Walsh, speaking of performances that highlight masculinities in crisis, foregrounds their ability to show "masculinity's contingency, its violent conditions of construction, its precarious modes of operation, and the effects of its expectations on male individuals".[23] The affective choreographies in *The Falling Song* communicated many of these aspects of masculinities in crisis, while also pointing towards the possibility of a re-scaffolding of these problematic constructs.

The Falling Song opens with four male dancers in their underpants and socks, walking around in a circle while getting dressed. The pace set for the circle dance does not slacken as they pull on their trousers and t-shirts, awkwardly bending over to put on, and tie, the laces of their shoes, all the while trying to keep up with the person in front. When they are dressed, their unrelenting rhythm is matched by an acceleration and crescendo of live, percussive music, and the quartet sweep through a series of partnering exchanges that involve flashes of recognisable moves and images that appear and then dissolve: rugby tackles and wrestling holds, breakdancing and ball throws; a man is lifted into the air, horizontal to the ground, face to the sky, and carried across the stage on the shoulders of pall-bearers; the four men divide into a brief, tug-of-war, strength-testing battle that pushes and pulls across the space; another man, wounded in battle, is swiftly carried by the group across a diagonal to safety; and a series of falls and catches of ever-increasing daring—in which dancers run and jump to be caught by each other, or simply fall towards and away from each other in an arcing pendulum motion that dangerously skirts the ground—always end in the safety of reciprocal weight exchange. Then the music and movement stops, and one man is left behind by the group as it exits the stage. The man climbs up the side of one of two, tall, ladder structures entwined with rope that dominate the set throughout the piece. The ladders curve at the top, trailing a tangled, knotted excess of rope dangling to the ground, which makes the structures look part-scaffold, part-adventure-park climbing frame. In contrast to the preceding frenetic dance of keeping-up, and falling and catching, the man's ascendance feels measured and deliberate. When he has climbed nearly to the top—maybe four or five metres from the ground—he carefully moves his position on the rung on which he is standing, so that he faces outwards to the audience. He shuffles sideways to the edge of the rung, and, without warning, lets go and falls forward into space, arms held tight by his side, body in a straight line, perfectly horizontal to the ground for impact. But this time there is no one to catch him, and a mattress painted to resemble grey, breezeblock bricks breaks his fall. The man lies prone on the mattress as two other men enter to begin a duet, and the piece continues.

Watching this body falling from a height causes a lurching sensation in the pit of my stomach that comes with a somewhat familiar mixture of feelings: both the excited fluttering that signals kinaesthetic empathy with a fleeting experience of weightlessness, and also the simultaneous fearful, clenching anticipation of an impending crash landing. This mixture of affect continues throughout the piece. In *The Falling Song*, the ladder/scaffold that looms above the action suggests the oppressive, ever-present nature of the constructs of masculinity that permeate the encounters between the men and children moving beneath it. The affective experience of a repeated fear of falling within an environment of foreboding and danger that is choreographed for the spectator, envelops the joyous displays of boisterous male camaraderie and physical derring-do. This affective environment brings awareness to the pain of non-belonging, of not being able to keep up, or measure up, and the falling dancer's jump becomes an escape from these pressures. As Gregg and Seigworth note, "[a]ffect marks a body's *belonging* to a world of encounters [...] but also, in *non-belonging*, through all those far sadder (de)compositions of mutual in-compossibilities".[24] *The Falling Song* shows the exhausting, physical repetitions required for "belonging" within a pressured affective environment of competitiveness, pressure to perform, and fear of inadequacy. This fear is made palpable through the dancer perpetually hovering precariously on the edge of a fall, leaving the spectator on the edge of their seat in anticipation of a fall. Yet the act of falling, as suggested in the description earlier, also (if however briefly) contains a moment of suspension, of in-between-ness between ascension and descent. Towards the end of the piece, all four dancers perform a series of falls from the scaffold, of ever-increasing daring and speed. A feeling of risk-taking pleasure builds to a joyous crescendo and the scaffold transforms into a platform for hopeful leaps into the unknown. The foreboding affective environment lifts in these moments of escape from a structuring order, eliciting a feeling of freedom and hope for future emancipation.

Tabernacle (2011)

In *Tabernacle*, by choreographer Fearghus Ó Conchúir, we also see a dance between bodies and oppressive structures of containment. Ó Conchúir set out to create a work "about the Catholic Church and the making of the Irish body", a work that "investigates authority, control and the individual search for purposeful living".[25] Within the context outlined earlier of the accelerated decline of the moral authority of the church following publications detailing the abuse of children in Catholic-run institutions, and in parishes by individual priests, Ó Conchúir felt that creating a work purely of condemnation was insufficient. Instead, he approached the subject by questioning the role of religion in contemporary Irish society and how it continues, despite recent developments, to influence the moulding of corporealities in Ireland. The creative process was a collaboration between Ó Conchúir, five dancers and co-choreographers (Mikel Aristegui, Elena Giannotti, Stéphane Hisler, Bernadette Iglich and Matthew Morris), sean nós singer and composer Iarla Ó Lionáird, and visual artist, Sarah Browne. The rehearsal process also integrated feedback generated from showings to various audience groups, including the Macushla Dance club for the over-50s. This open, collaborative and questioning process translated into a performance that sought to allow the spectator to engage with the questions posed by the work, rather than providing answers or judgements.

In the Catholic Church, a tabernacle is a cabinet above the altar that contains a box (the pyx) in which the sacrament (the consecrated bread that symbolizes the body of Christ) is kept. As with the ladder/scaffold sculptures in *The Falling Song*, *Tabernacle* contains objects that resonate with some of the affects associated with the subject of the work. In *Tabernacle*, these are three wooden structures that resemble tall, open cabinets containing a row of square shelves, but which transform into a number of different bodies and structures throughout the work, including benches and church pews, a rag tree for votive offerings,[26] a confessional box, and a bed. Building on Spinoza's ideas of how affect shapes and modifies bodies, Sara Ahmed suggests that bodies can "take the shape of the very contact they have with objects".[27] As the performers encounter the wooden structures throughout *Tabernacle*, and "partner" them in various manipulations through space, the architecture of their form necessarily imprints on the movement of the dancers, as the two bodies, wooden and flesh, come into contact with each other. As in *The Falling Song*, the dance of the performers with these structures works in an affective capacity. At times my experience of the encounters elicited feelings of discomfort, as when the cabinets seem to restrict movement and freedom of expression. This occurred, for example, when two dancers, a man and a woman, stand on either side of one of the cabinets, and try to touch each other through the openings. Their struggle to connect through the restrictions placed on their movement by the cabinet and their inability to see each other properly, results in awkward, blind gropings for each other's bare skin. Earlier in the piece, the same couple tries to embrace by lying down along a "bed" created by a cabinet on its side. The wooden structure groans and creaks with their weight, adding an acoustic dimension to the feeling of discomfort. The awkwardness of the imprint of this encounter is retained in a prolonged continuation of the embrace across the performance space, as the couple tie themselves in uncomfortable knots, limbs trapped at impossible angles.

Here, the affective experience of the encounters between dancers and the wooden cabinets echo the strain and constraint placed on the expression of sexuality by oppressive Church morality. The wooden structures, experienced as immobile body-objects, elicit feelings of containment and the petrification of corporealities. However, the tabernacle as container of the corporeal is also encountered in a supportive sense in the piece. The work highlights sensual aspects of encounters between bodies and religious iconography, and here the cabinets function, for example, as a platform for stolen kisses during duets that play with images of the pietà, or for caresses inspired by the proffering of wounds, such as the image of the sacred heart. Throughout the piece, one of the cabinets is used to contain items of clothing that are used by the dancers in various ways. In one sequence, a woman, who has covered herself with every item of clothing so that I had the feeling she was mummified and laden down with the weight of them, uses a cabinet as a launch pad or diving board to propel herself into the air. As she jumps, she sheds her outer skin of garments, as if transcending the weight of earthly problems, as she calls "catch me" to the other dancers, who then carry her in a joyous partnering exchange across the stage. Similarly, in the penultimate scene of the work, a man stuffs the top and bottoms of his tracksuit with all of the clothing, creating a frightening, misshapen figure that lurches, seemingly painfully, through an arduous dance, until he finally finds rest, and help, on cabinets functioning as a supportive bed and bench. This figure seems, through the distortion of his form by the excess clothing, to have internalized the "baggage" that the woman freed herself from. She assists him in removing the excess clothing from his body, and he repeatedly embraces her with gratitude.

The excess clothing in these two examples connects on one level with the weight of emotional and psychological trauma that now attends contemplation of contemporary relationships with religion and the Catholic Church in Ireland. In the scenes where the excess clothing is shed, a suggestion seems to be made that the potential for a new relationship with religion (as a structure for the "purposeful living" that Ó Conchúir investigates, or for the Spinozan "good") might be possible for those who wish for it, structured through the encounters of individuals meeting each other in supportive ways in the aftermath of trauma; a meeting of like-spirited bodies building stronger self-knowledge through the shedding of oppressive habits and constraints, and the rebuilding of trust through an experience of repeated supportive encounters. The affective experience of the danced encounters with the cabinets, both as constraining and containing/supportive structures, creates space for thought about how the church and religious bodies mould Irish corporealities. The experience of the cabinets *as* bodies, lends them a potential to also be affected (moved) by their encounters with others—a potential for a malleability that proposes that they are also in a process of becoming. This opens up the possibility for imagining a future restructuring of Ireland's relationship with the Catholic Church, in which religious bodies and institutions do not only operate as "architectures of containment".[28]

Dancehall (2016)

Building on the analysis of the choreography of affective encounters between organizing social structures and the corporealities that they mould, the focus of analysis for the final dance theatre piece discussed is on the dancing body itself. Choreographer Emma Martin explains of her work, *Dancehall*, that it grew out of a "wish to reconnect the primacy of the dancing body with the psyche and to explore the influences that society and its conventions (religious, political and ideological) has had on our body's rapport with the world", and that the show is, "about the essential connection to the Self".[29] The work for five dancers (Oona Doherty, Alistair Goldsmith, Arad Inbar, Anna Kaszuba and Kevin Quinaou) also included music composed by Andrew Hamilton, which was performed live on stage by a trio of keyboard, percussion and cello (William Butt, Lance Corburn and Alex Petchu from contemporary music group Crash Ensemble). As the title of the work suggests, the piece was also inspired, in part, by Ireland's Public Dance Halls Act, which was passed in 1935, and which continues (with some amendments) to be in operation today. This act regulates social dance meetings through a system of licensing and the taxation of tickets, and it was introduced by the government, with fervent support and policing from the Catholic Church, as an attempt to control spaces that might encourage "degenerate dances", and "occasions of sin". Of particular concern, as they were seen as a threat to morality and the "purity" of the national body politic, were "foreign" dances; for example, anything from the waltz and the foxtrot, to the myriad of dances that came under the umbrella term, "jazz" dance.[30] After the passing of the Dance Halls Act, if a public dance was to be held, a licence had to be obtained from the District Court. The District Justice decided whether applications were successful or not, and, as Barbara O'Connor points out, only people considered to be "reputable" were given licences, and only under controlled conditions.[31] The act commercialized social dancing, and curtailed the traditional practices of house dances and crossroad dances in Ireland, as they effectively became unlawful. There are stories of parish priests bursting uninvited into house dances and chasing the dancers out onto the street with sticks. Parishioners caught dancing were also denounced from the pulpit at Sunday mass, and there were several prosecutions under the act.[32]

Dancehall begins with the three musicians entering and taking up their instruments, upstage right. Then the five dancers, wearing casual, rehearsal clothing (t-shirts, shorts, tracksuits), enter to stand in a line downstage, with their backs to the audience. They change out of their rehearsal clothes into formal suit shirts, trousers and jackets, and then make their way to a row of seating along the back wall of the theatre. The dance space is scattered with empty drink cans and plastic bags; the detritus seen on a nightclub floor when the lights go up for closing time. Three giant, yellow curtains are tied up off the floor behind the musicians, and the lighting (by Stephen Dodd) is a mixture of deep shadow and stark brightness, often leaving the dancers faces in shadow and anonymity. A lone dancer begins to move to the rhythm of a bass drum and extremely long, drawn-out, synthesizer chords, which, due to the length of time they are sustained, sound like a mixture between a church organ and an accordion. The atmosphere created feels artificial, vaguely ominous, formal and stifling. One by one, the dancers enter the space to perform synchronized, slow-motion, controlled, but sometimes jerky, movement phrases. Then they line up, holding hands raised overhead, with their backs again to the audience, to perform a phrase of synchronized steps reminiscent of folk dances. As the tempo increases, the dancers move in and out of formation, internalizing the insistent rhythm of the bass drum with pulses in their torsos, and making sudden leaps into deep lunges, echoing seemingly erratic and didactic interjections of discordant notes from the cello. Then the musicians leave the performance space, but the dancers continue, except now the rhythms are produced by the sound of their footsteps as they beat the floor in a stepped dance of unison, and tight, almost military formations. Gestures appear, such as a patriotic hand over breast, or a raised fist; the dancers' corporeality has been regimented and moulded to the internalised rhythms of national expression.

After this sequence, a lone dancer separates from the group. He stands facing the group and begins, at first almost imperceptibly, to move the ball of his right foot back and forth in a tiny, joyful, twist movement to his own, internal rhythm. The group observes in stillness and silence. He moves closer to them and starts his right foot twist experiments again. A dancer from the group rushes at him, leaning against him with her shoulders in a tackling pose, as if trying to stop his movement, or maybe in an awkward embrace of the unknown. But his dance and rhythm is contagious, and spreads through the encounter to the tackling dancer, whose body has been moved by the twist dancer's rhythm through contact. She then moves away, carrying the initial rhythm to further develop it in her own repeated phrase. This contagion of personal rhythm spreads on to the rest of the group through danced encounter. In a kind of silent disco, recognisable social dance moves appear and disappear as if illuminated by strobe lighting: rock and roll poses, jazzy shimmies and more contemporary club dancing shapes,[33] all combined in idiosyncratic dance phrases. Some partnering and synchronised movement occur, but it now feels like these are happening through the chance proximity of bodies and individual choice, rather than through controlled orchestration. From this point on, a powerful feeling of release, freedom and joy builds incrementally through the rest of the performance. In these exchanges I read the building of agency through connection with an internal, rather than imposed external, motivation and capacity for action. As Philipa Rothfield explains in relation to Spinoza's affect theory, "power grows through the body's increasing ability to act. This is not because some external value is satisfied. Rather, it has to do with what a particular body becomes as a manifestation of its own singular essence."[34] In *Dancehall* the capacity to affect and be affected is made visible in the building—through imprints retained from affective encounters—of an increased capacity for individual agency and expression that moves the corporeal away from internalised structures of oppression.

Concluding Thoughts: Affective Accumulations and Action for Change

A century on from the moulding of an "Irish" body, corporeal matters are again at the forefront of the social consciousness. Dance creates a platform to think about corporealities in Ireland; to think about the capacity to move towards an understanding of corporeal traumas caused by state and church abuse, and to think about the ability to find a way to move towards a transcendence of the insecurities, fears and prejudices that caused them. Martin's aim in *Dancehall* to connect with an "essential essence of Self" that has been alienated through the oppression of certain corporeal expressions in Ireland is also at the heart of danced questioning in *The Falling Song* and *Tabernacle*. In each of these works, external societal values and ideals placed on bodies are shown to reduce the bodies' agency and capacity and power for action for change (the fear of falling in *The Falling Song*, the constraint of movement in *Tabernacle*, the regimented control of the dancing body in *Dancehall*). However, in rehearsing and repeating affective encounters within oppressive social constructs, we can also see how affect accumulates, and how the imprint experienced through these encounters signifies change and possible future transformation. Spinoza famously claims, "nobody has yet determined the limits of a body's capabilities".[35] The capacity of the body, "what a body can do", is also "never determined by a body alone but is always aided and abetted by, and dovetails with, the field or context of its force-relations".[36] The "force-relations" are the affects experienced in the encounters between bodies; the push and pull of transitions, through the feelings of sadness or joy, to a corresponding diminished or increased capacity/agency to act. The "good", for Spinoza, is achieved through a release from the influences of passions/affects on body and mind (such as sadness) that reduce the capacity for action. The striving for a better knowledge of self in the world increases the capacity to be affected, and through positive affective encounters, the capacity for action. Dancing, as Rothfield suggests, is an activity that, engaging explicitly with the unknowns of bodily capacity, pushes the body, through the joy generated by action, into developing its agency.[37] Alternatively, sadness is experienced when encounters with other bodies and force relations decreases an individual's "creative self-differentiation".[38] Deleuze, writing of the "sad passions" in Spinoza's theory of affect, suggests that they "represent the lowest degree of our power, the moment when we are most separated from our power of acting, when we are most alienated, delivered over to the phantoms of superstition, to the mystifications of the tyrant".[39] This description of the impotence and alienation engendered by the separation of a body with its power to act, resonates with the oppression of marginalized corporealities in Ireland through the ideologies of church and state. When individuals lose their ability for creative self-differentiation, they lose their agency to act for the "good" in Spinozan terms. In the dance theatre works discussed here, I argue that we see the "terrible inheritance" of the oppression caused by this policing and determining of "acceptable" corporeal expression danced into visibility. Yet I also experience—through the affective encounters between dancers, and between the dance and the spectator—a possibility for creative corporeal expression and action beyond the limitations of societal pressures and determinations.

Notes

1. I use the term affective encounters here to describe moments in dance performance in which the sensing, exchanging and imprinting of affect takes place between the dancers, and between the dancers and the spectators.
2. André Lepecki, "Skin, Body, and Presence in Contemporary European Choreography", *The Drama Review*, *The Drama Review* 43.4 (1999): 139.
3. For example, the report by the Commission to Inquire into Child Abuse investigating the abuse of children in industrial schools (known as the *Ryan Report*), and the *Murphy Report* investigating sexual abuse in the Catholic archdiocese of Dublin, both published in 2009 (http://www.childabusecommission.ie/rpt/pdfs/) (http://www.justice.ie/en/JELR/Pages/PB09000504) (accessed 1/1/2017), and the *Report of the Inter-Departmental Committee to establish the facts of State involvement with the Magdalen Laundries* (http://www.idcmagdalen.ie/

en/MLW/Magdalen%20Rpt%20full.pdf/Files/Magdalen%20Rpt%20full.pdf) (accessed 1/1/2017). Reports continue to be commissioned. Following the publication of an article by Catherine Corless documenting the deaths of 796 children at the Tuam Mother and Babies Home in Galway, which concluded that many were buried in a mass grave in a septic tank on the site of the home, the government ordered the "Mother and Baby Homes Commission of Investigation" chaired by Judge Yvonne Murphy. Excavations at the site in January and February 2017 have proven Corless's claims to be correct. The investigations are ongoing. http://www.mbhcoi.ie/MBH.nsf/page/index-en (accessed 28/3/2017).

4. Benedict Spinoza, *Ethics*, in *Spinoza: The Complete Works*, trans. Samuel Shirley, ed. with an introduction and notes by Michael L. Morgan (Cambridge: Hackett Publishing, 2002), 278.
5. Brian Massumi, *The Politics of Affect* (Cambridge: Polity Press, 2015), viii.
6. As Massumi notes, "[a]ffect is proto-political. It concerns the first stirrings of the political, flush with the felt intensities of life. Its politics must be brought out" (Massumi 2015, ix).
7. For example, Deleuze and Guattari (1987) and Massumi (2002).
8. Megan Watkins, "Desiring Recognition, Accumulating Affect", in *The Affect Studies Reader*, eds. Melissa Gregg and Gregory J. Seigworth (Durham: Duke University Press, 2010).
9. Deleuze's explanation of this distinction is useful in understanding the difference between the two terms as used here: "[i]t has been remarked that as a general rule the affection *(affectio)* is said directly of the body, while the affect *(affectus)* refers to the mind. But the real difference does not reside there. It is between the body's affection and idea, which involves the nature of the external body, and the affect, which involves an increase or decrease of the power of acting, for the body and the mind alike. The *affectio* refers to a state of the affected body and implies the presence of the affecting body, whereas the *affectus* refers to the passage from one state to another, taking into account the correlative variation of the affecting bodies" (Deleuze, 1988, 49).
10. Massumi, *The Politics of Affect*, 4.
11. Speaking of the debates about what "Irish" dancing was, and—more crucially for the project of decolonisation, perhaps—what it was not, Brennan suggests that the arguments that ensued were, "in essence, a cultural civil war with dance as the arena of combat" (Brennan, 1989, 31).
12. See Declan Kiberd, *Inventing Ireland: The Literature of a Modern Nation* (London: Vintage, 1996).
13. See Barbara O'Connor, *The Irish Dancing: Cultural Politics and Identities, 1900–2000* (Cork: Cork University Press, 2013).
14. See Aoife McGrath, *Dance Theatre in Ireland: Revolutionary Moves* (Houndmills: Palgrave, 2013).
15. Carolyn Swift, "Contemporary Dance Theatre at the Gate", *The Irish Times*, 23 March 1983.
16. McGrath, *Dance Theatre in Ireland*, 66.
17. Emma, Meehan, "Dublin Contemporary Dance Theatre: Body, Language and Fleshing out the Bones of Irish Cultural Heritage." In *Contemporising the Past: Envisaging the Future*. Edited by C. F. Stock & P. Germain-Thomas. 2015. Conference proceedings of the 2014 World Dance Alliance Global Summit, Angers, 6–11 July 2014, accessed March 12, 2017, http://www.ausdance.org.au

18. Ann Lovett gave birth alone, outside, in a grotto on her way home from school in the Longford town of Granard. Her baby died at the grotto, and she died a short time later from a post-partum hemorrhage and shock from exposure during childbirth. Her death occurred four months after the 1984 abortion referendum (in which two-thirds of voters agreed to amend the constitution to protect the life of the unborn, leaving the rights of mothers in jeopardy), and is a shocking example of tragedies that have occurred due to the shaming and exclusion of unmarried mothers in Irish society. For further discussion of Ann Lovett and *Giselle* see McGrath (2012).
19. Oona Doherty, from her website (accessed 31-3-2017): https://www.oonadohertyweb.com/hope-hunt#
20. From the description of the work on the Junk Ensemble website (accessed 15-12-2016): http://www.junkensemble.com/the-work/4
21. Related to the author in a public interview and post-show discussion following the performance of *The Falling Song* at the MAC Theatre in Belfast, 24 October 2012.
22. Ciarán Darcy, "Suicide Rates are 'Stabilising' After Increasing During Recession", *The Irish Times*, 26 April, 2016.
23. Fintan Walsh, *Male Trouble: Masculinity and the Performance of Crisis* (Houndsmills: Palgrave, 2010), 4.
24. Melissa Gregg and Gregory Seigworth, *The Affect Theory Reader* (Durham: Duke University Press, 2010), 2.
25. From the description of *Tabernacle* on Ó Conchúir's website (accessed 10-11-2016): http://www.fearghus.net/projects/tabernacle/
26. The performance of *Tabernacle* was accompanied by a printed artwork, entitled *Appendix*, by Sarah Browne. The text entries in *Appendix* connected with certain visual influences on the work, for example, a description of how hawthorn trees were used as so-called "rag" trees in Ireland. People would tie ribbons, or strips of the clothing of sick people, onto the tree branches, and the tree was believed to grant wishes, or absorb the illness. One of the cabinets was hung with strings and clothing in the manner of a rag tree, connecting the idea of superstition with the performance of religion (see Sarah Browne, *Appendix*, 2011).
27. Sara Ahmed, *The Cultural Politics of Emotion* (Edinburgh: Edinburgh University Press, 2004), 1.
28. The term "architecture of containment" is used by James M. Smith to describe how the Irish state used imprisonment in institutions, such as the Magdalen Laundries, to "contain" and discipline deviant bodies (see Smith, 2007).
29. Emma Martin from her essay, "Dark Days Need Ceremony" available on her website (accessed 20-12-2016): http://unitedfall.com/work/view/dancehall
30. See McGrath, *Dance Theatre in Ireland.*
31. See O'Connor, *The Irish Dancing.*
32. Helen Brennan, *The Story of Irish Dance* (Dingle: Brandon, 1999), 121–33.
33. Martin notes that one of the early influences for the piece is Mark Leckey's *Fiorucci Made me Hardcore*, a film that documents UK club dance culture from northern soul to the rave scene of the 1990s (see Martin, 2015).
34. Philipa Rothfield, "Embracing the Unknown: Ethics and Dance", in *Ethics and the Arts*, ed. Paul Macneill (London: Springer, 2014), 91.

35. Spinoza, *Ethics*, 280.
36. Gregg and Seigworth, *The Affect Theory Reader*, 3.
37. Rothfield, "Embracing the Unknown".
38. Ibid.
39. Gilles Deleuze, *Spinoza: Practical Philosophy* (trans. Robert Hurley) (San Francisco: City Lights Books, 1988), 28.

Bibliography

Ahmed, Sara. *The Cultural Politics of Emotion*. Edinburgh: Edinburgh University Press, 2004.

Brennan, Helen. *The Story of Irish Dance*. Dingle: Brandon, 1999.

Browne, Sarah. *Appendix*, 2011, available to view online: http://www.fearghus.net/wp-content/uploads/Sarah-Browne-Appendix.pdf

Darcy, Ciarán. "Suicide Rates Are 'Stabilising' After Increasing During Recession." *The Irish Times*, April 26, 2016. Accessed November 20, 2016. http://www.irishtimes.com/news/social-affairs/suicide-rates-are-stabilising-after-increasing-during-recession-1.2621438

Deleuze, Gilles. *Spinoza: Practical Philosophy*. Translated by Robert Hurley. San Francisco: City Lights Books, 1988.

Deleuze, Gilles, and Félix Guattari. *A Thousand Plateaus: Capitalism and Schizophrenia*. Minneapolis: University of Minnesota, 1987.

Gregg, Melissa, and Gregory Seigworth. *The Affect Theory Reader*. Durham: Duke University Press, 2010.

Kiberd, Declan. *Inventing Ireland: The Literature of a Modern Nation*. London: Vintage, 1996.

Lepecki, André. "Skin, Body, and Presence in Contemporary European Choreography." *The Drama Review* 43.4 (1999): 129-140.

Martin, Emma. "Dark Days Need Ceremony." Essay about *Dancehall*, 2015. Accessed December 20, 2016. http://unitedfall.com/work/view/dancehall

Massumi, Brian. *Parables for the Virtual: Movement, Affect, Sensation*. Durham: Duke University Press, 2002.

Massumi, Brian. *The Politics of Affect*. Cambridge: Polity Press, 2015.

Meehan, Emma. "Dublin Contemporary Dance Theatre: Body, Language and Fleshing Out the Bones of Irish Cultural Heritage." In *Contemporising the Past: Envisaging the Future*. Edited by C. F. Stock & P. Germain-Thomas. 2015. Conference proceedings of the 2014 World Dance Alliance Global Summit, Angers, 6–11 July 2014. Accessed March 12, 2017. http://www.ausdance.org.au

McGrath, Aoife. *Dance Theatre in Ireland: Revolutionary Moves*. Houndmills: Palgrave, 2013.

Nadler, Steven. *Spinoza's Ethics: An Introduction*. Cambridge: Cambridge University Press, 2006.

O'Connor, Barbara. *The Irish Dancing: Cultural Politics and Identities, 1900–2000*. Cork: Cork University Press, 2013.

Roche, Jenny. *Reshaping the Landscape: A Pathway to Professional Dance Training of International Standing in Ireland*. Dublin: The Arts Council, 2016.

Rothfield, Philipa. "Embracing the Unknown: Ethics and Dance." In *Ethics and the Arts*. Edited by Paul Macneill. London: Springer, 2014.

Ruddick, Susan. "The Politics of Affect: Spinoza in the Work of Negri and Deleuze." *Theory, Culture and Society* 27.4 (2010): 21-45.

Smith, James M. *Ireland's Magdalen Laundries and the Nation's Architecture of Containment*. Indiana: University of Notre Dame Press, 2007.

Spinoza, Benedict. Ethics. In *Spinoza: The Complete Works*. Translated by Samuel Shirley. Edited with an introduction and notes by Michael L. Morgan. Cambridge: Hackett Publishing, 2002.

Swift, Carolyn. "Contemporary Dance Theatre at the Gate." *The Irish Times*, March 23, 1983.

Walsh, Fintan. *Male Trouble: Masculinity and the Performance of Crisis*. Houndsmills: Palgrave, 2010.

Watkins, Megan. "Desiring Recognition, Accumulating Affect." In *The Affect Studies Reader*. Edited by Melissa Gregg and Gregory J. Seigworth, 269–285. Durham: Duke University Press, 2010.

Artistic Vision and Regional Resistance: *The Gods Are Angry, Miss Kerr* and the Red Kettle Theatre Company, a Case Study

Richard Hayes and Úna Kealy

Regional Theatre Practice and Irish Theatre in Transition

Christopher Murray, writing in 1979, maintains that Irish theatre of the late 1970s bridged two worlds, "the old or traditional and the new, in constant mutation".[1] The anxieties that arose in the Irish theatre in this transitionary period, the late 1970s through the 1980s—the unease that both manifested and created those conditions of "constant mutation"—are the subject of this essay. This essay engages with the period of the 1980s in particular through a consideration of the anxieties that relate to theatre practice described as "regional", a theatre that may be considered as a counterpoint to one defined in national terms. Theatre practice emanating from regional centres in the 1980s recognized tensions and anxieties within the emerging neoliberal state that oriented itself in such a way as to de-emphasize the small, the voluntary and the local; this theatre practice was radical and served to contradict and disrupt established narratives. While the chapter considers theatre practice island-wide, we focus on the work of Waterford playwright Jim Nolan and the Red Kettle Theatre Company as a means of clarifying some aspects of the history of Irish theatre of the period.

The Irish national theatre (as the framework for discourse about theatre practice in Ireland) and its institutional form (the Irish National Theatre, the Abbey) dominate the Irish theatrical landscape and the landscape of Irish the-

R. Hayes (✉) • Ú. Kealy
Waterford Institute of Technology, Waterford, Ireland
e-mail: rhayes@wit.ie; UKEALY@wit.ie

E. Jordan, E. Weitz (eds.), *The Palgrave Handbook of Contemporary Irish Theatre and Performance*,
https://doi.org/10.1057/978-1-137-58588-2_48

atre studies. (Irish Studies in general may be said to be preoccupied, to a greater or lesser extent, by the "national question".) Regional theatre practice, both theoretically and practically, is much more amorphous, more difficult to define, and less useful as an organizational principle around which to cluster critical remarks. Regional theatre practitioners, indeed, can be said themselves to have struggled to think of their own practice in regional terms. Thus, Field Day Theatre Company (founded 1980) chooses, tellingly, to define itself in relation to national questions. Its manifesto reads:

> All the directors [of the Company] felt that the political crisis in the North and its reverberations in the Republic had made the necessity of a reappraisal of Ireland's cultural and political situation explicit and urgent [...] They felt that Field Day could and should contribute to the solution to the present crisis by producing analyses of the established opinions, myths, and stereotypes which had become both a symptom and a cause of the current situation.[2]

Field Day's engagement with the landscape of Irish theatre (studies) is with the unified landscape, the nation in all its complexity and multiplicity, notwithstanding its regional base. Similarly, Druid (founded in 1975) which began "as a bold idea: to create Ireland's first professional theatre company outside of Dublin"[3] positions itself as a national and international theatre producer:

> Over the years, Druid has worked with actors, designers, directors, writers, producers and administrators, many of whom have each gone on to play leading roles in Irish and international theatre and all of whom have contributed to the shape of the company.[4]

By their own testimony both Field Day and Druid have prioritized, albeit in different ways, national and international questions and audiences rather than regional concerns. In other words (though the crudity of this argument is recognised), a regional company may fail, in one respect, *as a regional company* when it chooses to orient itself *in national terms.*

Regional theatre companies emerged in Ireland during the 1980s as a new force in Irish theatre history. These companies provided opportunities for theatre practitioners emerging from arts, drama and theatre studies programmes and community drama and participatory arts initiatives in the United Kingdom and in the Irish Republic to make a significant impact on the landscape of Irish theatre. Charabanc, formed in 1983 by Carol Moore (also Carol Scanlan), Eleanor Methven, Marie Jones and Brenda Winter, originated as a response to the actresses' frustration at the scarcity and nature of the work available to them.[5] Following an arts degree in University College Cork, Emelie Fitzgibbon founded Graffiti Theatre Company in 1984, creating the only theatre in education company outside Dublin.[6] In the west, Macnas was founded by Páraic Breathnach, Tom Conroy, Ollie Jennings and Pete Sammon to bring large-scale popular theatre to the streets of Galway in 1986.[7] Up north, Jill Holmes, Kate Batts and Zoe Seaton founded Big Telly Theatre Company in 1987 after

Seaton and Holmes returned to Portstewart having graduated from a Theatre Studies programme in the University of Kent; a year later, Lalor Roddy, Tim Loane and Stephen Wright founded Tinderbox Theatre Company to present "challenging theatre not ordinarily seen in Belfast".[8] Such companies, through their commitment to commissioning and producing new drama and regional stories, made important contributions to the ways in which life and culture was expressed on the island. Additionally, many of these companies developed audiences in other regional centres, paving the way for companies such as Gallowglass in Clonmel (1990), Corcadorca in Cork (1991), Blue Raincoat in Sligo (1991), Prime Cut in Belfast (1992) and Waterford Spraoi (1993). While the local circumstances differ, Red Kettle is typical in many ways of contrary regional theatre practice in the 1980s and is, in many respects, representative of the general case—and will therefore form the focal point for the following remarks.

The Local and the Centralized

In 1976, An Chomhairle Ealaíon published *Provision for the Arts*.[9] This report, an audit, in some senses, of all aspects of arts provision in the country, notes a number of peculiarities about the Irish situation that inform any enquiry into the "state of the arts". Two of these "certain conditions peculiar to Ireland, arising from the country's geographical and economic situation and its political and cultural history" come about because there is "too small a population to provide the degree of support for certain of the arts which is taken for granted in other countries" and, secondly, "a distribution of population and centralization of administration which leads to the majority of the arts being concentrated in the capital city".[10] These peculiar conditions set the terms of the ensuing discussion in the report as an exploration of a future arts strategy for the country. The future role of An Chomhairle Ealaíon forms part of the discussion and that future role is considered in terms of potential impact on the arts in the regions. The report recommends an urgent and "systematic extension of the Council's services into the regions outside Dublin" and offers a number of solutions to how best this could be done: "an extravagant method" that would involve the appointment of regional arts officers; an alternative, "to have one or more itinerant arts officers, based in Dublin and travelling through the regions"; or still another solution would be to "link up with other organizations which, unlike the Arts Council, already have representatives in the regions", specifically the Regional Development Organizations established in the late 1960s. James Richards, the report's author, qualifies all this, however, with an interesting remark: "It is important that arts officers working in the regions should report directly to the Arts Council in Dublin and to the Directors of the Regional Development Organizations, and not to any local committees."[11] Significantly, two of these proposals retain the centrality of the council and the other, in which greater devolution of power is considered, retains a fundamental centrality of state governance and is described as an "extravagant" idea. Finally, there is blatant recognition in Richard's qualifying remarks of the desire to refuse "local committees" access to decision-making power.

This tension between the local and the centralized is also reflected in Richards's account of a debate in the Dáil relating to the anomalous situation in which some activities were funded by An Chomhairle Ealaíon and others on the back of a particular relationship with the Department of Finance. Deputy Colley asks the then Minister for Finance, Richie Ryan, "Will the Minister state if arrangements have yet been made to co-ordinate the payment of various sums paid by the State by way of assistance to the arts under An Chomhairle Ealaíon?" Ryan replies:

> I am endeavouring actively to promote this, but there have been a number of arrangements directly under the auspices of the Minister for Finance for many years and some are loath to forego that special relationship and have it dealt with by An Chomhairle. I am hopeful that the necessary centralization and unification will take place.[12]

Evident here is a discourse of unification, and the national(ist) agenda that it speaks to (the title of the report is explicit in its reference to the twenty-six counties and the Republic, highlighting by omission Northern Ireland). More important, however, is the tension at the heart of *Provision for the Arts* between the distributed and the centralized, a tension also reflected in the Dáil exchange above which suggests the difficulty the Council itself had in achieving autonomy from the Department of Finance. What emerges within the documentation and public discussion is the fact that the arts in the Republic of Ireland (and indeed in other centres of global free-market capitalism) was caught up in a debate around autonomy that involved complex negotiations around the national decentralization of power and wealth, a central aspect of which was the sustainable economic viability of small-scale cultural organizations within an ever-increasingly neoliberalist social, cultural and economic infrastructure.

A number of years later, these tensions crystallize as primarily economic when, in the 1985 An Chomhairle Ealaíon *Annual Report*, the Council note "the general lack of appreciation of the financial return which the arts make to the community"[13] and their decision to commission an economic analysis of the impact of the arts in the Republic of Ireland. This analysis was published in 1987 as *The Performing Arts and the Public Purse*[14]; through referencing Richards it frames the debate in new terms, declaring:

> The most important contribution, initially, that economics can make to the question of the public funding of the performing arts in Ireland is to provide a coherent and logically consistent framework within which the debate can take place: in particular, it can throw considerable light on such issues as the objectives of public funding, the appropriate channels for such funding and the allocation of this funding by, for example, size and type of company.[15]

The Performing Arts and the Public Purse established the neoliberal credentials of An Chomhairle Ealaíon in its very title by asserting a connection between the arts and the public purse, and by promulgating the economic analysis of the arts as a viable means of valuing and developing arts activity. David Harvey contends that "the neoliberal state needs nationalism of a certain sort to survive. Forced to operate as a competitive agent in the world market and seeking to establish the best possible business climate, it mobilizes nationalism in its effort to succeed".[16] The discourse that finds expression in *The Performing Arts and the Public Purse*, and its version of the public thought of as national, is in service in Harvey's analysis of neoliberalism. Competition produces ephemeral winners and losers in the global struggle for position, and this in itself can be a source of national pride or of national anxiety and soul-searching. But this eschews the local and regional, and diminishes the power of locally oriented discourse in favour of grander national (neoliberal) narratives. Moreover, in this context, the local and the regional *cannot* succeed in the terms defined by the (neoliberal) state: the local, regional public does not have enough significance in this narrative to be considered successful, to compete in the game.

"Anxieties and Agitations" and the Waterford Response

This anxiety and soul-searching manifested in the emergence of participatory theatre practice throughout the island in the 1970s and 1980s.[17] In 1973, Ireland joined the EEC and the social and political ramifications of this decision had far-reaching effects on all aspects of Irish life, not least on the area of arts and cultural policy, funding structures and the evolution of theatre provision both in the capital and regional towns and cities. The tensions evident in the publications of An Chomhairle Ealaíon during the 1970s and 1980s indicate that there were multiple Irelands that needed to be brought into unity and that this passage to unity was problematic. Titling a postscript chapter "The Uncertain Eighties" to *Ireland: A Social and Cultural History 1922–1980*, first published in 1980 and republished in 1985, Terence Brown analyses the persistent political instability and increasingly worsening economic situation in the Republic in the mid-1980s as presenting a "new Irish reality [that was] ambiguous, transitional, increasingly urban or suburban, disturbingly at variance with the cultural aspirations of the revolutionaries who had given birth to the state".[18] Diarmaid Ferriter forensically charts inequalities in relation to education and wealth as exhibiting a disturbing coexistence of "squalor and neglect in the midst of a new-found opulence".[19] Similarly, Roy Foster identifies the early 1980s as a peak of inflation and unemployment explaining this as an evolved disparity between the incomes and educational qualifications of the wealthiest and the most poor.[20] The lived experience of this rapidly changing environment throughout the island was dominated by the Troubles in Northern Ireland and increasing levels of emigration, dependency on social welfare payments, and rising crime statistics and drug abuse leading Joe Cleary to describe the decade as one dominated by "tremendous anxieties and agitations".[21] In an increasingly educated, multicultural, globalized society many on the island were experiencing the "anxieties and agitations" of sharply decreasing standards of living, education and employment prospects.

Developing economic and social agendas often meant that regional areas struggled to survive this period of transition and the south-east of the island and the city of Waterford provides a good case in point. Waterford in the 1980s was a city traumatized by economic hardship that had begun in the previous decade. A four-day strike in Waterford Crystal in 1974 resulted in over 2000 employees taking strike action. Later that year Goodbody's Jute Factory closed, resulted in 500 job losses. In 1978 the National Board and Paper Mills factory shed 281 jobs and Munster Chipboard closed in 1979 with the loss of 186 jobs. The Paper Mills closed completely in 1980 and the remaining 200-plus jobs were lost. Clover Meats closed in 1984: 600 jobs went there and, in 1987, over 1000 jobs were lost from Waterford Crystal reducing the workforce by almost a third.

Somewhat surprisingly, perhaps, that decade of economic difficulty coincided with a time of remarkable cultural activity within the city. In the early 1900s theatre in Waterford consisted, in the main, of occasional touring productions from Britain and visiting variety performances and, from 1925 up to the 1970s, productions by Anew McMaster's company visited the city.[22] In addition to these professional productions, from the mid-1940s amateur dramatic societies began performing in the city. However, the most popular form of theatre within the city, in the years leading up to the 1980s, was the annual Festival of Light Opera (1966–2014). Although the festival, programmed in the city's Theatre Royal, involved participation from numerous local groups and businesses it became identified in the public consciousness with corporate evenings where patrons in evening dress could meet and mingle. Arguably, the performances of the patrons in the foyer were as important as those onstage. This was, at least, the perception of some Waterfordians as will be evidenced later.

However, in the mid-1970s an initiative facilitated by the Combat Poverty Agency to combat social exclusion and improve the social and cultural fabric of the city created the Waterford Arts for All Project (WAFA). WAFA originated as a multidisciplinary community arts organization which aimed to promote arts practice within the city by coordinating community arts festivals and campaigning to establish an arts centre. From WAFA two community theatre organizations arose, Ciotóg and the Arts For All Theatre Company, both of which occupied and created new cultural spaces within the city performing in housing estates, pubs, schools, women's and community centres and local pirate radio stations. In 1985 Red Kettle Theatre Company was formed and between the 4th and the 6th of May *The Gods are Angry Miss Kerr*, a play by local writer Jim Nolan, was staged in the Theatre Royal. The formation of Red Kettle Theatre Company and the decision to commission a new play by a local writer to be staged in the Theatre Royal can be read as a manifesto of resistance, an antidote of sorts, to the "anxieties and agitations" of an explicit neoliberalist direction within state policy.[23]

The Gods are Angry, Miss Kerr

Nolan's work examines and re-examines "anxieties and agitations" with each play presenting a new challenge to what Harvey describes as the "limits on democratic governance" imposed by neoliberal policy makers.[24] His oeuvre offers a sustained critique of neoliberalism beginning with when *The Gods are Angry, Miss Kerr* premiered in Waterford in 1985.[25] Set in 1956, primarily in Waterford city, *The Gods* explores individual and collective identity and expresses anxiety around issues of access to the places and spaces of Waterford city for a disenfranchised community. Opening literally with a snapshot of factory life where the characters pose for a photograph during a morning tea break the day before a factory outing to the seaside, *The Gods* presents two days in the lives of seven characters from Waterford, each of whom work in the weaving sheds of the city's jute factory. Central to the storyline are the middle-aged character of Albert the Liar O'Brien, two younger male characters, Tommy and Cottons, and Cottons' sister Julia. Albert is training Tommy to box in the hope that he will qualify for the Melbourne Olympics, though aware that this is an unlikely eventuality Tommy continues to train, resigned to the fact that there is little else to occupy him. However, while Tommy is stoical Cottons is dissatisfied with life in Waterford and decides to leave for London to find his father who left the city following the temporary closure of the jute factory in 1944. As Cottons leaves he recognises that the economic and unemployment malaise of Waterford is a global phenomenon and that he is moving from one disenfranchised and impoverished community for another.

Cleary describes the 1980s as "haunted by an uncanny sense of the 1950s" and *The Gods* reframes 1980s anxieties around emigration, unemployment, pregnancy outside marriage, and a general lack of opportunity to a 1956 setting.[26] Waterford city is an ambiguous place in the play—on the one hand, it allows the creation of communities such as the factory, the boxing club and the city's brass band but, on the other hand, it offers little in the way of opportunity. Mentions within the play of other cities such as Melbourne, Paris, Ankara and Luxembourg suggest exotic escapes from the narrow-minded church-controlled environment of Waterford or Ireland where the cinema and streets are closed for Eucharistic processions on the edict of the parish priest. However, in practice, the play demonstrates that this escape is more fanciful than real and a recognition that the neoliberal agenda is a global, and therefore inescapable, phenomena are explored in relation to mentions of London in particular. Several characters in *The Gods* flee to London, but that city, it transpires, merely offers identical indignities and hardships. Tommy says at one point:

> Tommy: The streets of London are just the same as here, Cottons. Walkin' up the Yellow Road to the Jute Factory or down some side street to a Bean Factory in Harlesden – there's no difference (21).[27]

The neoliberal agenda is endemic: Julia and Cotton's father goes to London when the jute factory closes in 1944, but although he is "alive and well" he lives "posin' as a war cripple and humpin' holy pictures in Leicester Square" (65). Pregnant at seventeen, Gertie, who had once dreamed of being an actress, escapes to a convent-run home for unmarried expectant mothers also in London. However, Gertie decides to keep her baby and finds a job and a flat but the baby dies and Gertie, fearing her inexperience has caused its death, secretly disposes of its body in a canal. London, then, represents a place of failure, isolation and tragedy where a child can be born, die and be discarded without anyone knowing. London might offer a freedom from repressive Irish Catholicism, but the price is the sacrifice of family, integrity and honesty and ultimately the freedom is merely an exchange of hardships and limitations. Cottons also makes mention of the Walsh brothers who return from London describing them as being "like somethin' you'd see in a gangster picture" (20). The Walsh brothers are direct descendants of John B. Keane's William Dee in *The Field* (1965) and, as such, offer an opportunity for Nolan to explore the national experience of the returned immigrant; this is not, however, the focus of *The Gods*. The play is interested instead in exploring the tensions of emerging globalization and the struggle to exist in communities experiencing diminishing levels of dignity, financial hardship, employment opportunities and creative and spiritual freedom. Paradoxically, in *The Gods* it is the community that attends the cinema, not the theatre, which expresses anger at this diminishing freedom.

The title of the play names a real person, an Ellen Kerr, who ran the local cinema, the Coliseum. "The gods" were the cheaper seats in that cinema—the people in these seats "were often angry, obstreperous even, and the long-suffering Miss Kerr was invariably called upon to quell their anger" (to quote from a contemporary review). *The Gods* references the Hollywood film *Fighting Father Dunne* (1948) in which the eponymous Father Dunne transforms the lives of impoverished news boys in St. Louis by providing them with shelter and quelling their violent rivalries. Significantly, the play does not reference a much more famous film of that era—John Ford's *The Quiet Man* (1952). Rather than escaping into an aesthetic conception of rural Ireland the play exposes the difficulties of urban life and suggests a need for leadership which recognises common adversaries while offering shelter and nurture as alternatives to competition. Both the titles of *Fighting Father Dunne* and *The Gods are Angry, Miss Kerr* suggest the legitimacy of anger and activism in the face of social and economic injustice and, in making reference to a restless, angry audience and the social and economic tensions of Waterford, *The Gods* draws attention to the conditions of its own performance highlighting the audience and the city as the centre of the play's attention. In this sense, then, the play implicitly refuses simply to map the landscape of a time past but actively engages an audience in self-empowerment in which the act of performance—in which the role of the audience is central—becomes an act of collective memory and an expression (perhaps) of collective anger. We refer to Michel de Certeau's metaphor of a map as "a totalizing stage on which elements of diverse origin are brought together to form the tableau of a 'state' of geographical knowledge".[28] *The Gods* can be regarded as a series of tableaux representing the "state" of social, political, cultural and economic conditions which acknowledge the subsumption of the nation into the global and advocate for an alternative.

In choosing Theatre Royal Waterford as the venue for *The Gods* Red Kettle Theatre Company extended participation in theatre in the city to a wider demographic. Red Kettle's production of *The Gods* in 1985 sought to tighten bonds not only between individual audience members but also between audience members and the theatre itself. Important within *The Gods* is the fact that the Coliseum has closed for a religious festival and this undemocratic closure is regarded as unjust. Democracy, access and activism are central preoccupations within *The Gods* and the title of the play recognises these as manifest within Waterford cinema audiences ("the gods" in particular), presenting an argument that theatre could offer a more effective cultural intervention than the cinema. Harvey characterizes urban areas as "divided and conflict prone" insofar as rich elites have taken control of planning and building—class conflict, therefore, is "indelibly etched on the spatial forms of our cities".[29] The reclamation of place in *The Gods* is not literal, in this sense, or not only so; it is also a class-inflected transformation of power relations from the haves to the have-nots, to put it crudely.

In its production of *The Gods* Red Kettle uses the location of Waterford city to play out the social politics, divisions and conflicts of which Harvey writes. The 1985 programme for the play includes a paragraph detailing the community credentials of the Red Kettle Theatre Company, outlining how it came into being, listing the names of Waterford-based writers and stressing the fact that they are local. Indeed, the word "local" is used in the paragraph four times in quick succession with the final lines stating:

> In fact Red Kettle is really just a new name for an old friend. We are pledged to consolidate and expand the work of the Arts-For-All Theatre Company; in particular we are dedicated to making the theatre a celebration in which all the people of Waterford can share.[30]

Another detail from this programme offers concession prices only to the "unwaged". What Red Kettle set out to do then was to reclaim the Theatre Royal as a space within the city accessible to the working and unwaged classes of Waterford. While the characters' social and economic circumstances are traumatic, the humorous and sympathetic portrayal of their interactions and the specific localized details of the setting lends a certain "old timey" feel to the play that is somewhat reflected in contemporary commentary. The play was described as "a review of Waterford in the early fifties" in *The Waterford Post*,[31] while a letter to the playwright from audience members for the original production confirms that it was received, by some at least, as a recreation of experience from the 1950s. The letter reads:

Hi Jim,

There is no way you know us. We would like to thank you for a brilliant play. The majority of our mothers worked in the jute factory at some time or another. All our lives we've listened to stories about their work. We decided as a group to go and see your play to be quite honest just for a laugh. Did we get a surprise. It was just as our Mammy's talked about factory work, and the way each worker got involved with the rest of those working with them. It was our first time at a play and in the Theatre Royal. We really enjoyed it. Congrats and keep them coming.

Your fans, who thought the theatre was only for snobs.[32]

The word "snobs" in the letter to Nolan suggests a (perhaps naïve) analysis of performance based on class. But part of Red Kettle's project was accessibility: the city is reclaimed through performance; and the theatre is reclaimed through the city. Though the play is, in many ways, a celebration of the camaraderie and solidarity between factory workers the sense of nostalgia does not dominate because the characters populating it have difficult social, economic and employment situations and struggle to exist within them. The play foregrounds—in looking back—the 1980s unemployment crisis by reminding audiences if not of better times then of times when at least the jute factory could be relied on for employment. It is an uncomplicated move: we are reminded of the jute factory's closure by hearing the sounds of the hooter indicating the end of a shift, a sound that would have been common in the area around Tycor where the factory was located. The performance of the sounds associated with the factory—the presence of actors pretending to be factory workers—is certainly an exercise in nostalgia; it is also, however, an exercise in repossession, a reclamation of different (if not better) times when factory hooters sounded over the city.

Another contemporary review of the production notes that this is a play "full of local colour and character".[33] Not only was the production performed by a local cast but the play makes specific and constant reference to places within the city. Streets, places and businesses are mentioned; references to the town's landmarks include the Theatre Royal, the Adelphi Hotel, the Coliseum Cinema, St Joseph's Boy's Club, Kiely's Brewery and St. Otteran's Psychiatric Hospital. Streets and laneways mentioned include the Yellow Road, the Mall, John Street, Bunker's Hill, Ballybricken, Broad Street, Millworth's field, Flaggy Lane and Sheep's Lane, the latter being two colloquial names that do not feature on maps—and which would have been familiar only to local, Waterford people. In naming these places, the play clearly seeks common ground (literally) with its audience; the recitation of real place names becomes an act not of mapping the city but of performing it. And in performing it, reclaiming it. It is to this, perhaps, that the audience members refer when they write of finding a new meaning in the theatre which before they thought was "only for snobs". The play acts out a sort of reclamation of the city through the theatre for those who are not "snobs".

The Gods dramatizes the emerging class divide associated with the developing neoliberal agenda as outlined above, expressed in part through the identification of people with particular places an example of which is when Julia, in conversation with Cottons, makes mention of a Mary Carney who ties sausages and streels "liver down in Sheep's Lane". In their conversation, Julia reacts fiercely to Cotton's insinuation that to be a factory worker is to be socially inferior, arguing:

JULIA: And anyway, I have news for you about shop assistants and office clerks.
COTTONS: What's that?
JULIA: Factory girls wages is twice as high as 'em. It's precious little money they get for a good name.
COTTONS: At least they have a good name.
JULIA: Just what do you mean by that?
COTTONS: Nothin'. I meant nothin'.
JULIA: You bloody well did! You meant a jute factory girl is some sort of a bloody second class citizen.
COTTONS: Don't be putting words in my mouth.
JULIA: 'Twas you who said it! Ye meant any self-respectin' gentleman from Newtown and the like wouldn't be seen dead with the likes of us (54).

Clearly, the play directs itself not at the "snobs", in the former words of the audience member (that is, the "self-respectin' gentleman from Newtown"—the location of a famous private school within the city), but at the jute factory girls and their ilk in the city; the kind of people who populate the places mentioned in the play and who would know the names of the lanes. In this moment Red Kettle's promise to make "the theatre a celebration in which all the people of Waterford can share" is realized. Performing this act of solidarity and inclusion provides the audience with cause to "celebrate" while the production itself offers an opportunity and reclaims an importance space in the city for communal celebration. Staging the play, about working-class life in Waterford Theatre Royal, a theatre building then synonymous with the Festival of Light Opera, and marketing the play specifically to working-class citizens enabled Red Kettle to offer a culturally and economically accessible alternative to the global phenomena that is the cinema. In this way *The Gods*, in its commissioning, title, thematic preoccupations, local references, production and premiere, can be regarded as a direct invitation to a specifically local audience to move from a global form of culture to a smaller, localized, community-oriented creative space—a manifesto in both literary and staging terms that opposed the neoliberal agenda and invited the "community groups" disenfranchised by *Provision for the Arts* to create local spaces and forge and strengthen the social bonds within these spaces.[34]

Theatre Practice and the Right to the City

Meanderinag though *The Gods* is the character of Janey Mac, a former resident of the city's St. Otteran's Psychiatric Hospital. Simultaneously feisty and vulnerable, Janey provides both comic and poignant moments within the drama as in one instance when she writes to Pope Pius XII asking him to refrain from instructing the local priest Father Coady "to stop the people going where they want to go" (21). Janey provides an example of the play's connection of people with places within the city and her character represents a community that was rarely seen on the stage up to or including the 1980s.[35] It is significant that, in the closing moments of the play, the characters gather around a whimpering Janey sheltering and protecting her thereby suggesting that, despite being on the outside of a hotel in which the official "Jewel of the Jute" beauty contest is taking place and symbolically, therefore, excluded from hegemonies of power and acceptability, the characters can create tightly knit localized communities that will protect the most vulnerable citizens. The final moments of the play can be interpreted as Nolan's characters wresting an "alternative from the meshes of the actual",[36] and constructing "weak voluntary associations" that, despite their fragility, seem to be the only possible alternative.[37]

In an earlier version of his essay "The Right to the City" Harvey introduces a concept of urban space which he terms "urban commons". He describes these public places (both geographical and philosophical) that require a collective effort in rolling back:

> that huge wave of privatization that has been the mantra of a destructive neoliberalism. We must imagine a more inclusive, even if continuously fractious, city based not only upon a different ordering of rights but upon different political-economic practices. If our urban world has been imagined and made then it can be re-imagined and re-made.[38]

In the mid-1980s, with *The Gods*, Jim Nolan and Red Kettle Theatre Company claim rights to the city for itself and its audience and created a form of radical art, a form of democratic performance and production that remained radical and democratic by remaining relentlessly local. Red Kettle refused to engage with the debate on the terms proposed by the neoliberal state, instead providing a formula by which citizens could imagine a new future for themselves in a city that was "uncompetitive" in neoliberal terms. Furthermore, the play and its production expose and critique the ways in which the city (and, by extension, other regional Irish towns and cities) was ideologically constructed as a cog within the neoliberal machine and offers a reimagining of the local for those unwilling to continue the unimpeded progression of the machine.

The Gods is important for another reason: it was the company's first (self-declared) "professional" production. A clear differentiation between the "professional" arts and other forms of arts practice is insisted on in successive Arts Council reports through the 1980s, summarized in *The Performing Arts and the Public Purse*. As that report notes, "[i]n a time of stringent finances, priority was given to the professional sphere, and to amateur organisations where it was hoped that improved standards would materialise".[39] By 1984, An Chomhairle Ealaíon had refined its understanding and set out the difference between the professional and amateur arts organisation in different terms:

> The first type of arts organisation is that which operates in a direct and close way with the community.... The second type of organisation is that which believes that the direct involvement of its audience in the *process of the arts activity* is at least as, and often more, important than the *finished object* such as the sculpture, video or novel.[40]

In declaring itself "professional", Red Kettle identified itself as the second type of organization above and thus made itself, importantly, eligible for Arts Council funding. But, as *The Gods* itself dramatizes, it is the first type of organization that seems to have a more vital, dynamic and radical role to play in local and regional contexts. As the 1980s developed, and as funding policy created by An Chomhairle Ealaíon hardened, directing funding towards professional organizations or those with an aspiration to be professional, the serious theatre reshaped itself throughout the island along neoliberal lines and there was a progressive sidelining of radical, resistant practice by both the Arts Council and the academy.

Notes

1. Christopher Murray, "Irish Drama in Transition 1966–1978", *Études Irelandaises*, 4, (1979): 301, accessed May 11, 2017, http://www.persee.fr/doc/irlan_0183-973x_1979_num_4_1_2605.
2. Richard Kearney, "Preface" to Seamus Deane *Ireland's Field Day* (London: Harper Collins, 1985) vii.
3. "The Druid Story", Druid, accessed May 17, 2017, http://www.druid.ie/about/the-druid-story.
4. "The Druids", Druid, accessed May 17, 2017, http://www.druid.ie/about/the-druids.
5. "Charabanc Theatre Company: One of the Major Irish Theatre Companies of the 1980s and Early 1990s", accessed May 17, 2017, http://www.culturenorthernireland.org/features/performing-arts/charabanc-theatre-company.
6. Roma Tomelty and John Keyes founded a theatre in education project in Belfast called 70s Productions in 1969 but this was short-lived due to Tomelty moving soon afterwards to the US. Dublin-based TEAM Theatre in Education Company was established in 1975 while Replay in Belfast was founded in 1988.
7. "About Us", Macnas, accessed May 17, 2017, http://macnas.com/about/history/.
8. "Tinderbox Theatre Company: Producing Challenging Performances", Culture NI, accessed May 17, 2017, http://www.culturenorthernireland.org/article/900/tinderbox-theatre-company.

9. James Maude Richards, *Provision for the Arts: Report of the Inquiry Carried Out During 1974–75 Throughout the Twenty-Six Counties of the Republic of Ireland* (Dublin: An Chomhairle Ealaíon, 1976).
10. Richards, *Provision for the Arts*, 8.
11. Richards, *Provision for the Arts*, 95.
12. Richie Ryan quoted in Richards, *Provision for the Arts*, 41.
13. An Chomhairle Ealaíon. *Annual Report 1985* (Dublin: An Chomhairle Ealaíon, 1986): 7, accessed May 17, 2017, http://www.artscouncil.ie/publications/?&Year=1986.
14. John W. O' Hagan & Christopher T. Duffy, *The Performing Arts and the Public Purse: An Economic Analysis: A Report Commissioned by the Arts Council/An Chomhairle Ealaíon* (Dublin: An Chomhairle Ealaíon, 1987).
15. O'Hagan & Duffy, *The Performing Arts and the Public Purse*, 5.
16. David Harvey, *A Brief History of Neoliberalism* (Oxford: Oxford University Press, 2005) 85.
17. See 'Participatory performance: spaces of creative negotiation' by Kate McCarthy and Úna Kealy also in this volume.
18. Terrence Brown, *Ireland: A Social and Cultural History 1922–1985* (London: Fontana Press, 1985) 314.
19. Diarmaid Ferriter, *The Transformation of Ireland 1900–2000* (London: Profile, 2005) 536.
20. Roy Foster, *Luck and the Irish: A Brief History of Change 1970–2000* (London: Allen Lane, 2007).
21. Joe Cleary, *Outrageous Fortune: Capital and Culture in Modern Ireland* (Dublin: Field Day Publications, 2007) 208.
22. Christopher Morash, *A History of Irish Theatre 1600–2000* (Cambridge: Cambridge University Press, 2002).
23. Cleary, *Outrageous Fortune*, 208.
24. David Harvey, *A Brief History of Neoliberalism* (Oxford: Oxford University Press, 2005) 69.
25. Henceforth referred to as *The Gods.*
26. Cleary, *Outrageous Fortune*, 208.
27. Henceforth all references are taken from the script of *The Gods are Angry Miss Kerr* revised edition (2011) held in the Red Kettle Archives in the Luke Wadding Library, Waterford Institute of Technology.
28. Michel DeCerteau, *The Practice of Everyday Life, Volume 1*, trans. Steven Rendall (Berkeley: University of California Press, 1984), 121.
29. David Harvey, "The Right to the City", *New Left Review*, no.53 (2008): 32, accessed May 17, 2017, https://newleftreview.org/II/53/david-harvey-the-right-to-the-city.
30. Red Kettle Theatre Company, *The Gods are Angry Miss Kerr Programme* (Waterford: Red Kettle Theatre Company Archives, Luke Wadding Library, Waterford Institute of Technology, 1985).
31. "Theatre Review: Premiere Success for Jim", *The Waterford Post*, May 7, 1985, 10.
32. Red Kettle Theatre Company Archives 1985–2014, "*The Gods Are Angry Miss Kerr*" (Waterford: Red Kettle Theatre Company Archive, 1985).
33. Publication unknown, "The Bull Post, 'Jute factory memories'", date unknown, 1985, 11 (Waterford: Red Kettle Theatre Company Archives, 1985).

34. Richards, *Provision for the Arts*, 95.
35. Patrick McCabe's powerful depiction of mental illness and isolation in *Frank Pig Says Hello* was first produced in 1992 and Pat Kinevane's *Silent* was first produced in 2011.
36. Cleary, *Outrageous Fortune*, 174.
37. Harvey, *A Brief History of Neoliberalism*, 69.
38. David Harvey, "The Right to the City", *International Journal of Urban and Regional Research*, 27, no. 4 (2003): 943, accessed May 17, 2017, http://onlinelibrary.wiley.com/doi/10.1111/j.0309-1317.2003.00492.x/abstract.
39. O'Hagan & Duffy, *The Performing Arts and the Public Purse*, 82.
40. An Chomhairle Ealaíon. *Annual Report 1984* (Dublin: An Chomhairle Ealaíon, 1985): 35, accessed May 17, 2017, http://www.artscouncil.ie/uploadedFiles/An_Chomhairle_Ealaion_1984.pdf

Bibliography

An Chomhairle Ealaíon. *Annual Report 1984* (Dublin: An Chomhairle Ealaíon, 1985) Accessed May 22, 2017. http://www.artscouncil.ie/uploadedFiles/An_Chomhairle_Ealaion_1984.pdf.

An Chomhairle Ealaíon. *Annual Report 1985*, Dublin: An Chomhairle Ealaíon. Accessed May 17, 2017. http://www.artscouncil.ie/publications/?&Year=1986.

Brown, Terrence. *Ireland: A Social and Cultural History 1922–1985*. London: Fontana Press, 1985.

Cleary, Joe. *Outrageous Fortune: Capital and Culture in Modern Ireland*. Dublin: Field Day Publications, 2007.

Culture NI. "Charabanc: One of the Major Irish Theatre Companies of the 1980s and Early 1990s." Accessed May 17, 2017. http://www.culturenorthernireland.org/features/performing-arts/charabanc-theatre-company.

Culture NI. "Tinderbox Theatre Company: Producing Challenging Performances." Accessed May 17, 2017. http://www.culturenorthernireland.org/article/900/tinderbox-theatre-company.

DeCerteau, Michel. *The Practice of Everyday Life, Volume 1*. Translated by Steven Rendall. Berkeley: University of California Press, 1984.

Druid. *Druid*. Accessed May 17, 2017, http://www.druid.ie.

Ferriter, Diarmaid. *The Transformation of Ireland 1900–2000*. London: Profile, 2005.

Foster, Roy. *Luck and the Irish: A Brief History of Change 1970–2000*. London: Allen Lane, 2007.

Harvey, David. 'The Right to the City,' International Journal of Urban and Regional Research. 27, no. 4 (2003): 939–41. Accessed May 17, 2017. http://onlinelibrary.wiley.com/doi/10.1111/j.0309-1317.2003.00492.x/abstract.

Harvey, David. *A Brief History of Neoliberalism*. Oxford: Oxford University Press, 2005.

Kearney, Richard. *"Preface" to Deane, S. Ireland's Field Day*. London: Harper Collins, 1985.

Macnas. "About Us." Accessed May 17, 2017. http://macnas.com/about/history/.

Morash, Christopher. *A History of Irish Theatre 1600–2000*. Cambridge: Cambridge University Press, 2002.

Murray, Christopher. "Irish Drama in Transition 1966–1978." Études Irlandaises 4 (1979): 287–308. Accessed May 11, 2017. http://www.persee.fr/doc/irlan_0183-973x_1979_num_4_1_2605.

Nolan, Jim. *The Gods Are Angry, Miss Kerr.* [Unpublished dramatic text] Red Kettle Theatre Company Archives, Luke Wadding Library, Waterford Institute of Technology, 1985 revised in 2011.

O'Hagan, John W. & Christopher T. Duffy, *The Performing Arts and the Public Purse: An Economic Analysis: A Report Commissioned by the Arts Council/An Chomhairle Ealaíon.* Dublin: An Chomhairle Ealaíon. 1987.

Red Kettle Theatre Company Archives. Luke Wadding Library, Waterford Institute of Technology, 1985–2014.

Red Kettle Theatre Company. *The Gods are Angry Miss Kerr Programme.* Red Kettle Theatre Company Archives, Luke Wadding Library, Waterford Institute of Technology, 1985.

Richards, James Maude. *Provision for the Arts: Report of the Inquiry Carried Out During 1974–75 Throughout the Twenty-Six Counties of the Republic of Ireland.* Dublin: An Chomhairle Ealaíon, 1976.

Cultural Materialism and a Class Consciousness?

Erika Meyers

This chapter examines how the depiction of working-class struggles in Dermot Bolger's *The Holy Ground* (1990) and Paul Mercier's *Home* (1988) are used not merely to illustrate social displacement, but, more significantly, to attack the level of complacency in Irish society that perpetuated its cycles of poverty, oppression and displacement. Although each play is underpinned by their protagonist's initial adherence to hegemonic structures, their prevailing narratives of disillusionment reveal an underlying mission to subvert the social inequalities their characters endure. Furthermore, I will illustrate how such inequality was a catalyst for what Ferdia Mac Anna has described as a "Dublin Renaissance"—a wave of Irish writing throughout the 1980s and early 1990s whose themes are diametrically opposed to the imposed social mores that influenced their work. Based on these notions, I will use these two plays in order to address Ireland's social and political landscape throughout this timeframe, the emergence of new writers and theatre companies and the ways in which their work has responded to sociopolitical issues within this timeframe.

With unemployment in the Republic of Ireland rising from 99,000 (8.2%) in 1978 to 217,000 (16.3%) by 1988,[1] and emigration rising from 40,200 in 1987 to 70,600 in 1989,[2] the country's depleting population and struggling economy throughout the 1980s presented a significant challenge to those striving for upward economic mobility. Such instability was also highlighted by the numerous changes of power within the role of Taoiseach, with Charles Haughey and Garret Fitzgerald succeeding each other several times throughout the 1980s and early 1990s.[3,4] However, it would be shortsighted to solely attribute the change in government leadership to Ireland's social and economic instability. Rather, the failure of those in power to appreciate the link between the Irish economy and external economic influences that precluded the

E. Meyers (✉)
The University of Edinburgh, Edinburgh, Scotland

E. Jordan, E. Weitz (eds.), *The Palgrave Handbook of Contemporary Irish Theatre and Performance*,
https://doi.org/10.1057/978-1-137-58588-2_49

government from making substantial changes to benefit Irish society[5] (health, education, equality, social mobility), alongside the bribery scandals that plagued Charles Haughey's career, underscored a recurring narrative of Irish citizens being ruled by those who did little to support them.[6] This can be recognised when the government used taxes to pay off government debt, which contributed little to the funds of working Irish citizens as their PAYE tax was used, "to pay this huge debt financed government strategy which saw the overall government debt to rise to 133 per cent of GDP in the early 1980s".[7] This strategy not only contributed to the rise of the level of debt, but also led to unfair advantages for the few over the many. For, although there was a tax increase, "(it) was used simply to pay government debt caused by unchecked spending on grant aiding industries and the offer of tax advantages".[8] Italian scholar Antonio Gramsci's theory of cultural hegemony identifies how oppressed groups are convinced to support the beliefs of the ruling class. This is driven by the concept "that man is not ruled by force alone, but also by ideas".[9] However, while citizens could be ruled by ideas, rather than mere force, Irish writing, particularly throughout the 1980s and early 1990s, also demonstrated that it was possible to attack complacence towards government corruption and expose its hegemonic underpinnings through the expression of counter ideas in poetry, plays and novels.

In his 1991 essay, "The Dublin Renaissance: An Essay on Modern Dublin and Dublin Writers", writer/director/lecturer Ferdia Mac Anna argued that a literary revival was developing, whereby working-class writers were using innovative techniques to actively address the consequences of corruption and inequality in the Republic of Ireland. Such writing, according to Mac Anna, was distinguished by "sources (that) are essentially non-traditional, even anti-literary (social issues, local environment, urban disillusionment, political corruption, rock music). (Y)ou could call it Dublin's answer to American dirty realism—a kind of 'Dirty Dublin Poetic Realism'."[10] "Dirty Realism", as it was identified in 1983 by *Granta*'s editor Bill Buford, was predominantly characterized by writing that is "prod down to the plainest of plain styles"[11] via sentences that have been "stripped of adornment, and maintain complete control on the simple objects and events that they ask us to witness; it is what's not being said—the silences, the elisions, the omissions—that seems to speak most".[12] According to this line of reasoning, accessible language provides the opportunity to draw greater attention to the content and the themes of American literature. Further, Buford posits, this style of writing presented a form of expression that distinguished itself from previous styles. However, by stating that this style of writing, "is not only unlike anything currently written in Britain, but it is also remarkably unlike what American fiction is usually understood to be",[13] Buford also inherently negates how sparse writing about everyday experiences as well as silences and gaps in society was developing in Irish literature. However, while Irish writing and dirty realism in America may have utilized similar styles and themes, Buford's contention that dirty realism is comprised of "stories not of protest but of the occasion for it",[14] writing during "The Dublin Renaissance" directly addressed the social ills to indict their society for its complacency towards poverty and abuse.

Founded in 1984, John Sutton, John Dunne and Paul Mercier's theatre company, Passion Machine, provided an outlet for writing focussed on themes of everyday life and working-class struggles.[15] These themes, according to Mac Anna, helped to incorporate new audiences into the theatre. Therefore, Mac Anna's contention that "Mercier's plays *Home* (1988), *Wasters* (1985), *Spacers*(1986) and *Studs* (1986) and Roddy Doyle's plays, *Brownbread* (1987) and *War* (1989), brought to the stage many aspects of life in an area of Dublin which had been virtually ignored by Irish media and mainstream theatre",[16] concurred with Mercier's own denunciation of representation in the media that buttressed apathy towards corruption and abuse. While Mercier contended that "a lot of what goes on in life never gets documented in newspapers or news programmes",[17] he maintained that this is not a sufficient reason for complacency, but rather, "(w)e should always combat mediocrity, ignorance, in this world".[18] So while the preoccupation with despair, poverty and crime could serve as a critique of Ireland's social ills, it also uses these themes to expose submerged narratives concerned with inequality.

Although many working-class stories have developed their narratives through explorations of competition for power within the workforce, which can be found in Colm Maher's *Cleaners* (2014), with welfare, as in *God of the Hatch Man* by Rita Ann Higgins (1993) or with the effect of growing up in areas with high unemployment in plays such as Joe O'Byrne's *Gerrup!* (1988), a driving force of this literature is the mentality of the people who take part, either willingly or unwillingly, in their own sense of stasis. In Paul Mercier's *Home* (1988), protagonist Michael Sheehy leaves Westmeath to live in a new bedsit in Dublin as he searches for a job in hotel management. His desire for upward mobility is perpetuated by his motivational self-talk, which leads to him giving others the benefit of the doubt rather than seeing things for what they really are. This is apparent not only through his own sense of importance, "If ye think big, then you're big. Think important, then you're important",[19] but also by his inability to apply critical thinking to his circumstances. This essential shortcoming subsequently allows others to take advantage of his naivety and precludes him from acting on possible inequities that occur around him. Instead, he decides he will be "putting it all down to experience"[20] and look to the future where he "may have to handle a similar crisis. The value of it all may come to bear. But today… No today, I'm writing off my losses and starting out afresh."[21] From Michael's perspective, his attitude and outlook control the outcome of his life. However, this mentality precludes him from addressing the cyclical nature of his experiences, which maintains a sense of stasis in his career and prevents him from enjoying upward mobility, regardless of where he lives. This is apparent as Valentine questions his desire to work as a waiter in Dublin, just as he did in Westmeath. So while Michael argues that "I just want to work… just to be part of things again. Anyhow, I was a waiter long enough at home. I'm no stranger to it",[22] such a claim demonstrates his inability to recognise how he will not progress by fulfilling the same role no matter where he goes, as Valentine points out that Michael "came all the way up to this dive just to be what you were already down home".[23] It is important to note that, while leaving Westmeath may have provided an illusion of change, it takes an outside observation for Michael to confront his inability to achieve a sustainable path towards personal and professional progress.

However, while Michael's positive self-talk may have helped to perpetuate his sense of stasis, his own realization of the monotony in his life further serves as a recognition of the lack of change that has occurred, despite his new residence. This notion is emphasized when Michael comes to the realization he has, "been inside more rooms than a hotel. I ended up not remembering one from the other",[24] suggesting a recognizable monotony within the setting of his life. While authors have used their settings to depict concentrated areas of poverty, which can be seen in Aodhán Madden's *The Dosshouse Waltz* (1985) and Heno Magee's *I'm Getting Out of This Kip* (1972) and *Hatchet* (1972), a play that interrogates how violence and crime can be perpetuated by one's environment, setting, in this instance, can be used to emphasize repetitious cycles of thought and living. This is evidenced through the rooms of a hotel as well as the metaphorical significance of the building in which Michael is living. For, although Michael is a newcomer to the flat initially, the play ends with another new tenant in the flat, therefore bookending the story in order to give a cyclical impression of Irish society, whereby major issues are not addressed so that they may recur: "Landlord (entering) Ah, it's your good self. The new tenant appears out of No. 3. He's going out for the night. He looks cheerful and gives the impression that this is his first flat and that he is a free man now. He descends the stairs; looking about at his new home and then exits out the front door."[25] While, on the one hand, this new tenant is described as a free man, by giving him a similar attitude and outlook towards his new home as Michael, Mercier is insinuating that there is still a level of naivety that recurs throughout his generation, as the forces that perpetuate their lack of critical thinking remain intact.

To balance these themes of stagnation and corruption, Passion Machine also sought to explore the ordinary experiences of everyday Irish people in an effort to find a relatable middle ground with audiences. This was achieved by incorporating common activities such as pub quizzes in Roddy Doyle's *War* (1989) and football through Alan Archbold's *A Little Bit of Blue* (2005). By encompassing ordinary experiences with working-class experiences, Passion Machine was not only able to help develop the careers of those in day-jobs outside of the theatre, such as Roddy Doyle, Paul Mercier and Brendan Gleeson, who all worked as teachers in Greendale Community School in Kilbarrack,[26] but also enticed a new audience to attend the theatre, therefore diversifying the theatre both on and off the stage. Anglo-Irish literary scholar Declan Kiberd contends that the effect of this was to allow working-class citizens to see their lives represented in ways in which they previously would not have. Therefore, "when Passion Machine put on plays on the north side of Dublin about the life of the working class living on estates, people attended those plays who would have never dreamt of going to the Abbey Theatre, or who did not feel that their lives were depicted in that theatre".[27] One way in which writers were able to diversify the level of performers and audience members was to incorporate rock music into their shows. This can be exemplified through plays such as Mercier's *Drowning* (1984), a rock musical set in a housing estate and Anto Nolan's *Too Much Too Young* (1995) where ska music presents a moment of unification for working-class individuals. More specifically, Wet Paint Theatre Company emerged to incorporate punk rock music and punk characters into productions such as: *Camberwell Beauty* (1982), where protagonist Netta is excommunicated from her punk rock community after she undergoes plastic surgery; *Plastic Zion* (1982), which centres on the experience of a washed-up musician; and *Cat Food* (1984), a play concerning female punk rockers who try to convert a squat into a women's refuge. Moreover, Wet Paint also emphasized the value of performing in venues that are easily accessible to working-class audiences. For example, Dermot Bolger's *The Lament for Arthur Cleary* (1989), a play, "Loosely having its origins in a re-imagining of the great Gaelic poem, Caoineadh Airt Ui Laoghaire (The Lament for Art O'Leary)",[28] was dominated by issues of emigration and poverty and was performed by Wet Paint Arts at the Project Arts Centre.[29,30] As such, Victor Merriman contends that the location of the performances reduces a gap between the theatre and those whose stories they tell. In this instance, *The Lament for Arthur Cleary* "was commissioned by Wet Paint Arts for performance to audiences in various locations in the many Dublin suburbs which subsist as economic, social and cultural wilderness. (T)he play accepts the challenge of testing the poem's assertions with audiences for whom dispossession, exile and fruitless return are experiences first, metaphor second."[31] As such, plays were emerging to incorporate alternative narratives and performed in locations that matched their respective themes and content. Therefore, a thematic link can be found amongst the writers via their focus on the hegemonic structures of Irish society and the attitude of the people that helped to preserve it.

Among the many examples of this is Bolger's 1990 play, *The Holy Ground*. Winner of the Edinburgh Fringe First Award, *The Holy Ground* is a one-act monologue told by Monica, a woman whose increasingly oppressive marriage to her sterile husband, Myles, serves as an indictment of the naturalization of received ideas used to silence women into predetermined roles as mothers and wives. While Bolger has explored the repercussions of social expectations endured by women in stories such as *A Second Life* (1994 and 2010), which illustrates the emotional ramifications of Ireland's adoption policies on both birthmothers and their children, and *The Family on Paradise Pier* (2005), which examines the downfall of a failed marriage in an age and place where divorce is still illegal, *The Holy Ground* (1990) demonstrates protagonist Monica's eventual retaliation against the expectations imposed upon her by the men in her life.[32] At twenty-three years of age, Monica meets Myles amongst a slew of men who either view women as objects or as prey.[33] By illustrating her experiences with abusive men, Bolger establishes an initial justification for her choice to be with the ostensibly innocent Myles, who is initially characterized through boyish features: "a little boy in a big jersey clutching your shin-pads like trophies".[34] Although Myles's youthful demeanour may appear to be his most attractive quality, another dynamic of his personality that enticed Monica is that their relationship conforms to received ideas of what women should want to want. This is demonstrated through the subsequent lack of fulfilment endured by conforming to pre-set expectations as Monica states that her home and her husband were "All I had ever been taught to dream of."[35] The word "taught" is significant insofar as it illustrates a recurring idea of not thinking for herself. This is demonstrated as Monica reveals a dissatisfaction with her life as she possessed "everything I had been taught to pray for… except a child and the love of a man."[36] A dichotomy has been created here, whereby, on the one hand, Monica is living according to the expectations that have been ingrained in her. However, on the other hand, her husband's sterility thwarts them from fulfilling these expectations completely. Such sterility serves as a catalyst for Monica to question the received ideas embedded in her society for women while also propelling Myles into a role as spokesman for conservative values, which he uses to overcompensate for his sterility. So while Monica may have previously asserted that "There was no harm in him",[37] politics, for Myles, provide him with the illusion of power and control where her choice of dress and makeup was increasingly scrutinized.[38] Such an indictment of Myles's conservative views recognizes the contrast between Ireland's moral and religious expectations and the underlying immoral acts used to perpetuate submission to these expectations.[39] As a result of her husband's staunch beliefs, Monica is plunged into a false sense of anonymity as she notes that her husband barely acknowledged her: "Did I exist at all? When we were alone you'd talk to the evening paper."[40] This is due, in part, to Myles's intent to assert his dominance by advocating Ireland's stringent censorship policies: "(O)h, you thrived on that anger, touring bookshops, being abused by cinema queues. No lover could have given you such pleasure".[41] Although sterility may have provided a catalyst for Monica and Myles to diverge in their sense of identity, their struggles with changing identity can also depict a larger struggle with Irish national identity. Moreover, it can also serve as an indictment of the Censorship of Publications Act 1929, which was created in order to ban literature, "as including suggestive of, or inciting to sexual immorality or unnatural vice or likely in any other similar way to corrupt or deprave",[42] therefore making it illegal "to print or publish or cause or procure to be printed or published in relation to any judicial proceedings—(a) any indecent matter the publication of which would be calculated to injure public morals".[43] This notion was bolstered by the work of the Catholic Church post-independence as, "The government of the Free State was shaky and insecure and, if it was to survive, it had to find a truly unifying theme to rally a divided population. The Catholic faith was to provide that required social glue."[44] From this point, censorship could primarily be seen as a result of "Church-driven attempts to manage the behaviours of the populace by controlling the communications landscape. The agenda pursued by the Church ensured that whilst the 1920s was an era of censorship across the whole of the Western world, Irish censorship was particularly punitive, at least in terms of a state with a democratic political system."[45] Consequently, some of Ireland's most celebrated writers, including James Joyce, Sean O'Casey, Frank O'Connor and Samuel Beckett, were on the list of banned authors,[46] therefore making it onto the list of censored writers became an "inverted badge of honour".[47] As such, Bolger's depiction of the conflict between Myles's avocation of censorship and Monica's dwindling sense of self, ironically, demonstrates the ability of theatre to illustrate the psychological effect of policies that seek to limit their rights of expression.

The ability to pinpoint the effect of social issues can subsequently lead to the notion that drama was developing a different role. Writing in reference to the drama from 1945 to 1970, literary scholar Ronald Peacock contended, "The drama continues to be evolved from the exacerbated criticism of a heavily imperfect individual and social world; and the disintegration of fixed moral points continues. There is no restoration of the old-established genres, which had their well-defined social function and moral colouring. The aim is always diagnosis",[48] suggesting that writers were deviating from established forms to, instead, use their work to determine the nature of their society. Therefore, drama, according to Peacock: "becomes now to a large extent a mimesis giving not rules, nor dogma, nor panaceas, but evidence. The function of the dramatist is to project this evidence, not as pleading for a specific principle but as unvarnished truth."[49] By contrast, Michael Riffaterre argues that "truth in fiction rests on verisimilitude, a system of representations that seems to reflect a reality external to the text, but only because it conforms to a grammar",[50] therefore maintaining that truth can be accepted as such when it adheres to pre-conditioned expectations. In regard to Bolger's work, however, describing a perspective of the truth about Ireland's social and legal restrictions is a side effect of illustrating how perceptions of truth both coincide with and work against the struggles endured by Ireland's underclass. So while writers can attempt to project the evidence they find to support their central ideas, Irish writing in the 1980s and early 1990s did not merely attempt to diagnose the psychological impact of enforced social norms that have been used to mediate perceptions of reality, but it also illuminated the potential for liberation from these socially and legally enforced restrictions.

For example, while Monica may have conformed to expectations that were historically enforced by her society as well as her marriage to Myles, it is important to note that Monica was not actually a receptacle for received ideas; rather, she was still seeking to fight the forces that oppressed her. As such, her attempt to kill Myles by putting rat poison in his stew[51] could demonstrate, among many things, her ability to act on her own volition. Though the violence in plays such as Peter Gowen's *The Stone Pickers* (1988) and Liam Lynch's *Voids* (1982) can be used to address how cyclical experiences can become a catalyst for violence, attempted murder in Monica's case allows Bolger to show that she is actually supporting the same hegemonic structures she thinks she is fighting against. This is supported by the realization that the Warfarin within rat poison "prevents clotting and thins out the blood",[52] and actually prolonged Myles's life since he suffered from thrombosis.[53] As a result of both her oppressive marriage to Myles and her inability to kill him, Monica submits to the feeling that she has not only lost her identity, but also her soul in the process noting that she "will die unmourned"[54] as Myles "had stolen my Christ away from me".[55] Although these dour final sentiments could address Monica's personal losses, Mireia Aragay contends that Myles's death is indicative of the death of traditional Ireland, and the values those traditions represent: "It is after Monica comes across the defiant little girl in the supermarket wearing the badge that says 'Spuc Off' that she publicly announces that it is a long time since Myles has been dead, that is, the ideology he embodies is obsolete. And as she recounts the story of her life, Monica is clearing the house of any trace of Myles and his stand for traditional Ireland."[56] While on the one hand, Myles's death may signify the end of his traditional values, it also heralds a new source of expression for Monica as, ironically, she is left to speak for him as the keeper of his memory.

Consequently, the monologue is intertwined with competing characters; they are embodied through Monica, who strives to tell her own story through the voices and accents of supporting characters.[57] The result of this is her lingering feelings of voicelessness that are expressed, in part, by her own voice. Taken further, this contrast extends beyond the text to the author himself, who founded Raven Arts Press in an effort to launch work that addressed submerged narratives in Irish society; a venture that also pervaded theatre via Wet Paint and Passion Machine.[58] Such a period with the fecundity for the production of writing that attacks complacency towards oppression during a period of political corruption and high unemployment underlines the potential for writers to combat stagnation by integrating voices and narratives that trouble conventional perspectives. Subsequently, with the dramatic socioeconomic fluctuations brought on by the Celtic Tiger and its crash, such narratives of disillusionment and hardship share continuing relevance that are bound to be incorporated by different voices as more people become effected by political corruption and economic instability. As such, inequality is the catalyst for direct action towards change, not the avoidance of it.

Notes

1. "Ireland and the EU 1973–2003 Economic and Social Change", in *Statistical Yearbook of Ireland 2004 Edition* (Dublin: The Stationery Office, 2004), xiv, doi: http://www.cso.ie/en/media/csoie/releasespublications/documents/statisticalyearbook/2004/statisticalyearbook2004.pdf.
2. "Population and Migration Estimates", *Central Statistics Office*, last modified September 15, 2011, doi: http://www.cso.ie/en/media/csoie/releases publications/documents/population/2011/Population_and_Migration_Estimates_April_2011.pdf.

3. Charles Haughey served from 1979 to 1981; 1982; and 1987 to 1992 and Garret Fitzgerald served from 1981 to 1982 and 1982 to 1987.
4. Nicholas Rees, "The Irish Economy and Europe", in *Europeanisation and New Patterns of Governance in Ireland*, eds. Nicholas Rees, Bríd Quinn, Bernadette Connaughton (Manchester and New York: Manchester University Press, 2009), 92, accessed February 15, 2016, doi: https://books.google.co.uk/books.
5. Nicholas Rees, "The Irish Economy and Europe", 92.
6. Several investigations, including the Tribunal of Inquiry into the Beef Processing Industry, the McCracken Tribunal and the Moriarty Tribunal investigated possible acts of corruption by Haughey. The Moriarty Tribunal, which took fourteen years, was eventually successful in identifying "a money trail leading to Haughey" (Murphy 2006, 101) who "received (about) £8.5 million in donations over a sixteen-year period" (Murphy 2006, 101).
7. Tom O'Connor, "The Structural Failure of Irish Economic Development and Employment Policy", *Irish Journal of Public Policy* 2, no. 1, (2010): par. 23, doi: http://publish.ucc.ie/ijpp/2010/01/tomoconnor/03/en.
8. Tom O'Connor, "The Structural Failure of Irish Economic Development and Employment Policy", par. 24.
9. Thomas R. Bates, "Gramsci and the Theory of Hegemony", *Journal of the History of Ideas* 36, no. 2 (1975): 351, accessed March 1, 2016, http://www.jstor.org/stable/2708933?seq=1#page_scan_tab_contents.
10. Ferdia Mac Anna, "The Dublin Renaissance: An Essay on Modern Dublin and Dublin Writers", *The Irish Review*, no. 10 (1991): 29, accessed March 1, 2016, http://www.jstor.org/stable/29735579.
11. Bill Buford, "Editorial", *Granta* 8, (1983): par. 3, doi: https://granta.com/dirtyrealism/.
12. Buford, "Editorial", par. 3.
13. Buford, "Editorial", par. 1.
14. Buford, "Editorial," par. 4.
15. Mac Anna, "The Dublin Renaissance: An Essay on Modern Dublin and Dublin Writers", 24.
16. Mac Anna, "The Dublin Renaissance: An Essay on Modern Dublin and Dublin Writers", 24.
17. Mercier in Declan Hassett, "Passion Machine: Playing in the Alternative League", *Cork Examiner* (1991): 13, accessed March 12, 2016, doi: http://www.corkpastandpresent.ie/culture/theatre/1991/newspapers/1991_10_29_studs.pdf
18. Mercier in Hassett, "Passion Machine: Playing in the Alternative League", 13.
19. Paul Mercier, "Home" (Dublin: Passion Machine Ltd., 1989), 78.
20. Mercier, "Home", 78.
21. Mercier, "Home", 78.
22. Mercier, "Home", 64.
23. Mercier, "Home", 64.
24. Mercier, "Home", 77.
25. Mercier, "Home", 106.
26. Ciara Dwyer, "The Cruel Business of Theatre", *Independent*, accessed February 11, 2016, doi: http://www.independent.ie/woman/celeb-news/the-cruel-business-of-theatre-26241686.html.
27. Declan Kiberd, "Declan Kiberd Interviewed by Jacqueline Hurtley", in *Ireland in Writing Interviews with Writers and Academics* (Amsterdam-Atlanta GA:

Rodopi, 1998), 160, https://books.google.co.uk/books?id=WgRFqupfW4IC&lpg=PA160&vq=passion%20machine%20ireland&dq=passion%20machine%20ireland&pg=PA160#v=snippet&q=passion%20machine%20ireland&f=false.

28. "The Lament for Arthur Cleary", Dermotbolger.com, accessed May 17, 2017, http://dermotbolger.com/plays_lamentforarthurcleary.htm.
29. Wet Paint Arts, a company devoted to promoting and increasing the accessibility of theatre to underprivileged young people, also functioned in conjunction with Wet Paint Theatre.
30. "The Lament for Arthur Cleary", Dermotbolger.com, n.d., http://dermotbolger.com/plays_lamentforarthurcleary.htm.
31. Victor Merriman, "Staging Contemporary Ireland: Heartsickness and Hopes Deferred", in *The Cambridge Companion to Twentieth-Century Irish Drama*, ed. Shaun Richards (Cambridge: Cambridge University Press, 2004), 249, https://books.google.co.uk/books?id=7LMZBAAAQBAJ&pg=PA245&lpg=PA245&dq=David+Byrne+wet+paint&source=bl&ots=-bbGSVO81F&sig=b-zbbyL1c1s14V6jPeSt6SI1Az4&hl=en&sa=X&ved=0ahUKEwiX0Yn5vuXKAhVEmg4KHU6IDg0Q6AEIIjAB#v=onepage&q=wet%20paint&f=false.
32. *A Second Life* was originally published in 1994 and rewritten and republished in 2010.
33. Dermot Bolger, "The Holy Ground", in *Plays: 1: "Lament for Arthur Cleary", "In High Germany", "The Holy Ground", "Blinded by the Light"* (London: Bloomsbury Methuen Drama, 2000), 103.
34. Bolger, "The Holy Ground", 105.
35. Bolger, "The Holy Ground", 114.
36. Bolger, "The Holy Ground", 116.
37. Bolger, "The Holy Ground", 117.
38. Bolger, "The Holy Ground", 118.
39. Damien Shortt, "'Who put the ball in the English net?': The Privatisation of Irish Postnationalism in Dermot Bolger's *In High Germany*", in *Redefinitions of Irish Identity: A Postnationalist Approach*, eds. Irene Gilsenan Nordin and Carmen Zamorano Llena (Oxford: Peter Lang, 2010), 116–17, accessed March 24, 2016, https://books.google.co.uk/books?id=Hj71Va_qefQC&pg=PA115&lpg=PA115&dq=the+holy+ground+play+bolger&source=bl&ots=eN-WjEmLnf&sig=egdLBIajRvV3aMO8ADAjszumWzQ&hl=en&sa=X&ved=0ahUKEwienoya1qbLAhXHtxoKHTzXAn4Q6AEINDAE#v=onepage&q=the%20holy%20ground%20play%20bolger&f=false.
40. Bolger, "The Holy Ground", 119.
41. Bolger, "The Holy Ground", 119.
42. "Censorship of Publications Act 1929", *Irish Statute Book*, par. 8, accessed February 15, 2016, http://www.irishstatutebook.ie/1929/en/act/pub/0021/print.html#sec6.
43. "Censorship of Publications Act 1929", par. 63–64.
44. Anthony Keating "Church, State, and Sexual Crime against Children in Ireland after 1922", *Radharc* 5, no. 7 (2004–2006): 157, accessed March 1, 2016, http://www.jstor.org/stable/pdf/25122348.pdf.
45. Keating "Church, State, and Sexual Crime against Children in Ireland after 1922", 159.
46. Donal Ó Drisceoil, "'The best banned in the land': Censorship and Irish Writing since 1950", *Modern Humanities Research Association* 35, (2005): 148. Accessed March 1, 2016, http://www.jstor.org/stable/3509330?seq=1&uid=3738032&uid=2&uid=4&sid=21103509944251.

47. Ó Drisceoil, "'The best banned in the land'", 157.
48. Ronald Peacock, "Drama and the Moral Connexion", *The Modern Language Review* 78.4 (1983): xxxi, accessed March 1, 2016, http://www.jstor.org/stable/pdf/3729598.pdf http://www.jstor.org/stable/pdf/3729598.pdf.
49. Peacock, "Drama and the Moral Connexion", xxxi.
50. Michael Riffaterre, *Fictional Truth*, (Baltimore: The Johns Hopkins University Press, 1990), xiii–xiv.
51. Bolger, "The Holy Ground", 122.
52. Bolger, "The Holy Ground", 124.
53. Bolger, "The Holy Ground", 124
54. Bolger, "The Holy Ground", 125.
55. Bolger, "The Holy Ground", 125.
56. Mireia Aragay, "Reading Dermot Bolger's *The Holy Ground:* National Identity, Gender and Sexuality in Post-Colonial Ireland", *Links & Letters* 4, (1997): 63, accessed March 1, 2016, http://www.raco.cat/index.php/linksletters/article/viewFile/49870/87845.
57. Bolger, "The Holy Ground", 106.
58. Bolger founded Raven Arts Press, which ran from 1977 to 1992.

Bibliography

Aragay, Mireia. "Reading Dermot Bolger's *The Holy Ground:* National Identity, Gender and Sexuality in Post-Colonial Ireland." *Links & Letters* 4, (1997): 53–64. Accessed March 12, 2016. http://www.raco.cat/index.php/linksletters/article/viewFile/49870/87845.

Bates, Thomas R. "Gramsci and the Theory of Hegemony." *Journal of the History of Ideas* 36, no. 2 (1975): 351–366. Accessed March 1, 2016. http://www.jstor.org/stable/2708933?seq=1#page_scan_tab_contents.

Bolger, Dermot. "The Holy Ground." In *Plays: 1: "Lament for Arthur Cleary", "In High Germany", "The Holy Ground", "Blinded by the Light"*, 101–125. London: Bloomsbury Methuen Drama, 2000.

Buford, Bill. "Editorial." *Granta*, 8 (1983). Accessed February 1, 2016. https://granta.com/dirtyrealism/.

"Censorship of Publications Act 1929." *Irish Statute Book*. Accessed February 15, 2016. http://www.irishstatutebook.ie/1929/en/act/pub/0021/print.html#sec6.

Dwyer, Ciara. "The Cruel Business of Theatre." *Independent*. Accessed February 11, 2016. http://www.independent.ie/woman/celeb-news/the-cruel-business-of-theatre-26241686.html.

Hassett, Declan. "Passion Machine: Playing in the Alternative League." *Cork Examiner*. Accessed March 12, 2016. http://www.corkpastandpresent.ie/culture/theatre/1991/newspapers/1991_10_29_studs.pdf.

"Ireland and the EU 1973–2003 Economic and Social Change." In *Statistical Yearbook of Ireland 2004 Edition*, v–xvii. Dublin: The Stationery Office, 2004. doi: http://www.cso.ie/en/media/csoie/releasespublications/documents/statisticalyearbook/2004/statisticalyearbook2004.pdf.

Keating, Anthony. "Church, State, and Sexual Crime Against Children in Ireland After 1922." *Radharc* 5, no. 7 (2004–2006): 155–180. Accessed March 1, 2016. http://www.jstor.org/stable/pdf/25122348.pdf.

Kiberd, Declan. "Declan Kiberd Interviewed by Jacqueline Hurtley." In *Ireland in Writing Interviews with Writers and Academics*, 143–176. Amsterdam-Atlanta, GA:

Rodopi, 1998. https://books.google.co.uk/books?id=WgRFqupfW4IC&pg=PA160&lpg=PA160&dq=passion+machine+ireland&source=bl&ots=nunmBAeMzT&sig=gK9aVHITR3FuS_nXv-K2-Ah2kMQ&hl=en&sa=X&ved=0ahUKEwjclqrY1f7JAhUCyRoKHcWaBzMQ6AEIQjAG#v=onepage&q=passion%20machine%20ireland&f=false.

"The Lament for Arthur Cleary." Dermotbolger.com. Accessed May 17, 2017. http://dermotbolger.com/plays_lamentforarthurcleary.htm.

Mac Anna, Ferdia. "The Dublin Renaissance: An Essay on Modern Dublin and Dublin Writers." In *The Irish Review*, no. 10 (1991): 14–30. Accessed March 1, 2016. http://www.jstor.org/stable/29735579.

Mercier, Paul. *Home*. Dublin: Passion Machine Ltd., 1989.

Merriman, Vic. "Staging Contemporary Ireland: Heartsickness and Hopes Deferred." In *The Cambridge Companion to Twentieth-Century Irish Drama*, edited by Shaun Richards, 244–257. Cambridge: Cambridge University Press, 2004. https://books.google.co.uk/books?id=7LMZBAAAQBAJ&pg=PA245&lpg=PA245&dq=David+Byrne+wet+paint&source=bl&ots=-bbGSVO81F&sig=b-zbbyL1c1s14V6jPeSt6SI1Az4&hl=en&sa=X&ved=0ahUKEwiX0Yn5vuXKAhVEmg4KHU6IDg0Q6AEIIjAB#v=onepage&q=wet%20paint&f=false.

Murphy, Gary. "Payments for No Political Response? Political Corruption and Tribunals of Inquiry in Ireland, 1991–2003." In *Scandals in Past and Contemporary Politics*, edited by John Garrard and James L. Newell, 91–105. Manchester and New York: Manchester University Press, 2006.

O'Connor, Tom. "The Structural Failure of Irish Economic Development and Employment Policy." *Irish Journal of Public Policy* 2, no. 1 (2010), doi: http://publish.ucc.ie/ijpp/2010/01/tomoconnor/03/en.

Ó Drisceoil, Donal. "'The Best Banned in the Land': Censorship and Irish Writing Since 1950." *Modern Humanities Research Association* 35, (2005): 146–160. Accessed March 1, 2016. http://www.jstor.org/stable/3509330?seq=1&uid=3738032&uid=2&uid=4&sid=21103509944251.

Peacock, Ronald. "Drama and the Moral Connexion." *The Modern Language Review* 78, no. 4 (1983): xxiii–xxxii. Accessed March 1, 2016. http://www.jstor.org/stable/pdf/3729598.pdf.

"Population and Migration Estimates." *Central Statistics Office*. Last modified September 15, 2011. http://www.cso.ie/en/media/csoie/releasespublications/documents/population/2011/Population_and_Migration_Estimates_April_2011.pdf.

Rees, Nicholas. "The Irish Economy and Europe." In *Europeanisation and New Patterns of Governance in Ireland*, edited by Nicholas Rees, Bríd Quinn, Bernadette Connaughton, 80–102. Manchester and New York: Manchester University Press, 2009. Accessed February 15, 2016. https://books.google.co.uk/books.

Riffaterre, Michael. *Fictional Truth*. Baltimore: The Johns Hopkins University Press, 1990.

Shortt, Damien. "'Who Put the Ball in the English Net?': The Privatisation of Irish Postnationalism in Dermot Bolger's *In High Germany*." In *Redefinitions of Irish Identity: A Postnationalist Approach*, edited by Irene Gilsenan Nordin and Carmen Zamorano Llena, 103–124. Oxford: Peter Lang, 2010. Accessed March 24, 2016. https://books.google.co.uk/books?id=Hj71Va_qefQC&pg=PA115&lpg=PA115&dq=the+holy+ground+play+bolger&source=bl&ots=eN-WjEmLnf&sig=egdLBIajRvV3aMO8ADAjszumWzQ&hl=en&sa=X&ved=0ahUKEwienoya1qbLAhXHtxoKHTzXAn4Q6AEINDAE#v=onepage&q=the%20holy%20ground%20play%20bolger&f=false.

The Utilization of Domestic Space in the Reflection of Social and Economic Struggles of Modern Living in Conor McPherson's New Translation of *The Nest*

Maha Alatawi

The portrayal of ordinary human emotions and struggles has long underpinned the work of Conor McPherson. In a co-production with the Young Vic Theatre, London, a new adaptation by McPherson of Franz Xaver Kroetz's *Das Nest* was premiered at the Lyric Theatre in Belfast on 1 October 2016. Kroetz's original play was performed in 1970s Germany in response to the post-war revival of the country's economy and the rise of capitalist consumerism. It is often analysed as a reflection on the rise of Nazism and contemporary inaction against tyranny. However, a contemporary version has been written by McPherson to correspond with the financial upheavals of contemporary Ireland and elsewhere, and the inequitable social impact of global economic growth.

Driven by human instincts of survival, an expectant couple Kurt and Martha, played respectively by Laurence Kinlan and Caoilfhionn Dunne, are struggling to make ends meet. Kurt is a lorry driver who, as Martha constantly complains, takes on any work he is offered: "Any chance of a few euros and you're gone."[1] Martha, on the other hand, works from home, conducting surveys on banking practices for Incorporated Research Group Limited. Their jobs are not lucrative or sufficient to sustain their fundamental needs. One window through which Kurt gets to gain more money is opened when his boss secretly offers him 200 euros for disposing unconsumed wine into a lake.

M. Alatawi (✉)
University College Dublin, Dublin, Ireland

E. Jordan, E. Weitz (eds.), *The Palgrave Handbook of Contemporary Irish Theatre and Performance*,
https://doi.org/10.1057/978-1-137-58588-2_50

The Nest explores the interplay of public and private spheres, reinforcing financial and social conflicts through the portrayal of a family home. On space in Irish theatre, Nicholas Grene states that "[t]he naturalistic home on the stage, as conceived by Zola and realised by Ibsen, figures both the outer world that surrounds it and the interiority of the private lives it houses".[2] In this performance, the home of the family is placed in the midst of a representational world of the exterior. On how she approached the set design, Alyson Cummins explains: "I was interested in the idea that no matter how we try to control everything we cannot live in a hermetically sealed and controllable environment. We must exist within the world and within society and the more Kurt and Martha fought against that the more difficult their lives were."[3]

Every spot of stage space is occupied by an engaging miniature of domestic and public places. Stage left, a long tree casts its shadow over the couple's small apartment which encapsulates the very essence of the play's title. Indicative of the couple's financial status, the apartment is poorly furnished, with a sofa bed serving a dual purpose and a small kitchen with a dining table. There is also a sky-blue curtain in the middle as a part of the bathroom which later appears to indicate the presence of a hospital. Cummins explains: "I started to think of all of the new-build developer-led apartment blocks which have cropped up in our cities and are often pretty uninhabitable places. These are buildings conceived as a money making exercise rather than a community driven development and their architecture reflects this."[4]

The stage-edge facing the audience is used to show a rocky side of a lake. The stage is continuous with the auditorium, as the audience space represents the lake itself. The couple's allotment is also within the scope of the audience's view; the spot is uncovered by two upward doors in the stage floor opened to reveal a small compartment. Una Chaudhuri proposes a kind of spatiality she calls "platiality" in which "the signifying power and political potential of specific places" and their relations are recognized.[5] Cummins' deft design captures a limitless image of the play and the spaces it occupies.

The represented living space is supplemented by materialized outside spaces. In this first production of McPherson's translation, the stage space is utilized not only to serve the different locales in the plot, but, more importantly, to show how Kurt and Martha's domestic nest is connected to other external environments and is influenced by them. The visibility of such private and public spaces on the stage, bearing in mind the possibility of using off-stage references instead, confirms the vicinities of their connection. Domestic life is inseparable from surrounding social and economic forces. During a blackout accompanied with music, Kurt appears holding a hose across the stage (the couple's apartment) to the auditorium (the lake) to enact the disposing of the wine while Martha is in the bedroom standing beside the baby's crib. By this, the outside world is brought into the home, which is also evident in the mould creeping up the bottom of the kitchen. The pollution of the lake in the play is not only environmental; in fact, its danger reaches their house, contaminating their private space and putting everyone's life in jeopardy; as his new-born son,

Stephan, suffers severe burns and Martha's hands are burned too, all from that poisonous lake. Greed, which can be seen as the motive behind Kurt's deed and also his boss's deceit, is a social disease and its menace exceeds that of simply polluting environment.

During the second scene, Martha sits at the dining table with a shopping list, files, laptop and commercial pictures of products. She is soon joined by her husband and their dialogue about maternity and baby gadgets, such items as they feel a need to purchase. The evolution of economy and the variety of products that makes life much easier necessitate finding ways to make money keep pace with mainstream living standards. Yet such up-to-date products are not clearly accessible to everyone. In this sense, the particular demands created by modernity and consumerism on parents are highlighted in this scene, and the desire to do one's best by their children. The more features buggies have, the more expensive they are. Bottle warmers save "loads of time apparently—especially in the middle of the night". At some point, they agree that their child will ask for "his own iPad so he can watch his programmes" and they will need a Samsung washing machine.

In *The Nest*, Kurt finds it difficult to keep up with the increasing needs of his family although he works relentlessly and, because he is so overworked, cannot enjoy days off work. In fact, his overwork is never sufficient to satisfy present-day financial requirements. In the scene when the couple are sitting on the lakeside, Kurt talks of how he prefers to work on the one day he has off in six months. Time, for Kurt, is money; a capitalist value imposed not only on Kurt but also on anyone of his social status. As such, he is tempted by the money he stands to get from the secret job he is doing for his boss, succumbs to the temptation of illegal financial gain, and unknowingly commits a crime by dumping the pollutant into the lake.

Because the whole story initially revolves around the financial implications of the coming of a baby, there is but the illusion of that baby created through the mimetic handling of an invisible child. Yet Dunne's Martha plays pregnancy very realistically. There is no doubt around the existence of a baby in the way she cuddles and speaks to him. (In the London production of 1986, the baby was played by a bunting, while in the New York production of 1989 it was a real baby.) Kinlan's Kurt displays all the characteristics essential to this role, bringing back to memory the skill with which he played Doc in McPherson's 2015 production *The Night Alive* (A Dublin Theatre Festival-Lyric Theatre co-production.) Amusing, pitiful, greedy, determined and understanding are qualities incorporated by Kinlan to build his likeable, engaging character. The most hair-raising moments in the performance are Kurt's screams during the drowning scene. This moment is very expressive of feelings of humiliation, regret, fear and helplessness. Kurt's suicidal acts, by hanging and cutting himself towards the end, creates such tension in the performance that I find it hard to exhale, but Martha's calm entrance puts an end to such tension. Suicide seems, at such a moment, to be a pathological response to problems and failures. Kurt's unsuccessful attempts at suicide are, thus, apparently attributable to his failure in his responsibilities as the breadwinner of his family as well as his feelings of guilt, humiliation and frustration, afflictions caused by the overwhelming pressures of twenty-first-century living, consumer capitalism.

As laughter flees the stage after the wounding of their son, humour is provoked again after Kurt's three attempts of suicide as he sarcastically comments "Yeah, well, I couldn't do it anyway. I've been dicking round here for an hour. An ape doesn't know how to kill himself". This particular shift from comedy to tragedy and then back to comedy has a key bearing upon the couple's reconciliation in final scenes. Kurt's apparent gullibility, evident in the way the actor speaks and acts, has been exploited by his boss who tricks him regarding the danger of the dumped wine. His somehow inadvertent complicity in this unlawful task has affected his own family. During a café scene, the comparison his boss makes between himself as a "big sausage" and Kurt as a "little sausage" has a double purpose. Not only does it illustrate the social disparity between the low status of Kurt compared to that of his boss, but it also provides a moment of humorous relief, provoking laughter from many in the auditorium.

Being a destitute lorry driver will cost him so much more compared to the losses accruing to his superior. When Kurt threatens to go to the police, his boss uses the condition of his injured son and his vulnerability regarding future employment to talk him out of it. Yet Kurt manages to somehow challenge the power of his boss when he informs the police. Kurt's intention is never destructive but rather corrective because, he realizes, "[i]t'll always be someone else. That is the problem!"[6] Both the prevention of such crimes alongside a desire for change incentives Kurt to take this action.

An appraisal of McPherson's work can never sidestep the congruity of his work to the ordinary cadences of contemporary life. Trapped in an endless cycle of poorly paid work and financial exploitation by superiors, couples like Kurt and Martha struggle to make a living. Yet human survival and resilience are obtainable endeavours; by the play's end as the seeds Kurt plants at the beginning start to grow in their small garden, as Stephan their son, who is now thriving, is watched playing around by his parents.

Typical of a McPherson play, audiences are urged to look beyond the domestic issues into the larger scale of current political, economic and social conditions. In his final words—"You've got to finish what you start"—Kurt strives for an honourable way to correct the wrong in a world where monetary assets are mostly valued over human dignity.

Notes

1. Conor McPherson, *The Nest* (Nick Hern Books: London, 2016), 24.
2. Nicholas Grene, *Home on The Stage: Domestic Spaces in Modern Drama* (UK: Cambridge University Press, 2014), 2.
3. Alyson Cummins, "Re: 5-minute interview," Received by Maha Alatawi. 30 April 2017. E-mail.

4. Ibid.
5. Una Chaudhuri, *Staging Place: The Geography of Modern Drama* (USA: The University of Michigan Press, 1997), 5.
6. McPherson, *The Nest*, 36.

Bibliography

Chaudhuri, Una. *Staging Place: The Geography of Modern Drama*. USA: The University of Michigan Press, 1997.

Cummins, Alyson. "Re: 5-minute Interview." Received by Maha Alatawi. 30 April 2017. E-mail.

Grene, Nicholas. *Home on the Stage: Domestic Spaces in Modern Drama*. Cambridge University Press, 2014.

McPherson, Conor. *The Nest*. Nick Hern Books: London, 2016.

———. *The Nest* directed by Ian Rickson. Perf. Laurence Kinlan and Caoilfhionn Dunne. Lyric Theatre, Belfast. October 16, 2013.

Audiences: Immersive and Participatory

Ciara L. Murphy

This chapter investigates contemporary participative and immersive audiences in Irish performance, examining performance companies located both north and south of the border. The relationship between the rise of immersive and participatory performance paradigms and the heightened focus on memory and performing memory is particularly pertinent to this study. This research builds on Emilie Pine's *The Politics of Irish Memory* by connecting remembrance in contemporary Ireland to the growing popularity of immersive and participative performance, thus establishing a link between the rise of both paradigms. This chapter will outline several examples of immersive and participative performance as a means of contextualizing its argument.

What constitutes an audience? Recognising that there is no definitive means of answering this question, I outline and analyse key critical theories in relation to audiences in order to interrogate and discuss criteria as to what constitutes participative and immersed audiences in contemporary performance contexts. Reflecting upon the changing performance paradigms in contemporary Irish performance since the 1950s, my analysis considers the rise of participative and immersive theatre practice from the 1990s onwards and the connection of this to the performance of memory. I note that the emergence of Performance and Live Art in the North of Ireland in the 1970s marked the true beginning of this rise and reflect on how the emergence of participative performance paradigms coincide with instances of cultural trauma on the island. Siobhán O'Gorman marks the 1950s as a "stage of revision",[1] citing the establishment of bodies like the Arts Council and the beginnings of the Dublin Theatre Festival as a turning point in Irish performance. I chart the changing role of Irish audiences from "viewer" to "witness", interrogating the impact of this redefinition of audience roles. It is vital to contemplate the genre of immersive

C. L. Murphy (✉)
NUI Galway, Galway, Ireland

E. Jordan, E. Weitz (eds.), *The Palgrave Handbook of Contemporary Irish Theatre and Performance*,
https://doi.org/10.1057/978-1-137-58588-2_51

theatre specifically, outlining and defining key aspects of this performance paradigm, and asking what constitutes immersion for an audience member. Central to my argument is the link between participative and immersive performance with site-specific or site-responsive settings, exploring the impact these have on audiences. I conclude by focusing on "audience agency", exploring the political value of audience agency, and interrogating what Louise Lowe, co-Artistic Director of ANU Productions, refers to as "moments of communion" between the audience and the performer.[2]

What Constitutes an Audience?

Before delving into the defining characteristics of "participatory" and "immersive" audiences, it must first be asked "what constitutes an audience?" Susan Bennett draws significantly from Grotowski in *Theatre Audiences*, where Grotowski poses and answers the question "can theatre exist without an audience? At least one spectator is needed to make it a performance."[3] By foregrounding his position in *Theatre Audiences*, Bennett is reinforcing the importance of the role of the spectator in performance, and Grotowski's claim that without the presence of at least one audience member, a performance cannot exist. Dennis Kennedy adopts a different approach to the definition of audience in *The Spectator and The Spectacle*. Kennedy begins his investigation of the spectator by stating "almost anything one can say about a spectator is false on some level".[4] Kennedy thus outlines the subjectivity of a spectator's response to a performance or spectacle. Differentiating between an "audience" and a "spectator", Kennedy uses the term "*audience* to refer to a group of observers of a performance, while *spectator* refers to an individual member of an audience" [emphasis original].[5] He also asks "does the solitary spectator really constitute an audience?",[6] thereby highlighting the difference between an audience consisting of a "crowd" or "group" of people and a single spectator. In relation to contemporary Irish participative and immersive theatre performance, these contrary definitions of "what constitutes an audience" become even more intriguing. Many of the examples outlined in this chapter employ performance structures that call for a "group" of audience members, a "single" audience member or spectator, or some combination of both. In Tinderbox's *Convictions* (2000), the audience experiences the production both as a collective large audience, and also in smaller groups.[7,8] The audience moves through the Crumlin Road Courthouse in Belfast, engaging with specific rooms and spaces throughout. The theatrical experience is peppered with visual art installations to accompany the audience while they are transitioning from space to space. In the work of ANU Productions it is commonplace for an audience member to experience the performance alone. In the case of *Laundry* (2011),[9] the three or four audience members enter the building together but are then split up for the performance, encountering each scene individually. In the case of contemporary Irish immersive performance practice, one audience member can indeed constitute an audience, but it is even more intriguing to ask why immersive theatre companies often privilege the one-on-one encounter or the small audience experience? This idea will be touched on in greater detail in throughout this chapter.

Audience Participation

Jacques Rancière queries the nature of the conversation between the audience and the playwright in contemporary theatre, stating that "[w]e no longer live in the days when playwrights wanted to explain to their audience the truth of social relations and ways of struggling against their capitalist domination".[10] He goes on to contend that "it might be that the loss of their illusions leads artists to increase the pressure on spectators: perhaps the latter will know what is to be done, as long as the performance draws them out of their passive attitude and transforms them into active participants in a shared world".[11] In order to transform the audience into what Rancière terms "active participants" a more diverse medium of theatre and performance is necessary, one that challenges the audience engaging them in the act of witnessing and participating. Commenting on the genealogy of Irish theatre in relation to their study on devised performance Siobhán O'Gorman and Charlotte McIvor state that "[h]istoriographical practice within Irish theatre studies has most frequently tended to valorize authors, the authority of the text and the history of culturally prominent, authorized venues".[12] This privileging of the text in Irish performance practice, and indeed in theatre and performance scholarship, has begun to wane since the 1990s, leaving room for a more active and physically engaging form of performance.

Gareth White argues in terms of audience participation that "of course all audiences are participatory. Without participation performance would be nothing but action happening in the presence of other people. Audiences laugh, clap, cry, fidget, and occasionally heckle; they pay for tickets, they turn up at the theatre, they stay to the end of the performance or they walk out."[13] Undoubtedly true, this chapter seeks to interrogate a specific, and very active, type of participation. This active participation, be it in immersive performance or otherwise, places the audience in a position whereby they can influence and act somewhat freely within the performance, going beyond White's descriptions above of a less active method of participation. Returning to Kennedy's assertion that an audience must be a "group" of people, White analyses the concepts of crowd community and individual audience agency, asserting that "[i]f the individual is so powerfully influenced by the crowd, then their responsibility for their actions is mitigated—they are not acting entirely as themselves, but as part of a larger organism. Their agency in the process appears to be undermined."[14] So what differentiates passive participation and active participation?

One defining characteristic of theatre audiences is their presence in the live event. In participative or immersive theatre the audience are not just privy to the live event but are complicit and active within it. Therefore, the actions undertaken by an audience member as part of a non-participative or non-immersive event, such as clapping, heckling, laughing, walking out, etc., will have a much less significant impact than the actions undertaken by audiences during a participative or immersive event. Brian Singleton recalls his experience of immersion at ANU Productions' *The Boys of Foley Street* as part of the Dublin Theatre Festival 2012.[15,16] Describing a moment during the play where spectators are asked by a performer to film a violent interaction between two other performers, Singleton states "[t]his was the first of the moral and ethical dilemmas for the spectator: should we film the violence? I did but what I did not realise was that I was filmed first being handed the iPhone so that my co-spectator, who has been in the bombed car, could see that I had been implicated in and contributed to an act of violence."[17] Kennedy states that

> in the case of live performance a further characteristic is its impermanence. Because it dematerialises in the moment of its accomplishment, live performance gains its power before an audience from its vanishing, its being here and then not being here in the flow of the now, regardless of its memory traces whether public or private.[18]

In Singleton's experience, the impermanence of the live event is undermined by the videotaping of his encounter by another audience member. He is complicit in the actions of the event. The experience of the participative or immersed audience member is multifaceted. The immersed audience member is not only watching the performance, she is experiencing it, witnessing it, but she is also being witnessed. Many of the examples that this chapter interrogates take place in public spaces. Members of the public, who are not part of the main performance, watch the active audience member perform with potentially no knowledge of the difference between the designated company "performers" and the audience. The experience is exposing and invigorating and is unique to immersive and participatory performance. I contend that White's audience are "passively" participating, whereas in participatory and immersive performance the audience are "actively" participating.

Changing Performance Paradigms in Contemporary Irish Performance

> To look at itself a society must cut out a piece of itself for inspection. To do this it must set up a frame within which images and symbols of what has been sectioned off can be scrutinised, assessed, and if needs be, remodelled and rearranged.[19]

The changing performance paradigms in Irish performance in the twentieth and twenty-first centuries are deeply informed by the impact of Ireland's changing cultural, political and social contexts. Since the 1950s, Ireland has seen the Northern Irish Troubles, the Peace Process, the Good Friday Agreement, multiculturalism, multiple instances of economic boom and bust, the legalization of contraception, divorce and the introduction of marriage equality and the introduction of the Gender Recognition Act. Currently, Ireland is in the middle of what has been termed "The Decade of Centenaries", where citizens in the republic are encouraged to come together and reflect on the Ireland of one hundred years ago and how this relates to present-day Ireland. This preoccupation with memory and commemoration is having a profound effect on the emerging paradigms of Irish theatre and performance, and the rise in popularity of participatory and immersive performance is one such example.

Emilie Pine argues, in her introduction to *The Politics of Irish Memory*, that memory is an ethical act. She argues that "[t]he cultural remembrance of the Irish soldiers of the Great War, or the children abused in Irish institutions, has provoked a social reaction and, in doing so, motivated acts of official remembrance, from governmental investigations to public commemorations. Memory can thus function as an ethical act, a moral duty that we exercise."[20] Memory and the act of performing memory has moved to the forefront of contemporary Irish performance practice, in particular within participatory and immersive performance. In his introduction to *"That Was Us": Contemporary Irish Theatre and Performance*, Fintan Walsh reflects on the role of Irish audiences in theatre and performance currently. Walsh also recognises the heightened focus on remembrance, stating "intense political, economic, and social disturbance over the past number of years has given rise to a sharp impulse to remember. On the one hand this is about dignifying past hurts and injustices, but it is also motivated by a desire not to repeat the same mistakes again."[21] Miriam Haughton surveys the relationship between truth and politics in the Dublin Fringe Festival, and refers to what she terms "a milieu of 'truth'", arguing that this "milieu" "pervades the work proposed to and produced by the Dublin Fringe Festival (DFF) [...] between 2008 and 2012".[22] Reflecting on the series of scandals that pervaded Irish society from the beginning of the twenty-first century, resulting from and leading to enquiries such as the Mahon Tribunal, the Moriarty Tribunal, the Ryan Report, the McAleese Report, and the Fennelly Commission, Haughton highlights how: "[i]n light of such momentous scandals of corruption and collapse in Ireland's national structures [...] the DFF received in recent years a multitude of proposals relating directly to these events, or ones which investigate the very notions of truth, ethics, morality, community, nation, and identity".[23] Connecting this to Pine's assertion that memory is an ethical act and returning to Walsh, who states that "[i]n theatre and performance, this phenomenon has frequently appeared in the form of work that constructs spectators as witnesses to textual, visual, or bodily artefacts, who are present not only to encounter the past, but to question their responsibility for the events presented",[24] a connection is made between the form of participative or immersive performance and the connection with memory or a "milieu of truth".

Walsh's assertion that the role of the audience in contemporary Irish performance has shifted from passive observer to active witness illustrates a drive to empower and activate audiences. This pre-dates the aforementioned 2008–2012 Dublin Fringe Festivals. Earlier examples of this are illustrated through theatre practice in the North of Ireland, with regard to which Performance art shares an interesting relationship with contemporary Irish theatre. Áine Philips introduces her volume *Performance Art in Ireland: A History* by observing the links in lineage between Irish performance art practice dating from the 1970s and the impact that the conventions of such had on contemporary Irish performance practice. She argues that:

> Theatre and dance forms in Ireland have been influenced profoundly by performance and Live Art in recent years. Theatre companies such as Pan Pan (directed by Aedín Cosgrove and Gavin Quinn) and Anu Productions (directed by Louise Lowe) have used structural performative processes such as extended durations, the use of improvised script and action, real actions (as opposed to simulated, "acted" gestures), nudity, expanded reality and identity, site-specific performance, real life testimony and audience participation. These companies have also used technical supplements to performance such as video, sound art, and live web streams. All of these strategies were employed by performance artists from the 1970s onwards while theatre in Ireland was still bound to the literary text and to the often rigid historical conventions of drama, acting, and characterisation.[25]

Indeed performance artist André Stitt notes in his essay in the same volume that "Conventional art mediums failed at a specific time and in the specific location of Northern Ireland because conventional practice separated art from everyday experience by operating in traditional terms, in neutered spaces such as galleries and art institutions."[26] This performance paradigm emerged in direct response to the "Troubles" and in response to the difficulty in representing these experiences through the then traditional art structures. Indeed, the need to engage audiences in an new and active way re-emerged in theatre in the north in the immediate aftermath of the Good Friday Agreement (1998) with trends of participatory and community theatre projects. The following year, 1999, saw the beginning of an intercommunity project, *The Wedding Community Play Project*, written by Marie Jones and Martin Lynch. This was "[a] much-celebrated event at the time, the Wedding Play took audiences into private houses inside Loyalist and Republican estates, then on to a public venue for the performance of a cross-community wedding".[27] In another development, Tinderbox Theatre Company produced *Convictions* (2000), a site-specific production that took place in the Crumlin Road Courthouse, Belfast. Both of these productions exemplify the changing roles of contemporary Irish audiences, engaging in the act of remembering, commemorating and moving forward. Audience members at *The Wedding Community Play* were guests at a mixed marriage (Catholic/Protestant) wedding. The journey begins "in the two houses across the peace-line in Shortstrand where the audiences witnessed the preparations of the two families for the wedding, whereas the actual church wedding scene was staged at the First Free Presbyterian Church in the City

Centre [of Belfast]."[28] After the wedding ceremony was finished, the audience, who are "brought to all of the locations on buses, and in separate groups",[29] finish their experience at a wedding reception. The audience in *The Wedding Community Play* are active participants in the performance of the day-long ritual of a wedding ceremony. Eva Urban argues that "[i]n the script of *The Wedding Community Play*, it becomes clear that Catholics and Protestants falling in love and getting married depend on the approval or disapproval of the paramilitary organisations".[30] In the aftermath of the Good Friday Agreement, and at a time of political turmoil in the North of Ireland, *The Wedding Community Play* encourages audiences from both communities to actively participate in diminishing these spatial and social boundaries that exist around the segregation of communities in Belfast. What is evident here is the need for modes of performance to engage with a suitable way of remembering and dealing with the difficulties of the past in the North of Ireland. This allowed for new and experimental modes of performance to emerge out of an area of Ireland that was coming to terms with its recent and troubled past by allowing audiences to actively engage with these themes.

Indeed, there has been no waning in the appetite for participatory and immersive performance that reflects and comments on moments in our nation's past. ANU Productions' most recent works, *Pals* (2015), *Glorious Madness* (2015) and *Sunder* (2016), are all commissioned by the state to commemorate the 1916 Rising and related histories. Utilizing historical buildings and landmarks in Dublin City, such as Collins' Barracks (*Pals*), Wynn's Hotel (*Glorious Madness*) and Moore Street (*Sunder*), ANU are encouraging their audiences to bear witness to political acts of commemoration through immersive performance. The focus on memory, and remembrance, in contemporary Irish performance calls for a more active role for audiences. The popularity of participative and immersive performance coincides directly with this heightened awareness of representing the past, illustrating that audiences are opting into this role of "witness" or "participant" rather than passive observer.

This diversification in the role of audiences is not exclusive to Ireland. Bennett has observed that "over the last thirty years [1960s to 1990s] many theatres have emerged which speak for dominated and generally marginalised peoples, and the proliferation of these groups demands new definitions of theatre and recognition of new non-traditional audiences".[31] The audiences may not be entirely "new", as Bennett suggests, but audiences are embracing a new diversity in their role as an audience member. The impetus Bennett places on exploring "marginalised peoples" is important in the Irish context. Walsh, in defining contemporary Irish theatre, outlines several common features; "(1) a deep engagement with space and place; (2) an insistence on remembering, bearing witness, and questioning responsibility; (3) the use of theatre as a platform for staging marginalised and seemingly minor stories; and (4) harnessing theatre's capacity to process powerful feeling and affect."[32] These criteria, outlined by Walsh, substantiate the arguments made by Pine (memory as an ethical act) and Haughton (a milieu of truth) and compound the proof that contemporary Irish society is seeking a means to digest our difficult histories in a more active way.

Who exactly is attending these participatory and immersive theatre performances? Bennett argues that "the survival of theatre is economically tied to a willing audience—not only those people paying to sit and watch a performance but increasingly those who approve a government, corporate, or other subsidy".[33] Therefore, a change (or lowering) in pricing allows for a different, and perhaps less "conventional" theatre audience to participate. ANU have explored the omission of ticket prices. During the 2013 Dublin Fringe Festival, the company programmed thirteen short immersive productions at various sites across Dublin city, including the Luas, Liberty Hall, Henrietta Street, and Dublin Castle, as part of the *Thirteen* series. The tickets to all of these events were free, with patrons only needing to book with the festival. The series aimed to reflect on the 1913 Lockout and what ANU deemed to be "[t]he closest thing Ireland has ever had to a socialist revolution".[34] This performance connects with both Haughton and Pine's focus on truth-seeking and ethical memory. ANU go on to state, in reference to *Thirteen*, that "[t]he current economic collapse [2013] and the resulting national distress pulls the issues of one hundred years ago sharply into focus. Echoes of mass meetings and marches, industrial unrest and the very rights of the citizen reverberate today as it did then."[35] ANU, through providing this series free of charge, ensured that it was, in theory, accessible to everyone. *Thirteen* connected its audiences to the city of Dublin, using the already present urban dramaturgy of the city to encourage audiences to participate in this durational event. I will return to *Thirteen* in greater depth later in the chapter.

The Art of Immersion: Immersed or Not?

Active participation can take place outside of immersive performance, yet immersive theatre has its own distinct defining features, which can transcend that of participatory performance. The term "immersive" has become a catch-all term for any performance or theatre event which happens outside of a theatre auditorium or venue; however, I would argue that this is a gross oversimplification of what is a growing and emergent performance paradigm. It is beyond the scope of this chapter to outline all competing assertions (of which there are many) surrounding what "defines" immersive theatre. Instead, I will utilize the research done by Josephine Machon, a leading scholar on immersive theatre practice, to analyse Irish immersive performance practice. There is often mention, when referring to immersive theatre, that it is "non-traditional" or "not conventional". It is complex, however, to determine what "traditional" and "conventional" refer to in theatre and performance practice as these are relative terms which will inevitably change depending on era, location or personal experience. Machon draws our attention to the conventions of both what she deems traditional theatre, i.e. a text directed for stage, and immersive theatre performance. Machon states that in the former the "audience/actor (us/them) relationship is defined by the delineation of space (auditorium/stage) and role (static-passive observer/active-moving performer) where the audience is viewing the action ahead of them".[36] She goes on to suggest that "it does not matter if you are there or not; the audience could get up and walk out and it would carry on".[37] Machon then contrasts this with what she describes, and outlines as, the conventions of immersive theatre, arguing that in this form

> the audience is thrown (sometimes even literally) into a totally new environment and context from the everyday world from which it has come. These environments are seemingly outside of 'everyday' rules and regulations and always have expectations of physical interaction. All elements of the theatre are in the mix, establishing a multidimensional medium in which the participant is submerged, blurring spaces and roles.[38]

Taking ANU Productions' *Thirteen* (DFF, 2013) as its example, this chapter will situate Machon's conventions for immersive theatre within this performance. This performance is foregrounded with this idea of remembrance as the overall production engages with, and commemorates, the 1913 Lockout. With thirteen productions to choose from as part of this series, the audience member is given a choice as to how many, and which productions to choose from. Machon argues above that in immersive performance "the audience is thrown [...] into a totally new environment" in the case of *Thirteen* the audience, if attending all productions as I did, were required to make their way to thirteen locations in Dublin City Centre. Many of the locations were in parts of the city that audiences may have been unfamiliar with; indeed, it was necessary to seek out some locations. The two weeks of these performances come across as an education in the geography of the city, and these locations, once found, even if familiar were represented in a uniquely performative way. In *Citizen X*, the audience are required to pre-load a soundtrack on to their music devices or phones, they are also required to purchase a Luas ticket for the red line service (Jervis Street to Spencer Dock). Once aboard the tram the soundscape encourages the audience to look for "The Girl in the Red Jacket", since it is her journey that we follow. The audience are undistinguishable from the rest of the commuters, who are oblivious to the performance going on alongside them. This new environment is, as Machon suggests, contextually different from the "everyday world from which it has come". Even though the audience are in a "public space" they are acutely aware of the performative nature of the event via the multimedia layering of the soundscape. Moving onto Machon's second point that "[t]hese environments are seemingly outside of 'everyday' rules and regulations and always have expectations of physical interaction" I will use *Protest Part I* as my example. The audience enters an old preserved tenement building, 14 Henrietta Street. Inside there is a woman, a table set out with props, and an envelope. The envelope is for the audience and sets out the rules of this engagement. It becomes clear that there is no possibility for inaction here as each audience member becomes responsible for how this performance plays out. Roles are assigned to certain, willing, audience members. I am given the role of "enforcer", for example, and must ensure that the rules of the game are observed. I am given the power to remove those audience members who do not comply. What follows is a game, the woman who has been present in this room is the subject of this encounter. One by one, the audience must pick up a piece of paper from the table and enact the written request on the body of the woman. Examples of these requests are: "Feed her", "Strip her", "Spit on her". The audience has options here, on the table is an array of food for example, so that when required to "feed her", one could choose to feed her chocolate, lemons or some coal. When the request "spit on her" was chosen, the audience member in question would not comply and so I removed them from the process. These acts of violence are not absolute; audience members, as in the previous example, can choose not to comply. However, the audience has the capacity in this moment to enact violence on the performing body, raising an ethical query regarding how far the company can let this go. ANU are testing their audiences with these situations, and the threat of removal hangs over the audience forcing their hand into some form of compliance. Connecting back with Machon's point about immersive performance environments being outside of the everyday rules and regulations this performance was foregrounded in such a way that the "rules" of that moment were distinctly separate from those of the everyday world. The audience's expectation of physical interaction was also challenged in this performance, as throughout the roughly forty-minute-long experience, several audience members experienced intimate contact with the performer, for example dancing with her, undressing her, and feeding her. Moving to the final point of Machon's definition of immersive performance, "[a]ll elements of the theatre are in the mix, establishing a multidimensional medium in which the participant is submerged, blurring spaces and roles", it is appropriate to comment on the piece in general. Across the thirteen performances the audience experience a constant "blurring" of roles and spaces. For example, I felt constantly connected to the performances of *Thirteen* even when I wasn't in one. An example of this is that I became increasingly suspect of all sorts of "unusual activities" that were taking place across the city centre. Every altercation that took place near one of the performance sites could have been part of the performance. In this series of performances the act of remembrance pushes at the boundaries of commemoration, encouraging audiences to draw parallels between 1913 and 2013 through the audience's own active participation in the performance of these memories. The combination of multimedia, dance, installation and theatre performance created a secret world within the 2013 Dublin Fringe Festival, an undercurrent of people engaging with history, memory and the politics of both through this mysterious subculture of events.

The immersive performance contract is central to these shifting paradigms of immersion and participation. Audiences attend the theatre with a certain expectation of what it will entail and what to expect. If one is attending a performance in an established, proscenium theatre, one might expect a clear delineation between "us and them" (the audience and the performers). In immersive theatre, the expectations are different. The audience is expected to participate, move, seek out an experience, and break down the barriers between "us and them". Machon refers to the process of creating a contract for participation in immersive work by stating "many [...] companies institute preparation techniques to gently immerse you [the audience] in the world [of the performance]: pre performance rituals and framing to acclimatise the guest participant within the work".[39] These "pre-performance rituals" can also be referred to as the "gathering process" which I will return to in greater detail farther on in this chapter. Bennett refers to the "theatrical contract" between the audience and the performance, arguing that "individuals can always refuse the collective contract by walking out of a production, or less dramatically, by falling asleep".[40] In immersive performance the contract can also be broken, but as the audience member is "participating" in the performance event it goes beyond merely walking out or falling asleep. Returning to liveness, the audience member in immersive theatre is also performing; therefore, the breaking of the immersive contract involves a different set of rules. Some audience members in immersive performances can overextend the reach of the performance contract, leading to what Adam Alston terms as being "errantly immersed". Alston defines "errant immersion" as a spectator

> who strays away from an intended course—'mis-takes' their environment as a designed or planned feature of an immersive world [...] The errantly immersed audience member plots her own path through a physically dispersed forest of things, acts and signs that are provided and that can be wandered through and at times interacted with, but they also extend the borders of this forest way beyond those intended by the theatre maker.[41]

What Alston is referring to here is a specific engagement with the immersive performance contract. This illustrates that although audiences are encouraged to participate actively in immersive work, the boundaries are at times difficult to see. The stumbling upon and entering of rooms and spaces not inhabited by the performance is enhanced by the performance's situation in the public sphere.

Audience and the Response to Site

Bennett states that "[t]he milieu which surrounds a theatre is always ideologically encoded and the presence of a theatre can be measured as typical or incongruous within it. That relationship further shapes a spectator's experience".[42] In immersive and participatory theatre, it is not only the relationship of the audience to the performance that is notable, but also the relationship of the audience to the performance site. Reflecting on Walsh's assertions on the relationship of Irish contemporary performance reflecting marginalized stories, Joanne Tompkins offers an interesting approach to the importance of site-specific theatre in general that can be related to this context. Tompkins argues that

> given that site-specific performance seeks a social activity in a social place, the theatre building can, for many reasons, sever the relationship between the idea of a specific social activity and a performance. Site-specific performance can provide a more appropriate forum for reflecting on and interpreting the relationship between performance, specific places in our worlds, and social contexts than theatre that takes place in conventional theatre venues.[43]

If the aim of immersive and participatory performance is to engage the spectator in the act of "witnessing" then a more engaging and active connection with the performance site is a necessary addendum to the performance. Kennedy reflects on the proscenium-style theatre and its relationship to spectators, suggesting that "all proscenium theatres discipline the gaze, but large auditoria amplify the separation between audience and performer by sheer force of distance".[44] He also suggests that there is a division of the audience in a proscenium theatre which is determined socio-economically, with the best seats more expensive and with seats priced less expensively the worse the spectator's line of sight becomes. In a proscenium theatre, whomever you are sitting beside is most likely going to be part of your class group.[45] The division of the audience in immersive theatre is often less structured. For example, in The Performance Corporation and ANU Productions' collaborative 2014 performance *Beautiful Dreamers*, the audience move as a group through Limerick City and into a vacated office building on the bank of the Shannon River. This performance is contingent on the audience being able to see what is occurring across the road in a hotel room, on a rooftop carpark, and on the streets below. The audience must create their own opportunities to see these moments through their willingness to engage and by exercising their agency in the performance. I will go into greater detail on this performance further on in this chapter.

ANU Productions foreground the majority of their performances in site-specific locales: to give a pertinent example, their award-winning "Monto Cycle"—comprising four performances: *World's End Lane* (2010), *Laundry* (2011), *The Boys of Foley Street* (2012), and *Vardo* (2014)[46]—all took place in the Foley street (previously Montgomery Street) area of Dublin City and used the site's urban dramaturgy to augment the immersive experience. Indeed, performing memory in spaces which are laden with past histories and contexts serves to consolidate an audience's engagement with the past and impacts on the performance of the past in these spaces. In this series of four performances audience members found themselves in close proximity to the performers and other audience members in a variety of site-specific locations: a taxi; a church confessional; the basement of Busáras; or an en suite bathroom in a brothel. As the audience in ANU Productions' performances often experience these situations as the only audience member, or one of two or three others, the sense of being part of a "larger" audience is often absent in these performances, leaving audiences open to interacting with the performance and the site as an individual rather than as part of a larger audience "group" and indeed members of the public. White argues that "a theatre crowd has norms of licensed behaviour that encourage simultaneous response that will draw people into intercorporeality. The physical relationship of an audience will often be encouraged to move as a crowd, physically enacting the process of "becoming one" with those around."[47] As suggested above, the nature of the audience's relationship to the site of the performance in immersive theatre removes the norms of licensed behaviour and thus the audience member is licensed to create or co-create a different set of behavioural norms.

Part of the negotiation of theatrical site is the experience of getting there and entering the performance, or what Bennett terms "the gathering process". As Bennett suggests, "[a]ll such elements of the gathering process are bound to influence the spectator's preparation for the theatrical event".[48] When attending a performance in a theatre building, this gathering process is a strictly coded event. The audience member collects their ticket from the box office, congregates in the foyer, perhaps she peruses the programme before taking her designated seat. In site-specific or site-responsive immersive performance this experience is altered. The act of leaving, or "the leaving process" is equally altered. In the absence of a curtain call, and with audiences often left waiting on the side of the street, how do we know when the performance has ended? The performance begins with the journey *to* the immersive performance. In the absence of a coded performance space the audience must treat everything as part of the experience. Machon argues that

> entering a traditional theatre or studio space makes us aware of the separateness of the world presented to us [...] in site responsive immersive practice, the space is integral to the experience of the work, we are not separated from it but *in* it, of it, surrounded by it, dwelling in it, travelling through it; the space is thus integrated within and as the world in which the audience-participants are immersed which ensures this sense of "rootedness" in the world the event is actively *felt*. [emphasis original][49]

In order for the audience to immersive themselves, and become active within the performance, they must feel rooted in its world. Similarly, the act of leaving the space is also problematized in immersive performance, as at times it is difficult to know when the performance has ended. On several occasions, I have found myself waiting aimlessly at the side of a street in Dublin wondering whether the performance is over or whether the next part of the performance is already underway. There is no applause or no curtain call. In the case of ANU Productions' *Vardo* (2014), I remained standing on the corner of Foley Street outside The LAB with the other three audience members for a significant period after the performance had "ended". So significant was the period of waiting that a member of the Dublin Theatre Festival staff had to tell us the performance was over. What ensued after this experience as I walked back though Dublin City was a heightened awareness of the pulse of the city and the stories contained within it. For me the performance was not yet over, only upon exiting the city did I begin to re-enter the "real world".

Further evidence of this relationship between audience and site in a participatory and immersive context can be seen in The Performance Corporation[50] and ANU Productions' collaboration *Beautiful Dreamers* (2014). The show, "[b]ased on interviews with Limerick's citizens [...] is an interactive performance that reflects the city's answers in surprising ways and through a variety of forms, including an FM radio frequency that you can tune into whether at the show, at home or in your car".[51] The audience were given instructions to meet outside the Belltable Arts Centre in Limerick City, from there the audience were brought to the top floor of an abandoned office building. The audience were encouraged to go to the windows and to look. Stories are relayed to them as they watch the city, below performers act out what is being narrated to them. Like voyeurs, the audience peers into the window of a hotel room across the road, observes a car on the roof of a multistorey car park, contemplates the intentions of two women on the bridge, and feels concern for a man's erratic behaviour on the banks of the Shannon River. Here The Performance Corporation and ANU Productions serve up Limerick City as the stage: the audience gets to choose what to watch, but they cannot watch it all. Another example of this relationship is in Kabosh Theatre Company's *Two Roads West* (2008).[52] Written by former hunger striker Laurence McKeown, this production was a performance of a black taxi journey travelling between Shankill and the Falls Road in Belfast City. In her scholarly examination of devised performance in an Irish context, the theatre historian, Eleanor Owicki, writes: "[b]y staging theatre in and explicitly about iconic locations, Kabosh hopes to enact a two-way transfer of meaning: audience's understandings of the play will be informed by their knowledge of the space, and their understanding of the space will be changed by the performance".[53] Certainly, the specifics of geography and location in Belfast will invoke a particular set of political and cultural identities and methods of remembrance. However, in *Two Roads West*, as Owicki suggests, Kabosh are interested in forging a two-way relationship which will expand the audience member's knowledge and perspective of these geographical locations. Kabosh are creating new memories and experiences on these sites that are laden with past conflicts, stories and memories. The Performance Corporation and ANU Productions are playing on past and present perceptions of Limerick City and also participate in what Owicki terms "a two way transfer of meaning" between their prior knowledge of the city of Limerick and their lived experience during *Beautiful Dreamers*. Here memory is being repurposed and altered by providing audiences with an experiential access to spatial memory.

Audience Agency: "Moments of Communion"

Co-Artistic Director of ANU Productions Louise Lowe refers in her descriptions of the company's work to the "moments of communion"[54] that can exist between the performer and the audience member. Lowe states "[t]he viewer for me is the vital element of the total production and in my opinion is not isolated from the creative process. The communion between the viewer and the performer in the space is the final piece of each production that I make and one that I consider deeply throughout all aspects of the build and development."[55] In order for the performance to be "immersive", the audience member must have the ability to act freely and individually within the event. Often these moments of interaction, where our agency can truly be witnessed, can be the defining moment in the experience of an immersive event. According to Machon, "participants in the event may be inspired to attend and interpret their own bodily experience of the work, while simultaneously orientating themselves to the bodies of co-participants in the event".[56] I will now refer to my own personal "moment of communion" in *Vardo* (2014). *Vardo* was the culminating performance of the "Monto Cycle" and focused on contemporary sex work in the Foley Street area. Once again, the audience experience the familiar sense of isolation as four audience members, myself included, were separated and led on an individual journey through the performances. The significant part of this journey was an encounter I had with a performer in the basement of Busáras. This performer, playing the role of a sex worker, beckoned me to her and initiated a conversation. It became clear over the course of our exchange that this woman had been a victim of human trafficking. She asked me to hold onto her passport to prevent it being seized by those who were holding her. Moments after I agreed to look after this document, a man arrived, and immediately requested the passport from me. I refused, vehemently, until his mannerisms become so aggressive and intimidating that I relinquished the document. This man led me and this woman upstairs to the lobby and upon approaching a vacant seat told me to sit down. He whispered a threat in my ear urging me not to follow, and as he disappeared with the woman who I had sworn to help, it caused me to reflect on the reality of human trafficking that had been represented so personally through performance. These "moments of communion" are important in terms of reinforcing the act of remembering by the audience members of immersive and participatory performance. In *Vardo* it is precisely in these moments that the audience member's active participation becomes a functional method of remembrance. By engaging with the past, through the reflection of 100 years of the "Monto" area, the audience member is encouraged to reflect on their own positionality in relation to the events described. Therefore, immersive and participatory theatre practitioners offer up an experiential mining of Irish history, an illuminating of traumatic histories, personal experiences, and events to their audiences. As seen earlier in this chapter, the emergence of experimental and experiential forms of performance stem directly from moments in Irelands past (the

"Troubles", the Peace Process, and moments of economic and political uncertainty) in order to allow audiences access to these moments in a way that text- and venue-based theatre cannot.

Conclusion

This chapter has illustrated that since the 1990s the emphasis on text and venue has shifted in Irish performance and become increasingly focused on experimental and participatory forms of performance. This has coincided, this chapter contends, with moments of trauma and of reflections on moments of traumatic history on the island. The emergence of this was signalled with reference to the forms of Live and Performance Art emerging in the North of Ireland in the 1970s, responding to the intensifying violence of the "Troubles". For a fuller enquiry into this form of performance, please see Una Mannion's contribution to this volume. The next emergence of forms of participatory performance came in the wake of the Good Friday Agreement (1998) when the island of Ireland was seeking a means of engaging with the violent events of the "Troubles" and the moving forward of the island towards peace. Performance companies, such as Kabosh Theatre and Tinderbox, chose site-responsive and participatory performance forms as a means of creating an inclusive theatrical experience. Indeed, several cross-community projects such as *The Wedding Community Play Project* (1999) emerged as a means to connect two historically segregated communities. In the south, the reaction to moments of momentous scandal, signalled by Miriam Haughton and her reference to a "milieu of truth", created a new avenue for performative exploration with companies such as ANU Productions and The Performance Corporation evolving in order to provide a means of dealing with these moment of social and political failings. Indeed, other forms of experimental and devised work also came to the fore with companies such as Brokentalkers, THEATREclub, and Pan Pan finding more abstract means of engaging with moments of current and historical traumas. The "Decade of Centenaries" (2012–2022) is one of the most significant markers of this performative focus on remembrance. Indeed, much of the available state funding in the arts sector has been earmarked for artists to engage specifically with the commemorative schedule. Many artists have responded by challenging dominant state narratives, choosing instead to comment on some of Ireland's less palatable histories. The work of ANU Productions transected the commemorative schedule and this challenging of dominant historical narratives with productions such as *PALS: The Irish at Gallipoli* (2015) and *Sunder* (2016).

This chapter also interrogated the function of audiences in immersive and participatory performance, highlighting an alternative form of spectating, of engaging with participatory and immersive performances. Prominent in this investigation was the audience's relationship to the site of these performances and the "moments of communion" between the audience and the performer in these productions. ANU Productions' "Monto Cycle", Kabosh Theatre

Company's use of the geographically segregated Belfast, and The Performance Corporation's exploration of Limerick City illuminated that these participatory performances utilized the urban landscapes and the urban dramaturgy of Ireland's major cities to locate their productions. For a fuller interrogation of performance taking place in "non-theatre" spaces refer to Charlotte McIvor's contribution to this volume.

This chapter also outlined, theoretically, definitions of immersive and participatory theatre and their relationship to Irish audiences and Irish performance practice. Through these investigations it is apparent that contemporary Irish audiences have sought a means of experiencing performance that removes the valorization of the well-established text–author–theatre relationship. This active role creates the opportunity for participation and witnessing and experiential engagement with these performances. Connecting back with Emilie Pine's assertion that memory can function as an ethical act, it becomes clear that the emergence of participatory and immersive performance forms since the 1970s (in the north) and the 1990s (in the south) connects into the need to ethically remember and reflect on moments of the past in an inclusive, experiential, and focused manner. Thus, by directly involving audiences, as agents, witnesses, voyeurs, and even at times performers, there is a democratisation of events, histories, spaces, and even artistic form which enables illumination, reflection, and remembrance.

Notes

1. Siobhán O'Gorman, "Scenographic Interactions: 1950s Ireland and Dublin's Pike Theatre, *Irisal* 3, no. 1 (Autumn 2014): 26.
2. Miriam Haughton, "From Laundries to Labour Camps: Staging Ireland's 'Rule of Silence' in Anu Productions' *Laundry*," *Modern Drama* 57, no. 1 (March 2014): 65, doi:10.3138/md.0595R.
3. Susan Bennett, *Theatre Audiences. A Theory of Production and Reception* (London: Routledge, 1990), 1.
4. Dennis Kennedy, *The Spectator and The Spectacle: Audiences in Modernity and Postmodernity* (Cambridge: Cambridge University Press, 2009), 3.
5. Ibid., 5.
6. Ibid., 6.
7. For more information on Tinderbox please see www.tinderbox.org.uk.
8. *Convictions*. By Daragh Carville et al. Directed by Mick Gordon et al. Courthouse, Crumlin Road, Belfast, Northern Ireland, October 30, 2000.
9. *Laundry*. By ANU Productions. Directed by Louise Lowe and Owen Boss. Magdalene Laundry, Sean MacDermott Street, Dublin, Ireland, 25 April 2011.
10. Jaques Rancière, *The Emancipated Spectator* (London: Verso, 2009), 11.
11. Ibid.
12. Siobhán O'Gorman and Charlotte McIvor, "Devising Ireland: Geneologies and Contestations," in *Devised Performance in Irish Theatre: Histories and Contemporary Practice* (Dublin: Carysfort Press, 2015), 3.
13. Gareth White, *Audience Participation in Theatre* (Basingstoke: Palgrave Macmillan, 2013), 3.

14. Ibid., 149.
15. For more information on ANU Productions' please go to www.anuproductions.ie.
16. *The Boys of Foley Street.* By ANU Productions. Directed by Louise Lowe and Owen Boss. Foley Street, Dublin, Ireland, June 17 2012.
17. Brian Singleton, "ANU Productions and Site-Specific Performance: The Politics of Space and Place," in *"That Was Us": Contemporary Irish Theatre and Performance* (London: Oberon Books, 2013), 33.
18. Kennedy, *The Spectator and The Spectacle. Audiences in Modernity and Postmodernity*, 15.
19. Victor Turner, "Frame, Flow and Reflection: Ritual and Drama as Public Liminality," *Japanese Journal of Religious Studies* 6, no. 4 (December 1979): 468.
20. Emilie Pine, *The Politics of Irish Memory. Performing Remembrance in Contemporary Irish Culture* (Basingstoke: Palgrave Macmillan, 2011), 13.
21. Fintan Walsh, "The Power of the Powerless: Theatre in Turbulent Times," in *"That Was Us": Contemporary Irish Theatre and Performance* (London: Oberon Books, 2013), 13.
22. Miriam Haughton, "A Theatre of Truth? Negotiating Place, Politics and Policy in the Dublin Fringe Festival," in *Devised Performance in Irish Theatre: Histories and Contemporary Practice* (Dublin: Carysfort Press, 2015), 128.
23. Ibid., 129.
24. Walsh, "The Power of the Powerless: Theatre in Turbulent Times," 13.
25. Áine Phillips, ed., *Performance Art in Ireland: A History* (London: Live Art Development Agency, 2015), 13.
26. André Stitt, "Performing Political Acts: Performance Art in Northern Ireland: Ritual, Catharsis, and Transformation," in *Performance Art in Ireland: A History* (London: Live Art Development Agency, 2015), 95.
27. Matt Jennings, "Aesthetics and Efficacy in Community Theatre in Contemporary Northern Ireland," *Research in Drama Education: The Journal of Applied Theatre and Performance* 15, no. 1 (February 2010): 111.
28. Eva Urban, *Community Politics and the Peace Process in Contemporary Northern Irish Drama*, Reimagining Ireland 31 (Oxford: Peter Lang, 2011), 250.
29. Ibid., 251.
30. Ibid.
31. Bennett, *Theatre Audiences. A Theory of Production and Reception*, 1.
32. Walsh, "The Power of the Powerless: Theatre in Turbulent Times," 10.
33. Bennett, *Theatre Audiences. A Theory of Production and Reception*, 4.
34. ANU Productions, "THIRTEEN," *ANU*, 28 July 2013, n.p., https://anuproductions.wordpress.com/2013/07/28/thirteen/.
35. Ibid., n.p.
36. Josephine Machon, *Immersive Theatres. Intimacy and Immediacy in Contemporary Performance* (Basingstoke: Palgrave Macmillan, 2013), 27.
37. Ibid.
38. Ibid.
39. Ibid., 84.
40. Bennett, *Theatre Audiences. A Theory of Production and Reception*, 165.
41. Adam Alston, "Making Mistakes in Immersive Theatre: Spectatorship and Errant Immersion," *Journal of Contemporary Drama in English* 4, no. 1 (2016): 6.
42. Bennett, *Theatre Audiences. A Theory of Production and Reception*, 135.

43. Joanne Tompkins, 'The Place' and Practice of Site-Specific Theatre and Performance," in *Performing Site-Specific Theatre. Politics, Place, Practice* (Basingstoke: Palgrave Macmillan, 2012), 7.
44. Kennedy, *The Spectator and The Spectacle. Audiences in Modernity and Postmodernity*, 134.
45. Ibid., 134–5.
46. For a more comprehensive description of the 'Monto Cycle' see Miriam Haughton's essay "From Laundries to Labour Camps: Staging Ireland's 'Rule of Silence' in Anu Productions' *Laundry*," *Modern Drama* 57, no. 1 (March 2014): 65–93.
47. White, *Audience Participation in Theatre*, 137.
48. Bennett, *Theatre Audiences. A Theory of Production and Reception*, 133.
49. Machon, *Immersive Theatres. Intimacy and Immediacy in Contemporary Performance*, 126–7.
50. For more information on The Performance Corporation see www.theperformancecorporation.com.
51. "Beautiful Dreamers—A Conversation with a City," *The Performance Corporation*, 1 December 2014, n.p., http://www.theperformancecorporation.com/theatre/beautiful-dreamers/.
52. For more information on Kabosh Theatre Company see www.kabosh.net.
53. Eleanor Owicki, "Reawakening Belfast's Streets: Tourism and Education in Site-Specific Northern Irish Theatre," in *Devised Performance in Irish Theatre: Histories and Contemporary Practice* (Dublin: Carysfort Press, 2015), 230–31.
54. Haughton, "From Laundries to Labour Camps," 65.
55. Louise Lowe, "You Had to Be There," in "*That Was Us*": *Contemporary Irish Theatre and Performance* (London: Oberon Books, 2013), 57.
56. Ibid., 142.

Bibliography

Alston, Adam. "Making Mistakes in Immersive Theatre: Spectatorship and Errant Immersion." *Journal of Contemporary Drama in English* 4, no. 1 (2016).

ANU Productions. *Laundry*. Dublin: ANU Productions, 2012.

———. *The Boys of Foley Street*. Dublin: ANU Productions, 2014.

———. "THIRTEEN." *ANU*, July 28, 2013. https://anuproductions.wordpress.com/2013/07/28/thirteen/.

"Beautiful Dreamers—A Conversation with a City." *The Performance Corporation*, 1 December2014. http://www.theperformancecorporation.com/theatre/beautiful-dreamers/.

Bennett, Susan. *Theatre Audiences. A Theory of Production and Reception*. London: Routledge, 1990.

Carville, Daragh, Damian Gorman, Marie Jones, Martin Lynch, Owen McCafferty, Nicola McCartney, and Gary Mitchell. *Convictions*. Belfast: Tinderbox, 2000.

Haughton, Miriam. "A Theatre of Truth? Negotiating Place, Politics and Policy in the Dublin Fringe Festival." In *Devised Performance in Irish Theatre: Histories and Contemporary Practice*. Dublin: Carysfort Press, 2015.

———. "From Laundries to Labour Camps: Staging Ireland's "Rule of Silence" in Anu Productions' *Laundry*." *Modern Drama* 57, no. 1 (March 2014): 65–93. doi:https://doi.org/10.3138/md.0595R.

Jennings, Matt. "Aesthetics and Efficacy in Community Theatre in Contemporary Northern Ireland." *Research in Drama Education: The Journal of Applied Theatre and Performance* 15, no. 1 (February 2010): 111–17. doi:https://doi.org/10.1080/13569780903481086.

Kennedy, Denis. *The Spectator and The Spectacle. Audiences in Modernity and Postmodernity.* Cambridge: Cambridge University Press, 2009.

Lowe, Louise. "You Had to Be There." In *"That Was Us": Contemporary Irish Theatre and Performance.* London: Oberon Books, 2013.

Machon, Josephine. *Immersive Theatres. Intimacy and Immediacy in Contemporary Performance.* Basingstoke: Palgrave Macmillan, 2013.

O'Gorman, Siobhán. "Scenographic Interactions: 1950s Ireland and Dublin's Pike Theatre." *Irish Theatre International* 3, no. 1, Autumn 2014: 25–42.

O'Gorman, Siobhan, and Charlotte McIvor. "Devising Ireland: Geneologies and Contestations." In *Devised Performance in Irish Theatre: Histories and Contemporary Practice.* Dublin: Carysfort Press, 2015.

Owicki, Eleanor. "Reawakening Belfast's Streets: Tourism and Education in Site-Specific Northern Irish Theatre." In *Devised Performance in Irish Theatre: Histories and Contemporary Practice.* Dublin: Carysfort Press, 2015.

Phillips, Áine, ed. *Performance Art in Ireland: A History.* London: Live Art Development Agency, 2015.

Pine, Emilie. *The Politics of Irish Memory. Performing Remembrance in Contemporary Irish Culture.* Basingstoke: Palgrave Macmillan, 2011.

Rancière, Jaques. *The Emancipated Spectator.* London: Verso, 2009.

Singleton, Brian. "ANU Productions and Site-Specific Performance: The Politics of Space and Place." In *"That Was Us": Contemporary Irish Theatre and Performance.* London: Oberon Books, 2013.

Stitt, André. "Performing Political Acts: Performance Art in Northern Ireland: Ritual, Catharsis, and Transformation." In *Performance Art in Ireland: A History.* London: Live Art Development Agency, 2015.

Tompkins, Joanne. "The 'Place' and Practice of Site-Specific Theatre and Performance." In *Performing Site-Specific Theatre. Politics, Place, Practice.* Basingstoke: Palgrave Macmillan, 2012.

Turner, Victor. "Frame, Flow and Reflection: Ritual and Drama as Public Liminality." *Japanese Journal of Religious Studies* 6, no. 4 (December 1979): 465–99.

Urban, Eva. *Community Politics and the Peace Process in Contemporary Northern Irish Drama.* Reimagining Ireland 31. Oxford: Lang, 2011.

Walsh, Fintan. "The Power of the Powerless: Theatre in Turbulent Times." In *"That Was Us": Contemporary Irish Theatre and Performance.* London: Oberon Books, 2013.

White, Gareth. *Audience Participation in Theatre.* Basingstoke: Palgrave Macmillan, 2013.

Sounding Affect in Pan Pan Theatre's Adaptation of *All That Fall*

Angela Butler

> *You don't have to understand everything. You can feel things.*[1]
> Gavin Quinn, Co-Director of Pan Pan Theatre

On entering the theatre space, we are led past the vacant seats of the Abbey Theatre, up the stairs and past the closed curtain, to sit on the stage of the national theatre. When I step onto the stage, I find myself under a dim light provided by countless bulbs suspended from the ceiling. A wall of rigged bulbs occupies an entire wall in the performance space. The seating is rocking chairs, which fill the room. Each chair has a cushion with an image of a skull on it. The floor is decorated with a carpet covered with simple drawings of roads and junctions. After the other audience members take their seats, sound begins to fill the space, and it quickly becomes apparent that we may be the only physically present performers in the piece.

February 2016—it has been five years since Pan Pan Theatre premiered their adaptation of Samuel Beckett's radio play *All That Fall* in 2011 at Project Arts Centre in Dublin. In an interview with Fintan Walsh for *Irish Theatre Magazine*, Gavin Quinn noted that this production of *All That Fall* is not concerned exclusively with meaning but rather places a strong emphasis on the performance's affective potential; Pan Pan wish to open a space in *All That Fall* "where you can feel things".[2] And this is never more apparent than their

A. Butler (✉)
Trinity College Dublin, Dublin, Ireland
e-mail: BUTLERAB@tcd.ie

E. Jordan, E. Weitz (eds.), *The Palgrave Handbook of Contemporary Irish Theatre and Performance*,
https://doi.org/10.1057/978-1-137-58588-2_52

decision to run the performance on The Abbey stage in 2016. While the design and overall structure of the piece remain more or less the same as when it was premiered at Project Arts Centre, placing the audience on the national stage, observed by vacant seats, accentuates the visceral and affective intention of the performance. When I saw *All That Fall* at Project Arts Centre, the enclosed performance space created the feeling of a sensory chamber, cut off from the rest of the world. However, choosing to place the performance space on the stage of The Abbey left me with an odd feeling of being observed and highlighted my role as both an audience member and performer in the piece. It had the effect, more so than in 2011, of diminishing concentration on the meaning of the piece and returned my attention to the presence and role of my spectating body.

All That Fall recounts the comic journey of the "long-suffering" Mrs. Rooney as she leaves her home to meet her husband, Mr. Rooney, at the train station. On the way she meets various locals, including Mr. Slocum who offers her a lift in his "limousine". On arrival at the station, she discovers that Mr. Rooney's train is delayed although the reason for the delay is not certain. Once the train arrives, Mr. Rooney and Mrs. Rooney begin to walk home, and the reason for the delay is revealed, that is, a child had fallen on to the tracks and died under suspicious circumstances. Pan Pan's adaptation of *All That Fall* presents the audience with a multi-form performance space in which programmed sound, diegetic lighting design, and a sculpture formed by audience members are the main points of information, as opposed to a set stage with physically present actor bodies. In this way, the regular conventions for communication with, and comprehension of, the performance are altered to present an affective, visceral, multi-form adaptation.

The play's sounds, which come through the speakers, blend with the human sounds of gentle rocking and the odd whisper or cough. Similar to the proposal that the listener of a radio play, cast as a collaborator, completes the production through visualization, in this production of *All That Fall* the physical presence of the audience make up a human sculpture rocking back and forth. Since we, the audience members, have become part of the performance as individual rocking sculptures, we are thus cast as collaborators, as listeners had been to the radio version, and our presence completes both the physical landscape and the soundscape of the performance. In this way, during *All That Fall*, the audience are located in the epicentre of the experience, surrounded by sound, light and sculpture. By choosing to seat the audience in rocking chairs, Pan Pan ensure that the performance space is never static and is seen from a number of points, perspectives and angles. We remain physically in dialogue with the rhythm of sound both internally and externally due to the nature of rhythm and sound perception in conjunction with the motion of rocking.

Lighting is one of the dominant features of Pan Pan's production and performs several significant roles. In addition to the wall of rigged bulbs and suspended bulbs, there is also a line of low-level lights on the floor opposite the wall of bulbs which occasionally casts a blue-white hue over the floor and chairs, creating shadowy outlines in the otherwise blacked-out space. Lights in this production play the role of human characters: Christy, Mr. Tyler, the Connollys who speed by in a van, Tommy and Mr. Barrell. They take on elemental roles of the wind and a storm. The lighting also inhabits the form of the train. Lastly, the lighting is employed in *All That Fall* for atmospheric purposes, for instance, the blue-white hue giving the impression of gloom, dreariness, and being caught in an everlasting dusk. Significantly, the lighting design in this production often escapes direct meaning. Lighting seems at times to be employed to distort spatial perception whereby, against the blacked-out surroundings, and working jointly with the unsteady balance of a rocking chair, my sense of structure, scale and perspective is challenged. It brings to mind a collection of essays on scenography by Arnold Aronson in which he suggests, "in our culture [we] have obliterated any true sense of darkness and our ability to comprehend it, while simultaneously eliminating logical and knowable motivation from lighting [...] light has drifted from its moorings, as it were. It is no longer tied to motivational sources but has taken on a physical force."[3] While the blue-white lighting evokes an eternal dusk, it also implies the light of the ever-present computer screen in our daily lives. In this piece, as Aronson suggests, light is no longer tied to nature but a reflection of a world that never sleeps, lit by artificial sources.

It is also noteworthy that *All That Fall* allows the audience large pockets of imaginative encounter intersected with several strategies of simulation and stimulation, almost imitating society's need to control our attention even when we are at rest. The wall of lights, and indeed the blue-white hue cast over the audience at various intervals, can be seen to be indicative of computer code, technological representations, staring at a screen of lights for information, and the ominous blue-white hue emitted by computers during darkness. The intersection of imaginative encounter and the imitation of artificial computer light presented in *All That Fall* seem to me to demonstrate a significant interrogation of the demands placed upon our attention from day to day, and they also present an examination of the information-intensive, multi-form environments we inhabit.

Similar to the way in which the rocking and the overhead bulbs against the black space can challenge audience members' spatial perspective of the performance space, the audience rocking back and forth while listening to the sounds of the piece affects their interpretation of the rhythm of language and, in turn, encourages a physical mimicking of the pace. We tip back and forth alongside Mrs. Rooney's traipsing dialogue. For instance, exchanges such as the following example, linguistically mimic a rocking chair movement, thereby inviting the audience to do so. Mrs. Rooney's rhythmic speech is presented in the structure of the first spoken line of *All That Fall*, "Poor woman, all alone in that ruinous old house."[4] Moreover, Mrs. Rooney reflects on the way she speaks during a conversation with Mr. Rooney:

Mrs. Rooney: No no, I am agog, tell me all, then we shall press on and never pause, never pause, till we come safe to haven. [*Pause.*]

Mr. Rooney: Never pause... safe to haven... Do you know, Maddy, sometimes one would think that you are struggling with a dead language.

Mrs. Rooney: Yes indeed, Dan, I know full well what you mean, I often have the feeling, it is unspeakably excruciating.[5]

Although she is not referring to her delivery of lines per se, I would propose, like many others who have written about this radio play, that her lines are inherently musical and designed to "consolidate the underlying rhythm... [one must] merge imperceptibly musical and realistic elements of the play",[6] as remarked by Donald McWhinnie, who produced the first broadcast of *All That Fall* on the BBC Third Programme in 1957.

The movement of the rocking chairs can also be seen as an abstract illustration of the constant transition of the technology-saturated world. We are, like technology, in constant transition; we have adapted to the play's rhythm. Notably, this design choice consolidates in an illustrative fashion the processes at work in digital culture, whether an intentional illustration on Pan Pan's part or not. Thus, while the image of the audience rocking may be reminiscent of a scene from the past of an elderly man or woman sitting in a rocking chair beside the radio, it also serves a much more dramaturgical and kinaesthetic purpose. Individually, each element—the light, sound and human sculpture—performs a significant and independent role. However, when they are considered together, their collective commentary and engagement with the influence of digital culture is apparent.

The sense of isolation that I experience during Pan Pan's production of *All That Fall*, alongside the feelings of intimacy and shared community that is instilled through the auditory nature of the performance, could also be regarded as a further comment by Pan Pan on our interactions with communication technologies. This is exemplified in the use of the skull image on the cushion that lies behind each audience member on their rocking chair—the solitary skull for the solitary listener, but a collective haunting of voices and rocking movement to provide a collective experience. Seated in my rocking chair, I was distinctly aware of the seating on the other side of the curtain, being seated on a stage, and the strange feeling of being observed. This served to underline the reference to haunting and point further to an omniscient figure that could move unseen through the sounds and seated spectators. Indeed, while it could be argued that this production of *All That Fall* harks back to an older tradition of gathering families and friends to listen to "the wireless", it also connects to the primarily individual and subjective experiences of new communication technologies. Sound designer for *All That Fall*, Jimmy Eadie, describes the process of sound design for the performance as follows:

> There are eight speakers surrounding the audience and also 4 subwoofers within the room. Each speaker is focused on a certain part of the audience [...] so that the audience can really get a sense of depth within the recording [...] I chose to keep the audio close to each member of the audience so they would look into just one speaker.[7]

Not only does this strategy deliver sound to each individual audience member's "inner ear", as portable devices connected to headphones do, it also speaks of the overall intention of the company to deliver an intimate, subjective experience to each spectator thereby engaging further with the experience of contemporary life.

Pan Pan's use of light as an actor, the formation of audience as a rhythmic moving sculpture, and the adaptation of space as a playground for the senses disrupt the regular conventions that guide our comprehension of performance to allow for an affective and more "felt" comprehension of the play. Beckett's radio play presented a significant challenge to the more traditional radio plays at the time of broadcast in 1957 due to its highly stylized form and use of abstract sound effects. However, I propose that Pan Pan's production of *All That Fall* challenges the form further through their creative adaptation which creates a curated, sensually immersive environment seeking to transform the relatively intimate form of the radio play into both a highly subjective experience and also a collective aesthetic experience.

The absence of a physical performer in conjunction with the techniques of simulation and stimulation that are used encourages high levels of introspection and communicates in a largely affective manner directly to the body of the spectator. The loss of emphasis on the visual as a primary communication point encourages the use of other senses for comprehension. *All That Fall* demonstrates that sound, rather than playing the traditional role of accompaniment or complement, can precede and render the image through visualization and imagination. While Pan Pan's adaptation of *All That Fall* may not seem like an apparent engagement with issues surrounding digital culture, on closer inspection, I would argue, it not only reveals the powerful, disruptive, immersive and intimate potential of sound as a way of encouraging a bodied response but also offers a valuable performative example of what it means to inhabit and engage with an information-intensive world. As suggested by the director of Pan Pan Gavin Quinn, as an audience member of *All That Fall*, "You don't have to understand everything. You can feel things."[8]

Notes

1. Fintan Walsh, "Pan Pan: A theatre of ideas," interview with Gavin Quinn for *Irish Theatre Magazine*, accessed November 10, 2015, http://itmarchive.ie/web/Features/Current/Pan-Pan---A-theatre-of-ideas.aspx.html.
2. Gavin Quinn,"Pan Pan: A Theatre of Ideas," Irish Theatre Magazine, last modified August 20, 2011, http://itmarchive.ie/web/Features/Current/Pan-Pan---A-theatre-of-ideas.aspx.html.
3. Arnold Aronson, *Looking into the Abyss: Essays on Scenography* (University of Michigan Press, 2005), 34–5.
4. Samuel Beckett, *All That Fall* (Faber & Faber, 1957), 7.
5. Ibid., 34–5.
6. Donald McWhinnie, *The Art of Radio* (Faber & Faber, 1959), 134.

7. "Interview with Jimmy Eadie—All That Fall—Pan Pan—Abbey Theatre," *No More Workhouse*, accessed 10 March 2016, https://nomoreworkhorse.com/2016/02/09/interview-with-jimmy-eadie-all-that-fall-pan-pan-abbey-theatre/.
8. Quinn, "Pan Pan: A Theatre of Ideas."

Bibliography

"Interview with Jimmy Eadie—All That Fall—Pan Pan—Abbey Theatre." *No More Workhouse*. Accessed March 1, 2016. https://nomoreworkhorse.com/2016/02/09/interview-with-jimmy-eadie-all-that-fall-pan-pan-abbey-theatre/.

Aronson, Arnold. *Looking into the Abyss: Essays on Scenography*. University of Michigan Press, 2005.

Beckett, Samuel. *All That Fall*. Faber & Faber, 1957.

McWhinnie, Donald. *The Art of Radio*. Faber & Faber, 1959.

Walsh, Fintan. "Pan Pan: A Theatre of Ideas." Interview with Gavin Quinn for Irish Theatre Magazine. Accessed November 10, 2015. http://itmarchive.ie/web/Features/Current/Pan-Pan---A-theatre-of-ideas.aspx.html.

Music in Irish Theatre: The Sound of the People

Ciara Fleming

When considering Irish theatre history, music is not usually the first thing that springs to mind. It would be easy to believe that our musical and theatrical traditions have largely evolved as separate entities, independent from one another. We have few examples of Irish opera, operetta or musical theatre, despite each of these art forms experiencing a significant period of popularity across Europe and America in the past century. As such, the field of study surrounding music in the history of Irish theatre is a slight one. It is perhaps a propensity towards the written word, and the musicality of the Irish command of language that is to answer for this. So suggests Harry White, one of the only scholars to write extensively on the subject, and someone whose ideas I investigate within this piece. He claims that Irish writers have adopted a "words for music" approach, and that the musicality of their written word is the reason for the scant number of integrated Irish musical works.[1] The extent of this argument is something that I will contend in this piece, which has led me to the discovery of many Irish plays that do in fact make significant and purposeful use of music within their pages.

The power of music to evoke feeling in an audience is something that dramatists have long made use of. Music allows dramatists to further explore ideas of identity, be they national, post-colonial, gendered or individual. This exploration of identity through music is at the centre of this piece. I have chosen three playwrights from within the Irish canon to focus on here, as they provide a microcosmic sampling of the broader journey that Irish art has taken with regards to the image of our identity. The work of W.B. Yeats, Brian Friel and Tom Murphy provide strong examples of the ways in which music has been employed within Irish drama across the years. In more recent times, the integrated musical and dramatic work has become a quiet presence within the

C. Fleming (✉)
Trinity College Dublin, Dublin, Ireland

E. Jordan, E. Weitz (eds.), *The Palgrave Handbook of Contemporary Irish Theatre and Performance*,
https://doi.org/10.1057/978-1-137-58588-2_53

output of Irish theatre companies. The very works of operetta and musical that are lacking in the historical canon of Irish drama have begun to occur with increasing frequency within the contemporaneous theatre scene.

Within this piece I will examine some Irish playwrights who have used music within their texts in a more traditional sense, as well as looking to the integrated musical works that we are increasingly seeing produced by Irish writers and theatremakers. Contemporary artists as diverse as Marina Carr, Arthur Riordan, Philip McMahon and many others are following on from the tradition that Yeats, Friel and Murphy have laid down within their musical texts. My study will take into account these artists in an attempt to chart the progression of music within Irish drama. In every case, however, my overriding concern will be what music has done to enhance the representation of identity within that particular play. In the course of this study, I hope to throw some more light onto the music employed by Irish dramatists to striking effect, and perhaps provide a new viewpoint on the role that music has played, and continues to play within the Irish dramatic canon.

Defining a Nation: W.B. Yeats

In order to examine clearly the ways in which music has been used in the Irish theatre, one must return to our early dramatists to receive an indication of how they used music to underpin the identity that they were trying to represent and evoke within their work. National identity within an anti-colonial or post-colonial state is always an emotive issue. Carefully constructed over time, there is often a level of performativity and intent with such national identities, and Ireland is no exception. The work of W.B. Yeats is integral to the cultural and artistic aspects of identity that the Irish people were encouraged to adopt in the lead-up to and directly following their independence. Yeats, along with the other members of the Irish Literary Revival, set about constructing their idea of an ideal national identity for the citizens of the Irish Free State to subscribe to, and the music that he employed within his dramatic works was a powerful tool used to achieve this. It was traditional and evocative, a true reflection of the cultural identity that Yeats was trying to inspire in his audiences. In writing about the "cultural bomb" of an imposed language Ngũgĩ wa Thiong'o claims that the effect of the English language is to annihilate pre-colonial identities, and that this happens across every sector of a population; physical, mental and spiritual.[2] As such, Yeats was tasked with creating a powerful identity for the Irish people, one that would operate not simply on a political or intellectual level, but also on an emotional and spiritual one.

The key ideals of this new culturally led national identity are noteworthy, and the ways in which Yeats used music in his work to advance these ideals is striking. The music that Yeats employs in his plays certainly serves this romantic depiction of pre-colonial Ireland, and paints a clear picture of the "ancient idealism" that Lady Gregory wished to inspire within her mission statement of the Abbey Theatre.[3] The lyrics are often nostalgic, and their sound invoked

Gaelic musicality in its most traditional sense. In *At the Hawk's Well* (1916), the musicians sing of the protagonist:

> He has lost what may not be found
> Till men heap his burial-mound
> And all the history ends.[4]

This certainly could not be classified as "buffoonery" or "easy sentiment", but rather expresses the heroic idea of Ireland that Yeats and Gregory were intent on showcasing. Yeats's music underlines this at every turn, and his final song of the same play truly emphasizes the ideals of the Ireland that he was trying to create.

The music of these early plays is described by Arnold Bax as being of a traditional folk sound, which echoes the themes of Yeats's plays, derived from folktales. Bax, a distinguished composer who spent considerable time studying music in Ireland, speaks of the "strange and startling richness" of the Irish folk music that was used in these pieces.[5] This strangeness was used to its emotive best in Yeats's final song of the play, which yearns for the familiar, human faces of the Irish people, rejecting the cold reception of the outside colonial forces:

> Come to me, human faces
> Familiar memories;
> I have found hateful eyes
> Among the desolate places,
> Unfaltering, unmoistened eyes.[6]

Derek B. Scott writes about the power of music within society and how it can become a formative force of that society: "because of its emotional impact, music also possesses a political power that can be exerted in the forging of national and social class identities".[7] He argues that music has powers that extend far beyond the emotional or superficial. This consideration of how music integrated within other art forms can operate as key to an understanding of why it is so important in the particular case of the Irish theatre.

The unity of the cultural idealism he was cultivating was something which Yeats used music to further, when he felt that language had exhausted its capabilities. Yeats had an intensely held belief in the "essential indivisibility of the two arts", drama and music.[8] He employed both his poetic dramatic tone, and the music of his productions to advance this cultural ideal which had far-reaching implications not only on the artistic landscape of the country but also on the political one. He wished to create what Anthony Bradley calls a "model of the nation" and to author a singular national identity that the whole population of the island would follow.[9] In speaking of this national identity, Yeats said: "I began to plot and scheme how one might seal with the right image the soft wax before it began to harden".[10] This is clearly evidenced in Yeats's works, and the music used within his plays further echoes this. The soaring melodies and lilting familiarity of the music used in Yeats's productions spoke to the specific sense of "Irishness" and identity that he was trying to draw out of the public at large.

There is much thought about the use of music to reclaim a voice for those who are otherwise omitted from the accepted narrative within a theatrical or cultural setting. The identity of women is often expressed and reclaimed through music within Irish theatre, something which is evident in Yeats's work. Nowhere is this more evident than with his use of the Cathleen Ni Houlihan figure, who appears in much of Yeats's dramatic works, most prominently, of course, in *The Countess Cathleen* and *Cathleen Ni Houlihan*, written with Lady Gregory.

The title character of *Cathleen Ni Houlihan* appears in the form of a mystical traveller, who manages to musically entice the young men of Ireland to follow her into battle to reclaim her "four beautiful green fields".[11] While her initial stories seem not to move the family whose cottage she has visited, it is Cathleen's song that wins over the heart and mind of Michael, their elder son. The words of her song seem to transfix him, and he will not be then distracted from her cause: "I do not know what that song means, but tell me something I can do for you."[12] The power of Cathleen's music to make Michael forget his own bride and wedding speaks to Yeats's belief in the power of the musical and cultural product in promoting an idea of Irish national identity.

Just as Cathleen's song inspired Michael to follow her into battle against the colonial powers, Yeats hoped that it would inspire contemporary listeners to do the same, if not in the physical sense then at least in political and ideological terms. Cathleen's song is heard after she has exited the stage, reminding us of the omnipresent nature of this newfound national identity. Yeats, however, was emphatic that it should be the experience of hearing these songs that would inspire action in his audiences, that listening to the words should be a secondary activity: "I say to the musician 'Lose my words in patterns of sound as the name of God is lost in Arabian arabesques. They are a secret between the singers, myself, yourself.'"[13] In this manner, Cathleen sings proudly of the virtuous men who will fight for retrieval of her four immaculate fields:

> They shall be remembered for ever,
> They shall be alive for ever,
> They shall be speaking for ever,
> The people shall hear them for ever.[14]

Here Cathleen uses the tool of music to express a uniquely female viewpoint that could not otherwise be expounded within the text. Yeats used music to embody the virtues of the Nation-as-Mother, and to elicit an emotional response from the Irish people that aligned with this new national identity, which was so influenced by the performance of an internal, domestic, feminine sphere. It is clear he wished for the music in his plays to have the same effect upon the Irish people as Cathleen's song had on Michael, whether this is expressed ideologically or through action. The use of music to express both the identity of the Irish nation, as well as the identity of its women who may not otherwise have been afforded the public space to speak about their lived experiences, is something to which I will return. This trait continues to be seen within the Irish theatre landscape and is a noteworthy aspect of the power that music has within drama to give a voice to the voiceless.

Exploring a Nation: Brian Friel

The use of music to explore themes of identity and belonging is a key feature in the work of Brian Friel, and a device that has endured within the work of contemporary theatremakers in his wake. The characters within Friel's plays often employ music as a powerful suggestion of personal identity; when we look in the broader sense at his body of work it gives us an idea of the national identity to which his characters contribute. He uses opposing styles of music within his plays to illustrate the emotional background of his characters and their communities. These varied sounds are often deeply evocative of a particular moment in time, and occur at pivotal points within his texts. The issues of identity and Irishness that his work has come to encompass are augmented and exemplified by the music of his texts, and it is this that I will investigate here. It can be suggested that within the "willed act" of nation-forming, or indeed re-forming, Friel's weapon of choice is music.[15] Specifically, his plays address the duality of the post-colonial position within an Irish identity which is still warring between the influences of the colonial powers and the post-colonial nationalists, both of which were essentially imposed upon the Irish people.

The music in *Dancing at Lughnasa* (1990) provides a succinct example of the duality that can occur within a post-colonial setting, as the Mundy sisters expose the conflicting influences that comprise their identities, and the Irish identity as a whole. Much of the music within this play has origins outside of Ireland, and the sisters' preoccupation with hearing these songs over "Marconi", the wireless radio, is a reminder of the omnipresent, unspoken desire to disassociate themselves with the rural sorts of Irishness of which they are in fact a product. "The Isle of Capri" and "Anything Goes" are the most enduring songs within the text, as each recurs sung by multiple characters. Their upbeat jazzy sounds distracting perhaps from lyrics that are in fact rather plaintive, they seem to form a source of distraction for the Mundy sisters. Although these non-Irish songs are the most numerous, the most significant musical moment within the text has an Irish tune, "The Mason's Apron", at its heart.

This section of wild abandon is one of the most momentous in the play. It begins with the traditional reel, which prompts the sisters to start their dance. Their movements become wild as they dance with reckless abandon to the increasingly exuberant music, fiddles soaring and becoming wilder and less constrained as the song goes on. This is the only moment within the text that the five sisters are truly spontaneous and, arguably, happy. They overcome the rigorous pressures of propriety that they have hitherto imposed upon themselves, and revert to an almost tribal method of untethered self-expression. The fact that the music accompanying this moment of freedom is Irish is a significant one, especially when we consider the implications within the post-colonial frame and how this affects the play's characters. Csilla Bertha notes that the use of indigenous musical moments within literature "with how-ever much self-irony and self-mockery they are performed—create a spiritual and emotional contact with a part of their heritage".[16] An indigenous sound is the one Friel has chosen to engender this moment of freedom and autonomy in *Lughnasa*, in stark contrast to the extraneous ones that occupy the characters throughout the rest of the play. This speaks volumes about the power that music affords the Irish national identity, in addition to the affect it has on the identity of the characters themselves.

The command and mastery of language forms a deeply rooted part of Ireland's national identity, and it is known as a country of poets and wordsmiths. Language and its employment, power and effect are one of the most notable recurring themes within Friel's work. Seen most vividly in *Translations* (1980), it is summed up by Richard Kearney, who says of Friel that "his overriding concern is to examine the contemporary crisis of language as a medium of communication and representation", and indeed music can be seen as one of Friel's tools in overcoming, or at least bypassing, this crisis.[17] His characters revert to musicality when words can no longer serve as adequate expressions of their inner selves.

The notion of Ireland's literary identity is taken one step further by White who suggests that this literary richness takes the place of a musical one within the Irish canon. In his book *Music and the Irish Literary Imagination* he seeks to examine "the extent to which literature has taken the place of music in the emancipation of an art form answerable to Ireland's sense of itself".[18] He argues, "Literature fills the void left by the absence of art music in Ireland".[19] This fails, however, to recognise the extensive use of music within much of Ireland's literary output, and the manner in which it has created a unique musical awareness within the nation's artistic consciousness. The manner in which White suggests that one can stand in for the other negates the significant effects that come from literary and musical influences coming together as indeed they do in Friel's plays, something which White's earlier work in fact recognises. Writing of Friel in 1999, White acknowledges that in Friel's work "the condition of music both absorbs and re-defines the condition of the drama itself".[20]

The protagonist of Friel's *Performances* (2003), Leoš Janacek, reminds us that music is "the language of feeling itself: a unique vocabulary of sounds created by feeling itself", which suggests that Friel too is opposed to the segregation of words and music as separate art forms that White describes.[21] Where White argues that the Irish theatre has developed a history of adopting "words for music", Friel's practice suggests the opposite: music fulfils a function that language cannot, owing, perhaps, to Seamus Deane's assertion that the Irish as a nation have been left with a linguistic aphasia following the erasure of Gaelic as our mother tongue.[22] Richard Pine would seem to support this, in his argument that musicality is "the overriding characteristic of what he (Friel) is writing" owing to the fact that "our modern society ... has exhausted our traditional strategies of speaking to ourselves, and ... some kind of 'music' is necessary even if only to give language a rest and an opportunity to reformulate itself".[23] Friel and other Irish writers must look to music when their language is restricted in such a manner, which proves a firm contention for White's argument regarding an Irish tradition of "words for music".[24]

Many post-colonial theorists expand upon Homi Bhabha's idea of the ephemeral "third Space"[25] between colonizer and colonized where the "incommensurable elements—the stubborn chunks—as the basis of cultural identification"[26] can yet be found. It has been suggested that Ballybeg is a "Fifth Province"[27] or "the non-physical centre of Ireland above borders, political, cultural, sectarian divisions".[28] Whether it is called a "third place" or a "fifth province", it is possible to suggest that this evanescent space between colonizer and colonized is best expressed in Friel's work through music. Where the demands of the society surrounding a voiceless individual make language impossible, music triumphs, and nowhere is this clearer than in the work of Brian Friel.

Reclaiming a Nation: Tom Murphy

So far this chapter has noted how Irish playwrights have used music to express identity, to give a voice to marginalized members of their communities, and to elicit emotional responses regarding the state of the nation. Tom Murphy mirrors these effects in his works, and the sound of a Murphy play is a key indication of a different form of Irishness that I have not yet interrogated. The evolution of Ireland's national identity as both a cultural and a post-colonial product is charted throughout Murphy's work, and he uses music to powerful effect to underpin this fact. The Ireland that Murphy depicts is one that has struggled with the various nuances of the Irish condition, which proves a noticeable contrast to the aspirational nature of Friel's work. In Murphy's plays are seen the bleak realities of the struggles that coincide with life in Ireland—struggles that Yeats, and to a lesser extent Friel, attempt to conceal from the spectator lest their belief in the nationalist ideal falter. This makes in Murphy's plays for a fascinating insight into the complexities of the Irish national identity and all the contradictions of which it is comprised. And nowhere is this clearer than when reflecting upon the sonic experiences of Murphy's audiences.

This growth in the complexity of representation can be seen if we contrast Friel's emigration story of *Philadelphia, Here I Come!* (1964), with those of Murphy's plays, particularly *A Whistle in the Dark* (1961). Friel provides an optimistic depiction of a bright young man leaving his troubled home life for happier climes, reflected in the cheery escapism of Gar's renditions of *Philadelphia, Here I Come!* Murphy, however, gives an insight into the difficulties that arise when an optimistic émigré is confronted with memories of home, something that is underpinned to no subtle effect when the audience hears the violence with which his brothers sing songs of their homeland. *A Whistle in the*

Dark explores the vulnerability of the Irish national identity in the newly post-colonial state, as well as the vulnerability of difference, of anyone who comes to be perceived as an outsider within their deeply traditional communities. This fragility is evident in the profound mistrust of Michael from those within his own family. The difficulties of such a position are highlighted with the music that Murphy uses in the text.

The music in this play comes to the fore at the climactic point of tension between the characters, a trait that can also be seen in many of Murphy's other works. When we reach the third act of *Whistle*, we have become familiar with the tensions of the performative masculinity that the brothers of the play are bound by. The sheer ferocity with which they try to uphold this image rises throughout the play, and by Act Three has reached boiling point. Dada holds the match under these tenacious flames by choosing to sing first a call to arms, then an evocative, romanticized depiction of Irish countryside. For Dada and the Carney brothers, no opportunity is lost to celebrate their national identity, thereby emphasizing the chasm that they perceive between it and that of Michael's whom they view as a traitor both to the family and to the country:

> Far away from the land of the shamrock and heather,
> In search of a living as exiles we roam,
> And whenever we chance to assemble together,
> We think of the land where we once had a home.[29]

The words of this piece are not dissimilar to those that Yeats used in his early plays, and yet the sound of this outburst is altogether more guttural and base than the music of Yeats's pieces. Here the sound of raucous drunken singing so familiar to many Irish people is what Murphy capitalizes upon to evoke feelings of tension in his audience. The words of Dada's song are idealistic, which contradicts the antagonistic manner in which they are performed. Michael, on the other hand, is a symbol of the hybridity that so often manifests itself in the Irish diaspora. We see that his new life in England has provided him with a different perspective than his brothers, one that they abuse him for with such doggedness that it eventually leads to the play's great tragedy in the final scene. His silence in the face of his brothers' musical outbursts further exemplifies his positioning as "other". Either he has forgotten the melodies of his homeland, or he has realized the manipulative intent with which they are being performed. In any case, it is his silence that once again sets him apart. Here Murphy manifests another of the emotional impacts that music has upon Irish theatre, in amplifying the impact of silence, when contrasted with the strong presence of musicality within his work.

Like Friel, Murphy also uses music to lend agency to the characters for whom it does not come easily. This is noted with Vera in *The Wake* (1998), who engineers the musical wake of the title to bend her family to her wishes. In this scene we see how far removed from a traditional heroine Murphy's Vera is, her silence like Michael's, proving both her strangeness and her strength in the face of the cacophonous sound of the play's musicality.

Murphy's skilful and evocative use of music is at its most notable in *The Gigli Concert* (1983), where the effects of his music become less political or practical, and more emotional. Here J.P.W. King, practitioner of the mystifying "dynamatology", encounters a so-named Irish Man who is an obsessive fan of tenor Beniamino Gigli. The play relies heavily on the music of Gigli for its dramatic arc and the music is integrated throughout the play in very regular intervals. The Man spends the entirety of the play attempting to imitate the talents of Gigli, and the audience can see how this very obsession has been wreaking havoc within his personal life. As noted above, White has suggested that the use of music within Irish plays can be linked firmly with the loss of the Irish language. He submits that Irish playwrights turn to music when they cannot glean satisfaction or representation from writing in the imposed English. If one agrees that this is true, the example of *The Gigli Concert* becomes a significant one in that it turns to music outside of Irish tradition for its expression of identity. Both this fact and the sheer volume and integration of music in this piece make it unique within Murphy's catalogue.

White describes the use of music in this piece as a moment "where the incantatory magic of Irish and the ineffable promise of music consort together as primary points of imaginative reference".[30] The fact that it is European art music that engenders this imaginative release proves perhaps, a growth in our Irish national identity, which need no longer be defined singularly within traditional Irish music. The openness to accept European influences as a significant contribution to the Irish national identity demonstrates a shift from the ways in which music was used to represent this identity within the works of Yeats and Friel. White's argument that Irish writers favoured "words for music" is one that has been questioned extensively here.[31] It is within *The Gigli Concert*, however, that the claim can no longer be merely questioned, but countered.

The way in which the music of Gigli overcomes JPW and the Irish Man is an overwhelming example of music and imagination finally triumphing over language and reality. They succumb to the music of their imaginations, relying on the otherworldly presence of Gigli that the Man has curated and venerated. Director Ben Barnes describes the men of the play as "middle-aged men in crisis"; however they find salvation within the music of the piece, most notably in the remarkable final sequence involving JPW.[32] Can the same be said, perhaps, of national identity? Murphy's writing tackles not only the middle age of these characters, but also the middle age of Ireland as a nation. The crisis of identity is one that has lessened, and with Murphy's use of non-indigenous music, perhaps we are seeing the security of this identity growing. No longer does the "symbolic force of music as an agent of nationalist discourse supervend any real concern with the thing itself", but rather the sole concern of this piece is the music itself.[33] Surely this must then indicate that the need for music to act violently as a nationalist discourse has lessened.

Now that the case has been ventured for the dramaturgical use of music evolving towards a more creative, imagined world, a link can be made to a gradually confident identity. Loomba argues that once tainted by imperialism "even our imaginations must remain forever colonised".[34] *The Gigli Concert*, however, is a powerful refutation of this claim; as we see, the music employed by Murphy allow his characters to transcend borders, language, and even reality, in favour of the realm of the imagination, which knows no boundaries; as Christopher Murray has proposed, "the music is finally imagined, and therefore real".[35]

Questioning a Nation: Contemporary Artists

The manner in which Yeats, Friel and Murphy have used music within their texts is something that has been echoed by many other playwrights in their wake. At the Abbey Theatre in 2014, *The Risen People* made a point of recreating the traditional, nostalgic sound favoured by Yeats in order to tell the story of the 1913 Lockout. Composer and musical director Conor Linehan used a mixture of traditional melodies and original pieces, achieving an effect not dissimilar to that employed by Yeats. Rousing choral melodies in a traditional style are augmented with haunting solo pieces. The plaintive "Only the Whores Have Money" brings contemporary language to the old practice of a female character singing a ballad of warning or despair. In Yeats and Lady Gregory's *Cathleen Ni Houlihan*, she begs, "Do not give money for prayers for the dead that shall die tomorrow".[36] The two pieces, written more than one hundred years apart, aim for similar effects upon the spectator via musical means. Both then and now, dramatists see the need to use music when language can go no further in the attempt to inspire feeling in their audiences.

Friel's use of traditional music to allow the dream of freedom to breathe is another characteristic that has been continued by contemporary playwrights. In Marina Carr's *On Raftery's Hill* (2009) we see a striking example of this in young Ded, whose use of music as a form of escapism comes to him while in the cornfield, the only place he can escape the tyranny of his father. Likewise, in Brendan Behan's *The Hostage* (1958) music is used to inspire dreams of freedom from oppression. Here Behan takes inspiration from Dublin's rich music-hall tradition, something that continues to inspire playwrights, as we can see from the 2017 revival of Michael West's *Dublin by Lamplight* (2004), also with music by Conor Linehan. Again we have examples of traditional music allowing characters to transcend their situation, proving that an indigenous Irish sound can be synonymous with change as well as tradition.

Contemporary playwrights have continued Friel's tradition of utilizing music where words can no longer function to masterful effect. Philip McMahon and Raymond Scannell's *Town is Dead* (2016) allows its characters to break into song when the grim nature of their reality can no longer be expressed in words. With a contemporary sound and continuous pulse, the music of this piece augments the characters' struggle to express the difficulties of life in present-day Dublin city. This sound becomes more wistful and innocent when Ellen sings of her love affair with "gorgeous George", becoming reminiscent of the simplicity of a traditional Irish work song, a repeated phrase used to pass the time and distract the mind. Both of these appositional sounds are reminiscent of the traits we have discussed within the work of Friel, and the ways in which he uses music to depict both the realities of home and the aspirations of leaving it.

Still today Irish playwrights are using music to allow their female characters a voice where the traditional methods of language may be lost to them, just as Murphy did before them. Arthur Riordan's *The Train* (2015) uses a vibrant score by Bill Whelan to bring life to the story of the forty-seven women who journeyed to Belfast in search of illegal contraceptives in 1971. As the women rousingly sing "now we're really gonna make the world listen", one wonders if they could have had the same autonomy were it not for the musical aspect of their storytelling.[37] Certainly, they could have told their story; however, as has been seen thus far, Irish dramatists have reached for music to elucidate upon women's narratives. Music allows them to transcend the usual strictures of narrative form, and thus tell their stories outside the patriarchal linguistic system. Nowhere is this more pertinent than in *The Train*. Stacy Wolf writes extensively on the musical as a feminist art form. She explains that historically, musicals exceed dramas in presenting women with "an identity that exceeds motherhood".[38] She also points out that music allows them this voice, and gives them the opportunity to "reclaim their experiences and their bodies through song".[39] Another example of utilizing a musical form to tell women's stories can be seen in Marina Carr's *Mary Gordon* (2016). This oratorio, with libretto written by Carr and music by Brian Irvine and Neil Martin, was one of the few pieces to focus on stories of women in the Easter Rising during Ireland's 2016 commemorative events, and was aided by a musical medium.

Murphy's use of non-Irish musical influences is also something that has been continued by contemporary writers. Emmet Kirwan's *Dublin Oldschool* (2014), for example, blends his uniquely colloquial writing style with a constant undercurrent of contemporary beats, hints of rap, and sections where the line between spoken and sung becomes indeterminable. Like Murphy, Kirwan has the confidence to utilize musical influences that are distinctly non-Irish, and yet both succeed wildly in capturing an essence of what Irishness was at their respective contemporaneous moments. In both pieces, the characters use music as a vehicle to search for the meaning that they crave, and after each it is the music rather than the meaning that is likely to be reverberating in the minds of the audience.

In addition to these echoes of how Yeats, Friel and Murphy used music, the contemporary Irish theatre landscape exhibits an increasingly varied and unconstrained exploration of music. No longer do playwrights simply add songs to pertinent moments within their plays rather, they are integrating music within their pieces in a more considered and effusive manner. Companies such as Rough Magic are known for their integration of music and theatre, with that element of wry self-awareness that audiences of contemporary musical theatre have come to expect. *Improbable Frequency* (2004), by Arthur Riordan and Bell Helicopter, could be seen as the height of their success within this genre.

The piece received multiple remounts and was praised by audiences and critics alike. Centring on the relationship between Britain and Ireland during the Second World War, this is another example of music being used to further political discussion among the theatrical audience. Rough Magic continue this political theme with more recent works such as the aforementioned *The Train*. Whether it be an integrated musical theatre piece or a more traditional drama with musical accompaniment, the commitment towards a musical form is always evident within the work of Rough Magic.

Following in the tradition of using music to voice the voiceless, THISISPOPBABY's *Alice in Funderland* (2012) uses music to allow an insight into the dark and twisted tale of one night out in Dublin's fair city. As an audience member one suspects that this topic could not be handled with a such tongue-in-cheek attitude were it not for the music, which allows us to suspend our cynicism and follow Alice on her madcap trip around the city. In a diametrically opposed manner, Kellie Hughes's *Death at Intervals* (2016) uses music to explore a much more elemental state. It deals with the murky line between death and her charges, using music to heighten this emotional impact upon the audience almost lulling them to sleep, only then to shake their nerves with an uneasy crescendo warning of the impending collapse. These hugely oppositional styles speak to the wide range of ways in which Irish theatre-makers are now using music to augment their works. All of this does not even speak to the commercial successes of conventional musicals such as *I Keano* (2005), *Once* (2015), *The Commitments* (2016), *The Girl from the North Country* (2017), written and directed by Conor McPherson, with music and lyrics by Bob Dylan, and *Angela's Ashes: The Musical* (2017), with music and lyrics by Adam Howell and book by Paul Hurt.

Why there are so few of them is a vital question. Perhaps, as White suggests, it is due to our rich literary history that was in such overflowing abundance that it did not leave room for a musical theatre tradition to grow. We have seen, however, that Irish dramatists have a long history of using music within their works to great effect. There is a suspected element of snobbery among audiences and artists, who see musical theatre as a lesser art form. This may be the reason for many of the contemporary pieces I have discussed being billed as a "play within music" (Philip McMahon's *Town is Dead*, 2016) or a "musical play" (Frank McGuinness's *Donegal*, 2016) rather than simply a musical. In his review of *Alice in Funderland*, Jim Carroll issues this caveat: "However, it is a musical and we were never going to get beyond mere surface in that context."[40] It is this very attitude that, perhaps, seeks to marginalize the aesthetic and artistic value of musical pieces, and is something that must be checked in order for our proud tradition of using music within the plays of the Irish canon to extend to a body of more integrated works of musical theatre.

Through this examination of the three playwrights and the works of contemporary artists that followed them, taking them as a microcosm of what was occurring within the Irish theatre scene at large, we can glean some small insight into the ways in which music has augmented the works of its canon.

The music used within our theatre has been instrumental in commenting upon issues of identity, belonging, politics and revolution. While integrated musical theatrical works such as operas or musicals may be underrepresented within the Irish tradition, in committing to the investigation of music within the dramatic canon one will note that this is an area abundant with material.

The theatre of Yeats was concerned with authoring a myth that would unify the nation's idea of its own identity. Whether we are speaking of Yeats's creation of this myth, Friel's reminiscing of it, Murphy's debunking of it, or contemporary artists' challenging of it, music has often been an integral tool in the process. Tom Murphy in interview has repeated Walter Pater's assertion that, "all art aspires to the condition of music", and while surrendering language to music may seem counterintuitive for a writer, this indeed is what Murphy does, proving the vast distance that Irish national identity has come from the days of Yeats needing to assert it through every phrase both musical and spoken.[41]

The question of the "music of language" versus the "language of music" is one that we now can see represented from both sides within the Irish dramatic tradition. There are few who would dispute the musicality of the writing of Irish playwrights, but we should note that while this is indeed significant, they have also exhibited a level of musicality and power in their works that is entirely wordless. These dramatists have used music in order to recover the Irish voice and to allow the subaltern, oppressed, colonized classes to speak. The journey to this point has been a meandering one, and is one that will continue to extend, helped along by the use of music to express what words cannot. Tom Murphy it seems, agrees with the power of music to affect such change in the human soul: "But it can be done. To sing. The sound to clothe our emotion and aspiration."[42]

Notes

1. Harry White, *Music and the Irish Literary Imagination* (Oxford: Oxford University Press, 2009), 8.
2. Ngũgĩ wa Thiong'o, *Decolonising the Mind: The Politics of Language in African Literature* (London: James Currey, 2011).
3. Mary Trotter, *Ireland's National Theatres: Political Performance and the Origins of the Irish Dramatic Movement*, (Syracuse: Syracuse University Press, 2001), 11.
4. W.B. Yeats, *Collected Plays of William Butler Yeats* (Bristol: Macmillan Library Reference, 1994), 217.
5. Declan Kiberd and Patrick J. Mathews, *Handbook of the Irish Revival: An anthology of Irish cultural and political writings 1891–1922* (Notre Dame: University of Notre Dame Press, 2016), 303.
6. Yeats, *Collected Plays of William Butler Yeats*, 219.
7. Derek B. Scott, *Musical Style and Social Meaning: Selected Essays* (Farnham: Ashgate, 2010), 235.
8. Paul Cohen, "Words for Music: Yeats's Late Songs," *The Canadian Journal of Irish Studies* 10(2) (1984): 16.

9. Anthony Bradley, *Imagining Ireland in the Poems and Plays of W.B. Yeats: Nation, Class, and State* (Basingstoke: Palgrave Macmillan, 2011), 12.
10. Ibid., 13.
11. Yeats, *Collected Plays of William Butler Yeats*, 81.
12. Ibid., 86.
13. Kiberd and Mathews, *Handbook of the Irish Revival*, 305.
14. Yeats, *Collected Plays of William Butler Yeats*, 86.
15. White, *Music and the Irish literary Imagination*, 208.
16. Csilla Bertha, "Brian Friel as Postcolonial Playwright", in *The Cambridge Companion to Brian Friel*, ed. Anthony Roche (Cambridge: Cambridge University Press, 2009), 163.
17. Richard Kearney, "Friel and the Politics of Language Play", *Massachusetts Review: A Quarterly of Literature, the Arts and Public Affairs*, 28 (3) (1987): 510.
18. White, *Music and the Irish Literary Imagination*, 21.
19. Ibid., 15.
20. Harry White, "Brian Friel and the Condition of Music", *Irish University Review* 29, Special Issue; Brian Friel (1999): 15.
21. Brian Friel, *Collected Plays; Volume Five* (Loughcrew, Oldcastle, Meath: Gallery Press, 2016), 207.
22. White, *Music and the Irish Literary Imagination*, 8.
23. Donald E. Morse, Csilla Bertha, and Mária Kurdi, *Brian Friel's Dramatic Artistry: "The Work has Value"* (Dublin: Carysfort Press, 2006), 62.
24. White, *Music and the Irish Literary Imagination*, 8.
25. Homi K. Bhabha, *The Location of Culture* (London: Routledge, 1997), 36.
26. Bertha, "Brian Friel as Postcolonial Playwright", 157.
27. Ibid., 155.
28. Ibid., 154.
29. Tom Murphy, *Plays: Four* (London: Methuen Drama, 1997), 69.
30. White, *Music and the Irish Literary Imagination*, 22.
31. Ibid., 8.
32. Christopher Murray, ed., *"Alive in time": The Enduring Drama of Tom Murphy: New Essays* (Dublin: Carysfort Press, 2010), 155.
33. Harry White, *The Progress of Music in Ireland* (Dublin: Four Courts Press, 2005), 67.
34. Ania Loomba, *Colonialism-postcolonialism* (London: Routledge, Taylor & Francis Group, 2015), 159.
35. Murray, "*Alive in time*," 147.
36. Yeats, *Collected Plays of William Butler Yeats*, 86.
37. Arthur Riordan and Bill Whelan, "The Train" (Dublin: Project Arts Centre, 2016).
38. Stacy E. Wolf, *A Problem like Maria: Gender and Sexuality in the American Musical* (Ann Arbor: University of Michigan Press, 2007), 16.
39. Ibid., 19.
40. Jim Carroll, "A Night in Funderland," *The Irish Times*, April 24, 2012, http://www.irishtimes.com/blogs/ontherecord/2012/04/24/a-night-in-funderland/.
41. Murray, "*Alive in time*," 139.
42. Tom Murphy, *Plays: Three* (London: Methuen Drama, 1994), 236.

Bibliography

Behan, Brendan. *The Hostage*. London: Eyre Methuen, 2000.

Bertha, Csilla. "Brian Friel as Postcolonial Playwright." in *The Cambridge Companion to Brian Friel*. ed. Anthony Roche. Cambridge: Cambridge University Press, 2009.

Bhabha, Homi K. *The Location of Culture*. London: Routledge, 1997.

Bradley, Anthony. *Imagining Ireland in the Poems and Plays of W.B. Yeats: Nation, Class, and State*. Basingstoke: Palgrave Macmillan, 2011.

Carr, Marina. *Plays Two*. London: Faber and Faber, 2009.

———, Brian Irvine, and Neil Martin, *Mary Gordon*. Dublin: National Concert Hall, 2016.

Carroll, Jim. "A Night in Funderland," *The Irish Times*, April 24, 2012. http://www.irishtimes.com/blogs/ontherecord/2012/04/24/a-night-in-funderland/.

Cohen, Paul. "Words for Music: Yeats's Late Songs." *The Canadian Journal of Irish Studies*, 10(2) (1984).

Doyle, Roddy. *The Commitments*. London: Palace Theatre, 2013.

Dwyer, Benjamin. *Different Voices: Irish Music and Music in Ireland*. Hofheim: Wolke Verlag, 2014.

Everett, William A. and Paul Laird. *The Cambridge Companion to the Musical*. Cambridge: Cambridge University Press, 2011.

Fay, Jimmy. *The Risen People*. Dublin: Abbey Theatre, 2015.

Fitzgerald, Mark and John O'Flynn, *Music and Identity in Ireland and Beyond*. Farnham: Ashgate Publishing Ltd, 2014.

Fleming, Ciara. "Abbey Theatre Dublin." 2016.

Friel, Brian and Seamus Deane. *Brian Friel: Plays One*. London: Faber and Faber, 1996.

———, and Christopher Murray. *Brian Friel: Plays Two*. London: Faber, 1999.

———. *Performances*. Loughcrew, Oldcastle, Meath: Gallery Press, 2003.

Grene, Nicholas and Tom Murphy. *Talking About Tom Murphy*. Dublin: Carysfort Press, 2002.

Helicopter, Bell and Arthur Riordan. *Improbable Frequency*. Dublin: O Reilly Theatre, 2004.

Hughes, Kelly. *Death at Intervals*. Galway: An Taidhbhearc, 2016.

Jennings, Jennifer and Philip McMahon, et al. *Alice in Funderland*. Dublin: Abbey Theatre, April 10, 2012.

Kearney, Richard. "Friel and the Politics of Language Play." *Massachussets Review: A Quarterly of Literature, the Arts and Public Affairs*, 28(3) (1987).

Kiberd, Declan and Patrick J. Mathews. *Handbook of the Irish Revival: An Anthology of Irish Cultural and Political Writings 1891–1922*. Notre Dame: University of Notre Dame Press, 2016.

Kirwan, Emmet. *Dublin Oldschool*. Dublin: Project Arts Centre, 2014.

Loomba, Ania. *Colonialism-postcolonialism*. London: Routledge, Taylor & Francis Group, 2015.

Matthews, Arthur and Michael Nugent. *I, Keano*. Dublin: Olympia Theatre, 2005.

McMahon, Philip and Scannell, Raymond. *Town Is Dead*. Dublin: Peacock stage, Abbey Theatre, 2016.

McPhearson, Conor. *The Girl from the North Country*. London: The Old Vic, 2017.

Morse, Donald E., Csilla Bertha, and Mária Kurdi, eds. *Brian Friel's Dramatic Artistry: "The Work Has Value"*. Dublin: Carysfort Press, 2006.

Mulcahy, Michael and Marie Fitzgibbon. *The Voice of the People: Songs and History of Ireland*. Dublin: O'Brien, 1982.
Murphy, Tom. *Plays: Three*. London: Methuen Drama, 1994.
———. *Plays: Four*. London: Methuen Drama, 1997.
———. *The Wake*. London: Methuen Drama, 1998.
Murray, Christopher, ed. *"Alive in Time": The Enduring Drama of Tom Murphy: New Essays*. Dublin: Carysfort Press, 2010.
O'Malley, Aidan. *Field Day and the Translation of Irish Identities Performing Contradictions*. New York: Palgrave Macmillan, 2011.
Riordan, Arthur and Bill Whelan. *The Train*. Dublin: Project Arts Centre, 2016.
Smyth, Gerry. *Music in Irish Cultural History*. Dublin: Irish Academic Press, 2009.
Thiong'o, Ngũgĩ wa. *Decolonising the Mind: The Politics of Language in African Literature*. London: J. Currey, 2011.
Trotter, Mary. *Decolonising the Mind: The Politics of Language in African Literature*. London: J. Currey, 2011.
Walsh, E. *Once, the Musical*. Dublin: Olympia Theatre, 2011.
West, Michael. *Dublin by Lamplight*. Dublin: Abbey Theatre, 2004.
White, Harry. "*The Sanctuary Lamp*: An Assessment." *Irish University Review* 17, Tom Murphy Issue, 1987.
———. "Brian Friel and the Condition of Music." *Irish University Review* 29, Special Issue; Brian Friel, 1999.
———. *The Progress of Music in Ireland*. Dublin: Four Courts Press, 2005.
———. *Music and the Irish Literary Imagination*. Oxford: Oxford University Press, 2009.
Wolf, Stacy E. *A Problem like Maria: Gender and Sexuality in the American Musical*. Ann Arbor: University of Michigan Press, 2007.
Yeats, W. B. *Collected Plays of William Butler Yeats*. Bristol: Macmillan Library Reference, 1994.

Sightings of Comic Dexterity

Eric Weitz

It would be a daunting prospect for any comic performer, welcoming the annual worldwide assembly of the International Society for Humor Studies on 27 June 2016, for which I was the host and organizer. A lecture hall in the Trinity College Dublin Arts Block is not the most congenial of performance spaces (although the blackboard may come in handy), and anyone looking for laughter from a roomful of humour scholars and practitioners from forty different countries is leaping headlong into unchartable territory.

Little John Nee had accepted the challenge several months earlier. Once a Gaelic clown poet, storyteller and minstrel who wandered city streets in the 1980s, he was by now a member of Aosdána. I first saw him in Barabbas' production of *Johnny Patterson the Singing Irish Clown* (2010) at the Project Arts Centre. I was taken on that occasion by the perfect marriage of historical figure and contemporary performer, neither of whom, incredibly, I had previously come across. Before me was a singular singing clown portraying a singular singing clown from another era, holding the stage with some superpower that seemed to derive from a palpably honest soul in the body of a consummate performer.

I had been reminded of Little John's plaintive composition, "The World Brings Fools Together", by Raymond Keane, who used it to break hearts at the end of *City of Clowns* (2010), the chorus of which goes like this: "The world brings fools together / So that they may help one another / Through the fear and the terror / The world will always bring fools together." I realized it would make a doubly fitting theme song for a conference of humour heads: a paean to the redemptive force of community with an ironic linking of foolishness to the attendees of a conference dedicated to humour. He skipped down the side

E. Weitz (✉)
School of Creative Arts, Trinity College Dublin, Dublin, Ireland
e-mail: weitzer@tcd.ie

E. Jordan, E. Weitz (eds.), *The Palgrave Handbook of Contemporary Irish Theatre and Performance*,
https://doi.org/10.1057/978-1-137-58588-2_54

aisle of the Synge Theatre and onto the quasi-stage—his sombre jacket and trilby made for a curious marking, at once gent of the countryside and classic clown.

In the event, Little John played the room like his ukulele, with insouciance and dexterity, and to endlessly charming effect. This was the practice as research no one had the presence of mind to preserve (least of all, I fear, the conference organizer), a lesson in the fishing technique of a consummate comedian, reeling in the laughter from a joke or facial expression and knowing precisely when to cast the next line to maintain discursive tension. The centrepiece of his routine was a song composed on the spot from a series of audience suggestions, the full folly of which he discovered in asking a roomful of wiseguys to supply a word for the last line. Some forty-letter word was hurled from the back of the lecture hall and the darkest recesses of academic language. (It may well have been made up on the spot; I had never heard it before and certainly cannot remember it now.) You could see right there and then how clowning loves a lost cause. Little John persevered painfully yet hilariously, intuiting on the fly an ideal balance between misery and persistence, with the occasional dash of feigned murderous ire. It may not be surprising to hear that, ultimately, he pulled the rabbit out of the hat—in this case a miracle of spontaneous invention and tripping articulation—to raucous applause and ensuing queries about his professional availability. He closed, as you might expect, with a starkly sincere rendition of the conference theme song, quite the anti-punch line in the overall scheme of things—but the conference was up and running in the best possible spirit.

If the opening slot posed literally a fool's errand, the closing plenary lecture to a conference audience registering toxic levels of accumulated analytical thinking called for a similarly intrepid comic sensibility. Up stepped Pauline McLynn, novelist and actor on stage, radio, screen and, of course, television, including her indelible portrayal of Mrs Doyle, the unrefusable bringer of tea on *Father Ted* (1995–1998). Ostensibly in conversation with Abie Philbin Bowman, writer, performer and journalist, McLynn responded to a question about her formative years as a comic actor. She embarked upon a recollection of how her family played a game based on the ritual re-enactment of John F. Kennedy's assassination, subtly sprinkled with a wistful yearning for the Sunday afternoons of childhood. A risk for a crowd of strangers, to be sure, but clearly one taken by a performer who had the measure of the group-wide sense of humour and its darker leanings—tapping into funerary Irish culture in one regard while inadvertently testing notions of what should and should not be joked about, which had emerged as a recurrent theme in the conference papers. Pauline went on to talk about appearances on the *Late Late Show*, early television work on RTÉ and later work on the BBC's satiric *Bremner, Bird and Fortune*, as well as her charity work for animal rights.

I wish I had taken notes—Trinity will not let you record any such proceedings in their lecture halls, and I hadn't the presence of mind to ensure someone would smartphone-video the performances without my knowledge. So it is largely in retrospect that these two wildly different slices of comic performance opened themselves to revelation about the key gift of a laughter-driven improviser. The extent to which humour is always radically beholden to the precise confluence of social, cultural and individual factors cannot be overemphasized. Neither can the performer's marshalling of technical skill nor precision accrued through rehearsal be undervalued. But clowns, stand-up comedians and, indeed, public speakers are beholden to a contract that opens a two-way channel with no fourth-wall protection. Little John and Pauline negotiated the route between narrative and its effects, adjusting to internal readouts of audience reaction by surfing a favourable response, extending a comic gambit with a look or a line, or glancing off an impending silence and onto a new thought.

This factor recalls the conceit of the "elastic gag", proposed by Richard Andrews regarding *commedia dell'arte*, and the continuous tension between a routine as rehearsed and its spontaneous regulation by the performer(s) on the spot, shortening, lengthening or otherwise departing from it according to audience reaction. In rhetorical tradition, the Greek word *chronos* is one of two time-related concepts, and refers to linear, sequential time. *Kairos*, by contrast, is taken to mean the "opportune moment" for spontaneous, well-judged action or utterance.[1] In a comedy context it is more than what we unscientifically call "timing", the rhythmic decisions aimed at maximizing the delivery of information and the springing of a punch line. It is a sort of comic dexterity in full spate, the ability to reach back or reach forward or snag something surprising yet inevitable from thin air, so the balls never actually clatter to the ground. It is a capacity to behold and to be held as the real magic of comic inspiration.

Notes

1. And I must thank Eddie Naessens for connecting me to this concept in a comic-practice context.

Theatre as Memory: Acts of Remembering in Irish Theatre

Emilie Pine

Memory plays many roles in Irish theatre; memory is both private and individual, and public and social; both material and measurable, and imaginative and elusive. Memory, as a way of making the past present, reconnects one with that past but also underlines its inherent past-ness. Yet perhaps memory's most frequent performance is as a tool to secure the identity of the individual and the family by creating a sense of continuity with the past.

Memory scholars such as Pierre Nora have previously commented on the risk of memory loss—that modern western culture forgets too easily, and loses contact with the past.[1] The dominant quality of many playwrights' representation of memory, however, is its excessiveness—and in Irish theatre there is often too much memory, so much so that it is inescapable, and its burden prevents characters from imagining their lives outside it. This chapter considers that excess-memory trend and traces the patterns of remembering in the work of Samuel Beckett, Enda Walsh, Brian Friel, Marina Carr, ANU Productions and Brokentalkers. It considers their exploration of the compulsion to remember, the refusal of memory to die, and the pressure on the dramatic form itself to represent painful memory.

Compulsive Memory: Samuel Beckett and Enda Walsh

We learn at the theatre that memory does not make us happy. In Beckett's *Krapp's Last Tape* (1958), Krapp begins the play with both a "*great sigh*",[2] and delight and child-like intrigue at language, "Spooool! [*Happy smile.*]".[3] Yet, as

E. Pine (✉)
University College Dublin, Dublin, Ireland
e-mail: emilie.pine@ucd.ie

E. Jordan, E. Weitz (eds.), *The Palgrave Handbook of Contemporary Irish Theatre and Performance*,
https://doi.org/10.1057/978-1-137-58588-2_55

the play progresses, Krapp switches from laughing to brooding and cursing, and from his initial energy to listless and "*motionless*" melancholy.[4] The play sees a sixty-nine-year-old man alone onstage, listening again to recordings that he made in earlier decades and facing the loneliness of no longer finding himself sufficient as an audience. And while Krapp's ritual of consulting the controlling devices of his personal archive: audio tapes (spools!), ledger and descriptive catalogue make him happy, as he listens to his younger self's "*pompous*" judgements,[5] he becomes despondent: "just been listening to that stupid bastard I took myself for thirty years ago, hard to believe I was ever as bad as that".[6] Dissatisfied with, and almost disbelieving, his earlier reflections on the intellectual rewards of life, Krapp instead dwells on the personal, repeatedly replaying a memory of lost love. This memory is not renewing, however; rather, it underlines the lonely isolation of the onstage Krapp. Memory has its limits—for Krapp, it functions as a link to the past, but not a conduit back into it—and so memory, paradoxically, both connects and disconnects past and present. Onstage Krapp's suggestion that in listening to his memories he finds a way to "Be again, be again" is contradicted by a range of factors, from the impossibility of ever being again as he was in the past, to his practice of the backward gaze as a substitute for being in the present.[7]

Krapp's response to the chaos of being is to preserve and codify his experiences—and so every year he records an audio tape to give an overview of his life. Unlike Vladimir and Estragon in *Waiting for Godot*, Krapp does not have to live with the uncertainty of yesterday—"I remember that. But when was it?"[8]—having devised a system that fixes the meaning of the past and allows him authoritative access to it. When his individual memory fails—Krapp cannot remember events or the meaning of certain words—the recorded and archived memory fills the gaps, providing an authenticated and reliable version of the past (the tapes, cross-referenced with the ledger). When Krapp is bored or unhappy with that version of the past, he simply moves the tape forward to another section, editing the past to his current tastes. For all this apparent control, however, Krapp's mood dis-improves the longer he remembers. Like May, in *Footfalls*, who will "never have done… revolving it all" in her "poor mind",[9] Krapp's ritualistic return to the past does not settle his existential questions but only reinforces his loneliness. Krapp cannot leave memory to chance and so he fails to allow for it to adapt—his life story becomes a fixed narrative and his attempted editing of the tape, fast-forwarding through the sections discussing his "work" suggests in fact a profound dissatisfaction with the fixity of this carefully produced archive. Krapp's mediation of the past (making notes and recording the significant events of a year on a single day) cannot be entirely resolved by his present attempt to remediate it, insofar as he cannot change the past, and can only partially edit the past to highlight certain fragments that interest him now. In *Krapp's Last Tape*, as "*the tape runs on in silence*" at the end of the play,[10] Beckett suggests a late and recriminating epiphany of the gap between memory and experience, a realization that losses cannot be restored by memory, and that the past self remains beyond reach.[11]

While a fixed narrative of the past creates certainty and a stable point of reference, the inherent failure of such a narrative to change or adapt to new circumstances arrests the self and exacerbates, rather than bridges, the distance between the past and the present. This distance is also identifiable in Enda Walsh's plays, wherein characters also archive memory, performances that reveal that the ritualistic repetition of a narrow canon of memories is problematic in the extreme.

In *The Walworth Farce* (2006), patriarch Dinny has invented a false memory narrative to cover up his murder of his brother and sister-in-law two decades before, and his resulting flight, with his two sons, Blake and Sean, from Ireland. Whereas Krapp indulges his memory reveries once a year, these three men enact this narrative every single day so that the false memory completely substitutes for both the present and the future. This obsessive attitude is mirrored in *New Electric Ballroom* (2005), in which Clara, Breda and Ada also perform a scripted memory narrative daily; in both plays, these performances are obligatory, not optional. Control of the memory narrative is understood in both plays to equal power as the obligation to perform, insisted on by the leaders in each play, prevents the others from making a break with either the past or the established power dynamic within the family home.

The *Farce* is a show about three Irish emigrants, a father (Dinny) and his two sons (Blake and Sean), and their bizarre life in a council flat on Walworth Road in London's Elephant and Castle. Each day the three men deliberately and self-consciously perform a "story" in which they re-enact their mythical last day in Ireland. The story the men perform is a fabulous farce of wife-swapping and money-grabbing, but it covers up a dark secret—that Dinny left Ireland because he had murdered his brother and sister-in-law.

Dinny is the creator of the story that the men enact daily, saying of the performance, "We're making a routine that keeps our family safe",[12] and projecting an image of memory as a defensive barrier. Though the story is almost entirely invented, Dinny accords it the status of "fact",[13] refusing to allow lines to be cut or even variations in the food—the men eat the same meal every single day, one of the elements of the "story" that suggests the labour involved in maintaining memory narratives. Dinny is a fierce director, insisting on the exactitude of the performance, which in turn suggests Susan Sontag's qualification that the term "collective memory" is better understood as "collective instruction", a less benign version of memory as a cultural performance.[14] In *The Walworth Farce*, the process of collective instruction is both explicit—Dinny's clear directions to his sons on the memory script—and implicit, for example, Dinny's use of memory cues, such as playing the same music at the beginning of the story ("An Irish Lullaby"), eating the same food every day and refusing to let the boys leave the flat (save Sean's daily shop in Tesco)—creating a totalizing culture of memory.

In *New Electric Ballroom*, much like the *Farce*, three sisters perform a single-memory narrative each day. Sisters Breda, Clara and Ada live in a rural village and, though Ada goes out to work at the local factory, the two older sisters never leave the house. This self-enforced isolation is their self-protective response to their teenage experiences of heartbreak at the hands of the womanizing Roller Royle in the Electric Ballroom. The two older sisters are unable to move on and each day they re-enact the stories of their failed seductions, directed by their younger sister, Ada. As in the *Farce*, the performance requires complex costuming, musical cues and a precise script. And again as in the *Farce* the play suggests that the manic memory performance is a compulsion that simultaneously entraps and secures the women's identities within the arrested time of the family home. The major divergence between the plays, however, is in the ability of the memory narrative to adapt in reaction to the entrance of an outsider. In the *Farce*, when Sean is followed home from Tesco by Hayley, Dinny responds to the disruption of the script by imprisoning Hayley within the flat and forcing her to join the action, "casting" her in the role of Maureen, the boys' mother and Dinny's absent wife. Dinny's subjection of Hayley to white face, by smearing her with moisturiser to make her up as a white Irish woman, and Hayley's unwillingness to become part of the performance, ultimately destabilizes the memory narrative so that the family's real history emerges. In the wake of this, Blake, who has believed the false-memory performance, kills himself and his father, in theory setting Sean free. Hayley flees the flat, but Sean chooses to remain inside, and begins performing "*a new story*".[15]

By contrast, in *New Electric Ballroom*, Breda realizes that Ada is becoming dissatisfied with the fixed daily performance and her equally lacklustre life and forcefully recreates the memory narrative in order to meet this challenge. Breda enlists outsider Patsy to temporarily join the women and to seduce Ada. Though this at first seems to promise a new direction for Ada, Patsy eventually flees the house out of a visceral fear of commitment, a moment which functions as a re-enaction of his father Roller Royle's decades-earlier rejection of both Breda and Clara. Ada's heartbreak adds a new dimension to the memory narrative, supplementing it rather than destabilizing it, and incorporating her into the "show" as a performer, leaving Breda space to take on the role of director: "BREDA *presses the tape recorder and a new story is told.*"[16] Breda thus understands what Dinny does not—that the memory narrative requires renewal in order to survive as a powerful force for maintaining the unity of the family. Breda also understands that there has to be a meaningful link between the memory script and the experience, so Ada's first-hand experience with Patsy (as opposed to learning second-hand her sisters' memories) in the *Ballroom* enables her to feel and thus form her own memory narrative: "*ADA gasps for air. For the very first time her eyes have filled with tears.*"[17] In contrast, Dinny's false-memory narrative and his refusal to allow the script to evolve according to present needs, exacerbates the natural fading of memory and undermines the power of the memory performance. As Blake says, "'Cause you'd say Dad's words and they'd give you pictures [...] And so many pictures in your head ... Sure you wouldn't want for the outside world, even if it was a good world! [...] But all them pictures have stopped. I say his words and all I can see is the word."[18] While the ritual of memory is unchanging, what is evoked by the performance, that is, the meaning of the past for the present, inevitably shifts and lessens. The interaction between the past and present in *New Electric Ballroom*, as the narrative is given first-hand relevance, renews the ritual and ensures its continuing relevance and meaning, where the memory is enriched by experience (rather than functioning as an empty ritual). Dinny's failure to do the same, insisting that the boys "Remember nothing! Say the line!",[19] results in his and Blake's death and, though Sean continues the family tradition of performing, the collective familial memory is also destroyed. For Krapp, the initial preservation and subsequent editing of the past (an example of active forgetting that suggests Krapp as an antecedent for Dinny) only serves to underline the pathetic contrast of his present isolation. For both Beckett and Walsh, the compulsion to remember is, at best, limiting, at worst, completely destructive. The message here is to move on.

Revenant Memory: Brian Friel and Marina Carr

Moving on is often not an option, however. For Beckett and Walsh's characters living-in-memory is a way of being, and the same is true for Brian Friel's characters in *Faith Healer*. This play, first performed in 1979, is a monologue play, consisting of four monologues by three characters: Frank Hardy (the faith healer of the title), his wife Grace, and their manager Teddy. The play is dominated by Frank—he delivers the first and last of the monologues, bookending Grace and Teddy, both of whom speak extensively about their relationship with him.

For Friel, the primary role of memory is in the construction of the self; its secondary and linked purpose is the projection of the self. In the first, memory functions to create a coherent and plausible inner identity; in the second, memory is used to project that inner identity outwards, to be validated by the audience. Validation, however, is a competitive process, driven by competing differences in the memory narratives that each character relates to the audience; differences due to the subjectivity of memory and the emotional cast of hindsight. For Frank, the defining conflict in his life is mastery of his faith-healing talent and the silencing of the "maddening questions" of his own identity.[20] For Grace, it is her erasure from Frank's emotional life that defines her. Teddy might then be the most objective of the rememberers; however, his memory is influenced by his position as outsider to their marriage, as well as by his intimated love for Grace. It is therefore up to the audience to decide, to choose a dominant narrative or, in a demonstration of a marketplace equality, to accept all three versions as conflicting yet subjectively "true" accounts of a past which cannot be objectively known.

The most striking differences in Frank and Grace's monologues centre on what happened in Kinlochbervie, "about as far north as you can go in Scotland".[21] This is where Grace gives birth to their stillborn son and where Teddy buries the child:

> Kinlochbervie's where the baby's buried [...] I had the baby in the back of the van and there was no nurse or doctor so no one knew anything about it except Frank and Teddy and me. And there was no clergyman at the graveside—Frank just said a few prayers that he made up. So there is no record of any kind.[22]

Grace remembers Frank being present at the birth and burial; however, in Teddy's version, Frank left them as soon as Grace started to go into labour and only returned after it was all finished. Though Grace says that "Frank made a wooden cross to mark the grave and painted it white and wrote across it *Infant Child of Francis and Grace Hardy*",[23] Teddy claims that role for himself: "I just said this was the infant child of Francis Hardy, Faith Healer, and his wife, Grace Hardy, both citizens of Ireland [...] And later that evening I made a cross and painted it white and placed it on top of the grave. Maybe it's still there." Both Grace and Teddy's accounts, however, are a major revision of Part One in which Frank remembers Kinlochbervie as the place where he learned of his mother's death. Though the place name evokes images of mortality and maternity, Frank entirely erases the stillborn child from his narrative.

Frank's and Grace's monologues often compete directly for the sympathies and belief of the audience, through their differing interpretations and versions of their shared past. However, in the Kinlochbervie memory the two versions are completely opposed. Grace's memory acts as a comforting myth, where she transposes Frank and Teddy, and chooses to remember Frank as having been present at the birth and burial. In contrast, Frank's version is a denial of the trauma, and a refusal to allow either himself or Grace the right to mourn their child. As Annette Kuhn argues, "such narratives of identity are shaped as much by what is left out of the account—whether forgotten or repressed—as by what is actually told".[24] This contradiction thus points up the reciprocity of memory and forgetting—both characters here actively choose to forget or mute certain aspects, in order to create a memory narrative that reassures them in the present (again, reminiscent of Krapp). This strategic interplay of remembrance and forgetting demonstrates not just the inevitability of subjective differences in memory, but their necessity. The plasticity of memory enables Frank and Grace, and indeed Teddy, to remake the past to secure identity in the present. Yet both Frank and Grace are ghosts—their identities are liminal at best and are now entirely dependent for existence on their nightly incantation of memory and on being remembered by others, that is, by Teddy and, implicitly, by the audience as witnesses.

Friel's creation of characters who are both haunting and haunted resonates with Marina Carr's Midlands Trilogy of plays—*The Mai*, *Portia Coughlan* and *By the Bog of Cats...*—each of which features a central female character who is so haunted by the past that she is unable to conceive of, let alone create, a future for herself. As in *Faith Healer*, death is no barrier to memory and, indeed, a surfeit of memory similarly grants Carr's characters a kind of deathly life, as Millie says, she is haunted by memories that persist "on and on till I succumb and linger among them there in that dead silent world".[25] In *The Mai*

(1994), Millie is haunted by the final stages of her mother's life before her suicide, driven by her despair at her husband's rejection of her. In *By The Bog of Cats...* (1998), Carr shows the reverse story, when the dead silent world invades the living as Hester Swane, who is haunted by her murdered brother and driven to kill herself and her daughter Josie, threatens in turn to haunt her former lover, "like a 'purlin' wind", elusive and inescapable, "Ya won't forget me now."[26]

The second play of the trilogy, *Portia Coughlan* (1996), is similarly haunted as Portia mourns the death of her twin brother Gabriel, who had committed suicide by drowning fifteen years earlier, and whose singing and ghostly presence now block her from living in the present. As she tells her husband Raphael, to "stay in" the world "has always been the battle for me".[27] Portia attempts to ignore Gabriel by drinking and taking a lover, recognising as Grace does that some memories are "restricted" and should not be "invited". Carr does not keep the audience guessing, revealing Portia's own suicide by drowning at the beginning of Act Two, before in Act Three reverting to the hours leading up to her death. This non-linear structure functions as a kind of pre-memory, a traumatic haunting of her living present by Portia's dead future, violating, like ghosts, the barriers of order and being. Portia's death is provoked by her guilt at Gabriel's death and by Gabriel's ghost, who is heard singing by Portia, and both heard and seen by the audience. Here the audience are given privileged access to a layer of being not available to characters other than Portia, suggesting an affinity between the audience and the ghost, as well as the audience's function as witnesses to validate Portia's experience.

Initially, Gabriel's voice has such power that it can "*come over and take her away*",[28] and Portia drinks and puts on loud music to "*drown*" him out.[29] However, in Act Three Portia is increasingly out of touch with Gabriel, so that his voice "*grows fainter, she strains to hear it*".[30] When Portia pursues the sound of his voice to the river, Gabriel disappears and his singing stops completely so that she is left with nothing. The fading of Gabriel's voice suggests the ephemeral and insubstantial nature of memory; since Gabriel's voice, however, sounds "*triumphant*" at Portia's admission of her need for him and decision to take her own life,[31] we can read here the emotional and affective power of memory to produce the present, and the manipulative power of the figure of the ghost. As Colin Davis argues in relation to psychoanalysis, the only thing greater than the fear of ghosts is the fear that we have been deserted by the dead; we might extend that to say that the only thing worse for Portia than remembering the past is the fear of forgetting it.[32]

Both Friel and Carr insist on the continued power of the dead to *live*—death is not the end but a shift to a different state of being, in which memory reanimates the past and the dead so that ontological divisions of being become irrelevant. If we consider Frank, Grace and Gabriel as a kind of embodied past that won't go away, then we see different kinds of memory being enacted from competitive to melancholy to vengeful. We also see striking similarities with Beckett and Walsh's work in which characters remember the past obsessively, performing narratives that are both creative and destructive. For all these characters, while they enjoy the illusion that they can control their memory narratives, they are inevitably also subject to them in ways that prevent them either engaging with the present or making peace with the past.

Experiments in Memory: Brokentalkers and ANU Productions

To an extent all memory plays manipulate form in order to embody and re-present the past, from the nostalgic narrator of Brian Friel's *Dancing at Lughnasa* (1990) and the storytellers of *Faith Healer* and Conor McPherson's *The Weir* (1997) to the non-linear devices of Marina Carr's work. Beckett deliberately exploits form so that it mirrors the character's interior landscape, as in the ritual sorting and editing of tapes and memories in *Krapp's Last Tape* and the ritualized pacing of May in *Footfalls*, which mimic the ritualized turning of their minds on the events of the past. Whether it is the direct address of the storyteller, the revelation of death in the midst of the play, or the refusal to share with the audience what it is from the past that traumatizes in the present, each of these devices has the effect of defamiliarizing the audience, alienating the spectator from the spectacle, from the plot, from the form. This defamiliarization has the further effect of suggesting memory as a disruptive force that cannot be contained within the traditional plot and that requires experiments in form to match the disruption in emotion. In recent years, it is devised theatre that has taken up the challenge to defamiliarize the form as a way of mediating painful pasts—and so in Brokentalkers' *The Blue Boy* (2011) and ANU Productions' *Sunder* (2016) spectators are consistently confronted with disruptive work which refuses to abide by the fourth wall convention.

The Blue Boy begins with Gary Keegan directly addressing the audience, telling a story about his grandfather's job as an undertaker, and how his grandfather would sometimes be called upon to measure and make a coffin for a boy who had died at Artane Industrial School. The Industrial Schools were part of a residential system operating in Ireland for the containment of thousands of (generally working-class) children who were thought to be at risk of "criminal" behaviour (often defined as truancy from school) or from families without the means to support them. The schools were administered by the Catholic orders, in the case of Artane by the Christian Brothers. In 1999, in response to widespread public outcry at revelations that the schools had been systematically abusive, the Irish government officially apologized to the children. And in 2009 the government published the Report of the Commission to Inquire into Child Abuse (the Ryan Report).[33] *The Blue Boy* is one of the strongest responses to these allegations and subsequent public apologies, exploring what they mean for individual and collective memory.

The Blue Boy is performed in a theatre space but is not a traditional theatre piece. The performance consists of several components (story, dance, multimedia, music), and the stage is divided into two—a small forestage is separated by a scrim (translucent screen) from the rest of the main stage. After his opening story, Gary walks to one side, and a projection onto the screen shows images from the 1932 Dublin Eucharistic Congress, while various recordings are heard, including two stories from people who had been incarcerated in Industrial Schools, one male, one female. At this point the screen, opaque until now, is lit from behind so that it becomes transparent and the audience can see seven masked performers dancing out a series of ritualized and repetitive tasks. The masks they wear are of blank, identical faces, and the dancers move awkwardly, shuddering, and obsessively repeating the same movements over and over; in the first production one dancer wore the mask on the back of her head so that all her movements were backwards, evoking the arrested development and active disabling of the child. These strategies suggest the flattening of individual difference by both the institutional system and the act of remembering; they further suggest the ways that the self is subjugated by the body within this system of incarceration, that the impact of the abuse (both psychological and physical) is felt and expressed by the body, and that through a combination of storytelling and non-verbal movement, the pain of abuse can be evoked and comprehended—or, at least, witnessed.

The role of the witness as validator is crucial here. As Gary's narrative is a direct address to the audience, the spectator is figured as an active witness from the beginning of the piece. The shifts from story to video to audio and then to dance and music are not seamless, rather they are very noticeable; for example, the footage of the smoothly ordered catholic ceremonies of 1932, projected behind the disturbing physical performance, calls on the audience to notice the discrepancies in the two performances of ritual. The audience must therefore make connections between different forms of performance, and also what they are seeing enacted in the present, which changes the meaning of the past in the present.

The role of the witness is doubly important here because for years the suffering of children within this system was not acknowledged, not "seen". This may be where Brokentalkers take the title for the work, from the local story of a blue boy (ghost) who haunted the area around Artane, which we can read as an example of how communities did talk about and express local fears of the institution without ever fully confronting what was happening to the living and breathing children within it. The scrim screen at the front of the stage space, both opaque and transparent, directly references the barriers to seeing, as well as symbolising the screens which have to be seen through in order to access these memories and histories.

The Blue Boy asks its spectators to imagine the link between the present (visible) and the past (invisible); this act of imagining—of imagination-as-memory—is even more fully embodied by ANU Productions' 2016 work, *Sunder*. This company has built a reputation for site-specific immersive work that takes the spectator out of the theatre—and out of her comfort zone. In the Monto Tetralogy (*World's End Lane* [2010], *Laundry* [2011], *The Boys of Foley Street* [2012] and *Vardo* [2014]) ANU used the Monto area of north inner-city Dublin as the set for work which performed the social history of the district, while simultaneously provoking spectators to "see" its current state. That simultaneity is the key to ANU's work as the company create pieces that consistently demonstrate the connections between the past and the present, and the necessary labour of the spectator in making these connections. Spectators experience this work either singly or in small groups, enhancing the sense of immersion; while the boundaries between performer and audience remain, the boundary between spectator and spectacle breaks down so that frequently spectators are required to react, verbally and physically, and interact with the scene.

In 2016, ANU's work focused on the centenary commemorations of the 1916 Easter Rising in Dublin against the British. As Brian Singleton argues, "The political power of ANU's performative acts stand as a direct challenge to the nation's desire to remember the past through an act of forgetting."[34] Indeed, ANU's interpretation of a theatre of memory is to create performances that challenge the audience member to do more than just watch. *Sunder* is set in the north inner-city area, the area where the Rising leaders had made their last stand, and from where they surrendered. Though initially the audience congregates in a group of four (outside the public library in the Ilac shopping centre), the group is immediately broken up (though it reforms at various points), so that each spectator has an individual journey through the show. At the start of the show, a young man, "Commandant General of the Irish Republican Army" (printed on his t-shirt), asks if we're "in".[35] When we say "yes", he gives each of us a mobile phone. And then the phone in my hand rings, I answer it, a voice asks my name and tells me to walk through the shopping centre towards the Moore Street Mall, and out the door onto the street. He asks me to name something I can see: "fruit stalls" I tell him. "You can see stalls, but what you can't see is the rubble, the melting glass…" He lists the signs of the fallout of the rebellion, describing the debris and telling me that though I can't see it, it's still there. The visible and the invisible interact, and the presence of the street, and my presence on the street, interact with all the absences. The voice tells me to greet a man in an old football shirt standing opposite me, who then takes the phone from me and walks me through the streets and alleys, describing where we are as if we were walking the streets of a hundred years previously. I am brought into two of the buildings to which the 1916 rebels retreated, and which are now fast-food places and a mini-supermarket; the contemporary (2016) decoration and costumes of the actors throughout underline the distance between these moments. But the actors' interactions with audience members, and the scenes they describe and enact, feel authentic: one woman asks me to help her carry her wounded and dying father; a man eats pears from a tin; another woman bemoans the destruction of her home. The smallness of the details, historically accurate, anchor the veracity of the performance so that this "memory" suddenly becomes first-hand.

The past as a palimpsestic landscape is a recurring feature of ANU's work, and here it is refracted by the political controversy over the redevelopment of this still economically deprived area, the plans for which would see these historic buildings bulldozed to make way for a new shopping centre and apartments. ANU's insistence that the past is present but invisible, and that it can be retrieved through an act of imagination-as-memory, is a powerful suggestion, but one that is nevertheless dependent on the continuity of the architecture—the idea that these bricks, this street, are an archive of the past. Without that archive the past becomes yet more distant and the act of imaginative remembering becomes a projection, rather than a summoning, of the ghostly invisible presence. Whereas for Krapp, the archive insists on the distance between then and now, so that listening to the tapes functions as both a bridge to a memory, yet underlines the difference between memory and experience, in ANU's work the archive, the memory and the experience are all brought together, so that the act of remembering—like the rebels' desperate tunnelling between houses to find an escape route—connects past and present and means that, in walking Moore Street in future, the past cannot be forgotten.

Though formally very different from more established memory plays, both Brokentalkers and ANU Productions maintain the consistent emphasis in memory theatre on the requirement of the audience to play their own role—as witnesses. Audiences are witness to the inequalities and injustices of the past, they are witnesses to the past's difference, and its sameness, they are witnesses to memory as a laborious, creative, subjective, liberating and restrictive performance. Irish memory theatre plays with the divisions between past and present, suggesting both the discontinuities of the past and present, and of identity, as in *Krapp's Last Tape* and *Sunder*. Both plays also suggest that even while observing the discontinuities, in their role as witnesses, the audience also work to close the gap between then and now, to understand the continuities of the memory performances that both underpin and undermine the self.

Coda

This chapter started with Beckett, so it seems fitting to revolve the argument back to the beginning and ask if Beckett has anything hopeful to say about memory. And I think we can answer with a very qualified "yes". In *Come and Go* (1965), three women sit on a bench observing each other and exchanging secrets. Though they resolve not to "speak" of the past, there is another performance of memory available to them. Vi suggests that they hold hands, "in the old way",[36] and the women arrange their hands in a criss-cross pattern so that they are holding onto each other. Flo's final line, "I can feel the rings",[37] is possibly evocative of both the marks of marriage bands upon their hands (though no rings are visible) and of the rings of grain that signify a tree's age. Ultimately, however, the line and the pose both seem to suggest the uniting circularity of the friendship and the act of memory. This physical enactment of memory, the handholding pose of their childhood, has none of the angst or uncertainty of other memory plays in which contact with the past is so unsettling. Indeed, this pose is echoed by a later play with an equally restful final tableau, Tom Murphy's *Bailegangaire* (1985), in which three women who have been in conflict—a grandmother and her two grand-daughters, resolve their differences by joining together to finish the story of the death of the grandson that the grandmother has been for years brokenly and guiltily trying to tell in full. Like Beckett's three friends, Mommo and Dolly and Mary are also physically reconciled, all of them settling peacefully for sleep in Mommo's bed at the end of the play, suggesting that the collective, rather than the individual, in witnessing and supporting each other, can produce a memory narrative that is redemptive. Instead of the disharmony, competition and oppression of the top-down narratives of Walsh's plays, or the individual struggles with memory in Beckett, Friel and Carr, in *Come and Go* and *Bailegangaire* the audience are left with an easeful final tableau free of haunting doubt, suggesting that through the physical practice of embodied and truly collective memory some reconciliation between self and other, present and past, may be possible.

Notes

1. Nora explicitly refers to French culture and "our depleted fund of collective memory" (20). See Pierre Nora (ed.), *Realms of Memory: Rethinking the French Past Vol. I: Conflicts and Divisions* (New York: Columbia University Press, 1996). Nora's work, while hugely ground-breaking, has not been uncontroversial.
2. Samuel Beckett, *The Complete Dramatic Works* (London: Faber and Faber, 1986), 215.
3. Ibid., 216.
4. Ibid., 223.
5. Ibid., 217.
6. Ibid., 222.
7. Ibid., 223.
8. Ibid., 57.
9. Ibid., 403.
10. Ibid., 223.
11. For discussion of similar gaps, see Diana Taylor's concepts of the distinction, distance and connections between the archive and the repertoire Diana Taylor, *The Archive and the Repertoire: Performing Cultural Memory in the Americas* (Durham: Duke University Press, 2003), 1–52.
12. Enda Walsh, *Plays Two* (London: Nick Hern Books, 2014), 70.
13. Ibid., 13.
14. Susan Sontag, *Regarding the Pain of Others* (New York: Picador, 2003), 67–8.
15. Ibid., 85.
16. Ibid., 129.
17. Ibid.
18. Ibid., 22.
19. Ibid., 65.
20. Brian Friel, *Plays One* (London: Faber and Faber, 1996), 376.
21. Ibid., 337.
22. Ibid., 344–5.

23. Ibid., 364.
24. Annette Kuhn, *Family Secrets: Acts of Memory and Imagination* (London: Verso, 1999), 2.
25. Marina Carr, *Plays One* (London: Faber and Faber, 1999), 184.
26. Ibid., 340.
27. Ibid., 255.
28. Ibid., 200.
29. Ibid., 195.
30. Ibid., 232.
31. Ibid., 255.
32. See Colin Davis, *Haunted Subjects: Deconstruction, Psychoanalysis and the Return of the Dead* (Basingstoke and New York: Palgrave Macmillan, 2007), 158–9.
33. See www.childabusecommission.ie for further information. For a longer discussion of this subject and the relationship between theatre and these scandals, see Emilie Pine, *The Politics of Irish Memory: Performing Remembrance in Contemporary Irish Culture* (Basingstoke: Palgrave, 2010).
34. Brian Singleton, "ANU Productions Monto Cycle: Performative Encounters and Acts of Memory," Lecture delivered at *Memory, Space and New Technologies* symposium, June 2015. Available as part of the Irish Memory Studies Network MemoryCloud: http://irishmemorystudies.com/index.php/memory-cloud/#singleton.
35. With ANU's work I have to describe the performance entirely from my perspective as it's impossible to speak of a general audience experience.
36. Beckett, *The Complete Dramatic Works*, 354–5.
37. Ibid., 355.

Bibliography

Beckett, Samuel. *The Complete Dramatic Works*. London: Faber and Faber, 1986.

Carr, Marina. *Plays One*. London: Faber and Faber, 1999.

Davis, Colin. *Haunted Subjects: Deconstruction, Psychoanalysis and the Return of the Dead*. Basingstoke and New York: Palgrave Macmillan, 2007.

Friel, Brian. *Plays One*. London: Faber and Faber, 1996.

Nora, Pierra, ed. *Realms of Memory: Rethinking the French Past Vol. I: Conflicts and Divisions*. New York: Columbia University Press, 1996.

Pine, Emilie. *The Politics of Irish Memory: Performing Remembrance in Contemporary Irish Culture*. Basingstoke: Palgrave, 2010.

Sontag, Susan. *Regarding the Pain of Others*. New York: Picador, 2003.

Walsh, Enda. *Plays Two*. London: Nick Hern Books, 2014.

Staging a Response: *No Escape* and the Rise of Documentary Theatre in Ireland

Luke Lamont

Mary Raftery's *No Escape* (2010) is a piece of documentary theatre which edits and condenses the report from Judge Sean Ryan's Commission to Inquire into Child Abuse—commonly referred to as the "Ryan Report"—into a stage performance. The show—commissioned by the Abbey Theatre—had a mixed reception: some criticized it for glorifying a report which they felt was an inadequate response to the decades of abuse committed in Industrial Schools, while others praised the show as a brave attempt to make such a daunting archive available and visible to Irish audiences. *No Escape* selectively edits the report, prioritizing certain voices while excluding others. Raftery uses the platform of the theatre to amplify the stories of those who have, in her eyes, been suppressed throughout history—offering a corrective to the hierarchy of memories presented in the report. Such a representation is not entirely unproblematic, and critics of *No Escape* have questioned the ethics of presenting—or exploiting—the voices of abuse victims for theatrical purposes.

More than a decade before *No Escape*, Raftery's documentary series *States of Fear*, aired by RTÉ in 1999, exposed the manner and extent of the abuse perpetrated at Industrial Schools in Ireland throughout the twentieth century. In response, Taoiseach Bertie Ahern made a public apology and announced the establishment of a commission of inquiry into the culture of institutional child abuse in Ireland. This inquiry yielded the Ryan Report, which outlines one of the darkest and worst-kept secrets in Ireland's history. It is notable that in spite of the countless persons involved or affected by this abuse, it took official declarations from establishment institutions—Ahern's Fianna Fáil government and the national broadcaster, RTÉ—for the people of Ireland to fully recognise this

L. Lamont (✉)
University College Dublin, Dublin, Ireland
e-mail: luke.lamont@ucdconnect.ie

E. Jordan, E. Weitz (eds.), *The Palgrave Handbook of Contemporary Irish Theatre and Performance*,
https://doi.org/10.1057/978-1-137-58588-2_56

awful reality. The Ryan Report ignited a debate as to how the Irish people should move forward, how to respond; those within the arts community were no exception. How could theatre try to intervene, to do justice to the contents of this chapter in Irish history? When the findings of the report were made public, the Abbey Theatre decided—as the national theatre of Ireland—it was its duty to provide an answer to this question.

Aideen Howard—then Literary Director of the Abbey Theatre—spoke about the decision-making process that ultimately led to Mary Raftery being commissioned to devise *No Escape*, making the point that the types of artists whom she would usually commission did not appear to be (in her opinion) "desperately interested in tackling that subject".[1] Hence, the Abbey began to take an interventionist approach. By October 2009, having trialled several different possible formats for such a production—from a start-to-finish reading of the report, to staging selected passages of the report but (crucially) leaving many out—the Abbey had still not come to a decision as to how to proceed. Howard was concerned that they had missed their window: "I started to think "actually, this is going to recede into the distance and our response is going to be so far behind the fact, that it will no longer have any currency".[2] It was at this point that the decision was made to approach Mary Raftery. In a personal interview, Howard explained how this partnership with Raftery developed from consultancy to collaboration: "she became an advisor to me as to how to deal with the content, and through those discussions I then asked her if she could shape the material and create an edit for the stage".[3]

Conscious of the potential ethical pitfalls with such subject matter, Raftery's presence provided a great deal of comfort and confidence in approaching this project. Despite her inexperience with theatre, Raftery was among the most respected journalists in this field, and had an encyclopaedic knowledge of the area, allowing them to "make sure that [they] didn't omit that which was absolutely non-omissible".[4] To bridge the generic gap between journalism and theatre, Howard brought in Roisin McBrinn to direct the production, and between the three of them they began to shape the format for what would become *No Escape*. From a textual perspective, however, Raftery was entrusted with the task of producing a script from this substantial and treacherous archive. Howard assured her that there was precedent for this process: indeed, the Abbey's then Artistic Director, Fiach Mac Conghail, was well versed in programming such productions, having served on the board of the Tricycle Theatre, London, between 1997 and 2001, at a time when it led the documentary theatre genre in the UK.

After the original two-week run on the Peacock Stage in 2010, a rehearsed reading of the show (directed by Conor Hanratty) was produced as part of the Theatre of Memory Symposium at the Abbey Theatre in January 2014. Attending this reading, I noticed that—almost five years on from the release of the Ryan Report—there remained an atmosphere of shock and anger amongst the members of the audience: it seemed we were still coming to terms with the findings of the report. The show presented a series of passages from the Ryan

Report's findings, witness statements and scenes from public hearings where members of the religious orders give evidence as to their appraisal of how these schools were run. These juxtaposed statements were read by the ensemble of seven actors. The original cast was Jane Brennan, Lorcan Cranitch, Alyson Cummins, Michele Forbes, Eamonn Hunt, Eleanor Methven, Donal O'Kelly and Jonathan White; for the reading in 2014, Cummins, Hunt and Methven were replaced by Helen Norton, Arthur Riordan and Don Wycherley. Only Cranitch remained constant—a narrator, of sorts—in his portrayal of Judge Sean Ryan. Both the full production and subsequent reading featured plain, non-frivolous costume (originally designed by Donna Geraghty), which gave the production surface realism. The set of the 2010 production of *No Escape* was designed by cast member Alyson Cummins: cardboard boxes containing the pages of the report littered the edges of a set which was surrounded by panes of glass, bearing facts and figures relating to the commission's findings in white marker.

The show is divided into seven parts: a prologue and six acts, each exploring a particular theme or finding of the report. Act Two, for example, focuses on the punishment methods used at these schools. Official Department of Education punishment regulations are juxtaposed with the reality of the punishment practices, as outlined by the findings of the report, and statements taken by witnesses to and victims of such punishments:

Dept. Ed.: The Manager must... remember that the more closely the school is modelled on a principle of judicious family government the more salutary will be its discipline, and the fewer occasions will arise for resort to punishment.

Sean Ryan: There were accounts of [boys] being hit or beaten with a variety of sticks, including canes, ash plants, blackthorn sticks, hurlers [*long list of weapons follows*].

Witness (male) 1: [...] You could hear the screams all over the whole building at night it was so quiet. Up to 4 Brothers would come and take a boy out of bed on some pretext and give him a hammering, make you take off your nightshirt, they would do what they wanted. They were like a pack of hunting animals.[5]

Occasionally, the show breaks from this pattern of direct address to scenes from public hearings presented as a duologue, followed by harrowing witness statements which conjure a dark irony. For example, Act III intersperses the questioning of Sr. Helena O'Donoghue—representing the Sisters of Mercy at St. Vincent's Industrial School, Goldenbridge—by Mr. Noel MacMahon SC and Mr. David McGrath SC, with statements from victims and survivors of Goldenbridge. O'Donoghue is asked why the Sisters of Mercy would apologize for their punishment methods, but at the same time deny they were excessive. She responds: "We would certainly apologise for the fact that we were in some way inattentive to the needs of the children and that the system, including corporal punishment, would not have addressed the children's needs and we regret that now."

This is followed directly by a witness statement, describing how the terrifying culture of punishment permeated her experience at Goldenbridge:

Witness 5 (Female): I can remember praying every night that I wouldn't wet the bed because I knew the next morning I would be severely beaten, reprimanded and I remember feeling very cold and standing naked and just the shame, the absolute shame of it...[6]

These temporal and textual shifts suggest a hybrid approach to the standard practices of documentary theatre: that is to say, rather than *either* recreating the events of the public hearings *or* presenting a series of excerpts from the report in the form of direct address, *No Escape* presents a combination of the two. This approach allows disparate aspects of the report to interact: Raftery creates a hypothetical and figurative scenario in which representatives of the religious institutions that carried out and covered up this abuse are asked to explain themselves, and the (generally inadequate) explanations are responded to by the detailed accounts of victims' experiences. All this, of course, is in front of an audience, who fulfil the role of "jury": there is a similarity, in this regard, between *No Escape* and the Tricycle Theatre's "Tribunal Plays". The Tricycle received great acclaim in particular for collaborations between Richard Norton-Taylor and Nicholas Kent, such as *Nuremberg* (1996), *Srebrenica* (1996), *The Colour of Justice* (1999) and *Justifying War* (2003), wherein public trials and inquiries were edited and re-enacted. However, rather than recreating an actual trial, as documentary theatre often attempts to do, Raftery is *imagining* one where all the voices—the voices of the clergy, of the commission and of the victims *especially*—are heard.

The structure of *No Escape* is crucial to its emotional affect: the narrative flow—what parts of the archive are included and when—is carefully constructed by Raftery in order to lead audiences to a desired conclusion. Such shows have an automatic appearance of "reality", making them at once compelling and ethically problematic: the archive has been adjusted to support a narrative that the writer wants its audiences to believe, to mark as being "true". The manner in which this show is constructed suggests that, within the archive of the report, there are certain parts that must be emphasized or remembered "better" than others. As Carol Martin notes in her essay, *Bodies of Evidence*, "Documentary theatre emphasises certain kinds of memory and buries others."[7] Given the unlikelihood that every (or any) audience member of *No Escape* had read the Ryan Report in full, many would assume, on some level, that the narrative of the show is "true"—not a calculated and *selective* version of the truth.

The hierarchy of memories presented in the production is intended as a corrective for the past: whereas before the victims were not heard or seen, now their stories finally come to the fore. At last, Ireland is witnessing its troubled past. It is not comprehensive, nor is it intended to be. What is intended is a restoration of balance to the hierarchy of memories. The Commission's report, for example, includes submissions from the schools under investigation, which outline the financial difficulties under which they operated: these have no place in *No Escape*. Raftery's show places the victims' stories above the excuses and explanations for their abuse. In this redressed hierarchy, it is now the voice of the victim that holds more credit than the voice of the Church. This is reflected by the final moments of the show, in which the witnesses—whose stories were ignored for so long by the majority of Irish society—are given the last word. The chorus chants the names of each town in Ireland in which these Industrial Schools were found, heightening an audience's sense of proximity to these events, before individually expressing how they continue to suffer from their experiences. The last words of the show are of defiance:

Witness (Male) 13: They all said "that couldn't have happened" but they can't say that to 5000 of us when we all have a similar story to tell.[8]

This ending insists that all audiences come away on the side of these witnesses, replacing responses of "that couldn't have happened" with "that *did* happen; it must never happen again". Both the 2010 production and the later reading of *No Escape* demonstrate the theatre's capacity to disseminate documents such as the Ryan Report, the contents of which—while publicly available—are often underrepresented in the cultural memory of a society.

The production was not universally well received: prominent amongst its critics was Gerrard Mannix Flynn, whose play, *James X* (2003), based on his own experiences of clerical abuse, was first produced in 2003 at the Project Arts Centre, Dublin by Farcry Productions. It was produced again alongside *No Escape* in the Abbey Theatre's *The Darkest Corner* series in 2010. Flynn, speaking at the Theatre of Memory Symposium in 2014, said he felt the production sanitized the already "whitewashed" contents of the Ryan Report, and labelled it "an excuse for the lack of artists' involvement in exposing state terror and church inhumanity as well as society's indifference to what went on in state institutions".[9] While Flynn's critique raises important questions about the ethics of this genre, the perceived weaknesses of the Ryan Report should not be conflated with responses to *No Escape*. The Abbey Theatre's mandate was to stage a response to the release of this report. By using a documentary approach, the Abbey Theatre made a mainstream contribution to the genre of documentary theatre in Ireland, engaging directly with the archive and disseminating its contents from the stage. Ultimately, *No Escape* succeeded in reopening and responding to a seminal moment in Irish history, lest it ever be forgotten or swept aside.

Notes

1. Irish Memory Studies Network, "Ways of Representing the Past—Documentary Theatre in Ireland and Brazil." *UCD Humanities Institute*, 2014. Podcast. https://soundcloud.com/ucd-humanities/representing-the-past-documentary-theatre-ireland-brazil?in=ucd-humanities/sets/irish-memory-studies-network.
2. Ibid.
3. Aideen Howard, Interview by author, Dublin, 2 March 2017.
4. Ibid.
5. Mary Raftery, *No Escape* (Abbey Theatre, 2010), 14–5. Unpublished.
6. Ibid., 26–7.
7. Carol Martin, "Bodies of Evidence," *TDR: The Drama Review* 50, no. 3 (2006): 11.
8. Raftery, *No Escape*, 55.
9. Abbey Theatre. "Theatre of Memory Symposium—New Memory." Filmed 30 January 2014. Posted 31 January 2014. https://www.youtube.com/watch?v=whalkq9gH-8.

Bibliography

Abbey Theatre. "Theatre of Memory Symposium: New Memory." Filmed January, 30 2014. Posted January 31, 2014. https://www.youtube.com/watch?v=whalkq9gH-8.

Howard, Aideen. Interview by author. Dublin, March 2, 2017.

Irish Memory Studies Network. "Ways of Representing the Past—Documentary Theatre in Ireland and Brazil." Podcast. *UCD Humanities Institute*, 2014. https://soundcloud.com/ucd-humanities/representing-the-past-documentary-theatre-ireland-brazil?in=ucd-humanities/sets/irish-memory-studies-network.

Martin, Carol. "Bodies of Evidence." *TDR: The Drama Review* 50, no. 3 (2006): 8–15.

Raftery, Mary. *No Escape*. Abbey Theatre, 2010. Unpublished.

Children of the Revolution: 1916 in 2016

James Moran

Come away, O human child!
To the waters and the wild
With a faery, hand in hand,
For the world's more full of weeping then you can understand[1]

Introduction

During the 2016 centenary celebrations of the Easter Rising, one of the best-known images of the rebellion was the face of Seán Foster. His image appeared in numerous online articles; on RTÉ television over Easter weekend itself; and on a commemorative postal stamp issued by *An Post* (Fig. 1).[2]

Seán Foster's image is that of a bonny boy of nearly three years of age. But it is also the image of a child who led a short and sad life. His father died on the Western Front in May 1915, and then, the following year, Seán himself was killed during the Dublin insurrection. On Easter Monday 1916, Seán's mother had been accompanying him along the junction of Church Street and North King Street, when she happened upon a rebel barricade (manned by her own brother) and upon a group of nonplussed British Army Lancers. In the brutal crossfire that followed, a single bullet hit Seán under the left ear, shattered his skull, and killed him instantly. He therefore became the first child casualty of the insurrection.[3]

J. Moran (✉)
University of Nottingham, Nottingham, UK
e-mail: James.Moran@nottingham.ac.uk

E. Jordan, E. Weitz (eds.), *The Palgrave Handbook of Contemporary Irish Theatre and Performance*,
https://doi.org/10.1057/978-1-137-58588-2_57

Fig. 1 The image of Seán Foster, as rendered on one of the sixteen commemorative stamps issued by *An Post* in January 2016 to mark the centenary of the Easter Rising

This long-dead child came to prominence in 2016, in large part because of the work of the broadcaster Joe Duffy, whose book, *Children of the Rising*, appeared in 2015 and told the story of the forty young people aged under seventeen who died during the insurrection. This volume became the highest-earning Irish book of 2015, shifting over 25,000 copies that year, taking in over €500,000 in sales, and thus achieving prominence in the midst of a very crowded field of commemorative publications about the Easter Rising.[4] This chapter will examine some of the public memorializing which accompanied or followed in the wake of Duffy's work, and will consider what this turn towards childhood might imply about how 1916 was depicted on the Irish stage at the time of the centenary.

"They Are of Us All"

One of the high-profile parts of the commemoration in 2016 was the opening of a new exhibition about the Easter Rising at the GPO. This "GPO Witness History" exhibition opened during Easter Week and was put together by Martello Media, with the guidance of Queen's University Belfast historian Fearghal McGarry, and these organizers opted to give a prominent place to the children of the Rising. Martello Media set about using images and graphs from Joe Duffy's book to show, for instance, how many children died as a proportion of the overall dead of 1916, and used artifacts to tell the story of particular children, including Seán Foster. The exhibition's designers also sought to emphasize how other young people may have been affected by the rebellion: at its inauguration, "GPO Witness History" displayed two affectionate letters written by the children of the British army captain, Frederick Dietrichsen. These letters were discovered in Dietrichsen's breast pocket after he had been killed at Mount Street Bridge, and were now loaned back to Dublin by his descendants.[5]

Indeed, anyone visiting the exhibition once it opened at Easter 2016 would have discovered that the whole presentation at the GPO culminated in a commemoration of the children of 1916. Visitors found that the "GPO Witness

History" exhibition concluded by leading them into an outdoor space that potentially recalled both the Stonebreaker's yard at Kilmainham and an urban children's playground. In this area, Barbara Knezevic had created an artwork entitled "They Are Of Us All", consisting of forty large stones upon a mirrored steel surface, with each stone designed to pay tribute to a young life lost during the insurrection. Those who had organized the space also ensured that this part of the exhibit had a sense of the redemptive about it, as the visitor's journey through the exhibition would conclude by moving up from the darkened main zone into the light of this outdoor area. And this final part of "GPO Witness History" was designed to be permanent. The rest of the exhibit may change in the future, but Knezevic's artwork was devised as a lasting memorial. Here, at least in theory, the stone's in the midst of all.

In 2016, the opening of the exhibition at the GPO was only one part of a broader national attempt to reclaim and rearticulate the experience of 1916 from the perspective of children. On 15 March 2016, Ireland witnessed "Proclamation Day", co-ordinated by the Department of Education and Skills, when each of the country's schools received national flags and copies of the 1916 proclamation. Although some of the elements of flag waving and parading looked old-fashioned and somewhat regressive, the day did include a focus on individual children's own aspirations for the future. In many classrooms, students not only parroted the 1916 proclamation, but also drafted and articulated new proclamations expressing their own hopes and wishes.[6] Such a focus on children's creativity perhaps dovetailed with the educational philosophy of Patrick Pearse himself, who had condemned the "mechanical" nature of education in Ireland in his essay "The Murder Machine".[7]

Similarly, during the centenary, RTÉ made available on their website a series of thirty one-minute-long films called "1916 Kidspeak", which used dramatic reconstructions to tell the story of everyday life in 1916 from the perspective of children rather than adults. This included the children of 2016 churning butter, and sewing clothes, and participating in various other relatively mundane activities that their counterparts would have been doing each day at the time of the Rising.[8]

Then, on Easter Monday itself, the official commemorations in Dublin determinedly focused upon, as the organizers put it, "8 family zones and 50 tents, with lots of activities for children and families".[9] Unfortunately, the day was rather cold, Easter in 1916 having fallen on almost the latest day it is possible to occur, and Easter in 2016 happening on one of the earliest dates. But nonetheless the "Reflecting the Rising" event (organized by RTÉ and the state body "Ireland 2016") occurred at locations including Merrion Square Park and St Stephen's Green, with circus activities, magic shows, musical performances, storytelling and other activities specifically designed for the active participation of children.

In many places across Ireland and elsewhere, urban space in the twenty-first century has been remodelled so the business of capitalism can be transacted more easily, so that the purpose of such space is not loitering or play but the swift movement of worker-consumers through to shops, offices, and eateries. By contrast, however, the Easter celebrations of Dublin allowed people to recover the central public spaces of their city, to bustle or dance or parade or protest as they saw fit.[10] As Declan Kiberd observed, “After the years of Tiger Ireland, in which everything from public transport to consciousness itself seemed to have been privatised, the community was learning once again how to use public space and reclaim the streets.”[11] Central to that reclamation was the encouraging of children to conduct relatively non-economic activity in the heart of Dublin, with families invited to spend time in the park with a hula hoop or face paints or a tin whistle. In 1900, James Connolly wrote his article “The Corporation and the Children” for *The Workers' Republic*, in which he condemned “the evil social conditions” that turn children into “embryonic capitalists”. A century later, he and his fellow insurgents were now being commemorated by children who had a comparatively large amount of space in central Dublin to enjoy what Connolly called the “sunshine” of freedom from such economic activity.[12]

Of course, 2016 scarcely marked the first time that children had been included in commemorations of the Easter Rising. For example, on the fiftieth anniversary in 1966, Bryan McMahon created a series of four television dramas specifically for children which had quite an earnest nationalist message. There was a well-remembered episode, for example, called “The Bicycle Man”, which revolved around an unpaid language teacher who travelled around, who taught Irish, and who criticized an imperial education system that saw pupils in Ireland parroting the phrase “We are happy English children”.[13]

Nonetheless, during 2016 children's experience became far more central to the commemoration of the Rising. This development relates, in part, to the fact that international cultural festivals, and particularly Edinburgh's fringe and book festivals, now tend to incorporate extensive outreach programmes and educational activities for children of various ages. Yet the child-centrism of Ireland's centenary commemorations also featured particular aspects that were unique to Ireland. National organizations that focused on the children of 1916 offered a relatively inclusive way of recalling the Rising, with those child casualties having been inflicted by *both* sides during the conflict. After all, for those who detest the Rising, the child deaths could be used as evidence of the folly of launching the entire rebellion: staging an armed insurrection in a highly populated urban environment was always likely to involve a great deal of “collateral damage”. Yet for those who admire the Rising, the sociopathic murders of Irish children by the South Staffordshire Regiment on North King Street, and the very presence of so many impoverished children in the centre of Dublin in 1916, might provide evidence of the injustices of colonial rule, and explain why that rule needed to be overturned in the first place. Besides which, in 2016, devoting time to the children of the Rising offered another kind of *mea culpa* for the systematic abuse of children in the institutions of the Irish church and state, with such abuse having been uncovered and widely publicized during the preceding three decades. Indeed, the child-focused nature of the Easter

Monday celebrations in 2016 proved successful enough to spawn *Cruinniú na Cásca* ("a meeting at Easter") the following year. Easter Monday 2017 provided the first of a planned annual day of culture and creativity focused, in its initial iteration, upon four public-festival spaces across Dublin, and featuring "a special focus on events for families and children".[14]

Waking the Feminists

The recent recovery of the children of the Rising dovetailed with a broader process of recovery of some of the hidden histories of Easter Week. One of the most widely reviewed Irish history books published in 2015, during the lead-up to the centenary of the Rising, was Roy Foster's compelling volume, *Vivid Faces*, which draws attention to various marginalized voices. For example, Foster highlights the fact that female couples were well known in Dublin's socialist and radical circles in the build-up to the insurrection, pointing to "Elizabeth O'Farrell and Julia Grenan; to a certain extent, lesbians may have been drawn to such organisations in order to meet each other". He goes on to describe how O'Farrell was stationed at the GPO during Easter Week and how the rebels' message of surrender was "carried by Nurse Elizabeth O'Farrell (under constant threat of gunfire) to Brigadier-General W.H.M. Lowe".[15]

Elizabeth O'Farrell had actually been with Patrick Pearse at the surrender, and had stood back when the famous photograph was taken so that only her feet were showing (Fig. 2).

Yet this image was notoriously retouched in some subsequent reproductions so that O'Farrell was missing entirely. Accordingly, when a Banksy-style parody of the image appeared in Moore Street at the start of 2016, with the British soldiers wearing high-vis builders' jackets, there was no sign of O'Farrell.[16] In this way, O'Farrell's fate has seemed to typify that of the 12% or so of participants in the Rising who were women, and whose experiences were subsequently expunged from the narrative.

Yet elsewhere, at around the time of the centenary, audiences did see Elizabeth O'Farrell being restored. For example, at the International Dublin Gay Theatre Festival in 2014, Brian Merriman's play, *Eirebrushed*, worked to highlight the story of O'Farrell and the other gay and lesbian participants of the Rising. Then, on Easter Monday 2016, when RTÉ broadcast the *Centenary* concert from the Bord Gáis theatre to a mass audience, there was a beautiful and telling moment about twenty minutes into the show, when the still image of Pearse and General Lowe was projected onto the stage. In front of that static image danced a woman dressed as O'Farrell, and holding a large white surrender flag. Here, then, was a deliberate reversal of the earlier positioning in the famous surrender photograph. During the *Centenary* concert, it was O'Farrell who became the lively, mobile figure who drew the eye, and the men were the static figures who now faded into the background (Fig. 3).

In the theatre, this issue of restoring the women of 1916 to prominence gained great attention because of the controversy over the "Waking the Nation"

Fig. 2 Patrick Pearse (far right) surrenders on 29 April 1916. He is accompanied by Elizabeth O'Farrell, but in this famous image nothing of her body can be seen apart from her feet, which appear next to his

commemorative programme which was announced by the Abbey Theatre in 2015, but which, upon examination, featured only one play written by a woman amongst the ten scheduled shows. The Abbey's director at the time, Fiach Mac Conghail, initially reacted on Twitter to the appalled reaction by writing "Them the breaks".[17] Ultimately, however, the Abbey's sidelining of women functioned, in a very welcome way, to encourage the public articulation of a broader set of concerns about women's position and status in the arts world, and in Irish society more generally. Indeed, on Easter Monday 2016, Mac Conghail himself spoke on the Abbey stage specifically in order to praise Helena Molony, the early twentieth-century actor and member of the Citizen Army. Mac Conghail declared that Helena Molony had emerged as what he called the "towering figure" of 1916.[18] Elsewhere, a number of television programmes and books highlighted the key contribution that women had made to

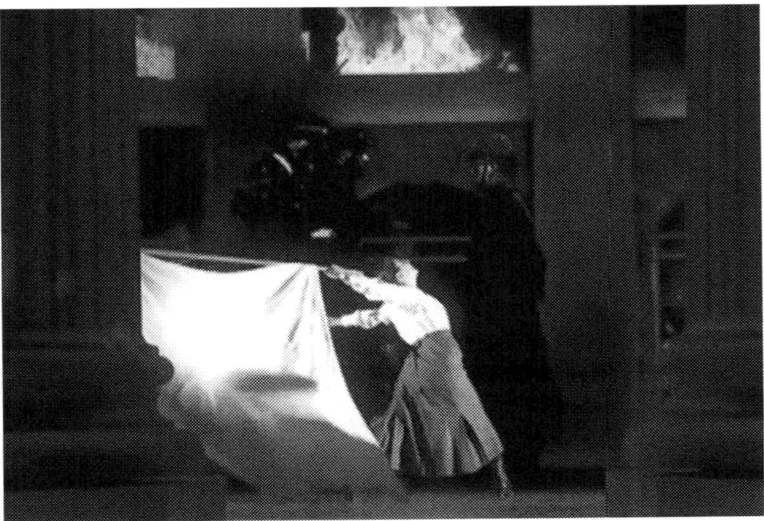

Fig. 3 Image from David Bolger's choreography for the "*Mise Éire*" part of the Centenary concert. (28 March 1916, *Bord Gáis* Energy Theatre, Dublin)

the insurrection. Such interventions included Lauren Arrington's fine monograph, *Revolutionary Lives*, and Fiona Shaw's well-produced television documentary, *Seven Women*.[19] Even the posters aboard Bus Éireann's fleet of vehicles highlighted the activities of female rebels. Perhaps, as Eleanor Methven put it, the Easter Rising was showing signs of mutating into an Estrogen Rising.[20] Indeed, on 31 March 2016 Victoria White wrote in the *Irish Examiner* to complain that this whole process had now gone too far, declaring, "I am sick, sore and tired of hearing about the women of 1916."[21] But that was the whole point of this recovery, to show that the women of the Rising were never just dilettante participants, but were seriously committed to the cause. If it had taken a great deal of effort to obliterate them from the narrative, then a great deal of effort had now been made to put them back.

The children of 1916 never had the same moment of public controversy as "Waking the Feminists", but the reclamation of children's experience of the rebellion clearly worked, and has worked in the theatre, in tandem with that movement to recover women's voices. After all, Ashis Nandy has suggested that the colonial relation is inevitably a profoundly gendered one, as the occupying power justifies its presence as civilizing and paternal towards the "underdeveloped" subjugated people, who are figured as feminized to make them seem passive and unthreatening.[22] Nandy also demonstrates that colonized human beings often come to be represented as children: he argues that colonized peoples have been recast by their oppressors as child*like* and thus open to reform, being "innocent, ignorant but willing to learn", and on the other hand colonized people have also been considered child*ish* and thus in need of firm-handed repression: the people "ignorant but unwilling to learn, ungrateful, sinful, savage, unpredictably violent, disloyal".[23] Thus, Nandy exposes not only the infantilizing of the colonized human being, but also the way that this devalues personhood in a fundamental way, distorting what any developmental stage theory would suggest as part of the normal process of growing up. Unsurprisingly, then, after independence the nationalist response to the colonial caricature of the feminized and childish Celt was to insist on adult Irish masculinity. Women and children were often considered solely in terms of the domiciliary, and when the machinery of the independent state remembered the uprising of 1916 there was a characteristic sidelining of any hints of female experience, child casualties, and the rights of women and children that had been articulated so insistently by James Connolly. Instead the state's public acts of remembering tended to be done in a male-dominated realm of anniversary parades and Catholic religious services.

The Abbey and O'Casey

The commemorations of 2016 revealed an attitudinal shift, and showed that a reclaiming of female involvement had now gone hand in hand with a reclaiming of children's experience. If "Waking the Feminists" showed how drama might assist with the recovery of women's voices, so the Irish stage also highlighted the children of the Rising. The one female-authored piece that was included on the Abbey Theatre's commemorative programme for 2016 was Ali White's play, *Me, Mollser*, effectively a single-hander inspired by Tim Crouch's recent dramas retelling Shakespeare's stories from the viewpoint of one particular character (*I, Peaseblossom* of 2006 and *I, Malvolio* of 2010). *Me, Mollser* therefore narrates the story of O'Casey's *The Plough and the Stars* from the perspective of the consumptive child Mollser, and had been touring Irish schools since 2012. White's show appeared in 150 primary schools during 2016 alone, and was staged in the Abbey main house itself on Easter Monday. The play includes an affecting moment when Mollser looks forward to her own future, anticipates both raising her own children and being a grandmother, before she then coughs and brings out a bloodied handkerchief that signifies her imminent death. The piece then ends by moving in the direction of Augusto Boal, initiating a discussion of children's rights amongst the young people in the audience. The show's female actor encourages spectators to become aware of the Irish children's minister and alerting them to the idea that young people should always complain to the ombudsman if they feel their rights are in any way infringed.

The Abbey Theatre's main-house production of *The Plough and the Stars*, staged over Easter in Dublin during 2016, likewise made the character of Mollser central to the drama. In this Brechtian rendering of the play, directed by Seán Holmes, Mollser began the entire drama by standing alone in the spotlight onstage, dressed in red sneakers and a red Manchester United shirt. She started performing the national anthem, but, in an opening *coup de théâtre*, the song was interrupted by her coughing and hacking up blood. Mollser then remained an almost ever-present figure on the stage throughout the play, only disappearing from view shortly before her death, after which her coffin took her place. Thus, Mollser retained an onstage presence almost from start to finish of the production.

This character's persistence on the stage served to heighten and draw attention to one of the most important and still-pertinent themes of O'Casey's script, namely, the way that children suffer in areas of cultural and economic impoverishment. For example, in Act Two of *The Plough and the Stars*, Mrs. Gogan brings a baby into the pub and feeds it with whiskey before getting into a fight and leaving without the child, provoking panic among the men who are left with it. But the 2016 Abbey version of the play allowed us to see what we do not usually have visualized: the fact that Mollser, Mrs. Gogan's other child, suffers from similar neglect. In this production, Mollser was shown at home, alone, through her period of sickening and dying, whilst her mother spent time brawling in the alehouse.

Furthermore, during the Dublin leg of this production, Mollser was being played at the Abbey by an Irish actor of Asian heritage, Mahnoor Saad. During act two, Saad remained onstage at the same time as the prostitute, Rosie Redmond, played by Nyree Yergainharsian, who yelled in Armenian across the bar at one particular moment of frustration. The casting of these actors, and the fact that they were clad in modern-day dress rather than in the fashions of 1916, like many of those around them, helped to make the point about the identity of the new economic victims of today's Ireland might be, and about the social positioning of women and children from the "New Irish" communities.

The production also repeatedly nodded towards contemporary images of childishness. For example, the pillaging of Noblett's sweetshop in 1916 found its echo at the Abbey in the looted shopping trolley onstage, filled with Chupa-Chups lollies and electronic-games equipment. The theatrical programme was decorated with the stylized image of a pram, as well as with a sports shoe (the starry plough becoming a variant on the Nike "swoosh"). Such a focus on childishness, and the particular focus upon Mollser—the child who was dying, who was a member of a minority community, and who was part of modern Europe's economic underclass—meant that the production kept asking an insistent question about the relevance of the Rising towards the injustices of 2016. After all, the production came in the wake of the death of three-year-old Syrian migrant Alan Kurdi; the reporting of a "mass grave" of babies at a Mother and Baby Home in Tuam; and the vigilante attack conducted by 200 people on a Roma house inhabited by children and toddlers in Waterford.[24] Indeed, on Easter Monday 2016, to her great credit, the actor playing Bessie Burgess, Eileen Walsh, interrupted the applause at the end of the show to say that the cast would be donating their bank holiday pay to a children's charity, and Walsh encouraged the audience to make a financial contribution too.

O'Casey himself, who was caring for his own dying mother at the time of the Easter Rising, had constructed a play in *The Plough and the Stars* that looks continually towards childhood and the way that it might be violated and ruined by prevailing forms of economic and political injustice. By the end of that script, after all, the revolutionary bloodshed and the imperial system under which it occurred has so stunted Dublin's life that the actual children of the tenement building are now either dead or miscarried, and in their place the grown-up characters themselves regress to infancy. The notion of childhood has gone so awry here that the British corporal at the end of O'Casey's play calls one of the Irish characters "mother" and another "daddy", and before being shot Bessie Burgess nurses the ailing Nora with all the delirious tiredness of a parent caring for a new-born baby.[25] This impulse within O'Casey's work was also drawn out, during Easter Week in 2016, by Mark O'Rowe's production of *Juno and the Paycock* at the Gate Theatre. O'Rowe's staging had none of the Brechtian hijinks of the Abbey production, but did give a similar thematic emphasis in highlighting O'Casey's depiction of ruined childhood. After all, although *Juno and the Paycock* is not set during the Rising, the effects of Easter Week upon the children of Dublin hang over the play, in the form of the doomed character of Johnny Boyle, who, according to his mother, "was only a chiselur of a boy scout in Easter Week, when he got hit in the hip".[26] Accordingly, after Johnny Boyle was dragged off to his doom in the Gate production, Mark O'Rowe added in a sound effect that is not specified in O'Casey's script: at that point at the Gate, there was a blackout and prolonged sound of a newborn baby crying.

Back to School

At around the time of the centenary, a group of theatre scholars also began to think afresh about the way that the Rising in 1916 had always been, from its very beginning, indebted to the realm of children's performance. Of course, Patrick Pearse's relationship with the children in his care has long been the subject of controversial (although likely unverifiable) speculation about his sexual predilections.[27] But between 2013 and 2017, Eugene McNulty and Róisín ní Ghairbhí published two co-edited books and organized a Dublin symposium, each of which helped to articulate the idea that Pearse's schoolroom theatrical work had made a significant impact on the overall philosophy and direction of the Easter Rising.[28]

As McNulty and ní Ghairbhí put it in their 2013 edition of Pearse's plays, Pearse became "an expert in marketing and public relations", having honed those skills after establishing St Enda's school in 1908:

> The founding of St Enda's provided Pearse with a space in which to convert his theories about education, the Irish language and history, and self-reliant identity into real-world practice. The school annals, published in *An Macaomh*, show that theatre played a very important role in wider school life from the beginning.[29]

When McNulty and ní Ghairbhí published their 2017 volume, *Patrick Pearse and the Theatre*, the curator of the Pearse Museum, Brian Crowley, contributed an essay that likewise emphasized how, at Pearse's school, "The plays were a great success, critically and ideologically. Pearse intended them to embody the school's mission to revive the Gaelic heroic tradition and impress upon both the audience and wider Irish society that Scoil Éanna represented nothing short of a rebirth of these ancient traditions."[30] What such scholarship did, then, was to show that, if the Rising had entered the realm of children's theatre in 2016, this was actually a return to origins, and not an entirely new departure. After all, something of the impulse of the Easter Rising was, according to these arguments, derived from the realm of children's theatre in the first place, and so the recent theatrical productions staged by the Abbey at Easter 2016 had simply been bringing it all back home.

Conclusion: *The Private View*

During the build-up to the centenary, a number of other stories emerged about the way that the other playwright-leaders of the Rising were associated with children and childrearing. For example, in February 2016 the *Irish Times* printed correspondence between Thomas MacDonagh and his son, Donagh. This included a letter written by the three-year-old child (or perhaps by his mother on the child's behalf) declaring, "Dear Daddy, I was a very good boy when you were out. Your loving little boy, Don xxxxxxxxxx."[31] Meanwhile, RTÉ made available the video testimony of James Connolly's daughter, Nora Connolly O'Brien, on the broadcaster's website in March 2014. This recording dated from 1965, but after RTÉ placed it on the internet the footage was widely reproduced on YouTube, making some of James Connolly's final words to his family more broadly known: "please don't cry, you'll unman me".[32]

Meanwhile, in 2015, a one-man show staged as part of the Dublin Theatre Festival focused on an intriguing father-son relationship not on the rebel side but on the imperial side of the conflict. For three days in October 2015, the director of the Little Museum of Dublin, Trevor White, staged his first play (directed by Gerard Stembridge) at the museum premises on St Stephen's Green, before giving three performances in the USA the following month. This drama, *The Private View*, begins by focusing upon the famous image of Pearse and O'Farrell's surrender that is reproduced as Fig. 2 in this chapter.

However, in *The Private View* O'Farrell and Pearse are not the main focus of attention. Instead, White's work tells the real-life story of the men to whom Pearse and O'Farrell were surrendering. As *The Private View* reveals, the British soldiers here were actually a father-and-son team, William and John Lowe. The older man, William Lowe, was commander of the British Forces in Dublin during Easter Week. The younger man, John Lowe, was an eighteen-year-old who had already fought during the war in Egypt and France, and who had taken what he thought was a break from combat to visit his parents in Dublin. But three days after he arrived, the Rising broke out, and John was co-opted as his father's Aide de Camp. Hence, as *The Private View* reveals, John Lowe and William Lowe are both present in the photograph, receiving the unconditional surrender.

Taking its cue from this image, Trevor White's play then continues—via a lecture-style delivery interspersed with various audio clips and visual images—to tell the unlikely (but true) story of how the son in that photograph, John Lowe, went on to become a major Hollywood film star and to get married, for a time at least, to Hedy Lamarr, one of the most glamorous actors of the age.

The biographical information about John Lowe in *The Private View* is largely culled from John Lowe's own memoir *Hollywood Hussar*, and audio clips from a recording of the book are played throughout the show. That 1977 volume explains how, to a large degree, John's career as a film star was triggered by his father's antipathy towards his son. As the memoir asserts, after the Easter Rising, John returned to fight in France, was captured by the Germans, and remained in Germany at the end of the war. Here he tried to run a condiments factory, but that venture soon failed and John reflected on how "[m]y father had been furious when I resigned my commission. I did not dare return home and face him now—a bankrupt pickle manufacturer".[33] With fear of his father keeping him from returning to his home country, John Lowe went to the Templehof film studios, introduced himself to the Hungarian producer Alexander Korda, and managed to get a part as an extra in a 1926 film starring Marlene Dietrich. But again, John knew that his father would be disgusted, writing in his memoir that:

> In those days the film world had a somewhat dubious aura [...] The prospect of my name being printed on a board outside a cinema would, I knew, meet with the unstinted disapproval of my very conservative father [...] My father was still rankling beneath my resignation from the only career he really approved of for a son of his. I had no wish to upset him any more.
>
> 'What shall I do about my name?' I asked Eric [Loder, an old schoolfriend].
>
> 'Simple, borrow mine', replied my friend who had always been a matter-of-fact character.[34]

Thus, John's relationship with his father grew so hostile that John had to change his name entirely, and it was under the adopted name of John Loder that he then went on to enjoy considerable success in the movie business for more than thirty years.

In Hollywood, John Loder even ended up acting alongside Arthur Shields, someone who had fought for the rebels in 1916 before himself becoming a famous Irish actor.[35] Loder and Shields were to act together in three films: *How Green is My Valley* in 1941: *Confirm or Deny* in 1941: and *Gentleman Jim* in 1942.[36] And it is surely tempting to wonder, as Trevor White's 2015 play does, about whether these two former combatants, from opposite sides of the Easter Rising, would have discussed their shared wartime experience in Ireland when shooting these films.

Indeed, although Trevor White's *The Private View* does not dwell on this particular movie, when John Loder and Arthur Shields starred in 20th Century Fox's *Confirm or Deny*, both actors had to perform as characters in London during the Blitz. Here, the two real-life veterans from opposing side in the conflict in 1916 were acting in a fictional scenario where bombs were exploding, where the buildings of a major city were being reduced to rubble, and where the plot concludes after the death of a twelve-year-old boy. In this film, the fictional Albert Perkins is killed in a German bombing raid on London, and is then celebrated with the lines:

> Single-handed, one of the Nazi squadrons mowed down an Englishman named Albert Perkins aged twelve. Albert Perkins, a volunteer, stuck to his post during the greatest bombardment in history. He will not be mentioned in orders. He will not get a citation or a Victoria Cross. But when they find his body and bury it in the ground of England the soil over his grave will be free soil.[37]

Did Loder and Shields talk to one another about this scene? Certainly, if we follow the thinking of Trevor White's *The Private View* of 2015, those two film stars may have spent some time reflecting on their experiences of Easter Week from the vantage point of the Hollywood hills.

Of course, during the Dublin Rising the children who died had generally not been sticking to any military positions, but had mainly been working-class boys and girls caught in pitiless crossfire whilst trying to go about their daily lives. Yet, just like the fictional Albert Perkins, for many years these real-life children were generally not mentioned in public memorials, were not given awards and honours, and found their stories obscured by a simplified narrative of adult conflict. The belated recovery, at around the time of the centenary, of the children of 1916 has now deeply affected and enriched our understanding of the Easter Rising. Moreover, this recovery work has offered a model for the retrieval of those other obscured narratives about 1916—including perhaps the gay, the lesbian, the socialist, the elderly, the disabled, and the transnational—which have still to be fully recognised, and have still to be adequately performed.

Notes

1. W.B. Yeats, "The Stolen Child," in W.B. Yeats, *The Collected Poems of W.B. Yeats*, ed. by Richard J. Finneran, rev. 2nd ed. (New York: Scribner, 1996), 18–19, 19.
2. *Children of the Revolution*, dir. Gerry Hoban, RTÉ, 27 March 2016.
3. Joe Duffy, *Children of the Rising: The Untold Story of the Young Lives Lost During Easter 1916* (Dublin: Hachette, 2015), 21–23.
4. John Spain, "Joe Duffy's Book," *Irish Independent*, 3 January 2016, http://www.independent.ie/entertainment/books/joe-duffys-book-focused-on-children-of-the-rebellion-is-the-biggest-irish-book-of-the-year-34331262.html.

5. For more about these letters, see James Moran, "Easter 1916: A British Soldier's Family Reunion and Death in Dublin," *Irish Times*, 6 April 2015, http://www.irishtimes.com/life-and-style/people/easter-1916-a-british-soldier-s-family-reunion-and-death-in-dublin-1.2162615.
6. See https://www.scoilnet.ie/proclamationtemplate/. I am grateful to Susanne Colleary for involving me "Proclamation Day" activities in Sligo.
7. Pádraic Pearse, "The Murder Machine," in Pádraic Pearse, *Political Writings and Speeches* (Dublin: Phoenix, 1924), 5–50, 11.
8. At the time of writing, only one of the films remains available to view, accessed 1 June 2017: http://www.rte.ie/player/ie/show/1916-kidspeak-30002276/.
9. Easter Monday, *Luan Cásca*, 28.03.2016, Event Guide, *Treoir na nImeachtaí*, fol. 1.
10. At one point on Easter Monday, those dressed in the paramilitary uniform of Republican Sinn Féin marched at one end of O'Connell Street, whilst, at the other end, Sharon Shannon and The High Kings performed music, and those dressed in Bloomsday-style costumes milled in between.
11. Declan Kiberd, "Acting on Instinct," *TLS*, 20 April 2016, 15.
12. James Connolly, "The Corporation and the Children," *The Workers' Republic*, 24 November 1900, https://www.marxists.org/archive/connolly/1900/11/children.htm.
13. Bryan McMahon, *The Bicycle Man*, RTÉ, 3 April 1966.
14. See "Cruinniú na Cásca—A Day for Culture and Creativity Nationwide", https://www.rte.ie/culture/2017/0323/862064-cruinniu-na-casca-celebrating-culture-and-creativity-this-easter/. The day was organized by RTÉ and Creative Ireland, with the support of Dublin City Council, OPW, and Transport for Ireland.
15. R. F. Foster, *Vivid Faces* (London: Allen Lane, 2014), 133, 243.
16. Hugh Linehan, "Moore Street Mural Is NOT By The Artist Banksy", *Irish Times*, 29 January 2016, http://www.irishtimes.com/culture/moore-street-mural-is-not-by-the-artist-banksy-1.2515144.
17. Mac Conghail quoted by Sara Keating, "Abbey Director 'Regrets Exclusions' in Programme", *Irish Times*, 6 November 2015, http://www.irishtimes.com/culture/stage/abbey-director-regrets-exclusions-in-programme-1.2419782.
18. Mac Conghail's words introducing Nell Regan's lecture, "Helena Moloney, Abbey Rebel", 28 March 2016, 3 p.m.
19. Lauren Arrington, *Revolutionary Lives: Constance and Casimir Markievicz* (Princeton: Princeton University Press, 2015). *Seven Women*, dir. Martin Dwan, RTÉ, 20 March 2016.
20. Methven quoted by Orla O'Sullivan, "Theatre Women Stage Uprising", *Irish Echo*, 9 March 2016, http://irishecho.com/2016/03/theatre-women-stage-uprising/.
21. Victoria White, "True Heroines of 1916 Forgotten in Attempt to Feminise the Rising", *Irish Examiner*, 31 March 2016 http://www.irishexaminer.com/viewpoints/columnists/victoria-white/true-heroines-of-1916-forgotten-in-attempt-to-feminise-the-rising-390207.html.
22. Ashis Nandy, *The Intimate Enemy: Loss and Recovery of Self Under Colonialism* (Delhi: Oxford University Press, 1988), 1–18.
23. Ashis Nandy, *Exiled at Home* (Oxford University Press, 1998), 16.
24. Helena Smith, "Shocking Images of Drowned Syrian Boy Show Tragic Plight of Refugees", *Guardian*, 2 September 2015, https://www.theguardian.com/

world/2015/sep/02/shocking-image-of-drowned-syrian-boy-shows-tragic-plight-of-refugees. Amelia Gentleman, "The Mother Behind the Galway Children's Mass Grave Story: 'I Want to Know Who's Down There'", *Guardian*, 13 June 2014, https://www.theguardian.com/world/2014/jun/13/mother-behind-galway-childrens-mass-grave-story. Sue Murphy, "Not Protests, But Vigilante Mobs", 28 October 2014, http://www.newstalk.com/Im-reluctant-to-call-them-protests-theyre-vigilante-mobs.

25. Sean O'Casey, *The Complete Plays of Sean O'Casey*, 5 vols (London: Macmillan, 1984), I, 250, 253.
26. O'Casey, *The Complete Plays*, I, 30–1.
27. See, for example, Ruth Dudley Edwards, *Patrick Pearse: The Triumph of Failure* (Dublin: Irish Academic Press, 2006), 127: "Pearse was an innocent, but there can be little doubt about his unconscious inclinations. His prose and poetry sing when he speaks of young male beauty."
28. See *Patrick Pearse: Collected Plays*, ed. Róisín ní Ghairbhí and Eugene McNulty (Dublin: Irish Academic Press, 2013); *Patrick Pearse and the Theatre*, ed. Eugene McNulty and Róisín ní Ghairbhí (Dublin: Four Courts, 2017). Ní Ghairbhí and McNulty also organized the symposium "Patrick Pearse and the Theatre" at St Patrick's College in 2013.
29. Róisín Ní Ghairbhí and Eugene McNulty, "Introduction", in *Patrick Pearse: Collected Plays*, ed. by Róisín ní Ghairbhí and Eugene McNulty (Dublin: Irish Academic Press, 2013), 1–63, 14–15.
30. Brian Crowley, "Escaping the 'Suburban Groove': Pearse, Theatre and the Landscape of Scoil Éanna", in *Patrick Pearse and the Theatre*, ed. by Eugene McNulty and Róisín ní Ghairbhí (Dublin: Four Courts, 2017), 50–66, 53.
31. Quoted by Ronan McGreevy, "Stories of the Revolution: The Thomas MacDonagh Letters", *Irish Times*, 6 February 2016, 4.
32. https://www.rte.ie/news/player/2014/0328/20552145-nora-connolly-obrien-talks-about-the-lead-up-to-the-1916-rising-and-her-last-meeting-with-her-father-before-he-was-executed/ and http://www.rte.ie/archives/exhibitions/1993-easter-1916/portraits-1916/793171-portraits-1916-nora-connolly-obrien/.
33. John Loder, *Hollywood Hussar: The Life and Times of John Loder* (London: Howard Barker, 1977), 70.
34. Ibid., 77.
35. Shields' career is detailed by Adrian Frazier in *Hollywood Irish: John Ford, Abbey Actors and the Irish Revival in Hollywood* (Dublin: Lilliput, 2011), 101–46.
36. Loder also performed in a 1936 film about the IRA, *Ourselves Alone*.
37. *Confirm or Deny*, dir. Archie Mayo and Fritz Lang, 20th Century Fox, 1941.

Bibliography

Arrington, Lauren. *Revolutionary Lives: Constance and Casimir Markievicz*. Princeton: Princeton University Press, 2015.

Connolly, James. "The Corporation and the Children." *The Workers' Republic*, November 24, 1900. https://www.marxists.org/archive/connolly/1900/11/children.htm.

Crowley, Brian. "Escaping the 'Suburban Groove': Pearse, Theatre and the Landscape of Scoil Éanna." In *Patrick Pearse and the Theatre*, edited by Eugene McNulty and Róisín ní Ghairbhí. Dublin: Four Courts, 2017.

Dudley Edwards, Ruth. *Patrick Pearse: The Triumph of Failure*. Dublin: Irish Academic Press, 2006.

Duffy, Joe. *Children of the Rising: The Untold Story of the Young Lives Lost During Easter 1916*. Dublin: Hachette, 2015.

Foster, R. F. *Vivid Faces*. London: Allen Lane, 2014.

Frazier, Adrian. *Hollywood Irish: John Ford, Abbey Actors and the Irish Revival in Hollywood*. Dublin: Lilliput, 2011.

Gentleman, Amelia. "The Mother Behind the Galway Children's Mass Grave Story: 'I Want to Know Who's Down There'." *The Guardian*, June 13, 2014. https://www.theguardian.com/world/2014/jun/13/mother-behind-galway-childrens-mass-grave-story.

Keating, Sara. "Abbey Director 'Regrets Exclusions' in Programme." *Irish Times*, November 6, 2015. http://www.irishtimes.com/culture/stage/abbey-director-regrets-exclusions-in-programme-1.2419782.

Kiberd, Declan. "Acting on Instinct." *TLS*, April 20, 2016.

Linehan, Hugh. "Moore Street Mural Is NOT By the Artist Banksy." *Irish Times*, January 29, 2016. http://www.irishtimes.com/culture/moore-street-mural-is-not-by-the-artist-banksy-1.2515144.

Loder, John. *Hollywood Hussar: The Life and Times of John Loder*. London: Howard Barker, 1977.

McGreevy, Ronan. "Stories of the Revolution: The Thomas MacDonagh Letters." *Irish Times*, February 6, 2016.

Moran, James. "Easter 1916: A British Soldier's Family Reunion and Death in Dublin." *Irish Times*, April 6, 2015. http://www.irishtimes.com/life-and-style/people/easter-1916-a-british-soldier-s-family-reunion-and-death-in-dublin-1.2162615.

Nandy, Ashis. *The Intimate Enemy: Loss and Recovery of Self Under Colonialism*. Delhi: Oxford University Press, 1988.

———. *Exiled at Home*. Oxford University Press, 1998.

ní Ghairbhí, Róisín and Eugene McNulty, eds. *Patrick Pearse: Collected Plays*. Dublin: Irish Academic Press, 2013.

———. *Patrick Pearse and the Theatre*. Dublin: Four Courts, 2017.

O'Casey, Sean. *The Complete Plays of Sean O'Casey*, 5 vols. London: Macmillan, 1984.

O'Sullivan, Orla. "Theatre Women Stage Uprising." *Irish Echo*, March 9, 2016. http://irishecho.com/2016/03/theatre-women-stage-uprising/.

Pearse, Pádraic. *Political Writings and Speeches*. Dublin: Phoenix, 1924.

Regan, Nell. "Helena Moloney, Abbey Rebel." Lecture. March 28, 2016, 3 p.m.

Smith, Helena. "Shocking Images of Drowned Syrian Boy Show Tragic Plight of Refugees." *Guardian*, September 2, 2015. https://www.theguardian.com/world/2015/sep/02/shocking-image-of-drowned-syrian-boy-shows-tragic-plight-of-refugees.

Spain, John. "Joe Duffy's Book." *Irish Independent*, January 3, 2016. http://www.independent.ie/entertainment/books/joe-duffys-book-focused-on-children-of-the-rebellion-is-the-biggest-irish-book-of-the-year-34331262.html.

Sue Murphy, "Not Protests, But Vigilante Mobs," October 28, 2014 http://www.newstalk.com/Im-reluctant-to-call-them-protests-theyre-vigilante-mobs.

White, Victoria. "True Heroines of 1916 Forgotten in Attempt to Feminise the Rising." *Irish Examiner*, March 31, 2016. http://www.irishexaminer.com/viewpoints/columnists/victoria-white/true-heroines-of-1916-forgotten-in-attempt-to-feminise-the-rising-390207.html.

Yeats, W.B. *The Collected Poems of W.B. Yeats*, edited by Richard J. Finneran. Rev. 2nd ed. New York: Scribner, 1996.

Postfeminism and Ethical Issues in Four Post-Celtic Tiger Irish Plays by Women

Mária Kurdi

Post-feminism, a term often regarded as a synonym for third-wave feminism, defies easy and unambiguous definition not unlike the other two major "posts", post-colonialism and post-modernism. In general, most critics assert that it has its roots within a neoliberal society and consumer culture, but their approaches to providing more details rest on different conceptualizations of its links with second-wave feminism and a range of social phenomena emerging with globalization. According to Fien Adriaens's summary, "Although embedded within neo-liberal society, proclaiming individualistic, late capitalist consumerist values, post feminist discourse can (paradoxically enough) be considered as a form of non-hegemonic resistance against neo-liberalism and its values … mainly expressed by means of humour, irony and through the practice of overemphasising".[1]

In *The Routledge Companion to Feminism and Postfeminism* (1998) the editor, Sarah Gamble, sums up the post-feminist debate as one that "tends to crystallise around issues of victimisation, autonomy and responsibility",[2] which also have strong ethical implications and ramifications. About the impact of the phenomenon and discourse of post-feminism on the post-modern self, Gamble adds that "because it is skewed in favour of liberal humanism, it embraces a flexible ideology which can be adapted to suit individual needs and desires".[3] While surveying definitions of, and approaches to, post-feminism across several

The first version of this chapter was delivered as a keynote lecture at the conference "Women Playwrights and Theatre Makers" in Limerick, June 2017.

M. Kurdi (✉)
University of Pécs, Pécs, Hungary
e-mail: mkurdi@dravanet.hu

E. Jordan, E. Weitz (eds.), *The Palgrave Handbook of Contemporary Irish Theatre and Performance*,
https://doi.org/10.1057/978-1-137-58588-2_58

other sources, Gamble airs the view that "the prefix 'post' does not necessarily always direct us back the way we've come. Instead, its trajectory is bewilderingly uncertain—while it can certainly be interpreted as suggestive of a relapse *back* to a former set of ideological beliefs, it can also be read as indicating the *continuation* of the ongoing term's aims and ideologies, albeit on a different level".[4] The diversity of interpreting post-feminism along with its paradoxical features is paralleled by the lack of consistency in the spelling of the term: by some authors it is spelt as two words while others use it as a compound word or a hyphenated one.

Cultural and literary manifestations of post-feminism are evidently shaped by the material and cultural conditions of the society and its media world from which they branch out. The so-called Celtic Tiger (ca. 1995–2008) was a period of hyperinflated super-growth in Ireland, which ultimately proved hollow and economically devastating. At the time it was dominated by neoliberal views and consumerism, the very context for post-feminism to be fostered by and thrive in. Wanda Balzano and Moynagh Sullivan begin their editorial to a special issue of *The Irish Review* on Irish Feminisms with a consideration of post-feminism in contemporary Ireland as a term "used liberally in the media", giving young women and men "the vague impression that we all live in an equal world—because, in the world of consumer choice, all seem to have equal opportunities".[5] What contradicts this and, concurrently, the securing of greater social justice in the early twenty-first century reveals itself in many consumers', women's as well as men's, irresistible desire

> to be at all costs modern, and post-modern, in other words progressive and trendy [… which] dangerously mirrors the more alarming aspects of a winning Celtic Tiger mentality. One cannot but remain unconvinced of this kind of entrepreneurial, self-congratulatory, *á la mode* feminism that follows the capitalistic model closely and is an indulgent form of bourgeois individualism, encoding a contradiction in terms that pits the group (women) against the self (woman).[6]

The contradictions of post-feminism in Ireland are perhaps more conspicuous than elsewhere, due to the uniquely inflected trajectory of feminism(s) in the Irish society which became post-modern and global too quickly after the prolonged span of the post-colonial years. Analysing Irish women's cultural products during the Celtic Tiger era in her *Irish Feminist Futures* (2016), Claire Bracken intimates that post-feminism involves "a contradictory problematics of subjectivity and objectivity, of negotiating the very fine lines between sexualisation and an articulation of sexual identity, of owning desire and being an object of desire".[7] In this light, post-feminism in Ireland can be defined as an intensely ambiguous discourse which, paradoxically, gives rise to forms, practices and embodiments of both conscious feminism and its opposite, acknowledged or latent and unrecognized anti-feminism or refocused backlash.

After 2008, with the collapse of economic prosperity and with it the apparent defeat of beliefs in the Celtic Tiger myth, post-feminism became transformed by the social costs of the recession. Writing about the gendered aspects and consequences of the post-boom situation, Diane Negra asserts that "the placement of intense economic austerity as an overriding imperative [...] nullifies the interest of gender equity". She implies that, in fact, it is men who are considered in need of more attention since, "[a]cross a wide rhetorical spectrum the notion of men as particularly and singularly impacted by the global recession has become culturally commonsensical and affectively potent".[8] In the circumstances, men's enhanced vulnerability and often concomitant self-regret may easily lead to the re-polarization of gender relations and the revival of male chauvinism. Negra cautions also of the alarming reappearance of certain phenomena originally dating back to the post-colonial period in the country, whose "rapid conversion from capitalist utopia to dystopia, a gendered logic of ascription/explanation for developments, the speed and scale of which nearly everyone finds overwhelming and disorienting, promises (sometimes implicitly, sometimes explicitly) stabilization through the restitution of essentialized gender dichotomies".[9]

Cormac O'Brien uses the tellingly coined phrase "post-feminist patriarchy" in reference to the latent refashioning of gender hierarchies and their destructive influence on day-to-day life in the present.[10] Discussing the pitfalls of making simplifications about the new-old patterns of differences, Eamonn Jordan calls attention to the entangled complexities of discursive formations like gender and class in the post-Celtic Tiger social landscape. He claims that "across all categories people can be radical on specific issues and deeply conservative on others, the allotment of an all-embracing 'non-hegemonic' status should be treated with caution",[11] which calls to mind the manifold fragmentation of the colonial/post-colonial Irish society along the lines of commitments and loyalties decades ago.

There is a burgeoning cultural production in contemporary Ireland, within which literature, film and theatre offer nuanced representations of the above paradoxes and complexities. Drama by women authors displays a high degree of sensitivity to the contradictions and problems related to the regendering of earlier achievements in women's emancipation as well as the courage to address these issues through innovative strategies of characterization and dramaturgy. Pinpointing significant changes in young women playwrights' attitudes, Melissa Sihra argues:

> Unlike many women during the 1980s and the 1990s, the younger generation of women in theatre now largely self-identify as feminists, due in part to the integration of feminist discourse in education, the visibility and vocalization of LGBTQ groups, the dismantling of its misogynist, bra-burning, 'man-hating' associations, and the move towards equality for all. There is a sense of self-worth and entitlement in this generation of women which was not inherent in the previous generation.[12]

Even though Sihra does not use the term, she does imply that post-feminism, understood as the continuation of feminism in the present, has embraced the potentially enabling goal of moving "towards equality for all", women and men alike, without the disadvantages and shackles of regarding binaries as inevitable and privileging the treatment of women's concerns isolated from those of men. In the plays themselves there is a visible move towards putting an increased emphasis on the issue of responsibility and solidarity or their lack, as well as the ethical implications and consequences of the ways in which these underpin the social interactions, family and gender relations the writers dramatize.

An "ethical turn" in literature and literary criticism has been identified and discussed for some years worldwide, not excepting the Irish scene. Werner Huber claims that in recent Irish literature "the signs of an 'ethical turn' begin to appear. Questions are being asked [...] concerning 'responsibilities' and the problem of being in accordance with moral/ethical standard of any kind".[13] The phenomenon is a notable element of Irish culture in the early 2000s because, Huber continues, "the enthusiasm that naturally goes with such progress [during the Celtic Tiger years] has evaporated and been replaced by sobriety".[14] Belatedly, if compared with the analysis of the ethical in other genres, an "ethical turn" has been recognized in the world of theatre studies too. Indeed, as several theorists emphasize, drama and ethics have always been intertwined; for instance, in Alan Read's view, "theatre has nothing to do with the political in any instrumental sense, but everything to do with ethics, it contributes to an ever-changing ontology of morals".[15]

Nicholas Ridout's *Theatre and Ethics* is a key source in the field, which departs from the premise that "Theatre dramatises ethical situations" and characters' ability to enter into "ethical relationships with others [which] depends on a suspension of self-interest".[16] Further on, Ridout claims that, "[f]or theatre and performance studies the appeal of Levinas' ethics seems to derive, at least in part, from the centrality of the encounter with the 'face'. For Levinas the 'face' is never any particular face but rather the otherness of the other as it appears to us in the encounter".[17] In the world of theatre, ethics involves orientation towards the other, which may be traced and analysed in the characters' incentives to act and the relational patterns thus invoked or, with joint and equal importance, between performances and their transformative effects on audiences.

This chapter is going to consider four post-Tiger Irish plays by women—Marina Carr's *Marble* (2009), *No Romance* by Nancy Harris (2011), *Shush* by Elaine Murphy (2013) and *Spinning* by Deirdre Kinahan (2014)—from the point of view of their dramatization of ethical issues in the context of post-feminism and economic recession. In the first two works, virtually none of the characters is able to suspend self-interest for the sake of another, while in the third and fourth there is progress, however tentative, towards an acceptance of otherness and the needs of others. Notably, in all the plays ethical issues appear through the characters' close relationships with partners, spouses, parents and children or old-time friends, while the plot focuses on both genders—with the exception of the all-female *Shush*.

Meadhbh McHugh explores the function of humour in *No Romance* and *Shush*, beside other plays by women that premiered in the Abbey between 2010 and 2014. She highlights that these works, conceived in a period she calls "fifth-wave feminism",[18] have one common factor, namely the use of humour. By means of comedy, McHugh argues, women authors expose shortcomings and failures within the society and make these the butt of the joke: "The inanity of sexism and misogyny; the absurdity of gender inequality, and the oppressive effect of patriarchy on both women *and* men, is now a cause for laughter, and by looking and laughing we might shake the foundations on which its culture stands."[19] Complicating this, the contradictions of post-feminism enhance the role of incongruities and absurdities through the mode of the grotesque in the four plays I have selected, to varying degrees. In the following, I will discuss the moral problems, disputes, moods and embrace of violent acts the characters embody related in some ways to the peak of the economic boom of the Celtic Tiger period and the aftermath of its collapse, as well as the strategic use of grotesque humour and the irrational as its kin.

Marina Carr's *Marble* focuses on marital relationships and their breakdown; the characters are two couples in their forties, who live in affluence: the men, Art and Ben, hold well-paid jobs and the women, Anne and Catherine, are housewives who look after the home and rear the children. There is no explicit mention of Ireland as the setting, yet some inferential references to the country appear in the text, for instance in Anne's rather cynical reaction to Art's mention of a newspaper article he has just read: "Don't tell me, something about what a happy little nation we are, a woman in a bikini telling us to invest so we'll be happier."[20] Belonging to the newly rich class, the characters can afford to buy anything they want or have a fancy for. For Ondřej Pilný, they exemplify the "overwhelming materialism and absence of value in the Celtic Tiger era".[21] At the same time their lives and marriages seem to be hollow at the core: the husbands, who are close friends, chat about superficial topics like fishing, while the wives feel bored and keep themselves alive by drinking wine and reading novels with plots set far away from their everyday experience. All four are deeply immersed in and have their share of what Carmen Kuhling and Kieran Keohane call "a liberal, affluent culture, but one that is shallow and vulgar; a new emancipated subjectivity, but one that is aimless and listless; a promiscuous and indiscriminate 'openness' to the new, a frailty and readiness to embrace the fashion, whatever it may turn out to be".[22] Likewise, having everything just makes the characters of *Marble* extremely possessive and hungry for more, tellingly expressed by Anne's story about purchasing a succession of sofas to pass the time, a grotesque image of the love of comfort and wealth turned into insatiability and meaningless excess.

The action begins with a casual meeting of the men. Art tells Ben, as if by accident, that he had dreamt of the other's wife, Catherine. In the dream, she had golden hair and they were making love on a marble bed in a marble room.

Learning about this from Ben, Catherine admits she had also had a dream with Art as her lover under the marble vaults. Art and Catherine dream more and more frequently about the amorous scene, and give a lot of thought to this desirable relationship with a new partner. Kuhling and Keohane argue that, paradoxically, while many successful middle-class Irish people embrace what is new they also feel a nostalgia for the past and pine for a kind of mystery missing from their life.[23] While the threads of action in the play become increasingly entangled, this polarity of extreme attitudes also seems to be borne out by Carr's characters. The "marble" dreams of Art and Catherine appear irrational in their congruence and also because the two people barely know each other. Taken metaphorically, the dream articulates their yearning for romantic love, passionate and exclusive, to be consummated in an exceptional place of beauty, which they cherish as a pathway leading out of everyday monotony and conformity. "Marble" and "gold" as images of perfect love date back to the *Bible* where, in *The Song of Songs*, the female voice describes her beloved including the lines "[h]is legs are pillars of marble / Set on bases of pure gold".[24] Viewed against the mysteriously gripping marble dream, Ben's and Anne's mundane possessiveness to keep their spouse as theirs by law has its roots in the revitalization of die-hard patriarchal norms as well as the most conservative beliefs about marriage.

The four characters never appear on stage altogether; each of the scenes confronts only two characters at a time, suggesting that they never think of discussing the situation openly and honestly by listening to all the affected parties' opinions and feelings. In the dialogues the participating characters show themselves to be selfish, even manipulative. Catherine visits Anne to learn how worthy, by her romantic ideals and standards, she is of her husband whom she, Anne, wants to have. Her vision of Anne and her wifely attitude sounds rather humiliating, even rude to the other woman: "So this is what Art is married to. What Art comes home to in the evening, kisses goodbye in the morning. This is what Art is so desperate to hold onto."[25] Although Anne admits that love between her and her husband is over, she insists on keeping up her conventional marriage of convenience and retorts to Catherine: "Art belongs here. You can't have him. He is necessary for my life and my children's lives to run smoothly, without event or upset. [...] you can cross as many lines as you want but I won't let you take Art with you".[26] Their dispute confirms Balzano and Sullivan's idea, quoted above, about the re-emerging division among women, which strikes the same chord as Luce Irigaray's argument that women under patriarchy "no longer relate to each other except in terms of what they represent in men's desire, and according to the 'forms' that this imposes upon them".[27] For his part, Ben imagines himself a good and loving husband. However, he looks upon women, and his wife seems not to take exception, as appealing or detestable objects or instruments when measured against his own well-being: "Women aren't allowed get old. I mean of course you're allowed but it's not mannerly. It's somehow not appropriate. Old women interfere with my sense of myself."[28]

While nursing their own dreams on the one hand and asserting their marital rights on the other, the characters are incapable of considering the otherness of the other in Levinasian terms, let alone forgetting about their self-interests and any sense of responsibility for anyone apart from themselves. Art's monologue in the last scene is revealing about the gap felt between the emptiness of the mundane and the attraction of the dreamlike, but solely from his own point of view, which he masks by using the third person: "There is nothing left, he said to himself as he watched his good-looking wife read a story about tasteful incest. He went to bed thinking that he could die that night and it wouldn't matter. But instead of dying he had a dream. He dreamt he was in a room full of marble and on the marble bed was a beautiful woman, her hair was spun gold ...."[29] The symbolism of marble in the play, visualized onstage in the form of a huge marble column which dominates the setting and dwarfs the characters, is given interesting consideration by Pilný: "The intertextual underpinning of the characters' story by Greek tragedy combined with the gradual shift in the meaning of the trope of marble thus suggests that when Art and Catherine leave in pursuit of their transgressive dream in the end and destroy both of their families, it means a move towards certain death, rather than liberation."[30]

Marble is also a superb trope because it condenses the fusion of beauty, material richness and emotional coldness towards fellow humans that the characters represent in an economically successful, yet culturally impoverished environment. Actually, Carr's play of 2009 is set on the cusp of the boom, the end of which is foreshadowed through the connotation of death one can associate with marble and the frequent and varied references to aging and death by the characters as the unavoidable fate they are aware of, lending the play a Beckettian tone in addition to its classical resonances.

The distinct yet combined plots of *No Romance* by Nancy Harris are set after the boom in Ireland. The play foregrounds newly emerging social problems linked to the economic recession, especially the resurfacing of traditionalist views on gender and family relationships which were dominant in Ireland earlier but also re-occur in both men's and women's attitudes and behaviour in the present. In *No Romance*, the communication of characters with close ties to each other is burdened with pretence, lies and the lack of solidarity because the circumstances of austerity and the concomitant changes in public discourse are pressing all of them to follow their own agendas, having no energy or wish to consider the interests of others, be they spouses, partners, parents or children. The novelty of the play is that it divides into three parts, loosely connected through the virtual realities most of the characters escape to from a state of powerlessness.[31] Adopting this discontinuous form the author manages to introduce the audience to the fragmentation of the Irish society during the post-Tiger recession period. However, if not the individual characters' traits, the problems they represent appear to be similar, largely because of their common roots.

The first and second parts of the play focus on failing partnerships, both homo- and heterosexual, and on a marriage that is dysfunctional at best. In scene one, Gail, a photographer and Laura, her new client, are in dialogue. Gail's ten-year-long lesbian relationship with her lover, Sarah, has just broken up, but she cannot afford to rent another place and move out because the financial recession has hit her so hard. For O'Brien, in this scene of *No Romance*, "the presence-through-absence of patriarchy becomes palpable on several levels".[32] He observes that Harris assigns typical male/female roles to the lesbian couple which emulate "heteronormative relationality",[33] thus prone to undermine equality in the circumstances: Gail is cast in the artist's feminine role whereas Sarah holds the traditionally male job of a doctor. Consequently, Gail remains dependent on Sarah, subjected to the inferior position of being tolerated and also trapped in Sarah's apartment.

At the time of the play's action, Ireland had not yet introduced same-sex marriage, so abandoned partners such as Gail had no access to any kind of legal arrangement to help them start afresh. Gail has to cope with the presence of Sarah's new girlfriend in the apartment, seeing the two women's gently touching silhouettes through the muslin curtain that separates her studio from the rest of the apartment. The unethical aspect of the situation shows itself primarily in the fact that Sarah seems to have no empathy for her former lover; she is too wrapped up in her new relationship to notice that the other woman might feel hurt and would need more privacy, an attitude which aggravates Gail's humiliation. On the other hand, Sarah's careless attitude is matched by Gail's conventional reaction as a victim who embraces the stereotypical role of the cheated and jealous woman: "I can't stand the thought of their love-making. Do you [Laura] think it means more to her than ours did?"[34] Hurt and powerless, Gail resorts to taking revenge on Sarah by defriending her on Facebook, an act which is reminiscent of the ineffectual attacks of the unequal Other under colonialism or patriarchal rule.

Gail's client, Laura, is emotionally dependent on her fiancé, Simon, who wants her to give up her job once they are married—a demand reminiscent of what had been the accepted norm in post-independence Irish society. Laura seems to be controlled by Simon even before their marriage: although having a cancerous lump in her body, she obeys him and wears a corset, an item with a history to emphasize femininity for the male gaze, which shapes her body to fulfil her fiancé's ideal of the female figure: "Simon bought me this corset. Picked out himself and everything, bless him. […] It's kind of a pain with all the laces and stuff but—if I could pull it off, he'd be in his element, I reckon. He loves the whole chorus-girl can-can thing."[35] To please him, Laura has come to Gail to be photographed in exotic costumes, an attempt to have her body eternalized in grotesquely erotic poses before she receives surgical therapy for breast cancer. The photos are intended to be a unique present for Simon's fortieth birthday. As O'Brien sums up her situation, Laura "willingly objectifies herself and embraces the patriarchal gaze economy of both her fiancé and society" as well as internalizing "post-feminist body politics".[36] Strangely, she is determined not to share her grave health problem with Simon and plans to leave him and thus save him from the coming troubles once he has got the photos. In fact, she fails to realize that by cherishing the dream that Simon will always remember her body in its pre-treatment beauty, she does damage to both of them. By not being honest she degrades herself and, concurrently, prevents him from expressing solidarity and offering help—which might have tested, yet strengthened their relationship as one of equal partners.

The second scene of *No Romance* involves a married couple, who are in a funeral parlour watching the corpse of the husband's mother's as it is laid out. Joe, the husband, is unemployed, while Carmel, his wife, holds a good job and has become the family breadwinner. Clearly, the shamefulness of depending on his wife has had a disastrous effect on Joe's ethical self, urging him to set the gender balance "right" by whatever means. For his feminized state, he seeks compensation by acting the authoritative judge of women in the family. He remembers his dead mother as "an old dragon"[37] and calls their daughter "an internet trollop"[38] because she has uploaded pictures of herself wearing only a wet T-shirt. Waiting in the sombre place, Harris's couple are having an increasingly heated row, leading to verbal and physical violence after Carmel reveals her recent discovery that Joe has received a pair of used stockings and an intimate letter by post from some woman blogger. Joe accuses his wife of violating his privacy by opening a parcel addressed to him. Infuriated, Carmel calls Joe a hypocrite and "*kicks him in the shin*",[39] unable (or, rather, unwilling) to realize that the motives of his behaviour might reach deeper than lying merely for the sake of convenient self-defence. As a man without any socio-economic status and agency Joe feels his manhood threatened and attempts to reclaim it by regressing to well-worn patriarchal attitudes and the assertion of his male rights.

To apply Negra's thoughts again, Joe is "the beset, recession-impacted man, whose anxieties are done away with via his transformation into the re-masculinized man",[40] a kind of anachronism in the circumstances that turns the spouses' exchange into a grotesque and fierce fight. One minute Joe falls on his knees like a medieval knight in front of his lady to plead for forgiveness; the following minute he becomes eager to take revenge on Carmel. He hides behind memories of his mother as a strong individual, who "was funny about most women",[41] suggesting that she felt no solidarity with them as representatives of the inscrutable and potentially disobedient or rebellious Other under male dominance. Adding more weight to the evocation of gender inequity, Joe throws at his wife that once his mother made a remark about the fatness of her legs after Carmel "got the job in the bank".[42] This intended humiliation only fuels Carmel: she strikes back by telling Joe about her sexual adventure with a Nigerian taxi driver, concluding that "I have never had a lover like him".[43] Next Joe rehashes age-old conventional beliefs about marriage according to which openness and sincerity had better be limited between men and women to avoid crossing certain fixed boundaries of living in peace and quiet: "I am not sure that all that knowledge will help me sleep easy at night. [...] What happened to discretion? What happened to keeping it to yourself? Maybe there are some things we are better off not knowing. Maybe we can love each other despite."[44] In her turn, Carmel stuffs "*the stockings inside the corpse's jacket*",[45] which ridicules Joe's secret dependence on internet pornography and its links with patriarchal resonances of post-feminist culture while desecrating the dead body of her mother-in-law for her previous criticism of her. Indeed, neither husband nor wife makes any effort to understand, let alone respect the other partner's emotions, resembling the alienated communication of Carr's couples; instead, the play revives a war between sexes known from earlier decades turned grotesque and (the second time) farcical.

The third scene of *No Romance* presents middle-aged Michael and his teenage son, Johnny, for whom he is now a weekend father after he has divorced. Michael sees himself as a victim deprived of authority and agency: "She [his ex-wife] wants him [Johnny] home tonight [...] despite the fact it's my weekend with him [...] Like all women she always gets what she wants in the end."[46] Like Joe in the second part of the play, Michael also chooses the compensation of exercising dominance over the weaker family members: his son, whom he orders about, but first of all over his eighty-year-old mother, Peg, the third onstage character in the scenario. He is determined to move her out of the country cottage where she lives and place her in an old-age home in Dublin. It is more than likely that Michael, worried about some post-boom financial loss, is looking to sell her house. Preoccupied with his own failures he does not realize that this country house symbolizes freedom for Peg, who thinks "it was a place I could be myself".[47] An old and lonely woman, Peg likes to chat about her life, and through memories of her ruined married life the joint subjects of gender inequity and domestic violence come to the surface. She had an unloving husband, who broke her nose out of frustration, since his real love was a male friend—homosexual inclinations he had to repress in the prudish sociocultural context of the time. Consequently, his wife and children suffered from the aggression he vented on them. Now the past revisits Peg in a new-old guise: she is treated like an object to be displaced at will by her son. Like Carmel in the second part of the play, she rebels by turning to violence; to fight against the renewal of male control she grabs the sweeping brush and, leaning out from her wheelchair, she hits her son with it, which enhances the grotesque effects of the scene.

While *Marble* and *No Romance* offer a rather negative picture of the characters' morals, in Murphy's and Kinahan's plays there are examples of sympathy and they also harbour a slow progress in reaching out to another human despite personally tragic circumstances. In *Shush*, the protagonist is Breda, a woman in her fifties who was left by her husband and made redundant at her workplace. There are hints about a period of depression she has recently experienced. The time of action is the evening of her birthday when two older women friends, Marie and Irene, together with Marie's daughter, Clare, arrive at Breda's house to celebrate with her and express sympathy for her present troubles. They are also joined by Ursula, a neighbour, who is desperate because her husband cheats on her. The play's action consists mainly of chatting about female experiences as well as eating and drinking. It becomes noteworthy that the two friends, Marie and Irene, women in their sixties, seem to have different ideas of how they could help Breda recover from her distress. In Breda's momentary absence they say:

MARIE: We have to do something.
IRENE: We'll be here for her.[48]

Marie suggests that they should find a way to give Breda relief without considering what she might really need. In contrast, Irene suggests that they should wait for Breda to let them know what her needs are. Her words echo Levinas's thought quoted in Ridout that just "to be there for someone" can be the starting point of a positive ethical act.[49]

Later in the drama the above polarization of attitudes extends further. Marie has brought a pair of ballroom dancing shoes for Breda as a birthday present because she "used to be a brilliant dancer".[50] Indeed, Breda got a cup at a dancing competition decades ago, so Marie's present reminds her of better days. However, when having put on the shoes Breda begins to waltz with Marie, after a few steps she loses balance, falls and sprains her ankle. Apparently, Marie's recipe to help Breda by reminding her of past glories awakens only nostalgia in her, which ends in a new disaster. The accident brings Breda back to the here and now, sobering her up enough to feel her abandoned state even more acutely. Her husband lives with another woman, which she feels unjust and deprivileging both for herself and her sex in general: "It's not fair how the men get to start over while the women are left to rot."[51] Some of her husband's belongings are still in the house, collected in a heap in the living room. Utterly helpless, Breda attempts to take revenge on her husband by breaking his golf club and preparing to cut the sleeves off one of his shirts. This grotesquely desperate act is even more senseless than Carmel's and Peg's attacks on the lying or oppressive husband or son in *No Romance*. It is Irene who shows real sympathy and undertakes responsibility for the other woman when she restrains Breda from such a useless move by convincing her that "[t]hey're only things, they don't mean anything".[52]

Breda's other friend, Marie, is loud and domineering; she offers help which Breda cannot but refuse since Marie tries to force it on her in an inconsiderate and quite peremptory fashion. Their friendship must have been superficial all along, and proves too fragile when tested by Breda's present distress. Irene, who lost a husband dear to her, is the one who offers wise grief counselling to Breda by saying "I'm not going to sit here and tell you it gets easier but the thing about grief, it catches up on you, waits patiently until you're at your lowest, then pounces and there's nothing you can do, you have to let the bugger beat you and hope the next time it strikes it'll be a little less severe".[53] Irene is able to suspend her own absorption in grief and to turn to Breda with genuine helpfulness. Left alone, Breda, as we learn from the telephone conversation with her son, is no longer afraid of the challenge involved by taking a flight to America and visiting him and his girlfriend there. She is beginning to undergo the kind of process which might change and also revitalize her, meaning a possible new turn after experiencing tragic loss, perhaps best described by Judith Butler in *Precarious Life: The Powers of Mourning and Violence*: "There is losing, as we know, but there is also the transformative effect of loss, and this latter cannot be charted or planned. [...] So when one loses, one is also faced with something enigmatic: something is hiding in the loss, something is lost within the recesses of loss."[54] Irene awakens Breda to this potential when she turns to her intuitively realizing the other's need and does not merely follow her own ideas about how to console a friend as Marie has done.

Partnerships gone wrong and the pitfalls of a parent–child relationship are also the subject of my last example, Deirdre Kinahan's *Spinning*, a memory play with a unique structure. The action starts with the encounter of the two protagonists, Susan and Conor, at the pier of a seaside village. Their exchange is periodically interrupted by short scenes they recall from various points of the past. In the present time they talk about the trauma they experienced four years earlier, when Conor drove his car into the sea with his own and Susan's daughter sitting in it. Susan's sixteen-year-old daughter, Annie, drowned while Conor and his daughter, six-year-old Kate, were rescued in time. The event took place after Conor and his wife, Jen, had divorced and the woman gained custody of Kate, making Conor a weekend father like Michael in *No Romance*. As he doted on the little girl this arrangement was unbearable for Conor, and he decided to bring Kate to the seaside village to hide themselves. Once the police started to watch their rented house and discovery was pending, in his utter distress he decided to commit suicide with his daughter as the only means to escape and have her to himself forever. Susan's daughter, Annie, raised without a father, met Conor accidentally and initiated friendship with him, a lonely-looking man who was about the age of her never-known father. She followed him everywhere and was unwilling to get out of his car on the fatal day until it was too late. After the tragic event Conor was sentenced to four years' imprisonment, and upon release he returned to the pier, again planning to commit suicide. Here he meets Susan, who works in the nearby café and often watches the pier, brooding on the incomprehensible death of her beloved daughter. Both protagonists are lonely and devastated, their sense of direction in life shattered by the loss of their respective daughters; Annie is dead while Kate is alive, but Conor's ex-wife no longer allows him to see the girl.

Spinning structures the recollected scenes by juxtaposing them alternately: the two characters act them out while the other protagonist remains on stage, watching. Susan's memories are evoked in the hope of finding peace through some kind of certainty about the reasons that led to the tragedy. As for Conor, it is Susan's relentless insistence on getting an answer to her questions that urges him to recollect scenes from his own personal history. Thus, the memory scenes emerge from the protagonists' wishes to understand and interpret the past through reliving some of its crucial moments, which results in the recognition of thus-far ignored or misunderstood signals.

The scenes in which Conor remembers his talks with Annie show that he had no sexual interest in the girl, but was engulfed by his own family problem. She was a teenager with a strong inferiority complex and having recently been abandoned by a boyfriend. She felt herself useful in the man's company, for instance, babysitting for Kate and undertaking the job of packing up before the fatal departure from the holiday house. During the recollected scenes with Annie, Conor realizes that although grateful for her services, he completely forgot about Annie in the crucial moment and did not make special efforts to prevent her from staying in the car before it hit the water. Annie's mother, Susan, recalls scenes with her daughter that confirm their devoted love for each other, but then also one about Annie's frustration because Susan does not help her search for her father:

ANNIE: I'm sure we could find him! [...]
SUSAN: For God's sake, Annie. He's probably married now with two kids and a mortgage ... he won't want to know about us.
ANNIE: How do you know?
SUSAN: I just know.[55]

Reliving this conversation allows Susan to realize that her discouraging behaviour might have been the cause of Annie's lack of sincerity, manifest in her never revealing the meetings with Conor.

Conor becomes increasingly aware that his loss of control and attempt at suicide with Kate had its roots in his failed relationship with Jen, therefore the play abounds in his memories of their married life, its conflicts and its ending in divorce. These recollected scenes reveal a widening gap between the couple despite their passionate love for each other at the start, showing a parallel with the couples in *Marble*. In Celtic Tiger Ireland, as sociologists observe, the "experience of accelerated modernization ha[s] produced a variety of cultural and social collisions between different and often incompatible forms of life, collision between 'traditional' and 'modern'".[56] It is just such a conflict that underpins the couple's drawing apart here, too: they have very different ideas about Jen's choice to be a working mother, the routine of spending the weekends with Conor's family and, most importantly, about childrearing. Conor plays the head of family whose dominance is beyond question, and he grows impatient with Jen when she dares to voice her own views. In one of the scenes Jen refuses to have sex with him and his reaction is characteristically patriarchal:

JEN: I'm tired of YOU! [...]
CONOR: What did you say?
JEN: I didn't mean it.
I don't mean it, I am sorry.

CONOR: I LOVE you.
And I WANT you all the time ... I don't think I like this change. [...]
JEN: [...] *She goes to leave. He grabs her arm quite violently. She stops, shocked.* Let go. [...] You can't touch me this way...[57]

Like Ben in *Marble*, Conor thinks of himself as a good husband who "let you [Jen] go back to work!", implying that they are not equal partners in marriage. Jen is provoked to strike back: "Did you hear what you just said? You let me? [...] You've always ... always made that difficult for me."[58] Recalling these scenes Conor is confronted with his own selfish, conventionally male-centred attitude to marriage.

The scenes about the couple's divorce and his life after that show Conor's feelings of being hurt and unjustly dispossessed. In an interview the playwright says that Conor's situation is quite common in the country: "We've only had the benefit of divorce in Ireland for about a decade, and there's still no system in place to support the emotional fallout, especially with the men. [...] usually custody is automatically granted to the mother, with fathers settling for visitation rights or weekend access, and it leaves them feeling powerless and even humiliated."[59] Conor is deeply affected by the collapse of his family life, while the business he runs with his brothers is also in financial trouble with the onslaught of the post-boom economic crisis, so much so that Jen offers him the chance to reduce his maintenance payments, a gesture that wounds his male pride even further.

Trying to take revenge on Jen and the whole hostile world, he acts in an irrationally self-destructive way when he drives his car into the deep water, with Kate and Annie fastened into their seats. In a sense Jen's reaction to the event is also extreme and potentially harmful: she refuses to look beyond the surface and understand the paradox that Conor loves Kate despite what happened, and she remains adamant in her refusal to let him see his daughter again. Unwittingly, by doing this she puts Kate into Annie's fatherless, emotionally vulnerable situation, which might lead to some kind of psychic problem or even tragedy in the future.

Having become aware of his self-centred behaviour and the consequences through recollecting the most crucial scenes, at the end of the play Conor manages to conjure his final memories of Annie (or just makes them up to serve a good cause), but this time not for the sake of acquitting himself, rather with the aim to give some comfort to the bereft mother:

CONOR: [...]
She called you.
She saw you.
Standing in the window.
You were with her, Susan.
You were with her as we hit the water. [...]
SUSAN *sees* ANNIE *now. She reaches out her hand to her.*

She whispers.

SUSAN: Annie.
ANNIE: *smiles at* SUSAN.
Thank you. Thank you Conor Bourke.[60]

Susan, in turn, advises Conor not to hurt Jen and Kate any more by committing suicide on this spot of tragic memories. From Susan's expressions of anger and hatred, and the self-absorbed, guilty inertia of Conor, the protagonists have proceeded to recognize the other's immediate needs and help each other to achieve some transformation in the sense of Butler's notion of transformative effect following the loss they had experienced. Now Susan can think of moving on, and, after some hesitation, Conor leaves the place, a sign that he is abandoning his suicidal thoughts.

My interpretation of the four plays discussed in this chapter is intended to demonstrate that there is a distinct concern with the ethical (and the lack of it) in contemporary women's drama, inspired by new phenomena linked with post-feminism and the alarming post-boom problems that are largely responsible for the chaotic moral state of present-day Irish society. These selected works contribute to the landscape of "ethics, politics, social justice" in contemporary drama, where, as Pilný writes, "the use of the grotesque [can be] a device of social and political critique".[61]

In addition, all four plays experiment with dramaturgical devices to highlight ethical concerns in the context of post-feminism and the warning signs preceding the economic collapse as well as the recession itself. *Marble* uses "marble" as a symbol to suggest wealth but also coldness and death, while the proliferating images of "sofa" in the play suggest inertia and comfortable passivity as an escape from making efforts to understand the human world surrounding the self and the concomitant reactions of others. By its discontinuous structure *No Romance* reflects an alienated social fragmentation, while *Shush* foregrounds objects which index the choice of methods in responding to the call from another human being. *Spinning* is particularly innovative in dramatizing self-reflexivity in a specific way: the protagonists, Susan and Conor, are the audience of each other's memories on stage, which points to the nature of theatre where playing and viewing are not only juxtaposed but also interact, with the potential outcome that all participants achieve an "ethical turn" towards each other and themselves as a workable foundation of "equality for all".

Notes

1. Fien Adriaens, "Post Feminism in Popular Culture: A Potential for Critical Resistance?", *Politics and Culture* 2009, 4, n.p.
2. Sarah Gamble, "Postfeminism" in *The Routledge Companion to Feminism and Postfeminism*, ed. Sarah Gamble (London and New York: Routledge, 2004), 36.

3. Ibid.
4. Ibid., 37.
5. Wanda Balzano and Moynagh Sullivan, "Editorial: The Contemporary Ballroom of Romance." in *The Irish Review*, 35 (summer 2007): 1.
6. Ibid.
7. Claire Bracken *Irish Feminist Futures* (London and New York: Routledge, 2016), 85.
8. Diane Negra, "Adjusting Men and Abiding Mammies: Gendering the Recession in Ireland" in *Irish Review* 46 (2013): 24.
9. Ibid., 31.
10. Cormac O'Brien, "Unblessed Among Women: Performing Patriarchy Without Men in Contemporary Irish Theatre" in *Ireland, Memory and Performing the Historical Imagination*, ed. Christopher Collins and Mary P. Caulfield (Basingstoke: Palgrave Macmillan, 2014), 200.
11. Eamonn Jordan, "Irish Theatre and Historiography," in *The Oxford Handbook of Modern Irish Theatre*, ed. Nicholas Grene and Chris Morash (Oxford: Oxford University Press, 2016), 691.
12. Melissa Sihra, "Shadow and Substance: Women, Feminism, and Irish Theatre," in *The Oxford Handbook of Modern Irish Theatre*, ed. Nicholas Grene, Chris Morash (Oxford: Oxford University Press, 2016), 557.
13. Werner Huber, "Introduction." in *Ireland: Representation and Responsibility*, ed. Werner Huber, Michael Böss, Catherine Maignant, Hedwig Schwall (Trier: Wissenschaftlicher Verlag, 2007), 9.
14. Ibid.
15. Alan Read, *Theatre, Intimacy and Engagement* (Basingstoke: Palgrave Macmillan, 2007), 69.
16. Nicholas Ridout, *Theatre and Ethics* (Basingstoke: Palgrave Macmillan, 2009), 13, 22.
17. Ibid., 53.
18. Meadhbh McHugh, "The Glass Ceiling and the Gag: Fifth Wave Feminism & Ireland's National Theatre, 2010–2014," in *For the Sake of Sanity: Doing Things With Humour in Irish Performance*, ed. Eric Weitz. (Dublin: Carysfort Press, 2014), 145.
19. Ibid., 145–6.
20. Marina Carr, *Marble* (Dublin: Gallery Books, 2009), 62.
21. Ondřej Pilný, "Whose Ethics? Which Genre? – Irish Drama and the Terminal Days of the Celtic Tiger", in *Ethical Debates in Contemporary Theatre and Drama*, ed. Mark Berninger, Christoph Henke, and Bernhard Reitz (Trier: Wissenschaftlicher Verlag, 2012), 177.
22. Carmen Kuhling and Kieran Keohane, *Cosmopolitan Ireland: Globalisation and Quality of Life* (London: Pluto, 2007), 127.
23. Ibid., 128.
24. Song of Songs 5: 15 in Holy Bible, New International Version. Biblica Inc., 2011 (1973). https://www.biblegateway.com/passage/?search=Song+of+Songs+5%3A15&version=NIV.
25. Carr, *Marble*, 52.
26. Ibid., 53.
27. Luce Irigaray, "Women on the Market" in *Literary Theory: An Anthology*. Second ed., ed. Julie Rivkin and Michael Ryan (London: Blackwell, 2004), 809.

28. Carr, *Marble*, 19–20.
29. Ibid., 65.
30. Pilný, "Whose Ethics? Which Genre?", 179.
31. About the role of the internet in the drama see my essay "Post-Celtic Tiger Crisis Genderized and the Escape to Virtual Realities in Nancy Harris's *No Romance*" in *Boundaries, Passages, Transitions: Essays in Irish Literature, Culture and Politics in Honour of Werner Huber*. Irish Studies in Europe 08, edited by Hedwig Schwall and Chiara Sciarrino. (Trier, Wissenschaftlicher Verlag, 2018), 113–125.
32. O'Brien, "Unblessed Among Women," 200–1.
33. Ibid., 201.
34. Nancy Harris, *No Romance* (London: Nick Hern Books, 2011), 37.
35. Ibid., 21.
36. O'Brien, "Unblessed Among Women", 201.
37. Harris, *No Romance*, 69.
38. Ibid., 45.
39. Ibid., 62.
40. Negra, "Adjusting Men and Abiding Mammies", 31.
41. Harris, *No Romance*, 70.
42. Ibid., 71.
43. Ibid., 74.
44. Ibid., 75.
45. Ibid., 76.
46. Ibid., 89.
47. Ibid., 102.
48. Elaine Murphy, *Shush* (London: New Hearne Books, 2011), 7.
49. Ridout, *Theatre and Ethics*, 56.
50. Murphy, *Shush*, 26.
51. Ibid., 55.
52. Murphy, *Shush*, 57. About the role of Irene in the play I totally disagree with Peter Crawley, whose review of *Shush* in the *Irish Times* writes her off as "supposedly the dimmest member of the group".
53. Murphy, *Shush*, 70.
54. Judith Butler, *Precarious Life: The Powers of Mourning and Violence* (London/New York: Verso, 2004), 21–22.
55. Deirdre Kinahan, *Spinning* (Dublin: Fishamble, 2014), 35–36.
56. Kuhling and Keohane, *Cosmopolitan Ireland*, 12.
57. Kinahan, *Spinning*, 42.
58. Ibid., 52.
59. Matthew, Roe. "An interview with SPINNING playwright Deirdre Kinahan." https://www.buzzonstage.com/chicago/wicker-park/irish-theatre-of-chicago/articles/an-interview-with-spinning-playwright-deirdre-kinahan.
60. Kinahan, *Spinning*, 86.
61. Ondřej Pilný, *The Grotesque in Contemporary Anglophone Drama* (Basingstoke: Palgrave Macmillan, 2016), 13.

Bibliography

Primary Sources

Carr, Marina. *Marble*. Dublin: Gallery Books, 2009.
Harris, Nancy. *No Romance*. London: Nick Hern Books, 2011.
Kinahan, Deirdre. *Spinning*. Dublin: Fishamble, 2014.
Murphy, Elaine. *Shush*. London: Nick Hern Books, 2011.

Secondary Sources

Adriaens, Fien. "Post feminism in popular culture: A potential for critical resistance?" In *Politics and Culture* 4 (2009): n. p.

Bracken, Claire. *Irish Feminist Futures*, London and New York: Routledge, 2016.

Butler, Judith. *Precarious Life: The Powers of Mourning and Violence*. London and New York: Verso, 2004.

Crawley, Peter. "A Sister Act That's Somewhere Between a Sitcom and a Kitchen Sink," In *The Irish Times*, June 13, 2013. http://www.irishtimes.com/a-sister-act-that-s-somewhere-between-a-sitcom-and-a-kitchen-sink-1.1427676.

Gamble, Sarah. "Postfeminism." In *The Routledge Companion to Feminism and Postfeminism*, edited by Sarah Gamble. London and New York: Routledge, 2004: 36–45.

Huber, Werner. "Introduction." In *Ireland: Representation and Responsibility*, edited by Werner Huber, Michael Böss, Catherine Maignant, Hedwig Schwall. Trier: Wissenschaftlicher Verlag, 2007: 9-12

Irigaray, Luce. "Women on the Market." In *Literary Theory: An Anthology*, 2nd ed., edited by Julie Rivkin and Michael Ryans. London: Blackwell, 2004: 799–811.

Jordan, Eamonn. "Irish Theatre and Historiography." In *The Oxford Handbook of Modern Irish Theatre*, edited by Nicholas Grene and Chris Morash. Oxford: Oxford University Press, 2016: 673–693.

Keane, Caomhan. "No Romance. Interview with Nancy Harris." http://entertainment.ie/theatre/feature/No-Romance-Interview-with-Nancy-Harris/210/1172.htm.

Kuhling, Carmen, and Kieran Keohane. *Cosmopolitan Ireland: Globalisation and Quality of Life*. London: Pluto, 2007.

McHugh, Meadhbh."The Glass Ceiling and the Gag: Fifth Wave Feminism & and Ireland's National Theatre, 2010–2014." In *For the Sake of Sanity: Doing Things with Humour in Irish Performance*, edited by Eric Weitz. Dublin: Carysfort Press, 2014: 143–158.

Negra, Diane. "Adjusting Men and Abiding Mammies: Gendering the Recession in Ireland." In *Irish Review* 46 (2013): 23–34.

O'Brien, Cormac. "Unblessed Among Women: Performing Patriarchy Without Men in Contemporary Irish Theatre." In *Ireland, Memory and Performing the Historical Imagination*, edited by Christopher Collins and Mary P. Caulfield. Basingstoke: Palgrave Macmillan, 2014: 190–206.

Pilný, Ondřej. "Whose Ethics? Which Genre?—Irish Drama and the Terminal Days of the Celtic Tiger." In *Ethical Debates in Contemporary Theatre and Drama*. Edited by Mark Berninger, Christoph Henke, and Bernhard Reitz. Trier: Wissenschaftlicher Verlag, 2012:175–188.

———. *The Grotesque in Contemporary Anglophone Drama*. Basingstoke: Palgrave Macmillan, 2016.
Read, Alan. *Theatre, Intimacy and Engagement*. Basingstoke: Palgrave Macmillan, 2007.
Ridout, Nicholas. *Theatre and Ethics*. Palgrave Macmillan, 2009.
Roe, Matthew. "An interview with SPINNING playwright Deirdre Kinahan." https://www.buzzonstage.com/chicago/wicker-park/irish-theatre-of-chicago/articles/an-interview-with-spinning-playwright-deirdre-kinahan.
Sihra, Melissa. "Shadow and Substance: Women, Feminism, and Irish Theatre." In *The Oxford Handbook of Modern Irish Theatre*, edited by Nicholas Grene, Chris Morash. Oxford: Oxford University Press, 2016: 543–58.

Reflections on Bernard Shaw and the Twenty-First Century Dublin Stage

Audrey McNamara

A prolific playwright, with an oeuvre of over sixty plays, George Bernard Shaw has been considered "the invisible man of Irish theatre".[1] A significant alteration in his status took place when three of his plays that had never been staged by the Abbey Theatre made their debuts: *Pygmalion* (1912) in 2011; *Major Barbara* (1905) in 2013; and *Heartbreak House* (1913–16) in 2014. *You Never Can Tell* (1897) was on its fifth outing in the Abbey in 2015, having been first staged in 1919 and again in 1921, 1933 and 1978. Prior to 2011, the last time a Shaw play was performed on the Abbey stage was 1998, when Patrick Mason directed *Saint Joan*. The Gate theatre, which has been more of a friend to Shaw's work, had reduced productions of his plays. After a ten-year gap, Alan Stanford directed *Arms and the Man* in June 2000. Two more plays were presented that same year, *How He Lied to her Husband* in Bewley's Café Theatre directed by Kelly Campbell and *Mrs Warren's Profession* in the Peacock Theatre directed by Brian Brady. This chapter will concentrate on the more recent Shaw productions, from 2004 to 2016, and examine the commonalities that prompted these stagings as relevant to a modern twenty-first century society.

Mrs Warren's Profession proved an appropriate choice in 2004, performed in the now defunct Andrew's Lane Theatre under John Breen's direction. This was the year that the *Gender Equality Policy 2004* was published. In the foreword to the policy, Minister for State, Tom Kitt stated:

> The Policy acknowledges that international recognition of rights of women has not been translated into practice on the ground. Women suffer sustained violations of their human rights, particularly in societies torn by conflict. Domestic

A. McNamara (✉)
University College Dublin, Dublin, Ireland

E. Jordan, E. Weitz (eds.), *The Palgrave Handbook of Contemporary Irish Theatre and Performance*,
https://doi.org/10.1057/978-1-137-58588-2_59

violence and other forms of violence against women, such as trafficking, forced prostitution and rape—including marital rape—are a common experience for women. Violation of women's human rights increases their vulnerability in many ways, not least by increasing their risk of contracting HIV. In this context, achieving gender equality is both a matter of human rights and of great urgency.[2]

There is no doubt that *Mrs Warren's Profession*, Shaw's third play, speaks to the ongoing struggle for women's equality. Its themes were just as relevant when it was performed some nine years later, in 2013, at the Gate Theatre (directed by Patrick Mason.) The *jounal.ie* reported in September 2013 that "more than 200 people were identified as victims of human trafficking in the previous three years [...] and that there was 'growing evidence' according to the Immigrant Council of Ireland that 'sex trafficking was going undetected'".[3] Shaw claimed when he wrote the play that it was intended

To draw attention to the truth that prostitution is caused, not by female depravity and male licentiousness, but simply by underpaying, undervaluing, and overworking women so shamefully that the poorest of them are forced to resort to prostitution to keep body and soul together.[4]

In essence, Shaw is creating a dialogue that places women as a medium of economic barter both inside and outside the confines of the law. In the case of both marriage and prostitution, the lack of economic protection for woman was the same—though marriage gave woman respectability. Mrs Warren's attitude to life is created by the poverty she was born into. Even in creating a wealthy life for herself and Vivie, her daughter, she fails to move on from age-old standards. The irony of Mrs Warren's rise in fortune is the way she made her money. She has used women whom Nelson O'Ceallaigh Ritschel describes as "products of extreme poverty".[5] She is indicative of society's responsibility for the poverty-stricken circumstances of some of its population. Unfortunately, very little has changed in 100 years. The ostensible topics of prostitution and the sex trade in the play are still very relevant in today's world, where they are very rarely out of the headlines. Vivie, at the end of the play, distances herself from the double standards of her mother and, as the door slams on her mother's back as she leaves, Vivie's expression becomes "one of joyous content". (286) Shaw has freed her from the constraints of a strait-laced Victorian society that sought to create a space for women behind their closed front doors. This space effectively ensured female silence and patriarchal control. The closed door symbolized the closing down, not only the female mind, but also her voice. Mrs Warren has internalized the values of patriarchy and has a false sense of her own freedom and a false sense of her own agency. Within a patriarchal order, she has supplied the sexual services of working class women to men—thereby providing a financially better life for herself and Vivie. However, Vivie comes to realize that her future—like the women her mother has exploited—has also been sacrificed and knows that in order to retain her independence she must cut all ties with her mother.

This theme re-appears in Shaw's later play *Pygmalion*, which was performed at the Gate Theatre (directed by Robin Lefévre) in 2004, later made its debut on the Abbey Stage in 2011 (directed by Annabelle Comyn) and was also performed at Smock Alley Theatre in 2016 (directed by Liam Halligan). Smock Alley Theatre's programme note describes it as "[a]n Ibsen-inspired tale of a woman's escape from class and gender oppression to a position of economic and personal freedom". In the programme note to the Gate production, G.S. Viereck quotes Shaw as stating that "until we sublimate the marriage relation, the difference between marriage and Mrs Warren's profession remains the difference between union and scab labour".[6] Roy Foster also aligned *Pygmalion* with *Mrs Warren's Profession* in the programme note to the Abbey 2011 production, stating that "[l]ike *Mrs Warren's Profession* twenty years before, *Pygmalion* provides among other things, a compassionate commentary on the limitations that patriarchy and capitalism impose on women—especially working class women".[7] The crucial scene that introduces Henry Higgins, Colonel Pickering and Eliza opens on a comedic note. Paranoia takes holds as the bystanders are made aware that there is somebody standing nearby taking notes of all that Eliza is saying, causing her to have a robust verbal interchange with Higgins that leads him to make the claim that he could pass her off as the Queen of Sheba (20). However, it is Eliza who initiates the change by appearing at Higgins" home the next day and demanding that he teach her to "talk more genteel" (30), in order that she can rise above her station in life. The Shavian construction of the feminine begins when Higgins rises to Eliza's challenge. This construction is illusory and designed to take the audience to a familiar and comfortable place, before Shaw exposes what his play is about. Quite differently to Galatea in the Greek myth—who is presented as a blank canvas, grateful for the life breathed into her by the wishes of Pygmalion—Eliza wishes to reject patriarchal governance and plans, and to take a degree of control over her own life and future with her newfound knowledge and education. Shaw, in breathing life into the character of Eliza, challenges the notion of the feminine construct. It can be argued that Eliza is a product of Higgins' conception, but ultimately it is her own power of reasoning that fashions the way her character develops. Unlike Galatea, who lived to obey Pygmalion, Eliza, with her new-found confidence and education, removes herself from Higgins, who does not believe that she will go. As she leaves, he issues her with instructions to order a ham and stilton cheese and to buy him gloves (128). Eliza replies to all his instructions and ends with, "What you are to do without me I cannot imagine" (128). Her mind is set. The stage directions state that "*she sweeps out*" (128); no slamming of the door for Eliza, rather a determined and forward movement as she gains control of her own life. Both Vivie and Eliza continue to represent the ongoing challenges of women in modern society. Although, great advances have been made to equalize the sexes, there is a natural patriarchal inclination that presents a barrier to true equality, especially in the workplace. According to figures released by the CSO in 2004

> The proportion of women at risk of poverty, after pensions and social transfers, was 23% in Ireland in 2001. This was the highest rate in the EU 25 [...] Female income liable for social insurance payments in 2002 was 63.3% of male income. After an adjustment for differences in hours worked, women's income was 82.5% of men's income.[8]

Women's positions changed very little in the intervening years, as the 2011 CSO report shows:

> Men were more likely to be in the labour force than women in Ireland in 2011, with just under seven out of ten men aged over 15 at work or unemployed while a little over half of women were in the labour force. More than half a million women in 2011 were looking after home/family compared with only 9,600 men.[9]

In both plays, Shaw is creating a dialogue that positions woman as a medium of economic barter within the constraints of the law. Undoubtedly, these plays speak to societal anomalies that persist in our so-called modern age.

The Abbey Theatre, under the directorship of Fiach Mac Conghail, continued its homage to previously neglected work by Shaw and premiered two of his plays over the following three years—as mentioned: *Major Barbara* in 2013, *Heartbreak House* in 2014 and the fifth Abbey production of *You Never Can Tell* in 2015. Mac Conghail states of *Major Barbara*, which was performed in the centenary year of the Dublin 1913 Lockout, that "Shaw has much to offer us [...] as a political thinker who can provoke us all".[10] Ironically, on 30 July 2013, the day before the play opened, the President of SIPTU, Jack O'Connor, stated at a meeting in Liberty Hall that "the approach of placing business interests above the common good [...] brought the country into a state of existential crisis for the third time in 80 years".[11] This statement could have been used as a form of introduction to the themes of *Major Barbara*. Conflicts around capitalism, morality, war, wealth, religion, salvation and poverty abound in the play. Major Barbara, the protagonist, faces the dilemma of whether to accept money from her father, Andrew Undershaft, to aid the poor. She cannot reconcile herself to taking "tainted money"; her father accumulated his wealth through his production of armaments. Lady Britomart, Barbara's mother and Undershaft's estranged wife, says of Undershaft to their son Stephen, "Your father must be fabulously wealthy as there is always a war going on somewhere" (345). Undershaft is unashamed of his wealth. In answer to Barbara's question on his religious beliefs, he tells her "I am a millionaire. That is my religion" (380). Shaw stated in his Preface to the play that "money is the most important thing in the world. It represents health, strength, generosity and beauty as conspicuously and undeniably as the want of it represents illness, weakness, disgrace, meanness and ugliness" (311–312). In 2013 in Ireland, as the country struggled to recover from the crash of the so-called Celtic Tiger, Shaw's words, though possibly unsavoury to purely socialist thinking, spoke to the lack experienced by so many citizens caused by the depraved capitalism of its bankers. In Undershaft, and by extension Barbara, Shaw created representations of the idea that wealth can be used intellectually and spiritually to counteract what he terms as the "greatest of our evils and the worst of our crimes [...] poverty" (305).

The Abbey premiere of *Heartbreak House* was staged in the centenary year of the start of the First World War. The play encapsulates the death of a way of life, but is more far-reaching than the ostensible subject of the demise of the big house. It symbolically uses the big house as a metaphor for the fractured society that existed during the war to end all wars. Shaw, in the Preface to the play, stated that "*Heartbreak House* is not merely the name of the play [...]. It is a cultured leisured Europe before the war".[12] This statement is loaded with irony and, as the play unfolds, the culture and leisure are revealed as mythical. *Heartbreak House* depicts a way of life—and a society—in a state of instability. Hesione Hushabye is preoccupied with money, as is Ellie Dunne, but for different reasons. Hesione worries that "money is running short" alluding to the deterioration of a way of life. The reaction of her husband, Hector, and her father, Captain Shotover, is somewhat apathetic and incredulous. Shotover's suggestion that Hector "invent something" is greeted by Hesione with dismay and highlights the fact that she, too, is unwilling to change the status quo in order to promote change (528). Ellie Dunne, on the other hand, is willing to marry for money in order to feed her soul. She tells Shotover that "Old-fashioned people think you can have a soul without money. [...] Young people nowadays know better. A soul is a very expensive thing to keep: much more than a motor car" (564). There is a sense of dislocation among the characters; they are strangers to each other in their way of thinking, even those related by blood. There is a lack of purpose within the house, which signals a sense of disconnect and alludes to the wider social problem of an archaic communal mindset. The way of life represented by the inhabitants of *Heartbreak House* resonates through to the twenty-first century. It shows that war can be as a much a product of boredom and greed as international tensions. Hector Hushabye's analysis of the problems with the house concludes that, "We are wrong with it. There is no sense in us. We are useless, dangerous and ought to be abolished" (578). There is no doubt that these words hold as much resonance today as they did when they were written in 1916, as wars continue to devastate communities and countries and cost tens of thousands of lives.

You Never Can Tell, staged from December 2015 to January 2016, had last been performed at the Abbey Theatre in 1978. As the Christmas showcase, Mac Conghail felt that "this unpredictable comedy was perfect for this time of year".[13] The play, despite having the unpredictability that Mac Conghail describes, deals with the very complex theme of marriage breakdown and a fractured family life. Shaw stated in the Preface that he wrote the play in response to "requirements of managers in search of fashionable comedies for West End Theatres", claiming that he "was more than willing to show that drama can humanize [...] things as easily as they, in the wrong hands, can dehumanize the drama".[14] Shaw once again portrays the thinking woman, in Mrs Clandon, a character who, for her period, has advanced ideas on her right to have agency. In line with Shaw's views on equality, the character of the waiter, William, is also bestowed with the same wisdom and becomes the centre from which the drama unfolds. Despite its comedic tones, the dialogue or action of the play is never farcical. It maintains a considerate if light-hearted respect for the depth of its themes. In essence, in true Shavian fashion, the subject of marriage and all its problems is dealt with in a pragmatic way, demonstrating that resolution and compromise are possible even in the most emotion-driven situations. In his preface to *Getting Married*, Shaw stated that "if marriage cannot be made to produce something better than we are, marriage will have to go or the nation will have to go" (328). Interestingly, 2015 was the year that Ireland became the first country to vote for same sex marriage in a public referendum. With the vote, the Irish people embraced the Shavian mindset and made marriage an equal opportunity for all members of society.

There is no doubt that new work and new drama has to be given space to breathe and grow, but it is well worth remembering that nothing comes from a vacuum and there is value in staying in touch with those dramatists who, like Shaw, revolutionized modern theatre. It is through the creative vision of their artistic directors that theatres in Dublin such as the Abbey, the Gate, Smock Alley, and others will continue to perform the work of the pillars of modern writing like Bernard Shaw whose plays still resonate in the twenty-first century in harmony with the work of the playwrights who have succeeded him.

Notes

1. Nicholas Grene, "Shaw in Irish Theater: An Unacknowledged Presence", in *Shaw and the Last Hundred Years*, ed. Bernard F. Dukore (University Park: Penn State Press, 1994), 15.
2. Tom Kitt, *Foreward: Gender Equality Act April 2004*, Department of Foreign Affairs and Trade.
3. Daragh Brophy, "45 people, including 23 children were trafficked into Ireland last year", *TheJournal.ie*, Sept 27, 2013, accessed September 12, 2016.
4. Nicholas Grene, *Bernard Shaw: A Critical View* (London: Palgrave Macmillan, 1984), 20, citing Shaw's 'Preface' to *Mrs Warren's Profession*, 181.
5. Nelson O'Ceallaigh Ritschel, "Shaw, Murder, and the Modern Metropolis", *SHAW, The Annual of Bernard Shaw Studies* 32 (2012): 105.
6. G.S. Viereck, *Sex, Love and Marriage* in "Shaw looks at Life at 70", *London Magazine*, December 1927 reprinted in the Gate Theatre Programme, 6 July 2004.
7. Roy Foster, "Pygmalion and Heartbreak", *Abbey Theatre Programme*, 27 April–11 June 2011.
8. Central Statistics Office *Women and Men in Ireland 2004 Press Release*. Accessed January 10, 2017, www.cso.ie.
9. Central Statistics Office *Women and Men in Ireland 2011 Press Release*. Accessed January 10, 2017, www.cso.ie.

10. Fiach Mac Conghail, "Welcome Fáilte", in *Major Barbara* Programme, 31 July–21 September 2013.
11. Jack O'Connor, *Result of the Lockout determined the future of Irish society* SIPTU News Archive. Accessed 10 January 2017, www.siptu.ie.
12. George Bernard Shaw, "Heartbreak House and Horseback Hall", in *Complete Plays with Prefaces Vols I–VI*, Vol I (New York, Dodd Mead & Company, 1963), 449.
13. Mac Conghail, "Welcome Fáilte."
14. George Bernard Shaw, "Preface" *Complete Plays with Prefaces Vols I–VI*, Vol III (New York, Dodd Mead & Company, 1963), 113.

Bibliography

Brophy, Daragh. "45 People, Including 23 Children Were Trafficked into Ireland Last Year." *TheJournal.ie,* Sept 27, 2013. Accessed September 12, 2016.

Central Statistics Office. *Women and Men in Ireland 2004 Press Release.* Accessed January 10, 2017. www.cso.ie

———. *Women and Men in Ireland 2011 Press Release.* Accessed January 10, 2017. www.cso.ie

Foster, Roy. "Pygmalion and Heartbreak." *Abbey Theatre Programme*, April 27–June 11, 2011.

Grene, Nicholas. "Shaw in Irish Theater: An Unacknowledged Presence." In *Shaw and the Last Hundred Years,* edited by Bernard F. Dukore. Pennsylvania: Penn State Press, 1994.

———. *Bernard Shaw: A Critical View.* Basingstoke: Palgrave Macmillan, 1984.

Kitt, Tom. *Foreward: Gender Equality Act April 2004.* Department of Foreign Affairs and Trade, 2004.

MacConghail, Fiach. 2013. Welcome Fáilte. *Major Barbara* Programme. July 31–September 21.

O'Connor, Jack. 2017. *Result of the Lockout Determined the Future of Irish Society.* SIPTU News Archive. Accessed January 10. www.siptu.ie

O'Ceallaigh Ritschel, Nelson. (2012). "Shaw, Murder, and the Modern Metropolis." *SHAW, The Annual of Bernard Shaw Studies* 32: 102-116.

Shaw, George Bernard. *Complete Plays with Prefaces Vol I* (Vols I–VI). New York, Dodd Mead & Company, 1963.

———. *Complete Plays with Prefaces Vol III* (Vols I–VI). New York, Dodd Mead & Company, 1963.

Viereck, G.S. *Sex, Love and Marriage* in "Shaw Looks at Life at 70", *London Magazine*, December 1927 reprinted in the Gate Theatre Programme, July 6, 2004.

"Endless Art": The Contemporary Archive of Performance

Barry Houlihan

In the 1991 song, *Endless Art*, by the Irish rock band, A House, the lead singer Dave Couse lists a necrology of past artists, reminding us through the refrain that those named are:

> All dead
> Yet still alive
> In endless time
> Endless art[1]

The refrain encapsulates the idea of how the archive of theatre and performance today facilitates this paradox—that all art, all performance, though essentially "dead" and past, is still alive in an endless archival purgatory.

As recently as 2004, performance theorist Richard Schechner warned that instead of too little material existing in the archives of performance, there is now too much. He warned that it had the potential to act as a flood of fact and incorruptible evidence that would stymie any space for creative thought and intellectual inquisition:

> The interplay between the past and the present was extremely active because so much of the past, in terms of hard evidence, was so partial. But with the advent of increasingly detailed first-hand archiving—I mean film, video, and digital memory—the whole archival enterprise has changed. Instead of too little, there is too much. Instead of an open net, there is now the record of the event itself. And

B. Houlihan (✉)
National University of Ireland Galway, Galway, Ireland
e-mail: barry.houlihan@nuigalway.ie

E. Jordan, E. Weitz (eds.), *The Palgrave Handbook of Contemporary Irish Theatre and Performance*,
https://doi.org/10.1057/978-1-137-58588-2_60

> the weight of these archived performances and other documents is only increasing over time. Digitization means that most probably even a great fire (such as destroyed the library of ancient Alexandria) would not have a great effect.[2]

By addressing Schechner's concern through the course of this chapter, I will discuss conceptual points regarding the archive of contemporary theatre versus the contemporary theatre archive (two disparate things), assess the structural make-up of the archive and how it reflects change in the theatre-making process witnessed in Ireland in recent years, and address how digital and technological interventions and the rise of "theatremakers" have resulted in a shift in provenance and classification of the archival record, particularly in an Irish context.

Alive in Time: The Performed Archive and Affect Today

In *Theatre & History*, Rebecca Schneider discusses the value of the archive as a reliable source for both historians and actors. It is dichotomous in terms of its reliability—as a collection of artifices, projections of works and actions onto the walls of Plato's cave, falsities within a form of embodied and verbal expression. "Isn't theatre, and theatricality, always essentially faux?", she asks.[3] In attempting to define the record itself, Schneider questions the essence of the theatrical source as reliable evidence, questioning the archive's ability to act as a reliable witness:

> But what is a truthful record? Can the living body be a recording machine, or a means of recording at all transmissible over time? And, even more thorny an issue, what are historical facts that could be said to correspond only to disembodied records?[4]

The archive of contemporary theatre comprises two main and central facets (and presents two questions). As Schneider presents frameworks about what constitutes history and the record, the same is needed for the archive—questions immediately arise, such as: is the original performance the same as a digitized recording? Peggy Phelan decisively argues no in her 1993 work, *Unmarked: The Politics of Performance*. But, in the absence of a recording, is an annotated prompt-script enough to remount exactly the events of the past? There is a duality of presence—of active recovery (moving towards the past) and active progression (moving towards the future)—where the archival present offers a compromise by seeking to stabilize both mediums within its repository. The separation between evidence, memory and the archive offers a space of and for reconstruction; digital means today allows for an active recovering of the sound and movement of actors, of the feeling of audience response, for intonation and accent of the text, animating multiple presences simultaneously.

Schneider also presents the question of the liminality of archival presences—the evidence in and between the here, the now, the past and future—and what has been performed live, what *is* live and what *will* be performed live in the future. This creates a tautology, the illusion of presence, within the contemporary theatre archive. The affect of the past, reconstituted in works such as those comprising *the Monto Cycle* by ANU Productions,[5] causes a tangential connection in the present through emotion, trauma, recognition or other responses to archival stimuli:

> Affect, and the liveness it seems to root around in, are thus the purview not only of the theatre maker, whose traffic in feelings crosses boundaries between stage and house, but of any encounter crossing the liminal borders separating a then from a now.[6]

Quantifying or deliberately intervening in the archiving of affect of liveness is problematic. Schneider contemplates that if affect is not a material remnant, but an immaterial residue at best... how can it be any way trustworthy as evidence? How can it be admissible and authenticated?

Diana Taylor situates the archive *as* repertoire and as a direct force in the geopolitical and post-colonial debate between colonizer and colonized between Europe and the Americas. This complex dichotomy between archive and repertoire and between historicizing power, privilege, and the act of recording itself. Repertoire is curated and conscious of its creators, and while the archive can also be so, it can act also act as a counternarrative to the dominant hegemonic event and its memory. Taylor further clarifies this by differentiating by positing:

> "the "event"—unique, verifiable, with protagonistic social actors—also poses problems of objectivity because what gets constituted and recognized as an "event," what qualifies as verification, who emerges as the hero, and how that vision of the past gets archived is determined by the analyst... events are not necessarily entered into history and archived because they are pivotal, but that they become pivotal by virtue of the fact that they are entered into history and archived."[7]

The power of the archive, then, is in fact directly relevant to the archive of contemporary performance where it can act as a powerful site of resistance and simultaneous "live" reaction by its very presence. Contested national histories in ANU's *Pals*,[8] or docu-archival works by Colin Murphy, such as *Guaranteed!*,[9] enabled audiences to stand as witnesses, active in the work's own re-situating of the historical affect, in place of being passive bystanders under more traditional audience–performer binaries.

Taking Taylor's position that the archive can alter the prescribed imperial privilege of the victor in history and offer restitutive order, then performing, witnessing and authoritatively redressing the archival absences through the act of theatre itself performs a form of archival redress. This can require the intervention of an archivist in the first instance to seek, reclaim and make available a body of records that act to counter previously accepted amnesias. Miriam Haughton exemplifies this in her article on the complicit silences and ANU's *Laundry* (2011): "The continual post-performance effect experienced by *Laundry*'s audience ensures that while the actual performance may be ephemeral, the memory and consequence of this performance lives on."[10]

The Archive of Contemporary Theatre and a Continuous Present: New Possibilities

To catch up on itself through digitization, better preservation practices, increased access and wider knowledge, the theatre archive may still only ever be running to stand still. The three-dimensional effect of the theatre archive, allowing scholars to see each layer of strata across a cross-section of the performance itself is allowing for new knowledge and new understanding of how works developed. These strata run through the devising/drafting process, through rehearsals and to final production and reception, but crucially also through the afterlife of the play—how it was received, remembered and how it impacted those who witnessed it. The archive of contemporary performance today is fluid and reactive in its form and constitution. It has moved long since past only the "text as archive", now comprising multimedia and mass-scale amalgamation of tangible items and intangible born-digital elements, such as e-mail, YouTube videos, podcasts and other social media posts as well as high-definition live recordings. Intervention is essential to ensure a comprehensive, democratic and impartial record, conscious of its shifting materiality and also of its reception and consumption as much as its production. It must include all matter of the act of performance.

The binary points of "beginning" and "end" are not always identifiable. Ric Knowles argues for the pursuit of "how meaning is produced" in order to gauge a clear understanding of performance through its cultural and material elements, thus efforts to locate a beginning and judge an end-point from one performance and also production from successive events. He argues for "developing modes of analysis that consider performance texts to be products of a more complex mode of production … rooted in specific and determinate social and cultural contexts".[11]

What is today being archived digitally has aroused questions upon what exactly typifies the form of Irish theatre in the last twenty years—what are we preserving? Looking at a point of foundation for the contemporary archive of Irish theatre, it is necessary to look at how and when Irish theatre has changed in and with Irish society over recent years. For instance, the Irish dramatic tradition historically has leaned heavily towards a playwright's theatre. That, of course, supports a canon of works that can be seen as diminutive in terms of the actual archived record of Irish contemporary performance, which far outstrips the select and few canonical works. The responsibility of the archive is to counteract memory gaps and also hegemonic biases in terms of who and what we actually remember in the first place. Patrick Lonergan detailed the most recent of all these noticeable changes in Irish theatre:

> Since the end of the Celtic Tiger period, we have seen the emergence of exciting new forms of theatre-making, and a resurgence in Irish playwriting and design. The boundaries between playwrights, actors and audiences are more porous than ever before—and it's no longer easy (or even useful) to define what exactly the "Irish play" might be nowadays.[12]

Writing in 2014, Fintan O'Toole describes playwright Mark O'Rowe, "with the possible exception of Sebastian Barry, actually the most fastidiously literary of contemporary Irish playwrights".[13] With the clear rise of devised and non-traditional site-specific productions, as well as a continuance of tradition in strong literary plays, the play itself is an art form that underwent radical change in the contemporary period. The archive of contemporary Irish theatre has and needed to undergo equal change for the archive to be as accurate a representation as possible of the act of performance itself; identifiable change in the latter results in subsequent change in the former.

Major archival projects, such as the Abbey Theatre and Gate Theatre Digital Archives at the James Hardiman Library, NUI Galway, allied with other archive collections, such as that of Druid Theatre Company, Thomas Kilroy, Siobhán McKenna and others, mean that never was so much material available for simultaneous interrogation and study. The National Library in Dublin makes available the archives of Brian Friel, Field Day Theatre Company, Hugh Leonard and Fishamble Theatre Company. Dublin City Library and Archive also holds a vast theatre collection, including archives of the Gaiety School of Acting, Anna Manahan and Storytellers Theatre Company and others from the contemporary period. Trinity College Dublin counts the archives of Tom Murphy, Rough Magic, the Pike Theatre and John B. Keane among their holdings. These few names are but very much the tip of the iceberg in terms of archival collections released in the last decade or so. However, these vast collections are, in the majority, available in paper format only, undigitized within respective institutions, which can ascribe perceived conditions of access restricted only to those who can attain entry to third-level education.

Where the paper archive meets the digital interface, as at NUI Galway, it is now possible to cross-search millions of items in a multiplicity of formats with instantaneous results. The video of an archived production can now be watched in sequence with the digital prompt-script, with enhanced photographs of productions with press reviews from across the globe, all accessible with the click of a mouse. The input and labour of an array of creative and administrative personnel behind each performance can be reclaimed.

Trace and Succession: Carrying on Performing

This multi-form approach affords a better visualization of the trace—the minutely perceptible element that links subsequent productions or performances of the same work across a wide timespan. The transmission of the present from one performance to another many years later, again creates a "second liveness," from one generation to another, each ascribing individual and personal social and cultural references and memories to respective viewings of a play, thus forming new production histories. For example, it is possible to study in detail Marie Mullen in the role of Mary in Druid's 1986 production of *Bailegangaire* by Tom Murphy, in which she played opposite Siobhán McKenna's Mommo to when Mullen assumed McKenna's character in the 2014 Druid production of the play. Likewise Mullen swapped her Tony-Award winning role of Maureen in Martin McDonagh's *Beauty Queen of Leenane* (1998) for the role of Mag Folan in the 2016 production, which was previously played by Anna Manahan. In this example, Peter Crawley commented on the 2016 *Beauty Queen* production as being a relatively faithful re-staging of the 1996 original:

> Druid's 20th anniversary production treats it [the 1996 original] with peculiar reverence. The lowing cellos and fretting piano notes of Paddy Cunneen's music suggest immense gravity to a drama without weight. Francis O'Connor's set, a grey bunker from which the orange lights of electrical sockets peek out like demonic eyes, is a perfect recreation of his 1996 original.[14]

The elemental succession retained cast members (Marie Mullen), set designers (Francis O'Connor) and, of course, Garry Hynes, as director, ensuring traces from twenty years previously, a work that heralded the mass global success of Druid, Hynes, McDonagh and others, would inevitably succumb to be seen as a continuing performance rather than a new production. As a much-marketed "Anniversary production", that production carried a much lighter comedic tone, portrayed by Mullen as the ghoulish mother in place of the late Anna Manahan, an actress of noted ominous physical and foreboding presence on stage. As Crawley further notes in his review:

> Some productions of McDonagh have seized that unreality, inflating his characters into Grand Guignol monsters, making gruesome goofiness more enjoyable. But though director Garry Hynes inscribes funny jokes in the margins, the stately pace of her naturalism seems more deferential, insisting the play has a soul. But it is not a subtle play; gags and intentions are clobbered home.[15]

The question of "trace" also presents opportunities to look for what may be absent in the archive. The evidence of exclusion of female voices by lack of direct access to the main stages of Ireland's theatres for female actors, playwrights, designers and technicians of all and any discipline, can now be traced and verified. Research conducted by Brenda Donohue reveals that from 1995 to 2014 only 11% of the plays staged by the Abbey Theatre, the national theatre of Ireland, were written by women. Donohue writes that:

> of 320 plays staged in this period, just 36 plays were written by a woman, 24 of which were new plays, while 12 were revivals. My analysis shows that women playwrights are significantly under-represented on the Abbey and Peacock stages in terms of full theatrical productions.[16]

The full report of the #WakingTheFeminists research group, entitled *Gender Counts* (2017), revealed the startling reality of an institutionalized sidelining of women practitioners, writers and others from professional theatre work in Ireland.

Fintan Walsh further adds to the debate on theatrical absence by maintaining that a gap exists in the performative representation of who actually lived and worked in contemporary Ireland and how immigrants to Ireland were assimilated into the performative narrative of our recent memory:

> One of the criticisms of Irish people often heard during the boom years was that we suffered from collective amnesia about the past, in the giddy rush to get ahead … Looking back over the last decade, what seems to have been particularly short lived in Irish theatre is any kind of sustained, coherent intercultural moment which seemed so assured at the turn of the twenty-first century in the work of Calypso Productions and Arambe Productions.[17]

Taking Donohue's and Walsh's points above, I would contend that within the archive of contemporary theatre and performance, a most ominous presence is, paradoxically, the element of absence. The archive of what is an inherently and utterly a live "thing" can therefore never fully capture or seek to replicate in full the accurate experience of witnessing theatre.

Following the March 1979 première production of Brian Friel's *Aristocrats* at the Abbey Theatre, Dublin, a letter appeared in the comment section of *The Irish Times*. The letter, from *The Irish Times* theatre critic David Nowlan, began by making a formal apology for his recent review of the play. The review was not a harsh or damning critique of the play, quite the opposite in fact. Instead Nowlan apologized for failing to remember to include any comment on the performance itself:

> I believe we owe an apology to our readers and particularly to the members of the Abbey Theatre Company who performed so well in the current production of Brian Friel's "Aristocrats." For reasons of space, all mention of the performance in this fine production (March 9th) was edited out of my review. May I, therefore, record that the playing of Niall O'Brien, Kevin McHugh, Bill Foley, John Kavanagh, Dearbhla Molloy, Stephen Rea, Ingrid Craigie and Kate Flynn was in the very best style and tradition of ensemble performance, finely disciplined yet individually distinct, and largely unforgettable? Like the play, the playing should not be missed.[18]

The simplicity by which the "official" record or review of a play, in this case by *The Irish Times*, is typical of the accidental nature by which essential memory of a performance may be lost or obscured. The actions of a diligent sub-editor in removing part of the review over concerns for print-space effectively erased the memory of the performance itself. The act of theatre may be recorded by virtue of a play title, playwright, theatre venue and production date being captured within the review, but the "liveness" was strangely absent by the omission of the actors themselves and of their labour in performance, though it was latterly described as "unforgettable" by Nowlan in his subsequent letter. This episode is a lesson for what the archive can forget and how essential it is for researchers to look beyond the initial layer of the archive for deeper meaning buried in subsequent layers which may not be immediately visible.

The nature of theatre production and performance and also that of archival curation emphasizes the interdisciplinary nature of the records resulting from performance and the skills required to preserve them. However, for such a process to be established and maintained as practice, debate and discourse on the theoretical framework for performance archives and for the preservation of memory must be undertaken.

The Archive in and as Part of Contemporary Theatre: Staging Memory and Experience

How modern living was presented theatrically is another key facet to understanding the archive of contemporary performance, whether the digital, digitized and physical. A trait of the style of work within the contemporary archive has been the direction of key plays that reflect contemporary living, especially within the past decade. Mark O'Rowe directed a remounting of his own play, *Terminus* at the Abbey Theatre, September 2010, while Annie Ryan directed Corn Exchange's *Freefall* by Michael West at the Project Arts Centre during the Dublin Theatre Festival of 2009. What this pair of plays reveal to audiences then and indeed now, over a decade later, is the immediate necessity for recent archival memory to be encountered. These plays offer a first-hand account of the devastation and isolation felt by the Irish population at the point of the onset of economic catastrophe. They provide the first ripple in the downward spiral of consequence for the Irish people from the demise of The Celtic Tiger, offering a form of 'acting out' personal memory and experience—a case in point of how Ric Knowles interrogates, "precisely *how* audiences produce meaning in negotiation with the particular, local, theatrical event".[19]

Emilie Pine further suggests that this confrontation between past and present leads us to question who we are now as much as who we were in the past: "The consequence of this revisiting of the past is that it creates new narratives—alternate and more complex narratives—taking account of memories that were for too long 'forgotten' or sidelined, by Irish history and culture."[20]

The plays which form the contemporary archive, consisting predominantly of works within the expanding theatrical canon, are also indicative, by their reliance on textual virtuosity, of a challenge between old and new styles, tradition and the future.

Fintan O'Toole, in an article discussing *Terminus*, said that "the play also highlights the struggle between form and language that needs to be resolved if Irish drama is to move forward".[21] O'Toole further argues that O'Rowe's play is taut with a direction style more akin to the Irish theatre archive canon of over one hundred years ago:

> There is also a narrative of freedom in the form—an ability to move from the mundane to the fantastical and from pathos to a final passage of breath-taking, outrageous and sublimely grotesque humour... Yet as a theatrical experience, the experience never matches the writing.[22]

O'Toole reasons that this physical stasis is in submission to linguistic extravagance and equates to the problem of Irish drama at the turn of the twentieth century where poets and playwrights wanted their words faithfully spoken and nothing more. "Yeats", O'Toole suggests, "had to look for new ways of music, dance and design to give physical expression to their words".[23] The battle for form and for expression of the production and its "theatre" is what makes the archive of contemporary performance such a complex entity. It is a constantly evolving body onto which is ascribed order, form and structure, either within a catalogued and organized form, or within the mass scale of the digital archive.

O'Rowe's trio of unrelenting intersecting monologues which comprise *Terminus* premièred at the Peacock Theatre, Dublin on 9 June 2007. The play is a linguistic and nightmarish journey from night-time Dublin docklands to rural Irish countryside and from demonic encounters to the deepest personal inner experiences of the individual within a contemporary and yet distorted vision of Irish life. The rhythmic and cadenced nuances of O'Rowe's monologue are rescued and preserved by the digital archive of the Abbey Theatre.[24] The digitized recording within the Abbey Theatre Digital Archive at NUI Galway allows one to hear accent, tone and diction which is critical to understanding the play on a deeper level. As O'Toole explains, the play is a lyrical representation of all things theatrical, from action, physicality and set design to place (the play features three characters each standing on a pedestal, black-out but with an illuminated spotlight on the speaker), so therefore the challenge to accurately archive the crippling world of O'Rowe's Celtic Tiger Dublin is dependent entirely on a digitized recording—the "illusion of presence", as O'Rowe writes in the play:

> The bus home then. The silent flat. No cat nor any kind of pet. The sofa—sit. The telly—hit the remote. Reward—the illusion of presence through voice.[25]

The Archive of Language and Place: Finding Voice in the Archive

In June 1997, Druid Theatre Company and the Royal Court Theatre staged the world première co-production of *The Leenane Trilogy* by Martin McDonagh. Comprising *The Beauty Queen of Leenane, A Skull in Connemara* and *The Lonesome* West, the production was a mammoth event in both scale and theatricality. The trilogy presented a production rich in inherited language and folklore of local people, place and language—a confrontation of past and present.

The first page within the 1997 *Trilogy* programme was not related to the finalized production that audiences were about to see. The opening page would normally offer the most lucrative placement for advertisements for what was the largest theatre event in Ireland that year. No advertisements, however, were present. Instead the programme included a feature on the private and unseen world of the rehearsal space for *The Leenane Trilogy*. The double-page black-and-white image featured a candid shot of the focused discussion taking place between actors Brian F. O'Byrne, Maeliosa Stafford, Marie Mullen, David Ganley, the playwright Martin McDonagh and the director Garry Hynes. The caption underneath the image stipulates that "the room in which the rehearsals take place is the heart of the project".[26]

The caption continues to state that within the rehearsal space, "here, finally, actors, writer, director and designers come together to create the production for the stage". In this ephemeral document, the theatre programme, often the most immediately disposable element of the process of going to the theatre, Druid set out to foreground the audience's experience of this production by exposing the bare bones of the rehearsal process. This allows the audience to witness the work and labour of actors, directors, designers, playwrights and all others who may be part of the utterly private and unarchived world of the ante-play—the unwilling and defiant former existence and iteration of the performance "proper".

Being acutely aware of "place" (being the physical geographical location and site of action) and "space" (the world and environment in which within the action takes place at a given time), within the programme note for *The Leenane Trilogy*, cartographer and writer Tim Robinson absorbs the idea of landscape (place) into the mind of those who live in the rugged and weather-beaten homes of its inhabitants (space). The article, entitled "A Connemara in the Skull", places the archive of landscape, which Robinson himself has documented, through his detailed cataloguing of the physical West—the landscape of Connemara, the Aran Islands and the Burren—and superimposes it onto the "linguistic West", as archived through the speech of McDonagh's characters.

This layering of the archive to include language and location is a key tool in unlocking further meanings of the archive of contemporary performance. Accent, diction, tone and language are all traits of the inherited identity of one's being. One's accent is often determined by one's location, retaining a flexible trait to allow change to match a change in location over time.

Abandoning of accent may allow one to sever ties with one's past, to move outside of the place of one past memory and experiences.

The conscious siting of this trilogy linguistically, socially and culturally in the heart of Connemara is furthered by the inclusion of an extract from *Connemara: A One Inch Map* also by Tim Robinson. In his article, Robinson suggests that what one most associates with Connemara, the rugged and inspiring landscape, the mountainous horizons and glistening lakes, are all unseen in McDonagh's trilogy. Instead what we are given in these plays are the contemporary results of over five hundred years of colonial interference, emigration, the decline of local Irish language and what Robinson terms "agrarian terrorism", which forced the British government to undertake the development of the West in the late nineteenth century. The archive of *The Leenane Trilogy*,[27] as described by Robinson, cannot exist outside of and separate from the archive of place of Leenane and Connemara itself:

> No need, I hope, for me to say that [McDonagh's Connemara] is not the only Connemara... but there is no doubt that this Connemara exists, this calamitous backdrop to the society McDonagh shows us, fled by its young, with its brutalised law and its old church gone in the teeth. The machine of the theatre forces us to laugh even as we pity and shudder at all of this, and the bare beauty of Connemara is one of the grim implicit jokes. Perhaps it is even close to "the crux of the matter".[28]

In his book of collected essays and articles, entitled *Navigations*, Richard Kearney describes the development of a modern Irish drama based on a typified form of verbal and linguistic structures, essentially how the voice of "The Self" was communicated and heard. The form of language and dialogue form the basis of communicative influence between the play and the individual, being the audience. For Kearney:

> The indigenous movement of verbal theatre boasts an august lineage extending from Goldsmith, Shaw, Synge, Yeats and O'Casey and to such contemporary dramatists as Murphy, Kilroy, Leonard and Friel. All these authors share a common concern with the place of language; they have created plays where words tend to pre-determine character, action and plot.[29]

For the non-verbal and "silent" archive, one which may only have textual records or remnants and for which no recording of the performance to listen to, the accent of a particular character places them in a distinct place, time or persona that may otherwise be lost. By trawling the archive of prompt-scripts of productions it is possible to counteract this silencing of the voice within performance. Within the archive of Druid Theatre's 1986 production of *Bailegangaire* by Tom Murphy, one can deduce the tone and verbal inflections added to the prompt-script by actress Siobhán McKenna in the role of the Mommo. Also detailed are facial expressions, physical reactions and intricacies of the "unarchivable" performance itself. Marginalia in a fragment of prompt-script detail that Mommo, the bedridden storyteller of Murphy's self-preserving but neverending tale, is "po-faced" and that Josie, her long-suffering daughter is "nasal" sounding.[30] Reading this archived prompt-script informs the aural experience of the rehearsal space and drafting of performance itself. The additional directions by Garry Hynes are extended to the sound of the auditorium itself as the noted "sound of the house" creates a soundscape to the babbling and talking of McKenna's Mommo and the nightly recounting of her own archived memory of how the town would find its name of Bailegangaire.

Similarly, in the Abbey Theatre's 1968 production of Tom Murphy's *Famine*, the actor's scripts reveal further the extent of the devising work that takes place in the private world of the rehearsal space. Within the Abbey Theatre Digital Archive, one of the files retained within the script archive is a typescript of *Famine*—but with the additional actor's marginalia the script reveals a much more collaborative and devised approach to characterization through sound and accent. The script, which is heavily annotated with drawing and sketches upon its cover page (perhaps revealing a somewhat drawn-out tedium to the lengthy rehearsal process), also features strike-throughs, underlining and additional manuscript notes, all referring to the character of Michael. Niall Buggy played this character in the Abbey production and so has "archived" his aural assumptions for this character onto the preserved script. The prompt-script allows for further aural reconstruction where "famine sound" is the only detail retained within the archive for the sound score to accompany the closing of Act One. As no sound recording of the production survives, one can but speculate as to what "famine sound" may have in fact sounded like.

The archive of place, people and memory itself is not restrained to rural wilds of McDonagh's Connemara. From the late 1990s and through writers such as Mark O'Rowe the archive of current day speech, sound and place is once more a central facet of the dramaturgy of contemporary theatre. *Howie The Rookie* by O'Rowe, is a play set in the working-class suburbs of North Dublin in 1999, also the year of its première, which was at the Bush Theatre, London. A subsequent tour of this production brought the play to the Civic Theatre, Tallaght, in Dublin. The play features two frenetic and interlinked monologues, one by the Howie Lee, the other by the Rookie Lee, which presents a literary, grotesque form of cartoonish violence and hellishly dark humour that roars its way across Dublin's streets.

The monologue format takes the play out of the present and out of the year 1999, as it is described in the play's opening notes, through a form of recounted memory. Linguistically and stylistically, the play is a retelling of past events, a memory play. It is a performance of an archive. Though part of an unspecific recent past, the events perpetrated by the Howie Lee and the Rookie Lee and their associated cast of dubious and equally delinquent associates, are acutely aware of, and reactive to, the onset of globalized culture and changing communication habits of Celtic Tiger Ireland and the social media generation that are about to blossom.

The playscript performs the role of a prompt-script. While one can easily purchase the published script, the private document of the prompt-script is the preserve of the archive and the repository. However, O'Rowe's language acts to embed the stage directions as dialogue, auto-archiving the physical actions of actors Aidan Kelly and Karl Shiels. The immense physicality and movement of both character and language is again in the realm of "unarchiveable", but O'Rowe blends his monologue into also "acting" as stage directions, setting notes and actor's movements:

> Part One. The Howie Lee.
> Smoke. Black smoke uphead there, north end of the field. Thick, billowin', curlin' up. Somethin' burnin'. Me, the Howie, south end, amblin'. Approachin'. A figure. A man ahead. Some fuck standin' there, stick in his hand, proddin' whatever's burnin'. Making sure it all goes up.[31]

O'Rowe maintains this synchronized past and present in place and language throughout the play. Howie lets the audience know where he is and where he is going at all times. "Me, The Howie Lee, getting' closer now. Passing through the field, me way home. Field, the back of the flats there, back of Ollie's flat, me mate Ollie's".[32] When mention of other witnesses to Howie's raucous tales and events are mentioned, they too are tracked by conventional wording reserved for printed stage directions usually archived within the prompt-script, never within the monologue/dialogue of the characters themselves: "Enter The Peaches. Youse Right? Enter the Peaches, Vámanos he says, exit the boys... ".[33]

Digital recordings of these works by Mark O'Rowe and Tom Murphy, within the Abbey Theatre Digital Archive and the Druid Theatre Company archive, offer the possibility for "second liveness" as described earlier and present the intersection of sound, text, place and language all within the digitized and reanimated performance archive.

The Digital Archive: Challenges and Opportunities

One of the first encounters between Irish theatre and of mass broadcasting and digital means can be traced to the early 1960s and the emergence of the national broadcaster and telecaster, Radió Teilifís Éireann (RTÉ). As Chris Morash notes, at this time Irish theatre was also engaging with this new medium. Some of the pioneering practitioners of Irish television included luminary figures of the Irish theatre and cultural scene: Hilton Edwards, Caroline Swift, Jack White, Wesley Burroughs, Shelagh Richards, among others. Morash points out that:

> Irish television drama became synonymous with studio-bound versions of stage plays, often with a minimal or stylised set. In this regard, the very first home produced drama broadcast by the station, a 1962 production of J.M. Synge's *The Well of the Saints*, was a sign of what was to come.[34]

For the first time, Irish theatre, or a form of the performance at least, was now able to be viewed by audiences within their family homes. The by-product of the process is a moving-image archive. The digital archive is continually going through physical redefinition in size, scope, accessibility and content. Aisling Keane and Martin Bradley describe the mass scale of data created during the Abbey Theatre Digital Archive project at NUI Galway: "Cloud storage (Amazon S3) was the chosen cloud host, which also served to minimize outlay on servers and infrastructure as on completion of the three-year project in August 2015, total data storage requirements exceeded 40TB. In comparison the Hubble Space Telescope Data Archive has amassed 1.2TB of data since 1993."[35]

Through digitization and digital access formerly inaccessible material can be made available. Reels, beta tapes, DV tapes, floppy disks, cassettes and mini-disks are all obsolete media which retain their original evidence. For instance, if one listens to the sound score of Tomás MacAnna's production of Brian Friel's *Philadelphia, Here I Come!* from the Abbey Theatre in 1972, one learns the play opens to the sound of a train whistle departing a platform, which then morphs into the sound of a jet engine.[36] This signifies the play and the theme of Irish emigration has been updated from the train/boat imagery of traditional Irish emigration to the modern arrival of transatlantic flights.

Text searching across the script archive of the Abbey Theatre by means of Optical Character Recognition (OCR) means every script (typescript at least) is word-searchable. This throws up a lot of interesting points about Ireland and various aspects of culture. For example, the depiction of drugs and drug taking in Irish (Abbey) playscripts: In the "Celtic Tiger" years (1998–2008) the word "heroin" appears fifty-eight times in the context of drug taking. By contrast the word "rape" appears eighty-four times on the national stage across thirty plays in that period while the word "immigrant" produced just twenty-two instances within Abbey Theatre plays between 1990 and 2008. A search of certain words and phrases reveal cultural moments regarding the representation of citizens and key social issues on the national stage. The digital archive can present a microcosm of Irish society in specific moments in both national and theatrical histories.

In the description of the second-generation iteration of the internet, "Web 2.0", according to Johnny Ryan, "evokes the programmer's convention of appending version number after the title of a piece of software to distinguish it from previous releases of the same package".[37] The same elemental description could apply to successions of productions over years and decades of classic plays. The archive of a play which has a long production history should make accountable the distinctions between re-mounting of a play and a new production of a past or classic play but which merits being recorded as being a "new production". The application of the idea of "production 2.0" into a theatre and performance context is akin to Ryan's point that the world wide web, though revolutionary, was limited in its first iteration to being a means of singular broadcast. It was a means of information exchange but only with a single channel and single direction of communication, from web to viewer. The future space of the archive of theatre will allow, and has already allowed, theatremakers to have second-generation two-way conversations between what is being disseminated in performance and what is being received through performance.

As Web 2.0 empowered users of the internet to create their own web and to comment upon, reply to, or edit the web posting of others, so too will the digital performance archive allow hitherto unknown or unattainable engagement with the recorded history of production. Users will curate their own performances archives. By digitization, previously "fixed" records of the past are transformed into malleable substances which are no longer constrained by the control of the originating format. Photographs can be enhanced, enlarged, cropped or artificially colourized from black and white to colour; long-lost recordings of sound scores allow the aural history to be heard once more; the text of scripts can be instantly searched en masse for trends and patterns of word use and placement. The entire oeuvre of playwrights or complete repertoires of theatres can be instantly cross-searched by keyword to reveal the minutest detail of overlap or separation.

Social media is a relatively young form of mass communication, defined by Patrick Lonergan as spaces where people perform identities, an inherently theatrical space.[38] Performed before live global audiences, online utterances are "archived" on one's personal YouTube channel, Twitter feed or Facebook page for possible preservation. Lonergan also comments on the transience of the form of the social media artefact: "The video itself may be altered, either by the original creator or by someone else. Different banner ads may appear as I log on from one day to the next. The comments on the website are likely to be added to. To watch something on YouTube involves seeing not just the video but also the various frames that contain the video."[39]

As Panti's Noble Call from the Abbey Theatre stage in February 2014 was delivered with passion and eloquence, the blurring of who was actually delivering the performance was less clear.[40] While it was clearly Panti speaking in the moment, the refrain within the speech "and that feels oppressive" related back to the personal experiences of homophobia with: experienced by Panti's alter ego, Rory O'Neill. The unstable medium of the viral video, instantly consumable and sharable within its format, is ultimately subject to the chance of deletion or alteration at the whim of internet users, counter to the premise of stability within the archive—a "final" version contained within its medium. Lonergan presents this argument in terms of Philip Auslander's treatise on "liveness", in the context of social media within and as performance: "Every posting to a social media platform is inherently unfinished, in the sense that is always open to being altered. Either directly or through the resources that frame it."[41] The Noble Call had a definitive impact in the campaign for the successful passing, in May 2015, of the referendum in Ireland to enable legislation to allow full same-sex marriage equality by virtue of many factors, not least its immediate international audience reached through retransmission on

YouTube. However, the Noble Call does not register as a production on the Abbey Theatre's online performance database. Within a narrow timeframe of only under two years, the Nobel Call video is already falling outside of the Abbey Theatre history and archive, dependent on YouTube for preservation but not searchable under the Abbey's records. Neither are Rory O'Neill nor Panti Bliss listed as performers or any person/character in the performance database of the Abbey Theatre's public website.[42] The true power of such a performance is found in the global reach and national political impact of Panti's performance. Taking this concept of shared experience, Tracy Davis contends that "the communal act of viewing normally helps us to forge a public realm, connecting private experience to the public; we reckon with our reactions privately but do so literally, in public".[43] Davis further draws on work by Baz Kershaw which equates preserving acts (in a case like the Noble Call) being committed to "YouTube" for communal consumption a reminder of the fragility and as yet, in archival terms, unstable medium of internet blogging sites and user-generated content.

Conclusion

Helena Grehan, writing on *Performance, Ethics and Spectatorship in a Global Age*, has observed:

> Performance engages its spectators emotionally, viscerally, and intellectually. It has the potential to generate a set of conditions within which linguistic or representational surfaces can be disturbed or interrupted in ways that allow spectators to reflect on and ask questions about the nature of any response to a work.[44]

The same judgement about how we assess our own spectatorship through the archive must form part of this future judgement. The digital reanimation of speech, dialogue, music, intonation, accent, laughter, gasps, ovation and other stimuli and responses can offer hitherto unknowable emotional and intellectual understandings of performances, audiences and reception. This runs counter to the fears, understandable as they are, by Richard Schechner and as outlined in the beginning of this chapter, concerned that the archive, as it progresses to accumulate the masses of information produced within the digital era, of collapsing under its own volume of "big data".

The efforts of archive repositories, archivists and technologists, along with the collaboration of researchers, academics and theatre practitioners and producing theatres themselves, will determine how much of what we see and experience in performance will be available for scrutiny in the future. Digital intervention has rescued vast sets of records from obsolescence and obscurity. It is now possible to be immersed in the active and reanimated memory of performances past and hear, see and experience what would otherwise be a forgotten archive of our own theatre.

Notes

1. *Endless Art*, A House, "Bingo" (1991) https://www.youtube.com/watch?v=cDo6Lgylsjg The song, the band's biggest hit and famous for its innovative stop-motion video, received heavy criticism at the time for the fact that all thirty-one artists named in the track (excluding "Walt Disney's Mickey Mouse") were men. An apology came later in the form of a "B-side" track entitled *More Endless Art*, which listed all women artists.
2. Richard Schechner, *Quo Vadis, Performance History*, Theatre Survey 45:2 (November 2004): 272.
3. Rebecca Schneider, *Theatre and History* (Palgrave Macmillan, 2014), 4.
4. Ibid., 13.
5. *The Monto Cycle* refers to a series of four plays presented by ANU productions and which premiered at the Dublin Theatre Festival between 2010 and 2014. These works, in order of production were *World's End Lane, Laundry, The Boys of Foley Street* and *Vardo*.
6. Schneider, *Theatre and History*, 44.
7. Diana Taylor, "Performance and/as History," *TDR: The Drama Review* 50, no. 1 (Spring 2006): 69.
8. *Pals* was staged at Collins Barracks, Dublin, by ANU Productions, Inspired by the previously untold stories of the 7th Battalion of the Royal Dublin Fusiliers. http://anuproductions.ie/pals/. Accessed 17 May 2017.
9. *Guaranteed!* premiered in June 2013 at the Riverbank Arts Centre, Newbridge, Co. Kildare. A dramatisation based on documentary sources about the bank guarantee scheme for Irish banks in the wake of global economic collapse. http://fishamble.com/guaranteed-by-colin-murphy/. Accessed 17 May 2017.
10. Miriam Haughton, "From laundries to labour camps: staging Ireland's 'Rule of Silence' in ANU Productions' Laundry," in *Radical Contemporary Theatre Practices by Women in Ireland*, eds. Miriam Haughton and Mária Kurdi (Carysfort Press, Dublin, 2015), 59.
11. Ric Knowles, *Reading the Material Theatre* (Cambridge University Press, 2004), 10.
12. Patrick Lonergan, "Was the demise of the Celtic Tiger the saviour of Irish theatre?," *The Irish Times*, February 20, 2015. http://www.irishtimes.com/culture/books/was-the-demise-of-the-celtic-tiger-the-saviour-of-irish-theatre-1.2109647. Accessed 22 March 2016.
13. Fintan O'Toole, "Vaughan- Lawlor finds humanity in savage tales of the Rookie," *The Irish Times*, July 13, 2013, accessed January 17, 2016.
14. Peter Crawley, "The Beauty Queen of Leenane review: old elemental conflicts meet new pop-culture obsessions," *The Irish Times*, September 21, 2016, https://www.irishtimes.com/culture/stage/the-beauty-queen-of-leenane-review-old-elemental-conflicts-meet-new-pop-culture-obsessions-1.2800066.
15. Ibid.
16. Brenda Donohue, "Letter to the Irish Times, *Women and the Abbey Theatre*", *The Irish Times*, November 4, 2015.
17. Fintan Walsh (ed.), *That Was Us: Contemporary Irish Theatre and Performance* (Oberon Books Ltd, London, 2013), 13–15.

18. Abbey Theatre. *Aristocrats*, 12 Mar 1979 [press cuttings]. Abbey Theatre Digital Archive at National University of Ireland, Galway, 0797_PC_0001, p. 11.
19. Knowles, *Reading the Material Theatre*, 17.
20. Emilie Pine, *The Politics of Irish Memory: Performing Remembrance in Contemporary Irish Culture* (Palgrave, London, 2011), 3.
21. Fintan O'Toole, *Stage for Action as Well as for Words*, *Irish Times*, 23 June 2007, Abbey Theatre. Terminus, 13 Jun 2007 [press cuttings]. Abbey Theatre Digital Archive at National University of Ireland, Galway, 4900_PC_0001, 40.
22. Ibid.
23. Ibid.
24. Abbey Theatre. *Terminus*, 13 June 2007 [video]. Abbey Theatre Digital Archive at National University of Ireland, Galway, 4900_V_001.
25. Mark O'Rowe, *Terminus* (London: Nick Hern Books, 2009), 9.
26. T2/241, Druid Theatre Company Archive, James Hardiman Library, NUI Galway., 2–3
27. Within the archive of Druid Theatre Company, James Hardiman Library, NUI Galway.
28. Tim Robinson, "A Connemara in the Skull", programme from *The Leenane Trilogy* by Martin McDonagh. T2/241, Druid Theatre Company Archive, James Hardiman Library, NUI Galway., 5.
29. Richard Kearney, *Navigations Collected Irish Essays, 1976–2006* (Syracuse University Press, 2006), 264.
30. T2/129, Druid Theatre Archive, National University of Ireland, Galway.
31. Abbey Theatre. *Howie The Rookie*, 09 May 2006 [video]. Abbey Theatre Digital Archive at National University of Ireland, Galway, 4893_V_001.
32. Abbey Theatre. *Howie The Rookie*, 09 May 2006 [video]. Abbey Theatre Digital Archive at National University of Ireland, Galway, 4893_V_001.
33. Abbey Theatre. *Howie The Rookie*, 09 May 2006 [video]. Abbey Theatre Digital Archive at National University of Ireland, Galway, 4893_V_001.
34. Chris Morash, *A History of the Media in Ireland* (Cambridge: Cambridge University Press, 2012), 176–7.
35. Martin Bradley and Aisling Keane, "The Abbey Theatre Digitisation Project at NUI Galway", *New Review of Information Networking* 20. 1–2 (2015): 37.
36. Abbey Theatre. *Philadelphia, Here I Come!*, 15 Feb 1995 [audio]. Abbey Theatre Digital Archive at National University of Ireland, Galway, 11009_A_001.
37. Johnny Ryan, *A History of the Internet and the Digital Future* (London: Reaktion Books, 2013), 137.
38. Patrick Lonergan, *Theatre and Social Media* (London: Palgrave, 2016), 2.
39. Lonergan, *Theatre and Social Media*, 33.
40. The "Noble Call" was a short performance of poetry, song, prose or speech delivered by artist, activist or other following each night's performance of *The Risen People* by James Plunkett at the Abbey Theatre, Jan.–Feb. 2014.
41. Lonergan, *Theatre and Social Media*, 33.
42. https://www.abbeytheatre.ie/archives/browse_performance_database/. Accessed 30 June 2017.
43. Davis, *Theatricality*, 37.
44. Helena Grehan, *Performance, Ethics and Spectatorship in a Global Age* (New York: Palgrave Macmillan, 2009), 2.

Bibliography

Archive Sources

The Abbey Theatre Digital Archive. James Hardiman Library. NUI Galway.
Druid Theatre Archive. James Hardiman Library. NUI Galway.

Published Sources

Abbott, Daisy, Sarah Jones, and Seamus Ross. "Redefining the Performing Arts Archive." *Archival Science* 8. 3 (2009).

Auslander, Phillip. *Liveness: Performance in a Mediatized Culture*. Routledge, London, 2009.

Bradley, Martin and Aisling Keane. "The Abbey Theatre Digitisation Project at NUI Galway", *New Review of Information Networking* 20 Issue 1–2, (2015).

Davis, Tracy C. and Thomas Postlewait, eds., *Theatricality*. Cambridge University Press, Cambridge, 2003.

Miriam Haughton and Mária Kurdi, eds., *Radical Contemporary Theatre Practices by Women in Ireland*. Carysfort Press, Dublin, 2015.

Grehan, Helena. *Performance, Ethics and Spectatorship in a Global Age*. Palgrave Macmillan, New York, 2009.

Kearney, Richard. *Navigations Collected Irish Essays, 1976–2006*. Syracuse University Press, 2006.

Lonergan, Patrick. *Theatre and Social Media*. Palgrave, London, 2016.

Morash, Chris. *A History of the Media in Ireland*. Cambridge University Press, Cambridge, 2012.

"Was the demise of the Celtic Tiger the saviour of Irish theatre?." *The Irish Times*, February 20, 2015. Accessed 22 March 2016. http://www.irishtimes.com/culture/books/was-the-demise-of-the-celtic-tiger-the-saviour-of-irish-theatre-1.2109647

O'Rowe, Mark. *Terminus*. Nick Hern Books, London, 2009.

Pine, Emilie. *The Politics of Irish Memory: Performing Remembrance in Contemporary Irish Culture*. Palgrave, London, 2011.

Ryan, Johnny. *A History of the Internet and the Digital Future*. Reaktion Books, London, 2013.

Sant, Toni. *Documenting Performance: The Context and Processes of Digital Curation and Archiving*. Bloomsbury, London, 2017.

Schechner, Richard. "Quo Vadis, Performance History?" *Theatre Survey, 45*(2), (2004): 271–274.

Schneider, Rebecca. *Theatre and History*. Palgrave Macmillan, 2014.

Taylor, Diana. *Performance and/as History*, The Drama Review, Volume 50, Number 1 (T 189), Spring 2006, pp. 67–86

Taylor, Diana. *The Archive and the Repertoire: Performing Cultural Memory in the Americas*. Durham: Duke University Press, 2003.

Walsh, Fintan, ed., *That Was Us: Contemporary Irish Theatre and Performance*. Oberon Books Ltd, London 2013.

Phelan, Peggy. *Unmarked: The Politics of Performance*. London, Routledge, 1993.

Newspaper Sources

Donohue, Brenda. Letter to the Irish Times, *Women and the Abbey Theatre*, *The Irish Times*, November 4, 2015.

Lonergan, Patrick. "Was the Demise of the Celtic Tiger the Saviour of Irish Theatre?," *The Irish Times*, February 20, 2015.

O'Toole, Fintan. "Vaughan-Lawlor Finds Humanity in Savage Tales of the Rookie". *The Irish Times*, July 13, 2013. Accessed January 17, 2016.

Websites

Abbey Theatre Performance Database

https://www.abbeytheatre.ie/archives/browse_performance_database/
www.youtube.com

Index[1]

[1] Note: Page numbers followed by 'n' refer to notes.

E. Jordan, E. Weitz (eds.), *The Palgrave Handbook of Contemporary Irish Theatre and Performance*, https://doi.org/10.1057/978-1-137-58588-2

N

S

Printed in the United States
By Bookmasters